# LET'S GO

# LET'S GO PUBLICATIONS

## TRAVEL GUIDES

Australia
Austria & Switzerland
Brazil
Britain
California
Central America
Chile
China
Costa Rica
Eastern Europe
Ecuador
Egypt
Europe
France
Germany
Greece
Hawaii
India & Nepal
Ireland
Israel
Italy
Japan
Mexico
New Zealand
Peru
Puerto Rico
Southeast Asia
Spain & Portugal with Morocco
Thailand
USA
Vietnam
Western Europe

## ROADTRIP GUIDE

Roadtripping USA

## ADVENTURE GUIDES

Alaska
Pacific Northwest
Southwest USA

## CITY GUIDES

Amsterdam
Barcelona
Boston
Buenos Aires
London
New York City
Paris
Rome
San Francisco
Washington, DC

## POCKET CITY GUIDES

Amsterdam
Berlin
Boston
Chicago
London
New York City
Paris
San Francisco
Venice
Washington, DC

# LET'S GO

# AUSTRALIA

**JAKE G. COHEN** EDITOR
**MARYKATE JASPER** ASSOCIATE EDITOR
**ANNA HALSEY STEIM** ASSOCIATE EDITOR

RESEARCHER-WRITERS

| | |
|---|---|
| **MOLLY FAULKNER-BOND** | **VICTORIA NORELID** |
| **CHARLES FISHER-POST** | **ANSLEY RUBINSTEIN** |
| **ANDREA HALPERN** | **ALEX SHELL** |
| **KYRA HILL** | **LAN ZHOU** |

**GRETCHEN MARINA KRUEGER** MAP EDITOR
**PATRICK McKIERNAN** MANAGING EDITOR

ST. MARTIN'S PRESS ✄ NEW YORK

**HELPING LET'S GO.** If you want to share your discoveries, suggestions, or corrections, please drop us a line. We appreciate every piece of correspondence, whether a postcard, a 10-page email, or a coconut. Visit Let's Go at **http://www.letsgo.com,** or send email to:

>  feedback@letsgo.com
>  Subject: "Let's Go: Australia"

**Address mail to:**

>  Let's Go: Australia
>  67 Mount Auburn St.
>  Cambridge, MA 02138
>  USA

In addition to the invaluable travel advice our readers share with us, many are kind enough to offer their services as researchers or editors. Unfortunately, our charter enables us to employ only currently enrolled Harvard students.

Maps by Let's Go copyright © 2009 by Let's Go, Inc.
Maps by David Lindroth copyright © 2009 by St. Martin's Press.

Distributed outside the USA and Canada by Macmillan.

ISBN-13: 978-0-312-38575-0
ISBN-10: 0-312-38575-7
Tenth edition
10 9 8 7 6 5 4 3 2 1

**Let's Go:** Australia is written by Let's Go Publications, 67 Mount Auburn St., Cambridge, MA 02138, USA.

**Let's Go**® and the LG logo are trademarks of Let's Go, Inc.

# ACKNOWLEDGMENTS

**TEAM AUS THANKS:** ▓Pat and Sam, for guidance and devotion, even during the low season; our brave, stellar RWs, who were everything we could have asked for; and Gretchen, for knowing where everything goes.

**JAKE THANKS:** Marykate and Anna, for being the smartest, funniest bookteam around; Pat, for being a better ME; AUK and vicinity for being a home; GAS, ELF, and RSB for food, drink, and shelter; EML for missing me back; and M/D for everything, as usual.

**MARYKATE THANKS:** Jake and Anna, for all the hard work, bubble tea, and veggies; the AUK-pod, for keeping it surly; Pat, for being a ray of sunshine in the pod that doesn't turn its lights on; the entire office, for making the summer more fun; Bing, for his grammar help.

**ANNA THANKS:** Jake, for just being the absolute best; Marykate, for her humor, and for introducing me to a new range of culinary delights; Pat, for his constant, reassuring, enthusiastic presence; Dwight, for the use of his chair and stapler; Mackenzie and Nan, for always asking about my day; Chrissie, for her shower; Kevin, for keeping my mornings interesting; the AUK pod, for its overwhelming peppiness and positivity; and Ella, for not letting me not apply.

**GRETCHEN THANKS:** Team Australia, for writing well, dancing, and bringing the Vegemite; my RWs, for indulging my wanderlust; Mapland, for being nothing to f*** with; Prince; Meg, shoop!; shorts and their aficionados; Becca and Elissa, for laughing, smiling and appreciating little things; Australia; Illiana, for giving advice about life after graduating; Derek, for the music and for teaching me about maps; Word; MNDC, for all the good times; Trish, Justine, and Eliz, for the love; my family; dinnuh.

**Editor**
Jake G. Cohen
**Associate Editors**
Marykate Jasper, Anna Halsey Steim
**Managing Editor**
Patrick McKiernan
**Map Editor**
Gretchen Marina Krueger
**Typesetters**
C. Alexander Tremblay, Jansen A. S. Thurmer

# LET'S GO

**Publishing Director**
Inés C. Pacheco
**Editor-in-Chief**
Samantha Gelfand
**Production Manager**
Jansen A. S. Thurmer
**Cartography Manager**
R. Derek Wetzel
**Editorial Managers**
Dwight Livingstone Curtis,
Vanessa J. Dube, Nathaniel Rakich
**Financial Manager**
Lauren Caruso
**Publicity and Marketing Manager**
Patrick McKiernan
**Personnel Manager**
Laura M. Gordon
**Production Associate**
C. Alexander Tremblay
**Director of IT & E-Commerce**
Lukáš Tóth
**Website Manager**
Ian Malott
**Office Coordinators**
Vinnie Chiappini, Jennifer Q. Wong
**Director of Advertising Sales**
Nicole J. Bass
**Senior Advertising Associates**
Kipyegon Kitur, Jeremy Siegfried,
John B. Ulrich
**Junior Advertising Associate**
Edward C. Robinson Jr.

**President**
Timothy J. J. Creamer
**General Manager**
Jim McKellar

# RESEARCHER-WRITERS

### Molly Faulkner-Bond
*Western Australia*

Molly may be the hottest travel-writer ever—after spending half her route in the scorching northwestern summer and ditching at least one melted shoe, she gave new meaning to the term "sweating it out." By the time she reached Perth, it was clear that there was absolutely nothing she couldn't conquer. A former resident of Byron Bay, Molly infused her copy with all the spunk and wit you would expect from her exuberant personality.

### Charles Fisher-Post
*Northern Territory, South and Western Australia*

Assigned what may have been the most extensive route in Let's Go history, veteran RW extraordinaire Charles knows Australia front to outback. From the scalding north to the frigid south, Charles drove and drove and drove, braving bugs and road bumps with brio. But the endless kilometers never got Charles down—the constantly blaring CCR kept him chill—and the book is fortunate to have benefited from his insight and iron will.

### Andrea Halpern
*New South Wales, Tasmania, and Victoria*

The definition of a world traveler, Dre took a look at her jam-packed Australian itinerary and took off without hesitation. Her love of travel took her through Asia and Europe after her route. A veteran Let's Go RW and Editor, Dre celebrated her birthday a whole day earlier than her friends and family did while revamping coverage of Tasmania and NSW. Never one for writing in the imperative, Dre leads by example—and what an example she is.

### Kyra Hill
*Southern Queensland*

They say Australians are friendly folk; no wonder Kyra fits in so well Down Under. Her buoyant spirit carried her throughout Queensland—she made friends and influenced people from the shores of Fraser Island to the mines of Mt. Isa. And all the while, she was delivering some of the most sparkling prose the book has ever seen. It should also be noted that Kyra rides a mean motorcycle.

### Victoria Norelid
*South Australia and Melbourne*

Victoria took her experiences as Associate Editor and Personnel Manager to Oz, where the locals took her in with open arms. Between swimming with wild dolphins, cuddling baby wombats, and (trying to) surf, Victoria personified her route, name and all. The copybatches were (really) long, but no one is complaining—the book is better for her detailed, thorough work.

# RESEARCHER-WRITERS

### Ansley Rubinstein
*Sydney and surrounds*

Excitable Ansley was perfectly suited to the hustle and bustle of Sydney; her background as a dancer gave her the energy necessary to get around Australia's largest city and its expansive outlying regions. From the exclamation points that enlivened all her copy, we can tell that Ansley had a good time Down Under, and we're happy we got a chance to enjoy her flawless research.

### Alex Shell
*Northern Queensland*

The King of Queensland, Alex easily made the transition from Austin, TX to Australia. His route came with its fair share of hardships, but resourceful and indomitable Alex got through them all. His hard work and dry wit paid dividends—his hilarious anecdotes and vibrant features go down as some of the richest and most entertaining in the book.

### Lan Zhou
*New South Wales*

Lan was all-business, all-the-time. Some researchers go to Australia in awe of the landscape and wildlife, but by the time Lan was through with Oz, the country was in awe of her. Lan absolutely owned her itinerary, and after weeks of interrogating hostel owners, she found time to return to nature, climbing every rock in sight. Lan rounded out an all-star cast of researchers and made us happy to come in to work every day.

# CONTRIBUTING WRITERS

**Tim Rowse** works in the History Program of the Research School of Social Sciences at the Australian National University. His publications on Australian history include studies of colonial policy and a biography of H.C. Coombs.

**Julie Stephens** is a graduate of Harvard College with a degree in Social Studies. A former Publishing Director for Let's Go, she took a year off during college and attended cooking school in Sydney, studied Indian art in Rajasthan, and worked on her honors thesis at the British Library in London. She is currently a PhD student in the history department at Harvard University.

# HOW TO USE THIS BOOK

**COVERAGE LAYOUT.** Australia has six states and two territories. Each state or territory gets its own chapter and begins with information on that region's capital city. The remaining towns and cities are organized by the "center-out" principle: they're listed in a clockwise, circular pattern, radiating outward from the capital city. The town or city located closest to the capital is listed first, and we continue from there. Our coverage begins with the Australian Capital Territory and proceeds through the states and territories in alphabetical order.

**TRANSPORTATION INFO.** Public transportation options are listed in tables for major hubs. In other, smaller towns, the duration and price of the journey is often given parenthetically after the destination listing. Due to the long distances that travelers frequently cover within Australia, most travelers find that a car is indispensible for getting around. **Essentials** (p. 9) has information on renting and buying cars, as well as insurance options, while **Great Outdoors** (p. 63) has important driving safety information.

**COVERING THE BASICS.** For a rough idea of when and where to go, check out **Discover** (p. 1). **Life and Times** (p. 48) gives a brief introduction to Australian history and culture, while **Essentials** (p. 9) contains practical information for traveling in Australia. **Beyond Tourism** (p. 81) lists short- and long-term work, volunteer, and study abroad opportunities. Our **Scholarly Article** (p. 62) offers a unique perspective on the Australian experience, while our **Beyond Tourism Article** (p. 95) showcases one of the many options available to travelers interested in studying or working Down Under. **The Great Outdoors** (p. 63) chapter covers important practical information to help you stay safe while camping and bushwalking. The **Appendix** (p. 767) has information you'll need to get around Oz, including tips on negotiating cafes and bars as well as a Glossary of 'Strine to get you talking like an Aussie.

**PRICE DIVERSITY.** Our researchers list establishments in order of value, with the best values listed first. Our absolute favorites are denoted by the *Let's Go* thumbpick (🖼). Since the best value doesn't always correspond with the lowest price, we've also incorporated a system of price ranges, represented from least to most expensive by the numbers ❶ to ❺. Symbols are based on the lowest cost for one person. Many accommodations in Australia offer different types of lodging, and those listed as ❶ may offer higher-priced options as well.

---

**A NOTE TO OUR READERS.** The information for this book was gathered by Let's Go researchers from January through August of 2008. Each listing is based on one researcher's opinion, formed during his or her visit at a particular time. Those traveling at other times may have different experiences since prices, dates, hours, and conditions are always subject to change. You are urged to check the facts presented in this book beforehand to avoid inconvenience and surprises.

# CONTENTS

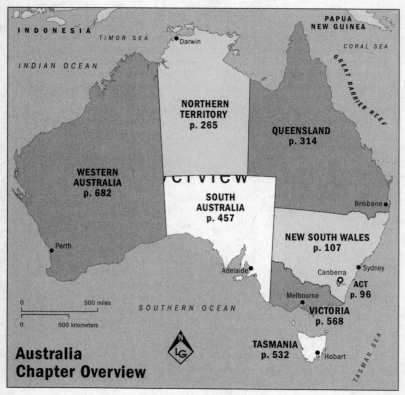

Australia
Chapter Overview

# ABOUT LET'S GO

## NOT YOUR PARENTS' TRAVEL GUIDE

At Let's Go, we see every trip as the chance of a lifetime. If your dream is to grab a machete and forge through the jungles of Costa Rica, we can take you there. If you'd rather bask in the Riviera sun at a beachside cafe, we'll set you a table. We write for readers who know that there's more to travel than sharing double deckers with tourists and who believe that travel can change both themselves and the world—whether they plan to spend six days in Bangkok or six months in Europe. We'll show you just how far your money can go, and prove that the greatest limitation on your adventures is not your wallet but your imagination.

## BEYOND THE TOURIST EXPERIENCE

To help you gain a deeper connection with the places you travel, our fearless researchers scour the globe to give you the heads-up on both world-renowned and off-the-beaten-track attractions, sights, and destinations. They dive into the local culture only to emerge with the freshest insights on everything from festivals to regional cuisine. We've also opened our pages to respected writers and scholars to hear their takes on the countries and regions we cover, and asked travelers who have worked, studied, or volunteered abroad to contribute first-person accounts of their experiences. In addition, each guide's Beyond Tourism chapter shares ideas about responsible travel, study abroad, and how to give back while on the road.

## FORTY-NINE YEARS OF WISDOM

Let's Go got its start in 1960, when a group of creative and well-traveled students compiled their experience and advice into a 20-page mimeographed pamphlet, which they gave to travelers on charter flights to Europe. Almost five decades later, we've expanded to cover six continents and all kinds of travel— while retaining our founders' adventurous attitude. Laced with witty prose and total candor, our guides are still researched and written entirely by students on shoestring budgets, experienced travelers who know that train strikes, stolen luggage, food poisoning, and marriage proposals are all part of a day's work.

## THE LET'S GO COMMUNITY

More than just a travel guide company, Let's Go is a community. Our small staff comes together because of our shared passion for travel and our desire to help other travelers see the world the way it was meant to be seen. We love it when our readers become part of the Let's Go community as well—when you travel, drop us a postcard (67 Mt. Auburn St., Cambridge, MA 02138, USA), send us an e-mail (feedback@letsgo.com), or sign up online (http://www.letsgo.com) to tell us about your adventures and discoveries.

**For more information, visit us online: www.letsgo.com.**

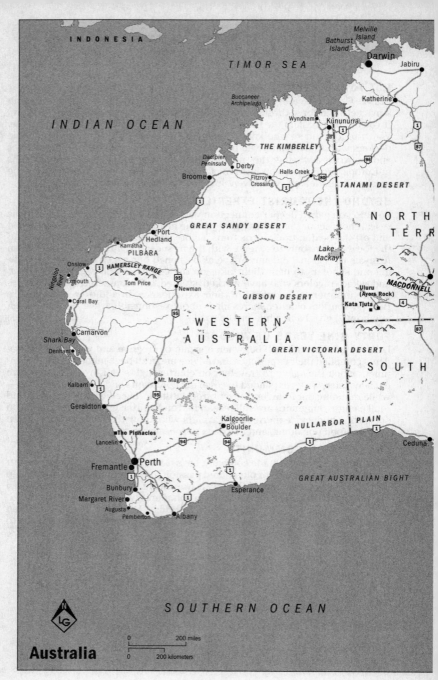

Australia

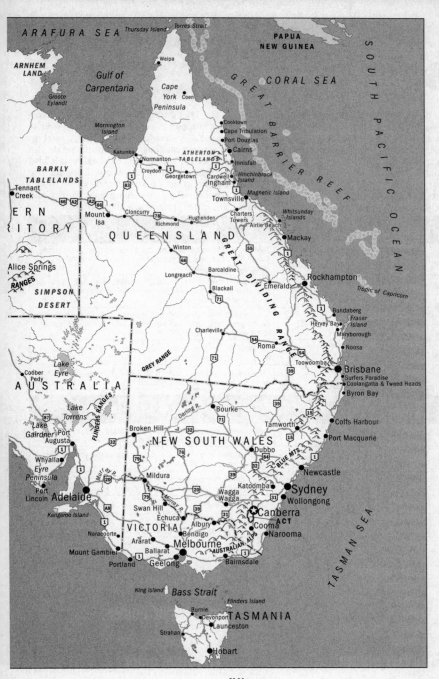

Our researchers list establishments in order of value, beginning with the best; our favorites are denoted by the Let's Go thumbs-up (🖒). Since cheap prices don't necessarily correspond to value, however, we've also designed a system of price ranges based on a rough expectation of what you'll spend. For **accommodations**, the costs indicate the cheapest price for which a single traveler can stay for one night. For **restaurants** and other dining establishments, we estimate the average amount a traveler will spend. The table tells you what you'll *typically* find in Australia in the corresponding price range; keep in mind that no system can allow for every individual establishment's quirks and that you might get more for your money in larger cities. Prices are all in AUS$.

| ACCOMMODATIONS | RANGE | WHAT YOU'RE *LIKELY* TO FIND |
|:---:|:---:|:---|
| ❶ | under $20 | The bare minimum; camping and dorm rooms or dorm-style rooms. Expect bunk beds and a communal bath. You may have to bring or rent towels and sheets. |
| ❷ | $20-30 | Upper-end hostels or small hotels. You may have a private bathroom, but don't be surprised if there's a sink in your room and a communal shower in the hall. |
| ❸ | $31-45 | A small but comfortable room with a private bath. Should have decent amenities, such as phone and TV. Breakfast may be included in the price of the room. |
| ❹ | $46-70 | Similar to ❸, but should ideally offer more luxury or be situated in a more upscale neighborhood. |
| ❺ | over $70 | Large hotels or upscale chains. If it's a ❺ and it doesn't have the perks you want, you've paid too much. |

| FOOD | RANGE | WHAT YOU'RE *LIKELY* TO FIND |
|:---:|:---:|:---|
| ❶ | under $12 | Mostly street-corner stands, pizza places, or fast-food joints. If you're lucky, a sit-down meal here and there. |
| ❷ | $12-16 | Some sandwiches and takeaway options; an increased number of sit-down restaurants available. |
| ❸ | $17-20 | Dishes are more expensive; chances are you're paying at least partially to enjoy the decor and atmosphere. |
| ❹ | $21-25 | Restaurants with better service and fancier meals. |
| ❺ | over $25 | If you're not getting delicious food with great service in a ritzy setting, you're paying for nothing more than hype. |

# DISCOVER AUSTRALIA

While people have been making the journey to Australia for over 40,000 years, the continent retains a magical, dream-like quality. Turns out, Australia is unlike anywhere else. Where else can you enjoy world-class wine tasting, get dangerously close to a saltwater croc, learn to play the didjeridu, snorkel in expanses of ancient coral reef, and dance the night away at the largest nightclub in the Southern Hemisphere? What other continent offers a bustling metropolis like Sydney on the same platter as the vast Outback, the rainforests of Cape York, and the colored sands of Fraser Island? You may need to pinch yourself, but rest assured: it's not a dream, it's Australia.

## FACTS AND FIGURES

**CAPITAL:** Canberra.

**WEST-TO-EAST DIAMETER:** 4000km.

**NUMBER OF ABORIGINAL LANGUAGES:** Over 200.

**HUMAN POPULATION:** 20.6 million.

**KANGAROO POPULATION:** 59 million.

**AUSTRALIANS WHO FOLLOW THE JEDI FAITH:** 70,509 (2001 census).

**NUMBER OF BEACHES:** Over 10,000.

**CLAIM TO LOCOMOTIVE FAME:** World's longest stretch of straight railway (478km), across the Nullarbor plain.

**NUMBER OF PLANT SPECIES:** More than 22,000.

**AMOUNT OF FOLIAGE KOALAS MUST EAT DAILY:** 500-600g (over 1 lb.).

**ANNUAL BEER CONSUMPTION, PER AUSTRALIAN:** 94.5L.

**JARS OF VEGEMITE PRODUCED PER YEAR:** 22.7 million.

**LARGEST CATTLE STATION:** 34,000 sq. km, outsizing the nation of Belgium.

**SPECIES OF FISH ON THE GREAT BARRIER REEF:** 1500.

# WHEN TO GO

Since Australia is huge and its climate can vary greatly between regions, the best time to visit should be determined by the things you'd like to do rather than by the calendar or season. Crowds and prices of everything from flights to hostel bunks tend to be directly proportional to the quality of the weather.

In southern Australia, the seasons of the temperate climate zone are reversed from those in the Northern Hemisphere. Summer lasts from December to February, autumn from March to May, winter from June to August, and spring from September to November. In general, Australian winters are mild, comparable to those in the southern US or southern Europe. While snow is frequent only in the mountains, winters are generally too cold to have much fun at the beach. In the south, high season falls roughly between November and April.

Northern Australia, however, is an entirely different story—many people forget that over one-third of the country is in the sweltering tropics. Seasons here are defined by wildly varying precipitation rather than by temperatures. During **the Wet** (Nov.-Apr.), heavy downpours and violent storms plague the land, especially on the north coast. During **the Dry** (May-Oct.), sections of Australia away from the temperate zone endure drought. Traveling during the Wet is not recommended for the faint of heart; the heavy rains wash out unsealed roads, making driving a challenge in rural areas.

**Great Barrier Reef** diving is seasonal as well. January and February are rainy, while the water is clearest between April and October. The toxic **box jellyfish** (p. 67) is most common off the northeast coast between October and April.

Ski season in New South Wales, Victoria, and Tasmania runs from late June to September, and the famous wildflowers of Western Australia bloom from September to December. To decide when and where to go, read below and see **temperature and rainfall** (p. 767) and **holidays and festivals** (p. 768).

# WHAT TO DO

## THE OUTBACK

Geographically contained by the continent's more developed coasts, Australia's Outback seems like the most infinite, empty place on earth. Every year, travelers and Aussies take on the Never-Never, looking for adventure or serious solitude. During the Dry, the **Kimberley** (p. 753) opens to those brave souls who dare to

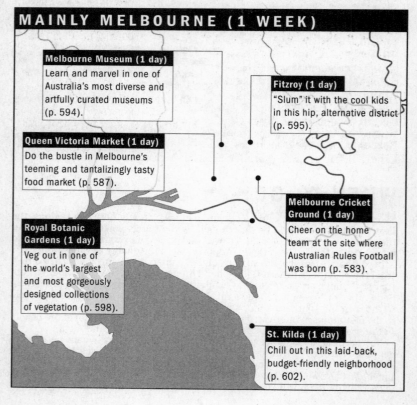

# MAINLY MELBOURNE (1 WEEK)

**Melbourne Museum (1 day)**
Learn and marvel in one of Australia's most diverse and artfully curated museums (p. 594).

**Fitzroy (1 day)**
"Slum" it with the cool kids in this hip, alternative district (p. 595).

**Queen Victoria Market (1 day)**
Do the bustle in Melbourne's teeming and tantalizingly tasty food market (p. 587).

**Royal Botanic Gardens (1 day)**
Veg out in one of the world's largest and most gorgeously designed collections of vegetation (p. 598).

**Melbourne Cricket Ground (1 day)**
Cheer on the home team at the site where Australian Rules Football was born (p. 583).

**St. Kilda (1 day)**
Chill out in this laid-back, budget-friendly neighborhood (p. 602).

rumble along the rough **Gibb River Road** (p. 762). In the Northern Territory, **Kakadu National Park** (p. 275) is the gateway to a world of thundering waterfalls, snapping crocs, and mystical beauty. The Aboriginal homeland of **Arnhem Land** (p. 294) may be the most well known Outback attraction. In Australia's Red Centre, imposing **Uluru** (Ayers Rock; p. 311) and its cousin **Kata Tjuta** (p. 312) keep watch over the rest of the Outback. Down in South Australia, **Coober Pedy** (p. 519), the "Opal Capital of the World," brings out the tough Down Under mentality—scorching temperatures force residents to carve out homes underground. The **Nullarbor** (p. 530) is an aptly-named stretch of empty plain. For travelers who don't make it out of the east, Queensland's outback mining towns and New South Wales's **Broken Hill** (p. 259) represent the limits of Australia's most-developed regions, offering just a taste of what lies beyond.

# THE OUTDOORS

Australia has a national park around every corner, preserving all types of landscapes—from rainforest to desert, mountain to coast. The **MacDonnell Ranges** (p. 304) have some of the continent's best hiking, and just next door is the spectacular **Kings Canyon** (p. 308). Up the track, the write-home-to-mum lookouts of **Nitmiluk** (Katherine Gorge; p. 291) are equaled by the spectacular waterfalls of **Litchfield** (p. 285). In Queensland, lush rainforest complements the nearby reef from the tip of **Cape York** (p. 444) all the way down to **Eungella** (p. 393). Further south, visitors flock to the watersports at **Surfers Paradise** (p. 345), and the world's best surfers catch a break off the Gold Coast's **Coolangatta and Tweed Heads** (p. 341). To see more pros in action, head to **Bells Beach** (p. 620) in Torquay, Victoria, every Easter for the Rip Curl Pro Classic. The **Blue Mountains** (p. 162) of New South Wales attract avid abseilers, and in winter, **Kosciuszko** (p. 240) becomes a haven for skiers. There are also a number of beautiful North Coast hinterland parks, such as **Mount Warning** (p. 217), which offer bushwalks for all skill levels. **Wilsons Promontory** (p. 671) is a gorgeous stretch of southern coast and part of a UNESCO Biosphere Reserve. Tasmania is Australia's hiking mecca, and the **Overland Track** (p. 552) is one of the best bushwalks in the world. South Australia's **Flinders Ranges** (p. 509) cater to the truly hardcore, while Western Australia showcases a number of marine species, including the whales and dolphins that call **Bunbury** (p. 704) and **Monkey Mia** (p. 740) home. Travelers to the region can also explore the off-the-beaten-track paradise of **Kangaroo Island** (p. 481), located close to the coast of South Australia.

## TOP TEN LIST

## TOP 10 ESCAPES FROM THE TOURIST TRAP

**1. Perth's West Coast Eagles vs. Freo's Dockers,** WA (p. 696). Melbourne and Sydney have nothing on this Aussie Rules rivalry.

**2.** The **unnamed road** leading from Bamaga to the Cape York Tip, QLD (p. 450). Bump along this track to the tip of the continent.

**3. The breaks** at Cooly and Tweed Heads, QLD (p. 341). Ditch Surfers Paradise and head south for renowned waves surfed by the sport's biggest names.

**4. North Stradbroke Island,** QLD (p. 337). Experience the beaches and world-class diving on this spectacular sand island.

**5. The Overland Track,** TAS (p. 552). A stunning six-day bushwalk over mountains, past waterfalls, and through unique ecosystems.

**6. Cape Conran Coastal Park,** NSW (p. 680). Stand on isolated beaches, or try your hand at windsurfing or rock pooling.

**7. The Torres Strait Islands** (p. 450). Approximately 274 naturally and culturally rich islands form the link between Australia and Asia.

**8.** Abseiling and rock climbing at **Grampians National Park,** VIC (p. 636). Rock out at the 60m abseil over "The Ledge," or any of the multi-pitch climbs.

**9. Camel Safaris,** NT (p. 309). Traverse the red center between two furry humps.

**10. WOMADelaide,** SA (p. 471). Enjoy the sounds of one of the world's largest and most diverse music festivals.

# DIVING

Whether you're a seasoned scuba diver or a determined beginner, you probably have "see the Great Barrier Reef" on your list of things to do in your lifetime. And for good reason—off the coast of Queensland, this 2000km reef system encompasses hundreds of islands, cays, and thousands of smaller coral reefs, all of which amount to a quintessential collection of Australian wildlife and natural beauty. Most choose to venture out from **Cairns** (p. 417), the main gateway to the reef. Farther south near **Townsville** (p. 403), the sunken SS Yongala is among the best wreck dives in the world. **Airlie Beach** (p. 395), considered the "heart of the Great Barrier Reef" by many visitors, draws backpackers ready to leave the bars for the thrill of the spectacular sights off-shore. Most of Australia's other coasts have good diving spots as well. In New South Wales, the diving in **Bateman's Bay** (p. 234) and **Coffs Harbour** (p. 200) is spectacular and highly accessible. In South Australia, **Innes National Park** (p. 508) provides access to the Southern Ocean's depths. In Western Australia, giant whale sharks patrol Ningaloo Reef in **Exmouth** (p. 742), making for an exhilarating dive among the largest fish in the world. The cheapest diving certification courses can be found in Queensland at **Hervey Bay** (p. 370), **Bundaberg** (p. 380), and **Magnetic Island** (p. 408). For additional diving information, see the **Great Barrier Reef** (p. 315).

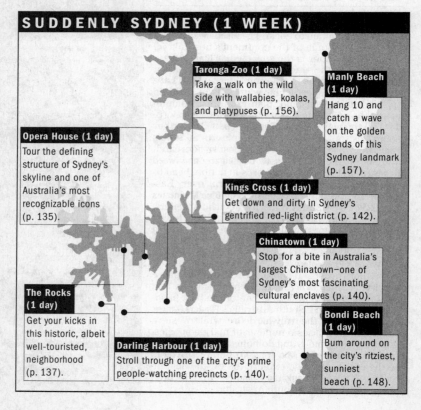

## SUDDENLY SYDNEY (1 WEEK)

**Taronga Zoo (1 day)**
Take a walk on the wild side with wallabies, koalas, and platypuses (p. 156).

**Manly Beach (1 day)**
Hang 10 and catch a wave on the golden sands of this Sydney landmark (p. 157).

**Opera House (1 day)**
Tour the defining structure of Sydney's skyline and one of Australia's most recognizable icons (p. 135).

**Kings Cross (1 day)**
Get down and dirty in Sydney's gentrified red-light district (p. 142).

**Chinatown (1 day)**
Stop for a bite in Australia's largest Chinatown—one of Sydney's most fascinating cultural enclaves (p. 140).

**The Rocks (1 day)**
Get your kicks in this historic, albeit well-touristed, neighborhood (p. 137).

**Darling Harbour (1 day)**
Stroll through one of the city's prime people-watching precincts (p. 140).

**Bondi Beach (1 day)**
Bum around on the city's ritziest, sunniest beach (p. 148).

# ABORIGINAL CULTURE

Indigenous cultures traditionally believe in a strong connection between the earth and its inhabitants. During the Dreaming, spirits are believed to have carved the canyons and gorges that contribute to Australia's amazing landscape and come to life as animals and trees. In New South Wales, **Mungo National Park** (p. 264) records the earliest Indigenous presence. Sacred regions and timeless rock art sites can be found everywhere from **Tasmania** (p. 532) to **Kakadu National Park** (p. 275) in the Northern Territory's Top End. **Tjapukai** (p. 428) near Cairns, the **Brambuk Centre** (p. 638) in Grampians National Park, and **Warradjan Aboriginal Cultural Centre** (p. 285) in Kakadu National Park attempt to present accurate representations of "Dreaming" stories and European interaction with Indigenous Australians. Modern Aboriginal art can be found in small galleries in many larger cities, but the National Gallery of Australia in **Canberra** (p. 96) has the continent's best collection; it should definitely be enough to please any visitor with an interest in art or the history of a captivating culture.

# CITY SIGHTS

Australia's cosmopolitan meccas are enticing enough to lure travelers away from the rugged beauty of the Outback. Multicultural **Sydney** (p. 110) enjoys a relaxed lifestyle while maintaining the excitement of a global center. **Melbourne** (p. 570) offers style and genteel grandeur—incredible nightlife, a thriving social cafe scene, incredible budget food options, and a sports-loving culture unmatched anywhere else in the world. Meticulously planned **Canberra** (p. 96) offers visitors insight into the heart of Australian government. Charming and historic **Hobart** (p. 534) is Tasmania's vibrant capital at the foot of Mt. Wellington. **Adelaide** (p. 459), though it moves at a slower pace, enjoys a monopoly on the tourist attractions of some of South Australia's most breathtaking coastline. **Perth** (p. 684) and **Darwin** (p. 267) have relaxed coastal stretches and hopping nightlife on the Western and Northern edges of the country.

## LET'S GO PICKS

**BEST VIEW:** Magnificent **Sydney Harbour, NSW** (p. 135), from the top of the Harbour Bridge, or the pristine **Franklin River, TAS** (p. 553) in a white-water raft.

**BEST PLACE TO SHOUT YOURSELF SILLY:** An Aussie Rules Football game at the **Melborne Cricket Ground, VIC** (p. 583), or by testing the astounding acoustics of **Jenolan Caves, NSW** (p. 176).

**BEST PLACE TO GET A BITE:** The land of wine and honey in **Mudgee, NSW** (p. 252), or with a shark at **Scuba World,** in **Mooloolaba Harbour, QLD** (p. 360).

**BEST UNDERGROUND SCENE:** Subterranean town **Coober Pedy, SA** (p. 519), or the artsy highlights of the **Adelaide Fringe Festival, SA** (p. 768).

**BEST PLACE FOR DREAMING:** Under the stars along the **Gibb River Road, WA** (p. 762), or in the Aboriginal art galleries of **Kakadu National Park, NT** (p. 275).

**MOST UNDERRATED: South Coast, NSW** (p. 227), **Perth, WA** (p. 684), or **Tasmania** (p. 532).

**BEST PLACE TO PONDER YOUR INSIGNIFICANCE:** The emptiness of the **Nullarbor Plain, SA** (p. 530), or the bustling **Great Barrier Reef, QLD** (p. 315).

**BEST PLACE TO GET WRECKED:** At one of the top 10 wreck dives in the world, the **SS Yongala,** off **Townsville, QLD** (p. 406), or for free in the vineyards of the **Hunter Valley, NSW** (p. 177).

**BEST PLACE TO ROCK OUT:** The amazing formations of **Devil's Marbles, NT** (p. 298), or Sydney's annual **Telstra Country Music Festival, NSW** (p. 225).

**BEST PLACE TO GET FRIED:** On the sunbaked shores of Sydney's **Manly Beach, NSW** (p. 129), or enjoying the famous fish and chips at Port Stephens' **John Dory's Seafoods, NSW** (p. 188).

# MIDDLE OF THE ROAD (6 WEEKS)

**Kakadu NP (5 days)**
Return to nature and explore the diversity of one of Australia's most deservedly famous parks (p. 275).

**Darwin (5 days)**
Get in one last party while visiting the capital of the rough-and-tumble Northern Territory (p. 267).

**Alice Springs (5 days)**
Stock up on supplies in this touristy outpost before delving into the dust of the Outback (p. 298).

**Uluru (5 days)**
Drop your jaw in awe in front of one of the world's most majestic natural wonders (p. 311).

**Flinders Ranges (5 days)**
Clamber around South Australia's largest and most beautiful mountain range (p. 509).

**Coober Pedy (5 days)**
Go underground in the tiny but fascinating opal city of the world (p. 519).

**Adelaide (5 days)**
Get clean in the low-key, urbane capital of South Australia (p. 459).

**Kangaroo Island (5 days)**
Hop across the Investigator Street and onto one of Australia's most thrilling tourist destinations (p. 481).

**Barossa Valley (5 days)**
Sip the country's finest wines in some of the world's most-celebrated vineyards (p. 490).

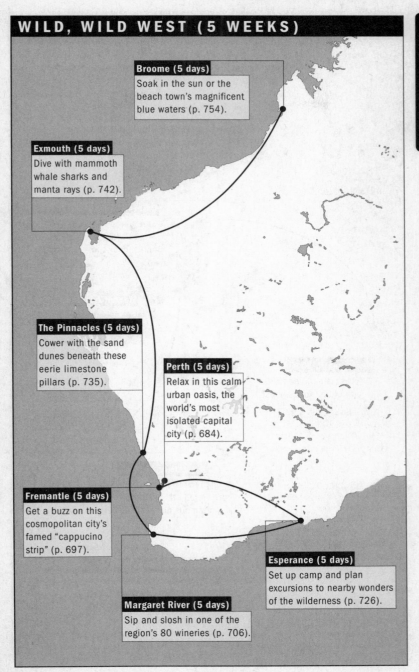

# WILD, WILD WEST (5 WEEKS)

**Broome (5 days)**
Soak in the sun or the
beach town's magnificent
blue waters (p. 754).

**Exmouth (5 days)**
Dive with mammoth
whale sharks and
manta rays (p. 742).

**The Pinnacles (5 days)**
Cower with the sand
dunes beneath these
eerie limestone
pillars (p. 735).

**Perth (5 days)**
Relax in this calm
urban oasis, the
world's most
isolated capital
city (p. 684).

**Fremantle (5 days)**
Get a buzz on this
cosmopolitan city's
famed "cappucino
strip" (p. 697).

**Esperance (5 days)**
Set up camp and plan
excursions to nearby wonders
of the wilderness (p. 726).

**Margaret River (5 days)**
Sip and slosh in one of the
region's 80 wineries (p. 706).

DISCOVER

# QUEENSLAND QUICKIE (4 WEEKS)

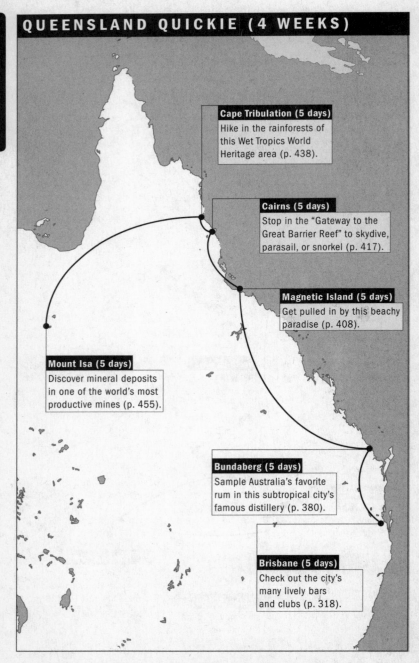

**Cape Tribulation (5 days)**
Hike in the rainforests of this Wet Tropics World Heritage area (p. 438).

**Cairns (5 days)**
Stop in the "Gateway to the Great Barrier Reef" to skydive, parasail, or snorkel (p. 417).

**Magnetic Island (5 days)**
Get pulled in by this beachy paradise (p. 408).

**Mount Isa (5 days)**
Discover mineral deposits in one of the world's most productive mines (p. 455).

**Bundaberg (5 days)**
Sample Australia's favorite rum in this subtropical city's famous distillery (p. 380).

**Brisbane (5 days)**
Check out the city's many lively bars and clubs (p. 318).

# ESSENTIALS

## PLANNING YOUR TRIP

**ENTRANCE REQUIREMENTS**
**Passport** (p. 10). Required of all visitors.
**Visa** (p. 11). Required of all visitors except holders of Australian and New Zealand passports. Eligible short-term visitors may alternatively purchase an **ETA** (p. 11) or apply for a Sponsored Family Visitor Visa.
**Working Visa** (p. 11). Required of foreigners planning to work in Australia.
**Student Visa** (p. 11). Required of foreigners planning to study in Australia.
**Recommended Inoculations** (p. 20). Hepatitis B, Japanese Encephalitis (for Northern Australia and the Torres Strait Islands), rabies, and boosters for tetanus and measles.

## EMBASSIES AND CONSULATES

### AUSTRALIAN CONSULAR SERVICES ABROAD

The Australian consulate in each of the following countries provides information to foreign nationals on obtaining visas or applying for citizenship.

**Canada:** High Commission, Ste. 710, 50 O'Connor St., **Ottawa,** ON K1P 6L2 (☎+1-613-236-0841; www.canada.embassy.gov.au). Consulate-general, Ste. 1100 South Tower, 175 Bloor St., East, **Toronto,** ON M4W 3R8 (☎+1-416-323-1155). For general visa information, call the Australian visa service at 1-888-990-8888.

**Ireland:** Embassy, 7th fl., Fitzwilton House, Wilton Terr., **Dublin** (☎+01 664 5300; www.ireland.embassy.gov.au).

**New Zealand:** High Commission, 72-76 Hobson St., Thorndon, **Wellington** (☎+04 473 6411; www.newzealand.embassy.gov.au). Consulate-general: Level 7, PriceWaterHouseCoopers Tower, 186-194 Quay St., **Auckland** (☎+09 921 8800).

**UK:** High Commission, Australia House, The Strand, **London** WC 2B 4LA (☎+20 7379 4334; www.uk.embassy.gov.au). Consulate: Euro Business Centre, 21-23 Hill St., **Edinburgh** EH2 3JP (☎131 226 8161).

**US:** Embassy, 1601 Massachusetts Ave. NW, **Washington, DC** 20036 (☎+1-202-797-3000; www.usa.embassy.gov.au). Consulates-general: 150 E. 42nd St., 34th fl., **New York,** NY 10017 (☎+1-212-351-6500) and Century Plaza Towers, 31st fl., 2029 Century Park East, Century City, **Los Angeles,** CA 90067 (☎+1-310-229-2300). For general visa information, call the Australian visa service at 1-888-990-8888.

### CONSULAR SERVICES IN AUSTRALIA

In Australia, foreign consulates can help their citizens obtain, renew, or replace a passport, or at least provide temporary travel papers to citizens who have lost their passport. They also provide information about money transfers, tax obligations when abroad, citizenship, travel cautions, and legal matters.

**Canada:** High Commission, Commonwealth Ave., **Canberra,** ACT 2600 (☎02 6270 4000; http://geo.international.gc.ca/asia/australia). Consulate-general: Level 5, 111 Harrington St., **Sydney,** NSW 2000 (☎02 9364 3000).

**Ireland:** Embassy, 20 Arkana St., Yarralumla, **Canberra,** ACT 2600 (☎02 6273 3022). Consulate-general: Level 26, 1 Market St., Sydney, NSW 2000 (☎02 9264 9635).

**New Zealand:** High Commission, Commonwealth Ave., **Canberra,** ACT 2600 (☎02 6270 4211; www.nzembassy.com/australia). Consulate-General: Level 10, 55 Hunter St., **Sydney,** NSW 2000 (☎02 8256 2000).

**UK:** High Commission, Commonwealth Ave., Yarralumla, **Canberra,** ACT 2600 (☎02 6270 6666; www.britaus.net). Consulates-General: The Gateway, Level 16, 1 Macquarie Pl., **Sydney,** NSW 2000 (☎02 9247 7521); 17th fl., 90 Collins St., **Melbourne,** VIC 3000 (☎03 9652 1670).

**US:** Embassy, Moonah Pl., Yarralumla, **Canberra,** ACT 2600 (☎02 6214 5600; http://canberra.usembassy.gov). Consulates-General: MLC Centre, Level 59, 19-29 Martin Pl., **Sydney,** NSW 2000 (☎02 9373 9200; http://sydney.usconsulate.gov); 553 St. Kilda Rd., **Melbourne,** VIC 3004 (☎03 9526 5900 http://melbourne.usconsulate.gov).

## TOURIST OFFICES

Government-backed **Tourism Australia** has an easy job: luring travelers to Australia. The organization's websites (www.australia.com; www.tourism.australia.com) and informational handouts provide tourists with a number of resources; more information is available from these office affiliates:

**Australia:** Darling Park, Tower 2, Level 18, 201 Sussex St., **Sydney,** NSW 2000 (☎02 9360 1111).

**Canada:** 111 Peter St., Ste. 630, **Toronto,** ON M5V 2H1 (☎+1-416-408-0549).

**New Zealand:** Level 3, 125 The Strand, Parnell, **Auckland** (☎+1 09 915 2826).

**United Kingdom:** Australia Centre, Australia House, 6th fl., Melbourne Place/Strand, **London** WC2B 4LG (☎+20 7438 4601).

**US:** 6100 Center Dr., Ste. 1150, **Los Angeles,** CA 90045 (☎+1-310-695-3200).

# DOCUMENTS AND FORMALITIES

## PASSPORTS

### REQUIREMENTS

Travelers need valid **passports** to enter Australia and to re-enter their home countries. Entrance to the country is not allowed if the holder's passport expires within six months of entry; returning home with an expired passport is illegal and may result in a fine.

### NEW PASSPORTS

Citizens of Australia, Canada, Ireland, New Zealand, the UK, and the US can apply for a passport at any passport office or at selected post offices and courts of law. Citizens of these countries may also download passport applications from the website of their country's government or passport office. In the US, new passport or renewal applications must be filed well in advance of the departure date, though most passport offices offer rush services for a very steep fee. Note, however, that "rushed" passports still take several weeks to arrive. In certain cases, making appointments and visiting passport offices in person can hasten the application process.

## PASSPORT MAINTENANCE

Photocopy the page of your passport with your photo as well as your visas, traveler's check serial numbers, and any other important documents. Carry one set of copies in a safe place, apart from the originals, and leave another set at home. Consulates also recommend you carry an expired passport or an official copy of your birth certificate in your luggage separate from other documents. If you lose your passport, immediately notify the local police and your home country's nearest embassy or consulate. To expedite its replacement, you must show ID and proof of citizenship; it also helps to know all information previously recorded in the passport. In some cases, a replacement may take weeks to process, and it may be valid only for a limited time. Any visas stamped in your old passport will be lost forever. In an emergency, ask for immediate temporary traveling papers that will permit you to re-enter your home country.

# VISAS, INVITATIONS, AND WORK PERMITS

## VISAS

Do not purchase your plane ticket before you have acquired a visa or an **Electronic Travel Authority (ETA).** Australia requires all visitors except Australian citizens and New Zealand passport holders to have a visa. If you are a citizen of one of 32 approved countries, including the US, the UK, Canada, and Ireland (see www.immi.gov.au/eta/countries.htm for the full list), you can obtain an ETA ($20) while purchasing your ticket at a travel agency, airport ticket counter, or online (www.eta.immi.gov.au). Quick and simple, the electronic ETA replaces a standard visa, allowing multiple visits within a one-year period provided that no single trip lasts longer than three months. An ETA is for tourist purposes; it doesn't replace a work visa. Travelers are encouraged to plan well ahead rather than attempt to obtain a new or extended ETA when in Australia. To extend a visit beyond the normal three-month period or to obtain a work visa, contact the **Department of Immigration and Citizenship** (www.immi.gov.au) in Australia before the end of your three-month stay.

Standard visa cost varies; the Department of Immigration requests that travelers consult form 990i (www.immi.gov.au/allforms/990i.htm) for a fee schedule. North Americans can also call the Australian embassy in the US (☎+1-888 -990-8888) with visa queries. Visa processing times average three weeks (when arranged by mail and in person), but can be highly variable.

Standard short-stay visas (under 3 months) and long-stay visas (between 3 and 6 months, extendable to a year) may be obtained from the nearest Australian high commission, embassy, or consulate. Visa extensions are not always possible. When they are, they come with a fee which varies depending on length of stay and type of visa. Contact the nearest Department of Immigration and Citizenship office before your stay period expires (go to www.immi.gov. au/contacts to find the relevant contact information). Otherwise, get in touch with an Australian consulate or embassy (p. 9).

US citizens can take advantage of the **Center for International Business and Travel** (CIBT; ☎+1-800-929-2428; www.us.cibt.com), which secures visas for travel to most countries for a variable service charge.

Be sure to double-check on entrance requirements at the nearest Australian embassy or consulate for up-to-date information before your departure. US citizens can also consult www.travel.state.gov.

## WORK PERMITS

Admission as a visitor does not include the right to work, which is authorized only by a work permit. Work permits can be obtained from the Australian embassy. For more information, see **Beyond Tourism** (p. 81).

# IDENTIFICATION

When you travel, always **carry at least two forms of identification** on your person, such as a passport, driver's license, or birth certificate. At least one of these should be a photo ID. Never carry all of your IDs together; split them up in case of theft or loss, and keep photocopies of them in your luggage and at home.

## STUDENT, TEACHER, AND YOUTH IDENTIFICATION

The **International Student Identity Card (ISIC),** the most widely accepted form of student ID, provides discounts on some sights, accommodations, food, and transportation; access to a 24hr. emergency help line; and insurance benefits for US cardholders (see **Insurance**, p. 21). Applicants must be full-time secondary or post-secondary school students at least 12 years old. Because of the proliferation of fake ISICs, some services (particularly airlines) require additional proof of student identity.

The **International Teacher Identity Card (ITIC)** offers teachers the same insurance coverage as the ISIC and similar but limited discounts. To qualify for the card, teachers must be currently employed and have worked a minimum of 18hr. per week for at least one school year. For travelers who are under 26 years old but are not full-time students, the **International Youth Travel Card (IYTC)** also offers many of the same benefits as the ISIC.

Each of these identity cards costs US$22. ISICs, ITICs, and IYTCs are valid for one year from the date of issue. To learn more about ISICs, ITICs, and IYTCs, try www.myisic.com. Many **student travel agencies** (p. 26) issue the cards; for a list of issuing agencies or more information, see the **International Student Travel Confederation (ISTC)** website (www.istc.org).

The **International Student Exchange Card (ISE Card)** is a similar identification card that is available to students, faculty, and children aged 12-26. The card provides discounts, medical benefits, access to a 24hr. emergency help line, and the ability to purchase student airfares. An ISE Card costs US$25; call ☎+1-800-255-8000 (in North America) or ☎+1-480-951-1177 (from elsewhere) for more information or visit www.isecard.com.

# CUSTOMS

Upon entering Australia, you must declare certain items from abroad and pay a duty on the value of those articles if they exceed the allowance established by Australia's customs service. Goods and gifts purchased at duty-free shops abroad are not exempt from duty or sales tax; "duty-free" merely means that you need not pay a tax in the country of purchase. Upon returning home, you must likewise declare all articles acquired abroad and pay a duty on the value of articles above your home country's allowance. In order to expedite your return, make a list of valuables brought from home and register them with customs before traveling abroad. Keep the receipts for goods acquired abroad.

Articles not automatically forbidden but subject to a possible **quarantine inspection** upon arrival may include camping equipment, live animals, food, animal and plant products, plants, and protected wildlife. Don't risk large fines or hassles when entering Australia—throw questionable items in the customs bins as you leave the plane, or at least declare them. The beagles in red smocks—members of the Australian Quarantine and Inspection Service (AQIS) Beagle Brigade—know their stuff and will sniff you out.

If you must bring your pets with you, contact AQIS (☎02 6272 3933; www. daff.gov.au/aqis) to obtain a permit. Visitors over 18 may bring into Australia up to 2.25L of alcohol and 250 cigarettes (or 250g of tobacco) duty-free. For other goods, the allowance is $900 (for visitors over 18) or $450 (under 18). Upon returning home, you must declare articles acquired abroad and pay a duty on the value of articles above the allowance established by your country's customs service. Australia recently implemented a Tourist Refund Scheme (TRS) refunding the Goods and Services Tax (GST) on items bought in Australia (see **Taxes,** p. 16). For more information on customs requirements, contact the **Australian Customs Service** (☎1300 363 263 or 02 6275 6666; www.customs.gov.au).

# MONEY

## CURRENCY AND EXCHANGE

The currency chart below is based on August 2008 exchange rates between Australian dollars (AUS$) and Canadian dollars (CDN$), European Union euro (EUR€), New Zealand dollars (NZ$), British pounds (UK£), and US dollars (US$). Check the currency converter on websites like www.xe.com or www.bloomberg.com for the latest exchange rates.

| CURRENCY | | |
|---|---|---|
| CDN$ = AUS$1.05 | | AUS$ = CDN$0.95 |
| EUR€ = AUS$1.70 | | AUS$ = EUR€0.59 |
| NZ$ = AUS$0.79 | | AUS$ = NZ$1.27 |
| UK£ = AUS$2.14 | | AUS$ = UK£0.47 |
| US$ = AUS$1.10 | | AUS$ = US$0.91 |

Australia's currency is **Australian dollars** ($) and **cents** (¢). Notes come in $5, $10, $20, $50, and $100 bills, and coins in 5¢, 10¢, 20¢, 50¢, $1, and $2 denominations. Credit cards are widely accepted in cities; in rural areas it's a good idea to carry cash. Personal checks are rarely accepted, and even traveler's checks may not be accepted in some locations.

 **IT'S NOT ABOUT THE BENJAMINS.** Unless otherwise noted, assume that all prices in this book are in Australian dollars.

As a general rule, it's cheaper to convert money in Australia than at home. While currency exchange will probably be available in your arrival airport, it's wise to bring enough foreign currency to last for at least 24-72hr.

When changing money abroad, try to go only to banks or bureaux de change that have at most a 5% margin between their buy and sell prices. Since you lose money with every transaction, it makes sense to convert large sums at a time (unless the currency is depreciating rapidly).

If you use traveler's checks or bills, carry some in small denominations (the equivalent of US$50 or less) in case you're forced to exchange money at poor rates, but bring a range of denominations since charges may be applied per

## TOP 10 WAYS TO SAVE IN AUSTRALIA

Australia is a backpacker paradise, and with some planning—and a touch of innovation—it's not hard to live within a budget. You won't even have to sacrifice food, fun, or fantastic experiences; use these tips to go wild without burning a hole in your pocket.

1. Buy food at markets and grocery stores instead of restaurants; try the Fremantle markets for Aussie oddities and groceries at rock-bottom prices.
2. Design your own bus pass, tailored to your itinerary, with Greyhound Australia.
3. Score a seasonal fruit picking job to offset travel costs.
4. Inquire at restaurants about backpacker specials or discounts affiliated with your hostel.
5. Take public transportation or walk as much as possible.
6. Find free Internet access in libraries and tourist offices.
7. If possible, avoid the ensuite double and opt for free bush-camping instead.
8. Build more outdoors experiences into your itinerary. (Brisbane, for example, is particularly stunning when viewed at the summit of Mount Coot-tha.)
9. Head to the show early and snap up student rush tickets at the Sydney Opera House
10. Work at your hostel part-time in exchange for accommodation.

check cashed. Store money in different forms. At any given time, you should be carrying some cash, some traveler's checks, and an ATM and/or credit card. All travelers should also consider carrying some US dollars (about US$50 worth), which are often preferred by local tellers.

# TRAVELER'S CHECKS

Traveler's checks are one of the safest means of carrying funds and are generally accepted in metropolitan areas of Australia. **American Express** and **Visa** are the most-recognized brands. Many banks and agencies sell them for a small commission. Check issuers provide refunds if the checks are lost or stolen, and many provide additional services, such as toll-free refund hotlines abroad, emergency message services, and stolen credit card assistance. Ask about toll-free refund hotlines and the location of refund centers when purchasing checks, and always carry emergency cash.

**American Express:** Checks available with commission at select banks, at all AmEx offices, and online (www.americanexpress.com). American Express cardholders can also purchase checks by phone (☎+1-800-528-4800). Checks available in Australian, British, Canadian, European, Japanese, and US currencies, among others. AmEx also offers the Travelers Cheque Card, a prepaid reloadable card. Cheques for Two can be signed by either of 2 people traveling together. For purchase locations or more information, contact AmEx's service centers: in Australia ☎02 9271 8666, in New Zealand +64 9 367 4567, in the UK +44 1273 696 933, in the US and Canada +1-800-221-7282; elsewhere, call the US collect at +1-336-393-1111.

**Travelex:** Visa TravelMoney prepaid cash card and Visa traveler's checks available. For info about Thomas Cook MasterCard in Canada and the US, call ☎+1-800-223-7373, in the UK +44 0800 622 101; elsewhere, call the UK collect at +44 1733 318 950. For information about Interpayment Visa in the US and Canada, call ☎+1-800-732-1322, in the UK +44 0800 515 884; elsewhere, call the UK collect at +44 1733 318 949. For more information, visit www.travelex.com.

**Visa:** Checks available (generally with a commission) at banks worldwide. For the location of the nearest office, call the Visa Travelers Cheque Global Refund and Assistance Center: in the UK ☎+44 0800 895 078, in the US +1-800-227-6811; elsewhere, call the UK collect at +44 2079 378 091. Checks are available in British, Canadian, European, Japanese, and US currencies, as well as a number of others. Visa also offers TravelMoney, a prepaid debit card that can be reloaded online or by phone. For more information on travel services offered by Visa, see http://usa.visa.com/personal/using_visa/travel_with_visa.html.

# CREDIT, DEBIT, AND ATM CARDS

Credit cards are accepted at most locations in Australia, though particularly small or rural accommodations, restaurants, and businesses may only accept cash. Credit cards should be used as often as possible, as they offer superior exchange rates—up to 5% better than the retail rate used by banks and other currency exchange establishments. Credit cards may also offer services such as insurance or emergency help, and are sometimes necessary to reserve hotel rooms or rental cars. **MasterCard** and **Visa** are most often welcomed; **American Express** cards work at some ATMs and at AmEx offices in large Australian cities and airports. Discover is generally not accepted in Australia.

The use of ATM cards is widespread in Australia. Depending on the system that your home bank uses, you can most likely access your personal bank account from abroad. ATMs get the same wholesale exchange rate as credit cards, but there is often a limit on the amount of money you can withdraw per day (around US$500). There is typically a surcharge of US$1-5 per withdrawal, unless explicitly stated otherwise.

Most ATMs charge a transaction fee paid to the bank that owns the ATM. However, **Bank of America** cards are accepted, with no fees, by Westpac ATMs in Australia. **Cirrus** (US ☎+1-800-424-7787; www.mastercard.com) is the most widespread ATM network in Australia; **PLUS** (US ☎+1-800-843-7587; www.visa.com) is almost as frequent, and **Visa,** though probably third best, is still fairly common. MasterCard and American Express are found less often and NYCE not at all. Though ATMs are increasingly prevalent in smaller towns and rural areas, they are scarce in northwestern Australia and remote interior areas.

**Debit cards** are as convenient as credit cards but have a more immediate impact on your funds. A debit card can be used wherever its associated credit card company (usually MasterCard or Visa) is accepted, and the money is withdrawn directly from the holder's checking account. Debit cards often also function as ATM cards and can be used to withdraw cash from associated banks and ATMs throughout Australia. Check with your credit card company to see if your credit card can also function as an ATM card. While in Australia, you might see references to **Electronic Funds Transfer at Point Of Sale (EFTPOS),** which works like a debit card and is a way in which Australians pay for goods.

# GETTING MONEY FROM HOME

If you run out of money while traveling, the easiest, cheapest solution is to have someone back home make a deposit to your bank account. Otherwise, consider one of the following options.

## WIRING MONEY

It is possible to arrange a **bank money transfer,** which means asking a bank back home to wire money to a bank in Australia. This is the cheapest way to transfer cash, but it's also the slowest, usually taking several days or more. Note that some banks may only release your funds in local currency, potentially sticking you with a poor exchange rate; inquire about this in advance. Money transfer services like **Western Union** are faster and more convenient than bank transfers—but also much pricier. Western Union has many locations worldwide. To find one, visit www.westernunion.com, or call in Australia ☎1800 173 833, in Canada and the US +1-800-325-6000, or in the UK +44 0800 833 833. To wire money using a credit card (Discover, MasterCard, Visa), call in Canada and the

US ☎ +1-800-CALL-CASH, in the UK +44 0800 833 833. Money transfers are also available to **American Express** cardholders and at selected **Thomas Cook** offices.

## US STATE DEPARTMENT (US CITIZENS ONLY)

In serious emergencies only, the US State Department will forward money within hours to the nearest consular office, which will then disburse it according to instructions for a US$30 fee. If you wish to use this service, you must contact the Overseas Citizens Services division of the US State Department (☎ +1-202-501-4444, from US +1-888-407-4747).

# COSTS

The cost of your trip will vary considerably, depending on where you go, when you leave, how you travel, and where you stay. The most significant expenses will probably be your round-trip (return) **airfare** to Australia (see **Getting to Australia,** p. 25). Before you go, calculate a reasonable **daily budget.**

## STAYING ON A BUDGET

A bare-bones day in Australia (camping or sleeping in hostels or guesthouses, buying food at supermarkets) costs about $50; a slightly more comfortable day (sleeping in hostels, guesthouses, or the occasional budget hotel, eating one meal per day at a restaurant, sightseeing, going out at night) costs about $70; and for a luxurious day, the sky's the limit. Don't forget to factor in emergency reserve funds (at least $200) when planning how much money you'll need.

## TIPS FOR SAVING MONEY

Some simple ways to keep cash include searching out opportunities for free entertainment, splitting accommodation and food costs with trustworthy fellow travelers, and buying food in supermarkets rather than eating out. Bring a **sleepsack** to save on sheet charges in hostels and do your **laundry** in the sink (unless you're explicitly prohibited from doing so). Museums often have days when admission is free; plan accordingly. Consider getting an ISIC or an IYTC if you're eligible for either; many sights and museums offer reduced admission to students and youths. For fast travel, bikes are an economical option; renting one is cheaper than renting a moped or scooter. But don't forget about walking; you can learn a lot about a city by seeing it on foot. Drinking at bars quickly becomes expensive; it's cheaper to buy alcohol and imbibe before going out. That said, don't go overboard. Though staying within your budget is important, don't do so at the expense of your health or travel experience.

# TIPPING

In Australia, tipping is not expected at restaurants, bars, taxis, or hotels, since service workers do not rely on tips for income. Tips are occasionally left at restaurants—especially fancier ones—when the service is exceptional. In this case, 10% is more than enough. Taxes are always included in the bill.

# TAXES

The New Tax System of 2000 provides for a **10% Goods and Services Tax (GST).** Some goods, such as basic foods and medicines, are not subject to this tax. However, the System also implemented a **Tourist Refund Scheme (TRS),** which may entitle tourists to a refund of the GST and of the **Wine Equalisation Tax (WET)** on purchases of goods bought from Australian retailers. The refund is good for GST or WET paid on purchases of $300 or more. Travelers can claim the refund at TRS booths in international airport terminals by presenting tax receipts from retailers, a valid passport, proof of travel, and the items themselves. See the Australian Customs Service website for details (www.customs.gov.au).

# PACKING

**Pack lightly:** Lay out only what you need, then take half the clothes and twice the money. Save extra space for souvenirs or other items that you might collect along the way. The **Travelite FAQ** (www.travelite.org) is a good resource for tips on traveling light. The online **Universal Packing List** (http://upl.codeq.info) will generate a customized list of suggested items based on your trip length, the expected climate, your planned activities, and other factors. If you plan to do a lot of outdoor activities, consult **Great Outdoors,** (p. 63) and **Camping and Bushwalking** (p. 69). Some frequent travelers keep a bag packed with all the essentials: passport, money belt, hat, socks, etc. Then, when they decide to leave, they know they haven't forgotten anything.

**Luggage:** If you plan to travel mostly by foot, a **sturdy internal-frame backpack** is unbeatable. (For the basics on buying a pack, see p. 70.) Unless you are staying in the same place for a large chunk of time, a suitcase or trunk will be unwieldy. In addition to your main piece of luggage, a **daypack** (a small backpack or courier bag) is useful.

**Clothing:** No matter when you're traveling, it's always a good idea to bring a **warm jacket or sweater,** a **rain jacket** (Gore-Tex® is both waterproof and breathable), **sturdy shoes** or **hiking boots,** and **thick socks.** Flip-flops or waterproof sandals are must-haves for grubby hostel showers, and extra socks are always a good idea. If you plan to go to bars and clubs in any major cities, pack a nice outfit and pair of shoes—many city bars don't allow sneakers or flip-flops at night (no matter how chic they are), and many clubs have dress codes. If you plan to visit any religious or cultural sites, remember that you will need to wear modest, respectful dress. See **Outdoors Essentials** (p. 70) for more details on packing for the Australian Outback.

**Sleepsack:** Some hostels require that you either provide your own linen or rent sheets from them. Save cash by making your own sleepsack: fold a full-size sheet in half the long way, then sew it closed along the long side and one of the short sides. Keep in mind that some of the bigger hostels in large cities prohibit sleeping bags.

**Converters and Adapters:** In Australia, electricity is 230-240V AC, 50Hz, enough to fry any 120V North American appliance. Hardware stores sell adapters (to change the shape of the plug; US$5) and converters (to change the voltage; US$10-30). Don't make the mistake of using only an adapter without a converter (unless appliance instructions explicitly state otherwise). For more info, check out http://kropla.com/electric.htm.

**Toiletries:** Deodorant, razors, tampons, toothbrushes, and condoms are often available, but it may be difficult to find your preferred brand; bring extras. Bring enough pairs of **contact lenses and solution** for your entire trip. Also bring your glasses and a copy of your prescription in case you need emergency replacements.

**First-Aid Kit:** For a basic first-aid kit, pack bandages, pain relievers, antibiotic cream, a thermometer, a multifunction pocket knife, tweezers, moleskin, decongestant, motion-sickness remedy, diarrhea or upset-stomach medication (Pepto Bismol® or Imodium®), an antihistamine, insect repellent, sunscreen, and burn ointment.

**Film:** Film and developing in Australia are available. But if you don't want to bother with film, consider using a **digital camera.** Although it requires a steep initial investment, a digital camera means you never have to buy film again. Just be sure to bring along a large enough memory card and extra (or rechargeable) batteries. Another option is to bring a few disposable cameras. Despite disclaimers, airport security X-rays can fog film, so buy a lead-lined pouch at a camera store or ask security to hand-inspect it. Always pack film in your carry-on: higher-intensity X-rays are used on checked luggage.

**ESSENTIALS**

**Other Useful Items:** For safety purposes, you should bring a **money belt** and a small **padlock.** Basic **outdoors equipment** (plastic water bottle, compass, waterproof matches, pocket knife, sunglasses, sunscreen, hat) are highly recommended. Quick repairs of torn garments can be done on the road with a needle and thread; also consider bringing electrical tape for patching tears. If you want to do laundry by hand, bring detergent, a small rubber ball to stop up the sink, and string for a makeshift clothes line. Other things you're likely to forget include: a rain poncho or umbrella (check region-specific weather trends), **sealable plastic bags** (for damp clothes, soap, food, shampoo, and other spillables), an **alarm clock,** safety pins, rubber bands, a flashlight, earplugs, garbage bags, long pants and hiking boots that cover your ankles (if hiking in the bush), and a small calculator. A **cell phone** can be a lifesaver (literally) on the road; see p. 36 for info on acquiring one that will work in Australia.

**Important Documents:** Don't forget your passport, traveler's checks, ATM and/or credit cards, government-issued ID, proof of ETA or visa purchase, driver's license (if you plan to drive less than three months) or international driving permit (if you plan to drive in the same state for more than three months), and photocopies of all of the aforementioned documents in case they are lost or stolen.

# SAFETY AND HEALTH

## GENERAL ADVICE

In any type of crisis situation, the most important thing to do is **stay calm.** Your country's embassy abroad (p. 9) is usually your best resource in an emergency. Registering with that embassy upon arrival is often a good idea. The government offices listed in the **Travel Advisories** box (p. 19) can provide information on the services provided their citizens in case of emergencies abroad.

| **EMERGENCY** | In Australia, dial ☎ **000**, or **112** from cell phones. |
| --- | --- |

## LOCAL LAWS AND POLICE

Ignorance is not an excuse with regard to Australian laws, which strictly punish drug and alcohol abuse (see below). In addition to local police officers, **park rangers** are a staple of Australian law enforcement.

### DRUGS, ALCOHOL, AND TOBACCO

Australia has strict drug laws, distinguishing between users and traffickers. While Australia is debating whether to legalize marijuana, the drug is currently illegal. Drivers may be asked to perform random saliva tests to detect drugs. If you carry **prescription drugs,** take a copy of the prescription with you.

There are very strict **drunk-driving** (or "drink-driving," as Aussies say) laws in effect all over the country. Random breath-testing is common. While road laws vary between different regions, the maximum legal blood-alcohol limit is 0.05% (the maximum limit for holders of learner or provisional licenses is 0% in most regions). Drunk-driving offenses may result in the cancellation of your license. You must be 18 or older to purchase alcohol or consume it in public. It's illegal to sell or give alcohol to a minor. Some public areas prohibit alcohol possession and consumption; obey any signs and postings.

**Smoking** is prohibited in nearly all enclosed public places in Australia, but smoking bans vary between states and territories.

# SPECIFIC CONCERNS

## NATURAL DISASTERS

**BUSHFIRES.** The threat of bushfire is a serious problem—especially in Western Australia—between May and September. Though Western Australia is particularly susceptible, most other areas are historically also affected. Fire-friendly conditions include low relative humidity, high wind, and low rainfall. Check out http://australiasevereweather.com/fires for more information.

**CYCLONES.** Most Australian cyclones form off the northeast and northwest coasts. The two most commonly affected states are Queensland and Western Australia. Destructive cyclones can even close roads and highways, so always check road conditions before starting a long drive, especially during cyclone peak season (February and March). Find more info online with the Australian Government Bureau of Meteorology (www.bom.gov.au/weather).

## TERRORISM

While Australian tourists in Indonesia have recently been targeted by terrorist attacks, there are currently no known terrorist threats to travelers in Oz.

**TRAVEL ADVISORIES.** The following government offices provide travel information and advisories by telephone, by fax, or via the web:

**Australian Department of Foreign Affairs and Trade:** ☎02 6261 1111; www.dfat.gov.au.

**Canadian Department of Foreign Affairs and International Trade (DFAIT):** ☎1800-267-8376; www.dfait-maeci.gc.ca. Call for their free booklet, *Bon Voyage...But.*

**New Zealand Ministry of Foreign Affairs:** ☎+64 4 439 8000; www.mfat.govt.nz/.

**United Kingdom Foreign and Commonwealth Office:** ☎+20 7008 1500; www.fco.gov.uk.

**US Department of State:** ☎+1-202-501-4444; http://travel.state.gov. Visit the website for the booklet, *A Safe Trip Abroad.*

# PERSONAL SAFETY

## EXPLORING AND TRAVELING

To avoid unwanted attention, try to blend in as much as possible. Respecting local customs may ward off would-be hecklers. Familiarize yourself with your surroundings before setting out and carry yourself with confidence. Check maps in shops and restaurants rather than on the street. If you are traveling alone, be sure someone at home knows your itinerary and never tell anyone you meet that you're by yourself. When walking at night, stick to busy, well-lit streets and avoid dark alleyways. If you ever feel uncomfortable, leave the area as quickly and directly as you can. To get medical, police, or fire assistance, dial ☎000 anywhere in Australia, or ☎112 from cell phones.

There is no surefire way to avoid all the threatening situations that you might encounter while traveling, but a good **self-defense course** will give you concrete ways to react to unwanted advances. **Impact, Prepare,** and **Model Mugging** can refer you to local self-defense courses in Australia, Canada, Switzerland, and the US. Visit www.modelmugging.org for a list of nearby chapters.

If you are using a **car,** familiarize yourself with Australian driving signals and road signs. Always wear a seat belt. Children under 40 lb. should ride only in specially designed carseats, available for a small fee from most car rental agencies. Study route maps before you get behind the wheel, and if you plan on spending a lot of time on the road or driving in the Outback, always bring spare parts, food, and plenty of water. If your car breaks down, stay near it and wait for the police to assist you. For long drives in remote areas, invest in a RFDS-compatible radio, a cell phone (not guaranteed to work in remote areas), and a **roadside assistance program** (p. 33). In urban areas, park your vehicle in a garage or well-traveled area, and use a steering wheel locking device. See **Driving in the Outback** (p. 73) for more info. Sleeping in your car is the most dangerous way to get your rest. For the perils of **hitchhiking,** see p. 34.

## POSSESSIONS AND VALUABLES

Never leave your belongings unattended; crime occurs in even the safest hostels and hotels. Bring your own padlock for hostel lockers, and don't ever store valuables in a locker. Be particularly careful on **buses** and **trains;** many thieves wait for travelers to fall asleep and then pilfer their belongings. Carry your bag or purse in front of you, where you can see it. When traveling with others, sleep in alternate shifts. When alone, use good judgment in selecting a train compartment: never stay in an empty one, and use a lock to secure your pack to the luggage rack. Use extra caution if traveling at night or on overnight trains. Try to sleep on top bunks with your luggage above you (if not in bed with you), and keep important documents and valuables on your person at all times.

There are a few steps you can take to minimize the financial risks associated with traveling. First, **bring as little with you as possible.** Second, **buy a few combination padlocks** to secure your belongings either in your pack or in a hostel or train station locker. Third, **carry as little cash as possible.** Keep your traveler's checks, ATM card, and credit cards in a money belt—not a "fanny pack"—along with your passport and ID cards. Fourth, **keep a small cash reserve separate from your primary stash.** This should be about $50 sewn into or stored in the depths of your pack. This is also an ideal location for your traveler's check numbers and photocopies of your passport, birth certificate, and other important documents.

In large cities, **con artists** often work in groups and may involve children. Beware of certain classics: sob stories that require money, rolls of bills "found" on the street, mustard spilled (or saliva spit) onto your shoulder to distract you while they snatch your bag. **Never let your passport or your bags out of your sight.** Hostel workers will sometimes stand at bus and train-station arrival points to recruit tired and disoriented travelers to their hostels; never believe strangers who tell you that theirs is the only hostel open. Beware of **pickpockets** in city crowds, especially on public transportation. Also, be alert in public telephone booths: if you must say your calling card number, do so very quietly; if you punch it in, make sure no one can look over your shoulder.

If you will be traveling with electronic devices, such as a laptop computer or a PDA, check whether your homeowner's insurance covers loss, theft, or damage when you travel. For more information, see **Insurance** (p. 21).

## PRE-DEPARTURE HEALTH

In your passport, write the names of anyone who should be contacted in case of a medical emergency, and list your allergies or medical conditions. Matching a prescription to an Australian equivalent isn't always easy; if you take prescription drugs, carry up-to-date, legible prescriptions or a statement from your doctor with the medication's trade name, manufacturer, chemical name, and dosage. While traveling, keep all medication with you in your carry-on. For tips on packing a basic **first-aid kit** and other essentials, see p. 17.

## IMMUNIZATIONS AND PRECAUTIONS

The Australian government recommends that travelers over two years of age have the following vaccines up to date: MMR (for measles, mumps, and rubella); DTaP or Td (for diphtheria, tetanus, and pertussis); IPV (for polio); Hib (for haemophilus influenza B); and HepB (for Hepatitis B). Flu shots are recommended for those visiting Australia between May and October. Vaccinations are not required unless you have visited a yellow fever-infected zone within six days prior to arrival. (See www.health.gov.au/pubhlth/strateg/communic/factsheets/yellow.htm for information.) For recommendations on immunizations and prophylaxis, consult your doctor or the **Centers for Disease Control and Prevention** (CDC; p. 22) in the US or the equivalent in your home country.

## INSURANCE

Travel insurance includes four basic coverage areas: **medical/health problems, property loss, trip cancellation/interruption,** and **emergency evacuation.** Though regular insurance policies sometimes extend to travel-related accidents, you may consider purchasing separate travel insurance if the cost of potential trip cancellation, interruption, or emergency medical evacuation is greater than you can absorb. Prices for travel insurance purchased separately generally run about US$50 per week for full coverage, while trip cancellation/interruption may be purchased separately for US$3-5 per day depending on length of stay.
**Medical insurance** (especially university policies) often covers costs incurred abroad; check with your provider. **US Medicare** does not cover foreign travel. Canadian provincial health insurance plans increasingly do not cover foreign travel; check with the provincial Ministry of Health or Health Plan Headquarters for details. Australia provides limited Medicare service in cases of "immediately necessary treatment" for nationals of the following countries (within certain time limits, and not applicable to visitors on student visas): Finland, Ireland, Italy, Malta, Netherlands, New Zealand, Norway, the UK, and Sweden (see www.medicareaustralia.gov.au for details).

  **Homeowners' insurance** (or your family's coverage) often covers theft during travel and loss of travel documents (passport, plane ticket, railpass, etc.) up to US$500. If you will be traveling with an electronic device (such as a computer or PDA) that is not covered by your homeowners' insurance, you might consider purchasing a low-cost separate insurance policy. **Safeware** (☎1800 800 1492; www.safeware.com) specializes in covering computers and charges $90 for 90-day comprehensive international travel coverage up to $4000.

  **ISIC** and **ITIC** (p. 12) provide basic insurance benefits to US cardholders, including US$100 per day of in-hospital sickness for up to 100 days and US$10,000 of accident-related medical insurance including $500 emergency dental coverage (see www.myisic.com for details). Cardholders have access to a toll-free 24hr. help line for medical, legal, and financial emergencies. **American Express** (☎+1-800-338-1670) grants most cardholders automatic collision and theft car rental insurance on rentals made with the card.

**ESSENTIALS**

### INSURANCE PROVIDERS

**STA** (p. 26) offers a range of plans to supplement your basic coverage. Other private insurance providers in the US and Canada include: **Access America** (☎+1-800-729-6021; www.accessamerica.com); **Berkely Group** (☎+1-800-797-4514; www.berkely.com); and **CSA Travel Protection** (☎+1-800-873-9855; www.csatravelprotection.com). Columbus Direct (☎+44 0870 033 9988; www.columbusdirect.co.uk) operates in the UK.

## USEFUL ORGANIZATIONS AND PUBLICATIONS

The American **Centers for Disease Control and Prevention (CDC)** maintains an international travelers' hotline and an informative website (☎+1-877-394-8747; www.cdc.gov/travel). Consult the appropriate government agency of your home country for consular information sheets on health, entry requirements, and other issues for various countries (see the listings in the box on **Travel Advisories,** p. 19). For quick information on health and other travel warnings, call the **Overseas Citizens Services** (from outside N. America ☎+1-202-501-4444, from US +1-888-407-4747; line open M-F 8am-8pm EST), or contact a passport agency, embassy, or consulate abroad. For information on medical evacuation services and travel insurance firms, see the US government's website at http://travel.state.gov/travel/abroad_health.html or the **British Foreign and Commonwealth Office** (www.fco.gov.uk). For general health information, contact the **American Red Cross** (☎+1-202-303-4498; www.redcross.org).

## STAYING HEALTHY

Common sense is the best prescription for good health while traveling. Drink plenty of fluids to prevent dehydration in the bright Australian sun, and always wear sturdy, broken-in shoes with clean socks. Be aware of special safety concerns associated with the Australian environment and wildlife. Remember: in the event of a serious illness or emergency, call ☎000 from any land line or ☎112 from a cell phone for the police, an ambulance, or the fire department.

## ONCE IN AUSTRALIA

### ENVIRONMENTAL HAZARDS

**Heat exhaustion and dehydration:** Heat exhaustion can be a serious concern in Australia, particularly in the Outback. Symptoms include nausea, excessive thirst, headaches, and dizziness. Avoid it by drinking plenty of fluids, eating salty foods (e.g., crackers), staying away from dehydrating beverages (e.g., alcohol and caffeinated drinks), and always wearing sunscreen. Also remember to always carry extra water in your car and, when hiking, on your person. Continuous heat stress can eventually lead to heatstroke, characterized by rising body temperature, severe headache, delirium, and failure to sweat. Victims should be cooled off with wet towels and taken to a doctor.

**Sunburn:** Australia has the highest rate of skin cancer in the world; about 8500 people are diagnosed with melanoma each year. Always wear sunscreen (SPF 30 or higher) when spending time outdoors. If you are planning on spending time near water, in the desert, or on long hikes, you are at a higher risk of getting burned, even through clouds. If you get sunburned, drink more fluids than usual and apply an aloe-based lotion. Severe sunburns can lead to sun poisoning, a condition that affects the entire body, causing fever, chills, nausea, and vomiting; it should be treated by a doctor.

**Hypothermia and frostbite:** A rapid drop in body temperature is the clearest sign of overexposure to cold. Victims may also shiver, feel exhausted, have poor coordination or slurred speech, hallucinate, or suffer amnesia. Do not let hypothermia victims fall asleep. To avoid hypothermia, keep dry, wear layers, and stay out of the wind. When the temperature is below freezing, watch out for frostbite. If skin turns white or blue, waxy, and cold, do not rub the area. Drink warm beverages, stay dry, and slowly warm the area with dry fabric or steady body contact until a doctor can be found.

**High altitude:** Give your body a couple of days to adjust to less oxygen before exerting yourself. Note that alcohol is more potent and UV rays are stronger at high elevations.

## INSECT-BORNE DISEASES

Many diseases are transmitted by insects—mainly mosquitoes, fleas, ticks, and lice. Be aware of insects in wet or forested areas, especially while hiking and camping; wear long pants and long sleeves, tuck your pants into your socks, and use a mosquito net. Use insect repellent and soak or spray your gear with permethrin (licensed in the US only for use on clothing). In especially bug-heavy areas, use a repellent that includes a small percentage of DEET. **Mosquitoes**—responsible for dengue fever, Australian encephalitis, Ross River virus, and Barmah Forest virus—can be particularly abundant in wet, swampy, or wooded areas like those found in national parks. **Ticks**—which can carry Lyme and other diseases—are particularly prevalent in rural and forested regions.

**Lyme disease:** A bacterial infection carried by ticks and marked by a circular bull's-eye rash of 2 in. or more. Later symptoms include fever, headache, fatigue, and aches and pains. Antibiotics are effective if administered early. Left untreated, Lyme can cause problems in joints, the heart, and the nervous system. If you find a tick attached to your skin, grasp the head with tweezers as close to your skin as possible and apply slow, steady traction. Removing a tick within 24hr. greatly reduces the risk of infection. Do not try to remove ticks with petroleum jelly, nail polish remover, or a hot match. Ticks usually inhabit moist, shaded environments and heavily wooded areas. If you are going to be hiking in these areas, wear long clothes and repellent with DEET.

## FOOD- AND WATER-BORNE DISEASES

Prevention is the best cure: be sure that your food is properly cooked and the water you drink is clean. If the region's tap water is known to be unsanitary, peel fruits and vegetables before eating them and avoid tap water (including ice cubes and anything washed in tap water, like salad). Watch out for food from markets or street vendors that may have been cooked in unhygienic conditions. Other culprits are raw shellfish, unpasteurized milk, and sauces containing raw eggs. Buy bottled water, or purify your own by bringing it to a rolling boil or treating it with iodine tablets; note, however, that some parasites have exteriors that resist iodine treatment, so boiling is more reliable. Always wash your hands before eating or use a quick-drying purifying liquid hand cleaner.

**Traveler's diarrhea:** Results from drinking fecally contaminated water or eating uncooked and contaminated foods. Symptoms include nausea, bloating, and urgency. Try quick-energy, non-sugary foods with protein and carbohydrates to keep your strength up. Over-the-counter anti-diarrheals (e.g., Imodium®) may counteract the problem. The most dangerous side effect is dehydration; drink 8 oz. of water with ½ tsp. of sugar or honey and a pinch of salt, try caffeine-free soft drinks, or eat salted crackers. If you develop a fever or your symptoms don't go away after 4-5 days, consult a doctor. Consult a doctor immediately for treatment of diarrhea in children.

**Dysentery:** Results from an intestinal infection caused by bacteria in contaminated food or water. Symptoms include bloody diarrhea, fever, and abdominal pain and tenderness. The most common type of dysentery generally only lasts a week, but it is highly contagious. Seek medical help immediately. Dysentery can be treated with the drugs norfloxacin or ciprofloxacin (commonly known as Cipro).

**Cholera:** An intestinal disease caused by bacteria in contaminated food. Symptoms include diarrhea, dehydration, vomiting, and muscle cramps. See a doctor immediately; if left untreated, cholera can be lethal within hours. Antibiotics are available, but the most important treatment is rehydration.

**Hepatitis A:** A viral infection of the liver acquired through contaminated water or shellfish from contaminated water. Symptoms include fatigue, fever, loss of appetite, nausea, dark urine, jaundice, vomiting, aches and pains, and light stools. The risk is highest in rural areas and the countryside, but it is also present in urban areas. Ask your doctor about the Hepatitis A vaccine or an injection of immune globulin.

**Giardiasis:** Transmitted through parasites and acquired by drinking untreated water from streams or lakes. Symptoms include diarrhea, cramps, bloating, fatigue, weight loss, and nausea. If untreated, it can lead to severe dehydration. Giardiasis occurs worldwide.

**Typhoid fever:** Caused by the salmonella bacteria; rare in Australia. While mostly transmitted through contaminated food and water, it may also be acquired by direct contact with another person. Early symptoms include high fever, headaches, fatigue, appetite loss, constipation, and a rash on the abdomen or chest. Antibiotics can treat typhoid, but a vaccination (70-90% effective) is recommended.

**Leptospirosis:** A bacterial disease caused by exposure to fresh water or soil contaminated by the urine of infected animals. Able to enter the human body through cut skin, mucus membranes, and ingestion, it is most common in tropical climates. Symptoms include a high fever, chills, nausea, and vomiting. If not treated it can lead to liver failure and meningitis. There is no vaccine; consult a doctor for treatment.

## OTHER INFECTIOUS DISEASES

The following diseases exist all over the world. Travelers should know how to recognize them and what to do if they suspect they have been infected.

**Hepatitis B:** A viral infection of the liver transmitted via blood or other bodily fluids. Symptoms, which may not surface until years after infection, include jaundice, appetite loss, fever, and joint pain. It is passed through unprotected sex and unclean needles. A 3-shot vaccination sequence is recommended for sexually-active travelers and anyone planning to seek medical treatment abroad; it must begin 6 months before traveling.

**Hepatitis C:** Like Hepatitis B, but transmitted differently. IV drug users, those with occupational exposure to blood, hemodialysis patients, and recipients of blood transfusions are at the highest risk, but the disease can also be spread through sexual contact or sharing items like razors and toothbrushes that may have traces of blood on them. No symptoms are usually exhibited. If untreated, Hepatitis C can lead to liver failure.

**AIDS and HIV:** For detailed information on Acquired Immune Deficiency Syndrome (AIDS) in Australia, call the US Centers for Disease Control's 24hr. hotline at ☎+1-800-342-2437. Note that Australia screens incoming travelers for AIDS, primarily those planning extended visits for work or study, and could deny entrance to those who test HIV-positive. Contact an **Australian consulate** (p. 9) for information.

**Sexually transmitted infections (STIs):** Gonorrhea, chlamydia, genital warts, syphilis, herpes, HPV, and other STIs are easier to catch than HIV and can be just as serious. Though condoms may protect you from some STIs, oral or even tactile contact can lead to transmission. If you think you may have contracted an STI, see a doctor immediately.

# OTHER HEALTH CONCERNS

### MEDICAL CARE ON THE ROAD

Most of Australia is covered by state emergency ambulance and hospital services; emergency medical care in rural Australia is provided by the **Royal Flying Doctor Service** (RFDS; www.flyingdoctor.net). If you plan on traveling in a remote area of Australia, see **Wilderness Safety** (p. 71) for general safety advice as well as specific information on remote communication devices.

If you are concerned about obtaining medical assistance while traveling, you may wish to employ special support services. The **MedPass** from **GlobalCare, Inc.** (☎+1-800-860-1111; www.globalcare.net) provides 24hr. international medical assistance, support, and medical evacuation resources. The **International Association for Medical Assistance to Travelers** (IAMAT; US ☎+1-716-754-4883, Canada 519-836-0102; www.iamat.org) has free membership, lists English-speaking doctors worldwide, and offers detailed info on immunization requirements and sanitation. If your regular insurance policy does not cover travel abroad, you may wish to purchase **additional coverage** (p. 21).

Those with medical conditions (such as diabetes, allergies to antibiotics, epilepsy, or heart conditions) may want to obtain a **MedicAlert** membership (US$40 per year), which includes among other things a stainless steel ID tag and a 24hr. collect-call number. Contact the MedicAlert Foundation International (☎+1-888-633-4298, outside US 209-668-3333; www.medicalert.org).

### WOMEN'S HEALTH

Women traveling in unsanitary conditions are vulnerable to urinary tract (including bladder and kidney) infections. Over-the-counter medicines can sometimes alleviate symptoms, but if they persist, see a doctor. Vaginal yeast infections may occur in hot and humid climates. Wearing loosely fitting trousers or a skirt and cotton underwear will help, as will over-the-counter remedies like Monistat or Gynelotrimin. Bring supplies from home if you are prone to infection, as they may be difficult to find on the road. And, since tampons, pads, and reliable contraceptive devices can be hard to find when traveling, bring supplies with you. Abortion laws vary in different states and territories.

# GETTING TO AUSTRALIA

## BY PLANE

When it comes to airfare, a little effort can save you a bundle. Courier fares are the cheapest for those whose plans are flexible enough to deal with the restrictions. Tickets sold by consolidators and standby seating are also good deals, but last-minute specials, airfare wars, and charter flights often beat these fares. The key is to hunt around, be flexible, and ask about discounts. Students, seniors, and those under 26 should never pay full price for a ticket.

## AIRFARES

Airfares to Australia peak between December and early February; holidays are also expensive. The cheapest times to travel are post-Easter, between April and early June, and late June and September. Midweek (M-Th morning) round-trip flights run US$40-50 cheaper than weekend flights but are generally more crowded and less likely to permit frequent-flier upgrades. Not fixing a return date ("open return") or arriving in and departing from different cities ("open-jaw") can be pricier than round-trip flights. Patching together one-way flights to out-of-the-way destinations is the most expensive way to travel. Flights between Australia's regional hubs—Sydney, Melbourne, Adelaide, Brisbane, and Perth—will tend to be cheaper.

If Australia is only one stop on a more extensive globe-hop, consider a round-the-world (RTW) ticket. Tickets usually include at least five stops and are valid for about a year; prices range US$1200-5000. Try **Northwest Airlines/KLM** (☎+1-800-225-2525; www.nwa.com) or **Star Alliance**, a consortium of 16 airlines including United Airlines (www.staralliance.com).

Fares for roundtrip flights to Sydney from the US or Canadian east coast cost US$2000, US$1350 in the low season; from the US or Canadian west coast US$1900/1350; from the UK, £1200/650; from New Zealand NZ$550/400.

**FLIGHT PLANNING ON THE INTERNET.** The Internet may be the budget traveler's dream when it comes to finding and booking bargain fares, but the array of options can be overwhelming. Many airline sites offer special last-minute deals on the web. **STA** (www.statravel.com) and **StudentUniverse** (www.studentuniverse.com) provide quotes on student tickets, while **Orbitz** (www.orbitz.com), **Expedia** (www.expedia.com), and **Travelocity** (www.travelocity.com) offer full travel services. **Priceline** (www.priceline.com) lets you specify a price and obligates you to buy any ticket that meets or beats it. **Hotwire** (www.hotwire.com) offers bargain fares but won't reveal the airline or flight times until you buy. Other sites that compile deals include www.bestfares.com, www.flights.com, www.lowestfare.com, www.onetravel.com, and www.travelzoo.com. **SideStep** (www.sidestep.com) and **Booking Buddy** (www.bookingbuddy.com) are online tools that can help sift through multiple offers; these two let you enter your trip information once and search multiple sites. **Air Traveler's Handbook** (www.faqs.org/faqs/travel/air/handbook) is an indispensable resource on the Internet; it has a comprehensive listing of links to everything you need to know before you board a plane.

# BUDGET AND STUDENT TRAVEL AGENCIES

While knowledgeable agents specializing in flights to Australia can make your life easier, they may not always spend the time necessary to find you the lowest possible fare, since many get paid on commission. Travelers holding **ISICs** and **IYTCs** (p. 12) qualify for big discounts from student travel agencies. Most flights from budget agencies are on major airline flights, but in peak season some may sell seats on less reliable chartered aircraft.

**STA Travel,** 5900 Wilshire Blvd., Ste. 900, Los Angeles, CA 90036, USA (24hr. reservations and info ☎+1-800-781-4040; www.statravel.com). A student and youth travel organization with over 150 offices worldwide (check their website for a listing of all their offices), including US offices in Boston, Chicago, Los Angeles, New York, Seattle, San Francisco, and Washington, DC. Ticket booking, travel insurance, railpasses, and more. Walk-in offices are located throughout Australia (☎03 9207 5900), New Zealand (☎+64 9 309 9723), and the UK (☎+44 8701 630 026).

**The Adventure Travel Company,** 124 MacDougal St., New York, NY, 10021, USA (☎+1-800-467-4595; www.theadventuretravelcompany.com). Offices across Canada and the US, including Champaign, New York, San Diego, Seattle, and San Francisco.

**USIT,** 19-21 Aston Quay, Dublin 2, Ireland (☎+353 1 602 1906; www.usit.ie). Ireland's leading student/budget travel agency has 20 offices throughout Northern Ireland and the Republic of Ireland. Offers programs to work, study, and volunteer worldwide.

# COMMERCIAL AIRLINES

The commercial airlines' lowest regular offer is the **APEX (Advance Purchase Excursion)** fare, which provides confirmed reservations and allows "open-jaw" tickets. Generally, reservations must be made seven to 21 days ahead of departure, with seven- to 14-day minimum-stay and up to 90-day maximum-stay restrictions. These fares carry hefty cancellation and change penalties (fees rise in summer). Book peak-season APEX fares early. Use **Expedia** (www.expedia.com) or **Travelocity** (www.travelocity.com) to get an idea of the lowest published fares, then use the resources outlined here to try to beat those fares. Low-season fares should be appreciably cheaper than the high-season ones listed here.

## TRAVELING FROM NORTH AMERICA

Basic round-trip fares to Australia range from roughly US$1300-3000, but they can hit $4500: from Los Angeles, US$1450-2500; from New York, US$1650-3500. Standard commercial carriers like American and United will probably offer the most convenient flights, but they may not be the cheapest, unless you snag a special promotion or airfare-war ticket. You will probably find flying one of the following "discount" airlines a better deal, if any of their limited departure points is convenient for you.

**Air Pacific,** Level 10, 403 George St., Sydney, NSW 2000 (☎1800 230 150; www.airpacific.com). Multiple U.S. stops but only one Canadian destination, Vancouver.

**China Airlines,** Suite 803, Level 8, 14 Martin Pl., Sydney, NSW 2000 (see website for regional contact info; www.china-airlines.com/en). Numerous stops in the US, but only one available in Canada (Vancouver, BC).

**Jetstar,** GPO Box 4713, Melbourne 3001 (☎131 538 or 03 9092 6401; www.jetstar.com). Run by Qantas. Single North American destination Honolulu, Hawaii. Offers service to many different Australian destinations.

**Qantas,** (☎13 13 13; in North America, +1-800-227-4500; www.qantas.com.au). Australia's largest airline. Operates primarily out of Sydney, but also offers service to other major cities. Most North American flights from the west coast of the US.

## TRAVELING FROM IRELAND AND THE UK

You can usually expect to pay £700-1400 if you're traveling down under from the UK, but prices will be significantly higher if you're flying out of Ireland. Although some European carriers such as British Airways and Air France will take you to Australia, Asian airlines are usually your best bet for both convenience and price. Many have one-night stopovers in major cities such as Singapore or Hong Kong. **Singapore Airlines** (www.singaporeair.com) and **Cathay Pacific** (www.cathaypacific.com) are both generally cheap.

# AIR COURIER FLIGHTS

Those who travel light should consider courier flights. Couriers help transport cargo on international flights by using their checked luggage space for freight. Generally, couriers are limited to carry-ons and must deal with complex flight restrictions. Most flights are round-trip only, with short fixed-length stays (usually one week) and a limit of one ticket per issue. Most of these flights operate only out of major gateway cities, mostly in North America. Round-trip courier fares from the US to Australia run about US$400-500. Most flights leave from Los Angeles, Miami, New York, or San Francisco in the US; and from Montreal, Toronto, or Vancouver in Canada. Generally, you must be over 18 (sometimes 21). In summer, the most popular destinations usually require an advance reservation of two weeks (you can usually book up to two months ahead). Super-discounted fares are common for "last-minute" flights (from 3 days ahead).

## STANDBY FLIGHTS

Traveling standby requires considerable flexibility in arrival and departure dates. Companies dealing in standby flights sell vouchers rather than tickets, along with a promise to get you to—or near—your destination within a certain window (typically 1-5 days). You call in before your specific window of time to hear your flight options and the probability that you will be able to board each flight. You can then decide which flights you want to try, show up at the appropriate airport at the appropriate time, present your voucher, and board if space is available. Vouchers can usually be bought for both one-way and round-trip travel. You may receive a monetary refund only if every available flight within your date range is full; if you opt not to take an available (but perhaps less convenient) flight, you can only get credit toward future travel. To check on a company's service record in the US, contact the **Better Business Bureau** (☎+1-703-276-0100; www.bbb.org). It is difficult to receive refunds, and clients' vouchers will not be honored if an airline fails to receive payment in time.

## TICKET CONSOLIDATORS

Ticket consolidators, or **"bucket shops,"** buy unsold tickets in bulk from commercial airlines and sell them at discounted rates. The best place to look is in the Sunday travel section of any major newspaper (such as *The New York Times*), where many bucket shops place tiny ads. Call quickly, as availability is very limited. Not all bucket shops are reliable, so insist on a receipt that gives full details of restrictions, refunds, and tickets. Try to pay by credit card (in spite of the 2-5% fee) so you can stop payment if you never receive your tickets. For more info, see www.travel-library.com/air-travel/consolidators.html.

### TRAVELING FROM CANADA AND THE US

Some consolidators worth trying are **Rebel** (☎+1-800-732-3588; www.rebel-tours.com), **Cheap Tickets** (www.cheaptickets.com), **Flights.com** (www.flights.com), and **TravelHUB** (www.travelhub.com). *Let's Go* does not endorse any of these agencies. As always, be cautious, and research companies before you hand over your credit-card number.

## CHARTER FLIGHTS

Tour operators contract charter flights with airlines in order to fly extra loads of passengers during peak season. These flights are far from hassle free. They occur less frequently than major airlines, make getting refunds particularly difficult, and are almost always fully booked. Their scheduled times may change and they may be canceled at the last moment (as late as 48hr. before the trip, and without a full refund). In addition, check-in, boarding, and baggage claim are often much slower. They can, however, be much cheaper.

Discount clubs and fare brokers offer members savings on last-minute charter and tour deals. Study contracts closely; you don't want to end up with an unwanted overnight layover. **Travelers Advantage** (☎+1-800-835-8747; www.

travelersadvantage.com; US$90 annual fee includes discounts and cheap flight directories) specializes in **European travel** and tour packages.

# GETTING AROUND AUSTRALIA

## BY PLANE

Because Australia is such a large country, most travelers will end up taking a domestic flight during their trip. Australian "uni" holidays are the worst times to do so; tickets will be most expensive then. Fares between big cities are cheapest and most convenient, but many flights run to smaller airports.

**Qantas** (☎13 13 13; www.qantas.com.au). Frequent flights between major cities and other destinations. Booking fee of $27.50 when reservations are made through telephone sales, Qantas outlets, and airports. Cheapest to purchase online.

**Rex (Regional Express)** (☎13 17 13, elsewhere ☎02 6393 5550; www.rex.com.au). Specializes in domestic travel across Australia, and offers more destinations than most other airlines.

**Virgin Blue** (☎13 67 89, elsewhere ☎07 3295 2296; www.virginblue.com.au). Sizeable selection of destinations, but slightly more expensive.

## BY BUS

Buses cover more of Australia's rural landscape than trains, but journeys off the beaten track may require a few days' wait. It may be more cost effective to buy a kilometer or multi-day pass if you're planning on a lot of bus travel.

### GREYHOUND AUSTRALIA

Greyhound Australia (☎1300 473 946; www.greyhound.com.au) is the nation's premier bus service, with travel options in every state. Fares booked over the phone include an additional fee; fares booked on the Internet are the least expensive (no additional fee) and may include discounts. They offer a standard 10% concessions discount and a number of passes. Their most popular options are **Aussie Explorer passes,** which include extensive travel along thematic or regional itineraries. These include the year-long **All Australian Pass** ($2968, concessions $2672), which allows you to hop on and off anywhere on Greyhound Australia's network; and the **Aussie Highlights Pass,** which gives you 365 days of travel to Australia's most popular spots, including everything from the wine country to the Great Barrier Reef ($1781, concessions $1603). A more flexible option is the **Aussie Kilometre Pass,** which allows travelers to purchase a set amount of kilometers (from 500 to 20,000km) and use them to explore Australia on any of Greyhound's bus lines until their pre-purchased kilometer package runs out; valid for one year. Shorter 30- to 45-day passes run between the major cities ($80-360, concessions $72-320).

### OZ EXPERIENCE

This popular bus company (☎1300 300 028, elsewhere ☎02 9213 1766; www.ozexperience.com) offers flexible backpacker packages and charismatic drivers who double as tour guides. The packages must be purchased for predetermined routes (cheaper if bought outside of Australia), and travelers can usually take up to six months to complete their route, often with unlimited stopovers. Oz Experience offers a variety of passes to suit any travel plan, including routes that run Cairns-Sydney, Adelaide-Darwin, Melbourne-Adelaide, and Alice Springs-Uluru. Be prepared for a younger, party-ready crowd.

# BY TRAIN

Australia does not have a comprehensive rail system, and with current airfare competition, a train ticket is not necessarily cheaper than flying. Nonetheless, trains can provide comfortable, scenic travel along certain routes. **Rail Australia** offers a **Backtracker Rail Pass** (www.railaustralia.com.au/railpasses.php) that includes unlimited travel on CountryLink Xplorer and Xpt trains and coaches (predominately in New South Wales) over consecutive days within a given period (14 days $218, 30 days $251); only open to foreign passport holders. The **Austrail Flexi-pass** allows you to purchase 15 ($950) or 22 ($1330) traveling days to be used over a six-month period through the Queensland, Countrylink, and Great Southern Railways, but you must present a valid passport and a return airline ticket to prove you're international. The **East Coast Discovery Pass** allows unlimited stops in one direction along the Eastern Seaboard within six months (Sydney-Melbourne $130, Sydney-Cairns $410.50, Melbourne-Cairns $500.50; other routes available).

Each state runs its own rail service, and transfers between services may require a bus trip to the next station. Wheelchair access on interstate trains can be poor, as the corridors are often too narrow. Some (but not all) larger stations provide collapsible wheelchairs. The main rail companies are:

- **Countrylink** (☎ 13 22 32; www.countrylink.info). Based in New South Wales. Ages 4-15 and ISIC card holders 50% discount.

- **Great Southern Railways** (☎ 13 21 47; www.gsr.com.au). Runs 3 routes—Ghan (Adelaide-Alice Springs-Darwin), Indian Pacific (Sydney-Adelaide-Perth) and Overland (Melbourne-Adelaide). Discount for students, backpackers, YHA, and children age 4-16.

- **Queensland Rail** (☎ 13 16 17; www.qr.com.au). Serves Queensland. Ages 5-15 and ISIC card holders 50% discount.

- **Transwa** (☎ 13 10 53; www.transwa.wa.gov.au). 50% discount for seniors, children.

- **V/Line** (☎ 13 61 96; www.vline.com.au). Serves Victoria. 50% discount on interstate travel for children, concessions; 10% discount for YHA/VIP; group discounts available.

# BY CAR

Australia's public highways are generally well-maintained, and most cities and towns are clustered around these routes. However, the majority of highways run along the coasts; only a few split the center of the continent. Many sparsely populated towns are only accessible via unpaved roads, and public transportation in these areas is spotty at best. National and state parks present similar problems, although some can be explored via tour buses. To travel on most outback roads and in national parks, you will probably need a four-wheel-drive vehicle (4WD or AWD), which can double the cost of renting or buying. Shop ahead of time and be aware that some trips may be quite expensive.

## RENTING

Most of Australia's popular coastal destinations are connected by train and bus companies. However, a sizable chunk of outdoorsy destinations are best accessed by car. A 2WD will suffice most of these sights, but if you're planning to hit the center of the country or do any serious driving through national parks, you're going to want a 4WD. This can be extremely expensive for an individual, but it can be relatively cost-efficient if split between a group. Despite the recent leaps in gas prices, car-rental is still pretty popular among Australia's tourists, and so it's usually possible to use a 2WD for most of the journey and only rent a 4WD when in areas that call for it.

## RENTAL AGENCIES

You can generally make reservations before you leave by calling major international offices in your home country. It's a good idea to cross-check this information with local agencies as well. The local desk numbers are included in town listings; for home-country numbers, call your toll-free directory.

To rent a car in Australia, you generally need to be at least 21 years old. Some agencies require renters to be 25, and most charge drivers 21-24 an additional insurance fee ($7-24 per day). Small local operations occasionally rent to people under 21, but be sure to ask about the insurance coverage and deductible, and always check the fine print. Rental agencies in Australia include:

**Avis** (☎13 63 33; www.avis.com.au).

**Budget** (☎02 9353 9399, 1300 362 848; www.budget.com).

**Europcar** (☎03 9330 6160, 1300 13 13 90; www.europcar.com.au).

**Hertz** (☎03 9698 2555, 13 30 39; www.hertz.com.au).

**Thrifty** (head office ☎02 8337 2700, reservations 02 8337 2790, from within Australia 1300 36 72 27; www.thrifty.com).

## COSTS AND INSURANCE

Rental car prices start at around $45 per day from national companies and $35 from local agencies. Expect to pay more for larger cars, and be prepared to empty your pockets for 4WD. Cars with **automatic transmission** can cost $3-10 per day more than cars with manual transmission (stick shift). It can often be difficult to find an automatic 4WD at all.

Remember that if you are driving a conventional rental vehicle on an unpaved road, you are almost never covered by insurance; ask about this before leaving the rental agency. Be aware that cars rented on **American Express** or **Visa/MasterCard Gold** or **Platinum** credit cards in Australia might not carry the automatic insurance that they would in some other countries; check with your credit card company. Insurance plans from rental companies almost always come with an **excess** of around $3000 for conventional vehicles; excess ranges up to around $5000 for younger drivers and for 4WD. This means that the insurance bought from the rental company only applies to damages over the excess; damages up to that amount must be covered by your existing insurance plan. Some rental companies in Australia require you to buy a **Collision Damage Waiver (CDW),** which will waive the excess in the case of a collision. **Loss Damage Waivers (LDWs)** do the same in the case of theft or vandalism.

National chains often allow one-way rentals (picking up in one city and dropping off in another). There is usually a minimum hire period and sometimes an extra drop-off charge of up to several hundred dollars.

# BUYING AND SELLING USED CARS

Buying and reselling used cars is a popular option for long-term travelers or those too young to rent. Automotive independence can cost under $5000. However, used car dealers have been known to rip off foreigners, especially backpackers. Do some research before hitting the lots or searching through classifieds. Alternatively, ask a trustworthy Aussie about reasonable prices; some people recommend bringing a local along when purchasing a car.

Buying from a private owner or fellow traveler is often a cheaper alternative. In many cities, private sellers rent space at used car lots where buyers are free to stroll around and haggle. Hostel or university bulletin boards are another good bet. In Sydney, check the weekly **Trading Post** on Thursdays (or online at www.tradingpost.com.au) for used car advertisements, and the **Daily Telegraph Mirror** and **Sydney Morning Herald** on Saturdays. Also check out **Craigslist** (http://geo.craigslist.org/iso/au) and **Gumtree** (www.gumtree.com.au).

Remember that seasons effect regional travel and therefore have an impact on vehicle prices. Vehicles are also easier to sell if they are registered in the state where they are being sold—**interstate registration transfers** can be a hassle. If you buy a car privately, check the registration papers against the license of the person who is selling the car. Australia's national consumer website also has good information about buying used cars (www.consumersonline.gov.au).

When buying a car, call the **Register of Encumbered Vehicles** (☎13 32 20) or check online at www.revs.nsw.gov.au to confirm that a vehicle is unencumbered—meaning that it hasn't been reported as stolen and has no outstanding financial obligations or traffic warrants. You'll need to provide the registration, engine, and VIN/chassis numbers of the vehicle.

Within two weeks of purchase, you'll need to **register** the car in your name at the local **Road and Traffic Authority (RTA).** Transferring the registration (or "rego") costs 3% of the price paid for the vehicle. Local automobile organizations can always help. Further information on vehicle registration in Australia can be found at www.australia.gov.au/Registration_&_Licences.

# DRIVING PERMITS AND CAR INSURANCE

### INTERNATIONAL DRIVING PERMIT (IDP)

Australian driving laws are managed by the individual state or territory. You can generally drive on your existing license for three months without penalty— if it's written in English. However, if you plan to drive a car for longer than three months, or if your home country's license is not in English, you must have an **International Driving Permit (IDP).** The IDP functions as a translation of your license, printed in 11 languages. Even if your home license is valid, it may be a good idea to get one anyway, as it doubles as a form of photo identification.

Your IDP, valid for one year, must be issued in your own country before you depart. An application for an IDP usually requires one or two photos, a current local license, an additional form of identification, and a fee. To apply, contact your home country's automobile association. You must be 18 to apply. Be vigilant when purchasing an IDP online or anywhere other than your home automobile association. Many vendors sell permits of questionable legitimacy for higher prices. Also be aware that an IDP is not valid by itself; you will also need to carry your actual license with it.

### CAR INSURANCE

Most credit cards cover standard insurance. If you rent, lease, or borrow a car, you will need a **green card,** or **International Insurance Certificate,** to certify that you have liability insurance and that it applies abroad. Green cards can be obtained at most car rental agencies, most car dealers (for those leasing cars), some travel agents, and some border crossings.

# ON THE ROAD

Australians drive on the left-hand side of the road. Therefore, in unmarked intersections, a driver must yield to vehicles entering the intersection from the right. By law, seat belts must be worn at all times by all persons riding in the vehicle. Children less than 40 lb. should ride in a car seat, available for a small fee at most rental agencies. Gasoline (petrol) prices vary, but average about $1.70 per liter in cities and around $1.60 per liter in outlying areas. The speed limit in most cities is 50kph and 100 or 110kph on highways. The Northern Territory has the most lenient limits in the country, with highway speeds capped at 130kph. State and territorial authorities, particularly those in Queensland, will sometimes use radar guns to patrol well-traveled roads, and some intersections are even equipped with cameras to catch offenders.

**DRIVING PRECAUTIONS.** When traveling in the summer or in the desert, bring substantial amounts of water (a suggested 5L of water per person per day) for drinking and for the radiator. You should always carry a spare tire and jack, jumper cables, extra oil, flares, a flashlight, and heavy blankets (in case your car breaks down at night or in the winter). If you don't know how to change a tire, learn before heading out, especially if you are planning on traveling in deserted areas. If your car breaks down, stay in your vehicle while waiting for help.

## DANGERS

While Australia's cities are plagued by typical urban traffic problems, its more rural routes present some extreme dangers. See **Great Outdoors** (p. 63) for an extensive list of hazards, like wildlife, road conditions, and car maintenance.

## CAR ASSISTANCE

The **Australian Automobile Association (AAA)** is the national umbrella organization for all of the local automobile organizations. You won't often see it called the AAA, though; in most states, the local organization is called the **Royal Automobile Club (RAC)**. In New South Wales and the ACT, it's the **National Royal Motorist Association (NRMA)**. In the Northern Territory, it's the **Automobile Association of the Northern Territory (AANT)**. Services—from breakdown assistance to map provision—are similar to those offered by automobile associations in other countries. Most overseas organizations have reciprocal membership with AAA (including AAA in the US; AA and RAC in the UK; NZAA in New Zealand). Bring proof of your membership to Australia, and you'll be able to use AAA facilities free of charge. If, for some reason, your membership is not honored, your AAA at home will usually reimburse you for fees incurred. It's possible to join AAA through any state's automobile organization. *Let's Go* lists the location of the regional automobile organization in each state or territory introduction.

# BY BICYCLE

Australia is an easy country to see via bicycle. Much of the country is flat, and most local authorities maintain **bike paths** for cyclists' convenience. In theory, bicycles can go on buses and trains, but most major bus companies require you to disassemble your bike and pay a flat fee of at least $25. (If you can't disassemble the bike, this fee can rise as high as $55.) You may not be allowed to bring your bike into train compartments. For this reason, many choose to rent a bike locally, from either a hostel or an adventuring company, instead of hauling the same bicycle around the country. Helmets are required by law in Australia. A quality **helmet** costs about $45—much cheaper than brain surgery or the cost of any injury out on the road. Travel with detailed maps from the state Automobile Associations, and obey all traffic laws and signals.

The **Bicycle Federation of Australia (BFA),** P.O. Box 499, Civic Sq., Canberra, ACT 2608 (☎02 6249 6761; www.bfa.asn.au), is a nonprofit bicycle advocacy group. The BFA publishes *Australian Cyclist* magazine (www.australian-cyclist.com.au) and offers a list of regional bicycling organizations and cycle tourism opportunities on its web page.

## BY THUMB

 **LET'S NOT GO.** Let's Go never recommends hitchhiking as a safe means of transportation; none of the information here is intended to endorse it.

Let's Go strongly urges you to consider the risks before you choose to hitch-hike. Hitching means entrusting your life to a stranger and risking assault, sexual harassment, theft, and unsafe driving. For women traveling alone (or even in pairs), hitching is just too dangerous. A man and a woman are a less dangerous combination; two men will have a harder time getting a lift, while three men will go nowhere. In more populous coastal states—Queensland in particular—hitchhiking is actively discouraged by the state government, and hitching on a motorway instead of a footpath is considered a traffic offense. Those who do hitchhike in Australia generally flag down giant **road trains** (see p. 79), which drive very fast and operate on a tight schedule.

# KEEPING IN TOUCH

## BY EMAIL AND INTERNET

Internet cafes are commonplace in most decent-sized cities in Australia. In most major cities, Internet shops will have booths offering discounted international calling as well. Access to the Internet ranges from as low as free at some libraries and accommodations, to as high as $10 per hour. Coin-operated Internet kiosks are an expensive (usually $2 per 10min.) and common option in cities and hostels. Many public libraries offer free access to the web, though sometimes you are restricted from checking email or must make a reservation with the library beforehand. This guide lists Internet availability in the **Practical Information** section of towns and cities. Other Internet access points in Australia can be found at www.gnomon.com.au/publications/netaccess. Although in some places it's possible to forge a remote link with your home server, in most cases this is a much slower (and thus more expensive) option; take advantage of free **web-based email accounts** such as ✉www.gmail.com or **www.hotmail.com.**

Increasingly, travelers find that taking their **laptop computers** on the road with them can be a convenient option for staying connected. Laptop users can call an Internet service provider via modem with a long-distance phone card specifically intended for such calls. They may also find Internet cafes that allow them to connect their laptops to the Internet. Lucky travelers with wireless-enabled computers may be able to take advantage of an increasing number of Internet "hot spots," where they can get online for free or for a small fee. Newer computers can detect these hot spots automatically; otherwise, websites like www.

jiwire.com, www.wififreespot.com, and www.wi-fihotspotlist.com can help you find them. For information on **insuring** your laptop while traveling, see p. 21.

**WI-FI WARY.** Wireless hot spots make Internet access possible in public and remote places. Unfortunately, they also pose **security risks.** Hot spots are public, open networks that use unencrypted, unsecured connections. They are susceptible to hacks and "packet sniffing"—ways of stealing passwords and other private information. To prevent problems, disable ad hoc mode, turn off file sharing and network discovery, encrypt your email, turn on your firewall, beware of phony networks, and watch for over-the-shoulder creeps.

# BY TELEPHONE

## CALLING HOME FROM AUSTRALIA

**Prepaid phone cards** are a common and relatively inexpensive means of calling abroad. Each one comes with a Personal Identification Number (PIN) and a toll-free access number. You call the access number and then follow the directions for dialing using your PIN. To purchase prepaid phone cards, check online for the best rates; www.callingcards.com is a good place to start. Online providers generally send your access number and PIN via email, with no actual "card" involved. You can also call home with prepaid phone cards purchased in Australia (see **Calling Within Australia,** p. 36).

**PLACING INTERNATIONAL CALLS.** To call Australia from home or to call home from Australia, dial:
1. The **international dialing prefix.** To call from **Australia,** dial 0011; **Canada** or the **US,** 011; and **Ireland, New Zealand,** or the **UK,** 00.
2. The **country code** of the country you want to call. To call **Australia,** dial 61; **Canada** or the **US,** 1; **Ireland,** 353; **New Zealand,** 64; and the **UK,** 44.
3. The **city/area code.** Let's Go lists the city/area codes for cities and towns in Australia opposite the city or town name, next to a ☎, as well as in every phone number. If the first digit is a zero (e.g., 02 for Sydney), omit the zero when calling from abroad.
4. The **local number.**

Another option is to purchase a **calling card** that's linked to a major national telecommunications service in your home country. Calls are billed either collect or to your account. To call home with a calling card, contact the operator for your service provider in Australia (**Optus** and **Telstra** are the main telecommunications companies) by dialing the appropriate toll-free access number (these are listed below in the third column).

| COMPANY | TO OBTAIN A CARD: | TO CALL ABROAD: |
|---|---|---|
| **AT&T (US)** | ☎800-364-9292 or www.att.com | ☎1800 551 155 (Optus) or 1800 881 011 (Telstra) |
| **Canada Direct** | ☎800-561-8868 or www.info-canadadirect.com | ☎1800 551 177 or 1800 881 150 |
| **MCI (US)** | ☎800-777-5000 or www.minutepass.com | ☎1800 551 111 (Optus) or 1800 881 100 (Telstra) |
| **Telecom New Zealand Direct** | www.telecom.co.nz | ☎1800 551 164 (Optus) or 1800 881 640 (Telstra) |

ESSENTIALS

Placing a collect call via international operator can be expensive, but may be necessary in case of an emergency. Often you can call collect without buying a company's calling card: dial its access number and follow the instructions.

## CALLING WITHIN AUSTRALIA

The simplest way to call within Australia is to use a coin-operated phone. Prepaid phone cards (available at newspaper kiosks and tobacco stores) usually save time and money in the long run. Phone rates typically tend to be highest in the morning, lower in the evening, and lowest on Sunday and late at night.

Public phones are everywhere in Australia. **Long-distance calls** within Australia use STD (Subscriber Trunk Dialing) services. You must dial an **area code** (listed next to town names in this guide) before the eight-digit number. Some public phones in Australia (mostly located at airports, in and around city centers, and at major hotels) will allow you to charge a call to your credit card.

For local and national **directory assistance** in Australia, you can call toll-free ☎1223 from any phone; for international assistance dial ☎1225 instead. Six-digit phone numbers beginning with **13** are information numbers that can be dialed from anywhere in Australia for the same price as a local call. Numbers beginning with **1300** operate similarly. Numbers beginning with **1800** are toll-free and can be dialed as such from public phones.

## CELLULAR PHONES

Cellular phones are common in urban Australia. Numbers are 10 digits long and always begin with 04. Incoming calls are usually free; caller charges run about $0.25 per minute. Major service providers include **Optus** (www.optus.com.au), **Telstra** (www.telstra.com), and **Vodafone** (www.vodafone.com.au).

The international standard for cell phones is **Global System for Mobile Communication (GSM)**. To make and receive calls in Australia, you will need a **GSM-compatible phone** and a **Subscriber Identity Module (SIM)** card, a country-specific, thumbnail-sized chip that gives you a local phone number and plugs you into the local network. Australia's GSM network is compatible with most phones used in Europe, but only with some of the phones commonly used in the US. Many SIM cards are prepaid, and incoming calls are frequently free. You can buy additional cards or vouchers (usually available at convenience stores) to "top up" your phone. For more information on GSM phones, check out www.telestial.com, www.orange.co.uk, www.roadpost.com, or www.planetomni.com. Companies like **Cellular Abroad** (www.cellularabroad.com) rent cell phones that work in a variety of destinations all over the world.

## TIME DIFFERENCES

Although there are formally only three time zones in Australia, keeping on schedule can be a bit confusing for travelers due to inconsistent observance of **Daylight Saving Time (DST)**, which happens every year from late October to late March or early April. Six of the eight Australian states/territories (excluding Queensland and Northern Territory) observe DST, meaning that Australia's time zones end up following state borders both vertically and horizontally (for **time zones,** see inside back cover). Greenwich Mean Time (GMT), also known as Universal Standard Time (UST), is not affected by DST, so it provides a standard to calculate differences in time zones.

In the table below, the column on the left represents your location. The values indicate the time in other regions relative to the time in your region. To calculate the time in a different zone, add or subtract the difference in hours between the two places. For example, if it is noon in GMT, then it is 10pm in

Victoria. Remember that sometimes the date is effected—Australia is ahead of the Western Hemisphere, so Monday evening in New York is Tuesday morning in Sydney. **All regions that observe DST have an asterisk (\*).** Therefore, during DST, if you start in a row with an asterisk, subtract 1hr. If you end in a column with an asterisk, add one hour. For example, if it is noon in GMT during DST, then it is 11pm in Victoria. South Australia, Victoria, New South Wales, Western Australia, and the Australia Capital Territory start DST on the last Sunday in October, while Tasmania begins its observation on the first Sunday in October. All states end DST on the last Sunday in March or the first Sunday in April.

| TIME ZONES | GMT | WA* | NT | SA* | QLD | ACT* NSW* TAS* VIC* |
|---|---|---|---|---|---|---|
| Greenwich Mean Time (GMT) | | +8 | +9.5 | +9.5 | +10 | +10 |
| Western Australia* (WA) | -8 | | +1.5 | +1.5 | +2 | +2 |
| Northern Territory (NT) | -9.5 | -1.5 | | 0 | +0.5 | +0.5 |
| Southern Australia* (SA) | -9.5 | -1.5 | 0 | | +0.5 | +0.5 |
| Queensland (QLD) | -10 | -2 | -0.5 | -0.5 | | 0 |
| ACT*, NSW*, Tasmania*, Victoria* | -10 | -2 | -0.5 | -0.5 | 0 | |

# BY MAIL

## SENDING MAIL HOME FROM AUSTRALIA

**Airmail** is the best way to send mail home from Australia. **Aerogrammes,** printed sheets that fold into envelopes and travel via airmail, are available at post offices. Write "airmail" or "par avion" on the front. Most post offices will charge huge fees or refuse to send aerogrammes with enclosures. **Surface mail** is by far the cheapest, slowest way to send mail. It takes from one to two months to cross the Atlantic and from one to three to cross the Pacific—good for heavy items you won't need for a while, such as souvenirs acquired in your travels. The *Australia Post* website (www.auspost.com) has a postage calculator for international deliveries. These are standard rates for mail from Australia to:

**Canada:** Allow 5-7 days for regular airmail. Postcards $1.30; aerogrammes $1.10. Letters up to 50g cost $2; packages up to 0.5kg $14.35, up to 2kg $47.65.

**New Zealand:** Allow 3-4 days for regular airmail. Postcards $1.30; aerogrammes $1.10. Letters up to 50g cost $1.35; packages up to 0.5kg $10.05, up to 2kg $30.75.

**UK and Ireland:** Allow 4-5 days for regular airmail. Postcards $1.30; aerogrammes $1.10. Letters up to 50g cost $2; packages up to 0.5kg $17.45, up to 2kg $60.35.

**US:** Allow 4-6 days for regular airmail. Postcards $1.30; aerogrammes $1.10. Letters up to 50g cost $2; packages up to 0.5kg $14.35, up to 2kg $47.65.

## SENDING MAIL TO AUSTRALIA

To ensure timely delivery of your correspondence, mark envelopes "airmail" or "par avion." In addition to the standard postage system, **Federal Express** (☎13 26 10, Canada and the US +1-800-463-3339, Ireland +353 800 535 800, New Zealand +64 800 733 339, the UK +44 8456 070 809; www.fedex.com) handles express mail services from the above countries to Australia. Sending small letters and postcards within Australia costs $0.50.

There are several ways to pick up letters sent to you while you are abroad. Mail can be sent via **Poste Restante** (known as General Delivery in the US) to almost any town in Australia with a post office, but should only be used if a street delivery address is unavailable. Address Poste Restante letters like so:

Mel GIBSON

Poste Restante

Sydney, NSW 2000

The mail will go to a special desk in the central post office unless you specify a post office by street address or postal code. It's best to use the largest post office, as mail may be sent there regardless. It is usually safer and quicker, though more expensive, to send mail express or registered. Bring your passport (or other photo ID) for pickup; there may be a small fee. If the clerks insist there is nothing for you, ask them to check under your first name. *Let's Go* lists post offices in the **Practical Information** section for each city and most towns.

**American Express's** travel offices offer a free **Client Letter Service** (mail held up to 30 days and forwarded upon request) for cardholders who contact them in advance. Some offices provide these services to non-cardholders (especially AmEx Travelers Cheque holders), but call ahead to make sure. *Let's Go* lists AmEx locations for most large cities in **Practical Information** sections; for a complete list, call ☎+1-800-528-4800 or visit www.americanexpress.com/travel.

# ACCOMMODATIONS

While it is generally easy to find accommodation while traveling in Australia, be aware that bookings (reservations) often need to be made months in advance at holidays, particularly school holidays. It is also not uncommon for accommodations to raise, or even double, their rates during these times.

| 2009 AUSTRALIAN SCHOOL HOLIDAYS BY STATE | | | | |
|---|---|---|---|---|
| **State** | **Easter/Autumn** | **Winter** | **Spring** | **Christmas/Summer** |
| **ACT** | Apr. 8 - Apr. 27 | July 4 - July 19 | Sept. 26 - Oct. 11 | Dec. 19 - Jan. 27 |
| **New South Wales** | Apr. 10 - Apr. 24 | July 13 - July 24 | Oct. 5 - Oct. 16 | Dec. 21 - Jan. 26 |
| **Northern Territory** | Apr. 6 - Apr. 13 | June 22 - July 17 | Sept. 28 - Oct. 2 | Dec. 12 - Jan. 24 |
| **Queensland** | Apr. 10 - Apr. 19 | June 27 - July 12 | Sept. 19 - Oct. 4 | Dec. 12 - Jan. 26 |
| **South Australia** | Apr. 10 - Apr. 26 | July 4 - July 19 | Sept. 26 - Oct. 11 | Dec. 12 - Jan. 26 |
| **Tasmania** | Apr. 10 - Apr. 17 | May 30 - June 14 | Sept. 5 - Sept. 20 | Dec. 18 - Feb. 10 |
| **Victoria** | Apr. 4 - Apr. 19 | June 27 - July 12 | Sept. 19 - Oct. 4 | Dec. 19 - Jan. 26 |
| **Western Australia** | Apr. 10 - Apr. 27 | July 4 - July 19 | Sept. 26 - Oct. 11 | Dec. 18 - Jan. 31 |

# HOSTELS

Many hostels are laid out dorm-style, often with large single-sex rooms and bunk beds, although private rooms that sleep two to four are becoming more common. They sometimes have kitchens and utensils for your use, bike or moped rentals, storage areas (many hostels allow guests to leave valuables in a safe at the front desk, but bring your own **padlock** for your storage locker), transportation to airports, breakfast and other meals, laundry facilities, and Internet. However, there can be drawbacks: some hostels close during certain daytime "lockout" hours, have a curfew, don't accept reservations, impose a maximum stay, or, less frequently, require that you do chores. In Australia, a dorm bed in a hostel will average around $20-25 and a private room around $30-40. A **membership card** offered by **VIP Backpackers** (www.vipbackpackers. com) gets discounts at many hostels. *Let's Go* designates these hostels with a VIP at the end of the listing. The two most common hostel chains in Australia are YHA and NOMADS (see below). A list of many hostels, regardless of affiliation, can be found at www.hostels.com.

---

**A HOSTELER'S BILL OF RIGHTS.** There are certain standard features that we do not include in our hostel listings. Unless we state otherwise, you can expect that every hostel has no lockout, no curfew, a kitchen, free hot showers, some system of secure luggage storage, and no key deposit.

---

## HOSTELLING INTERNATIONAL

Joining the youth hostel association in your own country (listed below) automatically grants you membership privileges in **Hostelling International (HI)**, a federation of national hosteling associations. Non-HI members may be allowed to stay in some hostels, but will have to pay extra to do so. The Australian branch of HI, **YHA Australia**, has hostels and agencies throughout Australia that are typically less expensive than private hostels. The website of HI's umbrella organization (www.hihostels.com), which lists the web addresses and phone numbers of all national associations, can be a great place to begin researching accommodation options in a specific region.

Most HI hostels also honor **guest memberships**—they should provide you with a blank card that has space for six validation stamps. Each night you'll pay a nonmember supplement (one-sixth the membership fee) and earn one guest stamp; six stamps make you a member. A new membership benefit is the FreeNites program, which allows hostelers to gain points toward free rooms. Most **student travel agencies** (p. 26) sell HI cards, as do all of the national hosteling organizations listed below. All the prices in these listings are valid for **one-year memberships** unless otherwise noted.

**Australian Youth Hostels Association (AYHA),** 422 Kent St., Sydney, NSW 2000 (☎02 9261 1111; www.yha.com.au). $52, under 18 $19.

**Hostelling International-Canada (HI-C),** 205 Catherine St., Ste. 400, Ottawa, ON K2P 1C3 (☎+1-613-237-7884; www.hihostels.ca). CDN$35, under 18 free.

**Hostelling International Northern Ireland (HINI),** 22-32 Donegall Rd., Belfast BT12 5JN (☎+44 28 9032 4733; www.hini.org.uk). UK£15, under 25 UK£10.

**Youth Hostels Association of New Zealand Inc. (YHANZ),** Level 1, 166 Moorhouse Ave., P.O. Box 436, Christchurch (☎+64 3 379 9970, in NZ 0800 278 299; www.yha.org.nz). NZ$40, under 18 free.

**Youth Hostels Association (England and Wales),** Trevelyan House, Dimple Rd., Matlock, Derbyshire DE4 3YH (☎+44 8707 708 868; www.yha.org.uk). UK£16, under 26 UK£10.

**Hostelling International-USA,** 8401 Colesville Rd., Ste. 600, Silver Spring, MD 20910 (☎+1-301-495-1240; www.hiayh.org). US$28, under 18 free.

## NOMADS

Another large hosteling chain in Australia is **NOMADS Backpackers** (www.nomadsworld.com). Every year, more than 1.5 million NOMADS beds are occupied in Australia and New Zealand, but you don't have to be a member to sleep in one. The NOMADS Travel Guide and Adventure Card is a complete guide for backpacker discounts in Australia. Priced at $34, it offers $1 off per night or seventh night free, discount international calling and Internet access, and hundreds of other adventure travel, touring, shopping, and transport discounts.

NOMADS also offers bargain and adventure packages into all Australian gateways; these packages organize accommodations and activities for the first few days of a trip. If you like to plan ahead, NOMADS also offers "Bed Hopper" accommodation vouchers that can be pre-purchased for five or 10 nights. Book online (www.nomadsworld.com) or with youth travel agencies worldwide.

# OTHER TYPES OF ACCOMMODATIONS

## HOTELS

While **hotels** in large cities are similar to those in the rest of the world, "hotels" in rural Australia—particularly in Victoria and New South Wales—are often simple furnished rooms above local pubs. Some resemble fancy Victorian-era lodgings with grand staircases, high ceilings, and wrap-around verandas. Others have been converted to long-term worker housing, and are thus less conducive to brief overnight stays. Singles in these hotels usually start at $50. This generally includes a towel, a shared bathroom, and a private room. The pubs downstairs can be noisy. **Motels** in Australia are mid-range accommodations. Quality and price varies, but most motel rooms will include private bathroom (ensuite), TV, and fridge. If you make **reservations** in writing, indicate your night of arrival and the number of nights you plan to stay. The hotel will send you a confirmation and may request payment for the first night.

## BED AND BREAKFASTS (B&BS)

A much more personal alternative to hotel rooms, Australian B&Bs (private homes with rooms available to travelers) range from acceptable to sublime. Hosts will sometimes go out of their way to be accommodating by giving personalized tours or offering home-cooked meals. On the other hand, many B&Bs do not provide phones, TVs, or private bathrooms. Rooms in B&Bs generally start at around $90, but are more expensive in heavily touristed areas. Check out **BABS** (www.babs.com.au) for a list of Australian B&Bs.

## UNIVERSITY DORMS

Many **colleges** and **universities** open their residence halls to travelers when school is not in session; some even do so during term time. Getting a room may take a couple of phone calls and require advanced planning, but rates tend to be low, and many offer free local calls and Internet access.

**Australian National University,** Bldg. 77, Brian Lewis Crescent, Australian National University, Canberra, ACT 0200 (☎02 6125 1100; http://accom.anu.edu.au).

**University of Melbourne,** Student Housing Services, Ground Fl., Baldwin Spencer Building, The University of Melbourne, VIC 3010 (☎03 8344 6550; www.services.unimelb.edu.au/housing).

**University of New South Wales,** Accommodations Services Central, UNSW Sydney, NSW 2052 (☎02 9385 4985; www.housing.unsw.edu.au).

**University of Sydney,** Services Building G12, The University of Sydney, NSW 2006 (☎02 9351 5865; www.usyd.edu.au/su/properties).

# HOME EXCHANGES AND HOSPITALITY CLUBS

**Home exchange** offers the traveler an opportunity to live like a native and cut down on accommodation fees in a variety of homes (houses, apartments, condominiums, villas, even castles in some cases). For more information, contact **HomeExchange.com Inc.,** P.O. Box 787, Hermosa Beach, CA 90254, USA (☎+1-310 -798-3864 or toll-free 800-877-8723; www.homeexchange.com) or **Intervac International Home Exchange** (☎02 9969 3169; www.intervac.com).

**Hospitality clubs** link their members with individuals or families abroad who are willing to host travelers for free or for a small fee to promote cultural exchange and general good karma. In exchange, members usually must be willing to host travelers in their own homes. **The Hospitality Club** (www. hospitalityclub.org) is a good place to start. **Servas** (www.servas.org) is an established, more formal, peace-based organization, and requires a fee and an interview to join. An Internet search will find many similar organizations, some of which cater to special interests (e.g., women, GLBT travelers, or members of certain professions). As always, use common sense when planning to stay with or host someone you do not know.

# LONG-TERM ACCOMMODATIONS

Travelers planning to stay in Australia for extended periods of time may find it most cost-effective to rent an **apartment.** A basic one-bedroom (or studio) apartment in Sydney will average $1500 per month. Besides the rent itself, prospective tenants usually are also required to front a security deposit (frequently one month's rent) and the last month's rent. Check apartment listings at www. realestate.com.au or www.rent-a-home.com.au.

# CAMPING

Camping is by far the cheapest way to spend the night. The ubiquitous caravan parks found throughout Australia offer basic camping sites, with or without power, for campers; in addition, some hostels have basic camping facilities or at the least allow guests to pitch their tents in the front or back yard. Unpowered campsites can vary in price, from free to $30 per night for a prime spot during Christmas holidays; most powered sites go for about $4-6 more. The **Great Outdoor Recreation Pages** (www.gorp.com) provide general information for travelers planning on camping or spending time in the outdoors.

**Caravanning** is popular in Australia, where many campgrounds double as caravan parks, consisting of both tent sites and powered sites for caravans. On-site caravans (also called on-site vans) are a frequent feature at caravan parks and are anchored permanently to the site and rented out. "Cabins" at caravan parks are often analogous to an on-site van, with a toilet inside.

In Australia, there is a distinction drawn between caravans and **campervans (RVs).** The former is pulled as a trailer, while the latter has its own cab. Renting a caravan or campervan is expensive, but cheaper than renting a car and staying in hotels. The convenience of bringing along your own bedroom, bathroom, and kitchen makes caravanning an attractive option, especially for older travelers and families traveling with children.

It's not difficult to arrange a campervan rental for your trip to Australia, although you should definitely start gathering information several months before your departure. Rates can vary widely by region, season (high season, Dec.-Feb. is the most expensive), and type of van. It pays to contact several different companies to compare vehicles and prices. **Maui Rentals** (☎03 8379 8891; www.maui-rentals.com) and **Britz Campervan Rentals and Tours** (☎03 8379

8890; www.britz.com) rent RVs in Australia. Check out **Family Parks of Australia** (☎02 6021 0977; www.familyparks.com.au) for a list of caravan and cabin parks across Australia belonging to their chain. For in-depth information on outdoor activities, wildlife, safety, and camping in the Australian Outback, see our **Great Outdoors** chapter, p. 63.

# SPECIFIC CONCERNS

## SUSTAINABLE TRAVEL

As the number of travelers on the road rises, the detrimental effect they can have on natural environments is an increasing concern. *Let's Go* promotes the philosophy of sustainable travel with this in mind. Through a sensitivity to issues of ecology and sustainability, today's travelers can be a powerful force in preserving and restoring the places they visit.

**Ecotourism,** a rising trend in sustainable travel, focuses on the conservation of natural habitats—mainly, on how to use them to build up the economy without exploitation or overdevelopment. Travelers can make a difference by doing researching in advance, by supporting organizations and establishments that pay attention to their carbon footprint, and by patronizing establishments that strive to be environmentally friendly.

**ECOTOURISM RESOURCES.** For more information on environmentally responsible tourism, contact one of the organizations below:

**Conservation International,** 2011 Crystal Dr., Ste. 500, Arlington, VA 22202, USA (☎+1-800-406-2306 or 703-341-2400; www.conservation.org).

**Green Globe 21,** Green Globe vof, Verbenalaan 1, 2111 ZL Aerdenhout, the Netherlands (☎+31 23 544 0306; www.greenglobe.com).

**International Ecotourism Society,** 1333 H St. NW, Ste. 300E, Washington, DC 20005, USA (☎+1-202-347-9203; www.ecotourism.org).

**United Nations Environment Program (UNEP),** 39-43 Quai André Citroën, 75739 Paris, Cedex 15, France (☎+33 1 44 37 14 50; www.uneptie.org/pc/tourism).

In Australia's giant island of endangered ecosystems, the greatest and rarest national treasures are ecological, so sustainable travel is particularly important. National parks are most susceptible to tourist damages; flocks of visitors hit these preserves every year, and some of them inevitably leave a mess behind. The best way to help with this problem in Australia is to simply do your part. When camping, hiking, or biking, don't litter, and be sure to clean up after yourself. See **Great Outdoors** (p. 63) for more detailed information.

## RESPONSIBLE TRAVEL

Your tourist dollars can make a big impact on the destinations you visit. The choices you make during your trip can have powerful effects on local communities—for better or for worse. Travelers who care about the destinations and environments they explore should make themselves aware of the social and cultural implications of their choices. Simple decisions such as buying local products, paying fair prices for products or services, and attempting to speak the local language can have a strong, positive effect on the community.

**Community-based tourism** aims to channel money into the local economy by emphasizing tours and cultural programs that are run by members of the host community. This type of tourism also benefits the travelers themselves, as it often takes them beyond the traditional sites of a given region. Visitors to Australia should consider visiting some of its seventeen **World Heritage sites.** The United Nations Educational, Scientific, and Cultural Organization (UNESCO) has designated these landmarks as essential pieces of the universal human heritage, and as such, entitled to protection. However, nature preserves are expensive to maintain, and pressure from developers can threaten efforts at conservation. The more revenue these locations can generate from tourism, the more plausible it is that they will continue to be protected. Luckily for the environmentally-concerned, the World Heritage list includes some of Australia's most popular tourist destinations, such as the Sydney Opera House and the Great Barrier Reef, but visitors should also consider visiting less-frequented spots, such as the Gondwana Rainforest, Fraser Island, Purnulu National Park, and Kakadu National Park. See http://whc.unesco.org for a complete list.

Visitors should also consider the social implications of their activity choices. Indigenous Australians are some of the most economically disadvantaged people in the country; socially conscious travelers will probably want to support any tours or adventure trips run by the local tribe. *The Ethical Travel Guide* (UK£13), a project of **Tourism Concern** (☎+44 20 7133 3330; www.tourismconcern.org.uk), is an excellent resource for information on community-based travel, with a directory of 300 establishments in 60 countries.

# TRAVELING ALONE

Traveling alone can be extremely beneficial, providing a sense of independence and a greater opportunity to connect with locals. On the other hand, solo travelers are more vulnerable to harassment and street theft. If you are traveling alone, look confident, try not to stand out as a tourist, and be especially careful in deserted or very crowded areas. Stay away from areas that are not well lit. If questioned, never admit that you are traveling alone. Maintain regular contact with someone at home who knows your itinerary, and always research your destination before traveling. For more tips, pick up *Traveling Solo* by Eleanor Berman (Globe Pequot Press; US$18), visit www.travelaloneandloveit.com, or subscribe to **Connecting: Solo Travel Network,** 689 Park Rd., Unit 6, Gibsons, BC V0N 1V7, Canada (☎+1-604-886-9099; www.cstn.org; membership US$30-48).

# WOMEN TRAVELERS

Women exploring on their own inevitably face some additional safety concerns. Single women might consider staying in hostels which offer single rooms that lock from the inside or in accommodations with single-sex rooms run by religious organizations. It's a good idea to stick to centrally located accommodations and to avoid solitary late-night treks or metro rides.

Always carry extra cash for a phone call, bus, or taxi. Hitchhiking is never safe for lone women or even for two women traveling together. Look as if you know where you're going and approach older women or couples for directions if you're lost or feeling uncomfortable in your surroundings. Generally, the less you look like a tourist, the better off you'll be. Dress conservatively, especially in rural areas. Wearing a conspicuous **wedding band**—whether you're married or not—sometimes helps to prevent unwanted advances.

Your best answer to verbal harassment is no answer at all. Feigning deafness, sitting motionless, and staring straight ahead at nothing in particular will usually do the trick. The extremely persistent can sometimes be dissuaded by a firm, loud, and very public "Go away!" Don't hesitate to seek out a police officer or a passerby if you are being harassed. Memorize the emergency numbers in places you visit, and consider carrying a **whistle.** A self-defense course will both prepare you for a potential attack and raise your level of awareness of your surroundings (see **Personal Safety,** p. 19). It might also be smart to talk with your doctor about the **health concerns** that women face when traveling (p. 25).

# GLBT TRAVELERS

The profile of the gay, lesbian, bisexual, and transgendered (GLBT) community in Australia has risen in recent years. The **Gay and Lesbian Mardi Gras** in Sydney is now the largest gay and lesbian gathering in the world (see p. 128). Though pockets of discrimination exist everywhere, the east coast is especially gay-friendly—Sydney ranks among the most diverse and accepting cities on Earth. The farther into the interior you get, the more homophobia you are likely to encounter, even though homosexual acts are now legal in every region of Australia. **Gay and Lesbian Tourism Australia (GALTA)** is a nonprofit nationwide network of tourism industry professionals dedicated to the welfare and satisfaction of gay and lesbian travelers to, from, and within Australia (www.galta.com.au). Listed below are contact organizations, mail-order catalogs, and publishers that offer materials addressing specific concerns. **Out and About** (www.planetout.com) offers a weekly newsletter addressing travel concerns and a comprehensive site addressing gay travel concerns. The online newspaper **365gay.com** also has a travel section (www.365gay.com/travel/travelchannel.htm).

**Gay's the Word,** 66 Marchmont St., London WC1N 1AB, UK (☎+44 20 7278 7654; http://freespace.virgin.net/gays.theword). The largest gay and lesbian bookshop in the UK, with both fiction and non-fiction titles. Mail-order service available.

**Giovanni's Room,** 345 S. 12th St., Philadelphia, PA 19107, USA (☎+1-215-923-2960; www.queerbooks.com). An international lesbian and gay bookstore with mail-order service (carries many of the publications listed below).

**International Lesbian and Gay Association (ILGA),** Avenue des Villas 34, 1060 Brussels, Belgium (☎+32 2 502 2471; www.ilga.org). Provides political information, such as homosexuality laws of individual countries.

**ADDITIONAL RESOURCES: GLBT.**

*Spartacus International Gay Guide 2008* (US$33).

*Damron Men's Travel Guide, Damron Road Atlas, Damron Accommodations Guide, Damron City Guide,* and *Damron Women's Traveller.* Damron Travel Guides (US$18-24). For further information, call ☎800-462-6654 or visit their website www.damron.com.

*The Gay Vacation Guide: The Best Trips and How to Plan Them,* by Mark Chesnut. Kensington Books (US$15).

# TRAVELERS WITH DISABILITIES

Those with disabilities should inform airlines and hotels of their disabilities when making reservations; some time may be needed to prepare special accommodations. Call ahead to restaurants, museums, and other facilities to find out if they are wheelchair-accessible. Guide-dog owners should inquire as to the quarantine policies of Australia.

After the 2000 Sydney Olympics and Paralympics, many locations in Australia (particularly the east) became wheelchair accessible, and budget options for the disabled are increasingly available. However, disabled travelers intending to use public transport should be wary: some of Australia's trains have extremely narrow corridors and will require a collapsible wheelchair (see **Getting Around Australia**, p. 29). Those looking to visit national parks should check the availability of wheelchair-accessible paths. Most parks try to maintain at least a few universal access trails, but some will only have one or two.

## USEFUL ORGANIZATIONS

**Accessible Journeys,** 35 W. Sellers Ave., Ridley Park, PA 19078, USA (☎+1-800-846-4537; www.disabilitytravel.com). Designs tours for wheelchair users and slow walkers. The site has tips and forums for all travelers.

**Flying Wheels Travel,** 143 W. Bridge St., Owatonna, MN 55060, USA (☎+1-507-451-5005; www.flyingwheelstravel.com). Specializes in escorted trips to Europe for people with physical disabilities; plans custom trips worldwide.

**Mobility International USA (MIUSA),** P.O. Box 10767, Eugene, OR 97440, USA (☎+1-541-343-1284; www.miusa.org). Provides a variety of books and other publications containing information for travelers with disabilities.

**Society for Accessible Travel and Hospitality (SATH),** 347 5th Ave., Ste. 610, New York, NY 10016, USA (☎+1-212-447-7284; www.sath.org). An advocacy group that publishes free online travel info. Annual membership US$49, students and seniors US$29.

# MINORITY TRAVELERS

Some would classify the majority of Caucasian Australians as racist in their attitudes toward Indigenous Australians, and this assessment may not be unfounded. Black travelers and other travelers of color may get a few stares or encounter some hostility in more remote Outback areas. As is the case in most parts of the world, cities tend to be more diverse and tolerant than far-flung, less populated destinations. Yet even Sydney has had recent troubles, most notably during the **2005 Cronulla Riots,** which garnered international attention when Caucasian youths clashed with youths perceived to be Middle Eastern. This was the most recent manifestation of the protests aimed at Muslim Australians that have brought issues of race relations back to the big cities. That said, Australia, like many nations, continues to deal with the advantages and disadvantages of a diverse populace. Increased tourism with its Asian neighbors has improved Australia's reception of Asian travelers, especially in the east.

# DIETARY CONCERNS

Fruits abound in Australia, so vegans and vegetarians shouldn't have too much difficulty keeping to their restrictions. Australia's environmentally-conscious population also works to ensure that organic and vegan options are available. The travel section of **The Vegetarian Resource Group's** website, at www.vrg.org/travel, has a comprehensive list of organizations and websites geared toward helping vegetarian and vegan travelers. They also provide an online restaurant guide. For more info, visit your local bookstore or health food store and consult

ESSENTIALS

*The Vegetarian Traveler,* by Jed and Susan Civic (Larson Publications; US$16). Vegetarians will also find numerous resources on the web; try www.vegdining. com, www.happycow.net, and www.vegetariansabroad.com, for starters.

Travelers who keep **kosher** should contact synagogues for information on kosher restaurants. Your own synagogue or college Hillel should have access to lists of foreign Jewish institutions. If you are strict in your observance, you may have to prepare your own food on the road. A good resource is the *Jewish Travel Guide*, edited by Michael Zaidner (Vallentine Mitchell; US$18). Travelers looking for **halal** restaurants may find www.zabihah.com a useful resource.

# OTHER RESOURCES

*Let's Go* tries to cover all aspects of budget travel, but we can't put everything in our guides. Listed below are books and websites that can serve as jumping-off points for your own research.

## USEFUL PUBLICATIONS

In addition to the printed travel resources listed already, there are a number of general publications that might be worth perusing before your arrival down under. Try *Culture Shock! Australia*, by Ilsa Sharp (US$15), to get you started. History buffs should also pick up *Australia: A New History of the Great Southern Land,* by Frank Welsh (US$38).

## WORLD WIDE WEB

 **LET'S GO ONLINE.** Plan your next trip on our newly redesigned website, www.letsgo.com. It features the latest travel info on your favorite destinations, as well as tons of interactive features: make your own itinerary, read blogs from our trusty researcher-writers, browse our photo library, watch exclusive videos, check out our newsletter, find travel deals, and buy new guides. We're always updating and adding new features, so check back often!

Almost every aspect of budget travel is accessible via the web. In 10min. at the keyboard, you can make a hostel reservation, get advice on hot spots from other travelers, or find out how much a train from Perth to Sydney costs.

Listed here are some regional and travel-related sites to start off your surfing; other relevant websites are listed throughout the book. As website turnover is high, use search engines (e.g., www.google.com) to strike out on your own.

### THE ART OF TRAVEL

**Backpacker's Ultimate Guide:** www.bugaustralia.com. Tips on packing, transportation, and where to go. Also tons of country-specific travel information.

**BootsnAll.com:** www.bootsnall.com. Numerous resources for independent travelers, from planning your trip to reporting on it when you get back.

**How to See the World:** www.artoftravel.com. A compendium of great travel tips, from cheap flights to self defense to interacting with local culture.

**Travel Intelligence:** www.travelintelligence.net. Travel writing from distinguished writers.

**Travel Library:** www.travel-library.com. Links for general info and personal travelogues.

**World Hum:** www.worldhum.com. An independently produced collection of "travel dispatches from a shrinking planet."

# INFORMATION ON AUSTRALIA

**Australian Tourist Commission:** www.australia.com. The low-down on Australia and traveling there, including information on its climate, economy, health, and safety concerns.

**Australian Whitepages:** www.whitepages.com.au. The place to go if you ever need a phone number or address in Australia.

**CitySearch Sydney:** www.sydney.citysearch.com.au. Enough rated bars, restaurants, museums, and events to help you navigate Australia's biggest city like a local.

**Travel Australia:** www.travelaustralia.com.au. A comprehensive, searchable source for accommodations, activities, attractions, and tours in every region of Australia.

**Embassy of Australia:** www.austemb.org. Facts about Australia and travel information related to Australian law and politics.

**World Travel Guide:** www.travel-guides.com/region/aus.asp. Helpful practical info about Australia, including the major national attractions.

ESSENTIALS

# LIFE AND TIMES

The Land Down Under may be inconveniently located, but it's got something for everyone. As the world's sixth largest country by area and one of its most sparsely populated, the vast empty expanses of Australia's Outback are ripe for exploration and ideal for the agoraphobic. But for those seeking to blend into the crowd, the continent boasts an impressive collection of teeming towns, including Sydney, which ranks among the world's most cosmopolitan and multicultural cities. Australia's many national parks are havens for outdoorsy adventurers and a variety of unique wildlife, such as kangaroos, emus, and dingoes. Known as Australia's cultural and sporting capital, Melbourne's the antidote for bush-weary city-slickers. Tourists camp out under the stars near Uluru or stay in a mega-casino in Queensland. Thrill-seekers can ski in the mountains of New South Wales or snorkel in the Great Barrier Reef. Australia boasts a continent's worth of opportunities for savvy travelers of all dispositions.

## HISTORY

### ABORIGINAL AUSTRALIA

**60,000 BC**
The first inhabitants are thought to have arrived in Australia.

**THE PEOPLE.** While **Indigenous Australians** are often thought of as a single, monolithic entity, the Aboriginal community actually consists of a wide variety of ethnic groups. It is estimated that the first humans reached Australia approximately 50,000 years ago. By the time the first Europeans landed, there may have been as many as 700,000 Indigenous people inhabiting Australia. These early residents were divided into nomadic groups, which migrated in search of food and resources. Indigenous Australians gained international visibility through the performance of track star **Cathy Freeman** in the 2000 Summer Olympics in Sydney. Freeman had the honor of igniting the Olympic Torch during the Opening Ceremonies, and, in winning the gold medal in the 400m dash, became the first Indigenous Australian to win a gold medal for Australia.

**35,000 BC**
Indigenous Australians are believed to have reached Tasmania.

**COMMUNITY LIFE.** Different Indigenous ethnicities were frequently separated from each other by territorial borders. Within their tribes, Indigenous Australians are often divided into smaller units made up of two or three families. Today, much of the Aboriginal population has been absorbed into cities, although over a quarter still live in isolated communities. While more than 200 Aboriginal languages once existed, many are endangered today.

**2000 BC**
The dingo becomes Australia's first domesticated animal.

**BELIEF SYSTEMS.** Although Aboriginal groups across Australia have developed separate legends, customs, and ceremonies, most of these groups share the same basic religious beliefs. Many indigenous people believe the world was cre-

**AD 5**
The didjeridu is invented.

ated during **the Dreaming,** or Creation Time, a mythological period when powerful ancestral beings shaped the land and populated it with humans, animals, and plants. The spirit ancestors provided the people with laws and customs, as well as the songs, dances, and rituals that form the basis of Aboriginal religious expression. There are three types of sacred land in Aboriginal culture: ceremonial sites, *djang,* and *djang andjamun.* Ceremonial sites are created by humans and used for burials, rites of passage, and other important events. At *djang* sites, a creator ancestor is believed to have passed through, taken shape, and entered or exited Earth, leaving the site safe for visitation. However, at *djang andjamun* sites, the ancestor still lingers, making for a spiritual hazard zone where human trespassing is prohibited.

# EUROPEAN SETTLEMENT

## COLONIZATION

**EXPLORATION.** In 1606, Dutch explorers became the first Europeans to set foot on the continent of Australia—or "New Holland," as they called it. The memorial at **Shark Bay** (p. 740), erected in 1616, marks the site of their first landing. In 1642, Dutch explorer **Abel Tasman** sailed forth to chart the southern coast of the continent, discovering the "new" island that now bears his name: Tasmania. In 1770, the English captain **James Cook** explored the eastern coast aboard the ship *Endeavor.* Cook and his crew of astronomers and scientists returned to England with stories of the strange plants and animals they had discovered in the area he went on to aptly name **Botany Bay** (p. 160). Though Australia's coasts were explored by numerous parties throughout the course of the 17th century, settlement was never attempted.

**THE FIRST FLEET.** Australia's first European settlement was a British penal colony. On May 13, 1787, the 11-ship **First Fleet** departed England with a cargo of over 700 convicts and 250 guards. Led by **Arthur Phillip,** the fleet arrived in Botany Bay after a grueling eight months at sea. When natural resources at the site of their landing were deemed insufficient, Phillip headed north to Port Jackson—around which later grew the city of **Sydney** (p. 110)—where he raised the British flag on January 26, 1788. In commemoration of the event, January 26 was named **Australia Day,** which is still celebrated in honor of the continent's first permanent colony.

## THE CONVICT ERA

**BEGINNINGS.** These first European settlers found themselves in an inhospitable land. The colony struggled to survive: the soil and climate proved uncooperative, the convicts were often petty criminals from London slums with little or no agricultural experience or acumen, disease was rampant,

**1606**
Willem Jansz makes the first recorded European landfall on Cape York.

**1788**
The English First Fleet arrives and founds the first European penal colony under Captain Arthur Phillip.

**1803**
Matthew Flinders completes the first-ever circumnavigation of Oz.

**1817**
Australia's first bank, the Bank of New South Wales, opens.

**1829**
The British Empire claims all of Australia.

**1850**
The University of Sydney, the country's first university, is founded.

LIFE AND TIMES

and relations with the Indigenous peoples rapidly took a turn for the worse. Supplies dwindled, and it wasn't until 1790 that the colony began to gain any kind of stability.

**1858**
Electric Telegraph links Sydney and Melbourne.

**1859**
Australian football becomes an official sport with the establishment of the Melbourne Football Club.

**1868**
The last convict settlers arrive in Australia.

**1873**
Europeans first come across Uluru.

**1880**
Bushranger Ned Kelly is hanged.

**1883**
The Sydney-Melbourne rail opens.

**1889**
Inventor Arthur James patents the electric drill.

**DEVELOPMENTS.** Though convicts were usually either employed by the government or "assigned" to private individuals during the early years of the penal colony, "tickets of leave" and pardons were granted relatively frequently, and freedom was obtainable. After the appointment of Lachlan Macquarie as Governor of New South Wales in 1809, opportunities for these freed convicts, or **Emancipists,** increased, and a balance of power with the **Exclusionists**—the colony's large-scale landowners—was reached. Macquarie encouraged exploration and expansion, and under his leadership, the settlement began to spread into the continent's interior.

# EXPANSION

**GROWTH.** While providing for the convicts had established the initial basis of the colony's economy (modest fortunes were often amassed through the sale of food and supplies to government stores), the continued influx of convicts became a source of tension. As the number of freed prisoners increased, the objective of the colony moved away from mere subsistence and toward economic prosperity, and caring for the convicts became an increasingly onerous chore for an already over-burdened population of settlers. By the 1830s, the Australian practice of **"assigning"** convicts to the service of individuals drew criticism from the English, who viewed it as one step removed from slavery. In 1840, assigning was abolished, and with it went the primary incentive for sending convicts to Australia at all. Settlers began to vehemently oppose the import of convicts, and they eventually got their way: in 1868, the last ship of prisoners unloaded its human cargo on Australia's soil.

**PROSPERITY.** The number of European settlers exploded from 50,000 in 1825 to 1,150,000 in 1861. The economy of the colony boomed in the 30 years between 1830 and 1860, thanks to major developments in **wool** and **minerals.** Australia's climate and resources proved remarkably well suited to the business of sheep farming, and by 1845, it had become the most profitable industry in the country. The growing national wealth that resulted from the increased export of wool as well as the **discovery of gold** in 1851 caused a mass immigration to the continent, increasing the population by over 1.1 million in the course of only three decades.

**CULTURAL RELATIONS.** Though the geographic, economic, and social growth of the Australian colony was excellent for the British, the same cannot be said for Australia's Indigenous people. The native population is estimated to have exceeded one million and to have sustained a high quality of life prior to European colonization, but due to the combination of conflict and disease, both the number and well-being of Indigenous Australians took a turn for the worse after 1788. Though initially relations between the two groups were cordial and even accommodating, the communication and cultural gulf gradually took its toll. European expansion inland encroached directly on both the territory and economic practices of the native people, leading to the displacement of scores of Indigenous Australians from their land and the desecration and destruction of many of their sacred sites. They responded with tenacious guerilla warfare but were ultimately defeated through force of arms. Many Indigenous Australians were killed; others were driven into the bush or fell in with the European "civilizing missions." **Disease** was an even greater factor than direct conflict in the decline of Australia's indigenous people in the 19th century. Newly introduced strains ran rampant throughout the continent, wiping out thousands of Aboriginal people. The alarming rate at which Australia's native people were disappearing prompted European settlers to pass certain laws for their protection and care. However well-meaning this gesture might have been, these laws designed to protect the Indigenous population only gave the Europeans greater power to restrict and control. Indigenous Australians were kept off their land and driven into poverty, and children of mixed descent were frequently taken from their Aboriginal families—a practice that continued well into the 20th century. The most tragic example of the **obliteration of indigenous society** occurred in the isolated territory of Tasmania, where an ancient culture was entirely exterminated over the course of only 70 years as a direct consequence of the presence of foreign settlers.

# TWENTIETH CENTURY

## UNIFICATION

**FEDERATION.** Before the formation of a central government, each of the six individual colonies that had developed over time had very little to do with one another, communicating directly with London instead. To unite the colonies, the **Commonwealth of Australia** was founded on January 1, 1901. Federation was a difficult process for Australia, and the new constitution was only ratified after a decade of debate among the colonies. The constitution united the colonies into six states, all of which are still in place: New South Wales, Queensland, South Australia, Tasmania, Victoria, and Western Australia. The Northern Territory and the Australian Capital Territory are self-governing regions but do not have state status.

**SUFFRAGE.** In Australia, **universal male suffrage** was granted in 1856. In 1902, the vote was extended to women, only nine years after New Zealand became the first country to approve women's suffrage. In 1921, Western Australia's Edith Dircksey Cowan became the first female elected as a representative to an Australian state parliament.

**1900**
The British Parliament passes the Australian constitution.

LIFE AND TIMES

**1901**
Australia becomes a federation on January 1.

**1902**
Women gain federal suffrage.

**1904**
Dalgety becomes the new capital.

**1907**
Photocopying is developed at the University of Sydney.

**1909**
The nation's first airplane takes off.

**1911**
Canberra becomes the nation's capital.

**1914**
Australia enters WWI.

**1915**
Duke Kahanamoku, famous Hawaiian swimmer, first introduces surfing in Australia.

**1920**
Qantas airline is founded.

**1923**
Vegemite is invented and quickly spreads its way across the nation.

**1926**
First Miss Australia contest is held.

**1929**
The Great Depression hits.

**1939**
Australia enters WWII.

**1942**
Daylight Savings Time is introduced as a wartime measure.

**1943**
Damien Parer, a wartime cinematographer, wins Australia's first Oscar.

**1946**
Oz's Norman Makin is voted first President of the UN Security Council.

**RACE.** During the gold rush of the mid-19th century, thousands of **Chinese miners** immigrated to the continent of Australia. In order to ensure a White Australia that was safe from non-European immigrants and—more importantly—free from the threat of cheap labor, the Australian Parliament passed the **Immigration Restriction Act** in 1901. This legislation required all non-European immigrants to pass a 50-word dictation test in any European language chosen by an immigration officer. As a result, non-white immigration into Australia took a sharp downturn for much of the early 20th century. While the act has never been officially repealed by the government, immigration policy has been amended significantly since World War II, and the number of non-Europeans in Australia has begun to climb again.

## WORLD WARS

**THE GREAT WAR.** At the outset of **World War I,** Australian prime minister Joseph Cook declared support for England, saying, "Our duty is quite clear—to gird up our loins and remember that we are Britons." An estimated 330,000 Australians went to war, 60,000 of which lost their lives and over 150,000 of which were wounded—a staggering percentage in light of the country's relatively small population of 5 million. At the **Battle of Gallipoli,** over 10,000 members of the **Australian and New Zealand Army Corps** (ANZAC) were killed, and 25,000 more were wounded during a campaign to gain control of the Dardanelles. In spite of these terrible losses, many look back at that day as a pivotal point of Australian nationalism. The government proclaimed April 25 **ANZAC Day** in 1916, and Australians still use this holiday as an opportunity to celebrate the heroism and memory of these soldiers.

**WORLD WAR II.** A generation later, the Royal Australian Air Force reaffirmed its commitment to Great Britain and its allies in **World War II,** and Australian troops celebrated victories at Tobruk and El-Alamein in North Africa. However, after the Japanese attack at Pearl Harbor on December 7, 1941—as well as the fall of British-protected Singapore on Feb. 15, 1942—Australian citizens became increasingly concerned about safety on their own shores. On February 19, 1942, Darwin, the capital of the Northern Territory, sustained the first of many **Japanese bombings.** Australia declared war on Japan independently of England (which, at the time, was battling Hitler in Europe) and turned instead to the United States for support and aid. The alliance between the US and Australia was strengthened by the war and culminated in a series of land and sea victories against Japan. All told, Australia lost roughly 34,000 men in the conflict.

## AFTER 1945

**POST-WAR BOOM.** Although Australia experienced relative peace and prosperity in the post-WWII era, the threat of

Communist China still motivated some aggressive and defensive social policies. Beginning in 1947, the Australian government extended a tempting offer to a devastated Europe: free passage to Australia in exchange for two years of labor for the Commonwealth. By 1970, more than **2.5 million immigrants** had been lured to the Land Down Under, including a wave of Asians during the late 60s.

**POWERFUL FRIENDS.** The Red Army also drove a wedge between Australia and the "Mother Country" of Britain. Unlike England, which socialized medicine in 1946, Cold-War Australia allied itself with the aggressive anti-communist and anti-socialist policies of the US. This westward shift of alliances was formalized in 1951 with the **Australia-New Zealand-United States (ANZUS)** pact. Consequently, when the US became embroiled in **Vietnam**, Australians were drafted alongside Americans, and a storm of anti-war sentiment slowly gathered. In the wake of major protests, Australian policy makers shifted their attentions eastward, focusing on opportunities and alliances in nearby Asia. Their efforts have tied the two cultures together not only economically but also demographically; Asian emigration to Australia is on the rise, and Australian restaurants have recently opened in Tokyo.

# TODAY

Australia may not make international headlines with great frequency, but no traveler should arrive in the country without brushing up on current events.

**TERRORISM.** The bombing of a nightclub in Bali's heavily touristed beach district in October 2002—one of the largest terrorist attacks since 9/11—carried grim significance for Australia. Bali is a popular destination for Australian tourists, and approximately half of the 200 victims of the attack were Australian. The bombing, which was followed by the 2004 car-bombing of the Australian embassy in Jakarta, was widely seen as a proxy attack on Australia, an active member of the US-led military force fighting the **Iraq War.** In 2003, Australia committed nearly 2000 troops to the conflict. The issue divided the nation, and protestors held massive peace rallies in all of Australia's capital cities.

**CRONULLA.** Several 2005 riots that occurred in the oceanside suburb of **Cronulla** challenged Sydney's reputation as a welcoming, muticultural metropolis. The events, spanning several days and involving the mass intimidations of Australians of Middle Eastern appearance, rocked New South Wales and revealed the hidden racial tensions that still exist between Sydney's many different ethnicities.

**PRIME OF HIS LIFE.** In November 2007, **Kevin Rudd** took over the post of Prime Minister after his **Australian Labor Party** ousted the conservative Liberal-National Coalition. Rudd replaced John Howard, who had served four terms and had

---

**1956**
Melbourne hosts the Summer Olympics.

**1958**
Australian researchers invent the Black Box Flight Recorder.

**1963**
Indigenous Australians are first granted full Australian citizenship.

**1964**
The Beatles tour Oz for the first (and only) time.

**1967**
Prime Minister Harold Holt disappears while swimming in Victoria.

**1977**
"Advance Australia Fair" becomes the national anthem.

**1995**
The Northern Territory momentarily legalizes voluntary euthanasia.

**2000**
Sydney hosts the Summer Olympics.

**2005**
Sixteen people are charged with planning terrorist attacks in Sydney and Melbourne

**2008**
Prime Minister Kevin Rudd delivers an apology to the Stolen Generation of Indigenous Australians.

LIFE AND TIMES

become the second-longest serving Prime Minister in Australian history. One of Rudd's first major actions in office was to deliver an **official apology** to the **Stolen Generations,** a phrase used to refer to the Indigenous children forcibly taken from their families by the Australian government in order to better "protect" them. Rudd's apology for this practice, which began in 1869 and lasted around 100 years, was an important step in removing the gulf that still divides Aboriginal from non-Indigenous Australians.

# PEOPLE

The Commonwealth of Australia is home to 20.6 million people, 2% of whom are Indigenous Australians. **Immigration** has defined the Australian narrative, and almost a quarter of the country's residents were born overseas. After WWII, an entire continent's worth of space needed to be filled, and formal legislation was passed as a means of doing so. The ensuing first wave of immigrants came primarily from Europe, the US, Turkey, and the former USSR. In recent years, Asians have immigrated to Australia in increasing numbers and currently account for about 7% of the Australian population.

**DIVERSITY.** Today, **multiculturalism** as a planned government project for promoting diversity is regarded as a cornerstone of the Australian national identity. Yet as much as immigration and cultural integration have defined Australia's history from the beginning, deep-seated racial tensions have become a reality and a widespread concern. From the beaches of Sydney to its inner-city neighborhoods, demonstrations against Muslim Australians—particularly those 300,000 of Lebanese descent—as well as widespread discrimination against Aboriginal groups have received international attention and caused a severe crisis of conscience in such a highly diverse nation.

**DEMOGRAPHICS.** Australia's population density is 2.6 people per sq. km. In comparison, the US averages 31 people per sq. km, and the UK a whopping 246. About 91% of Australians live in urban areas, and the suburbs are still growing. The vast majority live on or relatively near the coasts, particularly the east coast. The massive, inhospitable desert in the center of the country is perhaps the main reason for this coastal population concentration.

**LANGUAGE AND RELIGION. English** (for some quirks of Australia English, see **Glossary of 'Strine,** p. 769) is Australia's only national language, spoken in over 80% of Australian homes. According to the 2006 census, about 64% of Australians declare themselves Christians; non-Christian religions comprise about 6%. The rest either identify with no religion or chose not to respond.

# CULTURE

# FOOD AND DRINK

Although Australian cuisine has been traditionally dismissed as an uninspiring offshoot of English "pub food," Oz menus have recently undergone a multicultural makeover. European and Middle Eastern immigrants spiced up Australian cuisine in the post-WWII boom, and today's Japanese, Thai, Malay, Vietnamese, and Chinese immigrants pepper the urban centers with ethnic restaurants.

LIFE AND TIMES

**ON THE MENU.** Foreign influences aren't the only new forces in Aussie diets. The emerging Modern Australian cuisine—**"Mod Oz"** in the culinary world—has taken Indigenous fare out of the bush and into the bistro. Native ingredients are prepared with a fusion of Asian methods, producing a unique and inventive culinary style. French, German, and Italian immigrants have left their mark in Australian **vineyards,** which are gaining more and more international renown.

Breakfast, or **"brekkie,"** is usually not eaten out, and most restaurants don't open until noon. Luckily, the ultimate Aussie breakfast can be made in a hostel kitchen. Just grab a piece of toast and slather on some **Vegemite,** the infamously salty yeast by-product of Oz's breweries. Be sure to save room for **"tea"** in the evening; it's the largest meal of the day. Also, beware of ordering an "entrée;" it's an appetizer in Australia. **Tipping** in Australian restaurants is rare; however, expensive, urban restaurants expect a 5-10% gratuity for good service.

# AUSTRALIAN CUISINE

**FRUIT, MEAT, AND SEAFOOD.** Luckily for vegetarians, Australia's carnivorous contingent is balanced by its hippie sector: **vegan and organic options** abound. The Australian continent boasts a cornucopia of exotic fruits, including custard apples, lychees, passion fruit, star fruit, coconuts, quandong, and pineapples. Its meats are inexpensive and high grade—especially the veal and lamb—but the contents of the popular meat pie are usually of a more dubious quality. The doughy shell of this dish is often doused with a ketchup-like tomato sauce to disguise the taste of the meat. **Seafood** is a less questionable Australian favorite, with regional specialties like king prawns (shrimp), Balmain Bugs (a type of lobster), and Barramundi (freshwater fish).

**BUSH TUCKER.** Coastal Indigenous Australians have eaten crayfish, yabbies (freshwater shrimp), and tropical fish for centuries, but urban Australia has only recently discovered the merits of its exotic indigenous food. With the advent of Mod Oz, menus are increasingly inclined to incorporate wild **"bush tucker"** like bunya nuts, Kakadu plums, and wild rosella plums. Specialty meats like crocodile meat, Northern Territory buffalo, and kangaroo are also making a showing. However, the average tourist will still probably find witchetty grubs (ghost moth larvae) and wild magpie eggs a bit too daring.

**CHEAP EATS. Self-catering** is surprisingly easy in Australia. Most budget accommodations offer kitchen or BBQ facilities, and public BBQs are available at parks, beaches, and campsites. Your best bet for an inexpensive midday meal out is a **pub counter lunch,** which usually includes generous portions of "meat and two veg." Fish and chips is another budget Aussie institution, but it's a bit more tropical than its English cousin. Although still battered, fried, and served with thick-cut french fries, Australia's version is made from "flake," slang for shark meat. Australian-style bakeries offer a similar mix of familiar and foreign. They sell breads baked with cheese, onion, or other savory additions; sandwich-ready rolls; and blue treats like the lamington (coconut-covered chunk of pound cake dipped in chocolate) or pavlova (giant meringue).

# BEVERAGES

**COFFEE AND TEA.** Ordering "just coffee" is nearly impossible in Australia, particularly in the **cappuccino culture** of the major cities. If you need help ordering, see **Cool Beans** (p. 768). Tea, often affectionately referred to as a "cuppa," is also very popular. Sweet-toothed cafe fans may opt instead for iced chocolate, a frothy, creamy concoction of ice cream, cream, and chocolate syrup.

**BEER.** Australia produces some delicious brews, and Australians consume them readily. The best place to share a "coldie" with your mates is at one of the omnipresent Aussie **pubs.** Traditional payment etiquette is the shout, in which drinking mates alternate rounds. If the beach is more your style, throw a **"slab"** (24-pack) in the **"Esky"** (ice chest) and head to the shore. Although Foster's was marketed worldwide with the slogan, "Foster's: Australian for Beer," other brews are far more popular domestically. For more beer terminology and information on the types of beer available, consult **Terms of Embeerment** (p. 768).

**WINE.** Australian wines are among the best in the world. Exporting started soon after the first vineyards were created in the early 1800s, and the industry gained renown after a post-WWII influx of European oenophilic talent. The **Hunter Valley** (p. 177), the **Barossa** and **Clare Valleys** (p. 490), the **Swan** and **Margaret Rivers** (p. 706), and **Huon Valley** (p. 546) boast some of the best Aussie vineyards. Many cafes and restaurants advertise that they are **BYO,** or "bring your own," meaning patrons should bring their own bottle of wine.

# CUSTOMS AND ETIQUETTE

**PUBLIC BEHAVIOR AND TABOOS.** Known for their friendly informality, Australians are quick to adopt a first-name basis with new acquaintances and difficult to offend. However, it's still best to avoid public pronouncements on **sensitive topics** like race relations or refugees, and you shouldn't make any jokes about Australia's origins as a penal country. "Aborigine" has also become somewhat politically incorrect; use "Indigenous Australian" to be safe. Smokers beware: Australia's states and territories have recently implemented stringent bans on **public smoking.** Public buildings are tobacco-free throughout the continent, and smokers in licensed establishments—including bars, pubs, and hotels—can only light up in the Northern Territory. **Littering** in Australia is not taken lightly by its environmentally-conscious populace.

**WHAT TO WEAR.** For women, almost any clothing is acceptable if it steers clear of indecency. Tube tops, halters, and tank tops are all common. For men, pants or shorts are the norm. Cossies, swimmers, and togs (affectionate terms for Australia's favorite garment, the swimsuit) are appropriate only at the beach.

# SPORTS AND RECREATION

Spectator sports keep the continent cheering year-round. In winter, Western Australia, South Australia, and Victoria catch "footy fever" for **Australian Rules Football,** while New South Wales and Queensland traditionally follow **rugby.** In summer, the entire country turns to **cricket** matches. To hear the latest scores and schedules, tune in to H. G. Nelson and Roy Slaven's Sunday afternoon parody of Australian sports culture, *This Sporting Life,* on Triple-J radio, or spend Sunday morning watching one of the hugely popular Footy Shows (AFL or NRL) on television's Channel 9.

**CRICKET.** The uninitiated may have trouble making sense of a sport in which players can "bowl a maiden or a googly to the stumps," but even a novice will get swept up in the riotous national enthusiasm for these contests, which can last anywhere from an afternoon to five days. International teams stir up excitement during the summer, when they arrive to battle it out with the Australian national team in five-match tours through Melbourne, Sydney, Perth, Adelaide, and Brisbane. This season is never crazier than when Oz faces its archrival, England, in the **Ashes** series; the '06-'07 series sold over 1.25 million tickets. Domestic cricket matches assume center stage toward the end of summer, ending with the Pura Cup finals in March.

**AUSTRALIAN RULES FOOTBALL.** For many Aussies, the Australian Football League (AFL) teams fill the winter void that the end of the cricket season leaves. Played on large cricket ovals between teams of 18 players, the game was originally designed to keep cricket players in shape in the off-season. The **AFL Grand Final,** in September, is a stunning spectacle at the home of Australian sport, the **Melbourne Cricket Ground** (p. 583).

**RUGBY.** According to legend, rugby was born one glorious day in 1823 when an inspired (or perhaps frustrated) student in Rugby, England, picked up a soccer ball and ran it into the goal. Since then, rugby has evolved into an intricately punishing game with two main variants: 15-player **rugby union** and 13-player **rugby league.** On the international level, Australia has had a long history of dominance in the sport, winning the World Cup in 1999 and reaching the finals in 2003. Major tournaments such as the Tri-Nation Series (Australia, South Africa, and New Zealand) pack stadiums and pubs and grab the attention of devoted fans around the world. At home, the National Rugby League (NRL) has a large following, especially in New South Wales and Queensland, culminating in the NRL final in September. The only match that approaches the intensity and popularity of the NRL final is June's State of Origin series, in which Queensland takes on New South Wales. Both games promise a mix of blood, mud, and beer.

**SURFING.** Punishing surf and big-time waves have made Australia's **Gold Coast** (p. 341) an important destination for the world's surfers, but prime surfing conditions are the norm at most of the continent's beaches. Local surf shops are generally the best sources of information on both competitions and wave conditions. Visit www.surfingaustralia.com.au for comprehensive coverage of competitions, camps, lessons, and conditions. Web surfers can also find information on the Association of Surfing Professionals (ASP) Australasia, the premier pro surfing circuit in the region.

**MORE SPORTS.** Since the Australian national team's 2006 World Cup appearance (their first since 1974), the **"Socceroos"** and their sport have become points of national interest and pride. Their performance, the best in the nation's history, instantly vaulted Australian soccer to a level of international prominence. To watch some more established sporting traditions, visit Australia's largest cities. Every January, Melbourne hosts one of the premier Grand Slam events in tennis, the **Australian Open,** and the city's race circuit is scorched each March by the Formula One **Australian Grand Prix.** Melbourne garners national attention once again on the first Tuesday in November, when the stylish and the sporting flock to the prestigious **Melbourne Cup** horse race. On Boxing Day (the day after Christmas), both amateurs and professionals fill Sydney Harbour for the Sydney Hobart yacht race. The grueling Ironman triathlons are held in smaller venues; Port Macquarie, NSW, and Busselton, WA, host Ironman Australia and Ironman Western Australia, respectively. The competitors in these races swim, bike, and run over 226km of surf and turf for the simple glory of finishing.

# THE ARTS

While Australia has been producing canvases and novels for only 200 years or so, art is woven into the fabric of the nation itself. The rock sculptures and paintings of Indigenous artists predate the arrival of Europeans by millennia.

Today, a bevy of artists—both native and otherwise—are continuing Australia's proud artistic tradition, working in disparate styles and genres that reflect the nation's diffuse identity and evolving national consciousness.

# LITERATURE

**THE DREAMING.** Indigenous Australians have developed their own brand of literature through 50,000 years of **oral tradition.** Their stories revolve around the Dreaming, their creation legend, which is set in a mythological time where the landscape is endowed with mythic and symbolic status. Narratives of the Dreaming speak to a complex network of beliefs, practices, and customs that define Indigenous Australians' spiritual beliefs and connection to the land.

**BUSH BALLADS.** Perhaps the first Western literary genre to emerge from Australia was the **bush ballad,** a form of poetry that celebrated the working man and the superiority of bush life to dreary urban existence. The most famous of these ballads is AB Banjo Paterson's **"Waltzing Matilda,"** often considered the unofficial Australian national anthem. Henry Lawson celebrated bush life in both poems and short stories, with works like **"The Drover's Wife"** providing a popular mythology for this heavily urbanized society.

**EARLY NOVELISTS.** Early colonial novels tend to focus on the convict experience, as exhibited by both convicted forger **Henry Savory's** autobiography *Quintus Servinton,* the first Australian novel, as well as perhaps the first real Australian classic, **Marcus Clarke's** *For the Term of His Natural Life.* In the early 20th century, two female writers highlighted the changing face of the newly independent nation. Early feminist **Miles Franklin's** *My Brilliant Career* is a portrait of an independent and strong-willed woman seeking emancipation, while another female writer, **Henry Handel Richardson,** documented an immigrant family's history in *The Fortunes of Richard Mahoney.*

## TRAVEL WRITING WITH A TWIST

**IN A SUNBURNED COUNTRY, BY BILL BRYSON (2001).** With an eye for detail, a matchless commitment to historical accuracy, and an incorrigible sense of humor to boot, Bryson takes—and takes on—the road less-traveled, heading into the Outback for an unforgettable journey. From the Nullarbor Plain to the cities of the coast, this accomplished traveler and prolific writer lends his dry, observational wit to an exploration of the Land Down Under.

**CONTEMPORARY LITERATURE.** Since WWII, Australian literature has adopted a more outward-looking, cosmopolitan voice. *Voss,* by Nobel Prize winner **Patrick White,** uses the bleak emptiness of Australia's center to illuminate the universality of individual isolation. **Thomas Keneally** writes with a strong social conscience: his *The Chant of Jimmie Blacksmith* takes on the issue of turn-of-the-century race relations, and his Holocaust epic *Schindler's Ark* was later made into the film *Schindler's List.* Two-time Booker Prize winner **Peter Carey** is known for *Oscar and Lucinda* and, more recently, *The True History of the Kelly Gang,* an imaginative account of outlaw and Australian folk hero Ned Kelly. **David Malouf's** work explores the relation between cultural centers and peripheries in the immigrant experience, and his background as a poet surfaces in novels like *Remembering Babylon.* Australia's unofficial poet laureate, **Les Murray,** celebrates the irreverent with his "larrikin" characters and brought much-deserved attention to Australian poetry from every era, while the late **Judith Wright** occupies a special niche with her uniquely feminine poetic voice.

# MUSIC

**INDIGENOUS MUSIC.** Australia's rich musical tradition stretches back centuries to a time when indigenous people sang **"karma"** songs that celebrated their ancestry. Different regions produced different styles and instruments, but the **didjeridu** is perhaps the most famous musical contribution of Indigenous Australians. Invented by northern people some 2,000 years ago, the prototypes of these droning wind instruments were created using tree branches.

**THE RISE OF ROCK.** While classical music and precursors of jazz dominated the modest Australian music scene throughout the 19th and early 20th centuries, the country came into its own with the discovery of rock and roll. Shortly after the sound of Bill Haley & His Comets swept through Australia, the country produced its own rock star. Hard-rocking, hard-living **Johnny O'Keefe** was a perennial presence on the Australian charts throughout the late 50s, and his fitting nickname, "The Wild One," was also the name of his first hit. The British Invasion of the 60s also had a major impact on Australia: the **Easybeats** hit the international scene with their infectious tune, "Friday on My Mind." The wholesome acoustic sounds of the **Seekers** led the folk bandwagon, and contributions from sibling supergroup the **Bee Gees** helped Australian pop stay alive through the 60s and 70s.

**THE PUB SCENE.** In the late 70s, **AC/DC** scored big with their brand of blues-influenced heavy metal. Other groups, such as the **Skyhooks, Cold Chisel,** and **Australian Crawl,** grew up out of the pub scene and gained local fame with Aussie-themed hits that refused to emulate sounds from across the seas. In the 80s, politically aware pub-rock bands like **Midnight Oil** became famous for their energetic live shows. **Men at Work** broke into the American music scene and paved the way for superbands like **INXS** in the late 80s and thereafter.

**FROM INDIGENOUS TO INDIE.** After the dance-rock success of Arnhem Land group **Yothu Yindi** in the 90s, Indigenous music became commercially viable. Examples of politicized Aboriginal "bush rock" artists include the **Coloured Stones,** the **Warrumpi Band,** and **Archie Roach.** Indigenous pop artists in the charts recently include **Shakaya** and **Christine Anu.** At the same time, indie rock was popularized by such artists as **Silverchair, Severed Heads,** and **Savage Garden.**

**RECENT DEVELOPMENTS.** International purveyors of pop include **Delta Goodrem** and pint-sized Aussie icon **Kylie Minogue,** and rock is currently well-represented with such bands as **The Vines, Jet,** and the increasingly world-popular **John Butler Trio. Nick Cave** is still churning out hard-driving Aussie rock, both with his Bad Seeds and Grinderman. Australia's nation-wide radio station, **Triple J** (www. triplej.net.au), plays contemporary local music and actively promotes newer acts, such as indie groups **Cut Copy** and **Architecture in Helsinki.**

# VISUAL ARTS

**ABORIGINAL ART.** The rock paintings of Indigenous Australians have covered much of the Outback for millennia, and many of their carvings and sculptures still exist. Today, many artists carry on Indigenous traditions. Australia's most well-known Indigenous artist, **Albert Namatjira,** is famous for his depictions of Outback landscapes. His work made him a pioneer in the Aboriginal community, and he received full Australian citizenship in 1957. More recently, the frequently abstract and colorful paintings of **Emily Kngwarreye** have soared in value; in 2007, her *Earth's Creation* sold for over a million dollars at auction.

LIFE AND TIMES

**THE HEIDELBERG SCHOOL.** Led by artists including **Arthur Streeton, Tom Roberts,** and **Frederick McCubbin,** the **Heidelberg School** of Australian painting that emerged in the late 19th century is considered to be the root of western art in Oz. Named for the rural area near Melbourne where its painters worked, the style focused on landscapes and depictions of everyday Australian life.

**CONTEMPORARY ARTISTS.** Possibly the most famous Australian work is **Sidney Nolan's** Ned Kelly series, which tells the story of the folk hero's exploits, final capture, and execution through a series of vibrantly colored paintings. Other artists in the last half-century who have developed distinctively Australian styles include the acclaimed, controversial **Brett Whitely, Russell Drysdale, Arthur Boyd,** and abstract artist **John Colburn.** First awarded in 1921, the **Archibald Prize** is the pinnacle of Australian art and is awarded for achievement in portraiture.

# FILM

**SILENT ERA.** Australians love a good yarn, so it's little wonder that the Land Down Under also boasts one of the world's most prolific, innovative film industries. The world's first feature film was an Australian production; written and directed by Charles Tait, *The Story of the Kelly Gang* lasted 70min. and cost slightly more than $2,000. The **Limelight Department,** which was run by the Salvation Army in Melbourne, was among the world's first production companies.

**POST-WAR AND NEW-WAVE.** Despite auspicious beginnings, Aussie films suffered budget woes until foreign financing picked up during the post-WWII economic boom. Films like Leslie Norman's *The Shiralee,* a joint British-Australian production about a fancy-free wanderer forced to assume responsibility for his child, relied on foreign funding. The Australian film infrastructure didn't really solidify until the 70s, when generous government support ushered in the Australian New Wave, characterized by films like **Peter Weir's** eerie *Picnic at Hanging Rock* and **Bruce Beresford's** war epic, *Breaker Morant.*

**A LIGHT EXTINGUISHED.** Both Australia and the world of film were struck a blow in January 2008 with the passing of **Heath Ledger.** After breaking into Hollywood with the teen romantic comedy *10 Things I Hate About You,* Ledger went on to star in a string of box-office successes, including *The Patriot, A Knight's Tale,* and *Brokeback Mountain,* which earned him an Academy Award nomination for best actor. He completed his role as the Joker in Batman film *The Dark Knight* shortly before his death; the film was a critical success, and enjoyed the biggest opening weekend ever. His ashes are scattered in Karrakatta Cemetery, west of Perth.

**BOX-OFFICE BLITZ.** After the critical successes of the 70s, the 80s brought Australian films into commercial favor at the box office, both at home and abroad. Hits like *Mad Max* and *Crocodile Dundee* were wildly popular the world over. Films of the 90s were personal, Australia-specific, and often quirky—especially in intriguing character studies like *Muriel's Wedding* and *Shine.* Recent productions, such as **Baz Luhrmann's** *Moulin Rouge!* and **Phillip Noyce's** *Rabbit-Proof Fence,* demonstrate the multiplicity of themes and styles present in contemporary Australian film. The Land Down Under has sent an astonishing number of its stars abroad; these include **Geoffrey Rush** (*Shine*), **Cate Blanchett** (*Elizabeth*), **Nicole Kidman** (*Moulin Rouge!*), the New Zealand-born but Aussie-raised **Russell**

Crowe (*Gladiator*), **Guy Pearce** (*Memento*), **Hugh Jackman** (the *X-Men* series), **Toni Collette** (*About a Boy*), and **Mel Gibson** (the *Lethal Weapon* series).

# ADDITIONAL RESOURCES

## GENERAL HISTORY

*The Fatal Shore: The Epic of Australia's Founding,* by Robert Hughes (1988). A vast, entertaining tableau of Australia's early history that examines the effects of the convict transportation system on colonists and Indigenous Australians.

*A Short History of Australia,* by Manning Clark (1987). A considerably condensed version of Clark's comprehensive, influential 6-volume history of the Land Down Under.

*Damned Whores and God's Police: The Colonization of Women in Australia,* by Anne Summers (1975). A landmark work that details the treatment of women in Australian society from the colonial era to contemporary times.

*Prehistory of Australia,* by John Mulvaney and Johan Kamminga (1999). Offers a detailed account of the development of Indigenous culture over the course of the last 40,000 years and explores the continent's initial colonization as well as more current issues of Indigenous control over archaeological sites.

*The Rush that Never Ended: A History of Australian Mining,* by Geoffrey Blainey (2003). A chronicle of an industry that has both shaped Australian history and culture and defined much of the continent's geography.

## TRAVEL BOOKS

*The Songlines,* by Bruce Chatwin (1987). Travel story based on the "dreaming-tracks" or "songlines" of Aboriginal Australia. Combines history, science, and philosophy.

*Sydney,* by Jan Morris (1992). An impressionistic, elegant account of Australia's largest city that provides a portrait of modern Sydney illuminated through historical details.

*Tracks: A Woman's Solo Trek Across 1,700 Miles of Australian Outback,* by Robyn Davidson (1995). Armed with 4 camels and accompanied by a National Geographic photographer, the author crosses the desert and lives to tell the tale.

*The Confessions of a Beachcomber,* by E.J. Banfield (2001). Following Thoreau's example, Banfield ditches a stressful life and heads for the sun and sand of Dunk Island.

# From Oppression to Reconciliation

In acquiring the Australian landmass in 1788, the British acted on two assumptions. First, though the native peoples (dubbed "Aborigines") evidently had "customs," these didn't

## "In Australia, old colonial prejudices compete with new understandings."

amount to a system of law and government, which would entitle them to sovereignty. Second, these Aborigines roamed the land hunting and gathering, and didn't grow crops; therefore, the land wasn't their "property." The British acted accordingly.

Australia's indigenous peoples, who had occupied the continent for 50,000 years, suffered under the British colonists. Investors in the wool industry rapidly dispersed flocks over native hunting grounds. When Aboriginals killed these animals, the colonists responded with punishments that ranged from imprisonment to summary execution.

Australia's pastoral and mining frontiers were often marked by greed, racism, misunderstanding, and suspicion. Lacking firearms, horses, and fortifications, Aboriginals were at a severe disadvantage. These "frontier" conditions existed in Australia as recently as WWII. The last known (unpunished) mass killing of indigenous people was in 1928, near Alice Springs. It's estimated that over 20,000 Aboriginals were slain during the 140-year war of invasion.

Aboriginals lucky enough to survive the violence and diseases faced confused colonial authorities. The first wave of Christian missionaries had found Indigenous Australians difficult to convert. Rangers cautiously began to employ them. "Half-castes"— usually children of white men and Aboriginal women—were trained in what were considered useful occupations so that they could be absorbed into the invading population.

Through it all, Aboriginals tried to maintain and adapt their communal

life. They sought land security, education, and health services; they even requested to learn about the colonists' agriculture. However, the efforts of Indigenous Australians to become members of their communities were hindered by both prejudice and restrictive laws. One form of governmental "help" is now recalled with particular shame by most Australians. From 1897, state after state took children from their indigenous parents, reasoning that it was the state's duty to "rescue" younger Aboriginals from their homes. The practice of racially-motivated removal finally ceased in the 1960s. It wasn't until 2008 that the government officially apologized for its actions.

Despite this treatment, some Aboriginals developed enough loyalty to "King and Country" to enlist for the World Wars. After WWII, the Australian government began to dismantle discriminatory legal and institutional devices. Indigenous people who had "risen" to white standards were now rewarded with assimilation. However, assimilation required indigenous people to renounce their claims to land and comply with prejudicial views of their heritage. Remote Aboriginals, as well as those with exposure to colonial authority, refused assimilation in favor of self-determination.

Since the 1970s, Australian governments have acknowledged Aboriginal title to about one-fifth of the continent. Most Aboriginals must find their opportunities in cities. There, old prejudices compete with new understandings, sincere regrets about the past, and affirmations of the worth of "Aboriginality." Disproportionately unemployed, imprisoned, and afflicted by physical and emotional disorders, Aboriginals still find that the colonial past weighs heavily on their shoulders. But a communal sense of being a "surviving" people remains strong.

Tim Rowse works in the History Program of the Research School of Social Sciences at the Australian National University. His publications on Australian history include studies of colonial policy in Australia.

**A CLOSER LOOK**

# GREAT OUTDOORS

Australia's myriad ecosystems provide unparalleled opportunities for intrepid explorers who don't mind getting a little dusty—or being hundreds of kilometers away from other human beings. The country's 50-million-year isolation has allowed a plethora of unique species to evolve, making Oz home to some of the most extraordinary plants and animals on earth.

Australia's relatively recent contact with the outside world, however, has thrown its delicate ecology into peril. In the past 200 years, 27 of Australia's mammalian species have gone extinct, and many plants and animals are threatened with the same fate. While the government and many private conservation groups are mobilizing to safeguard Australia's biodiversity, issues such as deforestation and global warming are daunting obstacles to overcome.

This section provides travelers with useful information about both identifying and preserving Australian wildlife and plants. It also includes important advice for navigating the country's rougher roads and avoiding tour scams, as well as a glossary of Australian outdoors terminology.

---

### THE AUSTRALIAN GREAT OUTDOORS AT A GLANCE

- The **Great Barrier Reef** is considered to be the largest living organism in the world; it covers an area larger than Italy and is visible from outer space.
- Over **800 species of birds** call Australia home.
- The **duck-billed platypus** is one of the few venomous mammals. Males have spurs on their hind feet that they use to inject poison into adversaries.
- The venom of the inland **Taipan snake,** found in Queensland and the Northern Territory, is probably the most deadly in the world. The venom from just one bite could be used to kill around 250,000 mice.
- The **Golden Orb spider** comes the closest of any animal to spinning gold. The golden silk with which they spin the world's largest webs is almost as strong as Kevlar.
- Twelve species of **eucalyptus** exist outside Australia, but Oz boasts over 700 varieties of the tree, which pops up everywhere, including the Outback.
- Australia's **largest cattle station,** Strangeray Springs Station in South Australia, is only a little bit smaller than the country of Belgium.
- The bite of the **Tasmanian Devil** is the strongest of any living mammal.
- Fitzroy Crossing and Wyndham on the Great Northern Highway in Western Australia have earned the dubious distinction of being the world's **hottest inhabited places,** with average high temperatures of 35.6°C (96°F).

---

# FLORA

**FLOWERS.** Wildflowers are abundant in Australia's more temperate regions. Western Australia in particular stands out for its variety; each year, the landscape is painted anew with **swamp bottlebrush, kangaroo paw, Ashby's banksia,** and over **12,000 others.** Yellow and pink **everlastings** cover fields across the country, while rare, threatened **spider orchids,** hidden away in the forest, are invisible to all but the most persistent flora-finders.

**TREES AND OTHER FLORA.** Dominating forests from coast to coast, the **eucalyptus** tree is one of Oz's most adaptable species, existing in hundreds of varieties in as many different environments. The majestic **karri**—one such eucalypt—soars up to 50m tall throughout the rain-soaked southwest, while the stunted **mallee gum** squats in low scrubland copses. The characteristic bulging trunk and splayed branches of the **boab tree** serve as icons of the **Kimberley** (p. 753), Western Australia's arid northern region.

In drier areas of the southeast, a common species of the acacia tree known as the **golden wattle** is distinguished by both its fragrant blossom and its status as Australia's official floral emblem. Perhaps the rarest, most unusual tree in Australia is the **Wollemi Pine**, which was discovered in 1994 and is the sole living member of its genus (see **Wollemi National Park**, p. 167). Other trees common to the bush and coastal thickets include **banksias, tea trees,** and **grevilleas.** Feathery and almost pine-like in appearance, **casuarinas** also exist in multiple habitats. Valleys of tall tree ferns loom in temperate, rain-fed stretches of Victoria and Tasmania. The **mangrove** is an obstinate adapter from Australia's tropical coasts, whose stilt-like trunks cling tenaciously to the briny mud of alluvial swamps. Australia also has wide expanses of land with few, if any, trees. The arid Outback is dominated by dense tufts of **spinifex** grasses. Hearty **saltbush** shrubs are commonly used to convert such harsh habitats into livestock pastures.

Most of Australia's large tree species have tall, light-colored trunks, and their darker leaves only grow high above the ground. The overall effect is quite different from that of European or North American forests; here, bushwalkers find themselves surrounded by white and gray rather than brown and green.

# FAUNA

**BIRDS.** Australia is home to over 800 avian species, from the large **emu** to the tiny **fairy penguin.** Noisy flocks of **galahs, budgies,** and colorful **rainbow lorikeets** fill Aussie skies, and popular rhymes have immortalized the unmistakable, humanoid laugh of the **kookaburra.** All of these native Australian animals can be seen, and many can be handled, at open-air zoos such as the **Healesville Sanctuary** (p. 609) in Victoria and the **Taronga Western Plains Zoo** (p. 254) in New South Wales.

**MAMMALS.** **Marsupials,** or mammals that nurse their young in pouches, historically had few competitors on the Australian continent and consequently flourished in their various ecological niches. Perhaps the best-known marsupial, the **kangaroo,** can grow up to 3m long, nose to tail, and is capable of propelling itself nearly 30 ft. in a single bound. The kangaroo's smaller cousin, the **wallaby,** is also common in the Outback. Australia's other iconic marsupial, the **koala,** sleeps 18hr. per day and feasts on eucalyptus leaves. Other native marsupials include **wombats** (a rare, rotund, and terribly cuddly-looking burrowing creature), **possums, bandicoots,** and **quolls.** Two families of **monotremes,** or egg-laying mammals, also call Australia home. **Echidnas** are small porcupine-like anteaters with protruding snouts. The **platypus** sports an odd combination of zoological features: the bill of a duck, the fur of an otter, the tail of a beaver, and webbed claws unique to its own species. British naturalists treated colonists' original reports of platypuses with scrutiny and believed stuffed specimens were frauds.

GREAT OUTDOORS

**MARINE MAMMALS. Fur seals, elephant seals,** and **sea lions** populate Australia's southern shores during summer breeding seasons. **Kangaroo Island,** South Australia (p. 481), is a good place to see sea lions in their natural habitat. Dolphins are also common sights on Aussie coasts, especially in **Bunbury** (p. 704) and **Monkey Mia** (p. 740) in Western Australia; and **Sorrento,** Victoria (p. 613). **Humpback whales** frequent the eastern waters of **Hervey Bay,** Queensland (p. 370) and swim near the **Great Barrier Reef** (p. 315) between July and November.

**REPTILES.** In addition to both saltwater and freshwater crocodiles, Australia's reptiles include **goannas** (large lizards that can grow to be longer than 2m—one made an appearance in the kids' movie *The Rescuers Down Under*), and a wide array of snakes, many of them poisonous (see **Dangerous Species,** p. 66).

**CORAL.** Remarkable **coral reefs** make Australian waters a haven for snorkelers and ocean animals alike. Corals are essentially large colonies of sea polyps, and the skeletons they leave behind are gradually compacted and consolidated to form giant reefs. The **Great Barrier Reef,** off the coast of Queensland, is the world's largest coral reef. It boasts over 700 species of coral and, covering nearly 350,000 sq. km, is so large that it can be seen from space. This ecological giant shelters an incredibly diverse blend of species, including about 2000 different kinds of fish, six of the world's seven species of **sea turtle,** and the planet's largest populations of manatee-like **dugongs.**

**FISH.** Australia's waters are swimming with rare fish species. These include the enormous **potato cod** and many species of **scorpionfish,** an extremely spiny, deadly family of fish. Many oceanside shops sell convenient fish identification cards, but there a few fish with which even casual beach bums might care to be familiar. The **butterflyfish** and **batfish** are both round, but the latter is larger and has a black stripe across the eye. While the **angelfish** and **surgeonfish** have similar oblong shapes, the latter has a pair of razor-sharp spines, one on either side of its tail. Then there's the **parrotfish,** which eats bits of coral by cracking them in its beak-like mouth and envelops itself in a protective mucus sac at night.

**EXTINCT FAUNA.** Some of Australia's most interesting life forms haven't actually lived for a number of millennia. A wide range of dinosaurs—including **ankylosaurs, allosaurs,** and even giant **titanosaurs**—have been found in Australia. Queensland in particular has been a rich source of dinosaur fossils; **Dinosaur Country** (p. 454) is a must for archaeology buffs. Giant marsupials also roamed the prehistoric Australian landscape. These megafauna, which included towering kangaroo ancestors called **diprotodons** (see p. 514), disappeared soon after the arrival of humans. One infamous marsupial carnivore has survived, however. Fierce **Tasmanian Devils** are nocturnal scavengers who hunt small prey and kill livestock with their extremely powerful jaws.

**INTRODUCED AND INVASIVE SPECIES.** Humans have been responsible for the introduction of animals to Australia since prehistoric times, and many of these introduced species are now considered pests. The **dingo** (see **Dangerous Species,** p. 67) crossed the Timor Sea via Aboriginal trade routes several thousand years ago and now survives as a scavenger in the wild. Accidental introductions such as European rats and cane toads present serious threats to native fauna. The overpopulation of rabbits, supposedly introduced to Australia as targets for marksmen, has become one of Australia's most serious wildlife problems. Foxes have also upset delicate Australian ecosystems by hunting native species, particularly in Tasmania.

GREAT OUTDOORS

Domesticated cattle and sheep have been of tremendous economic importance in Australia since European settlement, and stations (ranches) can be found throughout the country. Vast tracts of land have been converted to pasture to support the meat and wool industries, resulting in a dramatic shift in the ecological balance. The farming of non-native honeybees has also become a growing part of the economy.

# DANGEROUS SPECIES

While Australia is home to some of the world's most deadly creatures, travelers who take adequate safety precautions have little reason to worry about feral fauna. Still, it's best to remember that some of the most dangerous animals are also some of the most harmless-looking. When exploring, keep a respectful distance from the wildlife.

Much of the danger associated with smaller land animals can be decreased by covering up skin, so wear boots, pants, and long sleeves while hiking. If bitten or stung, it's best to take the offending creature to the hospital with you (if you can safely capture it) so that doctors can administer the correct treatment. The following list highlights an array of potentially harmful Australian critters and details the appropriate safety precautions to be taken with each.

**IF YOU GIVE A CROC A COOKIE, HE'LL BITE YOUR ARM OFF.** While some animals may be safer to approach than others, introducing domestic habits to wildlife is never a good idea. In addition to provoking attacks, feeding or interacting with wild animals can make them less fearful of humans and more likely to venture into both cities and campsites. It can also make them less self-sufficient and more dependent on humans.

**Ticks and mites:** Sure, snakes are scary, but smaller animals can be harmful too. Mites and ticks vary in size: some are barely visible while others are a centimeter across. They are found all over Australia, particularly in eastern coastal areas, and can carry **scrub typhus.** Visitors should also be alert for **paralysis ticks,** which can, in extreme cases, paralyze human victims with their toxin. Be particularly vigilant when camping or hiking in the bush. Symptoms of a tick bite vary, but can include headache, nausea, swelling, and itchiness. **Safety information:** Wearing light-colored clothing makes it easier to spot ticks. Always keep bug repellent handy. Don't touch dead or rotting wood, and avoid sitting directly on the ground or on logs. Check your skin for lumps or swelling when hiking or camping. Seek medical attention if you develop symptoms of tick paralysis (weakness, swollen lymph nodes, fever, flu-like symptoms, partial paralysis) or scrub typhus (headache, muscle pain, fever, gastrointestinal discomfort).

**Snakes:** While Australia is home to the world's most poisonous snakes, the majority of these species are terrified of humans and will slither away at the sound of footsteps. If cornered, however, some will attack in self-defense. Snakes are of greatest concern in the Wet (see **When to Go,** p. 1). **Safety information:** Avoid walking through brush or grass too tall or dense to allow you to clearly see where you are walking. Step on (rather than over) logs, as snakes often bask next to them. If a snake is spotted, don't make any sudden moves; back away slowly. If bitten, tightly wrap the wounded area, working the bandage down to the tip of the limb and back up to the next joint to help slow the spread of venom. Seek medical attention immediately, and keep the affected area immobile. Do not try to suck out the venom or clean the bite, and don't panic—most snake bites can be treated effectively if dealt with quickly. Bites from unidentified snakes should always be treated as potentially dangerous.

**Spiders:** The famous **golden orb spider** can grow to be as big as a child's head but poses little threat to humans. The **funnel-web, redback,** and **white-tailed spiders** are among the most dangerous arachnids Australia has to offer. The funnel-web is oval-shaped with brown or gray markings; favors cool, wet places in eastern Australia (including Tasmania); can cause serious illness and death. The redback (common throughout Australia, especially in urban areas) gets its name from its red-striped back (sometimes brown or orange-striped). The white-tailed spider is found throughout Australia—sometimes in urban areas—and can be identified by its lighter-colored rear end. **Safety information:** Funnel-web bite symptoms include pain, sweating, excessive salivation, abdominal discomfort, vomiting, and mouth numbness. Redback bites can be treated with an antivenom, and white-tailed bites are often accompanied by nausea and burning pain. If bitten, apply an ice pack and seek immediate medical attention. Symptoms include pain, swelling, sweating, fever, headache, and nausea.

**Crocodiles:** Saltwater crocodiles, a.k.a. estuarine crocodiles or **"salties"** (some Aussies refer to them as "snapping handbags"), actually live in both salt and freshwater and can grow to lengths exceeding 5m. Freshwater crocodiles (**"freshies"**) are found only in freshwater. Though they will bite if provoked, they generally present little danger to adults. Crocodiles are found almost exclusively in the tropical north of Australia, although they range farther inland than you might expect (hundreds of kilometers, especially during the Wet). **Safety information:** Salties are difficult to see and will attack without provocation. When in croc territory, always camp, prepare food, and wash dishes more than 50m from water and at least 2m above the high-water mark. Do not swim in croc territory unless the state parks service has posted signs indicating that it is safe. Be particularly careful during the breeding season (Sept.-Apr.) and at night, when crocs are most active. A good way to identify dangerous areas is to look for mud slides where crocs have entered and exited the water. When **crossing a stream** in a 4WD, stay inside your vehicle—even if stuck, you're better off waiting for another car to provide assistance than attempting to dislodge your vehicle amid snapping crocs (if you're stuck in a stream in a remote area—well, good luck, mate).

**Sharks:** While sharks generally don't bother humans unless provoked or attracted by blood, several shark attacks occur each year in Australia. **Safety information:** Lifeguards at popular beaches generally keep good watch, but stay inside the flagged areas. Exit the water immediately if you are cut or bleeding, or if you see a suspicious-looking fin.

**Dingoes:** Believed to be descendants of wild Asian dogs, dingoes probably found their way to the continent 5000 years ago as the result of trade between Aboriginal and Indonesian peoples. Only 4975 years later, they found their way into pop culture when the parents of 10-week-old Azaria Chamberlain were charged with the infant's murder and blamed wild dingoes for her death instead. Dingoes pose little threat to adults but can injure or even kill small children. **Safety information:** When in dingo country, pack away all food and keep fishing bait off the ground.

**Blue-ringed octopus:** At rest, the blue-ringed octopus is normally yellow or brown; the bright blue rings appear only when the animal is about to attack. Though small (from the size of a pea to 10 in. across) and often pretty, they carry enough poison to kill 25 adults (roughly one marine biology class) at any given time. Their painless bite can penetrate a wetsuit and is followed by paralysis, respiratory arrest, and death. **Safety information:** Blue-ringed octopi can vary in color and size. Be careful when walking on the beach. Do not walk through tidal rock or coral pools, and avoid darkened areas. If stung, seek immediate medical attention.

**Box jellyfish:** Box jellyfish are unfortunately both attractive and lethal. These *femmes fatales* of the ocean are large, translucent white, and have tentacles up to 2m in length. They are hard to spot and inhabit the waters of the Top End Oct.-Apr. and the northern shores on the west and east coasts Nov.-Apr. **Safety information:** Warnings to stay out of the water should be strictly observed. Box jellyfish that have washed up on shore are still dangerous. Stings can be fatal; the pain alone causes immediate shock. Do not attempt to remove jellyfish tentacles, as this can increase the amount of toxin absorbed. Vinegar should be poured over affected areas as quickly as possible to prevent further discharge of toxins, and immediate medical attention is crucial.

**Irukandji jellyfish:** The Irukandji sting is not necessarily lethal, but it can cause the incredibly painful "Irukandji syndrome." The Irukandji is tiny (2cm), and swimmers sometimes don't realize they've been stung, even though stings are often characterized by a rash. Symptoms can develop any time from an hour to a few days after the sting. As always, seek medical attention if you have any doubts. **Safety information:** Many jellyfish stings can be treated by dousing the stings with vinegar. Calamine lotion and antihistamines can help to relieve the pain.

**Cassowaries:** Imagine, if you will, a gigantic, brightly colored turkey on stilts. Now, imagine it has huge, velociraptor-like claws. You should now have a good mental image of a cassowary. These large, flightless birds are found mainly in Queensland and can grow up to almost 2m in height and run 50kph. When threatened, they strike out with both sets of claws (which can slice through wood). **Safety information:** Cassowaries are most likely to attack during mating season (winter). Do not approach a cassowary; rather, watch it quietly, then back away slowly. If threatened, try to put something big between you and the cassowary, like a tree, a car, or your least favorite travel companion.

**Cone snails:** Killer snails? Proof that everything in Australia has it out for humans. Cone shell snails are often beautiful, with plain, spotted, or striped cone-shaped shells, but they can seriously injure and even kill humans. They are most often found in reef waters, sand flats, tidal pools, and mud. **Safety information:** Wear water shoes or sandals when exploring any of the aforementioned areas. Be careful about picking up shells, and keep a close eye on children. If you experience pain, blurry vision, disturbed speech or hearing, swelling, numbness, or nausea, seek immediate medical attention.

**Stonefish:** The stonefish is the most venomous fish in the world, with 13 toxin-filled spines lining its back. They are found on the seabed and in tidal inlets. True to their name, stonefish are virtually indistinguishable from rocks. **Safety information:** Wear water shoes, watch where you step, and tread lightly. Contact with stonefish spines causes intense pain and muscle weakness and requires immediate medical attention.

**Plants:** As if the animals weren't enough, Australia also has poisonous plants in its arsenal of dangerous organisms. The **Gympie bush**—a large shrub with heart-shaped leaves—is found throughout Queensland and can sting anyone who gets too close with its tiny, toxic hairs. Symptoms include a stinging sensation and redness; in extreme cases, the plant may cause death. **Safety information:** To remove the stinging hair, affix plaster or a bandaid to the area of the wound and then peel it off. As always, seek immediate medical attention.

# NATIONAL PARKS

Land is a tremendous source of national pride for Australians, so it follows that the government has designated over 28 million hectares of land as national parkland. From the great sandy beaches of the east coast to the mountains of the southwest, Oz offers a dramatic landscape, much of which is accessible to campers, climbers, and bushwalkers of all levels.

## GREAT BARRIER REEF MARINE PARK

The **Great Barrier Reef** (p. 315) is one of Australia's most popular attractions. The longest coral formation in the world, it is actually a series of many reefs that stretches more than 2500km along the eastern coast of Queensland, from the Tropic of Capricorn to Papua New Guinea. There are strict national marine park rules against removing any living creatures from the sea (including sedentary corals); there are hefty fines for removing any piece of a coral reef.

## NATIONAL PARKS ON LAND

Most national parks require visitors to pay modest fees; day passes are normally $6-12 per vehicle (more for week passes), while Parks Passes allow you to make unlimited visits to selected parks within a given period of time. Some state parks require camping permits (usually around $5-10), which can be obtained from the local ranger station. The list below contains contact information for each state's parks service, most of which provide free publications on state and national protected areas. For direct links to individual parks across Australia, visit www.ea.gov.au/pa/contacts.html.

**NatureBase (CALM),** Locked Bag 104, Bentley Delivery Ctr. WA 6983 (head office ☎08 9442 0300, general inquiries 9334 0333; www.calm.wa.gov.au).

**South Australia National Parks and Reserves,** addresses and phone numbers vary by region (☎08 8340 2880; www.parks.sa.gov.au).

**Natural Resources, Environment and the Arts,** P.O. Box 496, Palmerston, NT 0831 (☎08 8999 4555; www.nt.gov.au/nreta/parks).

**New South Wales Department of Environment and Climate Change,** P.O. Box A290, Sydney, South NSW 1232 (☎02 9995 5000; www.environment.nsw.gov.au).

**Parks Victoria,** Level 10, 535 Bourke St., Melbourne, VIC 3000 (☎03 8627 4699; www.parkweb.vic.gov.au).

**Queensland Parks and Wildlife Service,** P.O. Box 15155, City East, QLD 4002 (☎1300 130 372; www.epa.qld.gov.au).

**Tasmania Parks & Wildlife Service,** G.P.O. Box 1751, Hobart, TAS 7001 (☎1300 135 513; www.parks.tas.gov.au).

# CAMPING AND BUSHWALKING

Camping, hiking, and bushwalking (hiking off marked trails) are the best ways to experience Australia's wilderness. Camping outside designated campsites is usually not permitted near campgrounds, trailheads, or picnic areas. But while bush camping lacks amenities, it's often free; in some cases, permits (up to $12) may be required. Bush camping is usually only allowed in specific sections of parks—check with a parks office or ranger before setting up camp. As tempting as it may be, avoid camping on sandy creek beds, as rains can turn your convenient camping spot into a raging river with little warning.

Campers should be careful to leave no trace of human presence. A portable stove is a safer (and more efficient) way to cook than using vegetation to build a campfire. If you must make a fire, keep it small and use only dead branches or brush instead of cutting down live plants. If there are no toilet facilities, bury human waste at least 15cm deep and 50m from any water source or campsite (paper should be carried out or burned with a lighter). Always pack and carry your garbage in a plastic bag until you reach a trash receptacle.

Two excellent web resources for travelers planning camping or hiking trips in Australia are www.camping.com.au and the **Great Outdoor Recreation Pages** (www.gorp.com). *Hiking Tropical Australia*, by Lew Hinchman and John N. Serio (Grass Tree Press; US$16) provides planning tips, directions, and trail descriptions. For topographical maps of Australia, contact **Geoscience Australia** (☎02 6249 9111 or 1800 800 173; www.ga.gov.au), or write to G.P.O. Box 378, Canberra, ACT 2601. Local visitors centres provide information on park-specific camping and wildlife, and have maps and brochures.

GREAT OUTDOORS

Australia has its share of long treks for the adventurous. Established in 1970, the **Bicentennial National Trail** stretches for 5330km through Queensland, New South Wales, and Victoria. For the less adventurous, the 220km **Larapinta Trail** (p. 304) winds from Alice Springs into the West MacDonnell ranges. The **Overland Track** (p. 552), perhaps Australia's most famous trail, connects Cradle Mountain and Lake St. Clair through 80km of World Heritage wilderness in Tasmania. For highlights of Australia's bushwalks, see **Discover Australia,** p. 3.

 **LEAVE NO TRACE.** *Let's Go* encourages travelers to adopt the "Leave No Trace" ethic and protect natural environments for future generations. Set up camp on durable surfaces, use cook stoves instead of campfires, and respect wildlife and natural objects. For more information, contact the Leave No Trace Center for Outdoor Ethics, P.O. Box 997, Boulder, CO 80306, USA (☎+1-800-332-4100 or 303-442-8222; www.lnt.org).

# EQUIPMENT

**WHAT TO BUY.** Good camping equipment is sturdy and light. Buy ahead, as it is generally more expensive in Australia than in North America.

**Swag and sleeping bag: Swags** are portable, tent-like shelters made of tough, water-resistant canvas, with built-in sleeping bags that usually contain foam mattresses. They are a popular, uniquely Australian option and start at around $100 (visit www.swag-saustralia.com.au for a variety of options). Bringing a **sleeping bag** from home is a cheaper—albeit less protective—option. Most sleeping bags are rated by season ("summer" bags work best at 30-40°F; "four-season" or "winter" are suitable for temperatures below 0°F). Prices range from US$60-200 for a summer synthetic to US$240-300 for a good down winter bag. **Sleeping pads** are also an essential; foam pads (US$10-30), air mattresses (US$15-50), and self-inflating pads (US$30-120) are all possible options. Bring a **stuff sack** lined with a plastic bag to keep your stored sleeping bag dry.

**Tent:** The best **tents** are free-standing (with their own frames and suspension systems), set up quickly, and only require staking in high winds. Low-profile dome tents are the best for variable conditions. Good 2-person tents start at US$100, 4-person at US$180. Make sure your tent has a fly and waterproof seams. Other useful accessories include a **battery-operated lantern,** a plastic **groundcloth,** and a nylon **tarp.**

**Backpack: Internal-frame packs** mold better to your back, keep a lower center of gravity, and flex adequately to adapt to difficult conditions. **External-frame packs** are generally easier to pack because of their large number of pockets, but are also far more unwieldy and less comfortable than their internal-frame cousins. The type of pack you choose depends on personal preference and the kind of hiking you are plan to do. When deciding on a pack, the best thing to do is go to a store where you can consult a professional and try a number of packs on for size. Regardless of the type though, one thing you should make sure your pack has is a strong, padded hip belt that will transfer weight from your shoulders to your core. Any serious backpacking requires a pack of at least 4000 cu. in. (16,000cc), plus 500 cu. in. to fit sleeping bags; generally, internal-frame packs are one large pocket, with space for a sleeping bag inside it. When it comes to backpacks, it doesn't always pay to economize: sturdy models cost anywhere from US$60-500. Before buying, fill the pack with something heavy and walk around the store to get a sense of how it distributes weight; many stores will even fit the pack to your back upon purchase. It is also recommended that you buy either a **rain cover** (around US$20) or store all of your belongings in **plastic bags** inside your pack.

**Boots:** Boots provide protection against snake bites, mites, and ticks, and are absolutely essential for Outback bushwalks. Be sure to wear sturdy leather hiking boots with good ankle support. They should fit snugly over 1-2 pairs of wool socks and thin liner socks. Start breaking in boots several weeks before you leave in order to spare yourself painful blisters. Treat your boots to some waterproofing before leaving on a hike.

**Water purification and transport:** On long hikes, you'll need to carry water or purify what you find along the trail. **Boiling** water for 3-5min. is the most effective—although not the most convenient—method of purification. **Iodine and chlorine tablets** are the cheapest alternative method, but they won't rid dirty water of its muck or its characteristic taste. Ideally you should collect water from clear, fast-moving sources, but even then, debris and dirt can end up clouding your water bottle. **Portable water filters** pump out crystal-clear water but often require careful maintenance and extra filters. Don't subject them to dirty water unless you want to repeatedly clean or replace clogged filter cartridges. For transport, **plastic water bottles** keep water cooler than metal ones do and are virtually shatter- and leak-proof. Large plastic **water bags** (bladders) can hold up to several gallons and are perfect for long-haul travel. When empty, bladders occupy virtually no space and weigh next to nothing.

**Other necessities: Synthetic layers,** like those made of polypropylene, and a fleece jacket will keep you warm even when wet. **Rain gear** is absolutely essential on any hiking trip; a waterproof—as opposed to water-resistant—jacket and pair of pants acts as protection against both wet weather and wind. A **space blanket** will help you to retain your body heat and doubles as a groundcloth (US$5-15). In Australia, fires are only permitted in designated fireplaces; to cook elsewhere you'll need a **camp stove** (the classic Coleman starts at around US$50) and a propane-filled fuel bottle to operate it. Also, don't forget a **first-aid kit, flashlight, pocketknife, insect repellent, calamine lotion,** and **waterproof matches** or a **lighter.**

**WHERE TO BUY IT.** The mail-order and online companies listed below offer lower prices than many retail outlets, but visit local camping or outdoors stores to get a good sense of the look and feel of necessary items.

**Recreational Equipment, Inc. (REI)** (US and Canada ☎+1-800-426-4840; abroad 253-891-2500; www.rei.com).

**Campmor,** (US and Canada ☎+1-800-525-4784; abroad 201-335-9064; www.campmor.com).

**Discount Camping,** 833 Main North Rd., Pooraka, SA 5095, Australia (☎08 8262 3399; www.discountcamping.com.au).

**Mountain Designs,** P.O. Box 824, Nundah, QLD 4012, Australia (☎07 3856 2344; www.mountaindesigns.com).

**Eastern Mountain Sports (EMS)** (☎+1-888-463-6367; www.ems.com).

# WILDERNESS SAFETY

Always stay warm, dry, and hydrated. It's simple advice, but following it will prevent the vast majority of life-threatening wilderness situations. Plan ahead; you'll need two liters of water per day, and coming by liquids in the Outback can be tricky. Avoid alcohol and coffee, which accelerate dehydration. Prepare yourself for emergencies by always packing **rain gear, warm layers** (including a **hat and mittens**), a **first-aid kit,** a **reflector,** a **whistle, high energy food,** and **extra water.** Also, bring along a **compass** and a **detailed topographical map** of the area you're exploring. In terms of layers, go for **synthetic materials** such as fleece, Gore-Tex®, or wool; never rely on cotton for warmth, as it doesn't dry once it's gotten wet.

Make sure to **check all equipment** for defects before setting out. Check out forecasts before leaving and pay attention to the skies while hiking, since **weather patterns** can change suddenly. Always let someone know when and where you are hiking, whether it be a friend, hostel, park ranger, or local hiking organization. Many larger parks offer registration services at their entrances.

**Sunglasses, sunscreen,** and a **brimmed hat** are musts in Australia. **Light-colored clothing** also helps reflect the sun's rays. Total fire bans are unique to Australia and are common in many parts of the country. Make sure to check on fire dangers before going hiking, as they can sometimes result in the closure of trails.

If you plan on bushwalking, it's an excellent idea to rent an **Electronic Position-Indicating Radio Beacon (EPIRB),** also known as a **Personal Locating Beacon (PLB).** EPIRBs use satellite tracking to pinpoint your location and send a distress signal to emergency workers. EPIRB rentals cost $50-100. If you need to be rescued, simply turn on (and leave on) the EPIRB; a helicopter will be sent to find you. A more expensive option is a **satellite phone.** Many car rental companies provide EPIRB or satellite phone rental options.

# WATER ACTIVITIES

Australia offers unmatched opportunities for surfing, scuba diving, kayaking, and whitewater rafting. Water skiing is also common in the southeast, while windsurfing and sailing are particularly popular in the **Whitsunday Islands** (p. 399). Most resorts and some hostels rent out equipment to guests. Put on waterproof, high-SPF sunblock before undertaking any water activities. Australia has the highest rate of skin cancer in the world, a testament to the strength of the Australian sun and the lure of the outdoors.

**SWIMMING.** Many of Australia's beaches are patrolled by lifeguards, especially during the summer months. Patrolled beaches will be clearly marked with yellow-and-red flags that designate areas safe for swimming; be sure to confine your swimming to the water between these flags. Rips (undertows) are very common. If you get caught in a rip, don't try to swim against it. Instead, swim parallel to the shore until you've escaped its pull. Make sure to check about water conditions if you plan on swimming at an unpatrolled beach.

**SURFING.** Australia's beaches offer excellent conditions for surfers of all levels. Beginners should look for sandy beaches, where waves break on sand bars rather than on sharp reefs. A 2hr. lesson should be enough to get you upright on a longboard, though practice is required to ride the more maneuverable shortboard. Sunburn is a serious concern—consider wearing a rash guard (a tight-fitting, lightweight shirt of swimsuit-like material) to protect yourself. As with swimming, watch out for rips and check conditions at unpatrolled beaches. For current surf conditions and live surfcams, visit www.coastalwatch.com. *Surfing Australia*, by Mark Thornley, Peter Wilson, and Veda Dante (Tuttle Publishing; US$25), is a comprehensive guide to catching waves in Australia.

**SCUBA DIVING AND SNORKELING.** Australia boasts a number of the world's best locales for scuba diving. For beginners, most dive operators offer introductory dives with a trained guide. For those who want to take it to the next level, the most common certification course is with an instructor from the Professional Association of Diving Instructors (PADI). The cheapest courses in Queensland can be found at **Hervey Bay** (p. 370), **Bundaberg** (p. 380), and **Magnetic Island** (p. 408); however, courses are generally even cheaper in less-touristed areas. A diving medical exam is required for certified dives and certification courses. These are usually cheapest (around AUS$40) in hotspots like **Cairns** (p. 417) and **Airlie Beach** (p. 395). Snorkeling is also popular: all you need is a mask, snorkel, and fins, available at most hostels and resorts for a small fee.

**RAFTING AND KAYAKING.** Following the rapids of Australia's rivers, white-water enthusiasts get to experience some of Australia's most spectacular wilderness areas. The **Franklin River** (p. 553) in Tasmania is a hotspot for white-water excursions. Sea-kayaking is an increasingly popular activity, perhaps because it involves stabler boats and calmer waters than its river equivalent. Sea-kayakers have the freedom to explore remote coastal areas that are often inaccessible by car or foot. Opportunities are widespread, particularly in the **Whitsunday Islands** (p. 399) in Queensland.

# ADVENTURE TRIPS AND TOURS

Organized adventure tours offer another way to explore the wilderness. Activities may include hiking, biking, horseback riding, skiing, canoeing, kayaking, and rafting. Tourism bureaus can often suggest trails and outfitters; camping and outdoor equipment companies are also good sources of information. Companies such as **Adventure Tours Australia** (☎08 8132 8230 or 1300 654 604; www.adventuretours.com.au) and **Adventure Company Australia** (☎07 4052 8300; www.adventures.com.au) inform their clients about subjects as diverse as ecology and Aboriginal culture in addition to leading trips through the Outback.

**SOUNDS TOO GOOD TO BE TRUE? IT PROBABLY IS.** Upon arriving in Australia's regional hubs, today's budget travelers are frequently bombarded with pre-packaged "deals." These tours promise to cover everything, from accommodations to food to adventure. Popular east-coast travel routes are especially overrun by these packages, which sometimes guarantee tours of the entire Queensland coast for under $300. But once tourists arrive at each destination, hidden extra charges start to add up. Of course, not all tour companies are out to fleece you; many reputable agencies offer decent savings. A little investigation will fend off disappointment. If a tour package sounds suspicious, look up the companies involved, ask around, and determine whether their descriptions match your expectations. Be sure to ask about the length of time spent in each place and if there are hidden charges associated with food, fuel, accommodation, insurance, upgrades, and park entrance fees (some tour companies will double "park fees," keeping half for themselves). Finally, be sure to get it all in writing.

# DRIVING IN THE OUTBACK

Driving is the easiest—and, sometimes, the only—way to get around the Australian Outback. Public transportation is limited in the areas outside major cities; offroading is a way of life there. However, if you plan to drive, be prepared for some very long roadtrips. Also, certain roads and national parks are inaccessible without a 4WD vehicle. If renting, be aware that rental companies have complicated policies. Be sure you fully understand how many kilometers you are allowed to drive, where you are allowed to drive (many don't allow clients to take 2WD vehicles on roads not maintained by the government, making some parks inaccessible), and what your insurance plan does and does not

**GREAT OUTDOORS**

**1 Litchfield National Park:** Marvel at the magnetic termite mounds, some approaching 7m high, which are surpassed only by the area's waterfalls.

**2 Kakadu National Park:** Observe massive 150m waterfalls set against Aboriginal rock art galleries.

**3 Arnhem Land:** Experience some of the roughest Outback excursions that Australia can offer in this Aboriginal homeland in the Top End.

**4 Nitmiluk National Park:** Canoe through 13 gorges on the beautiful Katherine River.

**5 Purnululu (Bungle Bungle) National Park:** Hike by the Bungle Bungle Range or through the narrow Echidna Chasm.

**6 Iron Range National Park:** Explore the dense rainforest at the tip of the continent.

**7 Daintree National Park:** Hike the walks of Mossman Gorge and witness the collision of rainforest and reef in Cape Tribulation.

**8 Great Barrier Reef:** Snorkel or scuba dive in and around the largest living organism in the world.

**9 Eungella National Park:** Walk misty slopes and valleys in the "land where clouds lie low over the mountains."

**10 Uluru-Kata Tjuta National Park:** Visit the iconic symbol of the Australian Outback.

**11 Fraser Island:** Roam the pristine dunes on the world's largest sand island.

**12 Lamington National Park:** Waterfalls, rainforests, and an ancient volcanic crater provide a scenic backdrop to this bushwalker's paradise.

**13 Border Ranges National Park:** Enjoy prime picnic areas and views that rival those of the more touristed neighboring parks.

**14 Mount Warning National Park:** Visit the largest caldera in the Southern Hemisphere, formed by an ancient volcano and named by Captain Cook himself.

**15 Dorrigo National Park:** Hike through lush rainforest filled with wildlife.

**16 Warrumbungle:** Enjoy long walks and excellent wildlife sightings among craggy volcanic peaks.

**17 Oxley Wild Rivers National Park:** Gaze at gorgeous gorges, endangered wildlife, and waterfalls in over 140,000 hectares of national park.

**18 Booti Booti National Park:** Climb the 20m tower for spectacular views of coastal wetlands.

**19 Wollemi National Park:** Encounter pockets of undiscovered land in the second largest park in NSW.

**20 Blue Mountains National Park:** Ride the world's steepest railway or bushwalk over 140km of trails.

**21 Kanangra-Boyd National Park:** Experienced bushwalkers will appreciate the remote solitude of this rugged wilderness.

**22 Royal National Park:** Tour the world's second-oldest national park with 16,000 hectares of diverse ecosystems.

**23 Leeuwin-Naturaliste National Park:** From deep whale watching spots to fossil-filled caves, anyone can find adventure here.

**24 Cape Leeuwin:** The southwesternmost point of mainland Australia boasts magnificent ocean vistas.

**25 Flinders Chase National Park:** Hang out at the Remarkable Rocks in the company of New Zealand fur seals on the western coast of Kangaroo Island.

**26 Kosciuszko National Park:** Ski, hike, or just marvel at Australia's tallest mountains.

**27 Grampians National Park:** Learn about Aboriginal culture in the midst of rugged beauty.

**28 Snowy River National Park:** Get a taste of true Australian wilderness.

**29 Croajingolong National Park:** Trek through 100km of temperate rainforest in this UNESCO World Biosphere reserve.

**30 Wilson's Promontory National Park:** Take day-long and overnight trails in this hugely popular, unspoiled marine park.

**31 Narawntapu National Park:** Sample a number of popular hiking tracks and enjoy the company of wallabies.

**32 Mount William National Park:** Lounge on some of the best beaches in Tasmania, or bushwalk among marsupials.

**33 Mole Creek Karst National Park:** Explore the park's yawning caves and become a true spelunker.

**34 Freycinet National Park:** Enjoy prime swimming or snorkeling in this picturesque park.

**35 Southwest National Park:** Take in endless kilometers of untouristed mountains and lakes.

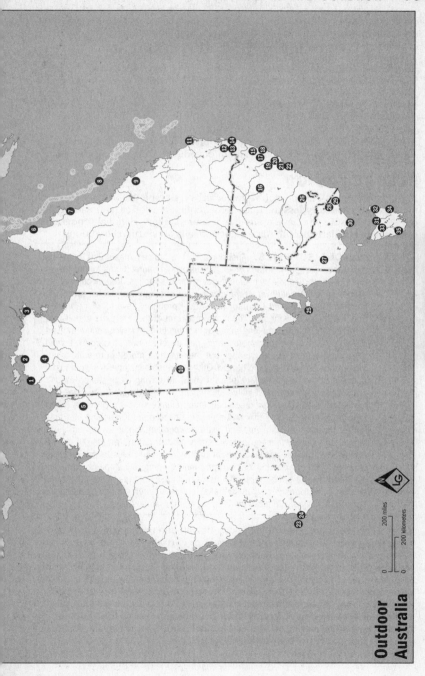

**Outdoor
Australia**

200 miles

200 kilometers

cover (windshield dings, scratches, underbody damage from sharp rocks, flat tires, and kangaroo collision damage are all common problems that can result in hefty fines). See **Costs and Insurance** (p. 31) for more info.

If you're spending a significant amount of time on the road, you might want to consider an automobile club membership, which can provide roadside assistance. The **Australian Automobile Association** (AAA) provides roadside assistance and has reciprocal relationships with automobile associations in other countries (see **Essentials**, p. 33). Roadside assistance is generally limited to sealed (bitumen) roads and is restricted to electrical and mechanical breakdown. An excess fee applies to most other problems (such as damage caused by rocks, trees, or animals). Extra charges also apply to assistance outside coverage zones. Talk to the state AAA office about coverage details before embarking.

## BEFORE YOU GO

If you're using a 4WD and you've never driven one before, it may be worth taking an introductory lesson. Many rental companies offer half- and full-day classes. Make sure you have up-to-date, accurate maps; regional topographic maps are particularly useful. Also, inquire locally about road conditions.

**VEHICLE SUPPLIES.** Australia's vast expanses mean that roadside assistance is often hundreds of kilometers away, making it crucial that travelers always carry their own emergency vehicle supplies. Rental companies should supply breakdown kits and may also offer survival packs, which are charged only if opened (around $90). You'll probably have to pick up additional supplies on your own. The most important of these is extra fuel. If your vehicle doesn't have one long-range or two regular fuel tanks, secure at least one extra tank of fuel in a metal safety can in your trunk (so it doesn't slosh around). Plastic cans are cheaper, but they are also more apt to spill, creating noxious fumes and a fire hazard. Other essentials include: two spare tires and a jack (as well as a jack plate if you'll be driving on unsealed roads); jumper cables; a wrench; Phillips and flat-head screwdrivers (both small and large, and long enough to reach concealed engine spaces); pliers (a bigger pair for gripping larger items and a needle-nosed pair for reaching into tight spots); a knife; a flashlight; and extra oil, coolant, clean water, and hose sealant. Also important are a new battery (if your current one is old or corroded) in static-resistant, absorbent packaging; road flares; a tire iron and pressure gauge; extra fan belts, rope, and sheeting; a compass; blankets; and food. Useful but nonessential items include duct tape, extra windshield washer fluid (for especially dusty treks), an ice scraper, a funnel, tow rope, a spray bottle filled with glass cleaner, rags, and matches.

One of the simplest ways to get yourself stalled in the middle of nowhere is to overlook your battery's charge. If it's old or corroded, get a new one before heading out. Roadside supply stops are rare, so self-sufficiency is a must. Water is most important; carry at least two liters of water per person per day. Also bring ample food. You'll need light clothing for the day, sturdy boots for hiking, and warm clothes for nights (when the temperature in some parts of the country can fall below freezing). Safety first: bring a first-aid kit and a fire extinguisher. Cell phones do not work in remote areas of the Outback, but smart bushwalkers swear by the Electronic Position Indicator Radio Beacon (EPIRB). For more info, see **Wilderness Safety**, p. 71.

# ON THE ROAD

If your vehicle breaks down, it's generally best to stay with it. It's likely you'll eventually be discovered by a passerby (although this doesn't necessarily pertain to especially isolated regions). Putting up your car bonnet (hood) is a universal signal of distress. If you decide to stop for other reasons, give passing cars a thumbs-up to let them know you're okay, and if you pass a stopped car, slow down and look for the thumbs-up sign before continuing.

Don't drive at night, while tired, or after drinking (Australia has strict drunk-driving laws; see **Essentials,** p. 33). Road conditions can change quickly, especially on 4WD-only tracks. For your safety and the safety of others, it's best to use your headlights at all times while driving.

## TIRES

Australia has a surprising number of unsealed (unpaved) roads, often covered with gravel and fallen branches. This virtually guarantees that you'll have at least one blown tire on longer trips. Petrol stations are often hundreds of miles apart, so tire-changing know-how is important.

**MAINTENANCE.** The best defense against tire problems is good maintenance. To ascertain the pressure to which your tires should be inflated, look on the tires, on the inside of your driver's side door, or in your vehicle's owner's manual. You can use a tire pressure gauge to determine the actual pressure of your tires. Both overinflation and underinflation are dangerous and can contribute to tire failure; you should check the pressure periodically throughout your trip. Since hot temperatures will give you inaccurate readings, readings should be taken when your tires have cooled down after driving.

**RUPTURES.** The first sign of a tire rupture will probably involve a significant change in the way the vehicle handles. You might notice that the car doesn't turn as easily or that it feels a bit more wobbly than usual. Pull over to a safe place at the first sign of trouble. Make sure that you stop somewhere off the road, away from blind corners, and on level ground. If your car sustains a tire blowout (or tread separation), you'll probably know right away. The car will suddenly become much more difficult to steer, especially through turns, and you may be tugged forcefully in a particular direction.

To handle a tire blowout, do not slam on the brakes, even though this may be your first instinct. A blown tire (especially a blown front tire) will reduce your braking capability, and slamming on the brakes will just send you into an uncontrollable skid. Grip the wheel firmly while you take your foot off the gas pedal, steering only enough to keep the vehicle in a straight line or away from obstructions. Let the vehicle gradually come to a complete stop.

## OVERHEATING

**PRECAUTIONS.** Always carry several liters of clean water. Impure stream or lake water can be used to top off your radiator, though you'll need to have the radiator flushed afterward. You should also carry additional coolant, which must be mixed with water after it's added to the radiator. On a cool day, you can prevent overheating by turning off your air conditioning. If your vehicle has a temperature gauge, check it frequently. If not, stop periodically and check for signs of overheating, such as odd noises coming from under your hood.

**SOLUTIONS.** If your car overheats, pull off the road and turn the heater on full force to cool the engine. If the radiator fluid is steaming or bubbling, turn off

**GREAT OUTDOORS**

the car for at least 30min. If not, run the car in neutral at about 1500 rpm for a few minutes, allowing the coolant to circulate. Never pour water over the engine, and never try to lift a hot car bonnet. If you need to open your radiator cap, always wait at least 45min. while the coolant loses its heat—otherwise, you may be splashed with boiling coolant. Even after waiting, you may still be spattered with warm coolant, so stand to the side. Remember that "topping off" your radiator does not mean filling it completely. Pour in a small amount of water and coolant (equal amounts) and wait for it to work its way into the system, and then add more. Continue to do so until the radiator is filled to the level indicated by the reservoir or your vehicle's manual. Coolant leaks are sometimes just the product of overheating pressure, which forces coolant out of the gaps between the hoses and their connections to the radiator. If this happens to you, allowing the vehicle and coolant to dump their heat may prove to be enough. If not, or if there are other holes in the hose, it helps to have hose sealant on hand. Treat sealant only as a short-term solution, and get the vehicle to a service station as soon as possible.

## OIL

There is dust everywhere in Australia. This means you'll need to change your oil and your filter more frequently than in most other parts of the world. Many service stations offer oil changes, but the price rises in remote areas. Check your oil level every few days by taking your vehicle's dipstick and sliding it into the engine's oil level test tube. To get an accurate measurement, wipe it off first and then slide it in and pull it out of the tube, checking the actual level against the level recommended on the dipstick or in your vehicle's manual. Test the level only after your vehicle has been at rest for several minutes. If your level is low, add more oil. The owner's manual will list appropriate grades of motor oil for your particular vehicle. Check these against the oil you pour into your engine—the grade is usually indicated on its packaging.

## HOSES AND BELTS

Hoses and belts are important to monitor for wear and tear. Even small problems with vacuum hoses, for instance, will prevent your vehicle from starting. Fan belts are notorious for snapping in the most out-of-the-way locations. It's worthwhile to carry a few extra fan belts, but it's most convenient to get failing belts replaced before setting out. Replace the fan belt if it looks loose, split, glazed, or shiny (all signs that your belt is dangerously close to cracking). In an emergency, pantyhose can serve as a very temporary substitute, allowing you to hobble back to a garage at low speed.

## AUSTRALIAN ROAD HAZARDS

The road signs come in all shapes and sizes, but they mostly mean one thing: pay attention. Signs often refer to possible driving or visibility obstructions.

**GETTING BOGGED.** Getting stuck in soft ground (or "bogged," as Australians say) is a common occurrence when off-roading or exploring unsealed roads. More often than not, the best way to extract your vehicle is to winch your car to a tree or rock. Unfortunately, some rental cars don't have winches, and travelers are left hoping that someone with a winch will stop to help. However, most rental companies will provide a snatch strap and D-shackles (used in tandem to de-bog vehicles) for a fee. If driving in particularly remote areas, be sure to bring a shovel and some boards. Use the shovel to dig mud or sand away from your tires. Place boards under each tire, which should give you enough traction to extract your car. If boards fail, you may want to try the "kanga-jack" method: with a large-enough jack and sufficient upper body strength, you can get one end of your car far off the ground, then push it forward so it lands a bit closer to where you want to be. Repeat the hopping motion until you are unstuck. A last resort method is to let almost all the air out of your tires (get down to 15-50psi), and then take advantage of the added traction flat tires provide to drive out of the sand. Do not attempt to drive far on a set of flat tires.

**KANGAROOS.** Kangaroos are a surprisingly common, quite serious hazard on Australian roads. Signs alerting you to their presence are common along highways but are less frequent on small roads. Dusk and dawn are particularly dangerous times, since kangaroos can jump in front of or into the side of cars, causing significant damage. Never assume that an animal will get out of your way. Many Australian drivers outfit their cars with metal bull bars or 'roo bars, which attach to bumpers and protect cars from kangaroo collisions.

**UNSEALED ROADS.** Unsealed roads are common in rural Australia and are made from varying substances, from smooth, hard-packed sand to a mixture of mud and stones. Locals are a good source of information about road conditions. When driving on unsealed roads, call regional tourist boards ahead of time for road conditions, especially in the north, as the Wet sometimes makes roads impassable even after the rains stop. When driving on unsealed roads, allow at least twice as much time as you would for travel on paved roads. Keep in mind that it's easy to skid on gravel. Loose gravel may feel comfortable at high speeds if you are traveling in a straight line, but as soon as you attempt to turn or brake, you'll realize that it's unwise to take things too quickly.

**ROAD TRAINS.** "Road train" refers to any truck with three or more trailers; some are over 150ft. long and have nearly 100 wheels. Keep a distance at least as long as the road train between you and the last trailer. They can kick up large clouds of debris which can damage cars or cause drivers to swerve. It's a good idea to roll up your window if you're heading toward one (even on sealed roads) so that your vehicle's cabin is not flooded by a cloud of dust.

**STREAM CROSSINGS.** On some northern roads, stream crossings are not bridged, meaning you will need to ford them. Before attempting this, scout the area as extensively as you can. Wade into the water and check the conditions of the bottom, removing any logs. Do not wade in if there is a risk of crocodiles in the area; storms during the Wet season bring salties far inland to even the most innocuous-looking streams. If crocs aren't a concern, feel for silt that could catch your wheels. Look for sharp, protruding rocks and entangling weeds. Choose your exit point on the other side of the stream and inspect the area. Use a stick to gauge how deep the deepest part of the crossing is. Compare this to your vehicle, and if it rises above the undercarriage, or if the water is especially violent, you may want to turn around. Be especially cautious during or after rain.

If you decide to ford the stream, do it relatively quickly to avoid becoming stuck in the streambed. Start driving toward the stream from a few dozen meters down the road and enter it in full motion, not stopping until you're across. If you are stuck in the middle of a stream during or after rain, remember that the water levels may rise very quickly and that it doesn't take much depth to lift your vehicle and send it downriver. If you experience a punctured tire while fording a stream, your best option is to keep on driving until you can get to flat, level ground on the other side. Throwing it into reverse might be all right if you've just entered the stream, but under most circumstances, it will just bog you down for good.

## GREAT OUTDOORS GLOSSARY

**ABSEILING.** The Aussie word for rappelling down a mountain or cliff with a rope.

**BITUMEN ROAD.** A paved road.

**BUSH CAMPING.** The cheapest way to get a night's sleep. Implies total self-sufficiency—generally no toilets, no fire pits, and no reliable sources of water. Bring your own supplies. Typically allowed only in specified sections of parks; check with a ranger or visitors center before setting up camp.

**BUSHWALKING.** Often used interchangeably with hiking, the term refers more specifically to exploring the wilderness without a trail to follow.

**CALM.** Conservation and Land Management, an organization that oversees Western Australia's national and regional parks and provides visitors with maps and info.

**EPIRB.** Electronic Position Indicator Radio Beacon, a safety device to call for emergency rescue where cell phone service is spotty. (see **Wilderness Safety**, p. 71.)

**FRESHIES.** The crocodiles that (probably) won't eat you. Freshwater crocodiles have long, thin snouts and are less aggressive than their saltwater kin; still quite dangerous and can be harder to spot.

**JACK PLATE.** Usually made of plywood or metal, used with jacks when replacing tires on unsealed roads and soft terrain. The plate distributes the weight of the car over a larger surface so that your jack doesn't get buried in the ground.

**MIDGIES.** Sandflies (gnats).

**MOZZIES.** Mosquitoes, commonly found in the Top End and Northern Queensland; kept at bay by using insect repellent.

**NEVER NEVER.** A slang term for particularly harsh, remote regions of the Outback.

**RIPS.** Strong currents that can pull a swimmer or surfer out to sea. If caught in one, don't panic—swim across (not against) it until free, or signal if help is nearby.

**'ROO BAR.** Also known as kangaroo or bull bars, these metal bars attach to bumpers, protecting cars from collisions with Australia's be-pouched wildlife.

**ROYAL FLYING DOCTORS SERVICE (RFDS).** Provides medical and emergency care to residents and travelers in remote regions of Australia.

**SALTIES.** The crocodiles that will eat you. Big, powerful, and hungry, these saltwater crocs have a shorter, wider snout than freshwater ones and often lurk just below the water's surface.

**SNORKELS (VEHICLE).** Essential for river and creek crossings, snorkels help keep water out of your 4WD's engine by raising the point of air intake. Look for them online or in Australian auto parts stores.

**SWAG.** A piece of heavy canvas, somewhat like a sleeping bag, with a foam mattress inside. Swags often replace tents and keep their owners warm and dry.

**TORCH.** A flashlight.

**UNSEALED.** Unpaved. Many roads through remote areas are gravel, dirt, packed sand, or some combination thereof. Corrugated roads (unpacked gravel) are the bumpiest.

GREAT OUTDOORS

# BEYOND TOURISM

## A PHILOSOPHY FOR TRAVELERS

### HIGHLIGHTS OF BEYOND TOURISM IN AUSTRALIA

**STUDY** acting at the **University of New South Wales**—make Sydney your stage (p. 87).

**RESCUE** endangered sea turtles on the coast of **Cape York** (p. 84).

**WORK** your way across the country **picking fruit** (p. 92).

**FLIP** to our **"Giving Back" sidebar feature** for a more region-specific opportunity to practice the Beyond Tourism philosophy (p. 751).

Hostel-hopping and sightseeing can be great fun, but connecting with a foreign country through studying, volunteering, or working can enrich your traveling experience far more than mere sightseeing can. This is what's different about a *Let's Go* traveler. Instead of feeling like a stranger in a strange land, you can understand Australia like a local. Instead of being that tourist asking for directions, you can be the one who gives them (and correctly!). All the while, you get the satisfaction of leaving Australia in better shape than you found it. It's not wishful thinking—it's Beyond Tourism.

As a **volunteer** in Australia, you can unleash your inner superhero by rescuing baby koalas, saving strangled sea turtles, or combating social injustice. This chapter is chock-full of ideas to get involved, whether you're looking to pitch in for a day or run away from home for a whole new life in Australian activism.

The powers of **studying** abroad are beyond comprehension: it can actually make you feel sorry for those poor tourists who don't get to do any homework while they're here. Australia's vast stretches of wilderness and wealth of national parks make it a haven for students of environmental science, sustainability, conservation, and public policy. But green doesn't have to be your favorite color to study in Australia; students can enroll in programs, or directly in various universities, in fields from Australian history to studio arts.

**Working** abroad immerses you in a new culture and can bring some of the most meaningful relationships and experiences of your life. Yes, we know you're on vacation, but these aren't your normal desk jobs. (Plus, it doesn't hurt that it helps pay for more globetrotting.) Get an internship in Sydney, Melbourne, or Perth, some of the most cosmopolitan and culturally rich cities in the world. Follow the harvest across the continent, picking everything from mangoes to apples to avocadoes. Work as an au pair for adorable Australian-accented kids. Live on a boat off the coast of Broome for a couple of weeks collecting some of the finest pearls in the world. Working from short-term job to short-term job is a great way for backpackers to finance their trip, and Australia is extraordinarily accommodating to travelers looking for temporary employment; it's a kind of culture down there. The possibilities are endless.

**SHARE YOUR EXPERIENCE.** Have you had a particularly enjoyable volunteer, study, or work experience that you'd like to share with other travelers? Post it to our website, www.letsgo.com!

# VOLUNTEERING

Feel like saving the world this week? Volunteering can be a powerful and fulfilling experience, especially when combined with the thrill of traveling to a strange land. Those looking to volunteer in Australia will find a tree-hugger's paradise of environmental service. Oz's enormous range of conservation projects includes wildlife rescue, rainforest rehabilitation, coastal clean-up, underwater reef research, and more. Most foreign volunteers choose one of these many recruit-happy ecological options. However, keep in mind that environmental work is not always as glamorous as it may sound. Cleaning and maintenance jobs play a significant role in the day-to-day of many volunteer positions, so plan on performing a fair amount of repetitive, strenuous labor rather than enjoying days of swimming with dolphins, comforting baby koalas, and swinging through the rainforest canopy. For those interested in social work, many Indigenous Australian communities now recruit volunteers for both community projects and educational positions.

Most people who volunteer in Australia do so on a short-term basis at organizations that only accept drop-in or once-a-week volunteers. The best way to find opportunities that match your interests and schedule may be to check with regional volunteer centers. The Australian government runs a series of online directories (see **Volunteer Opportunities,** p. 83) that can connect you to any one of a number of local conservation projects and environmental groups. State park services can also be a great resource for those in search of service opportunities. Australia is positively stuffed with national parks, which are almost always in need of volunteers for park maintenance works. Although these positions are generally reserved for locals, certain groups are open to travelers willing to make a minimum time commitment. Volunteer listings can be found on **Parks Department** webpages for New South Wales (www.environment.nsw.gov.au), the Northern Territory (☎08 8999 4825; www.nt.gov.au/nreta/parks), Queensland (www.epa.qld.gov.au), South Australia (www.parks.sa.gov.au), Western Australia (☎08 9334 0251; www.naturebase.net), Tasmania (www.parks.tas.gov.au), and Victoria (www.parkweb.vic.gov.au). Regional parks offices are also good places to inquire about local volunteer opportunities within Australian national parks. For general Australian Parks links, visit www.environment.gov.au/parks/links. Go Volunteer (www.govolunteer.com.au) and Volunteer Western Australia (www.volunteeringwa.org.au) are some other good resources. Read up before heading out.

Those looking for longer, more intensive volunteer opportunities usually find a parent organization that takes care of the logistical details and often provides a group environment and support system—for a fee. There are both religious and secular organizations that perform these services, although it's rare that either places restrictions on participation. Websites like **www.volunteerabroad.com, www.servenet.org,** and **www.idealist.org** provide information on volunteer openings both in your country and abroad.

# VOLUNTEER OPPORTUNITIES

Unless otherwise specified, assume that the volunteer listings in this section expect volunteers to be responsible for their own food, transportation, insurance, accommodations, and incidentals.

## LAND CONSERVATION

From the clearing of native forests to the draining of tropical wetlands, Australia's urban expansion is laying waste to its wilderness. Nearly 3000 natural habitats and almost 1500 species are predicted to disappear in the coming century, so it comes as no surprise that environmental conservation is by far the most popular field for volunteers. Check out www.afconline.org.au for general information from the Australian Conservation Foundation.

**Bush Heritage Austalia,** P.O. Box 329, Flinders Ln., Melbourne, VIC 8009 (☎1300 628 873; www.bushheritage.org.au). This organization purchases wild bushland and converts it into reserves for the public to enjoy. "Working Bees" volunteers weed, plant, and build fences in a particular reserve for 1 weekend to 1 month; $10 per day provided for meals. Longer "Volunteer Ranger" positions usually require outdoors experience, but accommodations can be provided upon request.

**Conservation Volunteers Australia,** P.O. Box 423, Ballarat, VIC 3353 (☎03 5330 2600 or nationwide 1800 032 501; www.conservationvolunteers.com.au). Offers travel volunteer packages ($40 per day; concessions available for students, pensioners, and members) that include service opportunities (wildlife and environmental work) as well as accommodation, meals, and project-related transport.

**Earthwatch,** 3 Clock Tower Place, Suite 100, Maynard, MA 01754, USA (☎+1-978-461-0081; www.earthwatch.org). Australian office 126 Bank St., South Melbourne VIC 3205 (☎03 9682 6828; www.earthwatch.org/australia). Arranges 1- to 3-week programs focused on conservation of native animals and ecosystems. Costs vary by location and duration but average $3500-4000. Total cost covers room, board, transportation (excluding airfare), basic insurance, and program cost.

**Landcare Australia,** P.O. Box 5666, West Chatswood, NSW 1515 (☎02 9412 1040; www.landcareonline.com). Serves as a network for hundreds of community-based environmental projects, including Coastcare and Bushcare. Also solicits corporate sponsors and donations for conservation. Contact regional headquarters or use the website's project directory to learn how you can help.

**Mareeba Tropical Savanna And Wetland Reserve,** P.O. Box 175, Mareeba, QLD 4880 (☎07 4093 2514; www.mareebawetlands.com). This 5000-acre wildlife sanctuary accepts volunteers to help maintain its savannas and wetlands. Expect to build walking paths, monitor animal activity, weed and plant. Alternatively, work indoors in the guest center. Tent accommodations provided. Minimum 2-week stay.

**Wet Tropics Volunteers,** P.O. Box 2050, Cairns, QLD 4870 (☎07 4052 0555; www.wettropics.gov.au). Numerous local programs offer options for helping out at this World Heritage rainforest, ranging from educating park visitors to caring for injured frogs. Check the online directory for specific group information.

## COASTAL PRESERVATION

Australia's coast runs for nearly 26,000km, stretching through sun-bleached sand, rainforests, grasslands, and mangrove swamps. Unfortunately, in a country where more than 80% of the population lives within 100km of the coast, these national treasures are very vulnerable to human development.

**Coastcare Australia** (http://coastcare.com.au). Working under the umbrella organization of Landcare, Coastcare provides a funding network for over 2000 community groups across Australia. Check the online directory for regional volunteer opportunities and contact info. Activities include building access paths, fencing off dunes, weeding clogged waterways, and educating the public.

**ReefCheck Australia,** P.O. Box 404, Townsville, QLD 4810 (☎07 4724 3950; www. reefcheckaustralia.org). This UN organization accepts certified advanced divers to monitor coral reef health. Training courses required ($774, students $648) but subsequent volunteer expeditions are usually free. Some 6-month volunteer positions available.

**I HAVE TO PAY TO VOLUNTEER?** Many volunteers are surprised to learn that some organizations require large fees or "donations." But don't go calling them scams just yet. While such fees may seem ridiculous at first, they often keep the organization afloat, covering airfare, room, board, and administrative expenses for the volunteers. (Other organizations must rely on private donations and government subsidies.) If you're concerned about how a program spends its fees, request an annual report or finance account. A reputable organization won't refuse to tell you how volunteer money is spent. Pay-to-volunteer programs might be a good idea for young travelers who are looking for more support and structure (such as pre-arranged transportation and housing) or anyone who would rather not deal with the uncertainty of creating a volunteer experience from scratch.

# WILDLIFE PROTECTION AND RESCUE

The Australian continent is known throughout the world for its strange, fantastic wildlife. Unfortunately, human expansion and the encroachment of non-native species have also saddled Australia with the highest mammalian extinction rate on the planet. Hundreds of animals currently occupy spots on the government's list of endangered or vulnerable species, including emus, bats, bandicoots, wallabies, parrots, and kangaroos.

**Birds Australia,** Suite 2-05, 60 Leicester St., Carlton, VIC 3053 (☎03 9347 0757; www. birdsaustralia.com.au). Call to register as a volunteer for the Threatened Birds Network; the national office sends updates about protecting endangered avian species.

**Cape Tribulation Tropical Research Station,** PMB 5, Cape Tribulation, QLD 4873 (☎07 4098 0063; www.austrop.org.au). Volunteers, students, interns, and researchers conserve threatened lowland tropical ecosystems and coastal environments. The station also works to save the spectacled flying fox. Min. 2-week commitment. Volunteers 25 and older preferred. All station members expected to assist with station cleaning in addition to conservation work. Inquire about fees. Cost includes 3 meals per day and accommodations. Transportation and insurance are not provided.

**Cape York Turtle Rescue,** P.O. Box 3352, Bangor, NSW 2234 (☎07 4069 9978; www. capeyorkturtlerescue.com). Work with the local Indigenous Australians to remove washed-up nets and other threats to the sea turtles while learning about indigenous culture. 5 nights $2125 per person; 3 nights $1275 per person. Accommodations, meals, and all transportation (minus flight) included.

**Koala Preservation Society Hospital,** P.O. Box 236, Port Macquarie, NSW 2444 (☎02 6584 1522; www.koalahospital.org.au). This group takes volunteers to help care for sick, diseased, and injured local koalas. Internationals will work the morning shifts for one month, assisting with rescues, releases, visitor info, yard work, and intensive care.

**Monkey Mia Reserve,** 89 Knight Terrace, Denham WA, 6537 (☎08 9948 1366; www. sharkbay.org). Wild bottlenose dolphins are hand-fed 3 times per day at this popular tourist spot. Volunteers can expect to clean the facilities and trails, provide information for visitors, and assist with dolphin feeds. Minimum 4-day commitment; maximum 2 weeks. Positions in high demand, so fill out the online application early.

# COMMUNITY-BASED PROJECTS

Although Australia has become one of the world's most developed countries, not all communities have benefitted equally. Indigenous regions are particularly affected by this disparity, and they offer most of the community-based service opportunities. Volunteers in these communities typically work to promote economic self-sufficiency through education and construction projects.

**Cape York Partnerships,** PMB1, Cairns TAFE, Room 120, J Block, Newton St., Cairns, QLD 4870 (☎07 4042 7200; www.capeyorkpartnerships.com). Facilitates placement of volunteers in Indigenous communities throughout Cape York. Volunteers work on projects in education, business, land management, preservation, and other projects. Offers a variety of programs from 4 weeks to 12 months of service. Provides basic accommodation only; volunteers are responsible for all other expenses.

**Habitat for Humanity Australia,** Level 1, 173 Pacific Hwy., North Sydney, NSW 2059 (☎02 9919 7000; www.habitat.org.au). Offers volunteer opportunities in Australia to build houses for needy families in a host community. Donation ($950, full-time student $750) and medical insurance (approximately $70) required.

**International Volunteers for Peace,** 499 Elizabeth St., Surry Hills, NSW 2010 (☎02 9699 1129; www.ivp.org.au). Arranges placement in Australian community work groups for members 17 and up. Membership $35. Work camp fee ($350; concessions $300) includes accommodations, food, and very basic insurance. Outside of Australia, contact IVP's affiliate Service Civil International (SCI) in your home country (www.sciint.org).

**Involvement Volunteers,** P.O. Box 218, Port Melbourne, VIC 3207 (☎03 9646 5504; www.volunteering.org.au). Offers volunteering options in animal care, education, and farming. Prices range from $1200-3360 and generally include room and board.

**Volunteers for Peace,** 1034 Tiffany Rd., Belmont, VT 05730, USA (☎+1-802-259-2759; www.vfp.org). Arranges placement in work camps in Australia. Camp projects vary each year, but usually include environmental and social work, as well as arts projects. Membership (US$30) required for registration. Programs average US$300 for 2-3 weeks; program fee includes room, board, and work materials.

# STUDYING

It's hard to dread the first day of school when Sydney is your campus and exotic restaurants are your meal plan. A growing number of students report that studying abroad is the highlight of their learning careers. If you've never studied abroad, you don't know what you're missing—and if you have studied abroad, you do know what you're missing. Either way, let's go back to school!

Study-abroad programs range from basic language and culture courses to university-level classes, often for college credit. In order to choose a program that best fits your needs, research as much as you can before making your decision—determine costs and duration, as well as what kind of students participate in the program and what sorts of accommodations are provided. Australia's study-abroad programs range from informal cultural courses to college-level classes. Unless you plan to complete your full degree in Australia, most undergraduate programs require current enrollment in a university. Although this section deals primarily with university-level study abroad, **International Student Exchange Australia** (www.i-s-e.com.au) features programs for high school students, and **Elderhostel, Inc.** (☎1 800 454 5768; www.elderhostel.org) has two-to five-week educational opportunities for seniors ages 55 and over. Back-to-school shopping was never this much fun.

If English is not your first language, know that there is a trade-off when you enroll in programs with large groups of students speaking your language rather than Australia's. You may feel more comfortable in the community, but you probably will not have the same opportunity to practice a foreign language or to befriend other international students. For accommodations, dorm life provides a better opportunity to mingle with fellow students, but there is less of a chance to experience the local scene. If you live with a family, you could potentially build lifelong friendships with natives and experience day-to-day life in more depth, but you might also get stuck sharing a room with their pet iguana. Conditions can vary greatly from family to family. **Study Abroad Links** (www.studyabroadlinks.com) lists the websites of a number of homestay programs spread throughout Australia.

**VISA INFORMATION.** See the Department of Immigration and Citizenship website (www.immi.gov.au) for information on how to apply for visas. Obtaining a student visa requires an application, a $450 fee, a valid passport, and an Electronic Confirmation of Enrollment (eCoE) and/or a letter of offer from the education provider for the courses to be taken. Students must also be able to finance their own travel, tuition, and living expenses during their time in the country; must be of good character and have no outstanding debts to the Australian government; and must declare respect for the Australian Values Statement. Depending on their intended activities and length of stay in Australia, as well as their personal medical history, students may also need to undergo a health examination. Health insurance is required. Students from the US and certain other countries may apply directly online for a visa; see the website for more information.

# UNIVERSITIES

One of the perks of studying abroad in Australia is that most classes are conducted in English. This makes it easier for students to enroll directly in a university abroad—which may be a cheaper option—although getting college credit may be more difficult. You can search www.studyabroad.com for various semester-abroad programs that meet your criteria, including your desired location and focus of study. Students of conservation and natural resource management may be particularly drawn to Australia, where they will be able to not only find a plethora of university programs in the field, but also conduct practical placements or volunteer in one of the country's many national parks. Contact **Parks Victoria** (☎03 8627 4699; www.parkweb.vic.gov.au) for more information on options for tertiary students.

If you're a college student, your school's study-abroad office is often the best place to start looking for a program, but if options are limited, the following list of organizations can help place you in a program that fits your needs.

# INTERNATIONAL PROGRAMS

**American Institute for Foreign Study (AIFS),** College Division, River Plaza, 9 W. Broad St., Stamford, CT 06902, USA (☎+1-800-727-2437; www.aifsabroad.com). Organizes programs for high school and college study in universities in Australia: semesters in Sydney and a summer program in Cairns. Cost for Sydney semesters is US$16,000; for Cairns in the summer: US$6000. Room and board included. Scholarships available.

**Arcadia University for Education Abroad,** 450 S. Easton Rd., Glenside, PA 19038, USA (☎+1-866-927-2234; www.arcadia.edu/cea). Offers undergraduate and graduate programs all over Australia. Costs range from US$13,500-20,000 (semester) to US$24,000-35,000 (full-year) and include room and board.

**Association of Commonwealth Universities (ACU),** Woburn House, 20-24 Tavistock Sq., London WC1H 9HF, UK (☎+44 20 7380 6700; www.acu.ac.uk). Publishes information about studying for degrees at Commonwealth Universities in Australia.

**AustraLearn,** 12050 N. Pecos St., Suite 320, Westminster, CO 80234, USA (☎+1-800-980-0033; www.australearn.org/programs/internship/intern.htm). Offers semester- and year-long abroad programs at 34 universities across Australia, New Zealand, and Fiji. Students enroll directly in the university of their choice. Semesters run between US$8000-12,500; years between US$15,000-25,500. Housing fees not included. Study Internship Combination Programs and scholarships available.

**Council on International Educational Exchange (CIEE),** 300 Fore St., Portland, ME 04101, USA (☎+1-207-553-4000 or +1-800-40-STUDY/407-8839; www.ciee.org). Among the most comprehensive sources for global work, academic, and internship programs. Sponsors university study in Perth, Sydney, and Wollongong. Costs range from US$11,000-18,000 (semester) to US$20,000-27,000 (year) and include housing.

**Institute for the International Education of Students (IES),** 33 N. LaSalle St., 15th fl., Chicago, IL 60602, USA (☎+1-800-995-2300; www.IESabroad.org). Offers semester and year-long programs for university study in Sydney and Adelaide and semester, year-long, and summer programs in Melbourne. Costs differ by location: Adelaide US$15,000/30,000 (semester/year), Sydney US$15,000-17,500/30,000-35,000 (semester/year), Melbourne US$17,500/35,500/5,250 (semester/year/summer). Room and board included. Scholarships available.

**School for International Training (SIT) Study Abroad,** 1 Kipling Rd., P.O. Box 676, Brattleboro, VT 05302, USA (☎+1-888-272-7881 or 802-258-3212; www.sit.edu/studyabroad). Semester-long programs with an environmental focus; in Australia, semesters run approximately US$22,000, including room and board, airfare, and personal expenses. Also runs the Experiment in International Living (☎+1-800-345-2929; www.usexperiment.org), with 3- to 5-week summer programs that offer high-school students cross-cultural homestays, community service, and ecological adventure (US$4500-7000).

## AUSTRALIAN PROGRAMS

Applying directly to Australian universities can be cheaper than using an outside program, though it's generally more difficult to receive academic credit (and often housing). A fairly comprehensive list of schools and services is available at www.studyabroadlinks.com/search/Australia. The Australian government's website, www.studyinaustralia.gov.au, is also a good tool, with information on institutions, requirements, the application process, visas, and living costs. **IDP Education Australia** (www.idp.com) is a non-profit organization that can help guide you through the process, with info on institutions, access to IDP counselors, and a free application and enrollment processing service.

Listed below are several Australian universities that run their own international study programs. Costs vary widely by program and field of study.

**University of New South Wales,** Level 16, Mathews Building, Kensington 2052, Sydney, NSW (☎02 9385 3179; www.studyabroad.unsw.edu.au). UNSW has both semester-long offerings ($9500), and 6-week study programs during the Northern Hemisphere summer for undergraduates and graduate students looking for a shorter study experience in Australia. Subjects include Australian history, media, environmentalism, biogeography, conservation, and others.

**University of Sydney,** Study Abroad and Student Exchange, International Office, Services Building G12, The University of Sydney, NSW 2006 (☎02 9351 2222; www.usyd.edu. au/fstudent/studyabroad). Choose from courses in a variety of fields and directly enroll using their Study Abroad program. Fees vary.

**University of Melbourne,** International Admissions, International Centre, John Smyth Building, The University of Melbourne, VIC 3010 (☎03 8344 4505; www.futurestudents. unimelb.edu.au/int/saex/index.html). Students may directly enroll in a wide variety of courses in a number of fields using their Study Abroad program. Fees vary.

# WORKING

Money trees don't exist (though *Let's Go's* researchers aren't done looking), but there are still some pretty good opportunities to earn a living and travel at the same time. As with volunteering, work opportunities tend to fall into two categories. Some travelers want long-term jobs that allow them to integrate into a community, while others seek out short-term jobs to finance the next leg of their travels. In Australia, agricultural work is a favorite for both long- and short-term employment. Other long-term options include interning, teaching, au pair work, waiting tables, bartending, and working in retail. While most backpackers in Oz seek jobs as fruit-pickers, many other short-term work possibilities exist, including construction jobs, pearling, and working on vineyards and at ski resorts. **Transitions Abroad** (www.transitionsabroad.com) also offers updated online listings for work over any time span.

If you plan to work in Australia in any capacity, you should apply for a **tax file number (TFN)** from the Australian Taxation Office (www.ato.gov.au). Without a TFN, you may be taxed at a much higher rate than necessary. Either before you leave or once you get there, you might also consider opening a bank account, which is usually easy for college students and temporary workers to do.

The following areas are known to be particularly good places for travelers to find jobs. Note that working in Australia requires a special work visa.

| WORK OPPORTUNITIES BY CITY AND TOWN | | | |
|---|---|---|---|
| **STATE** | **CITY OR TOWN** | **PAGE** | **TYPE OF WORK** |
| **ACT** | Canberra | p. 96 | Hospitality, retail, vineyards. |
| **New South Wales** | Katoomba | p. 165 | Hospitality, fruit picking. |
| | Jindabyne | p. 237 | Hospitality, ski work. |
| | Riverina | p. 246 | Farm work, fruit picking. |
| | Sydney | p. 110 | Hospitality, construction, retail. |
| | Tamworth | p. 225 | Ranches. |
| **Northern Territory** | Alice Springs | p. 298 | Office and computer work. |
| | Katherine | p. 289 | Fruit and vegetable picking. |
| **Queensland** | Bowen | p. 402 | Fruit and vegetable picking. Considered by some to be QLD's best stop for short-term employment. |
| | Brisbane | p. 318 | Hospitality, retail, construction. |
| | Bundaberg | p. 380 | Fruit and vegetable picking. |
| | Emerald | p. 451 | Cotton, fruit picking. |
| | Maroochydore | p. 358 | Fruit picking. |
| | Stanthorpe | p. 355 | Fruit picking. |

| WORK OPPORTUNITIES BY CITY AND TOWN | | | |
|---|---|---|---|
| South Australia | Adelaide Hills | p. 474 | Fruit picking. |
| | Barossa Valley | p. 490 | Vineyards. |
| Tasmania | Huon Valley | p. 545 | Fruit and vegetable picking. |
| Victoria | Gelantipy | p. 678 | Cattle farming. |
| | Mildura | p. 655 | Fruit and vegetable picking. |
| | Melbourne | p. 570 | Hospitality, retail, construction. |
| Western Australia | Broome | p. 754 | Hospitality, pearling. |
| | Carnarvon | p. 741 | Fruit and vegetable picking. |
| | Kalgoorlie | p. 729 | Mining. |
| | Margaret River | p. 706 | Vineyards. |
| | Perth | p. 684 | Hospitality, retail. |

# LONG-TERM WORK

If you're planning on spending a substantial amount of time (more than three months) working in Australia, search for a job well in advance. International placement agencies are often the easiest way to find employment abroad, especially for those interested in teaching. Online employment databases such as **CareerOne** (www.careerone.com.au) also provide thousands of listings for jobs throughout Australia. Although they are often only available to college students, internships are a good way to ease into working abroad. Many say the interning experience is well worth it, despite the low pay (if you're lucky enough to be paid at all). Some traditional Australian jobs may be easier to obtain with proper training. **Leconfield Jackaroo and Jillaroo School** offers 11-day training packages on traditional bush methods necessary for work on outback cattle stations. While they do give references and endeavor to assist graduates with finding employment, job placement is not specifically included in the course. (☎02 6769 4230; www.leconfieldjackaroo.com. Courses start at $895; $150 deposit required.) Be wary of advertisements for companies claiming to be able get you a job abroad for a fee—often the same listings are available online or in newspapers. Some reputable organizations include:

**BUNAC,** 16 Bowling Green Ln., London, EC1R OQH (☎+44 020 7251 3472 or +1-203-264-0901 in US; www.bunac.com). Helps organize working holidays, arranges visas, bank accounts, and tax file numbers, and helps find jobs and accommodations. US$595 (visa fees included) plus mandatory travel insurance.

**Travellers Contact Point,** 7th Floor, Dymocks Building, 428 George St., Sydney, NSW 2000 (☎02 9221 8744; http://travellers.com.au). Organizes visas, flights, travel insurance, and hostel bookings for working holiday travelers and helps find work and accommodations in Australia. Open M-F 9am-6pm, Sa 10am-4pm.

**Visitoz,** Springbrook Farm, 8921 Burnett Hwy., Goomeri, QLD 4601 (☎07 4168 6106; www.visitoz.org). Offers training and job placement in 2 areas: agriculture and hospitality. English-language instruction on a farm is also available. Program fee of $1890 includes job placement, a training course, and help with travel arrangements, visas, insurance, and obtaining a Tax File Number.

**Work Adventures Down Under,** 2330 Marinship Way, Ste. 250, Sausalito, CA 94965, USA (☎+1-415-339-2728; www.ccusa.com). Organizes travel arrangements and job placement for the duration of your visa. Services include visa processing, tax registration, pre- and post-arrival aid, and access to their Job Service. The programs cost US$560-1650, plus an additional $35 application fee and $65 per month for mandatory insurance. American passport holders can choose to apply for just the "Basic" package, which does not cover visa, flight, or insurance arrangements. THe package costs US$360 plus $35 application and $65 insurance fees.

# INTERNSHIPS

The most economical way to plan an internship is to organize placement on your own, but this can sometimes be difficult for someone without connections. Listed below are several internship and work experience placement programs that will help take care of the leg work.

**MORE VISA INFORMATION.** See the Department of Immigration and Citizenship website (www.immi.gov.au) for more information on visas. The following visas are required for temporary work in Australia.

**Work and Holiday Visa.** For tertiary-educated 18- to 30-year-old citizens of the US, Chile, Thailand, and Turkey. Valid for 12 months. You must have a valid passport, no dependents, English language proficiency, and, in some cases, a letter of government support and a health examination. You must also meet character requirements, respect the Australian Values Statement, complete an application, and pay a $180 fee. Holders of a Work and Holiday Visa can't work for the same employer for more than 6 months.

**Working Holiday Visa.** For 18- to 30-year-old citizens of Canada, the UK, Belgium, Republic of Cyprus, Denmark, Estonia, Finland, France, Germany, Hong Kong, Republic of Ireland, Italy, Japan, Republic of Korea, Malta, Netherlands, Norway, Sweden, and Taiwan. Valid for 12 months. Interested parties must have a valid passport and no dependents, meet health criteria and character requirements, promise to respect the Australian Values Statement, possess adequate funds to finance the trip and a return ticket, complete an application, and pay a $190 fee. Holders of a Working Holiday Visa generally cannot work for the same employer for longer than 6 months. Note: if you have a Working Holiday Visa and have been employed as a seasonal worker in regional Australia for at least 3 of your 12 months, you may be eligible to apply for a second Working Holiday Visa, which allows you to remain in Australia a full 24 months after your initial entrance.

**Australian National Internships Program (ANIP),** Building 3, 1 Block, Old Administration Area, Tennis Court Ln., Australian National University, Canberra, ACT 0200 (☎02 6125 8540; www.anu.edu.au/anip). Arranges internships in public policy for college and graduate students from Australia and abroad. Costs between $5500-8700.

**AustraLearn,** 12050 N. Pecos St., Suite 320, Westminster, CO 80234, USA (☎+1-800-980-0033; www.australearn.org/programs/internship/intern.htm). Offers not only study-abroad options, but internship opportunities in a variety of fields as well. Unpaid. Anywhere from 6- to 16-week internships available; costs range from US$3500-5500. Housing in a homestay or shared apartment included. Scholarships available.

**Australia Internships,** Suite 1, Savoir Faire Park Rd. Milton, Brisbane, QLD 4064 (☎07 3305 8408; www.internships.com.au). Organizes internships lasting anywhere from 6 weeks to 12 months in fields ranging from accounting to forestry. Some internships can be completed for academic credit. Costs vary greatly depending on the program, length of the internship, and any optional additional services requested, but include the development of a custom-designed internship, assistance with the visa process, and counseling support services. Non-refundable $500 application fee.

**Council on International Educational Exchange (CIEE),** 300 Fore St., Portland, ME 04101, USA (☎+1-207-553-4000 or 800-407-8839; www.ciee.org). This program doesn't just assist in study abroad but in working abroad as well; tucked into their study-abroad listings is a resource for international internships.

**International Association for the Exchange of Students for Technical Experience (IAESTE),** IAESTE Australia, Swinburne University of Technology, P.O. Box 218, Hawthorn, VIC 3122 (☎03 9214 8577; www.swinburne.edu.au/spl/iaeste). Your home country might have a local office; apply for hands-on technical internships in Australia. You must be a college student studying science, technology, or engineering. "Cost of living allowance" covers most non-travel expenses. Most programs last 8-12 weeks.

**International Cooperative Education,** 15 Spiros Way, Menlo Park, CA 94025, USA (☎+1-650-323-4944; www.icemenlo.com). Finds summer jobs for students in Australia. Semester and year-long commitments also available. Costs include a US$250 application fee and a US$700 fee for placement.

# TEACHING ENGLISH

While some elite private American schools offer competitive salaries, teaching jobs abroad pay more in personal satisfaction and emotional fulfillment than in actual cash. Perhaps this is why volunteering as a teacher instead of getting paid is a popular option. Even then, teachers often receive some sort of a daily stipend to help with living expenses. In almost all cases, you must have at least a bachelor's degree to be a full-fledged teacher, although college undergraduates can often get summer positions teaching or tutoring. Finding a teaching job in Australia, however, can be tough. There's plenty of competition for a limited number of posts, many of which pay poorly. Still, candidates with experience shouldn't have too much trouble securing a job.

The vast majority of schools require teachers to have a **Teaching English as a Foreign Language (TEFL)** or **Teaching English to Speakers of Other Languages (TESOL)** certificate. You may still be able to find a teaching job without one, but certified teachers often find higher-paying positions. Placement agencies or university fellowship programs are often the best resources for finding vacant teaching posts. The alternative is to contact schools directly or to try your luck once you arrive in Australia. In the latter case, the best time to look is usually several weeks before the start of the school year. The following organizations are extremely helpful in placing teachers in Oz.

**Teach International,** Level 2, 370 George St., Brisbane, QLD 4000 (☎1300 558 890 or 07 3211 4633; www.teachinternational.com). Provides information on securing TESOL training and offers extensive job listings.

**Australian College of English (ACE),** Level 4, 11 York St., Sydney, NSW 2000 (☎02 9389 0133; www.ace.edu.au). Established in 1981, ACE offers English courses through programs operating out of Sydney, Brisbane, Perth, Cairns, and Darwin.

**English Language Company (ELC),** 495 Kent St., Sydney, NSW 2000 (☎02 9267 5688; www.englishlanguagecompany.com). Located in the heart of Sydney, this program gets high marks for the many classes it offers.

**ESLBase,** (www.eslbase.com). This website features a comprehensive list of Australian schools that specialize in teaching English to foreign-language speakers.

# AU PAIR WORK

Au pairs are typically women (although sometimes men) aged 18-27 who work as live-in nannies, caring for children and doing light housework in foreign countries in exchange for room, board, and a small spending allowance or stipend. One perk of the job is that it allows you to get to know Australia without the high expenses of traveling. Drawbacks, however, can include both mediocre pay and long hours. The average weekly pay for au pairs in Australia generally falls between $150-250. Of course, much of the au pair experience depends on the family with which you are placed. The agencies below are a good starting point for most job hunts.

**Au-Pair Australia,** P.O. Box 1164, Glebe, NSW 2037 (☎02 9571 6121; www.aupairaustralia.com.au). Matches applicants to families in need of au pairs; based in Oz.

**InterExchange,** 161 6th Ave., New York City, NY 10013, USA (☎+1-212-924-0446 or +1-800-287-2477; www.interexchange.org). This American group has been arranging au pair placements for over 20 years.

**Childcare International,** Trafalgar House, Grenville Pl., London NW7 3SA, UK (☎+44 20 8906 3116; www.childint.co.uk). A British group that specializes in placing au pairs.

# SHORT-TERM WORK

Traveling for long periods of time can be hard on the wallet. Many travelers try their hand at odd jobs for a few weeks at a time to help pay for another month or two of touring around. In Oz, fruit and vegetable picking is generally a backpacker's best bet, as climatic diversity across the continent ensures that picking jobs are available year-round. The popularity of the work has in fact created a kind of fruit-picking subculture. Many hostels in picking areas cater specifically to workers, offering transportation to worksites and other such amenities. Pay varies from crop to crop, but pickers can expect to be paid by the hour and work approximately 40hr. weeks.

| PICKING OPPORTUNITIES BY REGION | | | |
|---|---|---|---|
| **STATE** | **LOCATION** | **AUSTRALIAN SEASON** | **WORK AVAILABLE** |
| **New South Wales** | Bathurst, Dubbo, Orange | Summer | Orchard and stone fruits, cotton. |
| | North coast | Year-round | Avocadoes, nuts, lychees. |
| **Northern Territory** | Darwin | Year-round | Bananas, citrus, vegetables, tropical fruits, melons. |
| **Queensland** | Stanthorpe | Summer | Orchard and stone fruits, grapes. |
| | Northern coast | Year-round | Bananas. |
| | Central coast | Winter | Sugar cane, cotton, grapes, citrus. |
| | Bundaberg, Childers | Year-round | Citrus, vegetables, melons, avocadoes, tomatoes. |
| **South Australia** | Barossa Valley | Fall | Grapes. |
| | Riverland | Summer, fall | Grapes, stone fruits. |
| **Tasmania** | Northern region | Year-round | Potatoes, vegetables. |
| **Victoria** | North-central region | Summer, fall | Orchard and stone fruits, citrus, vegetables, grapes. |
| **Western Australia** | Southwest | Summer | Grapes, berries. |
| | West coast | Year-round | Grapes, mangoes, tomatoes, vegetables, bananas, melons. |
| | Northeast | Year-round | Stone fruits, mangoes, citrus, vegetables, melons. |

Pearling has also emerged as a favorite occupation for those looking for short-term work. Broome, on the continent's northwest coast, produces some of the finest pearls in the world. Backpackers who try pearling experience Australia's diverse marine life up close; meet, swim, fish, and socialize with other travelers; and earn a nice, round $1000 paycheck for 10 days of work.

Some tour companies take workers in exchange for a trip or adventure experience. Those who can't afford the expense of a Whitsunday sailing safari, for example, may be able to see the islands by volunteering on a boat. "Vollies," as volunteers are affectionately called, do much of the cooking and cleaning but still get a little time to enjoy the beach. These positions are competitive, however. Some companies have waiting lists for volunteers, while others may offer jobs on an informal basis. The best way to find work is to ask around.

Another popular option is to work several hours per day at a hostel in exchange for free or discounted room and/or board. Most often, these short-term jobs are found by word of mouth or by expressing interest to hostel or restaurant owners. Due to high turnover in the tourism industry, many places are eager for help. *Let's Go* lists temporary jobs of this nature whenever possible; look in the **Practical Information** sections of larger cities or see below.

Many employers also join nationwide job-listing networks. These services often charge a membership fee, but their (free) websites alone can be helpful. The following resources provide information and access to job networks.

**Australian Job Search** (www.jobsearch.gov.au). A government agency with tens of thousands of employment listings. The website includes "Harvest Trail," a resource that provides information for backpackers on how best to find harvesting work in Australia.

**Ready Workforce** (☎02 8913 7777; www.readyworkforce.com.au). Industrial specialist recruiting for Australia and New Zealand. Their harvest and agriculture division, "Go Harvest," places beginner and experienced agricultural workers alike in permanent and temporary positions, including picking, truck driving, and machinery operating.

**Harvest Hotline Australia** (☎07 4922 6033; www.harvesthotlineaustralia.com.au). Recruits seasonal backpackers for picking work and provides members with assistance in filing taxes and setting up medical insurance and bank accounts, discount travel packages, and phone cards. Membership $60 for 3 months, $120 for a year.

**Jobaroo** (www.jobaroo.com). Offers online job listings and general information and advice for those looking for work in Australia. Includes a helpful section for backpackers in the market for harvesting, construction, hospitality, and pearling jobs.

**Willing Workers on Organic Farms (WWOOF)** (☎03 5155 0218; www.wwoof.com.au). Exchange labor for food and accommodations. Work is generally at farms or cooperatives, where workers learn about organic growing skills. Average expectations are 4-6hr. of service per day. Membership costs $55, or $65 for 2 people.

**Workabout Australia** (☎02 6884 7777; www.workaboutaustralia.com.au). Website at which one can buy *Workabout Australia*, a book containing seasonal and casual employment info by state. One can also join the Workabout Australia Club here; membership costs $55, and provides individuals with job opportunities, employment contacts, tips, hints, and general advice and information. The site offers a free preview list of short-term employment vacancies by state, including employers' contact information.

**Workstay** (☎08 9226 0510; www.workstay.com.au). Arranges live-in work at country pubs, farms, and cattle stations in WA. Open M-F 9:30am-5:30pm.

# SHORT-TERM HOUSING

The short-term nature of most work opportunities for foreigners in Australia, combined with the desire for mobility, means that the majority of visitors who come on working holiday or student visas live in hostels or dorms. Hostels that cater to working travelers by offering job transportation help and low weekly rates are noted throughout *Let's Go: Australia*. Some hostels even provide free room and board to travelers willing to work a few hours per day for them. Many hostels don't advertise these opportunities, but it's always worthwhile to ask. Similarly, those volunteering in a national park may find that the park is able to provide reasonably priced housing in a cabin or caravan. Another option for students and volunteers is a homestay with an Australian family. **Study Abroad Links** (www.studyabroadlinks.com) gives websites for a number of homestay programs throughout Australia.

If you're looking for something on the more permanent end of temporary, apartments are generally referred to as "units" in Australia and are advertised for rent under the "To Let" heading in the classified section of newspapers. Additionally, universities, cafes, and hostels often have notice boards advertising rentals, sublets, and shares. Finally, **Craigslist** (www.craigslist.org) is a great resource for finding rentals, shares, and furnishings.

---

### FURTHER READING ON BEYOND TOURISM

*Alternatives to the Peace Corps: A Guide of Global Volunteer Opportunities,* edited by Paul Backhurst. Food First, 2005 (US$12).

*The Back Door Guide to Short-Term Job Adventures: Internships, Summer Jobs, Seasonal Work, Volunteer Vacations, and Transitions Abroad,* by Michael Landes. Ten Speed Press, 2005 (US$22).

*Green Volunteers: The World Guide to Voluntary Work in Nature Conservation,* by Fabio Ausenda. Universe, 2007 (US$15).

*How to Live Your Dream of Volunteering Overseas,* by Joseph Collins, Stefano DeZerega, and Zahara Heckscher. Penguin Books, 2001 (US$20).

*International Job Finder: Where the Jobs Are Worldwide,* by Daniel Lauber and Kraig Rice. Planning Communications, 2002 (US$20).

*Live and Work Abroad: A Guide for Modern Nomads,* by Huw Francis and Michelyne Callan. Vacation Work Publications, 2001 (US$20).

*Volunteer Vacations: Short-Term Adventures That Will Benefit You and Others,* by Doug Cutchins, Anne Geissinger, and Bill McMillon. Chicago Review Press, 2006 (US$18).

*Work Abroad: The Complete Guide to Finding a Job Overseas,* edited by Clayton A. Hubbs. Transitions Abroad, 2002 (US$16).

*Work Your Way Around the World,* by Susan Griffith. Vacation Work Publications, 2007 (US$22).

# Sydney Culinary School

When I told people that I was heading to Sydney for ten weeks to attend French culinary school, I got more than a few puzzled looks. Friends asked why I wasn't traveling to Paris to bake croissants; others wanted to know why I would spend my time in Australia in a hot kitchen rather than surfing at Bondi Beach. I myself can't fully explain how I ended up at the Cordon Bleu in Sydney, but my experience there speaks for itself.

The Cordon Bleu, founded in 1895, is one of the most famous culinary schools in the world. It has a presence in over 20 countries, including France, Korea, Canada, Japan, and, of course, Australia. Though the flagship school is in Paris, the Sydney site offers several attractive advantages. Courses are taught in English, rather than in French with translation, as in Paris. Aspiring chefs can find true inspiration in Australia's world-famous restaurants, where chefs are known for their innovative Mod Oz fusion cuisine. And Sydney offers an amazing variety of quality raw materials, from local seafood to wine.

Sydney is one of the Cordon Bleu's less expensive locations. Tuition runs AUS$7600, as compared to €7750 in Paris, a difference of almost US$5000. Additionally, the cost of living in Australia is lower than in France. And to offset tuition bills, Sydney students can work in Australia. Unlike normal tourists, they can apply for student visas, which allow foreign students to work 20hr. per week during the school term and unlimited hours during vacations.

The Cordon Bleu in Sydney offers six courses: basic, intermediate, and superior levels of both cuisine and pastry. Each course consists of three 6hr. lessons per week and lasts ten weeks. While the school is designed to provide professional training, many students in the basic class are there to become better home cooks, not five-star chefs. In each class, the chef instructor cooks the day's menu in a special kitchen equipped with lecture seating and cameras. After the demonstration, students individually prepare the same dishes.

Although the classes were wonderful, it was the other students that made the experience memorable. We each had our own workstation, but professional kitchens rely on teamwork, and the classroom experience was no different. After class, we explored Sydney together, particularly the city's restaurants and markets. I've never had a more interesting meal than the one I shared with fellow students at Bécasse, one of Sydney's top restaurants. We ordered a tasting menu, took pictures of the presentation of each dish, and carefully critiqued everything as we ate.

Though I spent more than a few afternoons at Manly soaking up the sun, being enrolled at the Cordon Bleu introduced me to a different side of Sydney. From my field trip to the auction room of the Sydney Fish Market to stories from the kitchens

## "It was the other students that made the experience memorable."

of Australia's best restaurants, I was given a unique glimpse into the Australian culinary world. Though I don't plan on becoming a chef, I hope to return to Sydney someday to wine and dine at the restaurants where my old schoolmates are working as the next generation of Australian chefs.

*The Cordon Bleu (☎ 08 8346 3700; www. cordonbleu.net) offers 10-week culinary courses in Sydney (beginning in January, April, July, and October) and advanced programs in Adelaide. Those wanting to learn more about Sydney's culinary scene without spending ten weeks slaving over a hot stove can attend any number of one-day cooking classes at the Sydney Fish Market.*

*Julie Stephens is a graduate of Harvard College. A former Let's Go Publishing Director, she took a year off during college and attended cooking school in Sydney. She is currently a Ph.D. student in history at Harvard.*

# AUSTRALIAN CAPITAL TERRITORY

Carved out of New South Wales in 1908, the Australian Capital Territory (ACT) was a geographic and political compromise between Sydney and Melbourne in the competition to serve as capital of the newly federated Australia. Although the ACT is not a fully qualified state, Canberra is the center and capital of the territory, not to mention the political heart of the country. The quiet metropolitan region is filled with neat commuter towns, creeping outward from Canberra toward the bush. The ACT's fusion of cosmopolitanism and outback flavor promises visitors a truly capital look at high culture and government.

## CANBERRA                                                                 ☎02

For a city that's home to 330,000 people and the government of an entire continent, Canberra's streets are remarkably quiet. There are few other places on the east coast with so many worthwhile free sights and tourist attractions, but the town still feels eerily deserted. This emptiness can be traced to Canberra's decentralized city plan and reputation for dullness. It certainly caters to a specific type of traveler, with more museums and history than adventure trips and beach bums, but locals are still rightfully proud.

---

### ◪ HIGHLIGHTS OF THE AUSTRALIAN CAPITAL TERRITORY

**OBSERVE** the political antics that ensue when **Parliament** debates (p. 103).

**LEARN** about the history of the nation through the **National Museum of Australia's** state-of-the-art exhibits that are at turns affecting and fanciful (p. 104).

**PERUSE** the massive **National Gallery of Australia's** Australian and International art, contemporary and ancient, for free (p. 103).

**WALK** by monuments on Anzac Pde. to reach the **Australian War Memorial** (p. 104).

**HIKE** through the **National Botanic Gardens** to the top of Black Mountain Tower for spectacular 360° views of the city (p. 104).

---

## ✈ INTERCITY TRANSPORTATION

### BY PLANE

Located in Pialligo, 7km east of the Central Business District (CBD), the **Canberra International Airport** is easy to get to by car. From Commonwealth Ave., take Parkes Way east past the roundabout at Kings Ave., which becomes Morshead Dr., then Pialligo Ave. On weekdays, **Deane's Buslines** (☎02 6299 3722; www.deanesbuslines.com.au) operates the Air Liner, a shuttle service that takes passengers between the airport and the City Interchange. (20min.; M-F 26 per day; limited weekend service. $9 one-way, $15 round-trip.) For weekend transit, a **taxi** (☎13 22 27) is your best bet. ($20-25 from the CBD.) The airport only offers domestic flights to five cities; international travel requires a stop in Sydney. All flights listed are one-way, unless otherwise specified: **Tiger Airways** (☎03 9335 3033; www.tigerairways.com) is an incredibly low-cost carrier servicing only Melbourne and Adelaide. **Virgin Blue Airlines** (☎13 67 89; www.virginblue.com. au) offers low fares to Adelaide, Brisbane, Melbourne, and other destinations. **Qantas** (☎13 13 13; www.qantas.com.au) connects to a similar range of cities.

## BY TRAIN

The **Canberra Railway Station,** on the corner of Wentworth Ave. and Mildura St. in Kingston, 6km southeast of the CBD, is on ACTION bus routes. **Countrylink** has an office located inside the railway station. (☎ 02 6208 9708; www.countrylink. info.au.) Buses go to Melbourne (9hr., 1 per day, $81), and Brisbane (24hr., 1 per day, $117) via Sydney (4hr., 2 per day, $43).

## BY BUS

Intercity buses meet at **Jolimont Tourist Centre,** 65-67 Northbourne Ave., north of Alinga St. in Civic. (Open daily in summer 6am-10:30pm; in winter 5am-10:30pm.) Bus companies and Qantas have desks in the building.

**Greyhound Australia** (☎13 14 99 or 13 20 30; www.greyhound.com.au). To: **Adelaide** (18hr., 1 per day, $185); **Albury-Wodonga** (4-6hr., 3 per day, $64); **Goulburn** (1hr., 3-4 per day, $19); **Griffith** (6hr., 1 per day, $68); **Gundagai** (2hr., 1 per day, $40); **Melbourne** (8hr., 3 per day, $81); **Parramatta** (3hr., 2 per day, $36); **Sydney** (3-4hr., 9 per day, $36); and **Wagga Wagga** (2-3hr., 2 per day, $52). June-Oct. buses run to: **Cooma** (1hr., 2 per day, $43), as well as **Skitube** and **Thredbo** for $75 including National Parks admission fee (3hr., 2 per day, 7am-6pm.)

**Murrays** (☎13 22 51; www.murrays.com.au). To: **Batemans Bay** (3hr., 1 per day, $24); Narooma (4hr., 1 per day, $37); Sydney (3-4hr., 3-5 per day, $37); **Wollongong** (3hr., 1 per day, $32). Ski-season service to: **Cooma** (1hr., 1 per day, $42); **Jindabyne** (2hr., 1 per day, $42); **Perisher Blue** (2hr., 1 per day, $42); and **Thredbo** (3hr., 1 per day, $53). Offers ski packages, which include round-trip transport, lift tickets, ski rental, and park entrance from $139. Open daily 7am-6pm.

**Countrylink** (☎13 22 32; www.countrylink.info). To: **Cooma** (1hr., 1 per day, $14); **Goulburn** (1½hr., 2 per day, $12). Discounts available for advance bookings online.

## BY CAR

The **National Roads and Motorists' Association (NRMA)** club offers 24hr. emergency road service; call ☎13 11 11. All rental companies (except Value) have offices in Braddon and the airport (the airport offices generally have longer hours).

**Avis,** 17 Lonsdale St. (☎02 6249 6088; www.avis.com.au). Open M-F 8am-6pm, Sa-Sun 8am-noon.

**Budget** (☎02 6257 2200; www.budget.com.au), in the Rydges Lakeside Hotel on London Circuit. Open M-F 8am-5pm, Sa 8am-noon.

**Europcar,** corner of Northbourne Ave. and Cooyong St. (☎13 13 90; www.europcar.com. au). Open M-F 8am-6pm, Sa 8am-1pm.

**Hertz,** 32 Mort St. (☎02 6257 4877 or 13 30 39; www.hertz.com.au). Open M-F 8am-6pm, Sa 8am-3pm, Su 9am-3pm.

**Value Rent-a-Car,** (☎1800 629 561) in the Rydges Capital Hill Hotel on the corner of National Circuit and Canberra Ave. Often has cheaper rates than the larger companies. Open M-F 8am-5pm, Sa-Su 8am-noon.

ACT

# Canberra

TO AUSTRALIAN INSTITUTE OF
SPORT (2km), O'CONNOR (1km)

TO DICKINSON (1km),
CANBERRA AND REGION
VISITORS CENTRE (700m)

Condamine St.

TURNER

Greenway St.
Haig Park
Masson St.

BRADDON

Girrahween St.

David St.

Ridley St.

Dryandra St.

Bogenwood St.

Frogdott St.

Nicholson Cr.

Barry Dr.

McCaulty Rd.

Watson St.

Gould St.

Moore St.

Northbourne Ave.

Lonsdale St.

Torrens St.

Fawkner St.

Farrer St.

Elder St.

Limestone Ave.

Chisholm St.

Clunies Ross St.

Daley Rd.

North Rd.

Barry Dr.

Cooyong St.

Rudd St.

Chapman St.

Elimatta St.

Batman St.

Allambee St.

Australian
National
Botanic
Gardens

Entrance to
Gardens

TO BLACK MT.
AND TELSTRA
TOWER (2km)

ACTON

Sullivans Ck. Rd.

University Ave.

Ellery St.

Childers St.

Marcus Clarke St.

Kalinga

West Row

East Row

Perrie Petrie St.

City Wk.

Bunda St.

Akuna St.

St. Mary's
Church

Ainslie Ave.

CIVIC

Ballumbir St.

Currong St.

REID

Elimatta St.

Australian
War Memorial

Reid Park

Fairbairn Ave.

Australian
National
University

National Film
and Archive

Gordon St.

Binara St.

Binara St.

Glebe
Park

Coranderrk St.

Euree St.

Booroondara St.

Anzac Pde.
Memorials

TO (4km)
MT. AINSLIE

TO NATIONAL
ZOO AND
AQUARIUM
(6km)

Garran Rd.

Balmain Cres.

McCoy St.

Edinburgh Av.

London Circuit

Lennox Cr.

Footbridge

Liversidge St.

Parkes Way

Amaroo St.

Constitution Ave.

Parkes

St. John
the Baptist

Springbank
Island

West
Basin

National Capitol
Exhibition

Regatta Pl.

Regatta
Point

Commonwealth
Park

Way

Northcott Dr.

West
Lake

Lawson Cr.

Captain Cook
Memorial Water Jet

National Museum
of Australia

Central
Basin

Blundells'
Cottage

Russell Dr.

RUSSELL

Lake
Burley Griffin

National
Library

Questacon (National Science
and Technology Centre)

Aspen
Island

Kings
Park

TO AUSTRALIAN
MEMORIAL (5km)

Commonwealth Ave.

Langton Cr.

King Edward Terr.

Parkes Pl.

PARKES

High
Court

National
Carillon

A'exandria Dr.

Flynn Dr.

King George Terr.

Parkes Pl.

National
Portrait
Gallery

National Gallery
of Australia

Grevillea
Park

Morshead Dr.

Sterling Park

Coronation Dr.

Parkes Pl.

East
Basin

United
Kingdom
New Zealand
Canada

Queen Victoria Terr.

Old Parliament
House

Kings Ave.

Macquarie St.

Blackall St.

Bowen Dr.

Hunter St.

Forster Cr.

Empire Circuit

Canberra Mosque

Perth Ave.

State Circle

Capital Circle

Federation Mall

Blackall St.

Brisbane Ave.

BARTON

Mundaring Dr.

Arkana St.

Ireland

United
States

Turrana St.

Schlick St.

YARRALUMLA

The Lodge

Adelaide St.

Parliament
House

Sydney Ave.

CAPITAL
HILL

State Circle

Melbourne Ave.

New South Wales Cr.

Wentworth Ave.

TO (1km),
CANBERRA DEEP SPACE
COMMUNICATION
COMPLEX (30km),
TIDBINBILLA
NATURE RESERVE (31km)

Grey St.

Hotham Cr.

DEAKIN

Hobart Ave.

National Circuit

Telopea Park

Jardine St.

Tench St.

Giles St.

Kennedy St.

Eyre St.

KINGSTON

Gawler Cr.

FORREST

Dominion Circuit

Franklin Ave.

Canberra Ave.

Manuka Ave.

Manuka
Park

Leichhardt St.

Oxley Dr.

Dawes St.

Cunningham St.

Canberra
Railway
Station

Empire Circuit

Collins
Park

Bougainville Way

Manuka Circle

Owens St.

Canberra Ave.

Tennyson Cr.

Red Hill Dr.

Mugga Way

Baudin St.

Dampier Cir.

Tasmania Circle

MANUKA

Flinders Way

Murray Cr.

St. Paul's

TO RED HILL
(6km)

Canberra
Nature
Park

Arthur Circle

GRIFFITH

Cook Cr.

TO LANYON
HOMESTEAD (255km),
NAMADGI NP (28km)

HUME
PLACE

SEE CIVIC DETAIL MAP p. 99

0    300 yards
0    300 meters

N

ACT

## Canberra Civic Detail

**ACCOMMODATIONS**
Canberra YHA
  Hostel, **15**
Victor Lodge B&B, **7**

Silo Bakery and
  Cheese Room, **4**
Tandoor House, **6**
Zen Yai, **13**
Supabarn, **18**

**FOOD**
Gus' Cafe, **8**
Uni Pub, **16**
Kingston National
  Bakery, **2**
Mama's Trattoria, **10**
The Pancake
  Parlour, **11**

**NIGHTLIFE**
ANU Student Uni
  Bar, **1**
Filthy McFadden's, **5**
Holy Grail, **3**
Phoenix, **12**
Uni Pub, **17**

## ⚜ ORIENTATION

As planned, Canberra is a decentralized city composed of multiple suburbs, each with its own central complex. When applicable, addresses list the street followed by the suburb. **Lake Burley Griffin,** formed by the damming of the Molonglo River, splits Canberra in two; on each side is a central hill with concentric roads leading outward. **Commonwealth Avenue** spans the lake and connects the two hills. To the north is **Vernon Circle,** marking the center of Canberra and the southern edge of the area known as **Civic.** Civic serves as the city's social center and bus interchange. Restaurants, shops, and nightclubs crowd the pedestrian mall known as **City Walk** in between Northbourne Ave., Akuna St., Bunda St., and London Circuit. Immediately north of Vernon Cir., Commonwealth Ave. becomes Northbourne Ave. To the south of the lake is **State Circle** and the governmental part of the capital. Within State Cir., **Capital Hill's** huge four-pronged flagpole reaches up from the new Parliament House. **Parliamentary Triangle** encloses most of the city's museums and government institutions.

If you drive, pick up a free map from the visitors center., since signs often refer to suburbs rather than streets. The railway station and an assortment of budget lodgings are found in **Kingston,** southeast of Capital Hill, which, along with neighboring **Manuka** (MON-ah-ka), is home to trendy restaurants and nightspots. Embassies fill **Yarralumla** (YAR-ra-LUM-la), west of Capital Hill. **Dickson,** northeast of Civic via Northbourne Ave. and Antill St., is known as the city's Chinatown, and has moderately priced restaurants and markets.

## ▐ LOCAL TRANSPORTATION

The primary hub for Canberra's public transit system centers on the city bus interchange, located at the junction of East Row, Alinga, and Mort St. Full maps and timetables for all routes are available, free of charge, at the ACTION information office on East Row, between Alinga St. and London Circuit. Route maps are also posted near the passenger shelters at the city bus interchange. Timetables are posted at bus stops. Buses generally run M-Sa 6am-midnight

ACT

and Su 8am-7:30pm, though some routes have more limited hours. Note that there are separate bus routes for weekends and public holidays.

**Public Transportation: ACTION bus service** (☎13 17 10; www.action.act.gov.au) has converted to a "1 fare, anywhere" policy: $3 (concessions $1.50) will buy 1 trip; ask the bus driver for a transfer ticket, which is good for 1½hr. A full-day ticket is $6.60, but a Shopper's Off-Peak Daily ticket is only $4.10, valid weekdays 9am-4:30pm and after 6pm, and all-day weekends and public holidays. Fare-saver tickets ($22) are available for 10 rides. Tickets can be purchased onboard or at most news agencies.

**Taxis: Canberra Cabs** (☎13 22 27) cover the city and suburbs 24hr.

**Bike Rental:** A superb system of ▨ **bicycle paths** criss-crosses the capital. A ride along the shores of Lake Burley Griffin is an excellent way to take in Parliamentary Triangle. Many hostels rent bikes ($15 per day). **Mr. Spokes Bike Hire,** on Barrine Dr. on the southeastern side of the lake, provides convenient bike rentals. (☎02 6257 1188. Open daily June-Aug. 10am-4pm; Sept.-May 9am-5pm. 3hr. $25, children $20; full day $38/28.) **Row 'n' Ride** (☎02 6228 1264) offers mountain bikes (3hr. $30, full-day $39; 2 days $65), with free delivery and pickup and puncture-repair service.

**Tour Bus: The Explorer Bus** circles most major attractions. Full-day discovery tour $35, children/concessions $25. They also run lake cruises. Call to book. ☎04 1845 5099.

# ▨ PRACTICAL INFORMATION

## TOURIST AND FINANCIAL SERVICES

**Tourist Offices: Canberra and Region Visitors Centre,** 330 Northbourne Ave. (☎02 6205 0044, accommodations booking 1300 733 228; www.visitcanberra.com.au), about 3km north of Vernon Circle, answers all your questions about Canberra and current happenings. Take bus #2, 6, 7, 30, 31, or 39. Open M-F 9am-5pm, Sa-Su 9am-4pm. Wheelchair-accessible. **Canberra Tourism Booth** is inside Jolimont Tourist Centre, 2 blocks from the city bus interchange. Open M-F 9am-5pm, Sa-Su 10am-2pm.

**Budget Travel:** There are 3 different STA travel locations in the Civic area. **STA Travel,** 13 Garema Pl., on the corner of City Walk (☎02 6247 8633; www.statravel.com.au). Open M-Th 9am-5pm, F 9am-6pm, Sa 10am-4pm.

**Embassies:** Unless specified, all locations listed below are located in Yarralumla. Getting there involves a 30min. walk from Civic or a complicated transport network, but bus route #2 (or #932 on weekends) will take you there. **Canada** (☎02 6270 4000), **New Zealand** (☎02 6270 4211), and **UK** (☎02 6270 6621) are all located on Commonwealth Ave. south of the lake. **Ireland** is at 20 Arkana St. (☎02 6273 3022), and **US** at 21 Moonah Pl. (☎02 6214 5600, emergency 02 6214 5900).

**Currency Exchange: Travelex** (☎02 6247 9984), inside Harvey World Travel in the Canberra Centre shopping mall, off Petrie St. Open M-F 9am-5pm, Sa 9:30am-12:30pm.

## LOCAL SERVICES

**Library: Civic Library** (☎02 6205 9000; www.library.act.gov.au), on London Circuit and Ainsile Ave. 1 of 9 branches. 15min. free Internet. Open M 8:30am-5:30pm, Tu-Th 10am-5:30pm, F 11am-7pm, Sa 9am-4pm. See **National Library of Australia,** p. 103.

**Ticket Agencies: Ticketek,** 11 Akuna St., Civic (☎13 28 49; www.ticketek.com). Tickets to sports and music events and Royal Theatre. Open M-F 9am-5pm. **Canberra Ticketing** (☎02 6275 2700 or 1800 802 025; www.canberratheatre.org.au), in Civic Square London Circuit, covers the Canberra Theatre, Playhouse, and Courtyard Studio. Open M-F 9am-5pm, Sa 10am-2pm, later on show nights.

**Travel Books and Maps: Map World** (☎02 6230 4097), is on Northbourne Ave. between the Salon and Kremlin Bar. Open M-F 9am-5pm. The **visitors center** (see **Tourist Offices,** above) also provides clear and helpful local maps.

**Public Markets: Gorman House Markets** (☎02 6249 7377; www.gormanhouse.com. au), on Ainslie Ave. between Currong and Doonkuma St., vend crafts, clothing, and miscellany. Open daily 9am-5pm. The **Old Bus Depot Markets,** 21 Wentworth Ave., Kingston (☎02 6292 8391; www.obdm.com.au), feature food and arts-and-crafts stalls, as well as live entertainment. Open Su 10am-4pm.

### MEDIA AND PUBLICATIONS
**Newspapers:** The main newspaper is the *Canberra Times* ($1.20, free copies at the visitors center). *The Chronicle* is a free local suburban newspaper.
**Entertainment:** *bma* is Canberra's free, alternative entertainment bimonthly. Times Out, in the Thursday Canberra Times, also lists entertainment options.
**Radio:** Top-40 104.7FM; Rock, Triple J 101.5FM; News, ABC 666AM.

## EMERGENCY AND COMMUNICATIONS

**Police:** ☎13 14 44. On London Circuit opposite University Ave., Civic.

**Drug and Alcohol Crisis Line:** ☎02 6207 9977. 24hr.

**Gay/Lesbian Counseling Service:** ☎02 6207 2800. Open daily 4pm-midnight.

**Women's Info and Referral Centre:** ☎02 6205 1075; M-F 9am-5pm.

**Pharmacy: O'Connor Pharmacy,** 9 Sargood St. (☎02 6248 7050), in shopping center. Open daily 9am-11pm. Pharmacies with more limited hours are located in the Canberra Centre across from Supabarn and in the Garema Plaza.

**Hospital/Medical Services: Canberra Hospital** on Yama Dr., Garren. ☎02 6244 2222, emergency ☎6244 2222. Follow signs to Woden southwest from Capital Hill.

**Internet Access:** Not many Internet cafes, but cheap access is available. The **ACT Library** Service offers free sessions in 15min. blocks; book ahead. The **National Library of Australia** (p. 103) also offers free Internet access.

**Post Office: General Post Office (GPO),** 53-73 Alinga St. by Jolimont Tourist Centre (☎13 13 18). Open M-F 8:30am-5:30pm. Branch near Canberra Centre Mall, on Bunda St. between Petrie Pl. and Akuna St. Open M-F 8:45am-5:15pm. **Postal Code:** 2600.

## ▐ ACCOMMODATIONS

**Canberra YHA Hostel,** 7 Akuna St., Civic (☎02 6248 9155). Near cafes and clubs, this hostel is family-friendly hostel. Kitchen, pool, sauna, BBQ, and free movies ($5 deposit). Internet ($2 per 20min.), bike rental ($20), and laundry ($3). Reception 24hr. Dorms $30-36; doubles $80-93; family room $135-142. 10% YHA discount. Book ahead. ❸

**Victor Lodge Bed and Breakfast,** 29 Dawes St., Kingston (☎02 6295 7777; www. victorlodge.com.au), 5min. walk from the train station. Bus #4, 5, 8; on weekends #980 and 938 stop 2 blocks away. This quiet lodge is 1 block from Kingston shops and restaurants. Kitchen, TV, laundry, Internet ($1 per 7min.; 24hr. Wi-Fi $10), bike rental ($15-20), and breakfast (7:30-9am) included. Key deposit $20. Reception 7:30am-9:30pm. Dorms $30; singles $69; twins and doubles $85. VIP discount. ❸

# ◘ FOOD

Cheap food isn't easy to find in Canberra. However, inexpensive cafes can be found near the city bus interchange in Civic. Another good bet is the food court at **Canberra Centre** (☎02 6247 5611), a three-story mall with main entrances off either City Walk or Bunda St. Opposite the Canberra Centre, the **City Market** complex packs in fruit stands, butcher shops, and prepared food stalls. You'll also find a huge **Supabarn** supermarket in the Canberra Centre. (☎02 6257 4055. Open M-F 7am-11pm, Sa-Su 7am-10pm.) Kingston has over 30 restaurants around its main commercial block, and nearby Manuka is a posh dining hot spot. Dickson, north of the CBD, is a miniature Chinatown.

## CIVIC

**Gus' Cafe** (☎02 6248 8118), corner of Bunda and Genge St. Trendy locals meet in this open-air cafe to chat over a cuppa or quick bite. Sample focaccia fingers with chili and garlic ($7), or sip a pineapple frappe ($5.50). Try a steaming bowl of porridge ($9) or poached eggs with mushrooms ($15) from the all-day breakfast menu. 10% surcharge on public holidays. Open daily 7:30am-late. AmEx/D/MC/V. ❷

**The Uni Pub's bistro** (see **Nightlife**, p. 105), on the 2nd floor. Allows you to grill your own steak to perfection. Main meals ($7-22) include roll and salad. Diners also have the option of sampling the chef's creations. Daily $5 meal specials. ❶

**Zen Yai,** 111 London Circuit (☎02 6262 7594). Sizzling stir-fries, noodle dishes, and spicy salads keep locals coming back to this fine Thai restaurant. Leaner cuts of meat and fresher vegetables than most area Asian eateries. BYO. Takeaway and delivery (min. $30) available. Open M-Sa 11:30am-3pm and 5-10pm. AmEx/MC/V. ❸

**Mama's Trattoria,** 7 Garema Pl. (☎02 6248 0936). Dishes up huge portions of home-style Italian favorites. Dig into a hot bowl of mushroom risotto while being serenaded by Sinatra. The friendly servers make Mama's a homey retreat from the pub scene. Lunch $8-15, dinner $14-21. Open daily 10am-latenight. AmEx/D/MC/V. ❷

**The Pancake Parlour,** 122 Alinga St. (☎02 6247 2982). A great place to satisfy late-night munchies and early-morning cravings, whether you opt for fruit pancakes ($13.50), creative crepes ($22-24), or more standard steak and fish fare ($24-28). Free Wi-Fi. 10% YHA discount. Early-bird specials 7-9am and 5-7pm. Open M-Th and Su 7am-10:30pm, F-Sa 7am-1am. AmEx/D/MC/V. ❸

## KINGSTON

▧ **Kingston National Bakery,** 56 Giles St. (☎02 6295 9646). Takeaway meat pies ($2-4) and fruit pastries ($1-3) can be enjoyed at the outdoor tables in front of this classic Aussie pie- and sweet-shop. Indulge in a rich apple turnover ($2.20). Open M-F and Su 6:30am-6:30pm, Sa 6:30am-6pm. Cash only. ❶

**Silo Bakery and Cheese Room,** 36 Giles St. (☎02 6260 6060). Lauded by locals as the best bakery in Canberra. Silo creates delicate appetizers and main dishes ($13-20) from imported cheese and freshly baked bread. Open Tu-Sa 7am-4pm. AmEx/MC/V. ❸

**Tandoor House,** 39 Kennedy St. (☎02 6295 7318). There's nothing too special about this little Indian restaurant except that it offers one of the few affordable finer dining experiences in Kingston. Sit back and savor subtly spiced curries, vindaloos, and masalas ($15). Open daily M-F noon-2:30pm, Sa-Su 5:30-10pm. AmEx/MC/V. ❷

# ◎ SIGHTS

## PARLIAMENTARY TRIANGLE

A showpiece of grand architecture and cultural attractions, Canberra's Parliamentary Triangle is the center of the capital. The triangle is bordered by Commonwealth Ave., Kings Ave., and Parkes Way across the lake.

▓**PARLIAMENT HOUSE.** The building is actually built into Capital Hill so that two sides jut out of the earth, leaving the grassy hilltop on its roof open to the public via an internal lift. The design intentionally places the people above Parliament. Balanced on top of this landmark is a four-pronged stainless steel flagpole visible from nearly every part of Canberra. Inside, free guided tours give an overview of the building's unique features and the workings of the government housed inside. Visitors can observe houses in action from viewing galleries. The House of Representatives allows advance bookings. The televised Question Time provides entertaining acrimony. When the House and Senate are sitting, the floor is opened up at 2pm for on-the-spot questioning of the Prime Minister and other officials. *(Take bus #2; #932 on weekends. Wheelchair-accessible. ☎02 6277 5399. To reserve tickets for Question Time, call ☎02 6277 4889; www.aph.gov.au. Open daily 9am-5pm, as late as 11pm when in session. Consult info desk for free tour times. House and Senate sit M-Th in approx. 2-week blocks, total of 20 weeks per year; recess Jan., Apr., and July.)*

▓**NATIONAL GALLERY OF AUSTRALIA.** On the southeastern end of Parkes Pl., near the intersection of King Edward Terrace. and Kings Ave., the National Gallery displays an impressive collection of Australian, Aboriginal, and Torres Strait Islander art. Keep your eyes open for a few big-name French Impressionists/post-Impressionists like Cezanne, Monet, and Matisse. After exploring the airy galleries on the first and second floors, take a stroll through the impressive sculpture garden. *(Take bus #2, 3; 934 and 935 on weekends. ☎02 6240 6502; www.nga. gov.au. Open daily 10am-5pm. 1hr. guided tours daily 11am and 2pm. Aboriginal art tour Th and Su 11am. Wheelchair-accessible. Free. Separate fees for special exhibits $15-20.)*

**OLD PARLIAMENT HOUSE AND NATIONAL PORTRAIT GALLERY.** This classic building is aligned with the front of its more modern counterpart, the Parliament House, and was Australia's seat of government from 1927 until 1988, when the current Parliament House was completed. The sitting rooms around the House and Senate chambers have been turned into galleries, complete with stories of the behind-the-scenes political maneuvering that used to take place there. The building will also house the new **Museum of Australian Democracy,** opening May 2009. *(On King George Terr. Take bus #2, 3, 6 and on weekends, 934 and 935. ☎02 6270 8222, gallery 02 6270 8236; www.oph.gov.au. Wheelchair-accessible. Daily tours of Old Parliament House every 45min. 9:30am-3:45pm. $2, concessions $1.)*

**NATIONAL PORTRAIT GALLERY.** This collection of famous Australian portraits and rotating exhibits—now an annex in the Old Parliament House—gets its own building in the Triangle in 2009. *(☎02 6102 7000; www.portrait.gov.au.)*

**NATIONAL LIBRARY OF AUSTRALIA.** The nation's largest library (5.7 million volumes) is the final stop on Parkes Way. Open for research and visitation, it houses copies of Australian publications on over 200km of shelving. The library also features rotating exhibits on Australian topics. Free Internet is available. *(Take bus #2, 3; 934 and 935 on weekend. Wheelchair-accessible. ☎02 6262 1111; www.nla.gov.au. Free tours Th 12:30pm. Open M-Th 9am-9pm, F-Sa 9am-5pm, Su 1:30-5pm.)*

ACT

**LAKE BURLEY GRIFFIN.** The last two attractions in the Parliamentary Triangle are actually located in the middle of the lake. The Captain Cook Memorial Jet blows a six-ton column of water to heights of up to 147m to commemorate Captain James Cook's arrival at the east coast of Australia. The bell tower of the National Carillon is located on Aspen Island at the other end of the lake's central basin. A gift from Britain on Canberra's 50th birthday in 1970, the Carillon, one of the largest musical instruments in the world, is rung several times a week and can be heard from anywhere in the Parliamentary Triangle. *(For info on the Jet or the Carillon, contact the National Capital Authority ☎ 02 6271 2888; concert schedule www.nationalcapital.gov.au/experience/attractions/national_carillon.)*

## PARLIAMENTARY TRIANGLE SURROUNDS

◪**NATIONAL MUSEUM OF AUSTRALIA.** A short trip from the CBD, this colorful museum is a post-modernist playground. The main hall is an inside-out rope knot, and the entire complex is circled by an orange roller-coaster loop sculpture. State-of-the-art multimedia components include Circa, a futuristic rotating theater that poignantly introduces visitors to the museum's themes of "Land, Nation, and People." The central Garden of Australian Dreams is a lesson in symbolism. *(Take bus #3, 934 on weekends, from Civic. On Acton Peninsula off Lawson Cres. ☎ 02 6208 5000 or 1800 026 132; www.nma.gov.au. Open daily 9am-5pm. Free; fees for special exhibitions. Tours daily 9:30am, noon, 1:30, and 3pm; 11am Aboriginal tour. $7.50, students/concessions $5.50, children $5, families $20.)*

◪**AUSTRALIAN WAR MEMORIAL.** Stories of Australia's heroes in combat and at home are retold with artifacts, photos, and depictions of wartime life by Australian artists. The expansive tribute and attached museum merit a half-day of exploration. The Hall of Memory holds the tomb of an unknown Australian soldier beneath a mosaic dome. Commemorative sculptures line the ANZAC (Australian New Zealand Army Corps) Pde. on the way up to the memorial. *(ANZAC Pde., on bus route #10, 930 on weekends. from Civic. ☎ 02 6243 4211. 1½hr. and 45min. tours daily; call for times. Open daily 10am-5pm. Free.)*

**GOVERNMENT BUILDINGS.** West of Capital Hill, on the south side of the lake, Yarralumla is peppered with the embassies of over 70 nations. The Lodge, home to the Australian Prime Minister, is on the corner of Adelaide Ave. and National Circuit, but hecklers be warned: it's closed to the public. At the Royal Australian Mint, on Denison St. in Deakin, you can watch coins being minted. Push a button to "press your own" dollar coin—for $2.50. *(Take bus #2, 932 on weekends. ☎ 1300 652 020; www.ramint.gov.au. Open M-F 9am-4pm, Sa-Su 10am-4pm; coin production M-F 9am-noon and 1-4pm. Wheelchair-accessible. Free.)*

**AUSTRALIAN NATIONAL BOTANIC GARDENS.** This living monument to the nation's biodiversity is divided into thematic planting groups like Eucalyptus Lawn and Rainforest Gully. A 30min. walk will take you through the gardens. Take a breather in the Rock Garden, or challenge yourself. The athletic can take the **Black Mountain Summit Walk,** a steep 2.7km path to Black Mountain Tower accessible from the garden path. *(Take bus #3, 981 and 934 on weekends to Daley Rd.; walk 20min. toward the lake along Clunies Ross Rd. ☎ 02 6250 9540; www.anbg.gov.au. Tours at 11am and 2pm, additional walks in the summer. Open daily 8:30am-5pm. Visitors center open 9am-4:30pm. Free. Parking $1.30 per hr.)*

**AUSTRALIAN INSTITUTE OF SPORT (AIS).** Tours led by resident athletes take you to see competitors in training. Stop at the hands-on Sportex exhibit, where you can try your hand at rowing, golfing, wheelchair basketball, simulated ski runs, and rock climbing. Bring a bathing suit to take part in one of the many underwater activities. *(On Leverrier Cres. in Bruce, just northwest of O'Connor. Take bus #7, 934 and 980 on weekends. ☎02 6214 1010. Open M-F 8:30am-5pm, Sa-Su 10am-4pm. Tours daily at 10, 11:30am, 1, 2:30pm. $15, students $10, children $8, families $40.)*

**NATIONAL ZOO AND AQUARIUM.** Unless you're a kid (or have one), you may have trouble justifying the long trip out; there is no direct public transport. The seven-hectare animal sanctuary does offer unique, up-close animal encounters, but they're a bit of a splurge. Special tours include a 2hr. hand-feed Zooventure Tour ($95 weekdays, $125 on weekends). Meet a Cheetah allows you to enter the cage and pet the impressive animals for $150. *(About 3km from the city. From Parkes Way, heading out of the city to the west, Lady Denman Dr. branches south toward the zoo at Scrivener Dam. Take bus #981 on weekends. ☎02 6287 8400. www.nationalzoo.com.au. Open daily 10am-5pm. $26.50, concession $21.50, children $14.50, families from $77.)*

**LOOKOUTS.** A stop at one of the city's lookouts can give you a general idea of what's in store on a sightseeing tour. On a hill in Commonwealth Park at Regatta Point, on the north shore of Lake Burley Griffin, the **National Capital Exhibition** is a great place to start your explorations. It provides a panorama of Canberra with a 5min. diorama lightshow about its history. Brochures are available for self-guided walking tours of the city. *(☎02 6257 1068; www.nationalcapital. gov.au. Wheelchair-accessible. Open M-F 9am-5pm, Sa-Su 10am-4pm. Free.)* North of Lake Burley Griffin and east of the CBD, **Mount Ainslie** rises 846m above the lake, the Parliamentary Triangle, and the Australian War Memorial, providing the classic postcard view down Anzac Pde. To reach the summit by car, turn right on Fairbairn Ave. from the Memorial end of Anzac Pde., to Mt. Ainslie Dr. Hiking trails lead to the top from directly behind the War Memorial.

# 🎭 🌺 ENTERTAINMENT AND FESTIVALS

In addition to the usual first-run cinemas, Canberra is home to several funky art-house alternatives, including **The Street Theater,** on the corner of University Ave. and Childers St. in City West (☎02 6247 1223; www.thestreet.org.au), with live plays and comedy acts ($12-35). The **Canberra Theatre** on London Circuit is the best place for live entertainment. (☎02 6275 2700; www.canberratheatre. org.au. $30-100; concessions available for most performances.) Canberra's calendar is packed with small festivals, but a few annual events temporarily transform the city. For 10 days in March, the **Celebrate Canberra Festival** (www. celebratecanberra.com) is filled with artistic displays, food showcases, hot-air balloon rides, and Canberra Day festivities. **Floriade** (from mid-Sept. to mid-Oct.) paints Commonwealth Park with millions of blooms and fills accommodations; book ahead. (☎02 6205 0666; www.floriadeaustralia.com.)

# 🌙 NIGHTLIFE

## CIVIC

🍺 **The Uni Pub** (☎02 6247 5576), on the corner of London Circuit and University Ave. 5 floors of partying have something for everyone. There's a pub on the ground floor, a bistro on the first (see **Food**, p. 102), and a laid-back pool hall ($2 games) on the second. Things get posh on the 3rd floor "executive level," and the 4th floor becomes a hopping night club F and Sa nights. Open M-Th and Su 11am-11pm, F-Sa 11am-latenight.

**Phoenix,** 21 East Row (☎02 6247 1606). This bohemian bar attracts a motley crew of artists, intellectuals, and locals. The mix of people matches the odd assortment of tables and seats. Frequent live music. Open M-Sa noon-latenight, Su 1pm-latenight.

**ANU Student Uni Bar** (☎02 6125 3660; www.anuunion.com.au), in the student union, near the corner of North Rd. and University Ave. This popular uni hangout is the cheapest pub in town and hosts big names in music. Check *bma* (p. 101) or the website for gig listing. Open M-F noon-latenight, Sa 4pm-latenight.

## KINGSTON

**Filthy McFadden's** (☎02 6239 5303), intersection of Jardine and Eyre St. Possibly the best-named pub ever, Filthy's boasts the largest whiskey collection in the Southern Hemisphere. This down-to-earth place epitomizes the Irish country pub. Pint of Guinness $6.50. Open M-Tu and Su noon-midnight, W noon-2am, F-Sa noon-3am. AmEx/MC/V.

**Holy Grail** (☎02 6295 6071), in Green Sq. at the intersection of Jardine and Eyre St. This colorful, trendy bistro and bar turns into a packed nightclub F-Sa nights, with live cover bands and DJs. Cover $5. Open M-F 4-11pm, W-Su 1-11pm. AmEx/MC/V.

# ▓ DAYTRIPS FROM CANBERRA

**▓TIDBINBILLA NATURE RESERVE.** This wildlife park is covered in spectacular walks, freely roaming kangaroos, emus, and countless other birds. Take a stroll through the Sanctuary wetlands to see diving platypuses and enormous flocks of magpie geese. Informative displays at the visitors center showcase Tidbinbilla's breeding programs and conservation efforts. *(On Paddys River Rd., 35km south of town, just beyond the Canberra Deep Space Complex turn-off. ☎02 6205 1233; www.tams. act.gov.au. Guided tours on weekends. Reserve open 9am-6pm. Visitors center M-F 9am-4:30pm, Sa-Su 9am-5pm. Free, but may charge after April 2009.)*

**CANBERRA DEEP SPACE COMMUNICATION COMPLEX.** One of the most powerful radio antenna centers in the world, the Complex communicates with the most distant satellites including Voyager I, currently 9.9 billion miles beyond the sun. The 70m dish is the largest in the Southern Hemisphere. The Space Centre has displays on the history of space exploration. *(Take Adelaide Ave., which becomes Cotter Rd., to Paddy's River Rd. Off Paddy's River Rd., 35km southwest of Civic. ☎02 6201 7880; www.cdscc.nasa.gov. Open daily in summer 9am-5pm, in winter 9am-6pm. Free.)*

**NAMADGI NATIONAL PARK.** The expansive Namadgi National Park fills almost all of southern ACT with alpine wilderness traversed by only one major paved route: the Naas/Boboyan Rd. The park has walking tracks for all experience levels, but it is most famous for the untrammeled recesses accessible only to serious hikers. Birdwatchers and fishermen are also drawn to this wildlife haven. **Campsites ❶** at Orroral River, Honeysuckle and Mt. Clear—with parking nearby—have firewood, untreated water, and toilets. The **Namadgi Visitors Centre,** on the Naas/Boboyan Rd. 3km south of Tharwa, has maps and info on Aboriginal paintings and camping options. *(☎02 6207 2900. Register at visitors center. 33km south of Civic. Sites $5 per person per night. Open M-F 9am-4pm, Sa-Su 9am-4:30pm.)*

ACT

# NEW SOUTH WALES

From a historical perspective, there's no disputing that New South Wales has been the site of many of Australia's seminal experiences. It was here that British convicts survived the first bitter years of colonization, dreaming of what might lie beyond the impassable Blue Mountains; it was here that explorers first broke through the Great Dividing Range, opening the country's interior for settlement and ensuring the stability of the colony. In the central plains and the rich land of the Riverina, merino wool and agricultural success provided the state with its first glimpses of prosperity. Then, in 1851, prospectors struck gold just west of the mountains, and Australia's history changed forever. New South Wales shook off its prison colony mantle overnight, transforming into a place that promised a new life and an inflated bank account. Though the gold rush days are long gone, New South Wales has continued to grow. Today, it's the most populous state and—thanks largely to Sydney—the sophisticated center of Australia.

Sydney, the nation's biggest and flashiest city, sits midway along the state's coastline. During the summer, a trip up the coast is the ultimate backpacker party, with epicenters in the large coastal towns of Port Macquarie and Byron Bay. The south coast is colder, but less crowded and just as beautiful. Some of the state's best getaways are found in the accessible Blue Mountains, just west of Sydney's suburban stretches. The New England Plateau, along the Great Dividing Range north of the Hunter Valley wineries, creates a lush setting for a cozy collection of small towns and stunning national parks. Just below the carved-out enclave of the Australian Capital Territory, the Snowy Mountains offer enticing winter skiing and superb summer hiking.

## ◆ HIGHLIGHTS OF NEW SOUTH WALES

**LOSE YOURSELF** in one of the world's most fascinating cities, **Sydney** (p. 110).

**ESCAPE** from urban life to Sydney's great outdoors, the **Blue Mountains** (p. 162).

**TOUR** some of the most respected vineyards in the world and taste the fine red and white wines of the **Hunter Valley** (p. 177).

**SKI** down the black diamond slopes of **Thredbo** (p. 243).

**INHALE** the counterculture of **Nimbin** (p. 214).

# ▐ TRANSPORTATION

The cities and towns of New South Wales are connected by the state's excellent public transportation system, as well as by numerous reliable private transportation companies. Route information for all bus, rail, and ferry systems in the Sydney metro area is available from the **Sydney Transit Authority** (☎ 13 15 00; www.sta.nsw.gov.au). For info on more extensive travel throughout NSW and beyond, call **Rail Australia** (☎ 08 8213 4592; www.railaustralia.com) or **Greyhound Australia** (☎ 13 14 99 or 13 20 30; www.greyhound.com.au).

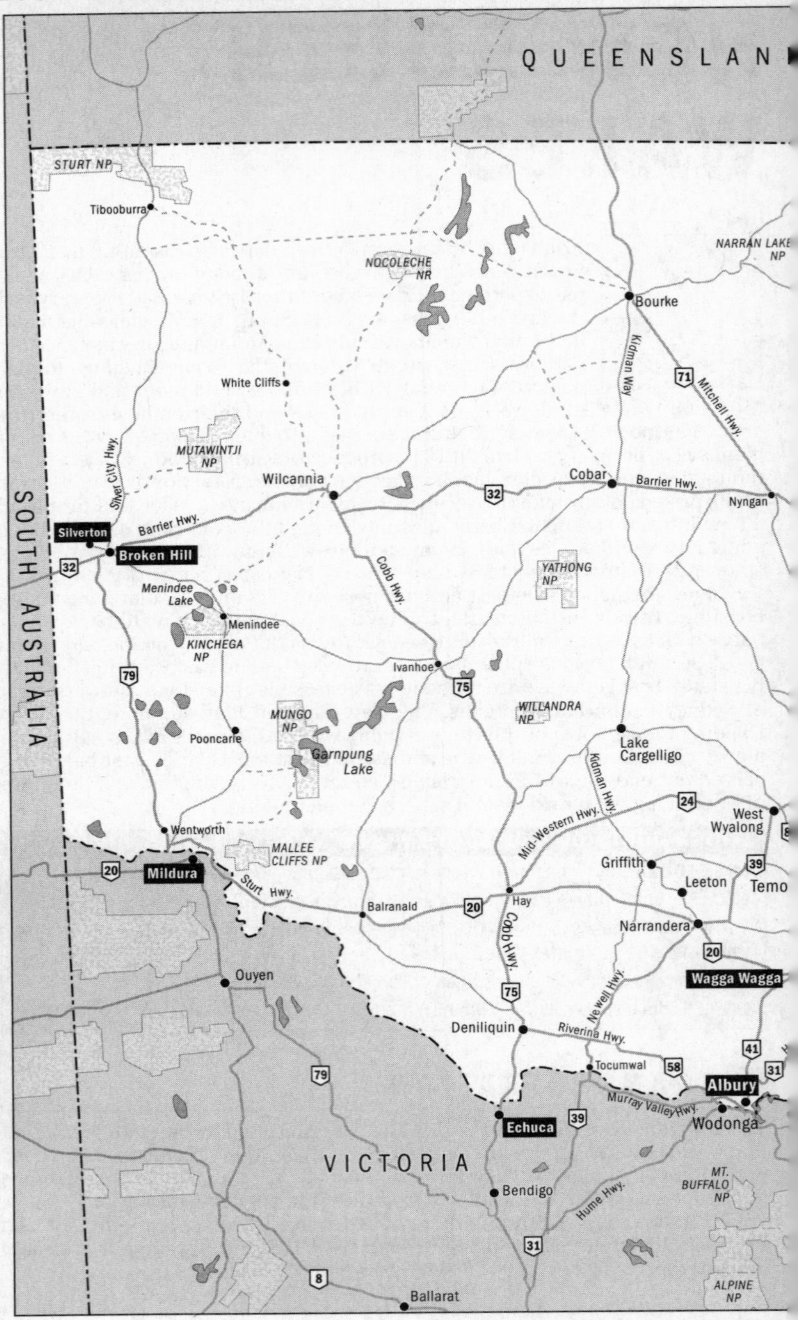
QUEENSLAN
STURT NP
Tibooburra
NOCOLECHE NR
NARRAN LAKE NP
Bourke
Kidman Way
71
Mitchell Hwy.
White Cliffs
MUTAWINTJI NP
Silver City Hwy.
Wilcannia
Cobar
Barrier Hwy.
32
Nyngan
SOUTH AUSTRALIA
Silverton
Barrier Hwy.
Broken Hill
32
Cobb Hwy.
YATHONG NP
Menindee Lake
Menindee
KINCHEGA NP
Ivanhoe
79
75
WILLANDRA NP
MUNGO NP
Pooncarie
Garnpung Lake
Lake Cargelligo
Kidman Hwy.
24
Mid-Western Hwy.
West Wyalong
Wentworth
MALLEE CLIFFS NP
20
Mildura
Sturt Hwy.
Griffith
39
Leeton
Temo
Hay
Balranald
20
Cobb Hwy.
Narrandera
20
Ouyen
Wagga Wagga
75
Newell Hwy.
Deniliquin
Riverina Hwy.
41
79
Tocumwal
58
31
Albury
Murray Valley Hwy.
Echuca
39
Wodonga
VICTORIA
MT. BUFFALO NP
Bendigo
Hume Hwy.
31
8
ALPINE NP
Ballarat

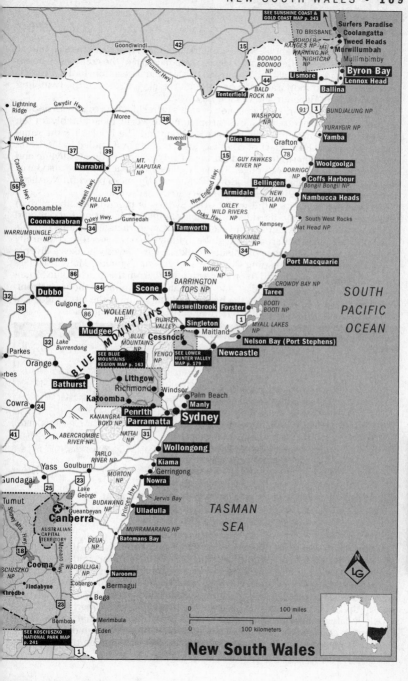

New South Wales

# SYDNEY ☎02

Australia's unofficial capital, Sydney blends liveliness and loveliness as one of the world's greatest cities. Home to more than one-fifth of the continent's population, Sydney is Australia's major urban center, and it certainly looks the part, from the elevated monorail snaking through the skyscrapers to the twinkling lights of Darling Harbour and Cockle Bay Wharf.

For all of Sydney's urban bustle, however, it's refreshingly in tune with nature. Its beautiful architecture is famous throughout the world, most notably for the astounding structures found in Sydney Harbour and The Rocks. It's the same harbor where the First Fleet of colonists and convicts first landed in 1788, and today, the iconic Opera House and Harbour Bridge define Sydney's skyline and draw visitors to the water's edge. Sydney's obsessive beach culture also lures tourists to the ocean; glamorous Bondi Beach and the more peaceful Northern Beaches above the harbor let Sydneysiders soak up the sun.

Like many major cities the world over, Sydney is much more liberal than the rest of the country. Its substantial gay population is out and about, and the annual Gay & Lesbian Mardi Gras celebration attracts enormous crowds of all persuasions from around the globe. Sydney also refuses to be culturally contained, as its wide range of cuisines makes clear. The city houses a diverse Asian population, and bustling Chinatown is growing quickly. Many travelers use Sydney as a springboard to other destinations, from the nearby Blue Mountains to the tip of Queensland's Cape York. But after dining by the waterfront, raging in the clubs, relaxing on the beach, and marveling at the city's vigor and dynamism, you might be ready to permanently relocate Sydney-side.

## ▨HIGHLIGHTS OF SYDNEY

**TOUR** the stunning Concert Hall at **Sydney Opera House,** the defining structure of Sydney's skyline and a masterpiece recognized the world over (p. 135).

**RIDE** the ferry to the friendly surfing suburb **Manly** for grand coastal walks and a glimpse of the utopia that is the Northern Beaches (p. 157).

**VISIT** Sydney's eden at the **Royal Botanic Gardens,** which offers spectacular views of Sydney Harbour at Mrs. Macquarie's Point (p. 138).

**EXPERIENCE Kings Cross,** Sydney's 24hr. neon den of sin, with active nightlife and seedy streets (p. 142).

**CHEER** at **Moore Park** for the Sydney Swans and Sydney City Roosters, the city's Aussie Rules Football and Rugby teams (p. 148).

## ✈ INTERCITY TRANSPORTATION

### BY PLANE

**Kingsford-Smith International Airport** (www.sydneyairport.com.au), 10km south of the **Central Business District (CBD),** is Australia's largest airport and serves most major international carriers. It is a primary hub for **Qantas** (☎13 13 13) and **Virgin Blue** (☎13 67 89), both of which offer the majority of domestic flights. Although locker storage is not available, **Smarte Carte** (☎02 9667 0926) will hold bags. (Up to 6hr. $7-14 per bag, 6-24hr. $9-20.) The **Sydney Airport Visitor Centre** kiosk, located on the arrivals level in the international terminal, offers booking service and free calls to area hostels. (☎02 9667 6050. Open daily 5am-last flight.) Transportation to the city is available directly outside the terminals.

**Airport Link** (☎02 8337 8417; www.airportlink.com.au) is part of the underground **CityRail** network, which runs trains M-Th and Sa-Su 5am-11:45pm, F 5am-12:30am along the green East Hills line to the City Circle, including Central and Circular Quay (15min.; every 10min.; $13.40-$13.80, same-day round-trip $18.40-20.80). If you're luggage-laden or just not in the mood for hauling bags on the CityRail, several companies operate airport shuttles that run to the city. **Kingsford-Smith Transport (KST)** operates small vans and buses to city and inner suburb accommodations. (☎02 9666 9988; www.kst.com.au. Every 20min. daily 5am-9pm. $12-13, round-trip $20-22). A taxi to the city center costs about $30 from domestic terminals, $35 from international. Additionally, many area hostels and hotels offer van service or free pickup; inquire with your accommodations to see if they can give you a ride.

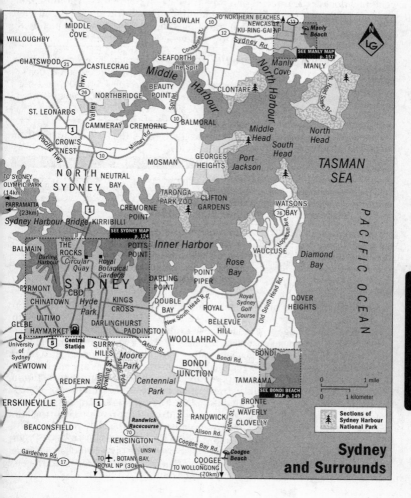

**Sydney and Surrounds**

NEW SOUTH WALES

## BY TRAIN

**Countrylink trains** (☎13 22 32; www.countrylink.info) depart from busy Central Railway Station on Eddy Ave. Tickets are sold in three classes: economy, first class, and first-class sleeper. ISIC members receive an automatic 50% discount. Combining the Countrylink and Queensland Rail options, the **Backtracker Rail Pass** provides passengers with unlimited travel on the entire Countrylink network for a period from 14 days to 6 months (passes available from Countrylink centers and selected travel agents; $232-420). For country-wide travel, the **Austrail Flexi-Pass** grants passengers 15-22 days worth of train travel to be used over 6 months at personal discretion ($950-1330). **Great Southern Rail** trains (☎13 21 47; www.gsr.com.au) provide routes across the south and one line through the Northern Territory, all with three ticket classes available. Round-trip fares are generally double the price of one-way fares. Great Southern also offers international backpackers/students a six-month unlimited travel card on all their services for $590. Please note that train times can and do change frequently, so call ahead or check their website for updates.

 **CUSTOMS CRACKDOWN** Australia's quarantine is very strict, so be prepared for long lines and thorough baggage checks upon arrival. Don't bring food or snacks of any kind, and cash exceeding $10,000 must be declared. For current regulations, contact the Australian Customs Service (☎02 6275 6666; www.customs.gov.au).

The table below lists information and adult fares for trains running from Sydney (fares will fluctuate based on season):

| DESTINATION | COMPANY | DURATION | DAYS | PRICE |
|---|---|---|---|---|
| Adelaide | Great Southern | 24hr. | W, Sa | $295 |
| Alice Springs | Great Southern | 40hr. | W, Sa | $650 |
| Brisbane | Countrylink | 15hr. | 2 per day | $95 |
| Byron Bay | Countrylink | 13hr. | 3 per day | $85 |
| Canberra | Countrylink | 4hr. | 3 per day | $40 |
| Coffs Harbour | Countrylink | 8hr. | 3 per day | $69 |
| Melbourne | Countrylink | 11hr. | 2 per day | $92 |
| Surfers Paradise | Countrylink | 14-15hr. | 2 per day | $88 |
| Perth | Great Southern | 3 days | Sa, W | $690 |

## BY BUS

Fifteen **bus** companies operate from the **Sydney Coach Terminal,** Central Station, on the corner of Eddy Ave. at Pitt St. (☎02 9281 9366. Open M-F 6am-6pm, Sa-Su 8am-6pm.) Luggage storage is also available ($5-10). The major national bus company, **Greyhound Australia** (☎1300 473 946, Sydney Terminal 02 9212 1500; www.greyhound.com.au) generally offers more frequent trips to major destinations than the smaller, regional carriers, but their rates are often higher. Greyhound Australia tickets can be purchased by phone, at the bus station, or online for pickup at any Australian post office. Check online for special deals and to see all types of available passes. Their **Aussie Explorer Passes** allows travelers to explore various parts of the country along pre-set routes; the Mini Travelers route, which runs along the east coast, is especially popular ($307-390, depending on route from Sydney; ISIC/YHA/VIP/NOMADS $279-351). **The Oz Experience** offers a similar service by also providing driver guides and travel agents to help along the way. Their main office is at 804 George St. in the city center. (☎02 9213 1766; www.ozexperience.com.)

The following table refers to the Greyhound Australia service and lists information and adult fares for buses running from Sydney:

| DESTINATION | DURATION | TIMES | PRICE |
|---|---|---|---|
| Adelaide (via Melbourne or Canberra) | 22-25hr. | 6 per day | from $140 |
| Alice Springs (via Melbourne, Canberra, or Adelaide) | 2 days | 6 per day | from $402 |
| Brisbane | 17hr. | 5 per day | from $124 |
| Byron Bay | 13hr. | 4 per day | from $112 |
| Cairns (via Brisbane) | 2 days | 4 per day | from $372 |
| Canberra | 4hr. | 8 per day | from $36 |
| Coffs Harbour | 9hr. | 4 per day | from $80 |
| Darwin (via Alice Springs) | 3 days | 1 per day | $738 |
| Melbourne | 12-15hr. | 6 per day | from $78 |
| Mount Isa (via Brisbane) | 2 days | 3 per day | from $300 |
| Surfers Paradise | 15hr. | 4 per day | from $119 |

#  ORIENTATION

The Sydney metropolitan area is immense and seems to be contained only by the forces of nature: **Ku-Ring-Gai Chase National Park** to the north, the **Blue Mountains** to the west, **Royal National Park** to the south, and the Pacific Ocean, the Tasman Sea, and Sydney Harbour to the east. Sydney's city center is of manageable size. The walk to **Circular Quay** along Pitt St. takes only 30min. from Central Station and only 20min. from Kings Cross. Outside the city center are the inner suburbs, like **Glebe** and **Surry Hills,** each of which has a distinctive feel. For a bird's eye view of it all, ascend **Sydney Tower** (p. 132).

> **OUR COVERAGE OF SYDNEY.** Each neighborhood in Sydney has unique features and a distinctive character. To give you the best of what each offers, we have grouped together each neighborhood's accommodations, food, sights, and nightlife. Information on entertainment, local activities, and area festivals can be found before the neighborhood coverage starts; for information on **daytrips** from Sydney, see (p. 159).

## NEIGHBORHOODS AT A GLANCE

| NEIGHBORHOOD | FEATURES | LOCAL BUS ROUTES |
|---|---|---|
| Bondi Beach | Home to most of Sydney's celebrities. | 380, L82 |
| CBD | Martin Place, Chinatown, Paddy's Market. | 380, 394 |
| Circular Quay | Sydney Opera House and all ferry wharves. | 380, 394 |
| Coogee Beach | Bondi's rival; youthful energy and vibrant nightlife. | 372, 373, 374 |
| Darling Harbour | Sydney Aquarium and Powerhouse Museum. Touristy, with a swanky nightlife scene. | Short walk from Town Hall or monorail |
| Darlinghurst and Paddington | Young, fashionable, creative types. | 378, 380, L82, 389 |
| Glebe | Bohemian cafes, pubs, and bookstores; neighboring student population. | 431, 432, 433 |

| | | |
|---|---|---|
| Kings Cross | Seedy center of Sydney back-packer culture, with hostels, cafes, strip shows, and crazy nightlife. | 324, 325, 326, 327, 311 |
| Manly | Friendly resort area with great beaches and surfing. | 175, 178, 180, L80, 185, L85 |
| Mosman | Taronga Park Zoo, other parks and gardens. | 247, 244 |
| Newtown | Vintage clothing, used books, and great eateries. | 423, 422, 426, 428 |
| North Sydney | Tree-lined financial district, upmarket cafes. | 202, 207, 208, 263, 273, 252, 253, 254, 261 |
| The Rocks | Historic neighborhood, upscale boutiques; perfect for an afternoon pint. | Short walk from Circular Quay |
| Surry Hills | Artsy cafes and clothing stores. | 301, 302, 303, 374, 376, 339, 372, 393, 395, 391 |
| Vaucluse/Rose Bay | Historic, upscale homes and Euro-style shopping. | 325, 324 |

# ⊟ LOCAL TRANSPORTATION

Sydney's well-oiled public transportation system makes it easy to travel within the city limits. The **Sydney Transit Authority (STA)** controls city buses, **CityRail** trains, and ferries; the network stops nearly everywhere. For information on any part of the STA system, call ☎ 13 15 00. Check prices for various passes, as they are frequently cheaper than paying multiple individual fares. The **DayTripper** ($16, ages 4-15 $8) grants unlimited use of Sydney ferries, local buses, and central CityRail lines. The **TravelPass** (Red $35, ages 4-15 $17.50; Green (two zones including Olympic Park and Manly) $43/21.50; Purple (premiere) $57/28.50) covers the four central zones and includes unlimited seven-day access to buses, trains, and ferries. The **Sydney Pass** includes unlimited use of buses, ferries, and Red Travelpass trains; round-trip Airport Link service; access to the Sydney, Bondi, and Parramatta Explorer buses; passage on Manly JetCats and Parramatta RiverCats; and discounts on selected Sydney attractions. (3-day pass $110, ages 4-15 $55, families $275; 5-day pass $145/70/360; 7-day pass $165/80/410.)

## BY BUS

Buses do not automatically stop at all bus stops; hail them from the sidewalk as you would a taxi. (Pay as you board; fares from $1.80-$5.80; ask for senior and student concessions). Color-coded **TravelTen passes** cover 10 trips at a discount and can be purchased from most news agencies. (Blue TravelTen for 10 trips from $14.40, concession $7.20.) **The Bus Tripper** ($12.10, children $6) covers one full day of bus travel. Most buses run between 5am and 11:30pm, but there is extended night service between the city center and some locales.

In addition to the local commuter bus service, the Sydney Transport Authority operates two **sightseeing buses,** the Sydney Explorer and the Bondi Explorer, which allow passengers to get on and off at major attractions along designated routes. The **Sydney Explorer** has 27 stops, covering sights between Sydney Harbour and Central Station, moving as far east as Woolloomooloo Bay and Kings Cross and as far west as Darling Harbour, originating in Circular Quay (every 20min. 8:40am-5:20pm). The **Bondi Explorer** has 19 stops, visiting the eastern bays and southern beaches down to Coogee, departing from Circular Quay (every 30min. 8:45am-4:15pm). The Explorer services are expensive but also an excellent way to tour the city. (1-day pass for both routes $39, ages 4-15

$19, families $97; tickets combining both routes over 2 non-consecutive days $68/34/170. Purchase tickets on a bus at any stop along the route.)

A **bus information kiosk** for STA bus services, labeled "Transit Shop," is located on the corner of Alfred and Loftus St. between the McDonald's and Circular Quay. (Open M-F 7am-7pm, Sa-Su 8:30am-5:30pm.) The STA info line (☎13 15 00; www.sydneypass.info) also has schedule details.

## BY SUBWAY AND TRAIN

Sydney's **CityRail train system** (M-Th and Su from 4-5am to midnight, F-Sa from 5am to 1:30-2am, depending on the line; www.cityrail.info) runs from Bondi Junction in the east to the most distant corners of suburban sprawl in the north, west, and south. Service is fast, frequent, and easy to navigate, but as with any public transportation, there are bound to be occasional delays. CityRail's lowest one-way fare within the city circle is $2.50, and as the length of your trip increases, the price increases accordingly. Round-trip fares are double the one-way price when purchased on weekdays before 9am. At all other times, the purchase of a round-trip "off-peak" ticket gets you up to a 40% reduction of the one-way fare. The combined **TravelPass** is a bargain for regular train users and has the added bonus of selected bus and ferry use. (Good for 1 week beginning on day of validation; Red Pass for city center and beaches $35; Green Pass, which includes Manly Beach and Olympic Park, $43.) **Train information offices** are at **Circular Quay** (open daily 9am-5pm) and at **Central Station** (☎02 8202 2000; open daily 6am-10pm).

**Monorail** and **Light Rail** (☎02 8584 5288; www.monorail.com.au or 02 8584 5250; www.metrolightrail.com.au), operated by the same company, provide transportation above the city bustle, which is a nice change if you are traveling directly and don't mind the slightly heftier fee. The Monorail links the City Center with Darling Harbour and Chinatown. (☎8584 5288. Every 3-5min. M-Th 7am-10pm, F-Sa 7am-midnight, Su 8am-10pm. $4.80, under 5 free, families $23, day passes with unlimited transport $9.50. Call in advance for reduced fares.) The more practical Light Rail connects Chinatown, Darling Harbour, Glebe, Star City, and Ultimo. (Daily every 10-15min. 6am-midnight; every 30min. midnight-6am. $3.20-5.70, seniors and ages 6-16 $2-4.20, families $20; unlimited day pass $9.)

## BY FERRY

**STA green and gold ferries** (www.sydneyferries.info) offer a scenic form of public transportation. Ferries leave from the Circular Quay wharves between the Opera House and the Harbour Bridge (daily 6am-midnight; check the timetables for schedules). Short one-way trips in the harbor cost $5.20. A **FerryTen pass** for the same area costs $33.50 and works like a normal bus pass. The fare for the JetCat to Manly is $8.20 (FerryTen pass $67.80). STA's fastest commuter ferry service, the RiverCat, sails to Parramatta ($7.70, FerryTen $54.30).

STA has several **Sydney Ferries Harbour Cruises:** the **Morning Cruise** (1hr.; daily 10:30am; $18, ages 4-16 $9, families $45); the **Afternoon Cruise** (2½hr.; M-F 1pm, Sa-Su and public holidays 12:30pm; $24/12/60); and the after-dark **Evening Harbour Cruise** (1½hr., M-Sa 8pm, $22/11/55). All depart from Wharf 4. Posher private ships, such as Captain Cook and Majestic Cruises, have slightly more comprehensive harbor cruises with meals and/or shows. Browse along East Circular Quay for the lowest fare; fares range from $25 to $50 per person, with some ships offering dinner cruises from $75 to $165. Ships depart from midmorning to evening. The **ferry information office** is located at Wharf 4. (☎02 9207 3170. Open M-Sa 7am-5:45pm, Su 8am-5:45pm.)

NEW SOUTH WALES

NEW SOUTH WALES

# Sydney CityRail Network

Western Line
(Emu Plains/Richmond–
North Sydney)

Northern Line
(Berowra–North
Sydney via Strathfield)

Carlingford Line
(Carlingford–Clyde)
*proposed line runs
St Leonard–Westmead

Northern Shore Line
(Berowra–Parramatta
via Central)

Eastern Suburb &
Illawarra Lines
(Waterfall/Cronulla–
Bondi Junction)

Inner West Line
(Liverpool/Bankstown–
City via Regents Park)

Bankstown Line
(Liverpool/Lidcombe–City
via Bankstown)

Airport & East Hills Line
(Macarthur–City via
Airport/Sydenham)

Cumberland Line
(Campbelltown–
Blacktown)

South Line
(Campbelltown–
City via
Granville)

TO NEWCASTLE

TO BLUE MOUNTAINS

TO SOUTH COAST

Interchange with other lines

◇ Suburban/Intercity train connections

Proposed Line

● Station does not have
bus stop/interchange

♿ Staffed handicapped accessible stops

Map reproduced courtesy of State Rail Authority of New South Wales

# Sydney Ferries

Proposed line

Handicapped accessibility stops

**Circular Quay Ferry Terminal**

Wharf 2
Wharf 3
Wharf 4
Wharf 5
Wharf 6

Manly — The Esplanade

Jetcat Service

Garden Island

Darling Point — McKell Park (stops M-F only)
Double Bay — Bay St.
Rose Bay — Lyne Park
Wilsons Bay — Military Rd.

Mosman Bay — Avenue St.
Old Cremorne — Green St.
South Mosman — Musgrave St.
Cremorne Point — Milsons Rd.
Taronga Zoo — Bradleys Head Rd.

Sundays Only

Neutral Bay — Hayes St.
Kurraba Point — Kurraba Rd.
North Sydney — High St.
Kirribilli — Holbrook St.

Harbour Sights Cruises

Milsons Point — Alfred St. South
McMahons Point — Henry Lawson Ave.
Balmain East — Darling St.
Balmain — Thames St.
Birchgrove
Greenwich — Mitchell St.
Greenwich — Valentia St.
Woolwich

Sunday Only

Darling Harbour — Nine St., Wharf 3
Balmain West — Elliott St.
Birkenhead — Henry, Marine Dr.

Darling Harbour — Aquarium
Pyrmont Bay — Casino & Maritime Museum (Only at high tide)

Cockatoo Island
Drummoyne — Wolseley St.
Chiswick — Bortwick Dr., Huntleys Point Rd.
Abbotsford — Great North Rd. (travel towards city only)
Bayview Park — Burwood Rd.
Cabarita — Cabarita Point
Kissing Point — Kissing Point Pk.
Sydney Point — John St.
Meadowbank — Bortefield Rd.
Sydney Olympic Park
Rydalmere
Parramatta

NEW SOUTH WALES

Map reproduced courtesy of The State Transit Authority of New South Wales

## BY CAR

Because of the extensive public transport system, renting a car to tour the city isn'tt necessary, and it can be confusing to navigate Sydney's numerous one-way streets. However, cars are useful for daytrips, and travelers planning an extended tour through more of Australia should investigate either renting or buying. All major **car rental** companies have offices in Kingsford-Smith Airport, and most appear again on William St. near Kings Cross. If you are traveling long-term to other parts of Australia after your stay in Sydney, consider investing in a used vehicle. Hostel notice boards overflow with fliers for privately owned cars, campers, and motorcycles selling for as little as several hundred dollars. When purchasing a car this way, it's a good idea to make sure it's registered to the seller so the registration can be transferred. For more information on car sales, see **Buying and Selling Used Cars**, p. 31. **Kings Cross Backpackers Car Market,** Level 2, Kings Cross Carpark, on the corner of Ward Ave. and Elizabeth Bay Rd., brings buyers and sellers together. They offer third-party insurance for travelers (see **Car Insurance,** p. 32), and their knowledgeable staff has valuable information on registration and other matters for car-buyers. (☎1800 808 188, www.carmarket.com.au. Open daily 9am-5pm.) **Travellers Auto Barn,** 177 William St., Kings Cross (☎1800 674 374), rents cars and offers guaranteed buyback agreements on cars they sell for over $3000. Buyback rates are 30-50% of purchase price, depending on how long you have the cars. There are six branches around the country, meaning that one-way rentals and buybacks are also offered. (Open M-F 9am-6pm, Sa 9am-5pm, Su 10:30am-3pm.)

## BY TAXI

Taxis (www.nswtaxi.org.au) can be hailed from virtually any street, although availability and frequency depend on the time and day of the week. Initial fare is $3 (surcharge with call-in request $1.60), plus $1.79 per km. Service is generally consistent among the different cab companies. Some of the bigger fleets are: **Taxis Combined** (☎13 33 00); **Legion Cabs** (☎13 14 51); **Silver Service** (☎13 31 00); **Premier Cabs** (☎13 10 17); and **St. George Cabs** (☎13 21 66, or their Elite Fleet 13 21 77). For up to five people, call to request a larger **Maxi Cab.**

## BY BICYCLE

Although biking is not the most popular option in Sydney's busy streets, it's a great way to take in lots of scenery. When combined with ferries, trains, and buses, it's possible to use a bicycle and tour Sydney Harbour and the northern and eastern beaches in a single day. Bikes are especially well-suited to nature-based routes in the area. Try cycling through the Olympic Park woodlands or Centennial Park. **Bicycle NSW,** Level 5, 822 George St., organizes weekly rides and events and gives rental advice. (☎02 9218 5400; www.bicyclensw.org.au. Annual membership dues $85.) For a coastal ride, visit **Manly Cycle Centre,** 36 Pittwater Rd., at Denison St. in Manly. (☎02 9977 1189. Open M-W and F-Sa 9am-6pm, Th 9am-7pm, Su 10am-5pm. $15 per hr., full day $35.)

# 🔢 PRACTICAL INFORMATION

## TOURIST SERVICES

**Tourist Office: Sydney Visitors Centre,** 106 George St. (☎02 9240 8788 or 1800 067 676; www.sydneyvisitorcentre.com), in the white historic sailors' building in The Rocks. Heaps of free brochures, as well as booking services for accommodations, tours, and harbor cruises. Internet service available ($1 per 15min.). Open daily 9:30am-5:30pm except Christmas Day and Good Friday. Wheelchair-accessible. Additional location, 33 Wheat Rd. (☎02 9240 8788), Darling Harbor. Open 9:30am-5:30pm.

**Budget Travel:** There are travel offices on practically every corner in Sydney.

**Travellers Contact Point,** Level 7, 428 George St. (☎02 9221 8744), between King and Market St. Internet access $1.50 for 30min., $3 for 1hr., ½-price before 11am. Mail forwarding and holding in Australia $50 per year. Employment board with recruiting officers for travelers with work visas. Open M-F 9am-6pm, Sa 10am-4pm.

**Australian Travel Specialists,** Jetty 6, Circular Quay (☎02 9247 5151; www.atstravel.com.au), and in Harbourside Shopping Centre, in Darling Harbour (☎02 9211 3192). Comprehensive info on trips around Sydney and beyond. Also books tours, ranging from a Harbour tour (all types) to a tour of the Blue Mountains ($65-165). Open daily 8:30am-6:30pm

**YHA Travel Center,** 422 Kent St. (☎02 9261 1111; www.yha.com.au), behind Town Hall. Also at 11 Rawson Pl. (☎02 9281 9444), next to Sydney Central YHA. Caters to backpackers' needs in particular. Open M-W and F 9am-5pm, Th 9am-6pm, Sa 10am-2pm

**Consulates: Canada,** Level 5, 111 Harrington St. (☎02 9364 3000). **Ireland,** 50th fl., 400 George St. (☎02 9231 6999). **New Zealand,** Level 10, 55 Hunter St. (passport ☎02 9225 2300, visa 9223 0144). **UK,** Level 16, Gateway Building, 1 Macquarie Pl. (☎02 9247 7521). **US,** Level 59, 19-29 Martin Pl., MLC Centre. Visitors report to security Level 10 (☎02 9373 9200).

---

### MEDIA AND PUBLICATIONS

**Newspapers:** The main papers are the *Sydney Morning Herald* ($2.20), *The Australian* ($2.20), and tabloid *Daily Telegraph* ($1.50).

**Entertainment:** The Metro section of Friday's *Sydney Morning Herald,* and free weeklies *Beat, Sydney City Hub, Streetpress,* and *Revolver,* which can be found in music and book stores.

**Radio:** Alternative, Triple J 105.7FM; pop, Nova 969 96.9FM; rock and pop, Triple M 104.9FM; classical, ABC Classic FM; sports, 2KY 1017AM; news talk, 2GB 873AM

---

## FINANCIAL SERVICES

**Banks: Commonwealth, Westpac,** and **National** pack the CBD. **ATMs,** located in convenience stores and many CityRail stations, usually accept MasterCard and Visa. Banks open M-Th 9:30am-4pm, F 9:30am-5pm.

**Travelex:** (☎02 8585 7000). Several locations in the international terminal of the airport. $9 charge on traveler's checks and currency exchanges. Open daily 5am-10:30pm. There are dozens of other offices, including on the ground fl. of the QVB. Open M-Tu and F 8am-6pm, W 9am-6pm, Th 8am-8pm, Sa-Su 10:30am-5:30pm.

## LOCAL SERVICES

**State Library of New South Wales** (☎02 9273 1414), next to the Parliament House on Macquarie St., houses galleries and research facilities, but doesn't lend books. Free Internet. Open M-Th 9am-8pm, F 9am-5pm, Sa-Su 10am-5pm.

**Ticket Agencies: Ticketek** (☎13 28 49; www.ticketek.com.au), has offices in multiple retail stores and an information kiosk at 195 Elizabeth St. Full-price advance booking for music, theater, sports, and select museums. Phone lines open for purchases by credit card M-Sa 9am-9pm, Su 9am-8pm. **Ticketmaster** (☎13 61 00; www.ticketmaster.com.au) has an information kiosk at 13 Campbell St. Open M-F 9am-5pm. Phones answered M-Sa 9am-9pm, Su 9am-5pm.

**CYBER SYDNEY**

**www.cityofsydney.nsw.gov.au** The Sydney homepage. Visitor guide and information on services provided by the local government.

**http://sydney.citysearch.com.au** A comprehensive business directory, entertainment listings, shopping, restaurants, and gay/lesbian info.

**www.sydney.com.au** Sydney's sights, accommodations, and transportation.

**www.visitnsw.com.au** In-depth neighborhood information.

## EMERGENCY AND COMMUNICATIONS

**Police:** 570 George St. (☎02 9265 6595). **Kings Cross police station,** 1-15 Elizabeth Bay Rd. (☎02 8356 0099), in Fitzroy Gardens. **Paddington police station,** 16 Jersey Rd. (☎02 8356 8299), off Oxford St.

**Crisis Lines: Rape Crisis, Mental Health, STD Clinic,** Darlinghurst Community Healthcare, 301 Forbes St. (☎02 8382 1911). **HIV/AIDS Information Line** (☎02 9332 4000. Open M-F 8am-6:30pm, Sa 10am-5pm). **Suicide prevention** (☎02 9331 2000). **Gay and Lesbian Counseling Service** (☎02 8594 9596 or 1800 184 527; open daily 5:30-10:30pm). **Sex Workers Outreach Program** (☎02 9319 4866).

**Late-night Pharmacy: Crest Hotel Pharmacy,** 91-93 Darlinghurst Rd., Kings Cross, 4 doors left of the rail station. (☎02 9358 1822. Open 8am-midnight.) **Wu's Pharmacy,** 629 George St., Chinatown. (☎02 9211 1805. Open M-Sa 9am-9pm, Su 9am-7pm.)

**Medical Services: Sydney Hospital** (☎02 9382 7111 or 9382 7009), on Macquarie St. opposite the Martin Pl. station. **St. Vincent's Hospital,** 390 Victoria St. (☎02 8382 1111). **Sydney Medical Centre,** 580 George St. (☎02 9261 9200), in the Pavilion Plaza. Consultation fee $60-80. Open daily 7:30am-9pm. **Contraceptive Services,** Level 1, 195 Macquarie St. (☎02 9221 1933). Consultation fee determined by medical insurance. Open M-F 8:30am-4:30pm. Sa 8:30am-1pm. Pregnancy consultations and abortions available M-F by appointment only.

**Telephones: Public pay phones** are common in Sydney; local calls cost $0.40. For international calls, invest in a cheap **calling card,** which can be found easily in Chinatown and at convenience stores in the CBD. **Apple** brand calling cards have been known to have particularly good rates, although deals change regularly within and between companies. Best to inquire about a few different types before making a choice. **Global Gossip** offers super-cheap rates ($0.01 per min. to the US and UK noon-6pm with pre-paid phone card, plus a $0.50 connection fee). Another good option is investing in a **pre-paid mobile phone,** which often allows you to accept calls for free (see **Cellular Phones,** p. 36). **Directory Assistance:** ☎1223.

**Internet Access:** Internet cafes abound, especially on George St. near Chinatown and the Sydney YHA, and in Kings Cross. Common charges in the CBD are $2-4 per hr., but rates fluctuate. **Global Gossip** (☎02 9212 4444; www.globalgossip.com) charges $3 per hr., and their shops are franchised across the city. Hours vary by location. Their main store is at 790 George St., near Sydney Central YHA. Open daily 9am-11pm.

**Post Office: Sydney General Post Office (GPO),** 1 Martin Pl. (☎02 9244 3710). Open M-F 8:15am-5:30pm, Sa 10am-2pm. *Poste Restante* available at 310 George St., inside Hunter Connection across from Wynyard Station; holds mail for up to 1 month. Enter up the ramp marked by the "Hunter Connection" sign. Open M-F 8:15am-5:30pm. Some hostels will also hold mail for up to 1 month. **Postal Code:** 2000.

Rooftop pool -
Sydney Central YHA

Railway Square YHA

Sydney Central YHA

Scubar -
Sydney Central YHA

Spa pool - Railway Square YHA

Carriage dorm-
Railway Square YHA

Glebe Point YHA

Bondi Beachouse YHA

Sydney Beachouse
Collaroy

Cronulla Beach YHA

# ♜ ACCOMMODATIONS

The city center is an obvious choice for accommodation because of its convenient location and the sheer abundance of options. The huge hostels near Central Station are more like hotels with dorm rooms, which usually means their facilities are excellent and noise levels high. More tight-knit backpacker communities exist in hostels on Pitt St., but the facilities are often less extensive. Well-located, traveler-friendly, and party-ready, Kings Cross is another established backpacker mecca, and the high concentration of steadily improving hostels ensures that beds are almost always available. However, the alleys and strip clubs make some travelers uncomfortable. If you do opt to stay in the Cross, be sure you feel satisfied with your hostel's security measures before letting your valuables out of sight. To stay close to the Cross and safe from its seedier side, consider booking a room in neighboring Darlinghurst. Good suburban bets include Bondi Beach, Coogee Beach, and Glebe, which offer many relaxed backpacker accommodations in close proximity to cafes, pubs, and student nightlife. Finally, if you're only in the city a few days and are willing to shell out the cash, consider staying in the historic Rocks, which provides close proximity to numerous sights and a trendier nightlife scene.

Unless stated otherwise, hostels and hotels accept major credit cards. Most dorm beds increase in price by a few dollars ($2-5) during high season (Nov.-Feb.) and Australian school holidays.

# ◪ FOOD

Sydney's multicultural makeup shines through in its variety of cuisines. Asian options, most notably Thai restaurants and small sushi shops, are abundant all over the city. The **CBD** is packed with the greatest range of options and prices. There are cheaper food courts, and the feeding frenzy of **Chinatown** lurks west of Central Station. However, the CBD is also home to many swanky Mod Oz restaurants and the city's top chefs. Likewise, there's classy dining along the waterfront at **Circular Quay** and **The Rocks**—be prepared to spend a bundle.

Outside the city center, the Oxford St. social artery that runs southeast from Hyde Park is lined with ethnic restaurants. A (very) **Little Italy** is located on Stanley St., between Crown and Riley St. in Darlinghurst; for a larger (and tastier) selection of Italian food, head out to Norton St. in **Leichardt**. Continuing east through Darlinghurst, the strip of restaurants on Oxford St. near St. Vincent's Hospital is a mix of cafes and Asian restaurants. Victoria St. runs north from Oxford St. at the hospital into the land of cappuccino chic before the coffee runs dry past the hostels of **Kings Cross.** In the Cross, Bayswater Rd. offers late-night bites and some of the cheapest prices in all of Sydney.

As usual, a large student population means good, reasonably priced cafes and restaurants on both Glebe Point Rd. in Glebe and King St. in **Newtown.** King St., in particular, is a foodie favorite for its prices, variety, and ambience. Blues Point Rd. on **McMahons Point,** Fitzroy St. in **Kirribilli,** and Military Rd. through **Neutral Bay** and **Mosman,** lead to the North Shore's stylish and affordable offerings, with well-loved local cafes and ethnic-inspired, family-focused eateries. At beach cafes in both the north and south, $8-11 generally buys a large cooked breakfast and an excuse to appreciate the view over the morning paper. Though the neighborhoods vary in their offerings, there is something for everyone, and your palate will never get bored. Unless noted otherwise, major credit cards are accepted everywhere in the many malls of the city center.

# ◎ SIGHTS

The main sights of Sydney are concentrated within the city's two main harbors—**Sydney Harbour** and **Darling Harbour**—and the historic district of **The Rocks** that's situated at the base of the Harbour Bridge. Sydney is also known for its spectacular beaches, particularly the trendy **Bondi Beach** and southern **Coogee Beach.** However, each of the city's neighborhoods has more than its fair share of entertainment, boutiques, and adrenaline boosts.

# ♫ ENTERTAINMENT

## THEATER

The iconic Sydney Opera House is the lynchpin of Sydney's creative culture. With five stages, the Opera House serves as the main venue for a variety of the city's artistic endeavors. (Box office for all venues ☎02 9250 7777; www.sydneyoperahouse.com.au. Open M-Sa 9am-8:30pm, Su 2hr. prior to show only for ticket pickup. Doors close at showtime. Student rush ticket policy differs from company to company; contact each for information.)

▨ **Concert Hall:** The 2679-seat Concert Hall, the most majestic of the Opera House's stages, is Sydney's primary venue for performances of symphony, chamber, and orchestral music. **Sydney Symphony Orchestra** (☎02 8215 4644; www.sydneysymphony. com) and the innovative **Australian Chamber Orchestra** (☎02 8274 3800; www.aco. com.au) both perform here throughout the year.

▨ **Opera Theatre:** The excellent Opera Australia (☎02 9699 1099, tickets 02 9318 8200; www.opera-australia.org.au) performs here. Reserved seats range from $89 (concession) to over $200 and sell out fast, even though there are 1547 of them. Standing-room and listening-only tickets are available after 9am on the morning of the performance, depending on availability; limit 2 per person. Leftover tickets are sometimes sold 1hr. before showtime as rush tickets (prices vary from show to show). Doors close promptly at showtime—be sure to arrive on time. The **Australian Ballet Company** (☎1300 369 741; www.australianballet.com.au) and the **Sydney Dance Company** (☎02 9221 4811; www.sydneydance.com.au) share the space.

**Drama Theatre:** This 544-seat theater frequently stars the Sydney Theatre Company (box office ☎02 9250 1777, administration 02 9250 1700; www.sydneytheatre.com.au). Advance seating from $50; standing-room tickets can be purchased at reduced rates 1hr. prior to show, depending on availability; also inquire about student rush tickets 30min. prior to show, depending on availability.

**Playhouse Theatre:** A traditional round-stage forum with 398 seats. Check out the Bell Shakespeare Company (☎02 8298 9000; www.bellshakespeare.com.au) for information on which of Will's classics they'll be presenting.

**Studio Stage:** This catch-all, transformable stage exhibits less-traditional Opera House offerings, including cabaret shows and contemporary performances. Number of seats vary according to the performance setup.

## MUSIC

Sydney's daily live music scene consists largely of local cover bands playing for free to pub crowds. The Metro section of the Friday *Sydney Morning Herald* and free weeklies such as *Beat* and *Sydney City Hub* contain listings for upcoming shows, along with information on art showings, movies, theater performances, and DJ appearances city-wide. Major concerts are held in the **Sydney Entertainment Centre,** on Harbour St., Haymarket (☎02 9320 4200; www.

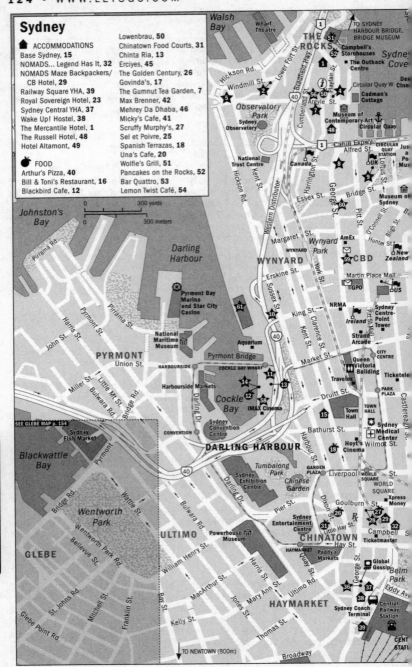

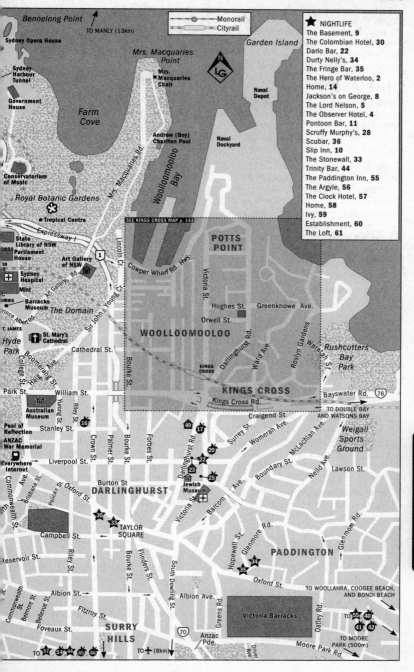

Monorail
Cityrail

★ NIGHTLIFE
The Basement, 9
The Colombian Hotel, 30
Darlo Bar, 22
Durty Nelly's, 34
The Fringe Bar, 35
The Hero of Waterloo, 2
Home, 14
Jackson's on George, 8
The Lord Nelson, 5
The Observer Hotel, 4
Pontoon Bar, 11
Scruffy Murphy's, 28
Scubar, 36
Slip Inn, 10
The Stonewall, 33
Trinity Bar, 44
The Paddington Inn, 55
The Argyle, 56
The Clock Hotel, 57
Home, 58
Ivy, 59
Establishment, 60
The Loft, 61

NEW SOUTH WALES

sydentcent.com.au; box office open M-F 9am-5pm, Sa 10am-1pm), and in the **Enmore Theatre,** 130 Enmore Rd., Newtown (☎02 9550 3666, www.enmorethe-atre.com.au). **The Capitol Theatre,** 13 Campbell St., Haymarket, has hosted Broadway shows and other top-notch acts for over 100 years. (☎02 9320 5000. Newly renovated. Box office open M-F 9am-5pm.)

## CINEMAS

Sydney's film scene contains a variety of independent movie houses, as well as mainstream cinemas showing American blockbusters. Mondays are often bargain days at arthouse cinemas, while larger cinema chains offer cheaper tickets on Tuesdays. The rest of the week, prices hover around $12-15 and $10-11 for children. For info on the **Sydney Film Festival,** see p. 128.

   **Dendy Cinemas,** 2 E. Circular Quay, CBD (☎02 9247 3800; www.dendy.com.au), and 261-263 King St., Newtown (☎02 9550 5699). All locations show a selection of quality arthouse films and mainstream films, while the adjacent cafes (esp. Newtown) serve delicious and affordable meals. Open daily based on movie showings.

   **Govinda's,** 112 Darlinghurst Rd., Darlinghurst (☎02 9380 5155). Shows 2-3 acclaimed contemporary films per day in a comfy, cushion-filled lounge; throws in a tasty all-you-can eat vegetarian buffet, too (see p. 144).

   **LG IMAX Cinema,** 31 Wheat Rd., Darling Harbour (☎02 9281 3300). At 8 stories high, this movie screen is the largest in the world. A different film is shown every hr., including recent releases and 3D features. Open daily 10am-10pm.

   **Greater Union,** 505-525 George St. (☎02 9273 7431). Sydney's largest mainstream cinema boasts 17 screens and is located halfway between Chinatown and the CBD.

## SPECTATOR SPORTS

Like Australians everywhere, Sydneysiders are sports mega-fans. All events below sell tickets through **Ticketek** (☎13 28 49; www.ticketek.com.au) and are played in stadiums in Moore Park, accessible by buses #373, 391, 393, and 395. The main number for all the stadiums is for the **Cricket Ground.** (☎02 9360 6601; www.sydneycricketground.com.au.) See **Sports and Recreation,** p. 56. Ticket prices vary from $20-150, depending on the sport and game.

   **Cricket:** To some, cricketers are men in sweater vests; to others, they're rough-and-tumble gods. Decide for yourself at the Sydney Cricket Ground, on Moore Park Rd.

   **Rugby League:** The **Sydney Football Stadium,** on the corner of Driver Ave. and Moore Park Rd., is home to the Sydney City Roosters. It draws rowdy, loyal fans throughout the winter season and in Sept. for the Telstra Premiership. **Rugby Union** (www.rfu.com) is the other popular "footy" league in NSW, though it does not field a Sydney team.

   **Australian Rules Football:** This head-crushing, uniquely Aussie game engages cross-state competition and is held at the Sydney Football Stadium. Root for the not-so-swan-like Sydney Swans. Tickets cost more and are harder to get than rugby tickets.

# ⬚ SHOPPING

Sydneysiders love to shop, and the city is outfitted accordingly: department stores, designer boutiques, factory outlets, and vintage stores are scattered throughout the streets. Fittingly, Sydney's commercial heart, the CBD, is also its shopping epicenter. Designer names like Chanel, Versace, and Louis Vuitton line Castlereagh St., while department stores like David Jones, on Market and Castlereagh St., and Grace Bros, 436 George St., link to the **Pitt Street Mall** (see **Malls** below). The Rocks holds small, upscale boutiques on Argyle and

George St., geared toward tourists but great for reliable opal and pearl jewelry. Paddington has pricey boutiques on Oxford St., while Newtown stores the city's best selection of secondhand clothing and artsy jewelry along King St. Leichhardt, Sydney's Little Italy, has fine Italian shoes and clothing on Norton St., though most of these designers can be found in the CBD and The Rocks. Shopaholics should pick up a free copy of *Sydney Shopping: The Official Guide* from The Rocks' visitors center or one of the arcade malls.

**MALLS.** You haven't been to a real mall until you've been to Sydney's humongous **Pitt Street Mall** multiplex, which is composed of several pedestrian-only blocks on Pitt St. and is lined with shopping complexes like Mid City Centre, Westfield Centrepoint, Skygarden, and Sydney Central Plaza. For high-end shopping in elegant, old-world atmosphere, head over to the ornate **Strand Arcade** and **Queen Victoria Building** (p. 133). Both of these shopping arcades feature upmarket Australian designer boutiques, ranging from the hypercolored Ken Done in the QVB to high fashion labels like Bettina Liano, Alannah Hill, and Third Millennium in the Strand. In Darling Harbour, Harbourside has Australian homewares; in Haymarket, Market City holds factory outlets and the famous **Paddy's Market** (see **Markets** below).

**MARKETS.** Sydney's year-round weekend markets tend to specialize in arts, crafts, and souvenirs. Some vendors fly all the way from Melbourne to showcase their goods at **The Rocks Market,** at the top of George St. in The Rocks, a quaint arts and crafts fair tucked away below the Harbour Bridge. Homemade preserves and handmade crafts (like stationery, jewelry, and boomerangs) are among the one-of-a-kind souvenirs available for purchase here. (Open Sa-Su 10am-5pm.) The **Sydney Opera House Markets,** at Bennelong Point at Circular Quay, are also known for their arts and crafts. They are more spread-out but just as touristy as The Rocks. (Open Su 9am-5pm.) **Glebe Market,** on Glebe Point Rd. in Glebe, is littered with clothing and housewares, sold for half the price of what you'll pay in most Sydney stores. Deliciously unusual food stands contribute to the overall bohemian feel. (Open Sa 9:30am-4:30pm.) With its elegant clothing, stunning jewelry, and pricey artwork, **Paddington Market,** on Oxford St. in Paddington, feels more like New York City's Park Ave. than a residential street. If you've got the funds, there's no better place to find an overpriced outfit—with an opal necklace to match—that's sure to turn heads. (Open Sa 10am-4pm.) **Paddy's Market,** in Haymarket, Chinatown, is perhaps the most famous of all of Sydney markets. This massive indoor display of wholesale goods is a bargain landmark. (See **Chinatown,** p. 140.) What the wholesale goods lack in quality, the fresh meat, fish, fruit and vegetable stands make up for in taste, presentation, and unbeatable prices. (Open Th-Su 9am-5pm.) The hip **Bondi Beach Market,** at Bondi Beach Public School on Campbell Pde., features local arts and crafts. (Open Su 10am-5pm, weather permitting.)

# ▣ NIGHTLIFE

Whether out on the town dancing or huddling around the latest sports telecast, many locals hit the pub and club scene as many as five times per week.

**Kings Cross** is the sloshing sanctum of weekend parties, crunching in herds of backpackers and locals. The area attracts a sizeable straight male contingent that quickly spills over from the strip joints into the pubs and dance clubs. Gay and lesbian Sydney struts its stuff on Oxford St., in **Darlinghurst** and **Paddington,** and also in **Newtown.** Some establishments are specifically gay or lesbian and many others are mixed. Because the gay clubs provide much of the city's best dance music, flocks of young, beautiful clubbers of all persuasions fill any extra space on their vibrant dance floors, which are often packed until dawn. Taylor Sq.—at the intersection of Oxford, Flinders, and Bourke St.—is the heart of this district. For more casual pub crawling, wander on Bourke and Flinders St. in **Surry Hills** or hang with the large student populations in **Glebe** and **Newtown**.

**Manly** holds up the North Shore's end of the nightlife equation, catering to a more chill partygoer. The city center is a bit more upscale, particularly in trendy Darling Harbour and the suit-filled **CBD**. In these clubs, the dress code slides from "smart casual" to cocktail, with women often in dresses and heels and men in button-downs and slacks. Shorts or sandals generally aren't allowed. The English-style pubs in **The Rocks** are more laid-back, though still expensive. The Sydney clubber's bible is *3-D World* (www.threedworld.com.au), a free weekly publication found in hostels, music stores, and clothing boutiques. Look for the free *Streetpress* or *The Revolver*, which highlight weekly dance hotspots; *Drum Media* covers music. *Sx News* (www.sxnews.com.au) and *Sydney Star Observer* (www.ssonet.com.au) focus on the gay community.

## ✳ FESTIVALS

**Sydney Festival** (☎02 8248 6500; www.sydneyfestival.org.au), throughout Jan. Over 300 arts and entertainment events. Check the *Daily Telegraph* for details on free concerts in The Domain, street theater in The Rocks, and fireworks in Darling Harbour.

**Tropfest** (☎02 9368 0434; www.tropfest.com), Feb. World's largest short film festival has outdoor screens in The Domain and Royal Botanic Gardens. Past judges have included Australia's own Russell Crowe and Nicole Kidman.

**Gay and Lesbian Mardi Gras** (☎02 9568 8600; www.mardigras.org.au), Feb.-Mar. This huge international event is always a rip-roaring good time. The festivities close with a giant parade and a gala party at the RAS Show Ground. Though the party is restricted and the guest list fills up far in advance, travelers can get on the list by becoming "International Members of Mardi Gras" for $25.

**Royal Agricultural Society's Easter Show** (☎02 9704 1111; www.eastershow.com.au), mid-Apr. At Sydney Olympic Park Showground. The carnival rides and cotton candy draw large crowds and create a fun atmosphere for children and adults alike.

**Sydney Film Festival** (☎02 9318 0999; www.sydneyfilmfestival.org), mid-June. The ornate State Theatre, 49 Market St., and 5 other cinemas throughout the city showcase documentaries, retrospectives, and art films from around the world.

**City to Surf Run** (☎1800 555 514; http://city2surf.sunherald.com.au), Aug. Draws 60,000 contestants for a 14km trot from Hyde Park to Bondi Beach. Some are world-class runners; others treat the race as a lengthy pub crawl. Entries ($40) are accepted up to race day, though early online entrants get a $10 discount.

**Manly Jazz Festival** (☎02 9976 1430; www.manly.nsw.gov.au/manlyjazz), early Oct. Australia's biggest jazz festival, showcasing both national and international artists.

**Rugby League Grand Final** (www.nrl.com.au), early Oct. The final game of the season brings massive crowds of fired-up fans to ANZ Stadium.

**Sculpture By the Sea** (www.sculpturebythesea.com), Oct.-Nov. This free, 24hr. outdoor art exhibit lines the beaches from Bondi to Tamarama with sculpture.

**Bondi Beach Party,** Dec. 25 (Christmas Day). Revelers from around the world gather for this foot-stomping toast to debauchery on Sydney's most happening beach.

**Sydney-to-Hobart Yacht Race** (www.rolexsydneyhobart.com), Dec. 26. Revives the hungover hordes with a healthy dose of water.

# ⚓ ACTIVITIES

## AIR ADVENTURES

**SKYDIVING.** Skydiving in Australia is comparatively cheap and the perfect outlet for those looking for some Aussie adventure. **Sydney Skydivers,** 77 Wentworth Ave., runs half-day tandem dives with magnificent views of Sydney, the coastline, and the Blue Mountains. (☎02 8307 3834; www.sydneyskydivers. com.au. From $250.) **Simply Skydive Australia** offers similar services, diving from up to 14,000 ft. (☎1800 759 3483; www.simplyskydive.com.au. From $309.)

**SCENIC FLIGHTS.** For aerial views of Sydney without a parachute, several companies offer scenic flights around the Sydney area. **Sydney by Seaplane** offers 15-60min. scenic flights over Sydney Opera House, the Harbour, and Ku-ring-gai National Park (☎1300 720 995 or 02 9974 1455; www.sydneybyseaplane.com. $145-175 per person). Flights depart from Rose Bay or Palm Beach.

## BEACHES

Sydney is home to many world-class beaches. Most are packed during the summer, especially the ever-popular Bondi and Coogee to the south. However, Sydney's equally surf-soaked Northern Beaches offer more secluded sunshine.

| BEACH | FEATURES | TAKE BUS |
|---|---|---|
| **SOUTH** | | |
| Bondi | "A-list" beach. Surfing makes the postcards. | 380, 382, L82 |
| Bronte | Quiet, family beach with strong undertow. | 378 |
| Coogee | Bondi's young rival, often just as packed. Good ocean pools. | 372, 373, 374 |
| Maroubra | Locals' beach gaining in popularity. Great surf. | 376, 377, 395, 396 |
| Tamarama | "Glamarama" is just beneath Bondi. Strong undertow. | 380, 382, L82 |
| **NORTH** | | |
| Avalon | Beautiful spot, almost chosen as set of *Baywatch*. | L88, L90 |
| Balmoral | Quiet, elegant harbor beach. Good for kids. | 238, 257, 258 |
| Collaroy | Attracts families and surfers, with sand running to Narrabeen. | L85, L88, L90, 185 |
| Manly | Popular beach with fantastic surfing and people-watching. | 151 or Manly ferry |
| Newport | Home to stunning waters, cliffs, and an ocean peak, surfable off both sides. | L88, L90 |
| Palm Beach | Glam set of TV soap *Home and Away* with easy access to great views from the Barenjoey Lighthouse. | L90 |

## WATER SPORTS

**SURFING.** While Bondi is Sydney's famous surfing beach, **Manly** and the more secluded **Northern Beaches** (including Freshwater, Curl Curl, Dee Why, Collaroy, Narrabeen, Newport, and Avalon) are also great options. The **Manly Surf School,** at the North Steyne Surf Club and at the Lifeguard Pavilion in Palm Beach, gives lessons to surfers of all skill levels and has been rated the number-one surf school in all of NSW. (☎02 9977 6977; www.manlysurfschool.com. Open for lessons year-round. 1 lesson $55; 5-day $200; 10-day $330. Private lessons $80 per hr., 2 people $60 per hr.; prices include gear. Booking required.) In Manly, **Aloha Surf,** 44 Pittwater Rd., rents boards and wetsuits. (☎02 9977 3777. Open daily 9am-5:30pm. Short and long boards ½-day $20, full day $40.) **Bondi Surf Co.,** 72-76 Campbell Pde., rents surfboards and bodyboards with wetsuits. (☎02 9365 0870. Open daily 10am-5:30pm. Credit card or passport deposit required. $15 per hr., $25 per 2hr., $50 per full day.)

**JETBOATING.** Several jetboat companies take their poncho-clad passengers on adventure rides in Darling and Sydney Harbours. Go for the exhilarating ride but don't expect gorgeous harbor views; the boat will be spinning, turning, and braking too fast for you to see much. **Sydney Jet,** located in Cockle Bay Wharf, Darling Harbour, is one of the cheapest options. (☎02 9807 4333. 45min. Jet Thrill ride departs daily 11am-sunset every hour. $65, children $45, family $190.) For a more leisurely ride, see **Harbour Cruises** (p. 136).

**DIVING. ProDive** offers the widest range of diving trips from one to five days (suitable for beginners or experienced divers), as well as a variety of certification courses. They have locations throughout Sydney and throughout Cairns and the Great Barrier Reef. Prices range according to length of trip. Check www.prodive.com.au or inquire at ☎1800 820 820 for more information.

**SAILING.** On any sunny day, white sails can be seen gliding across the water. **East Sail Sailing School,** at d'Albora Marina on Rushcutters Bay, caters to all levels and offers small courses, trips, and boats for chartering. (☎02 9327 1166; www.eastsail.com.au. Morning Adventure Cruise with tea 10am-12:30pm $99; 2hr. Sunset Cruise $129. Introductory sailing course from $475.) **Sydney by Sail** runs intro lessons from the National Maritime Museum. (☎02 9280 1110; www.sydneybysail.com. Max. 8-12 person. 3hr. harbor sail to Port Jackson $150. 2-day, 4-lesson introductory course $425. Book ahead.)

**WHALE WATCHING AND FISHING.** Whale watching season runs June-July and September-October. **Halicat,** 5 Manning Rd., Double Bay, has fishing, nature-watching, and whale-watching tours. (☎04 1131 1236; www.sydneywhalewatch.net.au. Tours include ½-day, full-day, and personalized trips. Depart from Rose Bay and Cremorne Point. Prices vary.) A number of charter boats run guided deep-sea fishing trips; groups get cheaper rates. Acclaimed **Broadbill,** departing from Sans Souci Wharf, runs a small operation (boat holds six) with competitive prices. (☎02 9534 2378; www.gamefishingcharters.com.au. $330 per person per day. Check website for multi-day packages and group deals.)

# TOURS OF SYDNEY

**WALKING TOURS.** The recently revamped walking tours of The Rocks depart from the **visitors center** at 106 George St. (☎02 9247 6678; see p. 118). Themed walks include ghost tours (some of which depart from Cadman's Cottage), historical tours, and pub crawls ($18-34 per person). The visitors center also provides information on self-guided walking tours and the best routes to take for getting the most out of your time in Sydney.

**SYDNEY BY DIVA.** Grab your falsies and get on board this 2½hr. comedy bus tour of Sydney, hosted by the most fabulous drag queens in town. As queens-in-training, guests are given both wigs and drag names before they head off to the

Opera House, Bondi Beach, and finally to Erskineville's Imperial Hotel (used in the 1994 film *Priscilla, Queen of the Desert*) for a final performance. Tours leave from the Oxford Hotel in Darlinghurst. (☎02 8004 0789; www.sydneyby-diva.com. Refreshments and mandatory dance lessons included. Tours daily 6pm or 8pm. $100 per person. Book ahead.)

## OLYMPIC PARK

The golden era of the 2000 Olympic Games in Sydney may be a thing of the past, but visitors are still welcome to visit the impressive **Homebush Bay Olympic Site**. From the 80,000-seat ANZ (formerly Telstra) Stadium to the Aquatic Centre, the stellar facilities are interspersed with interesting urban art and futuristic fountains. To take advantage of the extensive surrounding woodlands, hire a bicycle (1hr. $12 , 2hr. $17) from the **Visitors Centre** (☎02 9714 7888; open daily 9am-5pm) and explore over 35km of nature paths. Walk along the colorful **Brickpit Ring Walk** (free admission, open sunrise-sunset), suspended 19m above the habitat of the endangered green and golden bell frogs. Although the skinny metal supports may seem as fragile as the frogs they're intended to protect, this innovative pathway rewards walkers with 360° nature views. Follow up a tour of ANZ Stadium with a picnic in the adjacent 100-hectare **Bicentennial Park** or the smaller **Wentworth Common**. If you are a football or rugby fan, or if you just want to see Sydney as its craziest, be sure to catch a live game and see ANZ stadium in an echo of its Olympic glory. *(Take CityRail to Olympic Park Station, 14km west of the city center or a ferry from Circular Quay Wharf 5 for a scenic journey along the Parramatta River.* ☎*02 9714 7888; www.sydneyolympicpark.com.au. Open daily 9am-5pm. Aquatic Centre general entry $3, swimming only $6.40, students $5.10. Tours of ANZ Stadium $15-27.50.)*

# CENTRAL BUSINESS DISTRICT

## ▐▛ ACCOMMODATIONS

The CBD offers some of the largest and most well-established hostels in all of Sydney. In fact, they function more like hotels, frequently lacking the personal welcome of smaller establishments, but with the most extensive and well-maintained facilities available. While the CBD is not Sydney's most charming area, it is terrifically convenient, only steps from the food of Chinatown, the shopping of the QVB, and the transportation hub of Central Station.

▧ **Railway Square YHA,** 8-10 Lee St. (☎02 9281 9666), next to Central Station. Newest 5-star hostel in Sydney. This former parcels shed is now a modern facility with a spa, pool, kitchen, and TV lounge—all of which are extremely well-maintained. Whether your room is in the main building or in 1 shaped like railway carriages, all have lots of light and are extremely clean. Retains a personal feel despite being large. Internet access $3 per hr. Daytour desk. Dorms $29.50-40.50; doubles $86-89, ensuite $96-109. ❷

▧ **Sydney Central YHA,** 11-23 Rawson Pl. (☎02 9218 9000). Top-of-the-line hostel isn't very personal, but has incredible facilities: pool, sauna, game room, in-house cinema, travel desks, TV rooms, multiple kitchens, bar, and cafe. Underground **Scubar** (p. 135) makes a great hangout. Lockers for rent. Internet access $3 per hr. Parking $14 per night. 2-week. max. stay. Reception 24hr. Check-out 10am. Dorms $30-41.50; twins $88-107; ensuite doubles $100-123. YHA. ❸

**Wake up! Hostel,** 509 Pitt St. (☎02 9288 7888; www.wakeup.com.au), opposite Central Station. Voted Best Large Hostel in the World 2005 and Best Hostel in Oceania in both 2004 and 2005 by HostelWorld, this spot lives up to its reputation. Themed floors, large windows, and high ceilings give this hostel a sleek, modern feel. Particularly good for long stays. Cafe and the popular SideBar boast big-screen TV and nightly events. Internet access ($4 per hr.), travel desk, and TV lounge area. Reception 24hr. Dorms $28-36; doubles $98, ensuite $108. ❷

**Legend Has It... Westend,** 412 Pitt St. (☎02 9211 4588 or 1800 013 186; www. legendhasitwestend.com.au), opposite NOMADS Maze Backpackers/CB Hotel. Makes up for its simple, small rooms—all ensuite—with the liveliest staff around and planned activities, like trips to the Blue Mountains (from $60) and Hunter Valley (from $94). There are also some free events like beach trips and pub crawls. Locker rental available. Laundry $8. Free airport pickup with 3-night stay. Reception 24hr. Dorms $22-32; doubles $80; double/triple ensuite $83-105, family $145. NOMADS. ❷

**Base Sydney,** 477 Kent St. (☎02 9267 7718; www.basebackpackers.com), between Druitt and Bathurst St., a block from Town Hall. Close to Darling Harbour, the heart of the CBD, and Chinatown. Best location and one of the most secure in the CBD. Clean rooms and 340 beds are not particularly homey, but the staff is friendly and the facilities are fine. Basic TV and pool rooms, employment and travel desks, and attached Scary Canary Bar with cheap meals and happy hours. Lockers $2-8 per day. Laundry $6. Internet access $5 per hr. Max 4-week stay. Reception 24hr. All-female floors available. Dorms $26-34; doubles $89, ensuite $110. VIP. ❷

**Maze Backpackers/CB Hotel,** 417 Pitt St. (☎02 9211 5115 or 1800 813 522; www. mazebackpackers.com), 3 blocks from Central Station toward Circular Quay. A favorite with "partypackers" near Chinatown. 500 beds and common areas are basic, but friendly staff creates welcoming social atmosphere. Employment desk, TV, and pool rooms. Lockers $3 per day, mini-safes $2 per day. Laundry $6. $20 key deposit. Free airport pickup for 3-night stay. 4-week max. stay. Reception 24hr. 4- to 6-bed dorms $25-33; singles from $55; doubles/triples $72-93. $20 key deposit. NOMADS. ❷

# 🌀 FOOD

The city center is packed with small restaurants and food stands for a quick takeaway lunch during the work day. Come lunchtime, droves of office workers fill the cafe booths and park benches. For an inexpensive bite, try one of the many food courts scattered throughout the city—you won't be disappointed.

**Bar Quattro,** 110 Elizabeth St. (☎02 9267 0299), in Hyde Park near St. James Station. This Italian eatery has the best views of Hyde Park and food to match. The pasta dishes are spectacular ($16-24), and the chefs are fine with substitutions. The outdoor tables are perfect for people-watching. Open M-F 7am-5pm, Sa-Su 8am-5pm. ❸

**Scruffy Murphy's,** 43 Goulburn St. (☎9211 2002; www.scruffymurphys.com.au). This Irish pub is the best place in the city to get a hearty meal without overspending. Big Australian breakfast (eggs, sausage, bacon, mushrooms, chips, toast, and tomato) is only $6. Steak, pasta, and chicken (also $6) served all day. Relatively quiet until the bar crowd moves in around 9:30pm. Restaurant open 8am-10pm. ❶

**Spanish Terrazas,** 541 Kent St. (☎02 9283 3046; www.spanishterrazas.com.au). An extensive list of tapas ($12-15) and mixed grill paella ($40-60 for 2) in the pricey Spanish Quarter makes this place best for a large group of people. Wash it all down with a mixed drink or a pitcher of sangria—the smoothest you'll ever taste—while enjoying a live flamenco band on Th or live Latin bands F-Sa. Open for lunch M-F noon-3pm; for dinner M-Th 5:30-10:30pm, F-Sa 5:30-11:30pm. ❹

# 🔘 SIGHTS

🔳**SYDNEY TOWER.** Rising 325m above sea level, Sydney Tower offers the most stunning panoramic view of the city and its surroundings. When the sky is clear, views extend as far as the Blue Mountains to the west, the central coast to the north, and Wollongong to the south. Be sure to take plenty of photos against this postcard-perfect backdrop. Tickets to the observation deck also include **Oztrek,** a 30min. virtual tour (large TV screen and moving seats included) that introduces Sydney and other parts of Australia. If 325m wasn't high enough, invest in the **Skywalk,** a 90min. tour that lets you stand on glass floors extending over the sides of the roof. Complete a 360° rotation around the tower as an entertaining guide points out the sights. The 40-second ride to the top of Australia's highest building is steep in grade and price, so don't waste the trip on a cloudy day. **Sydney Tower Restaurant ❺,** the city's revolving restaurant, spins on the second-highest floor. *(100 Market St. ☎ 02 9333 9222; www.sydneytoweroztrek.com.au. Open M-F and Su 9am-10:30pm, Sa 9am-11:30pm. Tower and OzTrek $25, ages 4-15 $15, families $45-75. Upgrade to Skywalk for $40 extra. Restaurant reservations ☎ 02 8223 3800.)*

**⬛ART GALLERY OF NEW SOUTH WALES.** Take a break from your walk through the Botanic Gardens to visit Sydney's major art museum, housed in a large Art Deco building overlooking Woolloomooloo Bay and Finger Wharf. It has an incredibly diverse collection of Australian and international art, although its strength lies in its 19th and 20th century Australian works. There is also an extensive display of 15th-19th century European art and some intriguing modern paintings and installations that add to the museum's impressive breadth. Don't despair if you can't make it through all five floors. Just come back another day—it's free! *(Northeast corner of the Domain, on Art Gallery Rd. ☎ 9225 1744; www.artgallery.nsw.gov.au. Open daily 10am-5pm. Free.)*

**⬛AUSTRALIAN MUSEUM.** This museum houses a unique mix of natural and indigenous cultural history that is fascinating for visitors of all ages. The skeleton exhibits, which include an Asian elephant and enormous sperm whale, are fascinating. There is also a dazzling display of natural minerals and gemstones and a particularly popular dinosaur exhibit. Be sure to check out the rotating exhibits; the recent "Surviving Australia" exhibition explored why and how Oz's species avoid extinction. *(6 College St., on the east side of Hyde Park. ☎ 02 9320 6000; www.amonline.net.au. Open daily 9:30am-5pm. $10, concessions and ages 5-15 $5, under 5 free, families $17.50-25. Special and temporary exhibits cost up to $15 extra.)*

**⬛QUEEN VICTORIA BUILDING.** An imposing statue of Queen Victoria suggests that this building is anything but cutesy, but Sydneysiders have still nick-named this impressive edifice the QVB. Extending

**TOP TEN LIST**

### STARSTRUCK

Australia has its fair share of celebrities, and Sydney is a destination for many who call Australia home. Here's where to stalk them.

**1. Bondi Icebergs Restaurant and Bar:** This world-renowned restaurant is a favorite of Nicole Kidman's. See p. 150.

**2. Tamarama:** The bronzed and beautiful favor this small, hidden beach, nick-named "Glamarama." See p. 129.

**3. Paddington Market and Oxford St. shops:** With pricey boutiques, it's a shopping hot spot for the young and wealthy. See p. 127.

**4. Tropfest:** The stars line up for the world's largest short-film festival. See p. 128.

**5. The Iguana Bar:** Famous musicians have signed pictures on the wall. See p. 145.

**6. Sydney Entertainment Centre:** Touring bands and singers perform here when passing through NSW. See p. 123.

**7. Tank:** Finagle your way into the swanky VIP lounge. (3 Bridge Ln. ☎ 02 8295 9950.)

**8. Tetsuya's:** Its degustation menu ($185) is fit for the pocketbook of a celeb. (529 Kent St. ☎ 02 9267 2900; www.tetsuyas.com.)

**9. ANZ Stadium, Olympic Park:** When Russell Crowe enters through the VIP entrance, you might catch a glimpse. See p. 131.

**10. Sydney Opera House:** Stars come out often to support the arts. See p. 135.

for an entire city block, this building of sweeping staircases and stained-glass windows is topped with a giant central dome. Upon its completion in 1898, the building was home to the plebeian city markets, but renovations have since brought in four floors of ritzy shopping venues. Fortunately, a stroll through the beautifully tiled interior still doesn't cost a cent. Sports shops and designer stores are featured side-by-side in this ultimate shopping destination. *(455 George St. ☎ 02 9264 9209; www.qvb.com.au. Open M-W and F-Sa 9am-6pm, Th 9am-9pm, Su 11am-5pm. Daily guided tours on the history and architecture of the building, $10. Booking ahead is essential.)*

**▨HYDE PARK AND SAINT MARY'S CATHEDRAL.** The green space between Elizabeth and College St. has been a hub of fun since 1792, but it wasn't an official public space until Governor Lachlan Macquarie set it aside in 1810. It remains Sydney's most structured public park, complete with memorial fountains, stately fig trees, and wide avenues. In the northwest corner of the park, a life-size chessboard amuses competitive visitors. In the southern half, below Park St., the Art Deco **ANZAC Memorial** sits behind the Pool of Reflection. This memorial commemorates the service of the Australian and New Zealand Army Corps in WWI, as well as all Australians who have fought in war. Although it's a buzzing urban oasis and family-friendly picnic spot during the day, Hyde Park should be avoided after dark. *(☎ 9267 7668. Open daily 9am-5pm.)* To the park's east is the Neo-Gothic **Saint Mary's Cathedral.** Built for the Catholic convicts in 1833 and rebuilt in 1928, this cathedral is most-widely known for its plethora of stained glass windows and the mosaic floor of its crypt. *(☎ 02 9220 0400. Cathedral open before first mass and until after last mass each day. For times visit www.stmaryscathedral. org.au. Crypt open daily 10am-4pm. Tours Su noon after mass or by arrangement.)*

**TOWN HALL.** The Italian Renaissance-style Town Hall was built in the prosperity of the late 1800s and stands today as a reminder of Sydney's rich architectural past. The Town Hall houses an impressive concert hall, which is often used as a performance venue. The hall is undergoing renovations until late 2009. *(483 George St. ☎ 02 9265 9189. Concert hall 9265 9007. Open daily 9am-5pm. Free.)*

**HYDE PARK BARRACKS MUSEUM.** An unusual display of artifacts from the days of convict immigration tells the story of Sydney's colonial heritage in this small three-story museum. The eerie building was once a barracks, a women's immigration depot, and an asylum. The third floor recreates the original barracks, even outfitted with 190-year-old floorboards, and invites visitors to lie in inmates' hammocks, listen to the stories of former convicts, and search for imprisoned ancestors in a database. *(In Queens Sq., on Macquarie St. ☎ 02 8239 2311; www.hht.net.au. Open daily 9:30am-5pm. $10, concessions $5, families $20.)*

**NSW PARLIAMENT HOUSE, SYDNEY HOSPITAL, AND THE MINT.** The three-building complex of the Parliament House, Hospital, and Royal Mint was once the Rum Hospital, so-called because of the rum monopoly offered to the developers of the hospital in exchange for its construction. The 1814 hospital building is a landmark of colonial architecture; the central section is still the main medical center, the entrance to which is guarded by a bronze boar statue. Visitors are welcome in the current NSW Parliament House, formerly the Rum Hospital's north wing. During parliamentary sessions, visitors can access public viewing galleries in the grand foyer or take a free tour, which really is the best way to take in this sight. *(Parliament faces Macquarie St. between Martin Pl. and Hunter St. ☎ 02 9230 2111, www.parliament.nsw.gov.au. Open M-F 9:30am-4pm. Free tour 1pm 1st Th of every month. No bookings necessary.)*

## 📷 NIGHTLIFE

Although hard-core backpacker revelry is an infamous CBD standard, plenty of other establishments provide casual, chill options for a less-wild night out.

**Ivy,** 330 George St. (☎02 9240 3000). This new venue in the CBD is the trendy place to be for those who want to dress up for a classy night out. Chill in the upstairs cocktail bar and lounge, bathed in green and white accents, or descend into the leafy downstairs courtyard for mingling and dancing as the night progresses. Open M-Sa 11am-late.

**Scruffy Murphy's,** 43 Goulburn St. (☎02 9211 2002). With live entertainment almost every night—from musical performances to trivia games to talent shows—it's no wonder that Scruffy's Irish pub attracts such a large, rowdy crowd. This local legend of messy nights out is mostly frequented by backpackers, but some Sydneysiders stop by as well. A must-see for its rough-and-tumble scene. Tu nights are particularly loose and last until dawn breaks. Main bar open 24hr. Nightclub open daily 11pm-morning.

**Slip Inn,** 111 Sussex St. (☎02 9240 3000). A stylish venue that somehow remains refreshing and unpretentious. Famous as the meeting place of Danish Crown Prince Frederik and his Australian princess. Bar area includes a ground-level bar and pool area, chill courtyard, and downstairs sandbar. Its underground streetwear-only nightclub, **Chinese Laundry,** hosts events like Th Slip Inn Time (complimentary bubbly for ladies at 5pm) and F Break Inn (progressive break beats). Cover F $15 before 11pm; $20 after. Open M-Th noon-midnight, F noon-4am, Sa 5pm-4am.

**The Basement,** 29 Reiby Pl. (☎02 9251 2797; www.thebasement.com.au), near Circular Quay. Arguably the hottest live music venue in the area. With acts ranging from jazz to rock, this landmark institution has been a music mecca since the 1970s. Loved by locals and travelers alike. Cover $10, up to $50 for the most exclusive acts. Open M-F noon-3pm for lunch and 7:30pm-late, Sa-Su 7pm-latenight.

**Establishment,** 252 George St. (☎02 9240 3000). This swanky bar and lounge boasts an impressive 42m white marble bar extending the length of the main lounge area. However, the best part is the intimate courtyard out back with a glass roof, tall bamboo, fountains, and candlelit tables. Dress nicely. Open M-F 11am-late, Sa 6pm-late.

**Jackson's on George,** 176 George St. (☎02 9247 2727; www.jacksonsongeorge.com.au), near Circular Quay. City-Center hotspot with a restaurant, dance club, lounge, and multiple bars spread out over 4 levels. While the 1st floor feels like a pub with slot machines, the nightclub and lounge upstairs are sleek and sultry. Fog machines and roaming neon lights add atmosphere as partygoers dance to a variety of pop, R&B, and house. Open M-F 7:30am-late, Sa-Su 10am-late.

**Scubar,** 4 Rawson Pl. (☎02 9212 4244; www.scubar.com.au), next to the YHA, 1min. from Central Station walking toward George St. Billiards competitions, big-screen TV, and the ever-popular M night hermit crab racing. Cheap booze and close proximity to many hostels bring the backpackers in droves. Not really a place to meet locals, but a hot spot for international travelers. Open daily 3pm-late.

# SYDNEY HARBOUR

## 📷 SIGHTS

 **SYDNEY OPERA HOUSE.** Built to look like a fleet of sails, the Opera House defines all harbor views of Sydney, whether from water, land, or air. Designed by Danish architect Jørn Utzon, Sydney's pride and joy took 14 years and more than $100 million to construct—a decade and 90 million dollars more than originally planned. When it finally opened in 1973, the Opera House endured a

NEW SOUTH WALES

rocky start but recovered through a diverse program of local and international performances, which to this day includes operas, ballets, classical concerts, plays, and films. Photographed daily by thousands of tourists, the Opera House lives up to its iconic majesty at any hour of the day. The **⬛Concert Hall,** which holds a massive pipe organ that took 10 years to build, is especially stunning. *(On Bennelong Point, opposite the base of the Harbour Bridge. ☎02 9250 7250; www.sydney-operahouse.com. For box office info, see **Entertainment,** (p. 123). 1hr. tours every 30min daily 9am-5pm. $35, concessions $24, families $74.)* For an in-depth look, take the **"Back-stage Tour"** which is limited to 8 people at a time and explores areas of the opera house reserved for cast and crew members only. *(2hr., $150 per person.)*

**⬛SYDNEY HARBOUR BRIDGE.** Spanning the entire harbor, the arching steel latticework of the massive Harbour Bridge has been a visual symbol of the city and the best place to get a look at the Harbour and the cityscape since its opening in 1932. The stone tunnels at either end were added later in response to (unfounded) complaints that the simplicity of the steel beam construction meant it was unsafe. Pedestrians can enter the bridge walkway from a set of stairs on Cumberland St. above Argyle St. in The Rocks. At the bridge's southern pylon, there is an entry on the walkway which leads up to solid photo-ops. **The Harbour Bridge Exhibition** inside the pylon tells the fascinating story of the bridge's construction. *(☎02 9247 7833. Open daily 10am-5pm. Lookout and museum $9.50, ages 8-12 $4, seniors $6.50.)* For high adventure, **Bridgeclimb** will take you up catwalks and ladders to the summit for a breathtaking view of the city and harbor. Similarly, the **Discovery Climb** takes climbers up the suspension arch and teaches about the structure of the bridge. Only mildly strenuous, these tours offer maximum bragging rights with minimum stress, though it will noticeably lighten your wallet. All climbers must first take a Breathalyzer test, so don't hit the pubs beforehand. *(5 Cumberland St. From Argyle St., go all the way up the Argyle Stairs and turn right on Cumberland St. ☎02 8274 7777; www.bridgeclimb.com. Open daily 8am-6pm. 3½hr. day or night climbs $189-220, ages 10-16 $119-140. Twilight climbs daily $249-270, children $189-195. Dawn climbs on the 1st Sa of each month $295/195).*

**CIRCULAR QUAY.** Between Dawes Pt. and Bennelong Pt., Circular Quay is the departure site for both the city ferry system and numerous private cruise companies. In the landlubber department, it is also a major bus hub and CityRail stop. The Quay is always a lively hub of tourist activity, with street performers, souvenir shops, and easy access to many major sights.

**SYDNEY HARBOUR CRUISES.** If you'll be in Sydney for a week or more, you can easily experience the harbor's beauty via much-cheaper public transit ferries. However, if your stay in Sydney will be short, ferry cruises are a great way to take in all the sights. Sunset cruises are particularly beautiful. In addition to **Sydney Ferries** (p. 115), **Australian Travel Specialists** books 1-3hr. harbor cruises from Circular Quay and Darling Harbour. *(Jetty 6, Circular Quay. ☎02 9247 5151 or 1800 355 537. Departs 10am-8pm. From $40 coffee cruise to $160 dinner cruise.)*

**SYDNEY HARBOUR ISLANDS.** The Sydney Harbour Islands, which include **Shark Island, Rodd Island, Clark Island, Goat Island, Cockatoo Island,** and **Fort Denision,** are scattered throughout the waters of the harbor and managed by the National Park of New South Wales. Visits to the islands must be on a guided tour and booked ahead through **Sydney Harbour National Park.** *(Info center in Cadman's Cottage, 110 George St., The Rocks. ☎02 9247 5033. Open M-F 9:30am-4:30pm, Sa-Su 10am-4:30pm.)* The most popular tour is the **Fort Denison Heritage Tour,** which explores the history of the island off Mrs. Macquaries Pt. *(Tours M-Tu 12:15 and 2:30pm, W-Su 10:45am, 12:15 and 2:30pm; $27, concessions $22, children 5-15 $20).* Shark Island (named for its shape, not its inhabitants), near Rose Bay, and Clark Island near Darling Point, are both lovely areas for picnicking. Rodd Island, in Iron Cove near Birkenhead Point, has summer houses from the 1920s and a historic colonial-style hall. *(For further details and booking, call ☎ 02 9247 5033.)*

# THE ROCKS

## ▗ ACCOMMODATIONS

Although staying in the Rocks is much more expensive than in other districts, the location and atmosphere simply can't be beat. Sydney Opera House becomes a part of your daily panorama, and you're only minutes away from the transportation hub of Circular Quay.

▨ **The Russell Hotel,** 143A George St. (☎02 9241 3543; www.therussell.com.au), 2min. walk from Circular Quay. Located in the heart of the Rocks, this charming boutique hotel offers a unique experience to each of its guests—every room has a style of its own. The warm staff, daily chocolates on your pillow, and unbeatable location near Circular Quay make the Russell your home away from home. Rooftop terrace and sitting room with TV. Breakfast included. Free Wi-Fi. Rooms $135-290. ❺

**The Mercantile Hotel,** 25 George St. (☎02 9247 3570). The Mercantile's 15 rooms are clean, comfortable, and conveniently located above a pub. The Rocks Market sets up shop on your doorstep every weekend, and dozens of restaurants and sights are within walking distance. Quiet, cozy, and simple. Free pickup from airport. Breakfast included. Singles $80, ensuite $110. Doubles and triples $110, ensuite $140. ❺

## ▗ FOOD

The Rocks features some of Sydney's most tourist-targeted eating, and you can be sure that these scenic restaurants will take both your breath and your money away. However, you can still find plenty of reasonably priced meals without losing out on the magnificent views of Sydney Harbour.

**The Gumnut Tea Garden,** 28 Harrington St. (☎02 9247 9591). Tucked away on the corner of Harrington and Argyle St., the Gumnut charms customers with assorted cakes and puddings all day ($3-8). The afternoon tea special gets you tea or coffee and a pastry for $6. Breakfast ($10-15) and lunch ($12-17) also served. Live music on the leafy garden terrace F nights and Su afternoons. Open M-Tu and Sa-Su 8am-5pm, W-F 8am-10pm. Breakfast until 11:30am. ❷

**Pancakes on the Rocks,** 4 Hickson Rd. (☎02 9247 6371). This 24hr. crowd-pleaser opened in 1975 and serves the same wide selection of fluffy pancakes and sweet crepes ($7-16) to this day. The menu has since expanded to include pizzas ($14-18), salads ($8-16), and large portions of ribs ($25). Open 24hr. ❸

**Lowenbrau,** 18 Argyle St. (☎02 9247 7785), corner of Argyle and Playfair St. This is the place for a bit of Bavarian fun. The waitstaff dress in traditional German and Swiss garb and dance daily to the sounds of the Oom Pah Pah Band while serving chicken schnitzel and Schnapps. The food's a bit pricey, so consider sitting back with a beer and enjoying the entertainment. Outside seating available. Open daily 9am-late. ❸

**Wolfie's Grill,** 17-21 Circular Quay W. (☎9241 5577). For a night of fancy dining with a view of the Opera House, Wolfie's offers 2 levels of elegant candlelit tables for lovers of Australian beef and fresh seafood. Supremely good eating, polished atmosphere, and priceless harbor views make up for the steep prices (grill items $32-40). Open daily noon-3:30pm and 5:30-9:30pm. ❺

**SIGHTS**

At the southern base of the Harbour Bridge, The Rocks is the site of the original Sydney Town settlement, where living spaces were once literally chiseled out of the face of the shoreline rock. Today, the neighborhood is an important part of Sydney's identity, so give yourself ample time to visit its many attractions. Colonial pubs, quaint restaurants, and historic homes dot the stone streets, which offer amazing views of the harbor and Opera House. Every Saturday and Sunday, the north end of George St. and Playfair St. comes alive with **the Rocks Market.** Stalls spring up selling salted nuts and hot corn on the cob, while tents full of jewelry, artwork, and homemade jams compete with street performers for your attention. It's the perfect place to pick up classy gifts for your family and friends. (Open Sa-Su 10am-5pm; see **Shopping,** p. 126.)

> **TIP** **VISITORS CENTRE.** Don't forget that the **Sydney Visitors Centre** is located in the Rocks, at 106 George St. Check for free brochures and information on things to do in Sydney. See **Practical Information,** p. 118.

**ROYAL BOTANIC GARDENS.** Located on the harbor around Farm Cove, the gardens provide Sydney with 30 hectares of leafy goodness. This urban Eden is full of pools, fountains, flowers, plants, and an extensive collection of domestic and international trees. Sydneysiders love to jog along the water's edge, and families picnic on the hillsides. While the gardens can certainly be explored independently, daily guided walks begin at the visitors center, in the southeast corner of the park near Art Gallery Rd. Within the gardens, the Aboriginal plant trail, formal rose garden, and cockatoo sightings are great, but the fruit bats are incredible. Admission to the gardens is free; however, the Tropical Centre greenhouse charges a small fee. (☎02 9231 8104. Open daily 10am-4pm. $3-6.) **The Government House,** in the northwest corner of the Gardens, serves as the home of the governor of New South Wales and has a gated garden and grounds open to public. (☎02 9931 5222. Grounds open daily 10am-4pm; free house tours every 30min. F-Su 10:30am-3pm.) Finally, on the eastern headland of Farm Cove, the Botanic Gardens end at **Mrs. Macquaries Chair.** The chair, which looks like a simple bench carved into the stone, is now a classic Sydney photo-op, though turning the camera around so that it faces the gorgeous view of the harbor makes more sense. (☎02 9231 8111; www.rbgsyd.nsw.gov.au. Gardens open daily 7am-sunset. Free. 1½hr. guided walks daily 10:30am; 1hr. lunchtime walks Mar.-Nov. M-F 1pm. Book ahead for tours.)

**MUSEUM OF CONTEMPORARY ART (MCA).** Despite the intimidating exterior, the installments and artwork in this museum are refreshingly fun. Explore four floors of interactive media and modern artwork designed to make you intrigued, amused, and sometimes just confused. The fourth floor hosts rotating exhibits, and every even-numbered year, the MCA also becomes a major venue for the **Biennale,** a city-wide contemporary art festival that runs from June to September. (140 George St. ☎02 9245 2400; www.mca.com.au. Open daily 10am-5pm. Free. The main entrance is on Circular Quay W.; entering on George St. puts you on Level 2.)

**JUSTICE AND POLICE MUSEUM.** This small museum dedicated to the last 150 years of Sydney crime is cleverly arranged to reveal the building's different historical iterations. Displays of weapons, a gallery of mug shots, and storyboards explaining gruesome murders like the "Pyjama Girl" and "Shark Arm" cases are all on the walls. Rotating exhibits include a history of violence in Sydney's early rough-and-tumble pubs, and "Femme Fatal," an exploration of female criminals in Sydney. Visitors can also take a look into an old court-

**N E W S O U T H W A L E S**

room, a police charge room, and prisoner holding cells. (*Corner of Albert and Phillip St. ☎ 02 9252 1144; www. hht.net.au. Open Sa-Su 10am-5pm. $8, concessions and children $4, families $17. Wheelchair-accessible.*)

**SYDNEY OBSERVATORY.** Built on the site of partially completed Fort Phillip, the observatory is part museum, part gardens, and part scenic lookout. Displays of early astronomical instruments and planet charts satisfy historical curiosities, and there are nightly assisted viewings of the stars through various telescopes. After a quick wander through the small gardens, don't miss **Observatory Hill,** which has magnificent views of the Harbour Bridge and Darling Harbour wharves. There are shady spots and benches that are perfect for picnicking. (*Observatory Hill, ☎ 02 9241 3767; www.sydneyobservatory.com.au. Open daily 10am-5pm.*)

**CADMAN'S COTTAGE AND CAMPBELL'S STORE-HOUSES.** Constructed in 1816, Cadman's Cottage is one of Sydney's oldest surviving buildings. Today, it holds the **Sydney Harbour National Parks Information Centre,** where park tour bookings can be made. Nearby in Campbell's Cove, eleven merchant warehouses that originally stored tea, sugar, and spirits from India now house a variety of waterfront restaurants. These sights are all perfect for history buffs. (*Cadman's Cottage, 110 George St. ☎ 02 9247 5033. Open M-F 9:30am-4:30pm, Sa-Su 10am-4pm; Campbell's Storehouses, 7-27 Circular Quay W.*)

**THE OUTBACK CENTRE.** This Aboriginal center is a vibrant arts and crafts museum, gallery, and gift shop with an impressive selection of hand-painted boomerangs and didjeridus. Live "Sounds of the Outback" performances happen daily, and all products include the biographies of their respective artisans. (*Corner of George St. and Hickson Rd. ☎ 02 9283 7477. Open daily 10am-6pm. Free.*)

## ⬛ NIGHTLIFE

Even in this historic part of the city, there is an abundance of nightlife—from the colonial pubs to swanky modern lounges. While the pubs attract an older, more sophisticated crowd, they are a good place to grab a pint and soak in the historic surroundings. However, if that's not your thing, there are also a few spots where the young and dapper line up outside the doors.

⬛ **The Argyle,** 18 Argyle St. (☎ 02 9247 5500; www. theargyle.biz). This stylish addition to Rocks brings a new edge to this historic district. The cobblestone courtyard bar, cozy interior lounges, and comfortable

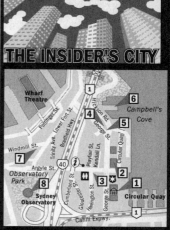

# THE INSIDER'S CITY

## A ROCKS RAMBLE

Numerous sights, eclectic shops, and quaint cafes make the Rocks Sydney's number one tourist stop.

**1.** The **Museum of Contemporary Art** has creative installations that will make your head spin.

**2.** Visit one of Sydneys oldest surviving buildings: **Cadman's Cottage,** just off Circular Quay.

**3.** Settle down at the **Gumnut Tea Garden** for tea and scones.

**4.** Satisfy all your jewelry, art, and collectible needs at the **Rocks Market** on Saturday or Sunday.

**5.** The **Outback Centre** has daily live dance and didjeridu performances.

**6.** Stop in **Campbell's Cove** for incredible views of the Opera House across the harbor.

**7.** Enjoy an early evening pint at the **Hero of Waterloo Pub,** a local favorite since 1845

**8.** Take in the views on **Observatory Hill** and explore the astronomical displays throughout the **Sydney Observatory.**

rustic vibe attract a stylish crowd. A DJ spins tunes in a glass booth each night. Open M-Tu and Su 11am-midnight, W-Sa 11am-3am.

**The Hero of Waterloo,** 81 Lower Fort St. (☎02 9252 4553). This pub has been a local favorite since 1843, and its popularity only increased when the underground tunnels were used for rum smuggling. Even today, the atmosphere oozes history, with exposed brick walls, wooden tables, and antique drawings on the walls. Great for an afternoon pint or for live Irish and folk music later in the evening. Open daily 9am-11:30pm.

**The Lord Nelson,** 19 Kent St. (☎02 9251 4044; www.lordnelson.com.au), at Argyle St. Sydney's oldest hotel and pub may be supported by wooden beams and draped with nautical flags, but this colonial landmark still attracts a young crowd. This is a great place for an after-work pint from one of Sydney's only microbreweries. Tours of the brewery available upon request. Try the award-winning Three Sheets, Nelson's Blood, or Old Admiral. Open M-Sa 11am-11pm, Su noon-10pm.

**The Observer Hotel,** 69 George St. (☎02 9252 4169; www.observerhotel.com.au). A mixed crowd packs this popular pub in the heart of the Rocks. Live music daily 8pm and even earlier on weekends. New bistro and courtyard. Sa Retro Night. Schooners $5.50 Open M-Th and Su 11am-11:30pm, F-Sa 11am-2:30am.

# DARLING HARBOUR AND CHINATOWN

On the west side of City Center, **Darling Harbour** is a popular tourist stop for movies, music, bars, clubs, restaurants, shopping, museums, and magnificent views of the city's skyline. The concentration of attractions in this small area makes it perfect for an afternoon of sightseeing, just as the waterfalls, carousels, and jungle gyms make it ideal for families with small children. Check harborside bulletins for schedules of **free concerts.** On foot, Darling Harbour is 5min. from Town Hall Station. Follow George St. toward Circular Quay, then turn left on Market St. to Pyrmont Bridge. From Circular Quay, a number of buses run down George St. and stop at the same Market St. intersection (#431, 432, 433, 434, 443). Finally, ferries run from Circular Quay to the aquarium steps. For transport as tourist-oriented as the destination, hop on the monorail from Pitt St., at Park or Market St. in the CBD.

As chock-full of attractions as Darling Harbour is, its restaurants can be expensive. Nearby **Chinatown,** with fewer attractions and less nightlife, is the best bet for cheap eats. However, Chinatown has its own sights, too. Don't miss the **entrance gates** flanking Dixon St. or the eclectic **Paddy's Market** (p. 127).

## 👁 SIGHTS

**■POWERHOUSE MUSEUM.** It takes time to explore this gigantic testament to the potentially boundless topic of human ingenuity. Exhibits and interactive displays focus on technology and applied science. An interesting permanent exhibit is **The Steam Revolution,** which traces the evolution of steam power from the 1600s to today through 12 life-size working engines and a merry-go-round. Temporary exhibits rotate every three to four months; some examples include the Princess Diana and Star Wars exhibits. For a taste of local talent, see the annual fashion design display from Sydney's University of Technology, the rising generation of Australian designers. (*500 Harris St., just south of Darling Harbour between Ultimo and Haymarket St. ☎02 9217 0111; www.powerhousemuseum.com. Open daily 10am-5pm. $10, students $6, ages 4-15 $5, under 4 free, families $25.*)

**SYDNEY AQUARIUM.** Over 12,000 Australian marine animals inhabit the tanks on the pier at Darling Harbour's eastern shore. Though Wildlife World may look more enticing, this is the sight to see. Seal, crocodile, platypus, and penguin exhibits are interspersed between colorful fish tanks. The three underground and underwater oceanariums, featuring huge enclosures of fish, sharks, and stingrays swimming overhead and around you, justify the hefty admission. Live feeds are open to visitors, so be sure to watch the seals, penguins, or sharks and rays munching their daily meals (usually at 9, 11am, and 3pm). Kids love the touchpools. (On Aquarium Pier. ☎ 02 8251 7800; www.sydneyaquarium.com.au. Open daily 9am-10pm; last entry 9pm. Seal sanctuary closes at sunset. $29.50, ages 3-15 $15, under 3 free, students and seniors $20.50, families of 4 $70. Discounted tickets available online.)

**PADDY'S MARKETS.** This huge warehouse market has become an iconic symbol of Sydney's Chinatown and the destination for any type of merchandise you can imagine—and we mean absolutely any. From clothes to cosmetics, cellphone covers to chintzy souvenirs, Paddy's wares include both the real and the ripped-off, but the prices can't be beat. (9-13 Hay St., in Chinatown. ☎ 1300 361 589; www.paddysmarkets.com.au. Open Th-Su 9am-5pm.)

**CHINESE GARDEN.** This serene garden designed and built by Chinese landscape artists was a bicentennial gift to New South Wales from her sister province of Guangdong, China. From the bubbling waterfalls to the koi fish in Lotus Pond, the garden provides a sheltered escape from the hubbub of the city. Each intimate courtyard and walkway is governed by the traditional principles of Yin-Yang and is sure to bring you peace of mind. As you explore, there are plenty of gazebos and benches to sit and relax. To complete the experience, stop for a leisurely pot of jasmine tea and a bite of lunch on the Teahouse patio overlooking the lake. (Corner of Harbour and Pier St. ☎ 02 9240 8888. Open daily 9:30am-5pm; teahouse open 10am-4:30pm. $6, under 15 $3, families $15.)

# ◪ FOOD

**Blackbird Cafe** (☎02 9283 7385), balcony level, Cockle Bay Wharf, in Darling Harbour. Trendy eatery with photo-op fountain, spiral staircase, lounging atmosphere, and delightful view of the harbor. The relatively lower prices will keep your bank account happy. Take advantage of the $12 days—each night of the week, one type of food is $12. For example, on Tu, all pastas are $12 (some originally up to $22). Open M-W 11:30am-10pm, Th 11:30am-11pm, F 11:30am-late, Sa 8am-late, Su 8am-10pm. ❷

**Chinta Ria: Temple of Love** (☎02 9264 3211), Roof Terr., Level 2, Cockle Bay Wharf, in Darling Harbour. A fantastic spot for soaking in the trendy wharf vibe amid funky Malaysian decor and brightly colored rice bowls. A big, stone Buddha statue greets you at the door. Authentic Malaysian fare ($15-27). Full bar and BYO option. Open M-Sa noon-2:30pm and 6-11pm, Su noon-2:30pm and 6-10:30pm. Lunch reservations only. ❷

**Chinatown food courts,** along Dixon St., all serve cheap, tasty meals ($6-10). **Dixon House Food Court,** 80 Dixon St., downstairs, at Little Hay St. Open daily 10:30am-8:30pm. **Sussex House Food Court,** corner of Little Hay St. and Dixon St. Open daily 9am-10pm. **Harbour Plaza Food Court,** on Dixon at Goulburn St. Open daily 10am-10pm; cash only. While you feel like you might be missing out on the outdoor Dixon St. seating of the pricier restaurants, grab a table or counter by the window and you can still watch some of the Chinatown bustle below. ❶

**The Golden Century,** 393-399 Sussex St. (☎02 9212 3901; www.goldencentury.com.au). This massive, 2-level Chinese restaurant is known for fresh seafood and long lines. Savvy customers, however, know it's well worth the wait. Pass the time by choosing your own entree from the huge tanks of crab, lobster, and fresh fish that line the walls. Meal costs are generally dependent on market prices. Open daily noon-4am. ❷

## NIGHTLIFE

If you thought Darling Harbour was just a tourist playground, stay and see who comes out to play at night. When the sun goes down, Darling Harbour offers a number of swanky lounge and club venues that are not to be missed. Dress up, fill your wallet, and prepare yourself for glittering harbor views.

**Home,** 101 Cockle Bay Wharf (☎02 9266 0600; www.homesydney.com). This UK-inspired nightclub hit Sydney with a vengeance. This is the ultimate swanky club; the scene is trendy and happening, so be prepared for huge lines. Despite a steep cover charge (from $20), the crowds keep coming. On F and Sa, 3 floors of dancing, DJs, and live music have the place grinding with everything from R&B to house until 7am. Club open F-Sa 9pm-late. Bar open daily 11am-late.

**The Loft,** 3 Lime St., King St. Wharf (☎02 9299 4770; www.theloftsydney.com). Ascend into this swanky bungalow with lantern-lit interiors and intimate booths. The views are spectacular, the tunes well-chosen, and the drinks perfectly mixed. Open M-W 4pm-1am, Th 4pm-3am, F-Sa noon-3am, Su noon-1am.

**Pontoon Bar,** 201 Sussex St., The Promenade, Cockle Bay Wharf (☎02 9267 7099; www.pontoonbar.com), right at the bridge. Sleek and stylish, the entire bar is an open terrace right on the harbor, so every seat has a great view. Slightly more casual than other venues on the wharf, with a younger, rowdier crowd. Go before 10pm on Sa to avoid the $10 cover charge. Open M-W and Su 11am-midnight, Th-Sa 11am-late.

# KINGS CROSS

## ACCOMMODATIONS

If you take up residence in the Cross, you can expect hopping nightlife, lots of backpackers, and seedy streets (most notably Darlinghurst Rd.). Some accommodations are fairly run-down, but plenty of clean, well-maintained rooms are available for the booking. CityRail runs from Martin Pl. in the city to Kings Cross Station. Buses also run from Circular Quay (#324, 325, or 326) and Chatswood (#200) to the Cross. The walk from City Center takes about 20min.

**Eva's Backpackers,** 6-8 Orwell St. (☎02 9358 2185; www.evasbackpackers.com.au). Guests rave about this clean, family-run hostel. Large, brightly colored rooms come equipped with large lockers, and the pleasant rooftop garden boasts spectacular views of the city. Newly refurbished bathrooms and the occasional hot breakfast give a homey, comforting feel. Free Internet access. Laundry $3. TV area. Breakfast, linen, and towels included. Reception M-Sa 7am-7pm, Su 7am-2pm. Dorms $26; doubles $75. 3-day stay $25/70 per night. Weekly $168/455. ❷

**Original Backpackers,** 160-162 Victoria St. (☎02 9356 3232; www.originalbackpackers.com.au). Spacious kitchen, TV lounge, dining area, and a courtyard with plants, fountains, and backpackers. Many planned activities; the enthusiastic staff will quickly get to know you by name. Constant cleaning keeps the old building well-maintained. Internet access $3 for 1hr. (can be used in intervals). Free luggage storage and small safe at front desk. All rooms have TV and fridge; some ensuite with safe in room. Key deposit $20. Reception 24hr. Check-out 10am. Dorms $26-29; singles/doubles $60-65, ensuite $70-75. Weekly $160-175/450/550. ❷

**O'Malley's Hotel,** 228 William St. (☎02 9357 2211), entrance to the left of the popular pub. 15 furnished rooms with TVs, bathrooms, coffee pots, and fridges are quieter than expected and well-secured from outside foot traffic. Perfect place to return home after a

**Kings Cross**

▲ ACCOMMODATIONS
Blue Parrot Backpackers, **1**
Eva's Backpackers, **3**
Jolly Swagman
    Backpackers, **6**
O'Malley's Hotel, **17**
Original Backpackers, **9**
Sydney Central
    Backpackers, **4**

🍎 FOOD
Dov Delectica, **5**
Govinda's, **19**
Little Penang, **8**
Macleay's Pizza, **2**
Roy's Famous, **12**
Thaipower, **7**

★ NIGHTLIFE
Iguana Bar, **14**
Kings Cross Hotel, **18**
O'Malley's Hotel, **16**
The World Bar, **15**

night of revelry at the nearby night-spots. Simple breakfast included. Check-out 10am. Reception daily 9am-noon. Doubles $79; triples (double with pull-down bed) $99. ❺

**Jolly Swagman Backpackers,** 27 Orwell St. (☎02 9358 6400; www.jollyswagman.com. au). Large eating area (indoor and outdoor) and common room with TV to help you meet new friends. Free drinks upon arrival and BBQs. Free airport pickup. Breakfast included, free Internet, reception 24hr., and travel desk with great ideas for sightseeing and trips. Laundry $3. Dorms $27; twins and doubles with TV $70. Weekly rates $162/420. ❷

**Sydney Central Backpackers,** 16 Orwell St. (☎02 9358 6600; www.sydneybackpack-ers.com.au), next to Eva's. Fun-loving atmosphere with jungle-themed decor and larger bedrooms with sink and fridge. Weekly entertainment. Free airport pickup. Simple breakfast included (7:30-9:30am). Lockers in rooms. Laundry $4. Free Wi-Fi (1hr. per day). Key deposit $20. Dorms $23; twins and doubles $60. Weekly $140/360. ❷

**Blue Parrot Backpackers,** 87 Macleay St. (☎02 9356 4888; www.blueparrot.com.au). Darlinghurst Rd. turns into Macleay St. past Fitzroy Gardens. Located on a larger street with shops and restaurants, this small, very blue hostel feels like a bungalow dormitory. Generally smaller facilities (bathrooms, courtyard, kitchen), except for large common room with TV and spacious lockers in rooms. Free Internet (30min. per day). Laundry $2. Reception 9am-8:30pm. Dorms $27-31; twins and doubles (only 1 of each) $89. ❷

**KINGS CROSS.** Make sure to stick to the well-lit streets at night. Darlinghurst, Victoria, and Bayswater Rd. are all well populated and relatively safe. Avoid narrow, dark lanes where unsavory characters might be lurking.

## FOOD

Though locals might look at you funny if you say you're going to Kings Cross for a meal, there are a few restaurants in the area that rival those in the City Center—and they're much less expensive.

**Govinda's,** 112 Darlinghurst Rd. (☎02 9380 5155; www.govindas.com.au). A unique restaurant and cinema where diners follow up a mostly Indian, wholly vegetarian, all-you-can-eat buffet with an arthouse or mainstream movie (depending on what's recent). The intimate, upstairs theater is equipped with cushy, couch-like chairs. Reservations strongly recommended. Open daily 5:45-10:30pm. ❷

**Thaipower,** 146 Victoria St. (☎02 8354 0434). Design your own noodle dish ($9.50-15) or stick to Thai favorites like garlic and pepper beef ($11) or basil vegetables and tofu ($9.50). Classic pad thai noodles with chicken ($11) are spectacular (and there's plenty for 2). Lunch specials (11am-4pm) bring everything on the menu down to $8. BYO. Open daily 11am-10:30pm. Cash only. ❶

**Dov Delectica,** 130 Victoria St. (☎02 9368 0600). Relaxed atmosphere for breakfast ($5-14), but they bust out candlelit tables in the evening. Lunch and dinner entrees include duck *pâté* ($14), seared lamb fillets ($23), and the Dov beef burger ($13). Don't miss the $10 early-evening menu 5-7pm. Open M-Tu 7am-4pm, W-F 7am-10:30pm, Sa 7:30am-10:30pm, Su 8:30am-3pm. ❷

**Little Penang,** 38 Llankelly Pl. (☎02 9356 2224). This cozy eatery is great for pre-partying munchies. Menu includes noodles ($8.50-13.50) and vegetarian dishes ($8.50-12.50). Try the beef-fried ho fun ($9.50) for something really flavorful and tasty. Open M-F 11am-3pm and 5-10:30pm, Sa-Su 4:30-10:30pm. ❶

**Macleay's Pizza,** 101a Macleay St. (☎02 9356 4262). The best pizza spot in the Cross, and long lines every night to prove it. The smell of freshly made dough makes it hard to pass by without grabbing a slice. Pizzas range from traditional margherita ($9.50) to topping-covered inventions like the Meat Lover's ($16). All pizzas available in medium and large sizes. Open M-Th noon-1:30am, F-Sa noon-3:30am, Su 3pm-1am. ❶

**Roy's Famous,** 176 Victoria St. (☎02 9357 3579). Huge portions and casual terrace seating make this a popular place to grab a sandwich ($11-16.50), some hearty comfort food ($17.50-19), or just glass of wine while watching the world go by. Steak, salad, and beer $15. Full bar. Open daily 7am-10pm. ❷

## NIGHTLIFE

Kings Cross is a constant buzz of activity, and its nightlife is the hub of the hive. Backpackers and locals cram the neighborhood hotspots nearly every night, but the weekend droves can make for a serious circus. Be sure to use caution late at night and try to avoid walking alone.

**The World Bar,** 24 Bayswater Rd. (☎02 9357 7700). Former brothel celebrates its roots with red mood lighting. Don't miss the teapots full of shots ($17) that can be shared in small shot glasses or consumed individually (responsibly, of course) right out of the spout. On the weekends, arrive early or be prepared to wait in a lengthy line. Live DJs daily. Open daily 1pm-late (up to 7am).

**Kings Cross Hotel,** 248 William St. (☎02 9358 3377), opposite the Coca-Cola sign. Centrally located; a prime liquor refuelling station. 5 floors of lounges and clubs with balconies make for great views of the streets below. Schooners $5, mixed drinks $6-9. Open daily 11am-4am. On weekends, the ground floor bar is open 24hr.

**O'Malley's Hotel,** 228 William St. (☎02 9357 2211). Take a break from the mixed drinks and recharge in this casual pub. The crowd gathers early to knock back a few schooners, but late arrivals will catch the music and dancing anyway—this place is sure to be hopping at any time of night. Open daily 10am-late.

**Iguana Bar,** 15 Kellett St. (☎02 9357 2609). Well-hidden bar has been a watering hole for many celebrities over the years; the walls lined with signed pictures prove it. The young and trendy converge here F and Sa for DJs and live bands. Great place to spend an evening or pick up a late-night snack (the restaurant is open until the bar closes). Mixed drinks $8-12.50. Beer $6.50. Open daily 9pm-late.

# DARLINGHURST

## ▟ ACCOMMODATIONS

Many of the old-school Aussie pubs in and around the greater Darlinghurst area double as hotels for travelers. Rooms are usually on the second and third floors above the pub.

**Royal Sovereign Hotel,** 306 Liverpool St. (☎02 9331 3672; www.royalsov.com.au), above Darlo Bar on the corner. All 19 pea-green rooms with TV, fridge, and coffee pots are doubles. Shared bathrooms are modern and well-maintained. Reception at Darlo Bar. All rooms from $77. Check seasonal rate changes. ❺

**Hotel Altamont,** 207 Darlinghurst Rd. (☎02 9360 6000; www.altamont.com.au). This boutique hotel's comfy leather couches and stone accents give it a classy bit of rock 'n' roll flair, so it's no suprise that its list of more famous guests includes Mick Jagger. The 14 ensuite rooms offer queen- and king-size bed options, and all come equipped with cable TV, air-conditioning and coffee pots. Free laundry and Internet. Boasts a Tuscan-style rooftop garden. Rooms from $129 per night. ❺

## ▐ FOOD

The suburbs of East Sydney have some of the city's best dining. Oxford St. offers a mix of cafes and ethnic eateries, Victoria St. has some charming bistros, and Stanley St. is crowded with sushi bars and a few classy Italian joints. Oxford St. addresses start at the street's origin on Hyde Park, but then the numbers begin again at the intersection with Victoria and South Dowling St., the dividing line between Darlinghurst and Paddington.

**Sel et Poivre,** 263 Victoria St. (☎02 9361 6530). Fancy French cuisine served in light, airy dining room or on the patio. Extensive wine list and impressive menu. Duck *pâté* on a baguette ($9). Steak au Poivre ($31.50) and braised beef cheek ($25) top the dinner menu. For something light, try a salad ($13-15) with cucumbers and creamy brie. Book ahead on weekend evenings. Open M-F 7am-late, Sa-Su 8am-11pm. AmEx/MC/V. ❸

**Bill & Toni's Restaurant,** 74 Stanley St. (☎02 9360 4702), between Riley and Crown St. Steak casseroles, traditional Italian fare, and huge pasta dishes ($9-15) are served in the upstairs dining room. Delicious takeaway sandwiches ($3-9) are available in the casual downstairs cafe. Tuna melt on Turkish bread ($9) can't be beat. BYO. Open daily noon-2:30pm and 6-10:30pm. Cash only. ❶

**Una's Cafe and Restaurant,** 340 Victoria St. (☎02 9360 6885). Austrian, Bavarian, and German food in a delightful wood and brick enclave with outdoor seating. Locals have been coming here for more than 35 years; you can (and will) wait for your table in the bar upstairs, giving you ample time to sample the great selection of imported beer and Schnapps. Great place for a big breakfast ($9). Vienna schnitzel lunch, sausages, or sauerkraut ($13-19). Open M-Sat 7:30am-10:30pm, Su 8am-9:30pm Cash only. ❶

## ☉ SIGHTS

**SYDNEY JEWISH MUSEUM.** Designed around a staircase in the shape of the Star of David, this museum is a moving exhibition of Australia's Jewish heritage and the horrors of the Holocaust. It's run entirely by volunteers—some of whom are Holocaust survivors themselves—that make this museum a truly unique place. As you are walking through the exhibits, take advantage of their willingness to share their stories of escape and survival. Many of them are personally connected to the displays presented, which makes the exhibits come alive as you view them. The Children's Memorial is particularly eye-opening. In it, there is a clear basin with one-and-a-half-million drops of water—each representing a tear for the one-and-a-half-million Jewish children murdered by the Nazi regime. *(148 Darlinghurst Rd. ☎ 9360 7999; www.sydneyjewishmuseum.com.au. Open M-Th and Su 10am-4pm, F 10am-2pm. $10, student and senior $7, children $6, families $22.)*

## ☉ NIGHTLIFE

Darlinghurst is known as the place where gay, lesbian, bisexual, and fun-loving straight people come to play at night. The artsy and alternative seem to outnumber the preppy and jockish two to one. Nightclubs in this area will provide the perfect amount of mixed drinks and mixed crowds.

**The Colombian Hotel,** 117-123 Oxford St. (☎02 9360 2151), corner of Crown St. With this hard-partying crowd of gay and straight alike, the drinking starts early and the dancing lasts late with DJs downstairs F-Su and upstairs Th-Sa mixing beats. Don't be surprised if the waiter who served you F night comes back as a fellow customer Sa. Vodka with anything, please ($11-15). Happy hour Th-Su 6-8:30pm. Open M-F 9am-late, Sa-Su 11am-even later (5-6am).

**The Stonewall,** 175 Oxford St. (☎02 9360 1963). A happening gay bar with buff bartenders and lots of live entertainment. Karaoke, go-go dancers, live music, and drag shows all rotate through the regular lineup. DJs spin funky dance music, while patrons mingle on couches upstairs and shake their booty to cookie-cutter pop downstairs. Open M-Th and Su 11am-5am, F-Sa 11am-6am.

**Darlo Bar,** 306 Liverpool St. (☎02 9331 3672), corner of Darlinghurst Rd. Retro lounge with bright funky furniture attracts a chill crowd. The upstairs terrace is particularly laid-back. Good for mingling over a glass of wine ($6-15) or a beer ($5-7) Rooms available (see **Royal Sovereign Hotel,** p. 145). Open M-Sa 10am-midnight, Su noon-midnight.

# PADDINGTON

## ⬒ FOOD

Fortunately, the cost of food in Paddington is far less than the cost of clothes sold in its fancy boutiques. That said, if shopping is your forte, then the Paddington section of Oxford St. is probably a must.

▨ **Chocolate by the Bald Man: Max Brenner,** 437 Oxford St. (☎02 9357 5055). Creator Max Brenner's policy on chocolate—"Get addicted. Be Happy"—is fitting, since his restaurant is perfect for creating cacao junkies. Try an innovative "choctail" ($7.50) or a classic hot chocolate ($5.50). Spend a bit more on dishes like banana-chocolate pizza or the yummy hot chocolate with crunchy waffle balls ($8-16). Open M-Th 9am-11pm, F-Sa 9am-midnight, Su 10am-10:30pm. ❶

**Arthur's Pizza,** 260 Oxford St. (☎02 9332 2220). This popular eatery serves up pizza in 21 topping combinations ($10-20, family size $25) and classic Italian pasta dishes ($8-13.50). Be prepared for lots of noise when a football game is on, and check ahead during peak hours. Open M-F 5pm-midnight, Sa-Su noon-midnight. ❶

**Micky's Cafe,** 268 Oxford St. (☎02 9361 5157). This average-looking cafe offers a surprisingly extensive menu, serving up everything from shepherd's pie ($25) to burgers ($15.50-17) to stir-fry noodles (16). Most meals $14.50-29. Splurge on the Mars bar cheesecake ($10). Breakfast served until 5pm. Open daily 8am-midnight. AmEx/V. ❸

## ◪ NIGHTLIFE

Compared to the boisterous nightlife of Darlinghurst, Paddington provides a tamer way to wind down the night. If you make it this far down Oxford St. before sunrise, be sure to hit these nightspots.

**Durty Nelly's,** 9-11 Glenmore Rd. (☎02 9360 4467; www.durtynellyssydney.com.au), off Oxford St. at Gipps St. Nelly takes her Guinness very seriously (schooners $4.40). Even on weekends when it's standing room only and impossible to hear the person next to you, the dark wood decor and jovial staff create a relaxing refuge from the Oxford St. melee. Open M-Sa 11am-midnight, Su noon-10pm.

**The Fringe Bar,** 106 Oxford St. (☎02 9360 5443). Though it might look like an old gentleman's smoking room, this dark bar attracts a good-looking 20-something crowd for drinking, dancing, pool, and comedy shows (M only). Every Th 2-for-1 creative mixed drinks and $10 all-you-can-eat pizza is the best deal around. Happy hour F 4-9pm. Open M-W and Su noon-midnight, Th-Sa noon-3am.

**The Paddington Inn,** 338 Oxford St. (☎02 9380 5913). In this bar, known for both its grub and grog, thirsty club-hoppers can enjoy the mixed drinks ($11-15) while hungry loungers snack on the Paddo Mixed Plate ($16). Don't come here looking for a wild party; instead relax by playing pool or chatting at the bars. Happy hour M-Th 4-7pm. Schooners $4.80. Open M-Tu and Su noon-midnight, W-Sa noon-1am.

# SURRY HILLS

Tucked beneath Oxford St. east of Central Station, the former industrial wasteland of Surry Hills is now a perfectly pleasant residential area. It's home to student-artist types, working-class old-timers, and recent immigrants—a diversity well reflected by the range of multicultural restaurants that line Crown St. and the fascinating mix of trendy boutiques and vintage clothing stores. Surry Hills is most easily (and safely) accessed by walking down Crown St. from Oxford St. instead of coming from Central Station.

## ◪ FOOD

▨ **Lemon Twist Cafe,** 393 Crown St. (☎02 9380 5242). Some of the best salads in Sydney—the mixed greens with mushrooms, olives, tomatoes, chicken, and pesto vinaigrette is unbelievable. Hearty burgers, sandwiches, and pasta also served. Don't be surprised if the tables are packed. Every Tu all salads $10.50, and every W all pastas and risottos $10. Cheaper takeaway is available. Open Tu-Su 8am-4pm. ❷

**Erciyes,** 409 Cleveland St. (☎02 9319 1309). This unassuming Turkish delight serves a wonderful array of *mezzes* (dips) with bread ($7-8) and traditional Turkish dishes such as chicken kebab with tabbouleh ($13). Welcoming and attentive staff. Don't miss the diamond baklava ($3) or rice pudding ($5) for dessert. Live belly dancing and music F and Sa evenings. Open daily 11am-midnight. ❷

**Mehrey Da Dhaba Indian Street Restaurant,** 466 Cleveland St. (☎02 9319 6260). The oldest dhaba in Sydney has a storied tradition of serving up inexpensive and filling East Indian meals ($9-16). While they specialize in tandoori dishes, they also serve a variety of vegetarian meals, naan, roti, and an extensive selection of flavorful curries. Open M-Tu and Su 5:30-11pm, W-F noon-3pm and 5:30-11pm, Sa-Su noon-midnight. BYO. ❷

## ◎ SIGHTS

**MOORE PARK.** Southeast of Surry Hills, Moore Park contains the **Sydney Football Stadium** and the city's major **cricket oval** (see **Sports and Recreation,** p. 56). Tours of the stadium take you through the dressing rooms, down the Players Tunnel, and out onto the field itself. You also get to visit a museum of Aussie sports history as part of the tour. (*☎ 1300 724 737. Tours M-F 10am, noon, and 2pm; Sa 10am; non-game days only. $25, concessions $17, family $65. Bookings essential.*)

## ◖ NIGHTLIFE

Crown St., the main drag of Surry Hills, is wide-awake at night and easily accessible from Oxford St., which it intersects in Darlinghurst.

**Trinity Bar,** 505 Crown St. (☎02 9319 6802), corner of Devonshire St. Modeled after Trinity College in Dublin and newly renovated in 2008, Trinity Bar is an Irish pub with a modern vibe. It boasts a fabulous outdoor terrace facing Crown St., and the walls are lined with jam-packed bookshelves. The mostly local crowd, however, is too busy socializing to read. Open M-Sa 11am-midnight, Su noon-10pm.

**The Clock Hotel,** 470 Crown St. (☎02 9331 5333; www.clockhotel.com.au). Easily recognizable by its distinctive clock tower, this hotel offers 4 bars spread over 2 levels. Watch the game in the street bar, play pool in the lounge, or chill at the balcony level's outdoor tables. The flavorful menu (dishes $12-22), which includes everything from mussels to burgers, is available throughout all 4 bars. Open daily 11:30am-midnight.

# BONDI BEACH

## ⌂ ACCOMMODATIONS

To reach Bondi Beach, take bus #380, 382, or L82 from Circular Quay via Oxford St., or drive east along Oxford St.; it's stop 12 on Bondi Explorer. CityRail runs to Bondi Junction, where buses #380, 381, and 382 run to the waterfront.

**GETTING TO BONDI.** For those who are traveling from the City Center to Bondi Beach, be aware that the train will deposit you at Bondi Junction, a bus ride away from the beach. However, the bus will drop you right on the waterfront and save you the extra fare.

**Bondi Beachouse YHA,** 36 Fletcher St. (☎02 9365 2088; www.bondibeachouse.com. au), corner of Fletcher and Dellview St. Although not directly on the beach, this is one of Bondi's largest and best hostels. The facilities are extensive and in tip-top shape, and surf and scuba diving rentals are included. Perks include: movie room, game room, large kitchen and dining area, BBQ, weekly activities, and a rooftop balcony with a view from Bondi to Bronte. Drinking in hostel only allowed 5-9pm. Internet $1 per 15min. Laundry $6. Key deposit $10. Dorms $25-30; twins and doubles $60-75, ensuite $70-85; family rooms $100-150. Discounts for YHA. ❷

**Bondi Backpackers,** 110 Campbell Pde. (☎02 9130 4660). Located in a prime spot just across the street from the ocean, this cosy little hostel has a great common room with a large TV and plenty of windows to take in the sun and views. Be sure to get a 4-6 share dorm room with a window facing the front; otherwise the rooms can be a bit dark. Breakfast (7:30-9am) and linen included. Laundry $5-6. Internet $1 for first 15min., then $2 per hr. Reception open 7:30am-10:30pm. Dorms $22; singles from $40; doubles $55-75. VIP/YHA discount. ❷

**Surfside Backpackers Bondi Beach,** 35A Hall St. (☎02 9365 4900; www.surfside-backpackers.com.au), 1 block inland from Campbell Pde. Surf scene murals and a sunny back patio will put you in the beach-bum mood. Has a kitchen, a common room with a TV, and a casual eating area. Free use of bikes, in-line skates, wetsuits, and boards. Breakfast included. Internet access $1 per hr. Laundry $6. Key deposit $30. Reception daily 8am-1pm and 5-10pm. Large dorms $25-28; doubles $80-85. Weekly $161-182/445-465. VIP/YHA discount. ❷

**Noah's Bondi Beach,** 2 Campbell Pde. (☎02 9365 7100; reservations 1800 226 662 or online at www.noahsbondibeach.com), on the beach's southern end. This large hostel has many rooms with beach views, and its spacious doubles all come with a TV, a fridge, and a sink. Dorms are a little cramped, so enjoy Bondi's beauty from the expansive rooftop. Free boogie board use. Connected to **The Shack Bar and Restaurant** (meals $6.50-9.50), which means non-guests are often in the building. Laundry $6. Key deposit $20. Reception 24hr. Internet $5 per 90min. Dorms $20-23; twins and doubles $50; beachside twins/doubles $60. Weekly $120-138/300/360. NOMADS. ❷

## 🄵 FOOD

Campbell Pde. is lined with take-away joints and fast food restaurants as well as a number of trendy cafes facing the beach. Hall St. and Roscoe St. (perpendicular to Campbell Pde.) and Glenayr Ave. (parallel) have cheaper sit-down restaurants but lack the ocean view.

**Bondi Tratt,** 34 Campbell Pde. (☎02 9365 4303), in Bondi Beach. This restaurant's outdoor terrace is high on Campbell Pde. and provides diners with excellent views of the beach. This restaurant will wow you with both its authentic Italian entrees and modern Australian cui-

**Bondi Beach**

🔺 ACCOMMODATIONS
Bondi Backpackers, **6**
Bondi Beachhouse
YHA, **9**
Noah's Bondi Beach, **8**
Surfside Backpackers
Bondi Beach, **3**

🍴 FOOD
Bondi Tratt, **4**
Sahnia, **11**
Gelato Bar Restaurant, **2**
Mojo's Cafe, **5**

⭐ NIGHTLIFE
Beach Road Hotel, **1**
The Eastern, **10**
Bondi Icebergs Club, **7**

**NEW SOUTH WALES**

sine. Pasta and pizza start at $15, while main dishes cost upward of $18.50. BYO and licensed. Open M-F 7am-10pm, Sa-Su 8am-10pm. ❸

**Mojo's Cafe,** 32 Campbell Pde. (☎02 9130 1322). Don't be deterred by the dark interior of this trendy tapas bar. Fruity house-made sangria ($7 per glass) and delicious meat, seafood, and vegetable tapas ($8-19) are the best you'll get without breaking the bank. Knowledgeable staff makes stellar suggestions. Packed in the evenings, so book ahead. Small seating area. Open M-Th 6pm-late, F-Su 4pm-late. ❷

**Sahnia,** 106 Campbell Pde. (☎02 9365 1546). This funky restaurant and bar is a great place for breakfast—whether in their outdoor seating area or tucked into an indoor table. Try the make-your-own pancakes ($9), a selection of eggs ($9-13), or the french toast with berries, carmelized banana, and maple syrup ($10). Also open for main meals and drinks. Check for deals through hostels in the area. Open daily 8am-midnight. ❶

**Gelato Bar Restaurant,** 140 Campbell Pde. (☎02 9130 4033). Serves a variety of chicken and steak dishes ($23.50-26.50), as well as basic sandwiches ($13-16), but the delectable cakes tortes and famous fruit strudels ($6.50-7.80) are the real highlights of this long-standing cafe. Open M-F and Su 8am-11pm, Sa 8am-midnight. ❸

## 🔊 NIGHTLIFE

Bondi's nightlife, like its beach, is more glamorous than that of its southern rival and ranges from beachside lounges to the clubs in Bondi Junction.

**The Eastern,** 500 Oxford St. (☎02 9387 7828; www.theeastern.com.au), near Bondi Junction. Built on the site of the historic Bondi Junction Hotel and spanning 4 floors, this club is the place to be on a W night in Bondi. The mid-week menu (W) features $3 drinks from 6-9pm to get the party started early. Then dance until dawn with a selection of music from electro-pop to R&B (depending on the floor), all the while cooling off with periodic drinks on the trendy terrace. Open M-Sa 10am-late, Su 10am-midnight.

**Beach Road Hotel,** 71 Beach Rd. (☎02 9130 7247). A staple of Bondi nightlife, this place fills up fast on weekends (Th-Sa), but even more so on Su. The ground-level sports bar is frequented by a slightly older crowd, while upstairs draws students and young travelers to its theme nights, live bands, dance floor, and pool tables. The hotel also houses 2 restaurants serving both Italian and modern Australian fare. Lower level open M-Sa 10am-11:45pm, Su 10am-10pm. Upper level open M-Sa 5pm-midnight, Su 5pm-10pm. Restaurants open M-Sa noon-11:45pm, Su noon-10pm.

**Bondi Icebergs,** 1 Notts Ave. (☎02 9365 9000). Just off southern Bondi Beach, this world-famous restaurant and lounge plays host not only to a great bar and cafe, but also to one of the best outdoor swimming pools in Sydney. (Pool ☎02 9130 4804; $4.50, child $2.50.) If the restaurant sounds pricey (meals $22-42), simply sit back with a pint and enjoy the cocktail lounge and amazing views. Bar Lounge open M-Sa noon-midnight, Su noon-10pm. Restaurant open daily for lunch at noon, dinner 6pm-late. Pool open M-W and F 6am-6:30pm, Sa-Su 6:30am-6:30pm.

# COOGEE BEACH

## ⌂ ACCOMMODATIONS

To reach Coogee, take bus #373 or 374 from Circular Quay, #372 or 374 from Central Station, #314 or 353 from Bondi Junction, or #400 from the Airport to change buses at Randwick Junction. Coogee is stop 14 on Bondi Explorer.

**Coogee Beach Wizard of Oz** (☎02 9315 7876, www.wizardofoz.com.au) and **Coogee Beachside Budget Accommodation** (☎02 9315 8511; www.sydneybeachside.com. au), 172 & 178 Coogee Bay Rd. Owned by the same local couple, these neighboring hostels have one building for dorms (Wizard) and one for doubles (Beachside). Hardwood floors and spacious dorms make this a great place for relaxation and socializing, especially during the free weekly BBQs. Dorms only have lockers in the hall. Also offers some family suites. Laundry $6. Key deposit $25. Reception daily 8am-1pm and 5-8pm. Dorms $27-45; doubles $65-100. ❷

**Surfside Backpackers Coogee Beach,** 186 Arden St. (☎02 9315 7888), across the street from Coogee Beach. This is the 2nd location of the Surfside Backpackers hostels, the 1st one being Bondi (see above). Open balconies make the rooms sunny, airy, and bright, and the common room balcony is particularly popular with its view of Coogee Beach. Key deposit $30. Laundry $6. Internet $2 per 30min. Reception daily 8am-1pm and 5-10pm. Dorms $25-30; weekly $161. Doubles $70-80. YHA/VIP discount. ❷

# ◖ FOOD

In Coogee, make sure to check out Coogee Bay Rd. for its active cafe social scene during the day. The street also has a great many Thai restaurants that regularly draw in big crowds for dinner.

**A Fish Called Coogee,** 229 Coogee Bay Rd. (☎02 9664 7700). This casual seafood emporium specializes in—you guessed it—fish. Definitely the best fish and chips place in Coogee ($9). Eat in or grab some takeaway for the beach. Open daily 11am-9pm. ❶

**Thai Eatery,** 244 Coogee Bay Rd. (☎02 9664 4700). Huge portions of steaming vegetables, meats, and sauces makes this *the* Thai restaurant along Coogee Bay Rd. Main dishes run $11-19, but all meals are ½-price on W, so reserve a table in advance. Come with a group of friends to enjoy the bustle and fun-loving atmosphere. BYO. ❷

**Coogee Cafe,** 221 Coogee Bay Rd. (☎02 9665 5779), in Coogee Beach. This modern cafe on bustling Coogee Bay Rd. is just the place for a quick lunch or a lazy breakfast over the morning paper. Offers a range of great sandwiches ($8.50-14) such as the BLAT—a twist on the classic BLT with bacon, lettuce, tomato, and spicy guacamole on toasted sourdough ($8.50). Open M-Sa 7am-5pm, Su 8am-5pm. ❶

# ◖ NIGHTLIFE

Though Bondi's glitzy cliques can afford to knock back their drinks in a wide range of venues, the younger, less pretentious Coogee crowds can also party just as hard in a number of happening nightspots.

**Coogee Bay Hotel** (☎02 9665 0000; www.coogeebayhotel.com.au), corner of Coogee Bay Rd. and Arden St. Backpackers, locals, and uni students alike come to Coogee Bay's multiple bars, beer garden, and nightly live music. **Selina's** nightclub, which has a capacity of 1800, is a top concert venue for local DJs and international acts ($5 cover on weekends.) Beach bar open daily 9:30am-3am. Sports Bar open M-Th 9am-4am, F-Sa 9am-6am, Su 9am-1pm. Selina's open F-Sa 9pm-late.

**The Palace,** 169 Dolphin St. (☎02 9664 2900), in Coogee Beach. The Palace features 3 levels of nighttime craziness: the ground-floor Beach Bar is your standard sports bar. The Mid-Palace dance club, popular with a well-dressed younger crowd, blasts R&B and dance music. The top-level Aquarium Bar features a much more casual, diverse crowd, live entertainment and great views of the beach. Beach Bar open M-Th 11am-1am, F-Sa 11am-3am, Su 11am-midnight. Dance club open W-Sa 9pm-late; Sa cover $5. Aquarium Bar open M-Th 11am-1am, F-Sa 11-3am, Su 11am-midnight.

# NEWTOWN

## 🗋 FOOD

In this young, bohemian neighborhood, cheap and tasty options are endless and include plenty of organic, vegan, and other healthy choices. Splitting Newtown in two, King St. is an entire thoroughfare of bargain meals. Asian restaurants and cafes wait for the adventurous diner.

**Green Gourmet,** 115-117 King St. (☎02 9519 5330; www.greengourmet.com.au). A great mix of Asian-inspired vegan cuisine awaits inside. Try a pair of delicious wheat-free Kumera Ginger Purses (a hearty sweet-potato pastry with ginger and vegetable filling; $3.20) or the Steamed Spicy Eggplant with sesame and tofu ($14.80). Won ton soup $5. No alcohol permitted. Open M-Th and Su noon-3pm and 6-10pm, F-Sa noon-3pm and 6-11pm. While you're in the area, be sure to check out the neighboring **Vegan's Choice Grocery,** 113 King St. (☎02 9519 7646). ❶

**Taste,** 235 King St. (☎02 9519 7944; www.tastenewtown.com). What this place does with chemical-free chicken is truly amazing, from BBQ plates to Thai chicken curry and char-grilled and satay dishes ($3.20-14). Vegetarians can enjoy salads such as chickpea and pumpkin and bean-avocado ($5.50-10). Steak burgers ($7) and vegetable pad thai ($5-9) are also on the menu. In winter, hot soup ($5) and the friendly staff will warm you up. Takeaway available. Limited seating. Open daily 10am-9pm. ❶

**Buzzzbar Cafe,** 349 King St. (☎02 9557 9191). Escape bustling King St. on the cozy velvet couches of this hanging-lantern-lit cafe. Salads ($6-15), pastas ($14-16) and other main dishes ($15-22) provide solid meals, but desserts like the chocolate truffle cake ($7.50) and baked cheesecake ($7.50) are truly delicious. Wash it down with a frothy cappuccino ($3). Open Tu-Sa 10am-late, Su 10am-6pm. ❷

**Sushi Train,** 316A King St. (☎02 9557 4435). Head here to snack on an extensive selection of freshly rolled sushi as 2-6 piece entrees ($3-$4.50) chug by on a train-like conveyor belt. The staff is friendly, the head chef is a sushi genius, and the prices are quite reasonable. Main dishes include tempura udon ($9). Open M-Th and Su 11:30am-10pm, F-Sa 11:30am-10:30pm ❶

## 🍸 NIGHTLIFE

After enjoying a steaming bowl of noodles or a gooey vegan pizza from one of the restaurants in Newtown and browsing the numerous specialty shops, join bar-hoppers of all types for a night out on King St.

**NO SUCH THING AS A MANIC MONDAY** To experience Newtown in full swing, avoid visiting on Monday or Tuesday, as many of the restaurants, shops, and bar are closed, and you might be left without much to do.

**Kuleto's Cocktail Bar,** 157 King St. (☎02 9519 6369). Deliciously fruity liqueurs go down smooth during happy hour (M-Sa 6-7:30pm, Th 9:30-10:30pm) at the newly refurbished Kuleto's. The Toblerone and the Red Corvette are by far the best. Long Island Iced Tea $14.50. Open M-Sa 4pm-3am, Su 4pm-12am.

**ZanziBar,** 323 King St. (☎02 9519 1511). On a warm evening, snag a table on the rooftop terrace and indulge in a fruity cocktail. While this late-night option offers tapas and meals, stick to the schooners ($4.50-7), daquiris ($13), and wine while schmoozing in the upstairs cocktail lounge furnished with a Moroccan flair. Happy hour M-F 5:30-7pm. Open M-Th 10am-4am, F 10am-6am, Sa 10am-5am, Su 10am-midnight.

**NEW SOUTH WALES**

**Marlborough Hotel,** 145 King St. (☎02 9519 1222). The "Marly" is the place to be after Kuleto's happy hour ends; come for pokies, casual boozing, dancing, and some decent local musical talent. Large venue with mirrored walls that sets the stage for a big party. Th DJ, F local bands, Sa cover bands, Su afternoon acoustic. Schooners $3.60-5. Open M-Sa 10am-3am, Su noon-midnight.

# ERSKINEVILLE

This small residential nook, just down the street from King St., Newtown, offers a way to interact with Aussie locals in more low-key settings. Follow your nose to the homey cafe ■Shenkin ❶, 53 Erskineville Rd, where the aroma of freshly baked pastries and breads wafts through the windows as you pass by. With colorful mugs, antique teapots, and a selection of newspapers and magazines to read, Shenkin offers breakfast all day ($4-14) as well as a lunch menu with unique dishes such as angel hair pasta with smoked salmon, snow peas, and dill cream sauce for $14. (☎02 9550 5511. Open M-Tu and Su 7:30am-6pm, Th-Sa 7:30am-late.) If passing through in the evening, have a drink and enjoy a game of trivia (Th) or live music (F-Sa) at the **Rose of Australia Hotel ❸**, 1 Swanson St., a popular colonial pub for locals. For a proper dinner, there are various Italian dishes ($16-22) in the hidden upstairs dining room. (☎02 9565 1441. Open M 10am-11pm, Tu-Sa 10am-midnight, Su 10am-10pm.

# GLEBE

## ♠ ACCOMMODATIONS

This bohemian knot of bookshops, pubs, and cafes is a low-key contrast to the frenzy of the Cross. Youthful energy from the nearby University of Sydney still infuses the club scene, and the student population also creates a convenient demand for cheap eats. The town is centered along **Glebe Point Road,** which can be accessed via bus #431, 432, 433, or 434 from George St., off Circular Quay. Or, from Central Station, follow George St., then go west on Broadway for 15min. to Victoria Park and turn right onto Glebe Point Rd.

**Verona Guest House,** 224 Glebe Point Rd. (☎02 9660 8975). This beautiful old mansion has been converted into one of the nicest—if not the single nicest—guesthouse in Glebe. 8 charming rooms, an elegant tiled kitchen, cozy common space with TV, and manicured courtyard. Guests eat their included breakfast at 1 long table in the kitchen, creating an intimate family setting. Free laundry and Internet. Wheelchair-accessible. Singles $145; doubles $165; triples $185. 10% discount for 3 nights or more. ❺

**Glebe Point YHA,** 262-264 Glebe Point Rd. (☎02 9692 8418), at the far end of Glebe Point Rd. This hostel may feel a bit secluded for those who want to be in the center of the action, but the rooms are spacious and have in-room sinks. Guests gather for an extensive list of activities, such as BBQs (F $5), movie nights (Tu), and gatherings at the A.B. Hotel. (See **Nightlife**). Internet access $0.75 per 15min. Laundry $6. Key deposit $10. Dorms $32.50, YHA $29.50, weekly $168. Twins and doubles $78/70/420. ❸

**Alishan International Guest House,** 100 Glebe Point Rd. (☎02 9566 4048; www.alishan.com.au). As its flyer says, "Near to everything but not in the middle of everything." This Victorian house is a perfect option for those wanting a more private setting in the heart of Glebe. The staff is multilingual and multinational, and the house has an open common area, backyard BBQ, and fully equipped kitchen. Private rooms have TV, fridge,

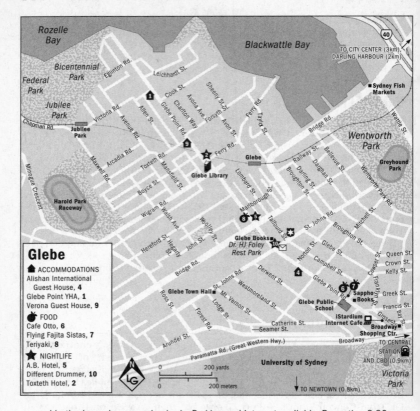

**Glebe**

🏠 ACCOMMODATIONS
Alishan International
  Guest House, **4**
Glebe Point YHA, **1**
Verona Guest House, **9**
🍴 FOOD
Cafe Otto, **6**
Flying Fajita Sistas, **7**
Teriyaki, **8**
★ NIGHTLIFE
A.B. Hotel, **5**
Different Drummer, **10**
Toxteth Hotel, **2**

and bath; dorms have wooden beds. Parking and Internet available. Reception 8:30am-10pm. Wheelchair accessible. Dorms $27-33; singles $88-99; doubles $99-115; 4-person family room $154. Extra person $16. ❷

# 🛏 FOOD

Glebe Point Rd. is packed with eclectic and inexpensive food. If you're in the mood for Thai, Indian, Italian, or some interesting combination thereof, you can find it on Glebe Point Rd., and it will definitely be cheap and tasty.

**Teriyaki,** 144a Glebe Point Rd. (☎02 9566 1625). This small Japanese restaurant can be easily overlooked if you walk by too fast, so turn around, take a seat, and order anything. The food is delicious and cheap, and the staff is eager to offer recommendations. The lunch specials are a particularly good value ($8-13). Try the "Lunch Box," which includes miso soup, chicken teriyaki, gyoza (dumplings), tempura veggies and prawns, and rice ($13). Open M-F noon-2:30pm and 5:30-10pm, Sa 5:30-10pm. ❶

**Flying Fajita Sistas,** 65 Glebe Point Rd. (☎02 9552 6522). Combination of Spanish and Tex-Mex flavors adds some experimental spice to the cuisine. Tamales ($23), burritos ($19), and enchiladas ($19) all make the cut. Don't miss Taco Tuesdays—$3 tacos and $3 tequila shots. BYO wine only ($4 per bottle). Open Tu-Su 6pm-late. ❸

NEW SOUTH WALES

**Cafe Otto,** 79 Glebe Point Rd. (☎02 9552 1519). High ceilings, old-fashioned furnace, and heated outdoor courtyard attract sophisticates of all ages. Everything from eggs benedict ($16) and pastas ($14.70-22.50) to meat dishes like shepherd's pie ($26). BYO wine only ($3 per person). Free Wi-Fi for 1hr. with any purchase. Open M-Tu 11am-11pm, W-Th 10am-11pm, F 10am-midnight, Sa 9am-midnight, Su 9am-11pm. ❷

## 🎱 NIGHTLIFE

Glebe's nightlife can be hit or miss depending on whether school is in session for University of Sydney students, but in general, the bars listed below tend to attract a steady crowd year-round. While there are a few cocktail lounges, Glebe's is much more of a pub culture. Young and old gather on leather couches and on wooden stools watching a rugby game or chatting over a pint. The atmosphere's fun, and the crowd is friendly.

**Different Drummer,** 185 Glebe Point Rd. (☎02 9552 3406). If you want to upgrade your schooner to a mixed drink without getting too upscale, this cozy lounge and tapas bar is the place to do it. The drink list includes the classic mojito ($16) to the raspberry beret ($14). Happy hour 6-7:30pm. Background tunes range from jazz to big band and house later in the evening. Music aside, it's really the quirky Glebe crowd that gives this party its different beat. Open Tu-Sa 5pm-late.

**A.B. Hotel,** 225 Glebe Point Rd. (☎02 9660 1417). At the center of Glebe Point Rd., this 7-room venue is the perfect place to bring all your friends. The Penthouse upstairs boasts a snazzy bar, while the Cantina downstairs offers pool tables and a nearby gaming lounge. The House of Poker tournaments and the prize pool of $1800 gets the whole town involved. Open M-Sa 10am-midnight, Su 10am-10pm.

**Toxteth Hotel,** 345 Glebe Point Rd. (☎02 9660 2370). Welcomes locals, students, and travelers alike. Slightly away from the main Glebe pulse, but good for a low-key early evening drink (especially if you are staying at the Glebe Point YHA nearby). There is a restaurant with steak and other pub food, though it's a little pricey for what you get. Their beer garden with bistro for warm days and big-screen TV for sporting events make this a stop for all seasons. Open M-Sa 11am-1am, Su 11am-midnight.

# LEICHARDT

With a Tuscan-inspired **Italian Forum,** 23 Norton St., and its own shop-lined piazza, Sydney's "Little Italy" is ideal for bookshopping and baked delights. After browsing through **Berkelouw Books,** 70 Norton St., sit down for a hearty Italian meal, or grab a sweet cannoli on the go for a stroll through **Pioneers Memorial Park** (formerly Balmain Cemetery).

## 🍴 FOOD

**Jolly Cafe,** 158 Norton St. (☎02 9560 2434). This small corner cafe is consistently busy but always delivers quality food. Chicken pesto penne, garlic prawns, and other main dishes $12-19. Bring a group of friends and eat, eat, eat. Outside dining area. BYO. Open M-F 10:30am-3:30pm and 5-11pm, Sa-Su 11:30am-midnight. ❷

**Mezzapica Cafe and Cake Shop,** 128-130 Norton St. (cafe ☎02 9568 2095, bakery 02 9569 8378). With a lavish display of baked goods to satisfy your sweet tooth, the cannoli should definitely win out. Small cannoli $1.60, large $2.50. Cafe open daily 7am-4pm; bakery open M-F 9am-5:30pm, Sa 8:30-1pm, Su 8:30am-noon. ❶

# NORTH SHORE

## 👁 SIGHTS

The Lower North Shore, between Sydney Harbour and Middle Harbour, is primarily home to wealthy Sydneysiders. Its residential neighborhoods and upscale boutiques are lovely but don't draw many travelers. The notable exception is **Mosman**, which holds the ever-popular **Taronga Park Zoo.** If you enjoy coastal walks, get acquainted with the area by starting at the Cremorne Pt. ferry stop and following the coastline around Mosman Bay to the Taronga Park Zoo. The popular **Northern Beaches** start in the lively suburb of Manly after the Spit Bridge and run up the coast to Palm Beach.

**TARONGA ZOO.** The suburb of Mosman is best-known for the **Taronga Park Zoo,** at the end of Bradley's Head Rd. Spanning 28 hectares, the impressive collection has animals from all over Australia and the world, including the magnificent snow leopard and Sumatran tiger, both of which are endangered. The zoo is perched on a hill, and the Sydney city skyline in the background provides a number of great photo-ops. You can also have your photo taken with a koala or giraffe at specified times during the day. Upon arrival, be sure to take the Sky Safari to the entrance of the zoo; it's a gondola ride over the park that gives you a preview of the gorillas and elephants, and the ride is included in the admission ticket. *(To reach the zoo, take a 12min. ferry ride from Circular Quay or bus #247 from Carrington St., Wynyard Station. ☎02 9969 2777; www.zoo.nsw.gov.au. Open daily 9am-5pm. $39, concessions $23, ages 4-15 $19, families $98.50. Discount tickets available online, or purchase a ZooPass at Circular Quay, which covers the ferry and admission.)*

**NORTHERN BEACHES.** A string of popular surfing beaches lines the Pacific Ocean on the North Shore, beginning with Manly and stretching all the way to Palm Beach. **Manly** (p. 157) is by far the most popular and accessible, although many of the others are also considered among Sydney's best. **Dee Why Beach,** 4km north of Manly, is a large family-friendly beach with plenty of restaurants and shops. Continuing north, the pounding waves of **Narrabeen** draw mostly experienced surfers. However, the gem of the northern beaches is serene **Palm Beach,** well-known as the location for the Aussie soap opera *Home and Away.* While there's no train access to the northern beaches, and bus rides from the CBD can take as long as 90min., the sun, surf, and sand can make the extra travel time worthwhile. *(For the fastest route, take the Northern Beach express bus L88 or L90 from Wynyard Station, Carrington St.; change at Warringah Mall for Manly services. www. sydneybeaches.com.au has tips on what to see and do in the Northern Beaches.)*

**COLLAROY BEACH.** Collaroy makes a great base camp for travelers looking to comb the northern beaches. **Sydney Beachhouse/Northern Beaches YHA ❷,** 4 Collaroy St., is a spectacular hostel located across the street from the beach. The TV lounge, large common space, and kitchen are modern and clean, and they loan out surfboards, snorkeling gear, and bikes for free. *(☎02 9981 1177; www. sydneybeachouse.com.au. Wheelchair-accessible. Internet $4 per hr. Dorms $26-40; doubles $70-110; ensuite family rooms $120-160.)* There are also plenty of places along Pittwater Rd. to grab a bite to eat, from traditional Aussie pies to Thai and Indian specialties. A few blocks down from the YHA hostel is 🔳**Sylvia and Fran's The Upper Crust Pie Shop ❶,** 1003 Pittwater Rd., winner of the 2001 and 2002 Great Aussie Pie Competition. They start on their delicious pies ($3.50-7.20) at 2am each day, and the scrumptious smell lasts until well after closing. *(☎02 9971 5182. Open daily 7am-5pm.)*

# MANLY

## ▐ TRANSPORTATION

The gorgeous **ferry ride** from Circular Quay sets the tone for the oceanside sub-urb of Manly, since its major activities are all water-related. The ferry leaves from Circular Quay (30min.; M-F 6am-11:45pm, Sa 8am-11:45pm, Su 8am-11pm; $6.40) or Jetcat (15min.; M-F 6-9:25am and 4:20-8:30pm, Sa 6:10am-3:35pm, Su 7:10am-3:35pm; $8.20). For more, see **Local Transportation,** p. 114.

## ▐▌ ORIENTATION AND PRACTICAL INFORMATION

The **visitors center** (☎02 9976 1430; www.manlyweb.com.au; open M-F 9am-5pm, Sa-Su 10am-4pm) is in front of the wharf near the enclosed Manly Cove swimming area. The cove is also the starting point of the famous **Manly to Spit Walk,** a 9.5km walk (3hr.) that offers views of harbor coastline, sandy beaches, national parklands, and bayside homes. **The Corso,** a pedestrian street lined with cheap cafes and fast food joints, connects the cove and wharf area to the sand and surf of Manly Beach. **Sydney Road** (off The Corso) also has a pedestrian-only portion,which turns into an arts and crafts marketplace on weekends.

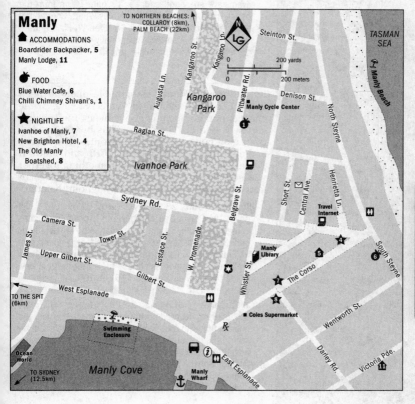

**Manly**

▲ ACCOMMODATIONS
Boardrider Backpacker, **5**
Manly Lodge, **11**

🍎 FOOD
Blue Water Cafe, **6**
Chilli Chimney Shivani's, **1**

★ NIGHTLIFE
Ivanhoe of Manly, **7**
New Brighton Hotel, **4**
The Old Manly
  Boatshed, **8**

TO NORTHERN BEACHES:
COLLAROY (8km),
PALM BEACH (22km)

TASMAN SEA

Manly Beach

Steinton St.

Kangaroo Ln.
Kangaroo St.
Augusta Ln.

Kangaroo Park

Pittwater Rd.

Denison St.

■ Manly Cycle Center

North Steyne

Raglan St.

Ivanhoe Park

Sydney Rd.

Short St.
Central Ave.
Belgrave St.
Henrietta Ln.

Travel Internet

Camera St.

Tower St.

Eustace St.

W. Promenade

Whistler St.

Manly Library

The Corso

South Steyne

James St.

Upper Gilbert St.

Gilbert St.

West Esplanade

TO THE SPIT
(6km)

Coles Supermarket

Wentworth St.

Swimming Enclosure

Ocean World

TO SYDNEY
(12.5km)

Manly Cove

Manly Wharf

East Esplanade

Darley Rd.

Victoria Pde.

## E VIEW FROM THE TOP

On my first day in Sydney, I climbed a hill to watch the sun set over the city. I didn't know the names of anything and the city seemed enormous. With the glow of an orange sky in the background, I could just make out 10 figures ascending the arch of the Sydney Harbour Bridge.

A month later, I wanted to bring my experience in the city to a close. I needed something that would surpass everything else I had seen or done. So even though the price was high, I decided to go on the **BridgeClimb**—a tour that takes you to the top of the Harbour Bridge.

BridgeClimb is a unique experience. The one-piece climbing suit has a large belt with a metal hook that attaches to a cable that then leads up the bridge. You ascend the arch until you are directly underneath the Australian flag at the top, a journey that takes about an hour and a half.

As I climbed up through the twilit sky, I saw the Opera House and the Botanic Gardens. The Rocks was lit by the glow of pubs and art galleries, while the waterfront restaurants in Darling Harbour had already opened their doors. Across the harbor, I saw Manly and the residential district of Mosman. From 134m in the air, the whole city was like a postcard beneath me. I was farther away, yet the skyline was more familiar than ever before.

—*Ansley Rubinstein*

# ACCOMMODATIONS

Lively, surfside Manly has a good range of accommodations and is the best base for travelers exploring the beautiful Northern Beaches.

**Boardrider Backpacker,** Rear 63, The Corso (☎02 9977 6077; www.boardrider.com.au). Manly's newest hostel is often booked solid due to its central location 80m from the beach and its top-notch features, which include private balconies, a large common area, a modern kitchen, and a rooftop BBQ. Nightly entertainment also adds to the great atmosphere of the place. Offers free luggage storage. Laundry $6. Internet $3 per hr. Key deposit $20. Dorms $23, $138 per week; twins and doubles $85/450; motel rooms $85/450 ensuite $100/500. Book well ahead ❷

**Manly Lodge,** 22 Victoria Pde. (☎02 9977 8655; www.manlylodge.com.au). All of the luxurious ensuite rooms come equipped with A/C, TV, and kitchenettes; some even have spas and saunas. It's only 100m from the beach and a 5min. walk from Manly Wharf. Continental breakfast included. Laundry $6. Free Wi-Fi. Standard $130-160; deluxe $180-210; family $180-210. Rates decrease with multiple-night stay. ❺

# FOOD

In and around Manly, fashionable open-terraced cafes line the beachfront on S. Steyne, while cheaper options, including several fast-food chains, can be found on The Corso. This buzzing pedestrian mall connects the beachfront to the harbor and also splits Steyne St. into north and south. If you are in the mood to throw something together yourself, head to one of the numerous supermarkets and smaller food stores throughout the area.

**Blue Water Cafe,** 28 S. Steyne (☎02 9976 2051), just below The Corso. One of many trendy oceanfront cafes lining the South Steyne waterfront, Blue Water serves dependable dishes, from bacon and eggs to burgers to Thai salmon. Large portions and reasonable prices make this the place to choose for a meal with a view of the beach. Main courses $15-29. 10% surcharge on Su. Open daily 7:30am-10pm. ❸

**Chilli Chimney Shivani's,** 26-28 Pittwater Rd. (☎02 9977 2890), located north of the town center, near the intersection with Denison St. With mouth-watering curry and tandoori dishes ($14-19), this is undoubtedly the best Indian food in Manly. The friendly staff and authentic atmosphere keep it chill. Cheaper takeaway available. BYO wine only. Open for lunch Th-Su 11am-3pm, daily for dinner 5:30pm-late. ❸

 **NIGHTLIFE**

**New Brighton Hotel and Sharkbar,** 71 The Corso (☎02 9977 3305). This hotel is home to a relaxed pub and lounge as well as the wild Sharkbar, which lures an energetic crowd. Each night brings something new, from M $5 drink specials and Tu $9 jugs for students to F-Sa DJs until late. Hotel open M-Sa, Su 10am-midnight. Sharkbar open M-F 3pm-4am, Sa noon-4am, Su noon-midnight.

**The Old Manly Boatshed,** 40 The Corso (☎02 9977 4443). A favorite haunt of the local pub-going crowd, this subterranean space is unassuming and great for a casual night out with a rowdy crowd. The best part is the live music on weekends and most week-nights. M comedy night is also popular. Open daily 6pm-3am.

**Ivanhoe of Manly,** 27 The Corso (☎02 9976 3955), opposite the fountain. This popular nightspot with 4 different levels fits any entertainment need. Downstairs, **Basebar Nightclub** spins techno, trance, and R&B on F and Sa nights, sometimes with a minimal cover charge. The ground-level lobby bar has live bands W-Sa (open M-Tu and Su 9am-midnight, W-Sa 9am-late). Upstairs, the dressier **Arriba Cocktail Lounge** plays house music. The top floor lounge welcomes a semi-trendy crowd. Open F-Sa 5pm-5am.

---

 **SYDNEY'S BEST CITY AND COASTAL WALKS**

**Opera House to Mrs. Macquaries Point.** This 20min. stroll along the edge of the lush Royal Botanic Gardens has one of the best views of the Opera House and the boat-filled harbor at Farm Cove.

**Across the Harbour Bridge.** You can cross the Harbour Bridge for free by foot, beginning in The Rocks near Argyle St. Once across the bridge in Kirribilli, walk downhill on Broughton St. for a spectacular harbor view.

**Hyde Park to Darling Harbour.** A 15min. walk down Market St. from either end leads you through the heart of the city and right by the Centrepoint Tower, Pitt Street Mall, Strand Arcade, and the Queen Victoria Building, as well as a number of designer shops.

**Bondi to Coogee.** This 1hr. coastal hike will take you along cliffs and through a cemetery for good views of Sydney's southern beaches.

**Manly to Spit.** A slightly strenuous 3hr. coastal walk that will give you a taste of bushland and the northern beaches.

**Mosman to Cremorne Wharf.** A picturesque 40min. walk along the harbor foreshore between 2 ferry wharves. Bring your swimsuit—the world's prettiest harborside pool is en route and open to the public year-round.

---

# DAYTRIPS FROM SYDNEY

Sydney's attractions are not limited to the city proper. The national parklands that encompass the surrounding hills and valleys are representative of the natural beauty for which the continent is known. If your stay in Oz is confined to Sydney, these daytrips offer a taste of the rest of the country.

**ROYAL NATIONAL PARK.** Just 32km south of Sydney's city center, Royal National Park is an easy escape from city life, with deserted beaches, quiet marshlands, and secluded rainforests. It's the world's second-oldest national park (after Yellowstone in the United States) and consists of more than 16,000 hectares of beach, heath, rainforest, and woodland, which contain 43 species of mammals and nearly 240 species of birds. **Escape Sydney Ecotours** (☎02 9664 3047; www.escapecotours.com.au) takes travelers from several pickup locations in

Sydney to the highlights of the park and offers a range of tour lengths and itineraries. Tours range from a half-day whale watching trek to a two-day coastal walking tour. Likewise, tours are offered through the **Royal National Park Visitors' Centre** located in the park in Audley, which is closest to the Engadine CityRail station. (☎ 02 9542 0648; www.npws.nsw.gov.au.) Again, a variety of tour lengths and difficulties are available, from a 3½hr. Aboriginal discovery tour to a rigorous 5hr. coastal hike. *(To get to the park by car, turn off the Princes Hwy. at Farnell Ave., south of Loftus, or at McKell Ave. at Waterfall. The route is clearly designated by signposts. $11 parking fee. CityRail trains run from Sydney to Loftus, Engadine, Heathcote, Waterfall, and Otford stations, which are located on the park's western edge and have trails leading into the park. $11. A ferry from Cronulla will get you to the park at Bundeena. ☎ 02 9523 2990.)*

**BOTANY BAY NATIONAL PARK.** Situated on the two peninsulas that form the entrance to Botany Bay, this historical national park is broken into a northern half **(La Pérouse)** and a southern half **(Kurnell)**. It's most well-known as the location of Captain Cook's landing in 1770, which can be seen on the 1.5km **Monument Track** in the southern Kurnell half. Also on this side, the **Banks-Solander Track** (1km), one of the most beautiful walks in the park, takes you past stunning sandstone cliffs and some of the same kinds of vegetation that Cook's botanist first studied. For a longer trek, take the **Cape Baily Track** (8km), which also passes many Cook-related sites. In the northern section, **La Pérouse Museum** documents the scientific expedition of French explorer the Comte de la Pérouse, who arrived in Botany Bay a mere week after Cook *(open W-Su, 10am-4pm)*. Finally, the **Bare Island Fort Tour** digs through the history of one of Sydney's earliest military forts, built in 1885. *(☎ 02 9247 5033. 45min.; meets at La Pérouse Museum; Su 1:30, 2:30, and 3:30pm. $10, concessions $8, family $25. Bookings not required. If you're arriving by car, drive to the end of Anzac Pde. to reach La Pérouse in the northern section of the park. To get to the park's southern end, take Rocky Point Rd. off the Princes Hwy., then Captain Cook Dr. in Kurnell. $7 parking fee. Buses #393 and 394 from Circular Quay run to La Pérouse in 55min., and bus #987 arrives at Captain Cook Dr. from Cronulla CityRail Station.)*

# PARRAMATTA                                                            ☎ 02

As Australia's second-oldest settlement, the bustling city of Parramatta is a mecca for lovers of Australian history. Several buildings from the early years of colonization have been refurbished to appear almost exactly as they did in the olden days. The **Old Government House** is located in Parramatta Park at the town's west end, and is the oldest public building in Australia. View the extensive collection of early colonial furniture by taking a tour. (☎ 02 9635 8149; www. nationaltrust.org.au. Open for guided tours only. M group bookings only, Tu-F 10am-4pm, Sa-Su 10:30am-4pm. $8, concessions $5, family $18. YHA discount available.) On the opposite side of town along the Harris Park Heritage Walk, **Elizabeth Farm,** 70 Alice St., was home to John and Elizabeth Macarthur, founders of the Australian merino wool industry. The farm is the oldest surviving European building in Australia. (☎ 02 9635 9488. Open F-Su 9:30am-4pm; group tours M-Th. $8, concessions $4, families $17.)

Parramatta has great dining options, with a variety of Lebanese, Vietnamese, and Thai cuisine, as well as numerous cafes. All of these are concentrated on Church St., where you're sure to find something that suits your fancy.

Parramatta is best reached from Sydney by way of a scenic 50min. **ferry** ride on the RiverCat pontoon (departs Wharf 5, $7.70). Otherwise the city is a 20min. drive along Parramatta Rd., which becomes the M4 Tollway at Strathfield, the most direct route to the Blue Mountains. CityRail also runs from the city center to Parramatta on the North Shore/Western Line and takes about 40min. Buses #L20 and 520 operate daily from Circular Quay to Parramatta

(1hr). Upon arrival, head to the **Parramatta Heritage Centre,** which has displays on Parramatta's history and people. The **Parramatta Visitors Centre,** 346 Church St., is conveniently located within the Heritage Centre. (☎02 8839 3311; www.parracity.nsw.gov.au. Open daily 9am-5pm.)

## PENRITH                                                              ☎02

Though the beauty of Penrith's outdoor offerings pales in comparison to that of the southern coast, the town is a good base for an introduction to the Blue Mountains. With a professional football team, a large shopping plaza, and commercial High St., Penrith maintains the urban feel of a city despite its diminutive size. Running through the western half of town, the placid Nepean River is a touch of beauty in an otherwise plain landscape. To get a first look at the Blue Mountains National Park, you can take a ride on the **Nepean Belle,** an old-time paddlewheel riverboat. (☎02 4733 1274; www.nepeanbelle.com.au. Departs Tench Reserve Park, off Tench Ave. in Penrith, with morning, afternoon, and dinner cruises. Shortest cruise 90min. $17.) For an aerial view of the Nepean River, follow Mulgoa Rd. south toward Wallacia and stop at **Rock Lookout.** Just across the river in Emu Plains, the **Penrith Regional Gallery & The Lewers Bequest,** 86 River Rd., showcases contemporary Australian sculptures in tidy gardens. (☎02 4735 1100. Open daily 10am-5pm. Free.)

**Explorers Lodge ❷,** 111 Station St., is Penrith's premier hostel, with spacious rooms, a kitchen, game room, TV lounge, BBQ, and payphone. (☎02 0419 229 473. Dorms $29; singles $48; doubles $70. Weekly rates available.)

To reach Penrith by car, travel west on the Great Western Hwy. (Hwy. 44). The North Shore/Western Line of the CityRail **trains** also runs to Penrith (1½hr.). The **Penrith Valley Visitors Centre,** on Mulgoa Rd., in the Panthers World of Entertainment Complex carpark, provides useful info on Penrith. (☎1300 736 836; www.penrithvalley.com.au. Open daily 9am-4:30pm.)

# KU-RING-GAI CHASE NATIONAL PARK

Founded in 1894, Ku-Ring-Gai Chase National Park is the second oldest national park in New South Wales (after the Royal National Park) and covers some 15,000 hectares of land traditionally occupied by the Guringai Aboriginal people. Today, visitors to the rugged park come for the numerous Aboriginal rock engravings, the bright wildflowers that bloom in early August, and the peace and quiet found beside hidden creeks and in the depths of the forest. Picnicking, sailing, and hiking are popular activities for visitors to the park.

**█▐ TRANSPORTATION AND PRACTICAL INFORMATION.** When visiting Ku-Ring-Gai Chase, it's much easier to access the park with a car, as public transportation will only get you to the park's entrances. Ku-Ring-Gai Chase Rd. from the Pacific Hwy. and Bobbin Head Rd. from Turramurra provide access to the southwest area of the park, while West Head Rd. runs through the eastern section. If you are arriving by public transportation from Sydney, you can reach the Bobbin Head Rd. entrance by taking the train to Turramurra (40min.), and then catching bus #577 from the station to the park gates at North Turramurra. Or from Wynyard, take bus #185 to arrive on McCarrs Creek Rd. or bus #L90 to Palm Beach Wharf, where you can catch a **ferry** to the park. Palm Beach Ferry Service (☎02 9974 2411; www.palmbeachferry.com.au) departs from Palm Beach and stops at The Basin, the park's camping area, every hour ($12.60 round-trip). Palm Cruises runs scenic cruises from Palm Beach to Bobbin Head. (☎02 9974 2411. Rates vary.) The Bobbin Head area in the southwest is home to the **Kalkari Visitors Centre,** on Ku-Ring-Gai Chase Rd., 3km inside the park gates. The center distributes free hiking maps and offers educational information on the park's wildlife. (☎02 9472 9300. Open daily 9am-5pm.) One kilometer farther, the **Bobbin Head Information Centre**, inside the **Bobbin Inn**, also distributes info about the park. (☎02 9472 8949. Open daily 10am-4pm.) Both centers run guided tours—call for schedule and details.

**♜ ACCOMMODATIONS.** The only place to camp is at **The Basin ❶.** You can get there on foot along **The Basin Track** (2.8km), by car on West Head Rd., or by the hourly ferry from Palm Beach. Campsites have cold showers, toilets, gas BBQ, and a public phone; all supplies other than bait and drinks must be carried in. Vehicles staying overnight require a special pass ($11). Booking is required and must be arranged through the NPWS 24hr. **automated reservation service.** (☎02 9974 1011. $14 per person, children $7). Certainly the most refreshing and remote hostel in the greater Sydney area, the **Pittwater YHA Hostel ❷** is set among greenery in a lofty, terraced perch over Pittwater. This open, outdoorsy hostel provides a secluded retreat where you'll need to bring your own food and linens. During the day, explore the national park, and at night, settle under the stars around the open fireplace or BBQ. To access the Pittwater YHA, take a ferry or water taxi from Church Pt. to Halls Wharf, then walk uphill along the path for 15 minutes. To reach Church Pt., drive along Pittwater Rd., take bus #156 from Manly (1hr.), or take bus #E86 from Wynyard (1hr.) in the city. (☎02 9999 5748. Dorms $25-28, twin/double $64.50-72. Booking ahead required.)

**⚲ OUTDOOR ACTIVITIES.** The **Discovery Walk** (20min.; wheelchair-accessible), just outside the Kalkari Visitors Centre, is a quick and easy way to spot a few kangaroos, emus, and some native plant life. A moderately difficult **bushwalk** (10km) begins at the Bobbin Head Rd. entrance to the park and follows the **Sphinx-Warrimoo Track** (6.5km) to Bobbin Head. The hike can be made into a circuit by taking the **Bobbin Head Track** (3.5km) back to the park entrance. The bushwalk passes through mangroves, along a creek, and near an Aboriginal engraving site. The **Basin Bay Track** and **Mackerel Track** at West Head are both moderately difficult hikes that feature stunning Aboriginal engraving sites accessible by West Head Rd. Rock engravings, up to 8m long, depict mythical beings and whales. For the best views of the Hawkesbury River as it feeds into Broken Bay, head north along West Head Rd. until you reach the ◪**West Head Lookout.** For an outstanding view of Sydney and Pittwater, head to the recently restored **Barrenjoey Lighthouse** back across the water at the tip of Palm Beach and tackle the steep climb to the top. (Tours are offered on Su every 30min. from 11am-3pm. $3, children $2.)

# BLUE MOUNTAINS

The gorgeous Blue Mountains region is Sydney's favorite escape, a tourist wonderland just outside the city, yet very much away from it all. Although a variety of adventure activities, such as abseiling and canyon rafting, have become popular in recent years, the primary draw of the Blue Mountains remains its excellent hiking. The remarkable blue color of the hazy valleys and ridges is the result of sunlight filtering through the eucalyptus oil in the air. From lookout points along canyon edges, the earth falls away to endless blue foliage speckled with white bark and bordered by distant sandstone cliffs.

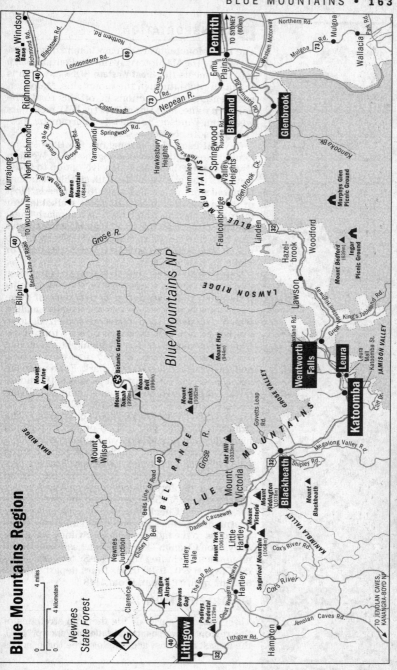

**Blue Mountains Region**

Newnes
State Forest

4 miles
4 kilometers

## LOCAL LEGEND

### THE THREE SISTERS

The Blue Mountains, spanning over 200,000 hectares, are beautiful to behold. Their name comes from the distinctive blue haze produced by a combination of tiny droplets of eucalyptus oil, dust particles, and water vapor, which scatter rays of light predominantly blue in color.

The unusual mist lends an eerie glow to the area, made more otherworldly by the myriad Aboriginal tales that explain the park's unusual formations.

Among the most famous of these stories is the legend of the Three Sisters, one of the mountains' main attractions. It tells the tragic story of "Meehni," "Wimlah," and "Gunnedoo," members of the Aboriginal Katoomba tribe. Legend has it that the sisters had fallen in love with brothers from another tribe, and tribal law forbade them to marry.

A battle ensued when the brothers tried to fight for their loves. Sensing the danger, a witchdoctor cast a spell over the sisters to protect them. He turned them into stone and set them high above the mountain valley, intending to return them to human form after the battle.

But it was not to be. The witchdoctor was killed in the battle, and the sisters are cast in stone for all eternity. They still preside over the valley today, their plight a symbol of the ancient battle and a sad reminder of the love they were never able to share.

## ▣ TRANSPORTATION

The Blue Mountains are an easy 90min. drive west of Sydney. The M4 Motorway runs to Penrith ($2.20 toll) and meets the **Great Western Highway,** which is the main route through the mountains. Many service centers and attractions lie off this road. The northern route, **Bells Line of Road** (p. 174), meanders west from Windsor, northeast of Parramatta, providing a more scenic passage.

CityRail **trains** stop throughout the Blue Mountains at most of the towns along the Great Western Hwy., offering the least expensive option to those travelers who are willing to walk sizable distances from rail stations and bus stops to trailheads. Most of the in-town distances are easily walkable. For more direct access to the trails at a similarly inexpensive price, use the local **Blue Mountains Buses** (for bus info, see **Katoomba,** p. 165). There are no public transportation options to Kanangra-Boyd or Wollemi National Park.

There are three above-average companies that run small bus tours into the Blue Mountains from Sydney. The advantage to using one of these companies is that the groups are usually smaller, which translates to a more personalized, less-touristy experience. **Wonderbus** offers a tour of the Blue Mountains that covers highlights including the mountains, a RiverCat ferry ride, wine tasting, and the Featherdales Wildlife Park. For a more leisurely pace, opt for the overnight stay in the mountains. (☎1300 556 357. Departs daily at 7:15am, returns 6pm. Blue Mountains tour $105, $129 with lunch. ISIC/NOMADS/VIP/YHA discounts.) The **OzTrails** tour takes you and 23 others to regional highlights and provides tea and lunch. (☎1300 853 842; www.oztrails.com.au. Departs 8am, returns 6pm. $68, $83 with lunch.) **Wildframe Ecotours** provides similar services and offers a trip into Grand Canyon, a rainforest-filled gorge in Blackheath. (☎02 9440 9915. $85, ages 14 and under $55, concessions $76.) Check with each company for their overnight offerings. Several companies run large-bus tours to the mountains from Sydney. **AAT Kings,** Jetty 6, on Circular Quay, offers a basic tour of the mountains, including the Three Sisters and Jenolan Caves. (☎02 9700 0133. Tours depart approx. 8:30am, return 6:45pm. From $148.)

## ▣ ORIENTATION

Three national parks divide the wild stretches of the region. **Blue Mountains National Park** (p. 172), the largest and most accessible of the three, spans most of the **Jamison Valley** (south of the Great Western Hwy. between Glenbrook and Katoomba), the **Megalong Valley** (south of the Great Western Hwy., west of Katoomba), and the **Grose Valley** (north of the Great Western Hwy. and east of Blackheath). The Grose and Jamison Valleys appeal primarily to hikers, while horseback riders favor the Megalong Valley (for more information on horseback riding, see **Blackheath,** p. 170). **Kanangra-Boyd National Park** (p. 175), tucked between two sections of the Blue Mountains in the southwest reaches of the park, is reserved for skilled bushwalkers. The park is accessible by partially paved roads from Oberon and from Jenolan Caves. **Wollemi National Park** (p. 175) contains the state's largest preserved wilderness area. It's so unspoiled that a species of pine tree thought to be long extinct was found here in 1994. Access to Wollemi, which abuts the north side of Bells Line of Road, is available at Bilpin and at several points north of the central Blue Mountains.

The national parks of the Blue Mountains region are administered by different branches of the National Parks and Wildlife Services (NPWS). If you are planning to bushcamp or drive into these parks, contact the appropriate NPWS branch a few days in advance to ensure that no bushfire bans are in place and that the roads are drivable (this is important; roads are closed fairly often). For a great all-in-one resource on the Blue Mountain region, including up-to-the-minute weather reports and detailed advice on all outdoor activities, go to www.bluemts.com.au. It is also highly recommended that you leave a bushwalk plan filed with the appropriate NPWS office before you go.

# KATOOMBA                                          ☎02

Quite possibly the best gateway to Blue Mountains National Park, Katoomba (pop. 9000) offers excellent hiking, climbing, and biking opportunities in a convenient, rail-accessible location. Though popular with the tourist crowd, Katoomba still harbors a distinctly alternative flavor in its quaint antique shops and fire-lit cafes. The image most widely associated with the Blue Mountains is that of the Three Sisters, a trio of towering outcroppings jutting out into the Jamison Valley, holding silent vigil over the blue-green expanse below. Visitors can marvel at the formation at Echo Point, in the south end of Katoomba.

## ▐▀ TRANSPORTATION

**Trains: Katoomba Railway Station** is on Main St., at the north end of Katoomba St. **City-Rail** (☎13 15 00) and **Countrylink** (☎13 22 32) trains run to: **Bathurst** (2hr., 7 per day, $13.60); **Blackheath** (13min., 17-23 per day, $3.40); **Glenbrook** (50min., 18-28 per day, $5.60); **Lithgow** (45min., 12-15 per day, $6.60); **Mount Victoria** (20min., 12-15 per day, $4); **Parramatta** (1hr., 20-29 per day, $10.60); **Penrith** (1hr., 19-26 per day, $6.60); **Sydney** (2hr., 20-29 per day, $12.20); **Zig Zag Railway** (45min., 2 per day, $5.60; be sure to request this stop with the guard at the rear of the train). **Mountainlink** (☎02 4782 3333) runs to Leura ($3) and Mount Victoria ($5.30).

**Local and Park Transportation: Blue Mountains Bus Company** (☎02 4782 4213) connects Katoomba to Wentworth Station, with stops near Echo Point, the Edge Cinema, Leura Mall, the Valley of the Waters trailhead, Scenic World, and Wentworth Falls. Regular service M-F approx. 7:30am-6pm, Sa-Su 7:30am-3pm. $2-8. The double-decker **Blue Mountains Explorer Bus** (☎02 4782 1866; www.explorerbus.com.au) runs a 27-stop circuit. Passengers to get on and off as often as they choose. Buses run daily every hr. 9:45am-5:15pm. Day pass $33, concession $28, children $16.50, family $82.50. Timetables for both services are at the Blue Mountains Tourism Authority on Echo Point. Stops opposite the Carrington Hotel on Main St.) **Mountainlink Trolley Tours** (☎1800 801 577; www.trolleytours.com.au) runs the cheapest area bus tours, with all-day

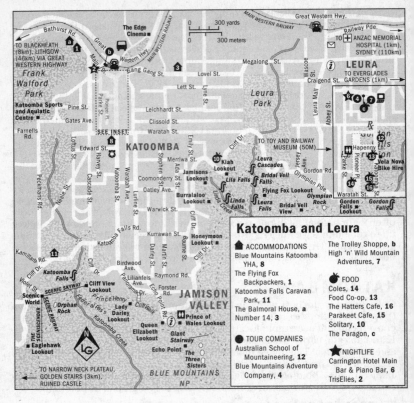

**Katoomba and Leura**

**⬛ ACCOMMODATIONS**
Blue Mountains Katoomba
YHA, **8**
The Flying Fox
Backpackers, **1**
Katoomba Falls Caravan
Park, **11**
The Balmoral House, **a**
Number 14, **3**

**⬤ TOUR COMPANIES**
Australian School of
Mountaineering, **12**
Blue Mountains Adventure
Company, **4**

The Trolley Shoppe, **b**
High 'n' Wild Mountain
Adventures, **7**

**◆ FOOD**
Coles, **14**
Food Co-op, **13**
The Hatters Cafe, **16**
Parakeet Cafe, **15**
Solitary, **10**
The Paragon, **c**

**★ NIGHTLIFE**
Carrington Hotel Main
Bar & Piano Bar, **6**
TrisElies, **2**

access and unlimited stops throughout the Leura and Katoomba areas for $20. Tickets are available at **The Trolley Shoppe,** 285 Main St. (☎02 4782 7999).

**Taxis: Katoomba Cabs** (☎02 4782 1311) picks up 24hr. anywhere between Wentworth Falls and Mt. Victoria.

**Bike Rental: Velo Nova,** 182 Katoomba St. (☎02 4782 2800). Mountain bikes ½-day $28, full day $50. Helmets, locks, and repair kits included. YHA/backpacker 10% discount. Open M and W-Su 9am-5:30pm.

## ▚ 🛈 ORIENTATION AND PRACTICAL INFORMATION

Katoomba sits just south of the Great Western Hwy., 2km west of Leura and 110km from Sydney. The town's main drag, **Katoomba Street,** runs south from the Katoomba Railway Station toward **Echo Point,** where Echo Point Rd. leads to the Blue Mountain's most touristed trio, the Three Sisters. **Main Street,** the hub for tourism and nightlife, runs along the north side of town by the rail station. It becomes Bathurst Rd. to the west and Gang Gang St. to the east.

**Tourist Office: Blue Mountains Tourism** (☎1300 653 408; www.bluemountainstourism. org.au), at the end of Echo Point Rd. Take Lurline St. south and veer left onto Echo Rd. While most of this center is a gift shop, there are stacks of free brochures on area activities in the back. Open daily 9am-5pm. For friendly hiking advice, talk to park rangers; try the NPWS Blue Mountain Heritage Center in **Blackheath** (p. 170).

**Hospital: Blue Mountains District Anzac Memorial Hospital** (☎02 4784 6500), on the Great Western Hwy., 1km east of the railway station.

**Internet Access: Katoomba Book Exchange,** 34 Katoomba St. (☎02 4782 9997). $2.60 per 15min., $1.70 per 10min. Open daily 10am-6pm.

**Post Office:** (☎13 13 18), 14 Pioneer Pl. Open M-F 9am-5pm. **Postal Code:** 2780.

# ♠ ACCOMMODATIONS

Although beds are plentiful, so are vacationers between November and April, as well as on winter weekends. Book ahead during these times.

▩ **Blue Mountains Katoomba YHA,** 207 Katoomba St. (☎02 4782 1416), 10min. walk downhill from the train station. With a kitchen, dining and common areas, pool table, TV and video lounge, and terrace, this hostel fills up fast. Helpful staff provides heaps of info. Internet access $2 per 30min. Key deposit $20. Linen included. Reception 7am-10pm. Dorms $26-30; doubles $73-84, ensuite $82-94. YHA discount. ❷

▩ **The Balmoral House,** 196 Bathurst Rd. (☎02 4782 2264), 5min. walk west of train station. This charming Victorian mansion is the oldest guesthouse in the Blue Mountains, offering superb hospitality and an unbeatable three-course breakfast. Ten stylish rooms, many of which open onto a wrap-around veranda, are expensive but worth the splurge. At night, curl up in the cozy parlor with some coffee and listen to tunes from the 1940s. Rooms M-Th and Su $130-170, F-Sa $150-190. ❺

**Number 14,** 14 Lovel St. (☎02 4782 7104; www.bluemts.com.au/no14). Small yellow house 5min. from train station. Quiet, friendly atmosphere with homey kitchen and comfortable furnishings. Offers a fully self-sufficient house for 10. Reception 9-11am and 5-8:30pm. Dorms $22-25; doubles $59-69, ensuite $69-79. ❷

**The Flying Fox Backpackers,** 190 Bathurst Rd. (☎02 4782 4226 or 1800 624 226; www.theflyingfox.com.au), 5min. walk west of the station. Fun, friendly, and aimed at a young crowd, this mellow hostel has a small kitchen, dining area with TV, common room with log fire, and outdoor chill-out hut with BBQ. Free luggage storage. Free Wi-Fi, Internet, and breakfast. Check online for last-minute discounts. Key deposit $10. Sites $17; dorms $25; twins and doubles $65. No ensuites. Weekly/VIP/YHA discounts. ❷

**Katoomba Falls Caravan Park** (☎02 4782 1835), on Katoomba Falls Rd., south of town via Katoomba St. Great location for bushwalks and Scenic World. Toilets, hot showers, indoor BBQ, laundry, and children's playground. No linen. Key deposit $20. Reception 8am-7pm. Sites $12.70 per person, $16.20 powered; cabins for 2 $77, ensuite $83-89; families $26.60/34.70/97.20/103. ❶

# ◖ FOOD

For small-town mountain shops, the eateries on Katoomba St. are incredibly varied—cozy cafes, organic markets, pizza spots, and kebab takeaway all line the street. A **Coles** supermarket is located next to K-Mart on Parke St., parallel to Katoomba St. (open daily 7am-midnight).

▩ **The Hatters Cafe,** 197 Katoomba St. (☎02 4782 4212). Attached to the Hattery store. Delicious meals, friendly waitstaff, and a pleasant atmosphere make this one of the best cafes in Katoomba. Caters to special diets including wheat-free, dairy-free, vegetarian, and vegan. Try the hotcakes with vanilla rhubarb and yogurt ($13) or the pumpkin-macadamia nut soup ($10). Open M-Sa 8am-5pm, Su 8am-4pm. ❷

**Solitary,** 90 Cliff Dr. (☎02 4782 1164), set on clifftop border between Katoomba and Leura. Tucked in at the end of a cliff walk, Solitary's kiosk-restaurant combo overlooks the Blue Mountain wilderness. Brunch ($9-11), salads, and sandwiches ($10-20) are common fare at the cafe, but it's an elegant affair in the restaurant, with meals such as lemon-garlic king prawns with linguine ($22.50). The restaurant menu changes seasonally. Kiosk open daily 10am-4pm, winter M-F 11am-4pm, Sa-Su 10am-4pm; restaurant open for lunch Sa-Su noon-3pm, dinner W-Su 6:30pm-9pm. ❹

**Parakeet Cafe,** 195b Katoomba St. (☎02 4782 1815), next door to The Hatters Cafe. With a cheery, colorful decor and brightly painted tables, this technicolor tearoom whips up sandwiches ($5-8), soup, and yummy, substantial schnitzel ($15). Internet and takeaway available. Open M-F 10am-5:30pm, Sa-Su 9am-6pm. ❶

**The Paragon,** 65 Katoomba St. (☎02 4782 2928). This iconic cafe, restaurant, and chocolatier opened in 1916, and its Art Deco interior carries the spirit of that decade. Perfect for a an afternoon coffee or tea ($4-6). On your way out, indulge in a box of chocolates. Open daily 9am-4:30pm. ❶

**Food Co-Op** (☎02 4782 5890), on Hapenny Ln. off Katoomba St. behind the post office. This mini-market scoops out heaping selections of organic fruits, nuts, and wheats (prices by kilo), and sells interesting energy bars. Open M-W and F 9am-5:30pm, Th 9am-6:30pm, Sa 8:30am-6pm, Su 10am-4:30pm. YHA 10% discount. ❶

## 🎵 🎭 ENTERTAINMENT AND NIGHTLIFE

**The Edge Maxvision Cinema,** 225 Great Western Hwy., a 10min. walk from the rail station, projects **The Edge**—a 38min. IMAX/3D film about the Blue Mountains— onto a six-story screen. The movie, which focuses on the fragile ecosystem of the Blue Mountains, shows viewers several places inaccessible to visitors, including the secret grove where the Wollemi Pine was discovered. The cinema also shows other giant-format and recent feature films. The Blue Mountains movie airs daily at 10:20, 11:05am, 12:10, 1:30, 2:15, and 5:30pm. (☎02 4782 8900. The Edge: $14.50; concessions $12.50; children, seniors, and YHA $9.50. Other films: M and W-Su $12.50/11.50/9.50, Tu $8.50.) **Outdoor markets**—where used clothing, flea market finds, and mountain-area produce are sold—run year-round in the Blue Mountains region. The markets tend to be hit or miss, but are a good place to stop by if you happen to be in town on the weekend. In Katoomba, they are held on the first and fourth Saturday of each month at the Civic Centre; the first Sunday of each month at the Leura Public School on the Great Western Hwy. in Leura; the second Sunday of each month at Wentworth Falls School of Arts, on the Great Western Hwy. in Wentworth Falls; the third Sunday of each month at the Community Hall on the Great Western in Blackheath; and on the second Saturday of each month on Macquarie Ave. in Springwood. Most open at 9am and close between 2 and 3pm.

Katoomba's nightlife revolves around the area by the rail station. The historic **Carrington Hotel,** 15-47 Katoomba St., runs two bars: a small, mellow piano bar with live music from Thursday to Sunday next to the Carrington Place on Katoomba St. (open M-Th noon-10pm, F-Sa noon-midnight, Su noon-8:30pm), and a large pub with an upstairs nightclub at 86 Main St. (☎02 4782 1111. Pub open M-Th 11am-1:30am, F-Sa 11am-5am, Su noon-10pm. Nightclub open Sa until 5am. Cover $5.) **TrisElies,** 287 Bathurst Rd., next to the rail station—not to be confused with the Greek restaurant by the same name on Main St.—is Katoomba's nightclub, drawing a younger crowd with DJs and live bands. (☎02 4782 1217. Open Th-Sa 9pm-late, Su until midnight. Cover F up to $20, Sa $7.)

## 🏞 LOOKOUTS, WALKS, AND ACTIVITIES

**ECHO POINT.** Nearly everyone who visits the Blue Mountains ventures out to Echo Point, at the southernmost tip of Katoomba, to take in the geological grandeur of the **Three Sisters.** According to Aboriginal legend, the Three Sisters are beautiful maidens trapped since The Dreaming (Aboriginal creation period) in stone pillars. After sunset, strategically placed floodlights lend a surreal brilliance to these three golden dames (dusk-11pm). There are numerous short trails and dramatic overlooks in the Echo Point area, but if you're up for a longer, more demanding circuit, descend the steep and taxing 860-step **Giant Stairway Walk** (2hr.) down the back of the Three Sisters and connect up with the **Federal Pass Trail.** At the trail junction, turn right and follow Federal Pass as it snakes its way through the Jamison Valley and past the base of Katoomba Falls and the beautiful, free-standing pillar known as **Orphan Rock.** Just beyond the base of Orphan Rock are three ways out of the valley. You can hike the seemingly endless **Furber Steps** and ascend through sandstone and clay rock formations, past the spray of waterfalls and through rainforest foliage; or you can buy a ticket for the adrenaline rush of the mechanized **Scenic Railway** (see below) or walk ten minutes along the boardwalk to the sleek, steady **Scenic Cableway** (see below). From the top of the canyon, it's also possible to return to Echo Point via the Prince Henry Cliff Walk.

**SCENIC WORLD.** At the corner of Violet St. and Cliff Dr., this touristy transportation hub offers three perspectives on the Blue Mountains region. The **Scenic Railway** (10min. one-way), the world's steepest inclined passenger-railway, is an attraction in its own right. Originally designed to haul unappreciative chunks of coal, its 52° pitch now thrills tourists and hikers during a very short trip in or out of the Jamison Valley ($10 one-way, children $5). The large, transparent **Scenic Cableway** cable car coasts from clifftop to valley floor and vice versa, offering passengers view of the Jamison Valley ($10 one-way). Both the Scenic Cableway and the Scenic Railway link up with popular hikes around **Echo Point** and down in the valley (see above). Finally, the **Scenic Skyway** is a cable gondola suspended over the Katoomba Falls Gorge. Passengers can watch the valley fly beneath their feet through the glass square on the gondola floor ($10 one-way). Visit the Scenic World Top Station to see a number of combined tickets. (☎02 4780 0200; www.scenicworld.com.au. Open daily 9am-5pm. Rides depart approx. every 10min.)

**NARROW NECK PLATEAU.** Jutting out and separating the Jamison Valley and the Megalong Valley, the Narrow Neck Plateau offers short and long walks, excellent mountain biking, and lookouts with spectacular panoramic views. To reach the plateau by car, follow Cliff Dr. west out of Katoomba. Just past the Landslide Lookout, turn right onto the gravel Glen Raphael Dr. You can drive about 1.5km along Narrow Neck up to a locked gate, but the next 7km is for walkers or cyclists only. One kilometer after the Cliff Dr. turnoff is the trailhead for the **Golden Stairs.** This track runs down the cliff face and intersects the Federal Pass track. To get to the Scenic Railway turn left at the bottom of the stairs. Reach **Ruined Castle** (5-6hr. round-trip), a rock formation reminiscent of crumbling turrets, by turning right at the bottom and following the path to the Ruined Castle turnoff on the right. At the Ruined Castle, a short climb to the top yields views of distant parts of the Blue Mountains and Kanangra-Boyd National Parks. On the return from Ruined Castle, some walkers avoid going back up the Golden Stairs and continue east instead to the Scenic Railway (see above). If you do this, add another hour to your itinerary.

 **TOURS**

Several companies in Katoomba organize adventure trips throughout the Blue Mountains. Most are clustered at the top of Katoomba St. across from the rail station. Prices are similar across companies.

NEW SOUTH WALES

**High 'n' Wild Mountain Adventures,** 3/5 Katoomba St. (☎02 4782 6224; www.high-n-wild.com.au). ½-day and full-day adventures in abseiling, rock climbing, mountain-biking, and canyoning. ½-day $100-150, full-day from $130. Winter ice-climbing courses by demand. Student/backpacker/YHA discounts. Open daily 8:30am-5:30pm.

**River Deep, Mountain High,** 2/187 Katoomba St. (☎02 4782 6109; www.rdmh.com.au), above Mountain Style Clothing. Offers a wide range of adventure trips including canyoning, bushwalking, photo safaris, abseiling, 4WD tours, and the 6-Foot Track Hike. Named a NSW Tourism Award Finalist in 2006-07 and 2007-08. Open daily 9am-5pm.

**Blue Mountains Adventure Company,** 84a Bathurst Rd. (☎02 4782 1271; www.bmac.com.au), opposite the rail station. Offers abseiling (full day $145), canyoning ($165-235), rock climbing ($175-185), and mountain biking ($190). Check the website for combined adventure packages and seasonal specials. Open daily 9am-5pm.

**Australian School of Mountaineering,** 166 Katoomba St. (☎02 4782 2014; www.asmguides.com), inside the Paddy Pallin outdoor shop. Offers introductory and advanced technical courses and tours in abseiling, canyoning, rock-climbing, ice-climbing, and survival and navigation. Check website for specific dates and fees. All-day abseiling or canyoning trips $175-190. YHA discount. Open daily 9am-5:30pm.

**Blue Mountains Walkabout** (☎04 0844 3822; www.bluemountainswalkabout.com). Evan, who is part Darug, leads a challenging 8hr. bushwalk to Aboriginal ceremonial and living spaces, with ochre body painting, sample bush tucker, and boomerang lessons along the way. Begins at Faulconbridge rail station, ends at Springwood rail station. Tours leave daily at 10am. 14+ $95. Bookings essential; max. 10 people per tour.

**Tread Lightly Eco-Tours** (☎02 4788 1229; www.treadlightly.com.au). One of few tour operators with National Advanced Ecotourism accreditation. Focuses on ecology, flora and fauna, history, and Aboriginal culture of Blue Mountains. Tours include wilderness walks, Grand Canyon walks, and 4WD tours. YHA discount.

# BLACKHEATH                                                            ☎02

Blackheath's location, sandwiched between two beautiful valleys, makes it a natural choice as a Blue Mountains gateway. However, its tiny town center has limited services and few adventure trips. Travelers without cars will probably prefer more-accessible Katoomba and Leura.

**🖂🔲 TRANSPORTATION AND PRACTICAL INFORMATION.** The Great Western Hwy. snakes 11km from Katoomba to Blackheath en route to Mt. Victoria and Lithgow. **Blue Mountains Buses** (#698) runs from Katoomba to Mt. Victoria via Blackheath and comes as close as possible to the town's major trailheads. (☎02 4782 4213. M-F 7:30am-6pm, Sa 6:30am-4:30pm.) **CityRail** train service connects Blackheath to: **Glenbrook** (1hr., 15-22 per day, $6.60); **Katoomba** (11min., 15-23 per day, $3.40); **Lithgow** (30min., 12 per day, $5.60); **Parramatta** (1½hr., 15-20 per day, $11); **Penrith** (1hr., 15-20 per day, $8.60); **Sydney** (2½hr., 15-20 per day, $13.60). Blackheath Station is 3km from the Govetts Leap trailhead.

Travelers can get regional tourist information from **Blue Mountains Tourism,** at Echo Point, Katoomba (☎1300 653 408). Questions about Blue Mountains National Park, Wollemi National Park, and Kanangra-Boyd National Park are best handled by the NPWS-run **Blue Mountains Heritage Centre,** at the roundabout near the end of Govetts Leap Rd. The center also has exhibits, detailed trail guides ($2-4), and refreshments. (☎02 4787 8877. Open daily 9am-4:30pm.)

**🖂🔲 ACCOMMODATIONS AND FOOD. The New Ivanhoe Hotel ❸,** at the corner of the Great Western Hwy. and Govetts Leap Rd., has clean, tasteful rooms. (☎02 4782 2652. Continental breakfast included; full breakfast $7. Reception at bar. Weekday single with shared bathroom $33; double $66; ensuite $44/$88. Weekend (F-Su) shared bathroom $66, ensuite $88.) Downstairs, the **Bistro** ❶ is a great place for a delectable meal, with pies and sandwiches ($6-9) and heartier main meals like lasagna ($14.50-17.50). Takeaway is also available. (☎02 4787 7507.) **Blackheath Caravan Park** ❶, on Prince Edward St. off Govetts Leap Rd., opposite Memorial Park, has toilets, showers, and BBQ. (☎02 4787 8101. Key deposit $10. Reception 8am-8pm. Sites $11.60, powered $15.05; cabins $46.30, ensuite (min. 3-night stay) $62.40. No linens or towels.) There are two NPWS **camping areas** ❶ accessible from Blackheath: **Perrys Lookdown,** 8km from the Great Western Hwy. at the end of the mostly unpaved Hat Hill Rd. (5 walk-in sites; max. 1-night stay), and **Acacia Flat,** on the Grose Valley floor, a 4hr. hike from Govetts Leap and a 2-3hr. hike from Perrys Lookdown. Both sites are free and lack facilities beyond pit toilets. Campfires are not permitted. Water from Govetts Creek is available at Acacia Flat, but must be treated. There is no reliable water source at Perrys Lookdown.

🖾 **HIKES AND LOOKOUTS.** Walks in the Blackheath area vary widely in length and level of difficulty. The **Fairfax Heritage Track** (1hr., 2km) is wheelchair-accessible and leads to **Govetts Leap,** one of the most magnificent lookouts in Blue Mountains National Park. From Govetts Leap, the moderate **Pulpit Rock Track** (3hr., 5km circuit) follows the cliff line north for spectacular views along the way of Horseshoe Falls and a fantastic view of the Grose Valley from the Pulpit Rock lookout. The **Cliff Top Walk** travels the other direction to Evans Lookout (1hr. round-trip) past the wispy Govetts Leap Falls, a thin stream that takes nearly 10 seconds to tumble all the way into the valley below. The moderate **Grand Canyon Walking Track** (5km; 3-4hr. round-trip) is undoubtedly one of the most popular hikes in all the Blue Mountains. You can start at either Neates Glen or Evans Lookout, but if you need to park a car, leave it at the Grand Canyon Loop Carpark along the Evans Lookout Rd. The circuit passes through sandstone cliffs, wet rainforest, and exposed heathland. Archaeological evidence suggests that Aboriginals occupied the Grand Canyon at least 12,000 years ago and used the route to gather chert (a quartzite rock) at the base of Beauchamp Falls. Six kilometers north of Blackheath along the Great Western Hwy. is Hat Hill Rd., a mostly dirt route that bumps and bounces to an excellent lookout and a popular trailhead for the **Blue Gum Forest** (5½hr., 5km, expert-only). Near the end of the road, the turnoff leading to the parking area for Anvil Rock and the magical features of the misnamed Wind Eroded Cave (water was the culprit, actually) is well worth the side trip.

The scenic drive into the Megalong Valley begins on Shipley Rd., across the Great Western Hwy. from Govett's Leap Rd. Cross the railroad tracks from the highway and take an immediate left onto Station St., following it until it turns right onto Shipley Rd. Megalong Rd. is a left turn from Shipley Rd., leading down to a picturesque farmland area that contrasts with the surrounding wilderness. In the valley, outfitters supply horses and conduct guided trail rides. **Werriberri Trail Rides** is 10km along Megalong Rd. near Werriberri Lodge. (☎02 4787 9171; www.australianbluehorserides.com.au. Open daily 9am-3:30pm. $48 per 1hr.; $65 per 1½hr.; $90 per 2hr. 2-9 day rides by request $190-230. Prices per person.) The **Megalong Australian Heritage Centre,** a bit farther south on Megalong Rd., is an aspiring cowboy's dream. The sprawling country-western ranch features upscale accommodations, an affordable restaurant that serves modern Australian cuisine, a friendly staff, livestock-lassoing shows, guided horseback riding tours, and guided 4WD bush trips. It also rents horses and 4WD vehicles for self-guided tours on more than 2000 acres of land. Inquire about job offerings. (☎02 4787 8188; www.megalong.

NEW SOUTH WALES

cc. Open daily 8am-5:30pm. Photo/4WD tours $125-195, depending on length. Horseback rides 30min. $30, 1hr. $45, 2hr. $80, ½-day to full day $100-195.)

# BLUE MOUNTAINS NATIONAL PARK

The largest and most-touristed of the Blue Mountain parks, the **Blue Mountains National Park,** is one of eight protected areas making up the World Heritage site collectively known as the Greater Blue Mountains Area.

| BLUE MOUNTAINS AT A GLANCE | |
| --- | --- |
| **AREA:** 208,756 hectares. | **GATEWAYS:** Blackheath (p. 170), Glenbrook (p. 172), Katoomba (p. 165). |
| **FEATURES:** Govetts Leap (Blackheath), Three Sisters (Katoomba), Wentworth Falls, Bridal Veil View (Leura) | **CAMPING:** Minimum-impact camping allowed; see individual regions. |
| **HIGHLIGHTS:** Over 140km bushwalking trails, horseback riding, canyoning, and riding the world's steepest railway. | **FEES:** Vehicles $7 (Glenbrook only). |

## ORIENTATION AND PRACTICAL INFORMATION

Blue Mountains National Park lies between Kanangra-Boyd National Park to the south and Wollemi National Park to the north. Two east-west highways partition the park into three sections: the section north of the **Bells Line of Road,** the section south of the **Great Western Highway,** and the section between the two.

    **Blue Mountains Tourism** operates offices in Glenbrook and Katoomba. (☎1300 653 408; www.australiabluemountains.com.au. Glenbrook open daily 9am-4:30pm. Katoomba open daily 9am-5pm.) The NPWS-run **Blue Mountains Heritage Centre,** at the roundabout near the end of Govetts Leap Rd. in Blackheath, handles questions regarding the parks. (☎02 4787 8877. Open daily 9am-4:30pm.)

## BLUE MOUNTAINS: A TOWN-BY-TOWN GUIDE

### ALONG THE GREAT WESTERN HIGHWAY

Leaving Sydney, the Great Western Hwy. passes Penrith just before the entrance to the Blue Mountains National Park. It extends to Lithgow, passing Katoomba and Blackheath on its way through the park.

**GLENBROOK.** Glenbrook is a gateway town just north of the easternmost entrance to the park. From the highway, take Ross St. until it ends, turn left on Burfitt Pde. (later named Bruce Rd.), and follow it to the park. The walking track to Red Hands Cave starts at the National Park entrance station and runs an easy 8km circuit that follows a creek through patches of open forest, leading ultimately to a gallery of hand stencils attributed to the Darug tribe. Along the way to the cave, the trail passes the turnoff for Jellybean Pool, a popular swimming hole near the park's entrance. You can reduce the length of the hike to a mere 300m stroll if you drive to the Red Hands carpark and begin there.

    The **Tourist Information Centre,** off the Great Western Hwy., is a convenient place to pick up maps and information about the Blue Mountains before heading further into the region. (☎1300 653 408. Open daily 9am-4:30pm.) Four kilometers beyond the Bruce Rd. entrance, over mostly paved roads, is the **Euroka Campground ❶.** The site has pit toilets and BBQ, and tap water is available at the park entrance. Kangaroos congregate in the area at dawn and dusk. The park entrance is locked in the evenings (in summer 7pm-8:30am; in winter

6pm-8:30am); campers are advised to bring ample firewood, food, and drinking water. Call the **NPWS** in Richmond to book ahead. (☎02 4588 5247. Open M-F 9am-5pm. Sites $10, children $5. Vehicles $7 per day.) On weekends, contact the **Glenbrook Office.** (☎02 4739 2950. Open Sa-Su 8:30am-3:30pm.)

**BLAXLAND.** At Blaxland, roughly 4km west of Glenbrook, Layton Ave. turns off onto a pleasant 2km detour toward Lennox Bridge, the oldest bridge on the Australian mainland. West of Blaxland (and the towns of Warrimoo, Valley Heights, and Springwood) lies Faulconbridge, site of the National Trust-owned **Norman Lindsay Gallery,** at 14 Norman Lindsay Cres. The gallery displays a large collection of sculptures, oil paintings, etchings, and marionettes by the multi-talented artist who once lived here. To get to the gallery from Sydney, turn right off the Great Western Hwy. onto Grose Rd., in Falconbridge, and follow the signs. (☎02 4751 1067. Open daily 10am-4pm. $9, concessions $6.) Public transportation to the site is limited to taxis from the Springwood Railway Station.

**WENTWORTH FALLS.** The town of Wentworth Falls is renowned for its picturesque waterfall walks and plant diversity—more varieties of plants are found in the Blue Mountains than in all of Europe. To find the trailhead at the Wentworth Falls Picnic Area, turn off the Great Western Hwy. onto Falls Rd. and continue to the end of the road. From this area, several viewpoints are within easy reach. The 15min. (1km, return) walk to **Princes Rock** offers the best views for the least effort. It ends at a lookout with views of Wentworth Falls, Kings Tableland, and Mt. Solitary. The 45min. (2km, return) walk to **Rocket Point Lookout** wanders through open heathland and has views of the Jamison Valley. Finally, the 30min. walk to **Weeping Rock and Queen's Cascade** also offers excellent views of the falls. (1km, return). To find the trailhead at the Conservation Hut, turn off the highway at either Falls Rd. or Valley Rd., turn right onto Fletcher St., and continue straight to the carpark.

For an ambitious and stunning loop hike, begin at the hut off Fletcher St. and follow the **Valley of the Waters Track** to Empress Lookout, head down the metal stairs, then follow the trail along the Valley of Waters Creek. Take the **Wentworth Pass** (6km, 5hr.)—a strenuous trail with major payoffs, including spectacular falls, rainforests, and views—through the valley to **Slacks Stairs,** where the steep steps take you up to Wentworth Falls and the Wentworth Falls Picnic Area. There are also a number of harder, lengthier bushwalks in the Wentworth Falls area. The **Undercliff-Overcliff walk** (4½hr., 6km) is a challenging circuit loop passing through the Valley of the Waters and accessing part of the National Pass trail. Spectacular scenery and lush hanging swamps will reward the extra effort. The one-way track from the Valley of the Waters to **Inspiration Point** is a slightly less-challenging 5km journey (2½hr.). To reach the **Ingar Campground ❶,** drive west past Woodford (and the towns of Hazelbrook, Lawson, and Bullburra), turn left off the highway onto Tableland Rd., travel 1.6km, turn left at Queen Elizabeth Dr., and proceed 9.5km along an unpaved road to Ingar. Set amid a grove of trees with trunks "scribbled on" by burrowing insects, the free campground has pit toilets and BBQs but no drinking water. The nearby creek and small pond make it a great spot for picnics and camping. No fees apply.

**LEURA.** The pleasant, affluent summertime town of Leura, 5km west of Wentworth Falls and adjacent to Katoomba, offers shops, cafes, and galleries along its central street, Leura Mall. **Everglades Gardens,** 37 Everglades St., is a lush example of the cultivation for which the town is known. Designed by Dutch master gardener Paul Sorensen, this 12½-acre estate in the Jamison Valley is a fountain-speckled oasis of European landscaping, with wild views of the mountains. (☎02 4784 1938. Open daily Oct.-Mar. 10am-5pm, Apr.-Sept. 10am-4pm.

**NEW SOUTH WALES**

$7, concession $5, children $3, customers of Explorer Bus, Trolley Tours, and selected hotels $4.) Near the gardens, Fitzroy St. intersects Everglades Ave. and leads east to Watkins Rd., which turns into Sublime Point Rd. before ending at the breathtaking overlook at Sublime Point. For travelers continuing toward Katoomba, the 8km **Cliff Drive**, beginning at Gordon Rd. near the south end of Leura Mall, provides a scenic escape from the road. In Katoomba, Cliff Dr. turns into Echo Point Rd. To experience Leura's beauty without a car, take the **Trolley Tour Bus** to Gordon Falls and walk back to town via the Prince Henry Cliff Walk. This section of the track is generally tourist-free, so it's peaceful. It runs past the **Leura Cascades**, the exhilarating **Bridal Veil View** (not to be confused with Bridal Veil Lookout), and the aptly named **Solitary Cafe** (see **Food, p. 167**). The staff at the **Blue Mountains Accommodation Centre**, 208 The Mall, books lodging and guided tours. (☎02 4784 2222. Open Tu-Sa 10am-5pm.)

# ALONG THE BELLS LINE OF ROAD

This 87km drive runs north of the Great Western Hwy. through the Blue Mountains and just below Wollemi National Park. It connects with the Great Western Hwy. in the town of Lithgow in the west, and runs east to Windsor.

**MOUNT TOMAH BOTANIC GARDEN.** 12km west of Bilpin, **Mt. Tomah Botanic Garden** is the cool-climate and high-altitude plant collection of Sydney's Royal Botanic Garden. With the exception of the formal terrace garden, the plants (including Jurassic-era Wollemi pines) thrive on the rich volcanic soil and grow in natural conditions. In spring (Sept.-Oct.), the large collection of rhododendrons and other flowers bloom, and in fall (Apr.-May), the deciduous forests change their colors. Free volunteer-guided tours daily at 11:30am. (☎02 4567 2154. Open daily Oct.-Feb. 10am-5pm; Mar.-Sept. 10am-4pm. $5.50, children/concessions $4.40, families $11. Call to confirm tour times.)

**MOUNT WILSON.** People come from far and wide to see the formal gardens and rainforest of **Mt. Wilson,** 8km north of Bells Line of Road, between Mt. Tomah and Bell. For a sample of the fern-laden rainforest, turn right onto Queens Ave. off the main road through town and proceed about 500m until you reach a park area on the left. Then follow signs to the moderate 45min. **Waterfall Trek** (with steep steps) that leads to the base of two waterfalls. The gardens stay open throughout the year, including **Sefton Cottage,** on Church Ln. (☎02 4756 2034; www.mtwilson.com.au; open daily 9am-6pm; $5) and **Merry Garth,** on Davies Ln., 500m from Mt. Irvine Rd. (☎02 4756 2121. Open daily 9am-6pm. $5.)

**LITHGOW.** The Great Western Hwy. and Bells Line of Road meet on the west side of the Blue Mountains at Lithgow, a medium-sized, semi-industrial town at the end of Sydney's CityRail line. The town provides a good base from which to explore nearby wilderness areas such as **Wollemi National Park** (p. 175) and the **Jenolan Caves** and **Kanangra-Boyd National Park** (p. 175). The highest lookout in the region (1130m) is well worth the 5min. detour along the Hassans Walls Link drive. **Blackfellows Hands Reserve,** 24km north of Lithgow, off Wolgen Rd. to Newnes, was a meeting place for Aboriginal tribes; paintings still adorn the walls of the cave. The 4WD-accessible **Gardens of Stone National Park,** 30km north of Lithgow, features pagoda-like formations created by millions of years of erosion. The spectacular granite formations of **Evans Crown Nature Reserve** (☎02 6354 8155), 32km west of Lithgow, make for a climbers' paradise.

Several hotels line Main St., but the **Grand Central Hotel ❷**, 69 Main St., is the pick of the litter. Take a left out of the train station and walk two blocks. (☎02 6351 3050. Bistro open M-F noon-2pm and 6-9pm. Key deposit $20. Breakfast included. $30 per person.) The **Blue Bird Cafe ❶**, 118 Main St., serves sandwiches ($3-7), fried dishes, and tasty milkshakes. (☎02 6352 1644.) The silver, lantern-shaped **visitors center**, 1 Cooerwull Rd. off the Great Western Hwy., just past the intersection with Main St., books accommodations and provides maps for Wollemi National Park. (☎1300 760 276; www.tourism.lithgow.com. Open daily 9am-5pm. Internet $2 for 30min.) The **library** at 157 Main St. also has Internet. (☎02 6352 9100. $1.60 for 30min. Open M-F 9am-6pm, Sa 9am-noon.)

## WOLLEMI NATIONAL PARK

Covering 4875 sq. km, Wollemi (WOOL-em-eye) National Park is the largest wilderness area and second-largest park in New South Wales. It extends north of Blue Mountains National Park all the way to the **Hunter and Goulburn River valleys** (see **Mudgee, p. 252**). Because 2WD access is limited, the park still has many pockets of undiscovered land. One such area yielded an amazing find in 1994: scientists found a species of pine tree, the Wollemi, known previously only through fossils. Fewer than 50 adult Wollemi Pine trees have been found in three remote locations in the region, but these few trees provide a link to the past that has helped researchers retrace evolutionary steps back to the era of dinosaurs. The grove location is a well-kept secret, and scientists studying the trees must sterilize instruments and clothing to avoid bringing disease to it.

The southernmost entrance to the park is at Bilpin on Bells Line of Road. In this corner of the park, also accessible from Putty Rd. north of Windsor, the Colo River slices the landscape along the 30km Colo Gorge. The picturesque, car-accessible **camping ❶** area at **Wheeny Creek** lies near good walking tracks and swimming holes. Entrance and campgrounds are free. Additional info is available at the NPWS office, 370 Windsor Rd., in Richmond. (☎02 4588 5247. Open M-F 9:30am-12:30pm and 1:30-5pm.) The NPWS office in Mudgee (☎02 6372 7199; open M-Th 9am-4pm) services the northwest section of the park and can supply info about **Dunns Swamp**, a beautiful picnic and **camping ❶** area with short 1-2hr. walks, 25km east of Rylstone, 8km of which are unsealed, into the park. (Compost toilets, no water. $5, children $3.) Farther west, a 37km unsealed road from Lithgow takes observers within 1.5km of **Glow Worm Tunnel,** an abandoned railway tunnel housing hundreds of tiny bioluminescent worms. Though the worms glow, it's still smart to bring along a flashlight. There are no marked trails in the northern section of Wollemi National Park.

## KANANGRA-BOYD NATIONAL PARK

Southwest of the Blue Mountains National Park, Kanangra-Boyd National Park stuns visitors with stark wilderness punctuated by rivers, creeks, caves, and the dramatic sandstone cliffs that mark the edges of the Boyd Plateau. The park's remote location and rugged terrain attract experienced bushwalkers.

The park is nonetheless worthwhile for casual visitors who follow its only 2WD access road, the unpaved **Kanangra Walls Road,** across the Boyd Plateau to the famous lookouts at **Kanangra Walls.** Use caution when driving; speeding accidents are common, as the roads are often unsealed and frequently crossed by wildlife. From the east, past Mt. Victoria, drive to Jenolan Caves off the Great Western Hwy. From there, a 5km dirt road will lead to the park and the junction with Kanangra Walls Rd. Turn left at the intersection and drive another 26km to the Kanangra Walls carpark. From the west, drive to the town of Oberon and follow the unpaved Jenolan Caves Rd. south to the junction with Kanangra Walls Rd. Turn right to reach the lookouts. The **NPWS office,** 38 Ross St., Oberon (northeast of the park), has details on the park's longer tracks. Call ahead, or you may find the branch unattended. NPWS cave permits must be obtained at least four weeks in advance. (☎02 6336 1972. Open M-F 9am-4:30pm.)

The **Boyd River Campground ❶**, on Kanangra Walls Rd. 6km before Kanangra Walls, has the park's only car-accessible camping. There are pit toilets and fireplaces. Bring your own wood or a camp stove. Water is available from the Boyd River but it should be treated before consumption. Camping is free, but park fees apply ($7 per vehicle per day). Most bushwalks in the park are not signposted, with the exception of three scenic walks, which begin at the Kanangra Walls carpark. **Lookout Walk** (20min. round-trip) is a wheelchair-accessible path leading to two viewpoints. The first gazes out across the Kanangra Creek gorge toward Mount Cloudmaker, and the other peers into the ravines at the head of the eight-tiered, 400m Kanangra Falls. The **Waterfall Walk** (20min. one-way with steep return) leads from the second lookout to a sparkling pool at the bottom of Kalang Falls. The moderate **Plateau Walk** (2-3hr.) branches off from the Lookout Walk between the carpark and the lookout on Mount Cloudmaker, descending briefly from the plateau before ascending to Kanangra Tops for views of Kanangra Walls. Along the way to the Tops, **Dance Floor Cave** contains indented floors and other signs of old-time recreation. A water container placed in the cave in 1940 catches pure, drinkable water that drips down from the cave ceiling. Longer walks are available in the park as well, including the three- to four-day hike from Kanangra Walls to Katoomba via Mt. Stormbreaker, Mt. Cloudmaker, the Wild Dog Mountains, and the Narrow Neck Plateau. These longer, more intensive walks must always be planned in advance with help from the NPWS.

## JENOLAN CAVES

The amazing limestone and crystal formations of the Jenolan Caves have intrigued visitors since they were opened to the public in 1838. All of the caves are stunning just to look at, and several adventure tours (see below) offer visitors the chance to explore further. The caves, which are 46km south of the Great Western Hwy. from Hartley, on the northwestern edge of Kanangra-Boyd National park, can be reached by bus from **Katoomba** (p. 165). The **Jenolan Caves Reserve Trust,** located at the bottom of the Jenolan Caves center, runs guided tours to nine different areas within the massive cave system. (☎02 6359 3911 or 1300 76 33 11; www.jenolancaves.org.au. Ticket office open daily 9am-4:45pm, with tours running continuously throughout the day.)

If you only have time to explore one cave, head to Lucas Cave, Imperial Cave, or Orient Cave. **Lucas Cave** (1hr., $25) displays a broad range of features including a 54m high cathedral, though the large crowds detract from the experience. Cello, guitar, and violin concerts are given twice a month in the cathedral; call ahead for dates. ($45, children $25; includes cave admission.) **Imperial Cave** (1hr., $25) has a more tolerable flow of visitors as well as fascinating stalactites and stalagmites. **Orient Cave** (90min., $33) showcases some of the most spectacular stalactites and stalagmites in its Egyptian Room and Indian Rooms. The **Temple of Baal** (1hr., $25) and the **River Cave** (2hr., $32) are also exciting options for spelunkers hoping to escape tourist mobs. Orient Cave and **Chifley Cave** (1hr., $25) are partially wheelchair-accessible. All cave tours include a free audio tour of Devils Coach House and Nettle Cave.

**Adventure tours,** run by the National Trust, takes small groups into some of the cave system's less-accessible areas. These trips involve moderate to strenuous climbing, crawling, and a healthy dose of darkness. The most popular adventure tour runs to the 🔲**Plughole** (2½hr., $60; departs daily 1:15pm), and allows spelunkers to abseil down to the cave entrance, squeeze through holes, and finally escape through the famous "S Bend." Visitors to the Plughole must be at least 10 years old; those venturing into Aladdin Cave (3hr., $65; departs 9am last Su every month) at least 12, and those into Mammoth Cave (6hr., $160; first Sa every month) at least 16. Check out the **Themes, Mysteries, Legends and Ghosts**

**Tour** to add entertainment to your cave exploration. (2hr., $38.) For those who prefer to stay above ground, many pathways amble along the surface and lead to **Carlotta Arch, Devils Coachhouse, McKeown's Valley,** and the **Blue Lake.**

Free overnight **camping ❶** is available at Jenolan Caves in parking lot 1. See **Jenolan Caves House Reception** for details. Serious outdoor enthusiasts might want to head off for a couple days of hiking along the dirt roadway that has connected Katoomba and Jenolan Caves since the late 1800s. Today there is the **Six Foot Track,** a 42km trail that runs from the Jenolan Caves to Nellies Glen Rd. off the Great Western Hwy., at the western end of Katoomba. The trail takes three days and is quite steep in places; hikers must bring their own water. Overnight camping is also available at four primitive sites along the way.

# HUNTER VALLEY

Located within a few hours' drive of Sydney and known for its famous wine exports, the Hunter Valley is a popular holiday destination for international travelers and Sydneysiders alike. Over 120 wineries take advantage of the region's warm, dry climate and sandy loam creek soils. Guesthouses and B&Bs dot the landscape, catering to the weekend tourist crowd. Though only 8-10% of all Australian wines are made from Hunter Valley fruit, local vintages claim more than their share of national wine trophies and medals. Chief among the varieties produced in the area are the peppery red Shiraz and the citrusy white Semillon. The region can be explored on a budget via free wine and cheese tastings, a rental car, and a designated driver. Most of the vineyards are clustered around Pokolbin in the lower Hunter Valley, just outside Cessnock's town center at the base of the Brokenback Mountains, but several notable labels are situated in the upper Hunter, centered around the small town of Denman.

## ◼ ◧ TRANSPORTATION AND TOURS

The best time to visit the Hunter Valley is mid-week, when there are fewer people and tours, and accommodations are less expensive. Countrylink (☎13 22 32) sends **buses** daily from Sydney to Scone (4hr., $40) via Muswellbrook (3½hr., $35). Rover Coaches, 231 Vincent St., in Cessnock, runs a bus from Sydney Central Station to Cessnock and the Cessnock Visitor Information Centre. (☎02 4990 1699; www.rovercoaches.com.au. Departs 8:30am. $40, roundtrip $6070. ISIC $30/50.) CityRail's Hunter Line runs between Cessnock and Newcastle (2hr., $15.80). **Bicycle** rental is available from **Hunter Valley Cycling,** at the Cessnock YHA. Free delivery and dropoff service are available. (☎04 1828 1480; www.huntervalleycycling.com.au. Mountain bikes $25 ½-day, 2 days $45; tandem bikes $50, 2 days $75), as well as **Grapemobile Bicycle Hire** in Pokolbin, at the corner of McDonalds Rd. and Palmers Ln. (☎04 1840 4039. One day $25, 2 days $35.) **Cessnock Radio Cabs** (☎02 4990 1111) can get you home safely.

Starting in Newcastle or Maitland, the standard 10- to 20-person tour generally lasts from 9am to 5pm (10am-4pm from Cessnock) and visits four or five wineries, with a cheese, olive, or chocolate stop along the way. The **Vineyard Shuttle Service** lets passengers request stops instead of following a strict itinerary. (☎02 4991 3655; www.vineyardshuttle.com.au. M-F $48, Sa-Su $50. Add $10 for evening restaurant, airport, and golf transfers.) **Hunter Vineyard Tours,** one of the longest running operations in the region that also offers customized itineraries, (☎02 4991 1659; www.huntervineyardtours.com.au) picks up from Cessnock ($60, with lunch $90), Newcastle, and Maitland (both $65/95). **Aussie Wine Tours** (☎02 0412 738 809; www.aussiewinetours.com.au) visits both boutiques and large wineries. **Trekabout** creates a more intimate setting by limiting tours to 12. (☎02 4990 8277; www.hunterweb.com.au/trekabout. ½-day $45, full-day $55.) Horse-drawn carriage tours generally start at $45 for half-day and $60 for full-day, available through **Pokolbin Horse Coaches** (☎02 4998 7305; www.pokolbinhorsecoaches.com.au), on McDonald's Rd. **Wonderbus** runs 20-person groups straight to the Hunter Valley from Sydney. It also offers a combo trip to the Blue Mountains in the morning followed by a wine tour in the Hunter Valley, a trip to a wildlife park, and a cruise on Sydney Harbour. (☎02 9630 0529 or 1300 556 357; www.wonderbus.com.au. Departs 7am, returns 7:15pm. $149 with buffet lunch, $105 tour only. Ask about the backpacker discount.)

## ⚡ WINERIES

Most wineries are open for free tastings and tours daily 10am-5pm (some 9:30am-4:30pm), although some of the smaller ones are only open on weekends. Of the over 100 wineries, the largest are **Drayton's, Lindemans, McGuigan's, McWilliams-Mount Pleasant Estate, Rothbury Estate, Tyrrell's,** and **Wyndham Estate.** Smaller boutiques, such as **Ivanhoe, Pokolbin Estate, Rothvale,** and **Sobel's,** sell their wines only on the premises. While not as glitzy, they are generally more intimate and relaxed. Check with **Hunter Valley Wine Country Tourism** about tours of individual wineries. Wine prices vary, but bottles typically start around $20.

> **★TIP** **MERLOT MATH.** A general guideline for drivers is that five tastings (20mL each) equals one standard drink.

# LOWER HUNTER VALLEY ☎02

Most visitors to the Hunter stay in the very accessible lower valley, where wineries are concentrated in the Pokolbin and Rothbury shires, just north of the town of Cessnock (pop. 20,000). Travelers who use Cessnock as a base to explore the wineries can save money by staying at one of the town's several budget motels or pub stays, but Cessnock lacks the distinct charm that lures many to the valley in the first place.

 **ORIENTATION AND PRACTICAL INFORMATION.** Those traveling by car should follow signs on the F3 Freeway (Sydney-Newcastle) to Cessnock, which is approximately 2hr. from Sydney and 50min. from Newcastle. **The Hunter Valley Wine Country Tourism Inc. and Visitors Centre,** 455 Wine Country Dr., 6km north of Cessnock toward Branxton, will book vineyard tours and accommodations, and has a daily specials board with cheaper standby rates at guesthouses and B&Bs (☎02 4990 0900; www.winecountry.com.au). The free *Hunter Valley Wine Country Visitors Guide* includes a map, as well as information on wineries, cellars, attractions, restaurants, and accommodations. (☎02 4990 0900; www.winecountry.com.au. Variable hours, but generally open M-F 9am-5:30pm, Sa 9am-5pm, Su 9am-4pm.) The **library,** 65-67 Vincent St., provides free Internet for research use and charges $2.75 for 30min. of email and chat. (☎02 4993 3499. Open M and F 9am-5:30pm, Tu-Th 9am-7pm, Sa 9am-1pm.)

🏠 **ACCOMMODATIONS.** The **Hunter Valley YHA ❷,** 100 Country Dr. between Cessock and the visitors center, offers very affordable backpacker accommodations close to the wineries. Facilities include a pool, sauna, BBQ area, outdoor pizza oven ($8 make-your-own pizza night), and on-site bar. (☎02 4991 3278. Laundry $6. Internet $8 per 2hr. Bike rental $30 per day, 20% YHA discount.

Organized vineyard tours at 11:30am for $40. Reception 8am-noon and 5-8pm. Dorms $29-30; doubles $77, ensuite $92. $10 YHA discount.) The **Hill Top Country Guest House ❺**, 81 Talga Rd., in Rothbury, is a 15min. drive from the visitors center via Lovedale Rd.; it offers horseback riding, a pool, billiards, and a view of the countryside. (☎02 4930 7111; www.hilltopguesthouse.com.au. Continental breakfast included. Twins and kings with shared bath M-Th and Su $90-180, F-Sa $312-500 for 2 nights.) Pub stays are scattered throughout Cessnock's town center. **Wentworth Hotel ❹**, on Vincent St., is one of the nicer ones. (☎02 4990 1364; www.wentworthhotelcessnock.com.au. Continental breakfast included. Singles M-Th $40, F-Su $60; doubles $70/95.)

⬛ **FOOD.** Though Cessnock has few, if any, noteworthy restaurants and cafes, there are a couple of cheap ways to eat well in the Lower Hunter. The **Wine**

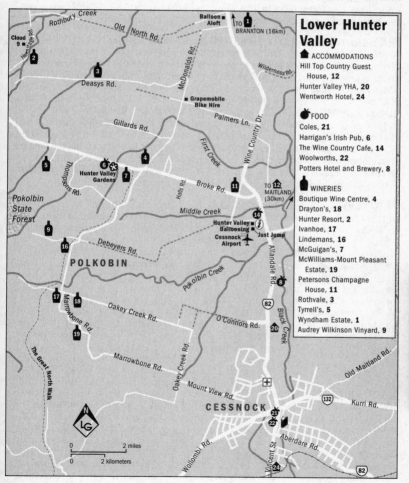

**Lower Hunter Valley**

🏠 ACCOMMODATIONS
Hill Top Country Guest House, **12**
Hunter Valley YHA, **20**
Wentworth Hotel, **24**

🍎 FOOD
Coles, **21**
Harrigan's Irish Pub, **6**
The Wine Country Cafe, **14**
Woolworths, **22**
Potters Hotel and Brewery, **8**

🍷 WINERIES
Boutique Wine Centre, **4**
Drayton's, **18**
Hunter Resort, **2**
Ivanhoe, **17**
Lindemans, **16**
McGuigan's, **7**
McWilliams-Mount Pleasant Estate, **19**
Petersons Champagne House, **11**
Rothvale, **3**
Tyrrell's, **5**
Wyndham Estate, **1**
Audrey Wilkinson Vinyard, **9**

NEW SOUTH WALES

**Country Cafe ❶,** at the Hunter Valley Wine Country Visitors Centre on Wine Country Dr., serves big breakfast meals ($5-14.50), delicious gourmet sandwiches ($10.50-13.50), hot drinks ($3-5), and sweet treats. (☎02 4990 9208; www.winecountrycafe.com.au. Open M-Sa 9am-5pm, Su 9am-4pm.) Many vineyards have restaurants and cafes. Both **Woolworths** and **Coles** supermarkets lie near Cooper and Darwin St. in Cessnock. ◪**Harrigans Irish Pub** is the center of Lower Hunter Valley nightlife. Friday and Saturday nights are packed with a mixed crowd partying to DJ mixes and live bands, while poker night ($10 buy-in) starts at 7pm on Tuesday night. (☎02 4998 4000; www.harrigans.com. au. Open M-W and Su 7:30am-11:30pm, Th-Sa 7:30am-2am.) For pub-going in Cessnock's town center, head to one of the local favorites that line Vincent St. **Potters Hotel and Brewery,** on Wine Country Dr. 3km north of Cessnock, has a lively night atmosphere with a DJ on Saturdays. They also offer a tour of their microbrewery for $10 daily at noon, 2, and 4pm. (☎02 4991 7922; www.pottersbrewery.com.au. Open daily from 7:30am to around 5pm.)

◪▨ **SIGHTS AND ACTIVITIES.** The **Hunter Valley Gardens,** on the corner of Broke and McDonalds Rd., is a touristy shopping complex that also contains 25 hectares of stunning sculpted gardens with 12 different themes. (☎02 4998 4000; www.hvg.com.au. Open daily 9am-5pm. $20, children $15.50, families $54.) The views are well worth the cost at the **Just Jump Skydive,** 210 Allandale Rd. (☎02 4322 9884; www.justjumpskydive.com.au. Tandem dives from $320.) **Balloon Aloft** (☎1800 028 568; www.balloonaloft.com), **Cloud Nine** (☎1300 555 711; www.cloud9balloonflights.com), and **Hunter Valley Ballooning** (☎1800 818 191; www.balloonsafaris.com.au) all have sunrise hot-air balloon flights lasting roughly 1hr. ($250-295, champagne breakfast usually $30 extra.) **Hill Top Country Guest House** (see **Accommodations,** p. 178) conducts 1½hr. horseback rides ($50), a fantastic sunset horseback trail ride ($65) as well as nighttime 4WD wildlife tours ($30, children $15) to observe nocturnal animals.

◪ **WINERIES.** The vineyards of the Lower Hunter are situated along a tangle of rural roads; the free map from the Hunter Valley Wine Country Visitors Centre is the best way to navigate them. Even so, the area's major intersections are marked with large billboard maps. A good place to start is the Hunter Resort, where the **Hunter Valley Wine School** gives wine tasting lessons (☎02 4998 7777. Daily 9-11am. $25. Book ahead.) The tour of its **Hermitage Road Cellar** ($5, daily 11am and 2pm) finishes with an evaluation of three whites and three reds. In addition to free tastings, **Tyrrell's,** on Broke Rd., gives free 1hr. tours at this 145-year-old, family-run business. (☎02 4993 7000; www.tyrrells.com.au. Tours M-Sa 1:30pm.) **McGuigan's** (☎02 4998 7402; www.mcguiganwines.com.au), on McDonalds Rd., is the valley's busiest winery. Also in the McGuigan complex, the **Hunter Valley Cheese Factory** (☎02 4998 7744) offers free tastings. **Wyndham Estate** (☎02 4938 3444; www.wyndhamestate.com), on Dalwood Rd., is the oldest winery in Australia, having first planted vines in 1828. Today, it has a huge tasting room and gives free tours at 11am. **Petersons Champagne House** (☎02 4998 7881; www.petersonhouse.com.au), at the corner of Broke and Branxton Rd., is the only place in New South Wales strictly devoted to the bubbly, and it also has an interesting selection of sparkling red wines. **Audrey Wilkinson Vineyard,** on DeBeyers Rd., has a proud range of award-winning wines, a museum, and the best views of the Hunter Valley from its hilltop vantage. (☎02 4998 7411; www. audreywilkinson.com.au.) Of the smaller boutique wineries in the lower valley, **Rothvale,** on Deasys Rd., consistently receives high praise. Groups can arrange for a free 1hr. wine education session (☎02 4998 7290; www.rothvale.com.au). Also notable, **Ivanhoe,** on Marrowbone Rd., is owned and operated by a member of the distinguished Drayton wine-making family. The vineyard produces gutsy reds and a deliciously fruity dessert wine (☎02 4998 7325; www.ivanhoewines. com.au). The **Boutique Wine Centre,** on Broke Rd., centers its extensive collection on the "rising stars" of the Hunter Valley (☎02 4998 7474).

# UPPER HUNTER VALLEY                              ☎02

A few towns northeast of Cessnock are popular bases for exploring Upper Hunter; budget accommodations and cheap food can be found in all of them.

**SINGLETON.** This sleepy town (pop. 21,000) is between Lower and Upper Hunter on the New England Hwy. Most notable for its massive sundial—the Southern Hemisphere's largest—Singleton is less upscale than Scone and less lively than Muswellbrook. Nevertheless, Singleton attracts visitors with its central location and numerous pub stays, specialty shops, and takeaway counters. Many of these line the town's main drags, John St. and George St. Clean, affordable rooms can be found at **Benjamin Singleton Motel ❺,** 24 New England Hwy. (At the start of George St., just as you exit the New England Hwy. ☎02 6572 2922. Singles $80-90; doubles $94-100. Extra person $12.) The **Visitors Information Centre,** 39 George St., on the New England Hwy., provides heaps of info about the Hunter. (☎02 6571 5888. Open daily 9am-5pm.)

**MUSWELLBROOK.** Farther northwest on the New England Hwy., **Muswellbrook** (MUSCLE-brook; pop. 12,000) is closest to Upper Hunter Valley attractions. The town has a large shopping center, and many historic buildings line the 4.5km **Muswellbrook Heritage Walk,** which begins at the Kildonan building just behind the historic Eatons Hotel on Bridge St. (New England Hwy.). The highway is also the site of a living Vietnam Memorial; each of its 519 trees represents an different Australian casualty suffered during the war. **Eatons Hotel ❸,** 188 Bridge St., has basic rooms in an 1830s building. (☎02 6543 2403. Reception and pub open M-Th 7am-midnight, F-Sa 7am-2am, Su 10am-10pm. Singles $40; doubles $50; triples $75.) **Pinaroo Leisure Park ❷** is 3km south on the New England Hwy. and popular with miners moving through town. A pool, laundry ($6), BBQ, and social room are available. (☎02 6543 3905. Powered sites for 2 $23; cabins $75.) The **tourist office** is located at 87 Hill St., just off Bridge St. (☎02 6541 4050; www.muswellbrook.org.au. Open daily 9am-5pm.)

**SCONE.** Scone, 26km north on the New England Hwy., is a more charming option than Singleton and Muswellbrook for Upper Hunter Valley accommodations. This small, pretty town prides itself on being the horse capital of Australia. Each year, the two-week **Scone Horse Festival** (www.sconehorsefestival. com) in mid-May culminates in two days of thoroughbred racing for the Scone Cup. The race course is 5min. from the town center. However, don't expect to find horseback riding opportunities here unless you're a professional jockey. The **Highway Caravan Park ❶,** 248 New England Hwy., is a decent place to pitch a tent, albeit next to the humming of road noise. The two-bedroom ensuite cabins and cottages are a nicer option than most of the pub stays. (☎02 6545 1078. Sites for 2 $16.50, powered $22; cabins and cottages from $77.) The **Scone Visitor Information Centre** is at the corner of Kelly St. (New England Hwy.) and Susan St., in front of the train station. (☎02 6545 1526; www.horsecapital.com. au. Internet access $2.50 per 30min. Open daily 9am-5pm.)

**WINERIES OF THE UPPER HUNTER VALLEY.** The Upper Hunter Valley has fewer wineries and tourists than the Lower Hunter, but its wines are fabulous, and the countryside is beautiful. Pick up the **Vineyards of the Upper Hunter Valley**

**brochure** with listings and a map from any area visitors center. The vineyards are all off the New England Hwy., beginning a few kilometers northwest of Muswellbrook, mostly around the Denman area. Unfortunately, no tour groups operate in Upper Hunter, so you need your own car. That said, one advantage to Upper Hunter is that you can easily visit all the wineries in a single day. Arrowfield, on the Golden Hwy. in Jerrys Plains, sits on the Hunter River and prides itself on producing respected, affordable wines (☎02 6576 4041; www. arrowfieldestate.com.au). **Two Rivers,** 2 Yarrawa Rd. at Denman, sells reasonably priced ($14-25), quality Semillons and Chardonnays (☎02 6547 2556; www. tworiverswines.com). **James Estate,** 951 Bylong Valley Way, in Sandy Hollow, produces a delicious White Sylvander and sells in bulk at a discount (☎02 6547 5168; www.jamesestatewines.com.au).

# CENTRAL COAST

These beaches are too often passed over by international tourists eager to reach the bright lights and holiday hot spots farther north. The region's pace lies somewhere between the metropolitan rat race and the eternal summer stroll of the Gold Coast. Thriving coastal cities like Newcastle and Port Macquarie draw locals with ample opportunities to sunbathe, water ski, or hang 10, as well as easy access to nearby national parks.

## NEWCASTLE                                                    ☎02

Newcastle, originally reserved for Oz's most troublesome convicts, is now a growing city. As the world's largest coal exporter, Newcastle ships out over one and a half million tons each week. However, the city is no longer the smog-choked industrial metropolis it was once reputed to be. High-adrenaline surfing, spectacular Pacific views, and proximity to the nearby Hunter Valley wineries and wetland reserves put Newcastle in sync with its vibrant, international student crowd and flourishing live music scene.

### ▛ TRANSPORTATION

**Trains:** Newcastle Railway Station (☎13 15 00), corner of Scott and Watt St. CityRail trains to Sydney (2hr., at least 1 per hr. 2:45am-9:20pm). The main transfer station for **CountryLink** (☎13 22 32) is Broadmeadow, a 5min. train ride on CityRail.

**Buses:** The bus depot abuts the wharf side of the railway station. Several bus lines including **Greyhound Australia** (☎13 14 99 or 13 20 30; www.greyhound.com.au) run to: **Brisbane** (14hr., 3 per day, $101); **Byron Bay** (11hr., 2 per day, $94); **Coffs Harbour** (8hr., 3 per day, $70); **Port Macquarie** (4hr., 3 per day, $57); **Surfers Paradise** (12½hr., 3 per day, $101); **Sydney** (2½hr., at least 3 per day, $44); **Taree** (3½hr., 1-2 per day, $37). **Rover Coaches** (☎02 4990 1699; www.rovercoaches.com.au) goes to **Cessnock**, a gateway for the Hunter Valley vineyards (1hr.; M-Sa 2-5 per day; $12). **Port Stephens Coaches** (☎02 4982 2940; www.pscoaches.com.au) shuttles to **Port Stephens** (1hr.; M-F 11 per day, Sa-Su 5 per day; up to $12, backpackers and students $6). Purchase tickets ahead from a Newcastle travel agency, online, or on the bus.

**Ferries:** Passenger ferries (☎13 15 00) depart from the wharf near the train station and cross the river north to Stockton. Ferries leave every 30min. M-Sa 5:15am-11:45pm, Su and holidays 8:30am-11:30pm. Tickets $2.10 one-way. Purchase onboard.

**Public Transportation:** City buses (☎13 15 00; www.131500.com) run along Hunter St. every few minutes during the day, less frequently at night, some as late as 3:30am.

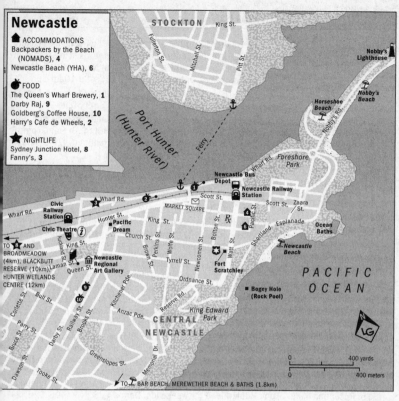

**Newcastle**

🏠 **ACCOMMODATIONS**
Backpackers by the Beach
(NOMADS), **4**
Newcastle Beach (YHA), **6**

🍴 **FOOD**
The Queen's Wharf Brewery, **1**
Darby Raj, **9**
Goldberg's Coffee House, **10**
Harry's Cafe de Wheels, **2**

⭐ **NIGHTLIFE**
Sydney Junction Hotel, **8**
Fanny's, **3**

STOCKTON   King St.

Fullerton St.
Mitchell St.
Pitt St.
King St.

Nobby's
Lighthouse

Nobby's
Beach

Horseshoe
Beach

Nobby's Rd.

Port Hunter
(Hunter River)

Ferry

Wharf Rd.   Foreshore
Park

Newcastle Bus
Depot

Newcastle Railway
Station

Scott St.
Scott St.   Zaara
St.

Civic
Railway
Station

Wharf Rd.

MARKET SQUARE

Esplanade   Ocean
Baths

Wharf Rd.

Hunter St.   Pacific
Dream   King St.   Bolton St.   Pacific St.   Shortland

Church St.   Perkins St.
Wolfe St.

Newcastle
Beach

Civic Theatre

Auckland St.   King St.

TO ⭐ AND
BROADMEADOW
(4km), BLACKBUTT
RESERVE (10km),
HUNTER WETLANDS
CENTRE (12km)

Laman St.   Queen St.

Newcastle
Regional
Art Gallery

Brown St.   Tyrrell St.   Newcomen St.   Watt St.

Fort
Scratchley

PACIFIC
OCEAN

Kitchener Pde.

Ordnance St.

Reserve Rd.

Bogey Hole
(Rock Pool)

Colette St.   Bull St.

Darby St.   Railway St.   Brooks St.

Anzac Pde.

CENTRAL
NEWCASTLE

King Edward
Park

Parry St.
Bruce St.

Greenslopes St.

Memorial Dr.

Dawson St.   Tooke St.

TO 🏖 BAR BEACH, MEREWETHER BEACH & BATHS (1.8km)

0   400 yards
0   400 meters

---

Tickets allow travel within a certain time limit and are for sale onboard (1hr. $3, 4hr. $6, all day $9). Routes within the CBD are free; just wave down a bus. Check at the tourist office for more information and a map.

**Taxis: Newcastle Taxis** (☎ 13 33 00).

**Car Rental:** All have locations in the city and at the airport: **Europcar,** 66 Hannell St., Wickham (☎02 4940 0364; www.europcar.com.au); **Thrifty,** 272 Pacific Highway, Charlestown (☎02 4942 2266 www.thrifty.com.au); **Budget,** 107 Tudor St., Hamilton (☎02 4927 6375; www.budget.com.au); **Avis,** 33 Maitland Rd, Mayfield (☎02 4940 2955; www.avis.com.au). Check websites for online specials.

## 🔦 ORIENTATION

**Hunter Street,** at the heart of the city, is Newcastle's commercial district and runs parallel to the wharf. On the eastern end of the main drag and atop a peninsular hill lies **Fort Scratchley** and a number of hostels and seaside bars, as well as the emerald-green **Foreshore Park. Darby Street** plays host to most of Newcastle's hipper happenings. For another dose of chic, take a significant trek farther west and reach **Beaumont Street** in Hamilton; or, take one of the free CBD buses that regularly runs there. From Newcastle, the New England Hwy. heads west toward the Hunter Valley wineries.

## ◪ PRACTICAL INFORMATION

**Tourist Office:** 361 Hunter St. (☎02 4974 2999 or 1800 654 558; www.visitnewcastle. com.au). From rail station, take a right on Scott St. and continue as it merges with Hunter St. Office is on left, just a block past Darby St. Free maps of Newcastle and Macquarie; accommodation and tour bookings. Open M-F 9am-5pm, Sa-Su 10am-3pm.

**Library:** (☎02 4974 5342), in the Newcastle War Memorial Cultural Centre on Laman St., next to the art gallery. Free Internet. Open M-F 9:30am-8pm, Sa 9:30am-2pm.

**Surf Shop: Pacific Dreams,** 7 Darby St. (☎02 4926 3355; www.pacificdreams.com.au). Rents short boards $50 per day; long $60. Open M-W 9am-5:30pm, Th 9am-7pm, F 9am-5:30pm, Sa 9am-4pm, Su 10am-3pm. Credit card deposit required. V/MC/AmEx.

**Police:** (☎02 4929 0999), corner of Church and Watt St.

**Post Office:** (☎13 13 18), corner of Scott and Market St. Open M-F 8:30am-5pm. **Postal Code:** 2300.

## ◤ ACCOMMODATIONS

With tourism on the rise, budget accommodations have become few and far between in Newcastle. Pub rooms abound (around $60), but the listings below are better bets. Book ahead in the high season.

**Newcastle Beach (YHA),** 30 Pacific St. (☎02 4925 3544). Around the corner from the beach and train station. Breezy building with a retro flavor. Spacious rooms and common area reminiscent of a country club with TV, pool table, fireplace, and kitchen. Free dinner at Finnegan's for YHA M-Tu and Su and at the Brewery Th. Internet $2 per 30min. Winery tour $50. Laundry $6. Free boogie boards. Reception 7am-10:30pm. Book ahead in summer. Dorms $30, YHA $27; doubles $65/73. AmEx/MC/V. ❸

**Backpackers by the Beach (NOMADS),** 34-36 Hunter St. (☎1800 008 972; www. backpackersbythebeach.com.au). 4min. walk north of train station, this hostel is on the corner of Hunter and Pacific St. Small rooms feel bigger than they are due to bright lights and high ceilings. Single-sex dorms. Surfboard rentals $8 per hr., bodyboards $2 per hr., bikes $3 per hr., snorkels $2 per hr. Th free BBQ. Internet $4 per hr. Key deposit $15. Reception 7am-11pm. Book ahead for weekends. Dorms $28, NOMADS $26; 2+ days $26/24; doubles $64/60. ISIC/NOMADS/YHA. AmEx/MC/V. ❷

## ◗ FOOD

Darby St. is the best place in town to hunt for eateries. Hunter St. has $7-8 lunch specials, but stick to the Pacific St. end if you want atmosphere. Though it's a 25-30min. walk southwest of the city center, Hamilton's less trendy Beaumont St. is lined with over 80 restaurants. Food-court options can also be found at Market Sq., in the center of a pedestrian mall on Hunter St., running from Newcomen to Perkins St. The huge 24hr. **Coles** supermarket (☎02 4926 4494) is in the Marketown shopping center at the corner of National Park and King St.

**Goldberg's Coffee House,** 137-139 Darby St. (☎02 4929 3122). Many meet here early in the evening for dinner or drinks before heading out for the night. Dark hardwood interior with a classy soundtrack and garden patio out back. Swing by for a late cup of coffee ($4) or a glass of wine ($6). Varied and reasonably priced menu; lunch and dinner dishes $7-20. Open daily 7am-midnight. AmEx/D/MC/V. ❷

**The Queen's Wharf Brewery,** 150 Wharf Rd. (☎02 4929 6333; www.qwb.com.au). Fine dining and hops at this popular wharf-side restaurant and multi-level bar. Attracting steak and seafood lovers for meals ($15-30) and a mixed crowd for evening drinks, there's something for everyone to enjoy here. Live entertainment and daily menu specials. Su live music starting at 1pm. Open M and Tu 10:30am-10pm, W 10:30am-1pm, Th 10:30am-noon, Sa 10:30am-2:30pm, Su 10:30am-midnight. AmEx/D/MC/V. ❸

**Darby Raj,** 115 Darby St. (☎02 4926 2443). With delicious North Indian curries to devour at one of the tables outside, Darby Raj is a choice budget eatery. Choose 1-3 curries on rice for $10, or for a light lunch grab a couple of samosas ($2.20 each) and cool your palate with a lassi ($2.50). Vegetarian-friendly. Takeaway available. Open M 4-10pm, Tu-W and Su 11am-10pm, Th-Sa 11am-10:30pm. AmEx/MC/V. ❶

**Harry's Cafe de Wheels** (☎02 4926 2165), on Wharf Rd. on the waterfront. What better place to sample a famous Australian meat pie than the longest-running takeaway joint in the nation? The "Tiger" is a hearty pie smothered in peas, mashed potatoes, and steaming gravy ($5.40). Open M-Tu 8:30am-9pm, W 8:30am-2pm, Th 8:30am-midnight, F 8:30am-3:30am, Sa 10am-4am, Su 10am-11pm. Cash only. ❶

##  SIGHTS AND ACTIVITIES

Though the ornate heritage buildings and the towering cathedral of the CBD are impressive, visitors come to enjoy the laid-back coastal lifestyle. Newcastle's a place to chill, with plenty of oceanfront parks, good surf, and the ever-present sound of crashing waves.

**BEACHES.** Newcastle's shore is lined with beaches, tidal pools, and landscaped parks. At the tip of Nobby's Head peninsula is a walkable seawall and Nobby's Lighthouse, in the middle of **Nobby's Beach,** a popular surfing spot. A walk down the coastline from Nobby's leads to a surf pavilion, then to the **Ocean Baths,** a public saltwater pool. Keep walking to find **Bogey Hole,** a convict-built ocean bath at the edge of the manicured King Edward Park. Farther along, you'll see the large **Bar Beach,** terrific for surfing. To tackle all the beaches, follow the **Bather's Ways** coastal walk from Nobby's at the peninsular tip to Merewether.

> **TIP**
> **FLAGS.** If your local beach is flashing flags, this means it's being patrolled. In Newcastle, these flags are often red and yellow.

**NEWCASTLE REGION ART GALLERY.** On a rainy day, stroll through this small museum's collection of contemporary paintings and multimedia presentations. *(Corner of Laman and Darby St. ☎02 4974 5100. Open Tu-Su 10am-5pm. Free.)*

**FORT SCRATCHLEY.** Famous as the only Australian fortification to return fire on the Japanese during WWII, Fort Scratchley had fallen into disrepair as a graffiti-scarred eyesore. Recently restored for the public, it now commands stunning views of the harbor. A fun-to-explore network of underground tunnels also runs below the fort. *(☎02 4929 3066; www.fortscratchley.org.au. Open M and W-Su 10am-4pm. Free general admission. Guided tunnel tours around $5.)*

**BLACKBUTT RESERVE.** A 182-hectare tree sanctuary with over 20km of walking trails and many animals along the way. Bring your own picnic to Black Duck Picnic Area where there's BBQ equipment, a jungle gym, a pioneer cottage that replicates the domestic life of 19th-century Newcastle settlers, a koala enclosure, and kangaroo, peacock, and emu reserves. If you're lucky, you can even pet a koala daily at 2pm for $3. *(Take bus #317, 224 or 225 from the city center for 30min. to the corner of Carnley Ave. and Orchardtown Rd. Walk up Carnley Ave. to the entrance on the right. By car, turn left on Stewart Ave., the Pacific Hwy., from Hunter St. After about 20min., hang a right on Northcott, and at the roundabout turn right on Carnley Ave. ☎02 4904 3344; www.ncc.nsw.gov.au. Open daily in summer 7am-5pm; wildlife exhibits 9am-5pm. Free.)*

**HUNTER WETLANDS CENTRE.** Founded in 1985 to provide sanctuary to birds and reptiles, these rehabilitated wetlands also offer respite to city-weary humans with walking paths and a creek for canoeing. Swans, egrets, ibis, blue herons, and parrots are just a few of the feathered fliers who call this place home. Monthly events include breakfast with the birds, twilight treks, and canoe safaris. Check website in advance for details. *(Take CityRail to Sandgate, in the suburb of Shortland, and then walk 10min. on Sandgate Rd. By car, take the Pacific Hwy. to Sandgate Rd. ☎02 4951 6466; www.wetlands.org.au. Canoe rental: 2hr. 2-person $10; 3-person $15. Open M-F 10am-5pm, Sa-Su 9am-5pm. $6, children $3, concessions $4, families $15.)*

**FESTIVALS. Surfest** *(www.surfest.com)*, Australia's largest surfing festival, rides into town in late March for a week-long international surfing extravaganza. The **Newcastle Jazz Festival** *(☎02 4973 2160; www.newcastlejazz.com.au)* plays out in late August at City Hall. **Newcastle Maritime Festival's** *(☎04 1227 5707 )* boat races and water sports are in October. **Mattara** spring festival *(☎02 4962 5648; www.mattarafestival.org.au)* celebrates cultural diversity in early October. The **This is Not Art Festival** *(☎02 4927 0470; www.thisisnotart.org.au)* brings together Newcastle's young musicians, artists, writers, media-makers, and troublemakers for five days of creative energy at the end of September and early October.

## 🎵 🎭 ENTERTAINMENT AND NIGHTLIFE

City Hall recently enforced a new 3am curfew, officially intended to curb street violence, but some locals grumble that there was never really a crime problem. Regardless, Newcastle is fast becoming one of Australia's major musical hubs. *The Post*, a free newspaper, publishes a weekly *That's Entertainment* guide to live music around the area; pick up a copy at the tourist office. Wednesday night is "Uni Night" all around town; keep your eyes open for special events and offers, as well as late closing times.

**Fanny's,** 311 Wharf Rd. (☎02 4929 5333; www.fannys.com.au). A happening dance club that caters to the R&B and techno crowds. Voted RALPH magazine's "easiest place to pick up in Australia." Probably should still hold the title. Drinks $6-10. 18+. Open W and F-Sa 8pm-3am. $10 regular cover. W Uni Nights: $5, students free.

**The Queen's Wharf Brewery** (see **Food, p. 184**). At night, the 2nd floor becomes a DJ-driven dance frenzy, while the lower level offers relaxed conversation. Live music Th 9:30pm; F live music 5pm, DJ 9:30pm; Sa live music 3pm, DJ 9:30pm.

**Sydney Junction Hotel,** 8 Beaumont St. (☎02 4961 2537; www.sjh.com.au), is a slick establishment with a packed line-up; it's an all-in-one cocktail lounge, dance club, and sports bar. Rock bands Th-Su. F and Sa live music in back room and DJ up front. W karaoke night. Free pool all day Su. Open daily 7am-late. AmEx/D/MC/V.

# PORT STEPHENS BAY ☎02

North of Newcastle, this ring of sleepy townships circles the placid blue-green water of Port Stephens Bay. A slew of outdoor activities near **Tomaree National Park** adds adventure to this otherwise relaxing destination. Most of the region's attractions, restaurants, and facilities are in the township of Nelson Bay, while Anna Bay and Shoal Bay offer beautiful and somewhat isolated beaches. During the summer, surfing beaches and luxury resorts draw backpackers and families alike, clogging central shopping areas with traffic. Dolphins are visible year-round in the harbor and are quite cheeky—they'll come right up and tag along with the daily dolphin cruises. The whale-watching season runs from June-Oct., when about 5000 giants head north to warmer waters to breed.

**TRANSPORTATION. Port Stephens Coaches** (☎02 4982 2940 or 1800 045 949; www.pscoaches.com.au) shuttles to and around Port Stephens and runs to Sydney (3hr.; 9:35am daily from Port Stephens Coaches Depot; $36, concessions $29). The Bay Rover Pack includes round-trip ticket and travel within and between Port Stephens's townships ($22/11.) The main stop in Nelson Bay is at the Coles supermarket on Stockton St. Local buses run all week. (M-F hourly, Sa and Su every 2hr. $3; 1-day unlimited travel $11.) It may be more convenient to rent a car from Newcastle in order to avoid being stranded in one township for hours. The **Port Stephens Ferry Service** (☎04 1268 2117) makes trips to Tea Garden, a fishing village across the water from Nelson Bay. (8:30am, noon, 3:30pm. Round-trip $20, children $10, concessions $18, families $50. Book ahead.) Call a **taxi** (☎13 10 08) for service around town. **Shoal Bay Bike Hire,** 63 Shoal Bay Rd., near the Shoal Bay Motel, is a cheap bike rental option. (☎02 4981 4121. From $4-8 per hr., $68 per week. Open daily 9am-5pm in summer; in winter M-W 9am-3pm, F-Su 9am-5pm.)

**ORIENTATION AND PRACTICAL INFORMATION. Nelson Bay Road** leads from Newcastle to four of Port Stephens' residential townships. The road forks onto **Gan Gan Road,** which leads to **Anna Bay,** where **Stockton Beach** boasts the largest sand dune area in the Southern Hemisphere. It's also close to the popular surf spot, **One Mile Beach,** called "The Big Beach" by locals. Gan Gan and Nelson Bay Rd. rejoin and lead to three other townships: **Nelson Bay** (the largest), **Shoal Bay,** and the rural **Fingal Bay.** The marina, shopping complex, and cafes are on Victoria Pde. and Stockton St. in Nelson Bay. The **tourist office** (☎02 4981 6900 or 1800 808 900; www.portstephens.org.au.), on Victoria Pde. by the wharf, arranges bookings for local attractions. (Open daily 9am-5pm.) **Tomaree Public Library,** in the Salamander Shopping Centre, has free Internet. (☎02 4982 0670. Open M, W, F 9:30am-6pm; Tu and Th 9:30am-8pm; Sa 9:30am-2pm.) Additional access is available at **Internet Cafe and Gaming Shop,** on Magnus St. in Nelson Bay. (☎02 4984 3225. $6 per hr. Open M-F 9:30am-7pm, Sa-Su 10am-8pm.)

**ACCOMMODATIONS AND CAMPING.** Budget accommodations abound in Port Stephens Bay. **Samurai Beach Bungalows Backpackers/Port Stephens YHA ❷,** is on Robert Connell Cir. Reached by Frost Rd. off Nelson Bay Rd., the hostel is nestled in dense bushland, making for a romantic and relaxing stay. Travelers riding a bus into town can ask for a dropoff at the hostel. Guests enjoy simple, stylish rooms, a volleyball court, an outdoor kitchen, a rec room with TV, a pool, free sand boards, and campfires. Bikes are also available for $5 per hr. (☎02 4982 1921; www.samuraiportstephens.com. Laundry $3. Internet available. Reception 8:30am-9:30pm. 5-bunk dorms with fridge from $25; doubles with TV, bar, and fridge from $75; family room with all amenities $89. Rates higher in the summer; book ahead.) **Shoal Bay Holiday Park ❸,** on Shoal Bay Rd., near the turnoff for Fingal Bay, has a new kitchen, two common TV areas, a rec room with ping-pong tables, and a tennis court. (☎02 4981 1427 or 1800 600 200; www.beachsideholidays.com.au. Laundry $3. Reception 8:15am-6pm. Powered sites for 2 $30-55; ensuite caravan sites $42-69; ensuite bungalows with kitchen and TV $59-180. Min. 2-night stay on weekends. Weekly rates available. Extra adult $10-15.) **Malaleuca Backpackers ❶,** 2 Koala Pl., is just 5min. from the beach and offers comfortable cabins and camping on an expansive lawn. Koala sightings are very common. Head down Gan Gan Rd. and turn left on Koala Pl. (☎02 4981 9422 or 04 2720 0950. Laundry $7. Sites $14-18; dorm beds $30-34; cabins $80. Book 2-3 months ahead for summer and holidays. VIP/YHA accepted.)

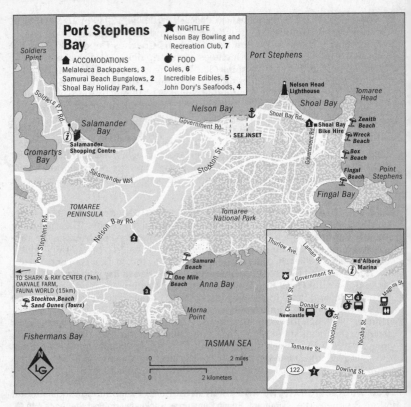

**Port Stephens Bay**

★ **NIGHTLIFE**
Nelson Bay Bowling and Recreation Club, **7**

🏠 **ACCOMODATIONS**
Melaleuca Backpackers, **3**
Samurai Beach Bungalows, **2**
Shoal Bay Holiday Park, **1**

🍎 **FOOD**
Coles, **6**
Incredible Edibles, **5**
John Dory's Seafoods, **4**

📸 **FOOD. Nelson Bay**—the Port Stephens hub—is the best place to find cheap food, particularly on Magnus and Donald St., parallel to Victoria Pde. **John Dory's Seafoods ❶**, 138 Magnus St., has unbeatable fish and chips ($8.20). Be prepared for a generous platter. (☎02 4981 3881. Takeaway available. Open M-Sa 10:30am-8pm, Su 11am-8pm. Cash only.) **Incredible Edibles ❶,** Shop 6 on Donald St., serves scrumptious sandwiches ($6.50-8) made with the freshest ingredients. (☎02 4981 4511. Open in summer daily 8am-4pm, in winter M-Sa 9am-3pm. Cash only.) A small **Coles** is located on the corner of Stockton and Donald St. in Nelson Bay (☎02 4981 1666) and a full-size **Woolworths** is in the Salamander Shopping Centre, which also holds a number of travel agencies and fast-food joints. Though Port Stephens is not known for its party scene, locals and backpackers alike enjoy good times and cheap drinks at **Nelson Bay Bowling and Recreation Club,** Stockton St., just up from the town center. (☎02 4981 1272. Live music F-Sa. Open M-F 10am-10pm, Sa-Su 10am-midnight.)

🎿🏄 **SIGHTS AND ACTIVITIES.** You've probably seen sport-utility vehicle ads on TV and wondered if anyone really drives off-road like that. Now's your chance to find out. The fun-loving folks at **Port Stephens Visitors Centre** (☎02 4981 1579) will let you buy a three-day pass ($10) so you and your 4WD can go play on **Stockton Beach,** the biggest sand dune in the Southern Hemisphere. (The fine sands of this 26km long dune not only move 10m inland every year but are also shipped to Waikiki Beach in Hawaii.) Eleven kilometers down from Anna Bay is **Tin City,** a collection of tin shacks that were featured in *Star Wars.* Don't let their simple exterior fool you: some are extremely well-furnished with cable, A/C, and other comforts. Passes are also available at the Mobil station in Anna Bay. Follow signs to Anna Bay from Nelson Bay Rd.; the Mobil is past the beach access sign. To get to the dunes, take Gan Gan Rd. and turn off onto James Patterson St. For renting or participating in more organized group-duning, try a 2hr. trip with **Port Stephens 4WD Tours.** The Beach and Dune Tour includes a trip to Tin City, *pipi* (clam) catch and release, and sandboarding down the dunes. (☎02 4984 4760; www.portstephens4wd.com.au. 10am daily, extra times Sa and holidays. $48, children $28.) **Quad Bikes** lets you motor through the dunes on a four-wheeler for $130. They also offer daily 4WD beach and dune tours from $45. (☎02 4919 0088; www.quadbikeking.com.au.) For a more tame sand activity, join **Sahara Trails** on spectacular 1½hr. dune and beach horse rides ($120) or a 1hr. bush ride starting at $50 per hr. (☎02 4981 9077; www.saharatrails.com. Open daily. Book ahead.) **Camel Rides** offers 20min. beach rides Su, and school holidays for $20. (☎04 2966 4172; www.oakfieldranch.com.)

Whale-watching and dolphin cruise boats depart throughout the day in the summer (winter trips run weather-permitting). The cheapest is the **Seascape,** which cruises the harbor for sightings of some of the 150 dolphins that live there year-round. (☎04 1882 2634; www.nelsonbaydolphinwatch.com.au. Cruises run daily noon and 1:45pm year-round. $19.50, concessions $18.50.) For a venture out of the bay and into the ocean, join the young crew aboard **Imagine Cruises** sailboats. Their popular 3½hr. Marine Discovery tour (Dec.-Mar.) includes sailing, swimming and snorkeling ($50, concessions $45), and their 3hr. whale-watching tours ($60, concessions $50), with afternoon tea, run June-November. (☎02 4984 9000; www.imaginecruises.com.au. Both depart Dock C, d'Albora Marina.) **The Shark and Ray Centre,** 686 Marsh Rd. in Bobs Farm township, invites intrepid visitors to feed the sharks and rays ($50, children $25) while snorkeling or standing in the tank. (☎02 4982 2476; www.ozsharkandray.com.au. Open daily 9am-5pm.) For less action and more cuddling, stop off at **Oakvale Farm and Fauna World,** 2828 Nelson Bay Rd., to pet or feed a koala or kangaroo. (☎02 4982 6222; www.oakvalefarm.com.au. Open daily 10am-5pm; feeding times 11am and 2pm. Wheelchair-accessible. $15, children $9.) For unparalleled views of Port Stephens Bay's rippling blue-green water and stark headlands, take the 20-40min. walk to the summit of **Tomaree Head** at the end of Shoal Bay. The Anna Bay shore offers opportunities for surfing and nude bathing; inquire at the Port Stephens tourist office in Nelson Bay for information.

# GREAT LAKES

This underrated region is home to some spectacular coastal scenery. The beautiful waters invite scuba exploration, and a host of little-known national parks provides opportunities for solitude and unusual wildlife sightings.

# FORSTER                                      ☎02

The small towns of **Forster** (FOS-ter) and **Tuncurry** are the most urban locales in the popular Great Lakes region. Although Forster's beaches pale in comparison to those just south, the town is a pleasant stop near Sydney or Byron Bay. It is also the most comfortable stopover for exploring the Great Lakes region.

📠 🛂 **TRANSPORTATION AND PRACTICAL INFORMATION.** Approaching the Pacific Hwy. from the south, exit at **The Lakes Way.** The Forster turnoff is 4km north of Buladelah and a 1hr. drive up The Lakes Way. From the north on the Pacific Hwy., turn east onto The Lakes Way in Rainbow Flat; Forster is a 15min. drive. Tuncurry is on the north side of The Lakes Way bridge, before you cross into Forster. **Busways** (☎1800 043 263) runs to Bluey's Beach (30min.; M-F 3 per day, Sa-Su 2 per day; $12, concessions $6, student/YHA $10), Newcastle (2hr.; 3 per day M-F, 2 per day Sa-Su; $35.50/17.50/28.40), Sydney (5hr.; 1 per day 7:15am; $55/37/44). **Eggins Comfort Coaches** (☎02 6552 2700) goes to Taree (1hr.; M-Sa 2-4 per day; $13.40, concessions $6.70). There's no public transportation to Myall Lakes. To get to Booti Booti, you can take the Busways to Bluey's Beach and request a stop at Tiona. Buses run 3 times a day, so you can take one to go there and catch another one coming back. See Busways info above.

The **Forster Visitors Centre,** 2 Little St., is by the wharf and is the bus terminal and a booking agency. Tickets can also be bought onboard. As the main visitors center for the Great Lakes region, this is the place to gather info on nearby beaches and national parks. Be sure to pick up a map of the area, since much of its charm lies in the many secluded beaches off main roads. (☎02 6554 8799 or 1800 802 692; www.greatlakes.org.au. Open daily 9am-5pm.) The **police station** (☎02 6555 1299) is on Lake and West St., and the **post office** is on the corner of Wallis Ln. and Beach St. in the center of Forster. You can rent bikes at **Holiday Hire** in the Dolphin Arcade across the river in Turncurry. (☎02 6557 2012; call to book in advance.) **Postal Code:** 2428.

📠 🛏 **ACCOMMODATIONS AND FOOD.** Lani's Holiday Island ❷, 33 The Lakes Way, offers value cabins and huts in a gated caravan park. Lani's owns an entire 100-acre island for bush camping. Amenities include pools and in-house movies. (☎02 6554 6273 or 1300 653 258; www.lanis.com.au. Internet $6 per hr., Wi-Fi $4 per hr. Linens $6. Cabins $40-75; ensuite powered sites $35-55, unpowered $22-39.) The tourist office can provide a list of budget motels in the area. To fuel up on a sumptuous all-you-can-eat dinner buffet—also called a smorgasbord in Australia—visit **Danny's Family Restaurant** ❷, 2 Strand St., in the Forster Bowling Club. Simply sign in at the front door to enter the club and proceed to Danny's Restaurant. (☎02 6554 6155; www.forsterbowl.com. M-Th and Su 6-9pm; F-Sa 5:30-9pm. $18.50 all-you-can-eat dinner buffet, $6.50 lunch (1 plate of food) noon-2pm.) **El Barracho Mexican Cantina** ❷, Wharf St. (☎02 6554 5573), was voted Best Mexican Restaurant of the Year in the Northern Region for its fun atmosphere and wholesome Mexican food (main dishes $13-17).

📷 🎯 **SIGHTS AND ACTIVITIES.** Tobwabba (taw-WAB-buh), 10 Breckenridge St., is an Indigenous studio and art gallery. The beautiful prints and canvasses are good alternatives to your usual ubiquitous stuffed kangaroos and koala souvenirs. (☎02 6554 5755; www.tobwabba.com.au. Generally open M-F 9am-5pm, but call and check before going.) At the south end of **Forster Beach,** three blocks north of town on West St., are toilets, a BBQ, and a saltwater swimming pool. The **Bicentennial Walk** runs from Forster Beach to Pebbly Beach, with rock pools and dolphin-spotting along the way. For better beaches, head south 20km on The Lake Way or to **Booti Booti National Park** (p. 191).

**Boomerange Rainforest Tour** (☎02 6554 0757) offers fun 4WD tours starting from $39. Call for a free hotel pickup. Boat and tackle rental sheds line the shore. **Forster's Dive School,** at Fisherman's Wharf opposite the post office, runs a variety of trips, including a swim-with-dolphins cruise ($60, non-swimmers $30) and a dive with gray nurse sharks. (☎02 6554 7478; www.diveforster.com.au. 2 dives with equipment approx. $140.) Consult the visitors center for more options.

# MYALL LAKES NATIONAL PARK

With 10,000 hectares of lake, 40km of beach, and walking tracks through a variety of ecosystems, **Myall Lakes National Park** has a lot to offer visitors. There are only two major vehicular access points to the area (with honesty boxes where visitors can pay the $7 vehicle entry fee): one from the south through **Tea Gardens** and the other from the north at **Bulahdelah.**

Located at Bombah Point, the office of the **Ecopoint Myall Shores Resort ❸,** right before the ferry crossing, rents canoes ($20 first hr., $5 every hr. thereafter), bikes ($10 per hr.), and outboards ($65 per 2hr.). It also sells petrol. Facilities include BBQ, laundry, store, pool, and restaurant. (☎02 4997 4495; www.myallshores.com.au. Powered sites $30-45; cabins $150-450. MC/V.) Paved Mungo Brush Rd. begins at Tea Gardens and runs 25km along the coast to the park's south edge, passing eight campgrounds. One of these is **Mungo Brush ❶,** with toilets, BBQ, and lake access, but no drinking water; Mungo Brush and **Yagon Campsite ❶,** on the headland, are both operated by park services. (Park offices ☎02 6591 0300. Sites $10 per day, $7 per day vehicle fee.) Facing the beach at Seal Rocks is **Seal Rocks Camping Reserve ❷,** with easy access to the powerful surf. (☎1800 112 234; www.sealrockscampingreserve.com.au. Sites $20-28, powered $22-32; cabins $95-115. MC/V.)

The northern entrance is accessible through Bulahdelah, 83km north of Newcastle on the Pacific Hwy. The **Bulahdelah Visitors Centre,** at the corner of Pacific Hwy. and Crawford St., serves as the park's only "interpretive center." (☎02 4997 4981. Open M-F 9am-4pm, Sa-Su 9am-3pm.) Pick up the free **Great Lakes National Parks Visitors Guide,** with a map and campsite information. To enter the park itself, take the semi-paved **Bombah Point Rd.** out of Bulahdelah. Beware of reckless cars, caravans, and boat tugs as you drive. Bombah Point Rd. eventually becomes Lakes Rd., which runs into **Bombah Point,** a center of activity for both Myall Lakes and Bombah Broadwater. A vehicle ferry connects the northern Bombah Point Rd. with the southern **Mungo Brush** area of the park (5min.; every 30min. 8am-6pm; $2). A third access point, leading to the very northern tip of the park, is found in Bungwahl on the The Lakes Way, 30km east of Bulahdelah and 34km south of Forster.

# BOOTI BOOTI NATIONAL PARK

Booti Booti features extensive coastal wetlands and heath communities, as well as palm forest along the edge of Wallis Lake. To reach the park, follow The Lakes Way south of Forster along the coastline of Elizabeth Beach. Bikers can use the same route (allow 1hr. each way), but there is no real bike path along the road, so use caution. Booti Booti's highlight is the spectacular view from **Cape Hawke Lookout,** just a few kilometers from Forster (follow Cape Hawke Dr. off of The Lakes Way until the carpark). A 420m climb up a wooded path leads to a 20m tower, from which the beautiful beaches and forests encompassing Forster can be seen. The ranger station is at **The Ruins Camping Area ❶,** by the soft white sand of **Seven-Mile Beach** and a mangrove forest. (☎02 6591 0300. Center open M-F 9am-4pm. BBQ, toilets, and showers. Pay fees in slots at the entrance to camping area. Sites $14, vehicle fee $7.) **Sundowner Tiona Tourist Park ❶,** 15min. south of Forster and 500m north of The Ruins, rents sites on both the Wallis Lake and Seven-Mile Beach sides of the road. (☎02 6554 0291; www.sundownerholidays.com. Sites $19-28, powered $22-32; cabins $55-400. MC/V.) On the west side of Tiona, the outdoor **Green Cathedral** overlooks Wallis Lake, its wooden altar and pews enclosed only by soaring palm trees. A walk around the lake through cabbage tree palms and eucalyptus trees leads to the ocean and Elizabeth Beach to the east.

NEW SOUTH WALES

# NORTH COAST

The north coast of New South Wales may be a well-trodden route, but it remains in top form with a seemingly endless stretch of bush, beach, and impressive tourist amenities. Inexpensive accommodations and a thriving adventure sports industry draw budget travelers to its lively beachside cities, while smaller oceanside villages offer first-rate surf and pristine rainforests.

## TAREE                                                           ☎02

Taree (pop. 20,000), off the Pacific Hwy. on the Manning River, is a small, convenient base for exploring nearby beaches and national parks. Taree and nearby Wingham's "country retreat" industries provide relaxing getaways.

**▐ TRANSPORTATION.** Taree's bus station, 58 Victoria St., is called the **Union Service Station.** Busways (☎1800 043 263), Countrylink (☎13 22 32), Greyhound Australia (☎13 20 30), and Premier (☎13 34 10) run **buses** to: Brisbane (9-10hr., 4 per day, $65-85); Byron Bay (8hr., 4 per day, $65-85); Coffs Harbour (4½hr., 2-3 per day, $48-57); Port Macquarie (1-1½hr., 2-3 per day, $32-49); Sydney (5-6hr., 3-4 per day, $57-85). Eggins Comfort Coaches (☎02 6552 2700; www.egginscomfortcoaches.com.au) is a regional line for the Great Lakes area, running routes between Taree and Forster, Kendall, Blackhead, Diamond Beach, Manning Point. A bus depot sits on Elizabeth St. **Holiday Coast Connection** (☎02 6581 5557) provides a daily service from Taree to Newcastle at 8:20am.

**▐▌ ORIENTATION AND PRACTICAL INFORMATION.** Taree's main road, **Victoria Street,** feeds directly into the Pacific Hwy. Most establishments are on Victoria St. or the streets between Pulteney and Macquarie St. The **Manning Valley Visitors Information Centre** on Manning River Dr., 4km north of town, is past the Big Oyster Ford car dealership. (☎02 6592 5444; www.manningvalley. info. Open daily 9am-5pm, public holidays and winter weekends 9am-4pm.) The **library,** to the right of the Fotheringham Hotel, Victoria St., offers free **Internet access.** (☎02 6592 5290. Open M-W and F 9:30am-5pm, Th 9:30am-6pm, Sa 10am-4pm.) The **post office** is on Albert St., near the intersection with Manning St. (Open daily 8:30am-5pm.) **Postal Code:** 2430.

**▐▐ ACCOMMODATIONS AND FOOD.** Accommodations are plentiful but not cheap; most hotels offer backpacker rates. **Namaste Beach House ❸,** 31 David St. in Old Bar, is a great alternative to staying in Taree. It has modern leather furniture, a meditation room, TV, and BBQ, and it's only a block from the beach. (☎02 6557 4224; www.namastebeachhouse.com. Singles $40; doubles and twins $70. VIP/YHA discounts available. MC/V.) **Exchange Hotel ❸,** on the corner of Victoria and Manning St., has well-kept rooms. (☎02 6552 1160. Reception at bar 10am-late. Singles $40; doubles $50-60. MC/V.) **Fotheringham Hotel ❸,** 236 Victoria St., has basic rooms. (☎02 6552 1153. Singles $45; doubles $55. Cash only.) **Twilight Caravan Park ❶,** 3km south of the town center on Manning River Dr., has laundry ($3), BBQ, and a kitchen. (☎02 6552 2857; www.twilightcaravanpark.com.au. Prices vary between seasons. Linen $7.50 per person.) Catch breakfast or lunch at **Raw Sugar ❷,** 224 Victoria St., for a modern Australian meal ($8-16) or a $4 cup of freshly brewed coffee. (☎02 6550 0137 Open daily 7:30am-3pm, until 4pm for the cafe. AmEx/MC/V.) **Delicious Noodle ❶,** 39 Manning St., (☎02 6551 1000) will wok ingredients of your choice into a bowl of noodles for $9-12. (Open daily 11am-9pm. Cash only.) Manning St. also has a large **Coles** supermarket. (☎02 6552 1611. Open daily 6am-11pm.)

**BEACHES.** The beaches near Taree are gorgeous and inviting but have unexpected currents, so swim only where patrolled. The closest is **Old Bar Beach,** a 15min. drive southeast from the town center on Old Bar Rd. **Wallabi Point,** to the south, offers great surfing and surfboard riding, and **Saltwater National Park** has a swimming lagoon. Farther south, **Hallidays Point** includes the well-known **Diamond Beach** and **Black Head Beach. Crowdy Head,** the site of a lighthouse lookout, is a 40min. drive to the north.

## FROM TAREE TO PORT MACQUARIE

There are two routes from Taree to Port Macquarie, each with its own distinct charm. Beach bums are advised to stick to the **Pacific Highway,** with a stopover in Crowdy Bay. Joy-riding daytrippers can take the scenic, bumpy 100km **Tourist Drive 8,** which curves inland before meeting back up with the Pacific Hwy.

**CROWDY BAY NATIONAL PARK.** Although the drive here is full of potholes, Crowdy Bay is worth every jolt. Crowdy Bay, 40km north of Taree off the Pacific Hwy., is home to some of the area's most popular beaches, bushwalks, and picnic areas, as well as an abundance of kangaroos. Coralville Rd., at Moorland on the Pacific Hwy., leads into the park's southern entrance. Wild eastern grey kangaroos live at each of its three campsites: **Diamond Head, Indian Head,** and **Kylie's Rest Area.** There are flush toilets and cold showers at Diamond Head; all other sites have composting toilets. *(Campsites adults $10, children $5.)* Groups of kangaroos hop within feet of astounded visitors, and whales can be seen off the headlands, but it often takes an expert to spot more elusive koalas at Indian Head and Kylie's Hut. There are three reasonably tame bushwalks in the park that pass through habitats stunted by exposure to wind and harsh salt sprays. The shortest walk is along the base of the headland cliff, accessible from Diamond Head at low tide. The longer **Diamond Head Loop Track** (4.8km) links Diamond Head and Indian Head, while a third track goes from Kylie's to the Crowdy Bay beach (1.2km return). Bring your own water into the park. The roads are 2WD-accessible dirt tracks. *(Daily vehicle fee $7.)*

> **TIP**  **RAIN ON MY PARADE.** If you're planning to drive down any unsealed 2WD drive roads, you may want to re-think your plans if it starts raining. Rain can quickly ruin these roads and make them impassable.

# PORT MACQUARIE  ☎02

Travelers often make the sad mistake of bypassing the pristine port town of Port Macquarie (ma-KWAR-ee; pop. 47,000), once a lock-up for Sydney's worst offenders. Today, killers have been replaced with koalas—Port Macquarie houses the world's largest urban population of cuddly marsupials. Adrenaline junkies are also at home here, as the meeting of the Hastings River and the Pacific Ocean provides a variety of adventure activities year-round.

## ⎘ TRANSPORTATION

Major **bus** lines, including Greyhound Australia (☎13 14 99 or 13 20 30) and Premier (☎13 34 10), pass through town three times a day on their Sydney-Brisbane routes. Check to make sure your bus stops at Hayward St. rather than out on the highway. Car rental outfits include: **Avis,** 166 Gordon St. (☎02 6584 5673); **Budget** (☎02 6583 5144 or 13 27 27), at the corner of Gordon and

Hollingsworth St.; **Hertz,** 102 Gordon St. (☎02 6583 6599 or 1300 132 607); and **Thrifty** (☎02 6584 2122), on the corner of Horton and Hayward St.

## ORIENTATION AND PRACTICAL INFORMATION

The **CBD** is bordered to the north by the Hastings River and to the west by Kooloonbung Creek. **Horton Street** is the main commercial drag. Perpendicular to Horton St. and running along the river to the Marina is **Clarence Street,** along which you'll find numerous restaurants and cafes as well as the **Port Central Mall.** The **Visitors Information Centre** is at the corner of Gordon and Gore St. (☎1300 303 155; www.portmacquarieinfo.com.au. Open M-F 8:30am-5pm, Sa-Su 9am-4pm.) **Banks** with **ATMs** line Horton St. between Clarence and William St. The **library,** on the corner of Grant and Gordon St., has **Internet access** (☎02 6581 8755; $4 per hr; open M-F 9:30am-6pm, Sa 9am-noon), as does **Port Surf Hub,** 57 Clarence St. (☎02 6584 4744. Open M-W and Su 9am-6pm, Th-Sa 9am-7pm. $2.50 initial access fee, plus $0.07 per min.) The **police station** (☎02 6584 0199) is on the corner of Hay St. and Sunset Pde. A **post office** is on the corner of William and Short St. (☎02 6588 3100. Open M-F 9am-5pm.) **Postal Code:** 2444.

## ACCOMMODATIONS

Port Macquarie has a range of good budget options, most of which offer weekly discounts. Book ahead during the high season, when motels and caravan parks sometimes choose to double their prices.

**Ozzie Pozzie Backpackers,** 36 Waugh St. (☎02 6583 8133 or 1800 620 020; www. ozziepozzie.com), off Gore St. between Buller and Bridge St. Friendly owner Richard organizes activities and offers personalized recommendations. Dorms are bright and clean; the center courtyard is an excellent place for BBQs and meeting other backpackers. Freebies include breakfast, bikes, boogie boards, and video collection (with deposits). Kitchen, Internet access ($1 per 15min.), and TV lounge. Free pickup from bus stop. Lockers $10 deposit. Dorms from $25; doubles from $58, ensuite from $65. Accepts VIP, NOMADS, and YHA discounts. MC/V. ❷

**Port Macquarie Hotel** (☎02 6580 7888; www.macquariehotel.com.au), at the corner of Horton and Clarence St. Location can't be beat: in the middle of the CBD and above some great bars, a block from the water. Outfitted in Art Deco design. Basic singles from $40; doubles $50, ensuite $55-70. AmEx/MC/V. ❸

**Beachside Backpackers (YHA),** 40 Church St. (☎02 6583 5512 or 1800 880 008). Close to the beaches and 5min. walk from CBD. Clean and friendly. Free boogie boards and fishing rods ($5 deposit). Internet access $2 per 20min. Bike rental $5 per day. Summer F night BBQs $8. Free pickup from bus stop. Reception 8am-10pm. Dorms from $28, YHA $$25; doubles from $72.50; twins from $67. AmEx/MC/V. ❷

**Sundowner Breakwall Tourist Park,** 1 Munster St. (☎02 6583 2755 or 1800 636 452; www.sundownerholidays.com). A huge waterfront park next to Town Beach and the Hastings River. Pool, BBQ, and 30min. free Internet access. Book ahead in summer. Dorms $25. Sites $25-47, powered $31-60; cabins and cottages for 2 $65-335. MC/V. ❷

## FOOD

Clarence St. is lined with affordable cafes and takeaways. The Port Central Mall, on Claren St., has a food court, deli, and supermarket. There's also a **Food for Less** on Short and Buller St. (☎02 6583 2364; open M-Sa 8am-9pm, Su 8am-8pm) and a 24hr. **Coles** supermarket one block up (☎02 6583 2544).

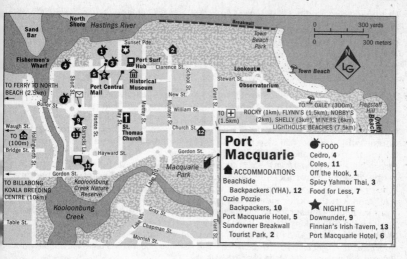

**Port Macquarie**

🍴 FOOD
Cedro, 4
Coles, 11
Off the Hook, 1
Spicy Yahmor Thai, 3
Food for Less, 7

🏠 ACCOMMODATIONS
Beachside
  Backpackers (YHA), 12
Ozzie Pozzie
  Backpackers, 10
Port Macquarie Hotel, 5
Sundowner Breakwall
Tourist Park, 2

⭐ NIGHTLIFE
Downunder, 9
Finnian's Irish Tavern, 13
Port Macquarie Hotel, 6

**Off the Hook** (☎02 6584 1146), on Horton St., off the town green. Cooks your choice of fish. Fish and chips $7.50. Fishburgers from $5. Open daily 11am-8pm. MC/V. ❶

**Cedro,** 72 Clarence St. (☎02 6583 5529). Scrumptious breakfasts and healthful salads and soups. Try the Cedro breakfast ($16.50) or a salad with roasted sweet potato ($14). Open M-F 7:30am-2:30pm, Sa-Su 8am-2:30pm. MC/V. ❷

**Spicy Yahmor Thai** (☎02 6583 9043), on Clarence St. in the middle of town. Offers spicy curries and noodle dishes ($13-17). Open daily 5:30-10pm. AmEx/MC/V. ❷

## 👁 SIGHTS

**KOALAS.** Port Macquarie is home to two of the best koala facilities in the state. The ▣**Billabong Koala Breeding Centre,** 61 Billabong Dr., 10km west of Port Macquarie at 61 Billabong Dr., allows visitors to pet and feed koalas, wallabies, and kangaroos. The center also has exotic birds, monkeys, and cassowaries, as well as the world's five most venomous snakes. By car, take Gordon St. west toward Wauchope; those without cars can reach the center by taking bus #335, which runs 2-6 times per day. The volunteer-led ▣**Koala Hospital,** south of the CBD on Lord St. at the **Macquarie Nature Reserve,** admits hundreds of sick koalas each year. Visitors can stroll around the grounds or watch the koalas receiving care through a viewing window. (Centre ☎02 6585 1060. Open daily 9am-5pm. Koala presentations 10:30am, 1:30pm, and 3:30pm. $15, children $10, concessions $13. Reserve ☎02 6584 1522; www.koalahospital.org.au. Feeding and tour daily at 3pm. Donations appreciated.)

**BEACHES.** The closest sand is at **Town Beach,** where the 8km long beach and headland walk starts. From the headlands overlooking Town Beach, you can see North Beach and Hasting River, across the inlet bay. Heading southeast along the coast, you'll find **Oxley Beach, Rocky Beach,** and **Flynn's Beach** (popular with families). From there, follow **Nobby's Beach** to **Nobby's Hill,** where an obelisk stands in memory of those who died swimming in the dangerous blowhole (let that be a lesson to you). Next in line is **Shelly Beach,** home to huge goannas and powerful surf. It's a perfect picnic spot, complete with BBQ area. The last part of the track leads to **Miners Beach** (an unofficial nude beach) and the **Tack-**

NEW SOUTH WALES

ing **Point Lighthouse,** a popular lookout over **Lighthouse Beach,** a great surf spot. Hostels are usually willing to drop off guests at the lighthouse if they want to take the walk back. *(To reach the beaches by car, drive along William St. to Pacific Dr., which hugs the coast. Turn left on Lighthouse Rd. to reach Miners Beach, the lighthouse, and Lighthouse Beach. Lighthouse, Flynn's, and Town Beach are patrolled during summer. Public toilets are located at Town, Flynn's, Shelly, Nobby's Hill, and the carpark just before the lighthouse.)*

**PARKS.** The **Sea Acres Rainforest Centre,** at Shelly Beach, preserves one of the largest stretches of coastal rainforest in the country. A 1.3km raised boardwalk circles through a portion of the 76-hectare reserve and allows glimpses of bush turkeys and flying foxes. You can explore on your own, but illuminating, volunteer-guided walks are also available. The **visitors center** has a free 20min. film and ecological display. *(☎02 6582 3355. Open daily 9am-4:30pm. $8, children $4. Accessible by bus #322 (hourly) from the town center. Shelly Beach Stop.)* At the end of Horton St. is one of several entrances to the **Kooloonbung Creek Nature Reserve,** a 52-hectare conservation area of peaceful bushland with footpaths through mangroves and wetlands. On the other side of the Hasting River, North Beach leads to Point Plommer and **Limeburner Creek Nature Reserve,** the site of Aboriginal artifacts and the **Big Hill walking track** (2km). *(Ferries take cars from Settlement Point, at the end of Settlement Point Rd. (called Park St. at the intersection with Hastings River Dr.), to North Shore Dr. From there, turn right onto the 16km coastal Point Plommer Rd., which is unsealed but bikeable. Those in 2WDs should take Maria River Rd. instead.)*

## ⬛ NIGHTLIFE

The **Port Macquarie Hotel,** on the corner of Clarence and Horton St., is a popular nightspot in town, with several bars and a dance floor. *(☎02 6583 1011. W karaoke. Su live music. M-Th and Su open 10am-midnight, F-Sa 10am-1am.)* **Downunder,** on Short St. next to Coles, has Trivia Wednesdays at 9pm. *(Open daily 9pm with last entrance at 1am.)* **Finnian's Irish Tavern,** on the corner of Gordon and Horton St., attracts a relaxed, older crowd. *(☎02 6583 4646. Th trivia, F DJ, Sa live music. Open M-Tu and Su 11am-11pm, W-Sa 11am-midnight.)*

## ⬛ OUTDOOR ACTIVITIES

**ON LAND.** Aussie adventurer Greg leads **Port Macquarie Camel Safaris.** Caravan along Lighthouse Beach and perhaps spot some whales or dolphins from your camelback vantage point. Pickup in the camel car can be arranged. *(☎04 3767 2080. 30min. Operates M-F and Su 9:30am-1pm. $25, children $20.)* Bikes can be rented from **Graham Seers Cyclery,** located at Shop Port Marina on Park St. *(☎02 6583 2333. $15 per hr., $40 per day, $70 per week. Open M-F 9am-5pm, Sa 9am-1:30pm.)* Most hostels also loan bikes. For mountain biking or abseiling, try **EdgeExperience,** with tours for cyclists and climbers for all levels. *(☎04 2732 4009; www.edgeexperience.com.au. ½-day mountain biking $65, or introductory abseiling $110. Free pickup.)*

**IN WATER.** Hang 10 with **Port Macquarie Surf School,** which offers classes for newbies and intermediate surfers. *(☎02 6585 5433; www.portmacquariesurf-school.com.au. 1½hr. group lessons $40.)* **Port Venture** runs 2hr. dolphin watching cruises in a large ship *(☎02 6583 3058; $25)* with daily tea and BBQ on W. **Kayak Tours** runs a variety of trip from 30min. *($15)* to 4hr. *($50)* through the mangroves or rapids. *(☎02 6584 1039; www.kayakinport.com.)*

**IN AIR.** **High Adventure Air Park** offers a variety of tandem flights. *(☎04 2984 4961. 30min. Coastal paragliding $160, mountains $220.)* To see the sky with your feet planted on the ground, visit the **Observatorium,** situated in Rotary Park on the corner of Stewart and Lord St., where a large telescope offers good views of the Southern Hemisphere's constellations. (☎02 6584 9164. Apr.-Oct. W and Su beginning 7:30pm; end of Oct.-early Apr. 8:15pm. Adult $8, concession $7.)

# NAMBUCCA HEADS ☎02

For the traveler in need of a break from tourist attractions and constant activities, Nambucca Heads (pop. 7000) provides a convenient stopover and welcome respite. Though it lacks hostels, Nambucca Heads has plenty of accommodations within walking distance of the charming river and the area's well-kept beaches. Nambucca is full of whimsical artwork; it's one of the few places where graffiti artists are welcomed and provided with an outdoor gallery.

**TRANSPORTATION.** The train station is 3km out of town. From Mann St., bear right at the roundabout to Railway Rd. Countrylink (☎13 22 32) goes to Coffs Harbour (40min., 3 per day, $4.80). The bus stop is at the visitors center, just outside town at the Pacific Hwy. and Riverside Dr. Busways (☎02 6568 3012) runs to Bellingen (45min., 3 per day, $8.50) and Coffs Harbour (1hr., 5 per day, $7.80). Greyhound (☎13 14 99 or 13 20 30) and Premier (☎13 34 10) together stop six times daily on Sydney-Brisbane routes.

**ORIENTATION AND PRACTICAL INFORMATION.** The main road in Nambucca Heads is Riverside Dr., which becomes Fraser St. and then Bowra St. as it passes through the town center. It then becomes Mann St., then Old Coast Rd., where it reconnects with the highway. Follow Ridge St. to Liston St., which heads toward the town's beaches. The **Nambucca Valley Visitor Information Centre** is at the intersection of the Pacific Hwy. and Riverside Dr. (☎02 6568 6954; www.nambuccatourism.com. Open daily 9am-5pm.) A **Woolworths** is in town off Bowra St., up the hill from the RSL (Returned Servicemen's League) Club. (☎02 6569 4505. Open M-Sa 7:30am-10pm, Su 7:30am-8pm.) For cheap **Internet access** ($3 per hr.), head to the **public library** on Ridge St. (☎02 6568 6906. Open M-F 9:30am-5:30pm.) The **post office** is on the corner of Bowra and Ridge St. (☎02 6598 7320. Open M-F 9am-5pm.) **Police** ☎02 6598 5399. **Postal Code:** 2448.

**ACCOMMODATIONS AND FOOD.** Nambucca and the surrounding townships of Bowraville, Scotts Head, and Valla Beach are overflowing with caravan parks situated near beaches or along the Pacific Hwy. **White Albatross Holiday Centre ❸**, at the ocean end of Wellington Dr., next to the V-Wall Tavern, is a sprawling caravan park with a gorgeous setting near a swimming lagoon and the Nambucca River. Amenities include picnic and BBQ areas, kitchen, laundry, game room, and a small store. (☎02 6569 4698; www.whitealbatross.com. au. Linens $6. Powered sites $32-55; cabins from $70-165. Book ahead in summer. MC/V.) **Aukaka Caravan Park ❶**, 2 Pacific Hwy., is fine for overnight stopovers, but the facilities are a bit on the old side. (☎02 6568 6647. Sites from $17-20, powered from $20-22; cabins from $35-59. MC/V.)

Bowra St. has an assortment of quick, cheap food possibilities. The **Bookshop and Internet Cafe ❶**, on the corner of Bowra and Ridge St., is the perfect place to trade in old books or have a delicious lunch. The cafe serves mouthwatering sandwiches ($5-12), soups ($9), and smoothies ($5.50). (☎02 6568 5855. Internet $7.50 per hr. Open daily in summer 9am-5pm, in winter 8:30am-4:30pm. Cash only.) The **V-Wall Tavern ❷**, at the mouth of the Nambucca River on Wellington Dr., has river views, televised sports, and a nightlife scene. (☎02 6568 6344. Meals from $12. Open daily noon-2:30pm and 6-8:30pm. MC/V.) **Nambucca**

**Tasty Tucka ❶**, 40 Bowra St., serves fish and chips (from $5) and burgers. (☎02 6568 7800. Open M-Th and Su 10am-7:30pm, F-Sa 10am-8pm. Cash only.)

**🏞 HIKES.** There are walks of varying difficulty throughout the beach and bush areas of Nambucca, some of which pass by the gorgeous Rotary, Captain Cook, and Lions Lookouts. For more structured exploration, **Kyeewa Bushwalkers,** a volunteer group, organizes free walks. Visit the **info center** or check online (www.nambuccatourism.com/events_monthly.asp) for an updated schedule.

# BELLINGEN                                                    ☎02

Beautiful Bellingen (pop. 3000) sits on the banks of the Bellinger River, 30min. from World Heritage-listed **Dorrigo National Park** (p. 199), and is halfway between Coffs Harbour and Nambucca Heads. "Bello," as locals call it, is a laid-back country town with friendly locals and great coffee shops.

**📠 TRANSPORTATION. Buses** stop at Hyde and Church St. Busways (☎1300 555 611) services Coffs Harbour (1hr.; M-F 3 per day, Sa 2 per day; $7.50) and Nambucca Heads (45min., 3 per day, $6.60). Keans (☎1800 043 339) travels to Port Macquarie (3hr.; Tu, F 1 per day; $35) via Coffs Harbour (35min., $28) and Nambucca Heads (1hr., $35); and Tamworth (4hr.; Th, F 1 per day; $73) via Dorrigo (35min., $28) and Armidale (3hr., $43). **Bellingen World Travel,** 42 Hyde St. (☎02 6655 2055; open M-F 9am-5pm, Sa 9am-noon), books transportation.

**📇 ORIENTATION AND PRACTICAL INFORMATION. Hyde Street** runs parallel to the Bellinger River and cuts through the center of town. The **Bellingen Shire Tourist Information Centre** is located on the Pacific Hwy., in the small town of Urunga. (☎02 6655 5711; www.bellingermagic.com. Open M-Sa 9am-5pm, Su 10am-2pm.) The smaller **Bellingen Visitor Centre** has friendly volunteers and has recently relocated into the old library in the center of town on Hyde St. (☎02 6655 5711; www.waterfallway.cm.au. Open daily in winter 9:30am-4:30pm, in summer 9am-5pm). The **library,** in the park in the center of town, has **Internet access.** (☎02 6655 1744. $3 per hr. Open Tu-W 10:30am-5:30pm, Th-F 10:30am-12:30pm and 1:30-5:30pm, Sa 9:30am-noon.) The **police station** is at 47 Hyde St. (☎02 6655 1444) and the **post office** is next door on the corner of Bridge St. (☎02 6655 1020. Open M-F 9am-5pm.) **Postal Code:** 2454.

**🏠 ACCOMMODATIONS. 🛏Bellingen Backpackers ❷**, 2 Short St., impresses with its huge verandas overlooking the Bellinger River. The patio lounge has a ping-pong table, floor pillows, didjeridus, and a TV. The friendly staff arranges day-trips to Dorrigo National Park ($35) and will pick up guests from Urunga train or bus stations. Bike rental ($5), laundry ($4), computer access ($5 per hr.), and Wi-Fi ($5 per day) are available. (☎02 6655 1116. Sites for 2 $25; dorms $28; doubles or twins $64-72. YHA discount.) The **Federal Hotel ❸**, 77 Hyde St., is a tidy pubstay with small fridges in every room. The bar and bistro downstairs often bring live music, featuring jazz on Wednesday nights. (☎02 6655 9345; www.federalhotel.com.au. 10-bed dorms $40; twins $80; triples $90. MC/V.)

**🍴 FOOD.** Scrumptious **🍽Riverstone ❷**, 105-109 Hyde St., serves big breakfasts and lunches in a modern, cozy atmosphere. (☎02 6655 9099; www.riverstone. com. Meals $12-16. Open daily 8am-2pm for breakfast and lunch, until 4pm for coffee. MC/V.) The **Lodge 241 Gallery Cafe ❷**, 117-121 Hyde St., on the western edge of town, is situated in a historical old masons' house and features some of the best panoramic views in town. Their blackboard menu rotates daily, but the food's always freshly prepared. (☎02 6655 2470; www.bellingen.com/thelodge. Breakfast and lunch $9-18. Open W-Sun 8:30am-4:30pm. MC/V.) **Swiss Patisserie ❶**, 7 Church St., is famous for its delicious Bee Sting ($3.40 per slice), custard-filled pastries, and wild berry dappers ($2.30). For those craving something salty, they also bake over 20 varieties of savory meat and vegetarian pies. (☎02 6655 0050. Open daily 7am-5pm. MC/V.) A well-stocked **IGA** supermarket is at 62 Hyde St. (☎02 6655 1042. Open daily 7am-8pm.)

🔲 📷 **SIGHTS AND ACTIVITIES.** Even if you're not necessarily in the market for a "didj" or have no idea how to circular breathe, **Heartland Didgeridoos**, 25 Hyde St. opposite the Shell Service Station, has an outstanding collection of homemade instruments and offers lessons and a didg-making course. (☎02 6655 9881; www.heartdidg.com. Didjeridus from $150 to $1000. Lessons $40 per hr. Inquire about lessons for making your own. Open M-F 9am-5pm, Sa 10am-4pm.) **Bellingen Canoe Adventures** (☎02 6655 9955) offers canoes for rent ($11 per hr.) as well as guided sunset champagne tours ($22) on the Bellinger River. Just across the Bellinger River on Hammond St. is the entrance to Bell-ingen Island, home to an active colony of "flying foxes," giant fruit bats with 3 ft. wingspans. A forest trail loops through the open understory for excellent views of the town. Turning right off Hammond St. onto Black St. leads to the showground, where an organic market is held the second and fourth Saturday of every month. A larger produce, crafts, and antiques community market with 250 stalls and live music takes place the third Saturday of the month. The three-day **Bellingen Jazz and Blues Festival** (☎02 6655 9345; www.bellingenjazzfestival. com.au) falls on the third weekend of August and brings more than a dozen performers to many town venues. **The Global Carnival** during the first week of October attracts talented musicians from around the world for a three-day music galore. Additional camping grounds are created for this event.

## DORRIGO NATIONAL PARK

It's best to begin your exploration of Dorrigo National Park, part of the World Heritage "Gondwana Rainforests," at the **Rainforest Centre**, 2km east of Dorrigo. The centre has a cafe and educational displays. Watch for red-necked pade-melons and brush turkeys in the lawns around the Center picnic area. (☎02 6657 2309. Open daily 9am-4pm.) Dorrigo is pure rainforest, with sections of multi-layered canopy and wet eucalyptus forest. When the rain makes things sloppy (not usually a problem on fully sealed trails), the leeches have a field day. Pick them off, or buy some insect repellent from the center. Behind the Rainforest Center is the spectacular 75m-long **Skywalk** that extends out and over the tree canopy, 21m above the forest floor. The **Lyrebird Link Track** is an easy 400m stroll that links the Rainforest Center to the 5.8km (2½hr., easy-medium) Wonga Walk loop that connects the Crystal Shower Falls and Tristania Falls. The Glade Picnic Area 1km further up Dome Rd is accessible by car.

From the park, follow Waterfall Way through the town of Dorrigo to visit the spectacular **Dangar Falls lookout.** A sealed pathway leads all the way from the viewpoint to the base of the falls, a swell swimming spot. Numerous picnic areas, walks, and attractions make this a pleasant day excursion. If you do decide to stay the night—and you'll have to if you take the bus—**Gracemere Grange ❸**, 325 Dome Rd., just 2km from the park, offers beautiful, B&B-style accommodations with continental breakfast included. (☎02 6657 2630; www. dorrigo.com/gracemere. Singles $35; doubles $70-80.)

Dorrigo is just 29km west of Bellingen and 64km west of Coffs Harbour. It's easiest to visit by car, but Keans also offers **bus** service from a number of local towns, including Armidale, Bellingen, and Coffs Harbour. (☎1800 043 339; www.keans.com.au. 1hr. Leaves for Dorrigo M, Th and returns Tu, F. $28.)

# COFFS HARBOUR ☎ 02

Situated along the coast, backed by the hills of the Great Dividing Range, and covered in lush banana plantations, Coffs Harbour (pop. 70,000) is a popular spot for partygoers, scuba divers, and adrenaline junkies. The town is also known for its proximity to **Solitary Islands National Marine Park.** The continuing expansion of Coffs has come at the expense of its coastal charm, but the town's tight-knit community and scenic harbor make it a worthwhile stop.

## ▮◗ TRANSPORTATION

**Trains:** The **station** is at the end of Angus McLeod Pl. by the jetty. From Harbour Dr., turn onto Camperdown St. and take the first left. **Countrylink** (☎13 22 32) goes to: **Brisbane** (6-8hr., 2 per day, $70); **Byron Bay** (4-5hr., 4 per day, $42); **Nambucca Heads** (40min., 3 per day, $6); and elsewhere. Prices vary by season. Student discounts.

**Buses:** The bus stop is off the Pacific Hwy., on the corner of Elizabeth and McLean St.

  **Greyhound Australia** (☎13 14 99 or 13 20 30). To: **Ballina** (2-3hr., 5 per day, $58); **Brisbane** (6-8hr., 5 per day, $81); **Byron Bay** (4-5hr., 5 per day, $67); **Newcastle** (8hr., 4 per day, $81); **Port Macquarie** (3hr., 3 per day, $58); **Sydney** (9-10hr., 4 per day, $91). ISIC/VIP/YHA 10% discount.

  **Keans** (☎1800 043 339). M, Th 1 per day to: **Armidale** (3hr., $43); **Bellingen** (35min., $28); **Dorrigo** (1hr., $28); **Tamworth** (5hr., $73). Return trips Tu, Fr.

  **Premier** (☎13 34 10). To: **Brisbane** (7hr., 2 per day, $54); **Byron Bay** (4hr., 3 per day, $46); **Newcastle** (6hr., 2 per day, $53); **Port Macquarie** (2hr., 2 per day, $43); **Taree** (2hr., 2 per day, $46); **Sydney** (8hr., 3 per day, $61). ISIC/VIP/YHA 15% discount.

**TAKE A LOAD OFF.** Coffs Harbour is nearly impossible to navigate on foot. Take advantage of free shuttles offered by hostels, or rent a bike.

**Car Rental: Coffs Harbour Rent-A-Car** (☎02 6652 5022), at the Shell Service Station, on the corner of Pacific Hwy. and Marcia St. Companies such as **Budget** (☎02 6651 4994 or 13 27 27) and **Europcar** (☎02 6651 8558 or 13 13 90) are at the airport.

**Taxi: Coffs District Taxi Network** (☎13 10 08).

## ▗▟ ◪ ORIENTATION AND PRACTICAL INFORMATION

As it passes through the city of Coffs Harbour, the Pacific Hwy. takes on three new names: **Grafton Street, Woolgoolga Road,** and **Bellingen Road.** Coffs is divided into two main clusters, each centered on a different end of Harbour Drive: the **Palms Centre,** on Vernon St. at the west end of Harbour Dr., is the Central Business District (CBD), while the **Jetty Village Shopping Centre** at the east end has a smaller strip of shops by the harbor. The **Muttonbird Island Nature Reserve** is accessible by walking along the breakwater boardwalk at the end of Marina Dr. The city can be difficult to get around on foot, but hostels will often provide rides to attractions that are more than a 15min. walk away.

  **Tourist Office: Visitor Centre** (☎02 6648 4990 or 1300 369070; www.coffscoast.com. au), on the corner of the Pacific Hwy. and McLean St. Open daily 9am-5pm.

  **Police:** 20 Moonee St. (☎02 6652 0299).

  **Hospital:** 345 Pacific Hwy. (☎02 6656 7000).

### Coffs Harbour
------- Nature Walk

▲ ACCOMMODATIONS
Aussitel Backpackers, **14**
Coffs Harbour Tourist
　Caravan Park, **6**
Coffs Harbour YHA, **11**
Hoey Moey Backpackers, **3**
Park Beach Holiday Park, **5**

🍎 FOOD
Bananacoast Bake House, **10**
The Crying Tiger, **13**
The Fishermen's Co-op, **12**
Rainforest Bar and Grill, **1**
The Blue Balloon, **4**

★ NIGHTLIFE
Ex-Service's Club, **8**
Greenhouse Tavern, **2**
Plantation Hotel, **7**
Coffs Hotel, **9**

TO BALLINA (175km),
BYRON BAY (205km)

TO BRUXNER PARK FLORA
RESERVE (1km), SEALY LOOKOUT
(3km), LEGENDS SURF MUSEUM
(8km)

Big Banana ■

Diggers Beach Rd.

Diggers
Beach

*Macauleys
Headland*

PACIFIC
OCEAN

*Little
Muttonbird
Island*

*Muttonbird
Island*

*Nature
Reserve*

Coffs Harbour

*Boambee
Beach*

*Corambirra
Point*

**Internet Access: Coffs Harbour City Library** (☎02 6648 4900), on the corner of Coffs
and Duke St., offers free 30min. sessions. Open M-F 9:30am-6pm, Sa 9:30am-3pm.

**Post Office:** (☎02 6648 7290) in Palms Centre; (☎02 6652 7499) in the Park Beach
Plaza; and (☎02 6652 3200) across from the Jetty Village Shopping Centre. All open
M-F 9am-5pm, Sa 9am-noon. **Postal Code:** 2450.

## 🏠 🏕 ACCOMMODATIONS AND CAMPING

Many motels are clustered along the Pacific Hwy. and Park Beach Rd. Caravan
parks and hostels often offer weekly discounts in the low season. For longer
stays and larger groups, you can book apartments at the visitors center. There
are also several urban camping options.

▨ **Coffs Harbour YHA,** 51 Collingwood St. (☎02 6652 6462). High-tech hostel near jetty.
Spacious rooms, kitchen, lounge area, TV, laundry ($6), Internet ($5 per hr.), ping-pong
table, and swimming pool. Free pickup and dropoff. Bikes, boogie boards, and surfboards $5-10 (with $50 deposit). Reception May-Sept. 8am-10pm; Oct.-Apr. 7am-
11pm. Dorms $23-33; doubles and twins $70-135. MC/V. ❷

**Aussitel Backpackers,** 312 Harbour Dr. (☎02 6651 1871 or 1800 330 335; www.
aussitel.com), 20min. walk from CBD and 10min. walk from the beach. Social and

clean. TV, pool, BBQ, foosball, luggage storage, laundry ($3.40), and Internet access. Free pickup and dropoff. Bikes for rent (prices vary) and free boogie boards. **Banana Coast Divers,** on premises, offers PADI certification $285; $55 medical waiver. Events nightly. Dorms $22-26, twins and doubles $55-65. NOMADS/VIP/YHA. MC/V. ❷

**Park Beach Holiday Park** (☎02 6648 4888 or 1800 200 111; www.parkbeachholiday-park.com.au), near the Surf Club on Ocean Pde. Very professional. On the beach, though not the best stretch. Sites $25-35, powered $28-44; cabins $61-280. MC/V. ❷

**Coffs Harbour Tourist Caravan Park,** 123 Pacific Hwy. (☎02 6652 1694; www.coffsharbourtouristpark.com) is another nearby camping option with clean cabins and facilities. Sites $21-24, powered $23-28; cabins $58-95. MC/V. ❷

**Hoey Moey Backpackers,** (☎02 6651 7966 or 1800 683 322), on Ocean Pde., at end of Park Beach Rd. 1min. from beach and 10min. to Park Beach Plaza. Hoey Moey, slang for "Hotel Motel," is a hostel, motel, and pub all rolled into 1. All rooms have bath, TV, and small fridge. Laundry $5.40. Key deposit $10. Free pickup and dropoff during reception hours. Free surfboards. Bikes $5 per day, $20 deposit. Reception in winter 8am-4pm; in summer 6am-11:30am and 1:30pm-7:30pm. Check-in at pub after hours. Dorms $26; motel rooms $50. Discounts for 1-week stays. VIP/YHA. MC/V. ❷

# 🍴 FOOD

Across from the Jetty Village Shopping Centre on Harbour Dr. is a row of expensive restaurants serving up Thai, Vietnamese, Indian, Chinese, Italian, and Mod Oz meals. The Palms Centre Mall, Park Beach Plaza, and Jetty Village Shopping Centre each have supermarkets. The **Plantation Hotel** ❶ has cheap pub meals, including an all-day steak special for $7 with any alcohol purchase.

**The Fisherman's Co-op,** 69 Marina Dr. (☎02 6652 2811), by the breakwater board-walk. Serves fresh seafood straight off the boat, with fish and chip meals ($8) and cajun-grilled hoki. Market open daily 9am-6pm; takeaway counter open daily in summer 10am-9pm, in winter 10am-6pm. MC/V. ❶

**The Blue Balloon,** 100 Harbour Dr. (☎02 6651 3333). This fun joint serves homemade gelato ($3.50-5.50) in decadent flavors like Turkish delight. Also offers breakfast, lunch, and dinner menus ($7-15). Open daily 7am-9pm. MC/V. ❶

**The Crying Tiger,** 384a Harbour Dr. (☎02 6650 0195), in the Jetty Village shopping area. Huge variety of contemporary Thai dishes amid colorful cushions and tall ceilings. Stir-fry and curries $18-25. Open M-F 7:30am-5pm, Sa 7:30am-2pm. Cash only. ❸

**Bananacoast Bake House,** 22a Gordon St. (☎02 6652 2032). Offers a traditional, no-frills bakery with cheap scones ($0.45), pies ($3), and sandwiches ($3). Open M-F 7:30am-5pm, Sa 7:30am-2pm. Cash only. ❶

**Rainforest Bar and Grill** (☎02 6651 5488), in the spacious, tropical Greenhouse Tavern at the corner of Bray St. and the Pacific Hwy. An extensive menu including hamburgers from $10 and steaks from $20. Open daily noon-2pm and 6-8:30pm. ❷

# 👁 SIGHTS

The **Coffs Harbour Jetty,** once bustling with local timber industry, is now a nexus of recreation with some commercial fishing. It has BBQ facilities and is an easy walk from Jetty Beach. The **breakwater boardwalk,** near the marina, connects the mainland to **Muttonbird Island** (named after its wedge-tailed inhabitants), a terrific lookout for spotting whales. The island was sacred to the region's Gumbaynggirr people; according to one story, a giant moon-man guarded the island and the muttonbirds. **Park Beach** and the beach immediately north of the marina are both popular hangouts, but they have dangerous currents. Since Coffs beaches are only patrolled in the summer, exercise caution. **The Botanic**

**Gardens,** on Hardacre St., one block north of Harbour Dr., is definitely worth the walk for the beautiful birds that flock to its exotic plants. (☎02 6648 4188. Open daily 9am-5pm. Donation requested.) The 4km **Coffs Creek Walk** connects Rotary Park, at the intersection of Gordon and Coffs St. in the CBD, with the Coffs Creek inlet near Orlando St.; it also has a detour to the gardens. Make the hike a 10km circuit by continuing on the **Coffs Creek Habitat Walk** (6km), which follows the northern bank of the creek.

The **Big Banana,** 4km north of town on the Pacific Hwy., embodies kitsch. Enjoy an interactive 3D movie and guided tour to learn more than you need to know about banana cultivation ($10.50, students $9.50, children $8). Go toboganing ($5, 5 rides $15), hike up through the plantation for a view over the city, or just snap photos in front of the giant banana. The cafe sells outstanding treats, including frozen, chocolate-covered bananas ($3.50) and banana splits ($7). A candy-maker, puzzle shop, ice rink, inflatable water slide park, and trike rental are also on the grounds. (☎02 6652 4355; www.bigbanana. com. Open daily 9am-4pm. Free.) For those who haven't gotten enough banana, drive another kilometer up the road and turn left at Bruxner Park Road. A 7km scenic road winds through banana plantations up to **Sealy Lookout** and **Bruxner Park Flora Reserve.** Farmers sell bags of bananas and avocados ($1-2) in wooden stands along the way; leave the money in metal courtesy boxes.

Advertisements all over town point to the **Pet Porpoise Pool,** on Orlando St. by Coffs Creek. Although they're geared toward kids, the dolphin shows at 10am and 1pm are still pretty fun. Come 30min. early and a dolphin will give you a peck on the cheek. (☎02 6652 2164; www.petporpoisepool.com. Open daily 9am-4pm. $27, backpackers $21, students $19, children $14, families $75.)

## ◀ AQUATIC ACTIVITIES

There's no shortage of activities in Coffs. Hostels generally offer good rates, but don't hesitate to call tour agencies to find commission-free fun. Nearly all companies operate year-round, and some offer discounts during the winter.

**DIVING.** ▣**Jetty Dive Centre,** 398 Harbour Dr., offers a four-day PADI course ($295 for backpackers staying at any Coffs hostel). The course is run off Muttonbird Island and not the Solitary Islands, making for better prices but less-exotic visuals. For $345, the half-and-half course offers two dives at Muttonbird Island and two in the Solitary Islands. An extra $88 is required for a medical check-up and textbook. (☎02 6651 1611; www.jettydive.com.au. Single intro-dive $165; double intro-dive $175; double boat-dive with gear from $160; snorkeling $55. Open daily 8am-5:30pm.) **Solitary Islands Marine Reserve** stretches 70km from Coffs Harbour to the Sandon River and encompasses nearly 100,000 hectares of protected beaches, headlands, creeks, and islands. Due to the unique mix of tropical waters from the north and cool, temperate waters from the south, the area has some of the most diverse marine life on the coast. Visibility is usually best during the winter, when the water is chilly. Swim with harmless gray nurse sharks year-round. The island is only accessible through dives and private boats. Contact the **NSW Fisheries and Marine Parks Office,** 32 Marina Dr., for more info. (☎02 6652 3977; www.mpa.nsw.gov.au. Open M-F 8:30am-5pm.)

**FISHING AND WHALE WATCHING.** Fishing boats **Adriatic III** (☎04 1252 2002) and **Cougar Cat 12** (☎02 6651 6715 or 04 1866 6715; www.cougarcat12.com.au) will set you up with bait, line, and tackle. (6hr. reef fishing $100; leave 6am-noon. Game fishing by appointment.) Whales swim past Coffs in June and July and again from September to November; spot them during the winter months with **Spirit Cruises**. (☎02 6650 0155; www.spiritofcoffs.com.au. 2hr. Leaves daily at 9:30am and also 1pm on weekends. $39-60.) Spirit Cruises also offers excursions to see or swim with dolphins from January to May ($19-40).

**WHITEWATER RAFTING AND JET-SKIING.** The **Nymboida River,** 2hr. west of Coffs, is the most popular place to raft. The rapids, mostly Class I-V sections, pass through dense rainforest. Various companies offer tours to the Nymboida. The **Goolang River,** a manmade kayaking course, is usually Class III, but flow depends on seasonal conditions. **Liquid Assets Adventure Tours,** the pioneers of surf-rafting, run unbeatable whitewater rafting on the Goolang and Nymboida, as well as slightly tamer but still adrenaline-charged sea-kayak and rafting tours. (☎02 6658 0850; www.surfrafting.com. Meals included with full-day tours. Goolang day $80; full day on the Nymboida $160. 3hr. sea kayaking $50; 3hr. surf-rafting $50; combo kayak and surf-rafting $50; "Big Day Out" combo of kayaking, surf-rafting, and whitewater rafting $135.)

**SURFING. East Coast Surf School** has a remarkable success rate with novices. Classes for advanced surfers are also available. Call to arrange pickup from hostels. (☎02 6651 5515 or 04 1225 7233; www.eastcoastsurfschool.com.au. 2hr. group lesson $55, 5 lessons $200; 1hr. private lesson $70.) **Liquid Assets** (see above) also offers a "learn to surf" class (3hr. $50). Most hostels provide surfboards and boogie boards for rental. The best surfing is at **Diggers Beach** (patrolled during school holidays), north of Macauleys Headland, accessible off the Pacific Hwy. From the **Big Banana** (p. 203), turn onto Diggers Beach Rd. and follow it to the end. **The Gallows Beach,** down at the Jetty, also offers good breaks. To learn about surfing without getting your feet wet, visit former surfing champ Scott Dillon's **Legends Surf Museum,** at 3/18 Gaudron's Rd. in Korora, about 2km north of Coffs Harbour on the Pacific Hwy. (☎02 6653 6536; dafin@key.net.au. Open daily 10am-4pm. $5, children $2.)

## 🎵 📷 ENTERTAINMENT AND NIGHTLIFE

Coffs nightlife, focused around Grafton St., isn't quite as active as the daytime scene, but finding a party crowd isn't too difficult in the summertime, and hostels sometimes organize nights out for their guests. Most pubs have cover bands or DJs on weekends. The **Plantation Hotel,** on Grafton St., caters to the younger college crowd with its lounge rooms, dance floor, and frequent big-name DJs. (☎02 6652 3855; www.plantationhotel.com.au. Cover F-Sa $5. Open M-Th and Su until 2am, F-Sa until 3 or 4am.). **The Coffs Hotel,** on the corner of the Pacific Hwy. and West High St., has a "Shamrock Bar" with Irish and Aussie brews. (☎02 6652 3817; www.coffsharbourhotel.com. Free karaoke W and Th at 8:30pm and in-house DJs most other nights.) The somewhat bland **Ex-Service's Club** (☎02 6652 3888), on the corner of Grafton and Vernon St., serves reasonably priced drinks (schooners $3.60). Non-members must arrive before 11pm. Although it is 20min. from town, the **Greenhouse Tavern,** on the Pacific Hwy. by Park Beach Plaza, has multiple bars and live music (☎02 6651 5488)

# BALLINA ☎02

Technically an island, Ballina (pop. 19,000) is a peaceful port and beach town 2hr. north of Coffs Harbour and 30min. south of Byron Bay. Getting around is surprisingly easy if you utilize the extensive network of bike paths linking Ballina and Lennox Head; pick up a map from the visitors centre.

📁 **TRANSPORTATION.** Greyhound Australia (☎13 14 99) and Premier (☎13 34 10) **buses** stop in Ballina on their Sydney-Brisbane runs. Greyhound departs from the **Transit Centre,** 4km from the town center in a complex called **The Big Prawn** because of the huge fiberglass prawn on its roof; tickets can be purchased inside the restaurant. Premier and other bus companies stop at the Tamar St. bus zone. Blanch's Bus Company (☎02 6686 2144) travels daily to Byron Bay (50min.; M-F 7 per day, Sa 6 per day, Su 3 per day; $9.40) with a stop in Lennox Head (20min.; $6). **Ballina Taxi Cabs** (☎13 10 08) take you into town for $10-12. **Jack Ransom Cycles,** 16 Cherry St., off River St., rents bikes. (☎02 6686 3485. Open M-F 8am-5pm, Sa 8am-noon. ½-day $10, full day $18, week $60.)

◢◪ **ORIENTATION AND PRACTICAL INFORMATION.** The **Visitor Information Centre,** on the eastern edge of town at the corner of Las Balsa Plaza and **River Street** (the main street in town), has info on regional activities. (☎1800 777 666; www.discoverballina.com. Open daily 9am-5pm.) Hop on the **Internet** at the public **library,** next to the visitors center. (☎02 6686 1277. Open M-Tu and F 9:30am-6pm, W-Th 9:30am-8pm, Sa 9am-noon, Su 1pm-4pm. $2.20 per 30min. Wi-Fi available.) **Woolworths** supermarket is at 72 River St. (☎02 6686 3189. M-F 7:30am-9pm, Sa-Su 7:30am-6pm.) Another is located in the Ballina Fair Shopping Centre on Kerr Rd. (☎02 6686 4825; open M-F 8am-9pm, Sa-Su 8am-8pm), and a **Coles** is directly across the street. (☎02 6686 9377. Open M-F 6am-10pm, Sa 6am-10pm, Su 7am-8pm.) The **post office** is at 85 Tamar St. on the corner with Moon St. (☎02 6626 8810. Open M-F 9am-5pm.) **Postal Code:** 2478.

▛▐ **ACCOMMODATIONS AND FOOD.** The **Ballina Travelers Lodge (YHA) ❷,** 36 Tamar St., is a motel and hostel in one. Go one block up Norton St. from the tourist office, then turn left. The owners run a tight ship. The YHA part of the complex has four basic rooms, a kitchen and TV area, BBQ, and laundry. The larger motel rooms have TVs. Courtesy pickup from the transit center is available by arrangement. There's a small saltwater pool, bikes ($5 per stay), limited fishing gear, and free boogie boards. (☎02 6686 6737. Dorms from $25; doubles $68-112.) **The Ballina Central Caravan Park ❷,** 1 River St., is just north of the info center. (☎02 6686 2220; www.bscp.com.au/central. Open daily 7am-7pm. Sites $24-30, powered $27-37; cabins $58-130. Weekly rates available. MC/V.)

Delicious deli food awaits at **Sasha's Gourmet Eatery ❶,** in the Wigmore Arcade, off River St. Takeaway selections like pasta salad, quiche, and gourmet sandwiches ($7) make perfect picnic fare. (☎02 6681 1118. Open M-F 8:30am-5pm, Sa 8am-12:24pm. MC/V.) **Pelican 181 ❷,** Wigmore Arcade, is an upscale restaurant with a takeaway breakfast and lunch counter. Try the yummy Thai fishcake and rice meals for $7.50. (☎02 6686 9181. M-Sa 7am-7pm, Su 7am-4pm. Cash only.) **Hotel Henry Raus ❷,** on the corner of River and Moon St., has a historic name and a modern menu. Although named for one of the shire's original settlers, the hotel still serves its dishes ($12-17) in a contemporary atmosphere. They also host live music acts F-Sa 9pm-midnight. (☎02 6686 2411; www.hotel-henryrous.com.au. Open daily 10am-10pm. MC/V.)

◪◪ **SIGHTS AND ACTIVITIES.** **Lighthouse Beach** is a great vantage point for whale watching. The 68-hectare reserve at **Angels Beach,** accessible from the Coast Rd. in East Ballina, sometimes has playful dolphins. In addition to being a fantastic surfing destination, **Flat Rock** possesses an incredible array of marine life including octopi, sea anemones, and sea stars.

Learn to surf or perfect your technique at **Summerland Surf School,** great for families. (☎02 6682 4393. In Ballina: private 2hr. lessons $100, small group lessons $45. In Evans Head: private 2hr. lessons $75, small group lessons $40. Ask about accommodation and lesson packages.) Swing by the **Ballina Naval and Maritime Museum,** on Regatta Ave., just down from the visitors center, to see one

**NEW SOUTH WALES**

of the three original rafts that crossed the Pacific from Ecuador to Australia on the 1973 Las Balsas Trans Pacific Expedition. (☎02 6681 1002. Open daily 9am-4pm. Donations encouraged.) For a leisurely afternoon, try **Richmond River Cruises.** (☎02 6687 5688 or 04 0732 9851. W and Sa 2hr. tours. $25.)

# LISMORE                                                                    ☎02

Forty-five kilometers inland from Byron Bay, Lismore (pop. 46,000) has soaked up nearby Nimbin's hippie vibe, offering visitors a laid-back atmosphere in a more urban environment. Students at Southern Cross University help to promote Lismore's first-rate art scene and vegetarian/vegan activism. Outside the town center, three World Heritage rainforests and the volcanic remains at Mt. Warning National Park beckon nature-loving backpackers. The disproportionately high number of rainbows (due to the position of local valleys) and a GLBT-friendly community have earned this area the nickname "Rainbow Region." Though not much of a tourist town, Lismore has great eateries.

**▐ TRANSPORTATION.** The **railway** station is on Union St. Countrylink (☎13 22 32) travels to Brisbane (3hr., 1 per day, $28) and Sydney through Casino (12hr., 2 per day, $81). The **Transit Centre** (☎02 6621 8620) is on the corner of Molesworth and Magellan St. Premier (☎02 9281 2233; www.premierms.com. au) sends two **buses** daily to Brisbane (5hr., $37) and one to Sydney (12hr., $90). The best way to get around is to rent a **car.** Options include **Avis,** corner of Three Chain Rd. and Bruxner Hwy. (☎02 6621 9002); **Budget,** 106 Conway St. (☎02 6622 1900); **Hertz,** 49 Dawson St. (☎02 6621 8855 or 13 30 39), and **Thrifty,** 2/31 Dawson St. (☎02 6622 2266 or 1300 367 227). For a **taxi,** call ☎13 10 08.

**▓▐ ORIENTATION AND PRACTICAL INFORMATION.** In the hinterlands west of Ballina, Lismore lies off the Bruxner Hwy. (called Ballina Rd. in town) just east of Wilsons River. Approaching the river from the east, **Ballina Road** crosses **Dawson, Keen,** and **Molesworth Streets,** the busiest part of town. Perpendicular to these streets in the town center are small **Conway** and **Magellan Streets.** One block past Magellan St., **Woodlark Street** crosses the river to **Bridge Street,** leading to the north side of town and Nimbin.

At the corner of Molesworth and Ballina Rd., the **Lismore Visitor Information Centre** has a small indoor tropical rainforest and social history exhibit. (☎02 6626 0100 or 1300 369 795; www.visitlismore.com.au. Open daily 9:30am-4pm.) **ATMs** can be found in the town center. Internet access is available at the **visitors center** for $6 per hr. and at **Armageddon Games,** 70 Magellan St., for $4 per hr. (☎02 6621 5432. Open Tu-Th 11am-6pm, F 11am-10pm, Sa 10am-6pm, Su 11am-5pm.) The **library,** 110 Magellan St., charges $4.40 per hr., and Wi-Fi is available. (☎02 6622 2721. Open M-W 9:30am-5pm, Th-F 9:30am-7:30pm, Sa 9am-1pm.) **Police** (☎02 6621 0599) are on Zadoc St., and the **Lismore Base Hospital** is at 60 Uralba St. (☎02 6621 8000). A **post office** is on Conway St., between Molesworth and Keen St. (☎02 6627 7316. Open M-F 8:30am-5pm.) **Postal Code:** 2480.

**▐▐ ACCOMMODATIONS AND FOOD.** Budget accommodations are nearly impossible to find in Lismore. For a motel room, the **Winsome Hotel ❺,** 11 Bridge St., rents newly renovated rooms at somewhat affordable rates, and live music rocks the downstairs nightly. (☎02 6622 1112; www.thewinsomehotel.com. au. GLBT-friendly. Doubles and triples $70-140. Weekly rates available. AmEx/MC/V). **Lismore Palms Caravan Park ❶,** 42 Brunswick St., offers basic rooms with an on-site kitchen and pool. Follow Dawson St. north and turn right onto

Brunswick St. (☎02 6621 7067; www.lismorepalms.com.au. Linen $5. Laundry $6. Sites for 2 $15-20; ensuite cabins $60-70. Weekly rates available. MC/V.)

Student demand for cheap vegetarian eats has resulted in some terrifically funky cafes. No cows are served at the vegan **20,000 Cows ❷**, 58 Bridge St. Surrounded by wild tablecloths, tall candlesticks, and comfy sofas, diners wolf down fresh pasta, and Indian and Middle Eastern food ($7-23). The eccentric menu reads, "All prices are suggested donations. Feel free to give yourself a discount," though most guests pay full. For the indecisive eater, try the best of everything in the $16 Middle Eastern Combo. (☎02 6622 2517. Open W-Su from 6pm.) **Goanna Bakery and Cafe ❶**, 171 Keen St., draws a devoted following, baking pies and making sandwiches for the gluten-free, vegetarian, and vegan communities. Especially popular is their ratatouille pie ($5, gluten-free $5.20). (☎02 6622 2629. Open M-F 8am-5:30pm, Sa 8am-3pm, Su 9am-2pm. MC/V.) For a meaty meal in an otherwise veggie town, try some pub grub at Winsome Hotel or another local spot. For groceries, head to **Woolworths** on Keen St., with a back entrance on Carrington St. (Open M-Sa 7am-9pm, Su 8am-8pm.)

◙ **SIGHTS.** The **Richmond River Historical Society**, 165 Molesworth St., in the Municipal Building, houses a natural history room with preserved baby crocs and mummified tropical birds, as well as a hallway of Aboriginal boomerangs. (☎02 6621 9993; www.richhistory.org.au. Open M-F 10am-4pm. $2.) Next door, the **Regional Art Gallery** hosts rotating exhibits. (☎02 6622 2209; www.lismore. nsw.gov.au/gallery. Open Tu-Sa 10am-4pm, Th 10am-6pm. Free.) **Tucki Tucki Nature Reserve**, which doubles as a koala sanctuary, is 15min. from Lismore on Wyrallah Rd. Lismore's water supply comes from the **Rocky Creek Dam**, home to a waterfront boardwalk and platypus lagoon. Look out for platypuses from the **Pontoon Bridge** during dusk hours. To protect the endangered Fleay's Barred Frog, don't go swimming. To get there, take Tweed St. from the north side of town about 30km. For fresh produce and organic goods, visit the **Rainbow Region Organic Markets**, held every Tuesday 8am-11am in the Lismore Showgrounds on the north side of town off of Tweed St. Every Saturday from 8am to noon, the **Lismore Farmers Market** takes place at the Showgrounds. For the antique dealers and bric-a-brac shoppers, the **Lismore Car Boot Market** (first and third Su of the month), in the covered Lismore Shopping Square, is a paradise.

**⭐TIP** | **KOALA TRACKS.** When trying to spy a napping koala, check the base of the trunks for scratch marks. The furry marsupials are most likely clinging to marked trees, nestled in the fork between two branches.

# BYRON BAY ☎02

A 1hr. drive south from the hipsters of Surfers Paradise and east from the hippies of Nimbin, Byron Bay (pop. 12,000) combines the best of both worlds. Though smaller than party-happy Surfers and less out-there than psychedelic Nimbin, Byron draws visitors of all types with its family- and surfer-friendly beaches, massage spas, palm readers, kebab shops, and bistros.

**▐ TRANSPORTATION**

**Buses:** Buses depart from the **bus depot** outside the visitors center on Jonson St. Buy tickets at **Peterpan Adventures** (see **Orientation and Practical Information, p. 208**).
  **Blanch's** (☎02 6686 2144; www.blanchs.com.au. To: **Ballina** (50min., 2-8 per day, $9.40), **Lennox Head** (30min., 2-8 per day, $6), and **Mullumbimby** (30min., 2-4 per day, $6).

Countrylink (☎13 22 32; www.countrylink.com.au). To **Ballina** (40min., 1 per day, $5); **Grafton** (3hr., 1 per day, $30); **Lennox Head** (35min., 1 per day, $5); **Lismore** (1hr., 3 per day, $7); **Murwillumbah** (1hr., 2 per day, $7); **Surfers Paradise** (1hr., 1 per day, $13); Sydney (14hr., 4 per day, $88). Prices vary by season. Student discounts available.

**Greyhound Australia** (☎13 14 10; www.greyhound.com.au). To: **Brisbane** (3-4hr., 7 per day, $41); **Coffs Harbour** (4hr., 4 per day, $57); **Lismore** (2hr., 1 per day, $43); **Murwillumbah** (50min., 2 per day, $16); **Port Macquarie** (7hr., 3 per day, $74); **Surfers Paradise** (1-2hr., 8 per day, $30); **Sydney** (13-14hr., 4 per day, $112). Backpacker discount 10%.

**Premier** (☎13 34 10; www.premierms.com.au). To **Brisbane** ($29) and **Sydney** ($90).

**Taxis: Byron Bay Taxis** (☎13 10 08). 24hr. Wheelchair-accessible taxis available.

**Car Rental: Earth Car Rentals,** 18 Fletcher St. (☎02 6685 7472; www.earthcar.com.au). Cars from $44 per day. $550 deposit. **Jetset Travel** (☎02 6685 6554), behind the bus station just off Jonson St., rents manual cars from $65 per day.

## ◼ 🛈 ORIENTATION AND PRACTICAL INFORMATION

Byron isn't directly on the Pacific Hwy., but it's accessible via nearby **Bangalow** (15km south) or **Ewingsdale Road** (6km north). Bangalow Road enters Byron Bay from the south. Turn off a roundabout on Browning St., which leads to Jonson St., the southern edge of the Central Business District (CBD). **Lawson Street,** north of town, runs along Main Beach. To the east, Lawson St. becomes **Lighthouse Road,** running past Clarkes Beach, the Pass surfing spot, Wategos Beach, the lighthouse, and the Cape Byron lookout. To the west, Lawson becomes **Shirley Street** and curves off to Belongil Beach. Farther west, it becomes **Ewingsdale Road** and passes the **Arts and Industrial Estate** before reaching the **Pacific Highway.**

**Tourist Office: Byron Visitors Centre,** 80 Jonson St. (☎02 6680 8558; www.visitbyronbay.com), at the bus station. Friendly staff books local adventure activities, hotel rooms, and sells bus tickets. Open daily 9am-5pm.

**Tours:** ◪**Jim's Alternative Tours** (☎02 6685 7720; www.jimsalternativetours.com) are led by Jim, a Byron Bay local since the 1960s. He offers a great 8hr. trip daily that travels through Minyan Falls, Nimbin, and Nightcap National Park. Includes a stop at Paul Recher's Fruit Spirit Botanical Gardens, reforested with 350 varieties of exotic fruit from around the world. $35. **Grasshoppers Eco-Explorer Tour** (☎02 6685 5068; www.grasshoppers.com.au) offers an all-day trip to subtropical rainforest, waterfalls, koala- and platypus-sighting spots, and Nimbin. Daily tours 10am-6pm. $39, includes BBQ lunch.

**Budget Travel:** Backpacker travel centers cluster around the bus station, and most hostels have travel desks that book trips and local activities. The friendly staff at **Peterpan Adventures,** 87 Jonson St. (☎1800 252 459; www.peterpans.com), does the same, and will book most local activities for free. Open daily 9am-9pm. **Wicked Travel,** 89 Jonson St., (☎1800 555 339; www.wickedtravel.com.au) offers similar services and Internet access for $3 per hr. Open daily 9am-7:30pm.

**Currency Exchange:** Banks on Jonson St. are generally open M-Th 9:30am-4pm, F 9:30am-5pm. **ATMs** are located across the street from the visitors center. The **Byron Foreign Exchange Shop,** 4 Byron St. (☎02 6685 7787), advertises low fees and good rates. Open M-Sa 9am-5pm, Su 10am-4pm.

**Police:** (☎02 6685 9499), on the corner of Butler and Shirley St.

**Hospital: Byron Bay Hospital** (☎02 6685 6200), corner of Shirley and Wordsworth St.

**Internet Access:** Internet cafes are everywhere in Byron; some pass out vouchers on the street for free or discounted access. Most activity-booking offices also offer free Internet access with bookings. Ask about the *Let's Go* discount at **Peterpan Adventures** (see above). **Global Gossip,** 84 Jonson St. (☎02 6680 9140), at the bus stop, has Internet for $3 per hr. Open daily in summer 8:30am-11pm, in winter 9am-10:30pm.

NEW SOUTH WALES

**Lockers:** The **transport booking center** next door to Global Gossip rents out lockers (large enough for 2 full backpacks) for $10 per day.

**Post Office:** 61 Jonson St. (☎13 13 18). Open M-F 9am-5pm, Sa 9am-2pm. **Postal Code:** 2481.

# 🏠 🏕 ACCOMMODATIONS AND CAMPING

In summer, especially around Christmas, Byron is saturated with thousands of tourists; some accommodation prices double accordingly. The best advice is to book early, but demand is so high that some hostels don't even accept reservations during the summer. Many would-be Byron visitors are forced to stay in Lennox Head or **Ballina** (p. 204), 10 and 20min. south, respectively. Sleeping in cars or on the beach is prohibited.

**Byron Bay YHA,** 7 Carlyle St. (☎02 6685 8853 or 1800 678 195); 300m from beach, 200m from bus stop, 100m from Woolworths. Clean, colorful, and cozy, this hostel has a large kitchen, heated pool, and a covered pavilion with billiards, hammocks, and picnic tables. Lockers $2-7 per day. Towel $1. Laundry $6. Internet $3 per hr., Wi-Fi available. Free parking. Surf boards $15 per day ($100 deposit). Free bikes ($50 deposit) and boogie boards. Reception 8am-9pm. Dorms $27-36; doubles $75-106, ensuite $85-117. Book at least 1 week ahead in the summer. MC/V. ❷

**Backpackers Inn on the Beach,** 29 Shirley St. (☎02 6685 8231; www.byron-bay. com/backpackersinn). Large and social with direct beach access; fantastic for surfers and sunbathers. Loft kitchen, volleyball, heated pool, BBQ, billiards, cable TV, and games. Free luggage storage. Blanket fee $1. Laundry $5. Internet access $4 per hr. Secure parking. Free bikes ($20 deposit) and boogie boards. Surfboards $16 per 3hr., $25 per day. W and Sa BBQ $5. W Sangria night $5. Wheelchair accessible. Reception daily 8am-8pm; check-in available until late. Dorms $23-30; doubles $65-74. Book ahead in summer. ISIC/VIP/YHA. MC/V. ❷

**Aquarius Backpackers,** 16 Lawson St. (☎02 6685 7663 or 1800 028 909; www. aquarius-backpackers.com.au), corner of Middleton St. This former 4-star motel has many spacious rooms with 2 levels, porch, and fridge. Poolside bar with happy hour, nightly meals ($9), travel desk, parking, kitchen, and cafe. Internet access $4 per hr., Wi-Fi available. Free boogie boards. Linen $2, blanket deposit $20. Laundry $4. Key deposit $20. Reception 24hr. Ensuite dorms $25-35; doubles $50-90; motel units $110-260. 3- and 7-day discounts. VIP/YHA discounts. ❷

**Arts Factory Backpackers Lodge** (☎02 6685 7709; www.artsfactory.com.au), on Skinners Shoot Rd., about a 10min. walk from beach. Sprawling grounds with teepees and island bungalows are a bit far from the action, but there's a heated pool (lit for nighttime pool parties), sauna, and cool cafe. Bring bug repellent. Lockers $2 per 12hr.; keyed wallet lockers $1. Laundry $6. Internet access $1 per 10min. Shuttles to town. Free didjeridu workshops. Pool and ping-pong tournaments. Yoga classes $5-10. Learn bush survival on free Bushtucker walks M-W at 4pm. Reception 7am-9pm. Sites $15-25; dorms and teepees $25-35; twins, doubles, and bungalows $50-80. Discounts for longer stays. NOMADS discount. MC/V. ❶

**Cape Byron Hostel (YHA)** (☎02 6685 8788 or 1800 652 627), on the corner of Middleton and Byron St. Pinball, pool table, TV, and VCR. Upstairs deck overlooks a solar-heated pool bordered by palm trees. Lockers $4 per day. Laundry $5. Internet $4 per hr. Free parking. Bikes and boogie boards free with deposit. Reception 6:45am-10pm. Dorms $25-35; twins and doubles $70-100, ensuite $80-130. MC/V. ❷

NEW SOUTH WALES

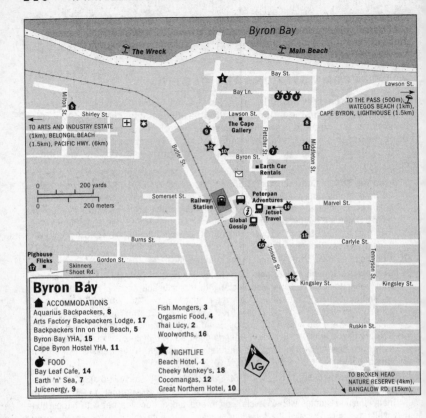

Byron Bay

The Wreck

Main Beach

**Byron Bay**

🏠 ACCOMMODATIONS
Aquarius Backpackers, **8**
Arts Factory Backpackers Lodge, **17**
Backpackers Inn on the Beach, **5**
Byron Bay YHA, **15**
Cape Byron Hostel YHA, **11**

🍎 FOOD
Bay Leaf Cafe, **14**
Earth 'n' Sea, **7**
Juicenergy, **9**

Fish Mongers, **3**
Orgasmic Food, **4**
Thai Lucy, **2**
Woolworths, **16**

★ NIGHTLIFE
Beach Hotel, **1**
Cheeky Monkey's, **18**
Cocomangas, **12**
Great Northern Hotel, **10**

TO ARTS AND INDUSTRY ESTATE (1km), BELONGIL BEACH (1.5km), PACIFIC HWY. (6km)

TO THE PASS (500m), WATEGOS BEACH (1km), CAPE BYRON, LIGHTHOUSE (1.5km)

TO BROKEN HEAD NATURE RESERVE (4km), BANGALOW RD. (15km),

Pighouse Flicks

Earth Car Rentals

Peterpan Adventures

Global Gossip

Jetset Travel

The Cape Gallery

Railway Station

## 🔷 FOOD

You can't take two steps in downtown Byron without stumbling into an out-door cafe, takeaway eatery, or upscale restaurant. A **Woolworths** supermarket is on Dawson St. (open M-F 8am-9pm, Sa-Su 8am-8pm), and the **Byron Farmers' Market** is held every Thursday 8-11am on Butler St. across the train tracks.

🔲 **Bay Leaf Cafe** (☎02 6685 8900) on Marvel St., 1 block from Jonson St. Scrumptious salads, sandwiches, and gourmet coffee in an open-air cafe ideal for lounging. Try the couscous salad (small $8.50, large $12.50). Open daily 7:30am-5pm. Cash only. ❶

🔲 **Fish Mongers** (☎02 6680 8080), on Bay Ln., in an alley off Jonson St. This fish and chips joint reels in hordes of customers with delicious grilled calamari, marinated octo-pus, tempura prawns, and hand-cut chips. Reasonable prices ($9-19) and non-greasy fish keep your wallet full and your fingers dry. Open daily noon-9pm. AmEx/MC/V. ❷

**Earth 'n' Sea** (☎02 6685 6029), in its new location on the corner of Fletcher and Byron St. Surfer decor makes this a great place to unwind. Serves 20 deliciously off-beat pizzas ($15-33), like the "Beethoven" combination of prawn, banana, and pineapple. Pastas from $12. Delivery available. Open daily 11am-late. AmEx/D/MC/V. ❸

**Thai Lucy,** 2/4 Bay Ln. (☎02 6680 8083). Every bite is worth the price (dishes $15-21) and the wait. Indoor and outdoor seating. Open daily 5:30-10pm. Cash only. ❷

**Orgasmic Food** (☎02 6680 7778), on Bay Ln. behind the Beach Hotel. Serves fantastic Middle Eastern food (from $9). Outdoor seating. Open daily 11am-9pm. Cash only. ❶

**Juicenergy,** 20 Jonson St. (☎02 6680 7780), fixes up fresh juices ($4.50-6.50), smoothies ($6), and fruit yogurt ($4.50-9). Open daily 8am-6pm. Cash only. ❶

## 👁 SIGHTS

**BYRON BAY LIGHTHOUSE.** Crowds assemble daily in the pre-dawn darkness to wait for sunrise along the paths leading to Cape Byron's crowning glory, the **Byron Bay Lighthouse,** at the end of Lighthouse Rd. Resting on cliffs above the easternmost point of the mainland and visible 50km out to sea, the lighthouse is one of the brightest in Australia. The last keeper left in 1989, long after the landmark became fully automated. His cottage is now an info center and shop, and assistant keeper cottages are available for private holiday rental. Parking at the lighthouse is $6, but there is a very small, free carpark 150m away off Lighthouse Rd. The walk to the lighthouse is 2km from Main Beach. (Grounds open daily sunrise-sunset. Tours Tu and Th 11am, 12:30, and 2pm, and during school holidays Sa 10, 11am, 12:30, 2, and 3:30pm; $8, children and concessions $6, families $25.) A boardwalk follows Lighthouse Rd. and continues past the lighthouse to the ⬛Headland Lookout, an excellent place for spotting dolphins and whales from May to September. From there, a **walking circuit** descends into the Headland Reserve, passing through Wategos Beach, The Pass, and Clarkes Beach, returning back to Lighthouse Rd. at the Captain Cook Lookout. Head here to catch the first morning rays at the easternmost point in Australia.

**ARTISTIC SIGHTS.** Byron's artistic community is flourishing; the best example is **The Cape Gallery,** 2 Lawson St., which exhibits local art and a fine pottery collection. (☎02 6685 7659; www.capegallery.com.au. Open daily in summer 10am-5pm; in winter M-Sa 10am-5pm, Su 11am-4pm.) West of town, the **Arts and Industry Estate,** off Ewingsdale Rd. (called Shirley Rd. in town), is a compound full of stores where local craftsmen sell industrial glass and metal, paintings, sculptures, crafts, and—oddly enough—shoes. **Farrell Glass Designs** blows glass at 6 Acacia St., and the gallery is filled with an impressive collection of their work. (☎02 6685 7044; www.farrellglassdesign.com. Gallery open M-F 9am-5pm, Sa-Su 10am-4pm; glass-blowing Tu-F 9am-4pm, F 9am-2:30pm.)

## 🎵 NIGHTLIFE

It's easy to avoid paying cover in Byron Bay. Many nightclubs come around to the hostels offering free entry stamps and other specials.

**Cheeky Monkey's** (☎02 6685 5886), on the corner of Jonson and Kingsley St. The tables are the best dancefloor at what promises to be a rocking venue any night of the week. Theme nights and frequent backpacker specials. The Cheeky Monkey Party Van scans the streets and swings past hostels to whisk you away. Call ☎1800 261 998 for free pickup. Dinner from $5 (F $2). Happy hour until 9pm. Open in summer M-Sa noon-3am, Su noon-midnight; in winter M-Sa 7pm-3am. Cover $5 after 10pm.

**Cocomangas,** 32 Jonson St. (☎02 6685 8493), features a smaller dance floor and affordable mixed drinks. Try the famous Jam Jar (juice, gin, Malibu rum, and Triple Sec; $4). Check for freebies in hostels. Happy hour 9-11:30pm. Cover $5 in summer after 10pm; in winter after 10:30pm. Open M-Sa until 3am.

**Beach Hotel** (☎02 6685 6402), on Jonson St., overlooking the beach. This posh establishment boasts a garden bar and huge patio. Large indoor stage hosts local and nationally recognized bands. Aquariums hang over 1 of the indoor bars and surf videos play in an adjoining room. Live music daily in the summer, Th-Su in the winter. Su live DJs starting at 4:30pm. Open until midnight.

**Great Northern Hotel** (☎02 6685 6454), on the corner of Jonson and Byron St. An incredible venue for live music, daily around 9pm. Everything from folk to punk. Cover varies depending on act. Open M-Th until 1:30am, F-Sa until 3am.

## ♫ 🌴 ENTERTAINMENT AND FESTIVALS

Byron nurses a thriving music scene, and ten or more acts hit the stage every night of the week. Check the gig guide in *Echo* magazine for information on the week's performances (found on the streets or online at www.echo.net.au every Tu morning). Music really takes over the town when the major music festivals arrive. The **Blues and Roots Music Festival** pulls in regional acts and some loosely folksy international superstars for a five-day fiesta over the Easter weekend (☎02 6685 8310; www.bluesfest.com.au), while **Splendour in the Grass** lights up the first weekend of August with a more alternative but still star-studded lineup. Both events almost always sell out, and accommodations prices invariably sky-rocket. **Pighouse Flicks,** at the Lounge Cinema in the Arts Factory, is a local favorite that screens classic, arthouse, foreign, and mainstream films in a funky blacklight-lit theater upholstered in comfy cow-print. (☎02 6685 5828. Opens 30min. before showtime. $10, daily specials $8.) **A Taste of Byron** (☎04 1917 0407) is a popular food festival that falls on the third week in September. The **Byron Bay Writers Festival** (☎02 6685 6262) takes place the third weekend in July and is a well-attended four-day literary event.

## ⌖ ACTIVITIES

For travelers seeking constant stimulation, Byron provides it on land (massages and meditation), in the water (boards and boats of every shape and size), and in the air (skydiving, ultralights, and hang gliders). Many packages include free pickup and dropoff. The **Byron Bay Visitors Centre** books activities, as do **Peterpan Adventures** (p. 208), **Wicked Travel** (p. 208), and many hostels.

### SURFING

Herds of bleach-blonde surfers trudge dutifully to Byron's beaches every morning at sunrise. Surf schools entice novices by providing all equipment; most guarantee you'll be standing on the board by the end of your lessons. Byron has excellent surfing spots all around the bay, so regardless of wind conditions, there are always good waves somewhere. **The Wreck,** just off Main Beach, is known for waves that break close to shore and is where many surf schools hold their lessons. Down the shore toward the lighthouse, **The Pass** promises long, challenging rides but can be dangerous because of overcrowding, sharp rocks, and boats. The water off **Wategos Beach,** close to The Pass, is best for longboards since the waves are slow and rolling. **Tallows,** on the other side of the headland from Wategos, has great northern-wind surfing, but watch for heavy rips. **Belongil Beach,** to the north of Main Beach, is long and sandy with clothing-optional sections. **Broken Head Nature Reserve,** 4km south of Byron on the Coast Rd., has verdant rainforest growing right down to its magnificent beaches. Take the track from Broken Head Caravan Park along the clifftop to **King's Beach,** or try **Broken Head** or **Whites Beaches** for serious surf.

**Black Dog Surfing** (☎02 6680 9828; www.blackdogsurfing.com), in Shop 8 next to Woolworths on Jonson St. They promise that if they can teach a dog to swim, they can certainly teach you. Offers the most-personalized surf school in Byron. 3hr. lesson $50-

60, including a snack; 2-day course $105, 3-day $135. Private or female-only lessons available. Surfboard rental full day $25, weekly $120. Wetsuits $10.

**Surfing Byron Bay,** Shop 5, 84 Jonson St. (☎02 6685 7099; www.gosurfingbyronbay. com), behind **Global Gossip** (p. 208). 3½hr. group lesson $60, 2hr. private lesson $120, 3-day group course $150, 5-day $225. Ask for board rental prices.

## MULTI-DAY SURF TRIPS

**Surfaris** (☎1800 00 SURF or 1800 634 951; www.surfaris.com), offers 5-day surf trips between Sydney and Byron (850km off coast). Departs M from Sydney ($549), Su from Byron ($599). All meals and camping included.

**Mojosurf** (☎02 6639 5100; www.mojosurf.com.au) is a popular choice for multi-day surf holidays. Most surf trips leave from Sydney heading towards Byron, but there are a few that depart from Byron. All-inclusive packages include 2-day trips ($195-245) and a 5-day excursion that connects Sydney and Byron ($595).

## DIVING AND KAYAKING

Most diving is done at **Julian Rocks Marine Park,** 2½km off Main Beach, widely considered one of Australia's best dive sites. It has both warm and cold currents and is also home to 500 species of fish and the occasional gray nurse shark. Required medical clearances cost $60. Dive certification courses can go up by $70-100 or more during the summer.

**Sundive** (☎02 6685 7755 or 1800 008 755; www.sundive.com.au), on Middleton St. behind Aquarius Backpackers. On-site pool. Courses usually start Tu or F, but 2-weekend certification courses are sometimes offered. 4-day PADI certification $395. Snorkeling $50; intro dives $150, day dives $70-80, additional trips $70.

**Byron Bay Dive Centre,** 9 Marvel St. (☎02 6685 8333 or 1800 243 483; www.byron-baydivecentre.com.au), between Middleton and Fletcher St. 4-day SSI certification courses start M and Th $395; 4hr. intro dives $150, day dives $80, additional trips $70; snorkeling $50. Seasonal 2hr. whale watching trips $75.

**Cape Byron Kayaks** (☎02 6680 9555; www.capebyronkayaks.com). 3hr. trips around the Cape with afternoon tea. Free return trip if you don't see dolphins, whales, or turtles. Free pickup from your accommodations. Trips in summer 8:30am-11:30am and 1pm-4pm; times vary May-Aug., so call ahead. Book 1 day ahead. $60.

## IN THE SKY

**Soaring Adventures** (☎02 6684 7572 or 04 1455 8794; www.byronbaygliding.com). Learn to fly a glider. Flights to lighthouse, Cape Byron, or Mt. Warning. $95-395.

**Flightzone Hang Gliding School** (☎02 6685 8768 or 04 0844 1742; www.flightzone. com.au). 30min. flights $140. 10-day certification course $1500. Cash only.

**Byron Bay Ballooning** (☎02 6684 7880; www.byronbayballooning.com), near the Tyagarah Airfield 6km north of Byron Bay. Offers sunrise flights over the beautiful Rainbow Region, followed by a champagne breakfast. 4hr. experience, 1hr. flight. Call about pickup from your accommodations. Adults $295.

**Circus Arts Byron Bay,** 17 Centennial Circuit (☎02 6685 6566; www.circusarts.com. au), in the Arts and Industrial Estate. You can run away to the circus after a 1½hr. flying trapeze class ($45), or work on the low trapeze, silks and aerial hoop in the $20 adult aerial session. Times vary by season. Call to arrange bus pickups.

## OTHER ACTIVITIES

**Byron Bay Bicycles,** 93 Jonson St. (☎02 6685 6067), in the Woolworths shopping plaza. ½-day $22, full day $28, $95 weekly. $50 deposit includes helmet and lock.

**Mountain Biking Tours** (☎1800 122 504; www.mountainbiketours.com.au), takes full-day guided mountain bike tours through the rainforest with lunch included. Adults $99. Mountain bike rentals $33 per day, $90 per week.

**Seahorse Riding Centre** (☎02 6680 8155; www.seahorsesbyronbay.com), 20min. west of Byron. Offers ½- and full-day packages. Available trips include rainforest rides, beach rides, and pony trots for children. $60-$100.

# NIMBIN ☎02

Once a small dairy farming town, Nimbin (pop. 800) is now Australia's cannabis capital. The town is a popular daytrip from Byron among backpackers looking for a taste (or whiff) of the nation's alternative culture. Though marijuana is illegal in Australia, visitors will find themselves solicited for "bush," "cookies," "pot," or any of a dozen other euphemisms for marijuana as they walk up Cullen St., the town's only avenue. The street is lined with eateries and markets specializing in organic and bulk foods, as well as half a dozen shops offering every imaginable piece of paraphernalia with pot-related puns. Guitars and bong(o) drums lie invitingly in cafes and accommodations, just waiting to be picked up for those with a penchant for impromptu jam sessions.

In 1973, thousands of university students descended on Nimbin Village for the Aquarius Festival, the antipodean answer to America's Woodstock, and ever since the community has retained its image as Australia's alternative/hippie hub. Some local residents resent the town's reputation and a surprising percentage don't partake, emphasizing instead Nimbin's earth-conscious agriculture ("permaculture") and alternative energy. The town is one of hundreds of shared communities that lie in the fruitful volcanic valley of Mt. Warning. WWOOF (see **Short-term Work,** p. 93) has a strong presence here, with many area farms accepting travelers for farmstays and organic farming opportunities. Residents' lives are closely intertwined with the land and its fruits.

 **NIMBIN TIME** Hours for Nimbin businesses are flexible. The town runs on "Nimbin time"—establishments open and close on their own schedules, which may not match customer demand or advertised hours of operation.

**TRANSPORTATION AND PRACTICAL INFORMATION.** The Nimbin Shuttle Bus (☎02 6680 9189; www.nimbintours.com) and The Happy Coach (☎02 6685 3996; www.happycoach.com.au) provide the only direct **public transportation** to the village from Byron. The shuttle departs daily from Byron Bay at 11am (1hr.), and leaves Nimbin at 3pm ($14, round-trip $30), and the coach leaves daily from Byron Bay at 10am (3hr.) and returns from Nimbin at 2:30pm ($15.) For visitors seeking just a glimpse of the place, **Grasshoppers Eco-Explorer Tours** stops in town for an hour or two as part of a day-long trip that includes the area's national parks (☎02 66855068; www.grasshoppers.com.au; $39 with lunch), as does Byron-based **Jim's Alternative Tours** (☎02 6685 7720; www.jimsalternativetours.com; trips daily 10am-6pm; $35).

Nimbin's town center is on **Cullen Street,** between the police station and the hotel on the corner—you can't miss the vivid murals, wild storefront displays, and thin wisps of smoke. The **Nimbin Visitor Centre,** 2/80 Cullen St., at the north end of town, has info on local activities and regional WWOOFing opportunities and membership; it also books shuttle bus transport, offers broadband Internet access ($2.50 per 15min., $6 per hr.), and sells local paraphernalia. (☎02 6689 1388; www.visitlismore.com.au. Open M-Sa 10am-4pm, every third and fifth Su 11am-3pm.) Find **police** (☎02 6689 1244) at the south end of Cullen St. and the **hospital** (☎02 6689 1400) at 35 Cullen St. The **post office** is at 43 Cullen St. (☎02 6689 1301. Open M-F 7am-5pm.) **Postal Code:** 2480.

**⌐◻ ACCOMMODATIONS AND FOOD.** Although many visitors come to Nimbin for just an afternoon, staying a few days at any one of the town's unique hostels provides the best chance to see through Nimbin's smoky haze. ▧**Nimbin Rox YHA ❶**, 74 Thorburn St., is worth the 20min. walk from town for its breathtaking views and a number of intricately decorated double rooms. Take a left onto Thorburn from Cullen St., just across the creek; the hostel is up an unpaved driveway through a horse pasture. Facilities include a pool, hammocks, a fruit garden, and an herb garden. (☎02 6689 0022; www.yha.com.au. Laundry $2 per wash. Internet access $6 per hr. Camping site $15; dorms $28, YHA $25; doubles and bungalows $62-72; 6-person teepee $22 per person. MC/V.) For the best idea of what town was like in the 1970s, spend the night in a mushroom bungalow or a gypsy wagon at the ▧**Rainbow Retreat ❶**, 75 Thorburn St., where horses wander the grounds and every room has a name like "Woodstock" or the "Love Shack." Amenities include a kitchen, an open-air cafe, and common rooms with a collection of musical instruments alongside a TV. (☎02 6689 1262. Sites $13; dorms $20; doubles $50. Cash only.) **The Nimbin Hotel and Backpackers ❸**, on Sibley St. in the town center, offers reasonably priced rooms and access to a pleasant veranda. (☎02 6689 1246; www.freemasonhotel.com.au. Singles $30; doubles $50.)

Nimbin cafes, pubs, and streets are home to a vibrant music scene. **The Rainbow Cafe ❶**, 64A Cullen St., has burgers ($8), fresh juices ($5), vegetarian options, and a sunny garden patio out back of the restaurant. (☎02 6689 1997. Open daily 7:30am-5pm. Cash only.) Late at night, share a pot of chai ($3) on the patio outside **Nimbin's Oasis Cafe ❶**, 80 Cullen St. (☎02 6689 0199). Just down the road, the **Nimbin Emporium,** 58 Cullen St., sells health and bulk foods and rents videos. (☎02 6689 1205. Open M-Sa 8am-7pm, Su 9:45am-7pm.)

### LET'S GROW

Though walking the center of Nimbin any time of the year gives new meaning to the phrase "main drag," reefer-induced revelry reaches its peak the first weekend in May, when Nimbin hosts its annual MardiGrass Cannabis Law Reform Rally. In 1988, public protest for marijuana legalization coincided with the Aquarius Festival, a celebration of counter-culture on a broader level. The 1993 rally ended with chanting pot-smokers brandishing a massive joint with "Let It Grow" inscribed in 4 ft. tall letters outside the Nimbin Hemp Embassy.

The following year, MardiGrass became an official event. Activities include the Hemp Olympics, in which contestants compete in everything from bong-throwing to joint-rolling contests. Judges score growers' products for aroma, size, and effect. It may seem like a party, but protesters say the real fun will begin only once political change is effected.

Local police have begun to weed out MardiGrass participants who flaunt the law. In 2006, increased vigilance meant roadblocks and vehicle checks. The press reported that a major crackdown had occurred, but the 50 arrests didn't extinguish Nimbin's party spirit. Despite the arrests, the festival still gives locals a green light to celebrate every year.

*Visit www.nimbinmardigrass.com for more information.*

**◉ SIGHTS.** The odd **🖼Nimbin Museum,** 62 Cullen St., redefines creativity and historical interpretation. The rooms relate the founders' version of regional history through myriad murals, stimulating quotes, and trinkets. The museum has proportional coverage of all three of the town's major historical periods: the first room is about Aboriginals, the second about European settlers, and the next six about hippies. (☎02 6689 1123; www.nimbinmuseum.com. Open 10am-dark. $2.) The Picture Factory north of town, a former butter factory, now houses the **Nimbin Candle Factory,** where artists craft colorful handmade candles for sale $0.50-$200. (M-F 9am-5pm. Sa-Sun 11am-4pm.) The Help End Marijuana Prohibition (HEMP) Party bases itself at the **Hemp Embassy,** 51 Cullen St., where racks of hemp clothing and a 1m high hemp wall proudly showcase the versatility of hemp. (☎02 6689 1842; www.hempembassy.net. Open daily 9am-6pm.) The attached **Hemp Bar** offers refreshments (www.nimbinhempbar. com). To see a bit beyond Nimbin's drug culture, swing by the **Nimbin Artists Gallery,** 49 Cullen St., which displays the work of local artists. (☎02 6689 1444. Open daily 10am-4pm.) Nimbin is also known for its earth-friendly lifestyle. The **Rainbow Power Company,** on your right after a 10min. walk from the town center down Cullen St. to Alternative Way, is a remarkable achievement in solar and wind energy production; it sells its excess generated power to the electricity grid for general consumption. (☎02 6689 1430; www.rpc.com.au. Open M-F 9am-5pm.) For a hands-on look at earth-conscious living, trek to **Djanbung Gardens Permaculture Centre,** 74 Cecil St. Take a left onto Cecil St. at the southern end of Cullen; the Djanbung Gardens are just after Neem Rd. Its resource center offers workshops on organic gardening, design, and community development. Ask about accommodation for workshop and class stays. (☎02 6689 1755; www.permaculture.com.au. Open W-Sa 10am-3pm. Guided farm and garden tours Sa 11am, $20.) Beyond Djanbung lies **Jarlanbah,** a community that lives by a permaculture (closed to outsiders) code.

# MURWILLUMBAH                                          ☎02

Located in a valley halfway between Byron Bay and Tweed Heads, Murwillumbah (mur-WULL-um-bah) is a charming country town. The town serves as a base for exploring several nearby national parks, including Border Ranges, Mebbin, Mooball, Mt. Jerusalem, Mt. Warning, Nightcap, and Wollumbin.

**▐ TRANSPORTATION.** To get to Murwillumbah by car, turn off the Pacific Hwy. onto Tweed Valley Way. Countrylink (☎13 22 32) offers **buses** to Casino (2-3hr., 3-4 per day, $18), where riders can reach Sydney by **rail.** Southbound buses stop at the railway station on the Pacific Hwy.; northbound buses stop outside the tourist info center. Premier Motor Services (☎13 34 10) run to Brisbane (2-3hr., 2 per day, $25), Byron Bay (1hr., 2 per day, $18), and other stops on its Brisbane-Sydney route. Greyhound Australia (☎1300 473 946) services Brisbane (2-3hr., 1-2 per day, $31) and Surfers Paradise (1½hr., 1 per day, $26). Local Surfside Buslines (☎13 12 30) runs to Tweed Heads (1hr., 9-12 per day).

**▐▐ ORIENTATION AND PRACTICAL INFORMATION.** Most of the town lies west of the Tweed River, but you'll find **Tweed Valley Way,** the visitors center, and the train station all on its east bank. To reach the town center, cross the Tweed River on the **Alma Street bridge. Alma Street** crosses Commercial Rd. before becoming **Wollumbin Street.** The **Tourist Information Centre,** in Budd Park, at the corner of Tweed Valley Way and Alma St., is located inside the **World Heritage Rainforest Centre,** which has a number of displays about the area's natural wonders. (☎02 6672 1340 or 1800 674 414; www.tweedcoolangatta.com.au.

Open M-Sa 9am-4:30pm, Su 9:30am-4pm.) Internet is at **Precise PCs,** 13 Commercial Rd. (☎02 6672 8300; $4 per hr.; open M-F 9am-5pm, Sa 9am-noon) and at the **library** (☎02 6670 2427; $2.20 per 30min; open M-W and F 9:30am-6pm, Th 9:30am-7:30pm, Sa 9am-noon). Find a **police** station at 81 Murwillumbah St. (☎02 6672 8300) and a **post office** (☎02 6670 2030) on the corner of Brisbane and Murwillumbah St. **Postal Code:** 2484.

**⌂◻ ACCOMMODATIONS AND FOOD.** The ▨**Mount Warning/Murwillumbah YHA ❷**, 1 Tumbulgum Rd., is a well-kept, colorful, homey lodge abutting the Tweed River 18km from the base of the mountain. From the tourist center, cross the Alma St. bridge, turn right on Commercial Rd., and follow the river around the bend about 150m. The lodge sits on the riverbank, with a wrap-around deck facing Mt. Warning. It offers free use of inner tubes and free nightly ice cream at 9pm. The incredible owner, Tassie, has been running this place for 28 years. (☎02 6672 3763. Laundry $7-9. Internet $6 per hr. Key deposit $10. Bike rental $10 per day. Canoes $20 per person. Bike, canoe, and transport to Mt. Warning free for guests staying 3 or more nights. Dorms $27-31; doubles $58-67.) The **Hotel Murwillumbah ❷**, 17 Wharf St., offers cheap pubstays on the second floor. (☎02 6672 1139. Dorms $20, weekly $100; doubles $50/120. MC/V.)

Most eateries are cafes and fish and chips shops on Main St., with a handful of multicultural restaurants on Wollumbin St. and Commercial Rd. ▨**Nam Yeng ❶**, 7 Wharf St., cooks up delicious Vietnamese and Thai specialties ($8-16) in a newly renovated space. The owner sold her former restaurant but missed cooking so much that she opened this new place. (☎02 6672 3088. Open daily lunch and dinner.) For lunch, locals love **Austral Cafe ❶**, 86 Main St., for its delicious pies ($3), milkshakes ($4), and sandwiches ($3-5), all served in large diner booths. (☎02 6672 2624. Open M-Sa 7:30am-5:30pm. Cash only.) For something different, try the unique combo at **Riverside Pizza Cafe and Thai ❷**, 6 Commercial Rd., which sells few Thai dishes ($13-18) alongside pizza ($11-20) and other Italian basics. (☎02 6672 1935. Open Tu-Su 5pm-9:30pm. Cash only.) A **Coles** supermarket is in the Sunnyside Shopping Center on the corner of Brisbane and Wollumbin St. (☎02 6672 4213. Open M-Sa 6am-10pm, Su 8am-8pm.)

If you don't mind a longer drive, **Tropical Fruit World,** Duranbah Rd., Duranbah, is just off the Pacific Hwy., 30min. north of Ballina and Byron Bay. This combination farm and park offers Australia's largest selection of tropical fruits. Over 500 varieties, including the famous chocolate pudding fruit, are here for the buying. (☎02 6677 7363; www.tropicalfruitworld.com.au. Open daily 10am-sunset. Entrance to sales pavilions free. Park has fruit-tasting shows, plantation safaris, and grounds tours. $33; children $16.)

# MOUNT WARNING AND BORDER RANGES     ☎02

The stony spire of Mt. Warning resembles a gigantic ▨**thumbs-up** from the south and an elephant's head from the north. Captain Cook named the promontory in 1770 to warn European travelers that they were approaching Australia's rocky shoals at Point Danger. Formerly a shield volcano, most of the ancient lava flows have eroded away, leaving behind an enormous caldera—the largest in the Southern Hemisphere. The prominent spire in the middle of the caldera represents the volcano's erosion-resistant central chamber, which serves as a plug over the volcano's core. Many hikers tackle the **Summit Track** (8.8km, 4-5hr. round-trip) on Mt. Warning in early-morning darkness in order to be the first on the continent to greet the dawn. The climb to the peak is moderate to strenuous. The last segment is a fun, frenzied 200m vertical rock scramble with a chain handrail, but the spectacular sunrise and fantastic 360° view make your effort more than worthwhile. The drier winter season (June-Nov.) offers the best chance for clear skies. You'll need a flashlight for the sunrise climb; though there are often fireflies, don't count on them to light the way. A good jacket or sweater and change of shirt and socks are advisable—you'll work up a sweat on the climb, but the summit can be chilly even when the sun is up.

Camping on Mt. Warning is not allowed. The nearest hostel is the **Murwillumbah YHA** (p. 217). **The Mount Warning Caravan Park ❷**, on Mt. Warning Rd., 2km from the junction with Kyogle Rd., also makes a great base for exploring the mountain and surrounding areas. (☎02 6679 5120; www.mtwarningholidaypark.com. TV room, pool, camp kitchen, BBQ, and a few friendly wallabies. Linen $5. Reception 8am-5pm. Sites $20, powered $24; cabins $65, ensuite $95. Extra person $6-8. Weekly rates available. MC/V.)

To reach the Summit Track from Murwillumbah, take Tourist Route 32 that follows Kyogle Rd. 12km west, turn on Mt. Warning Rd., and go about 6km to Breakfast Creek. The peak is also accessible by **bus** from Murwillumbah Town Centre, leaving at 7:10am and returning at 5pm (inquire at the information center for more details). The Murwillumbah YHA offers free transport to the mountain base for guests staying three or more nights. The incredibly fit could also **bike** the track, a 30km round trip with an 8.8km hike.

If you find Mt. Warning too overrun, the 32,000 gorgeous hectares of **Border Ranges National Park** offer extravagant views that rival those of its more-touristed neighbor. (Call the parks office at ☎02 6632 0000 for more info.) Though farther than some other parks, Border Ranges rewards intrepid travelers with the shade of a lush canopy and great vantage points for viewing the volcano region. To get to Border Ranges, take the Kyogle Rd. west from Murwillumbah for 44km; 5.2km past the turnoff to Nimbin marks the start of the signposted **Tweed Range Scenic Drive** (60km, 4-5hr.). The Barker Vale turnoff leads 15km along gravel road to the park entrance. The drive exits the park at Wiangaree, 13km from Kyogle and 66km from Murwillumbah. The first picnic area in the park is **Bar Mountain,** with a lovely beech glade. Less than 1km away is the remarkable **Blackbutts picnic area,** with striking views of Mt. Warning and the basin. Another 8km north, **Pinnacle Lookout** offers a similarly spectacular view. To reach the **Forest Tops camping area ❶**, travel 4km past the lookout, turn left at the junction, go another 4km, and turn left again ($5, children $3). If you turn right instead of left at this last junction, you'll wind up at the **Brindle Creek picnic area,** the departure point for the **Brindle Creek Walk** (10km round-trip; 3-4hr.), a track that winds among rainforests and waterfalls and ends at the **Antarctic Beech picnic area,** home to 2000 year-old trees. For a shorter scenic trip, turn off Kyogle Rd. at Doon Doon Rd., 1km past Uki Village, and head to **Cram's Farm picnic area,** a delightful spot on the lake. Travel farther down Doon Doon Rd., turn right at Doon Doon Hall, and follow the path down to its deadend to catch a glimpse of **Doughboy,** a smaller volcanic plug.

# NEW ENGLAND

The New England Highway begins just northwest of Brisbane, swinging south through Queensland's wine country before entering the New England region via Tenterfield. On its way south to Tamworth, the highway branches off to Waterfall Way and later to the Oxley Hwy., leading to lovely national parks.

## TENTERFIELD AND NEARBY PARKS                                    ☎02

It was in Tenterfield (pop. 3500) that Sir Henry Parkes cried out, "One people, one destiny," in an 1889 speech that foresaw Australia's federation. The town clings to its history with preserved buildings and a Sir Henry Parkes celebration. While known by locals as the "Birthplace of Our Nation," as the northern point of entry to the region, it is also called the "Gateway to New England."

**TRANSPORTATION.** Greyhound Australia (☎13 14 99 or 13 20 30) runs **buses** to Brisbane (5½hr.; 2 per day; $87, students $71) and Sydney (12hr., daily at midnight; $104/93). Kirklands (☎02 6622 1499) runs to Lismore (3hr.; M, W, F 2pm; $30). Crisp's Coaches (☎07 4661 8333) runs to Brisbane (4hr.; M, W, F, Su; $75, students $64). Buses stop at various points on Rouse St.; call for details. Countrylink runs buses to Armidale (2hr., daily 5:50am, $27).

**PRACTICAL INFORMATION. The Tenterfield Visitors Centre,** 157 Rouse St. (New England Hwy.), has info on all New England destinations. (☎02 6736 1082; www.tenterfield. com. Open M-F 9:30am-5pm, Sa-Su 9:30am-4pm.) Rouse St. is home to **ATMs** and the public **library**

**New England**

(☎02 6736 6060. Open M-F 10am-5pm, Sa 9am-noon. Free Internet access.) The **police station** is at 94 Molesworth St. (☎02 6736 1144), and the **parks office** is at 10 Miles St. (☎02 6736 4298; open M-F 8am-4pm). The **hospital** (☎02 6739 5200) is at 1-5 Naas St. The **post office** is at 225 Rouse St. (Open M-F 8:45am-5pm.) **Postal Code:** 2372.

**ACCOMMODATIONS AND FOOD.** For cheap accommodations, you can try the **Tenterfield Lodge Caravan Park ❷,** 2 Manners St., which houses a hostel with a friendly host who helps travelers find seasonal work. Most guests are male or fruit pickers, but female rooms are also available. Call in advance for free pickup from the bus station. (☎02 6736 1477. Sites for 2 $20, powered $22; cabins $40, ensuite $65. Extra adult $4. Dorms $25. Weekly rates available. MC/V.) A couple of hotels exist in town; try the **Telegraph Hotel ❷,** 133 Manners St., for basic rooms. (☎02 6736 1015. Singles $25, doubles/twins $30. MC/V.) Three unsealed kilometers north of Bald Rock National Park on Mt. Lindesay Rd. is the wonderful **Bald Rock Bush Retreat ❹,** which includes a stunning Spanish hacienda, a backpacker guest house, and luxurious waterfront cabins. Wander through the trails among the horses and kangaroos by day and enjoy a night sky so bright that a guest once termed this place the "5 million stars hotel." (☎02 4686 1227; www.baldrockbushretreat.com. Doubles $60-150; ensuite cabin $150. 8-person bunk house for min. 4-person group from $120, extra adult $30. MC/V.) **The Willow Tree ❷,** 274 Rouse St., serves delicious sandwiches on thick toasted bread ($9-16). Warm up by the crackling fire or enjoy the sun on the patio. (☎02 6736 2135. Open daily 8:30am-5pm. MC/V.) The

**NEW SOUTH WALES**

**Famous Pie Shop ❶,** on Rouse St., earns its name with the yummy "Wagyu Beef Pie" ($4.35), which recently won the National Aussie Pie Contest. (Open M-F 6am-5:30pm, Sa 7am-4pm. Cash only.) Both the Royal Hotel and the Telegraph Hotel offer reasonably priced counter menu lunches ($8-10) noon-2pm.

**🔦 OUTDOOR ACTIVITIES.** Tenterfield lies near three national parks ($7 entry fee). To reach them, take Rouse St. north, turn right on Naas St., then quickly bear left onto Mt. Lindesay Rd. Before reaching the parks, history buffs might want to take a look at the remains of Tenterfield's **WWII tank traps,** about 11km from town. These traps were part of the Brisbane Line, Oz's second line of defense in case the northern part of the country was defeated. Tenterfield was a major strategic center; during the war, up to 10,000 troops were camped in the area. About 3km farther, a narrow, gravel lane leads to **Basket Swamp National Park,** a preserved woodland area with picnic and bushcamping sites.

For a less-touristed look at a giant monolith, skip Uluru and head to **Bald Rock National Park,** home to the largest exposed granite monolith in the Southern Hemisphere. To reach it, head down Mt. Lindesay Rd. for 29km to a sealed road that runs 5km to the park's camping and picnic areas. Two paths lead to the 1277m summit and its great views of the McPherson Ranges. The **Burgoona Walk** (2.5km) is a scenic, moderate hiking path, while the **Summit Direct Path** (1.2km) is a steep scramble up the rock face (follow the white dotted trail). Combine the Burgoona ascent and the Summit Direct descent for a 3hr. round trip.

The entrance to **Boonoo Boonoo** (BUN-na buh-NOO) **National Park** is 24km north of Tenterfield, with another 14km of gravel leading to the stunning, carved-granite Boonoo Boonoo Gorge and Falls. From the carpark, one path leads to a lookout over the mammoth falls (300m) and another accesses a swimming hole above the cascade (200m). Camping is available at **Cypress Pine Camping Area ❶** and includes water, toilets, picnic tables, and BBQ ($10, children $5; vehicle entry fee $7). Pay the $7 vehicle entrance fee only once to access both Boonoo Boonoo and Bald Rock National Parks. Girraween National Park is just west of Bald Rock, across the Queensland border. Take the New England Hwy. to Wyberba and follow Pyramids Rd. for 9km. There is no public transportation to either park, but caravan park owners will sometimes drive their guests.

# GLEN INNES                                                                  ☎02

Glen Innes (pop. 10,000) is a standard town with a historic twist. Giant standing stones and an annual Celtic festival hark back to the ancient past, while mining activities and a pioneer museum celebrate Australia's beginnings.

**🚆 TRANSPORTATION.** Countrylink (☎13 22 32) has **bus** service to Sydney (9hr., 1 per day, $98), as well as direct service to nearby towns. The Countrylink station is next to the visitors center, where bookings can be made for a $5 fee. Greyhound Australia (☎13 14 99 or 13 20 30) sends buses to Brisbane (6hr.; 2 per day; $88, students $80); Sydney (11hr., 1 per day, $113/103); Tamworth (3hr., 1 per day, $71/64); and other small regional centers. Contact individual bus companies for details about local service. Greyhound stops at the 24hr. Caltex station on the New England Hwy. Call **taxis** at ☎02 6732 1300.

**⚹ 🛈 ORIENTATION AND PRACTICAL INFORMATION.** The main commercial street in town is Grey St., parallel to and one block west of the **New England Highway** (called **Church Street** in town), which runs north 93km to Tenterfield and south 95km to Armidale. The **Gwydir Highway,** known in town as **Meade Street**

and **Ferguson Street,** runs east-west. The **Glen Innes Visitors Centre,** 152 Church St., is near the intersection of the New England and Gwydir Hwy. (☎02 6730 2400; www.gleninnestourism.com.au. Open M-F 9am-5pm, Sa-Su and public holidays 9am-3pm.) Grey St. is home to several **banks** with **ATMs, supermarkets, pubstays,** basic **eateries,** and a **library** with free Internet access. (☎02 6732 2302. Open M and F 10am-5pm, Tu-Th 8:30am-5pm, Sa 9:30am-noon.)

**▗▖ ACCOMMODATIONS AND FOOD.** Cheap rooms are available at the **pubs ❸** on Grey St. (singles $30-40; doubles $45-55), and motels on the New England Hwy. Your best bet may be the **Club Hotel ❸,** on the corner of Grey and Wentworth St., which has rooms with sinks and some with electric blankets. (☎02 6732 3043. Breakfast $10. Singles $35; doubles $45. MC/V.) More charming stays are found a bit west of town. **Bullock Mountain Homestead ❺,** on Bullock Mountain Rd., 15km north of Glen Innes toward Emmaville, is a horse ranch with B&B-style accommodations and meals. (☎02 6732 1599; www.bullockmountainhomestead.com. Can arrange free pickup from bus stop. Sites $10 per adult, powered $12. Caravans $40. B&B rooms $95.) The Homestead also runs a variety of splurge-worthy horseback rides, including the popular horseback pub crawl. (Weekend $395, 4-day trip $1490; meals and accommodation included. Book ahead. AmEx/MC/V.) Next door, the **Three Waters High Country Holiday Park ❶** offers 1200 acres of secluded countryside perfect for camping, riding, and fossicking. Unpowered campsites line the river, and access to the new recreation center, showers, toilets, laundry, and gas BBQ is available. Free accommodation and meals are also possible for backpackers willing to do a bit of work around the property. Be sure to ask the owner Steven for some of his stories. (☎02 6732 4863; www.gleninnes.com/3waters. Fossicking $8, horseback riding $35 per hr. Sites $15 for 1, $20 for 2; cabins $65. Cash only.)

For good eats, try **Crofters Cottage ❶,** at Centennial Parklands next to the Standing Stones. Crofters serves gourmet main dishes ($9-13) and terrific toasted sandwiches. (☎02 6732 6516. Open M-W and F 10am-5pm, Th 9:30am-4pm. MC/V.) The local pubs, including the **Great Central Hotel ❶** and the **Club Hotel ❶,** offer hearty counter lunch deals ($8-12). If you're in the mood for Chinese, head to **Dragon Court ❶,** at 173 Grey St., for the $9 smorgasbord lunch special from noon-2:30pm (☎02 6732 1368. Also open for dinner 5:30-8pm).

**◐ ※ SIGHTS AND FESTIVALS.** Glen Innes celebrates its Celtic heritage every first weekend in May with the three-day **Australian Celtic Festival** (☎02 6730 2400, or call the visitors center; www.australiancelticfestival.com.) Many of the festivities are set in the shadow of the **Standing Stones,** a series of massive granite blocks in the tradition of an ancient Celtic form of timekeeping, erected on Martins Lookout, 1km east of the visitors center on Meade St. (Gwydir Hwy.) Every conceivable piece of pioneer equipment, from 150 types of barbed wire to an entire 19th-century slab cottage, can be found at the **"Land of the Beardies" History House Museum,** in the historic hospital building on the corner of West Ave. and Ferguson St. (☎02 6732 1035. Open M-F 10am-noon and 1-4pm, Sa-Su 1-4pm. $6, students and children $1, seniors $4.) **Fossicking,** or panning for sapphires, and fishing are both very popular; there are many opportunities to do both in and around Glen Innes. **Glen Rest Tourist Park,** 9807 New England Hwy, 3.5km south of the town center, offers $10 fossicking (☎02 6732 2413). **Reddeston Sapphires,** next door to the info center, will cut your sapphire for $25 per carat while you wait. (☎02 6732 5173; www.reddestone.com. Open daily 8:30am-5pm.) **Equine Ability** offers first-rate lessons in horsebreaking and training. Call to book. (☎02 6732 5295; www.equineability.com.au.)

# ARMIDALE ☎ 02

The highest city in Australia at 980m above sea level, Armidale (pop. 25,000) is conveniently located at the beginning of Waterfall Way, making it a great base for exploration of the magnificent countryside. A healthy pub scene is kept lively by students from the University of New England.

**⊞ TRANSPORTATION.** The bus terminal is attached to the visitors center at 82 Marsh St. (☎02 6772 4655 or 1800 627 736; www.armidaletourism.com.au. Open daily 9am-5pm.) Greyhound Australia (☎13 20 30) runs to Brisbane (8hr., 1 per day, $100); Newcastle (7hr., 1 per day, $89); and Sydney (10hr., 1 per day, $109). Countrylink (☎13 22 32) connects by coach to Tenterfield (2½hr., daily 6:30pm, $25). One block south of the visitors center on Marsh St. is the beginning of the Beardy Street Mall, an outdoor cluster of shops and cafes. **New England Travel Centre,** 188 Beardy Mall, is helpful for booking buses and trains. (☎02 6772 1722. Open M-F 9am-5pm, Sa 9am-noon.) For a taxi, call **Armidale Radio Taxis** at ☎ 02 6771 1455 or 13 10 08.

**◪⁊ ORIENTATION AND PRACTICAL INFORMATION.** The **visitors center** is located at 82 Marsh St. The Armidale **parks office** (☎02 6776 0000), in the W. J. McCarthy Building at 85-87 Faulkner St., has info on area parks. (Open M-F 8:30am-4:30pm.) The **library,** on the corner of Faulkner St. and Cinders Ln., has free Internet terminals for booking. (☎02 6772 4711. Open M-F 10am-6pm, Sa 10am-1pm.) The **police station** (☎02 6771 0699) is at 1 Moore St. Internet access is also available at **Civic Video,** 119 Rusden St., for $1 per 10min. (☎02 6771 1113. Su-Th 9am-9pm; F-Sa 9am-9:30pm.) **ATMs** are available on Beardy St. between Marsh and Dangar St., and the **post office** is at 158 Beardy St. **Postal Code:** 2350.

**⊞⊡ ACCOMMODATIONS AND FOOD.** ◪**The Pembroke Caravan Park ❷,** 39 Waterfall Way (also known as Grafton Rd. and Barney St. in town), is 1.5km east of town and has a **YHA hostel ❷** with a recreation room and TV lounge area. Tennis courts, a heated pool, kitchen, and laundry ($8) are among the hostel's offerings. (☎02 6772 6470 or 1800 355 578; www.pembroke.com.au. Reception 7:30am-6pm. Internet $1 for 10min. Wi-Fi available. Sites $21, powered $26; dorms $25-29; vans $39-47; cabins $60-101. AmEx/MC/V.) Formerly the Teachers College, **Smith House ❸,** 100 Barney St., north of Central Park, now welcomes tourists and students in its long halls. Each room is equipped with fridge, microwave, TV, and free Internet. (☎02 6772 0652. Free continental breakfast. Laundry $3. Singles $40, students $35; doubles $55. Reception 9am-5pm. Discounts available for longer stays.)

Reasonably priced cafes line the Mall. **Rumours on the Mall ❶,** 190 Beardy St., serves breakfast ($5-18) and lunch ($6-16). Try one of their Turkish bread sandwiches ($12) or the popular chicken minestrone soup for $9. (☎02 6772 3084. Open M-F 8am-5pm, Sa-Su 8am-2pm. Cash only.) Grab traditional pub grub at the **New England Hotel ❸,** on the corner of Beardy and Dangar St. "Newie's" serves main dishes that range from $14-25. To sample the uni pub scene, stop by Newie's upstairs later in the evening. (☎02 6772 7622. Open M-Sa noon-2pm and 6-9pm. MC/V.) A **Coles** supermarket is on Marsh St. between Beardy and Dumaresq St. (Open M-Sa 6am-midnight, Su 8am-8pm.)

**◪⚒ SIGHTS AND ACTIVITIES.** The visitors center provides a free 2½hr. heritage tour of Armidale daily at 10am; call to book. Following Marsh St. south uphill to the corner of Kentucky St. leads you to the **New England Regional Art Museum,** which features works from classic Australian painters in its $45 million collection. (☎02 6772 5255. Open Tu-Su 10:30am-5pm. Free.) Next door at 128 Kentucky St. is the **Aboriginal Cultural Centre and Keeping Place,** which has permanent and rotating art galleries of boomerangs, carved kangaroos, dot paintings, message sticks, and more. (☎02 6771 3606; www.acckp.com.au. Open M-F 9:30am-4pm. Donations appreciated.)

# NATIONAL PARKS IN THE NEW ENGLAND TABLELANDS

Tucked between the red dirt roads of Big Sky country and the crashing surf of the coast, the New England Tablelands' national parks offer travelers an easy wilderness escape. Bike the subtropical wilderness or simply gaze at cascading waterfalls. Waterfall Way (Rte. 78) stretches from Armidale to the Pacific Highway just south of Coffs Harbour. Straddling the southern side of the parks, Oxley Highway connects Walcha to Port Macquarie. These roads link to more than a dozen forests and reserves, providing a range of rugged terrain.

## ARMIDALE AREA NATIONAL PARKS

**WATERFALL WAY.** The World Heritage site Waterfall Way runs east-west between Armidale and the north coast of New South Wales. Along the way, the tourist route passes four excellent national parks with campgrounds, several tiny hamlets, and the charming town of **Bellingen** (p. 198). In addition to the parks below, ▇**Ebor Falls** (approximately 4km east of Cathedral Rock, 42km west of Dorrigo, and 600m off the highway) provides an gorgeous photo-op year-round. A 600m walk from the carpark leads to a breathtaking lookout.

**OXLEY WILD RIVERS NATIONAL PARK.** This World Heritage site is full of waterfalls tumbling into expansive gorges and is home to a variety of endangered species like the brush-tailed rock-wallaby. Pamphlets can help you choose a camp or picnic site; contact the **Armidale NPWS** (☎02 6776 0000) or **Armidale Visitors Centre** (☎1800 627 736) for more info. The Port Macquarie (☎02 6584 2203), Dorrigo (☎02 6657 2309), and Walcha (☎02 6777 4700) NPWS offices have info as well. To find out more on **Apsley** and **Tia Gorges** at the more remote western end of the park, see p. 224.

Two of Oxley's best vistas are not far from Armidale. Less than 20km south of the city lie the 120m high **Dangar Falls,** but be aware that they are sometimes dry. Take Kentucky St. east to Dangarsleigh Rd. and drive 8km south; 10km of gravel road leads to the gorge. The rest area is the trailhead for a series of walks ranging in length from the **Gorge Lookout path** (100m) to half-day treks; it is also equipped with BBQ, firewood, and pit toilets. After passing the grid, take the first left into the park for **campgrounds ❶** ($5). **Gara Gorge,** also a popular daytrip from Armidale, is the site of Australia's first public hydro-electric scheme, built in 1894. East from Armidale, Waterfall Way leads to Castledoyle Rd.; it's only an 18km trip, with about 3km of gravel as you approach the gorge. The **Threlfall Walk** (an easy 5.5km) circles the edge of the gorge, surveying leftover sites from the historic engineering scheme.

Long Point is a secluded wilderness area, nestled in a eucalyptus forest next to a rare dry rainforest. The turnoff for Long Point appears 40km east of Armidale along Waterfall Way. A 7km stretch of sealed track passes through Hillgrove, where a left turn leads to a dirt track that reaches the park 20km below. The attached campsite has pit toilets and fresh water. It's also the trailhead for the excellent **Chandler Walk** (5km, 2hr.), which leads through a grove of mosses, vines, and yellow-spotted Hillgrove Gum trees, unique to the area. Tremendous lookouts along the walk survey the valley and Chandler River.

The **Wollomombi Falls** gorge, located 40km east of Armidale, is the easiest part of Oxley to access from the east. 75km west of Dorrigo, the Falls are just 2km south of Waterfall Way. **Wollomombi Lookout** (150m), **Checks Lookout** (500m), and **Chandler Lookout** (1.5km) all provide stunning views. The moderately strenuous **Wollomombi Walk** (2km round-trip) takes you around the rim of the gorge and to a series of spectacular lookouts. There is a campsite with gas BBQ near the entrance to the gorge area. **The Dutton Trout Hatchery,** 3km off the New England National Parks turnoff, breeds 1-2 million rainbow and brown trout for release into Australian waterways and has an informative 8min. video and self-guided hatchery tours. (☎02 6775 9139; www.dpi.nsw.gov.au. Open daily 9am-4pm.)

## OXLEY HIGHWAY NATIONAL PARKS

**APSLEY AND TIA GORGES.** The must-see highlights of the southwestern end of **Oxley Wild Rivers National Park** (p. 223) are the waterfalls in the Apsley and Tia Gorges, which are most easily accessed from the Oxley Hwy. The larger part of the park is usually accessed from Waterfall Way, closer to **Armidale** (p. 222). About 83km south from Armidale and 20km east of Walcha is the turnoff for the **Apsley Gorge,** 1km off the highway. The waterfall is not only one of the most spectacular in the park, but also one of the easiest to view. A staircase leading down into the gorge provides an outstanding, unobstructed lookout. The **Oxley Walk** (2.7km, 2hr. round-trip) takes you around the rim of the gorge and across a bridge over the Apsley River. Campsites and fresh water are available at **Lions Lookout ❶,** one of the area's most scenic camping spots. 19km south of the Apsley Falls entrance is a 5.5km unsealed road leading to the small picnic and camping area of **Tia Falls ❶.** Tia Gorge is a short 650m walk, and the **Tiara Walk** (5km return) crosses the river by footbridge and follows the gorge's western bluff. (Both sites $3 per person plus $7 entrance fee.)

Small and charming, **Walcha** (WAL-ka; pop. 1800) is still a useful starting point for Apsley and Tia Gorges and the rest of Oxley Wild Rivers National Park, though the town lacks excitement. You'll find info on the local parks at the **Visitor Information Centre,** on the corner of Fitzroy and South St. (☎02 6774 2460. Open M-F 9am-5pm, Sa-Su 9am-4pm), and the NPWS outpost at 188 W. North St. From the only roundabout in Walcha, turn north onto Darby St., then left at the showground onto North St. (☎02 6777 4700. Open M-F 8:30am-4:30pm.) The newly renovated **Commercial Hotel ❹,** on Meridian St. off the highway, has food and large, clean rooms with TVs. (☎02 6777 2551. Free continental breakfast. Singles $55; doubles $65; twins $75.)

**WERRIKIMBE NATIONAL PARK.** More rugged than its neighbors, Werrikimbe is home to temperate and subtropical rainforest, eucalyptus forest, and snow gum woodlands. District managers in **Walcha** (☎02 6777 4700) or **Port Macquarie** (☎02 6586 8300) offer extensive information. The first 15km of this track aren't too bad, but the twisting, loose gravel path may be difficult for conventional vehicles, especially after rain. Inside the park, the tracks to the campground and visitor facilities are maintained to a 2WD standard (any further travel into the park will require a 4WD). Upon entering, travelers may choose to turn left into the **Mooraback Rest Area** or right to **Cobcroft's Rest Area;** both trailheads have parking, picnic tables, and toilets; Mooraback also has **campsites.** Mooraback is set amid snow gum woodlands by the Mooraback Creek, where the Hastings River begins its descent to Port Macquarie. The **Platypus Pools track** (2hr. round-trip) meanders past a series of pools where, if your timing is right, you might catch a glimpse of a monotreme or two. The rest area is the starting point for the 15min. **Mooraback Track** and the popular 3- to 4-day **Werrikimbe Trail.**

The rest area at Cobcroft is set in an open eucalyptus forest sprinkled with tree ferns. The **Carrabeen Walk** (1hr. round-trip) passes through an adjacent temperate rainforest. Longer walks into the **Werrikimbe Wilderness Area**, including the 8hr. **Mesa Trail,** are possible, but you should consult the NPWS office first.

Three spots are accessible from the Oxley Hwy. on the eastern side of the park, along Forbes River Rd. or Hastings Forest Way (though these are more conveniently reached from Port Macquarie): **Grass Tree Rest Area, Brushy Mountain Camping Area,** and **Plateau Beech Camping Area.** All three are trailheads. The passage from the Plateau Beech Camping Area crosses through gullies of Antarctic beeches, with gnarled bases that take on crazy shapes, before the trail heads on to **King Fern Falls** and **Filmy Ferns Cascades** (1hr. round-trip). The eastern and western sides of the park are linked by the 4WD-only **Racecourse Trail.**

Ten kilometers farther down the Oxley Hwy. from Werrikimbe (65km east of Walcha) is **Cottan-Bimbang National Park.** The park's main feature is the 15km **Myrtle Scrub Scenic Drive,** a looping, 2WD, dry-weather track that stops at a picnic ground, adjacent to a magnificent timber bridge over Cells River.

# TAMWORTH       ☎02

Every January, Tamworth (pop. 37,500) hosts the **Country Music Festival** (begins the third F of Jan. and lasts for 10 days. www.tcmf.com.au), drawing famous crooners and hordes of fans. A more recent tradition, the **Hats Off to Country Festival** brings smaller crowds every July but promises a full slate of live music for four straight days. The country spirit is otherwise upheld by 10-gallon-hatted cowboys and tie-in tourist attractions, like the giant golden guitar and a concrete slab with handprints of country artists. Though the town is a destination for country-music lovers, it is also a pleasant stopover for those headed to nearby national parks or Brisbane. It's also close to several of the popular Jackaroo and Jillaroo schools in the area.

**TRANSPORTATION.** The train station, on Marius St. between Brisbane and Bourke St., has a **travel center** that books tickets. (☎02 6701 9050. Open M-F 9am-5pm.) Countrylink (☎13 22 32) runs express **trains** to Sydney (6hr.; 1 per day; $60, concessions $42). All **buses** run from the coach terminal outside the visitors center. Greyhound Australia (☎13 14 99 or 13 20 30) travels to Brisbane (10hr.; daily 8am and 8:55pm; $197, concessions $93) and Sydney (7hr., daily 4:45am, $99/88) via Newcastle (5hr., $78/70). Keans Travel Express (☎02 6543 1322) also travels to other destinations; call or check at the visitors center for details. For **car** rental, **Avis** (☎02 6765 2000), **Budget** (☎13 27 27 or ☎02 6766 7255), **Hertz** (☎02 6762 3545), and **Thrifty** (☎02 6765 3699) have branches in town. Call **Tamworth Radio Cabs** (☎13 10 08) for a **taxi.**

**ORIENTATION AND PRACTICAL INFORMATION.** Tamworth is 412km north of Sydney on the New England Hwy. (which, from Armidale, enters town from the east and departs south) and is a convenient rest stop for those journeying to Brisbane (578km). The town's CBD lies along **Peel Street.** The main intersection is with **Brisbane Street (New England Highway),** which crosses the Peel River, becoming **Bridge Street** in West Tamworth. The **visitors center** is at the corner of Peel and Murray St. (☎02 6767 5300; www.visittamworth.com. Open daily 9am-5pm.) The **library,** 466 Peel St., has free Internet access. (☎02 6755 4460. Open M-Th 10am-7pm, F 10am-6pm, Sa 9am-2pm.) **ATMs** are all along Peel St. **Police** (☎02 6768 2999) are located at 40 Fitzroy St. The **post office,** 406 Peel St. (☎13 13 18), is on the corner with Fitzroy St. **Postal Code:** 2340.

**▆▐▊ ACCOMMODATIONS AND FOOD.** Beds are generally plentiful, except during January's Country Music Festival (book a year ahead). Several hotels offer pubstays for $35-60 per night. The **Tamworth YHA ❷**, 169 Marius St., offers cheap beds and spotless bathrooms just across the street from the train station. This hostel generally serves as the gateway to the Jackaroo and Jillaroo schools. Breakfast is available for $3.50. (☎02 6761 2600. Laundry $6. Internet $1 per 15min. Dorms $23-28; doubles $55-124. MC/V.) **Paradise Tourist Park ❶**, next to the visitors center along the creek on Peel St., has electric grills, a pool, and a playground. (☎02 6766 3120; www.paradisetouristpark.com.au. Linen $5 for singles, $8 for doubles. Laundry $6. Key deposit $10. Reception daily 7am-7pm. Sites for 2 $21-30, powered $27-36; bunk rooms $46-90; cabins $55-124. Extra person $9-12. MC/V. 7th night free in the low season.) For a true Aussie farm experience, stay at friendly **Castle Mountain Farmstay ❸** in Quirindi, about 45min. south of Armidale. This 2000-acre homestead has comfortable rooms—in dorms, doubles, or cottages—and homecooked meals. (☎02 6746 2102; www.castlemountain.com.au. 3 meals and accommodations $45.)

**The Vault ❷**, 429 Peel St., serves gourmet pizzas cooked in a wood-fire oven ($14-19). Live music fills the high ceilings of this refurbished 1892 former bank, on Th and Sa nights in the summer, F and Su afternoons in the winter. (☎02 6766 6975. Open M and Su 8am-4pm, Tu-Sa 8am-late. AmEx/D/MC/V.) The **Old Vic Cafe ❶**, 261 Peel St., is frequented by a laid-back clientele and fixes gourmet main courses ($10-18) as well as Turkish bread sandwiches ($10-11), freshly squeezed juices ($4), and homemade sauces and vinaigrettes. All-day breakfast is available. (☎02 6766 3435. Open M-F 8am-5pm, Sa 8:30am-3pm. MC/V.)

**▆▐▊ SIGHTS AND ACTIVITIES.** You don't have to be a country music fan to enjoy Tamworth; you just need a high tolerance for kitsch. The **Big Golden Guitar Complex** is worth the 10min. trip south on the New England Hwy., as much for the gift shop as for the 12m guitar itself. A realistic "Gallery of Stars" wax museum dresses 27 replicas in clothes donated by the stars themselves, including Slim Dusty, "The Man Who is Australia." In odd juxtaposition, an impressive gem and mineral display shares the complex. (☎02 6765 2688; www.biggoldenguitar.com.au. Open daily 9am-5pm. Wax museum $8, children $4, families $18.) The popular **Hands of Fame Cornerstone**, on Brisbane St. at Kable Ave., bears the handprints of Australian country music celebrities. The **Walk a Country Mile Interpretive Centre** at the visitors center takes you through an interactive history of country music in Australia. ($6, children $2, families $15.) Bring out your inner cowboy or cowgirl at one of the **Jackaroo and Jillaroo schools** in the Tamworth area, with crash courses in horse-riding, dog-training, cow-milking, lassoing, and mustering cattle from the saddle. Certificates and job placement assistance are given upon completion. **▊Leconfield** runs an excellent school 1hr. out of Tamworth. (☎02 6769 4328; www.leconfield.com. Free pickup at Tamworth YHA. 5-day course begins every M. Book a month ahead $550 includes food and accommodation. Cash only, $200 advance deposit required.)

**▐▊ ENTERTAINMENT AND NIGHTLIFE.** Tamworth is definitely a country town, and its nightlife has a tangible local flavor. Most establishments close well after 2am, but the standard Australian 1 or 1:30am curfew means you must be in the establishment door by that hour. The **West Diggers Club** (☎02 6766 4661), on Kable Ave., off Brisbane St., has live music on most weekends. The **Imperial Hotel**, on the corner of Marius and Brisbane St., draws a younger crowd that's generally uninterested in its country music heritage. (☎02 6766 2613. Live music Th-Sa. Curfew 1:30am.) **The Central Hotel,** on the corner of Brisbane and Peel St., features live rock and country live music Thursday-

Saturday. (☎02 6766 2160) Check out a free copy of *Tamworth City News* from the tourist office, for details and other venues.

# SOUTH COAST

While the path from Sydney up the North Coast has been well-worn by hordes of backpackers, the South Coast has only recently been discovered by tourists. Local residents proudly proclaim that it's one of Australia's best-kept secrets, and many city-weary visitors will be inclined to agree. The region's beaches are only minutes away from lush rainforests and are usually far less crowded than those in the north. Princes Hwy., south of Sydney, links South Coast destinations like Bateman's Bay, Jervis Bay, and Kiama.

# WOLLONGONG                                                    ☎02

About 80km south of Sydney, Wollongong (pop. 260,000) is the coastal gateway to scenic **Shoalhaven** and is a great place to stop for water sports or a night of partying. As the third-largest metropolitan area in New South Wales, Wollongong is anxious to push its cosmopolitan city appeal, but it's still essentially a small, friendly university town. While its foundations lie in industry, the 'Gong—bordered by steep mountains and miles of coastline—can't help but support outdoor activities. In addition to world-class surfing, there are adrenaline-pumping activities in nearby Stanwell Park.

**🖪🔢 TRANSPORTATION AND PRACTICAL INFORMATION.** CityRail **trains** (☎13 15 00) stop at **Wollongong City Station** on Station St. and run to Bomaderry (1hr., 4-10 per day, $8.60), Kiama (45min., 11-16 per day, $5.60), and Sydney (1hr., 12-28 per day, $10.60). Premier Motor Service (☎13 34 10; www.premierms.com.au) **buses** run to: Batemans Bay (3-3hr., 2 per day, $41); Bermagui (6hr., 1 per day, $55); Melbourne (15hr., 1 per day, $83); Narooma (4-5hr., 2 per day, $54); Sydney (1-2hr., 2 per day, $16); Ulladulla (2hr., 2-3 per day, $30). Murrays (☎13 22 51; www.murrays.com.au) runs to Canberra (3hr., 1 per day, $31). The **Princes Hwy.** runs into Wollongong, becoming **Flinders Street** north of the city and merging into **Keira St. ATMs** are available at the pedestrian **Crown Street Mall**, between Keira and Kembla St. **Tourism Wollongong,** 93 Crown St., is on the corner of Crown and Kembla St. (☎02 4227 5545; www.tourismwollongong.com.au. Open M-F 9am-5pm, Sa 9am-4pm, Su 10am-4pm.) **Network Cafe**, 157 Crown St., has Internet access for $3.50 per hr. (☎02 4228 8686. Open M-W and F 9:45am-6pm, Th 9:45am-8:30pm, Sa 9:45am-4pm.) The **post office** is at 110-116 Crown St., in the mall. (☎13 13 18. Open M-F 9am-5pm.) **Postal Code:** 2500.

**🖪 ACCOMMODATIONS.** 🖾**YHA Wollongong ❷** (also known as **Keiraview Accommodation**), 75-79 Keira St., is Wollongong's most impressive place to stay. The spacious rooms all contain fridges, and guests have BBQ equipment and a TV lounge at their disposal. (☎02 4229 1132; www.keiraviewaccommodation.com. au. Internet access $2.50 per hr. Wheelchair-accessible. Dorms from $26-29; twins from $36; ensuite singles and doubles $73-81; family rooms $78-87.) The **Keiraleagh hostel ❷**, 60 Kembla St., is also located in the city center, but is neither as spacious nor as well-maintained as the YHA. However, it's convenient, within walking distance of beaches, restaurants, nightclubs, and the Crown St. shopping mall. (☎02 4228 6765. Dorms $20-25; singles $30; doubles $50.)

NEW SOUTH WALES

Map legend:

**Wollongong**

▲ ACCOMMODATIONS
Keiraleagh, **1**
YHA Wollongong, **3**

🍎 FOOD
Trang, **6**
Harbourfront, **8**
Woolworths, **4**

★ NIGHTLIFE
Ivory, **2**
One Five One, **5**
Glasshouse Tavern, **7**

**FOOD AND NIGHTLIFE.** The restaurants lining Keira, Corrimal, and lower Crown St. offer a variety of Asian cuisines, with the cheapest entrees starting at around $10. There are also a number of Indian and Italian restaurants. **Trang ❶**, 165 Keira St., serves delicious Vietnamese food at affordable prices, including vermicelli spring rolls ($7), grilled pork, lemongrass beef, and prawns with salad (meat dishes $12, seafood $15). The recently redone dining space creates a stylish yet laid-back atmosphere. (☎02 4229 6883. Open daily 11am-3pm and 5-11pm.) If you're in the mood for seafood at the water's edge, hunker down in the relaxed atmosphere at **Harbourfront ❸**, 2 Endeavour Dr., and enjoy your view of the lighthouse. (☎02 4227 2999; www.harbourfront. com.au.) The **Woolworths** supermarket is on the corner of Kembla and Burelli St. (☎02 4228 8066. Open M-Sa 7:30am-10pm, Su 8am-8pm.)

Weekday nightlife is pretty quiet in Wollongong, but things get exciting when the uni students come out to play. The **Glasshouse Tavern,** 90 Crown St., between Kembla and Corrimal St., attracts a young crowd eager to impress, on weekends, when its back room transforms into a dance club. (☎02 4226 4305. Open M-Tu 10am-9pm, W-Sa 10am-4:30am, Su noon-midnight; nightclub opens W-Sa at 7 or 8pm.) **One Five One,** 150 Keira St., is Wollongong's brand-new venue, attracting hot DJs and live acts (☎02 4226 1215; open W and Sa

NEW SOUTH WALES

8pm-late), while **Ivory,** 77 Crown St., has a smaller dance floor and funky fun atmosphere (☎02 4226 1844. Open W-Sa 8pm-late).

**SIGHTS AND ACTIVITIES.** Like most of the South Coast, Wollongong's best features are found outdoors, particularly in and around **Wollongong Harbour.** The small, convict-built cove shelters sailboats and the local fishing fleet, and the two lighthouses, both visible from the beach, add an air of vintage charm. Visitors and residents alike enjoy the beautiful walking and cycling path along the harbor's edge to **North Beach,** a popular surf spot. Wollongong's other surfing beach is **City Beach,** only a few blocks from the Crown St. mall. For more info on bikes, boards, and extreme sports, contact the **Tourism Wollongong** activities hotline (☎1800 240 737; www.tourismwollongong.com) and consider heading to nearby **Stanwell Park,** another hot spot for outdoor activities. For an afternoon indoors, the **Wollongong City Gallery,** on the corner of Kembla and Burelli St., creatively displays regional, Aboriginal, and contemporary art. (☎02 4228 7500. Open Tu-F 10am-5pm, Sa-Su and holidays noon-4pm. Free.)

## DAYTRIPS FROM WOLLONGONG

**NORTHERN SCENIC DRIVE.** The winding **Bulli Pass** track twists and turns inland to the **Southern Freeway,** 12km north of Wollongong, and leads to **Bulli Tops,** a magnificent panoramic view of the coastline and bordering beach towns. Stopping points along the way, like **Bulli Lookout,** offer fantastic views of the mountains, sea, sand, and white-capped waves. Down at sea level, Wollongong's biggest attractions await at **Bulli Point** (also known as **Sandon Point Headland**), **Thirroul Beach** to the south, and, farther north, **Austinmer Beach.** The daring flock to Bulli or Thirroul for some of the area's best surfing, whereas more family-oriented beachgoers head to Austinmer. For those without a car, **CityRail** runs from Wollongong to Thirroul ($3.40). For several months in 1922, English writer **D.H. Lawrence** lived in Thirroul and described the area in his novel *Kangaroo.* His home is privately owned and inaccessible to the public, but the beach is open for strolling. North of Bulli Pass, **Lawrence Hargrave Drive** winds along the coast, providing tantalizing glimpses of the shore below before reaching the lookout at **Bald Hill,** north of Stanwell Park, considered by many to be the best view on this stretch of coast. You can get a bird's-eye view of Stanwell Park in the air; both **HangglideOz** (☎04 1793 9200; www.hangglideoz.com.au) and **Sydney Hang Gliding Center** (☎02 4294 4294; www.hanggliding.com.au) have tandem hang gliding trips starting at $195. Inquire about 10% backpacker discounts.

# KIAMA ☎02

Lovely Kiama (KAI-amma) is well worth a stop for its craggy cliffs, turbulent surf, and friendly, small-town feel. Kiama, whose name appropriately means "sound of the sea," is a B&B-filled town known for its geyser-like **Blowhole.**

**TRANSPORTATION.** From the CityRail station, on Bong Bong St. off Blowhole Pt., **trains** (☎13 15 00) run to Bomaderry/Nowra (30min., 10-15 per day, $4.60), Sydney (2hr., 12-16 per day, $13.60), and Wollongong (45min., 13-17 per day, $5.60). From the **Bombo Railway Station,** Premier Motor Service (☎13 34 10, www.premierms.com.au) runs **buses** to: Batemans Bay (2-3hr., 2 per day, $41); Bermagui (5hr., 1 per day, $55); Melbourne (15hr., 1 per day, $83); Narooma (4-4hr., 2 per day, $54); Nowra (40min., 2 per day, $16); Sydney (2hr., 2 per day, $23); Ulladulla (2hr., 2 per day, $30); Wollongong (35min., 2 per day, $16).

**◼◼ ◼ ORIENTATION AND PRACTICAL INFORMATION.** A **visitors center** is on Blowhole Pt. (☎02 4232 3322; www.kiama.com.au. Open daily 9am-5pm.) The **Kiama Library,** 7 Railway Pde., has Internet for $5 per hr. (☎02 4233 1133. Open M and W-F 9:30am-5:30pm, Tu 9:30am-8pm, Sa 9:30am-2pm.) A **post office** is at 24 Terralong St. (☎13 13 18. Open M-F 9am-5pm.) **Postal Code:** 2533.

**◼◼ ◼ ACCOMMODATIONS AND FOOD.** Thanks to Kiama's popularity, particularly its reputation as an ideal spot for romantic getaways in upscale accommodations, it's difficult to find an affordable room in town. The small **Kiama Backpackers Hostel ❷,** 31 Bong Bong St., is next to the train station. (☎02 4233 1881. TV and kitchen. Internet access $4 per hr. Key deposit $10. Dorms $20; singles $25; doubles $49.) Next door, the **Grand Hotel ❷,** 49 Manning St., offers simple accommodation upstairs with a common TV room and shared bathrooms. (☎02 4232 1037; rooms $30.) **Saltwater ❶,** 104 Terralong St., is a good choice for takeaway or sit-down seafood. The classic fish and chips ($10) can be cooked however you specify—grilled, beer-battered, or tempura-battered—and then devoured at the outdoor tables overlooking the park. (☎02 4232 1104. Open daily from 11am to around 7pm). There are also a number of other eateries along Terralong St., from fancier cafes to Thai restaurants to pizza joints. If you make it down to the Little Blowhole, dine at the **Little Blowhole Cafe ❷,** 4 Tingira Cres., which offers a selection of breakfast, lunch, coffee, and cakes. (☎02 4232 4990. Open M and W-Su 8am-4pm.)

**◼◼ ◼ SIGHTS AND ACTIVITIES.** Under the right conditions, when the wind is high and the waves surge from the southeast, water washing into a sea cave is forced noisily upward through a hole in the rocks to heights of 20-35m. This phenomenon is **Kiama's Blowhole.** At Marsden Head, at the end of Tingira Cres., near the Endeavour Lookout, the **Little Blowhole** erupts when the ocean swell comes from the opposite direction. It's worth the extra trip if its big brother proves to be a disappointment, but only if you've got a car. For swimming, check out the natural rock pool on the north side of Blowhole Point or the deeper rock pool, north of Kiama Harbour at Pheasant Point. To the north of Pheasant Point, experienced surfers brave the riptides at Bombo Beach. Here, sightseers can discover the **Bombo Headlands**, where there are a number of sandstone cliffs and fascinating rocks formations, including the striking **Cathedral Rock,** just north of the headland. Less-experienced surfers and swimmers should head south to popular **Surf Beach,** where the waters are patrolled. For those who get tired of gazing idly out across the ocean, **Kiama Charter Service** (☎02 4237 8496), **Kiama Harbour Game and Reef Fishing Charter** (☎02 4232 1725), and **MV Signa** can send you out to the deep sea for some sportfishing. (☎04 2325 1603; www.mvsigna.com.au). Their fishing expeditions generally last 7-8hr. and cost around $100, including bait and gear. Lastly, if you're in Kiama and are a surfing fan (or just a beach-lover), you'd be wise to make the 10km trip south to South Australia's largest and most famous surf shop, **Natural Necessity Surf Shop,** opposite Town Hall at 115 Fern St. in neighboring Gerringong. (☎02 4234 1636. Open daily 9am-5pm.) From there, continue 4km to exquisite **Seven Mile Beach** in the small town of Geroa. A local **craft market** is hosted on the third Sunday of every month from 9am to 3pm at Black Beach (☎02 4237 6111).

# NOWRA AND BOMADERRY ☎02

Each sign along the Princes Hwy. directs you to Nowra, falsely implying that there's something to see there. Truth be told, Nowra is best used as a base for exploring more scenic areas like **Kangaroo Valley** (p. 231) and **Jervis Bay** (p. 232).

**NEW SOUTH WALES**

It shares a railway stop with its smaller neighbor-to-the-north, Bomaderry. To see some wildlife without traveling too far, the nearby **Nowra Wildlife Park** has wombats, koalas, and kangaroos. (☎02 4421 3949. Open daily 9am-5pm. $16, student $12, children $8.) Area climbers recommend **Thompson's Point,** on the southern shore of the Shoalhaven River and find PC, Grotto, and South Central to be challenging. Climbers must supply their own gear. **The Gym** (☎02 4421 0587), at the corner of McMahons and Illaroo Rd., takes climbers to locations in North Nowra. **Skydive Nowra** (☎04 1944 6904) offers tandem skydives ($410 with video) and freefall courses ($450 with video). Be sure to book ahead.

**▣▨ TRANSPORTATION AND PRACTICAL INFORMATION.** CityRail's (☎13 15 00) last stop is in Bomaderry (Nowra) on Railway St. **Trains** run to Kiama (30min., 12-15 per day, $4.60), Sydney (3hr., 12-15 per day, $18), and Wollongong (1-2hr., 9 per day, $8.60). Premier (☎13 34 10; www.premierms.com.au) **buses** run from Nowra (Stewart Place) to: Batemans Bay (1hr., 2 per day, $25); Bega (4hr., 2 per day, $45); Bermagui (4hr., 1 per day, $42); Kiama (40min., 2 per day, $16); Melbourne (13hr., 1 per day, $80); Narooma (2hr., 2 per day, $39); Sydney (3-3½hr., 2 per day, $23); Ulladulla (1hr., 2 per day, $18); Wollongong (1hr., 2 per day, $16). Kennedy's Coaches (☎02 4421 7596 or 04 1123 2101) services Fitzroy Falls (1hr., 1 per day, $13.60) and Kangaroo Valley (30min., 1 per day, $4.80). The **Shoalhaven Visitors Centre** lies on the corner of Princes Hwy. and Pleasant Way, south of the bridge to Nowra. (☎02 4421 0778 or 1300 662 808; www.shoalhaven.nsw.gov.au. Open daily 9am-5pm.) The **National Parks and Wildlife Service,** 55 Graham St., Nowra, has park info. (☎02 4423 2170. Open M-F 8:30am-5:30pm.) The **Shoalhaven City Library,** at 10 Berry St., has Internet access. (☎02 4429 3705. $1.25 per hr.) The **police station** (☎02 4421 9699) is on the corner of Plunkett and Kinghorne St. The **post office** is at 59 Junction St. (☎13 13 18. Open M-F 9am-5pm.) **Postal Code:** 2541.

**▛ ACCOMMODATIONS.** The cozy, bungalow-style **M&M's Guesthouse ❸,** 1A Scenic Dr., on the right off Bridge Rd. just across the bridge into Nowra, has a backpackers' building and motel. (☎02 4421 2044; www.mmguesthouse. com. Laundry, TV, fireplace, and kitchen. Dorms $30; motel rooms $70-85.) For camping sites next to a wildlife park, head for **Shoalhaven Ski Park ❶.** From Bomaderry, take a right on Illaroo Rd., just before the bridge to Nowra; follow McMahon's Rd. left from the roundabout, and take a left at the first stop sign onto Rock Hill Rd. Toilets and hot showers. Sites $13, powered $17.)

# KANGAROO VALLEY
☎02

More than just a place to spot kangaroos, tiny Kangaroo Valley (pop. 500) is a good launching point for canoe trips down the Kangaroo and Shoalhaven Rivers. It has the pleasant feel of a rural area, which makes it popular for camping retreats, and its main street, Moss Vale Rd., is dotted with arts-and-crafts shops, restaurants, and cafes. At the northwest end of town, the Hampden Bridge spans the Kangaroo River. Built in 1898, it's Australia's oldest suspension bridge. With two locations on the north side of the bridge, **Kangaroo Valley Safaris,** 2210 Moss Vale Rd., organizes beginner to intermediate canoe camping trips to Kangaroo and Shoalhaven, including a 25km overnight canoe trip. A shuttle picks boaters up from the rail station. (☎02 4465 1502; www.kangaroovalleycanoes.com.au. Open daily 8:30am-5pm. Canoes and kayaks $30 per day, overnight sea kayaks $80, tents $40 per day. Bookings required.) **Fitzroy Falls** greets visitors at the northern entrance of **Morton National Park,** 20km from Kangaroo Valley on Moss Vale Rd. The **Bendeela Campground ❶,** 7km outside town, provides free camping with toilets, BBQ, and water. Reach it by driving north of town and turning left on Bendeela Rd., following signs to the entrance. The **Fitzroy Falls Visitors Centre**, run by the NPWS, has bushwalking trail maps. (☎02 4887 7270. Open daily 9am-5:30pm.) If you're driving, avoid the steep, winding Kangaroo Valley Rd. leading west from Berry and opt for Moss Vale Rd., which leads northwest from Bombaderry, off the Princes Hwy. Caution should still be used on the narrow, winding Moss Vale Rd. though; check road conditions ahead of time for both routes. Tourist info is available at **Newsagents,** next to the post office. (☎02 4465 1150; www.kangaroovalley.net. Open daily 10am-6pm.)

## HUSKISSON                                                            ☎02

Twenty-four kilometers southeast of Nowra along the coast of Jervis Bay lies the tiny town of Huskisson (pop. 1600). "Husky" is only slightly off the beaten track and is the perfect place to stop for fish and chips overlooking the bay or to start one of the cycling/walking trails up and down the coastline. The **Husky Pub ❺,** 73 Owen St., entertains a surprisingly mixed crowd. Families, backpackers, and pensioners all come to chow down and play pool in the bistro and pub below the rooms. Although they only offer basic pub-style accommodations, with ensuite sinks and fridges and shared bathrooms down the hall, the fun atmosphere and incredibly friendly staff make these plain rooms feel almost homey. (☎02 4441 5001; www.thehuskypub.com.au. Singles $50; doubles $70). The downstairs **bistro ❷** serves up fish, burgers, and fries ($11-15), all of which can be enjoyed on the terrace out back. Come evening, the pub turns into a Jervis Bay latenight hot spot. There are a few other cafes along Owen St. **Kiosk ❶,** 66 Owen St., offers dinner meals ($9-25), breakfast, and light lunches (☎02 4441 5464), and the Husky Bakery Cafe at 11 Currambene St. provides all sorts of sweeter snacks (☎02 4441 5015). Heading south from Huskisson, on the way to **Booderee National Park** (an area that can only be accessed by car) through Vincentia, many beautiful beaches lie hidden down side streets just off the main road. Almost any street will lead to a scenic bit of coast. Especially beautiful are **Greenfields Beach** and **Hyams Beach,** said to have the world's whitest sand. For tourist info, visit the antique-filled **Huskisson Trading Post** on the corner of Tomerong and Dent St. (☎02 4441 5241. Open daily 9am-5pm.)

## JERVIS BAY                                                           ☎02

The jewel of the South Coast, ◪**Jervis Bay** is a serene body of water surrounded by striking white beaches and magnificent national parks. Full of marine life and underwater rock formations, the bay offers some of the best diving in Australia outside of the Great Barrier Reef. Divers rave about the massive archways and rock shelves (**Cathedral Cave** and **Smuggler's Cave** are popular for cave diving), bushwalkers hunt for hidden creeks and waterfalls, fishermen boast about their catches, and animal lovers marvel at dolphins, penguins, and a large variety of colorful birds. Back in the water, the **Arch, Stoney Creek Reef,** and the **Ten Fathom Dropoff** are known for deep diving. **Steamers Beach Seal Colony** is great for dives and snorkeling. Visibility is best from April to early August.

Organize your day of diving or wildlife-watching at a number of shops in Huskisson. **Deep 6 Diving,** 64 Owen St., offers a variety of dives for certified divers as well as a four-day PADI course. Call to inquire about pricing. (☎02 4441 5255; www.deep6divingjervisbay.com.au.) **Jervis Bay Sea Sports,** 47 Owen St. (☎02 4441 6665; www.jbseasports.com.au), offers slightly more expensive services. For those who want a drier vantage point, **Dolphin Watch Cruises,** 50 Owen St. (☎02 4441 6311 or 1800 246 010; www.dolphinwatch.com.au), and **Dolphin Explorer Cruises,** 62 Owen St. (☎02 4441 5455 or 1800 444 330; www.dolphincruises.com.au), offer 2-2½hr. dolphin cruises with views of the cliffs daily at 10am, 12:30 and 1pm ($24-31, concessions $20-25, children $14-15, family

$68-88). Call to inquire about each company's specific times and rates. Most of them also offer 3-3½hr. whale watching trips during peak whale migrations. (Daily June-Nov. 9 and 9:30am. $60-62, concession $47, children $27-28, family $150-160.) **Jervis Bay Kayak Company,** Shop ½ at 13 Hawke St., leads guided kayak tours from 7:45am-1:15pm. Cost includes equipment and snack (☎02 4441 7157; www.jervisbaykayaks.com. $96 per person, $66 with own equipment.) Kayaks are also available for rent (2 hr. $36-46, 1 day $66-90).

# ULLADULLA                                                    ☎02

Moving south through the Shoalhaven, the next major town is Ulladulla (uh-luh-DUH-luh; pop. 17,000). Outdoorsy and beautiful, this town has plenty of diving, surfing, and fishing opportunities. Off the coast between Jervis Bay and Ulladulla Harbour lie shipwrecks that divers frequently explore, including the famous 1870 wreck of the *Walter Hood*. Still, the most beautiful draw is the **Pigeon House Walk,** a 5km hike with steep climbing and knock-out views at the top. (Allow 3-4hr. Turn off the Princes Hwy. onto Wheelbarrow Rd. 3km south of Burrill Lake. The trailhead is 27km farther on an unsealed road at a picnic area.) **One Track for All** is a gentle 2km trail dotted with hand-carved stumps, statues, and logs depicting Aboriginal and post-settlement history. The trail, which winds about the North Head cliffs near Ulladulla Harbour, affords several staggering ocean views. (Turn off Princes Hwy. onto North St., across from the police station. Take a left onto Burrill St., then a right onto Dolphin St.; the trailhead is at the end and is wheelchair-accessible.) The **Ulladulla Dive and Adventure Centre,** 211 Princes Hwy., at the southern end of Ulladulla near Dolphin Point, offers diving, snorkeling, canoe, and kayak lessons. PADI courses are also available. (☎02 4455 3029; www.ulladulladive.com.au. Open M-Tu and Th-Sa 8:30am-5:30pm, Su 8:30am-5pm.) Nearby Lakes Burrill and Conjola have nice swimming beaches, and Mollymook Beach, just north of town, is especially good for surfing and dolphin-spotting.

Cheap motels line the Princes Hwy. The local guest house, **Travellers Rest Guest House ❷,** 63 Princes Hwy., between Narrawallee and North St., is a small, impeccably tidy operation with beautiful hardwood floors, brightly colored walls, and a great sundeck and hammock area. (☎02 4454 0500. Dorms $20-25; doubles $45-55.) At the end of South St., **Holiday Haven Tourist Park ❷** has camping space with some amenities, but be aware that the site slopes slightly. (☎02 4455 2457 or 1300 733 021. Showers, toilets, laundry, BBQ, minigolf, and pool. Sites $22, powered $30; cabins M-F $55-110, Sa-Su $70-135.)

Premier (☎13 34 10; www.premierms.com.au) **buses** stop at both the Marlin Hotel (southbound) and the Traveland Travel Agency (northbound) en route to: Batemans Bay (45min., 2 per day, $14); Bermagui (3hr., 1 per day, $30); Kiama (2hr., 2 per day, $30); Melbourne (13hr., 1 per day, $80); Narooma (1hr., 2 per day, $24); Nowra (1hr., 2 per day, $18); Sydney (5hr., 2 per day, $33); Wollongong (3hr., 2 per day, $33). The **Visitors Centre** is located on the Princes Hwy. (☎1300 662 808. Open M-F 10am-5pm, Sa-Su 9am-5pm.) Internet access is available at the adjacent **library;** however, there are only 3 computers, so booking is advised. (☎02 4455 1269. $1.25 per 30min. Open M-F 10am-5:30pm, Sa 9am-2pm.) The **police station** (☎02 4454 2542) is on the corner of Princes Hwy. and North St. at 73 Princes Hwy. The **post office** is at the corner of Princes Hwy. and Green St. (Open M-F 9am-5pm.) **Postal Code:** 2539.

# MURRAMARANG NATIONAL PARK

With expansive views of the Pacific, the coastline of the Murramarang National Park makes a great detour. It is also a superb spot to check out the surprisingly tame kangaroos and parrots that play on the grass at ◪**Pebbly Beach.** A number of campgrounds and caravan parks are speckled throughout the park, but **tent camping ❶** sites are cheapest at the **Pebbly Beach camping area** (Pebbly Beach Rd.), which boasts even more kangaroos than the beach does. (☎02 4478 6023. Sites $10 per person plus $7 per vehicle; cabin from $85.) At the southernmost point in the Shoalhaven half of Murramarang National Park, **Durras North** looks onto Durras Lake and a windswept ocean beach. Pick up a brochure on self-guided bushwalks from the tourist office in Batemans Bay. The **Murramarang Beach Resort ❷,** on Durras Rd. off the Princes Hwy., has "Ocean Front Luxury" cabin suites, a camping area, and extra facilities such as a swimming pool and reception kiosk with newspapers and basic groceries. (☎02 4478 6355 or 1300 767 255; www.murramarangresort.com.au. Sites $15-49, powered $23-65; ensuite $49-86; 4- to 6-person garden villas from $92; cabin suites from $272.)

# BATEMANS BAY                                                ☎02

South of the junction at the mouth of Clyde River, Batemans Bay—and its picturesque harbor—begins where the Kings Hwy. from Canberra meets the Princes Hwy. at the coast. One of Australia's largest colonies of gray nurse sharks circles the islands, making Batemans Bay a popular dive spot. If you're not impressed by fish, zombie-eyed or otherwise, join backpackers and celebrities in gawking at the 'roos and parrots at Murramarang National Park.

**🔲🔽 TRANSPORTATION AND PRACTICAL INFORMATION. Buses** leave from outside the Promenade Plaza on Orient St. Premier Motor Service (☎13 34 10; www.premierms.com.au) goes to: Bega (3hr., 2 per day, $26); Bermagui (2hr., 1 per day, $22); Kiama (3hr., 2 per day, $41); Melbourne (12hr., 1 per day, $71); Narooma (1hr., 2 per day, $18); Nowra (2hr., 2 per day, $25); Sydney (5hr., 2 per day, $43); Ulladulla (45min., 2 per day, $14); Wollongong (3hr., 2 per day, $41). Murrays (☎13 22 51; www.murrays.com.au) offers a 10% YHA discount; they go to Canberra (2hr., 1-2 per day, $24). The staff at **Batemans Bay Tourist Information Centre,** on Princes Hwy. at Beach Rd., will book your accommodation in town for free and give you brochures and suggestions. (☎02 4472 6900 or 1800 802 528. Open daily 9am-5pm.) Access the Internet at **Total Computer Care,** Shop 10 in Citi Centre Arcade, for $4 per hr. (☎02 4472 2745. Open M-F 9am-5pm.) The **police station** is at 28 Orient St. (☎02 4472 0099). The **post office** is at 7 Orient St., next to the bus stop. (☎13 13 18. Open M-F 9am-5pm.) **Postal Code:** 2536.

**🏠🍴 ACCOMMODATIONS AND FOOD.** Plenty of motels sit on Orient St. and Beach Rd.; rooms usually start at $60-70 in winter. The **Batemans Bay Backpackers (YHA) ❷,** inside a caravan park on the corner of Old Princes Hwy. and South St., offers tidy facilities as well as trips to Pebbly Beach and Mogo ($5-30) when there's enough guest interest. (☎02 4472 4972; www.shadywillows.com. au. Laundry, kitchen, TV, pool, and boogie boards. Call to arrange pickup from the bus stop in town. Dorms $22-27; doubles $48-55. YHA discount.) The **Clyde River Motor Inn ❺,** 3 Clyde St., offers basic rooms in the heart of the town with amenities such as A/C, TV, and pool. (☎02 4472 6444; www.clydemotel.com.au. Singles from $81; doubles from $85; family rooms from $125.) Fish and chips seems to be the town's favorite meal; try **The Boat Shed ❶,** opposite the Clyde River Motor Inn on Clyde St., where basic fish and chips runs $11. (☎02 4472 4052. Open M-Th and Su 9am-7pm, F-Sa 9am-8pm.)

**🔷🔶 SIGHTS AND ACTIVITIES.** The 1880 wreck of the **Lady Darling** is a fantastic dive suitable for all skill levels. Other dives include the Burrawarra Wall, the Maze, and, for scoping out the nurse sharks, Montague Island. **The Dive Shop,**

33 Orient St., can be your link to the water world; they offer beginner and advanced diving at a variety of sites as well as special interest courses with trained professionals (☎02 4472 9930). The compact **Opal and Shell Museum,** 142 Beach Rd., owned and operated by a veteran miner, showcases an extensive display of opals and shells from Australia and around the world; for those interested in buying a souvenir opal, prices are much more affordable here than in larger cities. (☎02 4472 7248. Open daily 10am-6pm. $1.50, families $3.) To bushwalk, join the locals from **Batemans Bay Bushwalkers** ($5 for non-members). Visit www.bushwalking.org.au/~batemansbay to request a schedule by email. Traveling south on the coastal road, **Malua Bay** and **Broulee** have good surf. **Broulee Surf School,** 77 Coronation Dr., offers private and group lessons. (☎02 4471 7370; www.brouleesurfschool.com.au. Lessons $40-175.)

# NAROOMA AND MONTAGUE ISLAND ☎02

With several parks and one stunning island nearby, the town of Narooma is a good base for outdoor exploration. Only 7km offshore, fur seals, crested terns, and fairy penguins inhabit the **Montague Island Nature Reserve.** The island was inhabited by indigenous people for over 4500 years. In 1770, Captain Cook was the first European to sight the island, but he mistakenly thought it was a point on the headland and named it Point Dromedary. It wasn't recognized as an island until 1790, when the passing convict ship *Surprise* named it after the ship's sponsor, George Montagu Dunk, Earl of Halifax (the "e" was added later). Settlers introduced goats and rabbits to Montague to feed shipwreck victims; horses and cows continued the destruction of the island's original habitat. Today, the parks service is working hard to preserve the island's amazing range of wildlife by restoring the natural habitat and managing the kykuyu grass that has choked much of the original vegetation, making it difficult for fairy penguins and other birds to nest.

The reserve is only accessible through NPWS-sanctioned tours; a percentage of the fee for the tour goes to the island's preservation. Be sure to ask about the Marx Brothers-esque story of the lighthouse's construction. In spring, watch for whales on the ferry to the island. (3-4hr.; 1-2 per day; $125-130, ages 2-15 $99, families $420-430. Max. 90 visitors per day; tours must have 8 to depart. Book through the visitors center.) The popular **Eurobodalla National Park** (☎02 4476 2888) protects a 30km stretch of coastline, from Moruya Head in the north to Tilba Tilba Lake in the south, and features lush spotted gum forest. The park has a free **campground ❶** at Congo, near the town of Moruya ($10 per person), and another at Brou Lake north of Narooma. (No drinking water. No fees.) On Wagonga Head, off Bar Rock Rd., ocean waves, coastal winds, and a bit of chiseling have left one rock, known as **Australia Rock,** with a hole the shape of Australia (minus a bit of the Cape York peninsula). Depending on the winds, surfers head to **Bar, Carters, Dalmeny,** or **Handkerchief Beach.**

**Lynch's Hotel ❹,** 135 Wagonga St. (Princes Hwy.), offers cozy pub accommodations upstairs with expansive views of the bay from the wooden balconies. Good pub grub is also available downstairs. (☎02 4476 2001. Kitchen, TV, lounge, tea, and coffee. Singles $50; doubles $70-75; triples $80-90.) **Narooma Golf Club and Surfbeach Resort ❷,** on Ballingala St., has fine views of the water and good facilities. (☎02 4476 2522. Sites for 2 $26-35, powered $30-46; cabins from $50-300. Rates vary depending on season.)

Premier Motor Service (☎13 34 10; www.premierms.com.au) **buses** goes from Narooma to: Batemans Bay (13-14hr., 2 per day, $18); Kiama (5hr., 2 per day, $54); Melbourne (11hr., 1 per day, $65); Nowra (3hr., 2 per day, $39); Sydney (7hr., 2 per day, $56); Ulladulla (2hr., 2 per day, $24); Wollongong (5hr., 2 per day, $54). Murrays buses (☎13 22 51; www.murrays.com.au) runs from

Narooma Plaza to Canberra (4hr., 1-2 per day, $36.25). The **Narooma Visitors Centre**, on Princes Hwy., books tours and accommodations, and houses a museum about the history of Montague Island. (☎02 4476 2881 or 1800 240 003. Open daily 9am-5pm.) The **NPWS office** is on the corner of Princes Hwy. and Field St. (☎02 4476 2888. Open M-F 8:30am-4:30pm.) The **post office** is just off Princes Hwy. at 106 Wagonga St. (☎13 13 18. Open M-F 9am-5pm.) **Postal Code:** 2546.

# SNOWY MOUNTAINS

While skiers and snowboarders make the Snowies their winter playground, the warmer months attract swarms of hikers to the nation's highest mountains. Kosciuszko National Park, home of magnificent Mt. Kosciuszko (2228m), Australia's tallest peak, covers most of this area. The Snowy Mountains Hwy. and the Alpine Way ramble past boulder-strewn countryside where the skiing industry is king, though compared to other mountain ranges around the world, the runs are shorter and less challenging. Conditions vary wildly by mountain: Thredbo is a black diamond paradise with challenging advanced slopes; Perisher, despite its ominous-sounding name, is the largest and most popular park; Charlotte's Pass is an elite luxury resort with the highest altitudes and most natural snow; and Mount Selwyn offers great deals and family-friendly slopes. Thredbo is the only area open in the summer, and it provides an adventurous wonderland for hikers and mountain bikers. Naturally, the price of accommodations in the Snowy Mountains jumps astronomically in the winter, so be sure to check rates before deciding where to stay.

## COOMA                                                                    ☎02

The self-proclaimed "Capital of the Snowy Mountains" links Canberra and the coast with the mountains. Because of its location on the eastern edge of the Snowy Mountains, Cooma is far enough from the price-inflated snowfields to permit reasonable ski-season rates for those willing to make the commute. Cooma is also a base for traveling to Mt. Selwyn and Perisher or Thredbo. The area is a regional center and stays busy all year round, snow or not.

### ▐ TRANSPORTATION

In summer, it's no longer possible to get to Thredbo by public transportation. School buses run through the area on school days, but they are not reliable and often do not go all the way to Thredbo. You can either rent a car, take a taxi ($120), or hitch—*Let's Go* never recommends hitching. If the ski season is bad, companies will start to dropoff services before the official end of winter cutoff, so be sure to check before making final plans.

**Buses:** Many buses come through frequently during ski season, but service is severely curtailed the rest of the year. **Countrylink** (☎13 22 32) runs to **Sydney** ($45 total from Cooma) via **Canberra** (1-2hr., 1-2 per day, $35). Transborder Alpinexpress (☎02 6241 0033; www.transborder.com.au) offers year-round service from Centennial Park next to the visitors center on Bombala St. to **Canberra** (1hr., 1 per day, $37), **Jindabyne** (50min., 1 per day, $20), and **Thredbo** (1hr., 1 per day, $35). Reserve tickets in advance, or purchase on the bus. Greyhound Australia (☎13 20 30) Ski Express buses run to: **Canberra** (1-1hr., 1-2 per day, $38); **Sydney** (6hr., 1-2 per day, $66); **Jindabyne** (55min., 1-2 per day, $22); **Thredbo** (1hr., 1-2 per day, $51) from June to Oct. Murray's (☎13 22 51) services the mountains once daily during ski season ($25). **Alpine Char-**

ters (☎02 6456 7340 or 04 1440 0378) whisks people to the mountains when public transport is hard to find. ($60-80 depending on the number of passengers.)

**Car Rental: Thrifty,** 60 Sharp St. (☎02 6452 5300 or 1800 552 008; www.thrifty.com. au). The only rental car option in town; book far ahead.

## 🛂 PRACTICAL INFORMATION

Cooma's main drag is **Sharp Street,** flanked on either side by Massie and Commissioner St. **Cooma Visitors Centre,** 119 Sharp St., is in the center of town. (☎02 6450 1742; www.visitcooma.com.au. Open daily from mid-Oct. to May 9am-5pm, from June to mid-Oct. 7am-5pm.) The visitors centre provides **Internet** access ($1 per 10min.) and will book accommodations, though some hotel owners charge extra if you use this service. The **police station** is on Massie St., just up the street from the **post office,** on the corner of Massie and Vale St. across from Dawson St. (☎02 6452 0099. Open M-F 9am-5pm.) **Postal Code:** 2630.

## 🏠🍴 ACCOMMODATIONS AND FOOD

Get groceries at **Woolworths,** at Vale and Massie St. (Open daily 7am-10pm.)

**Cooma Bunkhouse Motel,** 28-30 Soho St. (☎02 6452 2983; www.bunkhousemotel. com.au), on the corner of Commissioner St. Great year-round hostel accommodations. Every colorful room at this former maternity ward is equipped with a bathroom, kitchen, and TV. Breakfast $12. Reception 24hr. Heated 4-bed dorms $30-35; singles without kitchen $35-45; doubles $50-55; family units from $65. VIP discount. MC/V. ❸

**Nebula Motel,** 42 Bombala St. (☎02 6452 4133). A pricier option with Austar TV, free Wi-Fi, tea and coffee, and large, clean rooms. Singles $80; doubles $110. ❺

**Snowtels Caravan Park** (☎02 6452 1828; www.snowtels.com.au), on Sharp St., 1.1km west of the town center. Kitchen, laundry, and tennis. Reception 8am-8:30pm. Sites for 2 $19, powered $23; basic cabins from $42; ensuite cabins for 5 $72-102. MC/V. ❶

**The Lott,** 178-180 Sharp St. (☎02 6452 1414). A trendy cafe with country touches, including antique skis on the wall. The scrumptious muffins ($3), carrot cake ($3), and tarts ($8) are a good deal; the capsicum and goat cheese tart is fantastic. Open M-W 7:30am-4pm, Th-F 7:30am-5:30pm, Sa-Su 8am-4pm. MC/V. ❶

**Rose's,** 69 Massie St. (☎02 6452 4512). An exotic option with juicy, authentic Lebanese kebabs ($8). The full banquet ($25) is a splurge, but it offers a taste of all things Middle Eastern, and for those arriving famished from the slopes, it's a big meal well earned. Dine-in or takeaway. Open M-Sa 11:30am-2:30pm and 6-10pm. AmEx/MC/V. ❷

## ⛷ SKIING

Because the ski resorts of Thredbo, Perisher, and Mt. Selwyn lie within 100km of Cooma, rental shops clutter the town's street, with flashing signs advertising "around-the-clock" rentals with cheaper rates than you'll find closer to the mountains. Skis, poles, and boot rentals run about $40 the first day and $10-15 per day thereafter; snowboard and boot rental cost about $45 for the first day and $10-30 for every day after; clothing rental $27; snowchains $20. The visitors center (p. 237) has brochures with 10% discount coupons.

# JINDABYNE ☎02

On the scenic shores of Lake Jindabyne, "Jindy" acts as a satellite ski town in-season, with corresponding services and high prices. After the ski season, prices and visitor numbers drop significantly while the town hibernates, and bushwalkers stop through while exploring vast Kosciuszko National Park.

**TRANSPORTATION.** During the ski season, Jindabyne Motors Alpine Express (☎02 6456 7340 or 0414 400 378) runs **shuttles** daily to the Skitube by reservation ($15 round-trip) and to Thredbo ($35 round-trip). From there, catch a **train** to Perisher Blue (round-trip $41, families $98). Transport into Jindabyne from the northeast goes through **Cooma** (p. 236). Transborder Alpinexpress (☎02 6241 0033; www.transborder.com.au) offers daily year-round service from Canberra to Jindabyne ($45). Greyhound Australia (☎13 20 30) offers limited **bus** service in the winter and summer, as does Countrylink (☎13 22 32). Snow and ski packages are a popular option. **Oz Snow Adventures** (☎1800 851 101; www.ozsnowadventures.com.au) runs trips from Sydney and Canberra from $225, including accommodation, transportation, meals, and park fees.

To get to Perisher by **car,** follow Kosciuszko Rd. (2WD vehicles must carry snowchains by law). Alternatively, follow the Alpine Way to the Skitube station at Bullocks Flat (21km from town), which serves the Perisher Blue resorts. The Alpine Way then continues 15km farther on to Thredbo (chains might be required in extreme weather). From Thredbo, the Alpine Way extends through the mountains to Khancoban, on the western edge of Kosciuszko National Park. The Shell station at the Perisher-Thredbo junction, outside Jindabyne, rents snow chains for $30 per day and has a dropoff program with the Khancoban roadhouse. Other service stations offer similar programs.

**PRACTICAL INFORMATION.** The **Snowy Region Visitors Centre,** on Kosciuszko Rd. in the center of town, is also a parks office. They have information on and sell entry passes for the national park. (☎02 6450 5600, road conditions 02 6450 5551, snow reports 02 6450 5553, weather 02 6450 5550. Open daily 8:30am-4:30pm.) **ATMs** are in the Nuggets Crossing Shopping Centre. The **police station** (☎02 6456 2244) is on Thredbo Terr. **Snowy Mountain Backpackers** (see below) has **Internet.** ($3 per 20min.) The **post office** (☎02 6456 2394) is on the corner of Gippsland St. and Snow River Ave. (Open in winter M-F and Su 8:30am-5pm, Sa 7am-5pm; in summer daily 8:30am-5pm.) **Postal Code:** 2627.

**Job opportunities** are everywhere in Jindabyne (mainly hospitality and ski-related work); many of the skiers and snowboarders who love Thredbo and Perisher find work in Jindabyne through postings and word of mouth. Two great places to look for postings are on the bulletin board of Snowy Mountain Backpackers (see below) and at the Snowy Region Visitors Centre.

**ACCOMMODATIONS.** Affordable accommodations in Jindabyne exist even in the height of ski madness, but availability may be a problem. Be sure to book well in advance. **Snowy Mountain Backpackers ❸,** 7-8 Gippsland St., behind the Nuggets Crossing Shopping Centre, combines an unbeatable location with new facilities, laundry, Internet access, TV room, and a kitchen. Cafe SuSu and a massage center are also on the premises. (☎02 6456 1500 or 1800 333 468; www.snowybackpackers.com.au. Laundry $3. Wheelchair-accessible. Reception June-Oct. 8am-8pm; Nov.-May M-Sa 9am-1pm, F-Sa 4-7pm, Su 11am-3pm. Dorms $30-42, weekend $35-44; doubles $90-120/90-130. VIP discount. MC/V.) The **Jindy Inn ❹,** 18 Clyde St., has private ensuite rooms with TV and fridge. There's a kitchen downstairs and an adjoining restaurant (winter only). During ski season, the inn functions more like a B&B. Bookings are required, and single-night stays are rare, especially on weekends. (☎02 6456 1957; www.jindyinn.com. Breakfast included in winter. Discounts for 3-day stays or longer. Twin-shares $59-95 depending on the season.) **Jindabyne Holiday Park ❶** is in the center of town on a choice stretch of Lake Jindabyne shoreline. (☎02 6456 2249; www.jindyhp.com.au. Laundry, kitchen, ski and snowboard rentals. Sites for 2 $22-25; powered June-July $35-40, Aug.-May $27-33. Extra person $10. On-site caravans June-July $100-105, Aug.-May $45-70. MC/V.)

**◘ FOOD.** Cheap food is generally hard to come by in Jindabyne. Preparing a flavorful range of traditional grub and some multicultural dishes, **Cafe SuSu ❷**, 8 Gippsland St., is part of the Snowy Mountain Backpackers and has decent prices (most meals $8-13) as well as a relaxed, funky interior. (☎02 6456 1503. Open M-Sa 8:30am-9pm, Su 8am-noon.) **Wrap-A-Go-Go ❷**, in Lakeview Plaza behind the Westpac at 2 Snowy River Ave., features spicy Mexican meals as well as its tasty titular wraps. (☎02 6457 1887. Main dishes around $12-15. Open daily noon-2pm and 6-9pm; closed M in summer.) **Mountain Munchies ❶**, 10a in Nuggets Crossing, serves up cheap comfort food, with all-day breakfast options averaging $5-15 and sandwiches that start from around $4. (☎02 6457 2255. Open daily 6am-4pm. Cash only.) A **Woolworths** supermarket is also in Nuggets Crossing. (Open daily 7am-8pm.)

**▨ ACTIVITIES.** The experts at **Wilderness Sports**, 4 Nuggets Crossing, rent a variety of outdoors equipment—including snowshoes, telemark and cross-country skis, and snowcamping gear—and organize cross-country skiing, snowboarding, snowshoe, and alpine touring adventures from $99 for 3hr. (☎02 6456 2966; www.wildernesssports.com.au. Open M-Th and Sa-Su 8am-6pm, F 8am-late. Prices generally depend upon group size.) Their **Snowsport Adventure Centre** in Perisher Valley also offers myriad rentals, as well as activity courses like snowcamping and rock climbing. (☎02 6457 5966. Open daily 9am-4pm. Snowshoe rental $25-35 per day; full-day abseiling $169; full-day Mt. Kosciuszko tour $149, includes lunch for min. 4 people.) **Rebel Sport** offers package deals with skis, boots, parka, and pants from $68 per day and a snowboarding package for $70. (☎02 6457 2166. www.rebelsport.com.au. Open M-F and Su 7am-5pm, Sa 7am-1pm.) **Mountain Adventure Centre,** next to the Shell station at the Perisher-Thredbo junction, offers similar services as well as mountaineering courses and mountain bike rentals. (☎02 6456 2922 or 1800 623 459; www. mountainadventurecentre.com.au. Open daily in summer 9am-5pm, in winter M-Th 8am-6pm, F 7:30am-noon, Sa-Su 7:30am-7pm. Full-day intro to mountaineering course July-Aug. $159; full-day Mt. Kosciuszko champagne ride $99. Min. 4-person. for bookings. Mountain bike and helmet $16 per hr., $36 ½-day, $50 full day.) **Rapid Descents Whitewater Rafting,** based in Canberra, runs rafting on the Murray River, but only in spring and summer. (☎02 6228 1264; www.rapid-descents.com.au. Make sure to book well ahead.)

**▨ NIGHTLIFE.** Nightlife roars in Jindy throughout most of the snow season, fueled mainly by those who work on the mountains. As Wednesday is payday at all ski-related spots in the area, people go out that night with the same intensity as on the weekend. Crowds of locals swarm to the **Banjo Paterson Inn,** 1 Kosciuszko Rd. (☎02 6458 2372; banjopatersoninn.com), which houses three full bars and casino tables, and features DJs many nights. The place reaches capacity quickly, so go early. (Bars open daily 10am-late. Nightclub W and F-Sa until 2am. No cover.) **Lake Jindabyne Hotel,** on Kosciuszko Rd. across from Nuggets Crossing, offers a quieter scene, betting, and a handful of pool tables. (☎02 6456 2203. Open M-Sa 11am-late, Su 11am-midnight.) The **Station Resort** throws the biggest parties and pulls in the biggest DJs throughout the season. You won't be able to miss the brochures and posters around town.

# KOSCIUSZKO NATIONAL PARK

Named after the revered Polish nationalist, Tadiusz Kosciuszko (incorrectly pronounced by many Australians as KOZ-ee-OSS-koh; should you happen to run into any Polish people on the mountain, use the correct pronunciation of Khaj-EESH-koh), Kosciuszko National Park contains Australia's highest mountains, the alluring Yarrangobilly Caves, several wilderness hikes, and NSW's premier ski fields. The park has a number of camping options, but visitors planning on spending some time in Kosciuszko's wilds would do well to bring their own food and water in with them.

### KOSCIUSZKO NATIONAL PARK AT A GLANCE

**AREA:** 6494 sq. km, about 700,000 hectares—the largest park in NSW.

**HEIGHTS:** Mount Kosciuszko: 2228m, Australia's highest peak.

**FEATURES:** Australia's tallest mountain, for which the park is named; the Snowy River; Yarrongobilly Caves; almost two dozen scenic camping sites.

**HIGHLIGHTS:** Skiing some of Australia's best slopes; camping and hiking during the warmer months.

**GATEWAYS:** Cooma and Jindabyne in the east, Khancoban in the west.

**CAMPING:** Free, except for one site just west of Lake Jindabyne that is privately owned and charges fees.

**FEES:** $27 per day vehicle fee during ski season, $16 in summer. Year-long pass $190. Motorists passing through non-stop on Alpine Way are exempt. Fees are strictly enforced by rangers.

**SKI SEASON:** June to mid-October.

**PRACTICAL INFORMATION.** The main tourist bureau is located in the **Cooma Visitors Centre,** 119 Sharp St. (☎02 6450 1742; open daily from mid-Oct. to May 9am-5pm, from June to mid-Oct. 7am-5pm). Other places to obtain information include the **Snowy Region Visitors Centre** on Kosciuszko Rd. in Jindabyne (☎02 6450 5600; open daily 8:30am-5pm), the **Tumut** (TOO-mit) **Visitors Centre** in the Old Butter Factory on Adelong Rd. (☎02 6947 7025; open daily 9am-5pm.), and the **Khancoban Information Centre,** perched at the corner of Scott and Mitchell St. at the west entrance of the Kosciuszko. (☎02 6076 9373. Open daily 9am-noon and 1-4pm.) For **weather information,** call ☎02 6450 5550, **road conditions** 02 6450 5551, and **snow report** 02 6450 5553.

**PARK FEES.** Visitors entering with their own vehicles are required to pay an entry fee ($27, in summer $16) valid for 24hr. upon purchase. Motorists who pass through the park without stopping along Alpine Way are exempt. If you enter the park after the ticketing stations have closed, you must purchase your pass in the morning at the nearest news agency. In summer, the northern section of the park is exempted from all fees. Fees are strictly enforced by park rangers who check automobiles daily. During ski season, 2WD vehicles must carry snow chains. The Snowline Caravan Park Shell station at the Jindabyne exit to Thredbo allows one-way chain rental and dropoff at the Khancoban roadhouse ($25; $50 deposit). Cars without snow chains will receive immediate fines starting at $135. Because many drivers with 4WD cars don't know how to use them properly in snow, it is advisable for all vehicles to carry chains; the parks service is currently considering making chains mandatory for 4WD.

**ACCOMMODATIONS.** Numerous camping areas are available throughout the park, and a system of over 80 regularly maintained huts are connected

## Kosciuszko NP

- - - - Unsealed Roads

▲ CAMP SITES

Braemar Bay, **6**
Buckenderra, **7**
Geehi, **11**
Half-way Flat, **18**
Island Bend, **9**
Jacob's River, **17**
Jindabyne, **14**
Jounama Creek, **2**
Khancoban, **8**
Kiandra, **4**
Leatherbarrel Creek, **16**
Ngarigo, **12**
Pinch River, **19**
Providence Portal, **5**
Running Waters, **20**
Sawpit Creek, **10**
Scotchie's Yards, **21**
Thredbo Diggings, **13**
Tom Groggin, **15**
Willis, **22**
Yarrangobilly, **3**
Yolde, **1**

NEW SOUTH WALES

by a network of trails designed for the area's long-term hikers. Bush camping is free in Kosciuszko National Park except at one privately run camping locale just west of Lake Jindabyne (**Kosciuszko Mountain Retreat ❶**; sites $18-23, powered $25-32; cabins $68-125). The many camping areas are popular and clearly delineated throughout the park and are available on a first come, first serve basis. Most lodges are self-contained, and most packages include lodging, lift tickets, breakfast, and dinner.

## ⚐ SKI SLOPE OVERVIEW

Cross-country skiing is always free on the following slopes:

| SKI SLOPE | THE LOWDOWN | FEATURES | PRICES |
|---|---|---|---|
| **Perisher Blue** | Australia's premier resort, with Perisher Valley, Blue Cow, Smiggins, and Guthega alpine villages. | 7 peaks, 51 lifts, and over 95 trails. | $98 per day, under 14 $54; night skiing (Tu, Sa) $25/14. |
| **Selwyn Snowfields** | Lacks the difficulty of other mountains in the park and experiences a shorter ski season due to lack of snow, but has 45 hectares of marked trails and beats the rest for value. | Beginner runs as well as a few expert runs; draws families and budget skiers. | $70 per day, under 15 $39. Lift pass and lesson $91/60. |
| **Thredbo** | Perisher's toughest and most worthy competitor. Home to Australia's longest slopes. Outdoor activities abound year-round. | 13 lifts of mostly intermediate runs. | $129 per 2 days, under 15 $45; night skiing (Tu and Sa) free with valid lift pass. Lift pass and lesson $110/75. First-timer $85/61. |
| **Charlotte's Pass** | The smallest, highest, and most elite of the resorts. A snow-bound village offers luxury packages and the most natural snow in the area. | Runs vary widely in difficulty and include a terrain park. | $89 per day, under 14 $53; group lesson $55/50. |

# PERISHER BLUE

New South Wales's premier ski resort, Perisher Blue (☎1300 655 811; www.perisherblue.com.au) is actually four resorts in one. One lift ticket buys entry to the interconnected slopes of all the resorts, leading down to the Perisher Valley, Blue Cow, Smiggins, and Guthega alpine villages.

**▣▤ TRANSPORTATION AND PRACTICAL INFORMATION.** Perisher is not exactly a full-service budget travel village; it has neither budget accommodations nor overnight parking. To get there by **car,** follow Kosciuszko Rd. (2WD are required to have snow chains on this road). The Perisher Valley day lot fills up quickly on busy days and is often entirely inaccessible due to road conditions, but the Skitube (☎02 6456 2010) is an all-weather **train** that makes the 8km journey underground into the Perisher Valley Alpine Village from Bullocks Flat, located along the Alpine Way (24hr. per day; press button to call; round-trip $41, children $23). You can either start your adventures in the village or keep riding the Skitube all the way up to the Blue Cow terminal. There, chairlifts take skiers and boarders of all levels to runs atop Guthega Peak and Mount Blue Cow. To get to the Skitube station at Bullocks Flat, take Jindabyne Coaches (☎02 6457 2117), which runs **shuttles** from Jindabyne (4 per day; round-trip $15). All lift tickets include unlimited use of the Perisher-Blue Cow segment of the Skitube. Purchase tickets at Bullocks Flat or at the **Perisher Blue**

**Jindabyne Ticket Office** in the Nuggets Crossing shopping center. (☎02 6456 1659. Open daily in winter 7am-7pm.) **Mojo Snow Transport** (☎1800 111 103) offers transport from Jindabyne, Canberra, or Sydney and helps manage all logistics, including equipment rentals, lessons, passes, and accommodations. By car, drive along the Alpine Way from Jindabyne until you reach the station. There's plenty of parking, a **post office,** a basic grocery store, and a few diners.

⛷ **SKIING.** Transfer between the seven peaks is relatively easy. Situated above the natural snow line, with a slightly higher elevation than its competitors, Perisher offers some of the best snow in the entire region. It is also a favorite with snowboarders, as it has a number of well-designed terrain parks. Another highlight is Double Trouble, the four double black trails on the backside of Mt. Perisher. There are four excellent, groomed cross-country ski trails, all of which start from the Nordic shelter, ranging 2-10km.

## SELWYN SNOWFIELDS

Along the Snowy Mountains Hwy., halfway between Cooma and Tumut, Selwyn Snowfields offers beginner and budget skiing, snowboarding, and other snow recreation options. (☎02 6454 9488; www.selwynsnow.com.au.) Primarily a family resort, Selwyn has a small number of trails, minimal amenities, and only a couple advanced runs. Toboggan and snowtube parks are a favorite with kids. The base elevation is 1492m and the summit is only 122m higher. The only resort in the north of the park, it also has the worst snow conditions. Selwyn bolsters its light snowfall with manmade snow used on over 80% of its terrain. On the bright side, lift tickets are inexpensive. ($70 per day, under 15 $39. Lift pass and 1hr. lesson $91/604. Lift value pack for 1 day $36/19.) Forty-five hectares of marked trails make cross-country skiing an attractive option. (Cross-country skiing is free on all mountains with the Kosciuzko Park entry fee.)

## CHARLOTTE'S PASS

At 1765m, Charlotte's Pass is the highest resort in the Snowy Mountains; with the most natural snow, it is a favorite with powder-crazy skiers. The resort can only be accessed by a snow cat from the Perisher Valley skitube terminal. For that reason, the resort has few day visitors and is mostly reserved for its 600 overnight guests, making it far more intimate than the other overnight resorts. Charlotte's Pass is by no means a budget resort; its mostly luxury accommodations are generally reserved as part of ski package deals. That said, if you were already planning on splurging on a lift package, the relative isolation and natural snow of Charlotte's Pass may make spending the extra money worth it.

# THREDBO

In 2000, Thredbo was named the NSW Tourist Destination of the Decade. Though it doesn't have as many runs as Perisher, it sports the longest slope (5.9km), the biggest vertical drop, and in summer it offers spectacular hiking and mountain biking. Due to a recent six-million-dollar upgrade in snowmaking, Thredbo's runs stay fresh for a good while. Its main resort is renowned for its nightlife, but it's a big splurge. If they're lucky enough to get a bed in the reasonably priced YHA hostel, budget-minded travelers stay there; otherwise, they tend to eat, sleep, and party in nearby Cooma and Jindabyne.

## ▣ ▯ TRANSPORTATION AND PRACTICAL INFORMATION

During ski season, Greyhound Australia (☎13 14 99) runs daily to Sydney (1hr., 1-2 per day, $45), and Transborder Alpine Express (☎02 6241 0033) runs daily to Canberra (1 per day, $35). In summer, you can't get to Thredbo by public transportation. Thredbo-bound hitchhikers stand at the roundabout outside Jindabyne—*Let's Go* does not recommend hitchhiking. **Thredbo Information Centre** is located on Friday Dr. (Accommodation booking and snow report ☎1800 020 589; www.thredbo.com.au. Open daily in winter 8am-6pm, in summer 8:30am-5pm.) Ski rentals at **Thredbo Sports** (☎02 6459 4119), near the base of the Kosciuszko Express chairlift, and at the east end of the village near the Friday Flat lift, are $20-40 higher than in Jindabyne or Cooma, averaging $92 for one day of skis, poles, and boots. Many find it worth the extra cost to rent near the slopes in case anything goes wrong. Check out www.transborder.com.au and www.mountainpass.com.au for additional transportation information.

## ACCOMMODATIONS

With nearby competition charging hundreds of dollars per night, the ▧**Thredbo YHA Lodge ❸**, 8 Jack Adams Path, is by far the best deal in town. Although the bright rooms are encased in cinderblocks, the common areas exude a cozy chalet feeling with a loft living room and fireplace. A large kitchen and Internet access ($6 per hr.) are available to guests. (☎02 6457 6376. YHA parking is located along the highway before the entrance to Thredbo; guests must trek down two flights of stairs to reach the entrance, although you can drive to the door to drop off bags. Pass the first entrance to town and make a right on Banjo Drive; then, make a right at the YHA sign. Reception 8-10am and 3-8pm. Nov.-May 4-bed dorms $29; twins $67, ensuite $78. June and Sept.-Oct. $50/120/140. YHA members only July-Aug.; min. $70; prices vary by number of nights; book as far ahead as possible.) Other lodges can be booked through the **Thredbo Resort Centre** or the information centre. (☎1300 020 589. Open daily May-Oct. 9am-6pm; Sept.-Apr. 9am-5pm; hours vary.)

## FOOD AND NIGHTLIFE

Eating on the mountain is expensive, though there is a range of options from takeaway to high-end restaurants with million-dollar views. The cheapest breakfast and lunch is at **Snowflakes Bakery ❶**, in Thredbo Village. (☎02 6457 7157. Pies, pastries, and sandwiches $3-7. Open daily May-Sept. 6am-6pm; Oct.-Apr. 7am-5pm.) **Alfresco Pizzeria ❸**, just below the Thredbo Alpine Hotel, serves pastas and pizza that will satisfy even the biggest appetite. (☎02 6457 6327. Small pies from $13, large pies from $16. Open in winter M-Th and Su noon-9pm, F-Sa noon-9:30pm; in summer Th-Su 5:30-8:30pm.) There is a small supermarket in Mowamba Pl. in the village. (Open in winter daily 8am-8pm; in summer M-Sa 8:30am-5:30pm, Su 9am-3pm.) After a day on the slopes, collapse at the **Schuss Bar,** in the village indoor center, for live entertainment. The **Keller Bar Nightclub,** in the Thredbo Alpine Hotel, provides riproaring nightlife.

## SUMMER ACTIVITIES

The **Kosciuszko Express** chairlift operates year-round for hikers. (One-way $20.50, round-trip $27. Open daily 9am-4:30pm, service ends at 4:30pm sharp.) Several excellent walks depart from the top of the chairlift, leading to panoramic perspectives of Kosciuszko National Park.

**KOSCIUSZKO SUMMIT.** The ▧**Mount Kosciuszko Walk** (13km round-trip, 4-6hr.) leads to the highest point on the entire continent and promises endless alpine views in all directions. One of the acclaimed "Seven Summits" of the world, the climb is significantly easier than the other peaks—especially considering that one is Mt. Everest—and offers a collection of unique flora indigenous only to the mountain. This is not undiscovered territory; hikers flock to the summit in summer, and the path is covered in a metal boardwalk to protect the delicate alpine terrain. However, the views are unspoiled, and if you leave before 8am, you may well have the summit to yourself. Hikers must bring warm clothes, water, a snack, lots of sunblock, and bug spray. The summit has notoriously fickle weather; it can snow in the middle of summer.

**OTHER HIKES.** For those interested in a shorter trek, visit the rather unimpressive **Kosciuszko Lookout,** which lacks sweeping vistas but has a picture-perfect view of the summit (4km round-trip, 2hr.). To admire the summit of Kosciuszko without leaving your car, take the sealed road from Jindabyne to **Charlotte's Pass,** the highest road in Australia. Charlotte's Pass is also the departure point for an alternative summit of Mt. Kosciuszko via the **Main Range Track** (18km, 6hr.), which traverses the ridgeline for spectacular views of rocky plains, verdant nooks, and mountaintops. The beginning section of the hike, the climb to the alpine Blue Lake, is the steepest bit, so don't get discouraged. After summitting, return by the same route or on a lower track through the forest; be aware that you will have to cross the Snowy River, which can be thigh-high after severe rains. Other options include the **Dead Horse Gap and Thredbo River Track** (10km), which ends in the village, and the **Porcupine Track** (5km round-trip, 2hr.), an easy, gradual trail that wanders through snowgums and wildflowers before ending at the Thredbo River with excellent views of Lake Jindabyne. Free maps of all trails with descriptions are available throughout Thredbo.

**MOUNTAIN BIKING.** The **Thredbo Activities Booking Desk** (☎02 6459 4119) arranges adventure activities during the summer, including mountain biking, horseback riding, abseiling, and rafting. **Raw NRG,** run out of the Service Station, offers wildly popular mountain biking excursions and initiation courses down the infamous 4.2km Cannonball Run. (☎02 6457 6234. 3hr.; departs daily 9:30am and 1:30pm; $99, with bike rental $199. Open daily 9am-4:30pm.)

# YARRANGOBILLY CAVES

Hidden on the valley floor in the beautiful northern scrub wilderness of the Kosciuszko National Park, the Yarrangobilly Caves attract curious visitors and hardcore spelunkers alike. The caves are well marked and located 6.5km off the highway on a winding, unsealed road. Over the last two million years, the churning waters of the Yarrangobilly River have been chewing their way through the dense limestone of the valley, creating some of the world's most breathtaking subterranean formations. The region is ever-changing as speleologists are uncovering newly formed caverns every year.

🛈 **PRACTICAL INFORMATION.** Visitors coming from outside the park must pay $3 if they haven't already paid the daily national park fee. The **Visitors Centre** at the site should be your first stop. (☎02 6454 9597. Open daily 9am-5pm. $3 site fee.) There is no camping at the caves; camping is available at **Yarrangobilly Village,** 15km north of the caves off the Snowy Mountains Hwy.

🄶🄽 **SIGHTS AND HIKING.** The surrounding area of northern Kosciuszko National Park offers a number of diversions that make the 2hr. trip to the caves well worthwhile. The best local hikes are detailed in the Kosciuszko Today newspaper. Many old buildings, including the **Coolamine Homestead** and the **Currango Homestead,** date from the gold rush and provide interesting insight into the heritage of the region. Turn off at Tantangara Rd. and then take the Port Philip Trail. The **Kiandra Heritage Walk** (1km) is an easy way to explore goldrush heritage; it starts at the RTA depot, the former courthouse. The fact that the area is less visited than the south also means that there is abundant wildlife. Unfortunately, severe wildfires swept through in 2003, and the extensive damage they caused is still evident; be extra careful not to stray from marked trails in order to give the flora a shot at recovery.

**◭ CAVES.** Of the dozens of navigable caves, only six are open to visitors—the rest have been marked for preservation. The ◪Jersey Cave is rather unremarkable upon entry, but visitors are soon treated to an amazing collection of colorful spires or "straws," which dangle incredibly close overhead (tours depart daily at 1pm; 1hr.; $13, children $8.50; there are 217 steps). The **North Glory Cave** contains similarly breathtaking sights. The **South Glory Cave** is about 100,000 years old and is the largest cave. It is the only cave open for a self-guided tour (45min., 206 steps), but you'll need a token from the tourist office to explore beyond the unusual "glory arch" entrance. (Open daily 9am-4pm. $10.50, children $6.50, families $29.) Handicapped individuals can access the two-million-year-old **Jillabenan Cave** with a special wheelchair provided by the visitors center (tours depart daily 11am and 3pm; 1hr.; $13, children $8.50). After wandering underground, head to the surface and try a short, very steep bushwalk on a maintained trail or take a load off in the 27°C (81°F) thermal pools near the river, a 700m steep downhill walk from the carpark (free).

# RIVERINA

A collection of sunburned towns rich in Aboriginal history and meandering waterways, the Riverina is a worthwhile sojourn on the trek from Melbourne to Sydney. The two main rivers are the Murrumbidgee, which starts as a trickle in the Snowy Mountains, and the Murray, which becomes significant at Albury-Wodonga and flows all the way to Adelaide. Although it lacks traditional tourist bait (like ocean views), the Riverina's plethora of farming and picking opportunities makes it a popular spot for backpackers (see **Beyond Tourism,** p. 81).

## ALBURY-WODONGA                                                      ☎02

On the border of Victoria and New South Wales, with one half of the dual city in the former state and the other in the latter, the metropolitan area of Albury-Wodonga (pop. 100,000) spans both sides of the Murray River. The Hume Hwy. rumbles through the center of town, making Albury-Wodonga an obvious pitstop for weary travelers. Many plan an extended stay because of its proximity to world-renowned wineries, ski slopes, and work on nearby farms, although the city itself does not offer many reasons to spend more than a night.

## ⊏ TRANSPORTATION

**Trains: Countrylink Travel Centre,** in the railway station, books Countrylink and V/Line transport. (☎02 6041 9555. Open M-F 9am-5pm.) Countrylink (☎02 13 22 32; open 6am-10pm) trains run to: **Goulburn** (5hr., 2 per day, $75); **Melbourne** (3hr., 2 per day, $60); **Sydney** (7hr., 2 per day, $100); **Wagga Wagga** (1hr., 2 per day, $25); **Wangaratta** (45min., 2 per day, $15); **Yass** (4hr., 2 per day, $50). Many trains run to **Cootamundra** and then switch to buses to their final destinations.

**Buses:** V/Line (☎02 13 61 96) services destinations in Victoria frequently and cheaply. Runs to: **Echuca** (3-4hr., 1-2 per day, $27); **Melbourne** (3hr., 4-6 per day, $50); **Mildura** (10hr.; M, W, Th, Sa mornings; $70); **Rutherglen** (40min.; M, W-Th, Sa mornings;

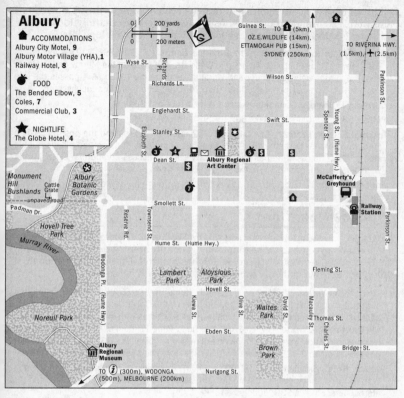

**Albury**

🏠 ACCOMMODATIONS
Albury City Motel, **9**
Albury Motor Village (YHA),**1**
Railway Hotel, **8**

🍎 FOOD
The Bended Elbow, **5**
Coles, **7**
Commercial Club, **3**

⭐ NIGHTLIFE
The Globe Hotel, **4**

Guinea St.   TO 🚂 (5km),
OZ.E.WILDLIFE (14km),
ETTAMOGAH PUB (15km),
SYDNEY (250km)

TO RIVERINA HWY.
(1.5km), ✚ (2.5km)

Wyse St.
Richards Pl.
Richards Ln.
Wilson St.
Englehardt St.
Swift St.
Stanley St.
Elizabeth St.
Dean St.
Albury Regional Art Center
Young St. (Hume Hwy.)
Spencer St.
McCafferty's/ Greyhound
Smollett St.
Reserve Rd.
Townsend St.
Hume St. (Hume Hwy.)
Railway Station
Parkinson St.
Monument Hill Bushlands
Cattle Grate
unpaved road
Padman Dr.
Albury Botanic Gardens
Hovell Tree Park
Murray River
Wodonga Pl. (Hume Hwy.)
Lambert Park
Aloysious Park
Hovell St.
Fleming St.
Kiewa St.
Olive St.
Waites Park
David St.
Macauley St.
Noreuil Park
Ebden St.
Charles St.
Thomas St.
Bridge St.
Brown Park
Albury Regional Museum
TO ℹ️ (300m), WODONGA (500m), MELBOURNE (200km)
Nurigong St.

$8); **Swan Hill** (6-7hr., 1-2 per day, $45); **Wangaratta** (45min., 4-6 per day, $15).
Greyhound Australia (☎ 02 13 20 30) runs from next to the railway station to: **Adelaide**
(16hr., 3 per day, $100); **Brisbane** (26hr., 5 per day, $150); **Canberra** (5hr., 4 per day,
$35); **Melbourne** (4hr., 5 per day, $40); **Sydney** (9hr., 5 per day, $50); **Wangaratta**
(45min., 2 per day, $50). Several companies, including Wayward Busline and Firefly
tours, offer service from Albury-Wodonga to **Melbourne** and **Sydney** while stopping in
various scenic locations along each route. Contact Firefly at www.fireflyexpress.com.au
or ☎ 1 800 631 164 for further information.

## 📋 🔢 ORIENTATION AND PRACTICAL INFORMATION

The **Hume Highway (Hwy. M31)** from Sydney enters Albury-Wodonga from the
northeast and winds through the center of town before resuming its southward
course into Wodonga. The **Murray Valley Highway (Hwy. 16)** runs along the Victoria
side and enters Wodonga from the southeast, running through town before
uniting with the Hume Hwy. Along the river on the New South Wales side, the
**Riverina Highway (Hwy. 58)** runs west to Corowa. The heart of Albury-Wodonga
can be found in the half-dozen blocks radiating from **Dean Street** in Albury. The
city's heart, main services, and few attractions are all in Albury. Wodonga, a bit
of a drive across the river, is missable. Because the area is more urban than

neighboring regions, temporary farming is scarce; look to the abundance of cafes and restaurants to provide hospitality work. The centrally located city can also be a useful home base while searching for fruit-picking jobs.

**Tourist Office: Gateway Visitors Information Centre** (☎1300 796 222) is located in the Gateway Village between Albury and Wodonga, just south of the Murray on the Hume Hwy. A bus runs between Albury and Wodonga and can be hailed as it passes the info center every 30min. Open daily 9am-5pm. 24hr. tourist information touchscreen.

**Currency Exchange:** Several **banks** and 24hr. **ATMs** line Dean St.

**Police:** 539-543 Olive St. (☎02 6023 9299), near Swift St.

**Internet Access:** ▓**Albury City Library** (☎02 6051 3470), behind the post office, is a modern black-and-white building with free, fast computers and cool red plastic bubble stools. Max. 1hr. Ask librarian for temporary card to access computers. Open M and W-Th 10am-7pm, Tu and F 10am-5pm, Sa 10am-4pm, Su noon-4pm.

**Post Office:** (☎02 6051 3633), at the corner of Dean and Kiewa St. Open M-F 9am-5pm. **Postal Code:** 2640.

# ACCOMMODATIONS

Budget accommodation is scarce in Albury-Wodonga. There are motels aplenty, but most are pricey, and those that aren't generally aren't worth the time either. The best bet is the motor village, which has a hostel. Unfortunately though, it is 5km out of town and only accessible to those with a car.

**Albury Motor Village (YHA),** 377 Wagga Rd., Hume Hwy. (☎02 6040 2999). 5km north of the city center in Lavington, just beyond Kaylock Rd. Only true budget option for backpackers. Calm, clean motor village mostly attracts families with their own transportation; you must have a car to get here. A/C and heat. Pool, TV lounge, kitchen, parking, and laundry. Reception 8am-8pm. Book ahead in summer. Dorms $23, non-members $27; powered sites for 2 $25; doubles $50-55; self-contained cabins for 2 $69-167. ❷

**Railway Hotel,** Smollett St. (☎02 6021 4700). Basic, clean rooms near the train station, as the name suggests. Bathrooms are slightly worn, but lace curtains brighten the atmosphere. Singles $30; doubles $40. ❸

**Albury City Motel,** 729 Young St. (☎02 6021 7699). Austar TV, a pool, and a BBQ offset the high price. Singles $75; doubles $100. ❹

# FOOD AND NIGHTLIFE

Culinary offerings in Albury are surprisingly excellent for the size of the city. While restaurants are mostly just limited to run-of-the-mill cafes and pub bistros, the quality is significantly better than in surrounding towns. Dean St. holds the majority of establishments. Find groceries at **Coles** in the City Centre mall off Dean St. (Open daily 7am-10pm.)

**The Bended Elbow,** 480 Dean St. (☎02 6023 6266). Offers high-quality food that almost erases the meaning of pub grub. Lovely dark hardwood decor and outdoor patio. Daily $10 lunch special noon-2:30pm. Entrees $15-19. Open M, Tu, Su 11am-10:30pm; W 11am-1am; Th 11am-midnight; F-Sa 11am-3am. ❷

**Q Cafe,** 555 Dean St. (☎02 6021 1994). Bright, hip cafe offering sandwiches, salads ($9), and fantastic fresh juices (watermelon and mint $3.50). Orange and white decor livens things up. Open M-F 7am-5pm, Sa-Su 7am-2pm. ❶

**Commercial Club,** 618 Dean St. (☎02 6021 1133). Stuff yourself silly on lunch and dinner buffets with a large selection of meats, vegetables, and desserts for only $13.

The enormous complex also houses live music and lots of gambling. All visitors must present a valid ID at the door. Open W-Su 8am-10pm, noon-2pm, and 6pm-late. ❷

**The Globe Hotel,** on Dean St. (☎02 6021 2622). Student crowd parties hard to the frequent live music. Take a break from the insanity in shiny red chairs in the hip lounge or soak up the safari atmosphere in hanging basket chairs in the front room. Pot of beer from $3; schooner $4.40. Open M-Tu 10am-midnight, W-Sa 10am-4am.

## 👁 🎿 SIGHTS AND ACTIVITIES

The ⬛Murray River is by far the most popular sight in Albury-Wodonga, and on hot summer afternoons, most of the town takes to the water. The river has a fairly strong current that carries swimmers westward through forests of gnarled red gum trees. A good place for a dip can be found just south of the botanic gardens in **Noreuil Park,** though this spot is popular among families with young (and often loud) children. **The Canoe Guy** (☎02 6041 1822) runs 17-37km canoe trips down the river (½-day $25, full-day $35, 2-day $70).

On Wodonga Pl. between Smollett and Dean St., the **Albury Botanic Gardens** (☎02 6023 8111) have pretty flowers and plenty of grassy picnic space. To take in a sweeping view of the region (or just to get some exercise), climb to the top of the **Monument Hill Bushlands** and gaze out onto Albury-Wodonga from the base of the Art Deco obelisk that is the **Albury War Memorial.** To find out more about the extensive trail and park system in Albury-Wodonga, visit the **Parklands Albury-Wodonga** office, behind the Gateway Visitors Information Centre. (☎02 6023 6714. Open M-F 8:30am-4:30pm.)

Just 15km north of Albury-Wodonga along the Hume Hwy., the goofy humor of the **Ettamogah Pub** caters to gawking tourists by satirizing and stereotyping all things Aussie. The late cartoonist Ken Maynard had been drawing a place like it for the *Australia Post* for years before someone decided to actually construct it. It may be kitschy, but it's also a lot of fun. (☎02 6026 2366. Pub open daily 10am-6pm. Bistro open daily 10am-10pm.)

Don't forget to make a stop at the nearby **OZ.e.wildlife.** It's a small, laid-back preserve filled with audacious kangaroos that will get up close and personal on their insatiable quest for food. Visitors can also feed wallabies and see penguins and koalas. Be sure to maintain a safe distance from the dingoes. (☎02 6040 3677; www.ozewildlife.com.au. Penguin parade 11am, 1, 3pm. Open daily 9am-5pm. $10, concessions $8, children $5, families $25.)

# WAGGA WAGGA ☎02

The largest inland city in New South Wales is known to most Australians simply as "Wagga" (WOH-guh; pop. 57,000). It derives its name from the local Aboriginal tribe for whom repetition implied plurality: *wagga* means crow, and therefore *wagga wagga* is the place of many crows. Locals proudly proclaim that their town is so good, they named it twice. Largely populated by students, Wagga is a surprisingly lively stop on the trek from Sydney to Melbourne. That said, it isn't a tourist draw and is mainly just a place for reconnecting with civilization after a lengthy stay in a nearby national park.

**🖅 🚻 TRANSPORTATION AND PRACTICAL INFORMATION.** The Sturt Hwy. (Hammond Ave. or Edward St. in town) intersects with **Baylis Street,** the town's main drag, and Baylis St. becomes **Fitzmaurice Street** once it crosses the bridge over Wollundry Lagoon. The center of the city is really only the very long Baylis St.; the side streets are residential. The bus stop and railway station are at **Station Pl.,** the southern terminus of Baylis St. Countrylink (☎132 232) and

Fearnes Coaches (☎ 02 6921 2316 or 1800 029 918) operate **bus** service to Canberra (3hr.; 2 per day; $32 and $41, respectively) and Sydney (6-8hr., 2 per day, $53/60). Greyhound Australia offers similar service ($43 to Canberra, $60 to Sydney), plus a route to **Melbourne** (7hr., 1 per day, $62). The **visitors center** at 183 Tarcutta St. provides maps and brochures about accommodations, restaurants, and sights. To find it, turn right at the Civic Centre, continue for one block, and follow the signs. (☎02 6926 9621; www.visitwaggawagga.com. Open daily 9am-5pm. 24hr. touchscreen information kiosk.) The **library**, in the Civic Centre, has free **Internet**. (☎02 6926 9700. Open M 11am-7pm, Tu-F 10am-7pm, Sa 10am-5pm.) A **post office** is in the Wagga Wagga Marketplace on Baylis St. (Open M-F 8:30am-5pm, Sa 9am-noon.) **Postal Code:** 2650.

## ACCOMMODATIONS AND FOOD.

The **Victoria Hotel ❷**, 55 Baylis St., is just a 5min. walk from the train station down Baylis St. Above the bustling pub and restaurant, the "Vic" has clean carpeted rooms. (☎02 6921 5233. Singles $40; doubles or twins $60.) **Romano's ❸** is another pub with accommodations located over the bridge where Baylis turns into Fitzmaurice St. (☎02 6921 2031. Singles $38; doubles $50, with shower $59, ensuite $78. Extra bed $13). **Wagga Wagga Beach Caravan Park ❶**, at the end of Johnston St., has sites and ensuite units with TV, A/C, and kitchen. Laundry and BBQ facilities are available. (☎02 6931 0603. Sites for 2 $17-20, powered $19-21; standard units $55-65.)

There are two large **supermarkets** along Baylis St. in the center of town: a **Coles** in the Sturt Mall (open M-Sa 6am-midnight, Su 8am-10pm) and a **Woolworths** in the Wagga Wagga Marketplace (open M-F 7am-midnight, Sa 7am-10pm, Su 8am-10pm), both near the intersection of Forsyth St. The main drag has a number of cafes and mediocre pub restaurants, but few stand out from the crowd. **The Baylis St. Bistro ❷** is on the ground floor of the Victoria Hotel and serves heaping lunch and dinner portions (from $8) at reasonable prices. (Open daily noon-latenight.) The **Bridge Tavern ❶**, 188 Fitzmaurice St., is a popular horse-racing pub and bistro attached to a plush steakhouse by the same name. Tavern bar fare is significantly less expensive than steakhouse grub. (☎02 6921 2222. Main courses $8-13. Open M-Sa 10am-late, Su 10am-10pm.)

## SIGHTS AND ENTERTAINMENT.

The **Wiradjuri Walking Track** features most of the Wagga's major landmarks, meandering through the city in a 30km loop starting at the visitors center, where you can pick up the detailed brochure. The **Civic Centre** at the north end of Baylis St. houses several galleries, including the **National Art Glass Gallery** and the **Wagga Wagga Art Gallery**. (Free. Open Tu-Sa 10am-5pm, Su noon-4pm.) The **Botanic Gardens** are small but lovely. (☎02 6925 4065. Open daily dawn-dusk. Free.) In summer, **Wagga Beach,** at Cabriata Park, is a popular spot, although the river is a bit muddy. The Capital is the only large nightclub venue in Wagga, catering primarily to the local university crowd. City officials have imposed a lock-down system; at 1:30am, all establishments lock their doors. If you're already inside, you can stay until the wee hours of the morning—you just can't switch pubs. (F dance club. Open W-Sa 9pm-3am.)

# BATHURST ☎02

Bathurst (pop. 37,000) features wide avenues and large, ornate lampposts, which suggest that it was once headed for greatness. However, it's the motorway in the southwest corner of town that has put the city on the map. Originally built as a scenic drive, the 6km loop up and down Mt. Panorama doubles as a public road and the track for the **V-8 Supercars Race,** held in early October, during which over 150,000 people descend on the usually low-profile town.

**▐ ▞ TRANSPORTATION AND PRACTICAL INFORMATION.** Bathurst is 100km west of Katoomba on the Great Western Hwy. **Trains** and **buses** leave the Railway Station at the corner of Keppel and Havannah St. Countrylink (☎02 6332 4844 or 13 22 32) goes to: Cowra (1hr., 2 per day, $13.80); Dubbo (3hr., 2 per day, $29); Forbes and Parkes (3hr., 1-3 per day, $24); Katoomba (2hr., 1-2 per day, $16); Lithgow (1-1½hr., 3-7 per day, $10); Parramatta and Penrith (3½hr., 2 per day, $24-25); Sydney (3-4hr., 1 per day, $32). For a **taxi**, call ☎13 10 08. The **Bathurst Visitor Information Centre**, 1 Kendall Ave., has brochures and maps. (☎02 6332 1444 or 1800 681 000. Open daily 9am-5pm.) **ATMs** abound on William and Howick St. Free Internet can be found at the **library** at 70-78 Keppel St. (☎02 6332 6281. Open M-F 10am-6pm, Sa 10am-5pm, Su 11am-2pm.) The **police station,** 139 Rankin St., lies between Russell and Howick St. (☎02 6332 8699). The **post office,** 230 Howick St., is between George and William St. (☎02 6332 4553. Open M-F 9am-5pm.) **Postal Code:** 2795.

**▐ ▐ ACCOMMODATIONS AND FOOD.** During the races, rates for all accommodations skyrocket faster than the cars themselves. Bathurst has a few pub stays downtown; the nicest affordable option is the backpacker-friendly **Commercial Hotel ❷**, 135 George St., which also serves up cocktails and mixed drinks ($5-10) in the downstairs bar. (☎02 6331 2712; www.commercialhotel.com.au. Dorms $25; singles $35; doubles $55.) The **Bathurst Motor Inn ❺**, 87 Durham St., on the corner of George St., offers rooms with TV, fridge, heat and A/C, and coffeemaker. (☎02 6331 2222. Reception 7am-10:30pm, Su 8am-8pm. Singles from $70; twins and doubles $80. extra person $15.)

A great departure from the town's greasy spoons, **Al Dente ❶**, on 886 Keppel St., is a regional produce deli serving great coffee ($3.50) and deli sandwiches. Gourmet foods (lunch $4.50-10) are also in its attached store. (☎02 6331 0531. Open M-F 6am-5pm, Sa 6am-1pm. MC/V.) A **Woolworths** supermarket is in the Stockland Mall off William St. (☎02 6331 9144. Open daily 7am-10pm.)

**◪ SIGHTS.** No trip to Bathurst would be complete without a spin (or even two) around the ▨**Mount Panorama circuit head,** southwest on William St., where it becomes Panorama Ave. As you twist up and down the steep hills, you'll gain an appreciation for the pros who do it in excess of 200kph during officially sanctioned races. Don't let the banner ads and tire piles seduce you; local police patrol the area frequently, looking for drivers who edge above the 60kph speed limit. The recently expanded **National Motor Racing Museum,** near the starting line, keeps the thrill of the race alive year-round. (☎02 6332 1872. Open daily 9am-4:30pm. $8, concessions $5.50, children $3.) The **Bathurst Historical Museum** in the court's eastern wing gives a more historical account of the town. Chock full of historic objects like shoe hooks, a concertina, and a ship's spar, the museum tells the story of the town's gold rush days. (☎02 6330 8455. $3, concessions/children $2. Open Tu-W and Sa 10am-4pm, Su 11am-2pm.) The **Chifley Home,** 10 Busby St., abode of Ben Chifley, prime minister from 1945 to 1949, is so unpretentious that it serves as a symbol of hope for political humility. (☎02 6332 1444. Open M and Sa-Su 10am-2pm. $7, children $4.50.)

Don't miss the **Abercrombie Caves**, part of the Jenolan Caves Trust, 70km south of Bathurst via Trunkey Creek. The majestic **Grand Arch** is the largest limestone archway in the Southern Hemisphere. (☎02 6368 8603. Open daily 9am-5pm. $10, with tour $15.) Fossicking—amateur mining, in this case for gold—is very popular in the area and its surroundings. **Bathurst Goldfields,** 428 Conrod Straight on Mt. Panorama, is a reconstructed mining area that allows you to try your hand at panning for gold (much as the company pans for the tourist dollar.) However, it's mostly intended for school groups, so it isn't always operational. (☎02 6332 2022. Call ahead for times. $20.)

# MUDGEE ☎02

A land of wine cradled in the foothills of the Great Dividing Range, Mudgee (Aboriginal for "nest in the hills;" pop. 8500) has over 40 vineyards and plenty of small town charm. Locals proudly proclaim that Mudgee is "tasting better each year," a claim confirmed by even a tipsy visit to nearby cellar doors.

**TRANSPORTATION.** Mudgee is a 3hr. drive from Sydney on Hwy. 86 (Castlereagh Hwy.), between Lithgow (126km) and Dubbo (133km). **Countrylink** (☎13 22 32) connects by **bus** to Mudgee and runs one to two times per day to Coonabarabran (3hr., $25), Lithgow (2-2½hr., $19), and Sydney (5½hr., $37). Book at **Harvey World Travel,** 68 Church St. (☎02 6372 6077. Open M-F 8:30am-5:30pm, Sa 9am-noon.) Because trains no longer pass through Mudgee, the old railway station on the corner of Church and Inglis St. is instead home to a cafe, gourmet local food shop, and gallery of local art. Countrylink coaches stop there and at the visitors center. There is no public transportation in Mudgee, and there's no hope of walking across this land of sprawling vineyards. For **taxis,** call ☎13 10 08. **Biking** is also an option for physically fit, and **Country-fit,** at 36-42 Short St., rents and provides helmets free of charge. (☎02 6372 3955; www.countryfitbicyclehire.com.au. $15 per hr., $25 per day, $30 per full day. Tandems available.) You can also look into a tour if you want to see the wineries (see **Sights and Wineries** below.) With transportation covered, choosing among the 40 area vineyards will be your big challenge.

**ORIENTATION AND PRACTICAL INFORMATION.** The **Mudgee Visitors Centre,** 84 Market St., has maps and free Wi-Fi. (☎02 6372 1020 or 1800 816 304. Open daily 9am-5pm.) The **NPWS office,** 160 Church St., across from the train station, administers the northwest section of Wollemi National Park. (☎02 6372 7199. Open M-F 9am-4pm, but call ahead to confirm that a ranger is there.) Free Internet is available at the **library,** 64 Market St. (☎02 6378 2740. Open M-F 10am-6pm, Sa 9:30am-12:30pm.) **Banks** and **ATMs** are on Church St. **Police** (☎02 6372 8599) are at 94 Market St. The **post office** (☎02 6378 2021) is at 80 Market St., on the corner with Perry St. (Open M-F 9am-5pm.) **Postal Code:** 2850.

**ACCOMMODATIONS AND FOOD.** Pub stay accommodations are readily available in town. The **Woolpack Hotel ❷,** 67 Market St., is located down the street from the visitors center, near the corner of Church St. A friendly, colorful cast of characters frequents the downstairs pub and TV lounge. Rooms include fridge, coffeemaker, and A/C. (☎02 6372 1908. Reception noon-midnight at bar. Backpacker rooms and singles $25; doubles $65. MC/V.) Another good option is the **Lawson Park Hotel ❸,** 1 Church St. The spacious, comfortable rooms for three all come with electric blankets and beds. There's a TV room with a kitchen at the end of the hall. (☎02 6372 2183. Continental breakfast included. Singles $40-44; doubles $50-65. AmEx/D/MC/V.) The **Mudgee Riverside Caravan and Tourist Park ❷,** 22 Short St., behind the visitors center, has showers and laundry. (☎02 6372 2531; www.mudgeeriverside.com.au. Linen $15. Laundry $6. Reception 8am-8pm. Sites for 2 $20, powered $23; ensuite cabins with A/C, kitchen, and TV $65-85. MC/V.) A number of motels are scattered through town, but the cheapest of them is **Central Motel ❸,** 120 Church St. (☎1800 457 222. Reception 8am-10pm. Doubles $60-120. AmEx/D/MC/V.)

NEW SOUTH WALES

The **Red Heifer ❸,** 1 Church St., inside the Lawson Park Hotel, is a great spot for live entertainment and good grub—grill your own steak ($17-20) and enjoy it with a bottle of local wine (from $10). Main dishes ($15-18) come with a salad or vegetables. (☎02 6372 2183. Open daily noon-2:30pm and 6-9pm. AmEx/MC/V.) Stop in at **Melon Tree ❶,** 71 Market St., to grab a gourmet sandwich ($6-9) or pick up a picnic pack for a day at the wineries. Breakfast for under $10 is a tasty and economical way to pad your stomach before you set out. (☎02 6372 4005. Open M-Sa 8am-4pm. MC/V.) A **Woolworths** supermarket is on Mortimer St. (☎02 6372 3377. Open daily 7am-10pm).

**◙ 🔏 SIGHTS AND WINERIES.** Mudgee's selling points are its viticultural venues, ranging from small, communal vineyards to large, self-sufficient wineries; consult the tourist office for guidance as to which best suits your tastes. The streets come alive during the **Mudgee Wine Festival** in September, but you can fill your glass with Mudgee's renowned reds year-round. If you want to do the wine-tasting circuit but also wish to avoid running afoul of drunk-driving laws, try **On the Bus Tours.** (☎04 1767 8619; www.onthebus.com.au.)

Not far from the center of town, **Frog's Rock** has an impressive range of earthy wines ready to be sampled. From town, take Cassilis Rd. to Edgell Ln. (☎02 6372 2408; www.frogrockwines.com. Open daily 10am-5pm.) **Botobolar,** 89 Botobolar Rd., 16km northeast of town, is Australia's oldest organic vineyard and offers daily tastings. (☎02 6373 3840. Open M-Sa 10am-5pm, Su 10am-3pm.) **Huntington Estate Wines,** 8km from town past the airport on Cassilis Rd., has an array of reds to taste on the free self-guided tour. (☎02 6373 3825; www.huntingtonestate.com.au. Open M-F 9am-5pm, Sa 10am-5pm, Su 10am-3pm.) The **Lowe Family Wine Company,** on Tinja Ln., the first left 2km down Craigmore Rd., is another organic wine producer, famous for its Zinfandels and eco-friendly composting techniques. (☎02 6372 0800; www.lowewine.com.au).

# DUBBO ☎02

The hub of central and western NSW and only a 4hr. drive from Sydney, Dubbo (DUH-boh; pop. 39,000) is a bustling, blue-collar service city and a common stop on journeys between Melbourne and Brisbane. In the middle of the town's buzzing CBD, it's possible to forget how close you are to the Outback, but a drive after dark in any direction (not recommended) will reveal how isolated you are. Dubbo has a smattering of attractions, but the city's headliner is the amazing menagerie at the Taronga Western Plains Zoo.

**▛ TRANSPORTATION.** Countrylink (☎13 22 32) **trains** and **buses** depart from the railway station on Talbragar St. to: Albury (7hr.; Tu, Th, Su 1 per day; $78); Broken Hill (8hr., 1 per day, $78); Forbes (2hr.; Tu, Th, Su 1 per day; $17); Melbourne (10hr.; Tu, Th, Su 1 per day; $116); Sydney (7-11hr., 1 per day, $79); Wagga Wagga (5hr.; Tu, Th, Su 1 per day; $57). Greyhound Australia (☎13 14 99 or 13 20 30) services: Adelaide (17hr., 2 per day, $192); Brisbane (12hr., 1 per day, $159); Coonabarabran (2hr., W-Sa 1 per day, $43); and Melbourne (12hr., 1 per day, $130). Tickets can be booked online, on the phone, or at the rail station (Open M-F 8am-5pm, Sa-Su 8-9:30am and 10:30am-2pm.) **Taxis** run 24hr. (☎13 10 08). **Darrell Wheeler Cycles,** 25 Bultje St., rents bikes for $15 per day. (☎02 6882 9899. Open M-F 8:30am-5:30pm, Sa 8:30am-1pm. Call ahead for Su rental.) Bike trails cross town, run along the Macquarie River, and head toward the zoo.

**◪ 🔁 ORIENTATION AND PRACTICAL INFORMATION.** Dubbo sits at the intersection of the **Newell Highway,** which runs between Melbourne (856km) and

Brisbane (895km), and the **Mitchell Highway,** which connects Sydney (414km) to western cities. The town's sprawling layout could make life difficult for the carless, though major sights are clustered around the zoo and CBD, which is marked by the intersection of Talbragar and Macquarie St. **Talbragar Street** runs east-west, parallel to the two major highways that sandwich the town. **Macquarie Street** is lined with **banks, ATMs, pharmacies,** and **supermarkets.**

The **Dubbo Visitors Centre,** on the corner of Erskine and Macquarie St. (Newell Hwy.) in the northwest corner of the small downtown area, is stocked with maps of biking trails. (☎02 6801 4450; www.dubbotourism.com.au. Open daily 9am-5pm.) The **police station** (☎02 6881 3222) is at 143 Brisbane St., across from the Grape Vine Cafe. Find Internet access at the **Dubbo Regional Library,** on the southwest corner of Macquarie and Talbragar St. (☎02 6801 4510. Free web searching. Email and chat $1.35 per 15min. Open M-F 10am-6pm, Sa 10am-3pm, Su noon-4pm.) The **post office** is at 65-69 Talbragar St. between Brisbane and Macquarie St. (☎02 6841 3210. Open daily 9am-5pm.) **Postal Code:** 2830.

**❢ ACCOMMODATIONS.** A mix of hostels and hotels is clustered near Talbragar St. in the CBD, with singles from $35-50; motels in the area generally run $70-120 for a double. The cheapest beds are at the **Dubbo YHA Hostel ❷,** 87 Brisbane St., near the corner of the Newell Hwy. The warm nightly fire, talking cockatoo, and verandas off each room add character to the hostel. Though this YHA is simpler than most, the friendliness of the managing couple is unparalleled. (☎02 6882 0922. Internet access $3 per 30min. Laundry $3. Bikes $8 per day. Reception 8-10am and 3-10pm. Dorms $25-28; doubles $49-55; family rooms from $56.) Swankier digs can be found at **Amaroo Hotel ❹,** 81 Macquarie St., in the middle of town. Amaroo features modern ensuite rooms with TV, fridge, electric blankets, heat, and A/C. (☎02 6882 3533. Ensuite singles $59; doubles $80. Extra person $30.) **The Dubbo City Caravan Park ❶,** on Whylandra St. just before it becomes the Newell Hwy., has beautiful shaded sites overlooking the Macquarie River. Call ahead, since it fills up during school holidays. (☎02 6882 4820; www.dubbocaravanpark.com.au. Linen $15 per bed. Laundry $6. Reception 7:30am-7:30pm. Check-in 1pm. Sites for 2 $18-20, powered $24-28, ensuite $32-38; caravans from $30; cabins $55-85; motel-style family units with linen and kitchen $85-125. Extra person $7-10. AmEx/MC/V.)

**❒ FOOD.** Sandwich shops and bakeries are plentiful in the CBD, but cheap restaurants are few and far between. For the best coffee concoctions, pastries, and light meals, try the chic **Grape Vine Cafe ❶,** 144 Brisbane St. When the weather's nice, regulars enjoy iced coffee on the patio out back; during colder months, sip hot chocolate at modern tables with cushioned banquettes. (☎02 6884 7354. Breakfast and lunch $8-15. Open M-F 8am-5pm, Sa-Su 9am-4pm.) There are local markets offering crafts, produce, and bric-a-brac at the showground on Wingewarra St. every second Sunday of the month. (Open 9am-1pm.) A **Woolworths** supermarket is in the Riverdale Shopping Centre on Macquarie St. (☎02 6882 1633. Open daily 7am-10pm.) For fresh produce, visit the **Macquarie Valley Farmer's Markets,** held every first and third Saturday of the month from 8am-noon behind the visitors center.

**DON'T GAZE AND GRAZE.** Bring a sack lunch, but don't eat while observing the animals—it gets them all riled up.

**◎ SIGHTS.** Dubbo's premier tourist attraction is the ▨**Taronga Western Plains Zoo,** on Obley Rd., 4km south of the city center off the Newell Hwy. Though perhaps not worth a special trip from Sydney, it's an awesome place to visit if you're in the area. In addition to Australian native species, the zoo houses Bengal tigers, lions, black rhinoceroses, and Australia's only resident African elephants, all wandering through loose enclosures. Exhibits are arranged by continent around a paved track suitable for driving or biking; BBQ and picnic areas abound along the way. Signs posted throughout the zoo announce feeding times and recent births. On weekends, and Wednesdays and Fridays during school holidays, 6:45am zoo walks provide a behind-the-scenes look at the animals ($10, children $5). For a real adventure, try the Big Cats Encounter, offered every day (except W) at 11:30am for $59. Wild Africa Encounters are daily at 10:45am for $29. (☎02 6881 1400; www.zoo.nsw.gov.au. Open daily 9am-5pm; last entry 4pm. 2-day pass $39, students $23, children $19. 4hr. bike rental $15 plus license or credit card deposit.)

Learn about aerodynamics, Aboriginal history, and woodcraft at **Jedda Boomerangs,** on Minore Rd, White Pines. As you head southwest to the zoo, turn right onto Minore and follow it for 4km. Watch the entertaining and knowledgeable staff craft a boomerang, then take a throwing lesson ($6) or design your own boomerang for $9-16. (☎02 6882 3110; www.jeddaboomerangs.com. au. Open M-F and Su 9am-5pm.) The **Tracker Riley Cycleway** offers an easy path along the banks of the Macquarie River for bikers and walkers alike. **Dundullimal Homestead,** on Obley Rd., 2min. past the zoo, is the oldest timber slab house in Australia. Built in the early 1840s, the house offers a glimpse of Dubbo's roots as a frontier town. (☎02 6884 9984. Open Tu-Th 10am-4pm. $8, children $4, families $20.) **The Old Dubbo Gaol,** 90 Macquarie St., features a holographic executioner's display and animatronic exhibits with inmates telling fascinating stories of crime and punishment. Theatrical performances at 10, 11am, 2:30, and 3:30pm. (☎02 6801 4460 Open daily 9am-4:30pm. $15, students and concessions $12, children $5. MC/V.) The **Western Plains Cultural Centre,** 76 Wingewarra St., is the Dubbo region's newest gallery and museum. (☎02 6801 4444. Open M and W-Su 10am-4pm. Free.) For a half-day trip from Dubbo, head south to Parkes to see the famous 64m diameter radio telescope dish. Made famous by the movie *The Dish*, this telescope has found over 1400 pulsars and helped work out the shape of our galaxy. (Turn off for the Parkes Radio Dish, 100km on the Newell Hwy from Dubbo, and drive in 6km. ☎02 6861 1770; www.csiro. au/parksdish. Free admission. Great film screenings; $6.50, children $5.)

# COONABARABRAN ☎02

Find answers to universal questions in the "Astronomy Capital of Australia," Coonabarabran (coon-a-BAR-a-bran; pop. 3000). Home to observatories and the country's two largest telescopes, the town is halfway between the lights of Melbourne and Brisbane, making it a great place to appreciate night skies.

**▐▀ ▐ TRANSPORTATION AND PRACTICAL INFORMATION.** Coonabarabran lies 159km northeast of Dubbo, 120km south of Narrabri and 182km west of Tamworth on the Newell Hwy. It's accessible from the northeast through Gunnedah, 105km away on the Oxley Hwy., which joins Newell Hwy. Countrylink (☎13 22 32) runs **buses** from the visitors center to Lithgow, where they connect with the train to Sydney (8hr., M-F and Su 1 per day, $65). Greyhound Australia (☎13 14 99 or 13 20 30), also at the visitors center, services Brisbane (10hr., Th-Su 9am, $134) and Melbourne (14hr., W-Sa 5:50pm, $154). **Teed Up Travel,** 79 John St., will book transport for a $5.50 fee. (☎02 6842 1566. Open M-F 9am-5pm, Sa 9am-noon.) For **taxi service,** try **Satellite Taxis** (☎1800 421 113).

The clock tower marks the intersection of John St. (Newell Hwy.) and Dalgarno St., which leads west to the observatories and Warrumbungle National Park. The **Visitor Information Centre,** at the south end of town on the Newell Hwy., has a display on Australian megafauna, including the skeleton of a 33,500 year-old giant diprotodon, the largest-ever marsupial. (☎02 6849 2144 or 1800 242 881; www.warrumbungleregion.com.au. Open daily 9am-5pm.) Other services include **ATMs** and a **library** on John St. (☎02 6842 1093. Free Internet. Email and chat $2.75 per 30min. Open M 10am-1pm, Tu-F 10am-5:30pm, Sa 9:30am-noon.) The **police station** (☎02 6842 7299) is on the southeast corner of John and Dalgarno St. The **post office** is right in the center of town at 71a John St. (☎02 6842 1197. Open M-F 9am-5pm.) **Postal Code:** 2357.

🏠🍴 **ACCOMMODATIONS AND FOOD.** A number of B&Bs and farmstays are also available in Coonabarabran and the Warrumbungle area, with singles from $55; inquire at the visitors center. Book ahead during school holidays. The **Imperial Hotel ❸,** a pubstay at the corner of John and Dalgarno St., has cheap rooms with heated blankets. (☎02 6842 1023. Reception 7am-midnight. Check-out 10am. Singles $30; doubles $35, ensuite $42-60. Extra adult $20.) More expensive motel options line John St. Halfway between town and the entrance to Warrumbungle National Park, the new **Warrumbungles Holiday Camp ❶** is 12km west of the clock tower on Timor Rd. Look for the big yellow signs on your right. (☎02 6842 3400. Reception 8am-dusk. On-site volleyball net, pool, kitchen, and BBQ. Sites $13, powered $15, extra person $3.50. Bunkhouse beds $16-22; cabins $50.) At **John Oxley Caravan Park ❶,** 1km north of town on Oxley Hwy., the affable owners run a tidy park with BBQ. (☎02 6842 1635. Linen $8 per person, $10 for 2. Reception 7am-7pm. Sites for 2 $17, powered $21; extra person $8. Ensuite cabins $45; extra person $10. AmEx/MC/V.)

The **Woop Woop Cafe ❷,** at 10 John St. in the Acacia Motor Lodge, offers healthful breakfasts ($6-14) and gourmet dinners ($17-28) in a high-ceilinged room flooded with light. Enjoy their great service and the sticky date nut cheesecake for $6. (☎02 6842 4755. Open M-F 7-10am and 6-9pm, Sa 7-10am and noon-2pm and 6-9pm; in summer, lunch W-Su noon-2pm. AmEx/MC/V.) The **Golden Sea Dragon Restaurant ❷,** next to the visitors center, features a huge menu, a golden Buddha, and a very impressive gold-inlaid interior. (☎02 6842 2388. 2-course Traveler's Lunch Special $12. Open M-F noon-2pm and 5-10pm, Sa-Su noon-2pm and 5-11pm. MC/V.) A **Woolworths** supermarket is located at 35 Dalgarno St. (☎02 6842 3510. Open M-Sa 7am-9pm, Su 8am-8pm.)

🔆 **SIGHTS.** The **Siding Spring Observatory,** Australia's largest optical astronomy research center and site of recent breakthroughs—including the discovery of several extrasolar planets—is open for visitors. Grounds and observatory entry are free, but for a small fee ($5.50, children and concessions $3.50), the observatory **visitors center** offers an exhibit about the work of resident astronomers. A short walk from the center leads to a colorful photo collection featuring shots of distant galaxies taken by the on-site telescope. (☎02 6842 6211. Open M-F 9:30am-4pm, Sa-Su 10am-2pm.) For those interested a magnified view of the sky, **The Warrumbungle Observatory** hosts nightly star-gazing shows (Apr.-Sep. 7pm; Oct.-Nov. 7:30pm; Dec.-Jan. 9pm; Mar. 8pm. $12, students $5), and $5 solar viewings on the weekends at 2pm. (9km from the tower on the road to Warrumbungle National Park. ☎04 8842 5112; www.tenbyobservatory.com. Bookings required. Max. 10 people per showing. Cash only.) **Pilliga Pottery** specializes in applying bright glazes and native Australian designs to terracotta. This complex is an open workshop, store, cafe, and farm homestay all in one.

Drive 35km north of Coonabarabran along the Newell Hwy. The last 10km are unsealed. (☎02 6842 2239; www.pilligapottery.com.au. Open daily 9am-5pm.)

 **DARK SIDE OF THE MOON.** The best time of the month to see the stars is during a crescent moon. When the moon is full, its glow brightens the night sky, making it difficult to see distant nebulae.

Impressive sandstone caves, hollowed out by wind and water erosion, can be found in the Pilliga Nature Reserve. They are tricky to locate and are a sacred site for local Aboriginal groups, so check with the tourist office for more info.

## WARRUMBUNGLE NATIONAL PARK ☎02

The jagged spires and rambling peaks of the Warrumbungle Mountains are the result of ancient volcanic activity. Softer sandstone worn away under hardened lava rock has left unusual shapes slicing into the sky above the forested hills. Resident kangaroos, koalas, and wedge-tailed eagles frequently appear above and beside the park's excellent trails.

Warrumbungle offers a range of short walks and challenging multi-day hikes. **The Whitegum Lookout,** 7km before the park office, offers a spectacular view of the spiky skyline along an easy 500m walk through the shade of eucalyptus trees. The most popular long walk is the **Breadknife/Grand High Tops Circuit** (12.5km, 4-5hr., steep grade), which passes the 90m high dyke known as the Breadknife, a narrow rock formation whose peaks seem to form the serrated edge of a knife. **Gould's Circuit** is a less strenuous hike (8km, 3hr., medium grade) that offers a view of the Grand High Tops and a turnoff to the summit of Macha Tor. Ideal for those pressed for time, **Fan's Horizon** is the shortest path to the Grand High Tops' best vistas. This steady climb over 1000 steps brings you to a view of the Breadknife, Crater Bluff, and other landmarks. (3.6km, 2hr., easy).

A 75km **scenic drive** (3km unsealed) branches off from the Newell Hwy. 39km north of Gilgandra and runs through the park, eventually circling back to the highway at Coonabarabran. The park entry fee ($7 per car) can be paid at the **Warrumbungle National Park Visitors Centre,** on the park road 33km west of Coonabarabran. The newly renovated Centre has informative displays and also provides free bush camping and rockclimbing permits for most peaks, though not Breadknife. (☎02 6825 4364. Open daily 9am-4pm.) On school holidays or by prior arrangement, the visitors center also offers informative and interesting **Discovery walks, talks, and tours** with Aboriginal guides. Tours include a **Tara Cave Walk, Breakfast with the Birds,** and a trip to the Sandstone Caves. Prices vary from $5 to 20 depending on the tour. Book with the visitors center.

The park has four camping areas (most without showers). **Camp Blackman ❶** is car-accessible and has toilets, hot showers, laundry tubs, and a pay phone, but bring your own drinking water. ($5, children $3; powered $10/4). Toilets and unpowered sites ($5, children $3) are available at **Camp Wambelong ❶,** accessible by car from both from the main park road and an unsealed road from Tooraweenah. **Camp Pincham ❶,** the start of the Breadknife hike, lies a short walk from a carpark and has toilets and unpowered sites ($5, children $3). Bring your own firewood or pack a fuel stove. Contact the visitors center for information on free bush sites and accommodations for large groups.

# NARRABRI ☎02

The roads to Narrabri (NEHR-uh-brye, meaning "forked waters;" pop. 7200) are lined with tufts of cotton, the region's "white gold." The town, equidistant from Sydney and Brisbane (560km) and 120km north of Coonabarabran on the Newell Hwy., is home to the new Australian Cotton Centre museum with exhibits about high-tech cotton production. Fiber facts may not interest you, but Narrabri is also conveniently close to the Southern Hemisphere's largest radio telescope array and the rugged beauty of Mt. Kaputar National Park. This is Australia's Big Sky country: watch the sunset with streaks of pink and orange as the sky fades from blue and lavender to pitch black.

**TRANSPORTATION AND PRACTICAL INFORMATION.** Countrylink (☎13 22 32) **trains** run to Sydney (8hr., 1 per day 9:25am, $84) from the station at the east end of Bowen St., four blocks from Maitland St. Greyhound Australia (☎13 14 99 or 13 20 30) **buses** leave for Brisbane (8hr., 1 per day 11am, $107) and Melbourne (17hr., W-Sa 2:50pm, $178) via Coonabarabran (2hr., 1 per day, $32) and Dubbo (4hr., W-Sa 3:50pm, $51). On the east side of town is Maitland St., which runs parallel to Tibbereena St. (Newell Hwy.), and traces the Narrabri Creek. The **Narrabri Visitors Centre** is opposite Lloyd St. on Tibbereena St., which veers north along the Creek. (☎02 6799 6760 or 1800 659 931. Open M-F 9am-5pm, Sa-Su 9am-2pm.) The **NPWS office,** 100 Maitland St., Level 1, offers info about outdoor activities. Enter around the corner on Dewhurst St. and go up the stairs. (☎02 6792 7300. Open M-F 8:30am-4:30pm.) The **post office** is at 140 Maitland St. (☎02 6799 5999. Open M-F 9am-5pm.) **Postal Code:** 2390.

**ACCOMMODATIONS AND FOOD.** Many of the pubs along the central stretch of Maitland St. offer inexpensive accommodations, and there are a number of motels on the highway leading into town. The **Dulcinea Holiday Retreat ❺,** on Mt. Kaputar Rd., has two cabins just 20km from the top of the mountain. Peacocks roam the property's gardens. Be sure to call ahead; they're likely to be booked. (☎02 6793 5246. Twin cottages $75. Cash only.) **BigSky Caravan Park ❶,** on Tibbereena St. just up the road from the visitors center, is next door to a community pool available for guest use ($2) in the summer. There are only four cabins, so call ahead. (☎02 6792 5799. Reception daily 8am-8pm. Tent sites for 2 $18, powered $21; ensuite cabins $57. Extra person $6. MC/V.) **The Tourist Hotel ❸,** 142 Maitland St., offers simple rooms, each with its own TV. Many workers stay here. (☎02 6792 2312. Singles $30; doubles $45, ensuite $55. MC/V.) Several B&Bs and farmstays are also available. **Dawsons Spring Camping Area ❶** is 21km inside, near the Mt. Kaputar summit, and has hot showers, toilets, and BBQ ($5, children $3); bring your own firewood. The **cabins ❺** each have four beds, a kitchen, and shower; a great deal for families or groups. (Book ahead at the NPWS office ☎02 6792 7300. $77; min. 2-night stay.)

Enjoy an outback meal ($10-25), complete with realistic thunderstorms every half-hour, at the authentically decorated **Outback Shack Bar and Grill ❷** at the RSL, 7 Maitland St. (☎02 6792 1202. Open daily noon-2pm and 6-9pm. MC/V.) Freshly baked bread at **Watson's Kitchen ❶,** 151 Maitland St., can be smelled halfway down the street. Stop in for a sandwich ($3-7), gelato, or pastry. (☎02 6792 1366. Open M-F 6am-6pm, Sa 6am-1pm, Su 7am-noon.) **Woolworths,** at 173 Maitland St., sells groceries. (Open M-F 7am-10pm, Sa 7am-9pm, Su 8am-8pm.)

**ACTIVITIES.** Narrabri's newest attraction is the **Australian Cotton Centre,** located next to the visitors center on the Newell Hwy. The center has interactive exhibits including a 3D theater and a giant cotton-picking machine. A self-guided tour takes you "from field to fabric" and explains the crop's varied uses, anywhere from textiles to explosives. (☎02 6792 6443 or 1300 663 853; www.australiancottoncentre.com.au. Open M-F 8:30am-4:30pm, Sa-Su 9am-2pm. $8, concessions $7, children $5.50, families $19.) Signs on the Newell Hwy. heading southwest toward Coonabarabran lead to the **Australia Telescope,** 24km west of Narrabri. This set of six large dishes comprises the largest, most powerful array of radio telescopes in the Southern Hemisphere. Interactive displays show how radio waves can be used to make visible images and explain how radio telescopes can "see" objects that normal optical telescopes cannot. The 22m diameter dishes are fenced off, but you can pick up radio waves emitted by the sun using a hand-operated telescope. (☎02 6790 4070. Open daily 8am-4pm. Free.) East of Narrabri, the peaks of the Nandewar Range beckon travelers to leave the road and scale the summit of **Mount Kaputar,** from which one-tenth (80,000 sq. ft.) of the entire state of New South Wales can be seen. The entrance to the central section of **Mount Kaputar National Park** lies 31km east of Narrabri; head south on Maitland St. and Old Gunnedah Rd. and continue for 20km. The park's most famous attraction is ◧**Sawn Rocks,** a basalt rock formation that looks like a pipe organ. It's in the northern section, accessible from the Newell Hwy. north of Narrabri (30min. drive northeast and 15min. walk from the carpark; not accessible from the rest of the park). Try the NPWS office in Narrabri for pamphlets on walking tracks and hiking info. The roads to and within the park are mostly unsealed, but generally 2WD-accessible; call the NPWS office (☎02 6792 7300) for conditions. **Pilliga Hot Artesian Bore Baths,** 100km west of Narrabri towards Wee Waa and then Pilliga (12km unsealed road), offer simple but free 37° hot baths. (☎02 6799 6760. Free entry and camping.)

# OUTBACK NEW SOUTH WALES

The heart and soul of the continent is its legendary outback interior, an expanse that begins where cities end. Fittingly, the empty stretches of northwest New South Wales are sparsely populated, difficult to reach, and largely untouched. The emptiness is so far-reaching that the curvature of the earth is often visible. Those intrepid few who venture into these arid lands can brag that they've been "Back o' Bourke," a small town that lies on the Mitchell Hwy. (Hwy. 71), 367km northwest of Dubbo and 142km south of the Queensland border.

# BROKEN HILL ☎08

Lying somewhere between the middle and the edge of nowhere, historic Broken Hill has authentic outback character. Located 1167km west of Sydney, the remote town came into being in 1883 when young Charles Rasp, along with six other surveyors, realized that an odd-looking craggy butte was in fact the biggest lode of silver-lead ore in the entire world. Almost overnight, over 20,000 fortune-seekers flocked to this "broken hill," even though work in the mines was frequently fatal and conditions in the burgeoning town were tough. Today, though mining continues in the local ore deposits, the town has also attracted artists, fascinated by the contrast between the land's natural beauty and the machines created to exploit it. This curious fusion of gritty labor, innovative art, and geographical isolation has made for an unusual town.

## ▐ TRANSPORTATION

While transcontinental trains chug through on a regular basis, buses and planes are limited. For any transportation queries, contact the visitors center or visit the helpful **Jetset Broken Hill** at 380 Argent St. (☎08 8087 8175).

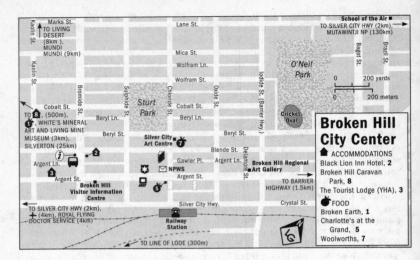

**Broken Hill City Center**

🏠 ACCOMMODATIONS
Black Lion Inn Hotel, **2**
Broken Hill Caravan Park, **8**
The Tourist Lodge (YHA), **3**

🍴 FOOD
Broken Earth, **1**
Charlotte's at the Grand, **5**
Woolworths, **7**

**Air:** The **Broken Hill Airport** is located 6km south of the CBD. **Rex Airlines** (☎13 17 13; www.rex.com.au) offers frequent flights from Adelaide (1hr., daily, $145) and Sydney (2hr., daily, $231).

**Trains:** The **train station** (☎08 8082 2550; desk open M-F 8am-5pm) is on Crystal St., near the intersection with Chloride St. **Great Southern** (☎13 21 47) runs the famous **Indian Pacific** train across the nation. Trains to Sydney depart every Tu and F at 6:30pm and arrive at 10:15am the next day (1-way $235, discounts for students and concessions vary). Trains from Sydney depart for Broken Hill on W and Sa at 2:55pm. Trains heading west to **Perth** and **Adelaide** depart every Th and Su at 8:20am and arrive at 3:05pm in Adelaide ($115, with discounts available) and in Perth approximately 2 days later ($495, with discounts available). **Countrylink's Outback Explorer** (☎13 22 32; www.countrylink.com.au) trains run daily to **Sydney**, though passengers leave in a coach at 3:45am with a 1hr. stop in **Dubbo** where passengers switch to the train ($145, with discounts available). On Tu, a direct train departs Broken Hill at 7:45am for the same price. Trains arrive from Sydney daily 8:50pm, Tu 7:10pm.

**Buses:** The **bus depot** (☎08 8087 2735; open M-F 9am-4pm) is just outside the visitors center (where tickets are sold), at the corner of Blende and Bromide St. **Buses R Us** (☎08 8262 6900; www.busesrus.com.au) offers service to and from Adelaide (7hr.; 1-way $78, round-trip $140; students $64/120; 3 buses weekly) and Mildura (3½hr.; $55/99, student $45/85; 3 buses weekly).

**Local Buses: Murton's Citybus** (☎08 8087 3311; office open M-F 8:30am-5pm) runs 4 routes through greater Broken Hill. M-F 8:30am-5pm, Sa only the Southern and Hillside routes. Timetables at the visitors center.

**Taxis: Yellow Radio Cabs** (☎13 10 08). **Independent Taxis** (☎08 8087 7744).

**Car Rental:** Expect to pay more than $65 per day. Try **Avis,** 195 Argent St. (☎08 8087 7532) or **Hertz** (☎08 8087 2719), at the visitors center.

**Bike Rental:** The **YHA Tourist Lodge** (☎08 8088 2086) rents bikes for $15 per day.

NEW SOUTH WALES

## PRACTICAL INFORMATION

**Tourist Office: Broken Hill Visitors Information Centre** (☎08 8080 3560; www.visit-brokenhill.com.au), corner of Blende and Bromide St. From the railway station, turn left onto Crystal St. and walk 2 blocks west, then turn right onto Bromide St.; the office is 2 blocks down on the left. The extremely helpful staff can answer any inquiries and assist with booking a multitude of outback activities. Be sure to pick up Broken Hill's comprehensive **visitor's guide** as well as the invaluable **Wide Canvas Country brochure,** which beautifully depicts the oddities of the region. Open daily 8:30am-5pm.

**Tours:** A wide variety of tours are available from several tour operators venturing to Silverton, the Living Desert Sculptures, nearby national parks, outback safaris, other mining towns, and stations a bit farther afield. Book through the tourist office.

**National Parks Information: New South Wales National Parks and Wildlife Service (NPWS),** 183 Argent St. (☎08 8080 3200). Open M-F 8:30am-4:30pm. The **visitors center** (see above) has considerable information as well.

**Banks: ANZ,** 357 Argent St. (☎13 13 14), is right next to **Commonwealth,** 338-340 Argent St. (☎13 22 21). Both open M-Th 9:30am-4pm, F 9:30am-5pm. 24hr. **ATMs.**

**Police:** 252 Argent St. (☎08 8087 0299).

**Internet Access:** Free 1hr. access is available at the **Broken Hill Library** (☎08 8088 3317), on Blende St. Book ahead to avoid waiting for a terminal. Open M-W 10am-8pm, Th-F 10am-6pm, Sa 10am-1pm, Su 1-5pm.

**Post Office:** 260 Argent St. (☎08 8087 7071). Open M-F 9am-5pm. *Poste Restante* available; pickup at the window around the side of the building. **Postal Code:** 2880.

> **TIME WARP.** Broken Hill uses the phone code of South Australia (☎08), as well as its time zone. That means it's 30min. behind the rest of NSW.

## ACCOMMODATIONS

**The Tourist Lodge (YHA),** 100 Argent St. (☎08 8088 2086), near the bus depot and visitors center. Has a clean kidney-shaped swimming pool, which is a lifesaver in desert summers. Although the cooking facilities are limited, ample common space with TV and a ping-pong table will satisfy backpackers. All rooms have A/C and heat. Dorms $30; singles $40; twins and doubles $50 per person. 10% YHA discount. ❸

**Black Lion Inn Hotel,** corner of Blende and Bromide St. (☎08 8087 4801), located across the street from the visitors center and coach terminal. Clean, carpeted rooms are stocked with antique-looking armoires. All rooms have A/C, some with TV and fridge. Reception 9am-latenight. Singles $33; doubles $48. ❷

**Broken Hill Caravan Park** (☎08 8087, 3841), on the Barrier Hwy., just as it comes into town and becomes Rakow St. The park offers a pool, playground, Wi-Fi, and standard camping facilities. Unpowered for 1 $19, for 2 $22; powered single $23, double $26; extra person $6; cabins $70-90 for 2, extra $10. ❶

## FOOD

The gastronomic assortment in Broken Hill is generally limited to the greasy spoons along **Argent Street** serving filling portions for reasonable prices. The Centro Westside Plaza, located on Galena St. near Blende St., has a huge **Woolworths** supermarket (☎08 8088 1711; open M-Sa 7am-10pm, Su 8am-8pm ).

**NEW SOUTH WALES**

**Charlotte's at the Grand,** 317 Argent St. (☎08 8087 2230). An endearing cafe with backpackers in mind. Savory homemade meals are all under $12. Try the massive "Miner's Brekky" ($12; served all-day), which includes eggs, toast, bacon, sausages, and tomatoes. Open M-F 7am-5:30pm, Sa 7am-2:30pm, Su 6am-2:30pm. ❶

**Broken Earth** (☎08 8087 1318), on Federation Way. On top of the area's main mining lode; offers sweeping views of the town and surrounding terrain. A self-proclaimed "gourmet experience," the restaurant offers its own brand of wine and interesting dishes incorporating local game (dinner $30). Lunch 11:30am-2pm, dinner 6-10pm. ❹

## ◉ SIGHTS

A trip to the **information center** is practically imperative, as it's an excellent resource for activities within the town and throughout the region. Several self-guided walking tours are available for purchase at the bureau, and most activities can be booked through the center as well. Pick up Broken Hill's comprehensive **visitor's guide** as well as the excellent **Wide Canvas Country guide** (both free).

**LIVING DESERT RESERVE.** In 1993, the Broken Hill Sculpture Symposium commissioned a group of local and international sculptors to create sandstone works atop a hill. The masterful pieces combine Aboriginal, modern, and international influences, each one blending seamlessly into the surrounding landscape without losing its thematic particularities. They are all best viewed at sunrise and ◪**sunset,** when the light plays on the colors. A 1hr. walking trail loops from the sculpture site past gullies, ledges, and outback animals. *(From Argent St., turn left onto Bromide, left onto Williams, then right onto Kaolin. Head north 8km along the northern segment of Kaolin St. You can drive all the way up the hill by obtaining a gate key from the tourist office for $10 with a $20 deposit, but the 15min. hike from a nearby carpark is free.)*

**MUNDI MUNDI LOOKOUT.** The über-flat terrain viewed from the west-facing lookout offers one of the only places on the planet where you can actually see the curvature of the earth. Visits at sunset yield particularly impressive vistas. Head northwest toward Silverton and you'll pass the lookout after traveling about 9km.

**WHITE'S MINERAL ART AND LIVING MINE MUSEUM.** Former miner Bushy White and his wife Betty teach the history of Broken Hill mining through dioramas and demonstrations. Over 250 of White's delicate mineral art works use locally mined minerals to depict mining equipment and techniques as well as landscapes and assorted

## THE LOCAL STORY

### PRICKLY PROBLEM

Since Australia drifted off as its own island over 200 million years ago, the continent's plants and animals have evolved separately from those of the rest of the world. The separation allowed unique animals like the echnida and platypus to develop and survive, but it also made the Australian ecosystem extremely vulnerable to non-native species.

Even the simplest of species can cause massive ecological crises. The infamous bitou bush originally arrived in New South Wales as discharged ballast from a South African ship, but this plucky plant quickly took root and stabilized Australia's usually mercurial dunes. The delighted government deliberately introduced bitou along the eastern coast, hoping for similar results. However, by 1982, the bitou bush had engulfed more than sixty percent of the NSW coast. It was restricting access to beaches, destroying bushland, and displacing native species. The government responded by introducing bitou-eating insects, but some Aussies had a more "hands-on" solution. In 1972, Crowdy Bay National Park began a proud tradition of "Bitou Bashing," in which enthusiastic volunteers tear up and cut down bitou plants, painting any remaining stems with herbicide.

Despite these efforts, bitou still remains a problem on the eastern seaboard. Keep your eyes peeled for rogue bitou mounds among the sands of New South Wales.

Australiana. Oddly intermixed with the mine exhibits are religious portraits and a collection of over 1000 dolls and teddy bears, making for a whole so deliciously weird it's mesmerizing. The Whites are proud to announce that there is "truly something for everyone" at this museum of sundry knick-knacks. *(1 Allendale St., off Brookfield Ave., about 2km west of the CBD. ☎ 08 8087 2878. Tours upon request. Open daily 9am-5pm. Wheelchair-accessible. $4, families $10.)*

**ROYAL FLYING DOCTOR SERVICE.** A museum and inspirational 20min. film detail the history of this noble institution, which provides health care to many out-of-the-way Outback residents. The display is as genuine a display of day-to-day heroism as you'll find in today's world of tourism. Guided tours of the facilities, including a peek inside the airplane hangar, are worth the extra time. *(At the Broken Hill Airport. ☎ 08 8080 1714 or 8080 1777. Open M-F 9am-5pm, Sa-Su 11am-4pm. 1hr. tour $5.50, concessions $4.40, children $2.20, families $15.)*

**SCHOOL OF THE AIR.** The School of the Air provides education for schoolchildren in Australia's more remote regions. Visitors can observe lessons conducted via Internet and satellite from M-F, but must book at the **info center** (p. 261) the day before and be seated by 8:30am—demerits for tardiness. The proceedings give authentic insight into the quirks of bush and outback life. *(On Lane St., 2 blocks east of Iodide St. ☎ 08 8087 6077 for booking, or book at the visitors center; www.schoolair-p.schools.nsw.edu.au. 1hr. school sessions $4.40.)*

# GALLERIES

With close to 40 art galleries, Broken Hill is much more than just a mining town. The galleries vary greatly in size and theme; some are privately run workshops, others are larger gatherings of indigenous work from around the country. Don't miss out on the several public buildings throughout the town that feature beautiful murals and are definitely worth a peek.

**BROKEN HILL REGIONAL ART GALLERY.** This collection's seven galleries constitute the oldest regional gallery in the state, showcasing local and 20th-century Australian painting, sculpture, and photography. The gallery's signature piece, Silver Tree, is a delicate arboreal sculpture commissioned for the 1882 Royal Melbourne Colonial Exhibition. *(At Sully's Emporium on Argent St., across from Hungry Jack's. ☎ 08 8088 5491. Open daily 10am-5pm. Donations appreciated.)*

**SILVER CITY ART CENTRE.** The gimmick here is *The Big Picture*, the largest canvas painting in the Southern Hemisphere. Created by local artist Peter Andrew Anderson, it took over two years to paint. At 100m long and 12m high, the wraparound work depicts the greater Broken Hill Outback. The gallery also includes an active silver workshop. *(☎ 08 8088 6166. Open daily 10am-4pm. Gallery free; admission to The Big Picture $5.)*

**BUSH 'N' BEYOND.** Artists Wendy Martin and Ian Lewis share a studio but create different types of pieces using oil, pastel, and watercolor. Their themes include Australian landscape, still life, and wildlife. *(4 Argent St. off of Gossan St. ☎ 08 8087 8807. Open M-Sa 10am-5pm, Su 10am-4pm. Donations appreciated.)*

# DAYTRIP FROM BROKEN HILL

**SILVERTON.** Located 25km west of Broken Hill, eerie Silverton is less of a ghost town than a cluster of dilapidated cottages. When silver, zinc, and lead ore were discovered nearby in 1876, Silverton burst into existence. After only nine years of mining, the supply was gone. Nearby Broken Hill was just beginning to boom, so many miners rolled down the road to the new lode. Today, Silverton is home to a handful of artists, and over a dozen movies have been shot on the bizarre terrain. The **Daydream Mine**, located 13km off the road connecting Silverton with Broken Hill, offers regular 1hr. tours through this antiquated mine. Sturdy footwear is recommended. (☎08 8088 9700. $20, concessions $19, children $8, families from $49.) Grab a beer at the **Silverton Hotel** and check out a replica of the futuristic car from *Mad Max II*, which was shot in Silverton.

## MUNGO NATIONAL PARK

From Mildura, 110km of rugged unsealed road terminates at Mungo National Park, where the oldest evidence of human life ever recorded outside of Africa was discovered. Long before the age of written records, hunter-gatherer communities flourished on the banks of Lake Mungo, in the extreme southwest corner of present-day New South Wales. Today, the lake is dry (and has been for 18,000 years); and Mungo has undergone spectacular weathering. Sand dunes around the lake bed have eroded into strange, ethereal landforms, accelerated over the past hundred years by settlers' introduction of grazing sheep and foraging rabbits. From a distance, the grand ▧**Walls of China** look like the crumbling fortifications of an ancient empire. Even today, the white-washed dunes continue to reveal fossils and artifacts, including the ancient remains of Mungo Man and Mungo Lady. The archaeological information uncovered here has earned the Willandra Lakes area status as a UNESCO World Heritage Site.

>
> **MUDDY MUNGO.** Roads to and within Mungo National Park are unsealed and subject to weather conditions; call ahead to the NPWS (☎08 5021 8900). Warnings should be taken very seriously, as wet weather instantly turns the sand tracks into thick gooey mud. Visitors are advised to carry their own food, drinking water, and petrol.

The park's infrequently staffed **visitors center** has pamphlets with info on the park's history, visitor regulations, and the incredible 70km self-guided drive tour that allows visitors to see the diverse wonders of the park at their own pace. This is also the place to pay camping and vehicle fees. (Camping $5 per night, children $3.) Nobody monitors payment, so consider the fee a donation to keep up park maintenance. The small museum display in the visitors center is worth checking out before rolling on to the self-guided tour. Fossils from Lake Mungo, artifacts and explanations relating to regional Aboriginal culture, a few mock-ups of extinct fauna, and ecological projections give an evocative impression of the surrounding area's history.

Camping facilities are available at **Main Camp ❶**, near the park entrance, and at **Belah Camp ❶**, farther into the park on the drive tour. Both sites have toilets and tables, but wood fires are only allowed at Main Camp. Between November and March, however, fires may be banned entirely; check at the visitors center before lighting up. The **Mungo Lodge ❺**, on the park road just before the park entrance, is the only available accommodation that doesn't require "roughing it." Clean ensuite cabins with heat and A/C are available. (☎03 5029 7297; www. mungolodge.com.au. Reception 7:30am-8pm. Book ahead. Cabins $240.)

# NORTHERN TERRITORY

The Northern Territory (NT) looms large in the heart of both the Australian continent and the adventurous traveler. The region's size belies its extreme lack of population: accounting for a sixth of the continent's land mass, the NT only contains 1% of its population. Over half of these intrepid "Territorians" crowd into the capital city of Darwin, located on the territory's northern coast.

From the lush and tropical **Top End,** where cyclones and floods are of constant concern, to the **Red Centre's** dusty desert expanses, where a drop of rain has everyone talking, the Northern Territory stretches into the country's most extreme regions. Still, the weather isn't nearly as dramatic as the landscapes over which it looms. It is no surprise that people often say the land rules the people in these parts; according to Aboriginal legend, Earth was sculpted by rainbow serpents, monsters, and blue-tongued lizards.

Traveling through the NT is becoming easier as the infrastructure improves. **Kakadu and Litchfield National Parks** in the Top End and **Uluru** and **Watarrka** in the Red Centre are accessible once the vast distances between them are overcome. Still, a trek across the Northern Territory is a foreboding prospect, even with the arrival of sealed roads, cell phones, road-crisis hotlines, and regular supply transfers. Far-flung ancient sites remind visitors that the traditional Aboriginal owners of the land have been at home here for millennia.

## ◪HIGHLIGHTS OF THE NORTHERN TERRITORY

**BOAT** past 150m high Jim Jim Falls, through croc territory, to a white-sand beach, complete with emerald plunge pool in **Kakadu National Park** (p. 275).

**COWER** beneath **Uluru** (formerly referred to as Ayers Rock), a symbol of Oz's natural beauty to which all else is compared (p. 311).

**EXPERIENCE** Darwin's creative side at **Mindil Beach Market;** crafts, culture, and delicious food emerge in festive form to greet the Top End twilight (p. 273).

**ROCK OUT** at the 7m in diameter granite **Devil's Marbles,** one of nature's most unusual rock formations (p. 298).

# ▐ TRANSPORTATION

The Northern Territory's vast expanses make transportation a big concern. Darwin, Alice Springs, and Yulara are most-commonly reached by air. **Trains** are also an option; The Ghan (☎13 21 47; www.gsr.com.au) connects Darwin to Adelaide through Katherine and Alice Springs (see below). Fares in the Day/Nighter Class range from $355 to Alice Springs (students $225) up to $710 (students $450) for the entire length. Greyhound Australia (☎13 14 99 or 13 20 30) **buses** service most major tourist centers, but not the farther reaches of the national parks. Renting a car is the best way to see these areas, but it's also the most expensive. Many national chains have offices all over the NT; **Territory-**

# Northern Territory

ARAFURA SEA

Cobourg Peninsula
Bathurst Island
Melville Island
Van Diemen Gulf
GARIG NP

Timor Sea

**Darwin**
Oenpelli
Nhulunbuy
Gove Peninsula
Cape Arnhem

LITCHFIELD PARK
Batchelor
Adelaide River
Arnhem Hwy.
Jabiru
KAKADU NP
Arnhem Land
Central Arnhem Rd.
Aboriginal Land

Gulf of Carpentaria

Daly R.
Pine Creek
Jim Jim Falls
Kakadu Hwy.
Daly River
21
NITMILUK NP

Joseph Bonaparte Gulf

Katherine
BESWICK
Roper R.
Roper Bay
Port Roper
Groote Eylandt

Maranboy
Roper Hwy.
Victoria R.
Victoria Hwy.
Timber Creek
Victoria River Roadhouse
1
Larrimah
ALAWA
NGANDJI
Sir Edward Pellew Group
Vanderlin Island

Kununurra
1
TO BROOME (1000km)

GREGORY NP
Victoria River Downs
80
Top Springs
Daly Waters
Carpentaria Hwy.
Borroloola

Buchanan Hwy.
Dunmarra
87
Cape Crawford

Buntine Hwy.
Kalkarindji
Newcastle Waters
Elliot

Barkly Tableland
WAANYI/ GARAWA
Nicholson R.

96
HOOKER CREEK
Lake Woods
Renner Springs
Tablelands Hwy.

WARLMANPA

Central Desert
Three Ways
**Tennant Creek**
Barkly Hwy.
MURCHISON RANGE
Camooweal
TO MOUNT ISA (200km)

Tanami Desert
Rabbit Flat
Devils Marbles
Wycliffe Well
Wauchope
Lake Nash

ABORIGINAL LAND
KARLANTIJPA SOUTH

Barrow Creek
Sandover Hwy.

Lake Mackay
Yuendumu
YUNKANJINI
Ti-Tree
Clarke's Creek
Plenty Hwy.

Aileron
Plenty Hwy.
Jervois

Lake Neale
WATARRKA NP
Hermannsburg
FINKE GORGE NP
**Alice Springs**
**MACDONNELL RANGES**
SEE MACDONNELL RANGES MAP p. MMM.

Kings Canyon
Lake Amadeus
Docker River
Valley of the Winds
Yulara
**Uluru**
Lasseter Hwy.
Curtin Springs
Erldunda
Finke R.
*Simpson Desert*

ULURU-KATA TJUTA NP
Kulgera
87
Finke

Great Victoria Desert
SOUTH AUSTRALIA
TO COOBER PEDY (400km), ADELAIDE (1250km)

WESTERN AUSTRALIA
QUEENSLAND

0    100 miles
0    100 kilometers

SEE TOP END MAP p. MMM.

**Thrifty Car Rental** (☎1800 891 125) and **Budget** (☎13 27 27) are the cheapest but limit kilometers (100-200km per day, each additional km $0.25-0.32), whereas **Britz** (☎1800 331 454) offers unlimited kilometers and rents 4WDs to customers under 25. **Europcar** (☎13 13 90) offers sedans from $58 per day, not including kilometer charges. Each company allows one-way rentals—at a high fee.

Major tourist centers are accessible by sealed or gravel roads. You'll need a 4WD to venture onto dirt tracks; this is necessary to see many of the spectacular sights of Kakadu National Park and the MacDonnell Ranges. Furthermore, rentals are rarely insured for accidents on unsealed roads. Rental companies determine their own restrictions, even for 4WDs. If going to remote areas, ask for a **high-clearance 4WD** with two petrol tanks. Also, make sure the 4WD you rent is not so top-heavy that it could flip over in rough terrain driving. If going beyond the highways, bring lots of extra water, food, emergency materials (tire, tools, rope, jack, etc.), and check in with a friend, visitors center, or ranger station. HF radios, compatible with the **Royal Flying Doctor Service** (☎02 8238 3333; www.flyingdoctor.net), offer security for drives through remote areas where cellular phones and other radios don't work. Avoid driving at dusk and dawn, when kangaroos and wild camels loiter in the road. Road trains can be up to 50m long and often leave dust storms in their wake. It is dangerous to pass road trains. When venturing onto unsealed roads, be sure to call ahead for road conditions (☎1800 246 199); some tracks may be washed out entirely. For weather reports, call ☎08 8982 3826. The **Automobile Association of the Northern Territory** (AANT; ☎13 11 11) provides valuable assistance.

## DRIVING TIMES AND DISTANCES

| FROM DARWIN TO: | DISTANCE | APPROXIMATE TIME |
|---|---|---|
| Alice Springs | 1490km | 15hr. |
| Batchelor | 98km | 1hr. |
| Kakadu National Park | 260km | 3hr. |
| Katherine | 315km | 3hr. |
| Litchfield National Park | 130km | 1hr. |
| Pine Creek | 226km | 2hr. |
| Tennant Creek | 986km | 10hr. |

| FROM ALICE SPRINGS TO: | DISTANCE | APPROXIMATE TIME |
|---|---|---|
| Darwin | 1490km | 15hr. |
| Kata Tjuta (Mount Olga) | 500km | 5hr. |
| Katherine | 1177km | 12hr. |
| Tennant Creek | 504km | 5hr. |
| Uluru (Ayers Rock) | 460km | 4hr. |
| Watarrka (King's Canyon) | 330km | 4hr. |
| Yulara | 444km | 4hr. |

# DARWIN                                                    ☎08

Founded in 1839, Darwin (pop. 110,000) has survived two major disasters, one deliberate (a Japanese bombing sustained during WWII) and one natural (Cyclone Tracy, which struck Christmas Eve 1974). Each time, the resilient city rebounded, and Darwin has evolved into the administrative capital of the NT. Anywhere else in the world it would be just another small city, but Darwin is not anywhere else—it's the gateway to the splendor of the Top End.

Seasons here are divided only into the wet season ("the Wet"; Nov.-Apr.) and the desert-like dry season ("the Dry"; May-Oct.). While the Wet washes away much of the tourist traffic, Darwin is awash in backpackers and beer during the Dry. Active populations of travelers and migrant workers give Darwin a shot of youthful DNA, and the beachside city boasts an unexpectedly vibrant and lively nightlife scene. Meanwhile, for those looking to explore Top End's fabulous national parks, Darwin is a natural base camp. Many tour companies operate out of the town, making getting out into the great outdoors easy and economical. Modern Darwin can provide you with whatever you missed while exploring the Outback, be it museums, refined cuisine, or a rip-roaring party.

# ✈ INTERCITY TRANSPORTATION

## BY PLANE

**Darwin International Airport** (☎08 8920 1811) is about 10km northeast of the CBD on McMillans Rd.; from the CBD, take a left on Bagot Rd. off the Stuart Hwy. **Qantas,** 16 Bennett St. (☎13 13 13); **Virgin Blue** (☎13 67 89); **Jetstar** (☎13 15 38); and regional carrier Airnorth, at 24 Cavenagh St. (☎1800 627 474), fly to destinations within Australia. For transport between the city and the airport, the **Darwin Airport Shuttle** is your best bet. (☎08 8981 5066. $11, round-trip $20.) Most accommodations will reimburse patrons for the ride from the airport if you've made a reservation. **Taxis** (☎08 8981 3777) run to the airport for $25-35.

## BY TRAIN

**The Ghan** (☎13 21 47; www.trainways.com.au) runs twice a week, departing W at 10am and Sa at 9am for Adelaide, Alice Springs, and Katherine. One-way "Day/Nighter" fares range $69-450 for students and $80-710 for adults. Sleeper cabins can cost thousands of dollars. Book ahead.

## BY BUS

The **Transit Centre** is at 67-69 Mitchell St., between Peel and Nuttall St. (☎08 8941 0911. Open M-W 6-9:30am and 10:30am-2:45pm, Th-F 6-9:30am and 10:30am-1:45pm.) Greyhound Australia (☎13 14 99 or 1300 473 946) runs directly to: Adelaide (2 days, 1 per day, $557); Alice Springs (1 day, 1 per day, $295); Broome (1 day, 1 per day, $373); Katherine (4hr., 2 per day, $80); Tennant Creek (14hr., 1 per day, $213). It's cheapest, although not necessarily most convenient, to buy a Greyhound pass based on distance that allows for stopovers.

# ⚔ ORIENTATION

Darwin is on a peninsula, with the CBD in the southeast corner. The tree-lined **Esplanade** and the rocky **Lameroo Beach** run along the western edge of the peninsula. The hub of the backpacker district is the

**Darwin and Surrounds**

CASUARINA

Casuarina
Shopping
Centre

Beagle Gulf
(Timor Sea)

Progress Dr.

Dariban Rd.

Rocklands Dr.

Vanderlin Dr.

Rapid Cr.

Trower Rd.

Lee Point Rd.

McMillans Rd.

TO CROCODYLUS PARK (2km)

Dick Ward Dr.

Charles
Eaton Dr.

Marrara
Swamp

East Point
Reserve

Mangroves

Bagot Rd.

Henry Wrigley Dr.

DARWIN
AIRPORT

Vestey's
Beach

East Point Rd.

Ross Smith Ave.

Stuart Hwy.

Fannie
Bay

Museum
and Art
Gallery of
the NT

TO LITCHFIELD (112km)
& KAKADU (211km),
NATIONAL PARKS

Tiger Brennan Dr.

Cullen
Bay

Mindil
Beach

Botanic
Gardens

Charles
Darwin
NP

LARRAKEYAH

McMinn St.

DARWIN

Lameroo
Beach

Frances Bay

SEE CENTRAL DARWIN
MAP, P. 271

N

LG

0        1 mile
0     1 kilometer

Transit Centre on the heavily trafficked Mitchell Street, which runs parallel to the Esplanade. The Smith Street Mall, a pedestrian zone occupying the block between Knuckey and Bennett St., runs parallel to Mitchell St. at the southern end of the city. At the tip of the peninsula, Stokes Hill and the Wharf area offer several sights and can be reached via Hughes Avenue off the end of Smith St., or down the waterfront access pedestrian staircase and path connecting Kitchener Drive with Harry Chan Avenue Moving northeast out of the city, Daly St. becomes the Stuart Highway and heads to the airport. Smith and Mitchell St. both continue north of the CBD before converging with Gilruth Ave. at Lambell Terr., leading to Skycity Casino, Mindil Beach, and the Museum and Art Gallery of the Northern Territory.

# ▛ LOCAL TRANSPORTATION

**Buses: Darwinbus** (☎08 8924 7666) runs to suburbs and beaches along the major thoroughfares. The terminal is between Harry Chan Ave. and Bennett St. just south of the Smith St. Mall. Stops along Mitchell and Cavenagh St. $2 for 3hr., concessions $0.50. Tourcards allow unlimited travel for a day ($5) or a week ($15).

**Taxis: Darwin Radio Taxis** (☎13 10 08).

**Car Rental:** Rental companies abound in Darwin, but demand frequently outstrips availability in the Dry, so make sure to book several weeks in advance. Always ask your rental company which roads are prohibited by your contract before setting out; even a 4WD can be banned from specific regions if road conditions are particularly poor. Sedans from $70 per day and small 4WDs from $170 per day, including 100km per day and $0.27 per extra km. Damage liability can usually be reduced for an additional daily surcharge. Rates and deals can vary widely, however. Large agencies include: **Avis,** 145 Stuart Hwy. (☎08 8981 9922); **Budget,** 3 Daly St. (☎08 8981 9800), at the corner of Doctors Gully Rd.; **Hertz** (☎08 8941 0944), at the corner of Smith and Daly St.; and **Territory Rent-a-Car,** 64 Stuart Hwy. (☎08 8924 2456). **Europcar,** 77 Cavenagh St. (☎08 8941 0300), offers good base rates (from $39 per day) and charges per km, while unlimited km are available at **Britz,** 44-66 Stuart Hwy. (☎08 8981 2081), and **Advance/Nifty,** 86 Mitchell St. (☎08 8981 2999 or 8941 7090). Europcar rents sedans to those over 21, but you must be 25 for a 4WD. The minimum age for rental is 21 at Britz and **Apollo** (☎08 8942 1255 or 1800 777 779, www.apollocamper.com), 75 McMinn St. Most major chains offer 4WD options, and Britz rents 4WDs with sleeper compartments ideal for long treks into the bush.

**Buying and Selling Used Cars:** The **Auto Barn,** 13 Daly St. (☎08 8941 7700 or 1800 674 374; www.travellers-autobarn.com.au), caters to backpackers. Sellers pay $40 per week to use the lot, but buyers can browse the merchandise for free. Cars sell fastest May-Oct. Open M-F 9am-5pm, Sa 9am-1pm. Also check with bulletin boards at hostels and Internet cafes for more auto options. Registration requirements vary for each state. See **Buying and Selling Used Cars, p. 31.**

**Automobile Club:** The **Auto Association of the Northern Territory (AANT),** 79-81 Smith St. (☎13 11 11). Open M-F 9am-5pm.

**Bike Rental:** Available through most hostels (average $5 per hr., $20 per day).

# ▟ PRACTICAL INFORMATION

## TOURIST AND FINANCIAL SERVICES

**Tourist Office: Tourism Top End,** 6 Bennett St. (☎08 8980 6000). Open M-F 8:30am-5:30pm, Sa-Su 9am-3pm. The main office of the **Parks & Wildlife Commission of the Northern Territory** (☎08 8999 4518; www.nt.gov.au/nreta/parks) is in Palmerston.

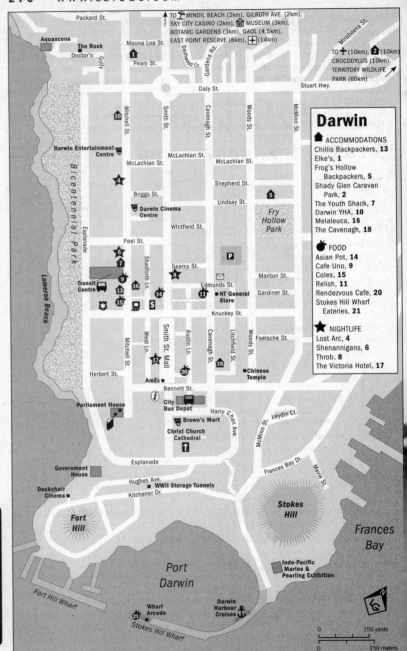

**Budget Travel:** Tours can be booked from many locations on Mitchell St. or the Smith St. Mall. **Flight Centre,** 24 Cavenagh St. (☎13 16 00; www.flightcentre.com.au), guarantees to beat any quoted airfare price. Open M-F 9am-5:30pm, Sa 9am-2pm.

**Currency Exchange: Bank South Australia,** 13 Knuckey St. (☎13 13 76). Open M-Th 9:30am-4pm, F 9:30am-5pm. **Westpac,** 24 Smith St., has an AmEx agency inside (☎13 20 32; AmEx ☎1300 139 060). Open M-Th 9:30am-4pm, F 9:30am-5pm.

## LOCAL SERVICES

**Backpacking Supplies: NT General Store,** 42 Cavenagh St. (☎08 8981 8242), at Edmunds St., has everything you need for the outdoors. Open M-W 8:30am-5:30pm, Th-F 8:30am-6pm, Sa 8:30am-1pm.

**Book Exchange: Read Back Book Exchange** (☎08 8981 8885), next to Star Village in Smith St. Mall. Open M-F 9am-6pm, Sa 9am-4pm, Su 10am-3pm.

**Work Opportunities: Backpacker Job Centre,** 69 Mitchell St., Shop 20 in the Transit center (☎08 8941 6969). **Grunt Labor Services** (☎08 8941 3700).

### MEDIA AND PUBLICATIONS
**Newspapers:** *NT News* (daily; $1.30); *Darwin Sun* (W).
**Entertainment:** The *Top End Visitors' Guide* monthly; *Arts Darwin* monthly; Entertainment section of *NT News* (W and F).
**Radio:** Rock, Triple J 103.3 and HOT-100 101.1 FM; News, ABC 105.7 FM.

## EMERGENCY AND COMMUNICATIONS

**Emergency:** ☎000.

**Hospital: Darwin Private Hospital** (☎08 8920 6011, after hours ☎08 8920 6055) and **Royal Darwin Hospital** (☎08 8922 8888), north of Darwin on Rocklands St.

**Police:** (☎08 8922 1503), Mitchell Centre, corner of Mitchell and Knuckey St. 24hr.

**Crisis Lines: General** ☎1800 019 116; **Sexual Assault** ☎08 8922 7156.

**Internet Access: Northern Territory Library** (☎08 8946 1434), in the Parliament building at the corner of Mitchell and Bennett St. Open M-F 10am-6pm, Sa-Su 1-5pm. Free Internet access, though not intended for long email sessions. Mitchell St. has many Internet cafes. Hostels also offer Internet at competitive rates (from $4 per hr.)

**Post Office: General Post Office Darwin,** 48 Cavenagh St. (☎13 13 18). *Poste Restante* held 30 days. Open M-F 9am-5pm, Sa 9am-12:30pm. **Postal Code:** 0800.

# ACCOMMODATIONS

Many of Darwin's hostels and budget accommodations are clumped around the Transit Centre on Mitchell St.; their offerings are pretty standard. High-end (and occasionally overpriced) accommodations sit along the Esplanade. For better prices, try the spots along Smith and Cavenagh St. Book ahead in the Dry; discounts are often offered in the Wet. During the Dry, many hostels have maximum stay limits, preferring short-term residents likely to book tours.

Camping options in central Darwin are limited. Camping and sleeping in cars is strictly forbidden around the Mindil Beach area. The **Shady Glen Caravan Park ❸** is closest to the city, about 10km from central Darwin at the intersection of the Stuart Hwy. and Farrell Cres. Patrons here are treated to a pool, kitchen, BBQ, and laundry. (☎08 8984 3330; www.shadyglen.com.au. Powered sites $29.50, $13.50 per extra person.)

**Melaleuca on Mitchell,** 52 Mitchell St. (☎08 8941 7800; www.momdarwin.com). MoM has 2 decks, a tiered pool, a hot tub with waterfall, and an undeniable energy emanating from its 2nd story poolside bar. Parties, movie nights, and BBQs spice up the week for guests, who rarely spend time in their small rooms. Bar open noon-midnight (happy hour 4-7pm). Key/linen deposit $20. Cutlery deposit $10. Dorm beds $20-30; doubles $65-115; 4-bed ensuites $95-150. YHA/VIP/NOMADS discounts. ❷

**The Cavenagh,** 12-16 Cavenagh St. (☎08 8941 6383). The best backpacker deal in town. Dorm rooms surround a central pool area. Its **restaurant** ❸ is open daily 11:30am-9pm. Meals $15-27. Internet $4 per hr. Key, cutlery, towel deposits $10 each. Bike rental $20. Su live band. All rooms ensuite with TV. 8- or 12-bed dorms $20-22; 4- or 6-bed dorms $22-27; doubles $109-159. ❷

**The Youth Shack,** 69 Mitchell St. (☎1300 792 302), next to the Transit Centre. Sparklingly clean and efficient—the most liveable of Darwin's downtown hostels. Independent, international crowd and competent staff. A/C, pool, kitchen, dining area, sun deck, and TV rooms. Lockers and luggage storage. Laundry $4. Internet $4 per hr. Reception 6am-10pm. Dorms $29; doubles $77. YHA $1 discount. VIP/YHA/ISIC discount. ❷

**Chillis Backpackers,** 69a Mitchell St. (☎08 9841 9722 or 1800 351 313; www.chillis.com.au). Chill with hip, friendly backpackers in the 2 hot tubs. Youth Shack pool available. Breakfast included. Internet access. Key, linen, and cutlery deposit $30. Clean and comfortable 4- and 8-bed dorms $28; doubles $77. VIP/YHA/ISIC discount. ❷

**Elke's,** 112 Mitchell St. (☎08 8981 8399), a 10min. walk from downtown. Caring staff lends a relaxed feel to this beautiful hostel with large outdoor spaces and a pool surrounded by lush greenery. 4-bed dorms $22-33; twins and doubles $65-80. YHA. ❷

**Frogs Hollow Backpackers,** 27 Lindsay St. (☎08 8941 2600 or 1800 068 686; www.frogs-hollow.com.au), 10min. from the Transit Centre. A good walk from the CBD. Solid backpacker-style facilities amid palm trees. Breakfast included. Lockers, luggage storage, and safe. Laundry. Internet $5 per hr. Key, linen, and cutlery deposit $20. Most rooms have A/C, pool, spa, spacious kitchen, and TV area. Reception 6am-9pm. Dorms $22-33; twins and doubles $80, ensuite $110. VIP/YHA/ISIC $1 discount. ❷

**Darwin YHA,** 97 Mitchell St. (☎08 8981 5385; www.yha.com.au). Removed from the lively end of Mitchell, the YHA attempts to rally a social scene with W pasta nights and F BBQs, each of which includes a free drink from the bar next door. On-site parking. Pool. Reception 6am-10pm. All rooms ensuite with fridges. 8-bed dorm $21-23.50; 6-bed dorm $23-26; 4-bed dorm $27-30; doubles $74.50-83; family room $88-98. ❷

# ⬛ FOOD

Darwin has no shortage of places to eat, though good, low-cost options are hard to find. The food stalls inside the Transit Centre serve decent food at reasonable prices. The eateries at ▧**Stokes Hill Wharf** serve good portions for low prices. You can get anything from pan-Asian noodles and fish and chips (from $6.50) to crocodile and kangaroo burgers ($6-8.50) and steaks ($10-15). Choose your meal and take your food out to the picnic tables that overlook the water. **Mindil Beach Market** (see **Sights, p. 273**) overflows with delicious pan-Asian food ($6-10). The **Parap Market** is smaller, more mellow, and popular with locals. Take bus #4 to Parap Shopping Plaza. (Open Sa 8am-2pm.) The **Victoria Hotel** (see **Nightlife, p. 275**) lures backpackers with buffet-style plates of food (around $6). Groceries are available at **Coles,** on the corner of Mitchell and Knuckey St. (Open 24hr.) All restaurants listed below accept major credit cards.

**Relish,** 35 Cavenagh St. (☎08 8941 1900), across from the general store. The best sandwich joint in town. Devour one of their wild creations or invent your own for $7.50.

Try it toasted on one of their melt-in-your-mouth rolls, on focaccia, or wrapped and ready to go as a snack. Lots of vegetarian options. Open M-F 7:30am-2:30pm. ❶

**Rendezvous Cafe,** (☎08 8981 9231), Star Village at Smith St. Mall. At the south end of Smith St. A great Malaysian restaurant. Main courses $12-18. Open M-W 10:30am-2:30pm, Th-F 10:30am-2:30pm and 5:30-9pm, Sa 9am-2pm and 5:30-9pm. ❷

**Asian Pot** (☎08 8941 9833), up and to the left off Smith from Knuckey St., Shop 6 in Arcade. Scrumptious pan-Asian fare and the best laksa in the Northern Territory ($8). Vegetarian, noodle, and rice dishes ($8-12). Open M-Sa 10am-2:30pm. ❶

**Cafe Uno,** 69 Mitchell St. (☎08 8942 2500), next to the Transit Centre. Though it serves everything from gourmet pizzas ($18.50-26) to huge sandwiches ($12-15), Cafe Uno's specialty is breakfast. Try any of the eggs served with thick-cut toast ($11.50) while people-watching from the outdoor seating. Open daily 8am-late. ❷

# 👁 SIGHTS

For many visitors, Darwin is merely a pit stop for a pint and a party before heading out to the vast natural wonderland beyond. However, the city has some interesting sights of its own. Many are a long walk or moderate bike ride from the CBD. The underappreciated bus system (see **Local Transportation,** p. 269) is also an option. The **Tour Tub** rounds up passengers at major accommodations and on the corner of Smith and Knuckey St., and takes them to 10 popular sights from Stokes Hill Wharf to East Point Reserve, offering discount admissions to many sites. (☎08 8985 6322; www.darwintours.com.au. Operates daily 9am-4pm. Full-day pass $30; buy on bus.)

🏖 **MINDIL BEACH SUNSET MARKET.** This collection of arts, crafts, and food stalls showcases the creativity of Darwin's cosmopolitan populace, too-often buried by backpacker-wooing travel agencies and bars downtown. As the sun sets over the waves, musicians entertain the mingling, munching crowds while vendors hawk crocodile skulls, saris, and laksa from their booths. *(Heading away from the CBD, take Smith St. past Daly St. and turn right onto Gilruth Ave. at the traffic circle. Take the 30min. walk, or catch bus #4. Open Apr.-Oct. Th 5-10pm and Su 4-9pm.)*

**MUSEUM AND ART GALLERY OF THE NORTHERN TERRITORY.** An extensive gallery traces the development of Aboriginal art from some of the earliest known rock paintings to its current kaleidoscope of styles. Pictures and a short film reveal the devastation wreaked on the city by Cyclone Tracy. Neon-lit exhibits investigate the history of natural life in Darwin, from ancestral megafauna to today. Nearby is the less-thrilling **Fannie Bay Gaol,** with self-guided tours through the facility that served as Darwin's jail from 1883 to 1979. *(Museum is along the shore toward Vestey's Beach; turn left on Conacher St. off East Point Rd. Gaol is 1km farther on the right. Wheelchair accessible. ☎08 8999 8264. Open M-F 9am-5pm, Sa-Su 10am-5pm. Free.)*

**MINDIL BEACH AND VESTEY'S BEACH.** These sunny spots lie north of the city, just off Gilruth Ave. Mindil Beach is on the left behind the casino, and Vestey's Beach is just north of the museum. Though the water may seem tempting, these beaches are best for sunbathing. Box jellyfish warnings (see **Dangerous Species,** p. 66) apply from October to March, but stings have been recorded all months of the year. Saltwater crocs are also a year-round concern. *(Bus #4.)*

**PARKS.** The area around Darwin is full of tranquil parks. Just north of Daly St., the shaded paths of the **Botanic Gardens** wind through a series of Australian ecosystems: rainforest, mangroves, and dunes. The hearty gardens survived cyclones in 1897, 1937, and 1974. *(Entrances on Geranium St. off the Stuart Hwy. and just past Mindil Beach on the opposite side of Gilruth Ave. Wheelchair-accessible. Gates open 7am-*

*7pm.)* The **East Point Reserve,** on the peninsula to the north of Mindil and Vestey's Beach, beckons with picnic areas, plus croc-and-jelly-free swimming in Lake Alexander. Wallabies are often spotted, especially in the evening. *(Access from East Point Rd. 45min. bike ride from city. No bus service.)* Walking trails, picnic areas, and views of Darwin Harbour lie in wait at **Charles Darwin National Park.** *(Bennett St. eastbound becomes Tiger Brennan Dr. Follow for 5km to the park entrance. ☎ 08 8947 2305.)*

**CROCODYLUS PARK.** This research and education center holds rheas, iguanas, and other assorted critters in addition to the featured reptiles. Sure, you might encounter crocs in the wild, but they probably won't let you hold them and pose for a picture. Come during the feedings for real action. *(Take local bus #5, which operates M-F, then walk 10min. ☎ 08 8922 4500. Open daily 9am-5pm. Feedings and tours 10am, noon, and 2pm. $27.50, seniors $22, ages 3-15 $13.50, family $70. YHA 10% discount.)*

**TERRITORY WILDLIFE PARK.** Learn all about the NT's wildlife and ecosystems at this park. See dingoes, crocs, wallaroos, buffalo, wallabies, and raptors at the "birds of prey" show. Park is a 45min. drive from central Darwin, 46km down the Stuart highway and then 11km down the road toward the Cox peninsula. *(☎ 08 8988 7200; www.territorywildlifepark.com.au. Open daily 8:30am-6pm. Last entry 4:30pm. $20, students/concessions $14, ages 5-16 $10.)*

# 🏔 OUTDOOR ACTIVITIES

Darwin also offers a selection of gravity-defying adventures. At **The Rock,** on Doctors Gully Rd. next to Aquascene, climbing connoisseurs can tackle a variety of wall climbs in the old tanker. *(☎ 08 8941 0747. Bouldering sessions $11; climbing $25; includes boot and harness rentals. M, W, F-Su noon-6pm; Tu, Th noon-9pm.)* Go skydiving from 10,000 ft. with **Top End Tandems.** *(☎ 04 1719 0140. www.topendtandems.com.au. From $310.)* Cruises in Darwin's harbor on the **Spirit of Darwin** are also a popular way for visitors to get a new perspective of the city. *(Afternoon and evening cruises depart from the Cullen Bay Marina down Marina Boulevard, opposite Smith St. at the traffic circle where it meets Gilruth Ave. ☎ 08 8981 3711; www.spiritofdarwin.net. 2hr. Apr.-Oct. daily 1:40pm and 5:30pm. Fully licensed bar on board. $40, concession $36, children $18.)*

# 🎵 🌸 ENTERTAINMENT AND FESTIVALS

The 🪑**Deckchair Cinema,** on a beautiful spot overlooking the ocean, has a mixed program, ranging from blockbusters to lesser-known arthouse films. Enjoy a beer while sitting on canvas benches under the stars. *(In Wharf Precinct below Parliament House, near Fort Hill. ☎ 08 8981 0700; www.deckchaircinema.com. Open in the Dry only. Daily 7:30pm, occasional shows F-Sa 9:30pm. $13, concessions $10.)* The **Darwin Entertainment Centre,** 93 Mitchell St., puts on a variety of theatrical productions. Call the box office for same-day 50% discounts and free shows. *(☎ 08 8981 1222. Open M-F 10am-5:30pm and 1hr. before performances.)* **Brown's Mart,** 12 Smith St. *(☎ 08 8981 5522),* near Bennett St., hosts shows in one of Darwin's oldest buildings. The **Botanic Gardens Amphitheatre** has open-air performances in the midst of lush gardens.

Darwin celebrates the Dry with a number of festivals. The **Darwin Beer Can Regatta,** held off Mindil Beach in early August, is about more than just sailing. Teams of devout beer-chuggers use their empties to make vessels and race them across the harbor. Full of parties and horse races, the **Darwin Cup Carnival,** begins in July and ends with **Cup Day** in August (around the same time as the Territory's **Picnic Day**). On the second Sunday in June, the city's Greek population stages the **Glenti Festival.** Held on the Esplanade, it is a musical and culinary celebration of heritage. Annual **Gay Pride Week** festivities also arrive in late-June (www.darwinpride.com). **Australian Football League** games occur every weekend in the Dry. Check the newspaper for a schedule. As the dry season dwindles, Darwin goes for broke with the 17-day **Darwin Festival** in mid-August.

# NIGHTLIFE

Central Darwin is full of party-starved backpackers from the surrounding Outback. Pubs and clubs advertise aggressively and even accost you by the hostel pool. Unfortunately, Darwin city law requires latenight clubs to charge a cover on weekends, but it's generally only a modest sum. Some don't start charging until midnight, making it possible to dodge fees entirely with some planning.

**The Victoria Hotel,** 27 Smith St. Mall (☎08 8981 4011). A guaranteed party every night. Sexually charged backpacker bar with inexpensive liquors, brews (beers from $4), and 2 dance floors. Cover $10 after 11pm on weekends. Open daily 10am-4am.

**Shenannigans,** 69 Mitchell St. (☎08 8981 2100). Irish pub packs in boisterous patrons. Live music draws locals into a backpacking crowd. M karaoke. Tu trivia night. Happy hour 4:30-6:30pm. Live music most nights after 10pm. Open daily 11am-2am.

**Throb,** 64 Smith St. (☎08 8942 3435). Escape Top-20 blues and break it down at one of Darwin's hippest venues with a stylish, chill crowd. Pool tables, friendly staff, and the best music in town. Drag shows nightly at midnight. Cover $5. Open Th-Sa 10pm-4am.

**The Cavenagh,** 12-16 Cavenagh St. (☎08 8941 6383). Fewer peanuts and beers, more oysters and wine. Swanky lounge with an outdoor bar attracts fashionable locals and tourists. Things get wilder on Su, with a pool party 2pm-late. Open 24hr.

**Lost Arc,** 89 Mitchell St. (☎08 8942 3300). Chill in the packed interior. Open daily 6pm-4am. Next door, the deservedly-hyped Discovery showcases talented local DJs. Cover $10 after 10pm, $20 after midnight. Open F-Sa 9pm-4am.

# TOP END

A lush tropical crown atop the vast, arid interior, the winterless Top End enjoys perpetually warm weather. In the Dry, backpack-toting pilgrims descend on Darwin and use this island of civilization as a base to explore the region's prime natural wonders—**Kakadu, Litchfield,** and **Nitmiluk National Parks.** During the Wet, the trickle of travelers who brave this monsoon season are treated to biblical rains and surging waterfalls. Eternal summer has its drawbacks, however; the heat can get overwhelming, and mosquitoes enjoy the tropical climates, too.

# KAKADU NATIONAL PARK

Located 155km from Darwin along the Arnhem Hwy., Kakadu, Australia's largest national park at an enormous 19,804 sq. km, is internationally recognized for the sheer breadth of attractions contained within its borders. Kakadu contains ancient Aboriginal sites dating back as many as 50,000 years, and the park is one of the rare World Heritage sites that qualifies for both its environmental and cultural significance. That Indigenous Australians chose to paint animal likenesses on rock walls so long ago is not surprising given the wealth of creatures that have adapted to handle the park's seasonal extremes. Home to over 1600 plant species, Kakadu also contains at least 280 species of birds, 60 species of mammals, 75 species of reptiles, 25 types of frog, and at least 10,000

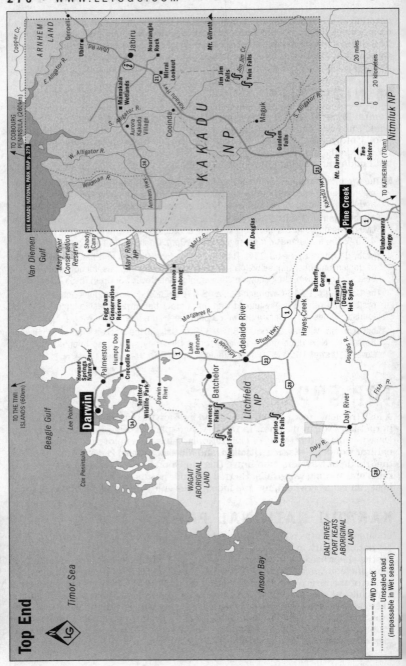

# Top End
## NORTHERN TERRITORY

varieties of insects, spread throughout a number of distinct ecosystems. Not all areas of Kakadu are accessible without permission. Land is systematically burned during the dry season, and group tours may be the only way for visitors without a 4WD vehicle to see some of the park's best sights. Still, the best way to experience Kakadu may be to explore the vast interior.

---

### KAKADU AT A GLANCE

**AREA:** 19,804 sq. km.

**FEATURES:** Stone country, floodplains of the Alligator River, the township of Jabiru.

**HIGHLIGHTS: Jim Jim** and **Twin Falls** (p. 282), galleries of Aboriginal rock art, sunset lookout points, riverboat cruises, 4WD treks to waterfalls, and plunge pools.

**GATEWAYS: Darwin** (p. 267) and **Pine Creek** (p. 288).

**CAMPING:** From free bushcamping to commercial campgrounds.

**FEES:** Free entrance. Additional fees are required for river cruises, Jim Jim tours, and Twin Falls tours ($159-79).

---

Intertwined with this awe-inspiring landscape is the living legacy of the Aboriginal community that resides in Kakadu. Aboriginal people have inhabited this land for approximately 50,000 years, but today the population has dwindled from the original European estimate of 2000 to a mere 400. The number of clans has likewise decreased from 20 to 12, and of the dozen languages once spoken here, only three survive. (However, the language of Gagudju, no longer spoken in Kakadu, lives on in the park's name.) Aboriginal people are active in the management and conservation of the park, and about 40% of the park's employees are of Aboriginal descent. Half of Kakadu is still owned by Aboriginal tribes that leased their land to the National Parks and Wildlife Service in 1978. Cultural sensitivity is a primary goal throughout the park, and the most sacred Aboriginal Dreaming sights remain off-limits to visitors.

---

 **TIP**

**WHEN TO GO.** Locals say they have a hard time describing wet-season Kakadu to dry-season visitors, and vice versa. Dry season, from April to October, is the most convenient and comfortable season in which to visit. Dry season temperatures are moderate (30˚C/86˚F highs and 17˚C/59˚F lows), and the humidity is low. It can get cold at night; travelers should carry an extra layer and repellent to ward off mosquitoes. Almost all roads are open except for a few unpaved ones. Check at the **Bowali Visitors Centre** for closures. Most camping, accommodations, and attractions operate during the dry season. Wet season dramatically alters the landscape with its monsoon rains and floods. Locals insist that the Wet is the most beautiful time of the year as the land teems with foliage and flowers. Still, the humidity, heat (35˚C/95˚F highs and 25˚C/77˚F lows), and bugs make the park harder to enjoy. The famous falls, particularly Jim Jim and Twin, are at their most powerful but can be seen only from the air. One bonus is that boat cruises run when Ubirr Rd. becomes a river (see **Sights and Hikes,** p. 282).

---

## 📂 TRANSPORTATION

Armed with *Kakadu National Park Visitor Guide and Map*, you can best see Kakadu in your own **car.** A 4WD is ideal, as it allows for a more personal, off-the-beaten-path experience. Renting a 4WD, however, is expensive, and rental companies might not allow access to certain sights even if the roads are open; check with them before you book. While ignoring rental rules may be tempting, companies have people report license numbers of rental cars seen on forbidden roads, so don't do it unless you're willing to risk a huge fine. A 2WD will get you to the top tourist destinations in the dry season, except Jim Jim and Twin Falls, which are prohibited even for 4WD rental vehicles. The only way to see Jim Jim and Twin Falls is on a tour or in a hardcore, non-rental 4WD.

**Flights: Jabiru Airport** (☎08 8979 2411), 6.5km east of Jabiru on the Arnhem Hwy., is the base for aerial tours of Kakadu. **Kakadu Air** (☎08 8979 2231) offers bird's-eye scenic flights of Kakadu ($120 for 30min., 195 per hr.). The **Scenic Flight Company** (☎08 8979 3432) also offers flights at comparable prices ($120 per 30min., $190 per hr.). Flights are popular during the Wet, since many roads are closed. Courtesy shuttles run between the airport and Jabiru.

**Buses: Greyhound** (☎1300 473 946) runs 3 buses per week to **Jabiru** ($59).

**Car Rental:** Rent out of Darwin if you can; options there are considerably cheaper. In Jabiru, **Territory Rent-a-Car** (☎08 8968 2552) is one option.

## ✈ ORIENTATION

Kakadu National Park is roughly rectangular. The two entries to the park are the **Arnhem Highway** in the north, which runs east-west, and the **Kakadu Highway** in the south, which runs northeast-southwest. These two paved roads converge in the park's northeastern interior near **Jabiru** (JAB-ber-roo; pop. 1100). The roads remain open year-round, except during severe floods. The park is divided into seven regions. Kakadu's north gate enters into the **South Alligator Region**. From here, the Arnhem Hwy. enters the **East Alligator Region** and arrives at Jabiru. and the Jabiru airport. To the north, the **Ubirr Road** runs to **Ubirr Rock.** The **Bowali Visitors Centre** is 5km from Jabiru to the southwest on the Kakadu Hwy. Running between Jabiru and Kakadu's south entrance, Kakadu Hwy. provides access to the remaining four regions, from east to west: **Nourlangie, Yellow Water, Jim Jim** and **Twin Falls** (4WD accessible only), and **Mary River.**

## ℹ PRACTICAL INFORMATION

**Tourist Office:** The **Bowali Visitors Centre** (☎08 8938 1120; www.environments.gov. au/parks/kakadu), 2km south of Jabiru on the Kakadu Hwy. A great 1st stop for all visitors, Bowali provides a thorough overview of the park, multi-day itineraries, maps, free permits for certain walks, and camping and cultural information. Bowali is also the only place in the park with cell phone reception. During the Dry, rangers give free daily talks and guided walks. Wheelchair-accessible. Open daily 8am-5pm. Just outside the park at the Southern Entrance and the Mary River Roadhouse is the **Goymarr Information Centre** (☎08 8979 6417), which is a privately owned Aboriginal Corporation that gives information about Kakadu as well as the local story, and can provide entry permits for Koolpin Creek. (Open daily 8:30-5pm in the Dry. Call for hours in Wet.)

**Tours: See Kakadu** (☎08 8979 3432), on Lakeside Dr. behind the Mobil, and **Kakadu Tours and Travel** (☎08 8979 2548), at Jabiru Plaza, can both book scenic flights, water cruises, and Arnhem Land and Kakadu 4WD tours. **Wilderness 4WD Adventures** specializes in tours geared toward fit nature-lovers with biology-savvy guides. (☎1800 808 288. 3- to 5-day tours $485-830.) **Kakadu Dreams** also offers 4WD safaris. (☎1800 813 266. 2- to 5-day safaris $350-6700.)

**Police and Park Rangers: Jabiru Police,** 10 Tasman Cres. (Emergency ☎000 or 08 8979 2122), across the street from Jabiru Plaza at the end of Flinders St. Ranger stations can relay information to the police and clinic from remote areas, but the stations open to the public only sporadically (daily 8am-4pm, but rangers are often away from

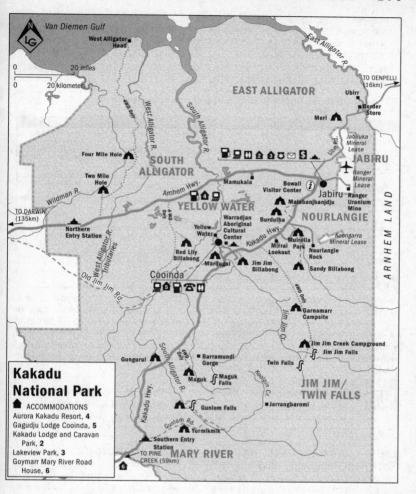

## Kakadu National Park

▲ ACCOMMODATIONS
Aurora Kakadu Resort, 4
Gagudju Lodge Cooinda, 5
Kakadu Lodge and Caravan
Park, 2
Lakeview Park, 3
Goymarr Mary River Road
House, 6

the office). Phone numbers are listed under the "Parks Australia North" entry in the phone book. A better bet is to find the nearest call box marked by an **Emergency Call Device (ECD)** pictogram on the free Kakadu Visitor Map. You will be immediately connected with emergency personnel. Boxes are located at the information bay on Arnhem Hwy., 17km from the western boundary of the park; they can also be found at various campgrounds (Waldak Irmbal, Gunlom, and Jarrangbarnmi), and at many of the more remote carparks (Jim Jim Falls, Twin Falls, and Maguk).

**Auto Services:** Fuel stations are at the **Aurora Kakadu Village, Jabiru, Cooinda,** and the **Mary River Roadhouse** at the south entrance. Jabiru's **Mobil** station (☎08 8979 2001) has auto repair. Open daily 6:30am-8:30pm.

**Banks: Westpac Bank** (☎08 8979 2432), at Jabiru Plaza, has **currency exchange** and a **24hr. ATM.** Open M-Th 9:30am-4pm, F 9:30am-5pm.

**Internet Access: Library** (☎08 8979 9459), at Jabiru Plaza. $3 per 20min. Open Tu 10:30am-5:30pm, W-F 10:30am-4:30pm, Sa 10:30am-1:30pm. **Kakadu Tours and Travel,** Jabiru Pl. $5 per hr. Open M-Sa 9am-5pm. **Gagudju Lodge Cooinda** (p. 280). $2 per 15min. Open 24hr.

**Post Office:** (☎08 8979 2727), at Jabiru Plaza. Operates out of Two Rivers News Agency. Open M-F 9am-5pm. **Postal Code:** 0886.

## ◢◣ KAKADU REGIONS OVERVIEW

| REGION | MAJOR SIGHTS | ACCOMMODATIONS | SERVICES |
|---|---|---|---|
| East Alligator | Ubirr, Guluyambi River Cruise | East Alligator Kakadu Hostel | Food and fuel at the Border Store |
| Jabiru | Bowali Visitors Centre | Kakadu Lodge and Cara-van Park, Lakeview Park | Food and fuel in Jabiru |
| Jim Jim/Twin Falls | Jim Jim/Twin Falls | Camping | None |
| Mary River | Gunlom, Barramundi Gorge | Mary River Road House | Food and fuel at Mary River Road House |
| Nourlangie | Nourlangie rock paintings | Camping | None |
| South Alligator | Mamukala Wetlands | Aurora Kakadu Resort | Food and fuel at Aurora Kakadu Resort |
| Yellow River | Gunlom Warradjan Aboriginal Cultural Centre, Yellow Water Cruise | Gagudju Lodge Cooinda (YHA) | Food and fuel at Cooinda |

## ◣ ◪ ACCOMMODATIONS AND FOOD

Aside from camping, Kakadu is sorely lacking in budget accommodations. Budget dorms generally leave much to be desired, and motel rooms are expensive, though prices generally drop in the Wet. Campsites tend to be situated in attractive spots with well-maintained, convenient facilities. However, sites with facilities are usually crowded in the Dry, and their close proximity to water means they swarm with mosquitoes. No matter where you go inside the park, bring your own food and plenty of water.

> **◢TIP◣ DRINKING WATER.** Clean, safe drinking water is available at **Bowali, Jabiru, Cooinda,** and **Aurora Kakadu Resort.** Rangers recommend boiling water from any other source, including the campgrounds listed below.

### JABIRU, NOURLANGIE, AND YELLOW WATER REGIONS

The Jabiru, Nourlangie, and Yellow Water regions are just a short drive from each other. **Lakeview Park ❺,** in Jabiru off Lakeside Dr., has rustic "bush bungalows" with canvas roofs, as well as two-bedroom cabins. (☎08 8979 3144; www. lakeviewkakadu.com.au. Bungalows $85-95, wet season $75; cabins $195/165.) Also in Jabiru, **Kakadu Lodge and Caravan Park ❷** is friendly, well-kept, and brimming with comforts such as a pool, A/C, linen, laundry, and a bistro. Occasional slide shows narrated by park rangers are a popular draw. (On the right on Jabiru Dr. before town. ☎08 8979 2422. Reception 7am-7:30pm in the Dry. Sites for 2 $26, $5 per extra person; powered $32/7; ensuite cabins with kitchens for 5 start at $200.) **Gagudju Lodge Cooinda (YHA) ❶,** down a 5km turn-off in the Yellow Water region, has motel rooms, a campground, and budget rooms. (☎08 8979 0145. Internet $2 per 15min. Sites for 2 $15, extra person $6.50; powered $35/7.50; dorms $35, YHA $31.50; budget doubles $80; motel doubles $280.)

The two standard-fee campsites ($5.40 per person) in the area have good facilities but are plagued by mosquitoes after dark. **Muirella Park Campground ❶,** is in Nourlangie, down a gravel turnoff 30km down the Kakadu Hwy. from

NORTHERN TERRITORY

Jabiru. **Mardugal Campground ❶** is 2km south of the turnoff for Yellow Water. Here you get shower, toilets, and amazing star-gazing. Free bush camping is available at **Sandy Billabong ❶**, just 5km of unsealed road past Muirella; **Jim Jim Billabong ❶**, on a 6km 4WD turnoff across from the Yellow Water turnoff; and **Malabanjbanjdju ❶** and **Burdulba ❶**, both around 16km south of the junction of the Arnhem and Kakadu Hwy. The last two camping areas give lovely views of Burdulba Billabong, but flies and mosquitoes can become unbearable at times.

Food and supplies are both available in Jabiru at the **Jabiru Plaza**. To get there, take a left on Castenzoon St. from Jabiru Dr. The **supermarket** is well stocked but expensive. (☎08 8979 2292. Open M-F 9am-5:30pm, Sa 9am-3pm, Su 9am-1pm.) The **Croc Bites Cafe ❷**, also in the plaza, has hot dishes for $9.50-14. (☎08 8979 2570. Open M 8:30am-7pm, Tu-F 8:30am-5pm, Sa 8:30am-2:30pm.) Farther south, **Gagudju Lodge Cooinda ❸** has petrol, basic groceries, and an on-site restaurant and bistro. (Restaurant open 6:30am-10am, 6pm-9pm. Breakfast $15-24, dinner $28-36. Bistro open 10:30am-9:30pm. Meals $17-29.) Petrol is also available at Cooinda and various places around Jabiru.

## SOUTH ALLIGATOR REGION

The impressive, well-run **Aurora Kakadu Resort ❺**, 40km west of Jabiru and 73km from the Northern Entry Station, has comfortable mattresses, A/C, laundry, and a swimming pool. (☎08 8979 1666 or 1800 818 845; www.aurora-resorts.com.au. Unpowered sites $12 per person; room for 2 $150-237; for 3-5 $214-325.) Just past the Northern Entry Station, a 4WD track extends north into the park. For 80km, it bumps its way to Van Diemen's Gulf. Along this road are two free, secluded campsites with refreshingly few campers. **Two Mile Hole ❶** and **Four Mile Hole ❶** are 8km and 38km from the Arnhem Hwy., respectively. They lack facilities but offer a peaceful place to pitch a tent right next to the Wildman River. Food, fuel, and beer can all be found at the Aurora Kakadu Resort.

## EAST ALLIGATOR REGION

**Merl Campground ❶** is 4km before Ubirr and has shaded sites ($5.40). Swarms of mosquitoes, however, make it inhospitable in the Dry. Alternatively, the more varied and cushy accommodations of Jabiru are a short half-hour drive away.

The **Border Store** has groceries, although it's only a short drive to Jabiru where there are both more supplies and lower prices. Buffalo, beef, or croco-

## LOCAL LEGEND

### WHAT'S IN A NAME?

You may not know it, but 'Strine has had a large impact on Australian pop culture.

**The Never-Never:** Although Never Never Land was introduced to a global audience by J.M. Barrie's *Peter Pan* and has since become associated with a dreamworld of child-like innocence, the term was originally coined to describe the remote regions of the Australian Outback. To this day, parts of Queensland and the Northern Territory are known by the moniker, and Aussie claims to the Never-Never have been immortalized in song and literature.

**Tasmanian Devil:** You may know it as a mischevious Looney Tunes character hidden in an omnipresent tornado of dust, but the real Devil is known less for its drooling destructive tendencies, instead earning its name through disturbing grunt-like bellows, rumored ill temper, dark color, strong odor emitted when under stress, and ferocious appearance. Interestingly, the carnivorous Devils are actually part of the marsupial family, along with the kangaroo and the koala.

**Van Diemen's Land:** Although popularly recalled in English and Irish folk songs—including a famous ballad written and recorded by U2's the Edge—this was the name that Abel Tasman bestowed upon Tasmania in 1642 to honor Anthony Van Diemen, the Governor-General of the Dutch East Indies.

dile burgers ($10) are all available at the store, and are good options if you're looking to inject some protein back into your diet.

## JIM JIM/TWIN FALLS REGION

Accommodations in this region are limited to a few campsites with well-kept facilities. **Garnamarr campground** ❶ is perhaps the best camping spot in the park, with few mosquitoes, a toilet, and views of the looming escarpment. It is located two-thirds of the way on the 4WD track to Jim Jim Falls. **Jim Jim Creek Campground** ❶, at the falls, is brilliantly located but often crowded. There are no services available along the 4WD track to the falls.

## MARY RIVER REGION

The only non-camping option in the Mary River region is just outside the park border. The **Goymarr Mary River Road House** ❶ is on the Kakadu Hwy., 11km from the Southern Entry Station. It is fairly priced, uncrowded, and has a pool, bar, and basic grocery store. (☎08 8975 4564. Reception 7am-8pm. Call ahead if arriving late and a staff member will wait for you. Sites $7 per person, children free; powered for 2 $25, extra person $7; bunks $17; budget rooms $40 per person; hotel doubles $100, family $140.) For bedding options further afield, **Pine Creek** (p. 288) is 59km south of the park entrance. Along the Kakadu Hwy. lie a few free campsites. **Maguk** ❶ and **Gungural** ❶ are roughly halfway from the southern entrance to Yellow Water. **Yurmikmik** ❶, perhaps the best of the bunch due to its slightly greater distance from water (and hence fewer mosquitoes), is halfway down the track to Gunlom, 24km north of the park's southern entrance. **Gunlom** ❶, meanwhile, has a small fee campsite by the falls ($5.40). Fuel, meals, and groceries are available at the roadhouse.

##  SIGHTS AND HIKES

Don't let Kakadu's subdivisions fool you: the most striking attractions (with the exception of Jim Jim and Twin Falls) are actually relatively close to each other. A route starting east of the Aurora resort at Mamukala and moving toward Ubirr traverses only 170km, all on sealed roads.

> **TIP**
>
> **HIKING SAFETY TIPS.** Self-sufficiency is the key to a safe adventure in Kakadu, as help and supplies are often hours away.
> **Bring:** Lots of water (at least 1L per hr. of walking), insect repellent, sunscreen, and sturdy shoes.
> **Beware:** These areas are full of **snakes** and **spiders**; long trousers and thick socks help protect against bites. **Crocs,** including salties, are common; keep a generous distance from the edges of bodies of water and don't swim. For more information on **Dangerous Species,** see p. 66.
> **Call:** Cell phones do not get reception in most of Kakadu. There are **emergency call boxes** at the carparks of some of the more remote hikes, such as Jim Jim. On tours, ask if guides carry satellite phones.

Walks and hikes range in difficulty levels. The main sights can be viewed from short, easy walking trails; a few are wheelchair-accessible. The climbs to the lookout points at Ubirr and Nourlangie are steeper. A number of excellent, longer walks reward the fit who choose to venture farther into the bush.

The visitors centers provide detailed information about each walk. For experienced hikers, unmarked overnight bushwalks are a great way to see Kakadu without the crowds. These routes generally follow creek lines and gorges along the escarpment. Routes and campsites on unmarked walks must be approved. For camping permits and route plan approval, contact the **Bowali Visitors Centre** (p. 278). Permits are free and take seven business days to process.

## SOUTH ALLIGATOR REGION

The squawks and whistles of hundreds of bird species greet you as you walk the 100m wheelchair-accessible path to the viewing platform at **Mamukala Wetlands,** on Arnhem Hwy., 29km west of Jabiru. In the Dry, the horizons of the floodplains surrounding Mamukala are thick with clusters of birds, from darting rainbow bee-eaters to plodding Jabiru storks. A 3km walk branches off from the path to wind along the edge of the wetlands.

## EAST ALLIGATOR REGION

Although it's no Uluru, **Ubirr Rock** is a popular substitute. Here, in the stone country of northeastern Kakadu, generations of Aboriginal artists have created some of the world's most intricate and extensive rock paintings in one of the Top End's most striking geological regions. A short **wheelchair-accessible circuit** (1km, 30min.) passes a few of the major galleries. Paintings in the natural rock shelters around the sandstone monolith document successful hunts, age-old ceremonies, and creation stories. They include depictions of long-extinct animals as well as more recent images, such as two silhouettes of early bushmen smoking pipes. A short ◪climb (250m; 15min.) leads to the top of Ubirr, with a spectacular view of the distant stone escarpment and the emerald floodplains. Sunsets on top of Ubirr are magical, but be prepared to share the experience with a crowd of tourists. (Open daily Apr.-Nov. 8:30am-sunset, Dec.-Mar. 2pm-sunset.) Free art-site talks are given during the Dry. Consult the *What's On* activity guide from the Bowali Visitors Centre for up-to-date schedules.

The **Guluyambi River Cruise** concentrates on educating guests about Aboriginal life. While drifting by the salties on the banks of the East Alligator River, Aboriginal guides explain local practices and demonstrate the use of traditional tools and preparation of Aboriginal foods. (☎1800 089 113. 45min. Departs daily Apr.-Nov. 9, 11am, 1, and 3pm. Call for schedules Dec.-May. $45, children $25.) The **Bardedjilidji Sandstone Walk** (2.5km, 40min.) passes by the intriguing weathered sandstone pillars, arches, and caves of the stone country. The trailhead is near the upstream boat ramp on a turnoff 1km south of the Border Store. The flat **Manngarre Monsoon Rainforest Walk** (1.5km, 30min.) leaves from the down-stream boat ramp and ambles through lush rainforest on a flat and easy trail to a viewing platform. The beautiful, tropical walk features occasional croc sightings along the East Alligator River.

## JABIRU REGION

The **Bowali Visitors Centre** (p. 278) provides an overview of the biology, geology, and cultural traditions of the park. A selection of nature films follows the region's wildlife through its annual cycle (half past every hr.). A nine-screen slide show with a soundtrack shows hundreds of colorful photographs of the park, progressing from the Wet through the Dry (every hr. on the hr.). The **Iligadjarr Walk** (3.8km, 2hr.) leaves from the Burdulba or Malabanjbanjdju campsites, crosses floodplains, and skirts the edge of Burdulba Billabong.

## NOURLANGIE REGION

The principal draw of this part of the park is Nourlangie itself, a huge rock outcropping used as a shelter and art studio by early Indigenous peoples. A winding **wheelchair-accessible track** (1.5km, 1hr.) connects the major art sites. Among the most engaging are the **Main Gallery,** with an extensive collection of layered work, and the **Anbangbang Rock Shelter,** a shady overhang beneath a large boulder that has been frequented by indigenous people since at least the last ice age. The walls are painted with the images of many spirits, including that of Nalbulwinj-bulwinj, who eats females after striking them with a yam. The farthest point on the loop is **Gunwarrdehwarrde Lookout,** a craggy climb to a view of the escarpment, where Lightning Man Namarrgon is said to live. Free talks are given during the Dry. Consult the *What's On* guide from the Bowali Visitors Centre for schedule information.

The stunning **Barrk Sandstone Bushwalk** (12km, 4-5hr.), one of the longest and most dramatic established trails in the park, branches off from the walk around Nourlangie. Strictly for the fit and sure-footed, it heads straight up Nourlangie's steep sides to spine-tingling vistas of the surrounding region. Along the way back, you'll pass the **Nanguluwur Art Gallery.** Some of the shorter walks in the region offer views of Nourlangie from afar. The **Nawurlandja Lookout** (600m, 20min.) and **Mirrai Lookout** (1.8km, 30min.) are short, steep climbs with stunning views. The **Anbangbang Billabong** track (2.5km, 30min.; accessible only in the Dry) is easy, circling lily-filled waters. The **Gubara Pools** are a good place to spend your time during the hottest hours of the day. One of the most accessible swimming-safe areas in the park, these cool pools can revitalize even the weariest hiker. Don't miss the second pool and small waterfall that lie around the corner from the first. (6km round-trip walk off a 9km unsealed road.)

## JIM JIM/TWIN FALLS REGION

The opening day of the 4WD-only access road (usually in early June) is eagerly awaited by tourists and tour guides, but is frustratingly uncertain. **Jim Jim** and **Twin Falls** are generally held to be the most breathtaking attractions in Kakadu. Located at the top of a tough 60km road, Jim Jim Falls cascades 150m down into a deep, clear green pool. In the Wet, the falls rush with roaring intensity, yet the same rain that causes the awesome spectacle also prevents road access to it; the only way to see the falls during this time is by air. There is a **lookout** 200m from the carpark. To get to the falls, first take a brief boat ride (every 15min., free) up the crocodile-filled river to a walking path. A boulder-laden walk (1km, 30min.) leads to the deep plunge pool, which remains quite cold for much of the Dry due to a lack of direct sunlight. Next to the plunge pool is a spectacular beach. The stunning **Barrk Marlam walk** (3km, 4hr.) branches off the path at the lookout, allowing experienced hikers to climb the escarpment and enjoy expansive views of the gorge.

The long journey to **Twin Falls** begins at the Jim Jim Campground. The first challenge is a formidable river crossing, which requires a 4WD with a snorkel system. A 10km rumble through the woods ends at the trailhead; an easy 400m stretch leads to a sandy beach. The double falls cascade over sandstone steps to a plunge pool. Although the water is clean, swimming is prohibited. For the 4WD-less, a few tour companies depart daily from both Jabiru and Cooinda. Try **Top End Explorer Tours** (☎08 8979 3615. $159, children $135; YHA discount) or **Kakadu Gorge and Waterfall Tours** (☎08 8979 0145. $179, children $143).

## YELLOW WATER REGION

**Yellow Water,** part of Jim Jim Creek, teems with bird life and salties. There are two ways to view the area. A **wheelchair-accessible path,** leaving from the Yellow Water carpark, leads to a platform with wetland views. The area is difficult to access on foot but is easily seen by boat. Try **Yellow Water Cruises.** (☎08 8979 0145. Book at the Gagudju Lodge Cooinda. 1½hr. cruises leave 11:30am, 1:15, 2:45pm in the Dry; 8:30, 11:45am, 1:30, 3:30pm in the Wet; $50, ages 4-15 $35. 2hr. cruises leave 6:45, 9am, 4:30pm in the Dry; $79/49.)

The **Warrandjan Aboriginal Cultural Centre,** 1km from the Gagudju Lodge Cooinda, is also a worthwhile stopover. The exhibits show the complexity of indigenous culture and do a good job of piecing together the disjointed bits of information found throughout the park. Built in the shape of a *warradjan* (turtle), the center contains wonderful displays on hunting techniques, Aboriginal arts, and the struggle to keep the culture alive, and screens free movies from a catalog of about 15 options (☎08 8979 0051. Open daily 9am-5pm. Free.)

## MARY RIVER REGION

**Mary River,** the region most recently incorporated into Kakadu National Park, lies in the far southwest corner of Kakadu, just inside the Southern Entry Station. Mary River boasts a collection of enjoyable walks as well as peaceful **Gunlom,** the only 2WD-accessible escarpment waterfall in the entire park. Mary River often gets short shrift—it is far from the major sights of the north and its attractions take a bit more effort to access.

Popular **Gunlom Falls** is the biggest draw in the Mary River region. An easy path leads to a plunge pool surrounded by rocky walls that's situated just beneath the falls. A steep trail (1km, 30min.) travels all the way to the top of the falls and has beautiful views of the surrounding area.

The secondary sights in the region provide greater challenges for cars and legs alike. **Maguk,** or **Barramundi Falls,** is a smaller cascade; the 4WD turnoff is 32km north of the Gunlom turn-off on the Kakadu Hwy. The falls are reached via 12km road and then a rocky hike (2km, 1hr.) through monsoon forest. Some hike to the top of the falls and swim in the beautiful waters there. The **Yurmikmik Walking Tracks** pass wet-season waterfalls. The trailhead is 21km down Gunlom Rd. off the Kakadu Hwy. There are three different circular tracks (2km, 45min.; 5km, 2hr.; 7.5km, 4hr.) and two longer tracks that require overnight permits; the 11km walk runs by a series of waterfalls, and the 13.5km walk has plunge pools during the Wet. Both of these longer walks are difficult, unmarked, and require good navigation and preparation. Near the Yurmikmik walks is **Jarrangbarnmi,** one of the *djang andjamun* areas that represent sacred spiritual sites to Aboriginal groups. Visitor numbers are restricted, and no one can enter the area without a permit and entry key. Ask at the **Southern Entry Station** (☎08 8975 4859) and the **Goymarr visitor center** (☎08 8979 6417).

# LITCHFIELD NATIONAL PARK

At Litchfield National Park, dusty roads wind through lush forests and massive termite mounds. A series of generally tame walks yields stunning vistas en route to inviting pools tucked into the bases of tumbling, roaring waterfalls. While its proximity to Darwin makes it busy, visiting Litchfield with a 4WD and staying for more than a day allow you to escape the crowds and explore the park's wonders on your own. Even without a 4WD, many of the park's highlights are accessible, making Litchfield a rewarding daytrip from Darwin.

| LITCHFIELD NATIONAL PARK AT A GLANCE | |
|---|---|
| **AREA:** 1460 sq. km. | **GATEWAYS:** Batchelor, Darwin (p. 267). |
| **CLIMATE:** Monsoonal, with distinct wet (Nov.-Apr.) and dry (May-Oct.) seasons. | **CAMPING:** Buley Rockhole, Florence Falls, Surprise Creek Falls, Tjaynera (Sandy Creek) Falls (4WD only), Wangi Falls, and Walker Creek. |
| **HIGHLIGHTS:** Spectacular waterfalls, tranquil walks, 4WD tracks, and towering termite mounds. | **FEES:** None. |

## ⚑ ⚐ ORIENTATION AND PRACTICAL INFORMATION

The park, 118km southwest of Darwin, is accessible by two routes. About 90km down the Stuart Hwy., **Litchfield Park Road** juts west, passing through Batchelor on its way to the eastern border of the park. On the other side of the park, it connects to an unsealed road that leads back to Darwin (115km). Most sights lie along Litchfield Park Rd. **Tjaynera Falls** and **Surprise Creek** are on a 4WD track just west of Greenant Creek. Litchfield Park Rd. is generally open to all vehicles in all seasons, while the 4WD tracks close in the Wet.

There is no ranger station, but information is available through the **Parks and Wildlife Commission of the Northern Territory** (☎08 8999 5511) in Darwin. Detailed maps are also available for free at the **Batchelor Store** (☎08 8976 0045), 20km from the park, and at the information hut across the street. Tours are available from a variety of agencies; most companies charge $80-150 for day tours. Call ☎08 8976 0282 for road conditions, especially during the Wet. Petrol is available at the Batchelor Store. The **post office** is in the Batchelor store. (☎08 8976 0020. Open M-F 9am-5pm.) **Postal code:** 0845.

## ⬛ ⬛ ACCOMMODATIONS AND CAMPING

Options within Litchfield are mostly limited to camping. In Batchelor, try the **Butterfly Farm and Petting Zoo ❸** with Balinese decor and a relaxing atmosphere. Turn off Batchelor Road onto Rum Jungle Road, and it will be on the left at the first road. (☎08 8976 0199; www.butterflyfarm.net. 2 people $60; 3 people $160; 4 people $95; 6 people $180; pricing can depend on specific rooms available.) Next door, the well-manicured **Rum Jungle Bungalows ❺**, next door to the Butterfly Farm in Batchelor, is a more upscale option. (☎08 8976 0555; www. rumjunglebungalows.com.au. Bungalows for 2 $160, extra person $10.)

**Litchfield Tourist & Van Park ❶** is 4km from the park border, on the way from Litchfield to fishing spots on the Finnis River. (☎08 8976 0070; www.litchfield-touristpark.com.au. Sites for 2 $18, powered $24, extra person $5, families $30; 2-person cabins $75, ensuite $105.) Just down the road is the family-run **Banyan Tree Caravan Park ❶**, with both phones and power. (☎08 8976 0330; www.banyan-tree.com.au. Sites $8.50 per person, powered for 2 $19.50; doubles $65; cabins for 2 $110. Breakfast included with rooms.)

**Camping ❶** in the park generally costs $6.60 for unpowered sites with showers and toilets. Pay at a drop box upon entering a campsite. The Wangi Falls campground fills up early in the day and can be uncomfortably crowded; more serene options lie near Florence Falls and Buley Rockhole. Visitors with a 4WD have more choices at Florence Falls and Tjaynera (Sandy Creek) Falls. Surprise Creek Falls and Walker Creek have toilets and are half the cost. Be prepared for ravenous swarms of mosquitoes. Caravan camping is allowed only at Wangi Falls and Surprise Creek, and generators are not permitted anywhere. Between Wangi Falls and Walker Creek, 4km from the Wangi turnoff on the Litchfield Park Road, a turnoff leads to **Litchfield Safari Camp ❷**. Technically outside the park, it offers accommodations close to the main attractions and boasts the best budget options in the area. (☎08 8978 2168; www.litchfieldsafaricamp. com. BBQ. Sites $10, child $5; powered for 2 $25-30, extra person $10, child $5; battery charge $35 per night; dorm bed $25; safari cabin $110, ensuite $130.)

## ◪ FOOD

In Batchelor, the **Butterfly Farm and Petting Zoo ❷** also serves hearty home-cooked meals with vegetables and herbs from on-site organic gardens. (☎08 8976 0199.

Breakfast $6-9, lunch $12-23, dinner $20-27. Cafe open daily 7am-8:30pm.) Basic groceries and propane are available at the **Batchelor Store.** (☎08 8976 0045. Open M-F 7am-6pm, Sa-Su 7am-5pm.) In the park, there's a **food kiosk** at **Wangi Falls.** (Open daily 9am-5pm.) Also, at the turnoff to Litchfield Safari Camp, a separate fork veers to **Monsoon Cafe ❷,** where park visitors can enjoy breakfast (bacon and eggs $12), lunch (sandwiches $4-6) and/or dinner (main dishes $16-23). (☎08 8978 2077. Open daily -Su 7am-9pm. Book ahead for dinner.)

## 👁 📷 SIGHTS AND ACTIVITIES

The following sights and activities are listed in order of appearance when driving into the park on Litchfield Park Rd. from north of Batchelor.

**MAGNETIC TERMITE MOUNDS.** Throughout Litchfield, termite mounds approaching 7m in height dominate the flat, open landscape. They are the handiwork of two species of termites; cathedral termites build towering conical mounds, while magnetic termites construct flat, gravestone-like homes. The magnetic mounds are all aligned with their faces pointing east and west for temperature regulation—they soak up the softer light of morning and evening and escape the midday glare. Information boards explaining termite life can be found at the Magnetic Termite Mounds site near the eastern edge of the park. Several mounds can also be viewed on the 4WD track to Surprise Creek.

**🏊FLORENCE FALLS.** The most impressive falls in the park are reached by a 15min. walk along the creek. Even in the Dry, copious amounts of water tumble 100m into a clear, calm pool. Nearby **🏊Buley Rockhole** is a series of small, deep pools perfect for quick dips, although others might have the same idea. A 3km drive or walk through verdant monsoon forest connects the two sights.

**LOST CITY.** A 10km 4WD track leads to this collection of eroded rock outcroppings. A maze of short trails winds among the twists and turns, arches, and turrets of the formations, allowing for endless exploration. In the early morning, a shroud of hazy mist lends the towers an air of mystery.

**TOLMER FALLS.** Only a short distance southwest from Florence Falls on the main road, a mild 1.5km walking loop winds past a natural stone arch and a lookout deck with a view of the falls and a peaceful creek, as well as the surrounding forests of Litchfield. Swimming is prohibited to protect the fragile ecosystem, home to several species of bats. Take the short (1km), surprisingly untrafficked creek walk from the carpark to get a peek at the stream above the falls and potentially a reclusive rock-wallaby or two.

**WANGI FALLS.** Converging streams cascade into a pool of clear water at the bottom of Wangi (WONG-guy) Falls. Come early to avoid the throngs of tourists. Salties sometimes like to swim here, and their presence recently forced a ban on entering the plunge pool and has made the falls less popular than before. A walking trail (1.6km loop, 45min.) passes through the forest atop Wangi, but affords no view of the falls themselves.

**🏊SURPRISE CREEK FALLS.** Twenty kilometers farther along the Tjaynera track from the Sandy Creek Falls, a series of pools connected by attractive falls create a refreshing oasis. A pond and two small bowl-shaped pools make for peaceful swimming; thrill-seekers often jump from the top pool into the bottom. The typically deserted falls are one of the best secrets in the Top End.

**THE LOCAL STORY**

## BOOMERANG BEWARE

Though examples have been found in ancient sites the world over, the boomerang remains an icon of Australia, where it's been used in sport, hunting, and ceremonies by Aboriginal people for thousands of years. The name "boomerang" originates from the Turuwal tribes from areas south of Sydney, but the instruments were employed and perfected for many different uses by Aboriginal people throughout the continent. It's theorized that boomerangs actual originated as hunting tools in numerous spots all over the world, but that the invention of the bow and arrow made them obsolete; indigenous people in Australia never developed the bow and arrow and instead perfected their boomerang techniques to devastating effect.

Indigenous Australians used many types of non-returning boomerangs, including some that weren't necessarily meant to be thrown. A few varieties were used for fishing or as clubs in close combat. A returning boomerang, meanwhile, was often used in the hunting of birds.

To throw a returning boomerang, don't toss it side-arm, but rather throw it from a vertical orientation—it will naturally correct itself on its course back to you if released properly. Of course, be careful to watch your head. These were originally hunting tools, not flying sticks, and you don't want to become your own prey.

## STUART HIGHWAY: DARWIN TO KATHERINE

The lonely Stuart Hwy. connects Darwin to Adelaide, slicing the continent down the middle. The first stretch runs 314km from Darwin to Katherine with several diversions along the way. About 35km south of Darwin, Cox Peninsula Road runs 11km west to **Territory Wildlife Park.** A nocturnal wildlife house, a reptile pavilion, and a number of pens feature a wide range of native fauna. The Birds of Prey presentation and enclosed tunnel aquarium are both highlights of the park. (☎08 8988 7200. Open daily 8:30am-6pm, last entry 4pm. $20, students and concessions $14, families $35.) Darwin Day Tours runs a half-day tour to the park. (☎08 8924 1124. Daily 7:30am-1:30pm. $64, children $32; includes entrance fee.) Berry Springs, next to the Wildlife Park, makes for a great stop. Watch the steam rise from these dolomite hot springs as you get a massage from the small waterfall in the first pool. (Open 9am-6pm. Free.)

Eighty kilometers south of Darwin, and 7km down an access road, lies **Lake Bennett Resort ❶**, an upscale lodge with budget accommodations next to a tranquil lake. Swim, rent a canoe ($13.20 per hr., $44 per day), fish, or play golf before watching the sunset. Guest rooms include fridge, A/C, and TV, with shared bath and kitchen facilities. The staff will meet bus travelers at the Stuart Hwy. (☎08 8976 0960; www.lakebennettwildernessresort.com.au. Sites $10 per person, powered $25; dorms $25; twins $170; triples $195.)

**Adelaide River** is the next town where you can refuel, and it happily boasts more than just a small BP station. The ⚑**Adelaide River Inn Pub** behind the BP serves heaping plates of "the original and the best" Barri and Chips in all of Australia. (☎08 8976 7047. Battered or breaded $16.50, grilled $19.50.) Between the fuel stations at Adelaide River and Hayes Creek, and 200km from Darwin, Tjuwaliyn (Douglas) Hot Springs is a worthwhile stop. The last 7km of the access road is gravel, but is tame enough for all cars in the Dry. In some areas, the springs can be too hot for comfort; head downstream if you're looking for cooler currents. Camping ❶ is available ($4.50, children $2, families $10). Pine Creek is the final stop on the route, 50km north of Katherine.

## PINE CREEK ☎08

Founded in 1870 shortly before Overland Telegraph workers discovered gold in the ground, Pine Creek (pop. 650) is located on the Stuart Highway, by the turnoff toward Jabiru and Kakadu National Park. It's still the small mining settlement it's been for over 100 years, but the price for authenticity is a lack of tourist diversions. Nonetheless, you'd be hard-pressed to find a better bed or bite in the area. The main street runs through Historic Pine Creek, past the ruins of Ah Toy's old bakery from 1908 to **Ah Toy's General Store** (since 1935), which doubles as a bus depot. (☎08 8976 1202. Open M-F 9am-5pm, Sa 9am-12:30pm.) **Greyhound Australia** runs to Darwin (3hr., 2 per day, $62) and Katherine (1hr., 2 per day, $40). The **post office** on Moule St.—just off Main—doubles as a **bank.** (☎08 8976 1220. Open M-F 9am-1pm.) Next door, **Mayse's Cafe** serves good meals for $6-12 and pizzas for $13.50-19.50. (☎08 8976 1241. Open daily 7am-3pm.) You can head next door to pick up some dinner ($20-32) and Sunday BBQ in the restaurant at the **Pine Creek Hotel,** 40 Moule St. The hotel also rents nice motel-style rooms ❺ (☎08 8976 1288. Singles $90; doubles $110; triples $125.) West of Moule Street, just off Main at the big sign, **Lazy Lizard's** has campsites ❶ and a happy hour (7pm-8pm, beer and spirits only) at its bar restaurant, as well as a pool. Book at the bar or at the service station out front. (☎08 8976 1019. Unpowered $15 per van/tent, powered $20 per caravan for 2, extra person $5. Service station open 5am-6pm). About 1km south of town on the Stuart Hwy., a turnoff leads to **Umbrawarra Gorge Nature Park,** 32km down an uneven dirt road. A fairly easy walk (1km, 10min.) leads to the creek at the foot of the gorge. A camping area with a toilet sits near the entry to the gorge (adult $3.30, child $1.65, family $7.70. Pay in honesty box).

# KATHERINE ☎08

A frontier town without the frontier mayhem, Katherine (pop. 9000) has lost its heyday rowdiness—and many of its local businesses. Now this outpost of the Top End—proud home of the only stoplight along the 1500km of the Stuart Hwy. between Darwin and Alice Springs—serves as a gateway to the national parks of the northern Outback. Restock along the main street at a host of suppliers, but unless doing nothing is your thing, it's probably best not to linger.

## ▐ TRANSPORTATION

The **Transit Centre** is located on the southern end of the main street through Katherine, near Lindsay St. Greyhound Australia **buses** (☎1800 089 103) stop at the Transit Centre on Katherine Terr. and run to: Alice Springs (15hr., 1 per day, $257); Broome (19hr., 1 per day, $298); Darwin (4hr., 2 per day, $91); and Townsville (30hr., 1 per day, $440). Local **car rental** agencies include **Thrifty,** 6 Katherine Terr. (☎1800 891 125), in the Transit Centre, and **Hertz,** 392 Katherine Terr. (☎08 8972 2511), which has 4WDs.

## ◼ ▐ ORIENTATION AND PRACTICAL INFORMATION

Katherine marks the intersection of three main roads. The **Stuart Highway** becomes **Katherine Terrace** in town; most shops and services are found here. The **Victoria Highway** leaves from the northern side of town, passing the town hot springs and heading toward the Kimberley region. Finally, **Giles Street** heads east from the middle of town toward **Nitmiluk National Park** (29km).

**Tourist Office: Katherine Region Tourist Association** (☎08 8972 2650), on the corner of Lindsay St. and Katherine Terr., across from the Transit Centre. Open Apr.-Oct. M-F 8:30am-5pm, Sa-Su 8:30am-5pm; Nov.-Mar. M-F 8:30am-5pm, Sa-Su 10am-2pm.

**Bank:** Several on Katherine Terr. All open M-Th 9:30am-4pm, F 9:30am-5pm.

**Work Opportunities: Grunt Labour Services** (☎1300 881 988), produces the *Harvest Workers Guide* and can arrange work with local mango farms from Sept.-Nov.

**Police:** (☎08 8972 0111), 2.5km south of town on the Stuart Hwy.

**Internet Access: Katherine Library,** on Katherine Terr. across the street from Woolworths, has the best connection. $4 per 30min. CD burning. Open Tu 8:30am-5pm, W-F 10am-5pm, Sa 10am-1pm. **The Didj Shop Internet Cafe** (☎08 8972 2485), on Giles St. a block west of Katherine Terr., $6 per hr.

**Post Office:** Katherine Terr. and Giles St. Open M-F 9am-5pm. **Postal Code:** 0850.

# ACCOMMODATIONS AND CAMPING

Motels are ubiquitous in Katherine, but budget bed options are mainly shabby options, even if they attract a youthful, colorful crowd. The cheapest, most comfortable accommodations may be the caravan parks outside town.

**Palm Court Backpackers YHA** (☎08 8972 2722 or 1800 626 722; www.travelnorth.com.au), on the corner of 3rd and Giles St. Shabby, often dirty rooms don't scare away the diverse, youthful crowd at Katherine's best option for a dorm bed. Pool and BBQ. All rooms ensuite. Free pickup and dropoff from transit center during business hours. Internet access $2 per 20min. Laundry $3. Key deposit $10. Bikes $10 per day. Reception 7am-7pm. Dorms $24; twins and doubles $54, with kitchen $82. ❷

**Coco's Backpackers,** 21 1st St. (☎08 8971 2889), to the east off Giles street. Behind the didjeridu, a ragtag mixture of musicians, Aboriginal artists, and international travelers mill about in the cluttered yard. The rooms are simple and a little run-down, but for those tired of the typical party hostel, it just might be a perfect fit. Coco is always willing to talk about Aboriginal culture. Call ahead. Sites $12 per person; dorms $23-24. ❶

**Riverview Caravan Park and Motel** (☎08 8972 1011), 2km west of town along Victoria Hwy. Pool, laundry, and BBQ. Wi-Fi $5 per hr.; Internet $3.50 per 30min. Reception 8am-6pm. Sites for 2 $21, powered $26, extra person $10.50; cabins for 1 $64, for 2 $79; ensuite for 1 $81, for 2 $95, extra person $13.50. ❷

# FOOD

**Bucking Bull Cafe ❶,** on Second St., which runs parallel to Katherine Terr. to the east off Giles St., serves up mouth-watering roasts (from $10), burgers ($9.50), and mango smoothies from $5. Breakfast specials from $9.50 are also available. (☎08 8972 1734. Open M-Sa 6:30am-6pm.) **Cinema Cafe ❶,** in the same building as the movie theatre at 20 First St., has no affiliation with the cinema, but does have $5 shakes (chocolate mint, banana, caramel, blue heaven, coffee—to name a few). A simple menu offers breakfast all day (french toast with jam and cream $8) and meals from $8.50. (☎08 8971 0594. Burgers $10-12.50. Open M 8am-3pm, Tu-Th 8am-5pm, F 8am-8pm, Sa 8:30am-8pm, Su 8:30am-11:30am.) A giant **Woolworths** supermarket is across from the transit center on Katherine Terr. (☎08 8972 3055. Open daily 6:30am-10pm.)

# ACTIVITIES

Two kilometers along the Victoria Hwy. from Katherine Terr., hot springs bubble along the Katherine River. The area is free, paved, and open to swimmers (8:30am-4:30pm). There are toilets nearby, and the springs are wheelchair-accessible along Croker St. and also off Murray St. **Coco's Place,** by **Coco's Backpackers** (see **Accommodations,** p. 290) is a didjeridu shop run by experts, making it a far better place to learn about the instrument than the backpacker-targeted shops in Darwin. **Travel North** runs a crocodile night tour along the Johnstone

River that includes wine and a BBQ dinner. (☎1800 089 103; www.travelnorth.com.au. Nightly 6:30pm. $55, children $29. Pickup $15/8.)

# NITMILUK NATIONAL PARK (KATHERINE GORGE)

A broad, majestic river runs through the chiseled walls and sandy embankments of the highly touristed Katherine Gorge, drawing visitors by canoe, car, double-decker tourist boat, and even helicopter. The 450 rock art galleries dotting the park, which include a series of paintings in the gorges themselves, are reminders that shutter-snapping tourists are not the area's first visitors. Since 1989, the park has been owned by its traditional residents, the Jawoyn people, who have leased it to the government of the Northern Territory for 99 years.

| NITMILUK AT A GLANCE | |
|---|---|
| **AREA:** 292,008 hectares. | **GATEWAYS:** Katherine (p. 289). |
| **FEATURES:** Katherine River, 13 gorges, Edith Falls, 17 Mile Creek. | **CAMPING:** Campgrounds near the visitors center and at Edith Falls; registered overnight bush camping. |
| **HIGHLIGHTS:** Canoeing, hiking up cliffs and through gorges. | **FEES:** Camping $9.50-12; bush camping requires additional $50 deposit. |

## ✴ ⁊ TRANSPORTATION AND PRACTICAL INFORMATION

The 13 gorges of the Katherine River form the centerpiece of Nitmiluk. The easiest, most popular way to access the park is by car, though tours can be arranged in Katherine. The gorges and all water sports can be accessed by boat or foot on the Southern Walks from the **Nitmiluk Visitors Centre,** at the end of the sealed Gorge Rd. 30km east of Katherine. A second entrance to the park lies 40km north of Katherine on the Stuart Hwy., where a 20km access road leads to Edith Falls. The 66km Jatbula Trail connects the two.

**WHEN TO GO.** The climate is most comfortable May-Sept., after the seasonal storms but before the unbearable humidity. Though greenery is most vivid during the Wet, floods limit activities in the park.

**Buses:** The **Jawoyn Association** (☎1300 146 743) runs buses from accommodations in Katherine to the visitors center. Book ahead. (25min., 2-3 per day, $24 round-trip.)

**Tourist Office:** The **Nitmiluk Visitors Centre** provides hiking information and camping permits. Tourist desk in the gift shop books canoe, helicopter, and boat tours, along with campsites. (Open daily 7am-6:30pm.) Free exhibits present a broad introduction to the park, from natural history to local Jawoyn culture. Licensed bistro serves $7.50-11 burgers and sandwiches. (☎08 8972 3150. Open daily 8am-8:30pm.) Contact the **Parks and Wildlife Commission** (☎08 8972 1886), which has a desk in the visitors center, for more information on Katherine Gorge and bush camping.

**Tours: Nitmiluk Tours** provides scenic helicopter flights and other creative ways to see the area. 3-gorge tour $75, 8-gorge $115, 13-gorge $165. Min. 2 people. Book at the visitors center (☎08 8972 1253; www.nitmiluktours.com.au). **Helimasters** (☎08 8972 2402), just outside of the park entrance, offers similar packages, as well as an extensive gorge tour that includes Edith Falls ($320). Book 1-2 days ahead. Min. 2 people.

## CAMPING

The shady, popular **caravan park** ❶ near the visitors center has toilets, showers, laundry, phones, and BBQ facilities. Be sure to clean up your campsite before bedding down for the night, or scavenging wallabies will do the job for you. Register at the visitors center. (Sites $9.50 per person, powered for 2 $24, extra person $10.) Sites are also available at a **campground** ❶ (☎08 8975 4869; sites $8.50) next to Edith Falls, with showers, BBQ, food kiosk, and picnic area. The falls are a pleasant, cool spot for relaxation. Beneath the waterfall, a lower pool is only a short walk away from the carpark.

Bush camping is permitted, but campers must register at the visitors center. ($3.30; $50 deposit.) Campsites are located along the **Jatbula Trail** and at the fifth, sixth, eighth, and ninth (toilets at fifth and sixth) gorges in the Southern Walks area. Fires are permitted along the Jatbula but not in the Southern Walks.

## NITMILUK BY WATER

Getting out on the Katherine River has many advantages; you can see much more of the gorges than you can along the trails, and it is often considerably cooler on the water than on shore. From May to September, quiet waters allow for canoeing and boat tours, but you must book several days in advance. **Nitmiluk Tours** (see above) is the only option for canoe rental and cruises, which can be booked at most accommodations in Katherine or at the visitors center. Canoeing affords some solitude despite the throngs of fellow paddlers and passing boat tours that encroach somewhat on the relaxing atmosphere.

**CANOEING.** Nitmiluk Tours rents Canadian-style canoes, which are a cross between a canoe and a kayak. This design was chosen for safety, not speed, and it can be awkward to operate. Consider taking a full-day trip, which allows you to get away from the stream of fellow paddlers at the third gorge, where you can climb from a sandy side beach to the pristine **Lily Pond Falls.** No more than 75 canoes are permitted in the gorge at once, so book several days in advance. (☎08 8972 1253. Single canoe ½-day $39.50, full-day $51, overnight $98; double canoe per person $29.50/38/110. $20 cash deposit. Overnight canoes require a $3.30 camping permit and a $60 deposit.)

**CRUISES.** Glide along the gorges in flat, shaded motor vessels. Be warned: the crowded arrangement sometimes makes it difficult to enjoy the natural tranquility of the area, and the hustling tours hurt any chance of moving at one's own pace. (Depart from the boat jetty. 2hr.; 4 per day in the Dry; $53, children $30.) Daily "adventure" and "safari" tours combine boating and hiking. Book in advance. (Depart in the morning. 4hr. $69, children $32; 8hr. $110.

## NITMILUK BY LAND

Although the walking trails are not as easy to access as the boating and canoeing trips, they tend to be less crowded, and the views of the gorge are truly phenomenal. However, unrelenting sun can make the trails uncomfortably hot (10°C hotter than areas near the water). Walking tracks in the park run the spectrum from strolls to struggles and range from 2.5km to 66km. The **Southern Walks** are usually open year-round; the **Jatbula Trail** is open only in the Dry. For overnight walks, register with the ranger station beforehand. Semi-detailed aerial maps are at the visitors center. Smaller trail maps are available for free.

## SOUTHERN WALKS

The main trail of the area starts at the visitors center and runs parallel to the rim of the gorge. Each side trail meanders toward the gorge. The main trail follows a riverbed past large boulders and eucalyptus saplings, providing photo-worthy vistas. Trails are listed starting with those closest to the visitors center.

**Lookout Loop** (3.7km, 2hr. round-trip, moderate). Steep, well-maintained climb up the side of the gorge offers views of the river and **Seventeen Mile Valley.** After the climb, the trail widens to an easy walk. Signs along the way detail the park's history.

**Windolf Walk** (8.4km, 3hr., moderate). Side trail of the Windolf Walk follows a riverbed almost to the edge of the gorge where it forks. The right trail leads to **Pat's Lookout** on the gorge rim, while the left descends to the **Southern Rock Hole.** Pat's Lookout overlooks a bend in the gorge with a sandy beach at the foot of a menacing cliff. The trail to the left passes a wet-season waterfall and plunge pool before reaching an inlet. A very steep, narrow trail leads to the right beyond Pat's Lookout to the base of the gorge. From here, bold hikers may swim across to the sandy beach and then walk along the right-hand canyon wall to reach an Aboriginal rock art gallery. The sure-footed can follow the bank up the river to the end of the first gorge; if the water is low enough, you can cross the natural rock bridge. With slippery rocks and raging water underneath, it is a harrowing experience. If you do cross, follow the footpaths to the galleries.

**Butterfly Gorge Walk** (12km, 4½hr., difficult). A good overview of the region, with woodlands and rock formations giving way to a dense, tranquil monsoon forest in a side gorge. The last few hundred meters take you through clouds of butterflies. After a short, strenuous scramble down the cliff face, the walk ends at a deep swimming hole.

**Lily Ponds Trail** (20km, 6½hr., difficult). A challenging scramble in sections; leads to a sheltered pool in the 3rd gorge. Few tourists.

**Eighth Gorge and Jawoyn Valley** (30-40km, overnight, very difficult). The longest of the Southern Walks takes a night in the bush with a return by midday. The terrain is fierce. Carry extra supplies. The Jawoyn loop passes a rock art gallery. All overnight treks require a $3.30 camping permit and a $50 deposit.

## JATBULA TRAIL AND OTHER TRAILS

The popular Jatbula Trail winds 58km over the 4- to 5-day journey from the visitors center to **Edith Falls.** Split into eight segments, the trail threads through pockets of rainforest and skirts waterfalls. The first section (8km, 4hr., moderate) is the only plausible day walk; it departs from the visitors center and winds through a valley before reaching the **Northern Rockhole** and adjacent rock face. The trail continues past **Biddlecombe Cascades** (day 1-2, 8km mark), beautiful **Crystal Falls** (day 2, 18.5km), an interesting **Aboriginal amphitheater** (day 2-3, 25km), **Seventeen Mile Falls** (day 2-3, 28km), the **Edith River Crossing** (day 3-4, 39km), **Sandy Camp Pool** (day 3-4, 43.5km), **Edith River South** (day 4, 50km), **Sweetwater Pool** (day 4, 54km), and finally into **Leliyn** (day 4-5, 58km). Two short walks leave from the Edith Falls car park at the end of the Jatbula Trail. The **Sweetwater Pool** walk (8.6km return, 4hr., moderate) leads to a waterhole and good camping. The **Leliyn Trail** (2.6km loop, 2hr., easy) heads to the smaller upper pools.

## ▣ ABORIGINAL ART

The first gorge harbors a series of impressive rock-art galleries, some of which are over 10,000 years old. Each gallery has layered images, with more recent paintings superimposed on older ones. Little is known about the paintings of the **West Gallery,** now faded to a faint red shadow. This indigenous art gives clues to the use and contents of different parts of the area. The mysterious **Central Gallery** depicts a hunt or ritual. Curiously, the figures are upside-down, signifying sleep, a ceremonial preparation, initiation, or death. The oldest, most-layered is **East Gallery**, which depicts a non-human male figure, a woman in a headdress, and a black wallaroo with joey.

# ARNHEM LAND

Take the expansive wilderness of Kakadu, multiply it by 10, and you still won't do justice to Arnhem Land. Sprawling across the entire northeastern region of the Top End, this Aboriginal homeland was established in 1931, and its geography and local law keep it isolated from the rest of the continent. Though much of Arnhem Land is uninhabited, it has two towns (Oenpelli and Nhulunbuy), several settlements, and around 150 indigenous outposts. Be aware that while many residents of Arnhem Land welcome tourism and its revenues, there are also those who would prefer to see their land free from swarms of outsiders.

Venturing into Arnhem Land is a serious matter. There are very few roads (those that do exist are navigable only in the Dry), and virtually no signs or services. Moreover, Arnhem Land is usually accessible only to indigenous peoples, so a destination-specific permit is required to enter. The **Northern Land Council** in the Jabiru Shopping Centre, next to the library, can issue permits for three locations close to Kakadu. (☎08 8937 3000. Open M-F 8am-4:30pm.) Permits for **Injalak** (IN-yaluk; $13.20 per day) and for **Sandy Creek** and **Wunyu Beach** (5 days, $88 per vehicle) take 10 days to process. To venture to the secluded beaches and wildlife of **Gurig National Park** on the Cooburg Peninsula, contact the **Parks and Wildlife Commission of the Northern Territory**. (☎08 8999 4814. 7 nights, $232 per vehicle.) If you're venturing to **Nhulunbuy** on the Central Arnhem Hwy., permits are available through the Northern Land Council in Katherine (see **Central Arnhem Highway, p. 294**). For permits to other sections of Arnhem Land, contact Darwin's **Northern Land Council** (☎08 8920 5100).

For those seeking experienced guides, tours of Arnhem Land are available. Multi-day tours with flights from Darwin can cost thousands of dollars; 4WD daytrips from Kakadu are cheaper. **Lord's Kakadu and Arnhemland Safaris** departs from Jabiru. (☎08 8948 2200; www.lords-safaris.com. $195, children $155.)

## CENTRAL ARNHEM HIGHWAY

The Central Arnhem Hwy. begins south of Katherine and passes through central and east Arnhem Land to the **Gove Peninsula**. Traveling on the road is difficult, but the reward is well worth the effort. *Let's Go* recommends using a 4WD vehicle for the journey from Katherine, though a high-clearance 2WD is adequate. Locals (and insane travelers) have been known to attempt the drive in low-clearance 2WD vehicles, but they run a high risk of flooding their engines or sustaining rock damage. If you decide to tempt fate, consider plugging your engine's air intake with a cloth and waiting for a 4WD to tow you through the deeper stream crossings; better yet, find some locals planning to make the drive and ask to follow them. The trickiest fords are at the **Wilton and Goyder rivers.** When crossing streams in this area, walk through before driving through to test for depth and bottom conditions—you can probably stand 2m of water, but your car can't. It's also a good idea to leave your engine running after crossing for as long as possible, since a flooded engine may not start again for quite some time. If you plan to visit Gove by road, your first phone call should be to the **Northern Territory Road Conditions Hotline** (☎1800 246 199).

Though the highway is not busy, there is some traffic; be alert for road-weary oncoming drivers at crests or around turns, and take breaks. Travel time from Katherine to Nhulunbuy is at least 10hr.; exercise caution and plan ahead.

Because the road passes through Aboriginal lands, you must have a permit from the **Northern Land Council** in Katherine (☎08 8971 9899). The permit is free but can take several days to process. You must be visiting a resident or have a booking at an accommodation in Nhulunbuy before you apply.

# NHULUNBUY AND GOVE ☎08

Nhulunbuy, a rugged bauxite mining town (pop. 4000), is an outpost of civilization in the vast frontier that is far northeastern Arnhem Land. Nhulunbuy is the sort of place where the speedway and motorcross track are the most visible icons, and nearly every house has a 4WD and a boat. The town is a popular base for exploring the stunning beaches, dunes, and pristine bushlands of the **Gove Peninsula**. Nhulunbuy is also a good place to learn about the culture of the **Yolngu people**, who have lived in this part of the world for many generations (perhaps as long as 60,000 years) and remained generally undisturbed by European influence. The **didjeridu** (called *yidaki* in local languages) is originally from northeastern Arnhem Land, and the Yolngu are its traditional custodians.

**☐ TRANSPORTATION.** The best way to visit Nhulunbuy and the Gove Peninsula is by air, and **flights** can be affordable with some advance planning. **Qantas** (☎13 13 13) flies to Nhulunbuy from Cairns and Darwin. **Airnorth** (☎08 8920 4000) flies from Darwin and often has fares under $300, though flights are in a small turbo-prop aircraft. Permits are still required to fly to Nhulunbuy.

The best way to get around Gove is in your own 4WD. A high-clearance 2WD will suffice for exploring the beaches closer to town. Most rental agencies in Gove are booked three or four months in advance, so plan ahead or rent in Darwin. **Manny's** (☎08 8987 2300) rents 4WDs and 2WD "utes" (utility vehicles). **Gove Rentals** has 4WD vehicles and 2WD utes. (☎08 8987 1700. 4WD $147-158 per day, utes $75, cars $86.) For **taxis,** call **Radio Taxis** (☎13 10 08).

**▟ ORIENTATION.** Heading toward town, the Central Arnhem Hwy. and the road from the airport converge to become **Melville Bay Road,** which runs past the large Aboriginal community of Yirrkala and **Matthew Flinders Way** in the direction of the harbor. On the drive into town along Matthew Flinders Way, the first left is **Arnhem Road,** the location of the **Captain Cook Shopping Centre.** In town, Westall St., off Matthew Flinders Way, borders **Endeavor Square,** the center of town.

**◪ PRACTICAL INFORMATION.** The **East Arnhem Land Tourist Association,** in Travel World in the town center, is a good source of information and has a wide variety of brochures. They also have a **free town map.** (☎08 8987 1111.) **Dhimurru Land Management,** in the Captain Cook Shopping Centre, is the Gove Peninsula's unofficial tourist office. An incorporated Aboriginal organization, it was established by Yolngu landowners to manage outside access to Yolngu land. (☎08 8987 3992. Open M-F 8:30am-noon and 1-4pm.) To leave town legally, a two-month **general visitor's recreation permit** ($35 per person; $20 for 7-day permit) is required. Some areas, such as **Cape Arnhem, Caves Beach, Oyster Beach, Wonga Creek,** and **Memorial Park,** require advance booking and special permits. The **Northern Land Council,** in Endeavour Sq. off the Woolworths carpark, grants permits for driving along the Central Arnhem Hwy. and anywhere not covered by Dhimurru permits. (☎08 8986 8500. Open M-F 8am-5:30pm.)

The **library,** 73 Matthew Flinders Way, has free **Internet.** (☎08 8987 0860. Open M-W and F 10am-5pm, Th 10am-7pm, Sa 10am-1pm.) The **police** (☎000 or 13 14 44) and a **hospital** (☎08 8987 0211) are on Flinders Way. **Postal Code:** 0880.

NORTHERN TERRITORY

▐▛▐█ **ACCOMMODATIONS AND FOOD.** Everything in Nhulunbuy is expensive. For most budget travelers, **camping ❶** is the best option. The least expensive place to stay is the **Gove Peninsula Motel ❺** on Matthew Flinders Way at Melville Bay Rd. All rooms are ensuite and have kitchenettes. (☎08 8987 0700. Rooms $154; twin share $172.) If you prefer an ocean view, try the **Walkabout Lodge ❺**, 12 Westall St. (☎08 8987 1777. Singles $160; doubles $185; triples $220.) The least expensive place to buy food is **Woolworths** (☎08 8987 1588) in Endeavour Sq. (Open M-Th and Sa-Su 8am-8pm, F 7am-8pm.)

◪ **SIGHTS.** The free **Mine Tour** (☎08 8987 5207) is thorough and engaging, offering a thoughtful, well-balanced view of the mine's impact on the land. The mine's construction outraged the local Yolngu people, and the legal battle over land rights went all the way to the Northern Territory Supreme Court. Though the mine won the case, the controversy led to the formation of the **Northern Land Council,** the entity responsible for reclaiming Aboriginal land and giving legal force to the traditional ownership system. The Mine Tour departs from the taxi stand on Westall St. every Friday at 8:30am. Book at least one day ahead and wear closed-toe shoes. The **Roy Marika Lookout,** on Mt. Saunders off Wuyal Rd., has a decent view of the town and the surrounding coastline. Take Matthew Flinders Way to Arnhem Rd. and then Arnhem to Wuyal Rd.

# DOWN THE TRACK

Heading south out of Darwin on the Stuart Hwy., vast stretches of road sprawl out between the few spartan settlements that offer refuge to parched travelers. Traffic may not roll by often, but roadside monoliths and stray marsupials try to keep lonesome drivers company. Expanses of scrubland stretch out in all directions, and the horizons only hint at the scale of the unoccupied space that surrounds Australia's major central corridor.

## VICTORIA HIGHWAY: KATHERINE TO KUNUNURRA

From downtown Katherine, the "Vic" careens westward 512km to Kununurra, Western Australia (p. 763). There's precious little between the two places to distract you from the startling escarpments and mountain ridges that run parallel to the highway. Located 200km west of Katherine, the **Victoria River Roadhouse** has petrol, a restaurant (burgers $6.50-10.50), and quiet campsites. (☎08 8975 0744. Sites for 2 $15, powered $20, extra person $7.50; singles $40; doubles $75; motel rooms from $95.) Scenic helicopter flights also depart from the roadhouse. (12min. $80, 20min. $135, 30min. $185.)

The highway cuts across the northern section of massive **Gregory National Park.** Call the **Timber Creek Ranger Station** (☎08 8975 0888) for road conditions. The Territory's second-largest national park (after Kakadu) occupies a swath of land that progresses from arid scrub to tropics and is most easily accessed by 4WD vehicles entering from the **Buntine and Buchanan unsealed roads.** Ten kilometers east of Timber Creek, adventure-seeking tourists can acquire a new red coat along the dusty and uneven **Bullita access road,** stretching for 42km into the heart of the park and the network of 4WD tracks, eventually forking toward either the **Limestone Gorge** or **Bullita Homestead and campground.** Campgrounds along the Victoria Hwy. and at the end of the Bullita road have honesty boxes to collect a minimal fee, while campgrounds off the 4WD-only roads are free. On these roads, frequent dips, ruts, and even potential creek crossings mean that those with 2WD, average-clearance vehicles should proceed with caution and opt for common sense rather than adventure. **Timber Creek,** a rowdy roadside settlement, is another 90km west of Victoria River. The **Wayside Inn** ❶ has a small, simple restaurant and a wide range of accommodations. (☎08 8975 0722. Sites $7.50 per person, powered for 2 $20; singles $45, ensuite $90-110. Book rooms at BP up the road.) **River cruises** depart from and can be booked at nearby **Victoria River Cruises** (☎08 8975 0850; M-Sa 4pm $80; children $40; 3½hr.; bus transfer to and from river 10min.). Four kilometers west of Timber Creek, a turnoff leads to a dirt, gravel, and paved path up to a lookout. There, a monument to the **Nackeroos**—Australia's northern army detachment during WWII—makes for a nice picnic spot. **Keep River National Park,** 45km east of Kununurra, is home to Aboriginal art sites and a few bushwalks through eroded sandstone sites. Camping is permitted at two sites (15km and 28km down a gravel road). Finally, about 480km west of Katherine (less than 40km from Kununurra) is the border crossing into Western Australia. There are strict quarantines against bringing fruits, veggies, or plants across the border.

> **! TIME TRAVEL.** Be aware that clocks in Western Australia are set 1½hr. behind those in the Northern Territory.

# TENNANT CREEK ☎08

Dusty Tennant Creek (pop. 3500), the self-proclaimed "Golden Heart" of the Northern Territory, appeals to most travelers as a welcome reprieve from the monotonous stretch of road between Alice Springs and Darwin. A product of Australia's last great gold rush in the 1930s, Tennant has remained small despite a $4-billion output of gold since the 1960s. The **Devil's Marbles** (p. 298) and the artistic flavor of Warumungu Aborigines make it worth a stop.

**TRANSPORTATION.** All **buses** stop at the **Transit Centre** on Paterson St., near the intersection with Stuart St., at the north end of town. (Open M-F 7:30am-5:30pm and 9-11pm, Sa 8am-12:30pm and 2:30-4:30am.) Greyhound Australia (☎13 14 99) serves Alice Springs (6hr., 1 per day, $151); Darwin (14hr., 1 per day, $213); Katherine (9hr., 1 per day, $157); Townsville (20hr., 1 per day, $257). Call **Tennant Creek Taxi Service** (☎08 8962 3626) for a cab.

**ORIENTATION AND PRACTICAL INFORMATION.** The **Stuart Highway,** called **Paterson Street** in town, runs north to south. Intersecting Paterson are **Stuart Street** (not to be confused with the Stuart Hwy.), **Davidson Street,** and **Peko Road** from the east, which becomes **Windley Street** west of Paterson. There's an **ANZ** bank (☎13 13 14), on Paterson St. between Davidson and Stuart St., and a **Westpac** bank, 64 Peko Rd. (☎08 8962 2801), at the corner of Paterson St. Both are open M-Th 9:30am-4pm, F 9:30am-5pm. The **police** (☎08 8962 4444) are on Paterson St. near Windley St. There is **Internet access** at the **Tennant Creek Public Library,** on Peko Rd. (☎08 8962 2657. $2 per 30min. Open M 9am-5pm, Tu 2-6pm, W-F 10am-5pm, Sa 10am-noon.) The **post office** is at the corner of Paterson St. and Memorial Dr. (☎08 8962 2196. Open M-F 9am-5pm.) **Postal Code:** 0861.

**ACCOMMODATIONS AND FOOD.** **Outback Caravan Park,** 600m from Paterson St. on Peko Rd., offers shady sites, neat lawns, and a swimming pool. Amenities include kitchen, BBQ, laundry, and friendly staff. (☎08 8962 2459. Sites for 2 $21, powered $27; deluxe ensuite cabins $61-115.) Reach **Tourists Rest Hostel** ❷, on Leichardt St., by walking south on Paterson St. and turning right on Windley St. This spacious, friendly hostel also has kitchen, pool, TV, and laundry. (☎08 8962 2719. Reception 24hr. Dorms $20, VIP/YHA $18; twins and doubles $42/38.) **Safari Backpackers YHA** ❶, 12 Davidson St., west of Paterson St., is small but comfortable. (☎08 8962 2207. Reception 7am-9pm across the street. Dorms $17; twins and doubles $40. YHA discount.)

Paterson St. is lined with takeaway snack bars and eateries. **Rocky's,** next door to the Transit Centre, provides takeaway-only pizza in a no-frills setting. (☎08 8962 1925. Open daily 4-11pm.) **Top of Town Cafe** ❶, just north of the Transit Centre, has veggie burgers and a sandwich bar for $3-6. (☎08 8962 1311. Open M-F 7am-4pm, Sa-Su 7am-2pm.) The **Tennant Food Barn** also sells cheap groceries. (☎08 8962 2296. Open M-Sa 8am-6pm, Su 9am-6pm.)

---

**FINDING YOUR MARBLES.** Geologists suspect water erosion. Aboriginal legend credits the Rainbow Serpent. Whatever created them, the boulders known as the **Devil's Marbles** are beautiful and baffling. Eighty kilometers south of Tennant Creek, just off the Stuart Hwy., the nearly spherical (7m in diameter) granite rocks balance precariously on one another.

---

# RED CENTRE

Though the Red Centre is home to less than 0.5% of Australia's population, it is considered by some to be the essence of the Australian continent. Everything in the Centre has a mythical, larger-than-life quality. The landscapes are nothing if not arresting; while massive **Uluru,** the world's largest monolith, draws your eyes skyward, the plunging depths of **Watarrka (Kings Canyon)** pull them down. In the endless skies, panoramic watercolor sunsets give way to millions of stars every night. **Alice Springs,** cradled between the craggy, decaying **MacDonnell Ranges,** is the only sizeable town in any direction, serving as the region's unofficial capital and gateway for many travelers. Those titles are more de facto than deserved, however; 5hr. drives to Watarrka and Uluru force time-strapped tourists to consider flying direct.

## ALICE SPRINGS                                                    ☎08

Local lore says that the founders of Alice Springs came looking for rubies in the surrounding mountain ranges. When the ruby deposit proved instead to be garnet, miners too lazy to leave the area helped found Stuart, now Alice Springs or Alice. Proximity to abundant natural wonders and precious little else has rendered the city an important center for commerce and tourism. With 30,000 residents, it dwarfs every settlement for nearly 1500km in all directions, and is the largest town between Adelaide on the Southern Ocean and tropical Darwin in the Top End. Other than the ubiquitous shops, desks, and kiosks offering tour options to Red Centre pilgrims, Alice Springs offers a wide variety of stores and suppliers for anyone passing through town looking to stock up for the unavoidably long journey to anywhere else. Still, those looking for depth below Alice Springs's surface aren't likely to find much; tourists rarely stay for more than a few days after their excursions to Uluru and Watarrka.

### 🔲 TRANSPORTATION

**Planes: Alice Springs Airport** (☎08 8950 3910), 10km south of the city on Stuart Hwy. **Qantas** (☎13 13 13) flies to: **Adelaide** (2hr., 2 per day); **Brisbane** (4hr., 1 per day);

**Cairns** (3hr., 1 per day); **Darwin** (2hr., 3 per day); **Melbourne** (3hr., 1 per day); **Perth** (3hr., 1 per day); **Sydney** (3hr., 1 per day); **Yulara** (45min., 3 per day).

**Trains: Alice Railway Station** is a 5min. walk from central Alice. From George St., take a left on Larapinta Dr., which crosses the Stuart Hwy. and runs into Alice. **The Ghan** (www.gsr.com.au) runs to **Adelaide** (22hr.; Th 12:45pm and Su 3:15pm; $355, student $225) and **Darwin** (24hr.; M and Th 6pm; $355, student $225). Make reservations through the tourist office or call direct (☎13 21 47). Several levels of accommodations available. Prices listed are for the least expensive level, Red Kangaroo Day/Nighter.

**Buses: Greyhound Australia** (☎08 8952 7888) runs from the corner of Gregory and Railway Terr. Service to: **Adelaide** (20hr., 1 per day, $262); **Darwin** (22hr., 1 per day, $295); **Tennant Creek** (6hr., 1 per day, $151); **Sydney** (2 days, 1 per day, $443).

**Public Transportation: ASBus** (☎08 8950 0500), the bus system, runs infrequently to the outskirts of town. Service M-F 8 or 9am-6pm, Sa only in the morning. $1.40-2.20.

**Taxis: Alice Springs Taxis** (☎8952 1877 or 13 10 18).

**Car Rental:** You must be 21 to rent a vehicle and 25 to rent a 4WD in Alice Springs. **Europcar** (☎08 8955 5994 or 13 13 90) at the airport has some of the best rates, with cars from $58 per day and a $13.20 per day under-25 surcharge. Open M-F 8am-5pm, Sa-Su 8am-1pm. **Territory-Thrifty** (☎08 8952 9999), on the corner of Hartley St. and Stott Terr., has cars from $78 per day with a $16.50 per day under-25 surcharge; 4WD from $145 per day. Open daily 8am-5:30pm. **Britz** (☎08 8952 8814 or 800 331 454), on the corner of Stuart Hwy. and Power St., has 2WDs from $55 and 4WDs or campervans with unlimited km from $100 per day. Open daily 8am-4pm. **Maui** (☎08 8952 8049), corner of Stuart Hwy. and Power St., has 4WD and campervans.

**Roadside Assistance: AANT** (24hr. ☎08 8952 1087).

**Road Conditions:** 24hr. ☎1800 246 199.

## ⚡ ORIENTATION

The **Stuart Highway** runs through Alice on its way from Darwin (1486km) to Adelaide (1570km). The dry **Todd River** bed provides an eastern border to the CBD; the **MacDonnell Ranges** form a natural border at the southern side of the city. The break between the east-west ranges, called **Heavitree Gap,** allows both the Stuart Hwy. and the Todd to pass through. The true commercial center of town is **Todd Mall,** a pedestrian-only stretch of Todd St. between Wills and Gregory Terr.; the two indoor malls are **Alice Plaza** (Todd Mall at Parsons St.) and **Yeperenye Plaza** (Hartley St. north of Gregory Terr.). Most tour agencies and small shops lie on **Todd Street,** just south of the Todd Mall.

## 🛈 PRACTICAL INFORMATION

**Tourist Office: Central Australian Tourism Industry Association** (☎08 8952 5800 or 1800 645 199; www.centralaustraliantourism.com), on Gregory Terr. at the end of Todd Mall. Books transportation, tours, and accommodations, sells maps, and has park info. Grab the excellent, free city map. Open M-F 8:30am-5pm, Sa-Su 9:30am-4pm.

**Budget Travel: Flight Centre** (☎08 8953 4081), Shop 18A, Yeperenye Center, guarantees the lowest airfares. Open M-F 9am-5:30pm, Sa 9:30am-12:30pm. **Travelworld,** 40 Todd Mall (☎08 8953 0488), near Parsons St. Open M-F 9am-5:30pm, Sa 9am-noon.

**Tours:** Many hostels run tours that include accommodations. Several agencies just off Todd Mall book tour packages. **Backpacker's World Travel** (☎08 8953 0666), on Todd St. and Gregory Terr. Open M-F 9:30am-6pm, Sa-Su 10am-4:30pm. Day tours from $99; 1-day, lightning-fast tours of Uluru start at $195; 3-day all-inclusive Uluru tours start at $275. **Mulga's** tours, run out of Annie's Place, are the cheapest.

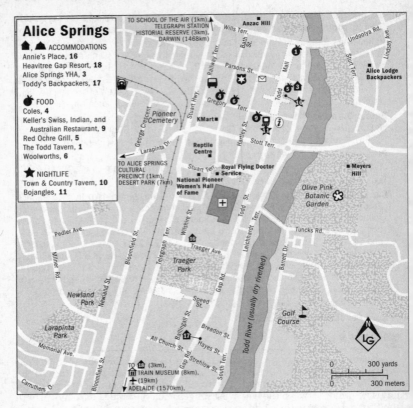

**Alice Springs**

🏠, 🏕 ACCOMMODATIONS
Annie's Place, **16**
Heavitree Gap Resort, **18**
Alice Springs YHA, **3**
Toddy's Backpackers, **17**

🍎 FOOD
Coles, **4**
Keller's Swiss, Indian, and
  Australian Restaurant, **9**
Red Ochre Grill, **5**
The Todd Tavern, **1**
Woolworths, **6**

⭐ NIGHTLIFE
Town & Country Tavern, **10**
Bojangles, **11**

**Currency Exchange: National Australia** (☎08 8952 1611) and **ANZ** (☎08 8952 1144) are in Todd Mall, along with **ATMs**. Both open M-Th 9:30am-4pm, F 9:30am-5pm.

**Work Opportunities:** Alice has a year-round labor shortage. Try **Centre Labour Force** (☎08 8952 3800). Hostel bulletin boards list short-term job opportunities.

**Library:** (☎08 8950 0555), on Gregory Terr. near Todd Mall next to the tourist office. Open M-Tu and Th 10am-6pm, W and F 10am-5pm, Sa 9am-1pm, Su 1-5pm.

**Book Exchange: Bookmark It,** 113 Todd St. (☎08 8953 2465). Open M-Tu, Th, F 9am-5pm, W 10am-5pm, Sa 10am-2pm, Su at Sunday Market.

**Emergency:** ☎000.

**Police:** (☎08 8951 8888), on Parsons St., at the corner of Bath St.

**Hospital: Alice Springs Clinic** (☎08 8951 7777), on Gap Rd. between Stuart Terr. and Traeger Ave. Dental and health clinic across the street.

**Pharmacy: Priceline** (☎08 8953 0089) in Todd Mall. Open M-F 8:30am-6pm, Sa 8:30am-3pm, Su 8:30am-1pm.

**Internet Access:** Numerous places along Todd St. between Gregory Terr. and Stuart St. Many services including digital photo processing. Rates $3-4 per hr., pro-rated. **Todd Internet,** 82 Todd Mall. Open M and F-Sa 10am-6pm, Tu-Th 9am-6pm, Su 9am-4pm.

**Post Office: GPO** (☎08 8952 1020), on Hartley St. south of Parsons St. Open M-F 8:15am-5pm. **Postal Code:** 0870.

# ACCOMMODATIONS AND CAMPING

All of the hostels listed below have A/C and pools; all recommend booking ahead and happily arrange tours. Most have bike rental from $25 per day.

**Annie's Place,** 4 Traeger Ave. (☎08 8952 1545, www.anniesplace.com.au). Clean dorms centered around a palm-lined courtyard. On-site bar serves meals (from $5) and drinks. Breakfast included. $8 airport dropoff. Dorms $22; doubles $55, with bath $65. ❷

**Heavitree Gap Outback Lodge** (☎08 8950 4444; www.auroraresorts.com.au), on Palm Circuit. Sparklingly clean rooms approx. 5km from CBD. Breathtaking location surrounded by bluffs inhabited by blackfooted wallabies. Shuttle bus runs to town ($1); the last shuttle from town is at 4:15pm. Dorms $27; ensuite doubles $135; family room $123. Sites $10 per person, powered for 2 $22, extra person $11. ❷

**Alice Springs YHA** (☎08 8952 8855), corner of Parsons St. and Leichardt Terr. Excellent facilities include a pool, TV lounge, and large kitchen. Safe and storage available. Internet access $4 per hr. Key deposit $20. Wheelchair-accessible. Reception 7:30am-8:30pm. 6- to 16-bed dorms $22.50-26.50; 4-bed dorms $29. YHA discount 10%. ❷

**Toddy's Backpackers,** 41 Gap Rd. (☎08 8952 1322), 10min. walk from the CBD. Many ensuite dorm rooms have their own kitchenette, TV, and balcony. Meals ($8-17) and beer (schooners $4.50) available in the **bar** ❷ (5:30-10:30pm; food 6pm-9pm), which features live music nightly after 8:30pm. Free breakfast included. Reception 6am-8:30pm. Dorms $20-24; singles, doubles, and twins with sink and fridge $60; budget motel rooms $60; ensuite motel doubles with TV and fridge $75. Extra person $10. ❷

**Alice Lodge Backpackers,** 4 Mueller St. (☎08 8953 1975 or 1800 351 925; www. alicelodge.com.au). Free continental breakfast, airport, train and bus pickups, free Wi-Fi, and a pool. Reception 8:30am-1:45pm and 4:30-7pm. 8- to 10-bed dorms $21; 3- to 4-bed dorms $25; singles $55; doubles $60. ❷

# FOOD

Food generally doesn't come cheap in Alice. Todd Mall, near Gregory Terr., has a handful of cafes where you can pick up basic sandwiches or snacks without breaking the bank. Cheaper still are the many supermarkets, including a 24hr. **Coles** on Bath St. at Gregory Terr. and a **Woolworths** in the Yeperenye Plaza. Unless noted, all restaurants accept major credit cards (AmEx/MC/V).

**Red Ochre Grill** (☎08 8952 9614), on Todd Mall near Parsons St. Sample what a top-notch chef can do with regional ingredients. Aussie Game Medley ($36) and marinated kangaroo pizza ($13.50) are popular. Check out the $10 lunch special or dine early at dinner for 20% off the menu. Open daily 6am-late. ❷

**The Todd Tavern,** 1 Todd Mall (☎08 8952 1255), near Wills Terr. Popular among tourists and locals alike, this pub/restaurant includes salad bar with every meal. Hearty specials $9-13. Sa all-you-can-eat buffet dinner $18.50. Open daily 10:30am-11pm. ❶

**Keller's Restaurant** (☎08 8952 3188), on Gregory Terr. east of Hartley St. Swiss and Indian fare come together in a portrait of diversity. Enjoy beef vindaloo ($25), Züscher Geschnetzeltes (veal in mushroom sauce, $27), or Kangaroo fillet stroganoff ($29.) No diverse menu would be complete without vegetarian options (Butcher's Rösti $25). Reservations recommended. Open M-Sa 5:30pm-late. ❹

**NO WORK, ALL PLAY**

## CAMEL DERBY

As beasts of burden, the camel has been a great friend of man's for hundreds of years. When they were imported to Australia in the mid-19th century to assist with railroad construction, they were highly prized because of their unique survival traits. Speed and elegance, however, were not among them. Still, in Alice Springs, where the river is dry and the major tourist attractions are hundreds of kilometers away, central Australians have adopted the stubborn creatures as the star sprinters in an annual July event called the Camel Cup.

The tradition began with a bet between two camel farmers who thought it would be fun to see whose humped steed could run faster. Eventually, it expanded into a full-day extravaganza with a series of races and events. These include a Rickshaw Race, a Mr. and Miss Camel Cup competition, and the Honeymoon Handicap race, in which new husbands stop midway to pick up their brides before continuing on to the finish line. Of course, there are also camel sprints. While the site of a heat of camels scampering around a track is less inspiring than bemusing, it does well to set the tone for a riotous day at Blatherskite Park.

*Adults $15, children $5, children under 12 free, families $30. For more information go to www.camelcup.com.au.*

## 🄶 SIGHTS

The **Alice Wanderer** shuttle circles around many of the major sights in the Alice Springs area. It's a cheap way to get out to some semi-distant attractions. However, its schedule requires that you spend an hour and ten minutes (or multiples thereof) at each sight that you want to see. (☎08 8952 2111 or 1800 722 111. Runs 9am-4pm, departs from the southern end of Todd Mall. All-day ticket $40, including second day free.)

### CITY CENTER

**ANZAC HILL.** Though the aerial view of Alice is often a little bit drab, Anzac Hill can offer a postcard-perfect sunset with the MacDonnells as a beautiful backdrop. *(Walk to Wills Terr. between Bath and Hartley St.; a metal arch marks the start of the easy 10min. "Lions Walk" from the base to the obelisk at the top. Vehicle access is around the corner on Stuart Hwy.)*

**REPTILE CENTRE.** With an impressive collection of local lizards and snakes—some of which you can hold, if you're brave enough—the Reptile Centre is a fun introduction to cold-blooded Australia. *(9 Stuart Terr., on the corner of Bath St. ☎08 8952 8900. Open daily 9:30am-5pm. Feedings 11am, 1, and 3:30pm. $12, children $6, family $30. YHA/VIP discount.)*

**NATIONAL PIONEER WOMEN'S HALL OF FAME.** This sight is an enjoyable tribute to over 100 Australian women who broke ground in fields ranging from sports to medicine. *(☎08 8952 9006; www.pioneerwomen.com.au. In the Old Gaol on Stuart Terr., across from the Reptile Center. Open daily 10am-5pm. $6.50, concessions $5, child 5-15 $3, family $16.)*

### OUTSIDE THE CITY CENTER

**🄼ALICE SPRINGS CULTURAL PRECINCT.** This collection of art galleries and museums is a great way to spend a few hours learning about all aspects of the region. The **Araluen Centre and Galleries** has rotating exhibitions, the largest collection of work by renowned Aboriginal artist Albert Namatjira, and displays of works completed by local artists. The **Museum of Central Australia** has a wonderful set of exhibits detailing the region's meteorology and biology. The **Central Australian Aviation Museum** tells the story of aviation's important role in the development of this remote region. The nearby cemetery contains Namatjira's grave. *(1km out on Larapinta Dr. ☎08 8951 1120. Open M-F 10am-4pm, Sa-Su 11am-4pm. $10, children $6, families $25.)*

**DESERT PARK.** An impressive collection of local flora and fauna. The nocturnal house is a great place to view such reclusive species as the bilby and dunnart. The **Birds of Prey show** is also popular. *(8km west of town on Larapinta Dr. Desert Park runs a shuttle from most accommodations to the park every 90min. 7:30am-6pm. Call for pickup ☎08 8952 4667. $38, concessions $28; includes admission. Park ☎08 8951 8788. Open daily 7:30am-6pm. Birds of Prey show 10am and 3:30pm. $20, children $10, families $55.)*

**SCHOOL OF THE AIR.** Central Australia's answer to the daunting task of educating children living on remote cattle stations, roadhouses, and Aboriginal lands. Using the Royal Flying Doctors' radio network, lessons are broadcast to 140 students over a network covering 1.3 million sq. km. *(Coming from Alice, before the turnoff to the Reserve, a sign on the Stuart Hwy. points down Head St. ☎08 8951 6834. Open M-Sa 8:30am-4:30pm, Su 1:30-4:30pm. $6.50, concessions $4, family $16.)*

**TELEGRAPH STATION HISTORICAL RESERVE.** From its early days as a relay station for telegraphs between Darwin and Adelaide, to its 10-year stint as a home for half-white-half-Aboriginal children, to its use as a camp by Aboriginal people banned from Alice Springs after dark, this station has an important history that is brought to life by tours and exhibits. *(Take the turn-off 3km north of the CBD on the Stuart Hwy. ☎08 8952 3993. 30min. walk from the CBD. $7.60, children $4.25.)*

## 🎵 🎭 ENTERTAINMENT AND NIGHTLIFE

The *Alice Spring News* ($0.90) has a "Dive Into Live" section listing upcoming events. The 500-seat **Araluen Centre,** on Larapinta Dr., presents indie flicks some Sundays and live theater performances. (☎08 8951 1122. Box office open daily 10am-5pm.) For mainstream movies, go to **Alice Springs Cinema,** at the north end of Todd Mall. (☎08 8953 2888. Tickets $14, Tu $10.) For those with more cash, **Red Centre Dreaming** offers a traditional three-course NT dinner with an Aboriginal cultural display that includes a dance troupe performance. (☎1800 089 616. Open daily 7-10pm. $105, children $60; includes pickup and dropoff.)

   **Bojangles,** 80 Todd St., has everything you could want in a saloon: a honky-tonk piano in the corner, great food, and a generous helping of outback cowboys. This is the kind of place where throwing peanut shells on the floor is appreciated. Be forewarned that your raucous night will be webcast (seriously, visit www.bossaloon.com.au) every night from 9pm-1am. (☎08 8952 2873. Open M-Th and Su 11:30am-1am, F-Sa 11:30am-3am. Frequent DJs. Su Blues Jam 3pm-late.) The **Town and Country Tavern** in the Todd Mall, meanwhile, is a great place to catch big sports events. Fosters schooners are $3.50 on Fosters Fridays. Last Friday of every month the jukebox is free and select drinks for $5. (Daily food specials from $15.50. Open M-Su 11am-2pm.)

## 🎪 FESTIVALS AND EVENTS

In April, **Heritage Week** features various historical reenactments and displays. Around the same time, Alice plays host to a month-long horse racing festival, the lavish **Alice Springs Cup Carnival,** which takes place at the town's **Pioneer Race Park** and culminates with the **Bangtail Muster parade** on the first Monday of May. On the **Queen's Birthday Weekend** in early June, the plucky cars and motorcycles of the **Finke Desert Race** traverse 240km of roadless dusty desert from Alice to Finke. The first Saturday in July hosts the traditional, agriculture-focused **Alice Springs Show.** The not-so-traditional **Camel Cup Carnival race** (www.camelcup.com. au), including a **Miss Camel Cup Competition,** is held the following weekend. The **Alice Springs Rodeo** and the **Harts Range Annual Races** are both held in August.

   The definitive Alice Springs festival is the **Henley-on-Todd Regatta** (third Sa in Sept.; www.henleyontodd.com.au). A good-natured mock celebration centered on the dry river; the "regatta" race is done in bottomless "boats" propelled Flintstones-style—by swift feet. The **Corkwood Festival,** on the last Saturday of November, resembles a gigantic garage sale, with daytime craft booths and energetic bush dancing at night.

# MACDONNELL RANGES

The MacDonnell Ranges are the craggy, eroded remains of mountains that once stretched as high as the Himalayas. Today, they cradle Alice Springs, and their sandstone precipices break up the plains of the rolling red center. Distant shots of their fuzzy shrubs and soft pastels have inspired watercolors and postcards for years, but get closer on a walking trail and you'll find sunburnt country—rusty orange earth, prickly ground cover, and glowing white ghost gums.

| MACDONNELL RANGES AT A GLANCE | |
|---|---|
| **AREA:** 460km. | **GATEWAYS:** Alice Springs (p. 298). |
| **FEATURES:** West MacDonnell NP along Namatjira Dr., Finke Gorge NP off Larapinta Dr., and several nature parks in the eastern ranges. | **CAMPING:** Available but limited. Check with a tour agency in Alice Springs before setting out for any camping trip. |
| **HIGHLIGHTS:** Hikes, swims, and views. | **FEES:** A small fee is charged only at Standley Chasm (p. 305) and the Hermannsburg Historical Precinct (p. 305). |

# WEST MACDONNELLS

## 🔆 ORIENTATION

To the north of the Uluru-Kata Tjuta and Watarrka area, immediately outside Alice Springs, lie central Australia's mountains. **Larapinta Drive** heads straight out of town, passing turnoffs to **Simpson's Gap** and **Standley Chasm.** After about 25km, the road forks into two branches, with Larapinta Dr. continuing on to **Hermannsburg** and **Finke Gorge,** and **Namatjira Drive** passing the **Ellery Creek Big Hole** and **Serpentine Gorge** en route to the **Glen Helen** area. The only road that runs between Hermannsburg and Glen Helen is the rough-and-tumble **Tylers Pass** loop, a rough 4WD track with extraordinary scenery.

## 🛶 ♿ HIKING AND TOURS

The **Larapinta Trail** stretches 223km from the Telegraph Station in Alice Springs to Mt. Razorback, beyond Glen Helen Gorge. Experienced hikers can make treks to the range's remote attractions on this trail, moving from gorge to gorge in individual two- to four-day chunks. Before attempting the long hikes, get information from the **Park and Wildlife Commission** in Alice Springs. (☎08 8951 8250. P.O. Box 2130, Alice Springs, NT 0870.) **Voluntary registration** (☎1300 650 730) is a good idea; the $50 deposit is refundable unless park rangers have to send out a search and rescue mission for you.

The **Glen Helen Lodge** (p. 306) has the only official accommodations in the West MacDonnells. The best bet for long visits is to take a tour. **AAT Kings Tours** does a daytrip to the range. (☎08 8952 1700; www.aatkings.com. Departs daily 7:30am. $110, children $55.) **Centre Highlights** makes a 4WD trek to some

area highlights, including Finke River and Palm Valley. (☎1800 659 574; www.
centrehighlights.com.au. Departs M, W, F 8am. Daytrips from $95.)

## ⚲ SIGHTS

The West MacDonnells' sights lie along two paved roads, Larapinta and
Namatjira Dr., heading out from the town of Alice Springs. The westernmost
parts of these roads, as well as the Mereenie Loop road, are 4WD-only. The distance from Alice is listed in parentheses after the description of each sight.

### LARAPINTA DRIVE

**JOHN FLYNN MEMORIAL GRAVE.** Just off the road is the grave of the minister
who created the Royal Flying Doctor Service. Sentiment that his gravestone
should be something symbolic of the Outback led to the selection of a massive
boulder taken from the **Devil's Marbles** (p. 298), near Tennant Creek—which in
turn led to a 20-year battle between the caretaker of Flynn's grave and Aborigines, for whom the Devil's Marbles are sacred. The dispute was settled in 1999
with the substitution of a stone from the East MacDonnells and the return of
the Devil's Marble to its original location. *(7km.)*

**SIMPSON'S GAP.** Simpson's Gap, located down a paved 8km turnoff, offers
some nice hikes and views of jagged red rocks. The **Gap Walk** is an easy 20min.
jaunt from the carpark. The **Cassia Hill Walk** is an equally simple 1.8km (30min.)
climb to a lookout. *(18km. Open daily 5am-8pm. Free.)*

**STANDLEY CHASM.** After traveling down a mostly flat, 30min. path along a
creek bed, crowds gather to marvel at the glowing orange walls when the sun
shines directly into this 80m fissure at midday. Venture past a shallow waterhole and up the rocky slide at the far end to enjoy a less crowded second
chasm and an aerial view of the first. *(46km. ☎08 8956 7440. Open daily 8am-6pm, last
entry 5pm. $8, concessions $7. Food and drinks available. Pay at cafe if kiosk unmanned.)*

**FINKE GORGE NATIONAL PARK.** This 46,000 hectare park contains the Finke
River, some stretches of which date back 350 million years. The park's main
attraction is Palm Valley, home to rare red cabbage palms. Two worthwhile
walks are the **Mpulungkinya Walk** (5km, 2hr.), which traverses the thickest growth
of palms, and the **Arankaia Walk** (2km, 1hr.), which climbs the valley rim. The
**Kalaranga Lookout** (1.5km, 45min.) offers 360° views of the park. *(125km. Accessed
via the 21km 4WD-only road that follows the path of the Finke River, off Larapinta Dr.)*

**HERMANNSBURG HISTORICAL PRECINCT.** Homes from the area's early
Lutheran mission and a gallery saluting the work of Aboriginal artist Albert
Namatjira are both here. The service station sells the **Mereenie Tour Pass** ($2.20)
for the 4WD track to **Kings Canyon** (p. 308), petrol, and groceries. *(126km. ☎08
8956 7402. Open daily 9am-4pm. $10, children $5, pensioners $8, family $25. Grocery store and
fuel open M-Sa 9am-5:30pm, Su 10am-5:30pm.)*

### NAMATJIRA DRIVE

**▨ORMISTON GORGE.** A 10min. walk leads to a few of the gorge's pools (some
14m deep). The wonderful **Ghost Gum Walk** (1hr.) climbs the side of the gorge
to an impressive lookout, then drops off further downriver, allowing hikers to
wander along the creek amid boulders stained silver, blue, and purple. During
late afternoon, the orange walls glow in the sinking sun and wallabies come out
to play. The **Pound Walk** (7km, 3-4hr.) is more peaceful, offering great views of
the surrounding hills before approaching the gorge from the back. *(130km.)*

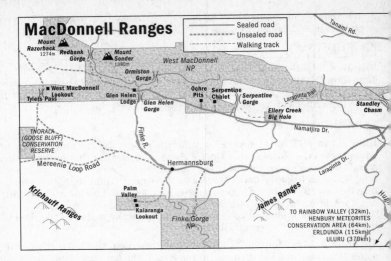

**MacDonnell Ranges**

Sealed road
Unsealed road
Walking track

Tanami Rd.

Mount Razorback 1274m
Redbank Gorge
Mount Sonder 1380m
Ormiston Gorge
West MacDonnell NP
West MacDonnell Lookout
Tylers Pass
Glen Helen Lodge
Glen Helen Gorge
Ochre Pits
Serpentine Chalet
Serpentine Gorge
Larapinta Trail
Standley Chasm
Ellery Creek Big Hole
Namatjira Dr.
Larapinta Dr.
TNORALA (GOOSE BLUFF) CONSERVATION RESERVE
Finke R.
Hermannsburg
Mereenie Loop Road
Krichauff Ranges
James Ranges
Palm Valley
Kalaranga Lookout
Finke Gorge NP
Hugh

TO RAINBOW VALLEY (32km),
HENBURY METEORITES
CONSERVATION AREA (64km),
ERLDUNDA (115km),
ULURU (370km)

**ELLERY CREEK BIG HOLE.** Down a rough 2km access road and a 100m wheelchair-accessible path, this waterhole makes for a nippy dip in the summer. The nearby **Dolomite Walk** (3km, 1hr.) traverses lush forest and spinifex.

**SERPENTINE GORGE.** A walk along a service road (1hr.) leads to this serene gorge. The highlight of Serpentine is the lookout walk, a short, steep climb starting near the gorge and ending with a great view of the West MacDonnells. Down a rough 3km road, the ruins of the **Serpentine Chalet** are unremarkable, but it's a great spot for bushcamping. *(99km.)*

**OCHRE PITS.** The cliffs are a key source of ochre, used in Aboriginal art. A wheelchair-accessible path leads to a platform overlooking the pits. From there, a walk along the riverbed provides views of the banded rock walls. *(111km.)*

**GLEN HELEN GORGE.** At the end of the paved road, the **Glen Helen Lodge ❷** sits at the foot of the gorge, illuminated at night with spotlights. It's the only place to fill up on gas and food this side of Alice. *(132km. ☎ 08 8956 7489. www.glenhelen. com.au. Sites for 2 $20; motel rooms for 2 from $130. Helicopter flights $45-295. Book ahead.)*

**GOSSE BLUFF.** You can see the site of the ancient crater up close from the 11km 4WD track, or take in the whole picture from the **West MacDonnell Lookout,** a turnoff near the north end of Tylers Pass. *(175km.)*

# EAST MACDONNELLS

## ✦ ⓘ ORIENTATION AND TOURS

Just beyond Heavitree Gap south of Alice, **Ross Highway** branches off the Stuart Hwy. and heads eastward into the East MacDonnells. The road narrows to a single lane at times, and wandering wild camels frequently travel down the center of the road. More varied, less crowded, and as fetching as their more lauded western neighbors, the East MacDonnells offer good 4WD tracks and rewarding

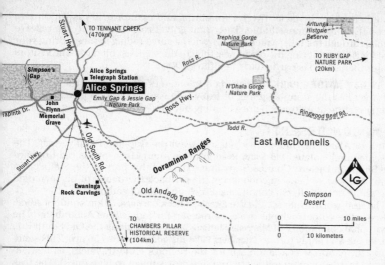

hikes. The range is accessed primarily through tours; campsites are not always open, so check with a tour agency in town before planning your trip.

## SIGHTS

The distance from Alice along Ross Hwy. to the turnoff for each listing is given in parentheses after the description of each sight.

**EMILY GAP.** Bold and unassuming, Emily Gap is an important site for the local Arrernte people. A gallery of Aboriginal rock paintings marks the spot where *Intwailuka*, an ancestral hero, cooked and ate caterpillars on his Dreamtime journey. Icy pools often obstruct the path into the gap and the gallery. If the water appears low enough, leave your shoes behind and cross in the center of the pool where it is most shallow. *(10km.)*

**TREPHINA GORGE NATURE PARK.** A partly paved 8km access road leads to the carpark and the **main campground ❶.** The **Trephina Gorge Walk** (2km, 45min.) follows the gorge rim before descending to the riverbed—pay careful attention: signs become less obvious as the walk continues. The **Panorama loop** (3km, 1hr.) leads to an excellent lookout over the park. At the **John Hayes Rockhole,** 4km down a 4WD-only track, there's more **camping ❶.** Here is the **Chain Ponds Walk** (4km, 1hr.), a sojourn past a great lookout and through a picture-perfect series of pools. The **Hayes Trephina Bluff Walk** is a 6hr. one-way hike that highlights both regions of the park. All campsites have pit toilets and BBQ. *(85km.)*

**N'DHALA GORGE.** An intermittently marked 11km 4WD track leads through a thigh-deep creek before intersecting a series of dry creek beds on its way to N'Dhala Gorge. An otherwise unspectacular **walking track** (1.5km, 1hr.) weaves through the gorge, passing a few Aboriginal rock carvings, some of which may be 10,000 years old. **Camping ❶** (without water) is available. *(90km.)*

**ARLTUNGA HISTORIC RESERVE.** A left turn off Ross Hwy. leads to the site of Central Australia's first town. Originally a ruby mine, Arltunga seemed doomed when the "fiery gems" were determined to be useless garnets. Gold was discovered in the area that same year, but the town was eventually abandoned nonetheless, as the lack of water for sifting and extraordinary isolation rendered the mining unprofitable. The 33km gravel road leading to the reserve climbs through the hills, a nice break from the surrounding flatness. Bring your flashlight for exploring the old mines; they're the slightest bit dark. The visitors center (8am-5pm) is particularly helpful. *(110km.)*

**RUBY GAP NATURE PARK.** Thirty-eight kilometers along a 4WD track beyond Arltunga lies the stunning gorge of Ruby Gap Nature Park. Register with the ranger station at Arltunga before heading out. *(150km.)*

## SIMPSON DESERT

South of Alice, the Stuart Hwy. passes Heavitree Gap and Palm Circuit. The unsealed and isolated **Old South Road,** off the Stuart Hwy., heads right toward the Simpson Desert. Charles Sturt first explored this part of the Simpson in 1845, and was so bent on conquering the Outback that many of his men died due to the desert's harsh conditions. Stock up before heading out.

The first worthwhile spot is the **Ewaninga Rock Carvings,** 37km south of Alice. The weathered petroglyphs are a sacred site for Indigenous Australians. The Aboriginal community of **Maryvale Station,** 82km more along the Old South Rd., marks the 4WD-only turn to **Chambers Pillar Historical Reserve** (58km). This sandstone formation was a landmark for the region's early travelers, as demonstrated by their carved initials (a practice now subject to high fines). The trek is far more taxing than it is rewarding, but the sunsets are usually masterpieces of color. (No water or facilities are available.)

---

**DRESSING FOR THE DESERT.** With scorching days and freezing cold nights, it is important to know how to dress to stay comfortable in the desert. Two general rules:

1. **Layers, layers, layers:** wear multiple layers that you can take on and off to adjust your temperature and stay comfortable.
2. **It's harder to get warm than to stay warm,** so don't wait until you are cold to put on another layer. Think ahead. If the sun is starting to set, grab a few extra pieces of clothing, and bundle up.

---

**Rainbow Valley** is a jagged, U-shaped ridge of bleached sandstone capped by more multicolored stone. The valley is famous for its winter sunsets, when the red-orange-yellow formation is illuminated at the ideal angle. A short walk leads to its base. It's a striking sight, but remember that there's 97km of nothing between here and Alice. Another 51km down the Stuart, the unsealed Ernest Giles Rd. heads west toward Watarrka; 11km past the turnoff and 4km north on an access road lie the **Henbury Meteorite Craters.** A 20min. trail leads around the rim of the circular indentation caused 4000 years ago by meteorites.

# WATARRKA NATIONAL PARK (KINGS CANYON)

The increasingly popular Watarrka National Park is centered around Kings Canyon. The views are postcard-quality, and the canyon-cradled greenery is a refreshing change of pace from the region's normally dusty terrain. Peering down from the upper rim, you can see this sandstone wonder plunge over 250m down to the forest floor. However, these dramatic views are only accessible after a long and difficult ascent.

---

**WATARRKA NATIONAL PARK AT A GLANCE**

**AREA:** 720 sq. km.

**FEATURES:** Kings Canyon, with cliffs over 250m high and 1-3hr. walks.

**HIGHLIGHTS:** Deep canyons, cool streams, and the "Garden of Eden."

**GATEWAYS:** Alice Springs and Kings Canyon Resort/Kings Creek Station.

**CAMPING:** Not allowed in NP. Available at Kings Canyon Resort and Kings Creek Station (see **Accommodations**).

**FEES:** None.

---

**■ TRANSPORTATION.** Watarrka is located on Luritja Rd., 2½hr. north of the junction with Lasseter Hwy. There are three different ways to drive to the park from Alice Springs. First, the fully paved route—the **Stuart Highway**—runs 202km south to the roadhouse settlement of **Erldunda ❶**, where it meets the Lasseter Hwy. Travelers changing buses here may end up spending the night. (☎08 8956 0984. Sites $10 per person, powered $8 per site; motel singles $89; doubles $107.) From the junction, take the Lasseter Hwy. west 110km and turn right on Luritja Rd., which goes north 167km to the Kings Canyon park entrance. Second, the "shortcut" along **Ernest Giles Road,** a 100km stretch of unpaved road that begins 132km south of Alice off the Stuart Hwy., can cut several hundred kilometers from your trip, though a 4WD is required. Third, Kings Canyon can be reached from Alice Springs via Hermannsburg in the West MacDonnells. Take Larapinta Dr. to the scenic, corrugated 4WD-only **Mereenie Loop Road,** which passes through Aboriginal land. There are no accommodations, and no camping is allowed on the Mereenie, so plan to do the drive in a single day. A $2.20 pass is required and can be obtained in Hermannsburg at the Larapinta Service Station, Glen Helen Lodge (at Kings Canyon Resort), or at the visitors center in Alice. Most tours to Kings Canyon are included in Uluru-Kata Tjuta multi-day packages from Alice Springs. **Emu Run** has 12hr. day tours from Alice. (☎08 8953 7057. $189, children $94.50.)

**■ ACCOMMODATIONS AND FOOD.** The **Kings Canyon Resort ❶**, 7km up the road from the canyon turnoff, is pleasant but expensive. Rooms have A/C, heaters, TV, fridge, shared bath, and kitchen. (☎08 8956 7442 or 1300 134 044; www. voyages.com.au. Reception 6:30am-9:30pm. Sites $13.50 per person, powered $16.50; 4-bed dorms $42. Book ahead.) The resort has a cafe (open daily 10am-3pm), a small grocery store (open 7am-7pm), and a petrol station. **Outback BBQ ❸** offers pizzas from $19.50 and steaks from $21.50 (open daily 6-9pm).

Camping is also available at the well-maintained **Kings Creek Station ❶**, about 30km south of the turn-off to the park. It's a low-key outpost with a friendly staff and cheap camel safaris, which start at $7 for a 5min. ride or $50 for a sunset trek. (☎08 8956 7474; www.kingscreekstation.com.au. Sites $14 per person, children $7, families $42; powered $17/7/44; cabin singles $88; twins $65.60 per person, includes breakfast.) No camping is allowed inside the park.

**■ HIKING.** The park was recently equipped with new water facilities, toilets, and dozens of informational signs along all paths. There are three walks to choose from, all of which are best enjoyed with insect repellent. The challenging **Kings Canyon Walk** (6km, 3hr.) has the most stunning vistas. The trail begins with a steep climb up the canyon before winding along the panoramic rim. Several side tracks are marked along the way. Not to be missed is the **Garden of Eden** (500m round-trip), a 30min. trail midway through the hike that runs down to a picturesque stream and reflecting pool where you can take a dip. The easy **Kings Creek Walk** (2.6km, 1hr.) along the bottom of the canyon provides views of the canyon's sheer walls from platforms. The quiet, wheelchair-accessible **Kathleen Springs Walk** (2.6km, 1.5hr.) winds through sandstone valleys to a rockhole sacred to local Aborigines. Those craving a longer hike can try the **Giles Track** (22km) for a relaxed two-day hike. The track winds over the southern rim of the range and connects Kings Canyon with Lilla and Kathleen Springs. Camping is permitted between the 3km and 20km markers.

# ULURU-KATA TJUTA NATIONAL PARK

At Uluru-Kata Tjuta National Park, the majestic rock monoliths formerly known as Ayers Rock and the Olgas (respectively) emerge from the earth and dominate the surrounding landscape. World-famous Uluru's red surface—smoothed and eroded in bands—is especially colorful at sunrise and sunset, when hordes of tourists armed with digital camera equipment descend on viewing areas to capture images of Australia's national icon. The 36 unique, rounded domes of Kata Tjuta, meanwhile, presents a different sort of monument. Today, the park is presided over by its traditional caretakers, the Anangu people, who for 20,000 years have treated the great monoliths as sacred sites and important relics of the Dreamtime. Accordingly, their customs dictate certain rules for the site's visitors; nevertheless, tourists don't always follow Anangu wishes. Walking trails around and among the monoliths, however, are an uncontroversial way to enjoy the magnificent natural wonders of the park.

## ULURU AND KATA TJUTA AT A GLANCE

**AREA:** 1325 sq. km.

**ULURU:** 348m high, 9.4km around.

**KATA TJUTA:** Mt. Olga peaks at 546m.

**HIGHLIGHTS:** Uluru's colors at sunrise/sunset, Valley of the Winds, Kata Tjuta.

**GATEWAYS:** Alice Springs and Yulara.

**CAMPING:** No camping within the national park. There is a commercial campground at Yulara.

**FEES:** 3-day pass $25.

**TRANSPORTATION.** Take the Stuart Hwy. to **Erldunda,** 202km south of Alice Springs and 483km north of Coober Pedy, then drive 264km west on **Lasseter Highway** past Yulara into the park. Long before Uluru, you'll see **Mount Conner** in the distance. It is often mistaken for Uluru, which it dwarfs in size; it has its own viewing area right off the road.

**ORIENTATION AND PRACTICAL INFORMATION.** The Uluru-Kata Tjuta National Park **entrance station** (☎08 8956 2252) lies 5km past the Yulara resort village, where all visitors must purchase a **three-day pass** ($25). The turnoff to Kata Tjuta is 4km ahead and well marked; Uluru is another 10km into the park. (Park open daily 1hr. before sunrise until 1hr. after sunset.) There are toilet facilities at the Cultural Centre, at the main carpark at Uluru, and at the sunset-viewing area at Kata Tjuta. Several water stations are located around the circular Uluru hiking and driving circuits. There are picnic tables at the Cultural Centre and the viewing area. As in the rest of the Red Centre, the bush flies can be unbearable from December to April; plan accordingly. In case of emergency, radio alarms located throughout the park can be used to contact a **ranger;** otherwise, call direct ☎08 8956 1128.

The fantastic **Uluru-Kata Tjuta Cultural Centre,** 1km before Uluru, gives the Anangu perspective on the region. (☎08 8956 1128. Open daily 7am-6pm. Information desk 8am-5pm. Free.) Constructed in shapes representing the park's spiritual ancestors, Kunyia (a python) and Liru (a venomous snake), the center is full of displays relating the Anangu stories of Uluru's origin. A video details the preparation of bush tucker, as thorough a catalog of Aboriginal ingenuity in the face of adversity as is to be found in Australia. There is also an information desk, a snack bar, bathrooms, and several Aboriginal art centers.

# ULURU

Uluru, long known as Ayers Rock, is more than just a big boulder, and while it may seem overrated, doubts disappear the moment it first comes into view. Towering elegantly over the surround scrub, Uluru just won't let you look away (which makes driving in a little dangerous). As you approach, small caves, gorges, and waterslides start to come into view. A walk around the base illuminates these seemingly infinite surprises, taking you past dozens of unexpected crevices and scores of rain-carved gullies. Sunset provides another unbeatable look at Uluru: most flock to a well-marked carpark 5km away to watch as Uluru becomes an explosive canvas of orange and red. Sunrise is equally stunning and, logically enough, best viewed from the opposite side of the rock.

## THE CLIMB UP

The Anangu prefer that guests do not climb Uluru because of its spiritual significance. The Cultural Centre will give you a better understanding of their reasons. If you decide to ignore their wishes, realize that the hike up Uluru is difficult (a full 2-3hr.), even for the young and able-bodied (35 have died in the past 20 years). Visitors should avoid climbing in the middle of the day or if they have medical conditions. Leave loose accessories behind; many of the deaths have resulted from chasing after hats or cameras. Bring at least 2-3L of water and wear sturdy footwear with ankle support. Due to the high level of risk, the climb is closed on excessively hot, rainy, or windy days. A fixed chain helps with the brutal initial uphill, the steepest part of the climb. Past the chain, the path, marked by white blazes, meanders along the top of the rock for over 1km. The trail is rugged and requires the scaling of near vertical sections (at times 2m high). When descending, use extreme care. Sliding down in a sitting position over the coarse rock is not recommended; grasp the chain firmly and take small steps backward, pulling on the chain for support. Despite the hazards, many tourists climb the rock daily.

## HIKES AROUND THE BOTTOM

There are less adventurous, less dangerous, and less intrusive hikes around Uluru. Grab *An Insight into Uluru* ($2), available at the Cultural Centre, for a self-guided tour highlighting the cultural creation features of these walks.

**Uluru Base Walk** (9.4km, 3-4hr.). Flat and level but long, this walk offers the best opportunity to study the innumerable dimples, grooves, and caverns of the rock. The path, which at times skirts the rock and also follows a road further from the base, is the only real chance to escape the throngs and contemplate the rock in solitude. As it is a circuit, the path can be picked up at many places around the base of Uluru.

**Mala Walk** (2km, 45min.). Part of the circuit walk, this wheelchair-accessible track leads from main carpark past Aboriginal art sites and a wave-shaped cave on Uluru's wall to Kantju Gorge, which holds a sacred Anangu waterhole. Free, engaging, ranger-guided walks along the path present an Aboriginal perspective on Uluru. Meet the ranger at the Mala Walk sign at the base. 1hr. Daily Oct.-Apr. 8am, May-Sept. 10am. Free.

**Kuniya Walk** (1km, 30min.). This flat, wheelchair-accessible track, served by a carpark to the right of the loop entrance, leads to a waterhole that is home to Wanampi, an ancestral watersnake. Signs along the way detail the battle between ancestral spirits Kuniya and Liru, the events of which are recorded in the rock's features.

# KATA TJUTA

While Uluru is stunning, many visitors find themselves twiddling their thumbs after staring at the rock for more than a few minutes. Luckily, the beautiful Kata Tjuta comes to the rescue, providing 36 awe-inspiring domes among which to wander for the remainder of the day. Anangu for "many heads," Kata Tjuta has many faces that adopt new characters and moods as you circle them or walk through their valleys. Rising from the surrounding flatness, the domes are both a mysterious and mystical sight.

## ■ HIKING

The 42km road to Kata Tjuta leaves the main road 4km after the park entrance. The **Dune Viewing Area**, 25km down the road, is at the end of a wheelchair-accessible walk (300m) and offers all-encompassing views of Kata Tjuta. The sunset-viewing area (toilets available) is near the starting points of the two walks.

- **Valley of the Winds Walk** (7.4km, 2-3hr.). This moderate-grade hike reveals spectacular views of stony countryside and picturesque valleys, viewed between the massive walls of the Olgas. The main circuit passes through the mountains, while a shorter circuit cuts across the trailhead of the main circuit and does not climb between the domes. Midway through the walk is the Karingana Lookout. With a sweeping view into the gorge, this spot is one of the best and least crowded in the entire park.

- **Walpa Gorge Walk** (2.6km, 45min.). An easy path that heads straight between a pair of the most daunting domes. The dome on the right is Mount Olga, the highest peak in the range at 546m. The lookout at the end is often crowded, and the view is no more spectacular than the views along the path.

# YULARA                                                ☎08

**Ayers Rock Resort** (the municipal name "Yulara" applies only because there is a small employee housing district) is a series of hotels and shops stretched along a side road just outside Uluru-Kata Tjuta NP. The resort is the only game in town and owns the supermarket, petrol station, hostel, hotel, and apartments. Prices are fairly high, especially for campsites.

■ **TRANSPORTATION. Connellan Airport** lies 5km north of town. **Airnorth** and **Qantas** (☎13 13 13) fly to Adelaide, Alice Springs, Brisbane, Cairns, Darwin, Melbourne, Perth, and Sydney. A free airport **shuttle** run by AAT Kings meets all flights and picks up from all accommodations. They also run a bus daily to Alice Springs, which picks up from all accommodations. (Approx. 5hr., departs 1:10pm, $135.) **Ayers Rock Resort** runs a free village shuttle around the resort loop. (Every 20min., daily 10:30am-12:30am.) **Territory Rent-a-Car** (☎08 8956 2030), **Hertz** (☎08 8956 2244), and **Avis** (☎08 8956 2266) have offices at the airport and at the Tourist Info Centre in the resort shopping center. Prices for cars start around $85 per day; you must book ahead, especially in the high season. Most backpackers come to Yulara on camping tours out of Alice Springs. Those without cars have several options for traveling to Uluru. Uluru Express (☎08 8956 2152) offers transportation to the rock ($45, children $25) and Kata Tjuta ($65, children $35). For a more comprehensive experience, **Anangu Tours**, owned by the Anangu, gives award-winning cultural tours of Uluru; book at the

Cultural Centre. (☎08 8956 2123. 2hr. tours $63, day tours up to $127.) Another option is to bike the 20km to Uluru (Kata-Tjuta is another 33km); rentals are available from the **Ayers Rock Resort Campground** (p. 313) from $20 per day.

**Ｚ PRACTICAL INFORMATION.** The **Tourist Info Centre,** in the shopping center, has general info and tour agencies. (☎08 8957 7324. Internet kiosks available; $2 per 10min. Open daily 8am-8pm; service desks maintain shorter hours.) The **Visitors Centre,** with a grand set of stairs rising from the road near the entrance to the village, has a gift shop and museum of desert animals, as well as a detailed history of Uluru. (☎08 8957 7377. Open daily 9am-5pm.) Petrol is available at the **Mobil station.** (☎08 8956 2229. Open daily 7am-9pm.) Other services include: **police** (☎08 8956 2166; open M-F 8am-4pm); ANZ **bank** with 24hr. **ATM** in the shopping center (open M-Th 9:30am-4pm, F 9:30am-5pm); and a **post office.** (☎08 8956 2288. Open M-F 9am-6pm, Sa-Su 9am-2pm.) **Postal Code:** 0872.

**ＲＣ ACCOMMODATIONS AND FOOD.** For all lodge bookings, call ☎1300 139 889. The **Outback Pioneer Lodge ❸,** on Yulara Dr., has simple barracks-style digs with a kitchen and large, clean baths. (☎08 8957 7605. Free storage. Reception 24hr. 20-bed dorms $34; 4-bed $42; budget doubles $184, ensuite $210. YHA 10% discount.) The **Ayers Rock Resort Campground ❶** is the only camping option in the area; camping is not permitted in the park. Campers have access to the same facilities as at the Lodge, including a pool, kitchen, laundry, hot showers, and BBQ. (☎08 8957 7001. Sites $15.50 per person, children $8.50, families $39.50; powered $18.) The only other alternative is 100km away at **Curtain Springs ❶,** which means either missing the sunrise/sunset at Uluru or driving in the dark. (☎08 8956 2906. Free unpowered sites. Powered $25, showers $2; singles from $60, ensuite $135; doubles from $80/135; tours on cattle station to Mt. Connor $60.) Food options are limited; the cheapest choice is to just take a shuttle to the supermarket (open daily 8am-9pm).

# QUEENSLAND

If the continent's natural attractions could be condensed into one state, the result would look something like Queensland, Australia's magnificently layered natural paradise. It encompasses reef islands, sandy shores, hinterland rainforest, and glowing red Outback. In the southeast corner of the state is Brisbane, the youthful, diverse state capital. Queensland's gorgeous coast crawls with backpackers year-round; with the same faces popping up in every town, the journey often feels like a never-ending party. The downside for those on this heavily touristed route is that real Aussie culture can be smothered by the young, international crowd that floods these shores. Moving from one hot-spot to another can be mind-numbing, as you'll be forced to wade through a never-ending swamp of brochures, billboards, and tourist packages.

However, travelers who escape the region's constant vortex of tourists find that Queensland is much more than one long beach party. Those willing to trade flip-flops for hiking boots can explore the rainforests of the far north and the Outback, where life moves at a koala's pace. The isolated inland is dotted with charming country towns, pockets of thriving indigenous culture, and plenty of adventures. Across the entire state, opportunities abound for travelers to both make money and enjoy camaraderie as part of the flourishing fruit-picking subculture. In Queensland, appreciating the real Oz can be as simple as driving toward Cape Tribulation and watching the dense layers of forest gradually give way to sand and ocean.

## HIGHLIGHTS OF QUEENSLAND

**DIVE** the **Great Barrier Reef** and swim among shimmering schools of fish (p. 315).

**DRIVE Fraser Island** and fulfill your 4WD fantasies on massive sand dunes (p. 375).

**SURF** the legendary breaks at **Coolangatta and Tweed Heads** (p. 341).

**HIKE** through lush rainforest and misty valleys in **Eungella National Park** (p. 393).

**CAMP** on a secluded rainforest beach in **Cape Tribulation** (p. 438).

# TRANSPORTATION

Comprehensive public transportation services Queensland all the way up through the far north and parts of its interior. Don't underestimate the distances involved; even within the state, many people choose to fly if they want to get from Brisbane to Cairns quickly. If you've got the time for a leisurely trip, taking a **bus** up the coast allows you to stop at fun spots along the way. The major busline is Greyhound Australia (☎13 20 30 or 13 14 99), and the train line is Queensland Rail (☎13 16 17). A popular bus line for those traveling up the coast is **Oz Experience,** which attracts backpackers almost exclusively and offers affordable passes that allow you to hop on and off wherever you want.(☎02 9213 1766; www.ozexperience.com.) If you have a few friends to chip in for costs, or if you're traveling with a family, **renting a car** is an affordable convenience that will provide you with a lot of freedom. All the major car rental agencies have offices in Queensland, as do dozens of cheaper local ones. You'll need a **4WD** to tackle the area from Cooktown north through Cape

York and some of the desert roads. It can be expensive, and finding an automatic transmission 4WD is tough. Even with a 4WD, roads in the tropics can be harrowing—and often impassable—during and immediately following the Wet season (Nov.-Apr.). It's best to call the **Royal Automobile Club of Queensland** (RACQ; ☎ 13 19 05, roadside service ☎ 13 11 11) for road conditions. For more information on driving in Australia, see **Essentials,** p. 9.

#  GREAT BARRIER REEF

> **WHEN TO DIVE:** Most divers prefer to make trips to the Reef from July to December, and during November spawntime. Avoid diving from January to March, in the aftermath of a major storm, south of a recent cyclone, or if the wind speed is above 20 knots.
>
> **WHERE TO DIVE:** **Cairns** (p. 417), **Port Douglas** (p. 433), **Cape Tribulation** (p. 438), Beaver Cay (in **Mission Beach;** p. 413), **Magnetic Island** (p. 408), the **SS Yongala wreck** (p. 406), and the **Whitsundays** (p. 399) from **Airlie Beach** (p. 395). The reef officially extends all the way to Bundaberg, but much of the reef is protected and off-limits to divers south of Airlie. Areas where it is permitted, however, tend to be much less crowded and less expensive than the more popular areas near Cairns.

The Great Barrier Reef is one of the world's most incredible natural wonders. It stretches for 2300km, from just off Bundaberg's shoreline to Papua New Guinea, encompassing hundreds of islands and thousands of coral reefs. This marine wonderland is easily accessible by boat from the Queensland coast. Diving and snorkeling sites and operators are described throughout our Queensland coverage, so that you can get a sense of what you are looking for before you decide on a specific dive operator.

## WHAT YOU'LL NEED
Queensland requires a **certification card** for all dives. **Hervey Bay** (p. 370) and **Bundaberg** (p. 380) have the cheapest PADI certification courses in the state. Before you begin a course or set out on an extended trip, you might want to try an introductory dive with a trained guide to see what it's all about. Some people find they have so much trouble stabilizing pressure that a multi-day course would be a waste. If you do decide on a course, try to get boat dives instead of shore dives; the sights are usually better offshore. An open water certification is the minimum qualification to dive without an instructor, but more advanced certification levels are available. Medical exams are required for all dive courses and can be arranged through local dive centers and area medical specialists for only $50-$60.

## ALTERNATIVES TO DIVING
Diving is the best way to get an up-close view of the reef, but it requires significant amounts of time and money. Snorkeling is a convenient alternative for swimmers; renting a mask and fins can be as cheap as $10 per day, though trips on the reef often run in excess of $130. Gear is sometimes free with sailing trips or hostel stays. Good snorkeling is often available just off the shore. When wearing fins, be aware of where you're kicking—you may destroy coral hundreds of years in the making. If you want to see the reef up close but don't snorkel or dive, many companies offer glass-bottom boat tours that glide over coral, fish, and even sea turtles and rays.

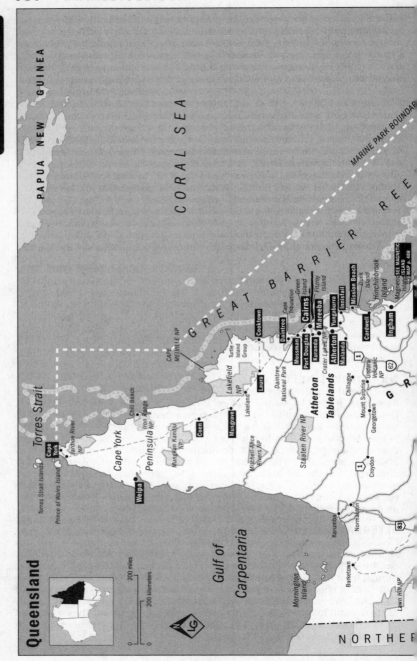

**Queensland**

0 ——— 200 miles
0 ——— 200 kilometers

PAPUA NEW GUINEA

CORAL SEA

MARINE PARK BOUNDARY

GREAT BARRIER REEF

Torres Strait

Torres Strait Islands

Prince of Wales Island

Cape York

Jardine River NP

Iron Range NP

Chili Beach

Lakefield NP

Lakeland

Laura

Cooktown

Cape Tribulation

Green Island

Daintree

Mossman

Port Douglas

Daintree National Park

Turtle Island Group

CAPE MELVILLE NP

Cairns

Fitzroy Island

Kuranda

Mareeba

Atherton

Malanda

Crater Lakes NP

Yungaburra

Innisfail

Mission Beach

Dunk Island

Hinchinbrook Island

Magnetic Island SEE MAGNETIC ISLAND MAP p. 408

Cardwell

Ingham

Atherton Tablelands

Chillagoe

Mount Surprise

Undara Volcanic NP

Georgetown

Croydon

Staaten River NP

Mitchell-Alice Rivers NP

Mungkan Kandju NP

Coen

Musgrave

Cape York Peninsula

Weipa

Gulf of Carpentaria

Mornington Island

Karumba

Normanton

Burketown

Lawn Hill NP

NORTHERN

CORAL SEA

QUEENSLAND

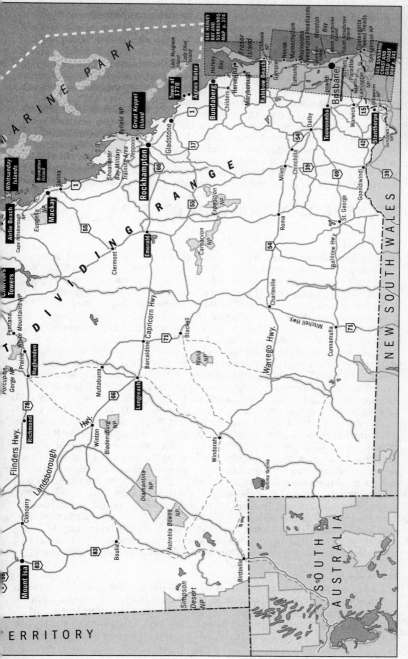

SEE HERVEY BAY AND SURROUNDS MAP p. 374

SEE SUNSHINE COAST AND GOLD COAST MAP p. 342

# BRISBANE ☎07

Often overlooked by those on a coastal pilgrimage, Brisbane (pop. 1.9 million) eschews glitz in favor of staying practical and clean. Its pedestrian malls radiate youthful energy, and the city's a safe bet for short-term employment.

The Central Business District (CBD) is full of everything a traveler could need, and it's only a 20min. walk from each of the city's four main neighborhoods. Excellent public transportation connects the CBD with the renowned nightlife of Fortitude Valley, the low-key residences of New Farm, the bohemian cafe culture of the West End, and the artistic highlights of the South Bank. The pleasant winter climate attracts those eager to shed their sweaters, and cultural events abound year-round. Visitors enjoy the serene waterfront, parklands, cafes, nightclubs, and the opportunity to tour famous Aussie breweries. For a break from the hustle and bustle of city life, the nearby islands of Moreton Bay offer unexploited sand, surf, and seaside hospitality.

## ✈ INTERCITY TRANSPORTATION

### BY PLANE

**Brisbane International Airport,** 12km northwest of the city, is served by seven domestic and 26 international airlines including **Qantas,** 247 Adelaide St. (☎13 13 13; www.qantas.com.au. Open M-F 8:30am-5pm, Sa 9am-1pm), and domestic budget airlines **Jetstar** (☎13 15 38; www.jetstar.com.au.) and **Virgin Blue** (☎13 67 89; www.virginblue.com.au). The **Visitor Information Centre** (☎07 3406 3190; open daily 5am-midnight) can be found immediately as you exit customs in the international terminal, 3km from the domestic terminal via the Airtrain (stops running at 8pm, $4) or the Coachtrans bus ($3) after 7:30pm.

To access the airport by car from the city, make your way to Sir Fred Schonell Dr. and follow the signs (25min. drive from the CBD). A **taxi** to the airport costs about $30-35. Privately owned **Airtrain** (☎07 3216 3308; www.airtrain.com.au) offers direct service to the airport until 7:30pm (until 8:00pm from the Airport to the CBD), making connections to Brisbane's Queensland Rail and **Citytrain** (p. 321) in the city (20min., every 30min., $13), and the Gold Coast (1½hr.; every 30min.; $24.70, concessions $20). To get to Surfers Paradise, get off at the second-to-last Airtrain stop, Nerang, and catch Surfside Bus #745 (30min., every 15-20min., $2.70) or Airtrain can arrange for a chauffeur to drive you from the station to your hostel ($37). Many hostels and information centers offer $3 discounted tickets to the airport on Airtrain. Timetables are available from Airtrain as well as from **Transinfo** (☎13 12 30; www.transinfo.qld.gov.au). **Coachtrans,** on level 3 of the **Roma Street Transit Centre,** runs a daily **shuttle** between the airport and Transit Centre and will drop you off at any hotel or hostel in Brisbane for no additional fee. (☎07 3358 9736; www.coachtrans.com.au. Every 30min. 5am-9pm; last bus to city 11:10pm. $12, round-trip $22; children $8/10.) They also run shuttles between Brisbane and the Gold Coast ($39; multiple day passes for travel within the Gold Coast available. Book ahead.)

### BY TRAIN

The **Roma Street Transit Centre,** 500m west of the CBD, is the city's bus and train terminal. (Open M-Th 3:45am-12:45am, F 3:45am-2:15am, Sa 3:15am-1:45am, Su 3:15am-12:30am.) Lockers ($6 per day) are on the first and third levels.

For rail travel, **Queensland Rail Travel Centre** (☎13 16 17 or 1800 872 467; www.traveltrain.com.au) can book full packages, including air travel and

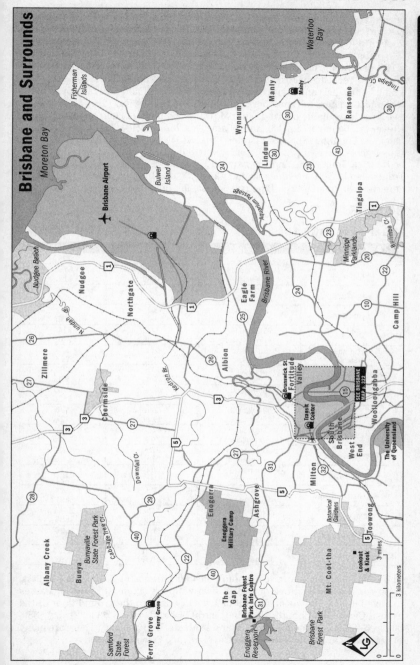

# Brisbane and Surrounds

*Moreton Bay*

accommodations. Offices are at Central Station on the corner of Ann and Edward St. (diagonally opposite **Palace Backpackers**, p. 326) and on the ground floor of the Transit Centre. Only students with ISIC qualify for student prices (50% off all adult fares, including those listed below) and YHA/VIP holders get a 10% discount. The sleek Tilt Train is the fastest way to travel; it runs north along the coast from Brisbane to Rockhampton (9hr.; M-Th 11am, F and Su 11am, 5pm; $105) and Maryborough West (3½hr.; M-F and Su 11am, 5pm; $58), with bus transfers to Bundaberg (1hr., $66) and Hervey Bay (1hr., $69). Transit to Cairns is available on Tilt (24hr.; M, W, F 6:25pm; $311) and on the cheaper, slower Sunlander (32hr.; Tu, Su 8:55am, Th 1:25pm; $213). These **trains** stop in Mackay (Tilt 13hr., $228; Sunlander 17hr., $154), in Whitsunday launch point Proserpine (Tilt 15hr., $238.70; Sunlander 18hr., $164), with bus transfer to Airlie Beach (25min., $10) and Townsville (Tilt 18hr., $270; Sunlander 24hr., $184). Trains also leave for Sydney (14hr.; daily 7:30am, 3:10pm; $92-$129); the later departure time includes a 12hr. train and a 3hr. bus. Book ahead.

## BY BUS

### FROM BRISBANE TO:

| DESTINATION | COMPANY | DURATION | PRICE |
|---|---|---|---|
| Adelaide | Greyhound | 35hr. | $295 |
| Airlie Beach | Greyhound | 18hr. | $183 |
| | Premier | 19hr. | $142 |
| Bundaberg | Greyhound | 7hr. | $78 |
| | Premier | 9hr. | $49 |
| Byron Bay | Greyhound | 3hr. | $41 |
| | Premier | 3hr. | $30 |
| Cairns | Greyhound | 29hr. | $248 |
| | Premier | 29hr. | $203 |
| Coolangatta and Tweed Heads | Greyhound | 2hr. | $29 |
| | Premier | 2hr. | $17 |
| Hervey Bay | Greyhound | 6-7hr. | $60 |
| | Premier | 7hr. | $38 |
| Mackay | Greyhound | 16hr. | $161 |
| | Premier | 17hr. | $126 |
| Maroochydore | Greyhound | 2hr. | $26 |
| | Premier | 1½hr. | $21 |
| Melbourne | Greyhound | 24-29hr. | $253 |
| | Premier | 34hr. | $176 |
| Mission Beach | Greyhound | 27hr. | $239 |
| | Premier | 27hr. | $193 |
| Mooloolaba | Greyhound | 2hr. | $26 |
| | Premier | 1½hr. | $21 |
| Noosa/Noosa Heads | Greyhound | 3hr. | $26 |
| | Premier | 2-3hr. | $21 |
| Rockhampton | Greyhound | 11hr. | $111 |
| | Premier | 12hr. | $88 |
| Surfers Paradise | Greyhound | 1½hr. | $26 |
| | Premier | 1½hr. | $17 |
| Sydney | Greyhound | 16-17hr. | $124 |
| | Premier | 15-17hr. | $93 |

Those with longer itineraries should consider purchasing a **Sunshine Rail Pass,** good for a given number of travel days within a six-month period. Passes are available at the Queensland Rail Travel Centre on the ground floor of the Transit Centre, or from the desk in Central Station. (14-day $336, 21-day $389, 30-day $488, half-price for children and students. Book ahead.) There are many other passes available to overseas travelers (see **Essentials**, p. 9).

QUEENSLAND

Bus coverage along the coast is excellent; **Greyhound Australia** (☎ 1300 473 946; www.greyhound.com.au) and **Premier Motor Service** (☎ 13 34 10; www.premierms.com.au) grant 10% discounts for ISIC/VIP/YHA. Both sell a range of two- to six-month travel passes. Although you may see **Suncoast Pacific** buses, they are officially owned and operated by Greyhound Australia.

# ORIENTATION

As it winds through the city, the meandering Brisbane River is spanned by five bridges: the **Merivale Bridge** is the westernmost bridge and is next to the **William Jolly Bridge; Story Bridge** connects Fortitude Valley and Kangaroo Point; the **Captain Cook Bridge** connects the southern edge of the CBD to southbound highways; and the **Victoria Bridge** connects the city to South Bank. The **Transit Centre** is located on Roma St.; a left turn out of the building and a 5min. walk southeast down Roma crosses **Turbot Street** and leads to the corner of Albert and Ann St. and the grassy **King George Square** (in front of the grand **City Hall**). **Adelaide Street** forms the far side of the square. Running parallel to Adelaide is the **Queen Street Mall.** This popular pedestrian thoroughfare is lined with shops and cafes and serves the center of Brisbane proper. Underneath the mall and the adjoining **Myer Centre** shopping complex is the **Queen Street Bus Station.**

Brisbane's neighborhoods radiate out from the CBD. A right turn out of the Transit Centre leads to **Petrie Terrace** and **Paddington,** with accommodations and mellow nightlife. North of Boundary St. is **Spring Hill,** bordered by **Victoria Park** and **Roma Street Parklands,** a 15min. walk from the Queen Street Mall up steep Edward St. A 20min. walk down Ann St., nightclub-heavy **Fortitude Valley** offers a hopping alternative scene and live music. The Valley is also home to a small, authentic **Chinatown.** Turning right down Brunswick St., a 10min. walk brings you to **New Farm,** with its free art galleries, not-so-free cafes, and excellent restaurants. Near the Botanic Gardens at the CBD's southern tip, the Victoria Bridge footpath turns into Melbourne St. and heads into **South Brisbane,** crossing Boundary St. six blocks later as it enters the **West End. South Bank** is to the east of the southern end of the bridge; farther along the riverside, **Kangaroo Point** is the long, narrow peninsula stretching into the River.

**BE SAFE.** Use caution in the areas around Fortitude Valley and the West End, especially at night. Also avoid city parks after dark; in particular, stay away from the Botanic Gardens, New Farm Park, and King George Square.

# LOCAL TRANSPORTATION

The **Translink** system coordinates transit on trains, buses, and ferries within Brisbane, extending all the way north to Noosa and south to Coolangatta. For inquiries, contact the helpful operators at **Transinfo** (☎ 13 12 30; www.transinfo.qld.gov.au). Off-peak (all day Sa-Su and holidays, as well as M-F 9am-3:30pm and after 7pm) travel within one zone costs $2.30 one-way; one zone daily passes are $4.60 for anytime travel on any form of public transit, $3.50 for off-peak. Two-zone travel is $2.70/$5.40/$4.10. Most travelers will stick to zone one, which incorporates all of central Brisbane, from the West End and Kangaroo Point up through the CBD to New Farm and Fortitude Valley.

**Trains: Citytrain,** Queensland Rail's intracity train network, has 2 major stations and numerous stops throughout the city. The main station is inside the **Roma Street Transit Centre;** the other is in **Central Station,** on the corner of Ann St. and Edward St. Citytrain

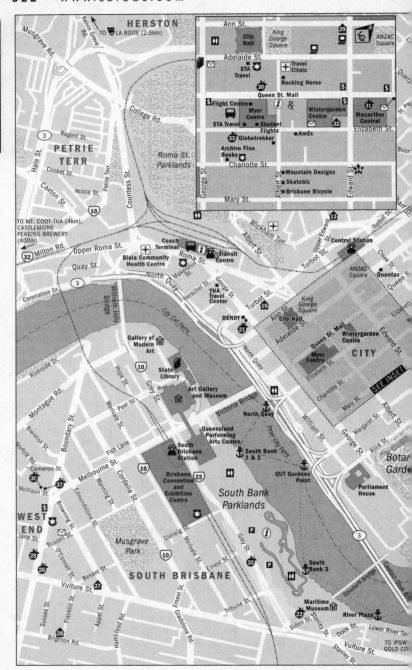

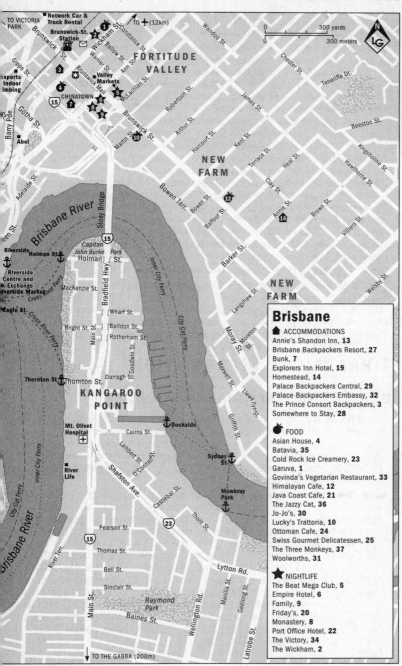

QUEENSLAND

## Brisbane

**ACCOMMODATIONS**
Annie's Shandon Inn, **13**
Brisbane Backpackers Resort, **27**
Bunk, **7**
Explorers Inn Hotel, **19**
Homestead, **14**
Palace Backpackers Central, **29**
Palace Backpackers Embassy, **32**
The Prince Consort Backpackers, **3**
Somewhere to Stay, **28**

**FOOD**
Asian House, **4**
Batavia, **35**
Cold Rock Ice Creamery, **23**
Garuva, **1**
Govinda's Vegetarian Restaurant, **33**
Himalayan Cafe, **12**
Java Coast Cafe, **21**
The Jazzy Cat, **36**
Jo-Jo's, **30**
Lucky's Trattoria, **10**
Ottoman Cafe, **24**
Swiss Gourmet Delicatessen, **25**
The Three Monkeys, **37**
Woolworths, **31**

**NIGHTLIFE**
The Beat Mega Club, **5**
Empire Hotel, **6**
Family, **9**
Friday's, **20**
Monastery, **8**
Port Office Hotel, **22**
The Victory, **34**
The Wickham, **2**

also connects to Airtrain, with service to the **airport** (p. 318). Trains generally run every 30min. Daily 6am-8:30pm. Check schedules for specific line info.

**Buses:** Buses going to the southern suburbs depart from the **Queen Street Bus Station,** a huge terminal beneath the Myer Centre and the Queen Street Mall. The bus stop for all other destinations is on Adelaide or Elizabeth St. Schedules organized by suburb and bus number are available from the helpful **Queen Street Bus Station Info Centre,** located on Level A of the Myer Centre. (Open M-Th 8:30am-5:30pm, F 8:30am-8pm, Sa 9am-4pm, Su 10am-4pm.) Most bus stops also post times and route maps. **CityXpress** runs from the suburbs to the CBD approximately every 30min. Free red buses operate every 10min. on the **Downtown Loop,** a circular service in the CBD (M-F 7am-7pm). Bus #199 offers convenient routes from West End to New Farm via the Valley.

**Ferries:** Brisbane's excellent ferry system offers affordable, practical transit with beautiful city views; look for colored signs that indicate service at ferry stops. The sleek **City-Cat** runs upstream to the University of Queensland and downstream to Apollo Rd. (every 15-30min. 5:40am-12:40am; blue sign). The CityCat also stops in Riverside, Queensland University of Technology, South Bank, and North Quay, near the Treasury Casino. The **Inner City Ferry** operates in the CBD and has more stops than the CityCat (every 30min. 6am-10:30pm; red sign). The **Cross River** runs 4 routes connecting Brisbane's banks, including 2 from Eagle St. to Kangaroo Pt. (every 10min. daily 6am-10:30pm; green sign). Schedules are posted at every dock and stop.

**Taxis:** Yellow Cab (☎13 19 24) and **Black and White Cabs** (☎13 10 08) run 24hr.

**Car Rental: Network Car and Truck Rentals,** 398 St. Paul's Terr. (☎1800 736 825; www.networkrentals.com.au), in Fortitude Valley, rents from $39 per day for 250km. Open M-F 7:30am-5:30pm, weekends 8am-3pm. AmEx/D/MC/V. **Abel** (☎1800 131 429; www.abel.com.au), on the corner of Wickham and Warren St., rents from $29 per day, with under-25 surcharge of $15 per day. Open daily 7am-7pm. AmEx/D/MC/V.

# ⁊ PRACTICAL INFORMATION

## TOURIST AND FINANCIAL SERVICES

**Tourist Office:** The very busy **visitor information center** (☎07 3006 6290; www.visit-brisbane.com.au), in the middle of the Queen Street Mall, provides info only on businesses that pay to advertise there. The center also has a Transinfo rep. Open daily 9am-6pm. Touchscreen available 24hr. The **Brisbane Transit Visitor Information** desk (☎07 3236 2020), on the 3rd fl. of the Transit Centre, provides information on accommodations and attractions. Open daily 7am-6pm.

**Budget Travel Offices:** Travel centers are everywhere, but the branches in the **Myer Centre** tend to have the best hours. **Flight Centre** (☎13 31 33 or 1300 733 867; www.flightcentre.com.au) has 50 offices in the city and a guarantee to beat any current quote. The Myer Centre branch, on basement level E, is open M-Th 9am-5:30pm, F 9am-8pm, Sa 9am-4pm, Su 10:30am-4pm. **STA Travel** (☎13 47 82; www.statravel.com.au) has 3 offices in the CBD, including one in the Queen Adelaide Building (90-112 Queen St.) and one at 243 Edward St. The Myer Centre branch is open M-Th 9am-5:30pm, F 9am-8pm, Sa 9am-4pm. **Student Flights** (☎1800 046 462; www.studentflights.com.au) has 3 offices in the city, including a bureau on Level A in the Myer Centre, and promises to beat any international fare for students. Open M-Th 9am-5:30pm, F 9am-8pm, Sa 9am-5pm. **YHA Travel,** 450 George St. (☎3236 1680; www.yha.com.au), near the Transit Centre, has budget travel rates and can help book hostels. Open M-Tu and Th-F 8:30am-6pm, W 9am-6pm, Sa 9am-3pm.

**Consulate: U.K.,** 1 Eagle St. Level 26 (☎07 3223 3200). Open M-F 9:30am-3pm. For after-hours emergency consular assistance, call ☎07 3830 5748.

**Banks:** Banks are found on Boundary St. in South Brisbane, Brunswick St. in the Valley, and Queen St. in the CBD. Most are open M-Th 9:30am-4pm, F 9:30am-5pm.

## LOCAL SERVICES

**Backpacking and Camping Equipment:** There are several equipment stores in the CBD and on Wickham St. between Gotha and Gipps St. in Fortitude Valley. **Mountain Designs,** 109 Albert St. (☎07 3221 6756; www.mountaindesigns.com) and **Globe Trekker,** 142 Albert St. (☎07 3221 4476; www.globetrekkers.com.au) offer 10% discounts to YHA members and students. Mountain Designs is open M-Th 9am-5:30pm, F 9am-8pm, Sa 9am-4:30pm, Su 10am-4pm; Globe Trekker M-Th 9am-6pm, F 9am-8pm, Sa 9am-5pm and Su 10:30am-4:30pm. AmEx/D/MC/V.

**Bookstores:** The Queen Street Mall area has many bookstores. The shelves of **Archive Fine Books,** 38-40 Charlotte St. (☎07 3221 0491; www.archives.com.au), are lined with 1 million used books. Open M-Sa 9am-9pm, Su 10am-4:30pm. There's a 3-story **Borders,** 162 Albert St. (☎07 3210 1220; www.borders.com.au), at the corner of Elizabeth St. Open M-Th 9am-7pm, F 9am-9pm, Sa 9am-6pm, Su 10am-5pm.

**WAIT TO WALK.** Brisbane police are quick to fine jaywalkers $200 or more for crossing without a signal. In this city, it seems, patience is a virtue.

**Library:** The beautifully renovated **State Library** (☎07 3840 7666; www.slq.qld.gov.au), part of the **Cultural Centre** (p. 329) in South Bank, has been converted into a popular destination with exhibitions and galleries. One of the few places that offers free Wi-Fi in Brisbane. Open M-Th 10am-8pm, F-Su 10am-5pm. The **Central City Library,** 266 George St. (☎07 3403 4166), occupies a beautiful new location. Book borrowing members only. Open M-Th 9am-6pm, F 9am-7pm, Sa-Su 10am-3pm.

**Public Markets:** Outdoor markets line the streets of Brisbane every weekend on a rotating basis; inquire at the Queen St. information booth for a full schedule. The **Valley Markets** (☎07 3854 0860; www.marketsonline.com.au) on Brunswick Street Mall, Fortitude Valley, have organic produce and second-hand items. Open Sa 8am-4pm, Su 8am-5pm. The **Riverside Market** (☎07 3870 2807; www.riversidemarkets.com.au), operates along the Eagle Street Pier. Open Su 8am-4pm. For fresh produce, the Farmers Market (☎07 3268 3889) takes place the 2nd and 4th Sa of every month at the Powerhouse Centre in New Farm. Open 6am-noon.

## EMERGENCY AND COMMUNICATIONS

**Emergency:** ☎000.

**Police:** Headquarters, 200 Roma St. (☎07 3364 6464). Branch stations are on 46 Charlotte St. (☎07 3258 2582) and Brookes St and Wickham St. in Fortitude Valley (☎07 3131 1055). There's also a police beat on 67 Adelaide St. (☎07 3224 4444).

**Crisis Lines: Statewide Sexual Assault Helpline** (☎1800 010 120). **Suicide Prevention Hotline** (24hr. ☎13 11 14). **Alcohol and Drug Information Service** (☎1800 177 833). **Pregnancy Advisory Centre** (☎1800 672 966).

**Late-Night Pharmacy: Queen Street Mall Pharmacy,** 141 Queen St. (☎07 3221 4585), on the mall. Open M-Th 7am-9pm, F 7am-9:30pm, Sa 8am-9pm, Su 8:30am-6pm.

**Hospital: Holy Spirit Northside Hospital,** 627 Rode Rd., Chermside (☎07 3326 3000). The **Travel Clinic,** 245 Albert St., offers dive medicals from $88 (☎3211 3611). Open M-Th 7:30am-7pm, F 7:30am-6pm, Sa 8:30am-5pm, Su 9:30am-5pm. AmEx/MC/V.

**Internet Access:** Internet cafes abound, especially on Adelaide St. and George St. There's free Internet and Wi-Fi at the **State Library** (p. 325). Most hostels offer a simple Internet or a Global Gossip connection for rates around $1 per 15min.

**Post Office: General Post Office,** 261 Queen St. (☎13 13 18). ½-block from the end of the mall. Open M-F 7am-6pm. Poste Restante available 9am-5pm. For weekend mail, try the branch at Wintergarden Centre Level 2. Open M-F 9am-5pm, Sa 9am-1pm. **Postal Code:** 4000 (city); 4001 (G.P.O. boxes).

### MEDIA AND PUBLICATIONS

**Newspaper:** *The Courier-Mail* ($1); *Brisbane News* (every W; free) and *City News* (every Th; free).

**Nightlife:** *Time Off, Scene,* and *Rave* magazines (free). For info on gay and lesbian nightlife, check out *Queensland Pride (QP).*

**Radio:** Rock, Triple M 104.5 FM and Triple J 107.7; Top 40, B105 FM; News, 612 AM (ABC Brisbane), 792 AM (ABC Radio National), and 936 AM (ABC Newsradio); Tourist Info, 88 FM.

# ACCOMMODATIONS

Accommodations cluster in several distinct districts of Brisbane. The CBD is a convenient—though perhaps slightly more expensive—area. Fortitude Valley is a mecca for nightclubs, and its quiet neighbor New Farm caters to long-term stays. The area near the Transit Centre is convenient for accessing both the CBD and clubs in the Valley. The West End and South Brisbane are a little removed from the action. Most of the accommodations listed below offer pickup and drop-off at the Transit Centre; call ahead.

## CBD

**Palace Backpackers Embassy,** (☎1800 676 340; www.palacebackpackers.com.au), at the corner of Edward and Elizabeth St. Because the original Palace Backpackers was so popular, the company opened up shop at a second, smaller location down the street. The atmosphere is less wild, and dorm rooms are just $1 more than at Palace Central. It also boasts a TV lounge that replicates a movie theater. VIP. MC/V. ②

**Palace Backpackers Central,** 308 Edward St. (☎07 3211 2433 or 1800 676 340; www.palacebackpackers.com.au), on the corner of Ann St. in the heart of the city. 5-level building is a backpacker landmark that fills to 400-person capacity in peak times. Its nightly rockin' pub, with cheap dinner specials ($6), makes for one of the best social scenes in the city. 3-story veranda, BBQ, and classy cafe with breakfast ($5-10). The $35 job club gives members a guarantee of finding work. Reception 24hr. 3- to 10-bed dorms $25-28; singles $45; doubles $65. VIP. MC/V. ②

**Explorers Inn Hotel,** 63 Turbot St. (☎07 3211 3488; www.explorers.com.au), near the corner of George St., 1 block from the CBD. One of the best budget hotels around. With its friendly staff and affordable restaurant (meals under $12), this place is great for families. The compact ensuite rooms have fridge, A/C, and TV. No kitchen. Reception daily 6:30am-10:30pm, latenight check-in with advance notice. Singles $95-$105; doubles $99-$109; triples $149. AmEx/D/MC/V. ⑤

**Annie's Shandon Inn,** 405 Upper Edward St. (☎07 3831 8684), Spring Hill. An escape from impersonal hostels is just outside the CBD. Like Grandma's house, with family snapshots, cozy beds, and pastels. No kitchen, but microwaves, a sink, and beverages in the downstairs lounge. Continental breakfast included. Reception 7am-8pm. Check-out 9am. Singles $65; doubles with shared facilities $75, ensuite $85. AmEx/MC/V. ●

# FORTITUDE VALLEY AND NEW FARM

■ **Bunk,** 11-21 Gipps St. (☎1800 682 865; www.bunkbrisbane.com.au), on the corner of Ann St. Among the best hostels in Brisbane. Rooms are well maintained and staff is friendly and helpful. A short walk from nightclubs. If you're traveling in a group of 4 or 5 and don't mind sharing big beds, ask for an apartment ($172). Attached to the impressively popular **Birdee Num Num** pub and nightclub. Reception 24hr. 4-, 6-, and 8-bed dorms with private bath $28-$31; singles $76; ensuite doubles $96. MC/V. ❷

**The Prince Consort Backpackers,** 230 Wickham St. (☎07 3257 2252). This inexpensive hostel has big rooms, shared facilities, and a great location in the heart of Fortitude Valley. On top of **The Elephant & the Wheelbarrow** pub. Free drink on check-in when you present a transportation receipt. 4- to 10-bed dorms $20-$28; doubles $65. NOMADS/VIP/YHA discount $1. AmEx/D/MC/V. ❷

**Homestead,** 57 Annie St. (☎07 3358 3538), New Farm. This hostel, situated on a quiet residential street about 10min. from the action on foot, is popular among relaxed, low-key backpackers. 4-bed female-only dorms available. Weekly BBQ and nightly outings. Free transportation to airport, Transit Centre, CBD, and F city job fairs. Free bike use. 3- and 4-bed dorms $20; doubles $69-$75. VIP/YHA. MC/V. ❷

# WEST END/SOUTH BRISBANE

**Somewhere to Stay,** 45 Brighton Rd. (☎1800 812 398; www.somewheretostay.com. au), Corner of Brighton and Franklin St. A homey hostel in a beautiful old Queenslander house with multiple balconies. Large rooms, some with city views. Lush greenery and swimming pool. Reception 8am-4am. Check-out 9:30am. Far from nightclubs and most nighttime activities, but an enticing option for its low prices: ensuite 4- to 6-bed dorms $19-$27; singles $39; doubles $49. VIP/YHA discount $1. MC/V. ❸

**Brisbane Backpackers Resort,** 110 Vulture St. (☎1800 626 452; www.brisbaneback-packers.com.au). A well-maintained hostel with nice amenities. A hike on foot from most activities, but easily accessed by public transportation and offers a free shuttle from the hostel. Rooms have baths, fridges, and balconies overlooking the courtyard; some have TV. Free bus to CBD and Transit Centre. Tennis court, swimming pool, bar, and cafe (breakfast $6-9, dinner $6-10). Reception 24hr. 4- to 8-bed dorms $25-29; singles and doubles $79. VIP/YHA discount. MC/V. ❷

# ◧ FOOD

The West End specializes in multicultural cuisine and small sidewalk cafes, particularly along Boundary St. and Hardgrave Rd. Fortitude Valley's China-town has cheap Asian fare, while trendier New Farm and the CBD have more expensive eateries. **Woolworths** supermarket is located downstairs at Macarthur Central in the Queen Street Mall (open M-F 8am-9pm, Sa 8am-5:30pm, Su 9am-6pm). For ice cream, try **Cold Rock Ice Creamery** opposite Little Stanley St., along the river in the Arbour View Cafes in the South Bank Parklands.

## CBD

**Jo-Jo's** (☎07 3221 2113; www.jojos.com.au), on the corner of Queen Street Mall and Albert St; sits amid skyscrapers and has a balcony overlooking the center of the mall. Attracts travelers, students, and businessmen to its 5 different kitchens, which include

Thai, Italian, and char-grill. Try the excellent pizzas ($12-25) or grilled sirloin and chips ($17). Gourmet sandwiches $14. Open daily 11:30am-10pm. AmEx/D/MC/V. ❷

**Govinda's Vegetarian Restaurant,** upstairs at 99 Elizabeth St. (☎07 3210 0255; www. brisbanesgovindas.com). Extremely popular among locals for its $10 all-you-can-eat buffet (students $9). Dining area is lined with Krishna flags, posters, and books. Vegan options available. Sunday's Krishna feast explores inner consciousness in the context of a vegetarian family meal (entry $5; starts at 5pm; students $7 from 2-3pm). Open M-Th 11am-3pm, F 11am-8:30pm, Sa 11:30am-2:30pm. Cash only. ❶

**Java Coast Cafe,** 340 George St. (☎07 3211 3040), near Ann St. One of our favorites among Brisbane's hundreds of coffee shops. The jungle-like courtyard dining area in the back is an inner-city sanctuary. Offers an array of specialty teas as well. Gourmet sandwiches ($7-8.50). Open M-F 7:30am-3:30pm. ❶

## FORTITUDE VALLEY AND NEW FARM

🖾 **Garuva,** 324 Wickham St. (☎07 3216 0124; www.garuva.com.au). Might be the most unique dining experience in Queensland. The trickling waterfalls, colored lights, and low-arching tropical trees that decorate the entrance are just the beginning of what makes this intimate eatery unique. Sit on a cushioned rug while a white curtain is drawn around your table to ensure privacy. Attentive service and international main courses ($18.50), from cajun blacked chicken to Turkish octopus. Book at least 2 days ahead. Open M-Th and Su 6:30pm-latenight, F-Sa 5:30pm-latenight. Happy hour F and Sa nights starting at 5:30pm. All mixed drinks are $10. AmEx/D/MC/V. ❸

**Himalayan Cafe,** 640-642 Brunswick St. (☎07 3358 4015). Call the number you scribbled on a coaster in the Valley last night and make a date to enjoy the distinctive Tibetan and Nepalese delicacies served in the relaxed atmosphere of this eatery. Veggie and vegan options abound. Open Tu-Su 5:30pm-latenight.

**Lucky's Trattoria** (☎07 3252 2353), behind the Central Brunswick Complex at the corner of Brunswick and Martin St. in New Farm. Excellent Italian favorites. Try the gnocchi with blue vein cheese sauce ($14-18). Open daily 6pm-latenight. AmEx/MC/V. ❷

**Asian House,** 165 Wickham St. (☎07 3852 1291) in Fortitude Valley. The best of the Chinatown restaurants. Excellent dishes and casual dining in a modern, clean interior. Try the chicken fillet and sweet ginger ($13) or curried Chinese vegetables ($11). Open daily 11:30am-3pm and 5-11pm; F open until 11:30. AmEx/D/MC/V. ❷

## WEST END AND SOUTH BANK

🖾 **The Three Monkeys,** 58 Mollison St. (☎07 3844 6045) in the West End. A Brisbane landmark, The Three Monkeys is much more than your run-of-the-mill coffee shop. Decorated with beautiful tapestries and tribal artifacts, its intimate, Eastern feel is complemented by the tropical garden area in the back. Choose from a mix of Greek-, Turkish-, and Italian-inspired food, or just sit and enjoy one of their teas, including their famous chai (from $3.60). Open M-Sa 9:30-midnight, Su 10am-midnight. AmEx/D/MC/V. ❶

**The Jazzy Cat,** 56 Mollison St. (☎3846 2544; www.jazzycatcafe.com.au) next door to The Three Monkeys. Funky feline decorations abound in this hip cafe. International cuisine, breakfast from $4, lunch from $12 and main dishes for dinner start at $18. Budget travelers should check out Budget Wednesday when meals start at just $3.50 all day. Open W-F 11am-10pm, Sa-Su 8:30-10pm. AmEx/D/MC/V. ❷

**Batavia,** 167 Grey St. (☎07 3844 4694) South Bank. This tea salon/shop sells over 57 specialty teas, including a variety of unique watergarden teas. Open M-Th and Su 10am-10pm, F-Sa 10am-noon. AmEx/D/MC/V. ❶

**Swiss Gourmet Delicatessen,** 181 Boundary St. (☎07 3844 2937; www.swissgourmet.com.au). This little gourmet deli packs a real punch; its prices and taste are hard to beat. Build your own sandwich (from $3.20) and top it off with a dessert made by the Italian owner. Open M-F 7:30am-5:30pm, Sa 7:30am-3pm. AmEx/D/MC/V. ❶

# 👁 SIGHTS

## CITY SIGHTS

**CITY TOURS. City Sights** is a 1½hr. bus tour of cultural and historical attractions that allows you to jump on and off as you please. Tickets are purchased on the bus. *(Tours officially leave from Post Office Sq., at Queen and Edward St., but you can start at any of the 19 stops. Call Transinfo ☎ 13 12 30 for timetables or check www.citysights.com.au. Daily every 45min. 9am-3:45pm. $25, concessions $20.)* For a tour of the Brisbane River, the large **Kookaburra River Queen** paddlewheel boat departs twice daily from the Eagle St. Pier. Includes commentary on sights and live accordion music. *(☎07 3221 1300; www.kookaburrariverqueens.com. 2hr. lunch cruise $20-55; 2hr. dinner cruise $75-85. Departs daily 12:15, 7:30pm.)* **Tours and Detours,** on the 3rd floor of the Transit Centre, offers a number of different city and river trips, including a half-day highlight tour *(☎ 1300 338 687; www.toursanddetours.com.au; departs 9:15am, returns 12:15pm; $72, concessions $70; children $42)*, an afternoon float to **Lone Pine Koala Sanctuary** and **Mt. Coot-tha** *(departs 1:45pm, returns 4:15pm; $57/55/38)*, and a moonlight tour of Brisbane *(departs 7pm, returns 9:30pm; $74/69/39)*. Those on foot can pick up a guide to the **Brisbane Heritage Trail.** The 3km path winds its way around the city's historical and cultural sights. *(☎07 3403 8888. Starts in King George Sq. Free maps and guides available at City Hall and the Brisbane City Council.)*

**CASTLEMAINE PERKINS BREWERY.** XXXX, which proudly proclaims itself "Queensland's beer," is brewed only 5min. from Caxton St. on Milton Rd., adjacent to the Milton train stop. The 1hr. walking tour ends with four samples. Meet at the **XXXX Ale House** off Milton Rd. on Paten St. *(☎07 3361 7597; www.xxxx.com.au. Tours M-F every hr. 10am-4pm, also W 6pm. $18, concessions $16.50, non-drinkers $10, children under 10 free. Book ahead. AmEx/D/MC/V.)*

**CARLTON BREWHOUSE.** Thirty minutes (41km) south of Brisbane are the brewers of VB, Fosters, and Carlton. The tour through the largest, most modern brewery in Queensland may be dry, but the three beers at the end sure aren't. *(In Yatala; by car, follow the Pacific Hwy. south of the city, and take exit #41. The brewery is inland from the highway. ☎07 3826 5858; www.carltonbrewhouse.com.au. Tours M-F 10am, noon, 2pm; Su noon, 2pm. $18, concessions $12, children $10. Book ahead. AmEx/D/MC/V.)*

**CITY HALL.** When it opened in 1932, it earned the nickname "Million Pound Town Hall" for the outrageous cost of construction. The restored **clock tower,** a landmark of the city skyline, is 92m high and has a free **observation deck.** The **Museum of Brisbane** hosts three small, well-organized exhibits; at least one display is usually by a local artist. *(Observation deck open M-F 10am-3pm, Sa 10am-2pm. Free. Museum ☎07 3403 6363, bookings for groups of 10 or more ☎07 3403 4048. Open daily 10am-5pm. Free. Museum admission $5, concessions $3.50, children $2.)*

**QUEENSLAND CULTURAL CENTRE.** In its numerous buildings on the south side of the Victoria Bridge, the Cultural Centre coordinates many of Brisbane's artistic attractions, including the art gallery, museum, **performing arts complex** (p. 332), **state library** (p. 325), and new museum of modern art. The **Queensland Art Gallery,** along with the newly opened **Queensland Gallery of Modern Art (GoMA),** has over 10,000 works, primarily Australian and contemporary Asian. *(☎07 3840*

7303; www.qag.qld.gov.au. Open M-F 10am-5pm, Sa-Su 9am-5pm. Free tours M-F 11am, 1, 2pm; Sa-Su 11:30am, 1, 2:30pm. Free admission. Special exhibits $8-15, ask for concession rates.) The **Queensland Museum** is home to the Sciencentre and a range of Australian artifacts of cultural and natural interest. (☎ 07 3840 7555; www.southbank.qm.qld.gov. au. Open daily 9:30am-5pm. $10, concessions and children $8, family $29.

## PARKS AND GARDENS

**SOUTH BANK PARKLANDS.** Built on the former site of the 1988 World Expo, South Bank offers tree-lined views of the river, a cafe-dotted boardwalk, and weekend markets. The man-made **lagoon** is surrounded by a real sand beach and fills with sun-seekers year-round. (Lifeguard on duty Dec.-Jan. 7am-midnight, Feb.-Mar. and from mid-Sept. to Nov. 7am-7pm, Apr.-Aug. 9am-5pm, early Sept. 9am-6pm.) The Parklands also contain the **Maritime Museum,** with wrecks and models. (At the old South Brisbane dry dock, south end of the Parklands. ☎ 07 3844 5361; www.maritimemuseum. com.au. Open daily 9:30am-4:30pm; last entry 3:30pm. $7, concessions $6, children $3.50.) The **South Bank Art & Craft Markets** has nearly everything, including crafts, jewelry, psychics, clothing, and massages. (Open F 5-10pm, Sa 11am-5pm, Su 9am-5pm.) The South Bank also organizes free events—including car shows, fireworks, and weightlifting championships—often held in the **Suncorp Piazza. South Bank Cinemas** movie theater shows recent releases at reduced rates and holds free showings on school holidays. Free BBQs are also available for use throughout the parklands, though you are responsible for bringing all utensils, food, and cleaning supplies. Obtain an event calendar and map from the visitors center in the park at the Little Stanley St. Plaza. (Accessible by foot, by bus to South Bank or Cultural Centre stops, by CityTrain to South Brisbane station, or by ferry to terminal stop at South Bank. Info Centre ☎ 07 3867 2051; www.visitsouthbank.com.au. Open daily 9am-5pm.)

**BOTANIC GARDENS.** Stroll among palm groves, camellia gardens, and lily ponds as you take in the exceptional birdlife. If you're lucky, you might see a large goanna lizard. (A 15min. walk from the CBD on Albert St., at the intersection with Alice St. ☎ 3403 7067. Open 24hr. Extremely dangerous at night and should be avoided. Free tours depart the rotunda near the Albert St. entrance M-F 11am, 1pm.)

**MOUNT COOT-THA.** Mt. Coot-tha, about 5km from the CBD, is split into two main sections: the botanical gardens and the summit. Bus #471 services both sections from Ann St., stop 11. (25min. to gardens, 30min. to summit. 1 per hr. M-F 8:45am-3:30pm, Sa-Su 10:15am-4:30pm.) The park is also accessible by car: drive down Milton Rd. and follow the signs. Queensland's premier subtropical **Botanic Garden** includes a Japanese garden, a library, a tropical dome, a bonsai house, and plenty of green space for holding afternoon picnics. (☎ 07 3403 2535. Gardens open 8am-5pm. Free tours M-Sa 11am, 1pm from the info center.) It also houses Queensland's first planetarium, the **Cosmic Sky Dome.** (☎ 07 3403 2578. Open Tu-F and Su 10am-4:30pm, Sa 10:30am-6:30pm. 45min. programs Tu-F 3:15pm; Sa 12:30, 3:15, 7:30pm; Su 12:30, 3:15pm. $12.10, concessions $10, children $7.10, families $32.70. Book ahead.) The casual **Kuta Cafe ❶** (most meals under $16) and the fancier **The Summit Restaurant ❹** (main courses $20-35) both have panoramic views. (www.brisbanelookout. com. Kuta Cafe ☎ 07 3368 2117. Open M-Th and Su 7am-11pm, F-Sa 7am-midnight. The Summit Restaurant ☎ 07 3369 9922. Open M-F 11:30am-2:30pm and 5pm-latenight, Sa 11:30am-latenight, Su 8am-10:30am and 11:30am-latenight. AmEx/D/MC/V.)

**BRISBANE FOREST PARK.** Picnic, camp, bird watch, cycle, ride horses, and hike on over 28,000 hectares of eucalyptus forest. The park headquarters offers bushwalking maps for several trails that originate near the office; the HQ also contains the **Walkabout Creek Wildlife Centre,** a small sanctuary that houses many of the animals for which Southeastern Queensland is famous. Bush camping is permitted in designated areas *($4.50 per person; book ahead).* Camping areas are remote and have no facilities; physical fitness, as well as navigational and bushwalking skills, is required. *(60 Mt. Nebo Rd. ☎ 13 13 04; www.epa.qld.gov.au/parks_ and_forests/. Take Musgrave Rd., which turns into Waterworks Rd., and then Mt. Nebo Rd., out of the city. Bus #385 ($3.60) from William St. outside the Treasury Casino (stop 113A) will take you the 14km to park headquarters, departing once per hr. 8:20am-3:20pm. Trails with camping are accessible by private transport only. Info center ☎ 1300 723 684. Open daily 8:30am-4:15pm. Wildlife Centre $5.30, concessions $3.70, children $2.60, families $13.20.)*

**ROMA STREET PARKLANDS.** The world's largest subtropical garden in a city center, the Roma Street Parklands comprise 16 hectares of gardens, lawns, and flora. Enjoy free performances, walk through recreated ecosystems, or ride the miniature train. *(☎ 07 3006 4545; www.romastreetparkland.com. Open from dawn to dusk. Train runs M-F 10am-2pm, Sa-Su 10am-4pm. $5, students $4, children $3.)*

# WILDLIFE

**★AUSTRALIA ZOO.** The late Steve Irwin used to make occasional appearances at this zoo, which he owned and operated. The park offers a schedule of feedings and info sessions every day. Cuddle a python, feed a kangaroo, ogle the world's 10 most poisonous snakes, and walk the well-maintained grounds of this 70-acre mecca for animal lovers. *(In Beerwah, 75km north of Brisbane. By car, take the Beerwah exit, Glass Mountains Tourist Rte., off the Pacific Hwy. 60km north of Brisbane, then follow the signs another 20km. By public transport, catch the Nambour Express from the Transit Centre at 8:02am. The train arrives at Beerwah at 9:30am where a free shuttle collects you for a short drive to the Zoo. Trains run to the Zoo all day, but only the express gets you there at 10am for the shows. Round-trip $17, weekends $13. Call ☎ 13 12 30 for timetables. A courtesy bus also runs to the Zoo from the Sunshine Coast; call Zoo for schedule. Zoo: ☎ 07 5436 2000; www.australiazoo.com.au. $46, concessions $36, children $29, families $139. Open daily 9am-4:30pm.)* **CC's Croc Connections** offers packages that include transit and Zoo admission. *(☎ 1300 551 249; www.crocconnections.com.au. $100, concessions $85, children $60.)*

**★LONE PINE KOALA SANCTUARY.** Lone Pine, the world's largest koala sanctuary, is home to over 130 of the beloved marsupials. If you're looking to get up close and personal with these cuddly creatures, this is one of the only places in the world that allows it. In addition to koalas, the Sanctuary houses crocodiles, wombats and kangaroos. *(By car, follow Milton Rd. to the Western Freeway, take the Fig Tree Pocket exit and follow the signs. A taxi should cost around $25 from the city. By public transport, take bus #430 from platform B3 in the Myer Centre, 1 per hr., or bus #445 from stop 45 on Adelaide St. opposite City Hall, 1 per hr. Sanctuary: ☎ 07 3378 1366; www.koala.net. Open daily 8:30am-5pm. $22, students $19, children $17, families $59. NOMADS/VIP/YHA.)* Make a day of the excursion and take the Mirimar Wildlife Cruise 19km upstream on the Brisbane River where you can not only see the city from the water, but also learn about its fascinating history from the friendly boatstaff. *(☎ 1300 729 742; www.mirimar.com. Round-trip including park admission $50, concession $45, children $30, family $145. Departs 10am South Bank from the Cultural Centre Pontoon, returns 2:45pm.)*

# ⚠ ACTIVITIES

## ROCK CLIMBING AND SKYDIVING

Join **★River Life** at the old Naval Stores at Kangaroo Point Cliffs for night kayaking with hot chocolate and marshmallows. *(Th 7-8:30pm; $45, includes equipment.)* The area is well lit. They also have rock climbing, abseiling, in-line skating, and boxing throughout the week. Book ahead. *(Lower River Terrace,*

Kangaroo Point. ☎07 3891 5766; www.riverlife.com.au.) If you need practice, try indoor climbing with **Rocksports Indoor Sports Climbing** (224 Barry Pde., Fortitude Valley. ☎07 3216 0462; www.rocksports.com.au. Open M-F 10am-9:30pm, Sa-Su 10am-5pm. $15 for unlimited climbing. $12 harness, shoes, and chalk rental. Bringing a partner is mandatory. MC/V.) A little higher up, the **Brisbane Skydiving Centre** will show you the city at 200kph from 12,500 ft. (☎5464 6111; www.brisbaneskydive.com.au. Tandem dive over Brisbane $499 per person, minimum 2 people. Tandem dive at Willowbank $300 per person. MC/V.) **Redcliffe City Skydiving** will drop you on the beach. (☎1300 788 555; skydiveredcliffe. com.au. Dives starting at $279; 14,000 ft. dive includes lunch and T-shirt. DVD $99, with photos $132. Free pickup.) Enjoy a more leisurely flight on a hot air balloon ride over the Brisbane countryside with **Balloons Above.** (☎1800 648 050; www.balloonsabove.com.au. Daily at sunrise. From $275, children $245; includes champagne breakfast. Book at least 2 days in advance. MC/V.)

### WATER ACTIVITIES

Brisbane has many waterways that are perfect for canoeing. Guides to the popular Oxley Creek and Boondall Wetlands are available from libraries or the City Council Customer Services counter, in the City Plaza, on the corner of Ann and George St. For rentals, try **Goodtime Surf and Sail.** (29 Ipswich Rd., Woolloongabba. ☎07 3391 8588; www.goodtime.com.au. Open M-F 8:30am-5:30pm, Sa 8:30am-4pm, Su 10am-3pm. Canoes and kayaks from $30 per day. Deposit $110. Includes paddles and life jackets.) **ProDive** goes to the area's reefs and wrecks. (☎07 3368 3766; www.prodive.com.au. Open M-W and F 9am-6pm, Th 9am-8pm, Sa-Su 9am-5pm. Daytrip with 2 dives from $159; gear rental $79; includes transit from shop to dive site, morning tea. Dives F-Su at 7am.)

# 🎵 ENTERTAINMENT

Brisbane continuously hosts festivals and an array of theatrical, artistic, and musical performances. Call the **Queensland Cultural Centre** (☎07 3840 7444) for a current schedule or visit www.ourbrisbane.com. For theater tickets, call **QTIX** (☎13 62 46; www.qtix.com.au). Most places offer discounts to students and backpackers; be sure to ask for concession prices.

## FINE ARTS

**The Queensland Performing Arts Centre** (☎07 3840 7444; www.qpac.com.au), just across Victoria Bridge in South Bank. Four theatres: the Concert Hall hosts symphony and chamber orchestras as well as contemporary music concerts; the Lyric Theatre sponsors drama, musicals, ballet, and opera; the Playhouse hosts drama and dance performances; and the Cremorne Theatre stages more intimate and experimental productions. Ticket office open M-Sa 9:30am-8:30pm and 2hr. before performances. Tour available F 11:30am; $7.50, $5 concessions. Book ahead.

**The Queensland Conservatorium,** 16. Russell St. (☎07 3735 6241; www.gu.edu.au/ concerts), has concerts ranging from classical to pop. Prices free-$20.

**Opera Queensland** (☎07 3735 3030; www.operaqueensland.com.au), adjacent to the Conservatorium. Produces 3 operas annually. Tickets from $45.

**La Boite,** 6-8 Musk Ave. (☎07 3007 8600; www.laboite.com.au), in Kelvin Grove. Contemporary Australian theater; 5 mainstage productions per year.

**The Queensland Ballet** (☎07 3013 6666; www.queenslandballet.com.au), the corner of Drake St. and Montague Rd. Presents around 100 performances each year; an impressive range of popular classics and full-length story ballets to contemporary works in a variety of dance styles. Tickets $20-65.

**Brisbane Powerhouse Centre for Live Arts,** 119 Lamington St. (☎07 3358 8600; www.brisbanepowerhouse.org), adjacent to New Farm Park. An alternative arts venue with 2 separate theaters, as well as art galleries and dining options. Box office open M-F 9am-5pm, Sa-Su noon-4pm, and 2hr. before performances.

## MUSIC, MONEY, MOVIES

The enormous **Treasury Casino,** at the top of Queen St., is a Brisbane landmark. It contains five restaurants, seven bars, and more than 1100 gaming machines. (☎07 3306 8888; www.treasurycasino.com.au. Open 24hr.) **Birch Carroll & Coyle** shows new films on level 3 of the Myer Center (☎07 3229 5949) and at Brisbane Regent, 167 Queen St. (☎07 3229 5949 or 3027 9999. $15, students $11, children $10.50.) Alternative films play at **DENDY,** 346 George St. (☎07 3211 3244; www.dendy.com.au. $13.50, students $10.50, children $9.50; M all films $9.50.)

## SPORTS

**Brisbane Entertainment Centre** is Brisbane's largest indoor complex for sports and events. Citytrain's Shorncliffe line runs to Boondall Station every 30min. (☎07 3265 8111; www.brisent.com.au. Tickets ☎13 28 49; www.ticketek.com.au.) The **Gabba,** at Vulture and Stanley St., Woolloongabba, is home to AFL's Brisbane Lions and the Queensland Bulls National Cricket Team.Take the bus to the corner of Main and Stanley St. ($2.70) or the train to Roma St. (☎07 3008 6166. For AFL tickets, ☎13 28 49; www.ticketek.com.au. For cricket, ☎1300 136 122; www.ticketmaster.com.au.) The new **Suncorp Stadium,** at the intersection of Hale and Milton St., is now home to all football matches, including those played by the rugby league "Brisbane Broncos." The stadium is accessible by foot from the CBD or from Citytrain's Milton and Roma stop. (☎07 3335 1777; www.suncorpstadium.com.au. Tickets ☎13 28 49; www.ticketek.com.au)

## FESTIVALS

The **Brisbane River Festival** (☎07 3846 7971; www.riverfestival.com.au) celebrates spring at the end of August or beginning of September with fireworks, concerts, and feasts. The **Brisbane International Film Festival** (☎07 3007 3003; www.biff.com.au) is held annually in mid-July; the festival features alternative and retrospective film releases. The **Valley Fiesta** (☎07 3854 0860; www.valleyfiesta.com), sometime

## THE LOCAL STORY

### POKIE PROBLEMS

Poker machines—or "pokies," as they have affectionately been renamed by Aussies—are ubiquitous in almost every region of the country. It's nearly impossible to find a bar or sports club that doesn't have at least a dozen of the machines beeping, flashing and twinkling away.

Aussies love the game, and—perhaps unfortunately—it seems that nothing can take them away from it. In 2007, Queenslanders alone lost $1.7 billion to pokie machines, which amounts to about $5 million in combined gambling losses per day. Pokie is much more than a game for many though. An estimated 30,000 Queenslanders are problem gamblers, and more than 80% of Australia's adult population gambles. That's the highest percentage of any country in the world.

Prime Minister Kevin Rudd has vowed to wean the country off its gambling addiction by banishing all ATMs from pokie venues in Victoria by 2012. But with revenues as high as they are, one can only imagine that it will be a long and difficult process—especially since Australian states have levied taxes on gambling profits. So if you're intrigued by all of the pokies around and want to give it a try, just be warned that you can easily find yourself with an empty wallet. And remember that, for many budget travelers, that also means an empty stomach.

between July and September, heats up Fortitude Valley with street festivals, local bands, and dance performances; check website for 2009 details. The **Australia Day Cockroach Races** are run every January 26 at the Story Bridge Hotel, 200 Main St., Kangaroo Point (☎3391 2266). This massive social event allows you to buy your own racing roach or cheer from the sidelines.

# ▧ NIGHTLIFE

Brisbane night-owls can choose between sweaty clubs, noisy pubs, or classy lounges. Fortitude Valley is home to Brisbane's best nightlife scene, with alternative bars, huge dance clubs, live music, and several gay establishments. In 2006, it was granted an exception to the city's strict noise regulations, allowing it to pump up the volume like never before. Caxton St. in Petrie Terr. has a great atmosphere for watching a rugby game on the telly, while the CBD is a big draw for backpackers with its Irish pubs, drink specials, and rocking Thursday nights. Expect long lines on the weekend.

## FORTITUDE VALLEY

▧ **Family,** 8 Mclachlan St. (☎07 3852 5000; www.thefamily.com.au). Brilliant neon laser lights fan out across the hip, the young, and the beautiful in what *Bartender Magazine* has named the "Best Club in Australia." Faux-industrial decor winds through a 5-story maze of lounges, bars, and dance floors; each new area features a different atmosphere, crowd, and music style. Cover varies with DJ, usually $8-15. Open F-Su 9pm-5am.

**The Beat Mega Club,** 677 Ann St. (☎07 3852 2661; www.thebeatmegaclub.com.au). Perhaps the best dance club in Brisbane, the 15 DJs keep all 5 dance floors and 7 bars packed on F and Sa. Popular with patrons of all kinds. Cover $10, free before 10:30pm. Tu night drag shows. Open M-Sa 8pm-5am and Su 5pm-5am.

**The Wickham,** 308 Wickham St. (☎07 3852 1301; www.thewickham.com.au). This club morphs into an outrageous dance party nearly every weekend. Costumes, cabarets— anything and everything goes. Shows Tu-F. Occasional cover charge $5-10. Open M-Tu 10am-1am, W-Th and Su 10am-2am, F-Sa 10am-5am.

**Empire Hotel,** 339 Brunswick St. (☎07 3852 1216). Downstairs, the **Corner Bar** and **Press Club** cater to a casual crowd. (Corner Bar M-Th 10am-2am, F-Sa 10am-5am, Su noon-3am. Press Club daily 6pm-5am.) The upstairs nightclub, consisting of the **Middle Bar** and **Moon Bar,** satisfies late-nighters of all types. To the right, comfy couches; to the left, fresh and funky chemical beats. Cover after 10pm $8-15. Open F-Sa 9pm-5am.

**Monastery,** 621 Ann St.(☎07 3257 7081; www.monastery.com.au). Pumps out techno and house music in a not-so-holy atmosphere. Back-lit stained glass and cushy leather couches recall old Europe with an irreverent twist. Rotating DJs and frequent special events. Occasional cover charge. Open Th-Su 9pm-5am.

## CBD AND RIVERSIDE

**The Victory,** 127 Edward St. (☎07 3221 0444), on the corner of Charlotte St. A massive complex with a classic Aussie pub, beer garden, nightclub, and karaoke lounge, spread out among 7 bars. Live music, DJ, and karaoke W-Su. M-Tu 10am-2am, W-Sa 10am-3am, Su 11am-1am. Nightclub open daily 8:30pm-3am.

**Port Office Hotel,** 38 Edward St. (☎07 3221 0072), on the corner of Edward and Margaret St. "Porto," as it is called by the locals, is a popular combination hotel, bar, and dance joint that makes for a great evening if the journey out to the Valley seems too far. The downstairs bar area and dance floor cater to a hip crowd. Venture upstairs for in-house techno that will keep your head bobbing. Open M-F 11:30am-late, Sa 2pm-late.

**Friday's,** 123 Eagle St. (☎07 3832 2122; www.fridays.com.au), next to Riverside Centre. This giant riverfront hangout attracts a diverse, young crowd. The maze of rooms offers a variety of entertainment, from a DJ spinning dance tunes to live performances. Live bands F-Sa; W $4 cocktail night 5pm-5am. Th-Sa $8-10 cover after 10pm. Open M-Tu and Su 11:30am-midnight, W-Sa 11:30am-5am.

# MORETON BAY AND ISLANDS

Many travelers heading north to Cairns or south toward the Gold Coast bypass beautiful, relaxed Moreton Bay and its islands; don't make the same mistake. The perpetually laid-back lifestyle of Manly is only a mere 35min. from Brisbane, at the mouth of the Brisbane River. North Stradbroke Island and Moreton Island are idyllic sites, offering diving, hiking, whale- and dolphin-watching, and swimming. Ferries run to the islands daily; several travel companies and hostels offer package deals that include transportation.

# MANLY                                     ☎07

There are more boats than people in the friendly harborside village of Manly. This hub for most local ferry services serves as the best base for exploring the islands of Moreton Bay, and it's a quiet place to return to after a long day of fishing, sailing, or scuba diving. If you prefer not to stay in a city, Manly is also a perfect base for exploring the streets of Brisbane.

**TRANSPORTATION.** From Brisbane, take Citytrain to the Manly stop on the Cleveland line (35-40min. from Roma St., daily at least every 30min., $3.20).

**ORIENTATION AND PRACTICAL INFORMATION.** With your back to the train station, take the second left turn at the "Boat Harbour" sign to reach **Cambridge Parade,** the main thoroughfare. Cambridge Pde. heads toward the harbor and the **Esplanade,** which runs along the water. The **Tourist Information Centre,** 43A Cambridge Pde., is across from the Manly Hotel. (☎07 3348 3524. Open M-F 9am-5pm, Sa-Su 10am-3pm.) There is a **Bank of Queensland** with a **24hr. ATM** located in the **Manly Harbour Village** shopping center on the corner of Cambridge Pde. and the Esplanade. (Open M-Th 9:30am-4pm, F 9:30am-5pm.) The **post office,** 222 Stratton Terr., is also in the shopping center. (☎07 3396 2735. Open M-F 9am-5pm, Sa 9am-noon.) **Postal Code:** 4179.

**ACCOMMODATIONS AND FOOD. Moreton Bay Backpackers ②,** 45 Cambridge Pde., is located across from Manly Hotel and is the only hostel in Manly. If you don't mind a little dust, this place offers a number of low-budget perks such as excursions to the islands and DVD rentals. You also get a free drink at the **High Tide Bar and Grill** (see below) upon check-in. (☎1800 800 157; www.moretonbaylodge.com.au. Free airport and train pickup. Key and linen deposit $20. 6- to 8-bed dorms $22; ensuite singles $55; ensuite doubles $70. 7th night free. Reception, inside High Tide Bar and Grill, open 24hr. in summer; in winter M-Th and Su 8:30am-8pm, F-Sa 8:30am-10pm. MC/V.) The clean **Manly Hotel ④,** 54 Cambridge Pde., is a favorite of businessmen and has several bars and a **restaurant ③** that serves food all day. Beer garden outside is packed every night. (☎07 3249 5999; www.manlyhotel.com. Th and Su karaoke, F-Su live music, W jam session. Restaurant open daily 7am-9pm; bars open M-Th 10am-midnight, F-Sa 10am-2am, Su 11am-9:30pm. Hotel singles $65-110; doubles $80-125.)

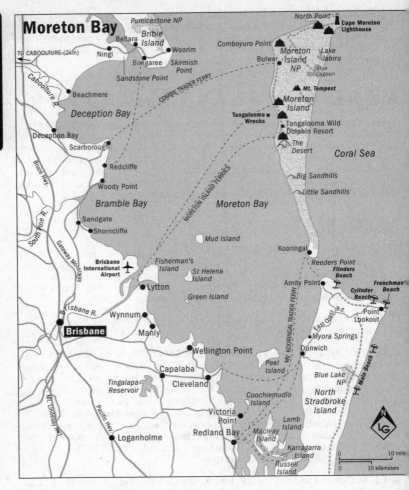

**Fish Cafe ❶**, 461 The Esplanade, at the intersection with Cambridge Pde., is great for quick seafood. The cod and chips ($7.50) and the fish cake panini burger ($6.50) are both delicious. Takeaway recommended; the place is crowded, and dining in is expensive. (☎07 3893 0195; www.fishcafe.com.au. Open daily 8-10:45am and 11am-8:30pm.) Across from Moreton Bay Backpackers is **High Tide Bar and Grill ❷**, offering large meals priced around $12 and nightly backpacker specials around $5. There is an **IGA** supermarket in the Manly Harbour Village shopping center. (☎07 3396 1980. Open daily 6am-10pm.)

**◉ SIGHTS.** Spot wildlife with **Manly Eco Cruises,** which runs several family-oriented daytrips around **Moreton Bay Marine Park.** The trip includes boomnet rides (which allows you to sit in a large open net and be dragged behind a boat), a tropical-themed lunch, short canoe rides, and commentary on the bay. (☎07 3396 9400; www.manlyecocruises.com. Daytrips M-Sa 9am-3pm $109. Su breakfast cruise 8:30-10:30am $35. Book ahead.)

# NORTH STRADBROKE ISLAND ☎07

North Stradbroke island is unique in its beauty and small, vibrant population. With stretches of sandy white surf beaches, famous blue inland lakes, world-class dive sites, and outdoor activity everywhere you turn, North Stradbroke ("Straddie") is the perfect place to step off the beaten path.

**TRANSPORTATION.** North Stradbroke is just a few hops away from Brisbane on public transportation. Take Citytrain to Cleveland (1hr., every 30min., $4.60); from Cleveland, three different **ferry** companies service the island. The Stradbroke Flyer Ferry is accessible from the train station via courtesy bus. Their "Gold Kat" passenger ferries arrive at One Mile Jetty in Dunwich. (☎07 3286 1964; www.flyer.com.au. 30min.; every 30-90min. Courtesy bus runs M-F 4:55am-6:25pm, Sa-Su 5:55am-6:25pm. Last ferry leaves 7:55pm, though there is no courtesy bus. $17 round-trip, students $12.) Alternatively, Stradbroke Ferries runs a **passenger water taxi** as well as a **vehicular ferry**. From the train station, take Veolia Transport Brisbane bus #258 (call Translink at ☎13 12 30. 6min.; runs every 30min., $2.30) to meet the ferry. (☎07 3286 2666; www.stradbrokeferries.com.au. Passenger ferry 30min.; 10-13 per day 6am-6:15pm; round-trip $17, students $12. Vehicular ferry 45-50min.; 11 per day 5:30am-6:30pm; round-trip $135 per car.) Sea Stradbroke runs a similar service from Cleveland. (☎07 3488 9777; www.seastradbroke.com. M-F 8-10 per day; $10, cars $122.) The **North Stradbroke Island Bus Service** runs between Point Lookout, Amity, and Dunwich; timetables make it easy to meet your ferry. (☎07 3415 2417; www.stradbrokebuses.com. 11-12 per day, less frequently to Amity, starting at 6:45am from Point Lookout and 7:25am from Dunwich. Adult $5, children and Queensland students $2.50.) A **taxi** from Dunwich to Point Lookout costs $30. (Stradbroke Cab Service ☎07 3409 9800.) Several companies in Cleveland provide rental **cars** to the island, but 4WDs are available only in Brisbane. A permit is necessary if you plan to drive a 4WD on island. These can be purchased from the tourist office or at most campsites. (Annual permits $30. MC/V.)

**ORIENTATION AND PRACTICAL INFORMATION.** North Stradbroke Island has three distinct townships: residential **Dunwich,** the ferry drop-off point on the western shore; **Amity Point,** north of Dunwich, with calm beaches and great fishing; and **Point Lookout,** 22km northeast of Dunwich, with most of the area's accommodations and tourist attractions. **East Coast Road** is the main road connecting Dunwich and Point Lookout; its name changes to **Mooloomba Road** in Point Lookout. The middle of the island consists of various lakes, swamps, national park land, and habitat reserves, while sand mines occupy a significant portion of the northern and southern ends of the island.

The **tourist office** is the yellow stone building on Junner St., at the base of the Dunwich football green, 250m from the Stradbroke Ferry Water Taxi. The incredibly helpful staff books tours and accommodations. (☎07 3409 9555; www.stradbroketourism.com. Open M-F 8:30am-5pm, Sa-Su 8:30am-3pm.) Although there's no bank on the island, **ATMs** are located in hotels in each of the towns. Other services include **police** (☎07 3409 9020) across from the tourist office in Dunwich, and **Stradbroke Island Medical Centre** (☎07 3409 8660) at Kennedy Dr., Point Lookout. (Open M-F 8:30am-5pm, Sa 9-11am, Su 10-11am.) The **post offices** in Dunwich and Point Lookout also provide some **banking services**

QUEENSLAND

for visitors. The Dunwich Post Office is located at 3 Welsby St. (☎07 3409 9010; open M-F 9am-5pm, Sa 9am-noon.) and the Point Lookout Post is at Meegera Pl., off Endeavor St. (☎07 3409 8210. Open M-F 9am-5pm.) **Postal Code:** 4183.

**🏠 ACCOMMODATIONS AND CAMPING.** The budget accommodations on the island consist of one hostel and six campsites—one in Amity, two in Dunwich, and three in Point Lookout. **◼Manta Lodge and Scuba Centre (YHA) ❷,** on the left side of East Coast Rd., at the entrance to Point Lookout and minutes from Home Beach, has an attached dive center and provides transportation from the Roma St. Transit Centre in Brisbane. (In summer M, W, F; in winter M and F. $25 round-trip. Call ahead.) The guesthouse rooms are simple and clean with shared facilities, and staff is friendly and welcoming. Amenities include Internet access, BBQ, laundry, kitchen, and a spacious common room. (☎07 3409 8888; www.mantalodge.com.au. Key deposit $10. Reception in summer 7am-late, in winter 8am-5pm. 4- to 8-bed dorms $28; doubles $70. YHA discount 10%. MC/V.) **Camping ❶** is also permitted on parts of Flinders Beach (from $13.50-$18.00) and at least 10km south of the paved causeway on Main Beach ($11.50-$13.50), both accessible by 4WD only. (Book through the Redlands Shire Council ☎1300 551 253. A range of powered and unpowered sites, as well as cabins, are available around the Island. Call for more information.)

**🍴 FOOD.** Most restaurants are in Point Lookout, along Mooloomba Rd. The cheap, yummy **Fins 'n' Fries ❶,** next to the post office at Meegera Pl., off Endeavor St., has excellent fish and chips and fish burgers ($5.50-$8). (☎07 3409 8080. Open Tu-Th and Su 11am-7:30pm, F-Sa 11am-8pm. Closed M except during holiday season.) **Point Lookout Bowls Club ❸,** on the right side of East Coast Road just past Manta Lodge coming from Dunwich, serves up large portions at fairly reasonable prices (main courses from $12-$23). It's also one of the only places to socialize in the evening. (☎07 3409 8182). **La Focaccia ❸,** at Meegera Pl. off Endeavor St., serves pasta and pizza ($12.50-17) in an open-air setting. (☎07 3409 8778. Open daily 6-9pm.) **The Stradbroke Island Beach Hotel ❸,** on the left at the top of the hill toward Point Lookout, has been recently renovated and is a romantic place to spend an evening looking out at the ocean. Their menu boasts a number of regional specialities; main courses cost around $23. (☎07 3409 8188; www.stradbrokehotel.com.au. Open for breakfast 7:30-11am, lunch 11am-5pm, dinner 6pm-late.) For groceries, try **Bob's Foodmarket,** Meegera Pl., Point Lookout. (☎07 3409 8271. Open daily 7am-9pm.)

**📷 SIGHTS AND ACTIVITIES.** Stradbroke's pristine beaches and untouched bush can keep a spirited traveler busy for days. Look for **Frenchman's Beach** as you head toward the end of Point Lookout on Mooloomba Dr., a popular surf and beachwalking spot. To get there, go past Snapper St. and look for signs before the Lookout Village Shopping Centre. For more exercise, continue past the Shopping Centre on your right; just beyond the public toilets on your left lies the entrance to the circular (and spectacular) **◼Gorge Walk,** a 30-45min. stroll past rocky headlands and gorges, white-sand beaches, and blue waters. This walk is famous for whale sightings from June to November, while dolphins, turtles, and manta rays can be seen feeding year-round. The Gorge Walk passes by **Whale Rock** and the **Blowhole,** where crashing waves are channeled up a narrow gorge in a rush of air that sounds exactly like the noise of a whale. **Main Beach** stretches 32km down the eastern edge of the island, luring surfers with some of Queensland's best waves thanks to the early summer's northerly winds. **Keyholes,** a swimming lagoon 6.4km down Main Beach, is a lovely picnic spot but can only be reached by car or vigorous hike. If driving by car, be aware that this is a private mining road that can be closed off at the owners' discretion. **Cylinder Beach,** which runs in front of the Stradbroke Hotel on the north side of the island, is more swimmer- and family-oriented, though good surfing breaks can be found there most afternoons. **Deadman's Beach,** just past Cylinder Beach, is more secluded and occasionally has good surf and fishing off the rocks. Though it may not seem appealing, a dip in **Brown Lake,** 3km east of Dunwich, is worth it. The water—dyed a rich amber by the surrounding tea trees and bushlands—leaves skin and hair silky smooth.

The island is known for world-class scuba diving and marine life. The friendly, professional **Manta Lodge and Scuba Centre,** attached to the hostel, has daily trips to 16 dive sites. (☎07 3409 8888; www.mantalodge.com.au. 2 dives with own gear $110, with gear rental $160; 3-day PADI $420.) **Straddie Kingfisher Tours** offers a variety of trips, including an eco-friendly, 4WD island tour. (☎07 3409 9502; www.straddiekingfishertours.com.au. $129, includes BBQ lunch and pick up from Brisbane accommodation.) **Straddie Adventures** offers popular adventure tours. (☎07 3409 8414 or 04 1774 1963; www.straddieadventures. com.au. Sandboarding daily 2-4pm, $30; sea kayaking and snorkeling 9:30am-12:30pm, $60; ½-day 4WD tour $55. Book ahead. Cash only.)

# MORETON ISLAND ☎07

Remarkably untouristed Moreton is a haven for adventurous souls. While Fraser Island is more popular with tourists, Moreton offers similar opportunities in a less-developed setting. Just 35km from Brisbane, visitors can snorkel among shipwrecks, toboggan down sand dunes, and spot whales and dolphins.

**E TRANSPORTATION.** The best way to get around the island is by 4WD; rent on the mainland or take a 4WD guided tour. There are a number of vehicular ferry options. **Moreton Island Ferries (MiCat)** leave from 14 Howard Smith Dr. in Lytton at the Port of Brisbane for the Tangalooma Wrecks on Moreton; take Citytrain from Brisbane to Wynnum Central (35min., every 30min., $3.60). On weekends, you will need a taxi to get there. (☎07 3909 3333; www.moretonad-venture.com. 30min.; daily 8:30am departure and 3:30pm return, F additional 6:30pm departure, Su additional 2:30pm departure, weekends 1 and 4:30pm return; round-trip $45, children $30, vehicles with 2 adults $190. AmEx/MC/V.) The **Combie Trader Ferry** also leaves from Thurecht Pde., Scarborough Harbor, and arrives at Bulwer. (☎07 3203 6399; www.moreton-island.com. 2hr. In summer M and Sa-Su 2 per day, Tu-Th 4 per day, F 3 per day. In winter M and W-Th 1 per day, F-Su 2 per day. Round-trip $40, concessions $35, children $25. Round-trip vehicles for 2 $165 in winter, $175 in summer. AmEx/MC/V.) Guests of the Tangalooma Wild Dolphin Resort can travel by the resort launch transfers.

**⑦ PRACTICAL INFORMATION.** Questions can be answered by the **national park office** (☎07 3408 2710; www.epa.qld.gov.au).

**Ⓒ Ⓒ ACCOMMODATIONS AND FOOD.** The massive **Tangalooma Wild Dolphin Resort ❺** promises that all guests can hand-feed dolphins, but at $260 for singles and $290 for doubles (prices vary according to season), you can decide whose dinner is more important. (☎1300 652 250; www.tangalooma.com. Pickup from Brisbane accommodations available for a fee. AmEx/D/MC/V.) Six designated **campsites ❶** with toilets and showers are located on Moreton ($4.50 per person), and **free camping** is allowed nearly everywhere on the island. You are not allowed to burn any native wood, so buy some firewood before arriving on the island. Pick up a map and pay any camp and 4WD fees ($33.40 per visit) at the ferry site on the mainland. For **campsite booking,** call ☎13 13 04. While the majority of the island is designated national park land, there is a resort and three small townships on the western side. **Fuel, food,** and **basic supplies** are available in the small village of Bulwer.

**◙ SIGHTS.** Hiking trails weave among the dunes and to the top of **Mount Tempest,** which at 282m stands as the world's highest compacted sand mountain. The **Desert** and the **Big Sandhills** are popular sandboarding and tobogganing spots. The tea tree tannins that dye the impeccably clear waters of the misnamed **Blue Lagoon** will rejuvenate your hair and skin. Around the northern headland is a walking track that leads to the **Cape Moreton Lighthouse,** built in 1857, and a panoramic view of the bay, with great opportunities for whale watching from June to November. On the eastern coastline, **Ocean Beach** stretches the full 38km length of the island, while the view from the western side is broken by the **Tangalooma Wrecks,** 16 ships that were intentionally sunk to create a small reef.

Tours of Moreton Island are the easiest, most economical way to see the island's highlights. ◙**Solo Adventure Sailing** (☎07 3348 6100) takes you sailing in a beautiful yacht around Moreton Bay, sandboarding at Moreton, snorkeling around the wrecks, and tube-riding. The $115 price tag includes tea, homemade lunch, and all snorkeling equipment. If you're traveling in a large group, the boat can be chartered for a pirate-themed treasure hunt. ◙**MiCat,** the company that runs the Ferry to Moreton, also offers daytrips to the island: travel around the sand and lakes in a 4WD or explore the wrecks. (☎07 3909 3333; www.moretonadventure.com. Tours $97-114. Book ahead.) **Moreton Bay Escapes** offers rugged, adventure-oriented 4WD trips to the island. (☎1300 559 355; www.moretonbayescapes.com.au. 1-day $149, 2-day $239; children $129/209; students $139/229. Book ahead. $35 round-trip ferry not included in two-day tour. MC/V.) **Dolphin Wild Island Cruises** also sends a powered catamaran from the mainland for an eco-daytrip full of wrecks, dolphins, and snorkeling. (☎07 3880 4444; www.dolphinwild.com.au. Tours 9:30am-5pm. Depart from Redcliffe, 30min. north of Brisbane. $110, students $100, children $60. Transportation from hotels in Brisbane $25, from Gold Coast $35. MC/V.)

## OTHER ISLANDS IN MORETON BAY

Moreton Bay is dotted with more than 300 islands, many of which make perfect daytrips. Cheap accommodations (other than camping) are sparse, but a day is enough to sample the islands' beaches—just be sure to start your day early.

**▥ BRIBIE ISLAND.** At the northern end of Moreton Bay, Bribie is the only island that can be accessed by car and thus is a great option for those who don't want to pay for a tour to the more secluded islands. From Brisbane, go 45km north to Caboolture, then 19km east to the Bribie bridge. Or take **Citytrain** from Brisbane to Caboolture, where Bus #640 runs to Bribie (1hr.; train leaves every 30min., bus every 1hr.; $6.70). The **tourist office** is just over the bridge from the mainland. (☎07 3408 9026. Open M-F 9am-4pm, Sa 9am-3pm, Su 9:30am-1pm.) Bribie is separated from the mainland by **Pumicestone Passage,** a marine park teeming with dolphins, manta rays, turtles, and over 350 species of birds. Bribie is also known for great fishing on the mainland side of the channel and surfing on the eastern side, which has lifeguards year-round. The Island also has a variety of galleries and art shops; visit the gallery at **White Patch.**

**▥ ST. HELENA ISLAND.** From 1867 to 1933, St. Helena was Australia's Alcatraz, with over 300 of the most dangerous criminals on an island surrounded by shark-infested waters. Today, St. Helena limits onshore visitors in order to preserve its national parklands. **A B Sea Cruises** runs day and night trips on its **Cat-o'-Nine Tails** vessel, where actors role-play St. Helena's colorful past. Its night cruise includes dinner and a ghost tour of the island; though it is a bit more expensive, it is well worth the money. Cruises run from Manly. (☎07 3893 1240; www.abseacruises.com.au. Day tours $69, concessions $59, children $39. Night tours $90/80/50. Book ahead. AmEx/D/MC/V.)

# GOLD COAST

Amazing beaches, nightclubs, and theme parks make the Gold Coast a vaunted destination. The region's population of around 500,000 increases to well over a million every summer as tourists flock to the sun, sand, and parties.

## COOLANGATTA AND TWEED HEADS ☎07

While Surfers Paradise has the name, Coolangatta, QLD, and Tweed Heads, NSW, provide the goods with some of the best surfing in all of Australia, if not the world. Only recently, "Cooly" and Tweed Heads were sleepy beachside towns popular among retirees from the southern states. But the unbelievable breaks couldn't be kept secret, and they have begun to attract the world's top surfers. The area is in fact home to two world surf champions, Stephanie Gilmore and Mick Fanning. Meanwhile, tourists have been making Cooly and Tweed Heads a popular alternative to the neon and skyscrapers of the Gold Coast. Development is occurring at a rapid pace, though, so this area may soon become indistinguishable from its glitzy neighbors.

### ▐▌ TRANSPORTATION

**Buses:** Greyhound Australia (☎13 14 99; www.greyhound.com.au) has a monopoly on distance travel from the twin towns. While the side of the bus may read Greyhound, McCafferty's, or Suncoast Pacific, they all fall under the same ownership. Buses leave from the bus shelter on Warren St. behind National Bank, about 100m from Griffith St. to: **Brisbane** (1-2hr., 5 per day, $29); **Byron Bay** (1-1hr., 7 per day, $26); **Noosa** (5hr.; 7:40am, 3:05pm; $41) via **Maroochy** (4hr.; 7:40am, 3:05pm; $41); **Sydney** (14hr., 4 per day, $112). Backpacker and student discounts available. Phone bookings have an additional fee of $6. Surfside Buslines (☎13 12 30) runs the only public transportation in the Gold Coast region. Bus 700 goes to **Southport** (1hr., $4.30) via **Surfers Paradise** (1hr., $4) and leaves every 30min. from the bus stop in front of the Twin Towns Resort. Bus TX1 runs to the theme parks, leaving from the Twin Towns Resort (1hr.; 8:10, 8:45am; $5). It returns from Dreamworld with stops at Wet 'N' Wild and Movieworld. 3-day Ezy Pass offers unlimited rides for $25. Timetables are posted at most stops.

**Taxis: Tweed-Coolangatta Taxi Service** (24hr. ☎07 5536 1144).

**Car Rental: Economy Rental Cars** (☎07 5536 8104 or 1800 803 874; www.economyrentalcars.com.au), at the Gold Coast Airport. Rentals start at $29 per day, including 75km per day and some insurance. Ages 21+. Major rental companies like **Hertz** (☎07 5536 6133) and **Europcar** (☎07 5569 3370) have airport offices. **Gold Coast Tourism Visitor Information Centre** can provide free transport to the airport for car pickup.

### ✦ ▐ ORIENTATION AND PRACTICAL INFORMATION

For a stretch of several kilometers, the Pacific Hwy. becomes the **Gold Coast Highway.** Ride it into Musgrave St., then bear left onto **Marine Parade,** which runs parallel to the beach through Kirra and Coolangatta. **Griffith Street,** the main drag in Coolangatta, runs parallel to Marine Pde. At the Twin Towns Service Club, turn right from Griffith St. onto **Wharf Street,** the main thoroughfare of Tweed Heads; continuing straight from this intersection, Griffith St. turns into **Boundary Street,** which divides the peninsula, terminating at the infamous **Point Danger** and the cliffs responsible for Captain Cook's shipwreck.

**Tourist Offices:** There are 2 accredited visitor information centers in town. **Gold Coast Tourism Visitor Information Centre,** at Shop 14B, Coolangatta Pl. (☎07 5536 7765 or 1300 309 440; www.verygc.com), on the corner of Griffith and Warren St., offers discounts on theme parks and attractions. Free maps also available. Open M-F 8am-5pm, Sa 8am-4pm. The smaller **Tweed and Coolangatta Tourism Inc.** (☎07 5536 4244 or 1800 674 414; www.tweedcoolangatta.com.au) has a desk inside the Centro Tweed Shopping Centre. Open M-Sa 9am-5pm.

**Banks:** Many **ATMs** are on Griffith St., including a **Bank of Queensland,** 84-88 Griffith St., and a **Westpac,** 4 Griffith St. All banks open M-Th 9:30am-4pm, F 9:30am-5pm.

**Backpacking Supplies: Sherry's Camping,** 43 Corporation Circuit, Tweed Heads (☎07 5513 1488; www.sherryscamping.com.au), offers backpacking gear at reasonable prices. Open in summer M-Sa 9am-5:30pm, in winter M-Sa 8:30am-5pm. MC/V.

**Bookstore: The Bookshop,** 26 Griffith St. (☎07 5536 7715), sells used books. Open M-Sa 8:30am-5:30pm, Su 9am-5:30pm. MC/V. **Billabong Bookstore,** 114 Griffith St. (☎07 5536 9986), has a slightly smaller selection. Open M and F-Sa 10:30am-4:30pm, Tu-Th 9:30am-5pm, Su 11am-5pm. Cash only.

**Pharmacy:** Pharmacies line Griffith St., including **Amcal Chemist,** 2 Griffith St. (☎07 5599 4419), attached to the post office. Open M-F 8am-5:30pm, Sa 9am-5pm.

**Internet Access: 3w C@fe,** 152 Griffith St. (☎07 5599 4536), charges $2 per 15min. and a bargain $5 per day for Wi-Fi. Offers fax service, digital camera photo downloading, and a wide range of phone cards in a relaxed, cafe atmosphere. They also offer a selection of teas, pastries, and coffees. Open M-F 7am-7pm, Sa-Su 8am-6pm. **Singapore Merlion Restaurant,** 25 McLean St. (☎07 5536 4678), at the intersection with Griffith St., has Internet for $2 per 20min. and a backpackers' special for $9 that includes 30min. of Internet and a choice of a chicken, beef, pork, or vegetarian plate. Open daily 10am-10:30pm. Winter hours may vary. Cash only.

**Post Office:** 2 Griffith St., at McLean St. Open M-F 9am-5pm. **Postal Code:** 4225.

# ACCOMMODATIONS

Finding a place to crash is not a problem, but budget digs are extremely limited, so consider booking ahead, especially in high season.

**Coolangatta Sands Hostel** (☎07 5536 7472), located on the corner of Griffith and McLean St., is brand new and right in the town center. The rooms are spotlessly clean, and many have balconies that look over the surf. Downstairs bar has discounted meals for backpackers, and the restaurant area turns into a hopping nightclub on F and Sa nights. 8-bed dorms $30, 4-bed $35. MC/V. ❸

**Coolangatta YHA,** 230 Coolangatta Rd. (☎07 5536 7644; www.coolangattayha.com), in Billinga, a 25min. walk north of Cooly; look for the large murals on the outside of the building. Sandwiched between the airport and Coolangatta Rd., the hostel is a short walking distance from decent waves; however, its location next to the airport and the ambulance station makes for some noise. Kitchen, laundry, game room, BBQ, TV lounge, pool, bikes, dropoff/pickup at the town center 4 times daily, and Internet ($2 per 20min.). Breakfast included. Lockers in the hall, $2-4 depending on size; free lockers in rooms. 8-bed dorms $27; 6-bed $28; 4-bed $29; singles $39; doubles $62.50. Weekly rates available. YHA discount 10%. ❷

**Coolangatta Ocean View Motel,** at the corner of Clark St. and Marine Pde. (☎07 5536 3722; www.coolangatta.net/oceanviewmotel), opposite Greenmount Beach. This motel has an excellent location and offers a roof-top deck (open daily 8am-8pm) that provides great views of the entire Gold Coast and a free BBQ to reserve. Its pink exterior is evocative of Floridian retirement communities, but all rooms come with private bath, A/C, refrigerator, TV, and toaster. Reception M-Sa 8am-8pm, Su 9am-7pm. High season singles $70; doubles $80; triples $90. Low season M-Th and Su $60/70/80; F-Sa $70/80/90. VIP and weekly discounts. AmEx/MC/V. ❹

**Kirra Beach Tourist Park** (☎07 5581 7744; www.gctp.com.au/kirra), on Charlotte St. in Kirra, near the airport. Great facilities: laundry, pool, TV room, and jungle gym for the kids. Linen $5 per person (free in cabins). Reception 7am-7pm. Unpowered sites for 2 $27-34; powered $30-$39. Rooms for 2 with TV and refrigerator, $85, low season

$59, extra person $10; spacious cabins for 4 with private bathroom and A/C $125-178. Discounts for longer stays. $15 charge for checkout after 4pm. MC/V. ❷

## 🍴 FOOD

Whether you want Italian, Mexican, Turkish, or Thai cuisine, your cravings will be satisfied by the many restaurants on **Griffith Sreet.** A **Coles** supermarket is located inside the Centro Tweed Shopping Centre on Wharf St. (Open M-Sa 6am-10pm, Su 8am-8pm.) **Night Owl** is a useful convenience store in the Showcase Shopping Centre on Marine Pde. (Open M-Tu 5am-11pm, W-Su 24hr.)

**Ocean Deck Restaurant,** 2 Snapper Rocks Rd. (☎07 5536 6390), atop the Rainbow Bay Surf Club, has a view that rivals those found on postcards. The entire Gold Coast, the Surfers Paradise skyline, and all the world-class surfers riding the waves lie right in front of you. Burgers from $15.50, mains from $13.50. Reservations recommended in summer. Balcony seating. Kitchen open daily 11:30am-2pm and 5:30-8pm. Surf club open M-Th and Su 10am-10pm, F-Sa 10am-midnight. Restaurant hours vary according to season. Weekend breakfasts from 8-11am. MC/V. ❷

**Dee and Paul's Rainbow Cafe,** 13 Ward St. (☎07 5536 4999), off Boundary St., provides walls of surf photos and a selection of wholesome breakfasts ($5-9), sandwiches ($5-6), and banana smoothies ($5.60). Open daily 7am-6:30pm. Cash only. ❶

**Little Malaya Restaurant,** 52 Marine Pde. (☎07 5536 2690), entrance on McLean St. Award plaques hang in the entrance of this Chinese-Malaysian restaurant. Palm trees, a thatched roof, and a wall depicting a Muslim city will make you forget you're in Australia.

The beef rendang ($18) and curry lamb ($19) are delicious. The chef uses a refreshingly small amount of oil. Reservations recommended. Open M and W-Sa noon-2pm and M-Sa 5:30pm-late, Tu and Su 5:30pm-late. AmEx/MC/V. ❷

##  SIGHTS AND BEACHES

The area's greatest attractions are the beaches that line its perimeter. **Rainbow Bay, Greenmount Beach, Coolangatta Beach,** and **Kirra** off Marine Pde., have some of the safest swimming on the Gold Coast but are susceptible to large swells. **Duranbah Beach,** famous among surfers for its reliable waves, lies on the southeast side of the peninsula. The best surfers in town can be found at **Snapper Rocks,** which hosts a professional tour event each summer.

> **! MIND THE FLAGS.** Swimmers should obey all posted warnings; details about up-to-date conditions can be found daily on a chalkboard located on the beach. Red flags mean the water is unsafe to enter. Yellow flags mean that visitors should exercise extreme caution. Red-and-yellow flags mean swimming is safe between the flags. Green flags are put up when the water is safe for swimmers within indicated areas. Since surfers cannot bring their boards inside the red and yellow flags, blue flags or signs indicate where surfing is permitted (although these indicators are not always posted).

The walkway facing the ocean, which begins to the left of Point Danger, is a beautiful route to Greenmount Beach. You'll trip over kangaroos, koalas, and saltwater crocs at the **Currumbin Wildlife Sanctuary,** 7km north off the Gold Coast Hwy. on Tomewin St. The sanctuary is also a surfside bus stop (take #700, 760, 765, or TX1 and ask the driver to announce the Currumbin stop). Help feed the wild rainbow lorikeets (daily 8-9:30am and 4-5pm) or take a nocturnal "wildnight" tour (daily 7pm-9:45pm; $49, children $27; book ahead). For more information about a daytrip to the sanctuary, call ☎07 5534 1266 or visit www.currumbin-sanctuary.org.au. (Open daily 8am-5pm. $32, children $21.) For great views of the ocean and the hinterlands, make your way up to either of two lookouts. **Razorback Lookout** is a small hike from the CBD (30min. on foot): follow Wharf St. inland from the Twin Towns Service Club and take a right on Florence St. At the top of the hill, take a left on Charles St., and follow Razorback Rd. to its end. Continue up the railed footpath for a fabulous panorama of Cooly, Tweed Heads, and Mt. Warning. The less-ambitious can head up the hill at the corner of Marine Pde. and McLean St.; the **lookout** on top provides unparalleled views of the entire Gold Coast. If the idea of walking uphill makes you cringe, stroll along the beach, either on the sand or the footpath right above, and take in the magnificent views of the coast. If you want a break, stop at any of the surf clubs along the beachside road (**Rainbow Bay, North Kirra, Kirra, Coolangatta,** or **Greenmount**) for a bite and a spectacular view.

The twin towns are surfer-friendly, and those who come to ride the waves will find plenty of shops that aim to please. **Surf X Cess,** near the Showcase Shopping Centre on Griffith St., is one of the few surf shops that rents surf gear. (☎07 5599 1164. Boards ½-day $20, overnight $30; bodyboards $15/20; flippers $5/7. Open daily 9am-5pm. Weekly discounts available.) For a 2hr. group surfing lesson that aims to get you standing in no time, contact **Walkin' on Water.** (☎04 1878 0311 or 07 5534 1886; www.walkinonwater.com. 2hr. group lesson $40. Call for information on group and private sessions.)

The annual **Wintersun Festival,** Australia's biggest rock-and-roll event, is held during the 10 days preceding the Queen's Birthday (the second M in June). In 2009, the festival is scheduled for May 29-June 8, with the party's climax occurring the final weekend. The 2010 festival will take place June 4-14. The twin towns will celebrate Elvis and the 1950s with retro cars, dancing, music, artists, and entertainers. (☎07 5536 9509; www.wintersun.org.au.)

## NIGHTLIFE

Though the waves are phenomenal, the nightlife is a bit lacking. For endless clubs and pubs, head to **Surfers Paradise,** the nightlife hub of the Gold Coast, just a quick bus ride away on **Surfside Buslines** (see **Transportation,** p. 341).

**Calypso Tavern,** 91-97 Griffith St. (☎07 5599 2677). Caters to an upscale crowd, featuring a downstairs bar with a plush club upstairs. Regular promotions and 3 DJs F and Sa night. Possible $10 cover upstairs. Open M-Th and Su 10am-midnight, F-Sa 10am-3am. Restaurant area downstairs offers meals with free drinks starting at just $7. MC/V.

**Balcony Night Club,** on Marine Pde., inside the Coolangatta Hotel (☎07 5536 9311; www.thecoolyhotel.com.au). A popular spot for young locals to jive to live music (tickets required, available at the hotel) or a DJ ($5-10 cover). Attracts local and international bands to their modern and newly renovated club. Downstairs, the hotel has promotional events, billiards, and live music or a DJ Th-Su. Open daily 9am-latenight.

**Twin Towns Service Club** (☎07 5536 2277), at Griffith and Wharf St., is like Las Vegas without the glamor. This gigantic club caters to an older crowd, with slot machines, cheap food, 5 eateries, 7 bars, live entertainment, and free movies M 10:30am and 6:30pm. On weekends, **Champions Bar** and **Images Bar** on Level 1 (open until 1:30am and 3am, respectively) are popular as cheap places to drink before heading to clubs.

# SURFERS PARADISE  ☎07

If you're looking for great surfing, Surfers Paradise is, ironically, not your best bet. The small breaks off Surfers are good for beginners, but serious surfers should head south to **Coolangatta** (p. 341). Nevertheless, the town draws thousands of backpackers with its wild nightlife, shopping, and proximity to theme parks and South Stradbroke Island. When the sun goes down, Surfers comes alive with an unrivaled choice of bars and nightclubs, making it the hottest scene on the Gold Coast. Boasting high-end fashion stores and cafes, all within walking distance of gorgeous beaches, it's no wonder that Surfers has become a premier East Coast holiday destination.

## TRANSPORTATION

**Buses:** The **Transit Centre** is on Beach Rd., just off Ferny Ave. (open daily 6:30am-8pm). Greyhound Australia (☎13 14 99; www.greyhound.com.au) offers service to **Brisbane** (1hr., 7 per day 4:45am-10pm, $26) and **Sydney** (15-16hr., 4 per day 8:20am-8:20pm, $119). Premier Motor Service (☎13 34 10; www.premierms.com.au) and Kirklands (☎1300 367 077; www.kirklands.com.au) offer very similar routes. J & B Coaches (☎07 5592 2655) has a fast, cheap **Byron Bay** express shuttle (70min.; every 2hr. 8:30am-2:30pm; $28, with student ID $25).

**Local Buses:** Surfside Buslines (☎13 12 30; www.translink.com.au), the local 24hr. bus company, runs to roadside stops along the Gold Coast Highway, as well as the Pacific Fair Shopping Centre (buses 704, 706, 745; 45min.; walk to the end of Cavill Ave. and turn left; runs every 15min.), local theme parks (bus TX2 services Wet 'N' Wild, Movieworld, and Dreamworld, every 15min., from Appel Park, just north of Cavill Ave. on Ferny Ave.; bus 750 goes to Sea World, every 20min., next to the WestPac Bank on the Gold Coast Hwy.) and Southport (buses 700, 702, 703, 706, 709; 20min. every 5-10min.; $2.70 one-way). If you are heading to Brisbane or the Brisbane airport, bus

QUEENSLAND

745, which picks up directly across from the Transit Centre, will you to Nerang Train Station where you can transfer. Bus leaves every 30min., and the journey takes 1hr. to Brisbane ($10) and 2hr. to the airport ($26). Ezy Passes provide unlimited use of all buses and can be purchased from drivers (3-, 5-, 7-, 10-, 14-day passes available; $25-60, children $13-30). Gold Coast Tourist Shuttle (☎07 5574 5111) offers transport to all theme parks with pickup and dropoff from accommodations and, with purchase of 3-, 5-, or 7-day travel pass, unlimited use of Surfside Buslines (3-day Gold Pass $44, ages 4-13 $22; 1 week $81/41). Also offers transfers to and from the Gold Coast airport.

**Taxis:** Regent Taxis (☎13 10 08) or Maxi Taxi (☎13 62 94), which also has vans.

**Car Rental:** Conveniently located inside the reception area of the Islander Resort Hotel, Dave's Car Rental (☎07 5504 5955 or 1300 130 242; www.davescarrental.com.au) has low prices. Cars start at $48 with 150km per day in high season; $35 low season. Insurance $12. Open daily 8am-5pm. Specials available, especially during low season. The transit center has a number of car rental services catering to backpackers.

## ⬛✴️🅐 ORIENTATION AND PRACTICAL INFORMATION

Maps of Surfers are long and thin, reflecting the fact that all the action is squeezed into a strip several kilometers long and just a few blocks wide, sandwiched between the ocean and the Nerang River. Three main avenues run parallel to the shore: the **Esplanade,** which skirts the beach; **Surfers Paradise Boulevard** (also known as **Gold Coast Highway**), a block farther inland; and **Ferny Avenue,** one more block inland. The heart of Surfers is **Cavill Mall,** a pedestrian street lined with restaurants, cafes, bars, souvenir shops, and the Centro Shopping Center. The Esplanade continues north past Main Beach to the **Marina Mirage** and the **Spit** at **Main Beach,** the end of the peninsula just past Sea World. **Southport** is located along the Gold Coast Hwy., past Main Beach and 3km northwest of the CBD. To the south is **Broadbeach,** home of the enormous Conrad Hotel Jupiter Casino and the gigantic Pacific Fair Shopping Centre.

**Tourist Offices: Gold Coast Tourism** (☎07 5538 4419; www.verygc.com), on Cavill Ave., is the only accredited visitor information center in the area. Open M-F 8:30am-5:30pm, Sa 8:30am-5pm, Su 9am-4pm. The **Backpacker's Travel Desk** (☎07 5592 2911 or 1800 359 830), in the Transit Centre, offers tourist information and arranges transportation to most area hostels. Open daily 8am-6pm.

**Banks: Westpac,** on the corner of Cavill Ave. and Gold Coast Hwy., has a 24hr. ATM, as does **Commonwealth Bank** next door. Both banks open M-Th 9:30am-4pm, F 9:30am-5pm. **ATMs** can also be found all over the center of town and in the shopping centers.

**Police:** 68 Ferny Ave. (☎07 5570 7888), at Cypress Ave. There's also a station (☎07 5583 9733) on the corner of Cavill Mall and the Esplanade.

**Medical Services: Gold Coast General Hospital,** 108 Nerang St., Southport (☎07 5571 8211). **Day Night Medical Centre** (☎07 5592 2299), in the Piazza Mall on the Gold Coast Hwy., is available for basic care. Open daily 7am-11pm.

**Internet Access: Peterpan Adventures,** a travel agency in the Transit Centre, offers Internet for $2 per hr. Open daily 10am-5:30pm. **Ozki Photo & Internet** (☎07 5538 4937), at the corner of Gold Coast Hwy. and Elkhorn Ave., is popular with backpackers. $3 per hr. Open daily 9am-8pm. **Chapters and Chinos** (☎07 5504 7731), a bookstore located at the Chevron Renaissance Centre on Surfer's Paradise Blvd., has a cafe with a mouthwatering selection of pastries and coffees, along with free Wi-Fi.

**Post Office:** The main branch is inside the Centro Shopping Center. Open M-F 9am-5:30pm, Sa 9am-12:30pm. **Postal Code:** 4217.

## ACCOMMODATIONS

In Surfers, hostel staff assume the role of camp counselors, providing backpackers with endless outdoor activities. Many staff members are backpackers themselves and love partying just as much as the guests do. Most hostels organize night-time activities as well, and many have bars that are arguably better and more social than the ones you'll find in town. Hostels and backpackers are all over Surfers, so this list is by no means exhaustive. Summer and Easter are peak times—book ahead and expect that listed prices could rise. Unless otherwise specified, hostels have free pickup from the Transit Centre (call before arrival), 10am check-out, and a pool. Internet access and laundry are usually available for a price. Be aware that towels are not provided at most hostels.

**Trekkers,** 22 White St., Southport (☎07 5591 5616 or 1800 100 004; www.trekkersbackpackers. com.au), 3km north of the CBD. An incredibly fun, friendly, and well-run hostel. Owners Cliff, Laura, and their little daughter Lottie do everything they can to make your stay enjoyable. 20min. walk to Main Beach. Courtesy bus goes to town every 2hr. Nightly club outings and a tour desk. Local buses travel between Surfers and Southport every 5-10min. ($2.70). Some dorms have private bath. Saltwater pool on premises. Break-fast included. Free BBQ. Reception daily 7am-10:30pm. 4-, 5-, 6-, and 10-bed dorms $27; doubles $70. VIP/YHA discount. MC/V. ❷

**Sleeping Inn Surfers,** 26 Peninsular Dr. (☎07 5592 4455 or 1800 817 832; www.sleepinginn.com.au), a 7min. walk from the Transit Centre across Ferny Ave. All 15 units are apartment-style with full kitchens, TV, private baths, and common area. Not as loud as other hostels; offers a mellow, friendly atmosphere and

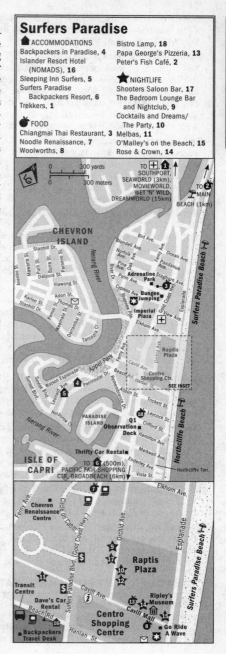

### Surfers Paradise

🏠 **ACCOMMODATIONS**
Backpackers in Paradise, **4**
Islander Resort Hotel
(NOMADS), **16**
Sleeping Inn Surfers, **5**
Surfers Paradise
Backpackers Resort, **6**
Trekkers, **1**

🍎 **FOOD**
Chiangmai Thai Restaurant, **3**
Noodle Renaissance, **7**
Woolworths, **8**

Bistro Lamp, **18**
Papa George's Pizzeria, **13**
Peter's Fish Café, **2**

⭐ **NIGHTLIFE**
Shooters Saloon Bar, **17**
The Bedroom Lounge Bar
and Nightclub, **9**
Cocktails and Dreams/
The Party, **10**
Melbas, **11**
O'Malley's on the Beach, **15**
Rose & Crown, **14**

superb comfort at low prices. Free pickup at Transit Centre in a limousine. Key deposit $20. Reception daily 7am-9pm. 4- and 8-bed dorms $27; doubles $65-78. ISIC/VIP/YHA $1 discount. MC/V. ❷

**Surfers Paradise Backpackers Resort,** 2837 Gold Coast Hwy. (☎07 5592 4677 or 1800 282 800; www.surfersparadisebackpackers.com.au), a 15min. walk south from the Transit Centre. Upbeat atmosphere and spotless facilities. All rooms ensuite. Kitchen, bar, tennis, basketball, small gym, and free laundry. As of early 2009, all of the self-contained apartment units will have been recently renovated. Free boogie board use. Sauna $4 per 45min. Reception daily 7:30am-7pm. 5- and 6-bed dorms $27; doubles $70; triples $93. VIP/YHA discount. MC/V. ❷

**Backpackers In Paradise,** 40 Peninsula Dr. (☎1800 268 621; www.backpackersin-paradise.com), just a 5min. walk from town; look for the murals. Friendly, fun, relaxed, and close to the beach, with simple dorms, spacious doubles, a bar, and even an on-site convenience store. Rooms have private bath. Organizes nightly trips to nightclubs. 20-bed dorms $21, 12-bed $23, 8-bed $25, 4-bed $26; doubles $65; apartments $75. Cheaper rates for longer stays. MC/V. ❷

**Islander Resort Hotel (NOMADS),** 6 Beach Rd. (☎07 5538 8000), adjacent to the Transit Centre. All the amenities of a resort at hostel prices. Practically in the CBD and just 1min. from the beach. The massive complex has rooms with TV, fridge, private bath, and balcony. Hot tub, bar, restaurant, coin-operated arcade, tennis, and squash courts. Not a member of Backpackers Association, but talk to reception about joining the club crawl. Reception 24hr. 4- to 8-bed dorms $28; doubles $85. AmEx/MC/V. ❷

# ▐ FOOD

Of Surfers's outdoor malls and arcades, **Cavill Mall** and **Chevron Renaissance Centre,** lined with mid-range bistros and cafes, are the most popular. For latenight eats, **Papa George's Pizzeria** (at the corner of Cavill and Orchid) is reliably greasy and delicious. For groceries, try **Woolworths,** in the basement of Centro Shopping Center, on Cavill Mall. (Open M-F 8am-9pm, Sa 8am-5:30pm, Su 9am-6pm.)

▨ **Bistro Lamp,** 3021 Gold Coast Hwy. (☎07 5538 4377; www.bistrolamp.com). A delicious, incredibly authentic Japanese eatery with a low-lit, romantic atmosphere. Open Tu-Su for lunch noon-2pm and 6pm-late for dinner. Lunch meals start from around $9, and dinner mains cost around $15. MC/V. ❷

**Chiangmai Thai Restaurant,** 5-19 Palm Ave. (☎07 5526 8891), across from Adrenaline Park. A restaurant with elaborate decor which includes wooden chairs with intricate elephant images, Buddha statues, and gold-plated items just about everywhere. The menu is comprehensive and delicious, with chicken and beef dishes ($17) and vegetarian plates ($14). Open daily 5:30-10pm. Reservations recommended. AmEx/MC/V. ❷

**Noodle Renaissance,** 3240 Gold Coast Hwy. (☎07 5504 5569), near Elkhorn St. Some of the best cheap lunch food in Surfers. Hong-Kong-style Asian food with curries and a large noodle soup menu ($7.70-10). Open daily 11:30am-4:30pm. Cash only. ❶

**Peter's Fish Cafe,** Shop 22, Mariner's Cove, Sea World Dr., Main Beach (☎07 5531 0077), has the best fish and chips in town (lunch $6, dinner $10; sauces $1-2) and other fresh seafood ($20-24). Open in high season Tu-F noon-3pm and 5-9pm, Sa-Su noon-9pm; in low season Tu-F noon-3pm and 5-8pm, Sa noon-9pm, Su noon-8pm. ❷

## ▚ BEACHES, SURFING, AND WATER SPORTS

White sand beaches stretch 25km from **Main Beach** on the **Spit** to Coolangatta's **Snapper Rocks.** Surfers Paradise is a bit of a misnomer, however. The best surfing is to the south, near **Coolangatta and Tweed Heads** (p. 341). Surfing conditions vary considerably, especially as shifting sand alters the breaks; locals sometimes drive up and down the coast looking for the best waves. For detailed info, go to www.coastalwatch.com or listen to 90.9 Sea FM's surf reports.

The most popular beach among boardless beachgoers is **Surfers Paradise Beach,** which runs a few blocks north and south of Cavill Mall. Farther south is **Broadbeach,** where you'll find **Kurrawa,** near the Pacific Fair Shopping Centre. **Burleigh Heads** offers a world-class break, which means large crowds during high season. Surfing is also popular at **South Stradbroke Island.** The beaches there are unpatrolled; use common sense.

For equipment, try **Go Ride A Wave,** a kiosk at the corner of Esplanade and Cavill Mall. (☎1300 132 441; www.gorideawave.com.au. Surfboards $25 per 2hr., $35 per 2-4hr., $45 per day. All types of boards and beach equipment available. Bag storage free with rental; otherwise $5.) **Learn 2 Surf,** on the corner of Hanlan St. and Esplanade, has the best deal in town. (☎1800 227 873. Open daily 10am and 2pm. 2hr. group lessons and equipment $35. Book a day ahead.) **Australian Kayaking Adventures** runs excellent sea kayaking tours from the Spit to South Stradbroke Island, including tea or breakfast, snorkeling, a bushwalk, and a chance of seeing dolphins on the early morning trip. (☎04 1294 0135; www.australiankayakingadventures.com.au. Tours leave at 6:30am and 11:30am. $75. Pickup and dropoff included. MC/V.)

## ⚠ ADVENTURE ACTIVITIES

Surfers Paradise boasts some of the best adventure activities anywhere on the continent. Tickets to all theme parks can be purchased at slightly reduced prices from the tourist info booths at Cavill Mall or in hostels. **Surfside Buslines** and **Gold Coast Tourist Shuttle** provide transportation to all parks (see **Local Buses,** p. 345). Call ahead and check hours.

**SKYDIVE BYRON BAY.** The friendly, funny staff make the jump unforgettable. They offer free transfers from any hostel in Surfers to Tyagarah Airport, 1hr. away. If you ask politely, the driver will drop you off at the Byron Bay lighthouse and town center for a few hours before your return. (☎07 6684 1323; www.skydivebyronbay.com. 8000-14,000 ft. jump $214-329, video $99-159. Book ahead. MC/V.)

**EXTREME JETBOATING.** For those looking for a fun (and nauseating) ride along the Nerang River. The capable handlers will spin you around 360° at 70kph. (☎04 1960 8978; www.extremejetboating.com. Adults $55, children $40. Book ahead. MC/V.)

## BEACH, BABES, AND BURNING RUBBER

While some countries hold their car races in massive stadiums, Australia brings the speed and fury right to the street. The Gold Coast Indy 300 is held in late October along the Surfers Paradise Esplanade. For four days and four nights, much of Surfers is shut down and turned into a gigantic urban racetrack as tires squeal and speeds exceed 270kph in Australia's largest racecar event.

With television cameras everywhere, jet planes performing acrobatic maneuvers in the sky, and over 320,000 spectators lining the streets, the atmosphere is electric. For many, the races are just a good opportunity to party. Nightclubs are packed wall-to-wall, and most even create extensions by setting up tents on the premises. In addition, clubs are permitted to remain open until 7am Sunday morning, catering to those who wish to party until they run out of gas.

*Hostels will be sold out during the weekend. Book at least a month ahead. Tickets for the event can be purchased online at www.indy.com.au, at Golden Casket News Agency, 2 Elkhorn Ave. between the Esplanade and Orchid Ave. in Surfers, or at the gate to the event at Elkhorn Ave. and the Esplanade. Pre-purchased tickets are cheaper than those bought at the gate.*

**THE Q1 OBSERVATION DECK.** The most spectacular view around lies atop one of the world's fastest elevators inside the world's tallest residential building. *(3003 Gold Coast Hwy., at the corner of Hamilton Ave. ☎07 5630 4700; www.qdeck.com.au. $18.50, concessions $13, children $10. Open summer M-Th and Su 10am-10pm, F-Sa 10am-midnight; winter M-Th and Su 10am-8pm.)*

**DREAMWORLD.** Australia's largest theme park will get your blood pumping with the tallest vertical free-fall in the world and the tallest high-speed gravity roller coaster in the Southern Hemisphere. The park also has one of only three interactive tiger exhibits outside the US. If you're lucky, you may even get to see some newborn cubs in the nursery. *(☎07 5588 1111 or 1800 073 300; www. dreamworld.com.au. Open daily 10am-5pm. $66, ages 4-13 $43.)*

##  ENTERTAINMENT AND NIGHTLIFE

If you're looking to party, you've come to the right place. The streets of Surfers are more crowded after midnight than at high noon. **Orchid Avenue** boasts Surfers's top nightclubs, but be aware that cover charges may rise during peak times. Since many of the clubs have theme nights, the crowd and the music may vary. Ask hostel staff about evening events or visit www.surfersparadise. com. Also check out www.goldcoastbackpackers.net to see if your hostel is part of the popular **Big Night Out club crawl**—it's a good time and a great deal. For $30, you get entry into four nightclubs, discounted drinks, pizza, transport on a coach bus, and the opportunity to make memories you may even remember.

> **TIP**
>
> **IN DA CLUB.** Clubbing is huge in Surfers, and the laws are strictly enforced. Passports are the best form of identification to carry, although if your driver's license is written in English, it normally doesn't present a problem. All bars and clubs are 18+, and according to Australian law, no one is permitted to enter or re-enter a club after 3am.

**Melbas,** 46 Cavill Ave. (☎07 5592 6922). A trendy restaurant downstairs, which turns into a Top 40 music nightclub. Another bumping club upstairs with dance music makes Melbas a popular spot for people of all ages. Happy hour 4-8pm downstairs, 7-10pm upstairs. There is often a long line and cover ($10-15) for entry upstairs. Restaurant open daily 7:30am-5am. Club open daily 7pm-5am. Hours may vary.

**The Bedroom Lounge Bar and Nightclub,** 26 Orchid Ave. (☎07 5538 7600; www. thebedroom.net.au). The dance floor is surrounded by beds. Great DJs and live hip-hop performances. $10-15 cover may apply. Open daily 9pm-5am.

**Shooters Saloon Bar,** Level 1, The Mark Building, Orchid Ave. (☎07 5592 1144). This place is country-western in decor, but don't let the saloon-like appearance fool you—mainstream dance and R&B music pack the dance floor. Free buffet dinner and drink on Su for backpackers. Cover F-Sa after 10pm $10-15. Open daily 8pm-5am.

**Rose & Crown,** Level 1, Raptis Plaza on Cavill Ave. (☎07 5531 5425; www.roseand-crown.com.au). Popular with a younger crowd. Dance, Top 40, and house play different rooms. Cover $5-10. Open in summer daily 8pm-5am; in winter Th-Su 8pm-5am.

**Cocktails and Dreams,** Level 1, Mark Bldg., Orchid Ave. (☎07 5592 1955). Packed club popular with backpackers. Head downstairs to **The Party,** one of few rock clubs in town. Separate cover (up to $10) for each. Open Th-Su 9pm-5am. Hours vary in summer.

**O'Malley's on the Beach** (☎07 5570 4075), at the end of Cavill Mall. Classic Irish pub with balcony views and live pub rock W-Sa. Open daily 10:30am-late

## ⚡ DAYTRIP FROM SURFERS

### SOUTH STRADBROKE ISLAND

*Ferries operated by the South Stradbroke Island Resort run from Gate C of the Runaway Bay Marina, 247 Bayview St., off the Gold Coast Hwy. past Southport. (☎07 5577 3311; www.ssir.com.au. 25min.; departs daily 10:30am and 4pm; returns M-F 2:30 and 5pm, Sa-Su 3:30 and 5pm; $35 round-trip, with BBQ and sandboarding $56; pickup from Surfers $7 extra.) If you don't have a car to reach Runaway Bay, Surfside Buslines bus #706 (☎13 12 30) connects Surfers Paradise to Runaway Bay ($3.50 one-way) and leaves from Appel Park on Ferny Ave. (30min., leaves 20 and 50min. past the hr.)*

Separated from the Spit by a thin channel, South Straddie is a treasure. Largely undeveloped and home to friendly, free-roaming wallabies, the long narrow island (22km by 2.5km) is lined by river beaches on the west and empty surf beaches on the east. The patrolled **Surf Beach** is on the ocean side, a 35min. walk from the resort. Check with the resort for current hours.

The **South Stradbroke Island Resort ❺** is the cheaper of the two resorts on the island. It boasts pools, spas, tennis courts, water sports, and restaurants. Individual cabins have TV and fridge. (☎07 5577 3311 or 1800 074 125. 4- to 6-person rooms from $145. Call for specials.) There are four **camping ❶** areas; all sites have toilets, showers, and cost $16 for two. **Tipplers campground** (☎07 5577 2849) is just 300m from the resort; the island's other sites are more private and require a water taxi. **Water taxis** (☎04 1875 9789) for up to four leave from Gate C of Runaway Bay to Tipplers (one-way $70), campgrounds at **Currigee** or **North Currigee** (☎07 5577 3932; one-way $40), and **The Bedrooms** (one-way $100).

# GOLD COAST HINTERLAND

Just a little over an hour from the bustling coast, the Hinterland lets nature-lovers bushwalk through subtropical rainforest, enjoy spectacular views, and stroll through tiny towns. It makes for a wonderful daytrip away from the glitz of the coast, and while there are limited budget accommodations, there are several great opportunities for camping.

Travel by car is the most flexible and enjoyable means to explore. Head south along the Gold Coast Hwy. and turn right at Hooker Blvd./Nerang (at Pacific Fair Shopping Centre). You will immediately see signs to **Springbrook National Park** (41km), **Binna Burra** (48km), and **O'Reilly's Plateau/Lamington National Park** (74km). Continue toward Nerang and then follow the signs. Many of the roads inland are not connected, and a fair amount of backtracking is inevitable. However, the parks are close enough to one another that two or more can be visited in just a few days. Look for kangaroos along the drive. For more info, contact **Queensland Parks and Wildlife Service** (☎13 13 04; www.epa.qld.gov.au).

There are group tours that can transport you to some of the parks. **Scenic Hinterland Tours,** 9 Beach Rd. (☎07 5531 5536; www.hinterlandtours.com.au.) across from the Surfers Paradise Transit Centre, picks up from Gold Coast resorts and has trips to both Lamington ($62) and Springbrook ($65) National Parks. While the guided tour is convenient, you will spend most of your time on the bus sitting next to Australian pensioners. Students get a $5 discount. You must book ahead. **All State Scenic Tours** accesses O'Reilly's Park in Lamington from the Transit Centre in Brisbane and will pick up passengers along the Gold Coast. (☎07 3489 6444; www.brisbanedaytours.com.au. Departs daily 9am, returns 4:30pm. $79, children $49. Includes morning tea and wine tasting.)

# LAMINGTON NATIONAL PARK

Lamington National Park is split into two accessible sections: **Green Mountains/ O'Reilly's** and **Binna Burra.** The park's 100km of well-trod paths lead to over 300 waterfalls, clear springs, subtropical rainforests, and the NSW border ridge, with magnificent views of Mt. Warning's ancient volcanic crater. Trails appeal to daytrippers and more serious bushwalkers, ranging in length from short walks and half-day hikes to strenuous full-day treks of 24km. If you're daytripping from Brisbane, **Rob's Rainforest Explorer Day Tours** will take you to Lamington and nearby Springbrook National Park, though you'll spend most of your day on the bus. (☎1300 559 355; www.robsrainforest.com. $99 includes pickup and transport, as well as morning tea, lunch, and afternoon tea. MC/V.)

**GREEN MOUNTAINS.** Green Mountains (and the privately owned O'Reilly's Park) can only be reached via Nerang and Canungra along a switchback road off the Pacific Hwy. After passing through Canungra, the last 30km of road is narrow and winding—there are 405 bends—and unsuitable for caravans. Stick to posted speed limits, as inches away from the road are hundred-foot dropoffs without guardrails. The **information center** is located 5km into the park; leave your car in the carpark below O'Reilly's, walk up the hill, and it will be on your left. The center provides maps, books campsites, and issues bush camping permits. (☎07 5544 0634. Open M and W-Th 9-11am and 1-3:30pm, Tu and F 1-3:30pm.) Accessible via the Booyong Walk, the 20m tall **Tree Top Canopy Walk** offers visitors a dizzying look at the rainforest, with explanatory placards and viewing platforms 24m and 30m high. From **O'Reilly's Rainforest Retreat** (see below), the popular **Toolona Creek circuit** (17.4km, 5-6hr. round-trip) will take you past numerous waterfalls and stands of native beech trees on its way to stunning panoramas. The tracks to **Moran's Falls** (4.4km, 1hr. round-trip) and Python Rock (3.2km, 1hr. round-trip) start about 800m downhill from the info center. The paved **Moran's Falls trail** descends deep into the rainforest before opening onto views of the waterfall, a gorge, and the Albert River. The **Python Rock** is a much easier trail that offers views of Moran's Falls, the Albert River Valley, and the impressive **Castle Crag.** On wet days in late spring and summer, listen for the guttural popping noise of the masked mountain frog.

On-site **camping ❶** includes toilets and hot showers, but campfires are not allowed. (☎13 13 04; www.qld.gov.au/camping. Book ahead. Bush camping permitted Feb.-Nov. $5, families $19.40). **O'Reilly's Rainforest Retreat ❺,** a guesthouse in O'Reilly's Park, has an excellent location just minutes from the trails and across from the info center. (☎07 5502 4911 or 1800 688 722; www.oreillys. com.au. Planned activities like bird walks and 4WD bus tours 6:45am-9:30pm. Book ahead. Singles from $215; doubles from $265. AmEx/MC/V.)

**BINNA BURRA.** To get to Binna Burra, follow the signs for Beechmont and Binna Burra from Nerang (37km). The **information center** provides bush camping permits ($5, families $19.40) and maps of the different hiking circuits. (☎07 5533 3584. Open daily 9am-3pm; rangers available M-F 1-3:30pm. Brochures and maps available at all times.) As trail and campsite conditions can vary throughout the year, always call ahead or visit the park office for information on camping and hiking before setting out.

The **Caves Circuit** (5km, 1hr. round-trip) is so popular that it has its own self-guided tour available at the info center, where the hike originates. The short trek provides sweeping views of Coomera Valley and the Darlington Range. Keep your eyes peeled for koalas in the open forest areas. Binna Burra's most popular full-day hike, **Coomera Circuit** (17.4km, 7hr. round-trip), leaves the Border Track 1.9km from the entrance; the path climbs beside the

Coomera Gorge and crosses the river several times. These crossings involve rock-hopping, which can be hazardous after heavy rain.

On-site camping is available at the **Binna Burra Mountain Campsite ❷**, on your left 1km past the info center. (☎07 5533 3622 or 1300 246 622; www.binnabur-ralodge.com.au. Book 2 weeks in advance. Reception open M-Th and Su 9am-5:30pm, F-Sa 9am-7pm. Sites $24; 2-bed safari tents $55, 4-bed $75, 6-bed $90.)

# SPRINGBROOK NATIONAL PARK

The Springbrook plateau lies on the northern edge of the ridge encircling the spire at the center of Mt. Warning's crater. Covering over 3,300 hectares of land, the park consists of three sections, all separated by a car drive: **Springbrook Plateau,** the **Natural Bridge** to the west, and **Mount Cougal** to the east. Springbrook's highlights are its striking rock formations and waterfalls.

**SPRINGBROOK PLATEAU.** Follow the signs to Mudgeeraba on the Pacific Hwy., also labeled as M1, and then head toward the mountains on Springbrook Rd. (30km). Follow signs to the unattended **information center** in the old school-house for maps of the park's walks, campsites, and picnic areas. (Ranger ☎07 5533 5147.) **Camping ❶** is available at the **Gwongorella picnic area.** (Book ahead. $5, families $19.40.) **Rosellas at Canyon Lookout ❸**, 8 Canyon Pde. (☎07 5533 5120) is a friendly bed and breakfast with rooms that each have a private bath, microwave, TV, fridge, DVD player, and electric blankets. (M-Th and Su singles $75; doubles $90. F-Sa singles $90; doubles $110. Follow signs to Canyon Lookout and you will see signs for Rosellas. MC/V.)

On a clear day at the **Best of All Lookout,** on the southern end of Springbrook Rd., you'll see Coolangatta, Byron Bay, and a huge shield volcano that dominated the region 23 million years ago. The 700m round-trip walk to the lookout passes by a grove of ancient Antarctic beech trees. The park's best walking tracks are accessible from the **Canyon Lookout,** off Springbrook Rd. Both the impressive **Twin Falls Circuit** (4km, 1hr. round-trip), and the popular day-long **Warrie Circuit** (17km, 5-6hr. round-trip) begin here. Both lead through rock wedge caves and behind, around, and under waterfalls.

**NATURAL BRIDGE.** The **Natural Bridge Circuit** (1km, 30min. round-trip) will take you into an arched cave created by the waterfall plunging from above. Go shortly after sunset to beat the evening crowds that flock to see the glowworms and bats. Look for signs for the **Natural Bridge** (30km from Nerang) en route to Springbrook National Park. There aren't any truly rugged routes here, so if you are looking to get off the beaten track, you may want to pass on this one.

# DARLING AND SOUTHERN DOWNS

West of the Great Dividing Range lies the Darling Downs, with fresh mountain air and breathtaking vistas. Its epicenter is Toowoomba, with beautiful parks that draw tourists to the area. The Southern Downs—visit standout city **Stanthorpe** (p. 355)—attracts hordes of backpackers in the fruit-picking season as well as year-round visitors to the region's wineries. Nearby Girraween and Sundown National Parks offer with dramatic rock outcroppings, spectacular views, rugged bushwalking, and brilliant wildflowers from September to March.

# TOOWOOMBA ☎ 07

With over 200 parks and gardens, many connected by bike and walking paths, Toowoomba (pop. 122,000) has long outgrown its name, which is (loosely) derived from an Aboriginal word meaning "where the water sits down" or "swamp." The metropolis is now called "the Garden City" for its gorgeous and varied green spaces. Toowoomba is Queensland's largest inland city, yet it clings to its rural charm. Just minutes outside the vibrant commercial center are hills that offer breathtaking views of the Great Dividing Range.

**TRANSPORTATION.** Greyhound Australia, 28-30 Neil St. (☎13 14 99), between Margaret and Russell St., runs to Brisbane (2hr.; nearly every hr. 5am-6pm; $26, students and backpackers $23), Melbourne (23hr., daily 8:50am, $259/231), and Sydney (15hr., daily 8:45pm, $132/118). Tickets booked over the phone are $8 more. For northern destinations, connect in Brisbane.

**ORIENTATION AND PRACTICAL INFORMATION.** Coming from Brisbane, **Warrego Highway** becomes **James Street;** the **Toowoomba Visitor Information Centre,** 86 James St., will be on your left. Coming from Warwick, take a right off Ruthven St. onto James St., and you'll see the Centre 1km on your right. (☎07 4639 3797 or 1800 331 155; www.toowoomba.qld.gov.au. Internet $2 per 10min. Open daily 9am-5pm.) Internet can also be found at **Ascension,** 455 Ruthven St., for $2.25 per 30min. (☎07 4638 1333. Open daily 10am-9pm.) Banks and 24hr. **ATMs** line Ruthven St. **Taxis** are available from **Garden City Taxis** (☎13 10 08).

**ACCOMMODATIONS AND FOOD.** Motels abound, but budget accommodations are difficult to find. The **Settlers Inn ❸,** at the corner of Ruthven St. and James St., offers a pub stay. Dorms in the back, off the street, are the quietest. (☎07 4632 3634. Shared facilities. Singles $40; doubles $50. AmEx/D/MC/V.) **Hotel National ❷,** 59 Russell St., is centrally located, and is the only place that provides three- and four-bed dorms (☎07 4639 2706. Shared facilities. Nice kitchen and common room. Laundry $2. Loud live band plays downstairs at the pub Th-Sa 9pm-1am. $25 per person, $120 per week. AmEx/MC/V.)

**SIGHTS AND FESTIVALS.** If you are seeking peace and tranquility, you won't find a better place than **Ju Raku En,** Australia's largest, most traditional Japanese stroll garden, adjacent to the University of Southern Queensland campus. To get there, take a left out of the visitors center carpark onto James St., then a left onto West St. Look for Wuth St. on the right after about 1km, and then turn left a few blocks up on Fleet St. For spectacular views year-round, head up to **Picnic Point,** a city park with short walking paths, a restaurant, and a cafe. From the visitors center carpark, exit right onto James St., and follow the signs. The Garden City is also home to the expansive **Queen's Park Gardens,** on Lindsay St. between Margaret and Campbell St., and **Laurel Bank Park,** on West St. and Herries St. All parks are free and open daily dawn-to-dusk; they're best visited in the full bloom of spring or summer. You can also pick up more extensive guides to the numerous parks and gardens at the visitors center. The **Carnival of Flowers** (☎07 4688 6912; www.thecarnivalofflowers.com.au), held the last full week of September, is Toowoomba's biggest draw. The carnival features a parade, flower shows, and an exhibition of prize-winning private gardens. Because Toowoomba is so big and contains so many parks and gardens, deciding exactly what to visit can be overwhelming. The **tourist information centre** offers a 2hr. tour with a local, with free pickup from any motel. (☎07 4687 5555. Tours are $35 per person and depart daily at 10am. Book ahead.) If you're not much into flowers, try the **Cobb + Co Museum,** 27 Lindsay St., which houses the **National Carriage Collection,** hands-on **Heritage Trade workshops,** and the **Toowoomba Gallery.** (☎07 4639 1971; www.cobbandco.qm.qld.gov.au. Open daily 10am-4pm. $9.50, concessions $7.50, children $5.50. MC/V.)

# STANTHORPE
☎07

If you are itching to leave the bustle of the city, the small town of Stanthorpe, nestled in the Granite Belt, may be just the place. Its location in the heart of Queensland's best wine country makes it a prime vacation spot, and backpackers swarm like locusts to pick fruit and vegetables in the summer months. If wine tasting and work is not enough, the town is also an ideal base for exploring the granite formations and wildflowers of the surrounding national parks: Girraween, Sundown, Boonoo Boonoo, and Bald Rock.

## TRANSPORTATION AND PRACTICAL INFORMATION

**Buses** stop on the corner of Maryland and Folkestone St. behind the Shell station. Bus information can be found across the street at Barry's Taxi Service. Crisps Coaches (☎07 4681 4577; www.crisps.com.au) and Greyhound Australia (☎13 14 99; www.greyhound.com.au) both serve Stanthorpe. Crisps is the faster, cheaper option, with buses to Tenterfield (45min.; M-Th 7:20pm, F 6:15pm, Su 12:45pm; $25, children $21) and Brisbane (3hr.; M-Th 7am, noon; F 7am, noon, 4pm; Sa 10:45am; Su 10:45am, 4pm; $60/51) via Warwick (45min., $26/22) and Toowoomba (2hr., M-F, $43/37). Crisps has guaranteed seating; tickets can be purchased on the bus. If you're staying north of town on High St., you can wave down the bus as it passes. Greyhound Australia tickets can be purchased via phone, online, or at **Harvey World Travel,** 1 Maryland St., across from the post office. If you're driving from the Gold Coast (245km, 3hr.), follow signs to Nerang, Canungra, Beaudesert, Warwick, then Stanthorpe.

To reach the **tourist information center,** 28 Leslie Pde., follow the information sign that leads you through town and over the bridge at Quart Pot Creek, then turn left immediately. (☎07 4681 2057. Open daily 8:30am-5pm.) **Banks** and 24hr. **ATMs** can be found in the center of town on Maryland St. Internet access is available for $2.50 per 30min. at the **library,** 56 Lock St., next to the park (☎07 4681 2141). The **post office** is at 14 Maryland St., on the corner of Railway St. (☎07 4681 2181. Open M-F 9am-5pm.) **Postal Code:** 4380.

## ACCOMMODATIONS AND CAMPING

Some accommodations help backpackers find picking jobs and also provide transport to and from work. Town pubstays don't offer placement services, but their central locations, low prices, and private rooms attract workers and travelers alike. If you plan on visiting during the summer, make a reservation before picking season begins—even a few weeks' notice may be insufficient.

**Backpackers of Queensland,** 80 High St. (☎04 2981 0998; www.backpackersofqueensland.com.au), on the right about 1km before you enter town. Backpackers rave about this hostel, which offers seasonal job placement and transportation in addition to excellent facilities and large, affordable dinners. Spacious co-ed ensuite dorms house 5 per room. Lockers and laundry. Free pickup and dropoff. Check-in by 7:30pm or call ahead. Call at least 2 days ahead during picking season (Sept.-May) to see if a bed is available. Weekly bookings only, $160. Shuts down for the winter. MC/V. ❷

**Top of Town Accommodation,** 10 High St. (☎07 4681 4888 or 1800 030 123; www.topoftown.com.au), on the right 2km before town. This extensive caravan park houses as many as 120 backpackers on its 20-acre estate during picking season. No job placement or transportation. Pool, ping-pong, Wi-FI, convenience store, common areas with TVs. Bring linen. Reception daily 8:30am-6:30pm. 2- and 4-bed dorms (open only during picking season) $25, weekly $125; campsite for 2 $22; on-site caravans $58/120. Bungalows and cabins also available, $75-120 per night. MC/V. ❷

**Country Style Tourist Accommodation Park** (☎07 4683 4358; www.countrystyleaccomodation.com.au), in Glen Aplin, 9km south of Stanthorpe on the New England Hwy. Don't let the distance deter you; Country Style offers free job placement and transportation to and from work for $40 per week. Each dorm includes kitchen, bath, and TV. Internet $5 per hr. Laundry $2 per load. $25 key deposit. Reception 9am-5pm. 4-bed dorms (open only during the picking season) $20, weekly $120; tent sites $60 per week; on-site caravans $100 per week. MC/V. ❷

**Country Club Hotel/Motel,** 26 Maryland St. (☎07 4681 1033). The best low-season budget accommodation. Travelers can stay in the cheaper hotel rooms with shared toilets above the pub (get 1 facing away from the street to reduce noise) or in a nicer motel room out back with private bath, TV, fridge, large beds, and 70s decor. No reception, just talk to the bartender. Hotel singles $20, motel $40; doubles $50/60. MC/V. ❷

## 🄵 FOOD

A **Woolworths** is on High and Lock St. (Open M-F 8am-9pm, Sa 8am-5pm.)

**Applejack's Coffee Shop,** 130 High St. (☎07 4681 0356). Popular among locals and travelers alike, Applejack's serves dirt-cheap food in a wonderfully homey atmosphere. The mushroom cheese omelette ($7.30) is not to be missed, and the pizzas ($6.50-18.50) are delicious. Pizza and pasta dinner F and Sa from 5:30-9pm. Takeaway available Tu-Su 5-8pm. Open M-F 9am-5pm. ❶

**Cosmo Cafe and Restaurant,** 18 Maryland St. (☎07 4681 3131), across from the post office. The Cosmo (cholesterol) Special of bacon, eggs, sausage, tomato, toast, and tea or coffee ($10) will leave you full for a week. The 3 daily specials ($8) and evening specials ($11) are nearly ½-off original price. Open in summer M-W 8am-5pm, Th-Sa 8am-8pm, Su 7am-3pm; in winter M-Sa 8am-5pm, Su 8am-2pm. Cash only. ❶

**Anna's Restaurant** (☎07 4681 1265; www.annas.com.au), on the corner of Wallangarra Rd. and O'Mara Terr. Some of the best food in town, with Italian buffets (F $30, Sa $35). Book ahead. Open daily 6pm-late, last seating at 8:30pm. AmEx/D/MC/V. ❸

## 🄵 WINERIES

More than 50 famous Granite Belt wineries line the New England Hwy. around Stanthorpe, and most offer free tastings. Unfortunately, they can't be reached by public transportation or on foot. The tourist office has info on local winery tours and provides a detailed local map for those driving. The roads and wineries are well marked. Tours ensure a jolly day and a late-afternoon nap. The best is **Fillippo's,** which imparts an endless stream of amusing local knowledge while covering eight of the best vineyards. Prices include pickup, dropoff, and lunch. (☎07 4681 3130; www.filippostours.com.au. M-F ½-day $55, full-day $69; Sa-Su $60/79.) Several other companies offer similar packages—check with the visitors center. **Ballandean Estate Wines** is Queensland's oldest family-operated winery and sponsors the **Opera in the Vineyard** festival, a black-tie wine-and-dine extravaganza the first weekend in May, and **Jazz in the Vineyard,** a more low-key event held the third weekend in August. (☎07 4684 1226; www.ballandeanestate.com.au. Free winery tours 11am, 1, and 3pm. Open daily 9am-5pm.) **Summit Estate** wines boasts the only female winemaker in all of Queensland, and she is an amazing talent. The wines at Summit are painstakingly crafted and have received numerous awards. Taste them in their candlelit cave filled with over 14,000 bottles of wine. (☎07 4683 2011; www.summitestate.com.au. Open daily 10am-4:30pm. MC/V). **Boireann Winery** appeals to the wine connoisseur, producing a small selection of high-quality red wines. If you're a fan of Shiraz or Cabernet Sauvignon, give this vineyard a try. (☎07 4683 2194. Open daily 10am-4pm, but call ahead. MC/V.) **Ravens Croft Wines,** on Spring Creek Rd., has world-famous wines, which you can taste in a beautiful cottage overlooking vineyards and mountains. Try the 2008 Verdelho if you like whites. (☎07 4683 3252; www.ravenscroft.com.au. Open F-Su 10am-4:30pm or by appointment.)

# NATIONAL PARKS OF THE STANTHORPE AREA

In addition to the parks listed below, two New South Wales national parks, **Bald Rock** and **Boonoo Boonoo** (☎02 6376 4298), are accessible from Stanthorpe. None of the parks can be reached by public transportation or by tour bus.

## GIRRAWEEN NATIONAL PARK

Girraween is a popular destination for bushwalkers, birdwatchers, campers, and picnickers. In contrast to the Hinterland's dense rainforest, Girraween's open eucalyptus forest is broken up by massive granite boulders balanced on top of each other. It's also home to Queensland's only common wombat population (though they are very shy and difficult to find). Girraween earns its Aboriginal name in the spring, when this "place of flowers" is coated in wildflowers.

Girraween features a number of well-maintained **walking tracks.** ▣**The Pyramid** (3.4km, 2hr. round-trip) has exhilarating views of immense, artfully stacked granite boulders. At the top, you'll be rewarded with panoramic views of the entire park, famous **Balancing Rock,** and **Bald Rock,** Australia's largest granite boulder. The last portion of the climb is up a steep granite face; wear appropriate shoes and don't even consider climbing when wet. A moderate level of fitness is required for the ascent, and the way down can be hazardous, so take it slow. The trail leaves from the picnic area just past the info center. **Castle Rock** (5.2km, 2hr. round-trip) is a moderate climb with a steep final ascent that yields an impressive 360° view. The final section should not be attempted in wet conditions. The trailhead is located in the **Castle Rock Campground,** just a short drive up the road to the right of the info center. For a more mellow hike, follow the flat trail out to **Underground Creek** (2.8km, 2hr. round-trip). This track provides spectacular wildflower displays and excellent birdwatching opportunities. The trailhead is located 4km down the road from the info center; while some of the road is unsealed, it is usually suitable for all cars.

To get to Girraween, drive 26km south on the New England Hwy. from Stanthorpe, turn left at the sign and then drive 9km on a sealed road. The **information center** (☎07 4684 5157), next to the carpark, is usually open daily; the rangers post the day's hours on a board near the center's entrance. Nearby there are picnicking, swimming, and rock climbing areas.

**Camping ❶** areas are available, with showers, toilets, and BBQ. (☎13 13 04; www.qld.gov.au/camping. $4.85, families $19.40. Register over the phone, online, at the information center, or at the park. Book ahead in high season.)

## SUNDOWN NATIONAL PARK

While Girraween is linked by well-marked paths, Sundown is less developed and caters almost exclusively to rugged bushwalkers and trailblazers. Those who make the journey will find chiseled gorges, high peaks, and panoramic views, as well as opportunities for swimming, fishing, and canoeing. Unlike the smooth hills and tenuously balanced granite boulders that characterize neighboring parks, the 16,000 hectares of Sundown are dominated by the sharp ridges and steep gorges of "traprock," dense sedimentary rock molded by faulting, folding, and erosion. The **Severn River** cuts the park in two.

The **Permanent Waterhole** is a pool on a major bend in the river where platypuses have been spotted. To get there, park 400m past the info center. There's a **walking track** ahead that cuts into the hills behind the river (45min. round-trip). The **Split-Rock** and **Double Falls** are well worth the 3- to 4hr. round-trip hike up McAllisters Creek. Cross the river east into the creek; don't be misled by the old 4WD track. The climb up **Ooline Creek** (the first deep gully to the left of the permanent waterhole) also runs by numerous waterfalls and gorges.

To get to Sundown from Stanthorpe, drive west on Texas Rd. and turn left at the signs for **Glenlyon Dam** (75km). Continue until you reach the dirt road marked by a Sundown National Park sign. You'll reach the park entrance after 4km on the rough dirt track; take it slow to avoid bottoming out. At the entrance, look for the left fork of the track and follow it to camp headquarters. From Tenterfield, head north for 5km, then west along the Bruxner Hwy. (52km) to Mingoola. Turn right and travel 12km to the park turnoff. Burrow's camping area is accessible only by 4WD from the east via Sundown Rd. Follow the signs to Ballandean Estate Wines. The 14km gravel road begins just past the winery. The camping area is another 20km inside the park. If taking this approach, call **Camp Headquarters ❶** (☎02 6737 5235), located at the southwestern edge of the park, to check road conditions. Campsites are available near Headquarters. All sites have pit toilets, fireplaces, and BBQ. (Bookings ☎13 13 04; www.qld.gov.au/camping. $5, families $19.40. Register over the phone, online, at the information center, or at the park.) To explore the park safely, use an official **Queensland Parks and Wildlife Services Map,** available at QPWS offices in Brisbane, Toowoomba, and Girraween, and bring a compass. The park is high, remote, and often cold, and visitors must be self-sufficient.

# SUNSHINE COAST AND FRASER ISLAND

The Sunshine Coast is a slightly warmer, less crowded, more relaxed alternative to the Gold Coast. Here, the sun shines 300 days a year, quiet beaches and national parks stretch into the distance, and resort towns like Noosa rise abruptly from the sand. Fraser Island, the largest sand island in the world, is a beach-and-rainforest playground crisscrossed by 4WD tracks. Its legendary dunes and freshwater lakes make it a mecca for adventurous backpackers.

## MAROOCHYDORE, ALEXANDRA HEADLANDS, AND MOOLOOLABA     ☎07

These three towns originally formed the township of Maroochy Shire. Though they have now officially joined the Sunshine Coast Regional Council, a down-to-earth attitude and endless surfing opportunities still connect them. The area is becoming popular with resort-dwellers and wealthy vacationers as well. An urban center located at the mouth of the Maroochy River, Maroochydore has thriving small industries. About 1km southeast, Alexandra Headlands is best known for its great waves. Another 2km south, a cafe-packed esplanade lines

Mooloolaba's family beach. This area is a popular base for fruit picking from June to October, when strawberries are in season.

**◘ TRANSPORTATION.** Greyhound Australia and Premier **buses** stop in Maroochydore. The bus terminal on First Ave., off Aerodrome Rd., has closed, but Premier still stops there, though it may move shortly. They stop in Mooloolaba at the Smith Street Car Park. If you are staying at the Mooloolaba Beach Backpackers, you can ask to be dropped off at their door (with prior notice). Greyhound stops in Maroochydore next to the tourist information office, off Aerodrome Rd. Greyhound (☎13 14 99; www.greyhound.com.au; phone-booking fee $8) runs to: Airlie Beach (17hr.; daily 4pm; $175, students $159); Brisbane (2hr., 7 per day, $27/$25); Cairns (28hr., daily 4pm, $242/$219); Gold Coast (3hr., daily 7:45am, $52/$48); Hervey Bay (4-5hr., 3 per day, $39/$35); Mackay (15hr., daily 4pm, $152/$138); Rockhampton (10hr., daily 4pm, $102/$92). Premier (☎13 34 10) runs daily to similar destinations at cheaper prices. The blue Sunshine Coast Sunbus (☎07 5450 7888) connects the three towns. Bus #600 and #601 run from the Sunshine Plaza in Maroochydore down Cotton Tree Pde. through Alexandra Headlands to Mooloolaba. (M-Sa every 15min., Su every 30min. $2.30.) Bus #620 heads to Noosa from Maroochydore (every 30min., every hr. on weekends, $5). Bus #610 departs every hr. passing through Mooloolaba and Sunshine Plaza, Maroochydore, for Nambour ($2.70).

**▦⚼ ORIENTATION AND PRACTICAL INFORMATION. Aerodrome Road** is the main commercial strip in Maroochydore. In Alexandra Headlands, it becomes **Alexandra Parade** as it curves along the ocean. Farther south in Mooloolaba, it becomes the **Mooloolaba Esplanade.** It eventually intersects with **Brisbane Road,** the main thoroughfare in Mooloolaba. **Sunshine Plaza** in Maroochydore is a large, clean pedestrian mall with cafes, shops, and department stores.

The **tourist office** is on Sixth Ave., off Aerodrome Rd. (☎07 5459 9050; www.discovermaroochy.com.au. Open daily 9am-5pm.) Mooloolaba has an **info kiosk** at the corner of First Ave. and Brisbane Rd. (☎07 5478 2233. Open daily 9am-5pm.) There are **banks** and **24hr. ATMs** on Horton Pde., Maroochydore, and a bank in Mooloolaba on the corner of Hancock St. and Brisbane Rd. Other services include: **taxis** (24hr. ☎13 10 08; about $15 from Maroochydore to Mooloolaba); **police** on Cornmeal Pde., Maroochydore (☎07 5475 2444); **7 Day Medical,** 150 Horton Pde. (☎07 5443 2122; open M-Th 8am-8pm, F-Su 8am-6pm); **Maroochy Day and Night Chemmart** pharmacy, 107-109 Aerodrome Rd., on the corner of Second Ave. (☎07 5443 6070; open daily 8am-10pm); and **Internet access** at All Systems Go, 25 First Ave. Maroochydore. (☎07 5443 6764. $3.50 per hr. Open M, W, Su 10am-8pm, Th-Sa 10am-10pm.) **Post offices** are at 22 King St., Cotton Tree; on the corner of Walan St. and Brisbane Rd., Mooloolaba; 17 Duporth Ave., as well as in the Sunshine Plaza, Maroochydore. (☎13 13 18. All open M-F 9am-5pm; Sunshine Plaza office also open Sa 9am-3:30pm, Su 10:30am-2:30pm.) **Postal Code:** 4557 (Mooloolaba), 4558 (Maroochydore and Cotton Tree).

**⌂ ACCOMMODATIONS.** Most hostels in the Maroochydore/Alexandra Headlands/Mooloolaba area arrange fruit-picking work. ▤**Mooloolaba Beach Backpackers ❸,** 75 Brisbane Rd., in a colorful modern building, is close to the nightlife and the beach. The pool and spacious, clean common area are always packed with friendly guests. The bunk dorms have kitchens and TV lounges on every level. Ensuite dorms with TV and large doubles are in a separate building. (☎07 5444 3399 or 1800 020 120; www.mooloolababackpackers.com. Cafe, Internet access ($6 for 5hr.), lockers, laundry, breakfast (included), and dinner ($6). Kayaks, bikes, and body- or surfboards free. Courtesy shuttle to bus stop and airport. Reception M-Th and Su 8am-8pm, F-Sa 8am-10pm. 4-bed dorms $26, ensuite $29; ensuite doubles $70. VIP. MC/V.) **Maroochydore YHA Backpackers ❷**, 24 Schirrmann Dr., is a hike from the center of town, but the relaxed atmosphere and freebies will blow you away: bikes, kayaks, canoes, bodyboards, and daily yoga sessions are all on the house, and movie nights are held 3-4 times per week. The YHA also has a large kitchen, common areas, a pool, and Internet access. (☎1800 302 855 or 07 5443 3151; www.yhabackpackers.com. Laundry $3 per machine. Arranges a variety of tours of the region. Call for free pickup from the bus stop. Reception 8am-7pm. 4- to 8-bed dorms $25-$28; singles $60; doubles $67. Weekly discount. YHA discount. Books up fast during picking season. MC/V.) **Suncoast Backpackers Lodge ❷**, 50 Parker St., off Aerodrome Rd., Maroochydore, is small, family-run, clean place, filled with laid-back fruit-pickers and surfers. (☎07 5443 7544. Outdoor common space, kitchen, pool table, and laundry. Reception 8:30am-noon and 5-6:30pm. 3- to 6-bed dorms $22; doubles $47. VIP/YHA. Books up fast during picking season. MC/V.)

**◑▣ FOOD AND NIGHTLIFE. ◪Fisheries on the Spit ❶**, along the Wharf at 21-23 Parkyn Pde., sells a spectacular variety of fresh and cooked seafood at fantastically low prices. Seared mahimahi or swordfish with salad and salsa is just $9; enjoy it in the outdoor seating area. (☎07 5444 1165. Open daily in summer 7:30am-8pm; in winter 7:30am-7:30pm. Fully licensed. MC/V.) **Buddha Asian Restaurant ❷** offers pan-Asian cuisine along the Riverwalk in Sunshine Plaza. Don't be deterred by the mall setting; the restaurant has outdoor seating next to the river. (☎07 5479 3382. Main courses $13-19. Open daily 11am-10pm. MC/V.) Maroochy has many good Thai restaurants; the best is **Som Tam Thai ❷**, on the corner of Fifth Ave. and Aerodrome Rd. (☎07 5479 1700. Main courses $11-21. Open M-Sa noon-2pm and 5-9pm, Su 5-9pm. AmEx/MC/V.) A **Coles** supermarket is on the ground floor of the massive Sunshine Plaza, off Horton Pde., along with a couple hundred shops and a plethora of eateries. (☎07 5443 4633. Open M-F 8am-9pm, Sa 8am-5:30pm, Su 9am-6pm.)

Of the three towns in this area, only Mooloolaba really comes alive after dark. **Zink Bar and Restaurant,** 77 Mooloolaba Esplanade, gets packed on the weekends with hip hop and house music booming onto the street. Authentic Spanish tapas and grill items are served until close. (☎07 5477 6077; www.zinkbar.com.au. W salsa and Latin night. Th and Su live music, F-Sa DJ. Open M-Th and Su noon-latenight, F-Sa noon-2am. Last entry 1:30am.) **Motown,** 121 Mooloolaba Esplanade, on the corner of Venning St., is a funky, retro lounge and nightclub with party beats and a gorgeous second-story deck with ocean views and a laid-back atmosphere. Come for a sunset dinner (burgers $7, pizza $10), or stay for a long happy hour (4-8pm; hamburgers $3), then hit the dance floor. (☎07 5444 5767. Open W-Su 4pm-midnight.) **The Wharf Tavern,** on the Wharf next to **UnderWater World** (see below), is a modern, laid-back bar downstairs and upstairs, a club with dance and R&B music that attracts young partygoers. (☎07 5444 8383; www.thewharftavern.com.au. Both open daily 10am-latenight, with W-Sa and Su live music. Nightclub open Tu and F-Sa 9pm-3am. Tu cover $2; F-Sa cover $5, entry into nightclub $8.)

**◱ ACTIVITIES.** Spending time in this area means spending time near the water. **Maroochydore Beach** has good breaks for short-board riders, while **Alexandra Headlands** has rips, large swells, and big crowds of mostly longboarders. **Mooloolaba Beach**, near the spit, is the safest beach for swimming. Along Aerodrome St., Alexandra Pde., and the Mooloolaba Esplanade, there are numerous surf shops that rent boards. **Alex Surf & Skate**, 158 Alexandra Pde., (☎07 5443 4839; www.alexsurfnskate.com) rents surfboards for $20 per hr. and $30 for the day. If you'd rather ride the pavement, **Skate Sauce**, 150 Alexandra Pde., Alexandra Headlands, offers in-line skates, bikes, and skateboards. A public skate park is across the street. (☎07 5443 6111. All rentals $12 per hr., $24 per day; includes basic safety gear. Open M-Sa 9am-5pm, Su 10am-4pm. MC/V.)

**Underwater World,** on the Mooloolaba Wharf at Parkyn Pde., has beautiful displays of sea creatures of all kinds. It's the largest tropical oceanarium in the Southern Hemisphere. In addition to billabong recreations and sea turtle displays, the aquarium has a fantastic moving walkway that glides underneath a 2.5 million-liter aquarium filled with sharks and giant manta rays. There are 14 shows daily, including shark and manta ray feedings. Don't miss out on the seals: swim with them or—better yet—kiss one. (☎07 5444 8488; www. underwaterworld.com.au. Open daily 9am-6pm; last entry 5pm. Kiss at 11am, 1, and 3:30pm; $10, with photo $22. Tour 11:30am and 2:30pm; $12, children $10. Swim after the 1pm show; $76 includes photo and 15min. swim. Book ahead for swim. General admission $26.50, students $19, children $16, families $73. Backpacker discounts.) If seals don't give you enough of an adrenaline rush, you can dive with the aquarium's sharks through **Scuba World**. (☎07 5444 8595; www.scubaworld.com.au. 30min. with sharks. Daily dive times vary. Certified divers $155 (plus a $10 entry), non-divers $195 (includes entry, equipment, and lesson). If you are certified, you can dive with Scuba World at the sunken **HMAS Brisbane**. (Meet at 7am, $120 with own gear, $140 for tanks and weights, $184 for all gear. Also offers 4-day diver certification courses starting at $495. MC/V.)

# NOOSA
☎07

Noosa is an eco-friendly spot with beautiful beaches, a relaxed atmosphere, and a large national park with plenty of wilderness. While there are open-air shopping centers, fancy hotels, and chic cafes to keep wealthy couples and pensioners occupied, budget travelers can easily avoid the glitz. The main drag, Hastings St., is perpetually crowded with tourists flocking to the restaurants, shops, and beach area. At Cooloola National Park, just north of Noosa, take advantage of abundant opportunities to 4WD, hike, canoe, and camp.

## ▉ TRANSPORTATION

**Buses:** Noosa doesn't have a bus terminal; coaches pick up and drop off passengers at the **Bus Interchange** on Noosa Pde. near Hastings St. Book ahead. Greyhound Australia (☎1300 473 946; phone booking fee $8) runs to: **Airlie Beach** (16hr.; daily 4:40pm; $167, concessions $150); **Brisbane** (2-3hr., 7 per day, $26/23); **Cairns** (27hr., daily 4:40pm, $240/215); **Gold Coast** (4hr., daily 6:40am, $41/37); **Hervey Bay** (3hr., 3 per day, $33/30); **Mackay** (15hr., daily 4:40pm, $147/132); **Rockhampton** (9hr., daily 4:40pm, $97/87). Premier (☎13 34 10) runs 1 service per day to the same destinations but at significantly cheaper rates.

**Public Transportation: Sunshine Coast Sunbus** (☎07 5450 7888) leaves from the bus interchange and offers service around Noosa. Bus #620 goes to **Caloundra, Maroochydore,** and **Mooloolaba** (every 30min.; $5.60-8). Bus #627 connects the neighborhoods of Noosa: service starts in Tewantin, continues through Noosa Heads, Noosa Junction, Noosaville, and terminates in Sunshine Beach. (Every 15-20min.; $2.30.) Bus #630 and #631 head to Eumundi every hr. or 2 while Bus #626 heads to Sunrise Beach every 30min. All buses run approximately 6:30am-6:30pm; later on weekends.

**Taxis: Suncoast Cabs** (24hr. ☎13 10 08).

**Car Rental: Europcar**, 66 Noosa Dr. (☎07 5447 3777; www.europcar.com.au.), rents from $45 per day with unlimited mileage. $14 per day age surcharge for those under

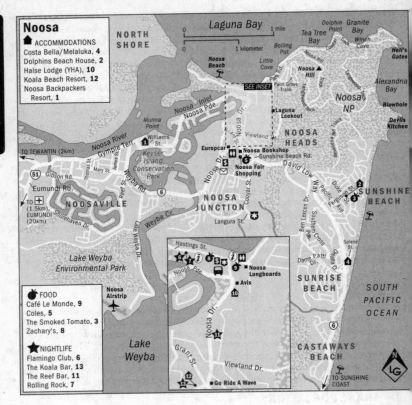

**Noosa**

🏠 ACCOMMODATIONS
Costa Bella/Melaluka, **4**
Dolphins Beach House, **2**
Halse Lodge (YHA), **10**
Koala Beach Resort, **12**
Noosa Backpackers
Resort, **1**

🍴 FOOD
Café Le Monde, **9**
Coles, **5**
The Smoked Tomato, **3**
Zachary's, **8**

⭐ NIGHTLIFE
Flamingo Club, **6**
The Koala Bar, **13**
The Reef Bar, **11**
Rolling Rock, **7**

25. Backpacker discount. (Open M-F 8am-5pm, Sa-Su 8am-1pm. AmEx/D/MC/V.) **Avis** (☎07 5447 4933; www.avis.com.au), on the corner of Noosa Dr. and Noosa Pde., has cars from $50. $27.50 per day surcharge for those under 25. Open M-F 8am-5pm, Sa 7:30am-3pm, Su 8:30am-1:30pm. AmEx/D/MC/V.

## ✈ ℹ ORIENTATION AND PRACTICAL INFORMATION

Be prepared to say Noosa a lot; nearly everything in the area carries the name. **Noosa Heads** is the main area; it encompasses **Hastings Street** and the commercial **Noosa Junction. Noosaville**, 3km west, is just off the Noosa River and is a bit quieter. The entrance to **Noosa National Park** is at the eastern end of Hastings St. Head one block away from the beach on **Noosa Drive** to find **Bus Interchange.** A 10min. stroll away from the beach on Noosa Dr. leads to the heart of **Noosa Junction,** the area's **Central Business District (CBD). Banks, supermarkets,** and the **post office** are all within 5min. of each other. **Noosaville** is a 1hr. walk (or a quick bus ride) down Noosa Pde. from the intersection with Noosa Dr. Its main street, **Gympie Terrace,** has several international restaurants, motels, and boat rentals. The **Sunshine Beach** area is around the point from Noosa Heads on a beautiful stretch of beach lined with magnificent houses. Both Sunshine Beach and nearby **Sunrise Beach** are popular spots, but the 40km stretch of sand leaves ample space for any number of sunbathers to spread out.

**Tourist Office: Tourism Noosa Information Centre** (☎07 5430 5000; www.tourism-noosa.com.au), at the intersection of Noosa Dr. and Hastings St. Open daily 9am-5pm.

**Currency Exchange: Banks** are on Hastings St., Noosa Heads; Sunshine Beach Rd., Noosa Jct.; Gympie Terr., Noosaville. Banks open M-Th 9:30am-4pm, F 9:30am-5pm.

**Bookstore: Noosa Book Shop** (☎07 5447 3066), in Suntop Plaza, Noosa Jct. Exchanges used books. Open M-F 9am-5:30pm, Sa 9am-5pm, Su 9am-4pm. MC/V.

**Police:** Main office on Langura St., Noosa Heads (☎07 5447 5888). Smaller Police Beat on the corner of Hastings St. and Noosa Dr., in Noosa Heads.

**Medical Services: Noosa Hospital,** 111 Goodchap St., Noosaville (☎07 5455 9200).

**Internet Access: Adventure Travel Bugs,** 9 Sunshine Beach Rd. (☎1800 666 720; www.oztravelbugs.com). Cheapest in town (15min. free, $2 per hr.). Book tours here as well. Open M-F 8am-8pm, Sa-Su 9am-7pm.

**Post Office:** 91-93 Noosa Rd., Noosa Jct. (☎13 13 18). Open M-F 9am-5pm, Sa 9am-12:30pm. **The Hastings St.** supermarket, located behind the Royal Copenhagen Ice Cream shop, also has postal service. Open daily 6am-8pm. **Postal Code:** 4567 (Noosa Heads, Noosa Junction); 4566 (Noosaville).

# ACCOMMODATIONS

Lodging in Noosa falls into one of three general categories: hostels, motels/hotels, and "holiday units," which are usually private homes or apartments. Hostels typically offer cheap meals, courtesy shuttle services, free surfboards, on-site bars, and tour-booking services. Because of Noosa's increasing popularity, there aren't always enough budget beds to go around during holidays, so be sure to book ahead. The best location is in Noosa Heads, near the beach and Hastings St. Families may find it more economical to rent units or homes— **Accom Noosa,** 41 Hastings St., can help you find affordable, long-term lodging. (☎1800 072 078; www.accomnoosa.com.au. AmEx/D/MC/V.)

## NOOSA HEADS

**Halse Lodge (YHA),** 2 Halse Ln. (☎1800 242 567; www.halselodge.com.au), across Noosa Dr. and up the hill from the bus interchange. Picturesque Queenslander home with large verandas and spacious common areas. Location close to the beach and Hastings St. can't be beat. Small bar is active until the common space lockdown at 11:30pm. The beautiful old building does have its drawbacks; some of the rooms can be noisy, and none of them have outlets (though you can purchase a locker with a built-in outlet for $3). However, the staff is friendly, and daily meet-and-greet sessions make it easy to meet other travelers. Laundry, Internet access, and kitchen. Free body boards. Reception 7am-8pm. 4- to 6-bed dorms $29-$35; twins and doubles $74-$96. NOMADS/VIP/YHA discounts. MC/V. ❸

**Koala Beach Resort,** 44 Noosa Dr. (☎1800 357 457; www.koalaadventures.com). 5-10min. walk from the bus interchange; take a right onto Noosa Dr. and follow it over the hill. Koala is on the right across from Go Ride a Wave. If you want to party in this sleepy town, Koala is the place. Spacious 7-bed ensuite dorms, courtesy bus, laundry, pool, volleyball court, basement kitchen, and outdoor eating area. Linen deposit system. Laundry available. Internet access $3 per hr. Reception 7:30am-8pm. Dorms $28; walk-through twins and doubles $62. VIP discount. MC/V. ❷

## SUNSHINE BEACH AND SUNRISE BEACH

**Dolphins Beach House,** 14 Duke St. (☎1800 454 456; www.dolphinsbeachhouse. com). Beautiful apartment-style dorms consist of 2 4-bed rooms that share a common TV area, bathroom, and kitchen. Just step outside your unit to enjoy the mellow hippie appeal of the spacious outdoor area. 3min. walk to Sunshine Beach. Laundry, Internet access, courtesy bus, surfboard rental ($25 per day), and free body boards. Reception 8am-8pm. Dorms $25; doubles $60. VIP discount. MC/V. ❷

**Costa Bella,** 7 Selene St. (☎1800 003 663; www.melaluka.com.au). Take the highway to Sunrise Beach; turn left at Vernon St. and make 2 quick rights down the hill. Choose from a variety of options ranging from standard hostel rooms to luxury apartments. Hostel composed of self-contained units and large common areas. Spacious Costa Bella unit has ocean views, kitchens, dining and TV areas, laundry, and patios or balconies. The less-expensive Melaluka building has dorm facilities and apartments. Free courtesy bus. Reception M-F 9am-5:30pm, Sa-Su 10am-10pm. Costa Bella rooms for 2 $75; Melaluka 2-bed dorms $26; doubles $60. MC/V. ❷

## NOOSAVILLE

**Noosa Backpackers Resort,** 9-13 Williams St. (☎1800 626 673; www.noosabackpack-ers.com). Located on a side street only 1min. from the river and close to Gympie Rd. 30min. walk to Hastings St. and Main Beach. Guests and locals alike crowd the **The Global Cafe** for its tasty food and reasonable prices. Courtesy van, game room, swimming pool, kitchen, bar, laundry, and 24hr. Internet access. Reception 8am-7:30pm. Dorms $28; doubles and twins $60. VIP/YHA and student discounts. AmEx/MC/V. ❷

## 🔲 FOOD

While there are a great many restaurants in Noosa, it can be all too easy to hover around only the popular Hastings St. district. Cheaper meals can be found around Noosa Jct., and the surf clubs are great places for cheap grub or a sunset beer; try **Noosa Heads Surf Life Saving Club ❶**, 69 Hastings St. (☎07 5423 3055. Open M-F 11am-midnight, Sa-Su 10am-midnight. MC/V.) Some area hostels also offer great meals for $12 or less. A **Coles** supermarket is located off Lanyana Way in the Noosa Fair Shopping Centre, Noosa Jct. (☎07 5447 4000. Open M-F 8am-9pm, Sa 8am-5:30pm, Su 9am-6pm.)

**Café Le Monde,** 52 Hastings St. (☎07 5449 2366; www.cafelemonde.com.au), Noosa Heads. A gathering place for surfer celebs. Try toasted baguettes (ft. long $9-14; noon-5pm). Pastas $14-23. Main courses $18-32. Live music 4 nights per week: Th from 6pm, F-Sa from 9pm, Su from 3pm. Open daily 6am-late. AmEx/MC/V. ❷

**The Smoked Tomato,** 36 Duke St. (☎07 5447 3913), Sunshine Beach. Offers terrific lunch specials from pastas ($5) to gourmet pizzas ($10). Lunch noon-3pm. Dine in or take out a few steps to the beach. Open daily 6:30am-late. MC/V. ❶

**Zachary's,** 30 Hastings St. (☎07 5473 0011; www.zacharys.com.au), Noosa Heads. Grab a gourmet pizza (from $15.50) topped with anything from pumpkin to duck. There are so many topping options, in fact, that if you asked for the works you'd end up paying $97 for a 7-inch high pie. Open daily noon-midnight. Winter hours may vary. Takeaway and delivery location at the Islander Resort in Noosaville. AmEx/MC/V. ❷

## 👁 📷 SIGHTS AND ACTIVITIES

**NOOSA NATIONAL PARK.** Just 1.4km from the city center, Noosa National Park covers over 400 hectares of rare and threatened vegetation and wildlife. It's the second-most visited park in Queensland, with over 1.5 million visitors each year. A short walk east from the Noosa info booth on Hastings St. will land you at the entrance. You can catch all of the park's highlights by walking or jogging along the five marked tracks, which range 1-7km in length. **Koalas** are most often spotted on the Coastal Track towards Tea Tree Bay and the foreshore picnic area; daily koala sightings are posted at the ranger station at the entrance to the park, where you can also find maps of the tracks. The track between Tea Tree Bay and Dolphin Point is paved and fully wheelchair-accessible. Rangers urge walkers never to walk alone and to stay on frequented paths. The best walk is the ■**Coastal Track** (2.7km), an easy trail which provides elevated views of the ocean and ends at the exhilarating **Hell's Gates.** Rather than return on the same path, jump on the **Tanglewood Track** (4.2km) to return to the park entrance. The easy 6.9km hike takes 2-3hr. There are also many places to surf along the path; **Tea Tree Bay** and **Granite Bay** are popular among surfers and body boarders alike. A beautiful stretch of beach on the eastern side of the park at **Alexandria Bay** is accessible primarily from Sunshine Beach. Be aware that there are no lifeguards at Alexandria Bay, and the rip can be extremely strong. The beach by Alexandria Bay is clothing-optional. Take the **Alexandria Bay Track** from **Parkedge Road** (4.6km round-trip, 1-1hr.) or from northern **Sunshine Beach** (2km, 30-40min. round-trip). Water and toilets are available, but camping is strictly prohibited. (☎ 07 5447 3243; www.epa.qld.gov.au. Office open daily 9am-3pm; closed for lunch.)

**SURFING.** Warm water, beautiful surroundings, and an active surfing community make the Sunshine Coast a great place to catch a wave. The most reliable breaks come during cyclone season (Dec.-Mar.). **First Point** is great for longboarders, while the western parts of **Main Beach** are better for beginners. Some of the best waves can be found at **National Park** and **Tea Tree,** where water breaks over granite into long lines and barrel sections. Unfortunately, this is no secret—in good conditions, both spots can be extremely crowded. To avoid the crowds, try **Double Island Point** to the north in Cooloola, but be wary of strong rips and bring a friend. Surfers are also spotted at **Sunshine Beach** and **Alexandria Bay,** but conditions are known to be erratic. Beginners should try **Learn to Surf** with world champion Merrick Davis; you're guaranteed to be standing on your board by the end of one lesson. (☎ 04 1878 7577; www.learntosurf.com.au. 2 classes per day. $55 per 2hr. includes wetsuit, board, and pickup and dropoff. Book ahead.) **Wavesense Surfing Academy** has twice been voted Australia's "Surf School of the Year." (☎ 04 1436 9076; www.wavesense.com.au. $55 per 2hr. Book through any hostel. $39.) Board rentals are available at **Noosa Longboards,** 62 Hastings St., Noosa Heads. (☎ 07 5447 2828; www.noosalongboards.com. Open daily 8am-5:30pm, later in summer. Body boards $15 per 4hr., $20 per day; shortboards $25/40; longboards $35/50. MC/V.) **Go Ride A Wave,** Shop 3/77 Noosa Dr., also rents boards and gives 2hr. intro lessons for $55. (☎ 1300 132 441; www.gorideawave.com.au. Open daily 9am-5:30pm. Surfboards $35 for ½-day; full-day $45; body boards $25/35, includes wetsuit or rash guard. MC/V.)

**OTHER ACTIVITIES. Kitesurf Australia** will show you what happens when kite meets surfboard in this serious adrenaline sport. (☎ 07 5455 6677; www.kite-surf. com.au. 2hr. lesson $150. MC/V.) **Clip Clop Horse Treks** takes you on a riding tour through the trails and bush around Lake Weyba. (☎ 07 5449 1254; www.clipcloptreks. com.au. 2hr. $70, ½-day $165. Also offers 2- and 4-day treks. Book ahead. Cash only.) **Aussie Sea Kayak Company** runs a variety of sea kayaking tours around the Sunshine Coast: Moreton Bay, Fraser Island, and longer tours up to the Whitsundays. (☎ 07 5452 7383; www.ausseakayak.com.au. Daily 2hr. sunset champagne tour $45, ½-day $65. ) If you want to see the Everglades (the dark tranquil waters of the upper Noosa River), **Beyond Noosa** will take you on a BBQ lunch cruise or combine it with a 4WD tour through Cooloola National Park. (☎ 1800 657 666; www.beyondnoosa.com. Tours M-F. Lunch cruise $84, children $50; combined $149/100. MC/V.) To fully experience

Noosa's "river of mirrors," go on a two- or three-day Everglades canoe safari with **Cooloola Canoe Safaris.** (☎ *1800 763 077; www.cooloolacanoes.com.au. 2 nights $154, overnight $129; includes park fees.*) If you've always wanted to jump out of a plane, the Sunshine Coast is the place to do it. Several companies offer tandem dives with views of Brisbane and beach landings.

## ◧ NIGHTLIFE

Noosa nights often passed in a laid-back manner typical of the down-to-earth ambience of this beachside town, but there are a few places that cater to those interested in engaging in some nocturnal debauchery.

**The Koala Bar,** 44 Noosa Dr. (☎ 1800 357 457), located in the hostel. Overflows with drunken, sun-kissed backpackers. Pool tables, happy hour (5-6pm and 8-9pm), DJs, and nightly specials. W night live bands are extremely popular. The fun ends promptly at midnight, but a shuttle runs to Rolling Rock after close. MC/V.

**Rolling Rock,** Upper Level, Bay Village on Hastings St. (☎ 07 5447 2255; www.rollingrock.com.au). The only nightclub serving a drop past midnight. Cover F-Sa $8, free before 10pm. Open daily 9pm-3am; no entry after 1:30am. Across the ramp is the exclusive **Flamingo Club,** the lounge part of Rolling Rock intended for a slightly older crowd. Open F and Sa night only. Must be 25+ to get in. Both Rolling Rock and Flamingo Club have a dress code that prohibits shorts or rubber flip-flops. MC/V.

**The Reef Bar** (☎ 07 5430 7500; www.reefnoosa.com), near the crest of Noosa Dr. A hip, spacious lounge with beautiful ocean views upstairs and a sports bar/thumping dance area downstairs. Lounge open M-Sa 10am-11pm; sports bar 8:30am-8pm—when it turns into a nightclub Th-Sa (summer) and F-Sa (winter). No cover charge except for once a month when special DJs come and spin at the club.

# RAINBOW BEACH ☎ 07

This small beach community is known to many as "The Backpackers Shortcut to Fraser Island." There really isn't much to do in this tiny town, but the hostels all arrange fabulous trips to Fraser, and the Coloured Sands and Carlo Sandblow are worth a visit. Its proximity to beautiful beaches and Cooloola National Park also make Rainbow Beach a wonderful launching pad for outdoor adventures ranging from wilderness hikes to skydiving.

## ◧ TRANSPORTATION

There is no proper bus station in Rainbow Beach. Greyhound Australia (☎ 13 14 99; www.greyhound.com.au) and Premier Motor Service (☎ 13 34 10; www. premierms.com.au) **buses** both stop on **Spectrum St.,** directly in front of the hostels. Greyhound has two buses daily that head north (12:30pm and 3:30pm) and two that go south (10am and 12:25pm). Premier has only one service in each direction (northbound 7pm; southbound 7:40am). Prices vary by distance, but Premier is significantly cheaper. If you are coming by car from Noosa, head toward Tewantin and Cooroy, at which point you will see signs to Bruce Hwy. The **Noosa Northshore Ferry** transports 4WD vehicles from Moorindal St. in Tewantin to the north shore of the Noosa River. (☎ 07 5447 1321. M-Th and Su 5:30am-10:30pm, F-Sa 5:30am-12:20am. $5 per vehicle each way. Cash only.) From the north shore, 4WD vehicles can cut across to the beach, which serves as the park's main thoroughfare. Check the tide tables to avoid getting stranded on the beach—or worse, swept out to sea.

Polleys Coaches (☎ 07 5482 9455; www.polleys.com.au.) travels to Tin Can Bay and Rainbow Beach from Gympie Return Services League (RSL) on Mary

St., Gympie. (M-F 1:20pm; returns from Rainbow
Beach 7am; one-way $15, student $7.50; returns
from Tin Can 8am, $11.70/5.85.) If you'd rather be
your own guide, try **Safari 4WD** at the corner of Carlo
and Karoonda Rd., Rainbow Beach (☎07 5486 8188;
www.safari4wdhire.com.au). The company is run
by locals who help tailor individual itineraries, do
great sand-driving training, and even show you
where you can go to camp with Indigenous Australians on the island. (Open 7am-5pm. 2- to 11-seaters
available. Cars range $90-170 per day.)

Several companies offer transport to Fraser
Island by **boat.** Fraser Explorer Barges runs from
Inskip Point (6km from Rainbow Beach) to Hook
Point, the southern tip of the island. (☎1800 227
437. 15min., operates continuously 6am-5:30pm.
No advanced bookings. Vehicles $85; walk-ons
$5.) You can also try Manta Ray Barge, a vehicu-
lar **ferry** that also runs from Inskip Point to Hook
Point on demand. (☎08 5486 8888; www.fraseris-
landbarge.com.au. 15min.; operates continuously
6:30am-5:30pm. Ferry leaves about every 20min.
Advance bookings possible but not required. Vehicles $85; walk-ons $5. MC/V.)

## PRACTICAL INFORMATION

The **Rainbow Beach Tourist Information Centre,** 8
Rainbow Rd., Rainbow Beach, gives out maps of
the tiny town. (☎07 5486 3227. Open daily 7am-
6pm.) There aren't banks in Rainbow Beach, but
look for an **ATM** at the **FoodWorks** supermarket or
at the **post office.** While the town's hostels all have
**Internet access,** you can also check your inbox for
nothing at the **Rainbow Beach Library,** 38 Rainbow
Rd. (☎07 5486 3705. Open M 9:30am-12:30pm, W
and F 2-5pm, Sa 8:30am-11:30am. Book ahead.)
For camping equipment, check out **Rainbow Beach
Cooloola Hardware,** 38 Rainbow Beach Rd. (☎08 5486
3444. Open daily 8am-5pm. AmEx/MC/V.) The closest **police station** is Tin Can Bay (☎07 5486 4125).
In case of emergency, contact the **Gympie Hospital**
(☎08 5489 8444). There is a **post office** at 6 Rainbow
Rd. (☎08 5486 3214; Open M-F 8:30am-5pm and Sa
8:30am-noon.) **Postal Code:** 4581.

## ACCOMMODATIONS

With about 95% of visitors in Rainbow Beach en
route to or from Fraser Island, the town's three
hostels make it a point to help you on your journey. All are a 5min. walk from the beach and
the town center. Each has a deal that includes
two nights accommodation, camping equipment (around $10 extra for sleeping bag), island

permits, and ferry passes. While prices vary, the initial quotes include differing amounts of insurance, food, and fuel. When all the extras are factored in, each package costs around $200. Book several days ahead.

The best of the hostels is ◪**Dingo's Backpackers Resort ❷**, 3 Spectrum St., Rainbow Beach. The common room and bar area are perpetually crowded, making it a great place to meet fellow adventurers headed for Fraser Island; traveling groups often form at the hostel. Excellent free pancake breakfast, though you have to get up early—it's at 7am. Kitchen, pool, bar, restaurant, laundry, and Internet are available. Tour agency and 4WD company attached. (☎1800 111 126. 7-bed ensuite dorms $22. MC/V.) **Fraser's on Rainbow Beach Backpackers ❷**, 18 Spectrum St., Rainbow Beach, has ensuite rooms, a huge lounge, outdoor pool, game room, kitchen, laundry, and a bar with restaurant. (☎1800 100 170; 6- to 8-bed dorms $24; doubles $68. Student and backpacker discounts. MC/V.)

**Camping ❶** is permitted at several sites in Cooloola National Park, as well as along a 15km stretch on Teewah Beach. **Freshwater** campground, at the end of a 16km sand path accessible by 4WD via Rainbow Beach, is the only developed site in the park, with drinking water, toilets, hot pay-showers, and a phone. (☎13 13 04; www.qld.gov.au/camping. $5 per person per night. Book ahead.) The **Upper Noosa River** has 11 undeveloped campsites that are accessible by foot or canoe only. **Poverty Point**, accessible by 4WD, is undeveloped. The **Cooloola Wilderness Trail** has four campsites; three are accessible by foot.

### ▮ FOOD

Restaurant options aren't plentiful in the tiny business center, but Dingo's and Fraser's hostels have cheap nightly specials that keep their guests happy. **The Groovy Grape ❶**, 14 Rainbow Rd., is extremely popular for its scrumptious Big Breakfast ($10), delicious "filled focaccia," and turkish bread sandwiches. (☎07 5486 3137. Open daily 5:30am-4pm. MC/V.) **The Shak Cafe ❶**, 12 Rainbow Rd., offers excellent burgers ($6-7.60) and cheap daily specials. (☎07 5486 3277. Open daily 7am-8:30pm. MC/V.) There is also a **FoodWorks** supermarket, 4 Rainbow Rd. (☎07 5486 3629. Open daily 5am-7pm.)

### ◉ ▮ SIGHTS AND ACTIVITIES

**COOLOOLA NATIONAL PARK.** Extending 50km north of Noosa up to Rainbow Beach is the sandy white coastline of Cooloola National Park. Together with Fraser Island, Cooloola forms the **Great Sandy Region,** the largest sand mass in the world. The rugged terrain and 4WD-accessible tracks make the park a great place to enjoy some windswept wilderness. There are no organized tours, and if you don't have your own 4WD vehicle, you will be limited to the **Carlo Sandblow** and **Coloured Sands**. Dingo's hostel runs a van to the area, but it is easily walkable. As you head out of town from Rainbow Beach Rd., turn left onto Double Island Dr. Then take a left onto Cooloola Dr. and follow it until the end. An easy 600m walk will bring you to the huge sand bowl of the Carlo Sandblow. Walk toward the ocean for unbelievable views of the 200m cliffs and Coloured Sands. For serious bushwalkers, the **Cooloola Wilderness Trail** presents the ultimate challenge. The 48km one-way trail connects East Mullen Carpark in the north to Elanda Point in the south. Pick up an information sheet and inform rangers of your itinerary before you set out. Information and maps are both available from a number of locations; try the **Rainbow Beach Tourist Information Centre** or the **Queensland Parks and Wildlife Service** in Rainbow Beach, on the right as you enter town. (☎07 5486 3160. Open daily 7am-4pm.) For more info, **Gympie Regional Council**, 242 Mary St., Gympie (☎07 5481 0800; open

*M-F 8am-5pm)* and **Great Sandy Information Centre,** at 240 Moorindil St. in Tewantin can be of assistance. *(☎07 5449 7792. Open daily 7am-4pm.)*

**SURF, SCUBA, AND SKYDIVE.** If bushwalking is not your cup of tea, there are plenty of other things to get excited about in Rainbow Beach. The **Rainbow Beach Surf School** will get you standing by the end of a 3hr. group lesson; you may even get to surf with dolphins. The same company also runs 3-5hr. **sea kayaking trips** to Double Island Point; they boast a 90% dolphin-sighting rate and good chances of seeing manta rays, turtles, and whales in season. *(☎04 0873 8192. Surf lesson $55; sea kayaking $65.)* **Wolf Rock Dive Centre** will plunge you 40m underwater and through vertical gutters, exposing the prolific fish life and grey nurse sharks. *(☎07 5486 8004; www.wolfrockdive.com.au. Introductory dive with gear $170; 2 certified dives with gear $170; 4-day dive certification course $500.)* If flying through the air seems more appealing than swimming with sharks, **Skydive Rainbow Beach** *(☎04 1821 8358; www.skydiverainbowbeach.com)* and **Rainbow Paragliding** *(☎07 5486 3048; www.paraglidingrainbow.com)* both offer spectacular views of Cooloola National Park and Fraser Island. *(☎04 0886 3706.)* **Surf & Sand Safaris** offers a tour that includes 4WD ride on the beach and through the national park, a short boat cruise, a boomnet ride, dolphin and whale watching (in season), and some surfing. *(☎07 5486 3131; www.surfandsandsafaris.com.au. $80, children $40.)*

# SUNSHINE COAST HINTERLAND

Just inland of the Sunshine Coast lies a smorgasbord of tourist delights: stunning national parks, roadside crafts markets, and kitschy-but-fun tourist traps. Most of the hinterland is inaccessible by public transportation. Several tour operators run trips to the region, but most involve more driving than hiking. **Noosa Hinterland Tours** offers several options, such as a tour of Montville, the Blackall Range, and the Glasshouse Mountains, a morning trip to the Eumundi Markets, and a "3-in-1 Tour" which includes the ginger factory, the Australia Zoo, and UnderWater World. *(☎07 5446 3111; www.noosahinterlandtours. com.au. Montville-Glasshouse $69, children $35, seniors $65. 3-hour trip to the Eumundi Markets with pickup and dropoff from accomodation $20-$22, children $10. $3 market discounts at select hostels. "3-in-1 Tour" $52/28/49 and discounted entry. Cash only.)* **Storeyline Tours** covers similar activities. *(☎07 5474 1500; www.storeylinetours.com.au. Montville-Glasshouse tour, including a visit to the town of Maleny $84, children $49, concessions $79. Markets with pickup and dropoff at Noosa accommodations $15, children $10. 3-in-1-type tour with a visit to the Big Pineapple and free or discounted entry $72/41/69. AmEx/ MC/V.)* **Off Beat Rainforest Tours** has exclusive access to **Conondale National Park's** untouched rainforest. *(☎07 5473 5135; www.offbeattours.com.au. Includes gourmet lunch and morning and afternoon tea. $149, children $99. MC/V.)*

**EUMUNDI MARKETS.** Every Saturday and Wednesday, the sleepy town of Eumundi comes to life, with more than 500 shops offering everything from local desserts to camel rides. Nearly everything is handmade, and the markets are a perfect place to buy presents for those back home. Get there early for the good stuff. The Markets are 20km southwest of Noosa Heads, via Noosaville and Doonan. Blue Sunbus #630 leaves Wednesday at 7:25am (25min.), and Bus #631 leaves at 8:45am (25-35min.); bus #631 leaves Saturday at 8 and 8:45am (40min.). Buses leave from the bus interchange on Noosa Pde. For those driving, parking is scarce; try the dirt lots downhill from the market. For more info, contact the **Eumundi Historical Association.** *(☎07 5442 7106; www.eumundimar-kets.com.au. Open W 8am-1:30pm, Sa 6:30am-2pm.*

**MONTVILLE AND BLACKALL RANGE.** The sheer Blackall Range escarpment rises from the plains, cradling green pastures, rainforests, and the old country villages of **Mapleton, Flaxton, Montville,** and **Maleny.** Before you reach Mapleton, take a left at the **Lookout** sign to take in the expansive view. Of the four towns, **Montville** has the most to offer tourists, with several blocks of antique and crafts shops, galleries, teahouses, and a cuckoo clock shop. From Noosa, follow the Bruce Hwy. south to Nambour and then turn toward the Blackall Range via Mapleton. The **information center** is on Main St., Montville, beyond most of the shops. (☎07 5478 5544; www.maroochytourism.com. Open daily 10am-4pm.)

**GLASSHOUSE MOUNTAINS. Glasshouse Mountains National Park** protects nine of the 16 distinctive peaks which puncture the otherwise flat surrounds. Most of the tracks are recommended for experienced climbers only, although there are a small number of easy- to medium-grade short hikes. Many of the rockier spires, like sharp **Mount Coonowrin,** are closed to the public. Coonowrin's beauty can be appreciated from an easy hike (20min. round-trip) to **Mountain View Lookout,** located in the Mount Tibrogargan Section just past the carpark. A more dramatic view can be seen from the **Glasshouse Mountain Lookout** off Old Gympie Rd. For those with limited experience but ample physical fitness, the best option is **Mount Ngungun.** The 1.4km round-trip path is shorter than the others, and the terrain is manageable. Nonetheless, the track shouldn't be attempted in wet weather. Some very good **rock climbing** can be found on Mt. Tibrogargan and Mt. Ngungun, but it's unsupervised, and you must bring your own equipment. In case of emergency, contact the **ranger** at ☎07 5494 0150. **Camping ❶** is permitted only on undeveloped sites in **Coochin Creek,** 9km east of Beerwah. (☎13 13 04; www.qld.gov.au/camping. $4.85 per person. Book ahead.) Bring your own car or join a tour group; signs on the Glass Mountain Tourist Rd. direct travelers to all sites. From the south, look for signs off the Bruce Hwy. just past Caboolture. From the north, exit the Bruce Hwy. at Landsborough.

# HERVEY BAY                                                    ☎07

The humpback whale's annual migration through Hervey Bay (pop. 52,000) and the town's proximity to Fraser Island have put it firmly on the tourist path. With booking agencies, tour companies, and 4WD rental shops jostling for travelers' attention, Hervey Bay is a jumping-off point for activity.

## ◘ TRANSPORTATION

**Trains: Trainlink bus** connects Hervey Bay to **Maryborough West** (☎07 4121 3719), the train station off Biggenden Rd. Bus leaves from Hervey Bay Coach Terminal 1hr. before trains depart Maryborough West ($10, students $5.50). Some services will pick up and drop off at accommodations on the Esplanade upon request. The **Tilt Train** (☎13 22 32) runs from Maryborough to **Brisbane** (3-4hr.; M-F 2 per day, Sa-Su 1 per day $57.20), **Bundaberg** (1hr., M-F and Su 2 per day, $26.40), and **Rockhampton** (5hr. M-F and Su 2 per day, $70.40, ISIC-carying students ½-price).

**Buses: Hervey Bay Coach Terminal** (☎07 4124 4000), in Centro shopping center on Boat Harbour Dr., Pialba. Open M-F 6am-5:30pm, Sa 6am-1pm. Lockers $6 per day. **Premier Motor Service** (☎13 34 10) runs 1 northbound bus (8:50pm) and 1 southbound bus (5:55am) per day, while **Greyhound Australia** (☎13 14 99; www.greyhound. com.au) has consistent but pricier service. Premier runs to: **Airlie Beach** (12hr.; $105 concessions $95); **Brisbane** (6hr., $38/34); **Bundaberg** (2hr., $15/14); **Cairns** (22hr. $192/173); **Mackay** (10hr., $89/80); **Maroochydore** (5hr., $24/22); **Noosa Heads** (4hr., $22/20); **Rockhampton** (5hr., $49/44). Most hostels offer free pick up and drop off to and from the bus station. **Wide Bay Transit** (☎07 4121 3719; www.widebaytransit.com.au) offers limited service. Route #5 connects Hervey Bay to Maryborough. Route #14 goes to Pt. Vernon. Routes #5, 16, and 18 connect Torquay and the Marina.

**Taxis:** Hervey Bay Taxi (24hr. ☎13 10 08).

**Bike Rental:** Bay Bicycle Hire (☎04 1764 4814; www.baybikehire.com.au). ½-day $15, full day $20. Tandem bikes $30/35. Open daily 7am-5pm.

## ✦ 🛈 ORIENTATION AND PRACTICAL INFORMATION

Hervey Bay consists of a cluster of suburbs facing north toward the Bay. From west to east, the suburbs are: **Point Vernon, Pialba, Scarness, Torquay,** and **Urangan.** Most action occurs along **The Esplanade** at the water's edge between Scarness and Urangan, which is lined with takeaway shops and tour booking agencies. The harbor and marina are behind **Buccaneer Drive** at the eastern end of town.

**Tourist Office:** The only official tourism bureau is the **Hervey Bay Visitor Information Centre** (☎1800 811 728; www.herveybay.qld.gov.au), located at the corner of Hervey Bay-Maryborough and Urraween Rd., about 5.5km from the Central Business District (CBD). Open daily 9am-5pm. There are also several booking agents on The Esplanade.

**Currency Exchange: Banks** and **24hr. ATMs** are located at the Hervey Bay Bus Terminal and on The Esplanade in Torquay. WestPac and National Bank, 414 and 415 The Esplanade, have **ATMs.** Open M-Th 8:30am-4pm, F 8:30am-5pm.

**Police:** ☎07 4123 8111; emergency ☎000. On the corner of Queens and Torquay Rd.

**Pharmacy: Beachside Pharmacy,** 347 The Esplanade, Scarness (☎07 4128 1680). Open M-F 8am-6pm, Sa-Su 8:30am-1pm.

**Internet Access:** At several tourist offices on The Esplanade. Also at **The Adventure Travel Centre,** inside the **Koala Beach Resort.** $4 per hr., guests $3. Open 7am-10pm.

**Post Office:** 414 The Esplanade, Torquay (☎07 4125 1101). Open M-F 8am-5:30pm. There is also an office at **Centro shopping center** in Pialba, across from the bus terminal. Open M-F 8:30am-5pm, Sa 8:30-noon. **Postal Code:** 4655.

## ⌂ ACCOMMODATIONS

No matter where you stay in Hervey Bay, you can be confident that reception will assist you in booking any and all tours. Some hostels have their own 4WD rental company, and nearly all match guests into groups before departing for Fraser Island. In addition, most hostels have a $10 key deposit, laundry facilities, BBQ, courtesy bus, Internet access, and communal kitchens.

▨ **The Friendly Hostel,** 182 Torquay Rd., Scarness (☎1800 244 107; www.thefriendly. com.au). This homey hostel certainly lives up to its name. Incredibly flexible owners will make sure that this place suits your needs. Apartment-style setup with impressively clean rooms, gorgeous kitchens, and teddy bears in all of the doubles and twins. Each unit has TV, DVD, games, and books. Free bike rental and Internet access. Reception 7am-7pm. Check-in 24hr. 3-bed dorms $23; doubles and twins $50. MC/V. ❷

**Next Backpackers,** 10 Bideford St., Torquay (☎07 4125 6600; www.nextbackpackers. com.au). Centrally located. This young business takes pride in its cleanliness. Kitchen sparkles, harwood floors shine, and bathrooms are spotless. Key deposit $2. Wheelchair-accessible deluxe dorm available ($27 per night). 6- to 12-bed dorms $24; 10-bed ensuite $27; 4- to 6-bed ensuite $30; doubles $69. Reception 7am-9pm. MC/V. ❷

**Colonial Village YHA,** 820 Boat Harbor Drive (☎07 4125 1844). Surrounded by tropical gardens, this hostel has clean rooms, games, a pool, and a bar. It is both backpacker- and family-friendly and is conveniently located near the marina. 4- or 5-share dorms $28-32, doubles $50-56. Reception 7am-8pm. MC/V. ❸

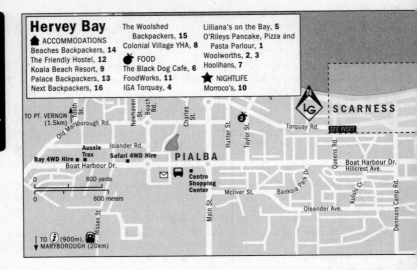

**Hervey Bay**

▲ ACCOMMODATIONS
Beaches Backpackers, **14**
The Friendly Hostel, **12**
Koala Beach Resort, **9**
Palace Backpackers, **13**
Next Backpackers, **16**

The Woolshed
 Backpackers, **15**
Colonial Village YHA, **8**
✦ FOOD
The Black Dog Cafe, **6**
FoodWorks, **11**
IGA Torquay, **4**

Lilliana's on the Bay, **5**
O'Rileys Pancake, Pizza and
 Pasta Parlour, **1**
Woolworths, **2, 3**
Hoolihans, **7**
★ NIGHTLIFE
Morroco's, **10**

SCARNESS

PIALBA

**Palace Backpackers,** 184 Torquay Rd., Scarness (☎1800 063 168; www.palaceback-packers.com.au). 5min. walk from the beach and The Esplanade. Most of their social self-contained units consist of a common room, kitchen, 2 bathrooms, a double, and 4 small dorms. A great setup for making new friends before heading to Fraser in one of their 4WD vehicles. If there's space, they'll allow you to go the morning you arrive. Swimming pool. 3- to 6-bed dorms $24; twins and doubles $50. VIP discount. MC/V. ❷

**Beaches Backpackers,** 195 Torquay Rd., Scarness (☎1800 655 501; www.beaches.com.au). Great 4-bed dorms, a lively bar and bistro, and spectacular packages which include trips to Fraser and the Whitsundays. Exclusive access to base camp at Cathedral Beach, which includes perks like hot showers and sheltered areas. 4- to 14-bed dorms $22; twins and doubles $60, ensuite $65. AmEx/MC/V. ❷

**The Woolshed Backpackers,** 181 Torquay Rd., Scarness (☎07 4124 0677; www.woolshedbackpackers.com). 5min. from the beach and The Esplanade. Small hostel surrounded by tropical gardens. Designed to resemble outback woolsheds, rooms and common areas are constructed of a dark wood with high ceilings and a very outdoorsy feel. Clean co-ed bathrooms and welcoming staff. Reception 7am-7pm. 3- to 6-bed dorms $20-22; twins and doubles $48, ensuite $64. MC/V. Credit card fee 2.5%. ❷

**Koala Beach Resort,** 408 The Esplanade (☎1800 354 535; www.koalaadventures.com.au). Party hostel in Hervey Bay. Dorms aren't the best in town, but the great location and thumping Morocco's nightclub (attached) mean that you spend little time in your room. Swimming pool in jungle-themed atmosphere. In-house 4WD tour agency. Linen $1.50. Reception 8:30am-9pm. Check-in available at Morocco's until 3am. 4- to 6-bed dorms $24, ensuite $28; doubles and twins $62. VIP discount. AmEx/MC/V. ❷

## 🏠🍴 FOOD AND NIGHTLIFE

For groceries, try **FoodWorks,** 414 The Esplanade (☎07 4125 2477; open daily 6am-11pm), **Woolworths,** on the corner of Torquay Rd. and Taylor St., Pialba (☎07 4128 3188; open M-F 8am-9pm, Sa 8am-5:30pm, Su 9am-6pm), or **IGA Torquay** (☎07 4125 2380; open 6:30am-7:30pm). Hostel bars dominate the back-

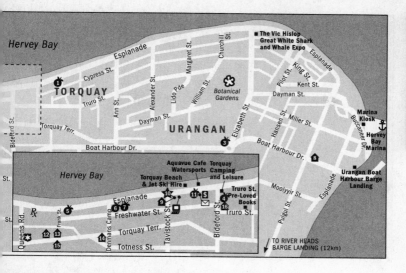

packer nightlife scene; **Koala Beach Resort,** with the attached **Morocco's,** is the closest thing to a nightclub the area has to offer (open until 3am; see above).

**The Black Dog Cafe,** 381 The Esplanade, Torquay (☎07 4124 3177). This trendy, relaxed eatery serves creative dishes with an Asian flair. Enjoy their delicious sushi rolls ($5.50-6.50) or outstanding teriyaki burgers ($9.50). Open daily 10:30am-2:30pm and 5:30pm-late; kitchen closes at 9:30pm. 10% YHA/VIP discount. MC/V. ❶

**O'Rileys Pancake, Pizza, and Pasta Parlour,** 446 The Esplanade (☎07 4125 3100). Serves some of the best pizza on the coast (2 for $16-22), excellent pastas ($9.50-14), and creative pancake concoctions ($6.50-10). Don't miss the Tu all-you-can-eat pizza and pancake buffet 5-9pm ($15). Open Tu 5:30pm-late, W-Sa 11:30am-2pm and 5:30pm-late, Su 7:30-11am, 11:30-2pm, and 5:30pm-latenight. AmEx/MC/V. ❶

**Lilliana's on the Bay,** 363 The Esplanade, Scarness (☎07 4128 1338). This coffee roastery and restaurant serves amazing coffee and loose-leaf tea along with an assortment of modern international cuisine. Lunches range $6-20 and dinner mains start at $18. BYOB with a corkage fee of $2 per person. Open W-Su 10am-10pm. MC/V. ❸

**Hoolihans,** 382 The Esplanade (☎07 4194 0099; www.hoolies.com). This Irish pub serves an array of lunch and dinner options, including traditional Irish fare like Guinness Pie. Tables are creatively perched on barrels, and the Irish music makes for an enjoyable experience. Main dinner courses around $15. Open daily 11am-late. After 9pm buy-one-get-one-free appetizers. MC/V. ❷

## ACTIVITIES

**WHALE WATCHING.** As Australia's premier whale watching destination, Hervey Bay is filled from late-July to early November with whale aficionados. It's the only place in Australia where boats guarantee sightings during the season. Eleven boats operate during high season, all out of the **Hervey Bay Marina** in Urangan—pick up an info sheet from the **Marina Kiosk** on Buccaneer Dr. (☎07 4128 9800. Open 7:30am-6pm.) The flagship vessel is the **Spirit of Hervey Bay,** built for whale watching and underwater viewing; it even has a whale-

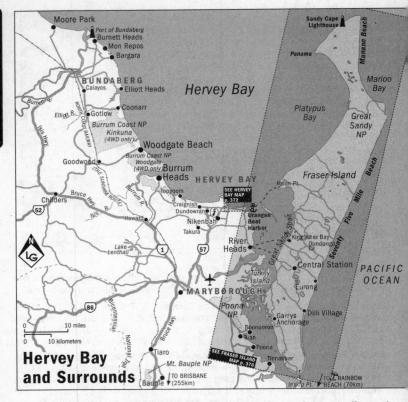

**Hervey Bay and Surrounds**

listening hydrophone. (☎1800 642 544; www.spiritofherveybay.com. 4hr. cruise departs 8:30am and 1:30pm. $99, concessions $94, children $55. MC/V.) **Quick Catt II** offers a ½-day, small-boat experience. (☎1800 671 977; www.hervey-baywhalewatch.com.au. Departs daily 8am and 1pm. $100/95/60.) If the whale season (July-Nov.) has passed, **Whale Song** guarantees dolphin sightings instead. (☎1800 689 610; www.whalesong.com.au. ½-day whale watching daily 7:30am and 1pm. $105/95/60. Dolphin watching Dec.-Jun. daily 9am-2:30pm. $75/65/50. MC/V.) The return of the humpback whales is celebrated annually in early August with the **Hervey Bay Whale Festival,** (☎07 4197 4441; www.herveybay-whalefestival.com.au) which consists of various events and parades.

**OTHER ACTIVITIES. Aquavue Cafe Watersports,** across from the post office and National Bank on The Esplanade, rents out equipment for a wide variety of beach activities. (☎07 4125 5528. Jet ski rental $40 per 15min. 2hr. guided tour for 1 or 2 to Fraser Island $320. Open daily 7am-5pm. MC/V.) **Hervey Bay Skydivers,** at the Hervey Bay airport, includes a scenic flight over Fraser Island. (☎07 4183 0119; www.herveybayskydivers.com.au. 10,000 ft. $250; 14,000 ft. $270. DVD $99, DVD and photos $120. Beach landing extra $30; $25 levy applied on day of jump.) If 4WD on the island isn't exciting enough, try some aerobatic adventure flights over the island with **Hervey Bay Air Adventures.** (☎07 4124 9313;

www.airadventures.com.au. Stunt planes seat only 1 passenger $130 per 20min. Peaceful scenic flights for up to 5 $160-450.) **Shayla Sailing Cruises** (☎07 4125 3727; www.shaylacruises.com.au) offers a variety of cruise options around Hervey Bay and Fraser Island ($80-255. Charters available. MC/V). If you want to catch some fish, **Hervey Bay M.V. Daytripper** can help you do so. (☎04 0180 4205; www.mvdaytripper.com. Open daily 9am-2pm. $59. Min. 5 people. Cash only.). The **Vic Hislop Great White Shark & Whale Expo**, 553 The Esplanade, Urangan, is a small museum with films, articles, and displays about a living shark-hunter, Vic Hislop, who is on a mission to inform the world about the dangers of the Great White. (☎07 4128 9137. Open daily in summer 8:30am-6pm; in winter 8:30am-5:30pm. $15, concessions $12, children $7. MC/V.)

# FRASER ISLAND                                              ☎07

Fraser Island, the world's largest sand island, is the only place on the planet where rainforest grows directly out of the sand. It's a World Heritage national park that attracts nearly every traveler passing along the East Coast. With freshwater lakes, beaches, and sandblows, it is clear why the island's Aboriginal name "K'Gari" means "Paradise." Though it is an ideal destination for bushwalkers, fishing aficionados, and 4WDers, Fraser is fun for the less-experienced as well. However, swimming is limited to its beautiful lakes, as tiger sharks and strong currents lurk in the surrounding ocean. Winds perpetually resculpt the topography, but Fraser's unique natural beauty is forever.

## ▐ TRANSPORTATION

### BY BOAT

Ferries run to Fraser from several locations and are owned by **Fraser Island Barges** (www.fraserislandbarges.com.au). Fares are as follows: round-trip walk-on $25, vehicles with 4 people $145, extra passenger $10.50.

**Fraser Dawn Barges** (☎1800 072 555), departs Urangan Harbor for Moon Pt. 55min., daily 8:30am and 3:30pm, returns 9:30am and 4:30pm. More services high season.

**Fraser Venture Barges** (☎1800 072 555), departs from Riverheads (20min. south of Hervey Bay) and arrives at Wanggoolba Creek. Ideal for independent travelers, given proximity to great tracks. 30min.; daily 9, 10:15am, and 3:30pm, Sa also 7am. Returns daily 9:30am, 2:30, and 4pm, Sa also 7:30am.

**Kingfisher Barges** (☎1800 072 555), leaves from Riverheads. Arrives at Kingfisher Bay Resort. 45min.; daily 7:15, 11am and 2:30pm; returns 8:30am, 1:30, and 4pm.

**Kingfisher Fast Cat Passenger Ferry** (☎1800 072 555), runs from Urangan Harbor to Kingfisher Bay Resort and the best walking tracks. 30min.; daily 6:45, 8:45am, noon, 4, 7, and 10pm; returns daily 7:40, 10:30am, 2, 5, 8, and 11:30pm. $55, children $28.

### BY PLANE

**Air Fraser Island** (☎07 4125 3600; www.airfraserisland.com.au) sells one-way ($70) and round-trip ($140). Also offers an overnight trip, including flight, 4WD, and camping equipment. $270. Scenic 30min. flights for 2-4 over island $70 per person. MC/V.

### BY GUIDED TOUR

Tours provide a structured, safe, and hassle-free way to see the island, though you'll have to forgo some freedom. Some buses seat 40 people, all of whom must shuffle in and out at each stop before continuing on to the next. Be sure to inquire about group size, accommodations, and meals before booking your

# Fraser Island

**CAUTION: Only 4WD vehicles are suited for the sand tracks on Fraser Island.**

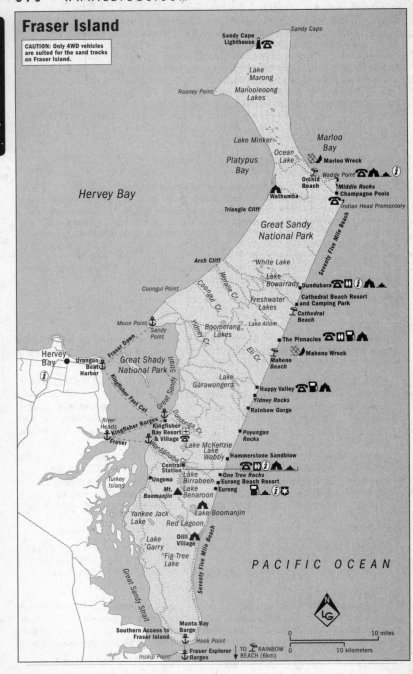

Sandy Cape Lighthouse

Sandy Cape

Lake Marong

Manooleoong Lakes

Rooney Point

Lake Minker

Marloo Bay

Ocean Lake

Platypus Bay

Marloo Wreck

Orchid Beach

Waddy Point

Middle Rocks

Champagne Pools

Wathumba

Indian Head Promontory

Hervey Bay

Triangle Cliff

Great Sandy National Park

Seventy Five Mile Beach

Arch Cliff

White Lake

Lake Bowarrady

Dundubara

Coongul Point

Woralie Cr.

Coongul Cr.

Freshwater Lakes

Cathedral Beach Resort and Camping Park

Moon Point

Sandy Point

Yidney Cr.

Boomerang Lakes

Lake Allom

Cathedral Beach

Fraser Dawn

Great Shady National Park

Eli Cr.

The Pinnacles

Maheno Wreck

Maheno Beach

Hervey Bay

Urangan Boat Harbor

Kingfisher Fast Cat

Great Sandy Strait

Lake Garawongera

Happy Valley

Yidney Rocks

Rainbow Gorge

River Heads

Kingfisher Barges

Kingfisher Bay Resort & Village

Dundonga Cr.

Poyungan Rocks

Fraser

Wanggoolba Cr.

Lake McKenzie

Lake Wabby

Hammerstone Sandblow

Central Station

Lake Birrabeen

One Tree Rocks

Eurong Beach Resort

Turkey Island

Ungowa

Mt. Boomanjin

Lake Benaroon

Eurong

Yankee Jack Lake

Red Lagoon

Lake Boomanjin

Lake Garry

Dilli Village

Seventy Five Mile Beach

Fig-Tree Lake

PACIFIC OCEAN

Great Sandy Strait

Manta Ray Barge

Southern Access to Fraser Island

Hook Point

Fraser Explorer Barges

TO RAINBOW BEACH (6km)

Inskip Point

0       10 miles

0    10 kilometers

tour so you know what you're paying for. Tour options are varied, but 2- or 3-day tours are the best way to get a feel for the island. Most tour groups are not subjected to the difficulties of serious camping or outdoor cooking, and instead sleep in cabins and eat prepared meals. While taking a tour can cost $100 more per person than an independent visit, there's no significant price difference once you've factored in food, permits, petrol, and stress for a self-driven tour. All hostels and 4WD companies can also organize guided tours.

**The Fraser Island Company** (☎1800 063 933; www.fraserislandco.com.au). Offers a variety of tours that are wonderfully run, eco-friendly, and the perfect way to experience the island. The One Day Safari explores the island's highlights ($155, children $95); the One Day Exclusive Tour is smaller and perfect for those seeking a more personalized experience ($195/141). To truly appreciate the island, stay the night in one of the company's luxurious tents at Cathedral Beach. 2 Day Northern Adventure explores the Northern part of the island and the 2 Day Wilderness Safari visits points farther south ($275/215). Splurge on a 3-day trip to really experience everything the island has to offer ($461/361). 1- and 2-day tours leave daily, 3-day leaves Tu, F, Su. AmEx/MC/V.

**Fraser Explorer Tours** (☎1800 249 122; www.fraserexplorertours.com.au). Their daytrips and 2-day safaris attract a younger set, but their various accommodation options make it ideal for any type of traveler. Accommodation in 4-person rooms at **Eurong Beach Resort** (p. 377). Day tour $149, children $89; 2-day safari $253-305. MC/V.

## 🔢 PRACTICAL INFORMATION

**Permits:** If you're traveling by car, you'll need a **vehicle permit** ($35; includes map and island details). Vehicle and camping permits are available from several places, including **Riverheads Information Kiosk,** which is at the carpark at the barge landing, the **Queensland Parks and Wildlife Service** in Rainbow Beach (☎07 5486 3160. Open daily 7am-4pm), and the **Marina Kiosk,** on Buccaneer Dr., Urangan, at the harbor. (☎07 4128 9800. Open daily 7:30am-6pm. MC/V.)

**General Supplies:** Stock up at **Eurong Beach Resort** (☎07 4194 9122; open daily 8am-5:30pm), **Fraser Island Wilderness Retreat** at Happy Valley (☎07 4125 2343; open daily 8am-6pm), **Kingfisher Bay Resort & Village** (☎1800 072 555; open daily 7:30am-6:30pm), **Frasers at Cathedral Beach Resort** (☎07 4125 2343; open daily 8am-5pm), or **Rainbow Beach's Fraser Island Bed & Breakfast** (☎07 4127 9127; open daily 8am-5pm). All take MC/V, and some can give you cash back.

**Telephones: Central Station, Dundubara, Waddy Point, Indian Head, Yidney Rocks.**

**Showers:** There are cold showers at most **campgrounds.** Coin-operated hot showers are at **Central Station, Waddy Point,** and **Dundubara.** $1 per 3min. $1 coins only.

**Emergency:** ☎000, cell phones ☎112. Limited medical assistance on the island; stand-by nurse at the **Kingfisher Bay Resort & Village** (☎1800 072 555). During peak tourist seasons, an **ambulance** is located at Happy Valley.

**Taxis:** ☎07 4127 9188 (Eurong).

**Tow Truck:** ☎07 4127 9449 (Eurong).

**Ranger Stations: Eurong** (☎07 4127 9128), the main station, is generally open 7am-4pm. Branches are found in **Central Station** (☎07 4127 9191), **Dundubara** (☎07 4127 9138), **Ungowa** (☎07 4127 9113), and **Waddy Point** (☎07 4127 9190), but these are only open daily 8-9am and 3-4pm.

## 🏠 🏕 ACCOMMODATIONS AND CAMPING

The Fraser Island Tour Company owns the only backpacking hostel on the island, **Fraser Island Backpackers** ❸ (☎1800 446 655; www.fraserislandco.com.

au/backpackers), located in Happy Valley. With an incredibly friendly staff, a variety of rooms, a bar and bistro, Internet, and a pool, this is the best option for budget travelers who want to avoid camping. (6-person dorms $39; 4-person $49; doubles $59. Packages available. MC/V.) **Eurong Beach Resort ❺** will make sure that you sleep comfortably in their expensive motel units and luxury apartments. (☎07 4127 9122; www.fraser-is.com. Motel doubles $150 in high season, $130 low season; apartments for up to 6 $270/180. MC/V.) **Yidney Rocks ❻** has family holiday units that sleep up to eight. (☎07 4127 9167; www.yidney-rock.com.au. High season $200, low season $180.)

**Camping ❶** is cheap and convenient and enables visitors to move easily through the island's different sights. There are three main QPWS camping areas, and camping is also allowed on designated beaches, including most of **Eastern Beach.** Pay close attention to the signs that designate camping areas, as camping outside of these areas will result in a fine. **Camping permits** ($5 per person) are good for all campgrounds except the privately run Cathedral Beach Resort and Dilli Village, both on the east shore. Some sites require pre-booking (☎13 13 04; www.qld.gov.au/camping). Each permit comes with a packet identifying camping areas; all developed campgrounds have 9pm noise curfews. Most campgrounds have taps and toilets, but only some have hot showers, BBQs, dingo fences, and picnic tables. Fires are not allowed, except for at Dundabara and Waddy Point. Only milled timber from the mainland can be used to build fires. **Cathedral Beach Resort and Camping Park ❷** has campsites and cabins. (☎07 4127 9177. Unpowered sites for 2 from $27. Powered sites for 2 from $47. Cabins for up to 6 from $140. 4-person ensuite cabins from $175.)

## 👁 🎒 SIGHTS AND HIKING

**INLAND.** With unbelievably clear waters and white sandy bottoms, Fraser's freshwater lakes are one of its biggest draws. **⬛Lake McKenzie** is the most popular, with two white sand beaches for bathers and water in three shades of gorgeous blue. **Lake Wabby** is at the eastern base of the steep **Hammerstone Sandblow,** which is gradually swallowing the lake and the surrounding forest. Some visitors run down the dune into the lake, but doing so has caused injuries and fatalities, so be careful. To get to Lake Wabby, follow the 1.4km track from the inland carpark via the massive sand dune (30min. walk one-way), or take the 5.5km round-trip circuit from the eastern beach (45min. one-way). Walking across the dunes is like crossing a desert; in fact, Fraser Island is alleged to contain more sand than the Sahara Desert.

The southernmost lake, **Lake Boomanjin,** is a wonderful place to take a dip in its honey-colored water. It also claims the title of "world's largest perched lake." Another series of lakes lies north of Boomanjin, but **Lake Birabeen** is by far the most impressive of these. There are also a number of freshwater creeks good for wading; among them Eli Creek and Wyuna Creek. Be sure not to miss the crystal-clear waters of **Wanggoolba Creek.**

**D-I-N-G-O.** Don't confuse the dingoes roaming Fraser Island with domesticated dogs; keep your distance, and never feed or pet them. By feeding the dingoes, visitors to Fraser have made them more aggressive and less fearful of humans. Now, dingoes routinely steal food from campsites; attacks on children have occurred in recent years. If you do happen upon a dingo, don't run; pick up some sand or an object and throw it near its front paws while yelling. At the same time, cross your arms over your chest and walk slowly backward, maintaining steady eye contact with the dog.

**EASTERN BEACH.** There is a lot of beach on Fraser Island, and most of it looks the same, bordered by raging surf and low-lying trees. Eastern Beach is perfect for 4WDing, but be careful (see **Driving on Fraser, p. 379**). The drive from Hook Point north to Indian Head takes a good 2hr. on a registered Queensland highway. Do not even consider swimming in the ocean, as tiger sharks and rip-tides are real dangers. Heading north from Eurong, patches of rocks decorate the beach, with short bypasses at **Poyungan Rocks, Yidney Rocks,** and a longer route around the **Indian Head promontory,** where one can spot dolphins, sharks, rays, and whales (on calm days from late-July to early Nov.). Near the top of passable beachland on **Middle Rocks,** a collection of shallow tide pools called the **Champagne Pools** make good swimming holes at low tide. Be careful at the pools, as the rocks are slippery and incoming waves can cause serious injury.

 ## DRIVING ON FRASER

Driving on Fraser is only possible in a 4WD vehicle. Rental agencies will brief you on island regulations and suggestions for safe travel—it's an insurance pre-caution for them—but listen up unless you enjoy being fined or pushing trucks through knee-deep sand. Speed limits are established on the island: 80kph on the Eastern Beach and 35kph on inland roads, though 60kph and 20kph, respectively, are recommended. Getting stuck happens often; have shovels handy. Allow at least 30min. to travel 10km on inland roads. The beaches themselves are registered national highways—all normal traffic rules apply, and breatha-lyzer- and speedgun-wielding police regularly patrol the roads, especially dur-ing fishing season and school holidays. Larger vehicles—buses in particular—will occasionally stay on the right, and the larger vehicle always has the right of way. If you want to pass, do so with caution. On the beach, keep to hard, wet sand, and don't try to cross washouts that are more than knee deep. Pay atten-tion to the tides; the best time for beach driving is within 3hr. of low tide.

> **CRASH COURSE: BEACH DRIVING.** Although beach driving is a lot of fun, reckless driving can lead to disaster. The most serious danger is creek cuts in the beach. Make sure to test the depth of a creek before attempting to cross, as the depth is often impossible to gauge from a dis-tance. Don't cross if the water is higher than your knees; wait for the tide to go down. Hitting washouts at high speed risks the vehicle rolling; it also can break the springs or cause front-end damage, leading to expensive repairs. Also, don't drive at night, when it is difficult to see and other drivers are more likely to be drunk. Location is important, as well; you're tempting fate by driv-ing north of the Ngkala Rocks, around Hook Point, or on the Western Beach.

Without a doubt, the most popular trip for backpackers is a self-driven three-day, two-night 4WD expedition. Most go through hostel-organized trips and nearly all come back with crazy stories, dirty clothes, and sand in places they didn't know they had. Unlike those on guided tours, guests camp out at night. Hostel self-drive safaris usually cost around $135, including 4WD rental, ferry passes, camping permits, access fees, camping equipment, and a full prepara-tory briefing. Petrol, insurance ($40-50), and food ($15-20) are not included. Hostels host either an afternoon meeting or an early-morning session before a short 4WD training. You must be over 21 to drive and at least 18 to ride. Bear in mind that the entire group assumes responsibility for vehicle damage regard-less of fault, so it's best to keep an eye on whoever is driving.

When choosing a hostel, there are a number of details to consider: first, look at the size of the tour group; most hostels cap group size around 11, although anything more than nine is uncomfortable. Check out the total cost, and be sure to add in the extras including insurance, bonds, and sleeping bag rental. Also, be aware that weather conditions can be harsh on Fraser, particularly in the winter; be prepared for difficult conditions. If hardcore camping is not for you, consider **Beaches Backpackers' base camp** or a **tour group** (p. 375).

**RENT YOUR OWN 4WD.** While hostels will help to create larger groups and develop a social cohesion among several cars, independent travelers will find renting a 4WD less expensive. Most rental companies offer similar deals, although prices appear to vary because of different advertising techniques. Cars seat 2-11 people, and rates range from $120-200 depending on vehicle size, length of rental, and season. While rental companies often assist in obtaining permits and ferry crossings, the price for such services is not included in the overall rental fee; be sure to ask for the grand total (car plus extras) before signing the paperwork. Camping gear is usually $15 per person per night, but competition is intense, so deals are common and bargaining is a definite possibility. Many rental agencies also offer discounts to card-holding backpackers. Operators in Hervey Bay include: **Bay 4WD Centre,** 54 Boat Harbour Dr. (☎07 4128 2981 or 1800 687 178; www.bay4wd.com.au), **Safari 4WD Hire,** 102 Boat Harbour Dr. (☎1800 689 819; www.safari4wdhire.com.au), and **Aussie Trax,** 56 Boat Harbour Dr. (☎1800 062 275; www.fraserisland4wd.com.au). All of these companies pick up locally, will help create a personalized itinerary, and hold safety meetings with clients prior to departure. They also offer guided tours. To ensure your safety, ask whether a rental agency belongs to the **Fraser Coast 4WD Hire Association,** a local watchdog group.

# BUNDABERG                                              ☎07

Bundaberg (pop. 60,000) is not a terribly exciting destination for east-coast travelers, but it does attract job hunters and prospective fruit-pickers. Fruit picking might sound fun, but many who stay to work complain about the relatively low pay and very hard labor. Some workers last a day; others, months. Unfortunately, locals and backpackers have a tense relationship, meaning that nearly all social events remain inside the hostels. If you do happen to come to Bundaberg during the Loggerhead hatching season, however, you can watch the newborn turtles make their trek from their eggs into the ocean.

## ▐ TRANSPORTATION

**Trains: Bundaberg Railway Station** (☎07 4153 9709) is at the corner of Bourbong and McLean St. Ticket office open M-F 4-5am and 7:45am-5pm, Sa-Su 8:45am-1pm and 2-4:15pm. Queensland Rail's Sunlander (☎13 16 17) trains go to: **Brisbane** (M-F 2 per day, Sa-Su 1 per day; $66); **Mackay** (1 per day; M and F $154; Tu, Th, Sa-Su $104.50); **Maryborough** (M-F 2 per day, Sa-Su 1 per day; $26.40), with bus connections to **Hervey Bay** ($10); **Rockhampton** (1 per day, $57.20). Children and ISIC 50% discount. Queensland Rail's Tilt train also runs through Bundaberg, but the fares are significantly more expensive than those of other trains.

**Buses:** The **Coach Terminal,** 66 Targo St. (☎07 4152 9700), between Crofton and Electra St. Premier (☎13 34 10) runs only 1 daily service northbound (11:10pm) and 1 southbound (3:30am). More expensive Greyhound Australia (☎13 14 99) has 4 buses daily and a 10% student and backpacker discount, but there's an $8 phone-booking fee, and trips are generally longer than with Premier. They both run to: **Airlie Beach** (10-13hr.; Premier $91, concessions $82; Greyhound $134); **Brisbane** (7-10hr.; $49/44; $78); **Cairns** (20-23hr.; $164/148; $211); **Hervey Bay** (1-2hr.; $15/14;

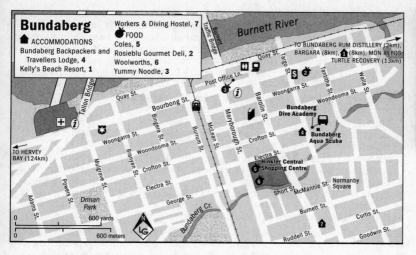

**Bundaberg**

ACCOMMODATIONS
Bundaberg Backpackers and Travellers Lodge, **4**
Kelly's Beach Resort, **1**

Workers & Diving Hostel, **7**
FOOD
Coles, **5**
Rosieblu Gourmet Deli, **2**
Woolworths, **6**
Yummy Noodle, **3**

Burnett River

TO BUNDABERG RUM DISTILLERY (2km),
BARGARA (8km), (8km), MON REPOS
TURTLE RECOVERY (13km)

Quay St.
Targo St.
Tantitha St.
Walla St.
Woondooma St.
Post Office Ln.
Woongarra St.
Barolin St.
**Bundaberg Dive Academy**
Bourbong St.
Bingera St.
McLean St.
Maryborough St.
Crofton St.
**Bundaberg Aqua Scuba**
TO HERVEY BAY (124km)
Woongarra St.
Woondooma St.
Branyan St.
Burrum St.
Electra St.
**Hinkler Central Shopping Centre**
**5**
**6**
Short St.
McMannie St.
Normanby Square
Crofton St.
Mulgrave St.
Electra St.
George St.
Bundaberg Cr.
Burnett St.
Curtis St.
Drinan Park
Powers St.
Adams St.
Ruddell St.
Goodwin St.
N
600 yards
600 meters

$18); **Mackay** (8-10hr.; $76/68; $112); **Maroochydore** (7-8hr.; $37/33; $63); **Noosa** (6-7hr.; $36/32; $59); **Rockhampton** (3-4hr.; $38/34; $61).

**Local Transportation:** Duffy's City Buses, 28 Barolin St. (☎07 4151 4226; www.duffys-buses.com.au) run around town, to local beaches, and to the **Bundaberg Rum Distillery** (p. 382). Buses M-Sa 8am-4pm, less frequent on Sa. Stewart & Sons Coaches, 66 Targo St. (☎07 4153 2646), departs the IGA supermarket on Woongarra St. for **Innes Park, Elliott Heads,** and **Moore Park** (M-F 3 per day, Sa 2 per day; fare varies depending on zone, $2-$4.60, ½-price concessions).

**Taxis:** Bundaberg Cab Co. (24hr. ☎07 4151 2345).

## 🔅🔢 ORIENTATION AND PRACTICAL INFORMATION

Most of Bundy's action takes place on **Bourbong Street,** which runs parallel to and one block south of the **Burnett River.** Crossing Bourbong from west to east are **McLean, Maryborough, Barolin,** and **Targo Street.**

**Tourist Office: Bundaberg Region Tourism,** 186 Bourbong St. (☎07 4153 8888; www.bundabergregion.info). Open M-F 9am-5pm, Sa-Su 9am-noon.

**Currency Exchange: ATMs** line **Bourbong Street** between Tantitha and Maryborough St.

**Police:** 256-258 Bourbong St. (☎07 4153 9111), just west of the CBD.

**Internet Access:** The **library,** on Woondooma St. allows 1hr. free Internet access. Wi-Fi available. (☎07 4153 9253). Open M-Th 9am-6pm, F 9:30am-5pm, Sa 9am-1pm. **The Cosy Corner,** on Barolin St. opposite the post office. $4 per hr.; free 15min. with each hr. Open M and F 8am-7pm, Tu-Th 8am-10pm, Sa-Su 11am-5pm. Other Internet cafes with similar prices and hours located on Bourbong St.

**Post Office:** 157B Bourbong St. (☎13 13 18). Open M-F 9am-5pm, Sa 8:30am-noon. **Postal Code:** 4670.

## ▚ ACCOMMODATIONS

Most of the hostels in Bundaberg will help you find work (usually within 24hr. of arrival) and will provide transportation.

**Workers & Diving Hostel,** 64 Barolin St. (☎07 4151 6097). From the bus station, call for a ride or walk down Crofton St., and take a left onto Barolin St. Despite the name, working is definitely the focus here. Self-contained units with 8 beds and dorm-style accommodations. The apartment beds are worth the additional cost. Social camaraderie among new and old pickers. Big outdoor common area, pool, and common room with movies. Reception 8:30am-noon and 3:30-7:30pm. 4- to 6-bed dorms in house $24, weekly $145; in units $25/150; doubles $50/300. NOMADS discount. MC/V. ❷

**Bundaberg Backpackers and Travellers Lodge,** 2 Crofton St. (☎07 4152 2080), across from the bus terminal. A no-nonsense hostel crowded with fruit-pickers. While the rooms are nothing to brag about, the A/C is especially nice during the humid summers. Free pickup at train station. Key deposit $20. Reception 8:30-10:30am and 3-6pm. 4- to 8-bed dorms $28, weekly $150. Student and backpacker discount. MC/V. ❷

**Kelly's Beach Resort,** 6 Trevors Rd., Bargara (☎07 4154 7200 or 1800 246 141; www. kellysbeachresort.com.au). The villas are expensive and far from Bundy, but the luxurious pool, tennis court, sauna, and trips to see turtles spawning justify the price. Great for groups and families. Pickup from Bundaberg $20; Duffy's bus #5 also passes alongside the resort. Free accommodation and food for 4½hr. daily resort work. Villas $99-$175 depending on season. AmEx/D/MC/V. ❺

## 🔲 FOOD

If you're searching for a healthful bite, try **Rosieblu Gourmet Deli ❶**, 90a Bourbong St. Lunch and breakfast are both prepared in-house using local produce, so there are many vegetarian and gluten-free options. Most lunches cost around $12. (☎07 4151 0957. Open M-F 8:30am-4pm and Sa 8:30am-1:30pm. MC/V.) **Yummy Noodle ❶**, 165 Bourbong St., serves up flavorful noodles, rice dishes ($9.20), and several vegetarian plates ($8.50) in large portions with less fat than many Chinese restaurants. (☎07 4152 8868. Open M-Th and Su 11:30am-9:30pm, F-Sa 11:30am-10pm. Takeaway available. Cash only.) Both **Coles** (☎07 4152 5222; open M-F 8am-9pm, Sa 8am-5pm) and **Woolworths** (☎07 4153 1055; open M-F 8am-9pm, Sa 8am-5pm) supermarkets are in Hinkler Central Shopping Centre, on the corner of Maryborough and George St.

## 🔲🔲 SIGHTS AND ACTIVITIES

Diving in Bundaberg is quite cheap, but be aware of hidden costs: books and required medical exams run about $105, and they may not be included in the quoted price. The most popular agency is **Bundaberg Aqua Scuba**, 66 Targo St. Shop 1, next to the bus terminal, which offers two shore dives for $60, two artificial reef dives for $135, and a PADI open-water course ($219) that includes four shore dives. (☎07 4153 5761; www.aquascuba.com. Accommodation $17 per night with course. Open daily 9am-5pm. AmEx/MC/V.) **Bundaberg Dive Academy,** 66 Targo St. Shop 3, located next to Aqua Scuba, will get you a PADI certification for $340. (☎07 4124 9943; www.bundabergdiveacademy.com. 4-day class begins weekly M and Th. 2 of 4 open-water dives at artificial reef.) If you're already certified, **Dive Musgrave** has incredible 3-day overnight cruises with 10 dives around various parts of the southern Great Barrier Reef. (☎1800 552 614; www.divemusgrave.com.au. $595; includes meals, air tanks, and weights. Environmental charge $6 per day.) Those who'd rather experiment with a different liquid can head to the **Bundaberg Rum Distillery,** where the tour includes two drinks. (☎07 4131 2900; www.bundabergrum.com.au. Duffy's service #4 drops off at the distillery. 45min.-1hr. tours M-F every hour 10am-3pm, Sa-Su 10am-2pm. $10, students $7.70, backpackers $4.40.)

Celebrating the start of the turtle nesting season, the week-long **Coral Coast Turtle Festival** in early November features a carnival, markets, and parades.

Fourteen kilometers east of Bundaberg is **Mon Repos Turtle Rookery,** the largest concentration of nesting turtles on the eastern Australian mainland. Night visitors can witness tiny hatchlings make their first journeys across the sand and into the water; an inspiring sight for anyone who gets the chance to watch it. (14km from the CBD; head east on Bargara Beach Rd. and follow signs to the rookery. ☎07 4159 1652. Open daily Nov.-Mar. 7pm-2am. $8.70, children $4.60. Book ahead; pre-paid tickets required. No guarantee of turtle viewing.)

# TOWN OF 1770 AND AGNES WATER ☎07

Named for the year of Captain James Cook's second landing, this area's natural beauty hasn't changed much since the days of its namesake. The water and wildlife remain unmarred by two centuries of sleepy village life. With exceptional outdoor-oriented tours at insanely low prices, the area is known to insiders as the hidden gem of the East Coast. No matter how many days you spend here, you will find yourself wanting to stay longer.

**TRANSPORTATION.** Greyhound Australia (☎13 14 99) and Premier Motor Service (☎13 34 10) buses serve the area. Greyhound's northbound service arrives at Fingerboard Rd. (30km from Agnes Water) at 8:45pm. The southbound service stops in front of **Cool Bananas** (p. 383) at 6:30am and at Fingerboard Rd. at 9:33am; tickets for the later bus are slightly more expensive. Greyhound's connecting shuttle is included in the price. Premier goes to Fingerboard Rd.; northbound 12:10am, southbound 2:15am. Hostels will arrange a $12 pickup. If you are continuing on, both Greyhound and Premier go to Brisbane (10-11hr.; Greyhound $111, Premier $57), Bundaberg (1hr., $24/9), Hervey Bay (3-4hr., $47/25), Mackay (7hr., $116/59), and Rockhampton (3hr., $66/30).

**ORIENTATION AND PRACTICAL INFORMATION.** Agnes Water is located 123km north of Bundaberg. The town center lies at the intersection of **Round Hill Road, Springs Road** (running south along the ocean), and **Captain Cook Drive** (running 6km north to the Town of 1770). Basic supplies and accommodations are available in Agnes Water; the Marina is in 1770. There is no public transportation between the towns. **Agnes Water Information Centre,** on Captain Cook Dr. across from Endeavor Plaza, books tours and accommodations. (☎07 4902 1533. Open daily 9am-4:30pm.) The only bank in town is the **Westpac** in Endeavor Plaza; it does not exchange currency. There are **ATMs** in the Endeavor Plaza **IGA** supermarket and **FoodWorks** in Agnes Water Shopping Centre. **Internet** can be found at the **Rural Transaction Centre and Library,** across from Endeavor Plaza. (☎07 4902 1515. $3 per 30min. Open M-F 9am-4:30pm, Sa 9am-noon.) There is a **laundromat** in Endeavor Plaza. (Wash $4, dry $1 per 10min. Open daily 7:30am-8pm.) The **police** (☎07 4974 9708) are in Agnes Water on Springs Rd. near Cool Bananas (see below). The **post office** is in the Agnes Water Shopping Centre. (☎07 4974 9900. Open M-F 9am-5:30pm.) **Postal Code:** 4677.

**ACCOMMODATIONS.** The two local hostels are both in Agnes Water, so if you want to stay in 1770 you will have to camp or pay resort prices. **Cool Bananas ❷,** 2 Springs Rd., Agnes Water, has a campfire, Internet, kitchen, and a bar. They also offer free shuttle tours, tea and coffee, and body boards. Many guests claim that this is one of the best hostels they've stayed in, with exceptionally clean, spacious dorms, a pretty patio, hammocks, and a chef who cooks fabulous meals for $5. (☎1800 227 660; www.coolbananas.net.au. Reception daily 7am-midnight. 6- to 8-bed dorms $25. Book ahead.) **1770 Backpackers ❷,** next to Endeavor Plaza on Captain Cook Dr., is a clean, friendly hostel only a

3min. walk to a surfing beach. There is a nice, outdoor common room, and as of January 2009, there will be a brand new unit of rooms. (☎1800 121 770; www.the1770backpackers.com. Reception daily 8am-9:30pm; after-hours arrival permitted. 4- to 12-bed ensuite dorms $25; doubles $55. VIP discount. MC/V.) **1770 Camping Grounds ❷**, on Captain Cook Dr. past the Marina, has beachfront camping with campfire and beautiful grounds. Other amenities include hot showers, BBQ, kitchen, and laundry. (☎07 4974 9268; www.1770campinggrounds.com. Reception and convenience store open daily 7:30am-6:30pm. Sites for 2 $24, powered $27; extra person $10. Book ahead. MC/V.)

**📇 FOOD.** Catch the sunset at **Saltwater Cafe ❸**, past the Marina on Captain Cook Dr., with some excellent potato wedges for two ($7.50) and large pizzas from $22.50. (☎07 4974 9599. Bar open daily 10:30am-late; food served daily 11am-2pm and 5-8pm.) **The Tavern ❶**, on Tavern Rd. at the top of the hill as you enter Agnes Water, has backpacker specials, like a bowl of spaghetti and a pitcher of beer ($10). A free courtesy bus is available for pickup and dropoff from hostels. Occasional bands and consistent good music make it a great hangout. (☎07 4974 9469. Open M-Th and Su 10am-midnight, F-Sa 10am-2am.) Groceries can be purchased at the **IGA** supermarket, in Endeavor Plaza (☎07 4974 7991; open daily 6:45am-7pm), or at the **FoodWorks** in the Agnes Water Shopping Centre (☎07 4974 9911; open M-Sa 6:30am-7:30pm, Su 7am-7:30pm).

**📷 SIGHTS AND ACTIVITIES.** Agnes Water and 1770 both have a slew of outdoor activities and charge some of the lowest prices in Australia. The towns are also located only 90min. from extraordinary Lady Musgrave Island, which is renowned for having some of the best snorkeling and diving on the coast. **Scooter-Roo Tours,** offers a 3hr., 60km motorbike ride with striking views of wild kangaroos and wallabies that is a fabulous way to see some of the area and learn how to ride a motorbike. The tour stops at the Saltwater Cafe to take in a spectacular view of the sunset and offers a chance to try some potato wedges and chili sauce. (☎07 4974 7697; www.scooterrootours.com. $45. Book through your hostel.) **Spirit of 1770 Great Barrier Reef Cruises,** in Endeavor Plaza, will take you to pristine and heavenly Lady Musgrave Island. (☎1800 631 770; www.spiritof1770.com.au. Operates a glass-bottom boat; snorkel gear included. $160, concessions $150, children $80. MC/V.) **Liquid Adventures** has two extremely popular guided sea-kayak tours. The 3½hr. kayak adventure explores local waterways where you can try your skills at kayak surfing. The 2½hr. sunset kayak includes a relaxing paddle, the opportunity to swim in the waterways, and a phenomenal sunset chased with a glass of wine. (☎04 2895 6630. 3½hr. tour $40, includes lunch. Sunset kayak $30. Book through your hostel.) **Dive 1770** benefits from the luxury of year-round warm water, and it is far less crowded (and cheaper) than Airlie Beach and Cairns. (☎07 4974 9359; www.dive1770.com. 4-day open-water PADI course $250; required medical check-up $60. Courses W, Sa, and by demand.)

# CAPRICORN COAST

Straddling the Tropic of Capricorn and squished between temperate and coastal zones, the Capricorn Coast is said to have 70% of all flora and fauna found on this massive continent. Sleepy seaside towns and secluded islands beckon travelers to the place known to "capture the true essence of Australia."

# ROCKHAMPTON                                              ☎ 07

The beef capital of Australia counters the backpacker routine of burgers, club beats, and beaches with outstanding steaks, country music, and rodeos. For the most part, Rockhampton (pop. 74,500) is a quiet town, and a pleasant place to take a short break from the fast-paced East Coast trek. Most travelers en route to Great Keppel Island stay in "Rocky" for at least a day.

QUEENSLAND

## ▛ TRANSPORTATION

**Trains: Train Station,** 320 Murray St. (☎07 4932 0453), at the end of the road. From the Central Business District (CBD), head away from the river on any street, then turn left on Murray St. Day lockers available $4-6. Queensland Rail (☎13 22 32; www.traveltrain.com.au) goes north and south along the coast, including stops at: **Brisbane** (8hr., $104.50); **Cairns** (16-19hr., $164); **Mackay** (4-5hr., $64); **Maryborough** (4hr., $70.40) with bus connection to **Hervey Bay** (45min., $10); **Proserpine** (6-8hr., $83.60) with bus connection to **Airlie Beach** (25min., $10); **Townsville** (9-12hr., $123.20). Northbound, expensive but fast Tilt Trains depart Tu and Sa 3:23am. The cheap but slow Sunlander departs Th 11:35pm and Sa-Su 8:25pm. Southbound trains depart daily 7:25am. ISIC 50% discount. Spirit of the Outback also leaves W 4:35am and Sa 11:20pm for: **Barcaldine** (11hr., $97); **Emerald** (5hr., $57.20); **Longreach** (13hr., $114.40). ISIC discount 50%; backpackers 10%.

**Buses:** Greyhound Australia (☎13 14 99) and Premier (☎13 34 10) depart from the Mobil station at 91 George St., between Fitzroy and Archer St. Greyhound has 3-4 services per day and Premier has 1 northbound (3:05am), and 1 southbound (12:15am). Both go to: **Airlie Beach** (6hr.; Greyhound $80, Premier $56); **Brisbane** (11-13hr., $111/88); **Bundaberg** (3-4hr., $61/38); **Cairns** (16-17hr., $174/137); **Hervey Bay** (5-6hr., $78/49); **Mackay** (4hr., $59/39); **Noosa** (9-10hr., $97/71).

**Public Transportation:** The blue Sunbus (☎07 4936 2133; www.sunbus.com.au) leaves from Kern Arcade, on Bolsover St. between Denham and William St., and covers most corners of the city. Runs M-F 6:30am-6pm, Sa 8:30am-noon. Route maps posted at most stops and available at tourist office. Fares $0.75-3.

**Taxis:** Rocky Cabs (24hr. ☎07 4924 9535), corner of the Denham and East St. mall.

**Car Rental: Europcar,** 106 George St. (☎07 4922 0044; www.europcar.com.au). Cars with unlimited mileage from $45. Under 25 surcharge $15 per day. Open M-F 8am-5pm. Additional location with longer hours at the airport. AmEx/D/MC/V. **Thrifty,** 43 Fitzroy St. (☎07 4927 8755; www.thrifty.com.au). Cars with 200km limit from $55. Under 25 surcharge $15 per day. Ages 21 and up. Open daily 7am-6pm. AmEx/D/MC/V.

## ▟ ▛ ORIENTATION AND PRACTICAL INFORMATION

The **Fitzroy River,** the second largest river in Australia, is the city's defining landmark. On its south side, the city has a flawless grid design, with most of the action near the river's edge along **Quay Street.**

**Tourist Office: Rockhampton Tourist Information,** 208 Quay St. (☎07 4922 5339; www.rockhamptoninfo.com). Open M-F 8:30am-4:30pm, Sa-Su 9am-4pm.

**Currency Exchange: Banks** and 24hr. **ATMs** line the East St. pedestrian mall. Most open M-Th 9:30am-4pm, F 9:30am-5pm. Free cash exchange at **Harvey World Travel,** on Denham and Bolsover St. (☎07 4922 6111. Open M-F 8:30am-5pm, Sa 9am-noon.)

**Backpacking and Camping Equipment: Campco's** (☎07 4922 2366; www.campco.com.au), on the corner of William and Kent St. AmEx/MC/V.

**Pharmacy: C.Q. Day and Night Chemist** (☎07 4922 1621), on the corner of Denham and Alma St. Open M-Sa 8am-9pm, Su 9am-9pm.

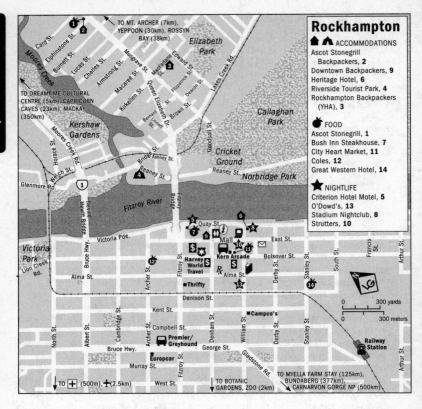

**Rockhampton**

🏠 ▲ ACCOMMODATIONS

Ascot Stonegrill
  Backpackers, **2**
Downtown Backpackers, **9**
Heritage Hotel, **6**
Riverside Tourist Park, **4**
Rockhampton Backpackers
  (YHA), **3**

🍴 FOOD

Ascot Stonegrill, **1**
Bush Inn Steakhouse, **7**
City Heart Market, **11**
Coles, **12**
Great Western Hotel, **14**

⭐ NIGHTLIFE

Criterion Hotel Motel, **5**
O'Dowd's, **13**
Stadium Nightclub, **8**
Strutters, **10**

**Internet Access:** Connect at **Cyberoz,** 12 William St. (☎07 4927 3633), for $5 per hr. Open M-F 9am-5:30pm, Su 10am-1pm. The **library,** 69 William St. (☎07 4936 8265), offers free access on 2 computers. Book ahead or prepare to wait. Open M-Tu and F 9:15am-5:30pm, W 1-8pm, Th 9:15am-8pm, Sa 9:15am-4:30pm.

**Post Office:** 150 East St. (☎13 13 18), located between William and Derby St. Open M-F 8:30am-5:30pm. **Postal Code:** 4700.

## 🏠 📷 ACCOMMODATIONS AND CAMPING

**Ascot Stonegrill Backpackers,** 117 Musgrave St. (☎07 4922 4719) atop Stonegrill. A cozy TV area, candy bowls, well-loved furniture, and pastels make you feel like you're spending a weekend at Grandma's, only with less cheek-pinching and more freedom. Friendly owners will do anything to see that you are happy, and guests have only positive comments. The restaurant downstairs has the best steaks in Rocky. Laundry, kitchen, and courtesy van to bus and train stations. Reception open 6am-10pm. 3- to 6-bed dorms $25; doubles $50. YHA/VIP discount. AmEx/D/MC/V. ❷

**Heritage Hotel** (☎07 4927 6996), on the corner of William and Quay St. This hotel offers terrific budget accommodations. The downstairs restaurant was recently redone, and the 3rd-floor backpacker area will soon undergo renovation. All rooms have A/C,

TV, and fridge. Key deposit $20. Shared bathroom. Check-out 11am. 4-bed dorms $20; singles $45; river-view doubles $60. Weekly rates available. AmEx/D/MC/V. ❷

**Downtown Backpackers,** (☎07 4922 1837; www.downtownbackpackers.com.au) on the corner of East and Denham St., above the Oxford Hotel. While it doesn't feel like a hostel, its location, small dorms, and price are difficult to beat. Light sleepers might be bothered by music from the bar downstairs. Kitchen, laundry, and Internet access. Reception is at the bar or at the Sidewalk Cafe next door; open M-Tu 8:30am-8pm, W-Th 8:30am-10pm, F-Sa 8:30am-midnight, Su 9:30am-7pm. Will leave keys at bus station for late arrivals. Check-out 10am. 2- and 4-bed dorms $20. AmEx/D/MC/V. ❷

**Rockhampton Backpackers (YHA),** 60 MacFarlane St. (☎1800 617 194). Clean, spacious hostel with A/C in most rooms. Kitchen, TV room, pool, laundry, and Internet. Pickup and dropoff at bus or train station. Reception 7am-9:30pm. Dorms $22; doubles $50; ensuite cabins for 2 $56. Backpacker and student discounts. MC/V. ❷

**Riverside Tourist Park,** 2 Reaney St. (☎07 4922 3779; www.islandcabins.com.au/rockhampton), along the Fitzroy River, right off the highway. Offers caravan and tent sites and well-maintained cabins. Very family-friendly. Pool, playground, Wi-Fi, BBQ, and laundry facilities. Reception M-Sa 7am-7pm, Su 8am-7pm. Sites for 2 $21, powered $28, extra person $7; on-site vans $50; cabins for 2 $60-80, extra person $10. MC/V. ❷

## FOOD

Unless you're a strict vegetarian, you can't leave Rocky without trying a steak. Buy your own at **Coles** supermarket, City Centre Plaza, at Archer and Bolsover St. (open M-F 8am-9pm, Sa 8am-5pm), and cook it on a riverside BBQ. The **City Heart Market,** in the Kern Arcade carpark on Bolsover St., has everything from crafts to fruits and vegetables. (☎07 4927 1199. Open Su 7:30am-12:30pm.)

**Ascot Stonegrill,** 117 Musgrave St. (☎07 4922 4719; www.stonegrill.com), at the Ascot Hotel. Amazingly tender, raw meat is brought out on hot slabs of stone, allowing you to cook it to personal perfection. The beef is so good, in fact, that it has transformed long-time vegetarians into devoted fans. Try the porterhouse steak with vegetables and excellent dipping sauces, or be more adventurous with kangaroo and crocodile ($26). Open daily noon-2:30pm and 5:30-8:30pm. AmEx/MC/V. ❹

**Great Western Hotel,** 39 Stanley St. (☎07 4922 2185; www.greatwesternhotel.com.au). A true display of outback pride, this restaurant offers delicious rump steaks ($19.50-29) in a superb atmosphere. F night practice bull-riding and monthly rodeos can attract up to 2000 people and should definitely not be missed. Entrance fees to bull-riding shows $15, students and concession $10. Open M-Sa 10am-latenight, Su 11am-late. Food served daily noon-2pm and 6-8pm. MC/V. ❸

**Bush Inn Steakhouse,** 150 Quay St. (☎07 4922 1225), in The Criterion Hotel. A local favorite for its excellent steaks. Main courses $15-27. Food served daily noon-2pm and 6-9pm. Book ahead on weekends. AmEx/D/MC/V. ❸

## SIGHTS AND ACTIVITIES

**CAVES.** The limestone **Capricorn Caves** offer natural acoustics and a light spectacle during the summer solstice (from early Dec. to mid-Jan. on the 11am tour). The 1hr. wheelchair-accessible **Cathedral Tour** covers highlights of the cave system The caverns also hosts the popular **Wild Caving Adventure Tours:** 2hr. of rock climbing, including sardine-style squeezes through tiny tunnels. *(23km north of Rockhampton. ☎07 4934 2883; www.capricorncaves.com.au. Book at least 24hr. in advance. Open daily 8:30am-6pm; tours 9am-4pm. Admission and 1hr. tour $18, children $9 Transport from Rockhampton M, W, F $40/20; adventure tour $60. Backpacker discount 10%. AmEx/MC/V.)*

**CARNARVON GORGE NATIONAL PARK.** This rugged national park encompasses Aboriginal rock art sites, deep pools, and soaring sandstone cliffs. The gorges, however, are the main attraction. The park **campsites** are only available during school holidays. Cool temperatures make March through November the best time to visit, but know that night temperatures fall below freezing. *(500km southwest of Rockhampton and Gladstone on Bruce Hwy. For more info, pick up a map in the tourist office or contact the ranger ☎ 07 4984 4505.)* **Takarakka Bush Resort ❷**, 4km from the park, has sites and cabins. *(☎ 07 4984 4535; www.takarakka.com.au. Linen $10. Sites $32 high season, $28 low season; powered $32/35; cabins from $90, extra person $15.)*

**DREAMTIME CULTURAL CENTRE.** The center provides an elegant and informative portrayal of the indigenous peoples of Central Queensland and the Torres Strait Islands, said to be among the oldest living cultures in the world. Take the guided tour and learn the arts of didjeridu-playing and boomerang-throwing. *(5min. north of Rockhampton by car, on the corner of Yeppoon Rd. and the Bruce Hwy. Sunbus #10 runs from the arcade carpark daily every hr. 8:35am-5:35pm; $3. ☎ 07 4936 1655; www. dreamtimecentre.com.au. Open M-F 10am-3:30pm. 1-1½hr. tours are best for seeing the center; tours 10:30am. $13.50, concessions $11, children $6.50. AmEx/MC/V.)*

**BOTANIC GARDENS AND ZOO.** The zoo has an enormous walk-through avian dome, chimpanzees, and of course, koalas, 'roos, and crocs (though the latter two might elicit some guilt if you ordered them for dinner last night at the Ascot Stonegrill). Tours of the garden can be arranged upon request. *(15min. ride from the city on Sunbus #4A; departs from the Kern Arcade carpark M-F 15min. past the hr. 7:15am-5:15pm, Sa 8:15-11:15am; one-way $2.05. ☎ 07 4922 1654. Feedings 3-3:15pm. Zoo open daily 8am-4:30pm; gardens open daily 6am-6pm. Both free.)* If you don't like the formality of botanic gardens, the **Kershaw Gardens,** stretching 1km along the Bruce Hwy. between Dowling and High St., recreate an Australian bush environment. *(☎ 07 4922 1654. Open daily 7am-6pm. Tours can be arranged upon request.)*

## 🅟 🎵 NIGHTLIFE AND ENTERTAINMENT

For a pint of Guinness ($7), live rock music on the weekends, and excellent $10 meals, hit **O'Dowd's,** 100 Williams St. (☎ 07 4927 0344. Open M-F 8am-2am, Sa 10am-2am, Su 10am-midnight. Restaurant open M-F 8am-3pm and 5pm-9pm, Sa-Su 10am-late.) If you want a more traditional nightclub, **Stadium Nightclub,** 228 Quay St. next to the Heritage Hotel, is the best in town. On the weekend, head upstairs to the glass bar to watch the heads bobbing down below. (☎ 07 4927 9988. Cover F-Sa after 11pm $7. Open W-Sa 8pm-5am; glass bar F-Sa 10pm-4am.) **Strutters,** on the corner of East St. and William St., hosts regular modeling contests and local concerts. (☎ 07 4922 2882. Cover W and F-Sa $7. Open W-Th 8pm-3am, F-Sa 8pm-5am.) **The Criterion Hotel Motel,** 150 Quay St., has a few bars. (☎ 07 4922 1225. Open daily 11am-3am.)

# GREAT KEPPEL ISLAND ☎ 07

Great Keppel Island was once the island party capital of Queensland, tempting tourists with the promise, "Come to Great Keppel and get wrecked." After the island's resort closed, almost 90% of the island's population disappeared, and much of the mainland is under the impression that the island has, for all intents and purposes, completely shut down. While this has made it difficult for those businesses still relying on tourists for income, it has actually made the island much more enjoyable for those who want to take advantage the outdoor activities that abound. The island boasts 17 beaches, clear waters, and fabulous snorkeling on the fringing reef right off shore.

**TRANSPORTATION.** From Rockhampton, it only takes a **bus transfer** (50min.) and a **ferry ride** (30min.) to reach the island. Check with your accommodations to see if they can arrange these for you: otherwise, call the companies directly. Young's Bus Service (Route #20) runs to the ferry from Kern Arcade, on Bolsover St., Rockhampton. (☎07 4922 3813; www.youngsbusservice.com.au. M-F 13 per day, Sa 6 per day, Su 5 per day. $8.10.) Rothery's Coaches will pick up and drop off at your Rocky accommodation. (☎07 4922 4320. Round-trip $16.50, children $8.25. Pay the driver; cash only.)

**Freedom Fast Cats** leaves from Keppel Bay Marina, Rosslyn Bay. (☎1800 336 244; www.keppelbaymarina.com.au. Tu 10:30am, return 2pm. W-Th and Sa-Su 9:15am, return 3:45pm. F transfers only, departs 9:15am and 3pm. Round-trip $45, students $37, children $25. AmEx/D/MC/V.) They also run fabulous day cruises that explore the bay through snorkeling, boomnet rides, and a glass-bottom boat tour of the reefs ($130/110/85). The fun, energetic crew makes the tour even more enjoyable. Those driving from Rocky should follow the signs to Yeppoon. From Yeppoon, follow signs for the Rosslyn Bay Marina. Free parking is available at the ferry terminal. There's also the **Great Keppel Island Security Carpark** on the Scenic Hwy., just before the turnoff to Rosslyn Bay; it has a secure lot and courtesy bus to the marina. (☎07 4933 6670. $8 per day, covered $10). The ferry lets passengers out on Fisherman's Beach, the island's main stretch of sand. Parallel to the beach is the red-tinted **Yellow Brick Road,** which leads to the island's few shops.

**ACCOMMODATIONS.** Packages that include bus and ferry transfers and rooms on the mainland don't save you much money, but they will spare you the hassle of arranging everything yourself. Camping is not allowed on Great Keppel but is available on the nearby Keppel Island Group. The **Great Keppel Island Holiday Village ❸** is friendly and relaxed, with one six-bed dorm, several powered tents, and more expensive cabins. Free snorkel gear is available for all guests. The managers run 3hr. sea-kayak adventures ($40) and canoe trips ($25) with snorkeling options. (☎1800 180 235; www.gkiholidayvillage.com.au. Kitchen, BBQ, and laundry. Reception and mini-grocery store 9am-1pm and 3:30-5pm. 11am check-out. Dorms $33; tents with hard floors and reed beds $76; cabins for 2 with shower $120. Extra person $20. Book ahead. MC/V.)

**FOOD.** Food on the island is expensive, so stock up prior to departure at **FoodWorks,** 18 James St., Yeppoon. (☎07 4939 2200. Open daily 6am-9pm.) Once on Great Keppel, all commerce is oriented around the **Yellow Brick Road. Island Pizza ❸** serves tasty but pricey pizzas from $17. (☎07 4939 4699. Check blackboard outside for hours. MC/V.) The nearby **Rainbow Hut ❷** has breakfast, lunch, and snacks in addition to a retail shop. (☎07 4939 5596. Open Tu-Su 9:30am-4pm. MC/V.) The adorable **Shell Shop ❷** has a huge collection of shells on display and for sale. You can also get sandwiches, morning tea, and ice cream. (☎07 4939 1004. Open Th-Su 9am-4pm. Cash only.)

**ACTIVITIES.** Keppel's calm beaches are perfect for swimming and snorkeling. **Shelving Beach** has easily accessible snorkeling. **Monkey Beach,** 20min. farther, also has great snorkeling opportunities. **Clam Bay,** on the island's south side, has the most vibrant coral and is reachable via the **Homestead Path** (3hr. round-trip). **Long Beach,** a 40min. walk past the airstrip, is splendidly isolated (3.6km round-trip). The hiking on the island is spectacular, but signs are sparse, so go with a friend and bring a map. Walks begin on the main track, which leaves from the water sports hut at the ferry dropoff. The uphill hike to ▓**Mount Wyndham** offers spectacular views of the heavily forested island (2hr., 7km round-trip). Other walks go to the Homestead (1hr., 5.6km round-trip) and across the entire island to the lighthouse (4hr., 15.4km round-trip).

The **Keppel Island Dive Centre,** on Putney Beach, offers dive and snorkel trips. (☎07 4939 5022; www.keppeldive.com. Introductory dive $120; certified dive $75, with tank and weight belt, $55. Snorkeling $38. Snorkel gear or wetsuit hire $15 per day.) The catamaran **Grace** runs a day-long cruise with lunch, tea, and snorkeling and fishing opportunities. (☎07 4933 6244; www.keppelbaymarina.com.au. Cruises run Tu and F-Su. $115, children $75. Book ahead. MC/V.)

## KEPPEL GROUP

The isolated islands in the Keppel Group are open for independent exploration, but getting there is difficult. Coconut-covered **Pumpkin Island ❷,** 16km from Yeppon's coastline, has coral and white-sand beaches. There are tents and five cabins available for rent; each cabin holds up to six people. Bring your own food and drink. (☎07 4939 4413; www.pumpkinisland.com.au. Toilets, showers, BBQ, and drinking water. Linen $10. Unpowered tent sites $20; cabins from $240.) The island's **Pumpkin Xpress** takes you to the island for $45 per person. To reach surrounding islands, take a pricey **water taxi** (☎07 4933 6133). **Humpy Island, Middle Island,** and **North Keppel** offer **camping ❶;** permits are available at the QPWS in Rosslyn Bay, adjacent to the Tourist Services office.

# WHITSUNDAY COAST

Stretching from Mackay to the small town of Bowen, the coast's moniker aptly highlights its greatest assets: the **Whitsunday Islands** (p. 399). This archipelago, accessible from Airlie Beach, draws a crowd but still offers ample opportunities to enjoy the solitude that is characteristic of northern Queensland. The sun, sand, diving, and tropical waters are a must for anyone exploring the region.

# MACKAY                                                   ☎07

Rising from a sea of sugar cane, the town of Mackay (mick-EYE; pop. 92,000) is a convenient gateway to Queensland's inland rainforests or a last stop before sailing off to the region's isolated islands. In this small, quiet city, eclipsed on the backpacker circuit by nearby Airlie Beach, most shops and services close just after dusk. Numerous outdoor attractions—hiking, swimming, and an abundance of wildlife are just a few—are within an hour's drive at **Eungella National Park** (p. 393). During the day, the town empties out as locals head to the booming coal mines. As a result, backpackers flock to Mackay to fill the well-paying jobs that open up throughout the town.

## ▆ TRANSPORTATION

**Trains:** The **train station** (☎07 4952 7418) is about 5km south of town on Connors Rd. There is no public transport from the station, but **Mackay Transit Coaches** is a 10min. walk and runs throughout town (under $5). **Taxis** to the station cost around $12. Purchase tickets at the station (open M-F 9am-4:30pm) or in town. Trains run less frequently and take longer than buses. Lockers available for $4-6.

**Buses:** Prices may vary depending on season and weather conditions. **Mackay Bus Terminal** (☎07 4944 2144) is on the corner of Macalister and Victoria St. **Greyhound Australia** (www.greyhound.com.au) is the most frequent bus service and runs to: **Airlie Beach** (2hr., 2-6 per day, $32); **Brisbane** (15-17hr., 1-7 per day, $161); **Bundaberg** (10-11hr., 1-3 per day, $112); **Cairns** (10-12hr., 1-7 per day, $136); **Hervey Bay**

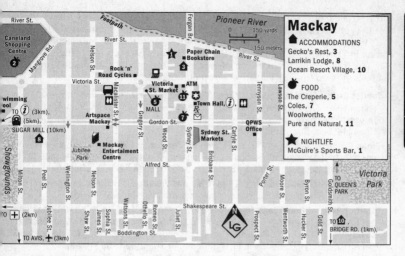

**Mackay**

▲ **ACCOMMODATIONS**
Gecko's Rest, **3**
Larrikin Lodge, **8**
Ocean Resort Village, **10**

◆ **FOOD**
The Creperie, **5**
Coles, **7**
Woolworths, **2**
Pure and Natural, **11**

★ **NIGHTLIFE**
McGuire's Sports Bar, **1**

(12-13hr., 1-6 per day, $125); **Maroochydore** via **Noosa** (12-15hr., 1-3 per day, $152); **Rockhampton** (4-5½hr., 1-7 per day, $59). **Premier Motor Service** is a cheaper option but runs less frequently, usually once a day to major destinations (☎13 34 10; www.premierms.com.au). **Ticket office** open M-F 7am-6pm, Sa 7am-2pm; ask about student discounts. The local bus service, **Mackay Transit Coaches** (☎07 4957 3330; www.mackaytransit.com.au) run throughout town and to the surrounding areas starting at Caneland Shopping Center. Schedules are available at the visitors center and in hostels; alternatively, call Mackay Transit Coaches for timetables.

---

**TIP**

**BOOK ONLINE.** Save money by booking buses online, as many travel agents charge as much as a 30% commission.

---

**Taxis: Mackay Taxi** (☎13 10 08). Available 24hr.

**Car Rental:** Rental companies are spread throughout the city. Many are located at the airport, but getting there can be a hassle (taxis are generally around $12-15; ask the visitors center or your accommodation for directions to the closest agency. **Europcar,** 174 Boundary Rd. (☎1300 131 390) offers cars from $59 per day with courtesy pickup. **Avis** (☎07 4951 1266 or 13 63 33) is located at the airport and has a high age surcharge ($27.50 per day). **Thrifty** (☎07 4942 8755 or 1800 818 050), at the corner of Bruce Hwy. and Sands Rd., has the lowest under-25 age surcharge around ($16.50 per day). Cars from $50 per day, 4WD $100 per day. Also offers courtesy pickup.

**Bike Rental: Rock 'n' Road Cycles,** 164 Victoria St. (☎07 4957 4484; www.rocknroad.com.au). As cheap as $10 per day or $50 per week for standard bikes. $100 security deposit required. Prices include helmet and lock.

## ✈📍 ORIENTATION AND PRACTICAL INFORMATION

Mackay's Central Business District (CBD) runs along on the southern bank of the Pioneer River. **River Street** hugs the waterfront, and the town's main drag, **Victoria Street,** runs parallel to it one block away. Nightspots and restaurants line **Sydney Street** and **Wood Street,** which run perpendicular to Victoria St. The **Bruce Highway** comes into the west side of town and exits to **Gordon Street,** the third street from the river, parallel to Victoria St. As the Bruce Hwy. curves south, it changes to **Nebo Road** and hits the town's major accommodations and the tourist office. The rest of the city is geared toward those with vehicles. The **marina** is 7km from the CBD (north along Sydney St. past the bridge over the Pioneer River), and there are **beaches** spread throughout the region—the closest is 4km from the CBD at the eastern end of Gordon St.

**Tourist Office: Mackay Tourism Office,** 320 Nebo Rd. (☎07 4944 5888); www.mackay-region.com), 3km southwest of the CBD. Open M-F 9am-5pm, Sa-Su 9am-4pm. A small **information booth** (☎07 4951 4803) is located in the Old Town Hall on Sydney St. Open M-F 9am-5pm, Sa 9am-noon.

**Parks Office: Queensland Parks and Wildlife Service** (☎07 4944 7800; www.epa.qld. gov.au), at Tennyson and Gordon St. National park info and camping permits for the Cumberland Islands (permits $4.85 per person). Open M-F 8:30am-5pm.

**Currency Exchange: Banks** and **24hr. ATMs** line Victoria St. between Gregory and Brisbane St. All offer traveler's check and currency exchange for a $5-11 fee.

**Internet Access: Hong Kong Importers,** 128 Victoria St. (☎07 4953 3188), has Internet for $5 per hr and Wi-Fi ($10 for 24hr). Open M-F 9am-5pm, Sa-Su 9am-noon. The **library** (☎07 4957 1787), behind the Civic Centre on Gordon St., has Internet for $6 per hr. Open M, W, F 9am-5pm, Tu 10am-6pm, Th 10am-8pm, Sa 9am-3pm.

**Market: Victoria Street Markets** feature arts and crafts. Open Su 8:30am-12:30pm.

**Police:** 57-59 Sydney St. (☎07 4968 3444), between Victoria and Gordon St.

**Post Office:** 69 Sydney St. (☎13 13 18). Open M-F 8am-5:30pm. **Postal Code:** 4740.

# ACCOMMODATIONS

Because Mackay is not a popular tourist destination, hostels are scarce. Budget motels line the streets of the CBD and are also found along Nebo Rd. Additionally, several caravan parks lie on the outskirts of town.

**Gecko's Rest,** 34 Sydney St. (☎07 4944 1230; www.geckosrest.com.au). Smack dab in the middle of the CBD, this well-maintained hostel offers a comfortable night's rest in spacious 4-bed dorms. Laundry facilities and A/C. Internet access $5 per hr. Key deposit $20. Reception 8am-9pm. Dorms $22; singles with fridge $35; twins and doubles $50. VIP discounts. AmEx/MC/V. ❷

**Larrikin Lodge,** 32 Peel St. (☎07 4951 3728 or 1800 611 953), a 10min. walk from the CBD. This small 31-bed hostel has a friendly atmosphere, comfortable mattresses, and thick pillows. The affable owners offer day tours to Eungella ($81 for guests) and will outfit you with complete camping gear. Laundry facilities. Internet access $4 per hr. Bike hire $8 per day or free with 2-night stay. Reception 7am-8:30pm. 3-, 5-, 7-, and 8-bed dorms available from $21; 1 double $50; twins $48. MC/V. ❷

**Ocean Resort Village,** 5 Bridge Rd. (☎07 4951 3200 or 1800 075 144). A 4km walk south of the CBD, Ocean Resort Village offers charming, self-contained cottages only seconds from the beach. Pool, BBQ, tennis court. Reception M-F 8am-5pm, Sa-Su 8am-1pm. Studios $93; family-rooms $103; 2-bed $135. Book 2-3 weeks ahead. ❺

# FOOD AND NIGHTLIFE

Travelers who are averse to name-brand grub and pub food will scoff at most Mackay menus. There are a few quality venues scattered throughout town, however. There is a **Woolworths** supermarket in the Caneland Shopping Centre, located inland on Victoria St. (☎07 4951 2288. Open M-F 8am-9pm, Sa 8am-5pm.) **Coles** supermarket is at the corner of Sydney and Gordon St. (Open M-F

8am-9pm, Sa 8am-5pm.) At night, local miners and backpackers hit the clubs hard. Most night spots run along or just off of Victoria St.

**Pure and Natural Mackay** (☎07 4957 6136), on Sydney St. across from the police station. Earns both parts of its name with its tasty low-fat and vegetarian options for breakfast and lunch. Try a baguette sandwich ($6.80), a fruit smoothie ($5.60), or the low-fat banana cake ($4). Open M-F 7:30am-3:30pm, Sa 8am-1pm. ❶

**The Creperie** (☎07 4951 1226), at the corner of Gregory and Victoria St. Serves up delightful French dishes in meal and snack sizes. Meat and vegetarian meal crepes ($13-16.30) come with salad, while dessert crepes ($7-9) are plump with fruits, liqueurs, and other sweets. Open M-F 11am-2pm, Tu-Sa 6pm-late, Su 6-9pm. ❷

**McGuire's Sports Bar**, 17 Wood St. (☎07 4957 7464). Attracts a young crowd, cheap jugs of Toohey's Extra Dry ($8) in hand. Live entertainment W-Su; usually no cover. Locals and backpackers shoot pool and watch football on the big-screen TVs. Cheap, tasty menu includes crumbed steak ($7) and rib fillet steak sanga ($8). Open M-W 9am-1am, Th-Sa 9am-2am, Su 10am-midnight. ❶

# ◉ SIGHTS

While most of Mackay's draw can be attributed to its surroundings, the town does offer a few interesting sights. Pick up the tourist center's free guide, **A Heritage Walk in Mackay,** which will direct you to historical and cultural attractions. Don't miss **Queen's Park,** on Goldsmith St. just north of Victoria Park, where the lovely **Orchid Gardens** overflow with flowers. The **Mackay Entertainment Centre,** next door to the library on Gordon St., is your one-stop destination for drama, comedy, and concerts. (☎07 4957 1777 or 1800 646 574. Open M-F 9am-5pm, Sa 10am-1pm; also 90min. before shows.) The centre also hosts the **Mackay Festival of Arts** (www.festivalmackay.org.au) in mid-July, a week-long celebration with concerts, fashion parades, food fairs, and comedy shows. Next to the Centre, **Artspace Mackay** displays traveling exhibitions by famous artists for free. (☎07 4961 9722. Open Tu-Su 10am-5pm.) Outside of town, **Reef Forest Tours** offers 2hr. tours of **Farleigh Sugar Mill** during the sugar-crushing season (June-Dec.). There is no public transport available. By car, take the Bruce Hwy. 9km north toward Proserpine, then turn right at Childlow St. (☎07 4959 8360). Tours daily 9am and 1pm. $22, children $12, families $59.) At sunset, in front of the boardwalk along the Pioneer River on River St., hundreds of starlings suddenly fly together over the golden water back and forth under the bridge.

# EUNGELLA NATIONAL PARK

Eighty kilometers west of Mackay on Pioneer Valley Rd. is the 52,000 hectare Eungella National Park, a range of drastic rainforest-covered slopes and deep misty valleys. At Eungella, the "land where clouds lie low over the mountains," 10 walking trails lead to spectacular hilltop and creekside views. Red cedars, palms, and giant ferns coat the slopes; platypuses are common in waterways.

**Walking tracks** are in two sections of the park: the **Finch Hatton Gorge area** and **Eungella/Broken River.** Trail maps are available at the **QPWS office** in Mackay or the **ranger station** at Broken River (☎07 4958 4552). Although no public transportation runs to Eungella, the park is easily reached via car and is only a 1hr. drive from Mackay. Ambitious day hikers can walk from the township to Broken River and beyond by stringing smaller hikes together; however, be prepared to hike the same trails back as there are no long circuit hikes. Behind the **Eungella Chalet** (p. 394), the **Pine Grove Circuit** (1.5km, 20-30min.) forks at 800m into the excellent **Cedar Grove Track** (2km, 40-60min.), which winds past stately red cedars to a roadside picnic area and lookout track. Two hundred meters down the road from the picnic area is the **Palm Grove trailhead** (1.5km, 30-45min.), which gives you the option of continuing on to Broken River via **Clarke Range Track** (5.5km, 2-3hr.). Five kilometers on Eungella Rd. from the Chalet, you'll cross **Broken River,** with an excellent platypus-viewing platform (see **Atherton Tablelands,** p. 429), picnic area, campground with toilets and hot showers ($4.50), and ranger station. (☎07 4958 4552. Open M-F 8:30am-5pm.) Several trails lead from Broken River, including the **Credition Creek Trail** (8.5km one-way), which follows the river's course, meandering in and out of the forest before reaching granite cascades and a scenic pool. For advanced hikers, intrepid intermediates, and beginners with a death wish, there's the popular, albeit daunting, **Mackay Highlands Great Walk** (56km). This three- to five-day expedition runs through deep ravines, thick and lush rainforest, vertical escarpments and remote farming villages. Rangers recommend this route be traversed between April and September only, when extreme climates are unlikely. They stress the importance of proceeding north to south to avoid steep dropoffs. Be sure to arrange a vehicle pickup from the southern end of the Great Walk. For directions to the pickup point, contact QPWS. **Camping permits** for Fern Flat, Credition Hall, Denham Range, and Moonlight Dam are required.

**FINCH HATTON GORGE.** After the Pinnacle Hotel is a well-marked turnoff to beautiful Finch Hatton Gorge (10km from Pioneer Valley Rd.). Nestled in a canyon where waterfalls meet undisturbed rainforest, this section of the park sees few visitors. Contact the **Finch Hatton Gorge Ranger** (☎07 4958 4552) or check with locals for the latest area road conditions, as the narrow track dips through several creeks that are sometimes too deep to cross after heavy rains.

On the dirt road to Finch Hatton Gorge is the rustic **Platypus Bush Camp ❶**, where open-air huts, abundant wildlife, and the adjacent creek (ideal for an afternoon dip) make for an authentic Aussie experience that you won't find at cookie-cutter resorts. There's also an outdoor kitchen, creek-side hot tubs forged from river rocks, and a snug enclosure surrounding a woodburning stove—the perfect venue for camp songs and traveler's tales. If you are weary of sleeping outdoors, crash in the old touring bus that has been converted into sleeping quarters. (☎07 4958 3204; www.bushcamp.net. Campsites $10 per person; dorms $35; twins/doubles $100.) Just past the bush camp, the **Finch Hatton Gorge Cabins ❺** have two small 4-bed dorms and two ensuite luxury cabins. Hot showers and a kitchen are also available. Just honk your horn for reception. (☎07 4958 3281. Self-contained double cabins $95.)

Finch Hatton's one **hiking track** leaves from the picnic area at the end of the Gorge Rd. The trail to **Wheel of Fire Cascades** (4.2km, 1hr.) follows rapids as they cascade down the rocky riverbed; the last kilometer is a steep stair-climb. To see the rainforest from above, book a trip with **Forest Flying**, which sends its customers whizzing through the canopy on treetop zip lines. (☎07 4958 3359; www.forestflying.com. Pickup from Gorge cabins or Kiosk. 2-3hr. depending on group size. Bookings required. $45, children $30.)

**EUNGELLA.** Twenty kilometers past the turnoff for Finch Hatton Gorge on Pioneer Valley Rd. is the Eungella township. The road is steep and curvy, climbing 800m in just 3km. At the top of the hill is the historic **Eungella Chalet ❸**. Overlooking the vast Pioneer Valley, this mountaintop resort has a large restaurant, swimming pool, extensive gardens, and a soaring view of the valley below. (Guesthouse singles $38; doubles $50, ensuite $85; 1-bed cabins $98. MC/V.) The Chalet's skytop restaurant, **Top of the Range ❸**, serves seafood, steak, and vegetarian dinners ($18.50-29.50) in heaping helpings. (☎07 4958 4509. MC/V.) Just past the Chalet on the right is **Suzanna's Hideaway Cafe ❶**, where friendly, German-born owner Suzanna invites guests to sit on her porch

QUEENSLAND

and enjoy fresh-baked treats from her oven. Famous for her apple strudel ($6) and coffee, she also cooks more filling meals, like frankfurters with sauerkraut ($14) and vegetarian options. She also found time between baking and conversation to construct a very curious jewel and rock garden in her backyard. (☎07 4958 4533. Open daily 9am-4pm.)

# AIRLIE BEACH ☎07

Airlie serves those seeking a gateway to the Whitsundays or a ticket to non-stop partying. This seaside port was nothing but mudflats until nearby Bowen decided it didn't want a manmade beach. The enterprising developer who'd suggested the project then turned his attention to Airlie. With truckloads of Bowen sand, he put the "Beach" into Airlie. Today, nonstop nightlife and the stunning beauty of the nearby Whitsunday Islands and Great Barrier Reef have made this village the biggest backpacker draw between Brisbane and Cairns.

## ▐ TRANSPORTATION

**Trains:** The **rail station** is in Proserpine, 25km outside the city. **Whitsunday Transit** (24hr. ☎07 4946 1800) picks up arriving train passengers and runs down Shute Harbour Rd., stopping in the center of Airlie and at some accommodations ($30); timetables available all over town. Book at least 24hr. ahead.

**Buses:** Travel offices and hostel desks book transport. Prices can vary depending on the season and weather conditions; the following are approximations. **Greyhound Australia** (☎13 14 99; www.greyhound.com.au) drops off at the end of the Esplanade; accommodations offer courtesy pickup, but most hostels are within walking distance. ISIC/VIP/YHA will save you up to $15 on some tickets. Buses run daily to: **Bowen** (1hr., 5 per day, $24); **Brisbane** (18½hr., 6 per day, $183); **Bundaberg** (10-11hr., 3 per day, $134); **Cairns** (10hr., 5 per day, $113); **Hervey Bay** (13hr., 4 per day, $139); **Mackay** (2hr., 6 per day, $32); **Maroochydore** (16-17hr., 3 per day, $180); **Mission Beach** (8hr., 3 per day, $101); **Noosa** (16hr., 3 per day, $180); **Rockhampton** (6-7hr., 6 per day, $80); **Townsville** (4½hr., 5 per day, $57).

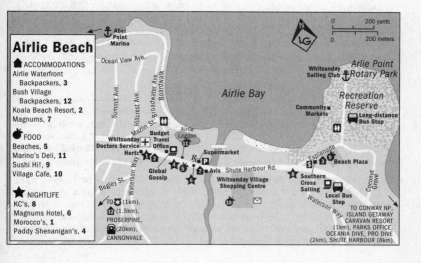

**Airlie Beach**

🏠 ACCOMMODATIONS
Airlie Waterfront
  Backpackers, **3**
Bush Village
  Backpackers, **12**
Koala Beach Resort, **2**
Magnums, **7**

🍴 FOOD
Beaches, **5**
Marino's Deli, **11**
Sushi Hi!, **9**
Village Cafe, **10**

⭐ NIGHTLIFE
KC's, **8**
Magnums Hotel, **6**
Morocco's, **1**
Paddy Shenanigan's, **4**

**Public Transportation: Whitsunday Transit** (☎07 4946 1800; whitsundaytransit.com) runs between Cannonvale and Shute Harbour daily every 30min. 6:20am-6:45pm, stopping in front of Global Gossip (257 Shute Harbour Rd.). Night service 7-11pm.

**Taxis: Whitsunday Taxi** (☎13 10 08).

**Car Rental:** There are several companies along Shute Harbour Rd., including **Hertz** (☎13 30 39) next to Morocco's (open M-F 8:30am-5pm, Sa-Su 9:30am-noon).

## ◄▶ ⚡ ORIENTATION AND PRACTICAL INFORMATION

The turnoff for Airlie Beach is at Proserpine, off the Bruce Hwy.; the road passes through Cannonvale and on to Airlie Beach (26km). The main road becomes **Shute Harbour Road,** running parallel to the water as it nears Airlie. Upon entering the town, you'll pass **Abel Point Marina**; at the opposite end, the road veers left to the **Esplanade** or continues straight toward the commercial **Shute Harbour** (8km). Picnic tables and BBQs adorn the waterfront area along the Esplanade while sunbathers lie on the beach or the grass around **Airlie Lagoon.**

**Budget Travel:** Many travel offices cater to backpackers. Some of the hostel tour booking offices offer free rooms if you book trips with them.

**Parks Office: National and Marine Parks Authority** (☎07 4967 7355), on the corner of Mandalay St. and Shute Harbour Rd., 2km outside town toward Shute Harbour. Info on camping and national parks. Open M-F 9am-4:30pm.

**Currency Exchange: ATMs** line Shute Harbour Rd. **King's Currency Exchange,** 293 Shute Harbour Rd., has low exchange rates and doesn't charge a commission fee. Wire transfers available. Open M-Sa 9am-7pm.

**Police:** (☎07 4946 6445), on Altman St., off Shute Harbour Rd. toward Proserpine.

**Medical Services: Whitsunday Doctors Service** (☎07 4946 6241 or 13 432 584 for emergencies), on the corner of Shute Harbour Rd. and Broadwater Ave. Open M-F 8am-5pm. Dive medicals $50. **ChemCoast Pharmacy** (☎07 4946 6156) is next to the shopping mart on Shute Harbour Rd. Open daily 8:30am-6:30pm.

**Internet Access:** Most shops offer Internet, and hostels have competitive rates. **Holiday-sallover,** 390 Shute Harbour Rd., charges $4 per hr. with all the frills: DVD/CD burning, printing, and copying. (☎07 4946 6399. Open daily 7:30am-7:30pm.) **Global Gossip,** 257 Shute Harbor Rd. (☎07 4946 6488), also charges $4 per hr. CD and DVD burning and printing. Open M-Th 9am-11pm, F 9am-10pm, Sa 10am-10pm, Su 10am-11pm.

**Post Office:** (☎07 4946 6515), in the Whitsunday Village Shopping Center on Shute Harbour Rd. Open M-F 9am-5pm. **Postal Code:** 4802.

## ⌂ ▨ ACCOMMODATIONS AND CAMPING

Airlie's plethora of budget lodgings barely keeps pace with backpacker demand, so book ahead. Ask about deals when booking tours through hostels; some offer free stays. The nearby Whitsundays have cheap camping, but space is limited. Try **Koala Beach Resort** (☎1800 800 421), on Shute Harbour Rd., or **Island Gateway Caravan Resort** (☎07 4946 6228), 1km past town on Shute Harbour Rd.

▧ **Bush Village Boutique Backpackers**, 2 St. Martins Rd., Cannonvale (☎07 4946 6177 or 1800 809 256), a 15min. walk from town. The ultimate in cleanliness and hospitality. Cabins with kitchen, TV, and bath flank a palm-lined driveway that leads to the pool, porch, and TV lounge. Relax in hammocks during the day, watch movies in the poolside lounge at night, and feed 'roos and wallabies in the backyard sanctuary. Though all are welcome, caters to females and couples. Continental breakfast with mouthwatering chocolate chip rolls. Free shuttles to town from early morning until late. Reception 7am–9pm. Dorms $27-31; doubles $78-108; triples $105. MC/V. ❷

**Airlie Waterfront Backpackers** (☎07 4948 1302; www.airliewaterfront.com), on the Esplanade. Very clean, quiet, and ideally located, with a quiet atmosphere, kitchens, and large balconies with great views of Airlie Bay. Dorms and doubles are arranged in suites around common rooms. Lounges and decks provide spectacular views. Luggage storage and key deposit $10. 10% discount at nearby restaurant. Reception 7am-8pm. 10-bed dorms $25; 4-bed $30; doubles $60. MC/V. ❷

**Magnums** (☎07 4964 1199 or 1800 624 634; www.magnums.com.au), on Shute Harbour Rd. Airlie Beach's centrally located party hostel. With 4 restaurants and over 400 beds in charming bungalows lining a faux-jungle footpath, this hamlet of hedonism is still somehow endearing—perhaps it's the live music and lively crowd of backpackers. All rooms clean and ensuite with A/C. Bring linen. Reception 6am-9pm. Campsites $18; dorms from $17 with 2-night stay; doubles $52. VIP. MC/V. ❶

## 🔲 FOOD

Cafes and mid-range restaurants line the main drag in Airlie. Several hostels (Magnums and Koala) have affiliated bars and nightclubs that double as restaurants before 9pm. There is a small **supermarket** right in the middle of town, across from Magnums on Shute Harbour Rd. (Open daily 7:30am-8pm.)

**Village Cafe** (☎07 4946 5745), opposite the post office in Whitsunday Village Shopping Center. A healthful alternative to Airlie's fish and chip joints. Breakfast served all day. Gourmet sandwiches ($11-14), meat, seafood, pasta, and vegetarian entrees. Fully licensed bar with extensive wine selection. Renowned coffee bar serves towering, toothsome mocha concoctions ($4-7). Open daily 8am-5:30pm. MC/V. ❷

**Marino's Deli,** 269 Shute Harbour Rd. (☎07 4946 4207). Serves up scrumptious sandwiches on bread of your choice ($6.30-8.70). Vegetarians will love the homemade potato gnocchi ($12-16) and other meatless options. Open M-Sa 11am-8pm. ❷

**Sushi Hi!** (☎07 4948 0400), in Beach Plaza on The Esplanade. The best raw fish joint in town. Massive seafood rolls fill you up without emptying your pocket (½-roll $7-8) Healthful smoothies ($6-7) make a perfect snack. For the less health-conscious, there's Japanese deep-fried ice cream ($2.50). Open daily 11am-late. MC/V. ❶

**Beaches,** 356-62 Shute Harbour Rd. (☎07 4946 6244). A perennially packed backpacker mecca that serves dinner on picnic tables. Counter meals ($10.50-18) are upscale and include fish dishes. Live music and dancing 7:30-late. MC/V. ❷

## 🔲 NIGHTLIFE

**Magnums Hotel,** 366 Shute Harbour Rd. (☎07 4946 6188), part of Magnums's metropolis. Nights here get sticky, soapy, noisy, and naughty. Indulge your more wicked fantasies by cutting it up in this Catholic-cathedral-themed club with a requisite towering cross. Frequent theme nights and live music outside daily 6-9pm. $5 cover after 11pm. Open W-Th until about 1am, F-Sa until 5am.

**Paddy Shenanigan's** (☎07 4946 5055), near Beaches on Shute Harbour Rd. A popular nightspot with Airlie dwellers and a great place to start the night off in style. Try their infamous green shooter teapots for $10. Boasts a dance floor and live music. W open mic night 8:30-10:30pm. Open daily 5pm-3am.

**Morocco's** (☎07 4946 6446), next to Koala on Shute Harbour Rd. Slightly upscale decor (the stripper pole being the only exception) with some outdoor tables and a huge TV screen inside. Frequent theme nights. Meals for $10-17, but you can usually get a $4 discount on the street or 20% off if you're staying at Koala's. Open daily 3pm-2am.

**KC's** (☎07 4946 6320), on Shute Harbour Rd., on the right before the turnoff for the Esplanade. If you're looking for a big piece of steak and some great live music, this is the place. A truly relaxing and intimate pub environment. Open daily 11am-3am.

## ACTIVITIES

Sailing the Whitsundays and diving the Great Barrier Reef are the two most popular reasons to visit Airlie, but they can be pricey. If you're in the market for something else, however, there are numerous alternative activities in this area that aren't quite as expensive.

### ON LAND

**Conway National Park** is a few kilometers east of Airlie Beach. A self-guided walk in the park lasts just over an hour and passes through a variety of Australian habitats. On the way, stop at the **QPWS** for a detailed leaflet. (☎07 4967 7355. Open M-F 8:30am-5pm.) Die-hard bush wranglers can try plowing through the bush on a four-wheeler with **Whitsunday Quad Bike Bush Adventures.** (☎07 4946 1020; www.bushadventures.com.au. Departs daily; $70 1hr. guided tours; $115 per 2hr.) If you have a car, go to any local tourist office and ask for some self-drive suggestions, as the area has several other swimming holes and scenic areas. **Whitsunday Crocodile Safari** cruises the Proserpine River in search of crocs and also offers open-air wagon ecotours and hikes through the wetlands. (☎07 4948 3310; www.proserpineecotours.com.au. $98, children $48. Family packages available. Free transfers to and from Airlie.)

### IN THE SEA

The scuba scene is amazing in the Whitsunday area. Dolphins, whales (in the winter months), turtles, manta rays, and even small reef sharks are common inhabitants of these crystal-clear waters. The most popular sites for overnight trips are on the outer reefs that lie just beyond the major island groups, including the **Bait, Hardy,** and **Hook Reefs.** Occasionally, boats will venture to **Black Reef** or **Elizabeth Reef. Mantaray Bay** is close by and also great for snorkeling. All trips incur an extra $5 per day reef tax. In addition to the companies listed below, **FantaSea Cruises** (p. 399) offers trips to the reef for marine-life viewing. For day-trips that won't break the bank, **Dive Time** (☎07 4948 1211 or 419 372 480; www.divetime.com.au) offers island trips from $110 (student $104; reef trips $130, student $124; intro dives $65; certified dives $60). **The Scuba Centre** (☎07 4946 1067; www.scubacentrre.com.au) offers three-day, three-night live-aboard trips. Dive and sail the Reef aboard the 16.4m *Kiana* (from $549, first dive free), which departs Monday and Friday mornings. Take a similar trip on the 65 ft. catamaran, the *Pacific Star* (from $479), or bask on the air-conditioned *Whitsunday Magic*, a majestic three-masted schooner (from $659).

Paddle or snorkel alongside sea turtles or camp on deserted island beaches with **Salty Dog Sea Kayaking.** Salty Dog offers half-, full-, overnight-, and 6-day tours around the islands. Adventurers can bring their own food or let the company handle the catering. (☎07 4946 1388 or 1800 635 334; www.saltydog.com.au. ½-day $70, full-day $125, overnight $365, 6-day $1490.) **Ocean Rafting's** speedy daytrip fleet can top 65km per hour, making this the fastest way to get to the islands. Trips include a chance to snorkel or dive, take rainforest walks, admire Aboriginal caves, or just tan on the beach. (☎07 4946 6848; www.oceanrafting.com. $103, children $66; lunch $13.) **FantaSea** (see p. 399) runs daily catered ferry trips to nearby islands. They also offer whale watches when the humpbacks are running back from Arctic feeding grounds. **Cruise Whitsundays** (see p. 399) has adventure packages, cruises, and resort ferries. If you're interested in diving the wreck of the **SS Yongala,** considered one of the world's premier dives of its kind, try **Yongala Dive** (p. 406). A relaxing fishing excursion is available aboard the **M.V. Moruya,** a local favorite. (☎07 4948 1029 or 0450 0111; www. fishingwhitsunday.com.au. Departs daily at 7:30am from Shute Harbour and returns around 4:30pm. Daytrip $150, concessions $130.)

# WHITSUNDAY ISLANDS

Over 90 islands constitute the Whitsunday group, a continental archipelago that was once a coastal mountain range until it was cut off from the mainland by rising sea levels at the end of the last ice age. The thousands of visitors who flock to this majestic area come to sail, enjoy the beaches and coral reefs, or just relax at one of the luxurious resorts. **Whitsunday Island** (p. 400), home to the famous **Whitehaven Beach** (p. 400), is the largest and most appealing to campers and hikers. Other backpacker favorites include: **Hook Island** (p. 400), with its choice snorkeling spots and Aboriginal cave paintings; **Daydream Island; Long Island**; and the **Molle Island Group,** of which **South Molle** (p. 401) is the best. At the posh resorts on **Hayman, Hamilton,** and **Lindeman Islands,** many guests arrive by private helicopter or plane, but the islands can make decent daytrips even for those who are strapped for cash. However, beware that public transportation to a number of the islands is very limited.

## ▐ TRANSPORTATION

Choosing which island to visit can seem overwhelming; one way to experience the group is by taking a multi-day sailing trip, but be aware that you'll be spending most of your time in transit. It's also possible to do island daytrips by ferry. One of the best ways to reach the islands is via one of the camping transfers listed below. Regardless of how you are traveling, if you only have time to visit one place, make it **Whitsunday Island** (p. 400).

**FantaSea** (☎07 4946 5111; www.fantasea.com.au). Offers direct transfers between the islands and mainland; departs several times daily from Shute Harbour. Schedules are available at almost any booking office or hostel. Multiple ferries leave the harbor daily to Hamilton Island Marina ($43 round-trip) and Daydream Island ($29 round-trip). Discounts for families and children available. MC/V.

**Cruise Whitsundays** (☎07 4946 4662 or 1800 426 403; www.cruisewhitsundays.com). Departs Abel Point several times daily to Daydream Island ($30, children $20) and Hamilton Island Airport ($55, children $35). Also offers adventure packages. MC/V.

**Camping Whitsundays** (☎07 4946 9330). Drops campers off at many of the island sites ($4.85 national park permit required), and has camping, snorkeling, kayaking, and camping equipment rental. Min. 2 people. To South Molle Island $60, to Whitehaven $60, to Hook Island $160. Prices include return and water supply. MC/V.

**Camping Whitsunday Islands** (☎07 4948 0933 or 1800 550 751; www.campingwhitsundays.com). Offers packages to: Whitehaven Beach ($270, with Crayfish Bay $330); Cockatoo Beach ($190); Denman Island ($190); Dugong Beach ($238); and many others. Shared accommodations available. MC/V.

**Air Whitsunday Seaplanes** (☎07 4946 9111; www.airwhitsunday.com.au). Offers 2½hr. scenic flight over reef and Whitehaven for $199. Flight to Hayman $490. MC/V.

## ▟ ISLANDS

The Whitsundays Island group has a variety of cheap camping options; there are 33 campsites on six different islands. Before embarking on your trip, you must get a permit from QPWS at the **Marine Parks Authority,** on the corner of Shute Harbour Rd. and Mandalay Rd., Airlie Beach. (☎07 4967 7355; book online at www.epa.qld.gov.au. Open M-F 8:30am-5pm. Permits $4.85 per night.) Walk-in applications are welcome, but you must book ahead to guarantee your spot.

**WHITSUNDAY ISLAND.** The most renowned destination in the Whitsundays is ◩**Whitehaven Beach,** a 7km strip along the western rim of the island. Sand swirls like fine snow from one edge of the island to the other; at low tide you can practically walk across the inlet opposite the longer portion of Whitehaven, where most day-tour companies moor and sailing trips stop for sunbathing and swimming. Make sure you get to **Hill Inlet Lookout** farther north on the island at Tongue Bay, an easy 650m walk. Beware: some tour companies will only take you to the portion of the beach that lies across the bay, but Whitehaven might seem a wasted trip unless you see it from above, so ask ahead and make sure the tour includes the lookout. Tour companies that make daytrips to Whitehaven and Hill Inlet Lookout (with snorkeling and lunch) include **Mantaray** (☎04 4946 4321 or 1800 816 365; www.mantaraycharters.com; $130, student $120, intro $75, certified dive $65) and **Reefjet** (☎07 4946 5366; www.reefjet. com.au; $130, student $120; rates lower in low season). **Ocean Rafting** speeds its guests to Whitehaven and Hill Inlet Beach in giant, yellow rafts (☎4946 6848; www.oceanrafting.com; $103, children $66; lunch $13).

The **campsite at Whitehaven Beach ❶** has toilets, picnic tables, and shelter (high season limit 60 people, low season limit 24). If you plan to camp in the Whitsundays, do it here. Three other campgrounds are available on the other side of the island at **Cid Harbour,** a common mooring site for two-night boat trips. The largest is **Dugong Beach** (limit 36 people), which has toilets, drinking water, sheltered picnic areas, and a **walking track** (1km, 40min.) that leads to the second campground at **Sawmill Beach** (limit 24 people). The same amenities are provided there. Bring a water supply if you're camping farther south at **Joe's Beach** (limit 12 people). All campsites cost $4.85 per night. The beach has excellent snorkeling; stingrays and turtles are common.

**HOOK ISLAND.** The beaches on Hook have beautiful stretches of coral offshore, literally a stone's throw from **Chalkies Beach** and **Blue Pearl Bay.** Blue Pearl Bay is arguably the best of the Whitsundays' popular snorkeling spots. It's also home to the islands' most popular fish, a gigantic 5 ft. tourist-loving wrasse named Elvis. On the south side of the island lies **Nara Inlet,** a popular spot for overnight boat trips. About 20min. up the grueling path is a cave shelter used by the sea-faring Ngalandji Aboriginals, bordered on both sides by middens (piles of shells). The rare paintings inside (dated to 1000 B.C.) provide fodder for an interesting Aussie myth. Legend has it that a boatload of exiled Egyptians washed ashore ages ago and left traces of hieroglyphics in various corners of Queensland. Although the story is unsubstantiated, it is true that at least one symbol in the cave is a good match for "king" in Hieroglyphic Luwian, the language of ancient Troy. **Maureens Cove,** on Hook's northern coast, is a popular anchorage and has **camping ❶** for $4.85 a night (limit 36 people). **Steen's Beach campground** (limit 12 people), is a good sea-kayaking site. **Hook Island Wilderness Resort ❷,** just east of Matilda Bay, offers a range of activities from snorkeling (full day $12) to fish and goanna feeding; there is also a reef 50m offshore. Remember to bring a towel, sleeping bag, and kitchen utensils. **Transfers** (round-trip $80) are available on the ferry Voyager with stops at Whitehaven Beach and Daydream Island. (☎07 4946 9380. Camping $25 per site; hut-style dorms $45 per person; beach-front cabins $120, ensuite $150.

MC/V.) One of the planet's oldest underwater reef observatories can be found at the end of the jetty; check at the resort for hours.

**SOUTH MOLLE ISLAND.** South Molle, just off the mainland, is a national park that offers some of the best bushwalking in Queensland. One of the best tracks is the hike to **Spion Kop** (4.4km, 1hr. round-trip), a rock precipice on one of the island's many peaks. Adventurous hikers scramble up the rocks for an astounding 360° view of the Whitsundays. Nearby **Sandy Beach** (limit 36 people) has over 15km of hiking trails. Many two-night sailing excursions moor offshore, and guests come ashore to bushwalk or use the pool at the **South Molle Island Resort ❺,** located in Bauer Bay. (☎07 4946 9433 or 1800 075 080. Packages from $148. Cheaper standby rates are often available. Open daily 7am-7pm. AmEx/MC/V.) All-inclusive packages are the cheapest and easiest way to enjoy the resort (includes room, meals, and non-motorized watersports). All island walks are accessible from the resort; reception can give you a map and information.

**OTHER ISLANDS.** **Hayman Island** is known as one of the world's premier resorts, but unless you have $500 for a night's stay, you're not going to visit for more than a day. **Hamilton Island** is the mini-metropolis of the Whitsundays, with high-rise hotels, the **Hamilton Island Resort,** and a main drag with **ATM, general store,** and over a dozen **restaurants.** Budget-friendly **North Molle Island** boasts the mammoth Cockatoo Beach Campground (limit 48 people), fully equipped with facilities and water supply. Other fully equipped campsites include **Gloucester Island's Bona Bay** (limit 36 people), **Henning Island's Northern Spit** (limit 24 people; no water), and the secluded sites at **Thomas Island** and **Armit Island** (limit 12 people). **Shute Harbour** offers basic grounds with bushcamping sites (limit 12 people).

## ☾ SAILING THE ISLANDS

Traveling to the Whitsundays without sailing the islands is like going to Paris without seeing the Eiffel Tower: a sailing safari is one of the most popular activities in Queensland. Although some hostels may save you money by offering a free night's stay if you book tours with them, it might not get you on the best boat. Make sure you get the full details on every trip before booking. Ask how much time is actually spent on the trip. Many boats offer "three-day, two-night" trips that leave at midday and come back only 48hr. later. Some multiple-day trips only offer an hour on each island; not nearly enough time to enjoy the white-sand beaches. Also make sure the company you go with has **"WCBIA" certification (Whitsunday Charter Boat Industry Association);** some companies will make up their own, unauthorized certification.

There are four classes of boats at play: the uninspiring **motor-powered** variety (boats that have sails but nonetheless motor everywhere); the stately **tall-ships,** with the riggings of yesteryear and the elegance of age; the **cruising yachts,** which offer more comfort, smaller numbers, and more sailing time; and the proper **racing yachts,** called **maxis,** which are usually past their racing prime, more expensive, and popular with young crowds and the adventurous. Discounts are greatest during low-season times (Oct.-Nov. and Feb.-Mar.), and as a result, sailing trips get filled up fast; book ahead.

**Southern Cross** (☎07 4946 4999 or 1800 675 790; www.soxsail.com.au). One of Airlie's premier sailing companies; trips have professional crews, spotless boats, gourmet meals, and free transfers. Their fleet includes: the *Southern Cross,* a former America's Cup finalist (max. 14 people); the *Siska,* a spacious 80 ft. maxi that is said to be one of the best (max. 22 people; 3-day, 2-night trip $429); and the *Solway Lass,* a gorgeous

127 ft. tallship built in 1902. (Max. 32 people. 3-day overnight trip starts at $519. 6-day overnight trip $889.) Open 7:30am-8:15pm. MC/V.

**Prosail** (☎07 4946 5433; www.prosail.com.au). Maxi yachts Condor and Broomstick offer 2-day, 2-night trips ($359). Crew creates an interactive experience, allowing guests to help steer the world-famous yachts through the Whitsundays. AmEx/MC/V.

**Oz Adventure Sailing** (☎07 4940 2000 or 1300 653 100); www.aussiesailing.com.au). With a wide range of sailboats, they serve a diverse group of customers. The maxi *Waltzing Matilda* takes 14 people and departs W and Sa (3-day, 2-night trip $520). MC/V.

# NORTH QUEENSLAND

Sandy beaches stretch along some of the world's oldest tropical rainforests as the Queensland coast extends farther north. To the west of the tropics, the earth becomes dry and the dirt turns red; much of this land sits high above sea level on former volcanic shelves. Tall green and silver fields, smoking mills, chugging trains, and Bundaberg rum all stand testament to north Queensland's greatest agricultural asset: sugar cane. Just off the coast of tropical Townsville, the region's economic and residential center, sits Magnetic Island, a haven for both koalas and urbanites alike. Between the island and Mission Beach, brilliant waters lap sands sheltered from rough seas by the Great Barrier Reef. Pockets of zealously preserved rainforest (and the inescapable "rainforest boardwalk") grow increasingly common in the tropical north.

## BOWEN ☎07

Dismissed as another bus stop on the coastal service, Bowen is regularly bypassed by travelers in favor of the party atmosphere of Airlie Beach 40min. to the south. Those who do stay are rewarded with gorgeous, secluded beaches on the outskirts of town and the tranquility afforded by its small size. Fruit picking and short-term work opportunities are available from April to November; working travelers praise Bowen as Queensland's best stop for short-term employment thanks to an abundance of beachside jobs.

**▐ TRANSPORTATION.** Greyhound Australia and Premier **buses** make daily stops in Bowen in front of **Bowen Travel,** 40 Williams St. (☎07 4786 2835 or 07 4786 1611. Open M-F 7am-5pm, Sa 7am-noon.)

**▐▐ ACCOMMODATIONS AND FOOD. Bowen Backpackers ❷** is a popular, social hostel on the corner of Dalrymple and Herbert St., on the opposite side of town from the bay. If you're looking to make some cash, owners Sian and Scott will set you up with temporary work in the area; buses to farms leave daily from here. Bowen offers a fully equipped kitchen, A/C, and is only minutes from the beach. It's always full during fruit-picking season, so book at least a week ahead. (☎07 4786 3433; www.users.bigpond.com/bowenbackpackers. Dorms $155 per week, with A/C $160-165. Minimum 1 week stay. May be closed Dec.-Mar., so call ahead. Reception 7:30-10:30am and 3:30-6pm. Cash only.) A block down on the corner of Herbert and George St. is the **Central Hotel ❶.** The rooms are clean and reasonably priced, and there is a restaurant and bar downstairs. (☎07 4786 1812. 1 week minimum stay from May-Nov. Reception open daily 10am-10pm. Rooms $120 per week, $150 with transport to and from work.) Backpackers looking for nightly rates should try **Grand View Hotel ❷** at the corner of Herbert St. and Richmond St. (☎07 4786 4022.) Dorms go for $30 per night or $130 per week without transport. Though you can't book ahead, it's the only place in town without a minimum stay. (Reception 10am-late.) At the other end of town is **Horseshoe Bay Resort ❷**, a family-friendly accommodation located at the end of Horseshoe Bay Rd. (☎07 4786 2564. Reception 9am-6pm. Sites $26, powered $30; cabins from $55; self-contained cabins $70-98. MC/V.)

Though pub food dominates Bowen's restaurant scene, **Blender Z Juice Bar ❶**, on Gregory St., is a culinary diamond in the rough (☎07 4786 5343). Wash the greasy fish and chips remnants out of your system with a mixed berry fruit crush or honeydew melon juice ($5-6). Cheap and delicious sandwiches on focaccia ($6.50) line the counter, and fruit salads ($3.50-$8) can be prepared in mere minutes. Free **Internet access** is available. (Open M-F 8am-6pm, Sa 9am-4pm, Su 10am-3pm. MC/V.) An **IGA** supermarket is at 57 Williams St. (☎07 4786 1844. Open M-F 7am-8pm, Sa-Su 7am-6pm.)

◪ **SIGHTS. Horseshoe Bay** is the town's biggest attraction. To get there, follow Soldiers Rd. out of town, take a right onto Horseshoe Bay Rd., and follow it to the end. Although it can be crowded, the clay, water, and coastal boulders create a picturesque setting in which to take a swim or catch the sunrise. **Murray Bay** is a less-frequented but equally beautiful beach. To get there, turn right off Horseshoe Bay Rd. onto unsealed Murray Bay Rd. From the end of the road, it's a 10min. walk to the beach. Most of the town borders **Queens Bay,** accessible via Soldiers Rd. Good fishing and calm water can be found at **Gray's Bay,** near Horseshoe Bay. **Bowen Transit** runs to the beaches from the library on Herbert Street. (☎07 4786 4414. Flag down the driver if you want a ride. $2.80.)

# TOWNSVILLE                                                    ☎07

Townsville (pop. 100,000), the largest city in the tropical north, was established long before the backpacking subculture infiltrated the region. The Central Business District (CBD) is surprisingly cosmopolitan and pedestrian-friendly and has done an excellent job of expanding to fill the needs of tourists. Shopping malls and office buildings mix with hostels and museums in the compact, revitalized CBD. Open-air eateries, night markets, palm-lined promenades, and endless stretches of uncrowded beach add tropical flavor to the mix. Just outside the city (and off the mainland) sits koala-filled **Magnetic Island** (p. 408) and the world-renowned dive site of the sunken **SS Yongala** (p. 406). Travelers can return from treasure-seeking expeditions to a sophisticated nightlife dominated by good wine and live music. Undervalued by the tourist circuit, Townsville is a lively port city with true Australian flair.

## ◪ TRANSPORTATION

**Flights:** The **airport** (☎07 4727 3211) is west of the city. Qantas (☎07 4753 3311), at the Dimmey's entrance in Flinders Mall, flies direct to: **Brisbane** (1hr., 5 per day, $132 one-way); **Cairns** (1hr., 5 per day, $142); **Mackay** (1hr., 2 per day, $141); **Sydney** (4hr., 1 per day, $224). An airport **shuttle bus** (☎07 4775 5544) runs to the city daily 5:30am-9pm. Bookings to the airport must be made 30min. before the scheduled pickup time. One-way $9, round-trip $13. To drive from the airport to the city, take John Melton Black Dr., which becomes Bundock St. Bear right onto Warburton St. and again onto Eyre St., then turn left on Denham St.

**Trains:** Trains depart from the new **train station** (☎07 4772 8288 or reservations 13 22 32; www.traveltrain.com.au) at the corner of Flinders and Morris St., a 15min. walk from the city. The Inlander train offers concessions rates and departs W and Su 3:30pm to: **Charters Towers** (3hr., $27); **Cloncurry** (16hr., $103); **Hughenden** (8hr., $60);

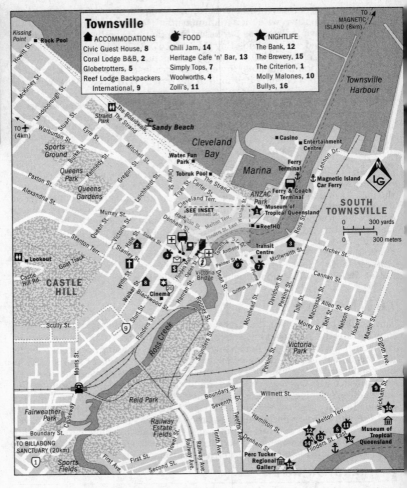

## Townsville

| 🏠 ACCOMMODATIONS | 🍎 FOOD | ★ NIGHTLIFE |
| --- | --- | --- |
| Civic Guest House, **8** | Chili Jam, **14** | The Bank, **12** |
| Coral Lodge B&B, **2** | Heritage Cafe 'n' Bar, **13** | The Brewery, **15** |
| Globetrotters, **5** | Simply Tops, **7** | The Criterion, **1** |
| Reef Lodge Backpackers | Woolworths, **4** | Molly Malones, **10** |
| International, **9** | Zolli's, **11** | Bullys, **16** |

**Mount Isa** (20hr., $124); **Richmond** (10hr., $74). The economy-class **Sunlander** provides coastal service as well as 50% discounts to ISIC cardholders. It departs Tu, Th, Sa at 4:35pm southbound to: **Brisbane** (24hr., $184); **Mackay** (7hr., $70); **Prosperpine** (4hr., $56); **Rockhampton** (13hr., $123). Northbound trains depart M and W at 2:25am and F at 5:35am for **Cairns** (8hr., $64). Tickets are available at the **Queensland Rail Travel Centre** (☎07 4772 8358), in the old train station at the corner of Flinders and Blackwood St. Open M-F 8:30am-5pm. They can also be purchased at the train station itself (Sa 12:15-4pm and Su 12:15-3:45pm).

**Buses:** The **Transit Centre** is on the corner of Palmer and Plume St., 5min. from town (open daily 6am-7:30pm). Greyhound Australia (☎13 14 99 or 13 20 30; open daily 5:30am-11pm) runs to: **Airlie Beach** (4hr., 6 per day, $57); **Brisbane** (20hr., 6 per day, $211); **Cairns** (4hr., 6 per day, $66); **Cardwell** (2hr., 6 per day, $39); **Charters Towers**

(2hr., 2 per day, $35); **Cloncurry** (10hr., 2 per day, $115); **Hughenden** (5hr., 1 per day, $60) **Ingham** (1hr., 6 per day, $33); **Innisfail** (4hr., 6 per day, $57); **Mackay** (5hr., 6 per day, $79); **Mission Beach** (3hr., 4 per day, $51); **Mt. Isa** (12hr., 2 per day, $140); **Richmond** (5hr., 2 per day, $78); **Rockhampton** (9hr., 6 per day, $118). Premier (☎13 34 10) stops in the city twice per day: northbound at 1:35pm, southbound at 1pm.

**Public Transportation: Sunbus** (☎07 4725 8482; www.sunbus.com.au) has its main terminal in the center of Flinders Mall. Most tickets run $3-6.

**Car Rental: Thrifty** (☎13 13 90), at the airport, rents from $55 per day. Avis, 81 Flinders St. (☎07 4721 2688 or 07 4725 6522), is open M-Sa 8am-5pm, Su 8am-noon.

**Automobile Club: RACQ**, 635 Sturt St. (24hr. ☎07 4721 4888). Open M-F 8am-5pm, Sa 8am-noon.

**Taxis: Taxi Townsville** (24hr. ☎07 4772 1555 or 13 10 08).

## ■ ⚡ ORIENTATION AND PRACTICAL INFORMATION

Townsville is a large city with a complex layout, but the CBD area is relatively easy to navigate. **Ross Creek** separates the mall side of the CBD from the Transit Centre side. Buses stop at the Transit Centre on **Palmer Sreet**, where you can also find several hostels. From Palmer St., it's only a 10min. walk over the Victoria Bridge to the open-air **Flinders Mall**. The beach and many restaurants line **The Strand**, a 5-10min. walk from the mall. Most of Flinders's cross streets will take you to The Strand; the easiest route is to walk east down Flinders toward ReefHQ and turn left. **Castle Hill** looms in the city's background and is accessible by road and a steep **walking trail** (the **"Goat Track"**); take Gregory St. from The Strand or Stanley St. from the CBD.

**Tourist Office: Visitors Centre** (☎07 4721 3660), the big circular kiosk in the center of Flinders Mall. Open M-F 9am-5pm, Sa-Su 9am-1pm.

**Reef and National Park Information Centre:** (☎07 4721 2399), outside the CBD in Cape Palerando. Open M-F 9am-5pm, Sa-Su 10am-4pm.

**Currency Exchange: Bank of Queensland,** 16 Stokes St. (☎07 4772 1799), often has the best rates. Commission $5. Open M-Th 9:30am-4pm, F 9:30am-5pm. **ATMs** are common in Flinders Mall and the CBD.

**Police:** (☎07 4759 9777), on the corner of Stanley and Sturt St.

**Hospital: The Doctors** (☎07 4781 1111), on the corner of Stokes and Sturt St., is open daily 7am-11pm. **Northtown Medical Centre** (☎07 4720 8100), in Flinders Mall, in front of the visitors center, offers bulk billing. Open daily 7am-11pm.

**Internet Access: Internet Den,** 265 Flinders Mall (☎07 4721 4500). $2 1st 30min. $4 1st 70min. $50 for 26hr. Printing $0.20 per page. Open daily 8am-9pm.

**Post Office: General Post Office** (☎13 13 18), in Post Office Plaza, on Sturt St. Open M-F 8:30am-5:30pm, Su 9am-12:30pm. **Postal Code:** 4810.

## 🛌 ACCOMMODATIONS

Townsville isn't a backpacker's city and, as a result, has only a few quality hostels. The best ones are on or near Flanders St. The lack of decent budget accommodations makes the city ideal for splurging on upscale lodgings.

■ **Coral Lodge B&B,** 32 Hale St. (☎07 4771 5512 or 1800 614 613; www.corallodge. com.au). From Flinders Mall, follow Stokes St. for 4 blocks, then turn left on Hale St.; it's on the left. Friendly and clean B&B; sits on the hillside over the city. Their plush bedding, old-world furnishings, and view make it well worth the price. All rooms have A/C, TV, and fridge. Singles $65, ensuite $85; twins and doubles $75/95. MC/V. ❹

**Civic Guest House,** 262 Walker St. (☎07 4771 5381 or 1800 646 619; www.civicguest-house.com). Family-run service with courtesy bus, F night BBQ, and Internet access. Kitchen, laundry, and TV lounge. Reception 8am-1pm and 4:30pm-7:30pm. 4- and 6-bed dorms $22, with A/C $24; singles $52; doubles $54. Ensuite $70. MC/V. ❷

**Globetrotters,** 121 Flanders St. East (☎07 4771 5000; www.globetrottersaustralia. com). Backpackers choose Globetrotters for its ensuite rooms with A/C and proximity to the city's pubs and clubs. Free continental breakfast and meal voucher to **Molly Malones** (see **Nightlife,** p. 407). Laundry, pool, BBQ, TV. Reception 8am-7pm. Must have passport. Dorms $24; doubles $70; family room sleeps 5 $120. VIP. MC/V. ❷

**Reef Lodge Backpackers International,** 4 Wickham St. (☎07 4721 1112), off Flinders St. E. Clean rooms with outdoor TV nooks. Gym, laundry, BBQ, A/C, and kitchen. Reception 7:30am-8:30pm. Dorms from $20; doubles $46-49. MC/V. ❷

# 🍴 FOOD

Most of the city's restaurants are located on The Strand, Flinders St. East, or Palmer St. **Woolworths** supermarket is on the corner of Stokes St. and Flanders Mall. (Open M-F 8am-9pm, Sa 8am-5:30pm, Su 9am-6pm.)

**Simply Tops** (☎07 4772 3028), on the corner of Plume and Palmer St. Fish and chips with flair. Serves sandwiches (from $5) and seafood. Looks more expensive than it is; main courses $10-22. Open M-F 9am-9pm, Sa 10am-9pm, Su 11am-9pm. MC/V. ❷

**Zolli's,** 113 Flinders St. E. (☎07 4721 2222). Enjoy Sicilian cuisine over red wine and Italian music in this cozy cafe. Many seafood and pasta ($12-17), and pizza ($8-18) choices in its beautiful dining area. Open M-Sa 5pm-late. AmEx/MC/V. ❷

**Heritage Cafe 'n' Bar,** 137 Flinders St. E. (☎07 4771 2799). Ultra-trendy scene with a large selection of Australian wines. Modern cuisine includes pasta, seafood, and meat dishes ($14-$25). Th bucket of cooked prawns $11.50; F same deal with bucket of oysters. Open T-Th 5pm-midnight, F 4pm-2am, Sa 5pm-2am. AmEx/MC/V. ❷

**Chili Jam,** 205 Flinders St. E. (☎ 07 4721 5199). Serves stir-fry ($12-17) and noodle plates ($10). Open Tu-F 11:30am-2:30pm and 5:30-10pm, Sa 5-10pm. MC/V. ❷

# 🤿 DIVING

The Townsville coast is often overlooked as a diving destination—a shame, since these are some of the best scuba spots in the tropical north. **Wheeler Reef,** Townsville's most exceptional spot on the Great Barrier Reef, is home to schools of fish and over 400 kinds of coral. **Davies and Kelso Reefs** are other popular dive sites. Townsville's best dive site, however, isn't on the reef. In 1911, the **SS Yongala** sunk off the coast; the shipwreck is considered one of the world's best wreck sites, but it requires advanced certification or a professional guide. Most Townsville certification programs include a dive to the *Yongala*. **Yongala Dive,** 56 Narrah St., Alva Beach, offers excursions to the wreck, departing from Ayr. (☎07 4783 1519; www.yongaladive.com.au. Departs daily. Offers Tu transfer from Airlie Beach, 6am, $40. 2 dives with full gear $220.)

**Adrenalin Dive,** 9 Wickham St. (☎07 4724 0600 or 1300 644 600; www.adrenalindive. com.au). A small operation that offers the only daytrip to the *Yongala* wreck, as well as daytrips to the Wheeler Reef. *Yongala* trip $225, not including a $25 levy fee. Picks up from Townsville and Magnetic Island. AmEx/MC/V.

**Sunferries** (☎07 4771 3855 or 1800 447 333; www.sunferries.com.au), at the ferry terminal on Flinders St. Makes daytrips to the Great Barrier Reef. Departs M-Tu and

F-Su at 8:30am; returns 5:30pm. $155, child $95, family $401. Certified dive $70 extra; discover dive $90. AmEx/MC/V.

## ◉ SIGHTS

Townsville's sizable population supports a variety of first-rate cultural and historical attractions, gardens, seaside parks, and unspoiled beaches. On the first Friday of the month (May-Dec.), head to the The Strand's night markets for food, crafts, rides, and entertainment (5-9:30pm).

**▨REEFHQ.** An extraordinary aquarium and reef education center, ReefHQ is home to a 2.5-million-liter aquarium that mimics the reef ecosystem. Tours and shows include shark feeds. *(2-68 Flinders St. ☎07 4750 0800; www.reefhq.com.au. Open daily 9:30am-5pm. $38.65, children and concessions $29.65, families $99.)*

**MUSEUM OF TROPICAL QUEENSLAND.** If you can't get to the *Yongala*, see the relics of **HMS Pandora,** displayed in this flashy museum. The museum also showcases Queensland's natural history, from dinosaurs to humans. Don't miss the great **deep sea creatures exhibit,** with its sculptures of the Loch Ness monster. *(78-102 Flinders St., next to the ReefHQ complex. ☎07 4726 0600. Open daily 9:30am-5pm. $12, concessions $8, children $7, families $30. MC/V.)*

**BILLABONG SANCTUARY.** The sanctuary runs daily presentations that allow you to take a hot pic with your favorite Aussie animal. *(17km south of Townsville. Coach service available. ☎07 4778 8344; www.billabongsanctuary.com.au. Open daily 8am-5pm. $28, students and seniors $25, children $17, families $88.)*

## ◤ ACTIVITIES

Townsville can sometimes feel like nothing more than a stopover en route to the oceanside attractions. If you're not here to dive, however, there are plenty of activities to keep you busy during your stay. Towering **Castle Hill** casts a dominating shadow over the city and offers some challenging walking paths that lead to views of Townsville and Magnetic Island; the best times to go are sunrise and sunset. Bring water and hiking boots; the paths are long, steep, and slippery. There's also a road to the top for the less aerobically inclined. **Coral Sea Skydivers,** 14 Plume St., leads tandem jumps daily, as well as two- and five-day certification courses for solo jumps. (☎07 4772 4889; www.coralseaskydivers. com.au. Book ahead. Tandem $315-415, depending on altitude.)

## ◪ NIGHTLIFE

*Remedy,* a free monthly nightlife publication, will lead you to all the hottest shows and bars in the city. **Molly Malones,** on the corner of Flinders St. E. and Wickham St., has live music, including a Wednesday jam session when locals take the stage. They also have a good restaurant with main courses around $15 and crumb steak, chips, and salad for $8.50. The clientele is a combination of locals and backpackers. (☎07 4771 3428. Open daily noon-2pm and 6-9pm.) Beer aficionados and partygoers alike start their nights at **The Brewery,** on the corner of Denham and Flinders St. E. Brewmaster Mitch Brady concocts delicious ales and lagers that consistently win international acclaim, and their gourmet pizzas ($14-15) and the roast of the day ($10) please discerning diners and thrifty backpackers. Substantial discounts are available at some hostels. (☎07 4724 0333. Open daily 11am-late.) **The Bank,** 150 Flinders St. E., is one of the most popular clubs in Townsville. Located in a stately old bank, it's frequented by locals and backpackers alike. (☎07 4721 1916. Open Tu-Su 9pm-3am. Cash only.) **The Criterion,** on the corner of Wickham St. and The Strand, is an old hotel pub that turns into a rowdy club late at night. It boasts an attached beer garden. (☎07 4721 5777. Open Tu-W 5pm-3am, Th-Sa 5pm-5am, Su 2pm-5am.) **Bullys,** across from Globetrotters (☎07 4771 5647) hosts revolving, risqué theme parties that consistently draw big crowds. A classy club where semi-casual dress is the norm, Bullys stresses acceptance of diversity and individuality. ($5 cover Fri-Sa 6pm-7pm. Open Tu-Su 8pm-5am. AmEx/MC/V.)

# MAGNETIC ISLAND ☎07

Named for interfering with Captain Cook's compass, the description "magnetic" now aptly describes the island's effect on visitors. Seduced by secluded bays, mountains teeming with wildlife, clear waters, and a relaxed atmosphere, many come for a day and stay for a week. Only a short ferry ride from Townsville, the large island is dominated by national parkland and is home to the largest concentration of wild koalas in Australia. The only inhabited area is a mere 20km of eastern coastline; the rest of the island is covered with tracks winding through tranquil wilderness. Averaging 320 sunny days per year, Maggie Island is paradise even when the rest of the tropics are wet and dreary.

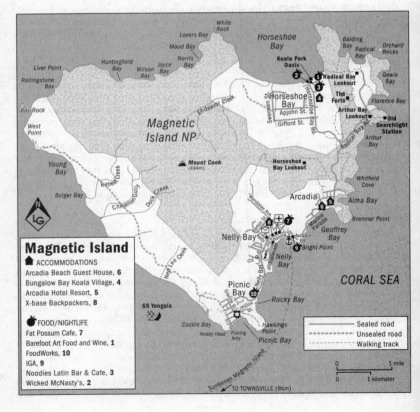

**Magnetic Island**

🏠 ACCOMMODATIONS
Arcadia Beach Guest House, **6**
Bungalow Bay Koala Village, **4**
Arcadia Hotel Resort, **5**
X-base Backpackers, **8**

🍎 FOOD/NIGHTLIFE
Fat Possum Cafe, **7**
Barefoot Art Food and Wine, **1**
FoodWorks, **10**
IGA, **9**
Noodies Latin Bar & Cafe, **3**
Wicked McNasty's, **2**

# TRANSPORTATION

The only public transportation to the island is Sunferries Magnetic Island, 168-192 Flinders St. East (☎07 4771 3855; www.sunferries.com.au). **Pedestrian ferries** leave from Townsville's **Breakwater terminal** (this is also the Greyhound Australia **bus station**) on Sir Leslie Thiess Dr. by The Strand (25min., 12-15 per day, $28 round-trip) and return from Magnetic Island's **Nelly Bay.** The only way to get vehicles across is on Fantasea, on Ross St. Six passengers and a car can travel for $156 round-trip. (Bookings ☎07 4772 5422; www.fantaseacruising-magnetic.com.au. M-F 8 per day, Sa-Su 7 per day). Book ahead.

There are less than 20km of sealed roads on the island, and the bus system covers all of them. **Magnetic Island Buses** (☎07 4778 5130) run roughly every 50min. from Picnic Bay to Horseshoe Bay; route stops are marked by blue signs. Tickets ($2-5), one-day unlimited passes ($6.50), and multiple-day passes are sold by drivers. Buses operate daily 6am-11pm. **Magnetic Island Taxis** (☎13 10 08) charges about $23 to cross the island.

Renting a "moke" (an open-air mini-car) is extremely popular. **Moke Magnetic,** opposite the ferry terminal, rents to ages 21 and over; rentals include 60km plus petrol ($73 per day). They also rent 4WD vehicles (from $80-85 per day) for those who want to make the trek to West Point or Radical Bay. When split among a group, this is an inexpensive way to enjoy some freedom. (☎07 4778 5377. Open M-F 8:30am-5pm, Sa-Su 8am-5pm. MC/V.) **Tropical Topless Car Rentals,** at the Harbour, has small, open-roofed, pink-and-yellow cars with 40km per day (plus fuel), perfect for indulging Barbie (or Ken) fantasies. (☎07 4758 1111. $83 per day. Book ahead.) But perhaps the best option is to see the island via quiet electric bikes. They can be taken off-road (scooters, mokes, and topless cars must remain on sealed roads), they're fast (up to 50kph), eco-friendly, and cheap. Rent from **Arcadia Beach Guest House** (see **Accommodations,** p. 410) or call ☎04 2524 4193 (www.goelectric.com.au. ½-day $15, full-day $25.) Bicycles can also be rented at most accommodations for $15 per day—but beware: there are some brutal hills between Nelly and Horseshoe Bays.

# ORIENTATION AND PRACTICAL INFORMATION

The island is triangular in shape, with all accommodations, restaurants, and activities along the east coast. The ferry arrives at the brand new **Magnetic Harbour** in **Nelly Bay.** The old port was to the south in **Picnic Bay,** and is now an upscale resort. From Picnic Bay you can also head west on an unsealed road (no mokes or scooters allowed) to **West Point,** a popular sunset spot. Continuing north from Nelly Bay will take you to **Arcadia,** a 15min. bus ride from the ferry; it boasts great beaches and a couple of nice restaurants. **Horseshoe Bay,** a 30min. bus ride from the ferry, is the island's northernmost populated area and has a water sports center. **Radical and Balding Bays,** near Horseshoe Bay, are accessible only by foot or 4WD; the treks are short and rewarding. **Florence and Arthur Bays** sit just a bit south and are closer to the main road.

**Tourist Office: Information Centre** (☎07 4758 1862), at the Ferry Terminal. Open M-Sa 8am-5pm, Su 8am-3pm.

**Banks:** The **post office** (see below) is the local agent for **Commonwealth Bank.** ATMs can be found at the **FoodWorks** in Horseshoe Bay, Arcadia, and Nelly Bay (see **Food,** p. 410); at the Express Food Store in Picnic Bay; at Maggie's Beachhouse in Horseshoe Bay; and additionally at Arcadia Hotel Resort.

**Police:** (24hr. ☎07 4778 5270), on the corner of Granite and Picnic St., Picnic Bay. Open M 8:30am-noon, W and F 8:30am-2pm.

**QUEENSLAND**

**Medical Services: The Magnetic Island Medical Centre,** 68 Sooning St., Nelly Bay (emergencies ☎000 or 07 4778 5107). Open M-F 9am-5pm, Sa 9am-1pm.

**Internet Access:** $6 per hr. at most hostels.

**Post Office:** On Sooning St. in Nelly Bay (☎07 4778 5118). Open M-F 8:30am-5pm, Sa 9-11am. **Postal Code:** 4819.

# ACCOMMODATIONS

Hostels are in **Picnic Bay, Arcadia,** and **Horseshoe Bay.** The **Magnetic Island Bus Company** offers discounted fares to accommodations from the Ferry Terminal.

**Bungalow Bay Koala Village,** 40 Horseshoe Bay Rd., Horseshoe Bay (☎1800 285 577 or 07 4778 5577; www.bungalowbay.com.au). Great atmosphere; cabins bordering a eucalyptus forest. Excellent amenities: large kitchen, pool, hammocks, and nightly tropical games like coconut husking and limbo. Try the **Bush Tucker Brunch** with "koalas on display" ($25, children $12.50). Wallabies and koalas run free at night. Winner of "Best Backpacker in Australia" award in 2007. $14 meal deals from on-site restaurant **Swenson's ❷.** Catch a guided tour of the attached **koala sanctuary** (presentations at 10am, noon, and 2:30pm; $19, backpackers $17). Get free accommodation and invaluable experience by volunteering at the sanctuary (min. 1 month). Sites $12.50 per person, powered $15; dorms $22; doubles $57. YHA. ❶

**Arcadia Beach Guest House,** 27 Marine Pde., Arcadia (☎07 4778 5668; www.arcadiabeachguesthouse.com.au). Essentially a B&B with a soft spot for backpackers; even claims to be the world's 1st hostel (est. 1947). Book ahead, as there are only 4 single beds available. Amenities include spa, kitchen, BBQ, TV, DVDs, F pizza night, free use of kayaks, snorkel equipment, canoes, and push bikes. Best of all, free pickup and dropoff in a Rolls Royce. Reception M-Sa 8am-6pm, Su 9am-5pm. Single bed $30-35 (2 per room; can be made into a double); queen-size bed $80; king-size bed $100; safari tents with queen-size bed and power $50. ❷

**X-base Backpackers,** 1 Nelly Bay Rd. (☎1800 24 2273; www.stayatbase.com/base-magnetic-island-hostel), between Nelly and Picnic Bay. Backpacker heaven just a 10min. walk from Picnic Bay. Located on Nelly Bay's gorgeous stretch of beach; diving school on-site (see **Reef Safari,** under **Activities,** p. 411), and scooter, motorbike, bicycle, and kayak rental. Barefoot DJs host parties almost every night with a sea breeze you won't find in any club. Campsites for 2 $25; dorms $27; doubles $62; cabins $110. ❷

**Arcadia Hotel Resort,** 7 Marine Pde., Arcadia (☎1800 663 666 or 07 4778 5177; www.magnums.com.au). Located 50m from the beach. New, huge, and chock full of amenities including swimming pools, bars, and a **restaurant ❷** (main courses $9-18). Lots of tidy, comfortable rooms in a relaxed setting. Due to its size, it's less intimate than some of its competitors. Reception 8am-8pm. Dorms $18-22; doubles $79-99. ❷

# FOOD AND NIGHTLIFE

Magnetic Island's few restaurants are innovative but expensive. For cheap food, try the supermarkets. There are two **FoodWorks:** one at 55 Sooning St., Nelly Bay, 1km past the post office (☎07 4778 5722; open daily 7am-7pm), and one in Horseshoe Bay (☎07 4778 5080; open daily 7am-6:30pm). The **IGA** supermarket at the Harbour is the best-priced and best-stocked (☎07 4758 1177; open daily 6am-8:30pm). The bar crowd tends to gravitate to Arcadia and Horseshoe Bay; be warned that the island's bus service ends in the early evening.

**Noodies Latin Bar & Cafe,** 2/6 Pacific Dr., Horseshoe Bay (☎07 4778 5786). When that nacho craving hits, get your fix here. The menu has tons of Mexican-inspired dishes;

try the vegetarian quesadilla ($18). Free sombrero with every "Pancho Villa" (pitcher of margarita). Open M-W and F-Su 11:30am-late. ❸

**Fat Possum Cafe,** 55 Sooning St., Nelly Bay (☎07 4778 5409). Offers great sandwiches, burgers, and cakes ($10); all-day breakfast ($10-15). M and Th-Su curry nights 5-9pm. Open daily 8am-5pm. AmEx/MC/V. ❷

**Wicked Mcnasty's** (☎07 4778 5861), on Pacific Dr., Horseshoe Bay. Far from nasty. Burgers ($7-10), sandwiches ($5-10), and salads. Open daily 8am-3pm. ❶

**Barefoot Art Food and Wine,** 5 Pacific Dr. in Horseshoe Bay (☎07 4758 1170). Add some culture to your cuisine at this classy restaurant/art-house hybrid. Barefoot Art serves up top-notch modern Aussie cuisine amid a variety of fascinating regional art exhibits. Find your center in the F guided meditation class (9am-10am) or enjoy weekly live jazz. Entrees run from $16.50-$19, while mains start around $18—but the quality of the dishes and the overall dining experience here more than makes up for the price. Open daily 11:30am-late. AmEx/MC/V. ❸

## ACTIVITIES

**TOURS.** Indulge the rock star within, and career around Magnetic Island with **Tropicana Tours,** 2/26 Picnic St. Guests tour the bush in Queensland-style luxury—a 10-seat stretch Jeep Wrangler. Cruise to loud music, feed lorikeets, see gorgeous beaches, and finish with wine at sunset. (☎07 4758 1800; www.tropicanatours.com.au. $75, children $40, family $196.)

**OUTDOORS ACTIVITIES.** Over 70% of Magnetic Island is composed of national parklands, with numerous bushwalks and plenty of opportunities to enjoy the natural beauty of the island. The most popular hike is the **Forts Walk** (4km, 1hr.), a hilly ascent to the ruins of a WWII command post and watch station. Koalas are often spotted along the way, so it's best to go during the evening when they are just waking up from their afternoon nap—walk slowly and listen carefully for the soft sounds of chewing in high treetops. Even if you miss the furry fellows, you can still catch a spectacular sunset at the fort. Another option is to take the **island path** (8km, 3hr.) that leads from **Picnic Bay** through wetlands and mangroves to **West Point.** From **Horseshoe Bay,** two great walks lead to secluded **Balding Bay** and **Radical Bay.** Don't miss the **Arthur Bay lookout,** a short walk past the bay on the Radical Bay Rd. At dusk, dozens of rock wallabies come to **Geoffrey Bay,** in Arcadia, for hand-fed snacks. For a list of other walks, go to the tourist office, ask the bus drivers, or grab a map at Maggie's. **Bluey's Horseshoe Ranch,** 38 Gifford St., Horseshoe Bay, will take you riding through the bush and cantering on the beach, then let you ride bareback or go swimming in the bay. The friendly staff matches riders with horses by skill level. Rides leave at 9am and 3pm. Cash only. (☎07 4778 5109. 2hr. $90; ½-day $120.)

**DIVING.** The small, friendly dive shops on Maggie Island offer some of the most inexpensive dive options in Queensland, while the small wrecks and reefs provide opportunities for endless exploration. Open-water courses, daytrips, and overnights are all available. **Pleasure Divers,** 10 Marine Pde., Arcadia, offers good deals on PADI certification classes from the shore (3-day course from $384) and also has four-day courses that include one day on the outer reef ($484). Other options include advanced courses to the Yongala wreck ($470) and a PADI open-water advanced Yongala package ($700). For those already certified, they offer shore dives (guided or unguided) with equipment for $65. (☎07 4778 5788 or 1800 797 797. Open daily 9am-5pm.) **Reef Safari,** located inside **X-base Backpackers** (see **Accommodations,** p. 410),offers a 4-day PADI open-water course ($279), an advanced course with 5 dives including a Yongala wreck dive ($440), single intro dives ($65, repeat dives $50) and certified dives ($50, repeat dives $30). Packages with free nights at X-base are also available. (☎07 4778 5777; www.reefsafari.com.) Note that some of the Townsville dive companies pick up from Magnetic Island.

**OTHER ACTIVITIES.** The **Magnetic Island Country Club,** corner of Yule St. and Hurst St., Picnic Bay, popular with Townsville and island residents, has a nine-hole golf course plus a licensed bar and restaurant. (☎07 4788 5188; www. users.bigpond.net.au/migolf. Open daily from 8am. $14, 18 holes $20.) Visit koalas, wombats, emus, and talking cockatoos at the secluded █Koala Park Oasis, on Pacific Dr., Horseshoe Bay. Follow Gifford St. past Bluey's Horseshoe Ranch for 2km and then make a right, following the signs to the Oasis for another 1.3km. (☎07 4778 5260. Open daily 9am-5pm. $10, children $5.)

# INGHAM AND SURROUNDS

Ingham, where over half the population is of Italian descent, is known as the "Little Italy of the North." Mediterranean influence infiltrates Ingham's architecture and customs, and the city celebrates its heritage on the second weekend in May during the Australian-Italian Festival. On Townsville Rd., the **visitors center** provides information about the area's national parks. (☎07 4776 5211. Open M-F 8:45am-5pm, Sa-Su 9am-2pm.) All parks in the Ingham area have self-registration huts (permits $5 per night), so it isn't necessary to buy permits in advance. The **Palm Tree Caravan Park ❶,** just 3km south of town on the Bruce Hwy., has basic campsites. (☎07 4776 2403. $19, powered $24.)

The region just west of Ingham has some of the most astounding natural attractions in Queensland. **Lumholtz National Park** (51km west of Ingham with 30km of unsealed road) is one of the world's oldest rainforests and home to **Wallaman Falls,** Australia's largest single-drop waterfall. The forest also shelters several species of endangered plants and animals, as well as the amethystine python, Australia's largest snake. Twenty-four kilometers south of Ingham, close to the Bruce Hwy., are the terraced **Jourama Falls.** Freshwater swimming holes, good turtle-spotting, and excellent birdwatching make this an ideal day-trip destination. Another 20km south, the **Mount Spec** section of **Paluma Range National Park** enchants visitors with crystal-clear streams that snake down the mountain. Camping is permitted only at **Big Crystal Creek.** Be aware that many sites can be difficult to access in the Wet.

# HINCHINBROOK ISLAND ☎07

Across the Hinchinbrook Channel is Hinchinbrook Island, one of Australia's largest island national parks. It offers unspoiled wilderness with looming granite peaks, mangrove swamps, and one of the few remaining populations of the endangered dugong. There are a few snorkeling opportunities, though most visitors devote their time on the island to the superb bushwalks. The famous **Thorsborne Trail** (32km, 3-7 days) is the most popular hike on the island. Only about 40 hikers are permitted on the trail at once, so obtain a permit several months in advance; book up to a year ahead if you plan to hike from April to September. (For permits, call ☎13 13 04 or go online to www.qld.gov.au.)

**Ferries** take visitors to two stops on the island, one at either end of the Thorsborne Trail. Hinchinbrook Island Ferries, at Port Hinchinbrook, docks at the north end of the island and offers day-tours, including walks to some of the pristine beaches. One-way tickets are useful if you have a camping permit and want to walk the length of the island. (☎1800 777 021; www.hinchinbrookferries.com.au. Transfers available from Cardwell. Day-tour $85, round-trip $125.) **Hinchinbrook Wilderness Safaris** goes to the south end of the island. The small boat leaves from George Point and will bring you back to Lucinda, south of Cardwell. (☎07 4777 8307. $46, transfer between Cardwell and Lucinda $28.)

Daytrips to the island don't require bookings, but overnight stays (camping or staying in the resort) always do. If you're planning to camp, obtain a permit in advance ($5 per night). Facilities include picnic tables, BBQ, water, and toilets. The folks at the **Rainforest and Reef Centre,** 142 Victoria St., Cardwell, on the north side of town near the jetty, are eager to help. The center has a free informational walk that details the science behind the rainforest and its inhabitants. (☎07 4066 8601. Open M-F 8:30am-5pm, Sa-Su 9am-3pm.)

# MISSION BEACH ☎07

Transformed virtually overnight into a major backpacker destination, this stretch of beach deserves every ounce of the hype surrounding it. The town experiences heavy traffic, but the expansive sands provide enough space for some peace and quiet. Reefs stuffed with untouched corals and sand cays make this one of the best diving spots on the Great Barrier Reef. In the rainforest, the many cassowaries make for unique nature hikes. Mission Beach flows with adrenaline, offering arguably the best white water rafting in the country on the Tully River as well as unbeatable skydiving.

## ▐▀ TRANSPORTATION

Greyhound Australia serves Mission Beach several times per day to Cairns (2½hr., 3 per day, $30) and Townsville (3hr., 2 per day, $51). Premier **buses** run twice per day. Once you arrive, a hostel courtesy bus will take you to your accommodation. You can also use these buses during your stay, or contact the Mission Beach Bus Service (☎07 4068 7400; www.transnorthbus.com), which runs about once per hr. (9am-6pm, $2 per section, day-ticket $10). **Sugarland Car Rentals** is 50m from the bus stop on 30 Wongaling Beach Rd. (☎07 4068 8272). Rentals are available from $55 per day (dropoffs in Cairns are $30 extra).

## ◢▐ ORIENTATION AND PRACTICAL INFORMATION

The region known as Mission Beach is actually a group of four communities lining a 14km stretch of waterfront property. From north to south, the towns are: **Bigil Bay, Mission Beach, Wongaling Beach,** and **South Mission Beach.** The main streets are **Porter Promenade,** which runs through Mission Beach proper, and **Cassowary Drive,** which runs through Wongaling. The massive **cassowary statue** in the center of Wongaling Beach, in front of the bus stop, is a popular landmark. Just off the coast are the **Family Islands,** including popular **Dunk Island.**

Pick up a map of the area, book tours and accommodations, and surf the net (Internet $5 per hr.) at **Mission Beach Information Station,** next to the bus stop. (☎07 4068 6899; www.missionbeachinfo.com. Open daily 9am-7pm.) The **Visitors Centre** is on Porter Pde. as you leave Mission Beach toward Bigil Bay. (☎07 4068 7099. Open daily 9am-5pm.) Local services include: **ATMs** at the supermarket in Mission Beach and the Mission Beach Resort; the **police** (☎07 4068 8422; open M, W, F 8am-noon; Tu and Th 8am-11am), 500m past the cassowary statue at the corner of Webb Rd. and Cassowary Dr. in Wongaling Beach; and Internet at **Intermission @ The Beach** ($5 for 1hr.; $15 for 5hr.) in the Village Green, off Porter Pde. (☎07 4068 117; open M-F 9am-6pm, Sa-Su 10am-6pm). No banks in Mission Beach exchange foreign currency. There's a **pharmacy** behind the bus stop in Wongaling (☎07 4068 8138; open M-F 8:30am-5:15pm, Sa 9am-noon). The **post office** is on Porter Pde. (Open M-F 9am-5pm.) **Postal Code:** 4852.

**QUEENSLAND**

## ACCOMMODATIONS

All hostels listed book tours, offer free pickup at the bus station, and provide courtesy buses around town. If you're camping, try **Mission Beach Caravan Park ❶**, at 53 Porter Pde. (sites on or near the beach from $12.50), or the conveniently located **Tropical Hibiscus ❷**, across the road from the bus station. (Unpowered sites $20 per night, powered $24 per night. MC/V.)

**Absolute Backpackers,** 28 Wongaling Beach Rd., Wongaling Beach (☎1800 688 316 or 07 4068 8317; www.absolutebackpackers.com.au). Excellent location 70m from the Giant Cassowary and bus station; only 400m from Wongaling Beach. A simple, relaxed, and clean place to crash; staff makes the place feel like home. Internet, pool, laundry, TV room, free parking, and free F BBQ. Reception 7:30am-7:30pm. Dorms $22-24; doubles $50. Female rooms $24. VIP/YHA discounts. MC/V. ❷

**Scotty's Mission Beach House,** 167 Reid Rd. (☎07 4068 8676; www.scottysbeachhouse.com.au). The hip staff at this lively hostel is friendly and helpful. Free wine and cheese Tu-Su. Every night is a party in **Scotty's Bar** (meals under $15; backpacker special $10), but it's removed enough from rooms to ensure a good sleep. Internet, laundry, pool, TV room, A/C, and free pickup from buses. Reception 7:30am-9pm. Sites $10; 12-bed dorms $21; 4-bed ensuite dorms $26; doubles $49, ensuite $59. MC/V. ❷

**The Treehouse** (☎07 4068 7137), on Bingil Bay Rd., Bingil Bay. The closest community in Mission Beach is perched high in the rainforest canopy. Guests lounge around on beanbags and hammocks in treehouse luxury, enjoying BBQ, pool, laundry, ping pong, and reading space. Internet $5 per hr. Rooms all around a common area where music (guests' choice) plays until 10pm. Reception 7:30am-8pm. Sites $13.50 per person; dorms $23; doubles $55. YHA. MC/V. ❷

## FOOD

There are several excellent restaurants on the Village Green in Mission Beach proper, as well as in nearby Wongaling.

**Piccolo's Paradise** (☎07 4068 7008), on David St. in the Village Green. A popular cafe that offers fresh baguette sandwiches, excellent pastas, pizza, and a selection of juices. Meals $12-17. Open Tu-Sa and Su 5pm-9pm. AmEx/MC/V. ❷

**The Shrubbery Tavern** (☎07 4068 7803), on the sea side of the Village Green, cooks up steak, seafood, and pasta from scratch, with wide views of the shoreline. Tourists and locals fill tables and flood the dance floor on Su, as surprisingly prominent Aussie bands take the stage. Open for lunch F and Su noon-2:30pm, for dinner W-Su 6pm-late. Lunch $14-17, dinner $18-30. Veggie options. AmEx/MC/V. ❸

**Mint Cafe** (☎07 4068 8401), on Cassowary Dr. between Mission Beach and Wongaling. Enjoy a healthful and tasty dish at Wongaling's grooviest eatery. Serves its acclaimed breakfast ($4.50-15) all day. Locals praise the zucchini and sweet corn fritter stack ($14.50) as well as the eggs Benedict ($12.50). For lunch, try one of the wide selection of sandwiches on bruschetta ($7.50-13), a wrap ($10-12), or salad ($11-15.50). Veggie options. Open daily 8am-4pm. Cash only. ❷

## SIGHTS AND ACTIVITIES

**DIVING.** Mission Beach occupies a unique spot on the Reef where coral drop-offs create long walls of underwater gardens. **Calypso Adventures,** around the corner from Woolworths in the Wongaling Shopping Centre, offers a range of dive courses and trips to the Reef (☎07 4068 8432; www.calypsoadventures.com.au). The cheapest option is a one-day snorkel/dive trip to Eddy Reef ($135;

children $80. Price includes lunch, transfers from accommodation, and snorkel equipment.) **Quick Cat** also makes trips to the reef, both directly and via Dunk Island. (☎07 4068 8707 or 04 0713 0137; www.quickcatscuba.com. $140, children $70; 1 intro dive $85, 2 certified dives $90.)

**HIKING.** Beautiful **walking tracks** criss-cross the area. On the back of the Mission Beach street directory (available for free around town), you'll find a list of readily accessible parks, forests, and walking tracks. There are several in the **Licuala State Forest,** including the **Rainforest Circuit Walk** (1.3km, 30min.), a nice stroll under a canopy of Licuala fan palms. Start at the Tully-Mission Beach Rd. carpark. **Licuala Walking Track** (7.8km, 3hr.) stretches north through coastal lowland rainforest to the El Arish-Mission Beach Rd. The **Cutten Brothers Walk** (1.5km, 30min.) snakes through mangroves between Alexander Dr. and Clump Point jetty. The **Bicton Hill Track** (4km; starts 3km past the Wet Tropics Info Centre) and the **Kennedy Track** (7km, 4hr.) are longer walks that pass by mangroves, beaches, and rainforest. For a less sweaty experience, visit **Garner Beach** at Marine Park. At low tide, visitors can embark on the so-called "rock pool walk," where they can marvel at coral and starfish on the sand. Just be careful about what you touch, as much of the marine fauna stings. Also, don't take anything from the beach, as it's a protected habitat.

**OTHER ACTIVITIES.** Adventure sports are quite popular in Mission Beach. **Jump the Beach** offers tandem skydiving and Queensland's only beach landing, complemented by incredible views of the rainforest, beach, reef, and islands. Many consider Mission Beach to be one of Australia's top jumps. (☎1800 444 568; www.jumpthebeach.com.au. 9000 ft. $210; 11,000 ft. $244; 14,000 ft. $295.)

## ▓ DAYTRIP FROM MISSION BEACH

### DUNK ISLAND

*A number of boats service Dunk Island. Those looking to maximize time there should opt for the* **Dunk Island Express Water Taxi,** *on Banfield Pde., near Scotty's in Wongaling Beach. (☎07 4068 8310. 10min., 6 per day, $30 round-trip.)* **Quick Cat** *departs from Clump Point Jetty, 1km north of the village green. (☎07 4068 7289 or 1800 654 242; www.quickcatcruises.com.au. Departs daily 8:30am, returns 4:30pm. $56.)* **Coral Sea Kayaking** *runs daytrips to Dunk, including lunch, environmental interpretation, and snorkeling gear. (☎07 4068 9154; www.coralseakayaking.com. Full day $118.)*

Due to their proximity to the mainland, the **Family Islands** are ideal escapes. **Dunk Island,** a.k.a. the "father island," is the most frequented, and really the only one that can be visited in a day. The island became famous because of E.J. Banfield's *Confessions of a Beachcomber,* an account of his life on the island from 1897 to 1923. Nearby **Bedarra,** a.k.a. "the mother," is uninhabited, save for a swanky resort. The "twins" are slightly farther out and the smaller land masses at the fringe of the group are the "brothers, sisters, and triplets."

The main attractions on Dunk, aside from the postcard-perfect beaches, are the hikes. A local favorite is the **walk around the island** (9.2km, 4hr.), which covers diverse landscapes and takes hikers to the island's highest point. An easier option is the **coastal hike** (1km, 15min.) up to **Muggy Muggy Beach** from the dock. Muggy Muggy is hidden in a pocket of 360-million-year-old rocks; find it and spend a few hours snorkeling. The hike directly to the **Mount Kootaloo Lookout** (2hr.), the highest point on the island, provides a good workout and a view.

The **Dunk Island Resort ❺** (☎07 4068 8199) monopolizes all island activities, and the rooms are rather expensive ($166 per person, including breakfast). Some of the best-equipped campsites in northern Queensland are only a short distance away (permits purchased on-site, $5). These sites are popular, so book well ahead. **Dunk Island Watersports** (☎07 4068 8199), near the jetty, issues the camping permits and rents a slew of water toys, including paddle skis ($20 per hr.), sailboards ($25 per hr.), snorkel gear ($15 per day), dinghies (½-day $90), wakeboards and waterskis ($25 per 15min.), and catamarans ($25 per hr.). Daytrippers can purchase the **Resort Experience Pass** ($40) at the Watersports shed, which entitles visitors to use of the resort facilities and a meal at the **Jetty Cafe ❷** or at the bar in the resort. The Jetty Cafe, next door to Dunk Island Watersports, is the only place to eat on the island that isn't the resort's upscale restaurant. It serves burgers, grilled fish, and salads. (Open daily 11am-4pm. Main courses $17-22, salads $9.50-15.50. No reservations.)

# NEAR MISSION BEACH

## PARONELLA PARK

Between Cairns and Mission Beach lies the Moorish castle of 🏰**Paronella Park** (☎07 4065 3225; www.paronellapark.com.au). Spaniard José Paronella built this elaborate complex for his fiancée in the 1930s. Uninhabited, the buildings degenerated into scenic ruins, carpeted by the green, encroaching rainforest. Winner of Queensland's highest tourism award, the park has served as the backdrop for three movies, eight TV shows, a music video, and an international magazine photo shoot. Enthusiastic guides give tours of the grounds, then leave you to explore on your own. The **"Darkness Falls Tour"** (starting at 6:15pm) is particularly breathtaking, as the castle and surrounding ruins are lit up at night. The admission ($30, children $15) includes all tours, a night's stay in the caravan park, and re-entry for 12 months. Early morning and overnight visitors should not miss the chance to enjoy breakfast by one of the park's stunning waterfalls, dining on tables José Paronella built 80 years ago.

Though Paronella Park is inaccessible by public transportation, it isn't hard to find a day tour from Cairns or Mission Beach that features the attraction as a destination. If you are driving, look for signs along the Bruce Hwy. (the South Johnstone exit is the fastest); from the Tablelands, follow the signs to South Johnstone and you'll come across the sign for the park. When you've finished gawking at Paronella Park's exquisite architecture, take some time to stroll down Kauri Ave., which offers a view of towering Kauri pines nearby. Or feed the fish and eels in the teeming waterfall pool nestled in the ruins of the castle's grand staircase. (Open daily 9am-7:30pm.)

## INNISFAIL

North of Mission Beach is the town of Innisfail. Although there are few tourist attractions, the Johnstone River and beautiful beaches make it a pleasant pit stop. There is also a high demand for fruit-pickers year-round; if you are looking for temporary work, this is a good place to visit. Just north of Innisfail, the road to the **Atherton Tablelands** (p. 429) branches inland toward Millaa Millaa.

There are four hostels in Innisfail, and all are chiefly for backpackers in search of work. Be sure to book ahead. The **Codge Lodge ❷**, 63 Rankin St., off Grace St. (which intersects Edith St.) is by far the best of them. Amenities include a huge pool, satellite TV, a nice lookout over the Johnstone River, free laundry, free Internet, transport, and the nicest rooms around. (☎07 4061 8055. Reception sometimes unattended; call ahead. Dorms $25, weekly $150; singles $25. AmEx/MC/V.) In a town with few appetizing options, **Roscoe's Piazza ❸**, on McGowan Dr., offers an entire all-you-can-eat buffet (lunch $16, dinner $22). Pasta, pizza, and salad comprise the top-notch smorgasbord.

(☎07 4061 6888. Open daily 10am-10pm. AmEx/MC/V.) When night falls, the town descends upon **Nite Rumors,** at 57a Ernest St., the only nightclub in Innisfail. It attracts all ages and is always packed. (Open F-Sa 10pm-3am. No cover.)

The bus station is on Edith St. (which becomes the Bruce Hwy. as it leaves Innisfail) in front of ANZAC Park. **Greyhound Australia** runs daily to Cairns (1½hr., $27) and Townsville (4½hr., $57). The railway station is off the Bruce Hwy. on Station St., west of town heading north toward Cairns (☎13 22 32; www.traveltrain.com.au). For information on Innisfail and the surrounding area, the **Canecutter Information Centre,** at the corner of Bruce Hwy. and Eslick St., just before the town center when entering from the south, has a friendly and knowledgeable staff and books tours. (☎07 4061 4361. Open M-F 9am-4pm, Sa-Su 10am-3pm; call Paronella Park after hours until 9:30pm.)

# FAR NORTH QUEENSLAND

The northeast corner of the continent is nothing short of heaven for outdoor adventurers. The Great Barrier Reef snakes close to shore, luring divers with its stunning views and sublime immensity. Vast tropical rainforests press up against the Coral Sea by the green-covered mountains of the Great Dividing Range. The variety of wildlife means that the Far North's greatest attraction is its natural beauty. While Cairns caters to travelers seeking urban comforts, the more remote parts of this land are untamed. The Captain Cook Hwy. leads modern-day trailblazers north into the rainforest, which becomes increasingly dense around Cape Tribulation. Wilder yet is the Cape York peninsula, which starts beyond Cooktown and stretches to the Torres Strait. Travelers daring enough to make the journey should anticipate very basic unsealed roads.

# CAIRNS                 ☎07

The last major city at the corner of the great tropical outback, Cairns (CANS) is both the northern terminus of the backpacker route and the premier gateway to snorkeling and scuba diving on the Great Barrier Reef. The countless neon signs and booking agencies that dot the Esplanade and Central Business District (CBD) betray Cairns's tourist identity. While tidal mudflats preclude traditional

## WORKIN' ROUND THE CROC

Damien Cowan is a 21 year-old croc handler in Innisfail, Queensland. He took a break to talk with *Let's Go* about his work.

**LG:** How did you get into crocs?
**DC:** I've been fascinated by crocs, snakes, and other reptiles all my life, so this is something I've always wanted to do.

**LG:** What sort of temperament is necessary to handle crocs?
**DC:** Handlers have to be cool, calm, and collected. You have to know what to do when a 5m croc is running after you.

**LG:** Are there any jobs at the farm more dangerous than yours?
**DC:** The most dangerous thing a croc handler can do is collect the eggs of a female croc. Hopefully I'll be doing that soon.

**LG:** Any close calls?
**DC:** The training is so extensive, I've been able to keep out of trouble. I know handlers who have lost their lives and limbs on the job.

**LG:** Your life insurance payment must be a killer.
**DC:** [Laughs] I tried to buy some life insurance as a joke once. The agent just stared at me and said she would get back to me. Her manager called me the next day and said they don't insure people in my "line of work." I told her I was mostly joking.

QUEENSLAND

beach activities, a dizzying array of reef and island excursions coupled with throngs of raucous, fun-loving backpackers leave few would-be beachgoers complaining. The atmosphere is friendly, relaxed, and outrageously touristy. A bustling city with a front-row seat to one of the ocean's most breathtaking treasures, Cairns is an ideal destination for travelers seeking thrills or just a chance to see nature at its most majestic.

# INTERCITY TRANSPORTATION

**Flights:** The airport (☎07 4052 3888) is 6km north of Cairns on the Captain Cook Hwy. Follow the signs. For the cheapest flights, try **Student Flights** (☎1800 046 462) or major regional carriers. **Virgin Blue** (☎13 67 89; www.virginblue.com.au) is a great domestic resource; also services New Zealand. **Qantas** (☎13 13 13; www.qantas.com. au) has daily flights to almost all domestic airports. Book online to avoid extra fees and commissions. Many hostels run a free airport pickup service; call for free from the kiosk in the terminal. To get back to the airport, you'll have to book ahead and pay $10 for the **Airport Shuttle** (☎07 4048 8355) or $15 for 2 people. Split a cab for a faster, more convenient ride at about the same price. **Buses** also run to town from the terminal ($10; $15 for 2). **Taxis** to town available 24hr. for $15-20.

**Trains:** The **train station** is between Bunda St. and the Cairns Central shopping mall. From the Esplanade, walk inland down Spence St. to Cairns Central. Walk to the back of the shopping center and then through the parking lot. The **Cairns Rail Travel Centre** (☎07 4036 9341, 1800 872 467 for bookings 7am-7pm), inside the train station, sells tickets. YHA discount 10% for long-distance trips. Open M 9am-4:30pm, Tu-F 8am-4:30pm, Sa-Su 8am-10am. The **East Coast Discovery Pass** (☎13 22 32) offers unlimited travel for up to 6 months on **Queensland Rail, CountryLink,** and **Traveltrain** and covers rail between Cairns and Brisbane ($281), Melbourne ($501), and Sydney ($411). With this pass, you can travel unlimited km in any direction (north or south) in 1 of 6 different travel sectors. Trains leave for **Brisbane** (31-32hr.; Tu, W, F-Su 8:30am; $187-281) and **Kuranda.** (Bookings ☎07 4036 9333. Trains daily 8:30 and 9:30am, Sa 8:30am; $37, $52 round-trip. Student, senior, and family discounts.)

**Buses:** The **bus station** is located at Trinity Wharf, on Wharf St. Luggage storage $9-12 per day. Open daily 6:15am-1am. **Sun Palm Coaches** (☎07 4087 2900) goes to **Cape Tribulation** (3½hr., 2 per day, $75) and **Port Douglas** (1hr.; several per day; $35, round-trip $60). **Greyhound Australia** (☎13 20 30) has 10% ISIC/VIP/YHA discounts and runs to: **Airlie Beach** (11hr., 5 per day, $113); **Brisbane** (28hr., 5 per day, $248); **Cardwell** (3hr., 5 per day, $37); **Ingham** (3hr., 5 per day, $61); **Innisfail** (1hr., 5 per day, $27); **Mackay** (12hr., 5 per day, $155); **Mission Beach** (2hr., 2 per day, $30); **Rockhampton** (15hr., 6 per day, $174); **Townsville** (6hr., 5 per day, $66). **Premier** (☎07 4031 6495 or 13 34 10) offers cheaper rates as well as VIP/YHA discounts but their buses tend to depart less frequently.

# ORIENTATION

Cairns is sandwiched in by forested hills to the west, a harbor to the east, and mangrove swamps to both the north and south. The **Esplanade** runs all the way along the waterfront. At the street's southern end is **The Pier,** with both a man-made lagoon and an upscale shopping center in the heavily commercial **Pier Marketplace.** Farther south, the Esplanade becomes **Wharf Street** and runs past **Trinity Wharf** and the **Transit Centre. Shields Street** runs perpendicular to the Esplanade and crosses **Abbott Street** before running into **City Place,** a pedestrian mall with an open-air concert space and coffee shops galore. From this intersection,

TO 🏠 (500m)
TO 🌼 FLECKER BOTANIC GARDENS (4km), TANKS
ART CENTRE (4km), MT. WHIFFIELD PARK (4km), ℹ️ ROYAL
FLYING DOCTOR VISITORS CENTER (6km), 🏖️ TRINITY BEACH,
MOUNT WHIFFIELD ENVIRONMENTAL PARK, AND ✚ (6km),
SKYRAIL AND KURANDA (25km)

**Cairns**

🏠 ACCOMMODATIONS
Cairns Girls Hostel, **4**
Caravella 149, **22**
Dreamtime, **17**
Gecko's Backpackers, **18**
Gilligan's, **12**
The Serpent, **1**
Traveller's Oasis, **19**
Tropic Days, **20**
Gilligan's, **21**

🍎 FOOD
Cafe Melt, **16**
Sushi Express, **9**
Tiny's Juice Bar, **15**
Woolworths, **7**
Little Aussie Bum, **23**

⭐ NIGHTLIFE
P.J. O'Brien's, **8**
Rhino Bar, **24**
Shenannigan's, **13**
The Woolshed, **5**

**Lake Street** runs parallel to the Esplanade. Continuing away from the water, Shields St. also intersects **Grafton Street** and **Sheridan Street** (called **Cook Highway** north of the city). The **Cairns Railway Station** is located on **McLeod Street** in front of **Cairns Central**, the city's largest mall.

# 🚍 LOCAL TRANSPORTATION

**Buses: Sunbus** (☎07 4057 7411; www.sunbus.com.au), on Lake St. in the market in City Place. Buses go south to the suburbs and north to Palm Cove, but not to the airport. Unlimited day pass for travel within the city $4.60; prices for other passes depend on where you go in Cairns. A $9.20 pass gets you from the CBD to the northern beaches.

**Taxis: Black and White** (24hr. ☎07 4048 8333 or 13 10 08).

**Car Rental:** The bigger companies in Cairns charge those under 25 a surcharge or significantly raise the deductible, which can increase the daily rental price by up to $50 or even disqualify you from purchasing insurance.

**A1 Car Rentals,** 141 Lake St. (☎1300 301 175), has weekly rates from $51 and a selection of high-end vehicles. Some of the lowest prices for 4WD rentals ($125+). Open daily 8am-5:30pm.

**Sargent 4WD,** 397-399 Sheridan St. (☎07 4032 3094 or 1800 077 353; www.sargent.com.au), specializes in providing cars for long-distance trips on questionable roads; if you want to drive to Cape York, they're among your best bets. More expensive than **A1 Car Rentals,** but has the toughest trucks available. 4WDs start at $175; there are no surcharges, but drivers under the age of 25 aren't allowed to buy damage reduction insurance.

**Europcar,** at the corner of Abbott St. and Shields St. (☎07 4051 4600 or 1300 131 407). Weekly rates from $31.50 per day, 4WD $68.40 per day. Open M-F 7:30am-6pm, Sa-Su 8am-5pm.

**Avis,** 135 Lake St. (☎07 4051 5911), has rates starting at $49 per day; 4WD $160 per day. Open M-F 7:30am-5:30pm, Sa-Su and public holidays 8am-4pm.

**Leisure Car Rentals,** 314 Sheridan St. (☎07 4051 8988), is a bit far from the CBD but has inexpensive rentals starting at $45 per day. Open daily 7am-5pm.

**Travellers AutoBarn,** 123-125 Bunda St. (☎07 4041 3722 or 1800 674 374), rents campervans with unlimited km, local or one-way, from $48 (2-person camper) per day. 5-day minimum; no under 25 surcharge. Open M-F 9am-5pm, Sa 9am-1pm.

**Bike Rental: Cairns Scooter and Bicycle Hire** (☎07 4031 3444; www.scoota.com. au), 47 Shields St. between Mcleod and Sheridan St. Rents bicycles for $20 per day, $60 per week; scooters (must be at least 21 years old and carry a driver's license) $55/175 per week. All rentals include a security deposit.

# 🔢 PRACTICAL INFORMATION

## TOURIST AND FINANCIAL SERVICES

**Tourist Offices:** The **Visitors Info Bureau,** on the Esplanade between Aplin and Florence St., has a 24hr. information line (☎07 4041 0007) and offers details for local accommodations, tour companies, and bike rentals.

**National Parks Office: Queensland Parks and Wildlife Service (QPWS)** (☎07 4046 6600), 5b Sheridan St. Provides helpful brochures and advice for visitors to national parks. Purchase the permits required for camping in national parks here ($4.50 per person per night). Open M-F 8:30am-5pm.

**Currency Exchange:** There are places to change currency and travelers checks throughout the city. The 2nd fl. of **Orchid Plaza,** 79-87 Abbot St., usually has the best rates for both, but be sure to shop around since rates change all the time. **Travelex** charges an $8 minimum for currency and traveler's checks but has negotiable rates for large transactions ($500+). Locations throughout the city: 69 Abbott St. (☎07 4031 6880; open daily 9am-9:30pm); Night Markets, Royal Harbour, 71-73 the Esplanade (☎07 4031 8280; open daily 5-10pm); 50 Lake St. (☎07 4051 6255; open M-Sa 9am-5pm).

**Ticket Agencies: TicketLink** in the **Cairns Civic Theatre** (☎07 4031 9555; www.ticketlink.com.au), at the corner of Florence and Sheridan St. Offers discounts for students and children. Box office open M-F 8am-6pm; Sa 9am-1pm.

## EMERGENCY AND COMMUNICATIONS

**Police:** (☎07 4030 7000) on Sheridan St., between Spence and Hartley St. Open 24hr. There's a police station next to the lagoon on the Esplanade. Open daily 8am-4pm.

**Crisis Lines: Alcohol and Drug Information** (☎1800 177 833). **Lifeline** (☎13 11 14).

**Pharmacy: Chemmart Pharmacy,** 119 Abbott St. (☎07 4041 0228). Open daily 9am-9pm. Gives advice to travelers continuing on to Asia.

**Medical Services: Cairns Base Hospital** (☎07 4050 6333), on the Esplanade past the Boardwalk. Emergency department. Open 24hr. More centrally located **Medical Centre** (☎07 4052 1119), on the corner of Florence and Grafton St. Open 24hr.

**Internet Access:** Internet access points are available all over the place in Cairns, but they don't really come cheap. Many places on the Esplanade and in City Place charge $4-5 per hr. **Global Gossip,** 125 Abbott St., offers low rates for members. $1 for first hr., $1 per 30min. after; free membership. Printing $0.35 per page, photocopies $0.25 per page, CD burning $7.50 for CDs, faxing, digital camera readers, and discount deals on international calls. Membership is free. For non-members, Internet is $4 for 1st hr., and $1 for every subsequent 20min. The best deal without membership is **Backpackers World,** 9-13 Shields St. (☎07 4041 0999), where you can access the Internet for $3 per hr., burn CDs for $2, and print for $0.50 per page. Also offers unlimited Wi-Fi deals ($15 for 1 day, $50 for 7 days, $150 for 30 days). The **Cairns City Public Library,** 151 Abbott St., charges $4 per hr. Wi-Fi available.

**Post Office: Cairns General Post Office (GPO),** 13 Grafton St. (☎07 4031 4303), on the corner with Hartley St. Open M-F 8:30am-5pm. Smaller branch located in **Orchid Plaza** just south of City Place between Abbott and Lake St. **Postal Code:** 4870.

#  ACCOMMODATIONS

Cairns may not be a big city, but its reputation as the gateway to far north Queensland's ecological wonders has established it as a favorite for backpackers. While many hostels are clustered along the **Esplanade,** there are plenty of others in the CBD and along the **Captain Cook Highway (Highway 1).** Hostels in these areas are generally large and are the best bet for last-minute bookings.

> **TIP**
> **COCKROACH MOTEL.** Some hostels are extremely cheap—but also extremely dirty. It's a good idea to check out rooms before booking them (if you're taking a taxi, ask the driver to wait). Make sure you'll be able to handle the grime before committing; this is especially important in the extremely humid tropical north, where mold can be a problem.

## CBD

**Cairns Girls Hostel,** 147 Lake St. (☎07 4051 2767), between Florence and Aplin St. This clean, friendly, women-only hostel has provided a safe haven for over 30 years. Renters praise the friendly staff, cleanliness, and privacy. No noise after 10pm. 3 kitchens, 3 bathrooms, 2 lounges, laundry, Internet access ($3 per hr.), free phone (incoming calls), BBQ, and TV. Free night's stay when you book certain dive courses through the hostel. Reception 7:30am-9pm. Dorms $20; twins $24. ❷

**Caravella 149,** 149 the Esplanade (☎07 4031 5680), has excellent doubles equipped with fridge and dressers. Flash your *Let's Go* guide and ask about a $5 discount on your 1st night's stay. Hostelers crowd in and around the large sparkling pool during the day and share food, music, and stories in the courtyard at night. For the cheapest digs on the Esplanade, try out the aptly named Aquarium. This 8-bed dorm is bright blue and substitutes windows for walls ($16), allowing residents a bird's-eye view of the hostel's goings-on. Free night's stay when you book $200+ in tours. Fridge in most rooms. Internet $5 per hr. Dorms $16-22; doubles $60. ❶

**Gilligan's,** 57-89 Grafton St. (☎07 4041 6566; www.gilligansbackpackers.com.au). This huge complex is a city within a city, stretching for half a city block. A 2000+ capacity bar (see **Nightlife,** (p. 428)) is attached, with a nightclub and more rooms above—just in case their 540 hostel beds fill up. You won't get the intimate feel of some of the smaller hostels, but here you'll have the advantages of an on-site restaurant ($8 meals), a free gym, several kitchens, free lockers, laundry, Internet ($4 per hr.), and a pool. Reception 24hr. 4-person dorms $28; 6-person dorms $24; 8-person dorms $22. ❷

QUEENSLAND

## JUST OUTSIDE THE CBD

**Traveller's Oasis,** 8 Scott St. (☎07 4052 1377 or 1800 621 353; www.travellersoasis. com.au). Off Bunda St., near **Dreamtime** and **Gecko's.** This hostel, with its brightly-colored, air-conditioned rooms, is a welcome respite from the backpacker factories throughout Cairns. The ever-resourceful and energetic owner, Cathy, is usually around and will get you some of the best deals possible on tours, car rentals, etc. Internet access ($1 for 15min., Wi-Fi $5 per day), laundry, pool, free coffee and tea, TV in doubles. Dorms $25; singles $42; doubles $59. ❷

**Dreamtime,** 4 Terminus St. (☎07 4031 6753 or 1800 058 440; www.dreamtimetravel. com.au). Located at the corner of Bunda St. and Terminus St. next door to **Cafe Melt** (p. 423), Dreamtime provides spacious, vibrantly colored rooms, breezy outdoor lounges, and an easygoing clientele that create the feel of a cozy resort rather than an urban hostel. Lounge away afternoons by the pool or surf the web with a cup of joe at the adjacent cafe (guests get free Internet access and meal vouchers). Daily shuttles to the Pier and bus station. Large, clean, bright rooms with comfortable beds. Pool, BBQ, kitchen. 3-, 4-, or 5-person dorms. Doubles have fridge. Reception 7:30am-noon and 4-8pm. Dorms $22; twins and doubles $55. Book ahead. ❷

**The Serpent,** 341 Lake St. (☎07 4040 7777 or 1800 737 736; www.serpenthostel. com), a 25min. walk north along the Esplanade from the CBD. The Serpent's cheap, cheery rooms and swanky lounge area make it worth the lengthy walk. Relax by the pool, strike up a game of sand volleyball, or nestle into 1 of the futons in front of the flat-screen TV. The free shuttle bus runs hourly except during early evening. Internet access ($4 per hr.), free evening meals at the hostel, $5 breakfast, laundry, kitchen, A/C, storage. Reception 7am-11pm. 12-bed dorms $14; 8-bed dorms $22; 6-bed dorms $23; 4-bed dorms $28; twins and doubles $65, ensuite $75; king deluxe $85. ❶

**Tropic Days,** 28 Bunting St. (☎07 4041 1521 or 1800 421 521; www.tropicdays.com. au). 20min. walk west from the CBD, behind the Showgrounds north of Scott St. Jungle-themed paintings, a neat tropical garden, and a sparkling pool. Fills up quickly, but anyone can pitch a tent in the backyard ($11, includes all amenities). M Australian BBQ with 'roo, croc, emu, and mackerel ($12) and a didjeridu competition ($8.) Free shuttle to the CBD (9 times per day, 7:30am-9:30pm) and free airport pickup (7:30am-2:30pm). Internet ($1 per 15min.) and TV lounge. Free evening meal at The Woolshed. Th all-you-can-eat pizza. Free guest telephone. $10 key deposit. Reception 7am-noon and 4-8pm. 3-bed dorms $24-25; twins and doubles $55-59. ❷

**Gecko's Backpackers,** 187 Bunda St. (☎07 4031 1344 or 1800 011 344). Offers clean, bright rooms with comfortable mattresses. Helpful staff make this small Backpackers seem like home. Free breakfast at hostel and vouchers for free meal in town. Free airport shuttle. Internet $2 for first 30min., $3 every subsequent hr. Pool, hammocks, BBQ. $10 key deposit. 10-day max. stay. Reception 7am-noon and 4-8pm. 3- and 4-bed dorms $22; singles $35; doubles $45. Extra for A/C. ❷

## ◨ FOOD

Cairns is overflowing with dining options, from all-night stalls on the Esplanade to upscale seafood restaurants. **Shields Street** is known by locals as "eat street." Some of the pricier restaurants offer discounts of up to 40% if you are seated before a certain time, which is normally 7pm. Most of the hostels in town hand out meal vouchers for one of the local watering holes, though you'll likely leave hungry unless you spring for one of the optional upgrades ($5-8 for full meals). Diners on a budget visit the **Night Markets food court,** 71-75 the Esplanade, for a variety of quick and cheap takeaways. (☎07 4051 7666. Open 5pm-late; full plates as little as $3.50.) Doing your own cooking is often the most economical dinner option. For basic groceries, try **Woolworths**, on Abbott St. between Shields and Spence St., **Bi-Lo and Coles**, in Cairns Central (both open M-F 8am-9pm, Sa 8am-5:30pm, Su 9am-6pm), or the smaller **IGA**, at Florence St. and the Esplanade, for latenight necessities (open 24hr.). You can also get wraps and sandwiches at their deli for less than $10.

**THE WAR BETWEEN THE STATES**

If visiting Australia in May, June, or July, don't be surprised if you find yourself engulfed in seas of Aussies clad in maroon or light blue. No, Cairns is not the vanguard of a puzzling fashion movement. When the streets turn light blue and maroon, Australia's most intense and divisive Rugby League series is likely looming.

The State of Origin, as it is called, is a fierce best-of-three rugby series held annually between the Queensland "Maroons" and the New South Wales "Blues." The matches captivate the entire continent for three months, pitting Maroon brothers against Blue sisters and dividing even the most remote towns.

The competition also provides tourists with a chance to get to know the grittier side of Australian culture. State of Origin festivals abound in Queensland and New South Wales from May to July, fanning the fiery rivalry but providing a more light-hearted atmosphere for passionate fans. Even tourists who don't know the difference between a pop pass and a rolling maul can't help but get caught up in the hoopla. If an entire festival devoted to a few rugby games doesn't sound all that appealing, at least try and squeeze your way into a pub to watch one game. Though the hordes of wild fans can be intimidating, the atmosphere (and drink specials!) are authentically Aussie.

🍴 **Cafe Melt,** 189 Bunda St. (☎07 4031 6754). This hip, airy restaurant next door to **Dreamtime** (p. 422) has good prices and one of the best deals in Cairns: huge "nightly revolving feature meals" featuring cuisine from around the world. Vegetarian options available. Wraps and salads $7.50. Pizzas $10. Internet access $3 per hr. Free Internet and discounted food for Dreamtime guests. Open daily 7:30am-late. ❶

🍴 **Tiny's Juice Bar,** 45 Grafton St. (☎07 4031 4331). This cheap, popular stop serves some of the healthiest food in Cairns. Try one of the refreshing energy drinks ($3-5.50), such as the soothing apple, papaya, orange, and watermelon. If you're confident in your creative abilities, order your own blends. The same goes for wraps, salads, and sandwiches made with ingredients like avocado, feta, cucumber, chicken, and hummus ($7-10). Tasty vegetarian and vegan options such as the Feta Avocado Salad ($8) and Tofu Pattie Salad ($7). Open daily 7:30am-4pm. ❷

**Sushi Express,** 79-87 Abbott St. (☎07 4041 4388), in Orchid Plaza. Tasty sushi at unbelievable prices. $2.70-5.70 per plate (transported to you by sushi locomotive). Most won't need more than 2 plates. Try the popular tuna Express Roll ($4.70) or stop in for their happy hour (daily 5-6pm; all plates $2.50). Ask about their frequent diner's card if you're staying in Cairns for a while. Open M-Sa 11:30am-3pm and 5-9pm. ❶

**Little Aussie Bum,** 29 Spence St. (☎07 4051 2100). In case its name leaves any doubt, this trendy new eatery flaunts its Aussie attitude with racy decor befitting a football team's locker room and a staff saucy enough to make its grittiest players blush. Stop in for a good time and a delectable Aussie Bum Burger ($13.50), a Chook Mango Salad ($14), or a True Blue Rump Steak ($21.50), and wash it all down with a Little Aussie Bum Margarita ($9). Theme nights abound: leave your inhibitions at the door and grab your skimpiest swim suit for Bikini and Budgy Smuggler Su ($12 for a meal and 2 drinks), or on Saucy Single Sa try a Love Pack ($25 for a meal and 4 drinks) and play Wheel of Love to win Reef trips with your new sweetie. Happy hour daily 5-7pm. Open M-F noon-late, Sa-Su 5pm-late. ❸

**Meldrums,** 97 Grafton St. (☎07 4051 8333). A fixture in Cairns for over 30 years, Meldrums main-

QUEENSLAND

tains a casual atmosphere, low prices, and a delicious menu. Try a focaccia sandwich ($6.50-8.50) or one of their signature gourmet meat pies—which won them the gold medal in the 2004 Great Aussie Meat Pie Show. Pie options include everything from steak or spicy Moroccan lamb to eggplant and zucchini or gnocchi pumpkin and sour cream. Finish off your meal with 1 of their irresistible, bakery-style desserts from behind the counter (pear and apple crumbles $4, mud cake slice $4). Order to go and save a few bucks. Open early-late. ❶

# 👁 SIGHTS

**◪TANKS ARTS CENTRE.** With exhibitions and stages housed in WWII oil tanks, this edgy art house feels more like a trendy urban gallery than a museum. Tanks displays all types of art and hosts a wide spectrum of performing arts and cultural shows. Their 600-person capacity concert stage is unlike any you've ever seen. Concerts usually run $15-30 and might be R&B, hip hop, country, blues, pop, or anything in between. On the last Sunday of every month from April to November, Tanks hosts **Market Day** (9am-1pm), a free bazaar with live music, arts and crafts workshops, and plenty of pottery, crafts, and herbs for sale. (46 Collins Ave. ☎07 4032 6600. Accessible by Sunbus #1B. Open daily 10am-4:30pm.)

**FLECKER BOTANIC GARDENS.** This Gondwanan garden is right next to Tanks. Take a moment to follow the meandering boardwalk through swampy jungle, and explore rare plant life and orchid houses. (☎07 4044 3398. Take Sunbus #1B from City Place or drive north on Sheridan St. and take a left onto Collins Ave. Guided walks Tu and Th 10am and 1pm. Open M-F 7:30am-5:30pm, Sa-Su 8:30am-5:30pm. Free.)

**MOUNT WHITFIELD ENVIRONMENTAL PARK.** This last bit of rainforest in the Cairns area is home to cassowaries, red-legged pademelons, and other jungle creatures. The park's shorter Red Arrow circuit is a steep climb to a breathtaking overlook and only takes 45min., while the more rugged Blue Arrow circuit is a 5hr. round-trip trek up and around Mt. Whitfield. Don't stay after dark—there's no camping, and finding transport back to Cairns might be difficult. (Wedged between the Tanks Art Centre and the Botanic Gardens on Collins Ave. Open 24 hrs.)

**KURANDA.** The Skyrail cableway coasts above the rainforest for 7.5km on its way to this popular mountain town. At the highest point, a boardwalk snakes through the trees; detailed information on the area is given one stop below that one. For more on **Kuranda,** see p. 429. (Trains leave regularly from the station. If you are driving, go north on the Cook Hwy. and follow the signs. ☎07 4038 1555; www.skyrail.com.au. 90min. one-way, 2½hr. round-trip; $40 one-way, $58 round-trip, children ½-price.)

# ◪ OUTDOOR ACTIVITIES

Cairns owes its tourist town status in large part to its warm winters and proximity to the Great Barrier Reef. At night, travelers stay in town and drink at local pubs, but when the sun comes up, the crowd dies down. From the break of dawn until early evening, the town empties as tourists head outside the city limits to enjoy thrills, bumps, and spills for reasonable prices. Activities can be booked through hostels or any one of the dozens of tourist centers in **Cairns** (p. 420). Most companies offer free pickup and dropoff. Booking isn't necessary, however, to enjoy open-air markets and bountiful outdoor dining.

**COMMISSION SUSPICION.** Be wary of booking agents who do not provide more than one tour option, as each tour pays a commission to its agents. Some low-quality tours survive by paying high commissions to agents talented at roping in unsuspecting tourists.

**CABLE-SKIING. Cable Ski Cairns** offers waterskiing, wakeboarding, and knee-boarding sans boat. Beginners are readily welcomed. (Off the Captain Cook Hwy. ☎07 4038 1304; www.cableskicairns.com.au. Open daily 10am-6pm; $34 per hr., under 16 $16 per hr., full-day $68.)

**CYCLING. Bandicoot Bicycle Tours** offers a day of cycling, wildlife-spotting, swimming in a volcano crater, and relaxing in the tablelands above Cairns. Guests enjoy trips to waterfalls, giant fig trees, and swimming holes. Lunch, tea, tropical fruit, and cold water are included. (☎07 4055 0155; www.bandicootbicycles. com. Trips depart M-F 8am, return 5:30pm. $99. Free pickup. Cash only.)

**BUNGEE JUMPING.** You may know it as "bungee" but to **AJ Hackett,** it's "bungy," slang in New Zealand for "elastic strap." This wild Kiwi knows a thing or two about the sport—ask him about bungy jumping off the Eiffel Tower (and getting arrested for it), then sign up for one of his (legal) Australian jumps. Try one of 16 styles of jumps, including one that requires jumping off of a speeding BMX bike, if you're feeling adventurous. Night bungy or parabungy (combination of parasailing and bungy jump) on request. $125 gets you a jump, transfer, certificate, and T-shirt. $5 insurance fee. (☎07 4057 7188 or 1800 622 888; www. ajhackett.com. Open daily 10am-5pm.)

**FISHING.** Fishermen can cast their own bait, then tow the line with **Fishing The Tropics,** which runs its 6m boat around the Great Barrier Reef, in the Cairns estuary, or in the Daintree River. (☎07 4058 1820. Reef $215; estuary ½-day $85, river full-day $170. Both include lunch, full bait, and tackle. Book ahead.) **VIP Fishing & Game Boat Services** offers similar packages, along with others featuring fly- and shark-fishing, or black marlin-hunting from June to December. (☎07 4031 4355. ½-day trips around $85, full-day around $160.)

**PARASAILING AND SKYDIVING.** This is your chance to parasail 300 ft. above Trinity Inlet. **North Queensland WaterSports** (☎07 4045 2735) offers parasailing and jet skiing from $199. **Skydive Cairns,** 82 Grafton St. (☎07 4031 5466 or 1800 444 568), runs solo and tandem jumps. (Tandem: 9000 ft. $210; 14,000 ft. $295. Solo: 14000 ft. $45). Reservations are recommended, but not necessary.

**WHITEWATER RAFTING. Foaming Fury** offers a portage-style rafting trip that begins with a hike through dense jungle to the wild rapids of the secluded Russell River. (☎07 4031 3460. $130, includes lunch.) They also lead tamer trips down the comparatively gentle Barron River. However, that's where most rafting tours operate; be aware that it can become crowded on busy days. **R'n'R Rafting** offers several options, including multi-day and family packages. (☎07 4035 3555, 24hr. reservations 4041 9444. ½-day $98, full-day on Tully River $155. $25 levy fee.) **Raging Thunder Adventures** boasts similar trips, including combination packages that offer activities like ballooning, bungee jumping, skydiving, and reef trips (24hr. reservations ☎07 4030 7990).

**MOTORCYCLING. Cape York Motorcycle Adventures** (☎07 4059 0220; www.capeyorkmotorcycles.com.au.) leads truly adventurous dirt-bike safaris. On their two- to eight-day trips into Cape York, Darwin, and Broome, you can ride through river crossings, along the ocean, up mountains into the rainforest, and across national parks. Enjoy a significantly cheaper adventure if you own your own bike. (2-day $848, 5-day $3400; camping and meals provided.)

# DIVING AND SNORKELING

The most popular way to see Cairns is through goggles, although experienced divers may prefer the less touristed reefs near Port Douglas. Every day, rain or shine, thousands of tourists and locals don masks, fins, and snorkels to slide beneath the ocean surface and glimpse the Great Barrier Reef. **Reef Teach**, 85 Lake St., on the top floor of the Main St. Arcade, offers an entertaining 2hr. lecture by marine biologists on the reef ecosystem. These witty scientists teach participants about the marine life they will encounter while diving or snorkeling and how they can interact with these Reef inhabitants without getting bitten, stung, stabbed, or pricked. Anyone planning to hit the Reef should stop in for this engaging, illuminating program; it will infinitely enhance your Reef experience. (☎07 4031 7794; www.reefteach.com.au; email or call for reservations. Lectures M-Sa 6:30pm. $15; ask about student discounts).

Because it's the main gateway to the reef, Cairns is studded with an overwhelming number of dive shops and snorkeling outfits. Making a decision can be daunting, given the excess of brochures and booking agents by which you'll be bombarded. Think about some questions in advance: how long do you want to dive? How big do you want your dive group to be? For personal dive instruction and a group atmosphere, smaller boats are usually the way to go. Are you going with other divers or with friends who may prefer other water activities? Unless you're all diving, you won't want a dive trip—maybe a cruise with diving options, such as **Noah's Ark Too** or **Passions of Paradise** (p. 426). Snorkelers are equally welcome aboard these day cruises.

To dive for more than a day in Australia, you need open-water certification (an aquatic driver's license). The only way to get this certification is to spend $370 for four days in scuba school, where you learn about scuba equipment and diving techniques. To enroll in dive classes, you need two passport-sized photos and a medical exam, which many diving companies arrange on-site.

## DIVING DAYTRIPS

Many divers prefer daytrips to multi-day trips, as they afford different views of the reef each given day. On multi-day trips, it is likely that you will visit only the section of the reef over which your diving company has the right to dive.

**Passions of Paradise** (☎07 4041 1600 or 1800 111 346; www.passions.com.au). Offers full-day cruises to Paradise Reef and Michaelmas Cay. Attracts a young, energetic crowd; spontaneous conga dancing may occur. Face-painting and chocolate cake for the youngsters. High-speed catamaran takes 60-70 passengers. Departs Marlin Jetty at 8am. Base price for snorkeling and lunch $125 (plus $10 reef levy). Introductory dive $70 extra ($45 for 2nd dive), certified dive $70.

**Ocean Free** (☎07 4050 0550; www.oceanfree.com.au). Sail to the reef in style on this stately ship. The tour anchors off Green Island on the Inner Barrier Reef, allowing for both reef and island exploration. The return sunset sail includes complimentary wine and a dessert. Lively crew and few passengers means lots of individual attention. Departs 8am, returns around 5pm. Base price $119 with lunch. Introductory dive $75 (2 dives $110), certified dive $55 (2 dives $75).

**Noah's Ark Too** (☎07 4050 0677), located at the Pier, finger E. The motto: "There are no rules." Relax on the boat (max. 32 people) and take the plunge on 2 of 10 outer reef destinations. After, sip a beer on the boat. A lively tour with a fun crew. Daily 8:30am-

4:45pm. Snorkel-only $70. Introductory dive including a free 10min. lesson underwater $109, additional dive $35. 2 certified dives $109. Buffet-style lunch included.

## MULTI-DAY TRIPS AND SCUBA SCHOOLS

**Pro-Dive** (☎07 4031 5255; www.prodivecairns.com), on the corner of Abbott and Shields St. Their most popular trip is the 5-day learn-to-dive course. Although the $695 price tag might seem hefty, it includes all diving equipment, 2 nights accommodation, and 9 dives. They also offer a 3-day, 2-night trip with 11 dives, including 2 night dives for certified divers (starts at $580). Meals included. Open daily 8:30am-9pm.

**Down Under Dive,** 267 Draper St. (☎07 4052 8300 or 1800 079 099; www.down-nunderdive.com.au). A 25m. catamaran runs daytrips ($85) with an introductory dive option ($65). Certified dives $65. The company also offers diver training; the 4-day courses include 2 days of pool training and 2 days on Hastings and Saxon Reefs (from $490). Meals included on both trips. Also offers daytrips on the faster, sleeker Osprey V starting at $119. Aussie BBQ lunch included. Open daily 7am-5pm.

**Cairns Dive Centre,** 121 Abbott St. (☎07 4051 0294 or 24hr. 1800 642 591; www.cairnsdive.com.au). Friendly, knowledgeable dive instructors offer some of the most affordable trips to the outer reef ($75 snorkel trip plus $75 for intro dive). Their fleet of vessels means you can book 4-, 5-, or 6-day dive trips; trips begin daily. 5-day liveaboard, learn-to-dive course $594; 4-day budget course $370. Open daily 7am-5pm.

# 🔳 NIGHTLIFE

Cairns's nightclubs, the last stop in a backpacker's day, cater to a young, rowdy crowd. Adrenaline-fueled days make for explosive nightlife. Hostels usually give out club vouchers to help draw the crowds. For the trendiest spots, editorials, and listings, pick up a free copy of *Barfly,* found all around town.

🔳**Ultimate Party** is the wildest, best time you'll have in Cairns. This bi-weekly pub crawl guides two double-decker buses of generally young, backpacker partygoers through five clubs and at least as many debaucherous couples competitions, leaving a trail of hazy memories and walks-of-shame in its wake. The ultimate party is held every Saturday and most Tuesday nights (high season). Pay $25 for entry into five bars and clubs, one all-you-can-eat meal and one pizza meal, entertainment, transportation, and a group photo that will likely be embarrassing in the morning. At the end of the night, pick up a book of vouchers for adventure trips, accommodations, food, and of course, more alcohol. Sign up at the Tropical Arcade on the corner of Shields and Lake St., online at www.ultimatepartycairns.com, or call ☎07 4041 0332.

**The Woolshed,** 24 Shields St. (☎07 4031 6304 for free shuttle bus until 9:30pm), is a rowdy all-night party and backpacker favorite. Travelers come here to dance on the tables, drink beer, and race goldfish (4 nights a week) or enter the M night Mr. and Ms. Backpacker contest. Practically every hostel in town offers free meal vouchers (upgrade to T-bone steak or other full meal $5-7) for this place. Show up early—because of these vouchers, there are lines out the door every night by 6pm. Escape the ruckus of the nightclub and relax downstairs with a drink in one of The Lounge's comfortable leather sofas. Cover M-Th and Su $5, F-Sa $7, free before 10pm every day. Open nightly 6-9:30pm for meals; club open until 5am, but no entry after 3am.

**P.J. O'Brien's** (☎07 4031 5333), in City Place, at the corner of Shields and Lake St., always finds a reason to celebrate. Tables are made from beer barrels and the pub is decorated with Irish memorabilia; this place looks like an Emerald Isle museum. Pints of Guinness ($7) and tasty food (meals $12-18) make this bar a hot spot. Try a pint of the famous Snake Bite ($6). Live bands some F. 4 themed nights per week with specials.

**Shenannigan's** (☎07 4051 2490), on the corner of Sheridan and Spence St. Boasts the best beer garden in Cairns. Watch the latest sports matches with locals and other backpackers on the 2 large TV screens, or listen to live music 4 nights per week. They also serve huge meals. Open daily 10am-2am.

**Gilligan's,** 57-89 Grafton St. (☎07 4041 6566; www.gilligansbackpackers.com.au). A 2000+ capacity nightspot attached to the hostel. Open-air beer hall, a nightclub, and a smaller dance club. Although this massive club can be desolate, there's no hotter spot when it fills up. Guest DJs. Open M-Th and Su 10am-2am, F-Sa 10am-3am.

**Rhino Bar** (☎07 4031 5305; www.cairnsrhinobar.com), upstairs on the corner of Lake and Spence St. A restaurant until 9pm, then transforms into a hot-spot nightclub. Boasts theme nights and a nightly happy hour 8:30-9:30pm. Open daily 6am-3am.

# 🔁 DAYTRIPS FROM CAIRNS

**TJAPUKAI.** The Indigenous cultural park of Tjapukai sits 15min. north of Cairns, off the Cook Hwy. in Smithfield. Pronounced "JAB-a-guy," this is one of the most rewarding and balanced presentations of Aboriginal myths, customs, and history in Queensland. Learn how to throw a boomerang or spear, see a cultural dance show, watch a film on Indigenous history, and more. Set aside at least half a day for the experience. Come back for a night of dancing and an international dinner buffet at Tjapukai by Night. (☎07 4042 9999; www. tjapukai.com.au. Open daily 9am-5pm and 7-10pm. Tjapukai by Day: $31, children $15.50; By Night: $90/46.50. 20% student discount; 10% YHA discount. AmEx/D/MC/V. Packages and evening events available. Transfers to and from Cairns and the Northern Beaches run $19 round-trip. Kuranda Scenic Rail and Skyrail also have service in the area.)

**CRYSTAL CASCADES.** Only 30km from Cairns's center, this freshwater swimming hole provides a refreshing break on hot, lazy days. The best part? It's completely free. Be careful on the slippery rocks in and around the cascades. There's also a short, breathtaking hiking trail through the surrounding area. (Drive north along Sheridan St., turn left on Aeroglen, head toward Redlynch, and follow the signs. Wheelchair-accessible. Restrooms available.)

**MOSSMAN GORGE.** Mossman Gorge is just a little further north of Crystal Cascades (near Port Douglas, p. 433). It's free, offers a more genuine introduction to the rainforest, and has better swimming holes.

# GREEN ISLAND ☎07

Diminutive Green Island barely pushes above the water's surface; its perimeter can be walked in 15min. Though it's dominated by a huge resort, a rainforest boardwalk and a beach path both provide access to its natural beauty.

Other than the snorkeling and beaches, the main attraction on the island is **Marineland Melanesia,** a combination oceanic art gallery, aquarium, and croc farm 250m left of the jetty when facing the water. Take a self-guided tour of the national park, which only takes 30min. (1.5km) and offers up-close views of the island's animal and bird life. Go at 10:30am or 1:45pm to watch a live feeding of huge crocodiles. If you're lucky (and he's hungry) you might even see Cassius: at 18 ft., he's the world's largest croc in captivity. There are also opportunities to hold yearling crocodiles. If that sounds too daunting, tour the art collection, which includes masks from New Guinea. (☎07 4051 4032. Open daily 9:30am-

4:15pm. $15, children $7.) Just off the end of the jetty is the **Marine Observatory,** where you can observe bits of the coral reef 1.5m below the surface ($10).

The cheapest way to the island is by ferry with **Great Adventures,** which offers a day on the island and a boat tour or snorkeling gear. (☎07 4044 9944 or 1800 079 080; www.greatadventures.com.au. Departs Cairns daily 8:30, 10:30am, and 1pm; departs Green Island noon, 2:30, and 4:30pm. $69, children $34.)

## FITZROY ISLAND                                              ☎07

Fitzroy Island is a picturesque island paradise, with coral beaches melting into mountainous rainforest. Unfortunately, most of the inland is under construction while a new high-end resort is being built. Meanwhile, there's still plenty of fun to be had on Fitzroy's magnificent beaches. For an adventure, try traveling to Fitzroy Island via sea kayak with **Raging Thunder Adventures.** A high-speed catamaran takes you most of the way, then spend a half-day on the island, complete with snorkeling and lunch. (☎07 4030 7990; www.ragingthunder.com.au. Daytrip $153.) Once there, you can rent kayaks ($15 per hr.; $20 per day. $50 deposit.), a catamaran ($45 per ½-day), or fishing rods and tackle ($10 per day). Raging Thunder also offers introductory dives for $75 and $60 for certified divers. Snorkel gear is available for $15 per day ($25 deposit).

Fitzroy Island has three main hikes. The best is the **Summit Trail,** a steep hike up the mountain (1.3km) with an incredible 360° view of the reef and coastline at the windy peak. You can turn around and head back the way you came (2.5km) or continue on to the lighthouse (an additional 4.2km round-trip, all downhill.) A walk up the **Secret Garden Trail** (1km round-trip) through a canyon is worth it if you haven't seen rainforest before. Another good walk (500m) cuts through the trees to pristine **Nudey Beach,** which offers great views of the surrounding mountain range. It is covered with pieces of coral from the reef offshore, and the snorkeling is great. Landlubbers can marvel at the bay between the beach and the mainland ranges, which was a green valley 6000 years ago.

# ATHERTON TABLELANDS

Although much of northern Queensland is picturesque, nothing compares to the Atherton Tablelands. Rolling hills meet unspoiled forests with hidden lakes, pockets of rainforest, and scattered waterfalls—all fringed by roaming herds of cattle and horses. Traveling northeast on the Kennedy Hwy., you'll find the farming village of Mareeba and touristy Kuranda. The southern route via Gilles Hwy. passes through the township of Atherton and charming Yungaburra.

## KURANDA                                                     ☎07

Many travelers can't escape the charm and beauty of this small mountain town, which serves as the gateway to the Tablelands. River cruises, street performers, and its famous markets draw hordes of tourists from Cairns by day, but when the last train leaves in the afternoon, quiet is restored. In the morning, the hustle and bustle begins again when the **Original Markets** (open daily 9am-3pm) and **Heritage Markets** (open daily 9am-3pm) transform the cozy village into a bazaar of arts, crafts, and clothing. Kuranda's outdoor amphitheater hosts a variety of concerts, including regular performances by local artists.

The **Kuranda Hotel Motel ❸,** on the corner of Coondoo and Arara St. across from the Skyrail, brings the Irish pub to the rainforest. The restaurant serves Guinness Pot Pie ($16) and other tasty concoctions on a patio that offers views of the rainforest. The tidy rooms with bath, fridge, and TV are perfect for couples. (☎07 4093 7206. Reception M-Sa 10am-10pm, Su 10am-4pm. Singles $65;

doubles $75. Extra adult $20. AmEx/D/MC/V.) Locals love **Frog's ❶,** 11 Coondoo St., with its spacious jungle porch out back. (☎07 4093 7405. ½-dozen oysters $10; gourmet pizzas from $11. Open daily 9:30am-4pm. MC/V.)

On the drive up the Kennedy Hwy. from Cairns, the road winds steeply through lush rainforest. Just outside Kuranda, the award-winning **Rainforestation Nature Park** offers everything from Aboriginal tours and walks to boomerang-throwing lessons. Hug a koala or ride in an amphibious Army Duck through the rainforest. Shuttles leave for the park daily from Kuranda village. (☎07 4085 5008. Aboriginal culture tours $18, children $9; wildlife park $13/6.50. Packages available.) Kuranda is also the gateway to the **Barron Gorge National Park,** located 2.5km outside of town. Follow the signs from the town center. A 3km boardwalk goes through dense rainforest to a lookout above **Barron Falls,** one of the largest waterfalls in the Tablelands. Another kilometer down the road is **Wright's Lookout,** providing a view down the gorge that spills out over the city of Cairns. The **Skyrail Rainforest Cableway** is a gondola that takes you up high above the rainforest canopy into Kuranda village, with stops at both the peak and Barron Falls (7.5km). A 2½hr. round-trip ride originates in Carovonica Lakes, 10min. northwest of Cairns. (☎07 4038 1555; www.skyrail.com.au. Open daily 8:30am-3:45pm. $58, children $29.) The **Kuranda Scenic Railway** runs an antique train that travels from downtown Cairns to Kuranda and stops in the park to let travelers hop off for a quick view. (☎07 4036 9333; www.ksr.com.au. From Cairns daily 8:30 and 9:30am; from Kuranda daily 2 and 3:30pm. $59 round-trip, children $29, concession discounts vary.)

## MAREEBA AND ATHERTON          ☎07

Mareeba and Atherton may lack the quaint atmosphere of Yungaburra and the views of Kuranda, but they are still nestled in the tropical Tablelands. The towns also boast over 300 days of sunshine a year. A short stop in Atherton will reveal much about the region's history, while the town of Mareeba has begun to garner attention for its growing industries—over 70% of Australia's coffee is produced here, as well as the world's only mango wine.

The **⬛Coffee Works,** 136 Mason St., in Mareeba, lures visitors with its aromatic homebrews and tasting tours. Admission ($19) includes a self-guided tour, a "bottomless cup" for tasting 43 different blends, entrance into the largest coffee and tea museum in the world, and hourly chocolate and liqueur tastings. (☎07 4092 4101 or 1800 355 526; www.coffeeworks.com.au. Open daily 9am-4pm. MC/V.) Don't miss the **Chocolate Works** inside; be sure to try samples of the lemon myrtle in milk chocolate. The **Golden Drop Winery,** only a short drive (9km) north on Hwy. 1 toward Mossman, is the world's only mango wine factory and farm. Stop by for a taste of their divine wines and tropical fruit liqueurs. (☎07 4093 2524. Bottles from $16. Open daily early-late.)

Atherton, propped on an extinct volcano, is a great base for exploring Lake Tinaroo and other Tableland destinations. There's a helpful **visitors center** (☎07 4091 4222) with friendly staff at the corner of Main and Silo St., across from McDonald's. The **Blue Gum B&B ❺,** 36 12th Ave. (☎07 4091 5149; www.atherton-bluegum.com) is an excellent place to stay, and it looks over the green hills of the Tablelands. (Continental breakfast, poolside BBQ, kitchen, TV in all rooms. Rooms from $120.) For budget accommodation, try the clean and welcoming **Atherton Travellers Lodge ❷,** 37 Alice St. (☎07 4091 3552. Dorms $25; singles $40; twins/doubles $60. AmEx/D/MC/V.) To indulge your sweet tooth, drive down the Gillies Hwy. between Atherton and Yungaburra until you see the sign for **Shaylee's Strawberry Farm** (☎07 4091 2962), which sells its titular fruit, ice cream, and fresh jam from $3. (Open daily June-Nov. 8:30am-5pm.)

# LAKE TINAROO AND CRATER LAKES NATIONAL PARK

**⬛🔋 ORIENTATION AND PRACTICAL INFORMATION.** The volcanic soil of the central Tablelands, nourished by crater lakes and waterfalls, sprouts lush forest that lines the shores of **Tinaroo, Barrine,** and **Eacham Lakes.** Lake Tinaroo can be accessed from Atherton or the gateway town of Tolga off Hwy. 1, a barren road that runs through farmland before reaching the forested area of the lake. Unsealed **Danbulla Forest Drive** circles this lake. The free **Danbulla State Forest Visitor's Guide,** available from **QPWS,** 83 Main St., Atherton (☎07 4091 1844), lists sights along the 40min. loop. If this QPWS office is closed, the **Info Center** in Atherton (p. 430) can offer you a detailed map of the region. Lake Barrine is located just off the Gillies Hwy. on the way into Yungaburra from Gordanvale. To reach Lake Eacham, continue on Gillies Hwy. from Gordonvale toward Yungaburra and turn left onto Lakes Dr. Contact the **QPWS Eacham District Office** (☎07 4095 3768) at Lake Eacham for info on paths around the lakes.

**🔋🏠 ACCOMMODATIONS.** At the entrance to Lake Tinaroo is the **Lake Tinaroo Holiday Park ❷,** which has a kiosk, petrol, and a game room. (☎07 4095 8232. Sites $20, powered $27; cabins from $70.) The road also passes five QPWS **campsites ❶** with toilets. ($5 per person.) Beyond the Tinaroo Dam, there are several excellent basic campsites off the walks that proceed from Danbulla Forest Dr. Register in advance, either by calling the QPWS office (☎13 13 04; M-F 8am-6pm) or going online at www.qld.gov.au/camping. At Lake Eacham, camping facilities are available at the **Lake Eacham Tourist Park ❶,** which has showers, laundry, a general store, and a petting zoo. (☎07 4095 3730. Open daily 7am-7pm. Sites for 2 $16, powered $19; cabins $72. MC/V.)

**📷🎿 SIGHTS AND OUTDOOR ACTIVITIES** The stunning 50m, 500-year-old 🌳**Cathedral Fig Tree** is on the east stretch of Dunbulla Forest Dr.; you can stand there gaping, or you can walk straight through it. (Dunbulla Forest Dr. can be accessed from a sealed road via the Gillies Hwy. en route to Cairns.) Two kilometers east from the Cathedral Fig Tree is the turnoff to **Gillies Lookout,** a popular hang-gliding spot. Go 4km down an unsealed road, past two cattle-holding gates that must be opened (and closed behind you), and you'll find one of the best lookouts in the whole region. At Lake Barrine, tour exotic gardens, dine at the teahouse restaurant, or cruise around the lake on a boat tour (departs daily from teahouse 9:30, 11:30am, 1:30, and 3pm. $14.50, children $7.25). The teahouse also has a **Wet Tropics Visitor Centre.** Make sure to check out the 1000-yearold **twin Kauri pines** only 100m from the teahouse. At Lake Eacham, you'll see a sign pointing toward the last of the great cedars, the **Red Cedar Tree.** The 600m path to the giant starts 8km past the lake. The 500-year-old tree fell during Cyclone Larry in 2006, and it takes 3-4min. to walk from its torn base to its tip. If you're in the mood for something even longer, walk the paved, 3.1km **Lake Eacham Track** around the lake and view for yourself the muskrat-kangaroos and giant iguanas that are often spotted there.

# YUNGABURRA                                        ☎07

Tiny Yungaburra (pop. 1400) is in the heart of the Tablelands, with Lake Tinaroo and the Danbulla State Forest to the north, Lakes Eacham and Barrine to the southeast, and the volcanic hills of the Seven Sisters to the west. The town seems untouched by tourism and is welcoming to visitors. Yungaburra hosts the largest **markets** in the north on the fourth Saturday of each month from 7am to noon, where shoppers can barter for homemade crafts, fresh produce, and even geese. From Cairns, take the Gillies Hwy. 60km west.

**THE BASHFUL PLATYPUS.** The best place to spot a platypus is the Atherton Shire Council Pumping Station. From Yungaburra, head past the bridge and down Gillies Hwy. toward Tolga. Five kilometers past the Curtain Fig turnoff, take a right onto Picnic Crossing Rd. (beware: the road sign is actually 10m beyond the turnoff). Then take the second right-hand turn. You'll find a concrete picnic table and—with some luck—platypus families near the bend in the river (you might need to walk left along the bank; head by foot along the path toward the road, then cut back in toward the river). The best times to see them are dawn or dusk: be quiet, as they're extremely shy. Another popular spot is at the bridge 300m before the Curtain Fig turnoff.

**⛺ ACCOMMODATIONS.** Yungaburra's sole hostel, **⚑On the Wallaby ❶,** is one of the best in northern Queensland. The common area feels like a mountain lodge with rustic furnishings and a wood-burning stove. The bathrooms are made of stone and are clean, and the bunk rooms are clean. Enjoy a BBQ ($10) or breakfast ($5). Internet is $5 per hr. Guests can also join hostel-run outdoor activities (day and night canoeing, biking, or hikes to swimming holes; all tours $30). Platypus-spotting trips are free. (☎07 4095 2031; www.onthewallaby.com. Full-day bike rental $15. Cairns transfer $25 one way. Reception 8am-noon and 4-8pm. Sites $10 per person; dorms $22; twins/doubles $55. AmEx/MC/V.)

**🍴 FOOD.** The coffee shop in the **Gem Gallery and Coffee Shop ❶,** 21 Eacham Rd., serves a huge breakfast on weekends for $6.50. The **Gem Gallery** itself specializes in inexpensive opals (earrings from $45, pendants from $40), and offers free opal-cutting. (☎07 4095 3455. Open daily 8am-late.) Next door is **⚑Flynn's ❸,** an award-winning French-Italian bistro run by owner and master chef Liam Flynn. Flynn assembles mouthwatering medleys of handmade pastas, home-grown veggies, and fresh seafood that will delight even the most discerning diner. Entrees start at $11 and mains at $27, but they're worth it; if you splurge once on your trip, do it here. (☎07 4095 2235. Open for dinner M-Tu and F-Su 5:30pm-late. AmEx/D/MC/V.) **Yungaburra Food Market,** on Eacham Rd., serves as the local supermarket. (☎07 4095 2177. Open daily 7am-7pm. MC/V.)

**🔆 SIGHTS.** To the west of Yungaburra is the **Curtain Fig Tree,** a monstrous strangler fig that forms an eerie curtain in the middle of the rainforest (to the left after the bridge, just outside of town en route to Tolga). About 25km south of nearby Malanda (south on the Gilles Hwy. from Yungaburra), the **waterfall circuit** leads past a series of spectacular swimming holes. From the north, a sign points to the falls. Catch the loop from the south by looking for the "Tourist Drive" sign. **Millaa Millaa Falls** is a picturesque jungle waterfall that thunders into a gorgeous, green pool. **Zillie Falls** starts off as a sedate creek; the best view is from the lip of the falls, as the small stream transforms itself into a large shower of water. A rocky, slippery path through the adjacent rainforest leads to the roaring drop where **Ellinjaa Falls** crashes over a tapestry of rocks. For more information, the **Malanda Falls Visitor Centre** is just past **Malanda Falls** on the way out of town toward Atherton. (☎07 4096 6957. Open daily 9:30am-4:30pm.) For a lesson in libations, try an interactive wine tasting at **Wild Mountain Cellars** on Eacham Rd. Affable owner Warwick guides tasters through a varied selection of wines, ports, and liqueurs, and teaches wine matching. All wines are made from tropical fruits found in northern Queensland, which gives them a wide spectrum of tastes, much broader than those at grape wineries. (☎07 4095 3000. Free tastings. Open daily 10am-6pm.)

# PORT DOUGLAS                              ☎07

This friendly outpost, between tropical rainforest and the Coral Sea, entertains dangerous box jellyfish populations during the Wet, but when these squishy guests leave in the Dry, Port Douglas plays host to wealthy tourists. Easy living in tropical surroundings entices even the most nomadic backpackers to stay longer than planned. Snorkel and scuba trips take travelers to the outer reaches of the Great Barrier Reef, while other adventures head up the coast to the world's oldest rainforest in Daintree National Park.

## ⌐ TRANSPORTATION

**Buses: Sun Palm Coaches** (☎07 4087 2900), at the Marina Mirage, runs door-to-door service daily to the **airport** (1hr., several per day, $35) and **Cairns** (1hr., same-day round-trip $70). A direct shuttle to Cape Tribulation costs $75 each way and originates in Cairns. **BTS** (☎07 4099 5665; www.btstours.com.au) services **Cairns** (1hr.; 7 per day; $28, $48 round-trip) and **Mossman Gorge** ($17 round-trip). **Sun Palm Coaches** also runs shuttles between the Rainforest Habitat and town. (Runs every 30min. 7am-midnight.) **Country Road Coachlines** (☎07 4045 2794; www.countryroadcoachlines.com.au) also runs daily to **Cooktown** (return $120) and **Cairns.**

**Taxis: Port Douglas Taxi,** Marina Mirage (☎07 4084 2600).

**Car Rental: Thrifty,** #2, 50 Macrossan St. (☎07 4099 5555), specializes in 4WD (from $135 per day). Must be 25 for 4WD. AmEx/D/MC/V. **Holiday Car Hire,** 54 Macrossan St. (☎07 4099 4999), rents compacts and beach-buggy "mokes" from $59 per day. **Avis** and **Budget** are on Warner St. between Grant and Wharf St.

**Bike Rental:** Biking is the best way to get around Port Douglas. Check with the hostels before renting, as some provide bikes or offer discounted rentals. Otherwise, visit **Port Douglas Bike Hire** (☎07 4099 5799), which has 2 locations: one on the corner of Wharf and Warner St., and the other at Davidson and Port St. All types of bikes are available: mountain, racing, child, and tandem. Rental includes lock and helmet. Open daily 9am-5pm. ½-day $15, full-day $19, weekly from $89. AmEx/D/MC/V.)

**Road Report: The Royal Automobile Club of Queensland** (☎13 19 05; www.racq.com.au) provides information on road conditions and closings.

**Port Douglas**

🔺 ACCOMMODATIONS
Dougie's Backpackers, 9
Parrotfish Lodge, 6
Port Douglas Motel, 7
Port O'Call Lodge, 8

🍎 FOOD
Central Hotel, 5
Coles, 3
Ironbar Restaurant, 2
Java Blue Cafe, 1
Mango Jam, 4
Soul n' Pepper, 11
Under Wraps, 10

(Map labels: Trinity Bay, Rex Smeal Park, Anzac Park, St. Mary's, Wharf Area, Court House Museum, Marina Mirage, Dickson Inlet, Warner St., Grant St., Mowbray St., Owen St., Midli St., Beryl St., Blake St., Davidson St., Port St., Crimmins St., Bally Hooley Tramway, Murphy St., Island Point Rd., Macrossan St., Davidson St., Garrick St., Esplanade, Four Mile Beach, CORAL SEA, TO RAINFOREST HABITAT (5km), MOSSMAN (25km), 0–600 yards, 0–600 meters)

## ✱ ❷ ORIENTATION AND PRACTICAL INFORMATION

70km north of Cairns, **Port Douglas Road** branches right off the Captain Cook Highway (Hwy. 1) and turns into **Davidson Street,** which then meets **Macrossan Street,** the town's main drag. Macrossan St. runs across the Port Douglas peninsula, ending at **Four Mile Beach** (on the Esplanade) to the east and **Marina Mirage** (on Wharf St.) to the west. Most shops are open until 5pm.

**Tourist Offices:** Port Douglas might have more tourist offices than residents. Two of the largest, **Port Douglas Tourist Centre,** 23 Macrossan St. (☎07 4099 5599), and **BTS Tours,** 49 Macrossan St. (☎07 4099 5665), have all the necessary tour and activity information and are also capable of booking transportation.

**Banks: National Australia, Commonwealth, ANZ,** and **Westpac** banks are within 200m of each other on Macrossan St. All are open M-Th 9:30am-4pm, F 9:30am-5pm. **ANZ,** 36 Macrossan St. (☎13 13 14), exchanges currency and AmEx Travelers Cheques for a $8 commission per transaction. Some hostels may exchange traveler's checks for free. If heading north, keep in mind that **ATMs** may be few and far between.

**Police:** (24hr. ☎07 4099 5220) Macrossan and Wharf St. Open M-Th 8am-2:30pm.

**Medical Services: Port Village Medical Centre,** Shop 17 in Port Village Centre on Macrossan St. (24hr. ☎07 4099 5043). Office open M-F 8am-6pm, Sa-Su 9am-noon. The nearest **hospital** (☎07 4098 2444) is located in Mossman, on Hospital St. Head north on Captain Cook Hwy. (Hwy. 1) into Mossman and then just follow the signs.

**Internet Access:** Try shops on Macrossan St. **Wicked Ice Cream,** 48 Macrossan St. (☎07 4099 6900). $5 per hr.; unlimited 1-day pass $15. Open daily 9am-10pm.

**Post Office:** 5 Owen St. (☎07 4099 5210). On the corner of Macrossan and Owen St., halfway up the hill. Open M-F 8:30am-5:30pm, Sa 9am-2pm. **Postal Code:** 4877.

## ▛ ACCOMMODATIONS AND CAMPING

There's no shortage of expensive beds in this resort town; luckily, hostels also abound. They tend to be reasonably priced and well-equipped; most have a pool, bar, and restaurant, and many offer free transport between Port Douglas and Cairns. These popular accommodations fill up quickly, so book ahead.

**Parrotfish Lodge,** 37/39 Warner St. (☎07 4099 5011 or 1800 995 011; www.parrotfishlodge.com). Close to the action on Macrossan St. Large, modern, and equipped with a bar, restaurant, Internet lounge, billiards, a pool, spacious decks, BBQ, and satellite TVs. Carpark underground. Breakfast included. Free bike hire. All rooms have A/C and are located on the 2nd fl. or above. Reception 8am-9pm. 8-bed dorms $25; doubles $86, ensuite $96. VIP discount. MC/V. ❶

**Port O'Call Lodge (YHA)** (☎07 4099 5422 or 1800 892 800), on Port St. Take a left off Port Douglas Rd. onto Port St. as you enter town. Incredibly comfortable motel-style hostel 15min. from town center. Amenities include laundry, kitchen, bike rental, A/C, and Internet. Free shuttle bus to and from Cairns M-Sa (departs Port O'Call at 8:45am; picks up anywhere in Cairns 10:30-11am). The hostel's popular **bistro** ❷ serves meals daily 6-9pm (main courses $14-22) and is hopping during happy hour (5-7pm). Free lockers. Reception 7:30am-7:30pm. Checkout 10am. 4-bed dorm with bath $28.50; doubles $77; deluxe motel rooms $99. YHA discounts; 25% off Haba dive trips. MC/V. ❷

**Port Douglas Motel,** 9 Davidson St. (☎07 4099 5504; www.portdouglasmotel.com). Only a 2min. walk to the beach. Great if you've got a few friends to share the cost. All rooms are clean and equipped with kitchenettes, bathrooms, TV, and A/C. Covered carpark, saltwater pool, BBQ. Prices $95-110 in high season; $70-85 in low season. ❺

**Dougie's Backpackers,** 111 Davidson St. (☎07 4099 6200 or 1800 996 200; www. dougies.com.au). 15min. from town center. A jungle-themed retreat. Toss back a few at the lively bar (open 4pm-midnight). Laundry, Internet, ATM, kitchen, pool, BBQ, bike rental ($2 per hr.), and employment information. Free bus to Cairns M, W, Sa 8:30am; free pickup in Cairns M, W, Sa 10:30am. Campsites $14 per person; tents with mattresses $23; dorms $27; doubles/twins $80. $1 off if you have a picture of your mother or your pet. Reception 7:30am-6:30pm. NOMADS/VIP/YHA discount. MC/V. ❶

## ☐ ☐ FOOD AND NIGHTLIFE

With the tourist offices closed and the affairs of sea complete, **Macrossan Street** lights the night with flame torches, courtyard restaurants, and live music. Trendy, upscale eateries crowd the street, offering everything from pizza to sushi, but at steep prices. Mixed into the fray are a few cheaper local eateries, but they're harder to spot. A **Coles** supermarket is located in the Port Village Shopping Centre on Macrossan St. between Wharf and Grant St. (Open M-F 8am-9pm, Sa 8am-5pm, Su 9am-6pm.)

**Ironbar Restaurant,** 5 Macrossan St. (☎07 4099 4776). With its rusty chandeliers and corrugated iron exterior, it could be an Outback bar—except that it's on Macrossan St. The main attraction is the nightly cane toad race at 8:15pm. Choose your own finely dressed amphibian; the winner (human, not toad) gets a prize. Ironbar offers a variety of Queensland delicacies such as the Aussie trio ('roo, croc, and emu) for $18. The only venue open past midnight, Ironbar becomes party central when the clock strikes 12. Live music W-F. Open M-Sa 11:30am-2am, Su 9am-2pm. AmEx/MC/V. ❷

**Soul n' Pepper,** 2 Dixie St. (☎07 4099 4499), by the markets. Ask where to find the best breakfast in town and you're sure to hear about this bubbly beachside bistro. Awarded "Best Breakfast Restaurant" in 2007 for its king-sized morning spread (3 eggs, sausage, and hashbrowns) that gets served in a frying pan ($15). For lunch, try the Tropical Chicken Salad with coconut, pineapple, mint, and mango salsa ($16). Great beach view. Dinner specials nightly ($17-29). Open daily 7:30am-9pm. MC/V. ❸

**Java Blue Cafe,** 2 Macrossan St. (☎07 4099 5814). Serves tasty sandwiches ($8-11), gourmet breakfasts ($4-13), and huge salads ($7-10). Pancakes with maple syrup for $7.50. Good coffee. Open daily 7am-3:30pm. Cash only. ❶

**Central Hotel,** 9 Macrossan St. (☎07 4099 5271). Spacious deck dining area with massive TV. Great for socializing over a game. Serves a predominantly local crowd and has area bands Tu-Su nights. If you work up an appetite during the drinking games, try burgers or fish ($10-16). Lunch special $9. Open daily 10am-midnight. ❶

**Mango Jam,** 24 Macrossan St. (☎07 4099 4661), with its lively terrace and good portions, is a good lunch option. Try a mango daiquiri or munch on one of the highly touted pizzas ($16-22). Meals $11-29. Open daily 7:30am-9:30pm. AmEx/D/MC/V. ❷

**Under Wraps,** 22 Macrossan St. (☎07 4099 5972), prepares scrumptious gourmet wraps ($6-11), salads ($9-11), and panini ($8) for reasonable prices. Tropical fruit juices for $5-6. Open M 8am-4:30pm, Tu-Sa 8am-6pm, Su 8am-3:30pm. ❶

## ☐ SIGHTS

Most of Port Douglas's historical sites are around the **Marina Mirage. Saint Mary's by the Sea,** a small white chapel next to the water, has a beautiful ocean view. Up the wharf, check out the **Courthouse Museum.** Built in 1879, it is the oldest building in town. (☎07 4099 4635. Open Tu, Th, Sa, and Su 10am-1pm. $2.) On Sundays (8:30am-1:30pm), there is a **craft market** in ANZAC Park near the Courthouse Museum, with stalls selling ice cream, fruit juices, and tropical fruits.

The **Rainforest Habitat,** located on Port Douglas Rd. as you enter town, has an impressive eight acres, three enclosures, and over 1000 animals that lack both cages and a discernible fear of people. Mingle with cockatoos and parrots, scratch a wallaby behind the ears, or ogle the endangered southern cassowary, a keystone species of the Dainsland rainforest. (☎07 4099 3235; www.rainforesthabitat.com.au. Wheelchair-accessible. Open daily 8am-5pm; last entry 4pm. $29, children $14.50, families $72.50. VIP/YHA/student discount 10%.)

## 🔺 OUTDOOR ACTIVITIES

### WATERFRONT ACTIVITIES

**Four Mile Beach,** at the east end of Macrossan St., is almost always quiet. This gorgeous stretch of sand attracts an array of locals, backpackers, and swanky resort-types. A netted portion protects swimmers from jellyfish during the Wet, and a lifeguard is on duty (M-Sa 9:30am-5pm).

**Extra Action Watersports** (☎07 4099 3175 or 04 1234 6303), is just north of Marina Mirage. Steve, owner and self-described "action man," runs the cheapest snorkeling trip available in town. Trips to Low Isle Reef last just over 2hr. and take 15min. to get to and from the reef. $100, children $80. MC/V.

**Wavelength** (☎07 4099 5031), next to Extra Action Watersports, is one of the few snorkeling-only operations. A boat departs daily at 8:30am for 8hr. trips to the outer reef with a marine biologist onboard. $180, children $130. Includes lunch and all fees.

**Dan's Mountain Biking** (☎07 4032 0066; www.cairns-aust.com/mtb) offers a burst of adrenaline that will leave you sweaty, dirty, and perfectly tired. Ages 12 and up. Departs Cairns 9am. ½-day $85, ¾-day $120, full-day $165.

### SCUBA DIVING

Experienced divers often prefer the untouched reefs near Port Douglas to the heavily touristed spots farther south in Cairns.

 **Haba Dive** (☎07 4098 5000), in the Marina Mirage. Offers up to 3 dives on each trip. The smallish group size (max. 40 people) makes for a relatively personal experience. Departs daily 8:30am, with free pickup and lunch. Returns at 4:30pm. Snorkeling $165, children $99; scuba, including 2 dives and gear, $225. MC/V.

**Poseidon Outer Reef Cruises** (☎1800 085 674 or 07 4099 4772; www.poseidoncruises.com.au), on the corner of Macrossan St. and Gant St. A 1-boat operation offering recreational snorkeling ($170), certified scuba including 2 dives ($230), and introductory scuba lessons ($220). Prices include lunch. Max. 80 people. Daily 8:30am-4:30pm. Office open daily 8:30am-7:30pm. MC/V.

**Quicksilver** (☎07 4087 2100; www.quicksilver-cruises.com), in Mirage Marina. One of the most respected operations in the business; immortalized in Peter Lik postcards. Offers a 5-star PADI Open Water course with group size limited to 8 per instructor. Packages for divers, non-divers, and snorkelers available. Introductory dives with gear $139; certified dives with gear $94, 2 dives $136. AmEx/D/MC/V.

## ◆ DAYTRIP FROM PORT DOUGLAS

### MOSSMAN GORGE

**BTS** (☎07 4099 5665; www.portdouglasbus.com) runs to Mossman (30min.; round-trip $17). Pickup from hostels at 8:20, 10:20, 11:45am, 2, and 3:45pm. Return at 12:45, 2:30, and 3:45pm. If driving, follow the Captain Cook Hwy. (Hwy. 1) north from the junction with Port Douglas for about 20km. Follow the signs for Mossman Gorge and turn left across from Mossman State High School. Drive about 4km to Kuku Yalanji, and 1km more to the carpark. If you intend to see Cape Tribulation or Daintree by rental car, Mossman Gorge is on the way, so don't bother using BTS.

Not all of Port Douglas's natural attractions require a pair of fins and a scuba mask. A ways outside town, the rainforest-covered mountains are easily accessible via Mossman Gorge, part of the Daintree National Park. The gorge has several **hiking paths** that originate in the visitors' carpark. Locals and tourists alike often make the easy 0.5km hike to the cool freshwater swimming holes (croc-free), while more adventurous hikers tackle the challenging 2.4km circuit track which travels up the river, over a swinging suspension bridge, and into the dark green canopy. Lizards, tropical birds, and bizarrely shaped trees are common sights, as are shoes soaked by overflowing creeks during the Wet.

Aboriginal tours can be arranged with **Kuku-Yalanji Dreamtime Walks,** which walks you through the plants used for traditional medicines and "bush tucker." The Aboriginal-owned operation also has a **visitors center** and shop. (☎07 4098 2595. Open M-Sa 8:30am-5pm. Tours M-Sa 9, 11am, 1, and 3pm; 1½hr. $32, children $18.50. Book ahead. Mini-bus pickup service from Port Douglas (pickup 8:30am, dropoff 11:30am) $55, children $36, including tour.)

### DAINTREE                                                    ☎07

Kingfishers, kookaburras, and friendly faces abound in this tiny village (pop. 150), a popular birdwatching destination. Most activities revolve around the **Daintree River**—a beautiful waterway teeming with rare wildlife. Daintree Township is about 6km north of the turnoff for the Daintree Ferry on the Cook Hwy. You'll need a car to get there. Beware that this portion of the road can flood; call **RACQ** (☎13 1905) or one of the local restaurants for road conditions.

The **Daintree General Store** (☎07 4098 6146) serves as the town watering hole and **post office.** Several companies run river excursions, which vary in length between 1 and 2hr. These generally start at $20; children travel for less. The quiet boats of **Daintree Electric Boat Cruises** (☎1800 686 103) make for a peaceful journey on the river and allow you to meet the wildlife. The cozy vessels are about the size of the estuarine crocodiles ("salties") you'll see as you meander down the Daintree River. **Daintree River Tours** also runs excellent morning wildlife- and bird-spotting tours from the jetty. (☎07 4098 7997; www.daintreerivertours.com.au. 2hr. $55. Departs 6:30am. Book ahead.) You can fish with **Far North River Safaris.** (☎07 4098 6111; www.daintreefishing.com.au. ½-day $90.)

A lush garden, bevy of exotic birds, and large, homemade breakfast are just some of the perks that convince many guests to stay an extra day at the wonderful ◆**Red Mill House,** a birdwatcher's sanctuary 50m up the road from the General Store. Breakfast is free and includes fresh tropical fruit with homemade yogurt and bread. The older part of the house has a two-bedroom family unit with lounge (4 people $240), and the new section offers ensuite doubles (multi-night $165). One suite is fully wheelchair-accessible. (☎07 4098 6233; www.redmillhouse.com.au. Free mountain bike use. Book ahead.)

# CAPE TRIBULATION ☎ 07

Cape Tribulation marks the spectacular collision of two World Heritage Parks. The rainforest crashes down onto the ocean surf, and every inch of forest and reef teems with life. About 15km north of the Daintree River, Cape Trib is a landmark in the heart of Daintree National Park.

## TRANSPORTATION

The best way to see Cape Trib is by car. Renting a vehicle will cost only slightly more than a tour package and will allow you the freedom to pick and choose between the many adventures available in and around Cape Trib. Many of the larger resorts have shuttles to sights and offer a number of activities on their premises. Sun Palm Coaches provides daily service from Cairns to Cape Trib at 7am and 1:15pm ($75 one-way; stops upon request). It returns to Cairns from **Cape Trib Beach House** (see **Accommodations**, p. 438) at 10:30am, 2, and 9pm. Travelers driving up the coast from Daintree will use the **Daintree Ferry,** which shuttles across the river 6am-midnight. (Walk-on passengers $1; cars $18 round-trip.) Access Cape Tribulation from the south via Cape Tribulation Rd., paved up to the carpark at Cape Tribulation Beach and crisscrossed by causeways and floodways at multiple points. If you're traveling during the Wet, call for road conditions (☎ 13 19 05). Given the number of river crossings, consider bringing a car with a snorkel (see **Great Outdoors,** p. 63).

## ORIENTATION AND PRACTICAL INFORMATION

When locals talk about Cape Tribulation, they're usually referring to a large general area served by **Cape Tribulation Road,** which runs north past **Cow Bay, Alexandra Bay, Thornton Peak,** and the **Cape.** There's no official information center in Cape Tribulation. The **Queensland Parks and Wildlife Service (QPWS) Ranger Station** has public info, but the hours are limited. (☎ 07 4098 9116.) Two other sources of info are the **Daintree Discovery Centre** and the **Bat House** (see **Sights and Activities,** p. 439). The **Rainforest Village,** a few kilometers before Cooper Creek, sells groceries and petrol and has a post box. (☎ 07 4098 9015. Open daily 7am-7pm.)

## ACCOMMODATIONS AND CAMPING

Hostels here reflect the active beach-going lifestyle and rainforest atmosphere of Cape Trib. Each has a slightly different theme, focusing on the beach, the rainforest, or a combination of the two. Those looking to cut costs can camp at several locations off Cape Tribulation for around $10 per person.

**Crocodylus Village** (☎ 07 4098 9166), on Buchanan Creek Rd., east off Cape Tribulation Rd. If heading north from Daintree Ferry, take a right after the Daintree Discovery Centre. This backpacker oasis offers open-air cabins scattered around a large wooden patio. Tour options include horseback-riding, sunrise paddle treks in a hybrid kayak/canoe, overnight kayak adventures, and guided bushwalks. ($16-179 depending on type and duration of trip). Laundry, pool, bar, restaurant. Organized bus transfers from Cairns or Port Douglas. Reception 7:30am-11:15pm. Cabin rooms $23, YHA $21; ensuite cabin for 2 $75, extra person $10, children $5. MC/V. ❷

**Cape Trib Beach House** (☎ 07 4098 0030 or 1800 111 124; www.capetribbeach.com. au), on the right after about 2km on the unsealed portion of Cape Tribulation Rd. Final stop on the Sun Palm bus between Cairns and Cape Trib. Relax on a pristine, private beach with forest dragons and butterflies. Free yoga on the beach daily 9am. Laundry, bar, restaurant, pool, Internet, bike rental ($10 per day), lockers ($5 per day), A/C.

Reception 7:30am-7:30pm. Some beachfront cabins, some 4-person ensuite with fridges. Dorms $25; doubles $79; private cabins $139-189. MC/V. ❷

**PK's Jungle Village** (☎07 4098 0400 or 1800 232 333; www.pksjunglevillage.com), about 400m past the "Welcome to Cape Tribulation" sign on Cape Tribulation Rd. Biggest, rowdiest hostel in Cape Trib. Backpackers drink and dance the night away. Bike rental (½-day $15, full-day $22). Laundry, kitchen, restaurant, and bar. Internet $6 per hr. IGA next door. 10min. walk to beach. Reception 7:30am-7:30pm. Check-out 9:30am. Campsites $10 per person; dorms $22; doubles $65. MC/V. ❶

**Lync Haven** (☎07 4098 9155; www.lynchaven.com.au), bordering the rainforest 16km from the ferry on the left. Sites $19, powered $24. MC/V. ❶

## 🍴 FOOD

**Lync Haven ❷,** with its wildlife exhibit full of orphaned 'roos and reptiles, is the most entertaining eating establishment in Cape Trib. Options include huge, tasty burgers ($7-18), sandwiches ($5-7), and a veggie-friendly menu ($14-16) at dinner. (☎07 4098 9155. Open daily 7am-7:30pm. MC/V.) **Cafe on the Sea ❷,** at Thorton Beach, serves up a hearty breakfast ($17), salads, burgers, and sandwiches. (☎07 4098 9118. Open daily 9am-5pm.) Most hostels and resorts also have their own bars and restaurants; the most hopping scene is **PK's Jungle Village,** where the bar is open daily noon-midnight. (ATM. MC/V.)

## 👁 ⚠ SIGHTS AND ACTIVITIES

For a unique taste sensation, visit the ▧**Cape Tribulation Exotic Fruit Farm,** where jungle expert Digby offers tasting tours of succulent and exotic fruits. (☎07 4098 0057; www.capetrib.com.au. Tour begins daily at 2pm. $20. Book ahead.) The **Daintree Discovery Centre,** just before Cow Bay, off Cape Tribulation Rd., is an informative and popular stop. It has an aerial boardwalk and 23m canopy tower, allowing visitors to view the rainforest from above. You can take a self-guided tour using the info booklet or rent an audio guide for $5. (☎07 4098 9171. Open daily 8:30am-5pm. $28, children $14, families $68, concessions for those lodging in the area $25.) A walk around **Jindalba,** just 450m up the road from the center, offers a look into some of the best-preserved, public rainforest in Cape Trib. The area has picnic facilities, bathrooms, and a sign-posted walk. The **Bat House,** opposite PK's Jungle Village on the west side of the highway, is a less extensive source of information than the Discovery Centre, but the all-volunteer staff will be happy to let you have a look at their giant flying foxes—Old Boy, Sunshine, and Pushkin—for $4. (☎07 4098 0063; www.austrop.org.au.)

**Cape Tribulation Wilderness Cruises** explores the mangroves of Cooper Creek. (☎07 4033 2052; www.capetribcruises.com. Daily departure times vary. Day cruises $25, under 14 $17.50; 1hr. Night charters $30, under 14 $20; 1½hr. Book ahead.) **Cafe on the Sea** (see **Food** above) sells tickets. MC/V.) **Rum Runner** is one of several Cairns-based tours running daily trips to the reef off the Cape, and departs from Cape Trib to explore the Mackay and Undine Reefs. The reefs visited on this tour are more pristine than those in over-touristed Cairns. (☎1300 556 332; www.rumrunner.com.au. Free bus to the beach from nearby resorts. Snorkeling equipment included. Snorkeling $120; ages 3-14 $90. Dives for certified and first-time divers. Max. 44 passengers.)

**Tropical Sea Kayaks** (☎07 4098 9166) offers a popular two-day, one-night trip to Snapper Island ($199; ask at **Crocodylus Village,** p. 438). The excursion features reef walking, snorkeling, and beach camping, and includes equipment and prepared meals. **Cape Trib Horse Rides**, at Cape Trib Beach House, leads horseback tours through rainforest, streams, riverbeds and along the Cape Tribulation

Beach. (☎07 4098 0030 or 1800 111 124. 3½hr. Departs daily at 8am and 1:30pm. $99. Transfers from all major Cape Trib resorts. Min. age 13. MC/V.)

# ROUTES TO COOKTOWN

There are two routes from Daintree to Cooktown—one inland, one coastal. Both offer stunning views and unique scenery; travelers should drive up one and down the other so as to take in the beauty of the far north in its entirety.

The coastal route, called the **Bloomfield Track,** beats through 150km of bush as it swerves and dips, carving its way through rugged coastal mountains. In rainy weather, it is impassable; rainforest creeks often become raging rivers. On a "good" day, however, the road is about as much fun as can legally be had in a 4WD. Thick rainforest canopy melts away to reveal coastal views, while steep inclines and river crossings keep the adrenaline pumping. Call ahead or check with locals for road conditions. Bring cash, as some places don't take credit.

The inland route to Cooktown doesn't offer the same kind of rugged adventure as the coastal track does; it's mostly sealed. That said, it's breathtaking, as it winds through rainforest ravines, over mountain passes, and finally into open savannah. In the late afternoon, drivers should look out for Brahma cattle and wild horses on the unfenced road. Country Road Coachlines (☎07 4045 2794) departs Port Douglas and Cairns via the coastal road M, W, and F, and Cairns via the inland road W-F and Su (from Cairns $72; from Pt. Douglas $60).

## BLOOMFIELD TRACK

This is a playground for those who desire an intense 4WD experience, and it's generally traveled enough that you probably won't have to wait long for help if you get stuck. From Cape Tribulation, the road turns to dirt and the fun really begins. The first part of the trip is the most difficult, as the track follows the coastal mountains up steep inclines and down sharp grades, and there are a half-dozen rivers to ford. A little over an hour's drive north brings travelers to **Wujal Wujal,** a tiny Aboriginal community. Between Wujal Wujal and **Ayton** (see below) is **Bloomfield Inn,** which has a service station. It stocks everything from food and meds to camping supplies and clothes. (☎07 4060 8174. Store open M-F 8am-10pm, Sa-Su 8am-midnight.) Beautiful **Bloomfield Falls** is only 5min. from Wujal Wujal. Take a left after the bridge over Bloomfield River; go in the opposite direction from the Cooktown arrow. Visitors who make the short (2min.) hike from the parking area to the falls are rewarded with a striking view of the 200 ft. torrent of crashing water. It's an excellent place for a picnic after a rough ride—just watch out for feisty crocodiles.

The mountains pull back from the coast between Wujal Wujal and Cooktown, and the wet tropics slowly yield to dry savannah. North of the bridge to Wujal Wujal, the road is smoother and occasionally paved, and travelers can count on passing the occasional store or small-town hotel. About 10km north of Wujal Wujal is the town of **Ayton,** where the local **IGA Express** has basic groceries, supplies, a cafe, a pay phone, and toilets. (Open M-F 8:30am-5pm, Sa-Su 8:30am-4pm.) **Bloomfield Cabins and Camping ❶** serves lunch and dinner ($17-26), and offers campsites and cabins. (☎07 4060 8207; www.bloomfieldcabins.com. Sites $10 per person, cabins for 2 from $75. MC/V.)

Four kilometers past the Lion's Den, the coastal road joins the sealed portion of the inland route (a.k.a. **Mulligan Highway**) and a tall, dark shadow appears on the horizon. The source of this silhouette is **Black Mountain National Park,** one of Australia's mysterious, lesser-known natural wonders. The two barren, black peaks (known as Kalkajakaare, or "Place of the Spears" in Aboriginal languages) are the subject of many **Dreaming** tales (p. 58), which are Creation Time stories of the Kuku Yalanji Aboriginal people. Signs at the park lookout explain that these jet-black rock piles are ringed with stinging bushes, house an intricate network of dangerous caves, and provide a habitat for three animal species found nowhere else in the world. Pilots passing over the rocks have supposedly reported experiencing turbulence and hearing loud bangs and mournful cries. The dark peaks (black from a film of fungi growing on the exposed rock) and surrounding area inspire many legends of those who have ventured into the mountain, never to return.

## INLAND ROUTE

Though the inland route is more developed and well-traveled than the coastal road, it's just as scenic. The first stop, **Mount Molloy,** is a 27km drive southwest of Mossman on the Peninsula Developmental Rd. (10min.) The **Mount Molloy National Hotel ❸** is a grand building built in 1901. The downstairs pub (with outdoor beer garden) has a varied menu, and the hotel offers Old-World style accommodations. (☎07 4094 1133. Reception at pub 10am-late. Meals $8-25. Rooms $30 per person, including breakfast.) Next door, the **Mt. Molloy Cafe ❶** serves acclaimed burgers ($8.50), calamari, pizza, and homemade meat pies (open daily 10am-late). Down the road, there are public toilets, a **post office** (☎07 4094 1135; open M-F 9am-1pm and 2-5pm), and a petrol station. (☎07 4094 1159; Open M-Sa 7am-7pm, Su 8am-7pm.) The picnic area at the junction entering town has toilets, hiking info, and **free campsites ❶** (max. stay 48hr.).

**Mount Carbine** sits 28km north of Mt. Molloy. Once a prosperous tungsten mining town, it now consists of three roadside buildings and an old miners' village, which has been converted into a caravan park and residential area. That village, the **Mt. Carbine Caravan Park ❶,** is the best place to stay on the inland route. It has basketball and tennis courts, a TV lounge, kitchen, and laundry facilities. Caravan parking is free if you stay for at least one night and are continuing up Cape York. (☎07 4094 3160. Reception 7:30am-8:30pm. One-bedroom houses with 2 beds, satellite TV, and fully-equipped kitchen $55; 2-bedroom $65; 3-bedroom $75; caravan sites $14, powered $16, each extra person $5. MC/V.)

As it continues north, the road cuts through the hills, exposing the cores of mountains now bereft of their once-famous gold deposits. The **Palmer River Roadhouse ❶,** 110km north of Mt. Molloy, proudly displays artifacts dating back to the gold rush. (☎07 4060 2020. Open daily 7am-10pm. Powered caravan and tent sites $16.50. Permanent tent accommodations can be arranged. MC/V.) Farther north (145km from Mt. Molloy), the road gives way to a snaky gravel descent through the hills with beautiful views. Just before reaching Cooktown the road passes the mysterious **Black Mountain National Park** (see p. 440).

# COOKTOWN ☎07

In the winter, southern winds sweep through Cooktown's dusty streets, bringing with them travelers who have abandoned the monotony of packaged tours and pre-paid holidays. Cooktown tends to act as traveler's quicksand, stopping passersby captivated by a place where bars are open until the last patron leaves and shoes are an infrequent addition to the daily wardrobe. The town dates back to 1770, when Captain James Cook of England ran his ship *Endeavour* into the Great Barrier Reef. The 239 years since have witnessed the settlement, abandonment, and resettlement of the area, along with a gold rush and devastating cyclones. Today, Cooktown (pop. 1500) is both a key gateway to the far north and an eccentric community full of small-town charm.

QUEENSLAND

## ⌐ TRANSPORTATION

**Buses: Country Road Coachlines** (☎07 4045 2794; www.countryroadcoachlines.com.
au) run between Cooktown and Cairns. One bus departs from each city every day except
M, alternating between coastal and inland routes. A round-trip ticket ($144) allows you
to get on and off as often as you like, but you will have to wait a day at each stop to
catch a bus continuing in the same direction. Buses run on the **inland route** (5hr.; W,
F, Su 2:30pm; $72) via **Lakeland** (1hr.); **Mt. Carbine** (4hr.); **Mareeba** (3hr.); **Kuranda**
(4hr.), or by the **coastal route** (7hr.; Tu, Th, Sa; $72) via **Cape Tribulation** (3hr.); **Cow
Bay** (3½hr.); **Mossman** (4½hr.); **Pt. Douglas** (5½hr.).

**Taxis: Cooktown Taxis** (☎07 4069 5387). Service from 6:30am until the pubs close ($6
fare anywhere within the city limits).

**Car Rental: A1 Car Rental,** 112 Charlotte St. (24hr. ☎07 4069 5775) has a small
selection. 4WDs start at $120.

**Road Report:** Call the **Royal Automobile Club of Queensland** (RACQ; ☎13 19 05).

**Service: Caltex Station** (☎07 4069 5354), at Hope and Howard St., has petrol. MC/V.

## ✷ ORIENTATION

The **Cooktown Development Road** becomes **Hope Street** as you enter Cooktown
proper and head toward **Grassy Hill,** where Captain Cook first spied the harbor.
Take a left off this street and continue two blocks to **Charlotte Street,** which runs
parallel to **Hope Street,** home to the majority of Cooktown's shops and services.
It intersects several streets, including **Boundary, Howard, Hogg,** and **Walker Street.**
Head east on Walker St. to visit the **Botanic Gardens** and **Finch Bay.** At the northernmost end of town, Charlotte St. runs along the water, curves eastward, and
becomes **Webber Esplanade** before coming to a dead end.

## ⁊ PRACTICAL INFORMATION

**Tourist Office: Cooktown Booking Centre** (☎07 4069 5381), on Charlotte St., across
from the post office, has a friendly and knowledgeable staff. Open M-Sa 9am-5pm in
high season. Also, **The Croc Shop,** 115 Charlotte St. (☎07 4069 5880), serves as an
info center, with a bookings office next door. Visit local legend Linda Rowe, author of *Paradise Found,* for tips on trekking to the Tip. Open daily 8:30am-6pm in high season.

**Bank: Westpac** (☎07 4069 6960), on Charlotte St., between Green and Furneaux St.,
next door to the post office. Open M-F 9am-4:30pm. Currency exchange at **ANZ** (☎07
4069 6522), on Charlotte St. next to The Croc Shop. $8 commission on note exchange;
$7 flat fee for traveler's checks. Open M-Th 9:30am-4pm, F 9:30am-5pm.

**Parks Service: Queensland Parks and Wildlife Service** (QPWS; ☎07 4069 5574), at
the end of Webber Esplanade. Open M-Th 8am-3:30pm, F 8am-3pm.

**Laundromat:** (☎07 4069 6799), under the Parks Office at Webber Esplanade.

**Police:** (☎07 4069 5320), across from the wharf on Charlotte St. Staffed M-F 8am-
12:30pm and 1-4pm; after hours, use the intercom at the office door.

**Medical Services: Cooktown Hospital** (☎07 4069 5433), on the corner of Ida St. and
Hope St., on the way out of town heading south.

**Internet Access: Cooktown Computer Stuff** (☎07 4069 6010), on Charlotte St. $2 per
20min. Open M-F 9am-noon and 1-5pm.

**Post Office:** (☎07 4069 5347), on Charlotte St., next to the bank and across from the
Sovereign Hotel. Open M-F 9am-5pm. **Postal Code:** 4895.

# ACCOMMODATIONS

**Pam's Place** (☎07 4069 5166), at the corner of Charlotte and Boundary St. Cooktown's backpacker hub. Amenities include a large kitchen, laundry, a bar, pool table, and morning shuttles to the bus station and airport. Internet access $6 per hr. Sites $11; dorms $25-$27; singles $55; motel rooms $90. YHA discount. MC/V, 2% surcharge. ❷

**Alamanda Inn** (☎07 4069 5203), across from the Ampol station on the corner of Hope and Howard St. Offers tidy guesthouse rooms among beds of flowers. Breakfast included. All rooms have A/C, fridge, TV, and sink. Singles $50; doubles $60. MC/V. ❹

**Cooktown Caravan Park** (☎07 4069 5536; www. cooktowncaravanpark.com), on Hope St., at the end of Cooktown Developmental Rd. Nestled in the trees at the base of Mt. Sorrow, this is one of the nicest places to camp in Cooktown, with arguably the best camp showers in all of Australia. Internet available. Sites $12, powered $19. ❶

# FOOD

Groceries can be purchased at the **IGA** supermarket, on the corner of Hogg and Helen St. (☎07 4069 5633. Open M-W and F-Sa 8am-6pm, Th 8am-7pm, Su 10am-3pm.) There's also a cheap fruit store called **Q-Cumber** behind the IGA (in an outdoor mall on Charlotte St., between Hogg and Walker St.).

**Vera's Cafe** (☎07 4069 6881), in the Botanical Gardens by Nature's Powerhouse. This tiny cafe serves what may be the best lunch in Cooktown. Sit on the patio overlooking the garden and enjoy bacon and cherry tomato quiche ($14). Excellent icy sodas made with local fruits, homemade syrups, herbs, and spices ($5-7). Open daily 10am-2pm. MC/V. ❷

# SIGHTS

**GUURRBI ROCK ART TOURS.** These tours present an amazing opportunity to view and experience the ancient rock art of the Nugal-warra tribe. Community Elder and Guide Wilfred Gordon weaves the ancestral story lines together with the lives of his guests, teaching the lessons of Aboriginal culture and history through a very personal and enlightening tour. *(Located in the Aboriginal community of Hope Vale, 45min. outside Cooktown. Take Charlotte St. out of Cooktown and follow the road all the way to Hope Vale (3hr.). ☎07 4069 6259. 3½hr. Great Emu tour $90, self-drive $60; 5½hr. Rainbow Serpent Tour $150/80. Book ahead.)*

## LOCAL LEGEND

### MOUNT MYSTERY

Legends abound in Cooktown about mysterious Black Mountain. Ask any local and you're sure to hear stories of cars and watches malfunctioning around its base, or about how friends of friends were seemingly swallowed whole while trying to reach the summit. Indeed, while official records of deaths caused by the mountain are as elusive as the ghosts that some believe inhabit it, pilots report turbulence when flying over the mountain to this day, and what sound like mournful cries and loud bangs can supposedly still be heard in its vicinity.

Though there may be more stories of climbers lost on Black Mountain than there are graves to substantiate them, climbing or even approaching the base of the mountain is prohibited. Pythons that spend their days sunning on the mountainside may look more menacing than they actually are, but the uncharted labyrinth of passageways and chambers underneath Black's exterior lend credibility to Cooktown folklore. If the pitch-black tunnels weren't hazardous enough, abrupt drop-offs bedevil would-be explorers.

Perhaps most menacing is the notorious "Queensland tiger," a large striped cat that supposedly roams Cooktown and takes most of its victims around the mountain. Descriptions of the ferocious feline are similar to those of the marsupial lion, which inhabited Queensland until it went extinct around 20,000 years ago.

**JAMES COOK HISTORICAL MUSEUM.** The crown jewel of a town obsessed with the landing of Captain Cook, this Catholic-convent-turned-museum even attracted Queen Elizabeth II to its dedication. Since then, it has drawn tourists intrigued by an assortment of Cooktown's historical relics, from Cook's anchor to a Chinese shrine to Aboriginal artifacts. Read entries from Cook's journal as well as those of his crew. (☎ 07 4069 5386. On the corner of Helen St. and Furneaux St. Open daily 9:30am-4pm. $10, discounts for children. MC/V.)

**OTHER SIGHTS.** The lush **Botanic Gardens,** off Walker St., is a great place for picnicking; you may even spot a kangaroo or two. Inside the garden, visit **Nature's Powerhouse,** an interpretive center with excellent croc and snake exhibits and the botanical artwork of Vera Scarth-Johnson. Locals swim at **Finch Bay** (reached by following Walker St. to its end), though recent croc spottings have kept would-be swimmers on land. Branching off the path to Finch Bay is a trail to **Cherry Tree Bay.** The trail from Cherry Tree Bay to the lookout is not well-marked at the beach and its challenging inclines are unsuitable for small children. However, the lookout and lighthouse on **Grassy Hill** can also be accessed via car or foot from the end of Hope St. The summit provides an astounding 360° view of hundreds of square hectares, including the entirety of Cooktown, the surrounding rainforest, and the Great Barrier Reef. There's an even better view at the top of **Mt. Cook** in **Mt. Cook National Park.** A 3-4hr. trail through rainforest to the mountain's summit starts at the end of Melaleuca St. See what Captain Cook saw when figuring out how to navigate out of the Reef; ask about it at The Croc Shop. Outside of Cooktown on the Cooktown Developmental Rd., the **Trevethan Waterfall** is tough to get to (4WD only) but is absolutely stunning and perfect for swimming—there's even a rope-swing. Take Mt. Amos Rd., a few kilometers after the turnoff for Archer Point (leaving Cooktown). It's 13km down the road, but the last 2km are rocky. During the Queen's Birthday weekend in June, the **Cooktown Discovery Festival** has truck-pulling competitions, reenactments of Captain Cook's landing, and other entertainment.

# CAPE YORK

Cape York is one of the last great wilderness frontiers in Australia; a forbidding and isolated Outback beckons adventurers to abandon civilization and make the journey of nearly 1000km to **Australia's tip.** Accessible only via the **Peninsula Developmental Road** (unsealed), the route is peppered with small towns and roadhouses every few hundred kilometers. During the Wet (Dec.-Apr.), most of the roads are impassable; the only way to see the Cape is by flying over it or into one of the small airports on the coast. During the Dry, the trip is arduous but manageable with a 4WD, and the reward is being witness to some of the most beautiful, diverse, and untouched landscapes in the world.

If you decide to undertake the journey, check out books specifically about Cape York, which offer logistical as well as historical and geographical information. This is particularly important if you're crazy (and insured) enough to drive the **Old Telegraph Track** (p. 449). *Cape York: An Adventurer's Guide* by Ron and Viv Moon (www.guidebooks.com.au) is a popular choice.

## THE TIP

During the Wet, the unsealed roads are muddy, flooded, and generally impassable. Though they vary in quality the rest of the year, they are mostly drivable (barring major tropical disturbances). According to locals, a 4WD is not essential if you're staying on the Peninsula Developmental Rd., but if you're accustomed to driving on paved roads with well-defined lanes, a 4WD with high ground clearance is strongly recommended. If trekking off the main roads (into the national parks, for example), a 4WD is essential, as river crossings, jagged rocks, and vegetation create plenty of driving hazards. Before tackling any new road, it is important to check with locals for advice.

Aside from renting a 4WD, tour packages and flights are often the only other option. **Regional Pacific** (☎07 4040 1400; www.regional-pacific.com.au) flies between Cairns and Bamaga from $776. **Qantas** flies from Cairns to Horn Island ($150-250), where **Aerotropics** (☎07 1300 656 110; www.aero-tropics.com.au) connects Horn to the outer islands of the Torres Strait (Horn Island-Badu $496). **John Charlton's Cape York Adventures** (☎07 4069 3302; www.capeyork-adventures.com.au) has comprehensive tours of Cape York, including an opportunity to fish in the Cape's renowned waters. **Bart's Bush Adventures** (☎07 4069 6229; www.bartsbushadventures. com.au) does outback daytrips out of Cooktown. **Billy Tea Bush Safaris,** an award-winning company, combines 4WD, flying, and boating in their trips to Cape York from Cairns. (☎07 4032 0077; www.billytea.com.au. 9-day fly/drive trips from $2750.)

This journey has long seemed out-of-reach for the budget traveler. Getting to the Tip requires relative self-sufficiency—you need tents and the ability to cook your own food. But if you can get a few people together, it can definitely be done, and it's usually a lot cheaper than going by boat, plane, or tour company. To see the national parks (which can be the best part of the journey), you'll need a 4WD with high clearance and a winch, in case you get stuck crossing any creeks or mud-holes. Problems can be avoided if you walk through creeks before driving through them, and if you stay to the packed-down tracks. Again, this is only necessary for national parks; the main roads (**Peninsula Developmental Road,** the **Telegraph Road,** and the **Bamaga Road**) strive to avoid the river crossings that are the heart of the Old Telegraph Track. Camping is generally inexpensive (about $10 per person). The area is also remote enough to allow for free camping: just stay away from the water, where crocs may be lurking.

There are plenty of supermarkets throughout the Cape, and cheap food is available. Fuel gets increasingly expensive as you head north; Bamaga has the most reasonable prices near the Tip. 4WDs can be rented in Cairns. **Britz** (☎07 4032 2611; www.britz.com) has a large range of 4WD campervans and 4WDs. **Sargent 4WD** (☎07 4032 3094 or 1800 077 353; www.4wdhire.com.au) has the toughest fleet of vehicles, but charges high rates with a large excess. They offer a winch for a set price in addition to the rental cost. These companies specialize in 4WDs, but other rental companies in Cairns may have a few available for less, so check around and plan ahead. You might also want to check out **A1 Car Rental** in Cooktown (p. 442), which has excellent 4WDs.

## BASE OF THE CAPE

If you don't have the time, money, or stamina for the full journey up the Cape, you can still have an exciting wilderness experience not too far from Cooktown. For a good two- to three-day trip, try a circuit around **Lakefield National Park** via the **Peninsula Developmental Road** and the **Battle Camp Track.** 4WD is highly recommended. From Cooktown, the Cooktown Developmental Road runs southwest to Lakeland, where it meets the northbound Peninsula Developmental Rd. This road travels along the edge of Lakefield National Park through the small town of **Laura** and then on to the outpost of **Musgrave,** the northern gateway to the park. On the Peninsula Developmental Rd., you can enter the park from either Laura or Musgrave (see **Lakefield National Park,** p. 446). You'll see a variety of wildlife, including kangaroos, wallabies, exotic birds, snakes, and crocodiles. At the southern end of the park, the **Battle Camp Track** returns to Cooktown. Although it's not a long drive, the rough terrain and river crossings (one of which is tidal and avoided by locals) will slow you down. Bring a spare tire, as the Lakefield region roads are known for their numerous sharp rocks.

In **Laura** (pop. 100), the **Laura Roadhouse ❶,** on Peninsula Developmental Rd. just after entering town from the south, offers fuel, food, an **ATM,** and **campsites.** (☎07 4060 3419. Open daily 6am-8pm. Sites $5, powered $8. MC/V.) Supplies are also available at the **Laura Store.** (☎07 4060 3238. Open daily 8am-5:30pm.)

# LAKEFIELD NATIONAL PARK REGION

| LAKEFIELD NATIONAL PARK AT A GLANCE | |
|---|---|
| **AREA:** 537,000 hectares. | **GATEWAYS:** The Battlecamp Track, from Laura or Musgrave. |
| **HIGHLIGHTS:** Seasonal billabongs bring an amazing assortment of wildlife; beautiful lily lagoons; historical homestead; birdwatching; excellent barramundi and catfish fishing. | **CAMPING:** Kalpowar, Hann Crossing, and many bush campgrounds. |
| | **FEES:** Camping $5. |

Laura is the gateway to the south of the park, while **Musgrave,** 138km north of Laura on the Peninsula Developmental Rd., is the closest point of contact with the northern reaches. Its only building is the **Musgrave Roadhouse ❶,** which has a restaurant, fuel, and a friendly staff. (☎07 4060 3229. Open daily 7:30am-10pm.) Accommodations are also available. (Sites $14; singles $32, doubles $55.)

**BEWARE CROCODILES.** Most of the swamps, lakes, and rivers in Lakefield NP contain saltwater crocodiles. Never camp within 50m of water or less than 2m above it. Never swim in the park, and exercise caution near the water's edge. (See **Dangerous Species,** p. 66.)

To reach the heart of the park from Musgrave, travel west toward Cooktown. As the name "Lakefield" suggests, the park and its roads are submerged during the Wet. During the Dry, all but a few billabongs evaporate, attracting the area's wildlife to these critical sources of water. Visitors during these months are treated to an animal extravaganza and world-famous birdwatching. Crocodiles, dingoes, wallabies, and feral pigs are commonly spotted in this area. After entering the park, travel east along the clearly marked track past **Lowlake,** a beautiful swamp covered in white lily flowers that is considered sacred to the region's traditional protectors. Farther down this road, **Nilma Plain** seems otherworldly with its endless expanses covered in tall, sharp termite mounds.

**Camping ❶** in these areas is by permit only ($5), which can be obtained by self-registering at one of three **ranger stations** in the park. The **Lakefield Ranger Station** is in the middle of the park, 112km from Musgrave; register here for the Kalpowar, Seven Mile, Melaleuca, Hanush's, and Midway sites. There are also boards announcing current road conditions. (☎07 4060 3271. Open daily 7am-4:30pm.) **Kalpowar** is the most developed campground, with toilets and showers; **Hann Crossing** is the only other campground with toilets. Camping in the southern section of the park requires a permit from the **New Laura Ranger Station,** while northern camping requires a permit from the **Bizant Ranger Station.**

Fishing and canoeing are the most popular activities in the park, with birdwatching close behind. Check out **Red Lily Lagoon** for some remarkable birdlife alongside the red lilies of the lotus plant. For fishing aficionados: Barramundi and catfish are the most common catches, but you can only keep a limited number, so be sure to consult a ranger when planning your trip.

You can access the **Princess Charlotte Bay** by boat, but not car. The Bizant boat ramp, 20km from the Bizant ranger base in the north of the park, provides the best access. Many of the other small lakes are suitable for small watercraft.

# COEN

North of Musgrave, the unexpected shifts in terrain and rapid directional changes of the Peninsula Developmental Rd. will test your reflexes. Fortunately, there aren't many other vehicles to contend with. After 109km on this "highway," you'll arrive in the tiny town of Coen (pop. 350).

The **Homestead Guest House ❹** is filled with goldrush memorabilia. (☎07 4060 1157. Laundry and kitchen. Reception 7am-9pm. Singles $60, doubles $80. Cash only.) The social center of Coen is the **Exchange Hotel ❺**. (☎07 4060 1133. Reception 10am-10pm. Motel rooms with A/C $99 per person.)

Most services are on Regent St. You can park your camper here or **pitch a tent ❶** in the lot next door ($15, powered $20). Across the street is the **BP Fuel Store** (☎07 4060 1144). Many establishments close or operate with restricted hours in the Wet. **Queensland Parks and Wildlife Service** (www.epa.qld.gov.au), on the left as you leave town heading north, has 24hr. info on nearby parks and campgrounds available to travelers. An **ATM** can be found at the Exchange Hotel. **Medical services** are available at the **Coen Clinic,** 2 Armbrust St. (☎07 4060 1166. Open M-F 8am-5pm, 24hr. emergency service.) The **Armbrust General Store** has groceries, petrol, a payphone, and a small **post office.** (☎07 4060 1134. Open M-F 8am-5pm, Sa 8am-3pm, Su 9am-noon. MC/V.)

# NORTH OF COEN

Another 65km north along the Peninsula Developmental Rd., a wet track of red earth and white sand leads to the **Archer River Roadhouse ❶**. A popular spot for those going to and coming from the Tip, this outpost is a welcome reminder that life does exist along these lonely roads. Those returning from the bush should fill their empty stomachs with a famous Archer Burger, stuffed with every topping that has ever been slapped between two buns—and then some. The kitchen also serves beer, sandwiches, and full meals ($9-25). Camping and limited **accommodations ❺** also available. (☎07 4060 3266. Reception 7:30am-10pm. Singles $60; doubles $100. MC/V.)

QUEENSLAND

# IRON RANGE NATIONAL PARK

| IRON RANGE NATIONAL PARK AT A GLANCE | |
|---|---|
| **AREA:** 34,600 hectares.<br>**WHERE:** On the remote eastern edge of the Cape York Peninsula.<br>**HIGHLIGHTS:** Australia's largest lowland rainforest; a diverse assortment of beautiful, endangered animals; picturesque Chili Beach. | **GATEWAYS:** 100km east of the Peninsula Developmental Rd.<br>**CAMPING:** Two rainforest bush camps; Chili Beach has pit toilets.<br>**FEES:** Camping $5. |

Iron Range National Park, Australia's largest lowland rainforest, is an unparalleled tropical fantasy land of exotic creatures, isolated beaches, and stunning views. Iron Range is a haven for those looking for the most pristine, untouched natural wonders Australia has to offer. The park is so remote that, aside from the Aboriginal Lockheart River community and the occasional safari group, there are no people for hundreds of kilometers. This kind of remoteness means the park has no substantial walking tracks, but it does offer strolls down pristine **Chili Beach** without a single footprint to mar the sand.

Travelers can access the route to the park 40km north of the Archer River Roadhouse on the Peninsula Developmental Rd. The small dirt track is a rough ramble over rocky creek beds, through two rivers, and down muddy hills, all while dodging wildlife. It begins in dry eucalyptus savannah and becomes increasingly tropical as you move eastward. The creek beds feed into a river so wide that the road's exit point on the opposite bank is not immediately obvious. It's recommended that you walk through the two rivers and choose the best path before driving through. Locals also recommend driving into washouts at an angle and then straightening out once in the water, rather than approaching them straight-on. This helps avoid being moved by rushing water.

From the Peninsula Developmental Rd., it is a 3hr., 95km drive to the entrance of Iron Range National Park. As you enter the park via Tozer's Gap, the path leads to an expansive scrub land with an impressive view of Mt. Tozer. A viewing platform just inside the park provides an excellent panoramic view. From there, the track descends into the heart of the rainforest; travelers can expect muddy downhill slides and rocky dips leading to small stream crossings. There is another entrance 65km beyond this entrance (from the Telegraph Road) called **Frenchman's Track.** The road has stunning views, but is not driven by many people because of its deep river crossing. It is 52km to the meeting of the track and the main road into the park and 27km to the ranger station.

The **ranger station** is a 30min., 15km drive into the park and is 110km from the Peninsula Developmental Rd. entrance. **Camping ❶** is available; all overnight campers must register here and pick up a permit ($4.85 per person). There are two rainforest campgrounds between the ranger station and the coast, but the most popular site is 45min. past the station at **Chili Beach,** a secluded white-sand expanse lined by coconut palms.

## WEIPA

The Peninsula Developmental Rd. bears west beyond the Archer River toward the bauxite-mining town of Weipa (pop. 2000). It's the only town of substantial size on the Cape York Peninsula, making it a good place to pick up supplies or find a comfortable bed. Bear in mind that a detour to this port on the Gulf of Carpentaria takes 2hr. and 145km, one-way. Unless you're heading there for fishing or a mine tour, you're probably better off continuing on to **Bramwell Junction** (see below) for fuel and supplies.

You can camp at **Weipa Camping Ground ❷.** The site also rents small fishing boats and cabins of various sizes, some ensuite and with kitchen. (☎07 4069 7871. Sites $24, powered $28; cabins $75-155. ½-day boat rental $100, full-day $150.) For something more luxurious, check into the **Heritage Resort ❺,** behind the shopping center on Commercial Ave. Clean rooms, a bar and restaurant, a pool with rock waterfall, and services including massage, babysitting, and a beauty salon are all welcome comforts after days in the bush. (☎07 4069 8000. Singles $150; doubles $160. AmEx/D/MC/V. 10% surcharge on AmEx/D.)

The **police** (☎07 4069 9119) are across the street from the hospital on Northern Ave. The **hospital** (☎07 4090 6225) is at the corner of Northern and Central Ave. Supplies are available at the shopping center on the corner of Commercial Ave. and Keer Point Dr., where you'll find a **pharmacy** (☎07 4069 7412), a **Woolworths** supermarket (open M-W 8am-7pm, Th 8am-9pm, Sa 8am-5pm), and a **post office** (☎07 4069 7110; open M-F 9am-5pm). **Postal code:** 4874.

## THE TELEGRAPH AND BAMAGA/BYPASS ROADS

The Peninsula Developmental Rd. forks at the junction to Weipa. For more adventures, head right on **Telegraph Road,** which is well-marked but rough. Dusty, bumpy tracks and river crossings characterize the remaining distance to the Tip. North of the Archer River, the Cape's jungle becomes wilder, the heat hotter, the tracks rougher, and the Wet wetter. **Moreton Telegraph Station** (☎07 4060 3360) lies 72km past the fork between Telegraph Rd. and Peninsula Rd. There are campgrounds here (powered and unpowered; power is turned off at 10pm), a pay phone, and some food, though no fuel and few supplies. **Bramwell Junction** (☎07 4060 3230), another 42km on the Telegraph Rd., has a service station, a garage for limited repairs, powered campsites, and limited accommodations (campsites $9 per person). **Bramwell Station** (☎07 4060 3300), 10k from Bramwell Jct., has DONGA rooms (singles $40; twins $60), plenty of campsites ($10), and meals. (Reception open 7am-7pm daily. MC/V.)

 **HEAD-ON COLLISION.** This is the most common type of accident south of the Jardine Ferry. Don't drive too fast, as the road is narrow and there are many blind curves, especially on **Bamaga Road.**

The road splits at Bramwell Jct., nearly halfway to the Tip from the Archer River. Continuing straight leads to the **Old Telegraph Track,** which is known throughout Australia as the ultimate 4WD experience. For those not willing to risk their necks on this stretch of harrowing road, the **Southern Bypass Road** (or **Bamaga Road**) is a much easier alternative.

Before reaching the Tip, travelers must pass the **Heathlands Resource Reserve** and then the **Jardine River National Park.** Campsites are available at **Captain Billy's Landing** on the coast and at the spectacular **Twin Falls,** just off Telegraph Rd. Both sites require pre-registration, which takes place at the **Heathlands ranger base** south of Eliot Falls, 12km off Bamaga Rd. There's a turnoff to **Fruit Bat Falls** and **Eliot/Twin Falls,** 110km past Bramwell Jct. where Bamaga Rd. intersects with the Old Telegraph Track again. **Fruit Bat Falls,** with its spa-like basin, is a great swimming spot—perfect after a dusty morning drive—and it's only 2km from Bamaga Rd. It also has toilets. Eliot/Twin Falls are 8km off the road and require some navigation on the Old Telegraph Track, but are worthwhile.

Returning to Bamaga Rd. (known as the **Northern Bypass Road** after the second intersection), it is 62km to the expensive **Jardine River Ferry.** (☎07 4069 1369. Vehicles $88 round-trip. Cash only.) The fare includes a permit for camping and fishing on the Jardine and Jackey Rivers.

## BAMAGA AND SURROUNDS

Before you get to the Tip, take time to observe the diverse communities on the last part of the peninsula; several distinct groups of Indigenous Australians and immigrated Islanders have made this area their home. The biggest community is **Bamaga,** essentially the last town before the Tip. It's on Bamaga Rd. after Injinoo. Alternatively, you can take the gravel road 28km after the ferry.

In Bamaga, there is a very helpful **information center** (☎07 4069 3777), with a small museum about the region, adjacent to the highway and next door to the BP fuel station. The center has facts about the entire area, including the Torres Strait Islands. Down the road is a **police station (emergency ☎000).** Farther along is a T-junction with Adidi St.; you'll find a well-stocked **supermarket** (open M-F 8am-7pm, Sa 8am-2pm, Su 9am-1pm), a **hospital** (24hr. ☎07 4069 3166), and a **post office** (open M-F 9am-12:30pm and 1:30-5pm). **Postal code:** 4876.

There are a few places to stay in **Seisia,** 5km from Bamaga. Follow Adidi St. past the supermarket, away from the T-junction. On your way check out **Loyalty Beach ❶,** which has powered and unpowered campsites, lodge-style accommodations, and a self-contained beach house. (☎07 4069 3372; www.loyaltybeach. com. Reception daily 8-10am and 4-6pm. Campsites $10 per person, $11 for power; single lodge $95; double $120; twin $75; 4-person beach house $195, extra person $20. MC/V.) **Seisia Holiday Park ❶,** 6 Koraba Rd., has a similar beachfront and rents small villas, rooms, and campsites for similar prices. (☎1800 653 243. Sites $8, powered $10. Singles $66; twins $106; cottage for 4 $185. MC/V.) Seisia also has a **supermarket** and a BP station (☎07 4069 3897; open M-F 6:45am-6pm, Sa-Su 7am-4pm). If you need to rent a car, look for **Seisia Car Hire.** (☎07 4069 3368. 4WDs from $110; must be over 25.) **Cape York Spares and Repairs** (☎07 4069 4803), across from BP, takes care of all your mechanical needs.

## GETTING TO THE TIP

From Bamaga, it's 34km to the absolute tip. Head toward Adidi St. in the Bamaga town center. After the BP service station, take a right onto the final, unnamed road to put the capstone on your trip to the edge of the continent. The road is gravel for the first 20km; after that, it turns to dirt, deteriorating until it becomes rocky, quite narrow, and full of small stream crossings—a fitting end to a toilsome journey. A 20min. hike gets you right to the Tip.

On the road, 10km from the Tip, is **Lockerbie's** (☎07 4069 3000; open daily 8am-5pm), which sells Aboriginal art, dramatic photographs of their own Lockerbie truck fighting (and sometimes floating) across rivers, horse rides through the rainforest, and a tour of India rubber trees. Lockerbie's also boasts a food stand and the only toilet for kilometers. Day tours go throughout the bush, crossing orchids, creeks, and all the wildlife you could hope for. ($60. 2hr. Departs daily but times vary; book ahead.) Three-day tours proceed from Lockerbie's, around the tip of the Cape and across the West coast. Camping supplies (except for bedding) and meals are provided. ($400; departure times based on bookings. V.) Across the road from Lockerbie's is the turnoff to **Punsand Bay ❶,** a 10km drive. Punsand has campsites, permanent tents, and cabins with A/C. Amenities include laundry machines, satellite TV, and a **bar/restaurant ❺** with meals starting at $25. (☎07 4069 1722; www.punsand.com.au. Campsites $10 per person, powered $1 extra per site; tents $60 per person, ensuite $90 per person; ensuite cabins $100 per person. AmEx/D/MC/V.)

If the top of the continent isn't quite enough, you can explore Torres Strait Island culture by catching a **Peddell's Ferry** (☎07 4069 1551; www.peddellsferry. com.au) from Seisia to the **Thursday** and **Horn Islands.** (Departs M-Sa 8am and 4pm, returns 6:30am and 2:30pm. One-way $48, children $24.) **Dato's Venture** (☎07 4090 2005) services Thursday and Horn Islands from Punsand Bay. Its departure times vary depending on bookings (Horn Island $115 round-trip, Thursday Island $100 round-trip). You can book most of these transportation options through the **Bamaga Tourist Office.**

# CENTRAL AND WESTERN QUEENSLAND

Central and Western Queensland are not frequented by backpackers, and they offer a very different experience of Australian culture from the coastal communities. The roads across Queensland's interior are long, flat, and straight, crossing immense distances dotted with tiny towns. Central Queensland is filled with coal mines, and the increased trade with Asia has led to a boom in the economy and job market. Western Queensland, on the other hand, suffers from a harsh, hot environment, which has led to a very slow pace of outback life. The drive offers varied topography, ranging from spectacular gorges and mountains to red dirt and vast expanses of bushland.

 **SHARING THE ROAD.** Driving through this region is an adventure; some of the highways require battles with roadtrains that demand more road than exists. Highways are graveyards for kangaroos; they line the pavement from collisions with the passing trucks. Don't drive between dusk and dawn when the marsupials are most active. While they are all too easy for the massive trucks to brush aside, they can be deadly for drivers in compact cars.

## CAPRICORN AND LANDSBOROUGH HIGHWAY

The road west from Rockhampton is heavily traveled by large trucks bringing their goods from the interior to the densely-populated coast. The route is known as Capricorn Highway until Barcaldine (essentially the beginning of the Outback) where it becomes the Landsborough Hwy., passing through Longreach and Winton before meeting the Flinders Hwy. 119km east of Mt. Isa.

### THE GEMFIELDS

Rather than hoping to win big with the ever-present pokies (slot-machines), thousands of hopeful souls bring their dreams of millions to the gemfields of central Queensland. The area is famous for its sapphires and zircon; about once a year, someone strikes it rich after stumbling upon an exceptional gem. Don't despair, though; most mines have bags of gravel you can sift through, and more often than not you will walk away with a few little stones of your own.

### EMERALD

The town of Emerald (pop. 15,500), named after a colorful, grassy property north of town, is an affluent community of surprising size; it draws its wealth from the nearby coal mines and high-yielding cotton and wheat fields. In fact, there is so much growth that those looking for work (in the mines or the office) are commonly placed within 24hr. of arrival. The town serves as a jumping-off point for the **Gemfields,** which are 30min. west. The best budget accommodation in the area is the **Central Inn ❹**, 90 Clermont St., which has rooms with TV and fridge, as well a communal kitchen and lounge area. (☎07 4982 0800. Shared bath. Breakfast included. Reception M-Th 8am-9:30pm, F-Sa 9am-9pm. Singles $55; doubles $65. Book several days ahead. MC/V.) The best place to eat in town is the **Emerald Hotel ❶**, 73 Clermont St., across from Central Inn. It dishes out exceptional specials for only $8.50. (☎07 4982 1810. Open daily noon-2pm and 6-8:30pm. MC/V.) The sandwiches (from $5.50) at **Theo's Coffee**

**Lounge,** 15 Anakie St., are excellent. (☎07 4982 3384. Open M-F 6:30am-5pm, Sa 8am-3pm, Su 8am-2pm. MC/V.) There's a **Coles** supermarket on the corner of Clermont and Opal St. in Market Plaza. (☎07 4982 3622. Open M-F 8am-9pm, Sa 8am-5pm.) Stop at the **Central Highlands Visitor Information Centre,** in the center of town on Clermont St. (☎07 4982 4142. Open M-Sa 9am-5pm, Su 10am-2pm.) Don't miss the world's biggest Van Gogh sunflower painting (25m high) behind the visitors center in Morton Park. Internet is available at the **Emerald Public Library,** 44 Borilla St. (☎07 4982 8347. $2 for 30 min. Open M noon-5:30pm, Tu and Th 10am-5:30pm, W 10am-8pm, F 10am-5pm, Sa 9am-noon.)

# LONGREACH

The micropolis of Longreach (pop. 4500) is the largest town in the Central West, and a good example of outback life. The town's biggest attractions are on the outskirts of town toward Rockhampton. The **Australian Stockman's Hall of Fame and Outback Heritage Centre,** off the Landsborough Hwy., is a massive multimedia museum that pays tribute to Australia's outback heroes. (☎07 4658 2166; www.outbackheritage.com.au. Open daily 9am-5pm. $22.50, students $18.50, ages 8-16 $12, under 8 free. AmEx/D/MC/V.) Across the street, under the giant 747, the **Qantas Founders' Outback Museum** showcases the role airplanes have had on outback life and commemorates the early pioneering days of Australia's largest airline company. (☎07 4658 3737; www.qfom.com. au. Open daily 9am-5pm. $19, children $10. Tours of Qantas 747, including walking on the wing; $85, children $55. Booking required.) Longreach is also famous for its **Billabong Boat Cruises** along the Thomson River. The 3hr. sunset cruise includes a campfire dinner, Billy tea and damper, and music from local bush minstrels. (☎07 4658 1776; www.lotc.com.au. Tours run Apr.-Oct. daily; Nov.-Mar. 3 per week. $50, concessions $46, children $36. Sold out many nights; book ahead at the Outback Travel Center, 115A Eagle St.)

There are a few pubs with budget accommodations upstairs, but you probably wouldn't even suggest most of them to your worst enemy. The best of the lot is **Commercial Hotel Motel ❸,** at the corner of Eagle and Duck St. across from the post office. It has rooms with A/C and a pub with excellent lunch and dinner specials from $6.50. (☎07 4658 1677. Restaurant open daily noon-2pm and 6-8pm. Reception 8am-6pm. Singles $35; twins and doubles $55. AmEx/D/MC/V.) The **Longreach Caravan Park ❷,** 180 Ibis St., at the street's end, is a small area with a lot of older couples. (☎07 4658 1770. Reception 7:30am-8pm. Tent sites for 2 $17, powered $20; on-site caravans with A/C for 2 $38; ensuite A/C cabins for 2 $58. Book ahead, especially in winter. MC/V.) For groceries, there is an **IGA** supermarket is on the corner of Eagle and Swan St. (☎07 4658 1260. Open M-W 8am-6:30pm, Th-F 8am-8pm, Sa 8am-4pm.)

Greyhound Australia buses leave for Brisbane (daily 3:25pm, $149) and Mt. Isa (daily 10:35am, $100) from the **Outback Travel Centre.** (☎07 4658 1776; www. lotc.com.au. Open M-F 9am-5pm, Sa 9am-noon and 3:30-4pm, Su 10-11am and 3:30-4pm.) There is a **visitors center** at **Qantas Park** on Eagle St. (☎07 4658 3555; www.longreach.qld.gov.au. Open M-F 9am-4:30pm, Sa-Su 9am-noon.) Free **Internet access** is available at the **library,** 96 Eagle St. (☎07 4658 4104. Open M 1-5pm, Tu and Th 9:30am-12:30pm and 3-5pm, W and F 12:30-5pm, Sa 9am-noon.) The **post office** is next door (☎07 4658 1887; open M-F 9am-5pm). **Postal Code:** 4179.

# CHARTERS TOWERS     ☎07

Although it is less than 1hr. from Townsville and the hectic coastline, Charters Towers feels much farther from the backpacker circuit. Once nicknamed "The World" for its cosmopolitan flair, Charters Towers is big on history and character. The 1871 discovery of gold helped the city develop into the second-largest in the state, with a population of 30,000 at its peak. When the gold ran dry in 1916, the town was nearly vacated; now the 8000 remaining locals live among extravagant architecture and well-celebrated ghosts.

**TRANSPORTATION AND PRACTICAL INFORMATION.** The **Charters Towers Railway Station** is on Gill St., on the east side of town. **Trains** (☎13 22 32; www.traveltrain.com.au) go to Townsville (3hr., departs Tu and Sa 7:02am, $26.40) and Mt. Isa (18hr., departs Th and Su 3:23pm, $112.64). Greyhound Australia (☎13 14 99; www.greyhound.com.au) **buses** leave the corner of Gill and Church St. and goes to Townsville (1hr., daily 5:15pm, $30) and Mt. Isa (10hr., daily 8:40am, $132). Douglas Coaches also goes to Townsville (1hr., M-F 8am, $22). Book tickets at **Travel Experience,** 13 Gill St. (☎07 4787 2622; www.travelexperience.com.au. Open M-Th 7:30am-5:30pm, F 7:30am-5pm, Sa 7:30am-noon.)

The Charter Towers **Historic City Centre** is created by the intersection of Mosman and Gill St. Government offices and the Royal Arcade Stock Exchange are found on Mosman St., while shops and restaurants line Gill St. The extremely helpful and straightforward **Charters Towers Information Centre,** 74 Mosman St., at the top of Gill St., provides a **"Ghosts of Gold" orientation tour** of local historical attractions and an excellent leaflet about local activities. (☎07 4761 5533; www.charterstowers.qld.gov.au. Open daily 9am-5pm.) There are several **banks** with **ATMs** along Gill St. **Internet access** ($3 per 30min.) is available at **Charters Towers Computers,** 59 Gill St. (☎07 4787 2988. Open daily 9am-5pm.) Internet is also available at the **information center** ($5 per hr.). There is a historical **post office** with a large clocktower on the corner of Gill and Bow St. **Postal Code:** 4127.

**ACCOMMODATIONS AND FOOD.** The **Royal Private Hotel ❸,** just up the street from the information center on Mosman St., offers budget and ensuite rooms in a beautiful old building in the center of town. The building is beginning to show its age, but in a town peopled by the ghosts of its past, creaky doors and worn armoires only add to the allure. (☎07 4787 8688. Shared facilities, A/C, laundry, Internet, and shared kitchen. Reception 7am-9pm. Singles $35, ensuite $66; doubles $45/70. AmEx/MC/V.) The **York Street Bed and Breakfast ❷,** 58 York St., is situated outside the town center, which gives it a relaxed atmosphere but makes it inconvenient if you don't have a car. Comfortable rooms in the main house are self-contained and include breakfast. Budget accommodations are impressive too, with TV and fridge. (☎07 4787 1028. 4-bed budget dorms $20; singles $26; doubles $50; main house singles $72; doubles $95. MC/V.) Most of the hostels in town have dirt-cheap lunch specials, but backpacker dinner rates can be found at **Sovereign Tavern ❶,** 180 Gill St., which serves up nightly specials for $10, or you can try some creative but more expensive items like the Mango and Chili Scallops for $16.50. (☎07 4787 3077. Lunch noon-2pm, dinner 6-8:30pm. AmEx/D/MC/V.) The better of the two Chinese restaurants in town is **Gold City Chinese Restaurant ❷,** 118 Gill St., which has freshly cooked meals plus an all-you-can-eat smorgasbord. (☎07 4787 2414. Smorgasbord Tu-F 11:30am-2pm, $10; dinner smorgasbord W and F-Sa 5-9:30pm, $14. MC/V.) **Woolworths,** on Gill St. at the corner with Deane St., has groceries. (☎07 4787 3411. Open M-F 8am-9pm, Sa 8am-5pm. MC/V.)

**SIGHTS AND ACTIVITIES.** A visit to Charters Towers is really a step into the past, since nearly all the activities are focused on the gold rush era. To understand how the town became so rich, check out the ▨**Venus Gold Battery,** the largest surviving gold battery relic in Australia. (☎07 4787 4773. 1hr. guided tours every hr. 10am-3pm. $12, children $6, concessions $11.) The lookout at the top of **Towers Hill** is spectacular; history buffs can take in the sunset and learn about the old mining town by watching the entertaining **Ghosts After**

Dark film. (25min. Nightly 6-7pm; times vary seasonally. Tickets available at the info center. $7, children $4, concessions $6.) **Geoff's City and Bush Safari** tours inform and entertain. (☎07 4782 0314. Departs daily 8am and 4pm. Free pickup and dropoff. Tickets available at info center. $20, children $10.) The **Zara Clark Museum,** at the corner of Mosman and Mary St., has a display of Charters Towers memorabilia that reflects the town's golden past. (☎07 4787 4161. Open daily 10am-3pm. $5, children $2.20.) **Bluff Downs ❷,** a 2hr. drive northwest of Charters Towers, is a working cattle station where sweat, hard work, and play are all part of a day on the farm. Guests are welcomed into the family homestead and can try traditional bush meals. (☎07 4770 4084; www.bluffdowns. com.au. All-inclusive special $100 per day. Powered and unpowered sites $20 per person; dorms $20. Additional charges for activities. Cash only.)

# DINOSAUR COUNTRY

## RICHMOND

West of Hughenden along the Flinders Hwy., Richmond packs an impressive prehistoric punch and promotes itself as the fossil capital of Australia. 🖳**Kronosaurus Korner,** 93 Goldring St., is home to the regional **visitors center** and the **Marine Fossil Centre,** which houses Australia's best vertebrate fossils, including the complete fossil remains of a pliosaur and an ankylosaur. (☎07 4741 3429; www.kronosauruskorner.com.au. Open daily 8:30am-4:45pm. $10, students $8, children $5.) After your visit, grab a meal at **Moon Rock Cafe ❷** inside the center, which has a limited but reasonably priced selection. Heading west toward Mt. Isa on the Flinders Hwy., you'll see the **BP Roadhouse,** which has an impressively extensive menu, hot showers ($2), toilets, and the last petrol station for 146km. (☎07 4741 3316. Open daily 6am-9pm.) Free Internet access is available at the **library,** 78 Goldring St. (☎07 4741 3077; open M-Tu and Th-F noon-4pm, W 9am-1pm); there's also a pay kiosk at the visitors center ($1 per 10min.). The **Lakeview Caravan Park ❶,** on your way into town from Hughenden before the visitors center, is perfectly located on a beautiful swimming lake. It boasts great facilities with A/C, shared bathrooms, swimming pool, and a communal kitchen. (☎07 4741 3772. Key deposit $10. Reception 7am-7pm. Sites $17, powered $24; twin-share bunkhouse with A/C $20 per person; ensuite cabin for 2 $80. Extra person $4-8. Book cabins ahead.) There is a **FoodWorks** supermarket at 78 Goldring St., down the street from the visitors center. (Open M-F 7:30am-5:30pm, Sa 7:30am-12:30pm, Su 7:30am-noon.)

## HUGHENDEN

Hughenden (HEW-en-den; pop. 1200) marks the eastern edge of Queensland's marine dinosaur fossil territory. You've probably imagined exactly this kind of landscape—vast, open, and empty—as the habitat for prehistoric creatures. Stop at **Flinders Discovery Centre,** 37 Gray St., to see the Muttaburrasaurus skeleton. The Centre also doubles as the town's **visitors center.** (☎07 4741 1021; www.flinders.qld.gov.au. Open daily 9am-5pm. $3.50, children $1.50.) **Porcupine Gorge National Park** (63km north of town) is known as "Australia's Little Grand Canyon" because of its towering sandstone cliffs and deep gorges inside a lush green vine forest. Follow the signs in town, but be warned that the paved road turns to well-kept dirt 29km out. The unsealed tracks are generally 2WD-accessible, but check with locals for current conditions. **Camping ❶** is available at the **Pyramid Lookout Campground.** (☎13 13 04; www.qld.gov.au/camping. Pit toilets and a shelter shed; bring your own water. Self-registration $4.50, pre-registration available.) If you plan to brave the mountains on your own, you are required to register at the QPWS office in town (☎07 4741 1113).

To get to the **Great Western Hotel ❷**, 14 Brodie St., from Flinders Discovery Centre, go down the hill and take your first right. The hotel has budget beds that will make you glad that you spent the night in this small town. The attached **pub** has cheap specials and Saturday-night disco. (☎07 4741 1454. Internet access and A/C. Reception 6am-1am. 2- to 7-bed dorms $25. AmEx/MC/V.) The **Allan Terry Caravan Park ❶**, 2 Resolution St., has a swimming pool, kitchen, laundry, and a BBQ spread out on their large grounds. (☎07 4741 1190. Reception M-F 7am-9pm. Sites $8 per person; budget rooms $25; cabins $60, with lounge $70. Extra person $10. Book cabins ahead. Credit card fee $1. MC/V.)

## WINTON

This little town forms the southern point of the Dinosaur trail triangle. It is known mostly, however, for the fact that Australia's unofficial national anthem, "Waltzing Matilda," was composed here in 1895. Winton is also home to the remains of Elliot, Australia's largest dinosaur (located at the heritage-listed **Corfield & Fitzmaurice Building** in the center of town; open M-F 9am-5pm, Sa 9am-1pm, and Su 11am-3pm). Most of the dinosaur-related attractions, however, are located 110km southwest of Winton at the **Lark Quarry Interpretive Centre.** Follow the signs from Winton to the **Lark Quarry Dinosaur Trackways.** At the Centre, you can go back in time to the Cretaceous and see the fossilized dinosaur tracks that inspired the stampede scene in Steven Spielberg's *Jurassic Park.* Contact the **Waltzing Matilda Tourist Information Centre** for all questions about the center and the town. (☎07 4657 1886; www.experiencewinton.com.au. Fully guided tours of the center daily at 10am, noon, and 2pm. Open daily 9am-5pm.)

# MOUNT ISA                                     ☎07

Mt. Isa (pop. 24,000) is one of the largest cities in the world, covering an area the size of Switzerland and with a main street stretching over 180km. It's also the birthplace of golf legend Greg Norman and tennis champ Patrick Rafter. The town owes its existence to the Mount Isa Mines, one of the world's largest mineral mining operations, which have huge smokestacks that loom over the city. Aside from these fun facts, there isn't a whole lot to "the Isa," as it's affectionately referred to by locals, although it's been claimed that you're not a real Aussie until you've been there. Backpackers commonly use it as a stopover when traveling between the Northern Territory and Queensland. Stock up on supplies, and make sure your car is full of fuel before leaving town.

**▐ TRANSPORTATION.** The **train station** is on Station St. (☎13 22 32; www.traveltrain.com.au. ISIC discount 50%. Open 24hr.) From the town center, cross the Isa St. bridge and turn right. The Inlander **train** departs M and F 1:30pm to: Charters Towers (17hr., $112.64 ); Hughenden (13hr., $80.08); Richmond (10hr., $68.64); and Townsville (20hr., $123.20). **Harvey World Travel,** 2A Marian St. (☎07 4743 3399), and **Travel World** at the **Irish Club** (p. 456), 1 19th Ave. (☎07 4749 1267), make bookings as well. Greyhound Australia has a small office in the Outback at Isa complex, 19 Marian St. (☎13 14 99; www.greyhound.com.au. Open 8:30am-5pm. Concessions 10%.) **Buses** heading to the coast (6:50am) and to the interior (7:30pm) leave daily from the complex with service to: Alice Springs (13hr., $277); Brisbane (26hr., $188); Charters Towers (10hr., $132); Darwin (22hr., $339); Richmond (5hr., $68); Rockhampton (23hr., $258); Townsville (12hr., $140). For 24hr. **taxis,** call United Cab (☎4743 2333).

**▐▐ ORIENTATION AND PRACTICAL INFORMATION.** The town center is a square grid, bounded by **Grace Street** to the north, **Isa Street** to the south, **Simpson**

Street to the east, and **West Street** to the west. The **Barkly Highway** enters from the Northern Territory and runs parallel to the **Leichhardt River** until the **Grace Street Bridge**, where it turns left over the water into the town center, becoming **Grace Street**. From Cloncurry in the east, the Barkly Hwy. becomes **Marian Street**.

The **Outback at Isa complex** contains the town **information center, the bus station, Internet, a cafe**, and two of the area's major attractions: the **Riversleigh Fossil Centre** (p. 456) and **underground tours**. (☎1300 659 660; www.outbackatisa. com.au. Open daily 8:30am-5pm.) Other services include: a **Westpac** bank, 23-25 Simpson St. across from K-Mart Plaza (☎07 4743 5344; open M-Th 9:30am-4pm, F 9:30am-5pm); **police**, 7-9 Isa St., at the intersection with Miles St. (☎07 4744 1111); and a **post office** on Simpson St. opposite the K-Mart Plaza (☎13 13 18; open M-F 8:45am-5:15pm, Sa 9am-noon). **Postal Code:** 4825.

**◪◩ ACCOMMODATIONS AND FOOD.** The only hostel around is **Travellers Haven ❷**, at Pamela and Spence St.; it has a kitchen, Internet access, a swimming pool, and a courtesy bus. The rooms and shared facilities in this old building are showing their age, and most of the guests work in the area. (☎07 4743 0313; www.users.bigpond.net.au/travellershaven. Key deposit $10. Reception 24hr. 3-bed dorms $25; singles $38; doubles $55. MC/V.) **Mount Isa Caravan Park ❷**, 112 Marian St., has nice, clean villas, cabins, and campsites. Up to 40% of guests are permanent residents. (☎1800 073 456; www.mtisacaravanpark.com. au. Reception M-F 7:30am-6:30pm, Sa-Su 8am-5pm. Sites $21, powered $25; cabins for 2 with shared amenities $75; ensuite villa for 2 with TV, A/C, and kitchen $90; extra adult $10, children $6. MC/V.)

The best places to eat are two casino-like clubs. The **Irish Club ❶**, on 19th Ave. off 4th Ave., has several bars, many food options, and an all-you-can-eat buffet (M and Su noon-1am, F-Sa 10am-3am). **◪Tram Stop ❶**, part of the Irish Club, boasts an enjoyable table atmosphere inside a restored Melbourne Street Tram; menu items are almost all under $10. (☎07 4743 2577. Free courtesy van picks up and drops off at any location in town. Open M and Su noon-1am, F-Sa 10am-3pm. Food served until 9pm. ) **The Buffs Club ❸**, on the corner of Grace and Simpson St., cooks up a lunch buffet ($13.50) and expensive dinners (from $17.50), but is most popular as a place to lounge around. (☎07 4743 2365; www. buffs.com.au. Restaurant open daily noon-2pm and 6-9:30pm, Su until 9pm.) There is a **Coles** supermarket in K-Mart Plaza, on the corner of Marian and Simpson St. (☎07 4743 6007. Open M-F 8am-9pm, Sa-Su 8am-5pm.)

**◪ SIGHTS.** The **Outback at Isa complex** offers a 3hr. **Hard Times Mine Tour** where visitors dress in authentic gear before descending into 1.2km of tunnels. The complex is also home to the **Riversleigh Fossil Centre**, which provides insight into the prehistoric inhabitants of the Outback, including life-size models of select beasts. Visitors are also allowed to peer into a working laboratory. (☎07 4749 1555; www.outbackatisa.com.au. Underground tour $45, concessions $38, children $26. Surface tour departs June-Nov. $27.50. Fossil Centre open daily 8:30am-5pm; $10, concessions $6.50. MC/V.) You can take a tour of the eerie **Underground Hospital** at the end of Joan St.; built in 1942, the structure was erected by the local government out of fear of Japanese air raids. (☎07 4743 3853. Open Apr.-Sept. 10am-2pm. $10, concessions $8, children $4.) **Australia's biggest rodeo** (☎1800 463 361; www.isarodeo.com.au) comes to Mt. Isa for three days over the second weekend in August. If you plan on attending, book accommodations at least one month ahead. **Lake Moondarra**, just 15min. northwest on the Barkly Hwy., is a nice place for a swim or BBQ, and **Lake Julius**, 30km on Barkly Hwy. toward Cloncurry and another 90km down a dirt track, is a great fishing spot. A 4WD is highly recommended. At night, view the lighted Mt. Isa Mines from the **lookout** off Hillary.

# SOUTH AUSTRALIA

As tourists zip around Oz carrying travel itineraries jam-packed with brief stops at the Opera House, the Great Barrier Reef, and Uluru, few leave room for South Australia, one of the country's best-kept secrets. About 80% of the state's population resides in the capital of Adelaide, an underappreciated metropolis with one of the country's best live music scenes. Stretching south from Adelaide is an expansive coastline leading east to the spectacular Limestone Coast, home to thousands of acres of national park. A hop, skip, and a jump from the mainland takes you to Kangaroo Island, a rustic, untouched paradise reminiscent of what the earth must have looked like before civilization. With opportunities to swim with dolphins and walk on the beach alongside fur seals, Kangaroo Island is a destination that no traveler should risk missing.

Harsh and vast, South Australia's stark interior will either capture your heart or send you running for the next bus back to the coast. Those who stick around soon adopt the local mantra of "save water, drink wine," and with good reason—the area's southern valleys are home to the nation's finest vintages, with world-famous vines grown in the Barossa and Clare Valleys. Farther away from civilization, the Flinders Ranges are a backpacker's paradise, a gallery of spectacular sculptures created over five billion years. Travelers ready for a more thorough introduction to the region often tackle the Stuart Hwy., which offers thousands of kilometers of otherworldly outback landscapes from the famous plains of the Nullarbor to Alice Springs. South Australia lures travelers by juxtaposing ocean, vineyards, and outback—all within a day's drive.

## HIGHLIGHTS OF SOUTH AUSTRALIA

**SAVOR** the secrets of Mod Oz cuisine in South Australia's capital **Adelaide,** also known as the culinary capital of the country (p. 459).

**SWIM** with wild dolphins on **Kangaroo Island,** home to the largest colony of Australian sea lions and thousands of waddling fairy penguins as well (p. 481).

**BE A BACCHUS** as you indulge in Shiraz in the **Barossa Valley** (p. 490), Rieslings in the **Clare Valley** (p. 495), and Cabernets in the **Coonawarra** (p. 503)—three of Australia's premier **wine regions** all in one state.

**TRANSPORTATION.** If you don't have a car, the best way to see South Australia is by **bus.** Greyhound Australia (☎13 14 99 or 13 20 30) runs between Adelaide and Melbourne, Sydney, Alice Springs, and Perth, stopping over at a few destinations in between. Premier Stateliner (☎08 8415 5555; www.premierstateliner.com.au) services smaller towns throughout South Australia; pick up a copy of their SA State Guide for an extensive map of bus routes and timetables. Three major **train** lines run through South Australia: the Overland to Melbourne, the Indian Pacific to Sydney, and the legendary Ghan to Alice Springs. Major **car rental** companies with branches in SA include **Hertz** (☎13

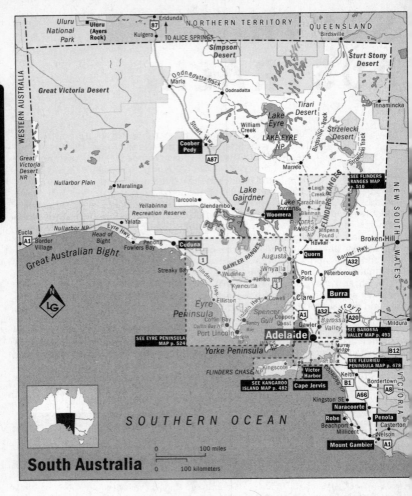

South Australia

WESTERN AUSTRALIA

NORTHERN TERRITORY

QUEENSLAND

NEW SOUTH WALES

VICTORIA

SOUTHERN OCEAN

0    100 miles

0    100 kilometers

30 39), **Avis** (☎13 63 33), and **Thrifty** (☎1300 367 227). A conventional vehicle is fine for wine and beach country, but a 4WD is recommended for forays into the Outback's rugged interior. If you're planning on saving money by sleeping at campsites and caravan parks, a popular option for backpackers is renting a campervan from **Wicked Camper** (☎1800 24 68 69 or 07 3634 9000; www.wicked-campers.com.au), with rates normally three times lower than those of major rental companies. Their Andy Warholesque paint jobs and funky furnishings will ensure that you'll be traveling in style.

Another good option is to book a tour. Many choose jump-on, jump-off backpacker buses that travel around South Australia, as well as the popular trek from Adelaide to Melbourne via the Great Ocean Rd. Book through the twenty-something favorites, **Wayward Bus/Adventure Tours** (☎08 8132 8230 or 1300

653 510; www.waywardbus.com.au or www.adventuretours.com.au/south-aus-
tralia-tour), or **Groovy Grape Getaways** (☎08 8371 4000 or 1800 661 177; www.
groovygrape.com.au). Plenty of organizations also run local trips, which are
listed in the Practical Information section of most towns in this chapter.

# ADELAIDE                                                          ☎08

Long overlooked by travelers in favor of Sydney, Melbourne, and Brisbane,
Adelaide has been under-appreciated for decades. Lately, however, the world is
waking up to discover all that this trendy, progressive—and cheaper—city has
to offer. Known as the Festival State, South Australia's capital city of Adelaide
also answers to the City of Churches, the City of Museums, and the Culinary
Capital of Australia. With more restaurants and world-class wines per capita
than any other Australian city, Adelaide can satisfy any palate on any budget.
Situated between the ocean and the outback, the city provides an excellent
base for ventures to the extensive coastlines of the Yorke and Fleurieu Peninsulas, Kangaroo Island, South Australian wine valleys, and dozens of wildlife
and conservation parks, full of hopping 'roos and cuddly koalas.

# ◼ INTERCITY TRANSPORTATION

## BY PLANE

The **Adelaide Airport** is 7km west of the city center. Many hostels offer free
pickup with advance booking. Failing that, the cheapest way to the city is the
**JetBus,** which leaves from Level 2 in the airport and runs to Grenfell St., adjacent to Rundle Mall. The **Skylink** shuttle ($7.50) leaves from the domestic termi-
nal and stops at several points downtown, including Backpack Oz, Hostel 109,
My Place Backpackers, and Shakespeare International Backpackers. From the
airport, a **taxi** into the city center averages $20.

International travelers can get discounted domestic one-way fares. **Regional
Express** (Rex, ☎13 17 13; www.regionalexpress.com.au) is the biggest local car-
rier, with flights to 35 South Australian cities, including Coober Pedy, Kangaroo
Island, and Port Lincoln. **Virgin Blue** (☎13 67 89; www.virginblue.com.au) and
**Qantas** (☎13 13 13; www.qantas.com.au) also offer competitive fares.

## BY TRAIN

All interstate and long-distance country trains use the **Adelaide Parklands Rail Terminal,** formerly known as Keswick Interstate Rail Terminal, off the southwest
corner of the central city grid about 1km west of West Terr. (Open M and W
6am-5pm, Tu 6am-6:30pm, Th 6am-7:30pm, Sa 5:40-6:30pm, Su 7:30am-7pm.)
The **Skylink** meets every incoming train at the Adelaide Parklands Rail Terminal and drops off at the Central Bus station, as well as several hostels downtown. (☎08 8332 0528. $4, round-trip $8.) **Taxis** from the city run about $15.
The rail terminal has **parking.** Only suburban commuter trains use the **Adelaide
Railway Station** (☎08 8218 2277), on North Terr.

**Great Southern Railway** owns the **Overland, Ghan,** and **Indian Pacific** lines. For
information, call ☎13 21 47. The **Overland** runs to Melbourne (10-12hr.; M, W, F
7:40am, Th-Su 9am; $89, students $50). The **Ghan** runs trains to Alice Springs
(19hr., W and Su 12:20pm, $355/225). The **Indian Pacific** runs to Sydney (24-25hr.,
W and Su 10am, $295/145). Be sure to inquire about the **RailSavers Pass,** which
could save you up to $100 on advanced-purchase, non-refundable tickets.

## BY BUS

Adelaide has two central **bus stations,** both located on **Franklin St.** Greyhound Australia has a station at 101 Franklin St., while V/Line, Firefly, and Premier Stateliner buses pull in to 111 Franklin St. National **bus companies** provide regular service to and from Adelaide at fares that generally beat rail and air travel; unfortunately, savings come at the price of comfort. Greyhound Australia (☎1300 473 946 or 13 14 99) runs to: Alice Springs (19hr.; daily 6pm; $210, concessions $189); Brisbane (29-30hr., daily 11am, $304/$274); Darwin (34hr., daily 6pm, $569/$512); Melbourne (10hr.; M, W-F, and Su 8pm; $60/$55); Sydney (24hr., daily 11am, $115). Prices listed are for booking at the Adelaide Greyhound terminal; booking through ☎13 14 99 has an added $2 processing fee. A newer budget-minded carrier, Firefly Express (☎1300 730 740; http://booking.fireflyexpress.com.au), runs directly to Melbourne (10-11hr.; daily 8am and 8:30pm; morning departure $45, evening $50), where it's possible to transfer and continue to Sydney for an additional $60-65. V/Line (☎13 61 96 or 08 8231 7620; www.vline.com.au) runs a daily coach and rail combination to Melbourne via Bendigo (12hr.; M-F 7:10am, Sa-Su 7:25am; $42.80, students $21.40). Within South Australia, Premier Stateliner (☎08 8415 5500) is the main bus carrier, serving over 200 destinations statewide, including McLaren Vale, Mt. Gambier, Naracoorte, and Victor Harbor. The free **State Guide,** available at the tourist office and many hostels, is indispensable for travel in this area.

## ✦ ORIENTATION

**Downtown Adelaide** is only one square mile in size, bordered by North, East, South, and West Terr. and centered on **Victoria Square.** The **CBD** is bisected north-south by **King William Street.** Streets running east-west change names when crossing King William St. **Rundle Street—**home to chic sidewalk cafes, top-notch eateries, and vibrant nightlife—runs from East Terr. west to Pulteney St. in the city's northeast quadrant (known as the East End). From there, it becomes the **Rundle Mall,** the city's main shopping area, then continues west to King William St. before changing names yet again to become **Hindley Street,** offering everything from adult stores to upscale restaurants. **Gouger Street,** in the southwest end, has a wide variety of multicultural eateries as well as the **Central Market,** a bazaar housing over 250 shops and restaurants. **Victoria Square** lies at the center of the city grid. **Light Square,** in the northwest quadrant, is where most hostels and a host of backpacker pubs are, while **Hindmarsh Square** in the northeast quadrant is another important landmark.

**BAD-ELAIDE.** Although the city of Adelaide is generally peaceful, the parklands are unsafe at night, especially near the River Torrens and Whitmore Sq. Do not enter the Botanic Gardens at dawn or dusk. The sidestreets off Hindley St. also demand extra caution at night.

A couple of kilometers north of the CBD and the River Torrens, swank **North Adelaide** comprises a smaller grid centered around the trendy bistros and shopping on upscale **O'Connell Street. Melbourne Street,** southeast of O'Connell, is another boutique strip with hip restaurants and funky shopping.

Just south of the city, in the suburb of **Hyde Park,** a number of chic cafes and some of Adelaide's best shopping line **King William Street.** The suburb of Keswick, which includes the Adelaide Parklands Rail Terminal, is about 1km southwest of the central grid, and the beach suburb of **Glenelg** is 12km southwest of the CBD via the **Anzac Hwy. (A5)** or the **Glenelg Tram. Henley Beach** lies 12km west of the CBD, while the northwest suburb of **Port Adelaide**, on the Port River, is another popular spot. The **Adelaide Hills**, including **Cleland Conservation Park** and the scenic **Mt. Lofty Lookout**, are visible just east of the city

#  LOCAL TRANSPORTATION

## PUBLIC TRANSPORTATION

Adelaide's buses and trains compose an integrated public transport system called the **Adelaide Metro** (☎08 8210 1000; www.adelaidemetro.com.au), which also runs two free services around the city: the **ShuttleTram** and the **99C.** The **ShuttleTram** runs in the city center, from the railway station on North Terr. and down King William St. to Victoria Sq. and back. (Daily every 5-15min. 8am-9pm.) The **99C** runs both directions around a loop that covers the northern half of the city, covering Light, Victoria, and Hindmarsh Sq. and the full length of North Terr., with stops at most major tourist attractions. (Every 15-30min. M-F 7:30am-7pm, Sa 8:30am-6pm, Su 10am-6pm.)

For travel beyond the ShuttleTram or 99C routes, **TransAdelaide's** bus and train transit system is a good option. For route schedules, visit the **Adelaide Metro Office,** at the corner of King William and Currie St., or call the info line. (☎1800 182 160, info line ☎08 8210 1000. Office open M-F 8am-6pm, Sa 9am-5pm, Su 11am-4pm; info line open daily 7am-10pm.) Single tickets work on any service for two hours and can be purchased from drivers or vending machines. (Single trip M-F 9am-3pm $2.50, concessions $1.20; all other times $4.10/2.) Daytrip tickets ($7.70, concessions $4) allow one day of unlimited travel on any service and can be purchased when boarding buses or trams, but must be bought beforehand for trains. Another option is the multitrip ticket (10 trips, $27).

---

**BUSTED.** If you are a student, you can often pay less at movie theaters, museums, and other attractions by qualifying for "concessions" fares. For the TransAdelaide transit system, however, you need to carry a South Australian Student ID or pre-approved government concessions pass. If you purchase a concessions ticket without an approved ID, you could be fined by the police.

---

For a guided tour of the area, **Adelaide Explorer** runs a 3hr. Adelaide-to-Glenelg hop-on, hop-off tour. Catch the small bus anywhere on the route, or join at 38 King William St., and pay onboard. (☎08 8293 2966. Daily 9:05, 10:30am, and 1:30pm. $30 per day, children 6-14 $10, 5 and under free.)

## BY CAR

All the major rental lines have offices at the airport and in town. The airport locations are open daily 6am-11pm. Major companies include: **Avis,** 136 North Terr. (airport ☎08 8234 4558, city ☎08 8410 5727; M-F 7:30am-6pm, Sa-Su 8am-2pm); **Thrifty,** 23 Hindley St. (airport ☎08 8234 3029, city ☎08 8410 3637; M-F 8am-6pm, Sa-Su 8am-4pm); **Budget** (airport ☎08 8234 4900, city ☎08 8418 7300; M-Th 7:30am-5pm, F 7:30am-6pm, Sa-Su 8am-2pm), on the corner of North Terr. and Frome St.; **Europcar,** 142 North Terr. (airport ☎08 8150 3090, city ☎08 8114 6350; M-F 8am-6pm, Sa 8am-4pm, Su 9am-4pm); **Hertz,** 233 Morphett St. (airport ☎08 8234 4566, city ☎8231 2856; M-F 7:30am-6pm, Sa-Su 8am-2pm).

Customers under 25 can sometimes get better deals from smaller agencies. One of the best outfits for 4WD rentals is **Complete Ute and 4WD Hire,** in the suburb of Findon, 10min. from the airport. Ute offers pick-up and drop-off anywhere in the city for $11 each way, and discounts for longer rentals. (☎08

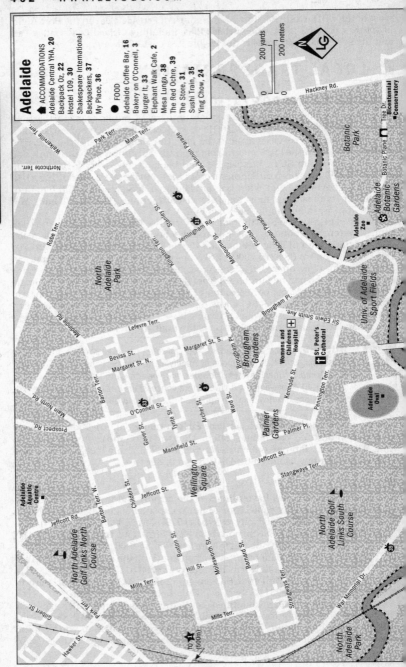

SOUTH AUSTRALIA

## Adelaide

▲ ACCOMMODATIONS
Adelaide Central YHA, **20**
Backpack Oz, **22**
Hostel 109, **30**
Shakespeare International
Backpackers, **37**
My Place, **36**

● FOOD
Adelaide Coffee Bar, **16**
Bakery on O'Connell, **3**
Burger It, **33**
Elephant Walk Cafe, **2**
Mesa Lunga, **38**
The Red Ochre, **39**
The Store, **31**
Sushi Train, **35**
Ying Chow, **24**

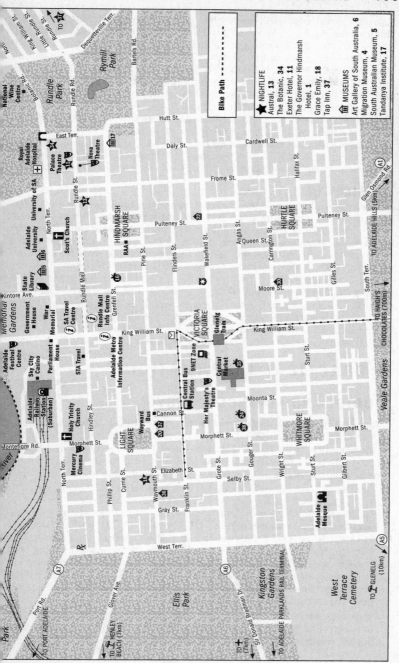

SOUTH AUSTRALIA

★ NIGHTLIFE
Austral, **13**
The Botanic, **34**
Exeter Hotel, **11**
The Governor Hindmarsh
  Hotel, **1**
Grace Emily, **18**
Tap Inn, **37**

🏛 MUSEUMS
Art Gallery of South Australia, **6**
Migration Museum, **4**
South Australian Museum, **5**
Tandanya Institute, **17**

- - - - - Bike Path

8244 5333; www.completeuteandvanhire.com.au.) **Koala Car Rentals,** 41 Sir Donald Bradman Dr., has some of the lowest rates in the city and also offers 4WD. (☎08 8352 7299; M-F 8:30am-5pm, Sa-Su 8am-3pm.) **Smile Rent-a-Car** (☎08 8346 8144), 141 Grange Rd. in the suburb of Beverly, has friendly service, but no 4WD. **No Frills Car Rental,** 296 Hindley St., is another local outfit. (☎08 8212 8333; open M-F 8:30am-5pm, Sa-Su 8am-noon). For **campervans** or **motor homes,** try **Britz** (☎08 8234 4701), 376 Sir Donald Bradman Dr., in Brooklyn Park.

**Taxis** are also an easy way to get around town, and there are a number of companies that service the city, including **Suburban Taxis** (☎13 10 08), **Adelaide Independent Taxis** (☎13 22 11), and **Yellow Taxis** (☎13 22 27).

The **Royal Automobile Association (RAA)** of South Australia is set up in Adelaide. (55 Hindmarsh Sq. ☎08 8202 4600. Open M-F 8:30am-5pm, Sa 9am-noon.) It provides free maps to members of the AAA and other affiliated organizations.

## BY BICYCLE

Adelaide is outstandingly bikeable, and most major roads are lined with designated cycling lanes. The **Linear Park Bike and Walking Track** (40km one-way) runs along the River Torrens from the ocean to the Adelaide Hills. **Linear Park Mountain Bike Hire,** located in a van on the south bank of the Torrens behind the Festival Centre, has high-quality bikes and extensive knowledge of the terrain. (☎04 0059 6065. Open daily 9am-5pm. Book ahead. $20 per day. Delivery, pickup, and weekly or family rates available.) Along with a number of hostels, **Flinders Camping,** 187 Rundle St., rents bikes in the city. (☎08 8223 1913. Open M-Th 9am-5:30pm, F 9am-7:30pm, Sa 9am-5pm, Su 11am-4pm. $20 per day includes maps and helmets. Lower rates for multi day rentals.) Keep your helmet on at all times as police are happy to issue tickets. You can take your bike on Adelaide's trams, but not on trains or buses.

## 🔢 PRACTICAL INFORMATION

### TOURIST AND FINANCIAL SERVICES

**Tourist Office: South Australian Travel Centre,** 18 King William St. (☎1300 655 276; www.southaustralia.com). Open M-F 8:30am-5pm, Sa-Su 9am-2pm. **Rundle Mall Visitor Information** (☎08 8203 7611), at the corner of Rundle Mall and King William St. Open M-Th 10am-5pm, F 10am-8pm, Sa 10am-3pm, Su 11am-4pm.

**Travel Agencies: YHA Travel,** 135 Waymouth St. (☎08 8414 3000). Open M-F 9am-6pm, Sa-Su 10am-1pm. **STA Travel,** 235 Rundle St. (☎08 8223 2426), open M-Th 9:30am-5:30pm, F 9:30am-7pm, Sa 10am-3pm; also at 36b James Pl. (☎08 8211 6600), open M-Th 9:30am-5:30pm, F 9:30am-8pm. Popular with students, the **Wayward Bus/Australia Adventure Tours,** 115-119 Waymouth St. (☎1300 654 604 or 8132 8230), organizes 2-8 day bus tours throughout SA. Open M-Sa 9am-8pm, Su 9am-7pm. Most travel agencies offer free Internet, usually 2hr., with tour booking. Many hostels in the city are partnered with travel agents that operate on the premises who can obtain excellent student and budget deals for tours throughout Australia; try **Peter Pan National Travel** next to **Shakespeare International Backpackers** (p. 465) or **YHA Travel** attached to **Adelaide Central YHA** (p. 466).

**Currency Exchange: Travelex,** 45 Grenfell St. (☎08 8211 7037). Open M-F 9am-5pm. Also at corner of Rundle Mall and King William St. (☎08 8231 6977). Open M-Th 9am-5:30pm, F 9am-7pm, Sa 9am-5pm, Su 11am-3pm.

**Work Opportunities: Centrelink,** 55 Currie St. (☎13 10 21). Open M-F 8:30am-5pm. Advertiser has classifieds W and Sa, and the free Messengers detail employment opportunities. Most hostels also have employment notice boards.

## LOCAL SERVICES

**Library: State Library of South Australia (SLSA)** (☎1800 182 013 or 08 8207 7250; www.slsa.sa.gov.au), on North Terr. at the corner of Kintore Ave. Book ahead for 30min. free Internet access, or wait for a first come, first serve 15min. slot. Open M-W 10am-8pm, Th-F 10am-6pm, Sa-Su 10am-5pm.

**Internet Access: iNet Zone,** 42 Grote St. (☎08 8410 2115), across from Central Market. Offers Internet access as well as computer repairs, accessories, and parts. $3 per hr., $10 per 5hr. Open daily 10:30am-11pm.

**Ticket Agency:** Most cultural and sporting events (especially football matches) are booked through **BASS.** (☎13 12 46; www.bass.net.au. Booking fee varies, usually around $3 per ticket. Call center open M-Sa 9am-8pm.) BASS Booths are spread all over Adelaide, including in the SA Travel Centre and the Rundle Mall, and the company's main office is located at the **Festival Centre** (p. 470). **VenueTix** (☎08 8225 8888; www.venuetix.com.au) also has tickets for major events and concerts and is the place to go for tickets to cricket and basketball events.

---

**MEDIA AND PUBLICATIONS.**
**Newspapers:** *The Advertiser* ($1.10), *Adelaide Review* (free).
**Nightlife:** "The Guide" in the Thursday *Advertiser. Rip it Up* (www.ripitup.com. au) and *dB* on the nightlife and alternative club scene (free). For gay nightlife, try *Blaze* or *Gay Times* (free).
**Radio:** Commercial-free alternative rock, ▣**Triple J** 105.5 FM; rock, 104.7 FM; pop, Nova 91.9 FM and 107.1 FM; club/house, Fresh FM 92.7 FM; easy listening, 102.3 FM; news, ABC 831 AM; tourist info, 88.1 FM.

---

## EMERGENCY AND COMMUNICATIONS

**Police: Adelaide Police Station,** 60 Wakefield St. (☎08 8463 7400 or 13 14 44). Another station at 26 Hindley St. (☎08 8303 0525). Both open 24hr.

**Late-Night Pharmacy: Midnight Pharmacy,** 13 West Terr. (☎08 8231 6333). Open M-Sa 7am-midnight, Su 9am-midnight.

**Medical Services: Royal Adelaide Hospital** (☎08 8222 4000), on the corner of North Terr. and Frome St.

**Post Office: General Post Office,** 141 King William St. (☎13 13 18; www.auspost.com. au), at the corner of King William and Franklin St. Open M-F 8:30am-5:30pm. *Poste Restante* be can be picked up M-F 7am-6pm, Su 8-noon. **Postal Code:** 5000.

# ▌ ACCOMMODATIONS

Hostels are scattered all over the city, but are concentrated near **Light Square.** Adelaide hostels are rarely full in winter, but book in advance in summer and during Adelaide's many festivals, including the **Fringe, Clipsal,** and **Womad** (p. 471). Travelers looking to escape the city should consider staying in the beach suburb of **Glenelg** (p. 472) or in the **Adelaide Hills** (p. 474).

▨ **Shakespeare International Backpackers,** 123 Waymouth St. (☎08 8231 7655; www. shakeys.com.au). At a spectacular location right in the middle of town, Shakeys occupies a genuine Victorian Era building, excellently restored with all the modern facilities including A/C, TV lounge with comfy couches, large kitchen with free rice, and clean communal baths. Job notice board. Reassuring security includes nightly guards and door codes. Internet access $4 per hr. Laundry $3, dry $2. Free luggage storage and lockers. Linen included. In-house **Peter Pan National Travel Agency.** Free accommodation in return for assistance with rooms and other cleaning activities. Single-sex and mixed dorms $26; singles and doubles $70. Ask about the *Let's Go* discount. MC/V. ❷

**Hostel 109,** 109 Carrington St. (☎1800 099 318 or 08 8223 1771), 10min. from Victoria Sq. For hotel quality at hostel prices, head to Hostel 109—the biggest "dorm room" at this hostel is a 4-bed room, making your accommodation feel more like a private hotel suite. The free, unlimited Internet access can't be beat. A/C and heat, new mattresses, modern kitchen, free luggage storage, security lockers, and great showers. Linen and breakfast included. Offers deals on trips to Kangaroo Island and Barossa Valley. Single-sex and mixed dorms $25; bunk twin $60; doubles $70; triples $84. $1 off when paying with credit card. AmEx/MC/V. ❷

**Adelaide Central YHA,** 135 Waymouth St. (☎08 8414 3010), just a few doors down from Shakespeare International Backpackers. The most popular hostel among backpackers, this clean 250-bed complex was recently renovated and has brand new mattresses. Unbeatable facilities include a huge kitchen (free tea, coffee, milo, and rice), an enormous TV and pool lounge, and a message board with current movies, concerts, and work opportunities. Internet and Wi-Fi $2 per 30min. A/C. Backpack-sized lockers by each bed. Conference room. Reception 24hr. In-house **YHA Travel** agency. Bike rental $10 per ½-day. Single-sex and mixed dorms $25; doubles $67.50, ensuite $81; family rooms $100. 10% discount for YHA members. AmEx/MC/V. ❷

**My Place,** 257 Waymouth St. (☎1800 221 529 or 08 8221 5299), one block from Light Sq. With free breakfast, sauna, City Tour, DVD collection, satellite TV, and rides to the beach, you'll want to make My Place yours. A/C and heat. Bikes for hire. In-house travel agency. Free pickup from bus and train station. Job recruitment agent on site. Internet $4 per hr. Laundry $5. Single-sex and mixed dorms $24; doubles $58. MC/V. ❷

**Backpack Oz and Guest House,** 144 Wakefield St. (☎1800 633 307 or 08 8223 3551; www.backpackoz.com.au), on the corner of Pulteney St., near Rundle St. Feels like a college dorm: party by night, post-raging party by day. Young backpackers chill out with beers in the TV lounge, shoot pool, and check email ($1 per 15min.; free Wi-Fi) in the sunny office. The newer Guest House across the street has a nicer kitchen and cable TV. Free pickup, employment info, and tour bookings. Laundry $5.40. Breakfast and W night BBQ included. Reception 6am-10pm. Mixed dorms $22, female-only $25; singles $50-65; doubles $60-70; triples $80-110. Discounted rooms July-Aug. MC/V. ❷

# 🍴 FOOD

Adelaide's reputation as the culinary capital of Australia is growing every day, and for a city its size, Adelaide is a gourmand's dream. **Gouger Street's** cheap, multicultural eats and **Central Market** (see below) are a backpacker's heaven. In the northeast section of the city, **Rundle Street** caters to the young hipster set with upscale dining, and nearby **Hindley Street,** flashy but cheap, appeals to hungry backpackers on tight budgets. For a splurge, the trendy restaurants on **O'Connell** and **Melbourne Street** in North Adelaide offer the best ambience. Supermarkets dot the city, particularly along **Rundle Mall, Hindley Street,** and **Victoria Square. Coles,** next to Central Market on Grote St., has convenient late-night hours. (Open M-F midnight-9pm, Sa midnight-5pm, Su 11am-5pm.)

## GOUGER STREET

Gouger Street, in the city center near Victoria Sq., offers a wide range of inexpensive, multicultural cuisine and houses the ⚑**Central Market,** whose stalls overflow with colorful fruits and vegetables, cheeses, and freshly baked breads. (Open Tu 7am-5:30pm, Th 9am-5:30pm, F 7am-9pm, and Sa 7am-3pm.)

**Ying Chow,** 114 Gouger St. (☎08 8211 7998). Specializing in regional Chinese cuisine, Ying Chow's is packed for lunch and dinner with locals who sing the praises of both the food and the prices. Entrees $7.50-16. Open M-Th and Su 5pm-12:45am, F noon-3pm and 5pm-1am, Sa 5pm-1am. Fully licensed and BYO. ❷

**Mesa Lunga** (☎08 8410 7617; www.mesalunga.com), on the corner of Gouger and Morphett St. The chef, trained in Madrid, prepares amazingly authentic Spanish food with an Italian zing. Try the popular paella or one of the excellent organic pizzas, like the Pizza Chorizo with cherry tomatoes, Spanish chorizo, and black olives. Extensive tapas menu ($3-14). Sangria carafe $30. Entrees $19-28. Open M-F noon-2:30pm and 6-11pm, Sa 6-11pm, Su noon-11pm (tapas menu only). AmEx/MC/V. ❹

**Sushi Train** (☎08 8231 3733; www.sushitrain.com.au), on Gouger St. in Central Market. Open M-Th 11am-9pm, F-Sa 11am-10pm, Su noon-9pm. It is always entertaining to sit and have food roll up to you. Choose what looks appetizing, which is basically everything on this incredibly inexpensive menu. Extensive takeout menu. Rolls $3-5.50. ❶

## NORTH ADELAIDE

Lined with Victorian mansions far out of the normal price range, North Adelaide has long been overlooked by budget travelers because of its expensive reputation. Don't judge a book by its cover, however—there are some cheaper spots along Adelaide's rich and famous **O'Connell** and **Melbourne Streets.**

⚑ **Burger It,** 110 O'Connell St. (☎08 8267 2612). You'd never guess this burger and chips joint would be featured in Adelaide's latest gourmet review. But as soon as you take a bite out of one of their 100% prime, hormone-free, South Australian angus beef burgers, you'll understand why. Try the "It'll Brie Good" burger with plum sauce and sliced brie ($9), or the vegetarian (vegan upon request) "Pump & Grind It" patty made from pumpkin, cashew, and ginger ($8). Open M-W and Su 11am-9:30pm, Th-Sa 11am-10pm. ❶

⚑ **Bakery on O'Connell,** 44 O'Connell St. (☎08 8361 7377). Under the motto "24/7 Heaven," this bakery combines delicious pastries, cakes, quiches, and pies with round-the-clock service. Pie floaters ($6), a South Australian specialty of steak pie floating in pea soup, are a must. If pie floaters don't float your boat, try the rocky road pastry. Internet $1 per 7min. Pastries $2.20-4.50. ❶

**The Store,** 157 Melbourne St. (☎08 8361 6999), on the corner of Jerningham Rd. Locally renowned for its satisfying organic breakfasts, The Store is always packed in the morning. The banana and honey smoothie ($5.50), blueberry pancakes ($14), and The Store BLT with tomato chutney and fontina ($12) are well worth the wait. Check out the attached gourmet organic food shop and its local products. Open daily 7am-10pm. ❷

**Elephant Walk Cafe,** 76 Melbourne St. (☎08 8267 2006). Tucked away among the chic bistros of North Adelaide, this quirky but cozy coffee lounge caters to the after-dinner crowd. Pair your espresso ($4.30) with one of the many delicious scones, puddings, or cakes ($8-11). Open daily 8pm-late. ❶

## BEST OF THE REST

**Adelaide Coffee Bar,** 73 Grenfell St. (☎08 8227 2001). Sip on one of the many delicious coffees served in this Italian-style coffee bar, and complement it with a home-

SOUTH AUSTRALIA

## LOCAL LEGEND

### OF CONVICTS AND CROWS

In a country of dubious origins, South Australia is proud to be the only state founded by free settlers. What South Australians aren't too keen to share is that the state was planned by a convict.

Imprisoned in London for kidnapping a young girl in the 1830s, Edward Gibbon Wakefield passed the time by dreaming of escape to the promised land. Eager to start anew after his release, Wakefield hatched a plan to found a colony of free men in Oz, drawing in honest investors with the lure of golden lands. Wakefield was eventually frozen out of the plan, but a fledgling colony named South Australia was nevertheless born as settlers flooded Adelaide.

The free men and their respectable wives didn't expect the harsh, sun-scorched desert of South Australia, and times were tough—so tough that, according to lore, the desperate and starving Adelaidians resorted to eating crows during the frequent famines. Melbourne and Sydney, sick of being looked down upon by snooty free Adelaidians, coined the name "croweaters," which still has currency. The term has lost its derogatory connotations, and one of Adelaide's premier footy clubs is named the Croweaters. Ask most croweaters the history of their name, and they'll shrug their shoulders. They probably don't know the answer—or, at least, they pretend not to.

made almond tart ($2.50). Fresh sandwiches $5.50-6.70. Wine served by the glass. Espresso $3. Open M-F 7am-4:30pm. ❶

**The Red Ochre,** War Memorial Dr. (☎08 8211 8555), overlooking the River Torrens. This elegant restaurant prepares Mod Oz cuisine with grace and finesse. The most popular dish by far is the Ochre Game Platter, featuring a selection of kangaroo fillet, wallaby skewer, marinated quail, emu chorizo sausage, lamb cutlet, and emu fillet ($38 per person, min. 2 people). Entrees $16.50-36. Open M-Sa 6pm-late. AmEx/MC/V. ❺

## ◎ SIGHTS

◪**ADELAIDE ZOO.** The Adelaide Zoo is home to more than 1300 animals, including an array of African wildlife. Don't miss the daily feedings of sea lions (11:45am), pelicans (2:30pm), and penguins (2:45pm). Ask about the **Boileau Animal Encounters** that take you behind the scenes with the keepers to help feed and care for the zoo's animals. *(Frome Rd., a 15min. walk from North Terr. through the Botanic Gardens or down Frome Rd. Take bus #271 or 273 from Currie St. Popeye boats, $6, from the Festival Centre also run to and from the zoo in summer. ☎08 8267 3255; www.adelaidezoo.com.au. Open daily 9:30am-5pm. Free guided tours leave from the Zoo Shop daily at 10:30am and 2:30pm. Admission $20, concessions $16, ages 4-14 $12; under 4 free. Boileau Animal Encounters have various prices, usually around $75, children $40.)*

◪**ADELAIDE BOTANIC GARDENS.** Acres of landscaping surround 19th-century heritage buildings, a small lake with black swans, and meandering walkways. The peaceful grounds contain the **Australian Forest,** the **Water Mediterranean Garden,** the **Amazon Waterlily Pavilion,** and the **International Rose Garden,** with over 5000 species from around the world. The **Bicentennial Conservatory,** the largest glasshouse in the Southern Hemisphere, recreates the tropical rainforest climates of Australia, Papua New Guinea, Indonesia, and the nearby Pacific Islands. In the summer, the gardens host the **Moonlight Cinema;** for more info, see p. 471. *(On North Terr. ☎08 8222 9311; www.botanicgardens.sa.gov.au. Gardens open Dec.-Jan. M-F 8am-7pm, Sa-Su 9am-7pm; Feb.-Mar. and Nov.-Oct. M-F 8am-6:30pm, Sa-Su 9am-6:30pm; Apr. and Sept. M-F 8am-6pm, Sa-Su 9am-6pm; May and Aug. M-F 8am-5:30pm, Sa-Su 9am-5:30pm; June-July M-F 8am-5pm, Sa-Su 9am-5pm. Conservatory open in summer daily 10am-5pm; in winter 10am-4pm; $4.70, concessions $2.50. Free 1hr. tours leave from the Schomburgk Pavilion outside the Visitor Information Centre daily at 10:30am.)*

**HAIGH'S CHOCOLATES VISITORS CENTRE.** Australia's oldest chocolate maker, Haigh's has been in business since 1915 and is proud to be one of only a few specialist chocolate retailers still making chocolate from raw cocoa beans. At the visitors center and factory, windows open onto areas where workers in white outfits and hairnets inspire comparisons to Charlie and the Chocolate Factory. With over 200 varieties to choose from, including Australian flavors such as Wattle Seed Crunch and Lemon Myrtle Cream, you can never sample enough. Haigh's has several shops dotting the city (including on Rundle Mall and in Central Market) whose staff will be more than happy to dole out free samples. (*153 Greenhill Rd., 1 block south of South Terr. between Pulteney St. and Hutt St. Bus #191, 192, 195, or 196 from C3 stop on King William St. to Stop #1 on Unley Rd. ☎08 8372 7000; www.haighschocolates.com.au. Open M-F 8:30am-5:30pm, Sa 9am-5pm. Free 20min. guided tours with tastings M-Sa 11am, 1, and 2pm. Book at least 2 days in advance; tours limited to 20 people. Self tours available when guided tours are not.*)

**OTHER SIGHTS.** At the eastern edge of the Botanic Gardens, the **National Wine Centre of Australia** hosts interactive exhibits that cover everything from grape varieties to Australian wine regions and even allow visitors to make virtual wine on a computer. At the end of the exhibits is an extensive cellar with a broad selection of wines. Courses and tastings available. (*Corner of Botanic and Hackney Rd. ☎08 8303 3355; www.wineaustralia.com.au. Open M-F 9am-5pm, Sa-Su 10am-5pm. Free; suggested gold coin donation. Guided tours with tastings included $15-30. Min. 10 people.*) The **Adelaide Gaol** was used for 147 years, and 45 inmates were executed and buried within its walls. These days, the only visitors to this creepy prison are tourists. (*18 Gaol Rd., Thebarton. From the corner of North and West Terr., take Port Rd. and turn right on Gaol Rd. Or take bus #115 or 118 and get off at Stop 1. ☎08 8231 4062; www.adelaidegaol.org.au. $8.50, concessions $7, children $5.50. Open for self-guided tours with audio M-F 11am-3:30pm, Su 1-3:30pm. 1hr. guided tours Su 11am, noon, and 1pm. Nightly ghost tours by appointment, $20 per person, min. 15 people.*)

# 🏛 MUSEUMS

**◪SOUTH AUSTRALIAN MUSEUM.** This stately building is the brilliant center-piece of the North Terr. cultural district. It features huge whale skeletons, displays on native Australian animals, rocks and minerals, an Egyptian mummy, and an exhibit on the life of the giant squid. The real highlight of the museum is the **Australian Aboriginal Cultures Gallery,** which has the largest collection of Aboriginal artifacts in the world. (*Between the State Library and the Art Gallery of SA, on North Terr. ☎08 8207 7500; www.samuseum.sa.gov.au. Open daily 10am-5pm. Free 45min. museum tours M-F 11am and Sa-Su 2 and 3pm. Wheelchair accessible. Free.*)

**◪TANDANYA NATIONAL ABORIGINAL CULTURAL INSTITUTE INC.** The oldest indigenously-owned and managed Aboriginal multi-arts complex in Australia, the Tandanya—which translates to Red Kangaroo place, the name given to the Adelaide city area by the Kaurna people—hosts rotating indigenous artwork exhibitions from around the country. Don't miss the free guided tour at 11am on Thursdays. The institute also has didjeridu performances (T-F noon) and a Torres Strait Islander Dance (Sa-Su noon), both free with gallery admission. (*253 Grenfell St., at the corner of East Terr. on the 99C bus route. ☎08 8224 3200; www.tandaya.com.au. Open daily 10am-5pm. $5, concessions $4, family $12.*)

**ART GALLERY OF SOUTH AUSTRALIA.** This impressive gallery showcases colonial and modern Australian, modern Aboriginal, Asian, and European prints, paintings, decorative arts, and ceramics. (*North Terr. near Pulteney St. ☎08 8207 7000,* *tours ☎ 08 8207 7075; www.artgallery.sa.gov.au. Open daily 10am-5pm. Free 1hr. tours daily 11am and 2pm. Wheelchair accessible. Free.)*

**MIGRATION MUSEUM.** Combining history and oral tradition to explain the patterns of immigration and exclusion that have shaped South Australian society, the museum's harrowing refugee stories and photographs are excellent, if sobering. The exhibits and interactive displays are particularly relevant now, as immigration policy has become one of the nation's most hotly contested political issues. Refreshingly, the museum does not shy away from the historical controversy surrounding Australian policy toward Aborigines during the 20th century. *(82 Kintore Ave., off North Terr., behind the state library. ☎ 08 8207 7580. Open M-F 10am-5pm, Sa-Su 1-5pm. Free, $2 donation suggested.)*

# ◪ ACTIVITIES

Easily accessible from the city center by tram, **Glenelg** (p. 472) is the perfect destination for beach bums, offering surfing, swimming with dolphins, scuba diving, and more. Those looking for a bit more action should visit the outdoor goods stores on Rundle St., most of which can point you toward the city's best purveyors of outdoor activities and fully outfit you for them. Try **Scout Outdoor** (192 Rundle), **Columbia Sportswear** (208 Rundle), **Super Elliotts Cycles** (200 Rundle), or **Anna Purna** (210 Rundle).

**BIKING.** Adelaide is a cyclist's paradise, with ample bike tracks and paths throughout the city. The world-famous **Tour Down Under** cycling race (p. 471) is held here every January. With the Adelaide **hills** (p. 474) on one doorstep and a **coastal bike track** between Glenelg and Henley (p. 473) on the other, the area provides the best cycling opportunities around. The 40km **Linear Park Biking and Walking Track** offers safe paths along the River Torrens, running the full distance between ocean and hills. For **bike rentals,** see **By Bicycle,** p. 464. For **self-guided cycling tours** running from Glenelg to coastal destinations farther south in the Fleurieu Peninsula, check out www.cyclingtoursaustralia.com.au.

**EARTH AND SKY. Rock Solid Adventure** offers abseiling, rock climbing, and a two-day hiking trip to the **Coorong** (p. 497). They also run various outdoor trips, including kayaking tours throughout southeastern Australia. Check their website for a list of upcoming trips. *(☎ 08 8270 4244; www.rock-solid-adventure.com. Full day of rock-climbing or abseiling $119. Ask about the Let's Go discount.)* **SA Skydiving** is pleased to assist in fulfilling your free-fall fantasies. With such an amazing view of Australia's southern coastline from above, you'll be too distracted to realize that you've just jumped out of a plane. *(☎ 08 8272 7888; www.skydiving.com.au. 8000 ft. tandem from $299, 10,000 ft. tandem from $449, video and stills $110-160. Ask about the Let's Go discount.)* **Adelaide Ballooning** offers 1hr. hot air balloon rides with a champagne breakfast for $250-280. *(☎ 1800 730 330; www.adelaideballooning.com.au. 10% discount with student ID, children 20% discount.)*

# ▣ ENTERTAINMENT

**PERFORMING ARTS.** A 2min. walk north on King William Rd. from its intersection with North Terr. at Parliament House leads to the huge, armadillo-shaped **Adelaide Festival Centre,** the epicenter of Adelaide's cultural life. You can pick up a calendar of events from inside the complex, access the schedule online at www.southaustralia.com, or call **BASS** (Centre ☎ 08 8216 8600; BASS 13 12

46. Centre open M-F 9am-6pm, Sa 2hr. prior to performance until 30min. after performance begins, Su 10am-4pm.) The **State Opera of South Australia** (☎08 8226 4790; www.saopera.sa.gov.au), the **Adelaide Symphony Orchestra** (ASO; ☎08 8233 6233; www.aso.com.au), and the **State Theatre Company of South Australia** (☎08 8231 5151; www.statetheatre.sa.com.au) all perform at the Festival Centre; it's also the place for big-name traveling musicals and theater performances. The ASO also performs in the town hall. Student rush tickets for the orchestra are available 30min. before the show at the Festival Centre.

**FESTIVALS.** As the capital of the Festival State, Adelaide hosts dozens of famous festivals, drawing Australians from all over to celebrate. January is the time for the **Tour Down Under,** where 100 cyclists from around the world race through 55 towns in South Australia with a finale in Adelaide. In March, the **Adelaide Festival of the Arts** (www.adelaidefestival.com.au), the eclectic **Adelaide Fringe** (www.adelaidefringe.com.au), the **Clipsal 500** (www.clipsal500.com.au), and the huge **WOMADelaide** (www.womadelaide.com.au) take to the streets. The **Adelaide Cabaret Festival** (www.adelaidecabaretfestival.com) occurs in mid-June, and the **Bartercard Glenelg Jazz Festival** hosts jazz bands from New Orleans as well as Australia in October. The **Feast Festival,** a three-week long GBLT cultural festival, takes place in November.

**CINEMAS.** Adelaide's two best alternative cinemas, the **Palace** and the **Nova,** are across from one another on Rundle St. near East Terr. Between the two, they cover most major international and independent films. (☎08 8232 3434; www.palacenova.com. Tickets $15, students $10). **Mercury Cinema,** 13 Morphett St., off Hindley St., has more artsy showings. (☎08 8410 1934; www.mercurycinema.org.au. $11, concessions $9; festival ticket prices higher.) December through February brings outdoor screenings of classics at the **Cinema in the Botanic Gardens.** (Tickets at gate from 7pm. www.moonlight.com.au, $3 booking fee; or through BASS ☎13 12 46. $14, concessions $12, children $10.)

> **TUNE IN ON TUESDAYS.** Most Australian theaters offer discount tickets on Tuesday nights, including the Palace and the Nova.

**SPECTATOR SPORTS. Australian Rules Football** is played in the suburb of West Lakes (Adelaide Crows) and in Port Adelaide (Port Power). **Cricket** (Oct.-Mar.) is played at the **Adelaide Oval,** north of the city along King William St. There is a 2hr. tour of the Oval that focuses on "Cricket's Greatest Batsman," the late Sir Donald Bradman. (☎08 8300 3800. Tours M-F 10am, non-match days only. Tours leave from Administration Office; from War Memorial Dr., pass through South Gate. $10, concessions $5. Tickets and schedules for footy and cricket available at BASS, ☎13 12 46, or VenueTix, ☎08 8225 8888.)

# ◢ PUBS

Adelaide has an excellent pub and live music scene, so take advantage of it while you can. There are plenty of nightclubs in town, such as **Zhivago, Mojo, Electric Circus, HQ,** and **Mars Bar** (the premier gay nightclub in town); however, to truly taste the flavor of Adelaide nightlife, the pubs are where you need to be.

>  **DRESS TO IMPRESS.** Bouncers at most of the city's dance clubs are very mindful of dress code. This usually means no sneakers, T-shirts, tank tops, flip flops, or hats, but can be extended to include no jeans.

The **East End,** which includes Rundle St. east of the mall, Pulteney St., and Pirie St., is the center of Adelaide's nightlife scene and teems with Uni students and twenty-something professionals on the weekends. The pub scene dominates this area, as students and others drink schooners, people-watch, and chat on the sidewalk. Rundle Mall is renamed **Hindley Street** in the West End, and is home to many X-rated venues and numerous fly-by-night dance clubs abutting stylish bars and bistros. Beyond the CBD, **North Adelaide** has swank hotels with pricey cocktails, while the beach suburbs, most notably **Glenelg** (p. 472), have a few watering holes right on the ocean.

**The Governor Hindmarsh Hotel,** 59 Port Rd., Hindmarsh (☎08 8340 0744; www.the-gov.com.au). North of town on Port Rd. From up-and-coming to big-name acts, the Gov is always grooving. Tu $5 pizza. W open mic, Th and Sa local bands in front bar, F Irish folk. If the music makes your mouth water, go for an excellent wood-oven pizza ($8.50-14.50), such as the lamb and rosemary pizza. Happy hour M-W 5-7pm: 2-for-1 sparkling white, red, and rose wine. Open M-F 11am-latenight, Sa noon-latenight; open Su only for events 2pm-late. Cover usually $2-5, more for well-known acts.

**Grace Emily,** 232 Waymouth St. (☎08 8231 5500). For great local, interstate, and international live music, join the chill crowd by the stage or around the pool tables. The Grace is the place on M nights for BBQ/Open Mic night. Open daily 4pm-late.

**The Botanic,** 309 North Terr. (☎08 8227 0799), on the corner of East Terr. right across from the Botanic Gardens. Dark and sleek, this chic bar caters to twenty-something professionals looking to wind down with a fine wine or cocktail. Th-Su live DJs, mostly R&B. Open Tu-Th 5pm-2am, F 4pm-3am, Sa 2pm-3am, Su 4pm-midnight.

**Exeter Hotel,** 246 Rundle St. (☎08 8223 2623). Live music club and curry bistro with eclectic, dreadlocked crowd. Live music is mostly local and always original. W and Th 6:30-9pm Curry Nights ($13) have a cult following. Open daily 11:30am-late.

**Tap Inn,** 76 Rundle St., Kent Town (☎08 8362 2116; www.tapinn.com.au). Bar/pub/restaurant/gambling lounge/driving range, the Tap Inn has it all. Really. Check out the tap fountain in the entrance hall and the glass floor in the pub. Visit the unique unisex bathroom in the restaurant. And, if nothing else, order a bag of chips for a good laugh. Pub happy hour Tu and F 5-7pm. Live music Sa. Buy 1 bucket of 100 golf balls, get one free daily 5:30-6:30pm. Driving range open M-Th and Su 9am-11:30pm, F-Sa 9am-midnight. Pub open M-Th noon-midnight, F-Sa noon-2am.

**Austral,** 205 Rundle St. (☎08 8223 4660). An unmistakable landmark, this old hotel draws a young crowd. If there's no night life happening here, there's probably not much going on anywhere in town. Open daily 11am-3am.

# ▶ DAYTRIPS FROM ADELAIDE

## GLENELG
*The best way to reach Glenelg is by the tram ($4.10), which runs every 15-20min. from Victoria Sq. to Moseley Sq.*

If you're sick of the city life, an easy beach escape is just 20min. away. The most famous of the beach suburbs, Glenelg (Gluh-NELG) is Adelaide's most-frequented weekend destination, with long stretches of coast, tons of restaurants and ice cream parlors, and ample ocean activities.

**Glenelg Scuba Diving** runs a four-day PADI certification class and weekend boat dives to Adelaide's wrecks and reefs. (☎08 8294 7744; www.adventureblue.com.au. Dives from $80, $45 for those with equipment. Ask about the broad range of PADI and SSI certification classes. Equipment hire available; PADI class $595.) **Eco-certified Temptation Sailing** brings you up close and personal with

St. Vincent Gulf dolphins. (Holdfast Shores Marina. ☎04 1281 1838; www.dolphinboat.com.au. Dolphin swim $98, children 8-15 $88. If you don't want to get your feet wet: $58, children under 15 $48. Full refund if no dolphins are spotted. Part of the proceeds go to dolphin research.) **Beach Hire Glenelg** (☎08 8294 1477), next to the Tourist Information Centre, rents out bikes ($12 per hr., tandem $18 per hr.), wave skis ($14 per hr.), and body boards ($9 per hr.). Deck chairs, umbrellas, volleyballs, towels, and cricket sets are also available.

**Glenelg Beach Hostel ❷**, on Moseley St. half a block from the action of Jetty Rd., offers clean, bright rooms, a beer garden and lively bar, and pool tables. (1-7 Moseley St. ☎08 8376 0007 or 1800 359 181; www.glenelgbeachhostel.com.au. Free breakfast. Linen included. Ceiling fans; no A/C. Internet access $3 per 15min. Laundry $3, dry $2. Mixed and female-only 4- to 10-bed dorms $25; singles $50; doubles $70; triples $100; quads $110.)

**Jetty Rd.,** the main strip in town, is chock-full of dining options, from takeaway fish and chips to classy Italian. One of the best pizza places around, **GoodLife ❸**, is located upstairs on the SW corner of the intersection with Moseley St. Using high quality local produce, GoodLife serves up delicious organic pizzas. (☎08 8376 5900. Open Tu-F and Su noon-2:30pm and 6pm-late, Sa 6pm-late. AmEx/MC/V.) A finalist for Adelaide's best fish and chips, the **Oyster Shop ❸**, at Jetty and Moseley St., has fresh seafood and home-grown oysters. (☎08 8376 7200. Dozen oysters $15. Fish and chips $10.50. Open M-Th and Su 11am-8:30pm, F 11am-9pm, Sa 10am-10pm.)

**Glenelg Tourist Information Centre** is on the foreshore (by the jetty), inside Dolphin Cafe. (☎08 8294 5833. Open M-F 9am-5pm, Sa 9:30am-3pm, Su 10am-2pm). The **Glenelg Municipal Library** offers free Wi-Fi and an hour of free **Internet** on their computers. (2 Colley Terr., half a block north of Jetty Rd. ☎08 8295 5045. Best to call ahead to reserve computer. Open M-Tu and Th-F 9am-5pm. W 9am-7pm, Sa 9am-1pm, Su 1-4pm.)

 **PARTY HARD.** If you're out late in Glenelg or Henley, there's an after-midnight bus into Adelaide, which costs as much as a regular Metro ticket. From Glenelg, it leaves every hr. 12:35-3:35am. From Henley, just add 4min.

## BEACHES

*The beaches and coastal spots below are listed from north to south. All can be easily reached via Adelaide's metro system of buses and trains. In addition, a coastal bike path runs south from Henley to Glenelg and the southern coast.*

The clear coastal waters of Gulf St. Vincent draw sunbathers, surfers, and sailors from far and wide. Glenelg is the most touristed, while the beaches of Henley, Noarlunga, and beaches further south provide a calmer getaway.

**HENLEY.** This quiet coastal town offers the perfect getaway in a less touristy beach scene than Glenelg, and it can be reached by bus #110 or 113. The clean sands' breathtaking, iridescent waters are perfect for working on your tan, and the long pier provides for great fishing. For a cheap Greek bite, **Estia Takeaway ❶**, on the foreshore next to the sit-down Estia Restaurant, has amazing gyros for $8 and beer-battered fish and chips for $3.50. (☎08 8383 5341. Open M-Th and Su 11am-8pm, F-Sa 11am-10pm.) For some latenight action, head to the renowned **Ramsgate Hotel,** one of the best pubs on the coast. (328 Seaview Rd. Open M-Th 11am-midnight, F-Su 8am-2am.)

**PORT ADELAIDE.** Port Adelaide, on the Port Adelaide River, is notable for a handful of historic pubs and a dolphin tour. It's accessible via the Outer Harbour Line or bus #118, 150, or 153. The visitors center, on Commercial Rd. at the corner of Vincent St., has plenty of information and maps. (☎08 8405 6560 or 1800 629 888. Open daily 9am-5pm.) The **Port Adelaide River** is famous for its own bottlenose dolphins colony, remarkable for its vicinity to urban waterways. Two river cruise companies run from the waterfront in Port Adelaide, with promotional fares on Sundays. (☎08 8447 2366; www.dolphinexplorer.com.au. 2hr. cruise departs at 11:30am and 2pm. $3.50.)

**PORT NOARLUNGA AND THE SOUTHERN BEACHES.** Closest to Adelaide, **Christies Beach** has a park and many small shops along **Beach Rd.** South from Christies, the **Port Noarlunga Aquatic Reserve** has a shallow reef accessible from the end of the jetty, and is the best diving and snorkeling spot in the Adelaide area. Farther south, **Seaford** has a walking and biking track along the cliffs. **Moana,** south of Seaford, has the best surf and is suitable for beginners, and **Maslin Beach** draws peeping Toms and free spirits with South Australia's largest nudist colony. (To reach Port Noarlunga, catch the Noarlunga train from Adelaide. To reach Seaford, Moana, and Maslin beaches from the port, take bus #740 or 741.)

# THE HILLS

Just a short drive from the city center, **Adelaide Hills** offers a perfect retreat, with wildlife parks, dozens of vineyards, and cozy villages.

**CLELAND WILDLIFE PARK AND MOUNT LOFTY SUMMIT.** Just 15km from the big city, ◼**Cleland Wildlife Park** provides a rare and spectacular opportunity to walk among 120 species of Australian wildlife. Kangaroos, wallabies, and emus wander freely throughout the open space enclosures, allowing you to approach, hand-feed, pet, and photograph the animals up close. Don't miss the **Koala Close-ups:** pet the koalas while they happily munch on eucalyptus (daily 11am-noon and 2-4pm) or cozy up and hug the cuddly creature (daily 2:30-3:30pm). There are also a variety of feeding times for the animals, including the Tasmanian devils (2pm), dingoes (2:30pm), and the most entertaining of them all, the pelicans (3pm). To make the most of the park, coordinate your visit with the Koala Close-up afternoon session and the various feeding times. (☎08 8339 2444; www.clelandwildlifepark.sa.gov.au. Open daily 9:30am-5pm; no admission after 4:30pm.) To get to Cleland by car (20min.), take Glen Osmond Rd. to Princes Hwy., exit at Crafers, and follow signs. Or, hop on bus #864 to Crafers, then change to the connecting #832 to Cleland.

Part of Cleland, **Mount Lofty Summit** is just down the road from the wildlife park. From the 710m summit, the city glitters all the way to the coast. On a clear day, the view stretches to Kangaroo Island. At the summit, the **Visitor's Information Centre** offers free maps of the nearby Adelaide Hills towns and advice about hikes in the park. One of the trails is a section of the 1200km **Heysen Trail** (www.hysentrail.sa.gov.au) which loops from the summit to the Botanic Gardens and back (6.5km, 2hr.). A 4km one-way trail leads from the summit to Waterfall Gully carpark up to Mt. Lofty; allow 2hr. for the return trip. A third hike leads to Cleland (4km, 1.5 hr round-trip). (☎08 8370 1054; www.environment.sa.gov.au. Tourist office open daily 9am-5pm. Cafe open M-Tu 9am-5pm, W-Su 9am-late. Free admission. Parking $1 per hr., $2 per day.)

South of the summit, the **Mount Lofty Botanic Garden** is a great place for a picnic or a leisurely stroll through rhododendrons, magnolias, ferns, and a national species rose collection. The garden has a very specific flowering calendar, with most species in full bloom August to November. The autumn foliage is particularly stunning April to May. (☎08 8222 9311; www.botanicgardens.sa.gov.au. Open M-F 8:30am-4pm, Sa-Su 10am-5pm. Parking $1 per hr., $2 per day.)

If you're looking for a solitary retreat with easy access to Cleland Wildlife Park, the summit, and the botanic gardens, **Mount Lofty YHA Wilderness Cottage ❶** is a great choice. Groups of 2-16 can rent out the stone cottage, equipped with basic kitchen/dining facilities, heating, showers, and toilets. (Book and pick up keys through Adelaide Central YHA, ☎08 8414 3010; www.yha.com.au. M-Th $80, F-Su $110; $10 YHA-member discount.)

**HAHNDORF.** Originally settled by East German Lutheran immigrants escaping religious persecution in 1839, Hahndorf is Australia's oldest German settlement, and has the bratwurst and polka to prove it. But even beyond the German fare, Hahndorf is a delightful village and provides the perfect base for taking advantage of all the Hills have to offer, with some of the Hills' best wineries at its doorstep as well as a strawberry picking farm and a charming cheese cellar. Most businesses and shops in town are on Main St., including the **Adelaide Hills Visitors Centre.** (41 Main St. ☎1800 353 323 or 08 8388 1185; www.visitadelaidehills.com.au. Internet $2 per 30min. Open M-F 9am-5pm, Sa-Su 10am-4pm.) To reach Hahndorf by car (40min. from Adelaide), take Glen Osmond Rd. to Princes Hwy. and exit at Hahndorf. Or, hop on bus #864F.

The Hills are famous for their wineries. The most contemporary and fresh of the bunch, **The Lane** offers the best view. (Ravenswood Ln. ☎08 8388 1250; www.thelane.com.au. Open M-Th 10am-4pm, F-Su 10am-5pm.) The cellar door at the **Hahndorf Hill Winery** is a nice mix of ancient and modern and overlooks the vineyards. (Pains Rd. ☎08 8388 7512; www.hahndorfhillwinery.com.au. Open daily 10am-5pm.) **Nepenthe Wines** is a hip winery with a number of premium wines. (Jones Rd. ☎08 8388 4439; www.nepenthe.com.au. Open daily 10am-4pm.) When you're done with the grapes and want to move on to strawberries, head to **Beerenberg** on Mt. Barker Rd. From the end of October to mid-May, you can pick your own strawberries. If you are visiting out of season, the shop stocks plenty of famous Beerenberg jams, pickles, chutneys, and sauces year-round. Visit www.beerenberg.com.au for recipes. (☎08 8388 7272. Open daily 9am-5pm, last entry for strawberry picking 4pm.)

To spend the night in Hahndorf, head to **Old Mill Hotel ❸.** (98 Main St. ☎08 8338 7888. Basic double M-Th $65, F-Su $90; spa double $105/120.)

**PARTY TIME.** The best time to visit the Adelaide Hills is during its yearly **Wine and Food Festival** in March, called **Crush.** With full fall foliage decorating the vineyards, cherry, apple, pear, and chestnut orchards, sip on boutique wines and enjoy delicious food and good music. To find out more, visit www.adelaidehillswine.com.au.

**SURROUNDING HILLS.** The tiny towns of **Stirling, Aldgate, Bridgewater, Strathalbyn, Balhannah,** and **Birdwood** embody the spirit of the hills with cute cafes and B&Bs tucked into the greenery of the landscape. The towns are perfect for a leisurely Sunday drive. If you prefer flying high, **Adelaide Ballooning** (p. 470) flies from Strathalbyn and provides an unforgettable aerial view of the hills.

The **Onkaparinga River Scenic Drive** (45km) starts just off the Hahndorf exit of Princes Hwy. and leads you through the beautiful Onkaparinga Valley, past vineyards, farmland, and historic towns like Balhannah, Oakbank, Woodside, Mount Torrens, and Birdwood. The **Angas Scenic Drive** (40km) starts in Stirling and winds its way through Aldgate, Mylor, Echunga, and historic Macclesfield, passing verdant farmland and tall gums on the way to Strathalbyn. Looping through vineyards, pine forests, and bushlands, the **Torrens Valley Scenic Drive** (28km) starts in Adelaide's northeast suburbs and winds its way past

Houghton, Inglewood, the Chain of Ponds reservoirs, Gumeracha (home to the Giant Rocking Horse), and historic Birdwood.

# FLEURIEU PENINSULA

The Fleurieu (FLOOR-ee-oh) Peninsula stretches southeast from Adelaide, encompassing the luscious vineyards of McLaren Vale, kilometers of coastline along Gulf St. Vincent and Encounter Bay, and dozens of charming seaside towns. The region's proximity to Adelaide has made it South Australia's most popular holiday destination for over a century, and affordable accommodations are harder to come by than in other parts of the state. Fleurieu's popularity, however, rarely translates into unwelcome crowding. Beautiful country roads weave past quiet pastures and jaw-dropping views. There are myriad water-based activities offered on the Fleurieu, including snorkeling, jet-skiing, and surfing. All tourist offices have a copy of the free and invaluable *Surfing Secrets on the Fleurieu Peninsula*, which provides a map of all the surf spots and detailed information including break descriptions and wind directions.

 **TOURIEU.** Camel Winery Tours, based between Kangarilla and McLaren Flat, offers a one-day winery safari on camelback with winery visits, a bottle of wine, and lunch. (☎04 0739 9808 or 04 0883 6246. $90.)

# MCLAREN VALE                    ☎08

A quick jaunt from the city, just 45min. (37km) south of Adelaide, the McLaren Vale wine region centers on the towns of McLaren Vale (pop. 5000), McLaren Flat, and nearby Willunga. Amid a Mediterranean climate and vast stretches of leafy, vine-dotted hillsides, countless vineyards have cellar-door sales and tastings en route to producing world-class wines. Make McLaren Vale a daytrip from Adelaide or stay longer to enjoy the beautiful coast of the Fleurieu.

## █ TRANSPORTATION

Having a car makes touring easier but imbibing harder. Common sense—and the law—makes designating a driver a must. It's not uncommon to find random breath-testing units on main roads to and from wine regions (the legal blood-alcohol limit is 0.05%). Alternatively, McLaren Vale is a beautiful area for a bike ride, though *Let's Go* does not recommend drinking and biking.

**Buses:** Premier Stateliner (☎08 8415 5555; www.premierstateliner.com.au) runs buses to **Adelaide** (1hr.; M-F 9:30am, noon, 3pm, Sa 9:30am, 4:30pm, Su 9:30am; $7.70). Loops around in the other direction through **Goolwa, Middleton,** and **Victor Harbor.**

**Bike Rental:** Oxygen Cycles, 143 Main Rd. (☎08 8323 7345). $5 per hr. Min. $15 rental. Open Tu-F 10am-6pm, Sa 9am-5pm, Su 10am-5pm.

## █ █ ORIENTATION AND PRACTICAL INFORMATION

This part of Australia has more wineries than you can shake a hangover at (and if you're not careful, it will be hard to shake that hangover). The road from McLaren Vale south to Willunga has vineyards at every turn, as does **Chalk Hill Rd. McLaren Flat,** on Kangarilla Rd. 3km east of McLaren Vale, is also surrounded by wineries. Just off **Main Road** in McLaren Vale, you can find **ATMs, the post office,** and a variety of other resources.

**Tourist Office: McLaren Vale and Fleurieu Visitors Centre** (☎08 8323 9944; www.mclarenvale.info), on the left as you come into town. Has a map of the wineries and handles B&B bookings. Their website also has useful information on local wineries and accommodations. Open M-F 9am-5pm, Sa-Su 10am-5pm.

**Police:** ☎08 8323 8330.

**Pharmacy: Chemmart,** in the Central Shopping Centre. Open M-W and F 9am-6pm, Th 9am-7pm, Sa 9am-4pm.

## ACCOMMODATIONS AND CAMPING

The majority of accommodations are rather expensive B&Bs. Most travelers make the area a daytrip from Adelaide, Port Elliot, or Victor Harbor.

**Southern Vales Bed and Breakfast,** 13 Chalk Hill Rd. (☎08 8323 8144; www.southern-vales.net), off the main street after the visitors center. Owner Allan provides 3 pleasant ensuite rooms with queen-size beds and 1 twin room with hall bath. Beautiful veranda overlooks the B&B's vineyards, and the wine produced from these grapes is available to guests. A/C and fireplace. Rooms $130. Ask about the *Let's Go* discount. MC/V. ❺

**McLaren Vale Lakeside Caravan Park,** Field St. (☎08 8323 9255). Turn north onto Field St. from Main Rd. Conveniently located for winery tours. Tennis, volleyball, and a pool. Reception daily 8:30am-6:30pm. Sites $21, powered $25-31; 2-person ensuite park vans $50; 2-person cabins $80-100. ❷

**Beach Woods Eco Tourist Park,** 2 Tuit Rd. (☎08 8556 6113; www.beachwoods.com.au), on Aldinga Beach. 15min. away from McLaren Vale and only a 5min. walk from the beach and the Aldinga Conservation Park. Has a volleyball court and a swimming pool. Internet access $3 per 30min. Reception M-W and F-Sa 8am-7pm, Th 8am-5pm. Sites $18, powered $25. Extremely basic budget single $25; 2-4 person studio cabin $60; 5-7 person ensuite cabins $80-100. MC/V. ❷

**Linear Way,** 41 Caffrey St. (☎08 8323 7328; www.thelinearway.com.au), just off Main Rd. Maureen and Thomas set you up quite comfortably in 1 of their 2 ensuite bedrooms, both with A/C, TV, and guilty pleasures (port and chocolates). Afternoon Devonshire tea included. Peaceful outside sitting area. Rooms $130. ❺

## FOOD

In McLaren Vale, the question isn't what wine goes with the food, but what food goes with the wine. A host of gourmet restaurants have menus designed to showcase the area wines. While most charge a hefty price, there are a few bargains in the area. Alternatively, beat the gourmet chefs at their own game at the **Coles** supermarket in the Central Shopping Center on Main Rd. (Open M-F 6am-9pm, Sa 6am-5pm, Su 11am-5pm.)

**Blessed Cheese,** 150 Main St. (☎08 8323 7958; www.blessedcheese.com.au). A trendy little shop that makes delicious pastries and sandwiches, milk shakes, and organic-egg omelettes. Cheese-making (and blessing?) classes are held most weekends. Classes 10am-5pm, $130 with lunch and wine tasting; book ahead. Breakfast ($6-10) served until noon. Open daily 8am-5:30pm. MC/V. ❶

**Carriage Cafe and Wine Bar** (☎08 8333 7689), on Main St. next to The Almond and Olive Train. Uniquely situated in a converted railway car. Selection of 40 premium local wines and 45 milkshake flavors. Breakfast all day. Lunch under $12.50; dinner $20-24. Open M, W-Th, Su 10:30am-7pm, F-Sa 10:30am-late. ❷

**Awganix Brasserie** (☎08 8323 8599; www.awganix.com.au), on the corner of Main St. and Chalk Hill Rd. Award-winning, elegant restaurant with delicious organic meals

SOUTH AUSTRALIA

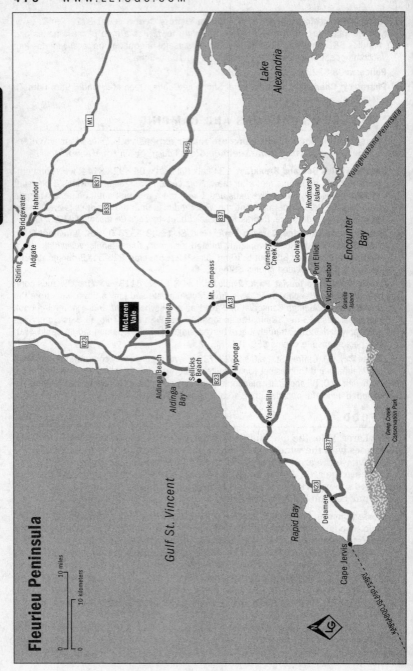

**Fleurieu Peninsula**

10 miles

10 kilometers

Gulf St. Vincent

Lake Alexandria

Younghusband Peninsula

Encounter Bay

Stirling
Bridgewater
Hahndorf
Aldgate

M1
B45
B37
B33
B37

Mt. Compass
A13

McLaren Vale
Willunga
B23

Currency Creek
Goolwa
Port Elliot
Victor Harbor
Granite Island

Hindmarsh Island

Aldinga Beach
Aldinga Bay
Sellicks Beach
B23
Myponga

Yankalilla

Deep Creek Conservation Park

Rapid Bay

B37

B23
Delamere

Cape Jervis

KANGAROO ISLAND FERRY

N  LG

at reasonable-ish prices (lunch $7.50-17; dinner $26-32). Regional wine suggestions with every meal. Open daily 10am-late. ❹

## WINERIES

McLaren Vale is the best-known wine area in South Australia after the Barossa Valley. There are over 50 wineries that offer free cellar-door tastings and sales. The cellars listed below are among the best in the region. Most of the larger vineyards operate cellar doors daily from 10am to 4:30 or 5pm, while smaller, family-run vineyards will open cellar doors only on weekends. The visitors center has maps and a complete list of hours for all vineyards.

**WINE ON A DIME. Blessed Cheese** (p. 477) offers a **Cheese & Wine Picnic Adventure.** For $55, get a picnic hamper for two, full of handcrafted cheeses that complements local wines. You also get a complimentary $20-25 bottle of wine from any featured cellar door as well as a $20 voucher, good at featured cellar doors, restaurants, and local food producers in McLaren Vale.

**Hugh Hamilton Wines** (☎08 8323 8689; www.hughhamiltonwines.com.au), on McMurtrie Rd. The 360° glass tasting area looks out on the Mt. Lofty ranges. The Mongrel is a delicious blend of 3 grapes, and the Jekyll & Hyde is their flagship Shiraz/Viognet. On Hugh's Oister Day, the 1st Su of each month Apr.-Nov., the man himself shucks huge oysters to complement the wines. Open M-F 10am-5:30pm, Sa-Su 11am-5:30pm.

**Kangarilla Road Wines,** on Kangarilla Rd. (☎08 8383 0533; www.kangarillaroad.com.au). A simple cellar door with some of the region's best wine values. The Viognet, a crisp and unique white, is unforgettable. Open M-F 9am-5pm, Sa-Su 11am-5pm.

**Primo Estate** (☎08 8323 6800; www.primoestate.com.au), on McMurtrie Rd. next to Hugh Hamilton Wines. The newest cellar door in McLaren Vale, Primo Estate is like a modern zen garden in the middle of beautiful vineyards. Their most outstanding wines are La Biondina (Colombard Sauvignon Blanc; $15 per bottle) and Moda (Cabernet Merlot; $55 per bottle). Open daily 11am-4pm.

**Hoffmann's** (☎08 8383 0232), on Ingoldby Rd. in McLaren Flat. Follow signs from Kangarilla Rd. A visit to this small, personal winery feels like sharing a glass in the home of a friend rather than tasting in a commercial venue. Guests are invited to lunch in the charming courtyard enclosed by grape arbors, and the vineyard almost comes through the front door of the tasteful cellar. Open daily 11am-5pm.

## BEACHES

Just a few kilometers west of McLaren Vale, the beaches near Aldinga are among the finest you'll find on the Fleurieu. A beautiful, popular stretch of beaches line **Aldinga Bay,** yet no beach in the area has waves bigger than a ripple, so surfers will have to be content with sunbathing. From the south, the first cluster includes **Sellick's Beach, Silver Sands Beach,** and **Aldinga Beach.** There is car access at each. The road to Port Willunga is farther north at the intersection of Commercial and Aldinga Rd. If you've forgotten your bathing suit, you're still covered, if only metaphorically: **Maslin Beach** has South Australia's oldest nudist colony (though hopefully not its oldest nudists).

# VICTOR HARBOR                              ☎08

Sheltered from the Southern Ocean by the sands of Encounter Bay, touristy Victor Harbor (pop. 11,500) was once used as the summer residence of South

Australia's colonial governors. Today, Victor's calm waves and its colony of fairy penguins on Granite Island draw most of the crowds. Victor embodies the peninsula's spirit of relaxed, oceanside living with its beautiful views, great food, and quality budget accommodations.

**TRANSPORTATION.** Premier Stateliner **buses** (☎08 8415 5555) run from Adelaide to Victor Harbor (1-2hr.; M-F 4 per day, Sa 2 per day, Su 1 per day; $18) and then Port Elliot, Middleton, and Goolwa. Purchase tickets on board. To get to Kangaroo Island from Victor Harbor, book at **Top Choice Travel/SeaLink,** which arranges SeaLink **coach services** to Cape Jervis and **ferry** tickets to the island. (Top Choice ☎08 8552 7000, SeaLink 13 13 01. SeaLink coach M-Tu, Th-F, Su at 7:25am to Cape Jervis $17, ages 3-14 $9. For ferry prices, see Kangaroo Island, p. 481. Open daily 9am-5pm.) Other services include **taxis** (☎08 13 10 08 or 08 8552 2622) and **RAA,** 66 Ocean Rd. (☎13 11 11 or 08 8552 1033).

**ORIENTATION AND PRACTICAL INFORMATION.** Victor Harbor is 85km down the Main South Rd. from Adelaide. The main commercial drag, one-way **Ocean Street,** runs parallel to the coast, becoming **Hindmarsh Road** at the intersection with Torrens St. Running along the ocean beneath massive fir trees, **Flinders Promenade** is parallel to Ocean St. The main street on the western side of the city is **Victoria St.,** which leads to the highway toward Cape Jervis. The helpful **Victor Harbor Information Centre,** near the causeway to Granite Island, is at the foot of Flinders Parade and has a map of town with shops and services on the back. (☎08 8551 0777; www.victor.sa.gov.au. Open daily 9am-5pm.) **Top Choice Travel,** in the same building, books horse-drawn tram rides, penguin tours, and **SeaLink** transport services to Kangaroo Island. (☎08 8552 7000. Open daily 9am-5pm.) Other services include: **ATMs** on Ocean St.; the **library,** 10 Coral St., just off Ocean St., with free **Internet** (☎08 8552 3009; open Tu-Th 10:30am-5:30pm, F 10am-6pm, Sa 10am-1pm); **police** (☎08 8552 2088) on George Main Rd.; and the **post office,** 54 Ocean St. (open M-F 9am-5pm). **Postal Code:** 5211.

**ACCOMMODATIONS AND FOOD. The Anchorage ❸,** 21 Flinders Pde., on the corner of Coral St., offers waterfront lodging at budget prices, along with a restaurant (lunch specials $7.50-12.50, entrees $12.50-17; 10% discount for guests) and funky, ship-shaped cafe/bar. (☎08 8552 5970; www.anchorageseafronthotel.com. Continental breakfast included. Singles $40; doubles $65-85; triples $70-105; 4- to 6-bed family rooms $100-150. Cafe open daily 8am-8:30pm. MC/V.) The 100-year-old **Grosvenor Junction Hotel ❸,** 40 Ocean St., has pleasant rooms and a balcony with a great view. Guests can request a second-floor room with balcony access. (☎08 8552 1011; www.grosvenorvictor.com.au. Lounge with TV, fridge, tea, and coffee. Shared baths but ensuite sinks. Continental breakfast included. 2- to 4-bed dorms $30; singles $35; doubles $60. MC/V.) **Victor Harbor Beach Front Caravan Park ❷,** 114 Victoria St., has beautiful sea views on the west side of the city, and all campsites are powered. (☎08 8552 1111. Reception daily 8:30am-7pm. Book ahead for cabins in summer. Sites for 2 $25-30; beachfront or ensuite sites $30-35. 2-4 person cabins $60-83.)

For fish and chips (up to $13) and cheap burgers ($5.50-9), **The Original Victor Harbor Fish Shop ❷,** 20 Ocean St., is the real deal. (☎08 8552 1273. Open M-Th and Su 10:30am-8pm, F-Sa 10:30am-8:30pm.) On the Esplanade, **Red Orchid Noodle Bar ❷,** No. 2-3, serves up modern Thai fare at great prices. (☎08 8552 8488. Lunch special M-F from $7. Open M-F and Su 11:30am-2:30pm and 5pm-late, Sa 5pm-late. MC/V.) A **Woolworths** supermarket is in Victor Central Mall, at the intersection of Torrens and Coral St. (Open daily 7am-10pm.)

◙ **SIGHTS.** **Granite Island** is the main attraction in Victor Harbor, and its 2000 fairy penguins take center stage. Access to the north shore of the island and the penguins that live there is limited to those on the **Granite Island Nature Park Guided Penguin Tours** at dusk. (☎08 8552 7555. Booking required. Purchase tickets through **Top Choice Travel**, p. 480. $12.50, concessions $11, children $7.50, families $36. Tours begin at dusk, so times vary seasonally.) The **Penguin Centre** is a rehabilitation clinic for rescued penguins where you can see the little waddlers get hand-fed and cared for. (Feeding times Jan.-Feb. W-Su 1, 2:30pm; Mar.-Dec. Sa-Su 1, 2:30pm. $6, children $4.)

⚲ **OUTDOOR ACTIVITIES.** From Victor Harbor, the **Encounter Bikeway trail** runs to the towns of Port Elliot, Middleton, and Goolwa. Rent a bike at **Victor Harbor Cycle and Skate,** 73 Victoria St. (☎08 8552 1417. $5 per hr., min. $10; 1st day $45, 2nd day $5, $20 per day thereafter. Open M-F 9am-5:30pm, Sa 9am-noon.) For an action-packed day, contact **Rock Solid Adventure,** which conducts rappelling and rock climbing out of Victor. (☎08 8270 4211; www.rock-solid-adventure. com. ½- and full-day adventures from $69.) Get your feet wet and learn to surf with **Surf Culture Australia.** While Victor doesn't get good waves and the rip tides at Middleton aren't suitable for beginners, nearby Goolwa (10min. drive from Victor) is perfect for all levels. (☎08 8327 2802 or 04 2779 6845; www.surfcultureaustralia.com. All equipment provided. Booking required. 2hr. class $40, 4-class series $120, 8-class series $160. Classes daily 10am, 1pm.) Jumping out of an airplane might be a stress-free way for you to take in the landscape. It might also be a stressful one. There's only one way to find out. Look into skydiving with **Skydive Goolwa.** (☎1800 813 557; www.skydivethecoast.com.au.)

## CAPE JERVIS ☎08

Cape Jervis serves as the jumping-off point for the Kangaroo Island ferry. Those who stay the night may be surprised by the quality of the **Cape Jervis Station ❷**, where options range from excellent cottage and homestead rooms ($120-160) to the backpacker digs in the Shearers' Quarters. The SeaLink bus picks up and drops off at the gate, and those who stay for two nights or more are entitled to free rides. (☎08 8598 0278 or 1800 805 288; www.capejervisstation.com.au. Sites $20, powered $25. Dorms $25; cabins $90.) The rest of the town consists of the pub/gas station/general store complex between the Station and the ferry. There is a **SeaLink** office at the ferry dock. SeaLink offers connecting **bus** service between Adelaide's central bus station and the Cape Jervis ferry dock (1hr.; daily 6:45am, 3:45pm; round-trip $40, ages 3-14 $20; book ahead) as well as service from Goolwa (1hr.; 6:50am; round-trip $34, ages 3-14 $18) and Victor Harbor to Cape Jervis (1hr.; 7:25am; $34/18). Book ferries well in advance (☎13 13 01). For more ferry information and prices, see **Kangaroo Island** (p. 481).

# KANGAROO ISLAND ☎08

If ever an island was well named, it is Kangaroo Island (locally known as KI; pop. 4500). One of the most spectacular destinations in Australia, Kangaroo Island has everything a nature lover could want in 4350 sq. km. With 21 national and local conservation parks on the island, you are sure to see kangaroos and koalas, snakes and seals, penguins and pelicans, and everything in between. KI has been isolated from the mainland for several long periods over the last 50 million years, giving its wildlife the chance to evolve on its own. You'll find species on KI that you won't find anywhere else in the world. The hikes through astounding landscapes showcase the wildlife as well as impressive

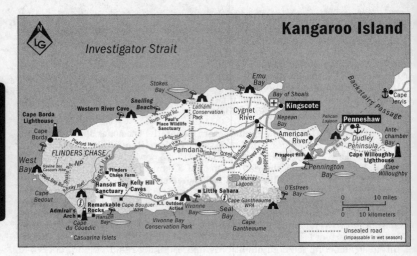

rock formations, limestone caves, and rugged sea cliffs. From lazing on near-deserted beaches to action-packed cave crawling, diving with leafy sea dragons to duneboarding and surfing, KI is a getaway that can't be surpassed. Budget travelers be forewarned: getting here is an expensive proposition, and there is no public transportation. While a car is the best way to see the island, many of the two- to three-day tours catch the highlights at reasonable prices.

## ✈ INTERCITY TRANSPORTATION

**Flights: Kingscote Airport (KGC),** 13km from the town of Kingscote at Cygnet River. The shuttle (☎04 2788 7575; $25) that runs to downtown Kingscote must be pre-booked. 4-5 arrivals per day from Adelaide on 2 airlines: **Air South** (☎1300 247 768; www.airsouth.com.au) and **Regional Express** (☎08 13 17 13; www.regionalexpress.com.au), which occasionally has good deals during the fall and winter.

**Ferries: Kangaroo Island SeaLink** (☎08 13 13 01; www.sealink.com.au), with offices in Victor Harbor and at the Cape Jervis ferry dock. Has a monopoly on ferry transport to Cape Jervis and KI, so prices are steep and discounts are hard to come by. Book very far in advance, especially during school holidays. Ferries (1hr.; 3-8 per day 8:30am-7:30pm; round-trip $80, ages 3-14 $44) cross the Backstairs Passage between Cape Jervis and Penneshaw. $2 discount each way with online booking. Fares with car (from $162) vary by size (the car's, not yours). Departures depend on sea conditions.

## ▦ ORIENTATION

KI is Australia's third-largest island (after Tasmania and Melville Island, Northern Territory). The ferry lands in **Penneshaw** (pop. 250), on the north coast of Dudley Peninsula. **North Terrace** in Penneshaw has a **petrol station, pub,** and a few small restaurants. **Hog Bay Road** heads southwest out of town to the narrow strip of land connecting the peninsula to the mainland before curving northwest toward American River and Kingscote. **Kingscote** (pop. 1800), KI's largest town, is about a 45min. drive from the ferry port. There, **Chapman St.** runs along the water, while most of the shops and services are on **Dauncey St.,** a parallel road one block away. **Playford Highway** heads west from Kingscote through the middle of the island, passing Parndana before ending at Cape Borda on the island's northwestern tip. **South Coast Road** diverges from the Playford Hwy. 15km west of Kingscote and swings through most of the attractions on the south coast, leading to the main entrance of **Flinders Chase National Park,** which spans most of KI's west end. The **West End Highway** runs north-south through Flinders Chase and connects South Coast Rd. to the Playford Hwy. All the main roads are sealed, but access roads to many sights along the way are unsealed. The very scenic but unsealed **North Coast Road** is accessible via the Playford Hwy. and leads to the north coast's tranquil beaches.

# ▐ LOCAL TRANSPORTATION

There is no taxi service on the island, but a lot of visitors still take to the roads. Most of the tourist thoroughfares are paved, and unsealed roads leading to major sights are generally in good condition. However, most rental companies do not insure vehicles on unsealed roads, so check ahead before bringing a car over on the ferry. A 4WD provides maximum flexibility. Rental companies on the island offer free shuttles to the airport in Kingscote and a ferry pickup option. Be sure to plan carefully when renting on the island, as most companies have limited kilometers and the island is larger than most visitors anticipate.

**Public Transportation:** Limited SeaLink **coach service** runs from the Penneshaw ferry terminal to **Kingscote** (1hr.; $14, children $7) via **American River** (30min., $11/5.50).

**Car Rental: Budget,** 51A Dauncey St. (☎08 8553 3133), in Kingscote. Arranges pickup anywhere on the island except American River. Ages 21 and up. **Hertz** KI (☎08 8553 2390 or 1800 088 296), on the corner of Franklin St. and Telegraph Rd. in Kingscote. Car pickup from the ferry by arrangement.

**Roadside Assistance: RAA** (☎08 13 11 11).

**MAKE WAY FOR THE 'ROOS.** Wildlife is plentiful in KI, and kangaroos, wallabies, and goats often dart across the road. Avoid driving at dusk and dawn when kangaroos are most active. If you find yourself within inches of a 'roo, go against your gut and avoid swerving out of the way. Swerving on unsealed roads can easily send the car into full roll. In case this dreadful scenario proves true, purchasing windshield insurance before you hit the road is an excellent idea.

# ▟ PRACTICAL INFORMATION

Penneshaw and Kingscote, KI's largest towns, lie on the northeastern coast of the island. Most of the south, west, and north ends of the island are relatively unpopulated and do not have basic services like hospitals, ATMs, and supermarkets (except for Parndana and Vivonne Bay). Before you venture away from the island's east end, make sure you've stocked up on cash, food, toiletries, and anything else you might need from the civilized world.

**Tourist Offices: KI Gateway Visitors Information Centre** (☎08 8553 1185), on Howard Dr. in Penneshaw. A 7min. walk from the port. After-hours board outside the office has maps and information. Open M-F 9am-5pm, Sa-Su 10am-4pm. **Kingscote Gift Shop,** 78 Dauncey St. (☎08 8553 2165), at the corner of Dauncey and Commercial

St. Open M-F 9am-5:30pm, Sa-Su 9am-5pm. **Flinders Chase National Park Visitors Center** (☎08 8559 7235), on South Coast Rd. Provides maps for the national park's drives and walks and sells day passes and camping permits. Park entry $8, concessions $6.50, children $4.50, families $21. Open daily 9am-5pm.

**Tours:** Most tours are led by friendly, knowledgeable guides and make sure to hit all the "must-see" sights. The majority are based out of Adelaide, and it's advisable to make arrangements before you even leave the mainland. However, the **YHA** in Penneshaw advertises last-minute or standby-option tours at a discount.

**Surf and Sun** (☎1800 786 386 or 0400 881 565; www.surfandsun.com.au) boasts 2- and 3-day 4WD wildlife tours, including sandboarding at Little Sahara, guided tours of Seal Bay, fishing, penguin tours, and beach time. The 3-day tour includes a surf lesson at Fleurieu Peninsula's Middleton Beach before heading to KI. 2-day $340, 3-day $399. Includes pickup from Adelaide, ferry, meals, accommodations, and park entrances. 13-person max.

**CampWild Adventures** (☎1800 444 321; www.campwild.com.au) offers 2- and 3-day RV adventure tours, including sandboarding at Little Sahara, snorkeling at Vivonne Bay, visits to Remarkable Rocks, and hiking in Flinders Chase. 3-day tour includes stops in the Fleurieu Peninsula. 2-day ($335) departs odd dates 6am; 3-day ($415) departs even dates 10am. Both include pickup in Adelaide, ferry, meals, accommodations, and park entrance. 13-person max.

**SeaLink KI Adventure Tours** (☎08 13 13 01; www.sealink.com.au/tours_backpacker) whisks you away on 2-day backpacker tours. The **Adventure Tour** hits all the major sights with fishing and surfing, while the **Beach Wilderness Tour** hits fewer sights with a more relaxed pace and tanning time. Adventure Tour ($379) departs Adelaide Dec.-Mar. daily 6:45am; Apr. and Nov. M, W-Th, Sa 6:45am; May-Oct. M, Th, Sa 6:45am. Beach Wilderness Tour ($257) departs Adelaide daily 3:45pm. Includes pickup from Adelaide, ferry, meals, and accommodations. 23-person max.

---

**TIP**    **YOUR ONE-STOP SHOP.** Great for those who plan to visit KI several times in one year, the **KI Tour Pass** allows unlimited access to Seal Bay, Kelly Hill Caves, Flinders Chase National Park, and the Cape Borda and Cape Willoughby lighthouse tours. However, do your entry fee calculations before purchasing the pass if you're planning on visiting KI just once—if you skip just one site, you will lose money. (Valid for 1 year. Available at park entrances. $46.50, concessions $36.50, children $28, family $126. Pass excludes Seal Bay's pre-sunset tour and Kelly Hill Caves adventure caving.)

---

**Library: Kingscote Library,** 41 Dauncey St. (☎08 8553 4516). Free Internet. Open M-W and F 9am-5pm, Th 9am-7pm, Sa 9am-noon.

**Police:** ☎13 14 44 or 08 8553 2018. At Dauncy and Drew St. in Kingscote.

**Pharmacy:** At the corner of Dauncey and Murray St. (☎08 8553 2153). Open M-F 8:30am-5:30pm, Sa 9am-noon.

**Medical Services:** The island's only **hospital** (☎08 8553 4200) is located in Kingscote, nestled into the town's Esplanade.

**Internet Access: Kingscote Library** (see Library). **Community Business Center,** in Penneshaw's Dudley Center, on the way to the KI Gateway Visitors Information Centre from the port. $3.50 per 30min.

**Post Office:** Penneshaw, in the Dudley Center. Open M-F 9am-5pm, Sa 9am-noon. Kingscote (☎08 8553 2122), on Dauncey St. Open M-F 9am-5pm. **Postal Codes:** 5222 (Penneshaw); 5223 (Kingscote).

#  ACCOMMODATIONS AND CAMPING

There are **campsites ❶** at **Western River Cove** ($3 per person or $5 per car, including passengers; pay at site) and **Stokes Bay** ($10; book through cafe).

## PENNESHAW

**Kangaroo Island YHA,** 33 Middle Terr. (☎08 8553 1344). 6-bed dorms with ensuite bath. Bikes $25 per day. Reception daily 9am-1pm and 5:45-7:45pm. Male-only and female-only dorms $28.50, YHA $25.50; doubles $75/67.50; ensuite $100/90. ❷

## KINGSCOTE

**KI Seaview Motel** (☎08 8553 2030; www.seaview.net.au), on Drew St. between Dauncey St. and Chapman Terr. Includes a guesthouse with rooms that share a bathroom and are cheaper than those in the main motel. Ask for a sea view. Continental breakfast included with motel. Reception 8am-8:30pm. Guesthouse singles $72; twins and doubles $82. Extra person $15. Motel singles $132; doubles $142. MC/V. ❺

**KI Central Backpackers,** 19 Murray St. (☎08 8553 2787). Cheapest digs in Kingscote. A little worn, but nothing out of the ordinary for a hostel. Dorms $22; doubles $55. ❷

## SOUTH COAST

**Hanson Bay Backpacker Accommodation** (☎08 8559 7344 or 04 2739 7344; www.hansonbay.com.au), conveniently located in the middle of the Hanson Bay Sanctuary. Easy access to Flinders Chase, Kelly Hill, and other sights along the south coast. Communal bath and kitchen. Linen included. Singles $30; doubles $60. ❸

> **TIP** **THEY'VE GOT THE GOODS.** Booking accommodations through SeaLink will actually save you your hard-earned dollars, as they have discounts on ferry-plus-accommodation bookings and can get you beds cheaper than booking directly with most KI hostels.

## FLINDERS CHASE NATIONAL PARK

Book ahead for Flinders Chase's four main **camping sites** ❶, all non-powered and with toilet facilities. Permits are available for all sites at Rocky River visitors center. As of winter 2008, only **Harveys Return,** on the north coast, was open after a devastating fire. When they reopen, **West Bay,** 20km west of Rocky River and 200m from the beach, and **Snake Lagoon** will join Harveys Return as the park's cheapest accommodations. However, caravans and campervans probably shouldn't tackle the unsealed roads that access them. ($5 per person, $10 per car, or $6 per motorcycle.) The fourth site, **Rocky River,** near the visitors center, also closed after the fire, offers convenience and the only showers in the park. Availability is posted outside the **visitors center;** call to check whether other sites have re-opened. ($6 per person, $21 per car, or $13 per motorcycle.)

**Flinders Chase Farm** (☎08 8559 7223 or 04 2772 2778), 15min. north of the park entrance on the West End Hwy. On a serene and secluded 800-hectare sheep and cattle farm. Wonderful owners offer self-contained cabins and spotless dorms with full kitchen, BBQ, and bathrooms. The perfect place to stargaze. Dorms $25; 2-person cabins $60; ensuite singles and doubles $100. Cash only. ❷

**Western KI Caravan Park** (☎08 8559 7201; www.westernki.com.au), 4km east of the Flinders Chase entrance on the South Coast Rd. Boasts a free koala walk. Campsites $20, powered $25. 2-person cabins ($110-140) can sleep up to 7. $20 per extra person. $20 more for single-night booking. MC/V. ❷

**KI Wilderness Retreat** (☎08 8559 7275; www.kiwr.com), on South Coast Rd. just before the entrance to Flinders Chase. Huge area with walking trails to be shared with the local wildlife. Luxury suites as well as more budget-friendly Eco Lodge rooms. Petrol available to guests and non-guests. Free Internet and Wi-Fi (guest use only). 2-person Eco Lodge rooms $150, with 3 people $180; luxury suites $215-420. MC/V. ❺

**Heritage Accommodation** (☎08 8559 7235), spread throughout the park. Rustic cabins at Flinders Chase's 3 lighthouse stations; pick up a pamphlet at any local visitors center for a listing. Linen $16.50 per person at Woodward Hut and Postmans Cottage; included elsewhere. Woodward Hut $18 per person, $8.50 per child. Postmans Cottage $24 per person, $8.50 per child. Other cabins $100-150 for 2 people. Extra person $23, extra child $15. Book well ahead. ❷

 **WE DIDN'T START THE FIRE.** South Australia is the driest state in the driest continent in the world, and KI is no exception. Much of the island's bush was torched by a massive fire in the summer of 2008. Be extremely careful with cigarette butts or other flammable objects, especially when camping. Only gas fires in the provided pits are allowed on the island, and no fires of any kind are allowed on **Total Fire Ban Days,** which are broadcast on local radio 891 ABC and 765 5CC as well as the hotline ☎1300 362 361.

# ◨ FOOD

## PENNESHAW

The **IGA** supermarket, on Middle Terr. across the street from the post office, sells groceries and toiletries. (Open daily 8am-8pm.)

**Penguin Stop Cafe** (☎08 8553 1211), on the corner of Nat Thomas St. and Middle Terr. Cooks up delicious food using fresh ingredients and meat from a local farm. Sandwiches $5.50-9. Open Aug.-May M-F 8:30am-5:30pm, Sa-Su 9am-5pm. Cash only. ❶

## KINGSCOTE

A **Foodland** supermarket is on the corner of Commercial and Osmond St. (Open M-W and F 8am-7pm, Th 8am-8pm, Sa 8am-5pm, Su 10am-4pm.)

**Roger's Deli and Cafe,** 76 Dauncey St. (☎08 8553 2053). An inexpensive selection of cafe fare including sandwiches, burgers, salads, and pies (from $7), as well as more formal mains ($15-16). Open M-F 8am-6pm, Sa 9am-5pm, Su 9am-4pm. MC/V. ❶

**Ozone Hotel** (☎08 8553 2011; www.ozonehotel.com), on the corner of Chapman Terr. and Commercial St. There are no holes in the impeccable service of this hotel restaurant. Fresh, local seafood from $14.50 with a beautiful view of the bay thrown in for free. Also holds free wine tastings; inquire at the bar for times. Open daily noon-2pm and 6-8:30pm. Bar open daily 11am-midnight. MC/V. ❷

## SOUTH COAST

Vivonne Bay has a good place on the island to fill up on fuel, supplies, and good tucker in the **Vivonne Bay General Store.** The whiting burger ($10.50) is famous among locals. (☎08 8559 4285. Open daily 7:30am-7pm.)

 **STOCK UP.** The west end of the island has no supermarkets and few restaurants, so pack any food you'll need before venturing westward.

## NORTH COAST

**Rockpool Cafe** (☎08 8559 2277), overlooking Stokes Bay. A fine kettle of fish and chips ($13). Also sells fishing bait. Open Sept.-May daily 11am-6pm. ❷

# 👁 ⚠ SIGHTS AND OUTDOOR ACTIVITIES

## PENNESHAW AND THE DUDLEY PENINSULA

**PENGUIN CENTRE.** Though Penneshaw also operates as the gateway to KI from the mainland, its fairy penguins attract their own visitors. The best time to see the penguins is from June to late December, during breeding season, when they spend more time on land. Each night after sunset, the little waddlers venture from the sea to their burrows along the coastline, their stomachs full from the day's catch. Though access to the boardwalk is free during the daytime, you must pay for a guided or self-guided tour to see the nightly sea-to-burrow voyage. *(Just east of the ferry dock, off Middle Terr. ☎ 08 8553 1103. Tours daily in summer 8:30, 9:30pm; in winter 7:30, 8:30pm. Guided tour $10, concessions $8.50; self-guided tour $8/7; includes admission to Penguin Centre, which opens at 8pm.)*

**PENNINGTON BAY.** Nestled in Pennington is an easily accessible beach with great beginner surf and soft sand. Swimmers, however, should beware of its notorious rip tides. Just next to the bay, **Prospect Hill's** 512 steps lead to a 360° view of the east end of the island, including American River, Pelican Lagoon, the Southern Ocean, Pennington Bay, and, on a clear day, Adelaide's Mt. Lofty. *(On the road to Kingscote, 32km out of town, on the south coast near KI's narrowest point.)*

**CAPE WILLOUGHBY.** On the eastern tip of the Dudley Peninsula and KI, the dramatic Cape Willoughby sees fewer visitors than the rest of the island. Explore the isolated and rugged **Cape Willoughby Conservation Park** to enjoy spectacular views across the **Backstairs Passage.** In 1852, the cape became the site of South Australia's first lighthouse, which now keeps daily guided tours from running aground. *(☎08 8553 1191. 45min. tours in summer and holidays 11:30am, 12:30, 2, 3, 4pm; in winter 11:30am, 12:30, 2pm. $12, concessions $9.50, children $7.50, families $33.)*

## KINGSCOTE

Kingscote has a variety of activities for the sea-loving traveler, from watching the island's famous fairy penguins to swimming among dolphins. Fishing and diving expeditions are also available from local tour companies.

**ISLAND BEEHIVE.** Since 1885, KI has been a Ligurian bee sanctuary, and, with its strict quarantine and importation laws, KI is proud to have the last remaining pure strain of Ligurian bees in the world. Honey pilgrims can taste free honey samples, take a guided tour, and peer into the glass beehive. No visit would bee complete without browsing the hundreds of bee products, including beeswax candles, honey ice cream, and honey-based body lotions. *(On the corner of Playford Hwy. and Acacia Dr. about 5min. from Kingscote. Give them a buzz at ☎08 8553 0080; www.island-beehive.com.au. Open daily 9am-5pm. Guided tours every 30min.)*

**KI MARINE CENTRE.** The wharf's Marine Centre is home to leafy sea dragons and cuttlefish. Guided tours begin at the center with a fish-feeding and aquarium tour and then head to the jetty to observe fairy penguins getting ready for bed. Don't miss the pelican feeding at 5pm, when members of the world's largest pelican species get up close and personal for their supper. *(☎08 8553 3112.*

*Penguin tours in summer 8:30, 9:30pm; in winter 7:30, 8:30pm. Building opens 30min. before 1st tour. $14, concessions $12, children $6, families $34. Pelican feedings daily 5pm; $2.)*

## SOUTH COAST

Many of KI's most traversed sights line the south coast and are accessible via the paved South Coast Rd., which heads to Flinders Chase from Cygnet River. The south coast has the island's best surfing, sandboarding, and kayaking.

**SURFIN' KI.** KI provides ample opportunities to hit the surf, but be aware that its waters host both rip tides and Great Whites. Visit the **KI Gateway Visitor Information Centre** in Penneshaw for the free **Surfing Guide** pamphlet, which details the breaks along the south coast at Hanson Bay, Vivonne Bay, and D'Estrees Bay as well as Pennington Bay on the east end and Stokes Bay on the north coast. The most convenient of these are Vivonne and Pennington Bays, both accessible via good roads and suitable for all levels. Hanson and D'Estrees are for advanced surfers, and Stokes only operates when there's a large swell. The water is cool year-round, so bring your wetsuit.

**SEAL BAY.** One of the most popular stops on the island, Seal Bay's excellent views would probably draw visitors even without the seals—a good thing, too, since the sand here is actually home to a large colony of Australian sea lions. With a total world population of only 12,000, the majority of these creatures live off the coast of South Australia. The conservation park's guided tour along the beach brings you within 10m of the sea lions for a chance to learn more about the rare species. From the boardwalk down to the beach, the skeleton of a humpback whale can be seen. *(To reach Seal Bay, take Seal Bay Rd. south from South Coast Rd. for 12km. ☎08 8559 4207; www.parks.sa.gov.au/sealbay. Guided tour $140, concessions $11, children $8.50, families $38. Self-guided boardwalk tour without beach access $10/8/6/27. Tours daily every 45min. 9am-5pm, last tour 4:15pm; summer holiday 9am-6pm. 1hr. pre-sunset tour on school holidays $32/25.50/19/86.50; 4-person min. Book far in advance.)*

**LITTLE SAHARA.** Just like the name suggests, this beach is a small-scale version of the Sahara. An Australian geological monument, the chain of sand dunes rises seemingly out of nowhere. The dunes are understandably popular with sandboarders, and the water is perfect for beginner surfers in need of balance training. Head to **KI Outdoor Action** (see below) for sandboard and toboggan rentals. *(The poorly marked left turnoff for Little Sahara is 7km east of Vivonne Bay on South Coast Rd. If you pass Crabbs Rd., you've missed the turnoff.)*

**VIVONNE BAY.** Recently voted Australia's best beach, Vivonne Bay hides a stunning stretch of sandy strand that's ideal for picnics and surfing. Swimming at Vivonne Bay should only be attempted near the jetty or in the mouth of the Harriet River—the rest of the waters have a strong undertow. The jetty is a popular fishing spot, while the beach near the Harriet River mouth has great waves for beginners. The surf gets larger the farther west you go along the beach break. *(Just west of Seal Bay and Little Sahara on South Coast Rd. To access the beach from South Coast Rd., turn left on Jetty Rd., which also has signs pointing to Harriet River and Point Ellen. Follow Jetty Rd. for 3km, past the picnic grounds; beach access will appear suddenly on your left. Farther down the road, you will reach the fishing jetty and a beautiful lookout point.)* Nearby, **KI Outdoor Action** can fulfill your outdoor needs. Rent surfboards, sandboards, and kayaks or go on the popular ATV tour. *(On Jetty Rd. ☎04 2882 2260 or 08 8559 4296; www.kangaroo-island-au.com/outdooraction. 75min. guided ATV tours $79 per person in daytime, $89 at dusk; 1st-time riders welcome. 4hr. rentals of: single kayaks $39, double $69; surfboards $39; sandboards $29; toboggans $39.)* Driving along the south coast is one thing, but how about flying over it? For a chance to see Vivonne Bay, the **Remarkable Rocks** (see below), and all the south coast's splendor from the air, take a scenic flight. (☎ 04 2777 6561. *Departs from Vivonne Bay Airstrip on South Coast Rd. Dec.-Feb. daily; bookings required. 30min. flight $120 per person, children $110. 2-person min., 3-person max.*)

**KELLY HILL CONSERVATION PARK.** Located on South Coast Rd., the **Kelly Hill Caves** lie halfway between Vivonne Bay and the Flinders Chase visitors center. Formed from a sand dune and soft limestone 2 million years ago, the cave is visually stunning. To see its smaller, more delicate formations, take the adventure caving tour and crawl through the cave's nooks and crannies. (☎ 08 8559 7231. *Conservation Park open daily 10am-5pm. 45min. tours daily 10:30, 11:15am, 12:15, 1:15, 2:15, 3:15, 4:15pm. $12, concessions $9.50, children $7.50, families $33. 2hr. adventure tours offered 2:15pm when there is interest, but you must attend the 1:15pm regular tour. $30, concessions $24, children $18, families $81.50. Book ahead.*) In addition to the caves, a number of trails start at the caves and wind through the conservation park, including the moderately difficult **Hanson Bay Hike.** (*18km, 6hr. round-trip.*)

# FLINDERS CHASE NATIONAL PARK

Numerous short hikes and excellent 2- to 7-day coastline treks are available in Flinders Chase. Hikers should pick up the all-inclusive **Bushwalking in Kangaroo Island Parks brochure** from any visitors center.

**SAFE TREKKING.** Long-distance bush walkers must discuss their route with a park ranger and complete a **Trip Intentions form** before heading off.

**REMARKABLE ROCKS.** Precariously perched on a 75m coastal clifftop are some huge—some might say remarkable—hunks of granite. Five hundred million years of erosion by ice, lichens, water, salt, and wind have sculpted them into bizarre shapes. The hooked beak of Eagle Rock is a perfect spot to snap a picture, but be careful—it's a long fall to the crashing waves below.

**CAPE DU COUEDIC.** West of the Remarkable Rocks lies Cape du Couedic (da COO-dee), with its 100-year-old lighthouse and the stunning cave of **Admiral's Arch.** From the lighthouse, several hiking trails wind around the cape, including the **Cape de Couedic loop.** (*2km, 40min.*) The trek to **Weirs Cove** is another tourist favorite. (*3km, 50min. round-trip.*) At Admiral's Arch farther down the cape, a few thousand New Zealand fur seals can be seen lazily sunning themselves, swimming through the ocean breaks, and playfighting. Sunsets seen through the arch can be absolutely breathtaking. To capture its hidden view, follow the wooden trail from the Admiral's Arch carpark. (*15min.*)

# NORTH COAST

Accessible only by unsealed roads and bypassed by most tours, the north coast remains one of KI's finest examples of unspoiled nature, with deserted beaches around every (rocky, unsealed) bend, rolling hills, and awe-inspiring views.

**WESTERN RIVER COVE.** The drive alone is worth the trip. The road leads down to sea level before ending up at the cove, where the Western River runs out to one of the north coast's best beaches. To reach the beach, cross the river's footbridge and head toward the cliffs. Sheltered by the jagged cliffs on either side, the cove's water is crystal clear and warmer than its neighboring beaches, making it perfect for swimming. (*Follow signs for the turnoff from Playford Hwy., 8km east of its junction with the West End Hwy.*)

**PAUL'S PLACE.** Paul's hands-on wildlife experience includes the opportunity to cuddle a koala, bottle-feed baby animals, get wrapped up by a snake, or carry a 'roo. *(On Stokes Bay Rd. ☎ 08 8559 2232; holiday@wavesandwildlife.com.au. Tours 1hr. Open school holidays daily noon-3pm; otherwise Tu, Th, Sa-Su noon-1pm. Call ahead, since tours may be canceled in extreme heat or rain. $12, children $8.)*

**STOKES BAY.** Stokes is a true escape into KI's raw beauty. Pulling up to the boulder-covered beach, you might not realize that the true prize lies behind the cliff to your right. Squeeze through the narrow rock formations and caves until it opens up to the beautiful oasis. The beach has big surf swells in the right conditions. *(At the end of Stokes Bay Rd. from Playford Hwy.)*

**EMU BAY.** Visitors to this cove 14km west of Kingscote will find yet another stunning beach. Emu Bay has plenty of opportunities to interact with underwater critters; you can finally live up to that "gone fishin'" sign you put on your desk at home. Although it can be a splurge, you'll never forget the experience on an **Island Explorer Tour** with the eco-certified **KI Marine Tours.** Friendly skipper Andrew whisks you around the northern coast's rugged cliffs to a quiet cove near Emu Bay, which is home to a pod of about 20 wild dolphins. Jump in: they are just as curious about you as you are about them. *(☎ 04 2731 5286; www.kimarinetours.com. Book online. Tours daily 9am, 1pm, weather permitting. 3hr. Island Explorer Tour $165, under 14 $110. Ask about the Let's Go discount.)*

**RAVINE DES CASOARS.** Heading east away from Cape Borda is the turnoff for the Ravine des Casoars hike. The challenging walk meanders through the woods before emerging at the mouth of a river that empties onto a beach surrounded by limestone cliffs and caves. Few visitors find the time to do the hike, so you'll most likely have the whole beach to yourself. *(8km, 4hr. round-trip.)*

# CENTRAL WINE REGIONS

The center of South Australia's wine universe is 70km northeast of Adelaide in the Barossa Valley. Grapes from the Barossa region produce some of Australia's best wines, particularly Shiraz. The Clare Valley, 45min. north of Barossa, is filled with smaller wineries that specialize in Rieslings and other cool-climate whites. For the budget traveler, wine tasting is not only a free buzz, but a cultural endeavor and a chance to take in the area's scenic rolling valleys.

## BAROSSA VALLEY ☎ 08

Steeped in history and a long tradition of winemakers, the Barossa Valley is arguably Australia's most well-known wine region. Johann Gramp, a German settler, produced the first crop in 1850 on the banks of Jacob's Creek; in the century and a half since, the Barossa's output has been prolific. Most of Australia's largest wine companies are based here, along with plenty of smaller family operations. Though the vineyards are a fine sight in any season, those visiting during the vintage (from mid-February to late April or early May) will see the vines laden with fruit and taste-test the different types of grapes. Vintage is also the best time to land a picking job (see **Short-term Work,** p. 92).

### ◰ TRANSPORTATION

Renting a car in Adelaide is strongly recommended for those bent on doing a serious wine tour, as many wineries are out of the way. The Barossa Way loop from Lyndoch north through Tanunda to Nuriootpa, then west to Angaston and south to Mt. Pleasant, is a breathtaking drive through the region, passing through the main towns and the bulk of the wineries. All of the area visitor centers stock the helpful **Barossa Valley brochure** which has region maps. In addition, Barossa Valley's police are vigilant when it comes to drunk driving, and the legal blood-alcohol limit is .05%. In Australia, random breathalyzing is normal, especially in areas where drunk driving is prevalent.

**Buses: Barossa Valley Coaches** (☎08 8564 3022; www.bvcoach.com) runs to and from **Adelaide** (M-F 12:45 and 5:45pm, Sa 9am and 5:45pm, Su 5:45pm), stopping at **Angaston** ($18.90), **Nuriootpa** ($17.40), and **Tanunda** ($16.10). Departs from the main bus terminal on Franklin St. in Adelaide. No need to prebook, pay driver on bus. **Barossa Dial-a-Ride** (☎08 8564 2212) runs to each township, but will not transport you to the wineries. M-F 9am-3pm, 2hr. notice. $5 each ride.

**Taxis: Goldstar Taxi** (☎08 8562 2778). Book early as Goldstar is the sole valley taxi service, with only 4 cars. About $15 from Nuriootpa to Tanunda. 24hr. service.

**Automobile Clubs: RAA,** in Tanunda. Call ☎13 11 11 for 24hr. roadside assistance.

**Bike Rental: Tanunda Caravan and Tourist Park** (☎08 8563 2784) rents bikes to the general public $10 per hr., $18.50 per ½-day, $30 per day. **Barossa Visitors Centre** rents bikes M-F $6.50 per hr., Sa-Su $8 per hr.; $22/30 per ½-day.

**Tours:** Most Barossa tours are full-day, round-trip outings departing daily from Adelaide in small buses of about 20 people. The visitors center in Tanunda has numerous brochures on tours departing from the valley, including helicopter rides, balloon rides, and forays across the countryside via vintage car. **Groovy Grape Getaways** is the most popular backpackers tour to Barossa, visiting four wineries, the Whispering Wall, Mengler Hill lookout, and the world's largest rocking horse along the way. (☎08 8371 4000 or 1800 661 177; www.groovygrape.com.au. BBQ lunch and pickup included. Departs Adelaide daily 7:45am. $75.) **Enjoy Adelaide** tours 4 wineries, the Whispering Wall, the Big Rocking Horse, Mengler's Hill, and the Australian Opal Company. (☎08 8332 1401; www.enjoyadelaide.com.au/barossa.htm. Lunch and Adelaide pick-up included. Departs M-Th and Sa-Su 9:15am, returns 5pm. $69, children $45.)

## ◢ 🛈 ORIENTATION AND PRACTICAL INFORMATION

The Barossa Valley's main reference points are its three small towns: Tanunda, Nuriootpa, and Angaston. Most of the wineries and tiny hamlets are clustered around them. From Adelaide (75min.), take King William St. north to **Main North Rd. (A1)** and branch off to A20. The **Sturt Highway (A20)** enters the Barossa from the north at Nuriootpa. For a more scenic drive, exit earlier at Gawler, where the **Barossa Valley Way (B19)** passes through Lyndoch (pop. 1300) and Rowland Flat before entering the main town of **Tanunda** (pop. 3800), meaning "water hole," 70km northeast of Adelaide. The highway's name then changes to **Murray Street** as it continues on to **Nuriootpa** (noor-ee-OOT-pah; pop. 5000), called "Nuri" by the locals. From there, **Nuriootpa Road** leads east to **Angaston** (pop. 2000).

The **Barossa Visitors Centre,** 66-68 Murray St. in Tanunda, handles B&B bookings, provides maps, and rents bikes. (☎1300 852 982 or 08 8563 0600; www.barossa.com. Open M-F 9am-5pm, Sa-Su 10am-4pm.) The **banks** in the valley all have **ATMs.** The **Tanunda Library,** in the Barossa Council building just across Murray St. from the post office, has free **Internet access.** (79 Murray St. ☎08 8563 2729. Open M and W-F 9am-12:30pm and 1:30-5pm, Tu 9am-12:30pm and 1:30-7pm, Sa 9am-noon.) For emergency services, contact the **police** (☎08 8568 6620) on Murray St., Nuri; an **ambulance** (☎1300 811 700); or the **hospital** (☎08 8563 2398) on Mill St., Tanunda. The **post office,** in Tanunda, is near the visitors center. (67 Murray St. Open M-F 9am-5pm.) **Postal code:** 5352.

## 🏠 ACCOMMODATIONS

Lodging in Tanunda tends to be more expensive than in Nuriootpa or Angaston as there are more upscale B&Bs to choose from. That said, there are still a few reasonably priced places to stay in the valley area.

🏠 **doubles d'vine** (☎08 8562 2260; www.doublesdvine.com.au), on Nuraip Rd., Nuriootpa. Stay in either the Cottage or the Lodge and enjoy the surrounding vineyard and garden-enclosed pool. Clean rooms with a wood-burning stove in the lounge area. Free laundry. Jan, the friendly owner, is always up for a chat and offers maps and advice. Linen and towels included. Bike rentals for guests $25 per day. Lodge doubles $70, multi-night $60. Cottage double $70/80. Extra person $25. Cash only. ❷

**Tanunda Hotel**, 51 Murray St., Tanunda (☎08 8563 2030), within walking distance of many shops and restaurants, has nice rooms and a popular bar on weekends. Doubles $70, ensuite $80. Extra person $15, rooms can sleep up to 4. AmEx/MC/V. ❹

**Barossa Valley Tourist Park** (☎08 8562 1404) on Penrice Rd., Nuri. Tranquil and shady park with BBQ, lakeside picnic areas, kitchen, playground, and tennis courts. Internet access $2 per 15min., Wi-Fi $6 per hr. Wheelchair accessible. Sites $21, powered $24; standard cabins $45, ensuite cabins $54-102, $15 per extra person. MC/V.

**Tanunda Caravan and Tourist Park** (☎08 8563 2784; www.tanundacaravantouristpark. com.au), just south of Tanunda on Barossa Valley Way. BBQ, laundry, and camp kitchen. Internet $2 per 15min., Wi-Fi $10 per hr. Key deposit $20. Tour booking and bicycle rental. Wheelchair accessible. Reception 8am-7pm. Sites $21, powered sites $26; 2-person cabins $62-125, $15 per person beyond 2 people; caravans $52. MC/V. ❶

## 🍴 FOOD

Barossa has a number of cellar doors that have cafes and bistros with food to perfectly complement your wine. The tourist office provides a list of all such wineries. For those hoping to have a picnic on one of the immaculate lawns, **Angas Park Shop,** 3 Murray St., Angaston, sells snack food, including dried fruit, chocolate, and dried fruit in chocolate. (☎08 8561 0800; www.angaspark.com. au. Open M-Sa 9am-5pm, Su 10am-5pm.) If you're in town on Saturday, make sure to swing by the weekly **Farmers Market,** held in Angaston on the corner of Stockwell and Nuriootpa Rd. (Sa 7:30-11:30am). For groceries, head to **Foodland** supermarket in Tanunda (119 Murray St. Open daily 7am-8pm).

🍴 **Maggie Beer's Farm Shop** (☎08 8562 4477; www.maggiebeer.com.au), on Pheasant Farm Rd., off Samuel Rd, Nuri. You can't leave Barossa without visiting Maggie Beer's, a valley institution. Maggie started from humble beginnings; she has worked herself up from owning a small pheasant farm to hosting her own nationally-televised cooking show. Taste-test Maggie's pates, spreads, and quinces, matched perfectly to Beer Bros. Wines; once you've picked your favorite things, enjoy your picnic platter by the river. Daily cooking demonstration at 2pm. Open daily 10:30am-5pm. MC/V. ❷

🍴 **Die Barossa Wurst Haus,** 86a Murray St., Tanunda (☎08 8563 3598). If you need to practice your beginner's German, this is the place to do it. The Radzevicius family has been serving up genuine German fare for years, so get your fill of mettwurst, cheeses, and cakes. Cornish pasties and quiches from $3.50. Fresh smoothies and milkshakes $5.50. Breakfast all day. Open M-F 7am-5pm, Sa-Su 7am-4pm. ❶

**Vintner's Grill** (☎08 8564 2488), on Nuriootpa Rd. between Nuri and Angaston. Very upscale and renowned for its cuisine. Immaculate outdoor patio. Main courses $28-32. Lunches around $18. Open daily noon-2:30pm and 6:30-9pm. ❺

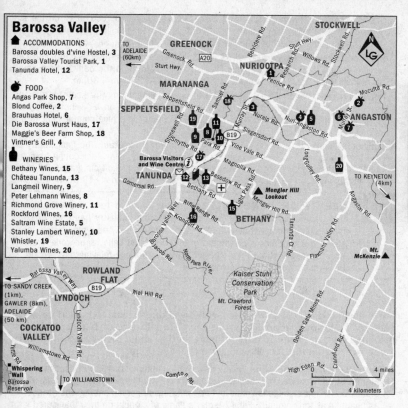

**Barossa Valley**

▲ ACCOMMODATIONS
Barossa doubles d'vine Hostel, 3
Barossa Valley Tourist Park, 1
Tanunda Hotel, 12

🍴 FOOD
Angas Park Shop, 7
Blond Coffee, 2
Brauhaus Hotel, 6
Die Barossa Wurst Haus, 17
Maggie's Beer Farm Shop, 18
Vintner's Grill, 4

🍷 WINERIES
Bethany Wines, 15
Château Tanunda, 13
Langmeil Winery, 9
Peter Lehmann Wines, 8
Richmond Grove Winery, 11
Rockford Wines, 16
Saltram Wine Estate, 5
Stanley Lambert Winery, 10
Whistler, 19
Yalumba Wines, 20

**Brauhaus Hotel,** 41 Murray St., Angaston (☎08 8564 2014). Serves one of the best pub meals in the valley. Try the homemade lasagna ($13.50) or the club sandwich ($9.50). Mains $9.50-23. Open daily noon-2:30pm and 6-8:30pm. MC/V. ❷

**Blond Coffee,** 60 Murray St., Angaston (☎08 8564 3444). Renowned among locals as the perfect breakfast spot ($2.80-8). Delicious coffee complements lunch too, like the roasted veggie panini ($8). Baguettes and sandwiches $8. Open M-F 7:30am-4:30pm, Sa-Su 8:30am-4:30pm. MC/V. ❶

## ⚡ WINERIES OF BAROSSA VALLEY

A complete tour of the 50+ wineries that offer free cellar door tastings requires effort and a Herculean ability to hold your liquor. The vintage lasts February through April and is the time to find picking jobs. (Call the visitors center for information on harvest work or the Australia-wide ☎1800 062 332). Most wineries in the valley are open daily from 10am to 4 or 5pm.

### BY FOOT

If you're worried about drunk driving, four wineries just north of Tanunda are connected by the bike- and pedestrian-friendly **Para Road Wine Path.**

**Stanley Lambert Winery** (☎08 8563 3375; www.stanleylambert.com.au), on the left side of Barossa Valley Way as you head north out of Tanunda. The first winery on the path, Lambert makes a chocolate Port. Open M-F 9:30am-5pm, Sa-Su 11am-5pm.

**Richmond Grove Winery** (☎08 8563 7303; www.richmondgrovewines.com). You can picnic among the gum trees at this Flemish-style chateau on the banks of the small Para River. Daily basket press tours $5.50. Open daily 10:30am-4:30pm.

**Peter Lehmann Wines** (☎08 8563 2100; www.peterlehmannwines.com). Lehmann showcases colorful, modern paintings that match the labels on his wines. They also have a beautiful, vine-shaded cafe, and the $20 platter is a nice complement to the wines. Open M-F 9:30am-5pm, Sa-Su 10:30am-4:30pm.

 **Langmeil Winery** (☎08 8563 2595; www.langmeilwinery.com.au). The final winery on the trail, Langmeil has a good tasting range in a historic cellar door dating from the 1840s. Try their flagship shiraz, "The Freedom," which is produced from grapes still growing on the original, 166-year-old vines planted in 1843. Open daily 10:30am-4:30pm.

**TIP** | **WEENIE OR OENOPHILE?** Don't be tempted to buy a wine just because it won an award. The efficient tourism industry has created so many competitions that virtually every winery has been recognized for some "outstanding" achievement or another. Most cellar door-workers are knowledgeable about their vineyard's wines and love relaying information. However, let your palate be your guide.

## BY CAR

For those not confined to wineries within walking distance, the options seem endless. While you're more likely to see familiar wines at the bigger producers, the small wineries offer a more intimate setting and a better chance to learn about wines from the people who actually make them.

**Château Tanunda** (☎08 8563 3888; www.chateautanunda.com), on Basedow Rd. off Murray St. in Tanunda. The largest château in the southern hemisphere, this winery blends its French architecture with its beautiful English garden setting. Their wines are as beautiful as their grounds. For $24, play a game of croquet on their manicured lawn and enjoy a cheese plate and 2 glasses of wine at the outdoor tables. This cellar door roots for the underdogs and also sells wines from the tiny, local vineyards without cellar doors: try Tin Shed. Basket press tour and barrel tastings $5. Open daily 10am-5pm.

**Yalumba Wines** (☎08 8561 3309; www.yalumba.com), on Eden Valley Rd. in Angaston. Established in 1849, Yalumba is the oldest family-owned winery in Australia. A friendly winery with beautiful grounds, Yalumba is renowned for their innovative wines, such as their new Viogniers. During the week, wander over to the cooperage to see the age-old traditional method to making wine barrels. Open daily 10am-5pm.

**Rockford Wines** (☎1800 088 818 or 08 8563 2720), on Krondorf Rd. east of Tanunda. With an emphasis on craftsmanship and quality, this small winery holds true to the tradition of winemaking. Hand-picked and basket-pressed, the grapes at Rockford boast freedom from the tainting of new-age contraptions. Enjoy their flagship Basket Press Shiraz or the superb 2007 Alicante Bouchet in the original 19th-century cottage-turned-cellar door. Tastings of local jams and spreads also offered. Open daily 11am-5pm.

**Bethany Wines** (☎08 8563 2099; www.bethany.com.au), on Bethany Rd. just east of Tanunda. Built into a former quarry overlooking the valley, this small, family-owned winery is the perfect place to relax with a view. Bethany's is the first winery to make a white port; enjoy their signature Old Quarry Fronti. At vintage time, watch as grapes are dumped into the cliff-top, gravity-fed crusher. Open M-Sa 10am-5pm, Su 1-5pm.

**Whistler** (☎08 8562 4942), on Seppeltsfield Rd. between Nuri and Tanunda. Set in a spectacular, cozy garden, this friendly, intimate winery hosts weekend picnics with the Whistler family to drink and chat about the vineyards and wine. It's a great opportunity to meet the people behind the grapes. Sa-Su picnics 12:30-1:30pm; bring your own lunch or use their BBQ and enjoy a complimentary glass of wine. Meet-and-greet the Whistler family Sa-Su 4:30pm as well. Open daily 10:30am-5pm.

**Saltram Wine Estate** (☎08 8561 0200; www.saltramwines.com.au.), on Angaston Rd., just outside Angaston. Smooth, fruity, and decadent, their Semillon is excellent. Has been making reds, whites, and Ports since 1859. Open daily 10am-5pm. For a delicious meal, try the attached **Salters Bistro ❺**. Open daily noon-3pm.

## 👁 🌸 SIGHTS AND FESTIVALS

Designated drivers, take heart: not every attraction in Barossa requires drinking. **Mengler Hill Lookout,** on Mengler Hill Rd. east of Tanunda near Bethany on Tourist Rte. 4, gives a bird's-eye view of all those grapes you've been tasting and also features a sculpture park. Take Tanunda Creek Rd. off Mengler's Hill Rd. to the **Kaiser Stuhl Conservation Park** for a guaranteed kangaroo sighting. An entire colony lives and breeds along the **Stringybark Loop Trail** (2.4km, 1hr. round-trip) and the longer **Wallowa Loop Trail** (6.5km, 2hr. round-trip). On the road linking Williamstown and Sandy Creek, the **Barossa Reservoir** retains over 4500 Olympic-size swimming pools' worth of water. It has the famous curved **Whispering Wall,** where sweet nothings can be heard 140m away.

Festivals abound in Barossa Valley. Foremost among these is the biannual **Barossa Vintage Festival** (☎1300 852 982; early Apr. 2009), the valley's largest, longest celebration of all things viticultural with over 100 events, including traditional barefoot grape-stomping. Also popular is **Barossa Under the Stars,** a weekend of wine and food enjoyed to the music of famous Australian bands. (☎1300 852 982. Feb.) For a full events calendar, visit www.barossa.com.

# CLARE VALLEY ☎08

Between Adelaide and the South Australian Outback, the Clare Valley is the final lush oasis before the earthy tones of the Flinders Ranges take command of the landscape. The valley's vineyards center around Clare, the largest town in the area (pop. 4000), with wineries dotting the landscapes of Sevenhill, Mintaro, Penwortham, Watervale, Leasingham, and Auburn. The higher altitude offers a respite from some of the lowland heat associated with the Yorke Peninsula, providing the perfect climate for the valley's famous Rieslings.

## 🌟 🛈 ORIENTATION AND PRACTICAL INFORMATION

**Main North Road** shoots straight through Clare Valley, passing Auburn, Sevenhill, Penwortham, Watervale, and Leasingham before reaching Clare. On Mintaro Rd., the heritage town of **Mintaro** is 8km off Main North Rd. At the north end of town, **Farrell Flat Road,** also known as Burra Rd., heads east through the hills toward **Burra** (p. 513). The **Clare Valley Visitor Information Centre** is south of town on the corner of Spring Gully and Main North Rd. (☎08 8842 2131; www.clare-valley.com.au. Open M-F 9am-5pm, Sa 9:30am-4pm, Su 10am-4pm.) The **banks** along Main North Rd. have **ATMs.** The **Clare Library** has free **Internet access.** (33 Old North Rd. ☎08 8842 3817. Open Tu-W and F 10am-6pm, Th 10am-8pm, Sa 10am-noon.) In case of emergency, contact the **police** (☎08 8842 2711) on Main North Rd. or the **hospital,** 47 Farrell Flat Rd. (☎08 8842 6500). The **post office,** 253 Main North Rd., is open M-F 9am-5pm. **Postal Code:** 5453.

# ACCOMMODATIONS

**Clare Hotel,** 244 Main North Rd. (☎08 8842 2816; www.clarehotel.com.au). This historic hotel's basic pub rooms are the cheapest accommodation in the valley. Pub singles with communal bath $30; ensuite motel rooms and singles $50, doubles $70. ❸

**Riesling Trail and Clare Valley Cottages** (☎04 2784 2232; www.rtcvcottages.com.au). All cottages along Main North Rd., just 2km south of Clare. Office: 6 Warenda Rd. For a delightful bed and breakfast experience, rent one of these many cottages with A/C, generous breakfasts, and wood fireplaces. Cottages for 2 $135-160, $50 per adult, can sleep up to 8. Min. 2-night stay during weekends. ❹

**Clare Caravan Park** (☎08 8842 2724; www.clare-caravan-park.com.au), 3km south of town on Main North Rd. next to the visitors center. The award-winning Clare has a pool and rents bikes to the general public. Cabins can sleep 6 people and have A/C and TV. Bikes $15 per ½-day, $25 per day. Reception 8am-7pm. Sites $20, powered $25; cabins for 2 $55-95, extra person $12. Min. 2-night stay on weekends. AmEx/MC/V. ❷

# FOOD

**Skillogalee Wines** (☎08 8843 4311; www.skillogalee.com). Follow signs 3km from Main North Rd., between Sevenhill and Penwortham. For an unforgettable dining experience in the midst of Skillogalee vineyards, enjoy a lunch or an afternoon tea on the verandah at this beautiful and rustic winery. The gourmet meals are all made with local valley produce complemented by their wines. Open daily 10am-5pm. MC/V. ❺

**Main Street Bake-house,** 269 Main North Rd. (☎08 8842 2473). This joint has been baking pies, pasties, and sausage rolls since 1879. Pasties $3.40-3.80. Foccacia and baguettes $7.50. Burgers $8. Open M-F 8am-5pm, Sa 9am-4pm, Su 10am-4pm. ❶

**Magpie and Stump Hotel,** 1 Burra Rd. (☎08 8843 9014). Bread is baked fresh here every day in an impressively large original 1854 wood oven. Lunch $3.50-15. Dinner mains from $13. Lunch daily noon-2pm. Dinner M-Sa 6pm-late. MC/V. ❷

# WINERIES OF CLARE VALLEY

The granddaddy of Clare wines is the famous Riesling, though nearly every other grape and wine variety in the region is starting to catch up. An old railway line, parallel to Main North Rd., has been converted into the 27km (one-way 2hr. bike, 7hr. walk) scenic ▧**Riesling Trail.** The trail runs between Clare and Auburn, and is suitable for walking and biking. Convenient carparks in Clare, Sevenhill, Watervale, and Auburn allow walkers to take shorter journeys (Auburn to Watervale 9km, Watervale to Sevenhill 9km, Sevenhill to Clare 7km). The trail passes farms, vineyards, quarries, a gum plantation and several art galleries, as well as a few wineries. Every January, Annie's Lane Winery hosts **A Day on the Green** (www.adayonthegreen.com.au), a concert tour that draws the biggest names in Australian music. The venue, a large outdoor amphitheater, makes for a night of good music and good wine. Tickets available through **Ticketmaster** (☎13 61 00; www.ticketmaster.com) and **Venuetix** (☎08 8225 8888; www.venuetix.com.au), as well as **Annie's Lane.** (Quelltaler Rd., Watervale. ☎08 8843 0003. Open M-F 9am-5pm, Sa-Su 10am-4pm.)

**Sevenhill Cellars** (☎08 8843 4222; www.sevenhillcellars.com.au), 6km south of Clare on College Rd. in Sevenhill. The Jesuit owners here have been producing wine since 1851. You can access the winery's underground storage cellar and the adjoining museum as well as the beautiful Jesuit church on the grounds. The large stone house, previously the priest's quarters, is now used for religious retreats. To experience a short

(.3km, 10min.) portion of the Riesling Trail, park your car at the historic Sevenhill Cemetery and meander through rusty farm appliances and original 19th-century cottages, now crumbling, before you reach the church and cellar door. Open daily 9am-5pm.

**Leasingham Wines** (☎08 8842 2785; www.leasingham-wines.com.au), just south of town center on 7 Dominic St. Established in 1895, this winery is a perennial medal-winner and venerable institution. If the Classic Clare range is out of your price range, try the Leasingham Bin range instead. Open M-F 8:30am-5pm, Sa-Su 10am-4pm.

**Jeanneret Wines** (☎08 8843 4308; www.jeanneretwines.com), on Jeanneret Rd. between Sevenhill and Penwortham. What Jeanneret lacks in history (it was started up in 1992), it makes up for in personality and intimacy. Try their "Fancy Pants" Sparkling Grenache. Open M-F 9:30am-5pm, Sa-Su 10am-5pm.

 **TOURS**

Bikes can be rented in Clare from **Riesling Trail and Clare Valley Cottages,** which has access to the north end of the Riesling Trail. (6 Warenda Rd. ☎04 2784 2232. ½-day $20, full-day $35; tandem $35/50. Open daily 8am-6pm.) **Cogwebs** in Auburn also rents out bikes and has direct access to the Riesling Trail. (30 Main North Rd. ☎08 8849 2380. Internet access $4 per 30min., $6 per hr. Bikes ½-day $25, full-day $40; tandem $35/65. Open M-Tu and Th-Su 8am-6pm.) The tourist office also has info on many private tours, including **Clare Valley Experiences** (☎08 8842 1880; www.clarevalleyexperiences.com/experiences; 3hr. tour in a Mercedes 4WD $220 per person, 4-person max.) and **Clare Valley Tours.** (☎08 8843 8066; www.cvtours.com.au. $50 per 4hr., $70 with lunch.)

# LIMESTONE COAST

The less-famous sister of Victoria's Great Ocean Road, the Limestone Coast offers all that a tourist could want: bushwalking in Aboriginal reserves, surfing along the Southern Ocean, and wine tasting in some up-and-coming vineyards. As the name suggests, limestone is the key to many of the region's attractions: it creates the beautiful formations in the Tantanoola and Naracoorte caves, lines the Mt. Gambier volcano crater, and gives the Coonawarra Cabernets their full-bodied flavor. South Australia is infamous for its unreliable public transportation, and the Limestone Coast, no exception to the rule, is best experienced by car. That said, Premier Stateliner **buses** (☎08 8415 5500; www.premierstateliner.com.au) pass through daily on the Adelaide to Mt. Gambier run.

# COORONG NATIONAL PARK

Taking its name from the Aboriginal word *karangh*, meaning "narrow neck," the Coorong—one of the most fragile ecosystems in the world—is a long, narrow stretch of pure-white sand dunes, dry salt lakes, and glittering lagoons. Providing temporary refuge for over 200 species of rare migratory birds, including the world's largest breeding colony of Australian pelicans, the Coorong is a haven for the famous Coorong mullet and hundreds of plant species. The Ngarrindjeri Aboriginal people have lived in the area for 6000 years, and several Aboriginal reserves are located in the national park, where the Ngarrindjeri offer medicinal plant bush walks, kayak tours, and talks about their culture.

**VIA THE MURRAY RIVER.** Australia's longest riverway, the Murray, passes through Coorong to the Murray Mouth and empties into the Southern Ocean. One of the most popular ways to access the Coorong's northern reaches is

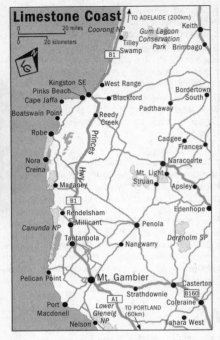

**Limestone Coast**

TO ADELAIDE (200km)

0 — 20 miles
0 — 20 kilometers

Coorong NP
Keith
Gum Lagoon
Tilley Conservation
Swamp Park Brimbago
B1
Kingston SE West Range
Pinks Beach Bordertown
Cape Jaffa Blackford South
Boatswain Point Padthaway
Reedy
Creek
Robe
Cadgee
Frances
Nora
Creina Naracoorte
Mt. Light
Maganey Struan Apsley
B1
Rendelsham Edenhope
Millicant
Canunda NP Penola
Tantanoola Dergholm SP
Nangwarry
Pelican Point
Mt. Gambier
Casterton
Strathdownie B160
Port A1 Coleraine
Macdonell Lower TO PORTLAND
Glenelg (60km)
Nelson NP Tahara West

by boat from Goolwa on the **Fleurieu Peninsula** (p. 476). **Spirit of the Coorong** offers half- and full-day eco-cruises. (☎1800 442 203; www.coorongcruises.com.au. Pickup from Adelaide available, $55 per person. ½-day Discovery Cruise year-round M and Th, plus Tu and Sa Oct.-May; $74, children $55. Full-day Adventure Cruise Oct.-May W and Su, June-Sept. Su; $88/60.) The **Signal Point Interpretive Centre** in Goolwa can book tours along the Murray River, and offers the *Limestone Coast Secrets* information booklet and *The Tattler*, the essential publication covering the Coorong and other area parks. (On Goolwa's wharf. ☎08 8555 3488. Open daily 9am-5pm.)

**VIA NARRUNG.** If a trip to Goolwa isn't in your travel plans, you can still access a remote, northerly section of the Coorong from the northwest. Traveling from Adelaide, turn left off Princes Hwy. before you hit Meningie and then follow signs to Narrung. This █road off Princes Highway to Narrung leads past freshwater Lake Alexandrina and spectacular, rolling farmlands before crossing a narrow inlet on the free 24hr. ferry. From there, a turnoff leads to Pelican Point, home to dozens of the large-beaked birds as well as more graceful swans. Though this area is remote, it can be reached easily with most 2WD vehicles.

**VIA MENINGIE.** The easiest—though least exciting—way to reach the Coorong is via the town of Meningie (pronounced with a hard g), a common Coorong gateway. From Adelaide, Princes Hwy. leads past Tailem Bend to Meningie, running along the western outskirts of the national park. The **Chambers Info Centre,** just past the entrance of town on the left-hand side, provides maps, brochures, and *The Tattler* for those heading into the depths of the park. (14 Princes Hwy. ☎08 8575 1770. Open daily 10am-4:30pm.)

**CONTINUING SOUTH.** The Murray River, Narrung, and Meningie paths all join at the base of Lake Albert, where Princes Hwy. continues its winding path along the national park. Point Hack, about 28km south of Meningie, is home to the Ngarrindjeri-owned **Coorong Wilderness Lodge ❶,** adjacent to their Aboriginal reserve. The Lodge provides camping and bunkhouse accommodation, as well as unique guided tours and activities led by the Ngarrindjeri. From Princes Hwy., exit right at the Coorong Wilderness Lodge sign; follow the dirt road to your right for about 10min. until you reach the Lodge at water's edge. Guided kayaking tours (3hr., $60 per person) and Aboriginal bush walks (approx. 30-40min., $10 per person; best enjoyed Nov.-Mar. when medicinal plants are in full bloom) are just a couple of the cultural activities that the Lodge provides to guests as well as the general public. (☎08 8575 6001 or 04 3875 6040. Licensed restaurant. Site $12, powered $22.50; dorm $25; double $70. Cash only.)

Midway down the long, petrol-station-less highway between Meningie (60km to the north) and Kingston (45km to the south), Salt Creek provides a welcome rest stop to fuel your body and car. The **gas station ❶** has cheap eats for take-away (pasty $2.70, hamburger $3.30) as well as a sit-down diner (steak sandwich $4.90, Coorong mullet $9.50). For a longer rest, take an overnight break at **Gemini Downs ❶**, just 3km before Salt Creek. (Turn left off Princes Hwy. ☎8575 7013; www.geminidowns.com.au. Sites $15, powered $20; cabins $60. MC/V.)

Continuing 18km south on Princes Hwy., a marked turnoff for the ▨**42 Mile Crossing** leads down an unsealed road past the spectral outlines of several lakes 3km to a campsite, where a 4WD track through the dunes leads to the beach. For those without a 4WD vehicle, this point also represents the most convenient pedestrian access to the beach (20min. one-way). **Campsites ❶** are available here, as well as at Parnka Point, along Loop Rd. and Old Coorong Rd. The sites at Parnka Point and the 42 Mile Crossing are among the few in the area that have water and toilets. Permits ($8 per car per night) are required for camping and can be obtained via self-registration or at most gas stations and info centers along the Coorong section of the Princes Hwy.

Many ventures through the Coorong come to a close at its southern base, **Kingston SE** (pop. 1600), voted best middle-size town in 2003. We don't know what that means, who voted, or which middle-size towns were Kingston's competitors, but we do know that Kingston is home to famous **Larry the Lobster,** a four-ton, 17m tall, red-metal crustacean. If Larry sparks a craving for crayfish, head to **Lacepede Seafood ❶** by the jetty for fresh seafood and take-away. After Larry on your left and Apex Park on your right, take your first right down Agnes St., then left on Holland St. which becomes Hanson St. You'll find the jetty on your right. (☎08 8767 2549. Open daily 9am-5pm. Cash only.)

# ROBE ☎08

Surrounded by water on three sides, Robe (pop. 1600) is the Limestone Coast's quintessential beach town. A trendy getaway for Adeladians, this upscale destination is still perfectly accessible to most budget travelers. With its beautiful Victorian buildings, what is arguably the best backpackers on the entire Limestone Coast, and great surf, you'll never want to leave.

## ▢ TRANSPORTATION

Premier Stateliner **buses** (☎08 8415 5555; www.premierstateliner.com.au) stop through Robe (Mobil Roadhouse) on their way to Mt. Gambier (M-Th 12:50pm, F 12:20pm and 10:05pm, Su 7:20pm) as well as Adelaide (M-Th 9:56am, F 9:56am and 4:26pm, Sa 1:26pm, Su 4:26pm).

## ▨ ▨ ORIENTATION AND PRACTICAL INFORMATION

The coastal highway winds through Robe, passing Long Beach on the right and the turn-off for Little Dip Conservation Park on the left (11km). In the town center, the road becomes the town's main drag **Victoria Street,** which is lined with chic cafes and restaurants and ending at the foreshore. From here, the road winds its way around Lake Butler until it reaches the point of the peninsula: **Cape Dombey** and the historic **Obelisk.**

The **Robe Visitor Information Centre,** at the town library, provides maps and free **Internet.** (Corner of Victoria St. and Mundy Terr., opposite the foreshore. ☎08 8768 2465. Open M-F 9am-5pm, Sa-Su 10am-4pm.) Just past the visitors center next to the post office, Bank SA has an **ATM.** In case of emergency, contact the **police,** Lord Syleham St. (☎08 8768 2118); the closest **hospital** is in Kingston

(☎08 8767 0222). The **post office** is past the visitors center, on Bagot St. (☎08 8768 2020. Open M-F 9am-5pm). **Postal Code:** 5276.

# ACCOMMODATIONS

The **Little Dip Conservation Park**, 11km from the center of town, has **camping areas ❶** with toilets but no other facilities at the Stony Rise campground and the Gums campground. ($8, on-site registration.) Stony Rise is down a remote, dirt road that is difficult without a 4WD, while Gums is easier to access. (Ranger's Office, Robe St. ☎08 8768 2543 or 04 2895 3169. Open daily 8am-5pm.)

**Lakeside Manor YHA,** 22 Main Rd. (☎08 8768 1995 or 1800 155 350; www.lakeside-manorbackpackers.com.au.) On the northern edge of town in a heritage-listed 1880s mansion. This amazing hostel—complete with rose gardens, spotless kitchen and bathrooms, flat-screen TV, and library stacked with old books and leather couches—is the perfect place to unwind. Internet $5 per hr. Free pickup from Robe bus station. Dorms $27, YHA $24; doubles $72.50/65, ensuite $100/90. MC/V. ❷

**Guichen Bay Motel,** 42 Victoria St. (☎08 8768 2001; www.guichenbaymotel.com), on the corner of Victoria and Robe St. Comfortable doubles in a beautiful, vine-covered building right in the center of town. Rooms have a TV and fridge, and there's an attached restaurant, pool, heated spa, and BBQ. Reception M-Sa 7:30am-9pm, Su 7:30am-7:30pm. Singles $65; doubles $79-89. AmEx/MC/V. ❹

**Long Beach Caravan Park** (☎08 8768 2237; www.robelongbeach.com), at Long Beach on the Esplanade. Camping and budget cabins. Perfect for a dip, either at the beach or in the pool. Reception daily 8am-9pm. Sites $26, powered $28; cabins $50-110. ❸

# FOOD

A **Foodland**, at the beginning of Victoria St., is open daily 7:30am-7:30pm.

**Wild Mulberry Cafe,** (☎08 8768 2488), at the corner of Robe and Victoria St. Famous for its homebaked pastries and cakes. Serves breakfast all day long as well as gourmet lunches. Breakfast $5-14. Lunch $6.50-16. Open daily 8am-4pm. MC/V. ❶

**Robe Seafood and Takeaway,** 21 Victoria St. (☎08 8768 2888). This town favorite offers famous southern-zone rock lobster and cheap fish and chips. Fish burger $5.50. Dozen oysters $13. Open M-Th 11am-8pm, F-Su 11am-8:30pm. Cash only. ❶

**Gallerie Restaurant,** 2 Victoria St. (☎08 8768 2256). Chic decor and unique fare. The "Front Room" section of the restaurant has a cheaper but more basic menu. Main dishes $11-29. Open daily noon-2pm and 6-8pm. MC/V. ❹

# BEACHES AND OUTDOOR ACTIVITIES

With all of the town's available waterfront property, there is certainly no shortage of underwater activities. The town foreshore, **Hoopers Beach,** and **Long Beach** are good for swimming and snorkeling, while **Stony Rise** in **Little Dip Conservation Park** has heavy surf for experienced surfers.

**Steve's Surf Shop,** 26 Victoria St. (☎08 8768 2094). Bodyboards and surfboards available for rent at the longest running surf shop in South Australia. The board outside gives the latest surf conditions. Discounts for weeklong rentals. Open in summer daily 9am-5pm; in winter M-F 9am-5pm, Sa 9am-1pm, Su 10am-1pm.

**South Coast Wind & Wave** (☎04 1982 1409; southcoastkitesurf@hotmail.com). Offers kitesurfing lessons. Ask for Anthony. Beginner lessons $50 per hr., min. 2hr.

**Robe Adventure Tours** (☎04 1915 8279). From Long Beach, operates guided kayaking trips through Robe's lakes and beaches. Contact Garch. 1hr. kayak rental: single $20, double $25. Guided kayak trip, 2hr., $40.

**Robe Deep Sea Fishing Charters** (☎08 8768 1807 or 04 2931 0052). Head out to sea and catch some dinner. Rods and bait are both supplied. ½-day $130 per person; full-day $240 per person, min. 5 people.

# BEACHPORT ☎08

Forty-eight kilometers south of Robe, Beachport (pop. 440), is a sleepy little town that forces guests to relax. Known as one of the Limestone Coast's must-sees, █**Bowman's Scenic Drive** curls around Beachport's coastal cliffs, with stupendous views of the breaking ocean from above. Situated on the scenic drive, the █**Pool of Siloam,** a sheltered swimming lagoon that's about seven times saltier than the ocean, draws visitors from all around country for its reputed healing properties. Breaking on the rocks below the dramatic coastal cliffs, Rivoli Bay has excellent—though challenging—surf.

Near the jetty, the friendly **Bompas ❸**, 3 Railway Terr., has views of the Southern Ocean from its wonderfully restored historic building dating from 1876. The restaurant serves great meals (lunch $9-21, dinner $14-29, cheaper takeaway prices) and is a local favorite on weekend nights for music and billiards. (☎08 8735 8333. Singles $30; doubles $60, deluxe ensuite doubles $145. Ask about the *Let's Go* discount. Cafe serves meals 8-11:30am, noon-2:30pm, and 6pm-late. MC/V.) The **Beachport Caravan Park ❶**, the first left off the beach road heading into town, has laundry, BBQ, and beach views. (☎08 8735 8128. No linen provided. Sites $19, powered $20; cabins for 2 from $60, extra person $5. MC/V.) **Beachport Takeaway ❶**, 18 Railway Terr., has cheap eats. The homemade burgers ($7.20) and fish and chips are good budget options. (☎08 8735 8180. Open M-Th 11am-7:30pm, F-Sa 11am-8:30pm. Cash only.)

The **Beachport Visitors Centre,** on Millicent Rd. as you enter town, hands out a useful map of the walking trails along the rugged coastline. (☎08 8735 8029; www.wattlerange.sa.gov.au. Internet access $3 per 30min. Open in summer M-F 9am-5pm, Sa-Su 10am-4pm; in winter M-F 9am-5pm, Sa-Su 10am-1pm.) Premier Stateliner **buses** (☎08 8415 5555; www.premierstateliner.com.au) stop through Beachport at **Jarmo's Automotive** on Railway Terr. on their way to Mt. Gambier (M-Th 1:28pm, F 12:58pm and 10:43pm, Su 7:58pm) and to Adelaide (M-Th 9:19am, F 9:19am and 3:49pm, Sa 12:49pm, Su 3:49pm).

# MOUNT GAMBIER ☎08

South Australia's second-largest city lies midway between Adelaide and Melbourne. Built on the slopes of an extinct volcano, the self-named "City of Craters, Lakes, Caves, and Sinkholes" is home to the brilliant **Blue Lake** (brilliant mid-Nov. to Mar.) as well as sunken gardens, underwater limestone caves, and hiking trails encircling the dormant volcano.

▌ **TRANSPORTATION.** Several intercity **bus** routes service Mt. Gambier during the week with stops near attractions. (☎08 8724 9978; www.mccormicksbus. com.au. Service M-F only. Bus schedules available at the visitors center.) For a **taxi**, call **Lake City Taxis** (☎08 8723 0000) or **Vears Taxis** (☎08 8725 0666). **V/Line buses** (☎08 13 61 96; www.vline.com.au). Buses travel from **Melbourne** to **Mt. Gambier** and back via the Great Ocean Road (5hr.) or the slower inland (6hr.) route ($32.40, concessions $16.20). **Premier Stateliner buses** (☎08 8415 5555; www.premierstateliner.com.au). run from Adelaide to Mt. Gambier via the Limestone Coast or the inland route (6hr.; $59.90). Both bus companies depart from and drop off at the visitors center. Book in advance by phone or online; the visitors center does not sell bus tickets.

**◪ PRACTICAL INFORMATION.** The coastal highway that travels through Coorong, Robe, and Beachport enters the city of Mt. Gambier from the east and becomes Jubilee Hwy. West. At the intersection with Penola Rd. in the center of the city, it turns into Jubilee Hwy. East, which then continues to Melbourne. Cutting through town north-south, Penola Rd. becomes Bay Rd., which meets up with John Watson Dr. to encircle Blue Lake.

Identified by a huge ship on its front lawn, the **Lady Nelson Visitors Centre** has tons of brochures, maps, and info on the city and its nearby attractions, including the Naracoorte Caves and the Coonawarra wine region. (Jubilee Hwy. East, before the intersection with Crouch St. North. ☎08 1800 087 187 or 8724 9750; www.mountgambiertourism.com.au. Free Internet. Open daily 9am-5pm.) The **library,** in the Civic Centre, near the corner of Commercial St. and Bay Rd., has free **Internet** and Wi-Fi. (☎08 8721 2540. Open M-W and F 9am-6pm, Th 9am-7pm, Sa 9:30-12:30pm.) In case of emergency, contact the **police** (Bay Rd., ☎08 8735 1020) or the **hospital** (267-300 Wehl St. North; ☎08 8721 1200). An extended-hours **pharmacy** is in the Lakes Village Shopping Centre on Helen St. (☎08 8725 8700. Open M-Sa 9am-9pm, Su 11am-9pm.) The **post office** is at 30 Helen St. (☎08 13 13 18. Open M-F 9am-5pm.) **Postal Code:** 5290.

**⌂⌂ ACCOMMODATIONS AND FOOD.** In the center of town, **Commercial Hotel ❸,** on Commercial St. West, provides simple but clean pub rooms for the cheapest prices in the city. (☎08 8725 3006; www.commersh.com.au. Singles $30; doubles $50. MC/V.) **Mount View Motel ❹,** 14 Davison St. is in a quiet location overlooking McDonald Park, with convenient access to the center of town. Going east on Jubilee Hwy., turn left on Davison St. (☎08 8725 8478 or 04 1782 6796; www.mountviewmotel.com. Double $50, with kitchen $60, with A/C and kitchen $65. Extra person $11. MC/V.) Spotless **Blue Lake Holiday Park ❷,** on Bay Rd. just south of the lake, has a pool, tennis and basketball courts, an 18-hole golf course, outdoor cooking facilities, and is a 2km downhill walk to the CBD. (☎08 8725 9856; www.bluelakeholidaypark.com.au. Sites $24-26, powered $29-32; cabins from $82. AmEx/MC/V.)

The CBD is packed with chip shops and takeaway joints, supermarkets and greengrocers. There is a **Coles** supermarket in the Lakes Village Shopping Ctr. (☎08 8724 9522; open M-Sa 6am-10pm, Su 9am-6pm) and a **Woolworths** on Commercial St. East. (☎08 8725 8088. Open M-Sa 6am-10pm, Su 9am-8pm.)

For a quality meal that won't break the bank, locals looks to ⬛**Caffé Belgiorno ❶,** on the corner of Percy and Mitchell St., next to the Oatmill cinema complex. Its wood-fired pizzas (small $11, large $15) have been annually voted among Australia's best. (☎08 8725 4455. Open daily noon-2pm and 5-9pm. MC/V.) Sip on gourmet coffee and fresh pastries amid potted roses and bougainvilleas at **Plants on Sturt ❶,** 34 Sturt St., a rare nursery/coffee shop combo. Heading south on Penola Rd., turn right on Helen St., which becomes Sturt after the roundabout; the coffee shop is just past the roundabout on the right. (☎08 8725 2236. Cappuccino $3.20. Scones $3.80. Open daily 10am-4pm. MC/V.) Next to the Commercial Hotel, the **Sage and Muntries Cafe Restaurant ❸,** 78 Commercial St. West, is locally renowned for serving excellent food. Dine on gourmet burgers, foccacia, and pastas for lunch, or treat yourself to an indulgent dinner. (☎08 8724 8400. Lunch $8-18. Dinner $12.50-40. Open M-F 10am-3pm and 5:30-late, Sa 11am-2pm and 6pm-late. AmEx/MC/V.)

**◪ SIGHTS.** Mt. Gambier's star attraction is the **Blue Lake,** a brilliantly colored lake filling a volcano crater that last witnessed an eruption around 4500 years ago. The nine million gallons of pure freshwater serve as the town's water supply; the water is transported with a basic system of pumps and gravity-fed water pressure. Bay Rd. loops around the right side of the volcano, and then becomes John Watson Dr., making the full circle at the crater's rim. Along the way, several excellent lookout points provide fantastic views into the volcano. The best time to visit the Blue Lake is from mid-November to early March, when its hue of sapphire is at its most beautiful; the rest of the year, the water turns steel gray, an effect that baffles scientists to this day.

To reach the lake's surface, embark on a 45min. tour down an elevator shaft and through tunnels with **Aquifer Tours;** the guide will explain the history of the lake, from indigenous stories of the volcano's creation to the modern water pumping mechanisms. The tour office is on the corner of Bay Rd. and John Watson Dr. on your left as you pull up to the Blue Lake. (☎08 8723 1199; www.aquifertours.com. Daily tours every hr. Nov.-Jan. 9am-5pm, Feb.-May 9am-2pm, June-Aug. 9am-noon, Sept.-Oct. 9am-2pm. $7, children $3, family $19.)

The Blue Lake's neighbors, the **Devil's Punchbowl** and **Valley Lake,** are connected by a large network of walking trails. You can reach the trails by turning right at the large stone signs marked "Wildlife Park" and "Valley Lake," located next to the caravan park. The now-dry **Leg of Mutton Lake Crater walking trail** (1.6km, 45min.) starts at the Leg of Mutton lookout on Bay Rd., which is the first lookout as you make the loop around Blue Lake.

While the nearby caves at Naracoorte get all the attention, there are a couple interesting holes in the ground right in the center of Mt. Gambier. A huge complex of limestone caves underneath the city, **Engelbrecht Cave,** on Jubilee Hwy. West, has two large, water-filled chambers available by 45min. tour. Cave diving is a particularly adventurous lure here; to learn more about it and the necessary qualifications (PADI is insufficient), check out www.cavediving.com.au. (Get permits at the visitors center. ☎04 1813 3407. Tours daily 9am-2:30pm. $7.50, children $4.) The **Cave Gardens,** at Bay Rd. and Watson Terr., is a beautifully lush and landscaped sinkhole, famous for its rose gardens and waterfalls; the scene is particularly enchanting in the evening, when the limestone walls are floodlit. (Open 24hr. Free.) Another beautifully landscaped and floodlit sinkhole, **Umpherston Sinkhole,** on Jubilee Hwy. E., draws visitors at night when the possums come out to feed. (Open 24hr., floodlit until 1am. Free.)

# COONAWARRA WINE REGION

If the **Barossa** (p. 490) and **Clare** (p. 495) **Valleys** are the grandaddies of Australian wine regions, the Coonawarra is the rebellious teenager. Labeling itself "Australia's other Red Centre," the Coonawarra is famous for its *terra rossa,* or red soil, which produces excellent Cabernets. The region lies 20km north of Mt. Gambier and 50km south of Naracoorte, making it the perfect place to stop between volcanoes and caves for some relaxed wine tasting.

# PENOLA

The oldest town on the Limestone Coast, Penola (pop. 1200) is also the Coonawarra region's biggest town, and has the most amenities. The wineries lie on the famed 12km *terra rosa* strip, starting just north of the township.

**⬛⬛ ORIENTATION AND PRACTICAL INFORMATION.** Riddoch Highway, which runs from Mt. Gambier to Naracoorte, passes right through the center of town, known as **Church Street.** All services are located on Church St., and the wineries line Riddoch Hwy just outside of town. The helpful **Penola/Coonawarra Visitor Centre,** 27 Arthur St., provides maps detailing the location of the region's 20-plus wineries. (☎08 8737 2855; www.coonawarra.org. Internet $1.50 per

15min. Open M-F 9am-5pm, Sa-Su 10am-5pm.) The **library,** in the Penola High School on the corner of Gordon and Cameron St., has free **Internet.** (From Church St., pass the visitors center and turn right on Cameron St. ☎08 8737 2838. Open M and W-F 8:30am-4pm, Tu 8:30am-8pm, Sa 9:30am-noon.) There are **ATMs** at ANZ (30 Church St.) and Bank SA (40 Church St.). In case of emergency, contact the **police** (☎08 8737 2315) or the **hospital** (☎08 8737 2311), both on Church St. on the south side of town. **Postal Code:** 5277.

**▚▐ ACCOMMODATIONS AND FOOD.** Popular with grape pickers, the **Eagles Nest Backpackers ❷,** 55 Portland St., has cheap bunks. Eagles Nest sets up harvesting jobs and provides transportation to and from the employing vineyards. (From Church St., turn east on John St. ☎04 1351 2559 or 04 1345 8740; www. eaglesnestpenola.com.au. No reception on-site; call to book a bed or discuss harvesting work. Communal kitchen and bathrooms. Linen supplied. Dorms $25. For harvesters, $125 per week for accommodation and transportation to work. MC/V.) For a luxurious stay in a beautifully restored 19th-century heritage hotel for a lot less than you'd think, **Heyward's Royal Oak Hotel ❹,** 31 Church St., is unbeatable. Doubles have four-poster mahogany beds, and the beautifully decorated period rooms are equipped with porcelain sinks. (☎08 8737 2322; www.heywardshotel.com.au. Communal bathrooms. Continental breakfast included. Singles $55; doubles $88. MC/V.)

A local favorite, **Windara Bakery ❶,** 35 Church St., sells homemade pastries ($3), pies ($3-3.50), and delicious fresh bread. (☎08 8737 2727. Pizza $2.90 per slice. Focaccia $3.40. Open M-F 6am-5pm, Sa 8am-2pm. Cash only.) In the tiny township of Coonawarra 10km north of Penola, **Red Fingers ❷,** on Memorial Dr. just off Riddoch Hwy., serves Mod Oz cuisine accompanied by local wines. Try the famous red dog pie (beef marinated in 3 bottles of shiraz, with mushrooms in a puff pastry; $17.50) or marinated kangaroo fillet for $25. (☎08 8736 3006. Coffee and cakes. Lunch $8.50-18. Dinner $25-29. Open M 9am-2pm, W-Su 9am-2pm and 6-8pm. AmEx/MC/V.) For the cheapest burgers and schnitzel in town, head to **Aussie Takeaway ❶,** 38 Young St. (From Church St., turn east on Young St. ☎08 8737 2331. Open daily 10am-9pm. Cash only.)

**▟ WINERIES.** The trick to these wines is all in the dirt: *terra rossa,* or red soil, gives the grapes a rich, earthy flavor. While the Barossa and Clare Valleys are famous for German vines (Shiraz and Riesling, respectively), the Coonawarra owes its reputation to Cabernet vines imported from France. Most wineries in the Coonawarra have only started up in the last few decades, and their winemaking is generally both contemporary and fresh, based on experimentation and blends. There are about 20 cellar doors in the region, with most opening hours running from 10am to 4pm daily.

Opened by descendants of the original founder of Coonawarra, **▨Rymill** whips up hybrids like the "mc²," a blend of Merlot, Cabernet Sauvignon, and Cabernet Franc, in its modern building. The observation decks overlook wine production on one side and the beautiful vineyards on the other. The Yearling ($13 per bottle) is an excellent value for its quality. (From Riddoch Hwy., turn west on Clayfield Rd. ☎08 8736 5001; www.rymill.com.au. Open daily 10am-5pm.) One of the only wineries with a restaurant overlooking the vineyards, **Hollick Wines** exemplifies the indulgent wine-and-dine. This company was one of the first in the region to experiment with Italian (Tempranillo, San Giovese) and Spanish (Alberino) grapes. The desserts are to die for: try the vanilla panna cotta with a berry and sparkling merlot sauce ($11), accompanied by a sparkling merlot, of course. (Ravenswood Ln. ☎08 8737 2752; www.hollick.com. Main courses $25.50-29. Cellar door open daily 9am-5pm. Restaurant open T-Th and

Su noon-2pm, F-Sa noon-2pm and 6:30pm-late.) The smallest boutique winery in Coonawarra, **The Blok Estate** is a simple, family-owned winery that spoils its grapes with a lot of TLC. Along with the wine tasting, try a local cheese platter ($10) or scones with Cabernet jam for $5. (On Riddoch Hwy., just north of Hollick Wines. ☎08 8737 2734; www.blok.com.au. Open daily 10am-5pm.)

# NARACOORTE ☎08

Fossils and limestone formations await you at the famed Naracoorte Caves. Though the town of Naracoorte itself isn't much, the caves 12km south of town are a magnificent network of hollows, tunnels, stalactites, and stalagmites, perfect for an adventure caving experience. The caves have been named a World Heritage site, as they provide the most complete fossil record of megafauna in the Pleistocene era (500,000 years ago) embedded into the limestone.

**TRANSPORTATION.** Premier Stateliner **buses** (☎08 8415 5500; www.premierstateliner.com.au) pass through town once per day in each direction (on the inland Mt. Gambier to Adelaide route).

**ORIENTATION AND PRACTICAL INFORMATION.** From the south, the Riddoch Hwy. from Mt. Gambier and Penola leads to the turnoff for the caves first, then, 12km later, the town itself. In town, the highway becomes **Gordon Street** before ending at the small park. Almost everything can be found on one of two streets: **Ormerod** (Commercial) and **Smith Street,** both running parallel on either side of the park. The **Visitors Centre,** 36 MacDonnell St., is located in the Sheep's Back Museum. (☎08 8762 1399; Internet free for 15min.; open M-F 9am-5pm, Sa-Su 9am-4pm.) Services include: **ATMs** on Ormerod and Smith St.; a **library,** next to the park, with free **Internet** (open M 10am-5pm, Tu-W and F 9:30am-5pm, Th 10am-8pm, Sa 8:30am-noon); **pharmacy,** 100 Smith St. (open M-F 9am-5:30pm, Sa 9am-noon); **police,** 66 Smith St. (☎08 8762 0466); and **post office,** 23 Ormerod St. (open M-F 9am-5pm). **Postal Code:** 5271.

**ACCOMMODATIONS AND FOOD.** Naracoorte Backpackers ❷, 4 Jones St., a few blocks up the hill from the park, is a hostel popular with backpackers doing local picking work. This isn't the place to get a good night's sleep, as the workers unwind (loudly) into the wee hours of the morning, but it is a great place to meet people. The rooms, kitchen, and bathroom seem to be in a constant state of disarray and are in need of renovations. (☎08 8762 3835 or 04 3982 3835. Dorms $20. Cash only.) The **Naracoorte Hotel-Motel ❸,** 73 Ormerod St., across from the park, offers standard-issue pub rooms as well as nicer ensuite rooms in the adjoining motel. (☎08 8762 2400. Singles $35; doubles $60, motel double $78-88. MC/V.) The **Wirreanda Bunkhouse and Campground ❶,** at the caves, has toilets, showers, BBQ area, free laundry facilities, and power. Follow signs for the Naracoorte Caves. The campground is 300m past the caves. (☎08 8762 2340. Car sites $21, motorcycle $13, hiker/cyclist $6; on-site registration. Dorms $15; no reception, book through Wonambi Fossil Centre at the caves. MC/V.) **Maddie's Cafe ❶,** on Smith St., has tasty, inexpensive sandwiches (from $4.60) and focaccia ($7.90) in an understated setting. (☎08 8762 3953. Cappuccino $3.10. Open M-F 8:30am-5pm, Sa 9am-2:30pm. Cash only.) In the Naracoorte Hotel-Motel, **Billy Mac's ❸** serves typical pub fare and local wines. The daily special is a bargain at $8.50. (Main dishes $10-22. Kitchen open daily noon-2pm and 6-8:30pm, later for drinks. MC/V.) Buy groceries at **Foodland** supermarket, next to the Naracoorte Hotel-Motel (Open M-F 8am-8pm, Sa-Su 8:30am-7pm.)

◪ **CAVE TOURS.** The **Naracoorte Caves National Park** consists of a large complex of caves, most available exclusively by guided tour. Only the Wet Cave is accessible without a guide. The most famous of the caves, the ◪**Victoria Fossil Cave,** carries 500,000-year-old fossils in its deepest chambers. (1hr. tours daily 10:15am and 2:15pm.) Victoria Fossil is also the only wheelchair accessible cave. (Call ahead to arrange.) Although access into the massive **Bat Cave** is not allowed, the guided tour will bring you to the Bat Observation Centre, where you can sit, relax, and watch some Bat TV—video of the cave taken with infrared cameras. The resident Southern Bentwing bat has recently entered the critically endangered species list. Tours to watch the colony fly out of the cave for its evening meal are conducted at dusk during summer holidays. (1hr. guided tours daily 11:30am and 3:30pm; Bat Cave tour includes a wander through the Blanche Cave.) The spindly limestone wonders in **Alexandra Cave** make for great photo ops. (30min. guided tours daily 9:30am and 1:30pm.)

For a more hands-on experience (that is, hands, knees, and elbows), try **Adventure Caving,** a trip that allows you to squeeze in and out of nooks on all fours. (☎08 8762 2340. $30, concessions $20, children $18. Book in advance.)

All guided tours and access to the self-guided Wet Cave and Wonambi display is arranged through the **Wonambi Fossil Centre,** the main info center at the entrance to the caves. The display recreates the environment thought to have surrounded the caves during the Pleistocene era. The center sells different combos for those who want to explore various caves, with up to four options. You can buy tickets to the guided tours of Victoria Fossil Cave, Bat Cave, and Alexandra Cave, as well as a ticket for the self-guided combo of Wet Cave and Wonambi. Pick one, two, three, or four of any of those options. (One $12, concessions $9.50, children $7.50; two $19.50/15.50/12; three $27/21.50/16.50; four $34.50/27.50/21. Fossil Centre open daily 9am-5pm.)

# YORKE PENINSULA

On boot-shaped Yorke, sandy flats punctuate rolling farmland, and the sheer cliffs that loom over the hinterland storm into the sea. Sometimes called the "golden plains," the area's extraordinary fertility has made it one of South Australia's leading grain-producing regions. While agriculture may not exactly captivate visitors, the isolated coastline and shipwreck diving spots certainly will. Native fauna still claims the bottom of the peninsula in Innes National Park, where rare birds take refuge from the fierce winds and surfers battle some of South Australia's biggest and baddest waves.

## COPPER COAST ☎08

Situated along the Copper Coast, the northern towns of **Moonta** (pop. 3500), **Wallaroo** (pop. 3800), and **Kadina** (pop. 4250) sprang up as a result of discoveries of large copper deposits in the 1860s. Today, the historic towns survive on the seasonal influx of Adelaideans during holidays. While Kadina is primarily useful for its services, a visit to **Wallaroo** (an approximation of the Aboriginal word for "wallaby urine") and **Moonta Bay** on the beautiful Copper Coast is more worthwhile, offering prime fishing, diving, and swimming opportunities. Besides the attractions of the coastline, Moonta plays its Cornish and mining heritage to the hilt and you can experience it firsthand through a mining expedition or during **Kernewek Lowender,** Australia's largest Cornish Festival in May.

**SOUTH AUSTRALIA**

## ⊞ ⁊ ORIENTATION AND PRACTICAL INFORMATION

Forming the bottom of the Copper Triangle, Moonta is 17km southwest of Kadina and 16km south of Wallaroo. Like Moonta, Wallaroo lies on the coast, while Kadina is the farthest inland. **Premier Stateliner** runs buses from the Adelaide via Port Wakefield to all three towns. (☎08 8415 5555; www.premierstateliner.com.au. Buses depart from Adelaide, 111 Franklin St., M-F 10:30am and 5:45pm, Sa noon, Su 7pm. $23.60, concessions $11.80.) **Copper Triangle Taxis,** based in Kadina, will charge about $18 to reach Wallaroo and $45 to Moonta Bay. The Copper Triangle, much like the rest of Yorke Peninsula, is best traveled via car, as public transportation within and between cities is practically non-existent. The **Moonta Station Tourist Office,** at the end of Blyth St. in the old railway station, stocks a number of handouts about local lore as well as local recipes for the much-touted cornish pasties. (☎08 8825 1891. Books Wheal Hughes Copper Mine tours. Open daily 9am-5pm.) The **Moonta Community Library,** offers free **Internet.** (Blanche Terr. ☎08 8825 1511. Open T-W and F 9am-4pm, Th 9am-6pm, Su 1:30-4pm.) All three towns have **ATMs.** The main **police station** is in Kadina (58 Graves St., ☎08 8828 1100), and the area **hospital** is in Wallaroo (Ernest Tce., ☎08 8823 0200). Each town has a **post office** (all open M-F 9am-5pm). **Postal Code:** 5554 (Kadina), 5556 (Wallaroo), 5558 (Moonta).

## ⚑ ACCOMMODATIONS

▨ **Cornwall Hotel,** 20 Ryan St. (☎08 8825 2304), in Moonta. The nicest pub rooms you'll ever stay in, with modern furniture and impeccable communal bathrooms. Continental breakfast included. Pub open daily noon-2pm and 6-8pm for meals. Lunch specials $7.50. Main dishes $11-17. Singles $30; doubles $50; discount for longer stays. ❸

**Weeroona Hotel,** 4 John Terr. (☎08 8823 2008), in Wallaroo. This hotel offers very basic pub rooms in a convenient location near the jetty. Continental breakfast included. Communal bathroom. Singles $25; doubles $40. MC/V. ❷

**North Beach Caravan Park,** (☎08 8223 2531; www.wallaroonorthbeachtouristpark.com.au). This is the nicest of the parks along the Wallaroo waterfront. Cabins sleep up to 6. Cabin linen not included, but available for rent. Internet access. Reception M-Th 8:30am-6pm, F-Sa 8:30am-7pm, Su 8:30am-5:30pm. Sites $16, powered $22; cabins $95-120, with spa $130-140, extra person above 2 $13. Min. 2 night stay. ❶

## ▯ FOOD

The entire Yorke Peninsula is famous for its Cornish cuisine, especially the pasties, but only Moonta is bold enough to claim the moniker "Australia's Little Cornwall." For groceries, head to Moonta's **Foodland** supermarket, 21 George St. (☎08 8825 2050. Open daily 7:30am-8pm.)

**Cornish Kitchen,** 10-12 Ellen St. (☎08 8825 3030). Cornish is impeccably kept and serves up some of Little Cornwall's best pasties ($3) as well as other light meals for $2-6. Open M-F 9am-3:30pm, Sa 9am-2pm. ❶

**La Cantina Cafe** (☎08 8825 3253), in Moonta Bay. This casual spot serves Italian fare (pizza $10-20, pasta $9-14, seafood main dishes $18-21) while overlooking the ocean. Tu-F all you can eat pizza and pasta $10, children $6. Delivery in Moonta and Moonta Bay; takeaway available. Open Tu 5-10pm, W-F noon-10pm, Sa-Su 10am-10pm. ❷

**The Boat Shed Restaurant,** (☎08 8823 3455), at the end of Jetty Rd., Wallaroo. The Boat Shed has a beautiful ocean view from its al fresco cafe and upstairs dining room. Seafood $7.50-11. 9" pizza $12-13; 12" $12-16. Prices increase for upstairs dining room (mains $18-30). Al fresco cafe and takeaway counter open daily 11am-late; upstairs dining room open Sa 6pm-late. ❷

## SIGHTS AND ACTIVITIES



To experience Moonta's mining history, don a hard hat and camp lamp and head 55m underground with the **Wheal Hughes Copper Mine** tour. (Bookings essential, made through Moonta Station Tourist Office. Tours W and Sa-Su 10, 11:30am, 1, and 2:30pm.) For more mining history, check out the **Moonta Mines Museum.** (Verran Terr. ☎08 8825 1891. Open daily 1-4pm.) Departing from the museum, the **Tourist Railway** takes you through tunnels, past the reservoir and ore-sorting floors, and stops for a visit at the Precipitation Works for an explanation on copper recovery. (50min. Runs W 2pm, Sa-Su 1, 2, and 3pm.) Beautiful **Moonta Bay** and Wallaroo's **North Beach** offer the best beaches in the area and calm, seaweed-free water. Both coasts of the peninsula running down to **Innes National Park** have a number of secluded beaches with excellent fishing and diving. Many are only accessible with 4WD. **Captain Cook Charters** runs fishing trips from the Wallaroo Marina, and outfits you with full fishing gear, tackle, bait, and soft drinks. Bring your own lunch. (☎04 2962 1557. Full-day charter, 7am-3:30pm, $150 per person. Min. 4 people.) **Sea SA Ferries** crosses the Spencer Gulf from Wallaroo to Eyre Peninsula's Lucky Bay six times daily. (☎08 8823 0777; www.seasa.com.au. Bookings essential. $32.50, children $15, vehicles $110.) Lovers of Cornish culture and baked goods rush to Moonta every May for **Kernewek Lowender** (www.kernewek.org), the largest Cornish festival in Australia. Few know what the festival title means, but that doesn't stop the crowds from enjoying its week-long lineup of activities.

# INNES NATIONAL PARK

Fantastic for surfing and bird-watching, **Innes National Park,** 300km from Adelaide at the toe of the Yorke boot, is the peninsula's most popular attraction. The Western Whipbird, which was rediscovered in 1962, is largely responsible for the area's designation as a national park. There are many other varieties of rare birds within the park; the visitors center has descriptions of them and advice on how to spot them. Buses go no farther south than Warooka, making the park practically inaccessible without a car. The main road through the park to Pondalowie Bay is sealed, and the unsealed roads can be accessed by 2WD; unless you plan on launching a boat from the Fisherman's Village boat ramp, there isn't too much need for a 4WD in the park.

**ACCOMMODATIONS AND FOOD.** Located just inside the park entrance, the **Rhino Tavern** ❸ serves up local seafood, curries, and schnitzels for $18-20. (☎08 8854 4078. Serves meals daily noon-2pm and 6-8pm, drinks 10am-10pm.) The attached general store has a petrol station, refills scuba tanks, and gives advice about fishing and surfing locations. (Open daily 8am-7pm.)

**BYOW.** In this area of low rainfall, small water reserves, and perennially drought-prone land, the availability and quality of water cannot be assured; visitors are advised to bring their own water supplies while in Innes NP.

Innes spreads its several primitive **campsites** ❶ over a few prime locations in the park. There are also three self-registration bays (Gym Beach, outside the general store, and outside the visitors center) for after-hours camping and travel within the park. Sites at **Pondalowie Bay** ($10 per car per night) have showers, toilets, phone and BBQ facilities. **Casuarina** ($15 per car per night) is the only campground that can be booked ahead. Several heritage accommodations of varying prices are available near Shell Beach and in the historic ghost town of Inneston within the park; the cheapest is **Shepherd's Hut,** with no facilities, electricity, or nearby toilets. (Sleeps 4; $35). Contact the visitors center if you're interested in booking a site. All bookings have a two-night minimum for weekends and school holidays. The **Marion Bay Caravan Park ❶** lies just before the park entrance. (☎08 8854 4094. Reception open daily 8am-6pm. Sites $17.50, powered $21. On-site vans $67-83.50. Extra person $7.50.)

📷 **OUTDOOR ACTIVITIES.** The **National Park Visitors Centre,** at Stenhouse Bay, sells day-passes and camping permits, and has guides for walking, fishing, and surfing in the park. (☎08 8854 3200; www.parks.sa.gov.au/innes. Open during holidays daily 9am-4:30pm; otherwise M-F 9am-4:30pm, Sa-Su 10:30am-3:00pm. Day-passes $7.50 per vehicle or $4.50 per motorcycle. Also available from self-registration station near entrance.) There are seven well-marked walking trails in the park ranging from 30min. to 5hr. in duration (pick up the *Innes Walking Trails* brochure at the visitors center). Highlights include the layered limestone cliffs at **The Gap,** views of the Althorpe Islands from **Chinaman's Hat** (a popular winter whale-watching spot near Cape Spencer lighthouse), and the sunset views from **West Cape,** which overlooks Pondalowie Bay. Shell Beach and Dolphin Beach are both beautiful beaches that afford lots of privacy.

Snorkelers should head to Cable Bay, while divers must check out the **Investigator Heritage Trail,** littered with 26 shipwrecks dating from 1849 to 1982. The national park provides some excellent fishing points. **Browns Beach** is one of South Australia's best salmon fishing areas, while you can catch squid, mullet, tommy ruffs, garfish, and whiting year-round at Stenhouse Bay jetty. **Reef Encounters** handles fishing charters from Marion Bay and Pondalowie Bay, famous for its snapper, sharks, salmon, and more. (☎08 8854 4102 or 04 0760 9988; www.reefencounters.com.au. Fishing 1-day charter $200 per person, 2-day $400.) The visitors center also has a comprehensive list of surf breaks within the park. **Chinaman's Reef** is the most challenging of these, with 1-2m swells that break on a shallow rock ledge. Pondalowie Bay provides an easier beach break, up to 3m with easterly off-shore winds. One of the biggest surfing competitions in the country, the **Cutloose Quiksilver Yorke's Classic** (☎04 2779 6845) is held here during a long weekend in early October.

# FLINDERS RANGES

The Flinders Ranges may not be the Himalayas or the Andes, but these ancient peaks belong in the pantheon of awe-inspiring ranges. The main road (Hwy. 47) drifts between kangaroo-filled flatlands and sagebrush-covered hills, while dirt-tracks (4WD-only) carve through timeless gorges. The Flinders are most popular from April to October, when the nights are chilly and the days sunny. It's hot in summer, but for hardcore hikers or drivers with A/C, it's a worthwhile trip. The Ranges begin at the northern end of the Gulf of St. Vincent and continue 400km into South Australia's northern Outback, ending near Mt. Hopeless. Towns and attractions in the region are listed from south to north, as they would be encountered if driving from Adelaide.

SOUTH AUSTRALIA

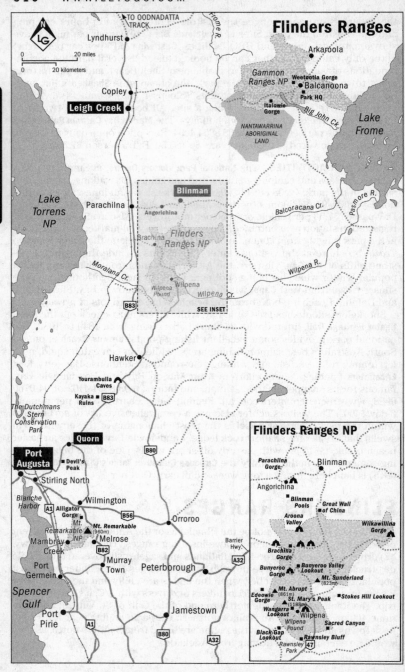

# Flinders Ranges

TO OODNADATTA TRACK

Lyndhurst

Frome R.

Arkaroola

Copley

**Leigh Creek**

*Gammon Ranges NP*

Weetootla Gorge
Balcanoona
Park HQ

Italowie Gorge

Big John Ck.

Lake Frome

*NANTAWARRINA ABORIGINAL LAND*

*Lake Torrens NP*

Parachilna

**Blinman**

Angorichina

*Flinders Ranges NP*

Brachina

Balcoracana Cr.

Pasmore R.

Wilpena R.

*Moralana Cr.*

*Wilpena Pound*

Wilpena

*Wilpena* Cr.

**SEE INSET**

B83

Hawker

Yourambulla Caves

Kayaka Ruins

B83

*The Dutchmans Stern Conservation Park*

**Quorn**

B80

**Port Augusta**

Devil's Peak

Stirling North

*Blanche Harbor*

A1

Alligator Gorge

Wilmington

B56

Orroroo

*Mt. Remarkable NP*

Mt. Remarkable (960m)

Melrose

B82

Murray Town

*Mambray Creek*

Port Germein

Peterborough

Barrier Hwy.

A32

*Spencer Gulf*

Port Pirie

A1

Jamestown

B80

A32

## Flinders Ranges NP

Parachilna Gorge

Blinman

Angorichina

Blinman Pools

Great Wall of China

Aroona Valley

Wilkawillina Gorge

Brachina Gorge

Bunyeroo Valley Lookout

Bunyeroo Gorge

Mt. Sunderland (823m)

Edeowie Gorge

Mt. Abrupt (861m)

St. Mary's Peak (1188m)

Stokes Hill Lookout

Wangarra Lookout

Wilpena

Sacred Canyon

*Wilpena Pound*

Black Gap Lookout

Rawnsley Bluff

*Rawnsley Park*

47

**TRAVELING THROUGH THE FLINDERS RANGES.** Before setting out on the unsealed roads of the Northern Flinders and the outback tracks, check road conditions. The website www.transport.sa.gov.au/quick-links/northern_roads/northern.asp has current road maps, showing closures, warnings, and 4WD only. Alternatively, call the **Road Conditions Hotline** (☎1300 361 033). Before hiking, listen to AM 639 for fire warnings.

# PORT AUGUSTA                                                    ☎08

Located at the intersection of Hwy. 1 and Hwy. 87, Port Augusta (pop. 14,800) is the self-described "crossroads of Australia," but it's little more than a stopover for travelers emerging from the Nullarbor or heading north to Coober Pedy and Alice Springs. Those who aren't in need of a rest would be best advised to continue north to Quorn or south to Whyalla.

**TRANSPORTATION AND PRACTICAL INFORMATION.** The **bus station** sits opposite the library on Mackay St. Premier Stateliner (☎08 8642 5055) runs **buses** to and from Adelaide and Whyalla five times daily.

Intersecting Hwy. 1, **Flinders Terrace** runs roughly east-west and connects to Commercial Rd. and Maryatt St., both of which lead into the town center. **ATMs** can be found on Commercial Rd. The **Tourist Information Office and Wadlata Outback Centre,** 41 Flinders Terr., at Maryatt St., books outback tours. (☎08 8641 0793. Open M-F 9am-5:30pm, Sa-Su 10am-4pm.) The **NPWS office,** 9 Mackay St., 2nd fl., provides information about local parks. (☎08 8648 5300. Open M-F 9am-5pm.) The **library,** on the corner of Mackay and Marryatt St., has free **Internet** and Wi-Fi access, available in 30min. blocks. (☎08 8641 9151. Open M, W, F 9am-6pm; Tu and Th 9am-8pm; Sa 10am-1pm; Su 2-5pm.) The **post office** is located on Commercial Rd. **Postal code:** 5700.

**ACCOMMODATIONS AND FOOD.** Port Augusta doesn't have much to offer in the way of unique budget accommodations. **The Flinders Hotel ❷** (☎08 8642 2544), on the corner of Commercial Rd. and Mackay St., has standard Aussie pub-style rooms (doubles $70). The backpacker rooms ($22 per person) with only two beds per room are the best bargain, though they lack a kitchen. The Flinders is also one of the town's best bets for a **budget meal ❶** (burgers, pasta and pizza from $10). A little north of town, **Shoreline Caravan Park ❷** (☎08 8642 2965) can be found on Gardiner Ave. Located on the water, Shoreline provides sites, cabins, and basic hostel-style rooms with access to a common kitchen and toilet area. (Reception 8am-7pm. Unpowered sites for 2 $22, powered $25. Hostel bed in 4-bed room $16, 2-bed room $36-40; doubles $55; 4-person suites $83-93.) An added bonus for patrons of the caravan park is access to the West Augusta Football Club. Take your drink voucher there for a true taste of Aussie culture—pokies (slot machines), a full bar, and pub meals on Th and F nights ($8.50). A **Coles** supermarket is on the corner of Jervis and Maryatt St., across the green from the library. (Open daily 6am-10pm.)

**SIGHTS.** The main attraction in Port Augusta, the **Wadlata Outback Centre,** located in the **Tourist Information Office** (see **Practical Information** above), introduces visitors to outback history and culture through hands-on exhibits. (☎08 8642 4511. Centre admission $11, concessions $10, families $24.50.) The **Arid Lands Botanic Gardens,** north of town off the Stuart Hwy., has bushwalking trails with instructive plant labels. (☎08 8641 1049. 1hr. guided tours M-F 10am. $6.50. Gardens open M-F 9am-5pm, Sa-Su 10am-4pm. Admission free.)

# SOUTHERN FLINDERS

## MOUNT REMARKABLE NATIONAL PARK

Mount Remarkable National Park, located halfway between Port Pirie and Port Augusta, is the pride of the southern Flinders. With excellent opportunities to bushwalk, observe wildlife, or just drive the winding scenic roads, Mt. Remarkable is a nice introduction to the red, arid peaks of the Flinders Ranges.

The **Port Pirie Regional Tourism Center** (see above) is a good place to get area information. Hwy. 1 runs along the west coast of the park and passes through **Mambray Creek,** 45km north of Port Pirie and home to the park headquarters. To reach nearby **Melrose,** take the winding road off Hwy. 1 by Port Germein 27km to **Murray Town;** from there it's another 14km on Hwy. B-82 to Melrose.

The park headquarters at Mambray Creek has a self-registration kiosk for day passes and camping permits and provides detailed maps of all park trails. (☎08 8634 7068. Day passes $7.50 per vehicle.) The **campground ❶** has 54 sites with water, toilets, showers, BBQ, and picnic areas ($10 per car, $6 per motorcycle, or $5 for hikers or cyclists). There are also 11 **bush camping ❶** sites deep within the park ($4). Bush camping is prohibited during the fire ban season (generally Nov.-Apr.). There is a simple **cabin ❸** for four at Mambray Creek that can be rented through the park service. (☎08 8634 7068. Linen not included. Book in advance. M-Th and Su $35, F-Sa $40.) Mambray Creek is also the site of numerous trailheads. Visitors on a tight schedule should consider the **Sugar Gum Lookout** (8km, 3hr. roundtrip), an easy trail following Mambray Creek that provides nice views of the surrounds. Those with more time can take a day to hike the ironically well-marked **Hidden Gorge** (18km, 7hr. roundtrip) and see the area red gums as well as some of the best views of Spencer Gulf.

Tiny Melrose, the oldest town in the Flinders, is a good base for hikes. All attractions are well-labeled off the main strip. The town's recently renovated **North Star Hotel ❺,** 43 Nott St., dating from 1854, has quirky and surprisingly classy chalets built into antique farm trucks. The hotel pool provides welcome relief. (☎08 8666 2110; www.northstarhotel.com.au. Reception 9am-5pm; call in advance to arrange other times. Standard room $90, boutiques $225, truck chalets $140-160.) The hotel **restaurant ❷** has occasional live entertainment. (☎08 8666 2110. Main dishes $10-22. Open W noon-2pm, Th-Sa noon-2pm and 6-8pm.) **Bluey Blundstone's Blacksmith Shop,** 30-32 Stuart St., was built in 1865, and reopened after a restoration as a **coffee shop ❶** (lunch $9.50-14; open M-F 10am-4pm, Sa-Su 10am-5pm) and rustic **B&B ❺** consisting of a cottage and barn. (☎08 8666 2173. Continental breakfast included. Cottage for 2 $135; barn for 2 $120, $40 each additional person up to 6 total.) The **Melrose Backpackers and Caravan Park ❶,** on Joe's Rd. off Stuart St., also provides tourist info and maps. (☎08 8666 2060. Linen $5. Sites $7.50 per person, powered $20, dorms $15, cabins from $45.) Melrose's **general store** (☎08 8666 2057; open M-F and Su 8:30am-6pm, Sa 8:30am-7pm) is on Stuart St., while the **post office** (☎08 8666 2014) is on the corner of Stuart and Nott St. **Postal code:** 5483.

Many hikes begin from the Melrose Caravan Park. The most well-known is the **summit trail** (12km, 5hr. round-trip), which doesn't actually have much of a summit view but does provide some nice vistas on the way up. For a shorter hike, try the **Melrose Nature Hike** (4.7km; 2½hr. return). Mountain bikers should pay a visit to ▓**Over the Edges.** They rent standard bikes for $25 per day but also rent out top-of-the-line cycles for $100 per day. The area has over 50km of tracks, although that total should more than double by 2010 with new paths under construction. (☎08 8666 2222. Open M and W-Su 9am-5pm.)

# CENTRAL FLINDERS

In the Central Flinders, the stark landscape of the arid red center transitions to the greener pastoral lands of the south. The most famous and accessible Flinders attractions, including the vast amphitheater of Wilpena Pound, are located here. Good roads and well-placed towns allow even the outback novice to marvel at the colorful mountains and plentiful wildlife. To reach Quorn, Rawnsley Park, or Wilpena Pound via public transportation, take **Stateliner** through Port Augusta. (Adelaide ☎08 8415 5555, Port Augusta ☎08 8642 5055.) Wilpena Pound marks the end of public transport into the range. Many private tours also explore the Central Flinders.

## BURRA                                                                ☎08

Once Australia's largest inland settlement, Burra (pop. 1200) hosted over 5000 miners and had one of the largest copper mines in the world. Today, Burra revels in its past. The town was declared a State Heritage area in 1993, and its crumbling buildings and historical focus give it a ghostly, albeit friendly, feel.

**ORIENTATION AND PRACTICAL INFORMATION.** Burra is 156km (2hr.) north of Adelaide and 42km (30min.) northeast of Clare on **Barrier Highway (A32),** the main route to Sydney via Broken Hill. The highway leads to **Market Square,** at the intersection of Market and Commercial St., before turning left in town. Commercial St. becomes Kingston St. on the other side of the highway. The **Burra Visitors Information Centre,** 2 Market Sq., books accommodations, dispenses the essential **Burra Heritage Trail Passport** key, and provides town maps. (☎08 8892 2154; www.visitburra.com. Open daily 9am-5pm.) **Bank SA,** on Market Sq., has an **ATM.** There is free **Internet access** at the **library,** which is in the school at the end of Bridge Terr., just north of the creek. (Open M-F 8:30am-6pm, during school holidays 11am-1pm and 2-6pm.) The **post office** (open M-F 9am-5pm) is on Market Sq., next to the **IGA** supermarket (open M-F 9am-5:30pm, Sa 9-11:30am, Su 10am-1pm). **Postal Code:** 5417.

**ACCOMMODATIONS AND FOOD.** The **Burra Hotel ❸,** 5 Market Sq., is a 154 year-old establishment with pub rooms and meals as well as a classier dining section with local produce and wines. (☎08 8892 2389. Communal bath. Singles $35; doubles $50; family rooms $70. Open daily for lunch noon-2pm, dinner daily 6:30-8:30pm. Lunch $12-16. Dinner mains from $13.) The **Lavender Cottage ❺,** in Burra, is the cheapest B&B in town and can sleep four people in its two cozy rooms. Book through the visitors center. ($95 for 2, extra adult $25; with breakfast $120.) **Gaslight Collectibles and Old Books ❶,** 20 Market Sq., is a unique cafe where visitors can sip on tea or snack on a homemade scone ($5) amid antiques and old books. (☎08 8892 3004. Open Tu-Th 10am-5pm.)

**SIGHTS.** Burra's tourist favorite is the **Burra Heritage Trail Passport,** a key that opens eight locked historical sites and allows visitors as much time as they need to complete the self-guided tour. (Basic passport $15, concessions $11; full passport with entrance to all 4 area museums $30/23.) Most sites are ruins, all are eerily empty, and some of them, including the **Unicorn Brewery Cellars** and the old **Redruth Gaol** (used in the 1979 movie *Breaker Morant*), are downright

Today, the Eastern Grey Kangaroo is the largest marsupial native to Australia, but as recently as 40,000 years ago, this wasn't the case. Fossilized remains discovered in Australia reveal that the country was once home to the giant emu *Genyornis,* the Australian "lion" *Thylacoleo,* and the biggest marsupial to have ever lived, the diprotodon.

The diprotodon, which resembled a cross between a wombat and a koala, stood about 6ft. tall at the shoulders, was around 10 feet long, and weighed over 6000 lbs. These hairy herbivores lived in forests and on open plains.

Theories for the extinction of the diprotodon—as well as other Australian megafauna—include climate change as well as human hunting. The exact date of the arrival of the first people to Australia is still somewhat disputed, but it is acknowledged that the first Aboriginals probably coexisted with a number of these species. However, some scientists maintain that there currently exists no strong evidence of human hunting in remains thus far uncovered to support this conclusion.

*To learn more about megafauna and see fossilized remains of diprotodon, visit the Red Banks, and take a 4km walk past excavation sites. For more information, visit the Burra visitor center.*

spooky. The most popular site, the large, open cut of the **Burra Mine,** a.k.a. the **Monster Mine,** is indicative of the importance of copper in Burra's history. The mine was one of the world's largest and was last used in the 1970s. **Morphett's Engine-house Museum,** on the site of Burra Mine, details its mechanical aspects. Be sure to go through the miners' underground tunnel; a mere 1.5m high, it was just tall enough for the miners to duck through en route to work. (Open daily 11am-2pm. $5, concessions $4.) Other sights on the tour include the old **Burra Smelting Works, Hampton Village** (archaeological remains of an old township), and the old **dugout homes** where the first miners lived. Just out of town, off the main road, **Thorogoods** is a small, privately-owned apple winery that uses an old Italian basket press to make wine, beer, cider, and liqueurs out of the apples grown in their orchards. The friendly owner and homey feel ensure you'll have a wonderfully personalized wine-tasting experience. The Misty Morning sparkling wine is particularly delicious. (☎08 8892 2669; www.thorogoods.com.au. Open daily noon-4:30pm.)

**FESTIVALS.** In late February or early March, Burra hosts **Jazz in the Monster Mine,** an annual performance held in the mine crater. (☎08 8892 2154; bvc@capri.net.au. $45.) The **Jailhouse Rock Festival,** held on the last weekend in February, celebrates the oldies. (☎08 8892 2154. $30, children $15.) Festival tickets are booked through the visitors center. Known for being the antique center of the Mid-North, Burra hosts a large **Antique and Collectibles Fair** every year in early May.

# QUORN  ☎ 08

An old railway town smack in the middle of the Flinders Ranges, Quorn (pop. 1400) is the outback town of the movies, both figuratively and literally. Its wide streets and hilly backdrop have appeared in at least nine films, including the WWII epic *Gallipoli.* Quorn's country hospitality, best found in the town's pubs, makes it an ideal base from which to explore the stunning **Warren Gorge** as well as the **Dutchman's Stern** and **Devil's Peak** bushwalks.

**TRANSPORTATION AND PRACTICAL INFORMATION.** Quorn is on Hwy. 83 (which later becomes Hwy. 47; the two are used interchangeably on signs), 40km northeast of Port Augusta and Hwy. 1. The historic Pichi Richi Railway runs a steam engine **train** from March to October every weekend and school holidays between Port

Augusta and Quorn, as well as to Woolshed Flat and back from Quorn. (☎08 8648 6598 or 1800 440 101. Tickets between Port Augusta and Quorn: $45 one-way, $71 round-trip; concessions $42/66; children $17/23; family $107/165. Quorn round-trip to Woolshed Flat: $42, concession $39, children $14, family $9.) The **Flinders Ranges Visitors Centre,** on 7th St., between First St. and Railway Terr., has Internet ($3 per 15min.) and area information. (☎08 8648 6419; www. flindersranges.com. Open daily 9am-5pm.) Other services include: **police** (☎08 8648 6060), 24 Railway Terr.; a small **IGA** supermarket, on 7th St., across from the visitors center (open M-F 8am-6pm, Sa-Su 9am-4:30pm); and free **Internet access** at the **library,** on West Terr. (☎08 8648 6101; open during school hours; during holidays Tu and F 1-6pm, W-Th 1-5pm, Sa 10am-noon.) The **post office** is at 21 Railway Terr. **Postal Code:** 5433.

**⌂ ACCOMMODATIONS.** The sprawling **Andu Lodge ❷**, 12 First St., is a family-run hostel that offers clean rooms, an ample kitchen, and a lounge area. Work exchange is possible. (☎08 8648 6020. Dorms $25; singles $30; doubles $55; families $65. Weekly rates available.) The **Quorn Caravan Park ❶**, at the east end of Silo Rd., is environmentally conscious, with knowledgeable owners and work-exchange opportunities. (☎08 8648 6206; www.quorncaravanpark.com. au. Reception 8am-8pm. Unpowered for 2 $18, powered $22, extra person $6. Hikers and cyclists $6 per person. Cabins $50-80.) There is bush camping with toilets but no water at **Warren Gorge ❶**, a beautiful spot 20km northwest of town off the Arden Vale Rd.; follow signs from West Terr. out of town.

**◖ FOOD.** The **Quandong Cafe and Bakery ❶**, 31 First St., offers home-cooked meals in a pleasant dining room adorned with local art. (☎08 8648 6155. Open daily 8:30am-4pm. Breakfast $11, sandwiches and salads from $5. Closed from mid-Dec. to mid-Mar.) The cook at the **Buckaringa Better Buy Market ❶**, 40 First St., has Thai takeaway for $8-12. (☎08 8648 6381. Internet $8.45 per hr. Open M and W-Sa 9am-5:30pm, Su 10am-5:30pm; takeaway 11am-5pm. Cash only.)

**◪ HIKES.** Quorn is a short drive from a number of rewarding hikes. Arguably the area's top hike, **◪Dutchman's Stern**, a bluff 10km north of Quorn, is the proto-typical Australian hike, spotted with hopping kangaroos and overlooking red-soil hills. Hikers can choose between two walks: a ridgetop hike (8.2km, 4hr. round-trip) and a loop walk (10.5km, 5hr.). **Devil's Peak** (2hr. round-trip) affords 360° views of the Flinders region. (Closed summer during fire ban season.) Another 10km north of Dutchman's, **Warren Gorge** is good for viewing yellow-footed rock wallabies, recognizable by their striped tails. **Mount Brown Conservation Park,** 16km south of town on Richman Valley Rd., contains (usually dry) **Waukerie Falls** and **Mount Brown.** Allow seven hours for the trip to the summit and back. (Closed in summer during fire-ban season. Contact a ranger at **Mambray Creek** ☎08 8634 7068 or **Port Augusta** ☎08 8648 5300 for hike availability.)

**◪ OUTDOOR ACTIVITIES.** Located at the base of Devil's Peak, 3km down Devil's Peak Rd., **Pichi Richi Camel Tours** offers short treks through the Flinders on their large, hardy camels. (Bookings required. ☎08 8648 6640; www.pichirichi-cameltours.com. 30min. tour $25; 1hr. tour $35; sunset tour $65; camel to candlelight dinner $175.) The tourist office has a map of many scenic drives. The 36km long Buckaringa Scenic Rd. is a charming, narrow dirt road that winds past the Buckaringa private reserve and ends at a lovely lookout on a hill—a perfect spot to watch the sunrise. The driving options off the scenic road offer "soft adventure" (read: less risky, same views) 4WD tracks. Access to tracks is granted through the **Austral Hotel,** 16 Railway Terr. (☎08 8648 6017).

# WILPENA POUND AND FLINDERS RANGES NATIONAL PARK

Wilpena Pound, a valley encircled by the soaring mountains of the Flinders Range, is the iconic site in Flinders Ranges National Park. A hilly syncline, or geological upfold, outlined in jagged quartzite and resembling a huge crater, Wilpena Pound is a fitting introduction to the Flinders with its rewarding hikes and scenic drives punctuated by gorges created millions of years ago.

**☎ ☷ TRANSPORTATION AND PRACTICAL INFORMATION.** Most of the tours through the Flinders stop by Wilpena Pound. The helpful **Wilpena Visitor Centre** is the park's headquarters, offering general park and hiking info, passes good for five days or until leaving the park ($7.50), camping permits ($10 per night), and bookings for scenic flights and 4WD tours. (☎08 8648 0048. Flights start at $95 per 20min. Open daily 8am-6pm. Day and camping passes can also be obtained from self-registration stations at the park entrances and the Rawnsley Park Station.) There's a **general store** just behind the center with a limited selection of food and supplies as well as petrol, an **ATM,** and **Internet access** ($6 per 30min.; open daily 8am-6pm, hours may vary in summer). Fifty-five kilometers south of Wilpena in Hawker, the **Hawker General Store** is a good place to stock up on fresh, decently priced hiking and camping essentials. Try out the delicious, thick steak sandwich ($9), or choose from among a variety of cakes, breads, and pastries. (Open M-F 8am-5:30pm, Sa 9am-1pm.)

**☎ ☷ FOOD AND ACCOMMODATIONS.** Camping is available in the park and can be paid for at the visitors center or at self-registration kiosks ($10 per vehicle). A few sites have water and toilet facilities; pick up a park map from the visitors center for a complete list of campgrounds and amenities. For a shower, hit the refurbished **Wilpena Campground ❷,** next to the visitors center. (Permits available at the visitors center. Sites for 2 $20, powered $28. Extra person $6.) The **Wilpena Pound Resort ❸** operates a restaurant, bar, pool, and motel down the road from the visitors center. The resort has nice rooms with A/C and TV. Big meals from the bar run $15-23. The lunch burger ($15.50) is particularly delicious and packed with extras. (☎08 8648 0004 or 1800 805 802. Restaurant open daily 7:30-10am, noon-2pm, and 6-8:30pm; 6:30-9pm in summer. Bar open 12pm-late. 4-bed dorms $35; doubles from $135.)

**☷ HIKING.** Walks of varying intensity lead to views of the immense Wilpena Pound. Be sure to pick up the thorough *Bushwalking in the Flinders Ranges National Park* brochure from the visitors center before heading out. All of the walks to the Pound begin at the visitors center and most follow the same flat path for 2-3km. No cars are allowed inside the park, but a shuttle bus service from the visitors center cuts 2km off the trip each way, leaving you 1.6km (about 1hr. round-trip) from Wangarra lookout (4-6 buses per day, 9am-5:15pm; one-way $2.50, round-trip $4). In an emergency, contact the **police** (☎08 8648 4028), the visitors center, or the **Wilpena Pound Resort** (☎08 8648 0004; open daily 7am-7:30pm) to be connected to emergency services.

For avid hikers, rangers recommend the high-intensity climb to the summit of **☷St. Mary's Peak,** which rewards the effort with sprawling views of the Pound. The St. Mary's **outside loop track** (14.6km, 6hr. round-trip) starts up the mountain from the resort and is the fastest way to reach the summit. The **inside loop track** (21.5km, 9hr. round-trip) to the peak is wide, flat, and boring until Cooinda Camp. Past Cooinda Camp, the remaining 3km (1hr.) become wild and overgrown. The return journey can be confusing; keep an eye out for the short stacks of rocks that serve as path markings when the signposts aren't visible.

**⚑ OTHER ACTIVITIES.** Those heading north to Parachilna, Leigh Creek, or the Oodnadatta Track should consider exiting the Flinders via the 50km ▓**drive through the park's gorges.** Their colored walls and geological ramparts are stunning, making every turn something of a surprise. The stretch through Bunyeroo Gorge and Brachina Gorge is the highlight, and geology buffs will be astounded by the well-labeled and diverse geological trail through Brachina Gorge. The road on the way to the gorges from Wilpena Pound passes the **Cazenaux tree,** which was made famous when an artist named Cazenaux photographed the tree to national and worldwide acclaim. The turnoff for the gorges is 4km north of the Wilpena junction on the road toward Blinman. **Stokes Hill Lookout,** 17km past the turnoff for the gorges toward Oraparinna and Arkaroola, provides more breathtaking sights and a great spot for a picnic.

Rock climbers should contact the **Edeowie Station** (☎08 8648 4714), to the west of the park, for information on accessing **Edeowie Gorge,** the area's top rock climbing spot. The gorge is visible from the park, but can only be accessed through the privately owned station.

# NORTHERN FLINDERS

The few visitors who arrive in Northern Flinders are welcomed by an impressive palette of colors. Sage-green shrubs dot the ground below while orange hills fade to red, blue, and purple mountains in the distance. After a rare rainfall, thousands of yellow flowers blanket the normally dry ground. The vastness of the Outback is apparent here: the mountains are large, the gorges deep, and the human company scarce. To cover the few hundred kilometers between **Flinders Range National Park** and **Gammon Ranges National Park,** drivers can either come up through **Wilpena** (p. 516) and Blinman or stick to the highway from Hawker and follow the paved road as far as Copley. The stops described here are located along the highway, though the dirt-road route to Gammon will show you what the "back of beyond" is all about.

Travelers looking to head north of Gammon and Arkaroola will need a **Desert Parks Pass.** For info, call the **Desert Parks Pass Hotline** (☎1800 816 078) or talk to the rangers at **Balcanoona** in Gammon Ranges Park or at the **Parks Office** in Port Augusta. (☎08 8648 5300. Year pass $95, day pass $11, overnight pass $20. Prices may vary.) The pass allows unlimited access to the Simpson Desert, Innamincka, Lake Eyre, and Dalhousie areas, among others. It comes with a packet of brochures and great regional maps.

## LEIGH CREEK                                               ☎08

Leigh Creek, 22km south of a coalfield and 110km from the start of the **Oodnadatta Track** (p. 521), was planned and built by the Electricity Trust of South Australia (ETSA), and it shows. Bizarrely sterile, the town consists of gently curving residential streets lined with gravel "lawns," all clustered around one central shopping center. The **visitors center** is in the Open Cut Cafe in the central mall. (☎08 8675 2723. Open M-F 8:30am-5:30pm, Sa 8:30am-2pm.) The school doubles as the town **library** and has free **Internet.** (Open during school term M and W-Th 8:30am-4pm, Tu and F 8:30am-4:30pm and 7-9pm, Sa 9am-noon; school holidays Tu 7-9pm, W-Th 10am-4:30pm, F noon-4:30pm and 7-9pm.) The landscaped downtown area has a pub and an **IGA** supermarket. (☎08 8675 2009. Open M-F 9am-5:30pm, Sa 9am-12:30pm.)

The **Leigh Creek Hotel ❺** in town isn't cheap, but all rooms are ensuite with TV, telephone, and fridge. (☎08 8675 2025. Cabins $95; motel singles $110; doubles $135.) Book through the Mobil Station for the **Caravan Park ❶**, on your right immediately after turning off the highway. (☎08 8675 2016. Sites $6 per person; powered $11, 2 for $18; cabins for 2 $80, $10 per extra person.)

## VULKATHUNHA-GAMMON RANGES NATIONAL PARK

This is where central Australia gets serious. The Gammons are even more craggy and remote than the Northern Flinders. The local Aboriginals, who co-manage the park with the National Park and Wildlife Service (NPWS), call the area Arrkunha, or "place of red ochre," after the deep colors of the mountains. The park is best explored on unsealed 4WD tracks or on foot. Be sure to bring enough food, water, and supplies to remain self-sufficient.

The **NPWS headquarters** in Balcanoona has up-to-date park info and sells the Desert Parks Pass; however, it is infrequently staffed. (☎08 8648 4829.) Arka-roola, to the northeast of the park, can provide information when the park office isn't open. All campsites have self-registration booths (free entry, $4 per car camping) and toilets. Most have rainwater tanks, but don't rely on them in summer. For emergencies, contact the **Leigh Creek Police** (☎08 8675 2004), **Hawker Police** (☎08 8648 4028), or the **Wilpena Parks Office** (☎08 8648 0049).

Driving the **Wortupa Loop Track** (80km, 4-5hr.) is the easiest way to see the park. Italowie Camp and Weetootla Gorge are accessible via 2WD and connect with shorter trails (2-16km) at the park's fringe. **Lake Frome**, 38km east of Balcanoona (4WD only), is a sprawling lake-bed covered in salt. No access is allowed after 3pm until 5am, when the area becomes a hunting ground.

For serious hikers, the park has a number of lengthy and challenging trails. **Italowie Gorge Hike** (15.7km, 8hr. one-way) is lauded by many as the region's best. The trailhead can be found on the park's eastern edge off the main road. There are several one-way options off the track of the **Weetootla Gorge Hike** (18.4km loop, 7½hr. round-trip) that traverse rugged territory. Start the hike from the Weetootla Gorge carpark. Be sure to check with the ranger before starting any hike. The terrain is dangerous if you are unprepared; feral goats aimlessly wear paths into the hills that can lead hikers in circles.

# OUTBACK SOUTH AUSTRALIA

If you've ever wanted to go off the grid, this would be the ideal place to do it. Outback South Australia's unsealed roads stretch endlessly across baked earth, punctuated only by intimidating "Next gas: 454km," or "Danger: Extreme Conditions Ahead" signs. The only living creatures on this sun-dried highway are wandering cattle and marauding bushflies. The sun is king; it burns the land from horizon to shimmering horizon during the day, and then plunges it into frigid, unsheltered nights. Summers are scorching, with temperatures reaching 45°C (113°F) in the shade. For most, a drive from one end to the other is enough, and the few who call the Outback their home are a rough and rugged crowd as intriguing as the landscape. The helpful (and difficult to find) *Remote Travel Hints for 4x4 Tourists* offers simple tips for novice drivers tackling the Outback. The two most important things to remember are to bring plenty of water, and never to leave your vehicle should something happen. For more tips and safety information, see **Driving in the Outback** (p. 73).

# STUART HIGHWAY: ADELAIDE TO COOBER PEDY

As the Stuart Hwy. winds its way northwest toward Coober Pedy, there is little to see other than the harsh, red terrain. This is pasture land, so beware of free-roaming horses and cattle. Fuel prices will increase the farther you venture north, so it's a good idea to make a pit stop in Port Augusta or Pimba before continuing on into the great red yonder.

## WOOMERA ☎08

Located 6km off the Stuart Hwy by Pimba, Woomera (pop. 300) was initially designated a "secret" town by the Australian and British militaries, a blank dot on maps until 1960. Created in 1947 as the unofficial capital of the Woomera Prohibited Area, the town is a long-range weapons testing area that once covered nearly 27 million hectares; it is still the largest land-locked military test site in the world. The pre-planned village sits at the edge of the area, known affectionately as "the range" by locals. From 1970 to 1999, the American military was the primary partner in the Joint Defence Facility-Nurrangar, a satellite and missile tracking center. Reassuringly, the base is currently geared more toward satellite launching than bomb testing.

The **Woomera Heritage Centre,** on Dewrang Ave. in the middle of town, details nuclear bombs, radio astronomy, and other aspects of Woomera's past. Strangely, the center is also home to a 10-pin bowling alley. Pick up a free pamphlet for a self-guided tour of the outdoor plane and rocket exhibit in the center of town. (☎08 8673 7042. Museum $6, concessions $4.50, 15 and under $3, families $20. Open daily Dec.-Feb. 10am-2pm, Mar.-Nov. 9am-5pm.) Because of the lack of light pollution, Woomera is great for star-gazing. Nightly astronomy tours are held at **Baker Observatory.** (☎08 8674 3227 or book at the visitors center. Adult $10, students and concessions $6, family $20.) The **Eldo Hotel ❺,** named after the European Launch Development Organisation (ELDO), was built for rocket scientists. (☎08 8673 7867; www.eldohotel.com.au. Continental breakfast included. Bar and restaurant on-site. Ensuite for single or double occupancy, $89 extra person $17.50.) Woomera also has a caravan park, the **Travellers Village ❶,** just as you come into town. (☎08 8673 7800. Reception 8am-7pm. Unpowered $10 per person; powered for 2 $24, $6 extra person. Motel rooms $75.) There's a supermarket as well as a petrol station just off the Stuart Hwy in Pimba, at **Spud's Roadhouse.** (☎08 8673 7473. Open daily 6am-10pm.)

## COOBER PEDY ☎08

The "opal capital of the world," Coober Pedy supports 80% of the world's opal industry. Unlike the gemstones that make it famous, Coober Pedy is rather low on aesthetic appeal, but even more colorful than its gems are the people hiding in the dirt. These hardy Aussies literally live "down under," since over half of the town's 3500 residents make their homes underground. Locals invariably impress tourists with stories of international opal-seekers—from Latvian crocodile-hunters-turned-opal-miners to fortune-squandering Italian playboys, these characters give Coober Pedy a wild edge and a diversity unseen anywhere else in central Australia—over 42 nationalities are represented in the area schools. This den of characters and carats is traveler heaven.

▓ **TRANSPORTATION.** Greyhound Australia (☎13 14 99 or 13 20 30) runs to Coober Pedy once daily from Adelaide and Alice Springs. The **bus station** is next to the police station on Malliotis Blvd. (☎08 8673 5151. Open daily 6-9am and

5-8pm.) In addition, virtually every tour between Adelaide and Alice stops off in Coober Pedy. The Stuart Hwy., the main north-south road through Australia's interior, goes straight through town. **Budget** (☎08 8672 5333) rents 4WDs.

**ORIENTATION AND PRACTICAL INFORMATION.** Coober Pedy is 685km (6-8hr.) south of Alice Springs, 744km southeast of Uluru, 166km west of William Creek and the Oodnadatta Track, 538km north of Port Augusta, and 846km (8-10hr.) north of Adelaide. The turnoff from the Stuart Hwy. leads into Hutchison St., the main street, where most points of interest are located. The helpful **Visitor Information Centre** (☎08 8672 4617 or 1800 637 076; open M-F 8:30am-5pm, Sa-Su 10am-1pm), at the south end of Hutchison St. across from the bus depot, has free 30min. Internet access. **Internet** and Wi-Fi are also available for free at the community **library**, on Paxton Rd., just off Wright Rd. (Open M-F 9am-5pm, Su 11am-4pm; school holidays M-F noon-5pm.) If the visitors center is closed, try the unofficial tourist office, **Underground Books**, on Post Office Hill Rd., left off Hutchison St. (☎08 8672 5558. Open M-F 8:30am-4pm, Sa 10am-4pm.) Other services include: **ATM** at Westpac Bank and at the Opal Inn Hotel; **RAA** (☎08 8672 5230), at Desert Traders; the **police**, on Malliotis Blvd. (☎08 8672 5056), the first left off Hutchison's from the Hwy.; a **pharmacy** on Hutchison St. across from the Umoona Mine (☎08 8672 3333; open M-F 9am-6pm, Sa 9am-2pm); the **Miner's Store**, a supermarket on Hutchison St., on the right after the roundabout (☎08 8672 5051; open M-Sa 8:30am-7pm, Su 9am-6pm); and a **post office** in the Miner's Store. **Postal Code:** 5723.

> **TIP**
>
> **GETTING SHAFTED.** Outside town boundaries, 1.5 million abandoned mine shafts make the danger of plummeting to your death very real. Mining practices make it unsafe to fill in the holes, so they are left open and uncovered. Signs around town, though co-opted by the tourist industry, are no joke; do not attempt to explore opal fields by yourself.

**ACCOMMODATIONS.** **Radeka's Backpacker's Inn ❷**, at Hutchison and Oliver St., on the right at the base of the hill after the roundabout, is an underground hostel, with a clean, comfortable maze of underground caves 6.5m below ground. If you're lucky, you can stay in the "dungeon," which is actually quiet and inviting. (☎08 8672 5223 or 1800 633 891; www.radekadownunder.com. au. Kitchen, pool table, TV room, courtesy bus pickup and dropoff, and a bar. Internet access $2 per 15min. Reception daily 8am-9pm. Dorms $22; doubles $55; motel singles and doubles $105.) **Riba's Underground Camping ❶** is on William Creek Rd., outside of town. Coming from Port Augusta, turn off 4km before Hutchison St. (☎08 8672 5614. Sites $8; subterranean sites $12; powered aboveground sites $22 for 2, $8 per extra person; budget singles $45; doubles $55.) The swankiest spot in town is the **Desert Cave Hotel ❺**, opposite Radeka's on Hutchison St. Equipped dugout rooms (TV, couch, phone, wine) are accompanied by a swimming pool, gym, and restaurant. (☎08 8672 5688 or 1800 088 52; www.desertcave.com.au. Reception daily 6:30am-11:30pm. Doubles $218.)

**FOOD AND NIGHTLIFE.** Run by an immigrant Sicilian family, **John's Pizza Bar ❶**, located in the strip mall on Hutchison St., is where Italian tradition meets Coober Pedy quirkiness. Pizzas run $8-29. (☎08 8672 5561. Open daily 9am-10pm.) On Hutchinson St., by the roundabout, **Tom and Mary's Greek Taverna ❶** has a hearty menu of sit-down and takeaway fare. (☎08 8672 5688. Gyros $8. Burgers $8-12. Chips $4. Open daily 5pm-late.) Coober Pedy has a rollicking pub, the **Opal Inn Hotel,** on the corner of the roundabout. (☎08 8672 5054. Schooners $3. Happy hour M, W, F 6-7:30pm. Open daily 10am-11pm.)

**TOURS.** The visitors center books all tours, but you can also contact operators directly. Those who prefer to go at their own pace should note that most destinations can be covered independently by car. The 12hr. **Mail Run** covers a triangular route, stopping at points of interest while delivering mail to cattle stations. (☎1800 069 911; www.mailruntour.com. Book ahead. M and Th 8:45am from Underground Books. $175.) **Radeka's Desert Breakaways Tours** is popular with backpackers and includes Crocodile Harry's, the opal fields, a trip out to the Breakaways (a set of mesas), and a chance to mine for your own opal. (☎08 8672 5223. Daily at 1pm. 4hr. $50.) The **Desert Cave Hotel's Tour** offers a similar trip for more money. (☎08 8672 5688 or 1800 088 521. Daily at 2pm. Min. 4 people. $85, discount for guests.) **Riba's Evening Mine Tours** takes guests underground for a 90min. mine tour. (☎08 8672 5614. Daily 7:30pm. $18.) **Radeka's Downunder Stargazing** tours take advantage of the clear night skies around Coober Pedy for some astronomy lessons and stargazing. (☎08 8672 5223. Nightly 8pm; 1hr.; $20, children $10.)

**SIGHTS.** The **Umoona Opal Mine and Museum,** on Hutchison St., is an award-winning museum with displays of local Aboriginal culture, town history, and, of course, opals. The underground complex includes a full-size home that contrasts early and modern dugout styles. Check out the display dedicated to Eric the Plesiosaur, a sea-dwelling creature whose fossilized skeleton (as well as the remains of his last supper) turned to opal. Eric himself is on display at the Australian Museum in Sydney. (☎08 8672 5288; www.umoonaopalmine.com. au. Mine and museum open daily 8am-7pm. Tours daily 10am, 2, 4pm. $10, children $5.) The town's underground churches are usually open to visitors. The oldest of these churches is the **Saints Peter and Paul Catholic Church,** next to Radeka's. The underground **Serbian Orthodox Church,** left off Flinders St. (look for the sign), with its Gothic design, is unusual and worth a visit. Another sort of underground shrine is **Crocodile Harry's Crocodile's Nest,** the lair of the late, legendary womanizer, adventurer, and crocodile-slayer who was one of the models for the character Crocodile Dundee. Originally from Latvia, Harry's croc-wrasslin' days are behind him, but his home, 2km west of town on Seventeen Mile Rd., is still sometimes open to the public. (Admission $2. If the signs are down, ask at the visitors center for directions.) Outside town, 17km north on the Stuart Hwy., the track on **Moon Plain** (70km return; 2hr.), a lunar landscape of glinting rocks and browned pieces of vegetation, is fun to explore. This is also the stretch of road featured in the movie *Priscilla, Queen of the Desert. Mad Max III* was also filmed out here. The famous **Great Dog Fence,** the world's longest fence, is about 15km outside Coober Pedy.

# OFF THE STUART HIGHWAY: OODNADATTA TRACK

The **Oodnadatta Track,** one of the most famous Outback tracks in Australia, runs 619km from Marree, north of Leigh Creek in the Flinders, through William Creek and Oodnadatta to Marla, 235km north of Coober Pedy on the Stuart Hwy. Without a doubt a great way to see the Outback, the track gives visitors a taste of the harsh realities of life in the center. The horizon shimmers in the heat, and carcasses of cars join those of animals that met the same fate. There is no cell phone service on the track, and there is no free water anywhere.

After a rare rainfall, the entire track can close, cutting residents off from the rest of civilization. Mostly following the route of the Old Ghan train line that used to connect Alice Springs with points south, the Oodnadatta passes the salt-beds of Lake Eyre, stretches of baked red nothing, ruins of ancient farm homes, and the legendary dog fence. The unsealed road can be driven in a 2WD vehicle, but drive slower than 40kph. Most rental companies do not insure their cars on unsealed roads. It's a good idea to call or check online with the **Northern Road Conditions Hotline** (☎1300 361 033; www.transport.sa.gov.au/quick-links/northern_roads/northern.asp) for road closures, though signs at each town provide conditions for the next segment of track. Be particularly careful around road trains, as they can kick up rocks that shatter windshields.

Various roadhouses carry a thorough ▨**mudmap guide** to the Oodnadatta Track that includes every detour and detail that a traveler could desire to know about. Try to pick it up before you leave **Adelaide** (p. 459) or the visitors center in **Port Augusta** (p. 511); otherwise, check the website.

Though larger tours, such as **Wayward Bus** (p. 458), incorporate the Oodnadatta into some of their itineraries, there are tour groups that operate exclusively in the area. Those who want to take in the vastness of the Outback from the air should try **Wrightsair** (☎08 8670 7962; www.wrightsair.com.au), a scenic-flight company based in William Creek. For a unique approach to traveling the Outback, the eco-friendly **Camel Safaris** (☎08 8634 7079 or 1800 064 244; www.austcamel.com.au) runs four-day camel treks along the Track from April to October. See the website for a schedule of tours and prices. Towns are listed below as they would be encountered traveling south to north on the Track.

**OODNADATTA.** Oodnadatta has precious amenities for drivers on the track, including car repair facilities and the unmistakable **Pink Roadhouse ❶**, which offers valuable info and services, including petrol, groceries, and emergency supplies. Longtime owners Adam and Lynnie are happy to help every traveler who passes through. Check road and weather conditions with Pink's or with the **police** (☎08 8670 7805). The roadhouse also has a **post office** (open M-F 9am-noon and 2-4pm; **postal code:** 5734), **Internet access** ($3 per 15min.), filling burgers ($6-9), and accommodations. They can arrange car repairs and vehicle recovery as well. Essentially, Pink's does everything except arrange marriages. (☎08 8670 7822 or 1800 802 07; www.pinkroadhouse.com.au. Open daily high season 8:30am-6pm; low season M-F 8am-5:30pm, Sa-Su 9am-5pm. Sites $17.50, powered $22.50; singles $45; hotel-style doubles $59; ensuite cabins for 2 $95.) From here, you can either continue northwest on the track to its end at Marla (210km) or head southwest to Coober Pedy (195km). Oodna is also a good base for those traveling to the oasis at **Dalhousie Springs** (190km north) and the **Simpson Desert,** both popular destinations (Desert Parks Pass required).

**MARLA.** Marla, where the Oodnadatta Track rejoins civilization, is an over-grown highway rest area that sits approximately halfway between Adelaide and Alice Springs. The **Traveller's Rest Roadhouse ❸** has petrol and a small supermarket (both open 24hr.), a bar, a restaurant, **Internet access** ($2 per 15min.), a free community pool, showers ($4), and pricey accommodations. (☎08 8670 7001. Camping $5 per person, power an additional $8; budget cabin singles $35; doubles $45; motel singles $85; doubles $90; extra person $35.) Those heading north toward Uluru and Alice should get fuel here: the next station is Kulgera, 180km north. Those heading south should push on to Cadney Homestead, 153km north of Coober Pedy, rather than staying over in Marla. Cadney's offers one-night camping and use of facilities for $3.

# EYRE PENINSULA

Although the landscape may not look promising from the highway, the Eyre Peninsula is as spectacular as it is underappreciated. It encompasses the stretch of coastline from Ceduna to the start of the Nullarbor Plain. Free from hordes of tourists, the tiny fishing villages remain picturesque, basking in the salty breezes of the Southern Ocean. While the east coast has gentle rolling dunes and calm waters, the aquamarine waves of the west coast caress rock faces and rough-hewn cliffs. An abundance of fish on both coasts makes the Eyre Peninsula Australia's premier fishing destination. The free *Seafood and Aquaculture Trail Guide* lists a series of interesting, unusual tours along the peninsula that highlight the importance of the sea in the local economy and culture. The trail includes visits to rock lobster colonies and a seahorse breeding facility in Port Lincoln. The Eyre is also home to several phenomenal national parks, most notably the three clustered at the southern tip of the peninsula: **Lincoln National Park, Coffin Bay,** and **Whaler's Way.** Towns are covered below from east to west, as they would be encountered coming from Adelaide on Alt. Hwy. 1.

## TRANSPORTATION

Premier Stateliner (Adelaide ☎08 8415 5555, Port Lincoln ☎08 8682 1288, Whyalla ☎08 8645 9911) is the only public **bus** carrier on the Eyre with anything approaching frequent service, though Greyhound Australia stops in Ceduna on the way to Perth. Stateliner runs between Adelaide and Whyalla (M-W 4 per day, Th-F 5 per day, Sa-Su 3-4 per day; $52.50, concessions $26.25). Buses also leave Adelaide bound for Port Lincoln, stopping in towns along the east coast. (M-F and Su 2 per day, Sa 1 per day; $92.10, concessions $46.05.) Traversing the Eyre Peninsula by car means diverging from the Eyre Hwy. (Hwy. 1), which runs 468km across the top of the peninsula from Whyalla to Ceduna. The highlights of the Eyre are on a triangular coastal route via the Lincoln and Flinders Hwy. (Alt. Hwy. 1), which takes 763km to connect the same towns.

# EYRE PENINSULA EAST COAST

As Alt. Hwy. 1 winds along the east coast, the land's rolling plains are dotted by small settlements separated by intervals of about 60km. Any of these small fishing hamlets is a good place to stop and rest, but **Cowell,** 111km south of Whyalla, has the most to offer visitors. Right on the Franklin Harbour, **Cowell** has a thriving oyster industry, the nation's only commercial jade mining, and a quiet foreshore with excellent fishing.

**ORIENTATION AND PRACTICAL INFORMATION.** After Cowell, from north to south, **Arno Bay, Port Neill,** and **Tumby Bay** are also good spots to visit. All towns have petrol stations and post offices; Cowell's **post** is located at 2 Main St. (Open M-F 9am-noon and 1-5pm). In addition, the **Ebb 'n Flow Cafe,** on Main St., has tourist information. (☎08 8629 2692. Open M-Th 9am-5:30pm, F-Su 9am-9pm.) The **School Community Library,** on Story Rd. just off Hwy. 1, has free **Internet** and Wi-Fi access. (Open M noon-5pm, Tu-F 9am-5pm; during school holidays Tu-Th 11am-5pm, F noon-5pm.)

**ACCOMMODATIONS.** All of the above towns have caravan parks and pub hotels (singles from around $30; doubles $40). The **Franklin Harbour Hotel ❸,** 1 Main St., in Cowell, has clean rooms and a balcony overlooking the harbor as well as the most character of any of the east-coast accommodations. Mountain

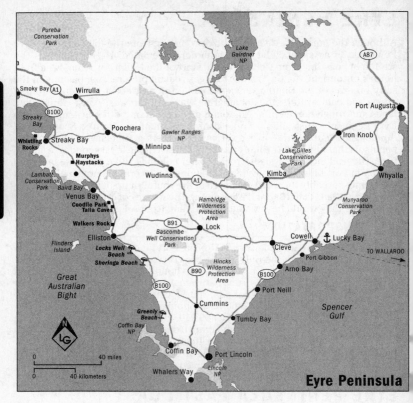

**Eyre Peninsula**

bikes and fishing rods are available for guest use. (☎08 8629 2015 or 1800 303 449. Continental breakfast included. Bar open M-Th and Su 10am-midnight, F-Sa 10am-2am. Singles $35; doubles $49.) **The Commercial Hotel ❸**, 24 Main St, in Cowell, has similar accommodations, but lacks the harbor views. (☎08 8629 2181. Singles $35; doubles $45; family rooms $60.) Farther south, the **Seabreeze Hotel ❸**, 7 Tumby Terr., in Tumby Bay, faces the water. (☎08 8688 2362. Singles $30, ensuite $65; doubles $40/75, extra person $10.)

**🍴 FOOD.** Visitors coming from the east can consider Cowell their introduction to Eyre Peninsula's extensive seafood menu. Those who really want the local seafood with local style can try their hands at fishing from any of the town's jetties. Otherwise, **Cowell Seafood Producers ❶**, 72 The Esplanade (follow 3rd St. out of town and then look for signs), sells fresh local seafood, including Cowell's signature oysters. (☎08 8629 2621. $5.50 per fresh ½-dozen oysters. Open M-F 7:30am-5pm.) **Cowell Bakery ❶**, 25 Main St., bakes pies and pastries (from $3.20), but oyster kebabs ($7.50) are the real standout on the menu. (☎08 8629 2034. Open M-F 8am-5pm, Sa 9am-4pm, Su 10am-4pm.)

**🔦 SIGHTS.** From Cowell, 3rd St. runs out of town and becomes unsealed (though relatively smooth and still 2WD-accessible) Beach Rd., so named because it provides access to numerous beaches down the coast. The various beaches are well labeled off Beach Rd. On the whole, the east coast beaches have calm waters perfect for swimming and fishing. ◪**Port Gibbons,** 22km south of Cowell, is arguably the best spot on the east coast with massive sand dunes overlooking the ocean. Follow the signs to get there.

# PORT LINCOLN                                                                    ☎08

Port Lincoln (pop. 15,000) is perched at the tip of the Eyre Peninsula and overlooks Boston Bay, one of the largest natural harbors in the world. There's no fresh water, but it's the salt water that has turned the town into the seafood capital of the region. Port Lincoln boasts both the largest fishing fleet in the Southern Hemisphere and more millionaires per capita than anywhere else in Australia. Beyond the sea, Port Lincoln is a popular resort town for its proximity to a few of the peninsula's most spectacular areas. **Lincoln National Park, Coffin Bay National Park,** and **Whaler's Way** are where the green fringe of the great southern Outback meets the ocean in a cacophony of pounding surf.

▚ **ORIENTATION.** Port Lincoln sprawls across the southern tip of the Eyre Peninsula, and smart travelers will stop by the visitors center for a map of the town. In general, most places of interest can be found on the waterfront strip near the jetty. Most restaurants and hotels are located on **Tasman Terrace,** which runs east-west along the waterfront. One block inland, parallel to Tasman Terr., **Liverpool Street** is the town's shopping district. About 3km southeast of the town jetty is the ritzy **Lincoln Cove Marina,** with a number of upscale restaurants.

▛▟ **TRANSPORTATION AND PRACTICAL INFORMATION.** Premier Stateliner **buses** depart from their booking office at 24 Lewis St., just south of Tasman Terr. (☎08 8682 1288. Open M-F 8am-6:45pm, Sa 8:30-11:30am.) Buses run to Adelaide (M-F and Su 2 per day; Sa 1 per day; $92.10) via Port Augusta ($65). Book ahead for buses. A **ferry** leaves from Lucky Bay by Cowell and crosses to Wallaroo. (☎08 8823 0777; www.seasa.com.au. Book at the visitors center. Leaves M-F 10:30am and 4pm; Sa noon; Su 2:30pm. Car $120. Caravan $27.50 per meter. Passengers $30, students $20, children $10.) If you need a **taxi,** try ☎08 8682 1222 or 13 10 08. Make your first stop in town the ◪**Visitors Information Centre,** 3 Adelaide Pl. The visitors center provides information on a variety of area tours, handles bookings, and sells permits for local national parks. (☎08 8683 3544 or 1300 788 378; www.visitportlincoln.net. Internet access $3 per 15min. Open daily 9am-5pm. Also rents aquatic equipment.) The **library,** in the Spencer Institute building, just off Tasman Terr., offers 1hr. blocks of free **Internet** and boasts Wi-Fi. (☎08 8688 3622. Open M-Tu and Th-F 9am-5pm, Sa 9am-7pm, Su 1-4:30pm.) The **Port Lincoln Hospital** is on Oxford Terr. (☎08 8683 2284), and a **pharmacy** can be found at 43 Tasman Terr. (☎08 8682 2664. Open M-F 9am-5:30pm, Sa 9am-noon.) Other services include: **banks** and **ATMs** on Tasman Terr. and Liverpool St.; a 24hr. **police station,** 1 Liverpool St. (☎08 8688 3020); and a **post office** at 68 Tasman Terr. (Open M-F 9am-5pm.) **Postal Code:** 5606.

▟ **ACCOMMODATIONS.** The **Pier Hotel ❸,** at the center of Tasman Terr., offers adequate rooms, some with bay views and all with cable TV. Night owls will appreciate that the raucous epicenter of Port Lincoln nightlife is just downstairs. (☎08 8682 1322. Happy hour F 4:30-6pm. Rooms $60-110.) Though not as centrally located, **Hotel Boston ❸,** 19-21 King St. near the silos at the west end of Tasman Terr., has decent rooms that saw their most distinguished guest in 1954 when Queen Elizabeth II stayed there. (☎08 8682 1311. Dining hall serves lunch from $7 and dinner from $10. Singles $35, ensuite with TV $45; doubles $45/70. Weekly rates available.) **Port Lincoln Caravan Park ❷,** 11 Hindmarsh St., at the end of London St., has sites and cabins (☎08 8621 4444. Bring own linen. Unpowered sites $23, powered $26; budget cabin $55, ensuite cabin $70, ensuite self-contained cabin $85, Holiday Unit self-contained cabin $99.)

**⬮ FOOD.** With a prime waterfront location, **Moorings ❸,** in the Grand Tasman Hotel, 94 Tasman Terr., is the best place to sample local seafood. Dishes are served with minimal seasoning, allowing the quality of the fish to stand out. The sashimi tuna ($25, entree $17) is tasty. (☎08 8682 2133; www.grandtasmanhotel.com.au. Vegetarian calzone $18. Main courses $20-32. Open M-Sa 6-8:30pm, Th-F noon-2pm.) The large fish and chips portions (from $6.50) at **Ocean Delights ❶,** 57 Tasman Terr., are delicious. (☎08 8682 4993. Open daily 10am-8pm. Shorter hours in winter.) A **Coles** is on Liverpool St. (☎08 8682 2700. Open M-W and F 6am-7pm, Th 6am-9pm, Sa 6am-5pm, Su 11am-5pm.)

**◉◪ SIGHTS AND ACTIVITIES.** **Fishery Bay,** just before **Whaler's Way** (p. 527), is a long stretch of sand with a consistent surf break and shallow waters that make it surfable for all ability levels. Whether for sunbathing or surfing, Fishery is a must for visitors. Be careful of sharks, as great whites live nearby. Rent bikes from **Cluster Cycles,** 60 Liverpool St. (☎08 8683 0822. ½-day $17-29, full-day $28-39, 24hr. $32-45.) Boat cruises leave daily from the Marina Hotel boardwalk. (90min. Book at visitors center. $26, concessions $21, children $12.)

**🎆 FESTIVALS.** Port Lincoln celebrates the sand and the salt in their **Tunarama Festival** (☎08 8682 1300), a three-day extravaganza of fireworks, sand castles, and seafood held annually the week before Australia Day in late January. The festival also features live music, a highly competitive tuna-tossing contest, and a seafood extravaganza at the yacht club (☎1800 629 911). The **Adelaide-to-Lincoln Yacht Race,** held the last weekend of February, is a chance to see some of the area's impressive fleet in action. Food, fashion, and general merriment are abundant during the **Port Lincoln Cup Carnival,** a horse-racing event held annually in the beginning of March (☎08 8682 3851).

# LINCOLN NATIONAL PARK AND MEMORY COVE

One of Eyre's best-kept secrets, **Lincoln National Park** is just 13km from Port Lincoln and offers outdoor enthusiasts breathtaking scenery, abundant wildlife, and pristine beaches. At the southernmost end of the park, Memory Cove provides the best views and camping in the area. Most major attractions and campgrounds within the park are 2WD-accessible in good weather. The difficult **Sleaford-Wanna Dune trail** is one of the few 4WD tracks in the park, traversing 14km of scorching sand dunes. At the northern tip of the park, **September Beach** is an excellent swimming spot with great camping facilities.

To reach the park, take Mortlock Terr. out of town, which will eventually become Verran Terr. Turn left after crossing the railroad tracks and follow Proper Bay Rd. toward Tulka and Whaler's Way. **Camping ❶,** with toilets and rainwater facilities, is available at designated park areas along the way. Park passes ($7.50) are available in kiosks at the camp entrance. Those looking to camp will have to pay for an additional camping permit ($5 per night). Groups might want to consider renting the five-room **Donington Cottage ❺,** at the north tip of the park. (☎08 8683 3544. Book through Port Lincoln's **visitors center** (p. 525). Full kitchen. $80 per night, min. 2 nights for up to 6 people. Bring own linen.) In addition to the Port Lincoln visitors center, the **Eyre District Parks Office,** 75 Liverpool St., Port Lincoln, has park information (☎08 8688 3111).

SOUTH AUSTRALIA

Memory Cove, in the southeast section of the park, is a remote wilderness area accessible by 4WD track. Visitors need a key and permit to access the cove; these are available from the **Port Lincoln Visitors Information Centre** (p. 525). The **Memory Cove campsite ❶**, 19km (45min.) from the locked gate, rewards visitors who made the effort to visit Memory Cove with a private stretch of beach and the chance to fall asleep to the sounds of the ocean. (☎08 8683 3544. Day pass, including camping $7.50. Bush camping is limited to 5 sites and must be booked ahead. $12 per night, 3-night limit. Key deposit $20.)

## WHALER'S WAY

Thirty-two kilometers from Port Lincoln, the most spectacular display of the peninsula's raw beauty is found in Whaler's Way. Access to this privately owned reserve requires a key and an expensive permit, but the experience is worth the extra cost. Purchase permits at the Port Lincoln Visitors Information Centre. (☎08 8683 3544. Map with detailed directions to lookout points included. Key deposit $10. $25 per car, includes 1 night of camping, each additional night $5.) The 2002 season of the American hit television show *Survivor* was filmed here, in South Australia's harshest, most rugged landscape. Roads are unsealed and may be difficult for 2WD vehicles depending on conditions—check with the visitors center. **Bush camping ❶** is allowed at Redbank and Groper Bay. **Groper Bay** has BBQ and toilets, while **Redbanks** has beach access. Be forewarned that all facilities are very basic. Those unwilling to pay admission to Whaler's Way should visit ⚑**Fishery Bay** (p. 526). Just before the turnoff for Whaler's Way, Fishery is a free beach and far more accessible, but still allows for a glimpse of the jagged cliffs and ocean swells that make Whaler's famous.

A 14km dirt road traverses the interior of the park, and numerous well-marked tracks lead to commanding views of the Southern Ocean. **Cape Carnot,** in the southwest, has a blowhole where waves crash against the rocks, often getting as high as the cliffs themselves. Just north of Cape Carnot, **Theakstones** is a narrow crevasse where water rushes in and ricochets off the walls. Emus and kangaroos roam throughout the park year-round, and seals can even be found lounging on rocks. To see the park's namesake, visit in September or October when the whales frequent the waters below.

## COFFIN BAY NATIONAL PARK                                   ☎08

A mere 47km from Port Lincoln toward Ceduna is the lazy town of Coffin Bay, gateway to the magnificent ⚑**Coffin Bay National Park.** Visitors to Coffin Bay will find the camping and accommodation options limited. The **Coffin Bay Caravan Park ❶** is on the Esplanade; turn left on Giles Rd. and follow signs. (☎08 8685 4170. Sites $10 per person, powered $24-6, extra person $7. On-site vans for 2 $45-55, cabins for 2 from $55-95, extra person $10.) The **Coffin Bay Hotel/Motel ❺**, on Shepherd Ave., is the sole hotel option and has one of the only **ATMs** in town. (☎08 8685 4111. Singles $85; doubles $95.)

Park information is available at the **Beachcomber store** on the left of the main road as you come into town. The same building houses a limited general store. (☎08 8685 4057. Open daily 7am-7pm. Burgers $5-8.50.) The **National Parks and Wildlife Service** (☎08 8688 3111) in Port Lincoln also provides information on Coffin Bay, as does Port Lincoln's **Visitors Information Centre** (p. 525).

Follow signs from the Esplanade to reach Coffin Bay National Park. This peninsular park is a 4WD enthusiast's dream. **Yangie Bay** (15km from the entrance) is the only campground in the park that is 2WD-accessible year-round; several bush hikes also originate here. Although **Almonta Beach** (16km from the entrance) and **Point Avoid** (18km from the entrance) are also generally accessible with 2WD, the rest of the park is 4WD-only, and Coffin Bay isn't really worth visiting unless you can explore it in an off-road vehicle. With 4WD, the park is nothing short of amazing; tracks lead to myriad hidden coves and private look-outs. If you are braving the 4WD tracks, be forewarned that they are mostly just markers on sand dunes designed for experienced 4WD drivers. Deflate tires to around 17psi to avoid getting bogged. Tell someone your planned route and have a shovel on-hand in case of a bogging.

**Camping ❶** is allowed at designated sites only, all of which have toilets and a limited rainwater supply (unreliable in summer months). Day passes, camping permits, and maps are available at the park entrance with self-registration. (Entry $7.50 per car; camping $5 per night.) All of the campgrounds are located in sheltered areas right on the beach. Arguably the most picturesque is 🄫**Black Springs,** 28km from the entrance (allow 3hr. round-trip for the drive). A short walk or drive down the road to the left of the campground entrance sign leads to a dead end and cliff area that is one of the most beautiful spots in the park.

# EYRE PENINSULA WEST COAST

The west coast of the Eyre Peninsula runs north from Port Lincoln to the town of Ceduna. With scenery comparable to that of the Great Ocean Road, these coastal drives are far less trafficked and fringed with secluded views of lime-stone outcrops, excellent surf and diving, and abundant fishing. With a still-fledgling tourism industry, the west coast lacks the tours and public transporta-tion that its scenery deserves, but here, the journey is half the fun.

🄫🄩 **ORIENTATION AND PRACTICAL INFORMATION.** The Eyre Peninsula booklet has an excellent map with beaches and points of interest labeled. In addition, signs on the Eyre Hwy. lead visitors to the prime coastal spots. The two main towns on the coast are **Elliston** and **Streaky Bay,** 169km and 294km northwest from Port Lincoln, respectively. The **Elliston Visitors Center,** on the right as you come into town, has **Internet** ($3 per 30min.) and area informa-tion. (☎08 8687 9200. Open M-F 9am-5pm, Sa-Su 10am-3pm.) Farther north, the **Streaky Bay Tourist Centre,** 21 Bay Rd., has information on the northwest coast. (☎08 8626 1126; www.streakybay.com.au. Open daily 9am-5pm.) Both Elliston and Streaky Bay have supermarkets, petrol, **ATMs, police stations,** and **post offices** in the town centers. **Postal code:** 5670 (Elliston); 5680 (Streaky Bay).

🄫 **ACCOMMODATIONS.** Most towns on the highway have hotel pub rooms and caravan parks. By far the best deal on the west coast, 🄫**Coodlie Park ❶,** a left off the highway about 50km. north of Elliston, has a wide range of stellar accommodations, and the owners ensure that each traveler sees the top spots the region has to offer, some of which are on their extensive coastal property. They also run a number of tours in the area, including $10 wombat night tours. (☎08 8687 0411; www.coodliepark.com. Bush camping $9 per car; $35 per week. Shearer's Quarters $15 per person or $25 per room. Self-contained units $65 per night. Work exchange possible; see **Beyond Tourism,** p. 81.) The **Elliston Hotel Beach Terrace ❹,** left off Memorial Drive, has self-contained rooms. (☎08 8687 9009. Rooms $60-80. Lunch M-Sa noon-2pm $8-10; dinner M-Th and Su 6pm-8pm, F-Sa 6pm-8:30pm $15-22. Book ahead in summer.) On Waterloo Bay at the end of Beach Terr., **Waterloo Bay Caravan Park ❷** has a convenient location and excellent facilities. (☎08 8687 9076. Sites for 2 $20, powered $24; cabins $50, ensuite $65-105.) **Venus Bay Caravan Park ❶,** approximately 65km north of Elliston near the jetty in Venus Bay, also has waterfront sites. (☎08 8625 5073; www.venusbaycaravanparksa.com.au. Unpowered sites $16, for 2 $18; pow-ered $22, extra person $6; cabins for 2 $40-100, extra person $6-10.)

◙ **BEACHES.** With so much relatively untouched coastline, you are practically guaranteed to find a pristine spot anytime you turn off the highway. **Greenly Beach,** a little north of Coulter, is one of the prime west-coast surf spots. To get there, turn onto Coles Point Rd. from the highway; the beach is about 12km down, and the scenic drive is marked with rocky outcrops over the ocean. Farther north, 8km off the highway (turn off just past Sheringa general store), **Sheringa Beach** has great salmon fishing and impressive sand dunes, though the strong waves prevent safe swimming or surfing. (Camping by permit $5.) You'll have to trek down almost 300 stairs to reach **Locks Well Beach,** about 15km north of Sheringa, 3km from the highway, which is renowned throughout Australia for its salmon fishing and is arguably the top fishing beach on the west coast. Just north of Elliston, **Walker's Rocks** has sand dunes and calm waters.

◙◙ **SIGHTS AND TOURS.** About 40km north of Elliston, **Talia Caves** affords a chance to go underground. Farther north, about 15km past Venus Bay after a 2km turnoff, the odd granite rock formations of **Murphy's Haystacks** will puzzle visitors. Quite literally in the middle of a field, the large granite structures seem picturesquely out of place. Entry is by donation at the gate ($2, family $5). Twenty-four kilometers down the unsealed but 2WD-accessible road, you'll reach a 17km turnoff to ◙**Point Labatt,** where visitors can look down on a sea lion colony. In Baird Bay, 10km off the highway north of Port Kenny, **Baird Bay Ocean Eco Tours** runs tours during which visitors can swim with dolphins and sea lions in their natural habitat. (☎08 8626 5017; www.bairdbay.com.)

# CEDUNA                                                         ☎08

Ceduna (pop. 3800) is the last town before travelers begin the harsh westward trek across the Nullarbor Plain toward Perth. The name is taken from the indigenous word "Cheedoona," meaning "a place to sit down and rest," but the town rewards the active with ample aquatic opportunities. Stock up on supplies at area shops before heading out; or, celebrate your return to civilization. Over the last long weekend in October, Ceduna celebrates **Oysterfest.** The champion speed-oyster-opener goes on to an international competition. **Decres Bay,** 10km east of town in the Wittelbee Conservation Park, is a good swimming beach; farther east, **Laura Bay** has more of the same.

The best of the five area caravan parks, **Shelly Beach Caravan Park ❷** is 3km east of town on the Decres Bay Rd., on picturesque Shelly Beach. The park offers Internet, a full kitchen, and a game room with a ping-pong table. (☎08 8625 2012. Internet $3 per 15min. Powered and unpowered sites for 2 $25; ensuite cabins for 2 from $77; $11 per extra person for sites and cabins.) **Bill's Chicken Shop ❶,** on Poynton St., serves mouth-watering fish and chips (from $10), spectacular lamb gyros ($8.50), and fried chicken. (☎08 8625 2880. Open daily 9am-8:30pm.) The well-stocked **Foodland** is on the corner of Kuhlmann and Poynton St. (☎08 8625 2021. M-F 8am-7pm, Sa-Su 8am-6pm.)

**Ceduna Gateway Visitors Information Centre,** 58 Poynton St., has information on tours and is your best source of info on the Nullarbor crossing. The info center also provides **Internet** and books bus tickets. (☎08 8625 2780 or 1800 639 413; www.cedunatourism.com.au. Internet $3 per 15min. Open M-F 9am-5:30pm, Sa-Su 9:30am-5pm.) The town has **police** (☎08 8626 2020) and a **hospital** (☎08 8626 2110). **Taxi** service is also available (☎13 10 08). **Postal Code:** 5690.

# GAWLER RANGES

For those coming from the Nullarbor, the scrub-covered stretch of Hwy. 1 running from Ceduna to Port Augusta will seem like a gradual re-entry into civilization. There are towns with petrol stations (beware 6-8pm closing times) every 100km or so along the way; most have a small general store and basic accommodations as well. From west to east, the towns are as follows: **Wirrulla** (92km from Ceduna), **Poochera** (140km), **Minnipa** (170km), **Wudinna** (210km), and **Kimba** (310km). Wudinna has an Internet cafe on the west side of town in the **Wudinna Telecentre,** 44 Eyre Hwy. The Telecentre also has park information and sells park permits. (☎08 8680 2969. Internet access $5 per 30min. Park permits $7, camping $4 per night. Passes also sold at park entry points. Open M-F 9am-12:30pm and 1:30-5pm.) There is also a food store in town. Kimba, the largest of the above, has a **caravan park ❶**. (☎08 8627 2222. Unpowered for 2 $18, powered for 2 $19, extra person $5; singles $65; doubles $75; triples $85; extra person $5). Kimba is also home to the 8m **Big Galah,** a huge pink bird that marks both the halfway point between one Australian coast and the spot where Galahs gather before chasing trucks departing the granary across the street.

Kimba, Wudinna, and Minnipa act as gateways for the **Gawler Ranges,** which is perhaps South Australia's least-appreciated natural park. Formed by huge volcanic eruptions 1.6 billion years ago, the park is a great place to observe a variety of birds, as well as kangaroos and wombats. From Wudinna the Granite Trail scenic drive showcases Gawler Ranges' claim to fame—its granite formations. One of the trail's many points of interest is **Mount Wudinna**, Australia's second-largest monolith. Just north of the park is typically dry **Lake Gairdner,** where land-speed records in rocket cars have been set.

# CROSSING THE NULLARBOR

Welcome to the Nullarbor—a treeless plain running from the town of Nullarbor west into Western Australia, before ending at Norseman. The Nullarbor could contain England, the Netherlands, Belgium, and Switzerland with 7000 sq. km to spare, and crossing the Nullarbor remains a badge of pride for visitors who are traversing Australia. Commemorative crossing certificates are available for free at tourist offices at either end of the journey.

The main road, Hwy. 1, sees fairly significant traffic compared to the empty stretches up north, so it's rarely more than 100km between roadhouses, but repair facilities are few and far between. Additionally, this is a road train route (see **Australian Road Hazards,** p. 78), so drivers should brace for turbulence from passing trucks. See **Driving in the Outback,** p. 73, before setting off.

Visitors crossing from Western Australia to South Australia or vice versa must pass through agricultural roadblocks where any organic matter will be confiscated. The roadblocks are located at **Border Village** (☎08 9039 3277), for those heading west, and **Ceduna,** for those heading east (☎08 8625 2108). Roadhouses and practical information for crossing the Nullarbor are listed below, as well as points of interest. Within each section, listings are from east to west.

**🖊🖹 PRACTICAL INFORMATION AND TRANSPORTATION.** Most of the roadhouses along the way accept major credit cards. Police are located in **Penong** (☎08 8625 1006) and Ceduna (☎08 8626 2020). **In case of emergency, dial ☎000.** Cellular phones do not work anywhere on the Nullarbor; Ceduna is your last hope for even so-so reception. The highly regarded **◪Nullarbor Traveller** is a backpacker-oriented camping trip that runs from Perth to Adelaide. Travelers snorkel, whale watch, explore caves, and camp under the stars. For those with the cash and the time, this is the way to cross in style. Tour prices include accommodations, activities, and meals. (☎08 8687 0455; www.thetraveller.net. au. 10-day Adelaide to Perth tour $1450, VIP/YHA/NOMADS $1350; 9-day Perth to Adelaide $1295/1195. Itineraries vary based on the point of departure.)

**ACCOMMODATIONS.** Roadhouses are relatively frequent on the Eyre Highway and generally provide food, fuel, and accommodations. The first roadhouse coming from Ceduna, 78km west of Penong, is **Nundroo Hotel Motel and Caravan Park ❶**. (☎08 8625 6120. Reception daily 7:30am-11pm. Sites for 2 $8, powered $18; backpacker beds $10 per person; motel doubles $90, extra person $12.50.) From Nullarbor, it's 188km to **Border Village ❶**, where there are cheap accommodations and a chance to pay your respects to the enormous fiberglass kangaroo, Rooey II (☎08 9039 3474).

**PENONG AND CACTUS BEACH.** Penong, 75km west of Ceduna, is the gateway to South Australia's most famous surf—**Cactus Beach.** To reach the beach, follow signs for Point Sinclair 21km south down an unsealed but 2WD-passable road; wood-carved signs stating simply "To Beach" lead to Cactus, where you can watch top-notch surfers. The beach has **bush camping ❶** available (call the groundskeeper at ☎08 8625 1036; $7.50), while back in Penong, the **hotel ❸** has proper rooms. (☎08 8625 1050. Singles $33; doubles $44.)

**FOWLER'S BAY.** With massive sand dunes, a fishing jetty, and a population of 10, Fowler's Bay is one of the best-kept secrets on the Eyre Hwy. From the highway, the 21km turnoff for Fowler's Bay is 33km east of Nundroo. The town's sand dunes provide excellent sandboarding and 4WD tracks, and **Back Beach,** on the other side of the dunes, has great swimming. The town has a **caravan park ❶**. (☎08 8625 6143. Office open 8:30am-6:30pm. Unpowered for 2 $19; powered for 2 $25; extra person $5. Takeaway food available, as well as meager grocery options.) Fowler's Bay also has a general store and petrol.

**THE NULLARBOR PLAIN.** The largest single block of limestone in the world, the plain encompasses over 250,000 sq. km in total and was formed around the same time that Australia broke away from Antarctica—about 50 million years ago. For today's visitors, this means a long stretch of jagged cliffs looking out over the Great Australian Bight. The intrepid traveler can veer off the highway on any one of a number of unsealed roads and arrive at what is sure to feel like the end of the Earth, with land meeting water in a stark boundary stretching to all horizons—keep an eye out for whales.

**SOUTH AUSTRALIA**

# TASMANIA

As the license plates suggest, Tasmania truly is Australia's natural state. A whopping one-third of the island is protected by government conservation projects, leaving plenty of space for bushwalkers to stretch their legs. They do so in a famously unique environment, populated with unique species such as the lovably voracious Tasmanian devil and the slow-growing Huon pine.

Encompassing the tranquil bustle of capital Hobart, a rainy and wild west coast, isolated beaches in the east, and a southern wilderness so far off the beaten path you may not see another soul, Tasmania offers a variety of truly extraordinary outdoor experiences. While many visitors come to hike the famous Overland Track and leave it at that, those who go deeper into Tasmania's wilds will be rewarded by amazing vistas, fascinating fauna, and a warm welcome from locals. Tassie, as it is affectionately known, is one of the traveler's best opportunities to meet Australians and get a sense of what it's like to live here. With so few visitors, Tasmania will welcome you with open arms.

Australia's least-visited state isn't for everyone. If hiking boots are a foreign idea or shops and pubs are more important to you than natural sights, the hop across the Tasman Sea probably isn't worth your while. Plus, the island is not always a budget traveler's paradise; transportation is tricky here, and it is often limited to rental cars or bus tours. However, the "Under Down Under" has a tremendous amount to offer to anyone willing to seek it out. Not many travelers can say they've been to Tasmania, and those who can often remember it as a highlight of their trip to Australia.

### HIGHLIGHTS OF TASMANIA

**SCORE** a bargain and enjoy street performances in **Salamanca Market,** Hobart's eclectic shopping district (p. 540).

**TOUR** the ruins of convict-built buildings at the **Tasman Peninsula** (p. 543).

**GET INTO** the bush on the world-famous **Overland Track** (p. 552).

## TRANSPORTATION

Tasmania has three principal gateways: the **Hobart Airport,** the **Launceston Airport,** and the **Devonport Airport.** Take a flight or, if you want an adventure, take the Spirit of Tasmania overnight **ferry** to Devonport or the Devilcat ferry to George Town Port in Launceston. Flying is certainly cheaper, but taking the ferry is a unique experience, complete with pubs on board the ship.

Getting around the island on a budget is a bit of a challenge. There is no rail network, and the main **bus** lines—Redline and TWT's Tassielink—are expensive, limited, and infrequent. Tassielink offers **Explorer Passes,** which are worth the investment when using their buses as a touring service (7 days $189, 10 days $225, 14 days $260, 21 days $299). On the bright side, many hostel managers offer reasonably priced **shuttles and tours** on a call-and-request basis. Seek local recommendations and check out hostel information boards.

The most popular way to travel in Tasmania is by **car.** Gateway cities host major national chains and many small companies offering cheaper, older cars,

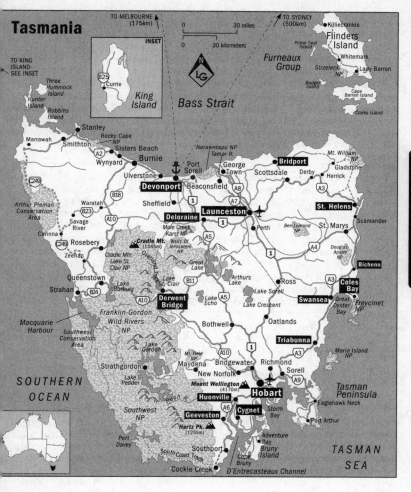

but they are often fully booked during the summer. Visitors unaccustomed to Tassie's narrow, winding roads should drive cautiously. Check with the rental company on its policy regarding unsealed roads; some prohibit driving on them altogether, others increase the liability excess. Four-wheel-drive vehicles, necessary for some of Tassie's backroads, come with better insurance policies on unsealed roads. Be aware that hidden speed cameras line roads. Petrol is rare outside towns, and even in urban areas petrol stations tend to close around 5pm. It's advisable to take spare containers of petrol to avoid getting stranded, as well as extra water in case you can't avoid getting stranded.

**Biking** is a satisfying alternative in Tasmania, especially on the more accessible east coast of the island. Attempting to cycle the west is only for the stronghearted and iron-thighed, as serious hills, unsealed roads, and cloudy, chilly weather will deter everyone else. The three major gateway cities have bike-rental outfits catering to touring, but gear will rarely be found elsewhere.

**Hiking** is the reason many travelers come to Tasmania, but it will not get you around the island unless you're planning on taking to the wilderness for many months. Some trailheads are serviced by public buses, but for most hikes you'll need a rental car or a tour bus to drop you off.

**Tours** also make seeing Tassie easy and enjoyable, allowing travel to places otherwise inaccessible. **Adventure Tours** (☎03 4124 9943; www.ozhorizons. au/tas/hobart/adventure/tour.htm; 3-day $440, 6-day $795, 7-day $810) and **Under Down Under Tours** (☎1800 064 726; www.underdownunder.com.au; 1-day $95-110, 3-day $410, 5-day $645, 8-day $925) offer touring options that include bookings for accommodations and meals, are geared toward a party crowd, and focus on ecotourism. Most tours leave from Hobart.

**PARK IT!** All of Tasmania's national parks charge an entrance fee. A 24hr. pass costs $11 (vehicles $22). Two-month passes are available for $28 (vehicles $56), and an annual all-parks pass for vehicles for $60-84 (1 park only $30-42). Passes are available at most park entrances or from the Parks and Wildlife Service offices. Parks and Wildlife prints two helpful pamphlets: *Tasmania: A Visitor's Guide* has a brief summary of every national park in Tasmania, and *Tasmania's Great Short Walks* outlines 30 fantastic walks, most under 1hr. (Both free.) The service also publishes a handy booklet to reduce your environmental impact called the *Essential Bushwalking Guide & Trip Planner*. For more information, contact the head office in Hobart, 134 Macquarie St. (☎03 6233 6191; www.parks.tas.gov.au.)

# HOBART ☎03

Tasmania's capital is a lovely, if not particularly exciting, place to begin or end your Tasmanian travels. Situated by the mouth of the Derwent River at the foot of Mt. Wellington, Hobart (pop. 205,000) is filled with vacationing Australian families, leading some backpackers to denounce it as dull. However, the city has affordable accommodations, is walkable, and boasts a fantastic farmer's market. It's easy to see Hobart as a mere stepping stone to the Tasmanian wilderness, but an extra day here is worthwhile for its charming architecture, laid-back atmosphere, and tours of its famous factories that produce two of life's greatest pleasures: chocolate and beer.

## ✈ INTERCITY TRANSPORTATION

**Flights: Hobart Airport** (☎03 6216 1600; www.hobartairpt.com.au), 17km east of Hobart on Hwy. A3. International flights must make connections on the mainland. Redline Airporter Bus (☎03 1938 2240; $12.50, round-trip $21) shuttles between the airport and lodgings. Virgin Blue (☎03 13 67 89; www.virginblue.com.au) to Melbourne (4 per day, $69-239). Qantas (☎03 13 13 13; www.qantas.com.au) to Melbourne (up to 9 per day, $90-247) and Sydney (2 per day, $156-231). TasAir (☎03 6248 5088) to Burnie (2 per day, $385). Also charters flights around the island.

**Buses:** Hobart has 2 major bus terminals serving 2 major bus lines.

**Central Transit Centre,** 199 Collins St. Timetables available for Redline Coaches (☎1300 360 000, line open daily 6am-10pm), which runs to **Launceston** (2hr., 2-4 per day, $31.50) with connec-

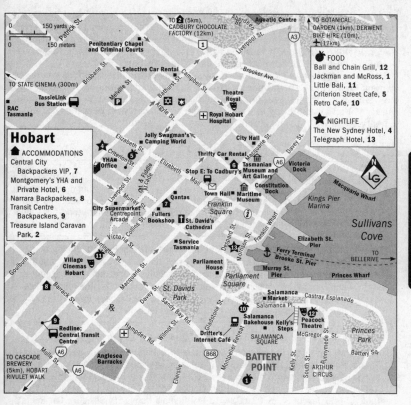

tions to: **Bicheno** (2hr., M-F 1 per day, $28); **Burnie** (2hr., 3 per day, $30); **Devonport** (1hr., 4 per day, $22.10); **Saint Helens** (2hr., M-F and Su 1 per day, $47). 20% student and YHA discount.

**Tassielink Terminal,** 64 Brisbane St., is the hub for Tassielink buses (☎1300 300 520). Rides to: **Bicheno** (3hr., W, F, Su 1 per day, $31.70); **Cockle Creek** via **Huonville** (3hr., M, W, F 1 per day, $65); **Devonport** (4hr., 1 per day, $51.40); **Dover** (2hr., M-F 2 per day, $18); **Launceston** (3hr., 1 per day, $30.20); **Mount Field National Park** (2hr., Tu, Th, Sa 2 per day, $29.60); **Port Arthur** (2hr., M-F 1 per day, $24.20); **Saint Helens** (4hr., F and Su 1 per day, $46); **Strahan** (9hr., Tu and Th-Su, $67.70); **Swansea** (3hr., M-F 1 per day, $26). In summer, inquire about Overland Track service including Hobart, Lake St. Claire, Cradle Mountain, and return ($119).

## ◼ ORIENTATION

Most tourist attractions are condensed into the downtown area west of the Sullivan's Cove wharf, which is contained by **Davey** and **Bathurst St. Elizabeth St.,** which intersects downtown, proceeds uphill to budget-friendly **North Hobart.** South of the cove, **Battery Point** is one of the oldest sections of the city and is packed with antique shops and cottages. The northern border of Battery Point is defined by **Salamanca Place,** a row of renovated Georgian warehouses that now houses trendy shops and restaurants. Nearby **Franklin Wharf** is the departure point for numerous harbor cruises. Hobart is set amid the Wellington Range with the imposing **Mount Wellington** on the western skyline and the smaller **Mount Nelson** to the south, both of which offer fine views of the region. The city proper can be easily negotiated on foot, while public buses run to the outer suburbs. Several well-maintained roads lead into the city center, including **Highway 1,** connecting Burnie, Devonport, Launceston, and Hobart.

Beyond the Queen's Domain north of downtown, the **Tasman Bridge** spans the **Derwent River.** There, the **Tasman Hwy. (A3)** heads east and connects to the A9 and the Tasman Peninsula. Brooker Ave. leads north up the Derwent Valley, becoming Hwy. 1 and connecting to the A10 to the west. Davey St. becomes the A6 as it heads southward to the Huon Valley and Bruny Island.

#  LOCAL TRANSPORTATION

**Public Transportation:** Metro city **buses** (☎03 13 22 01) run through Hobart and the suburbs daily 6am-10pm. Purchase tickets on board ($2-4, depending on the number of route sectors you plan on traveling through). Exact change is required. **The Metro Shop,** 9 Elizabeth St., in a corner of the post office, has a complete (and free) timetable, as does www.metrotas.com.au. Open M-F 8:30am-5:15pm.

> **TIP**
>
> **BUSY BUSES.** Check in with the tourist office before attempting to get anywhere by public bus. Hobart is very well served by local transport, but the many bus lines are confusing, and the timetables change between December and February, when schools are out for the summer holiday. The tourist office can get you on your way and, if you're going to the Cascade Brewery or Cadbury Factory, can ensure you make your tour on time.

**Taxis:** City Cabs (24hr. ☎03 13 10 08 or 03 6234 3633). City to airport $35-40.

**Car Rental:** Car-rental agencies are everywhere in Hobart, particularly along Harrington St., but advance bookings are required in summer. Low season rates run as low as $17 per day. Listed companies rent to ages 21-24 with no surcharge. Autorent Hertz, 122 Harrington St. (☎03 6237 1111). High season $55-85 per day, low season $40-70. Thrifty, 11-17 Argyle St. (☎03 6234 1341). Rentals from $59. Selective Car Rentals, 47 Bathurst St. (☎03 6234 3311 or 1800 300 102). High-season rentals from $55, low-season $25. Range/Lo-Cost, 105 Murray St. (☎03 6231 0300). Rents older cars, including minibuses and campervans, from $35. The tourist office has deals with Budget and Europcar, so if you're interested in using either of those companies, book through the info center. Rentforless (www.rentforless.com.au) and Bargain Car Rentals (www.bargaincarrentals.com.au) are good websites to check for special deals.

> **TIP**
>
> **YOU'LL DRIVE YOURSELF CRAZY.** If you flattened all of the hills in Tasmania, the island's area would be the same as that of mainland Australia. The bumpy topography makes for great hiking and challenging biking, but it also adds a certain dread to driving. Be extra careful cresting hills when you can't see far ahead of the car; Tassie's ubiquitous wildlife or speeding trucks may be waiting for you on the other side.

**Automobile Club: RACT** (☎03 6232 6300, 24hr. roadside help 03 13 11 11, insurance queries 03 13 27 22), at the corner of Murray and Patrick St. 1-year coverage $82, plus a $40 joining fee. Open M-F 8:45am-5pm.

**Bike Rental:** Derwent Bike Hire (☎03 6260 4426). Follow directions to the Botanical Gardens until you get to the Aquatic Centre, then follow the road downhill. Turn right under the underpass and right on the other side of the highway. Rents bikes, tandems, and in-line skates from $7 per hr., $20 per day, and $100 per week. Open Dec.-Mar. daily 10am-4pm; Sept.-May Sa-Su 10am-4pm.

# ⚡ PRACTICAL INFORMATION

## TOURIST AND FINANCIAL SERVICES

**Tourist Office: Hobart Tasmanian Travel and Information Centre,** 20 Davey St. (☎03 6230 8233), at Elizabeth St., might employ the friendliest people in Australia. Books accommodations and cars for $3, tours for free. Also sells excellent national-park maps for $5-10. Open M-F 8:30am-5:30pm, Sa-Su 9am-5pm. **Service Tasmania,** 134 Macquarie St. (☎1300 135 513), in the Service Tasmania Bldg. The office for the Tasmanian Parks and Wildlife Service. Open M-F 8:15am-5:30pm.

**Tours:** Day tours organized by **Tasmania Smash and Grab** (☎1800 777 103) or **Experience Tasmania** (☎03 6234 3336; www.grayline.com.au), run by Grayline, are good if you're short on time. Both offer pickup and combo tours highlighting Hobart, Cradle Mountain, and southeastern Tassie. Book through the **info center** (☎03 6230 8233), at hostels, or direct with the company. Tours $38-145. **Gregory Omnibuses** (☎03 6236 9116 or 6224 6169; www.reddecker.com.au) sends its fleet of bright-red double-deckers on hop-on, hop-off tours around the city, including to Cascade Brewery. $25, with Brewery $44. M-F only. Book at info center.

**Budget Travel Office: YHA's Tasmanian Headquarters,** 28 Criterion St., 2nd fl. (☎03 6234 9617; www.yhatas.org.au). Travel insurance, bus and tour tickets, and travel advice in addition to YHA memberships and hostel bookings. Open M-F 9am-5pm.

**Banks:** Many **banks** and **ATMs** crowd in and around Elizabeth Mall and line Collins St.

## LOCAL SERVICES

**Bookstore: Fullers Bookshop,** 140 Collins St. (☎03 6224 2488). Funky local hangout boasts aquamarine bookshelves, an excellent collection of local literature, and a loft cafe with free newspapers for your perusal. Pumpkin, spinach, and lentil lasagna $12. Scrumptious chocolate-chip cookies $2.70. Open M-F 9am-6pm, Sa 9am-5pm, Su 10am-4pm. Cafe open W 9am-5pm, Sa 9am-4:30pm, Su 10am-3:30pm.

**Library: State Library of Tasmania,** 91 Murray St. (☎03 6233 7481). Internet $5.50 for 30min., but travelers report that they are not charged; there is often a line, so book early at the main information desk. Also has a cafe that serves coffee and smoothies. Open Dec.-Jan. M-Th 9:30am-6pm, F 9:30am-8pm, Sa 9:30am-12:30pm; Feb.-Nov. M-Th 9:30am-6pm, F 9:30am-8pm, Sa 9:30am-2:30pm.

**Outdoor Equipment:** Elizabeth St. near Liverpool St. teems with gear stores. These are the only places to rent gear outside Launceston and Devonport. **Jolly Swagman's Camping World,** 107 Elizabeth St. (☎03 6234 3999), has a superb inventory. Rents stoves ($25, $100 deposit), packs ($30-100), and sleeping mats ($5-15). Open M-F 9am-6pm, Sa 9am-3:30pm. **Service Tasmania** (below) has a list of all gear-rental options.

**MEDIA AND PUBLICATIONS**
**Newspapers:** *The Mercury.*
**Entertainment:** *The Mercury* runs *Gig Guide* on Thursday and *EG* on Friday.
**Radio:** Rock, Triple J 92.9FM; News, ABC 747AM.

## EMERGENCY AND COMMUNICATIONS

**Emergency:** ☎000.

**Police:** 37-43 Liverpool St. (☎03 6230 2375). Call for lost and found.

**Fire Watchdog Line:** Call ☎1800 000 699 to report a wilderness fire.

**Crisis Lines: Crisis Watchline** (24hr. ☎03 13 11 14). **AIDS Hotline** (☎1800 005 900). Staffed M-F 9am-5pm. **Alcohol and Drugs Hotline** (24hr. ☎1800 811 994).

**Pharmacy: Macquarie Street Pharmacy,** 180 Macquarie St. (☎03 6223 2339). Open daily 8am-10pm.

**Medical Services: Royal Hobart Hospital,** 48 Liverpool St. (☎03 6222 8423). Emergency entrance on Argyle St. Open 24hr. **Hobart Private Clinic** (☎03 6214 3080), on the corner of Argyle and Collins St. Open 24hr.

**Internet Access: State Library of Tasmania** (see **Library** above). **Service Tasmania,** 134 Macquarie St. (☎1300 135 513). Has 10 free terminals. 30min. max. Open M-F 8:15am-5:30pm. **Drifters Internet Cafe,** 9/33 Salamanca Pl. (☎03 6224 6286). Sweetens its Internet deal ($5 per hr.) with coffee ($3), smoothies ($5), fresh juice ($5), and (Hobart native) Errol Flynn-themed decor. Open daily 8am-6pm.

**Post Office:** 9 Elizabeth St. (☎03 1313 1818), at Macquarie St. From this post office, Roald Amundsen sent a telegram announcing his accomplishment as the 1st man to reach the South Pole. Open M-F 8:30am-5:30pm. **Postal Code:** 7000.

# ꭅ ꭅ ACCOMMODATIONS AND CAMPING

**Montgomery's YHA and Montgomery's Private Hotel,** 9 Argyle St. (☎03 6231 2660), downtown. A quiet, well-maintained, and well-equipped hostel. Clean kitchen and common room with TV. All rooms have phones; hotel rooms have towels, TV, and refrigerator. Luggage storage. Laundry. Internet $5 per 30min. Reception 8am-11pm. Dorms $29, YHA members $26; hotel twins and doubles $90/81. ❷

**Central City Backpackers VIP,** 138 Collins St. (☎03 6224 2404 or 1800 811 507; www.centralcityhobart.com), on the 2nd fl. through the Imperial Arcade. The name says it all. Large, social hostel has small, plain rooms with comfortable mattresses, but the central location is hard to beat. Linen $3. Key deposit $10. Reception 8am-9pm. 8-bed dorms $23, 6-bed $25, 4-bed $27; singles $55; doubles $69. ❷

**Narrara Backpackers,** 88 Goulburn St. (☎03 6231 3191). Turn left off Harrington St. This 3-story house in North Hobart has clean, bright rooms with thin mattresses and a lived-in common area, complete with industrial stove. Reception 8am-10pm. 8-bed dorms $23, 6-bed $25; twins $60. ❷

**Transit Centre Backpackers,** 199 Collins St. (☎03 6231 2400), above the bus terminal. Spacious common area done all in purple. Friendly proprietors live on-site. Tiny rooms crammed with bunk beds. TV, kitchen, laundry, pool table. Free storage. Internet $4 per hr. Reception M-F 8am-9pm, Sa-Su 8am-1pm and 4-9pm. 10-bed dorms $21, 8-bed $22, 6-bed $23; twins $26; doubles $60. ❷

**Treasure Island Caravan Park,** 1 Alcorso Dr., Berriedale (☎03 6249 2379), 12km north of the city center on Hwy. 1. Challenging to reach by public transport; take the X1 bus, but check in with the tourist office first, as service is often patchy. Situated on the Derwent River. Facilities include showers, laundry, and kitchen. Reception 8am-10pm. Sites $13-21, powered $18-24; on-site caravans $48; cabins $72-80. ❶

# ⬛ FOOD

Hobart won't let you go hungry, although few restaurants here have menus designed for budget travelers. Your best bet for cheaper fare is local produce and baked goods, displayed at their best in a number of cafes located in Battery Point. Restaurants downtown serve meals from nearly every region of Asia, while the pubs and grills of Salamanca Pl. provide their clientele with more traditional Aussie dishes. Elizabeth St. in North Hobart is home to a cluster of restaurants that showcase a variety of cuisines—from Indian to Mexican to Vietnamese. **Woolworths,** 179 Campbell St., North Hobart, is the only fully stocked supermarket near the city center. (Open daily 7am-10pm.) For a decent selection of groceries smack dab in the heart of Hobart, **City Supermarket,** 148 Liverpool St., has everything you need. (Open M-F 8am-7pm, Sa 9am-5pm, Su noon-5pm.) The Saturday ⬛**Salamanca Market** is your best option for wonderful produce, sauces, spreads, honey, cheese, and more. The market has cheap takeaway vendors with surprisingly good food and offers excellent people-watching to boot. (Open Sa 8:30am-3pm.)

> **⭐TIP** **DEVILISHLY DELICIOUS.** Traditional Tassie tucker is abalone or salmon with a cold Cascade beer. The many seafood restaurants along the waterfront are your best bet, but expect to pay $15 or more.

**⬛ Jackman and McRoss,** 57-59 Hampden Rd. (☎03 6223 3186). Bright cafe in Battery Point offers delicious breakfast pastries ($4.50), innovative lunch pies (lamb shank and rosemary pie $6.50), and excellent coffee ($3). Treat yourself to the berry-and-cream-cheese tart ($5). Exposed brick walls and worn wood floors complete the picture. Open M-F 7:30am-6pm, Sa-Su 7:30am-5pm. Cash only. ❶

**Little Bali,** at the corner of Harrington and Collins St., next to Little India and Little Salama. Follow your nose to this little restaurant with decidedly non-little servings of Indonesian curry dishes ($8.50) for eat-in or takeaway. Most expensive dishes ($10.50) comfortably satisfy 2. Open M-F 11:30am-3pm and 5-9pm, Sa-Su 5-9pm. ❶

**Retro Cafe,** 31 Salamanca Pl. (☎03 6223 3073), on the corner of Montpelier Retreat. Enjoy fine food and coffee in an atmosphere that matches the cafe's name. It can be hard to get a seat, but their all-day brekkie (scrambled eggs with smoked salmon and melted cheese; $14.50) is worth the scramble. Open daily 8am-6pm. Cash only. ❸

**Criterion Street Cafe,** 30 Criterion St. (☎03 6231 0890), just up from the YHA office, is one of the best lunch bets in the city center, with daily soup specials ($4.50-6.50), healthful smoothies ($4.50-5.50), and excellent muffins ($3.50). Grilled beef salad with zucchini makes a great splurge ($14.50). Open M-F 7:30am-4pm. ❶

**Ball and Chain Grill,** 87 Salamanca Pl. (☎03 6223 2655). Plates of char-grilled meats cover wood tables. Although not cheap (steaks $15-42), the meats are specially aged and expertly cooked to order. Open M-F noon-11pm, Sa-Su 5:30-11pm. ❹

# 👁 SIGHTS

Hobart's best sights are a bus ride away: the fantastic tours of the Cascade Brewery and Cadbury chocolate factory, as well as the famous peaks of Mt. Wellington and Mt. Nelson, are outside of central Hobart. However, the city itself will provide you with a few hours of sightseeing downtown, and Salamanca Pl. and Battery Point are wonderful places to wander.

# CENTRAL HOBART

**SALAMANCA PLACE.** This row of beautiful Georgian warehouses contains trendy galleries, restaurants, and the shops of the much-celebrated ◼**Salamanca Market**, a definite highlight of Hobart. On Saturdays, the popular outdoor market delights with a wonderful hodgepodge of crafts, produce, food, and performers. Bringing together local farmers, outspoken environmentalists, craftspeople, and tourists from the mainland, it's a wonderful mixture of local meeting place and display of Tasmanian culture. There is also a huge array of mouthwatering food that will keep your wallet happy. *(Open Sa 8:30am-3pm.)*

**TASMANIAN MUSEUM AND ART GALLERY.** The Tasmanian Museum explores the island's early convict history, unique ecology, and artistic heritage. The exhibit on Aboriginal culture, including a beautiful display of shell necklaces, is excellent. Frequent exhibitions highlight the cultural and artistic history of the region. *(40 Macquarie St., near the corner of Argyle St. ☎ 03 6211 4177. Open daily 10am-5pm. Guided tours leave from the bookstore W-Su 2:30pm. Free.)*

**PENITENTIARY CHAPEL AND CRIMINAL COURTS.** One of the oldest, best-preserved buildings in Tasmania is worth a stop, although you can visit only by guided tour. The chapel for prisoners was erected in 1831, ironically built over solitary confinement cells. View the courtrooms and gallows built during the grim 1850s and used until 1983. *(6 Brisbane St. Enter on Campbell St. ☎ 03 6231 0911. Admission by tour only. Tours daily 10, 11:30am, 1, 2:30pm. $8, concessions $7, ages 5-18 $6, under 5 free. Ghost tours ☎ 04 1736 1392. Daily 8pm. Book ahead. $8.80.)*

**WATERFRONT.** At Sullivan's Cove, the Elizabeth, Brooke, and Murray St. Piers harbor most of Hobart's large vessels. Constitution and Victoria Docks are teeming with fishmongers and boast popular seafood restaurants. Several companies run harbor cruises from this area. *(Free.)*

**MARITIME MUSEUM.** This facility highlights Tassie maritime heritage, with a focus on local shipping and whaling. Its model ships and an old-time diving suit are nice to look at, but its size (two rooms) doesn't quite match up to the ocean's. *(16 Argyle St., in the Carnegie Building on the corner of Davey St. ☎ 03 6234 1427. Open daily 9am-5pm. $7, concessions $5, ages 13-17 $4, under 13 free.)*

# OUTLYING REGIONS

◼**CADBURY CHOCOLATE FACTORY.** There are no Oompa-Loompas, and Gene Wilder won't take you for a ride in his glass elevator, but the Cadbury Chocolate Factory is just the (golden) ticket for entering the world of Willy Wonka. One of Hobart's most popular attractions, the factory offers tours that take you through the entire chocolate-making process. There's nothing between you and vats of molten chocolate, wrapping conveyor belts, and mounds of Cherry Ripe filling. The strong smell of sweet chocolate will make you glad there's a bargain shop at the end of the tour. *(In Claremont, north of Hobart and the Derwent River. From Metro stop E, on the corner of Elizabeth and Murray St., outside the post office, take the Claremont service to the Cadbury factory stop. Check with the driver and, if the direct bus is not running, change at Glenorchy. ☎ 03 6249 0333 or 1800 627 367. Tours every 30min. M-F Sept.-May 7:30am-4pm; June-Aug. 9am-1:30pm. Advance booking required. Long pants and closed shoes required. No jewelry, cameras, or bags; a locker is provided at the beginning of the tour, but it is recommended to leave valuables at home. $15, concessions $11, ages 5-15 $7.50, under 5 free.)*

◼**CASCADE BREWERY.** Fed by the clear waters of Mt. Wellington, the magnificent Cascade Brewery, Australia's oldest, was built in 1832 based on designs by a convict in debtors' prison. (After enjoying the result, you'll wonder whether he was paroled on very, very good behavior.) Tours cover the brewery's process and history and include a stroll around the beautiful surrounding gardens. If the image of giant vats of churning beer makes you thirsty, never fear; the tour is followed by a free tasting of three glasses of beer, hard cider, or sparkling fruit juice. *(140 Cascade Rd. From the Franklin Sq. Metro stop M, take the South Hobart/ Cascades bus. Ask the driver to let you off at the brewery, as there is no official stop. If driving, follow Davey St. out of the city, staying in the right lane. When the road connects with the A6, turn right and then left on Macquarie St., which becomes Cascade Rd. ☎ 03 6224 1117. 2hr. tours M-F Dec.-Mar. every 30min.; Apr.-Nov. every hr. Advance bookings required. Long pants and flat, fully enclosed shoes required. $20, concessions $18, under 18 $11.)*

**▓ BONORONG WILDLIFE PARK.** If you're looking to satisfy your craving to pet a kangaroo, see the tremendous fangs of a Tasmanian devil up close, and support the island's conservation efforts all at the same time, this is the place to be. The park, which also features wombats, wallabies, emus, and echidnas, has all the benefits of a zoo without many of the downsides. These critters were rescued from injury; the rare eagles can no longer fly because of shooting incidents. Kangaroo food is scattered around the park in green buckets; Tasmanian Devil feedings, which take place at 11:30am and 2pm, are another park highlight. *(North of Hobart in Brighton. Metro bus X1 from Hobart to Glenorchy Interchange connects with #125 or 126 to Brighton, 1hr. The bus stops 2km shy of the park; from the terminus, you have to walk—1hr. following signs to the park. Or take the Mt. Wellington shuttle service, which offers trips to Bonorong daily 10:15am-1:30pm. ☎ 04 0834 1804. $30 round-trip. 2-person min. To drive, take Rte. 1 north out of Hobart, following signs to Launceston, and then follow signs to Brighton. Once in Brighton, follow signs for the park. ☎ 03 6268 1184; www.bonorong.com.au. Wildlife tours 11:30am, 2pm. Open daily 9am-5pm. $16, under 18 $10.)*

**MOUNT WELLINGTON.** Several kilometers west of Hobart, Mt. Wellington (1270m) is a must-see. The top is extremely windy, cold, and often snowy. On a clear day, the peaks of the Wellington Range (all clearly marked on signs in the observation shelter) are visible. Although the summit is home to a huge telecommunications tower that mars the natural beauty, the surrounding walking tracks are spectacular. The road to the top is occasionally closed due to snow and ice. **Mt. Wellington Shuttle Bus Service** provides narrated van trips to the top for $25 round-trip. *(☎ 04 0834 1804. 2-person min.)* Another van option is **Captain Fell's.** *(☎ 03 6223 5893. $21 round-trip; $12 one-way, if you want to walk back down.)* **Fern Tree,** on the lower foothills of the mountain, is a picturesque picnic area with walking tracks up the slope. *(40min. from Hobart on B64 Huon Rd. By bus, take the Fern Tree bus from the Franklin Sq. Metro stop M to stop 27, at the base of the mountain; from there, you have to hike to the top, which is a solid 2hr. of sweaty climbing. To drive, follow Davey St. south out of town; it becomes C616 and goes straight to the top of the mountain. Observation shelter open daily 8am-6pm. For track details, get the $4 Mt. Wellington Walk Map from the tourist office.)*

**ROYAL TASMANIAN BOTANICAL GARDENS.** With 13 hectares and 6000 species, the Royal Tasmanian Botanical Gardens are the largest public collection of Tasmanian plants in the world and the largest collection of mature conifers in the Southern Hemisphere. The wildly popular **Al Fresco Theatre** puts on an outdoor play in January and "Shakespeare in the Garden" in February. *(North of the city, near the Tasman Bridge. Take any bus, including the MetroCity Explorer, headed to the eastern shore to stop 4 before the bridge or take the X3-G express to Bridgewater, which stops at the main gate. Alternatively, for a 50min. stroll, walk down Liverpool St., away from the city center, and take the underpass at the roundabout. Take the stairs to the left up to the Aquatic Centre, then stay right along the highway, curving uphill to a gravel walking path. After 30min., at the paved road, cross the road and turn right down the gravel path; turn right again when you hit the carpark, and the entrance will be on your left. ☎ 03 6236 3050. Open daily Oct.-Mar. 8am-6:30pm; Apr.*

T A S M A N I A

*and Sept. 8am-5:30pm; May-Aug. 8am-5pm. Gardens free; donations encouraged. Book theater tickets through Centertainment ☎03 6234 5998. Outdoor theater $22, concessions $11. Shows Feb.-Mar. Tu-Sa 7pm. Outdoor cinema $13/8. Showings Dec.-Mar. Sa 8:50pm.*

# 🎭 ENTERTAINMENT

Find entertainment listings in the "EG" insert of Friday's *Mercury* newspaper.

**State Cinema,** 375 Elizabeth St. (☎03 6234 6318; www.statecinema.com.au), in North Hobart. Tasmania's oldest running and only independent movie theater. Indie films screened in glamorous facilities. $15, concessions $13, seniors $11.

**Peacock Theatre,** 77 Salamanca Pl. (☎03 6234 8414; www.salarts.com), in the Salamanca Arts Centre. Experimental theater with a lovely interior. $15-30.

**Theatre Royal,** 29 Campbell St. (☎03 6233 2299). The oldest theater in Australia. Stages plays, musicals, song and dance shows, comedy festivals, and a variety of other crowd-pleasers. Box office open M-F 9am-5pm, Sa 9am-1pm. $25-50.

**Tasmanian Symphony Orchestra,** 1 Davey St. (☎1800 001 190), in the Federation Concert Hall at the Grand Chancellor. Over 50 years old and holds performances every few weeks. Box office open M-F 9am-5pm, Sa concert days from 5pm, and all concert nights from 6pm. $35-49, concessions $20.

# 🎵 NIGHTLIFE

Hobart's nightlife only really gets going on Wednesday, Friday, and Saturday nights. Those looking for nocturnal diversions the rest of the week should arrive at pubs early, as most close between 10pm and midnight. Nightlife centers on the waterfront and Salamanca areas, although North Hobart also boasts a number of pubs. If you go out in North Hobart and are returning late to central Hobart, it's advisable to take a cab; the area between the two neighborhoods is relatively deserted. For a bite while out on the town, go to the 24hr. **Salamanca Bakehouse ❶**, behind Salamanca Pl. in Salamanca Sq. (Pastries $2-5.)

**Telegraph Hotel** (☎03 6234 6254), at the corner of Brooke and Morrison. A party hot spot for college-aged youth. The best beer selection in town, with 110 imports. Cheap beer W and Su, when you can get jugs for the price of the hour ($5 at 5pm, $6 at 6pm, etc.). W "Toss Your Boss" lets customers flip for a free drink. Sa live music. Open W-F noon-late, Sa-Su 3pm-late. Neat dress required.

**The New Sydney Hotel,** 87 Bathurst St. (☎03 6234 4516). A popular Irish pub and proud member of the Irish Association of Tasmania. Pint of Boag's $7.50. Live music, mainly cover bands, F-Su. Open M noon-10pm, Tu noon-midnight, W-F 11:30am-midnight, Sa 1pm-midnight, Su 4-9pm. Kitchen open M-Sa noon-2pm and 6-8pm, Su 6-8pm.

# THE SOUTH

The South is dotted with picturesque towns. To the east, the Tasman Peninsula and Port Arthur testify to Tassie's fascinating colonial history. To the west, the entrance to the vast Southwest National Park welcomes visitors to the Tasmanian Wilderness World Heritage Area. Between the two lie the hop vines of the Derwent Valley and the vast apple orchards of the D'Entrecasteaux Channel region, which don't have many attractions but can offer temporary work.

# TASMAN PENINSULA AND PORT ARTHUR

The narrow Eaglehawk Neck isthmus connects the Tasman Peninsula to the rest of Tasmania. One of the island's first attractions, which drew a steady stream of early settlers, was the line of guard dogs stationed at Eaglehawk Neck to alert guards of any escape attempts. Military units once dumped repeat offenders over the peninsula's steep cliffs into shark-infested waters. The ruins of the convict-built sandstone buildings at █**Port Arthur** are still Tasmania's most-popular tourist attraction, drawing 250,000 visitors annually, and for good reason. Less-heralded are the walking tracks and gorgeous views afforded by the Tasman Peninsula's unique geography. Port Arthur makes an excellent daytrip, especially as budget accommodations are scarce. Be forewarned, however, that bus schedules may force you to spend the night. Luckily, the Historic Ghost Tour and wonderful local walks may make a sleepover a palatable proposition.

**☐ TRANSPORTATION.** There is no real Port Arthur town, just businesses and government services affiliated with the historical site. Tassielink (☎1300 300 520) is the only **bus** company servicing the tourist attraction. Buses depart the depot in Hobart (in summer, M, W, F 10am and M-F 4pm). Only 1hr. to the north, **Sorell** is the main stop en route to the Suncoast (via the A3).

**⛊ PRACTICAL INFORMATION.** There's a helpful tourist office in the **Port Arthur Historic Centre** with an expensive cafe and restaurant. (☎03 6251 2371. Open daily 8:30am-10pm.) By the Eaglehawk Neck Historic Site on the A9, the **Officers' Mess** has a few groceries and takeaways, as well as pricey Internet access. (☎03 6250 3635. Internet $3 per 15min. Open daily 9am-8pm.) In Sorell, the Westpac bank, which has a 24hr. **ATM**, is at 36 Cole St. at the junction of the A3 and the A9. (Open M-Th 9:30am-4pm, F 9:30am-5pm.) **Internet access** is available for free at **Service Tasmania**, 5 Fitzroy St., just down the street from the Sorell tourist office. (Open M-F 9am-5pm.) There's a **post office** at 19 Gordon St., the main drag in Sorell. (☎03 6265 2579. Open M-F 9am-5pm.) **Postal Code:** 7172.

**⛺ ACCOMMODATIONS AND CAMPING.** Budget accommodation is scarce near Port Arthur. The only true hostel in the area is the tiny, quirky, and environmentally conscious **Eaglehawk Neck Backpackers ❷**, 94 Old Jetty Rd. Look for signs as you

## IN RECENT NEWS

### SYMPATHY FOR THE DEVILS

Unfortunately, the Tasmanian Devil may be going the way of Tassie's previous icon, the now-extinct Tasmanian Tiger. Devils are dying at an alarming rate due to Devil Facial Tumor Disease (DFTD), which produces a rash of gruesome tumors in its victims that gradually make feeding impossible.

Scientists think the malady may be a type of cancer, but it seems to be communicable through physical contact. The fatality rate of DFTD at this point is 100%; devils usually die within six months of contracting the disease. The entire wild population is at risk for the disease, since DFTD has spread to affect Devils from all over the island.

Local conservationists, terrified at the idea of losing this prized species and source of Tassie pride, are experimenting with captive Devils who have not been exposed to the disease in order to try to find a cure. One of the main areas of such research is the Tasmanian Devil Conservation Park on the Tasman Peninsula, not far from the popular tourist site of Port Arthur. There, scientists are studying healthy specimens in hopes of finding genetic defenses against the scourge of DFTD. As of yet, no major breakthroughs have been reported, but conservationists are keeping their fingers crossed that science can give the Devil a break.

pass Officer's Mess. The hostel is rustic: there is a compost toilet, as much water as there is rain, and no heat. It also only has four beds, so be sure to book ahead. It is a 20min. drive to Port Arthur. If you choose to camp, you will be sharing your tent site with sheep. (☎03 6250 3248. Key deposit $10. Dorms $20. Tent sites $8 per person.) The **Port Arthur Garden Point Caravan Park ❶** is left off the A9, 1km before the historic site; it is convenient but basic. (☎03 6250 2340. Extremely basic dorms $18; sites for two $18, powered $20.)

**🖪 🖾 SIGHTS AND TOURS.** The penitentiary, hospital, and church associated with the 🖾**Port Arthur Historic Site** are vivid reminders of Australia's convict heritage. From 1830 and 1877, over 12,000 male convicts were transferred to cold, desolate Port Arthur, many sentenced to years of hauling timber and breaking rocks. These weren't your average baddies; they were repeat offenders, men who had committed crimes in Australia, where they were already serving a transport sentence for crimes committed in Britain. That said, Port Arthur was not a colony of murderers: 5% of the convicts were there for being "inveterate drunkards." The complex is large and can be explored over two days, although it needs at least 3hr. to do it justice. When you buy your ticket at the tourist office, you will be booked onto the next available walking tour and harbor cruise. The museum is in the basement of the tourist office building. The rest of the complex is best explored simply by wandering around. Don't miss the Separate Prison, reserved for the worst of Port Arthur's convicts, where you can experience the punishment cell and understand firsthand why solitary confinement drives men to madness. The excellent museum brings this turbulent story to life by having each visitor pick a convict and follow his history. Don't miss the opportunity to try on leg irons and see how hard the labor really was. The **walking tours** (40min.; 9:30am-4:30pm every hr. on the ½-hr.) of the grounds and the free **boat tours** (11, 11:40am, 1, 1:40, 3, 3:40pm) provide further insight into convict life. A 20min. harbor cruise past the Isle of the Dead, the colony's cemetery, and Point Puer, the convict boys' colony, is included in the price of admission; book at the visitor complex. Cruises that actually land on the Isle of the Dead (6 tours daily) cost an extra $10 (children $6.50). Tours of Point Puer are 2hr., with 3 tours daily, also $10/6.50. The popular Historic Ghost Tour (1hr.) runs nightly, delighting tourists with spooky stories, shadows, and history. (Bookings required. 9 and 9:30pm; earlier during daylight savings time. $17, children $10.) Tickets can be purchased from local accommodations or the tourist office. (☎1800 659 101; www.portarthur.org.au. Open daily 8:30am-dusk, though most tours end and some buildings close at 5pm; others stay open until 7pm. 2-day admission $25, concessions $20, children $11.)

## AROUND THE TASMAN PENINSULA

Peter and Shirley Storey's handy *Tasman Tracks*, available at tourist shops on the peninsula, maps out many walks around Tasman National Park. A great way to view the spectacular cliffs of the park is with **Port Arthur Cruises** on the Tasman Island Wilderness Cruise. This 2hr. cruise views the highest sea cliffs in Australia. (☎03 6231 2655 or 1300 134 561. Book 24hr. in advance. Departs Oct.-May M and Th 8:15am. $65, concessions $59, children $49.)

One of the region's most intriguing sights is the **Tessellated Pavement,** just before Eaglehawk Neck. The grooves and splits across this natural rock platform were etched by salt crystals left behind as sea water evaporated. The crystals dried in the cracks and expanded, cutting open the rock and giving it the appearance of tile. The carpark is 500m up Pirates Bay Dr., an easy 15min.

round-trip walk to the beach. Nearby, just behind the Officer's Mess, is the magnificent **Pirates Bay,** perfect for a stroll across the sand.

Just past Eaglehawk Neck, the C338 intersects the A9 and leads to the Devils Kitchen and Tasman Arch carparks. Both remarkable cliffside sights were carved by centuries of waves and are easy 10-15min. round-trip walks from both their respective carparks and each other. Continue along the moderate gravel track to Patersons Arch (15min.) and Waterfall Bay (45min.), where it links up with the steep Tasman Trail (1hr.) to the falls and Waterfall Bluff (1hr.). Walking from Devils Kitchen to Fortescue Bay is a breathtaking 6-8hr. walk. **Basic camping ❶** is available, with drinking water, showers, and toilets ($5.50, park fees apply). The campsite manager (☎03 6250 2433) has details. To get to Waterfall Bay by car, take the first right off the C338 and follow the road 4km to the cul-de-sac; for Fortescue Bay, follow the sign-posted, unsealed road east off A9, south of the B37 Taranna junction.

# D'ENTRECASTEAUX CHANNEL

The channels, islands, and caves south of Hobart were first charted by Frenchman Bruni d'Entrecasteaux in 1792, more than a decade before the first English settlement in the area. The valley's cool climate and fertile soil, nourished by the Huon River, make the area perfect for growing berries, pears, and apples. These fruits are what bring backpackers to Cygnet, as they can work short-term to finance their travels (see **Beyond Tourism,** p. 81). The main attractions of the area for those who don't want to farm are near Geeveston, the tiny launching point for the southwest wilderness. The other draw is simply driving down the local winding roads, passing picturesque farmland, forest, and lakes.

## CYGNET AND THE HUON VALLEY ☎03

The Huon Valley has two attractions: fruit and wine. The first draws hordes of backpackers looking to make an extra buck, while the second is a relatively undiscovered but lovely way to explore the area. If neither of these things is on your list, the valley isn't worth the trip. Near the mouth of the Nicholls Rivulet on Port Cygnet and 60km southwest of Hobart, the artsy, tourist-friendly community of Cygnet hosts many seasonal fruit-pickers. Testaments to the region's booming fruit trade pop up repeatedly along the A6, from Hobart to Huonville, but the small town of Cygnet is the heart of the fruit-picking industry.

 **GRIN AND BERRY IT.** Fruit picking is not for everyone. Farming is hard work, and you get paid by the barrel, bushel, bucket, or basket, so just putting in a certain number of hours isn't enough; hard labor is what counts. More importantly, not all fruits pay the same. Blueberries and cherries pay much better than strawberries, so if only strawberries are in season, picking may not even be worthwhile. It is advisable to try picking for a day before settling in for the long haul or, more to the point, before paying a full week's non-refundable rent at the local hostel.

🚍 **TRANSPORTATION.** Hobart Coaches' **buses** depart from 21 Murray St. in Hobart for the Cygnet carpark. (☎03 6233 4232. 1hr., M-F 1 per day, $10.)

**ACCOMMODATIONS AND FOOD.** The **Balfes Hill Huon Valley NOMADS Backpackers** ❷, 4 Sandhill Rd., Cradoc, 4.5km north of Cygnet, caters to workers willing to pick berries or prune orchards from November to May. The hostel managers will help find employment and provide transportation to work and a weekly trip into town ($30 per week). Make sure you don't hate fruit picking before paying the non-refundable weekly rent. The sizable compound houses comfortable bunks, clean bathrooms, kitchens, a video lounge, ping-pong, billiards, a pay phone, laundry ($10), and Internet access ($6 per hr.). Call ahead for pickup from the bus stop. (☎03 6295 1551. Key deposit $10. Reception M-Sa 9:30-10am and 6-8:30pm, Su 7-8pm. Dorms $25; doubles $60-90; 1 week in dorms $140. Weekly rent requires passport deposit.) **Cygnet Caravan Park** ❶, on Slab Rd. off Mary St. in Cygnet, is tidy and well managed, with few facilities but centrally located grassy sites. (☎03 6295 1267. Sites $15, powered $25. See the staff at Cygnet Hotel, across Mary St. from the caravan park, to pay.)

**Red Velvet Lounge** ❷, 87 Mary St., is part art gallery, part Whole Foods store, and part cafe, serving good coffee and vegetarian-friendly dishes among comfortable couches. (☎03 6295 0466. Veggie burger $14. Coffee $3. Occasional live music. Open daily 9am-5pm.) Both **supermarkets** in town, located on Mary St., are open daily 8am-8pm, but **Festival** has the larger selection.

**WINERIES.** The Huon Valley is known for its cool-climate wines, and a host of local vineyards offer tastings, providing a theme for a tour around the countryside. Just don't forget to use the spittoon; Australia has very strict blood-alcohol level limits for drivers. The high-end **Home Hill Winery**, 38 Nairn St., Ranelagh, inside a modern stone, glass, and wood building, has free wine tasting and local fruit, along with delicious, if expensive, lunches. Home Hill's 2006 Pinot Noir was a champion at the Cool Climate Wine Show. (☎03 6264 1200. Cellar door open daily 10am-5pm. Restaurant open M-Th and Su noon-3pm, F-Sa noon-3pm and 6pm-late.) The small **Hartzview Vineyard and Wine Centre** is 10km east of Cygnet near Gardners Bay, via B68 and C626; keep an eye out for the grape sign. Hidden away off an unsealed road, the winery vends its own Pinot Noir and fruit wines as well as affordable coffee and even desserts. B&B accommodations are available on-site. (☎03 6295 1623. Open daily 10am-5pm. Tastings $2, refunded on purchase. 3-bedroom house $180-220.) With views over its vineyards, **Panorama Vineyard**, 1848 Cygnet Coast Rd., Cradoc, features excellent Cabernet Sauvignon, Pinot Noir, and a unique pear liqueur. (☎03 6266 3409. Wines $20-25. Open M and W-Su 10am-8pm.)

**FESTIVALS.** On the second weekend in January, Cygnet comes alive with the **Cygnet Folk Festival** (www.cygnetfolkfestival.org/index.shtml), an open-air celebration of both folk music and food. Book lodgings ahead if you plan to visit during the festival, as the town gets crowded.

# GEEVESTON AND THE FAR SOUTH ☎03

Featuring magnificent countryside, terrifying winding roads, and isolated wilderness, the far south has almost no services but boasts plenty of natural wonders. Twenty-five kilometers south of Huonville along the winding d'Entrecasteaux Channel is Geeveston, a hamlet teetering on the edge of the wilderness. A small town (pop. 800) with only one main street and limited accommodations, Geeveston serves primarily as a gateway to the **Hartz Mountains, Southwest National Park** (p. 547), and nearby forest reserves.

**▐▼ TRANSPORTATION AND PRACTICAL INFORMATION.** Tassielink **buses** (☎1300 300 520) run from Hobart to: Cockle Creek (3hr.; M, W, F 8:30am; $60.70), Dover (2hr., $18.10), and Geeveston (1hr., M-F, $13.70). The tourist office is the Forest and Heritage Centre on Church St. (☎03 6297 1836. Open daily 9am-5pm.) Church St. is also home to a few **ATMs** and the **post office.** (☎03 6297 1102. Open M-F 9am-5pm.) **Postal Code:** 7116.

**▐▐ ACCOMMODATIONS AND FOOD.** The best part of Geeveston is the fantastic hostel; ▨**Bob's Bunkhouse/Geeveston Backpackers ❶**, on the corner of Huon Hwy. and School Rd. just past the center of Geeveston, is a home away from home at reasonable prices. The bright blue kitchen, extensive DVD collection, and comfortable bunks will make you want to stay forever. (☎03 6297 1069 or 04 2930 0665. TV lounge, kitchen, board games, BBQ. Laundry $2. Free Internet. Free parking. Campsites $10. Dorms $20.) The region has many **camping ❶** options, including **Arve River picnic and camping area,** 15km west of Geeveston, and secluded spots at gorgeous **Cockle Creek,** 25km south of Lune River. Both are off unsealed roads and offer pit toilets and drinking water. Cockle Creek also has a phone. For showers and flush toilets, **Dover Beachside Caravan Park ❷**, 20min. from Geeveston in Dover, is an option. (☎03 6298 1301. 13 powered sites, all 2-person, $25; caravans from $43. Cabins from $50.)

**Kyari ❶**, on Church St., is a nice cafe with sandwiches ($6) and coffee ($3) for the road. (☎03 6297 1601. Open M-F and Su 9am-4pm.) An **IGA** supermarket is also nestled on Church St. (Open daily 7am-7pm.)

**▐▼ DAYTRIP FROM GEEVESTON: ARVE ROAD FOREST DRIVE.** This beautiful sealed road leads from Geeveston to the Huon River and the Tahune Forest Reserve with its famous **Airwalk.** This walkway, set in the tree canopy 48m (157 ft.) above the ground, passes over dazzling patches of temperate eucalyptus rainforest, the Huon and Picton Rivers, and native Huon pines and is only slightly vertigo-inducing. Nearby, the easy **Huon Trail** (20min.) meanders through these ancient pines, which take 500 years to mature and live up to 2500 years. (☎03 6297 0068. Open daily 9am-5pm. $22, under 17 $10.) While many people speed directly to the Airwalk, there are a number of overlooks, picnics, and short walks that are well worth a stop as well. The **Big Tree,** alleged to be the biggest tree in Australia, is an 87m (285 ft.) swamp gum of enormous girth only a minute's walk off the main road. The **West Creek Lookout** is another great stop, providing amazing views over the surrounding temperate rainforest, including gushing waterfalls after it rains. (The entire road is 25km. All sites are clearly posted.)

**▐▼ DAYTRIPS FROM GEEVESTON: COCKLE CREEK.** The carpark past the free camping area in Cockle Creek marks the end of Australia's southernmost road, which is unsealed but well-maintained. An easy walk (4hr. round-trip) from the camp goes to South Cape Bay, the closest you can get to Australia's southernmost tip and Antarctica. The area west of Cockle Creek is part of the **Southwest National Park** (p. 547). Park passes are available from the tourist office.

# SOUTHWEST NATIONAL PARK ☎03

There are three things to do in Southwest National Park: hike, fish, and gape. The largest of Tasmania's immense national parks, the park is mostly inaccessible by car, making it perfect for hikers who want to forget civilization. For getting around on four wheels, there is one road that runs through the park: Hwy. B61, better known as **Gordon River Road,** grants easy access to the awesome surrounds of **Lakes Gordon and Pedder.** Unless you're using the road as a starting point for hiking or fishing, it's a drive for the drive's sake, but the immensity and magnificence of the wilderness around you may make it worthwhile.

**TRANSPORTATION AND PRACTICAL INFORMATION.** From Maydena, the B61 traverses nearly 90km of mountainous terrain, running through the settlement of Strathgordon (pop. 15—please say "hello" for us) 12km before its end 2hr. down the road at the Gordon River Dam. Tassielink (☎ 1300 300 520) runs summer **bus** service between Hobart and Scotts Peak (4hr.; Tu, Th, Sa 1 per day; $68) via Timbs Track (2hr., $64.40), Mount Anne (2hr., $68), and Red Tape Track (3hr., $55). Extensive information about the Gordon River Dam's construction, as well as advice on the park's variety of hikes, are available from the sfaff of the **Lake Pedder Chalet** (p. 548).

**CAMPING AND FOOD.** Picnic tables and free **campsites** ❶ are everywhere at various points off the B61. Sites at **Edgar Dam,** 8km before the end of Scotts Peak Rd., **Huon Campground,** and **Teds Beach,** east of Strathgordon, all have pit toilets, tank water, and firewood. Scotts Peak offers bushcamping. Strathgordon's **Lake Pedder Chalet** ❹ is the only park accommodation with a roof as well as the only food option within 80km of the dam. It has the only petrol in the park. (☎ 03 6280 1166. Continental breakfast included. Free Internet. Twins and doubles $55-90. Excellent restaurant open daily noon-2pm and 6-9pm.)

**SIGHTS.** Carved out of the Tasmanian Wilderness World Heritage Area, the manmade **Lake Gordon** and **Lake Pedder** are captivating. Those looking to get up close and personal with the dam can rappel down it with **Aardvark Adventures,** which runs the world's highest commercial rappel as part of a daytrip from Hobart. (☎ 04 0812 7714. Booking required. $160.) Lake Pedder can be viewed from both the main road and the unsealed Scotts Peak Road; the contrast between the lake and the soaring mountains behind it breathtaking.

**HIKING.** If Mt. Field is relatively untouristed, then the Southwest is completely uncharted territory; the low ratio of hikers to excellent hikes makes the park one of the best bushwalking spots in the entire state. The unsealed **Scott's Peak Road,** off Gordon River Rd. 28km into the park at Frodshams Pass, showcases a number of the park's best hikes before ending 38km later at the Huon Campground. The arduous hike up to the **Eliza Plateau** (5-6hr. round-trip), which has great views of central Tasmania, is a favorite. Along Gordon River Rd., 13km from the Scotts Peak Rd. junction, is the enjoyable forest **Wedge Nature Walk** (30min.), and the trailhead to **Mount Wedge** (5hr.), whose summit affords an overwhelming panorama of the park. Consult with a Tasmania Forestry office or guide before heading out on your trip; a map, compass, and Tasmania bushwalking guide are recommended for all hikes.

**UNDER THE WEATHER.** Attempt to hike only in good weather and always bring all-weather gear, as the plateau is completely exposed and conditions can change rapidly for the worse.

**FISHING.** Trout are plentiful on Lake Gordon and Lake Pedder from August to April; boat-launch sites can be found at Edgar Dam and Scotts Peak Dam and along the road to Strathgordon (license required). For park info, contact the **entrance station** (☎ 03 6288 1283) or **rangers** at Mt. Field (☎ 03 6288 1149).

# WESTERN WILDERNESS

The scenic splendor of Tasmania's western wilderness is carved out by the dramatic: the deep glaciers of Lake St. Clair, the magnificent slopes of Cradle Mountain, and the epic Overland Track that runs between the two. One of the world's great temperate zones, it's also one of its last. Most of the land in this region of Tasmania is protected as part of the UNESCO Tasmanian Wilderness World Heritage Area, but logging and mining still threaten the areas just outside the official national park borders. While the region's well-trammeled trails justifiably attract plenty of visitors, most of the west is unspoiled; lush rainforest, forbidding crags, windswept moors, and swirling rivers have been left almost untouched by civilization.

 **TENSE TIMES FOR THE TENTLESS.** Less-touristed areas of Tasmania—including many of the national park areas in the west—are often the most difficult places to find a cheap bed. The budget accommodation options that do exist are usually smaller than their city counterparts and book up quickly in high season, forcing budget travelers into overpriced alternatives. While tent sites are usually available on short notice (except during holiday weekends), be sure to book ahead whenever possible when traveling tentless into Tasmania's western wilderness.

**TASMANIA**

# CRADLE MOUNTAIN ☎03

One of the most popular natural attractions in Tasmania (and with good reason), Cradle Mountain rises majestically above Dove Lake. The surrounding area is a complex fabric of creeks and crags that shelters the state's rugged gems: sweet-sapped cider-gum woodlands, rainforests of King Billy and celery-top pine, and lush carpets of cushion plants. Endowed with extensive walking tracks, Cradle Mountain is well worth a multi-day visit.

**▐ TRANSPORTATION.** The towns of Launceston and Devonport serve as the urban hubs of public transportation to Cradle Mountain, although it's also possible to make the long trip from Hobart by connecting in Queenstown. The **Cradle Mountain Transit Terminal,** in the same building as the **Information Centre,** has the most up-to-date **bus** and **shuttle** schedules (open 8am-5pm). **Tassielink** (☎1300 300 520) runs daily from Launceston (3hr., $53.30) and Devonport (1hr., $36.70), and on the west coast from Strahan via Queenstown (3hr.; Tu, Th, Sa 11:15am; $34.20). A free shuttle to the visitors center and Dove Lake runs from both the Information Centre and the Cosy Cabins campground across the street. The shuttle operates every 20min., from early morning until late throughout the summer tourist season; it's free for all parks passholders except those with a 24hr. pass, in which case it costs $7.50. In the winter, **Maxwell's Coach and Taxi Service** (☎03 6289 1141 or 04 2830 8813) offers expensive service to the northwest (see **Lake Saint Clair,** p. 551; book ahead). For more information on transportation for the **Overland Track,** see p. 552.

If you're traveling by car, the park is a 1hr. drive south from Devonport on B19 and B14, and then west on C132 to the park entrance. From Launceston, it is a 2hr. drive on A1 to B13, and C156 through Sheffield. From the west, follow A10 for 2hr. to C132 into the park. There is no direct road through the park. Visitors can reach Lake St. Clair most easily via the Belvoir Road (C132) and the Murchison and Lyell Highways (A10). Be sure to display your parks

## SO OVER THE OVERLAND TRACK

Most people take their day off to relax. I decided to climb a mountain. Tasmania is famous for its rugged Overland Track, a six-day hike through the midst of the Cradle Mountain-Lake St. Clair Wilderness, and every bit of my outdoors-loving self wished I could do it. However, I was awake and working, which left me looking forlornly at the many trekkers embarking on the Track with overburdened backpacks.

Luckily for me, the Overland Track is not Tassie's only hiking jewel; a number of intense day hikes give those of us without the time for a multinight trip the opportunity to explore the wilderness. I chose to summit Cradle Mountain, a famous day hike that includes the beginning of the Overland Track and provides stupendous views over the entirety of Cradle Mountain National Park. At 7am, I was the only hiker on the path, and the amazing vistas seen from the Cradle Plateau nearly blew me away.

The end of the hike involved some tough boulder scrambling that left me with bloody palms, but the incredible feeling of solitude and having mastered the universe that I felt upon reaching the summit made it worth it. I don't envy the Overland trekkers anymore; I feel bad for them because the summit of Cradle Mountain isn't on their route.

—*Andrea Halpern*

pass on your car's dashboard, because you can be hit with a $50 fine for failure to do so.

Parking can be tricky. There is always parking at the information center, from which you can take a shuttle to the park, but parking within Dove Lake is possible only before 10am or after 3pm. Between those hours, the lots in the park are almost always full, and there is a line to enter.

**◪ PRACTICAL INFORMATION. Cradle Mountain-Lake Saint Clair National Park** is the northernmost end of the **Tasmanian Wilderness World Heritage Area**. Park fees apply. There is extensive parking just outside the park limits at the information center, but this lot serves primarily as a jump-off for the free shuttle (see above) into the park proper. The **visitors center**, 3km farther, features displays with helpful layouts of the walking tracks and registry for the Overland Track, as well as a public telephone. (☎03 6492 1110. Open daily in summer 8am-5:30pm, in winter 8am-5pm.) A 7.5km sealed road, often one-lane, runs south from the visitors center to Waldheim and Dove Lake. The **Cradle Mountain Lodge**, just outside the park, can arrange for bike rentals (½-day $20, full-day $30; deposit $200), walking tours (1-3hr., $10-89), canoe trips (3hr., $53), and fly fishing trips (3hr., $60).

 **H2-UH-OH.** Cradle Mountain National Park, like so much of Australia, suffers from frequent water shortages and droughts. It's a restricted water area, meaning that visitors should significantly limit their water usage. Make sure to stay hydrated while hiking, but try to limit shower time.

**⌂⌂ ACCOMMODATIONS AND FOOD.** In high season, accommodations fill up quickly, so book ahead. On the entrance road, opposite the Cradle Mountain Cafe, **Cosy Cabins Cradle Mountain ❶** provides tent sites, alpine huts, bunk rooms, powered caravan sites, and cabins. There's an unequipped cooking shelter with BBQ and sinks, and a kitchen for hostelers. Reception has a limited, expensive supply of groceries. (☎03 6492 1395. Reception 8am-6pm. Free Internet. Tent sites $15, caravan sites $45; bunks $40; family room $85; cabins for 2 $145. VIP/YHA discount $2.) The visitors center runs **Waldheim Cabins ❺**, 5km inside the park. The eight family cabins offer heating, a basic kitchen, showers, toilets, and power. (☎03 6492 1110. Book at the visitors center. Bedding $7.50. Bunk cabins $70 for 2, extra adult $25.)

The cheapest way to feed yourself in this area is to bring your own food. There is no grocer at Cradle Mountain, and while a few places have a small selection of goods, you pay dearly for the convenience. The only food option near the park is the **Cradle Mountain Cafe ❷**, 2km outside the park and across from the Cosy Cabins campsite; it also has the only petrol for 40km. (☎03 6492 1024. Sandwiches $5.50. Coffee $3.50. Open daily 8am-5pm.) The **Cradle Mountain Lodge General Store,** right outside the park, sells basic supplies and meals. The swanky lodge itself has painfully slow dial-up Internet access ($2 per 15min.) and a pay phone. (Open 24hr.)

**◪ HIKING.** Cradle Valley is the northern trailhead for the **Overland Track** (p. 552), Tasmania's most famous bushwalk. This tough hike traverses the entire length of the Cradle Mountain-Lake St. Clair National Park, but the Cradle Mountain area also has a web of tracks to accommodate all degrees of fitness and ambition. The free park map is useful only to those hiking the **Dove Lake Circuit** (2hr.), justifiably the most popular walk, consisting of a beautiful, mostly boardwalked lakeside track through old-growth forest. Short trails around the visitors center and the Cradle Mountain Lodge include **Pencil Pine Falls** (10min.) and a rainforest walk. The map for sale at the visitors center ($5) is crucial for longer dayhikes. The first stage of the Overland Track and its side tracks offer more arduous climbs: the hike up to **Marions Lookout** (1223m) begins along the **Dove Lake track,** continues steeply to the summit, and returns via **Wombat Pool** and **Lake Lilla** (2-3hr.); the ascent to **Cradle Mountain** (1545m) is a difficult hike from Ronny Creek or Dove Lake past Marions Lookout, involving some boulder-climbing toward the summit (7-6hr.).

# LAKE SAINT CLAIR ☎03

Half the headline act of the Cradle Mountain-Lake St. Clair National Park, Lake St. Clair is Australia's deepest lake and the source of the River Derwent. The lake anchors the southern end of the famous **Overland Track** (p. 552), with Cradle Mountain at its northern end. The trip to Lake St. Clair and its surrounding forests is one of the most popular activities in Tasmania.

**▐ TRANSPORTATION.** Tassielink (☎1300 300 520) **buses** run from Hobart (3hr., 1 per day, $43.30), and Strahan via Queenstown (4hr.; Tu, Th-Su 1 per day; $34.40). From Launceston and Devonport, connect in Queenstown in winter (6hr., M-Sa 1 per day, $63); in summer, take the direct wilderness shuttle (3hr.; W, Th, Su 1 per day; $86.10). Overland Track routes include Lake St. Clair and Cradle Mt., with return to Hobart or Launceston available ($80-110; inquire at Tassielink). For group travel, **Maxwell's Coach and Taxi Service** (☎03 6289 1141 or 0428 308 813) operates a charter service in the Cradle Mountain-Lake St. Clair region to Devonport, Hobart, Launceston, and Queenstown. Call ahead for prices, which vary by destination and number of passengers.

**▨ PRACTICAL INFORMATION.** The **visitors center** at Cynthia Bay, on the southern end of the lake, is accessible via a 5km access road that leaves the Lyell Hwy. just west of Derwent Bridge. **Register** for any extended walks, especially the Overland Track. (☎03 6289 1172. Open daily 8am-5pm.) Next door, Lakeside St. Clair, which runs the park's ferries and the nearby campground, is an **info center, restaurant,** and **booking agency;** they also sell fishing licenses, which are required. (☎03 6289 1137; www.lakesidestclaireresort. com.au. Open daily in summer 8am-8pm, in winter 10am-4pm. Fishing gear

$25 per day; fishing licenses $18 for 24hr.; canoes $25 per hr., full-day $75.)
**Ferries** (daily; in summer 9am, 12:30, 3pm; in winter 10am and 2pm) run the
length of the lake from the Cynthia Bay jetty, on the southern end of the lake
by the tourist office; many travelers choose to take a ferry out and then walk
back to the visitors center. A return cruise to Narcissus Bay is also available.
The 12:30pm ferry is a shuttle for hikers; the other two are scenic tours.
(Book ahead at the tourist office. 1hr.; Cynthia Bay to Narcissus Bay $25,
children $15; Cynthia Bay to Echo Point $18/15; scenic tour $35/18. Minimum
$120 in bookings for tour to operate.)

**ACCOMMODATIONS AND FOOD.** The park has **free camping ❶** sites
within the entrance at **Fergys Paddock,** with pit toilets and walking access (10min.
from Cynthia Bay toward Watersmeet) only. Other sites are located at **Shadow
Lake** (no toilet), **Echo Point,** and **Narcissus Bay.** Travelers can also stay at the **Lake
Saint Clair Wilderness Resort ❶,** just outside the park entrance. (☎03 6289 1137.
Coin-operated showers $1; a pay phone. Sites Sept.-Apr. $10 per person, May-
Aug. $8; powered sites for 2 $25/20; doona $5; heated backpacker bunks $28.)
The **Derwent Bridge Wilderness Hotel ❷,** opposite the Lake St. Clair access road on
the Lyell Hwy., offers backpacker rooms in small modular units detached from
the main, barn-sized building. (☎03 6289 1144. Also has petrol. Hotel doubles
$95; budget rooms $25 per person. The hotel serves meals at reasonable prices.
Open daily 8-9:30am, noon-2pm, and 6-8pm.) If you're hungry (regardless of
whether or not you're a wombat), travel the kilometer or so south to Derwent
Bridge and try **The Hungry Wombat Cafe ❷.** (☎03 6289 1125. Nice breakfast menu
$10-13.50; $10 make-your-own burgers. Open daily 8am-6pm.)

**HIKING.** All tracks branch off from the **Watersmeet Track,** which starts at
the carpark a few hundred meters to the west of the visitors center. If you
only want a stroll, the lake in all its magnificence is accessible from a viewing
platform right next to the visitors center. A little over an hour's walk from the
visitors center, at Watersmeet, the **Platypus Bay Trail** (20min.) makes an enjoyable
loop through the woods to the water. Longer hikes head west to the sub-alpine
forests and watarah (flowering Nov.-Dec.) of **Forgotten and Shadow Lakes** (4-5hr.);
over the ridge, you can tackle steep **Mount Rufus** (7hr. round-trip). If you take
the ferry out in the morning, the lakeside hike to **Cynthia Bay** from Narcissus Bay
amid rainforest and buttongrass takes 5hr.; it's 3hr. from Echo Point.

**TEMPERAMENTAL TASSIE.** Weather in this national park is wildly
unpredictable. It can rain or snow at any time in any season—summer
included—and even the weather forecasters can't always predict what's coming. When snow's not a problem, heat is. Take the following precautions:
**Register** for any walks longer than 2hr.
**Rent an EPIRB (Electronic Position Indicating Radio Beacon),** recommended by Forestry Tasmania. There's no cell service in the wild.
**Drink water continuously,** even when you're not particularly thirsty. Dehydration can exacerbate hypothermia.
**Wear the right clothing.** Pack a raincoat, solid boots, wool socks, sunhat,
sunglasses, sunscreen, thermal long underwear, gloves, hat, rainpants, and
a sweater or fleece. Avoid cotton and denim, since they will not dry easily.
Instead, wear wool or synthetics.

# OVERLAND TRACK

The most famous bushwalk in Australia and among the most beautiful in the world, the Overland Track draws adventurers straight to the Tasmanian wilderness. The track, spanning 65km of World Heritage wilderness and taking most travelers five to eight days over astonishing scenery, is a mandatory part of any outdoors lover's Australian itinerary.

**TRANSPORTATION.** If you're driving, park at Lake St. Clair and take a **bus** to Cradle Mountain to begin the track; it's a bummer to take a bus back to your car after a week in the bush. Getting to and from the Overland Track by bus requires some advance planning, as shuttles between the trailheads and the rest of the island are either sporadic or expensive. Tassielink (☎03 6272 6611) runs from: Hobart to Cradle Mountain via Queenstown (8hr.; Tu, Th, Sa 7am; $105, students $94.50); Lake St. Clair to Hobart (2hr.; M, W 12:30pm; Tu, Th, Sa 4:15pm; F 6:25pm; Su 4:25pm; $65/58); and Launceston to Cradle Mountain (3hr.; M, W, F, Su 12:30pm; $80/72). Fares and times subject to change.

**PRACTICAL INFORMATION.** All walkers starting the Overland Track during the high season (Nov.-Apr.) must purchase a permit before setting out. With the purchase of a permit, walkers lock themselves into a certain start date for their hike, after which point they are free to walk the track at whatever pace they choose. You can make a booking in July of the year before you plan to trek at www.overlandtrack.com.au, by calling ☎03 6233 6047, or by asking the visitors center at Lake St. Clair, Cradle Mountain, Mt. Field, or Freycinet national parks. Permits cost $150. Pick up your permit at the Cradle Mountain visitors center before 3pm (in Apr. by 2pm). Be warned: your pricey Overland Track permit does not guarantee space in any of the five sleeping sites along the track; they're first come, first served. Thus, all hikers should bring a tent with two layers as well as a four-season sleeping bag and cooking stove to combat the cold. If you're lucky enough to get one, the five sleeping sites are equipped with tent platforms, toilets, and water tanks.

The *Essential Bushwalking Guide* is available at kiosks, as is *The Overland Track* ($12). If you are planning to walk the track, read the walking notes online at www.dpiwe.tas.gov.au and request an info kit from the **Parks and Wildlife Service.** (☎03 6492 1110. Cradle Mountain Enterprise and Waldheim Huts, P.O. Box 20, Sheffield TAS 7306.) The track can be undertaken from **Cradle Mountain** (p. 549) or **Lake St. Clair** (p. 551); starting from Cradle Mountain is most common, as it gives a downhill advantage and allows for a ferry trip if you don't want to hike the 15km lakeside track at the end of the Overland Track.

# FRANKLIN-GORDON WILD RIVERS NATIONAL PARK ☎03

Immense and pristine, Franklin-Gordon Wild Rivers is rightfully part of the Tasmanian Wilderness World Heritage Area. This extraordinary expanse can only be seen on foot or by air; timeless glacial mountains, fast-flowing rivers, deep gorges, and endless rainforest reward the determined traveler. Those just passing through will be able to get a taste of the park's grandeur through a number of short, pleasant walks leading off from the highway.

**TRANSPORTATION AND ORIENTATION.** The **Lyell Highway (A10)** runs from Hobart to Strahan, passing **Lake St. Clair** as it winds between the Derwent Bridge and Queenstown within the park, which is otherwise roadless for kilometers.

"Highway" is a bit of a misnomer; the two-lane road twists and turns up and down mountains, so don't expect to go much faster than 70kph.

 **CAMPING.** Between Queenstown and Nelson Falls, **Lake Burbury** has swimming, boating, trout fishing, and **camping ❶** surrounded by mountains. (No showers or laundry. Sites $5.) Between Nelson Falls and Donaghys Hill, the **Collingwood River** also has free **camping ❶** with fireplaces and picnic facilities.

**SIGHTS AND HIKING.** We can use words such as "magnificent," "awe-inspiring," and "extraordinary" only so many times; the short walks off the Lyell Hwy. will give you an idea of what we mean. Three in particular stand out. The **Nelson Falls Nature Trail** (10min.), hidden in wet rainforest 25km east of Queenstown, leads to a lovely cataract. **Donaghys Hill Lookout** (40min. round-trip), 50km east of Queenstown, should not be missed. Renowned for sunset views, the track offers incredible 360° views of the Franklin River Valley and Frenchman's Cap, its principal peak (1443m; 3- to 5-day round-trip hike to the top). The **Franklin River Nature Trail,** 60km east of Queenstown, is a well-maintained 20min. circuit through rainforest.

# THE NORTHWEST

The Northwest is often overlooked by travelers, and frankly, for good reason. It's a center of agriculture, industry, and mining, with some boring towns thrown in for good measure. However, the region has two saving graces. First, it's a convenient gateway to the Western Wilderness, including Cradle Mountain; second, the Northwest boasts magnificent stretches of coastline.

## DEVONPORT                                                    ☎03

Lured by visions of rainforest, ancient peaks, and wild rivers, travelers arriving in Devonport (pop. 25,000) are confronted with an unpleasant surprise. Its grim waterfront on the Mersey River, dominated by a cluster of huge gray silos, is an unremarkable gateway to Tasmania's wild charms; the marvelous nearby **Rocky Cape National Park** is the city's one highlight, and it's not even in the city.

**TIP** | **DEVOIDPORT.** Devonport is perhaps best seen from the rearview mirror of whatever transport you've booked to other parts of the state. If at all possible, minimize the time you'll be spending in Devonport; it's the rarest of travelers who regrets not prolonging his or her stay in what is one of the least appealing cities in the state.

## ▣ TRANSPORTATION

The **airport** is 8km east of the city center on the Bass Hwy. Qantas (☎13 13 13) flies four times per day from Melbourne (1hr., $140). A **shuttle** (☎03 0400 5995; $10) transfers passengers between the airport and downtown. **Taxis Combined** is a more expensive but more convenient alternative. (☎03 6424 1431. $18-23.)

Most popular with those transporting a car, the **ferries** *Spirit of Tasmania I* and *II* sail to Melbourne and, new as of 2004, the *Spirit of Tasmania III* sails to Sydney; breakfast, dinner, and accommodations are all provided. (☎1800 634 906; www.spiritoftasmania.com.au. *Spirit I* and *II:* 11hr.; depart nightly at 8pm from Melbourne and Devonport; Dec. 17-Jan. 25 also 9am; $114-418.

*Spirit III:* 20-22hr.; departs from Sydney Tu, F, Su at 3pm, and from Devonport M, Th, Sa at 3pm; $180-340. Car surcharge $61, bike $6.) The Mersey River Ferry Torquay takes passengers from east Devonport back to the Devonport city center. With your back to the Spirit of Tasmania terminal, turn left and head down the first street to reach the water; the shuttle ferry wharf is located straight ahead. (☎03 1835 0142. Runs M-Sa 9am-5pm on demand; $2, children and students $1.20; bike surcharge $0.50.) MerseyLink (☎03 6423 3231; www. merseylink.com.au) also **buses** around town M-Sa and links the ferry to local accommodations ($2-3.10). The Spirit Shuttle transports travelers daily to both Launceston ($21.20) and Hobart ($51.40).

## ❄ 🛈 ORIENTATION AND PRACTICAL INFORMATION

The port of Devonport is the mouth of the **Mersey River,** with the ferry terminal on its eastern bank. Devonport is bounded to the west by the **Don River** and to the south by the **Bass Highway (Hwy. 1),** which has the only bridge across the Mersey. The city center lies on the western bank, with **Formby Rd.** at the river's edge and the **Rooke Street Mall** one block inland, both intersected by **Best Street** and **Stewart Street;** most essentials lie within a block of these four streets. To the north, Formby Rd. leads to **Mersey Bluff** and **Bluff Beach.**

The **Devonport Visitor Centre,** 92 Formby Rd., around the corner from McDonald's, books accommodations and transport. (☎03 6424 4466. Open daily 7:30am-5pm.) 🔲**The Backpackers' Barn,** 10-12 Edward St., has all the information and gear you need to engage in environmentally friendly bushwalking throughout Tasmania, including the famed **Overland Track** (p. 552). The building also offers a restroom, showers, and announcement board. (☎03 6424 3628; www. backpackersbarn.com.au. Open Nov.-Mar. M-F 8am-6pm, Sa 8am-3pm; Apr.-Oct. M-F 8am-5pm, Sa 8am-3pm. Gear can be sent back by **Redline Coaches** for a fee. Lockers $1 per day, $5 per week, with free backpack storage for 1 day.)

## 🏠 🏕 ACCOMMODATIONS AND CAMPING

🔲 **Mersey Bluff Caravan Park,** (☎03 6424 8655), a 30min. walk from town on Mersey Bluff. Situated on a lovely, quiet spot next to the lighthouse with stunning views of the Strait. Laundry $2. Reception 7:30am-noon, 4-6pm, and 7-9:30pm. Sites $7.50 per person; powered for 2 $18; caravan $40; cabin $62. ❶

**Tasman House Backpackers,** 169 Steele St. (☎03 6423 2335). The interior is nicer than the institutional exterior suggests; a well-stocked kitchen with brightly painted cupboards, a pool table and wood stove in the lounge, and clean dorm rooms are all draws. Doona $3. Laundry $4.40. Key deposit $10. Free parking. Reception 7am-1pm and 3-10pm. Dorms $16; twins $18 per person; doubles $40, ensuite $50. ❶

**Molly Malone's,** 34 Best St. (☎03 6424 1898). The only budget accommodation convenient to the city center. Standard 4-bed dorms have sinks and heat; a nice kitchen, balcony, and TV lounge sweeten the deal. Linen $5. Internet $2 per 15min. Key deposit $10. Check-in at the pub. Dorms $15; doubles $30, ensuite $50. 4-night max. stay. ❶

## 🍴 FOOD

Good eating is difficult to come by in Devonport, although those looking for fast food have come to the right place. The tastiest meals in town can be found at 🔲**Rosehip Cafe ❶,** 12 Edward St., attached to the Backpackers Barn. A focaccia sandwich stuffed with three fillings of your choice ($7) and a fresh fruit smoothie ($4.50) make for a delicious and healthful lunch. (☎03 6424 1917. Open M-F 7:30am-3pm.) **Coles** and **Woolworths** supermarkets share a carpark on Best St., a few blocks up from the waterfront. (Both open daily 7am-10pm.)

## SIGHTS

**Tiagarra Aboriginal Cultural Centre and Museum,** a 30min. walk from the city center to Mersey Bluff on Formby Rd., near the lighthouse, explores 40,000 years of Tasmanian Aboriginal history in basic but informative displays. The Aboriginal Tasmanians are thought to have been the most isolated peoples of the world, having had no outside contact until the 19th century. (☎03 6424 8250. Open M-Sa 9am-5pm. $4, children and students $2.50.) The nearby ◪**lighthouse** provides a prime view of the shimmering blue Bass Strait. A pleasant bicycling and walking path connects the point to the city and approaches Back Beach.

## DAYTRIPS FROM DEVONPORT

**Rocky Cape National Park,** a worthwhile 2hr. drive from Devonport, features a magnificent mountainous coastline offset by sparkling turquoise waters, rare flora, and Aboriginal cave sites, the latter of which are unfortunately closed to the public. The two ends of the park are accessible by separate access roads. The 9km eastern access road turns off A2 12km west of Wynyard and leads to walking tracks and the truly spectacular—and surprisingly isolated—◪**Sisters Beach.** The unsealed 4km western access road, 18km farther down A2, ends at a lighthouse with great views of **Table Cape** and the **Nut,** a 152m volcanic plateau. The **Coastal Route** track traverses the length of the park along the undeveloped coast (11km, 3hr.) while the **Inland Track** heads in the same direction with somewhat better views. There is no visitors center, but the shops near both entrances stock park brochures. The small park is geared toward day use; the low-growing vegetation is still recovering from a severe bushfire and offers little protection from the sun during extended walks.

    **Narawntapu National Park** is a small coastal heathland reserve, about an hour from Devonport and Launceston, has ample fishing and swimming opportunities at Bakers and Badger Beach. The reserve is also popular for its walking tracks and abundant wildlife, including wombats and Forester kangaroos. Register to camp just past the park entrance at **Springlawn ❶**, with flush toilets, BBQ, tables, water, and a public telephone. Two more scenic **camping ❶** areas are 3km farther down the road on the beach near Bakers Point, and have pit toilets, fireplaces, tables, water, and wallabies. (The park is accessible by car only via three gravel roads. From Devonport take B71 to C740, which heads north between Devonport and Exeter. Take care driving at dawn and dusk, as wallabies abound. Park office ☎03 6428 6277. Book ahead in summer. Springlawn: sites $10, extra person $5. Baker's Point: Sites $5.50, families $15.)

# DELORAINE AND SURROUNDS    ☎03

In the foothills of the Great Western Tiers, huddled in the agricultural Meander Valley between Devonport and Launceston, Deloraine functions as a perfect base for exploring the World Heritage Area to the southwest.

## TRANSPORTATION AND PRACTICAL INFORMATION

Redline (☎1300 360 000) **buses** run out of **Cashworks,** 29 W Church St., with daily service to: Burnie (2hr., 1-2 per day, $23.60), Devonport (1hr., 1-2 per day, $15), and Launceston (1hr., 3 per day, $11.10). **Deloraine Visitor Information Centre,** 98 Emu Bay Rd., doubles as the folk museum. (☎03 6362 3471. Open daily 9am-5pm. Museum $7.) Deloraine's services include: **ANZ** with a **24hr. ATM** on Emu

Bay Rd.; **police** on Westbury Pl. (☎6362 4004); a **pharmacy** at 62-64 Emu Bay Rd. (☎03 6362 2333; open M-F 8:45am-5:30pm, Sa 9am-12:30pm); **Internet access** at **Online Access Centre,** 21 West Pde., behind the library (☎03 6362 3537; $7 per hr.; open M-Tu and Th-Sa 10am-4pm, W noon-4pm, Su 1-4pm); and a **post office** at 10 Emu Bay Rd. (☎03 6362 2156; open M-F 9am-5pm). **Postal Code: 7304.**

## ACCOMMODATIONS

**Deloraine Highview Lodge YHA,** 8 Blake St. (☎03 6362 2996). On Emu Bay Rd. turn right at Beefeater St., then left at Blake St. This is the best hostel around, with amazing views of Quamby Bluff and the Great Western Tiers, comfy bunks, and a refreshing family atmosphere. A great outdoor deck and lovely kitchen don't hurt either. Reception 8-10am and 5-10pm. Dorms $21, YHA $18. ❷

**Apex Caravan Park,** (☎03 6362 2345). On West Pde., parallel to Emu Bay Rd. off the roundabout. Check-in at the house on the corner across from the park. Showers for non-guests $4. Sites $11, powered $15; sites for 2 $19/22. ❶

## FOOD

**Deloraine Deli,** 36 Emu Bay Rd. (☎03 6362 2127). This delicatessen serves a number of excellent lunch dishes. Especially delicious is the zucchini and bacon frittata ($14). Open M-F 8:30am-5pm, Sa 8:30am-2:30pm. ❷

## SIGHTS

**WALLS OF JERUSALEM NATIONAL PARK.** A 1hr. drive southwest from Deloraine, ending in 19km of unsealed road, will take you to the arterial walking track that leads to the Walls of Jerusalem National Park. The mostly boarded track begins from a carpark with a pit toilet off Mersey Forest Rd. (C171) and continues to the dolerite walls over the course of a moderate 3-4hr. one-way trek. The first hour is a steep walk to the park's border and to an old trapper's hut. From there, the path becomes relatively level. A compass, a $10 park map (available for purchase at the Deloraine visitors center), and overnight equipment are required even for day hikes due to the region's highly variable weather and changing elevations. Despite the moderate inclines and boarding, the Walls are not to be taken lightly, especially as the park has no ranger station for emergencies; rangers recommend the hike only to experienced backpackers and warn against the potential dangers of hiking alone. *(☎03 6363 5133. Call ahead. Park fees apply. Register for all walks at the Walls.)*

**MOLE CREEK KARST NATIONAL PARK.** About 35km west of Deloraine off B12, Mole Creek Karst National Park is home to over 300 caves and two spectacular spelunking opportunities. The enormous **Marakoopa Cave** features a glowworm chamber (don't be frightened—though the brighter the worms glow, the hungrier they are) and the famous, immense **Cathedral Cavern;** the magnificent, million-year-old rock formations inside are worth the 250 steps you'll take during the tour. **King Solomon's Cave** is much smaller and has fewer steps with more colorful formations. Temperatures in the caves can drop to a chilly 9°C (48°F). A few pleasant walking tracks traverse the park. **Alum Cliffs,** from a turnoff 1km east of the town of Mole Creek, is a 1hr. hike to a lookout over the cliffs. *(☎03 6363 5182. Park fees do not apply to those visiting the caves, though most area walks require passes. Park rangers run tours every hour from 10am to 4pm at Marakoopa and from 10:30am to 4:30pm at King Solomon's; buy tickets for both at the ranger station at Marakoopa. $15 per cave, concessions $12, children $8, families $38.)*

**TASMANIA**

# THE NORTHEAST

Tasmania's northeast is blessed with a sunny disposition. The pleasant coastline is dotted by quiet fishing and port towns, the weather is a pleasant counterpoint to the rain and clouds of the Western Wilderness, and the area's main city, Launceston, is a pleasant place to soak up a bit of civilization.

## LAUNCESTON                                                     ☎03

Built where the North and South Esk rivers join to form the Tamar, Launceston (pop 103,200) is Tasmania's second-largest city and Australia's third-oldest, founded in 1805. The intense historic rivalry between Hobart and Launceston manifests itself most clearly in beer loyalty: Boag's is the ale of choice in the north, Cascade in the south. Launceston itself is charming, with the vibrancy of a university town set in beautiful Victorian architecture, and the surrounds, which include nearby **Cataract Gorge** (p. 561), are truly spectacular.

### ▉ TRANSPORTATION

**Flights: Launceston Airport,** south of Launceston on Hwy. 1 to B41. VirginBlue (☎13 67 89; www.virginblue.com.au) flies 4 times daily to **Melbourne** (1hr., $49-305) and once per day to **Sydney** (2hr., $59-334). **Qantas** (☎13 13 13) also flies to **Melbourne** (1hr., 5 per day, $131-347) and **Sydney** (1hr., 1 per day, $112-332). The reliably low-cost **JetStar** (☎13 15 38) flies 3 times daily from Melbourne to **Launceston** ($89-199). An airport **shuttle** connects the airport with city locations. (☎03 6343 6677. Runs 8am-8pm. $12, children $6.) A **taxi** to town will run $25-30.

**Buses:** Redline Coaches depart the **bus terminal** at Cornwall Sq. (☎1300 360 000 daily 6am-10pm; www.tasredline.com). Their buses run to: **Burnie** (2hr., 1-2 per day, $29.30); **Devonport** (1hr., 3 per day, $22.10); **Bicheno/Swansea** (2hr., 1 per day, $30); **St. Helens** (2hr., M-F 1 per day, $27); and **Scottsdale/Derby** (2hr., M-F 1 per day, $15-21). Tassielink buses (☎1300 300 520) run to: **Hobart** (2hr., 1 per day, $30); **Devonport** (1hr., 1 per day, $19.20); **Cradle Mountain** (3hr., in summer 3 per day, $53.30); **Strahan** (9hr., M-Sa 3 per day, $73.90) via **Queenstown** (6hr., M-Sa 3 per day, $64.70); and **Bicheno** (2hr.; F-Su 1 per day, $23.70).

**Public Transportation: Metro** (☎13 22 01) buses run daily 7am-10pm. Fares $1.70-4. All-day ticket $4.40.

**Tours:** The red, double-decker **City Go Round Bus** (☎03 6336 3733) hits major tourist stops including the museums, brewery, and gorge. 1hr. Daily 10am and 1pm. $20.

**Taxis: Taxi Combined** (☎13 22 27 or 13 10 08). Free taxiphone in Transit Centre.

**Car Rental: Budget** (☎03 6391 8566), at the airport, from $31 per day, depending on length of rental. $24 surcharge for ages 21-24. **Economy,** 27 William St. (☎03 6334 3299), from $31 per day, 17+.

**Automobile Club: RAC Tasmania** (☎13 27 22, 24hr. 13 11 11), at the corner of York and George St. Open M-F 8:45am-5pm.

**Bike Rental: Arthouse,** 20 Lindsey St. (☎03 6333 0222). $15 per day.

### ◪ ▉ ORIENTATION AND PRACTICAL INFORMATION

The town is best explored on foot, since most attractions are within four blocks of the **Brisbane Street Mall,** many of the streets are one-way, and virtually all parking near the city center is metered. However, there is limited ▉**free parking** along the Esplanade. The city center is bounded on the north by the **North Esk**

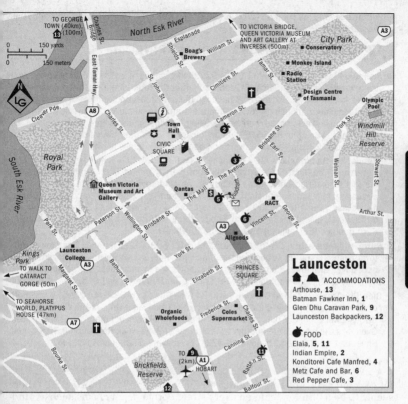

**River** and on the west by the **South Esk,** which flows through the **Cataract Gorge.** From here, the A8 runs north to George Town; Hwy. 1 heads south to Hobart through the Midlands and west to Deloraine and Devonport; and the A3 snakes east to St. Helens and the east coast.

**Tourist Office: Launceston Travel and Information Centre** (☎03 6336 3133), on the corner of St. John and Citimiere St. 90min. walking tours M 4pm, Tu-Sa 10am; $15. Open M-F 9am-5pm, Sa 9am-3pm, Su 9am-1pm.

**Bushwalking Equipment: Allgoods,** 71-79 York St. (☎03 6331 3644; www.allgoods. com.au), at St. John St. Inexpensive, with a great selection that includes army surplus and maps. Basic equipment rental at their Tent City annex, 60 Elizabeth St. Tent $4.50 per day, stove $2 per day. Open M-F 9am-5:30pm, Sa 9am-4pm, Su 10am-2pm.

**Currency Exchange: Commonwealth Bank,** is at 97 Brisbane St. The mall has **ATMs.**

**Police: Station** (☎03 6327 1471) on Cimitiere St. Enter through Civic Sq.

**Internet Access: Service Tasmania** (☎1300 366 773), in Henty House, Civic Sq., has 3 free terminals. Open M-F 8:15am-5pm. The **library,** 1 Civic Sq. (☎03 6336 2625) also has free Internet with a 1hr. limit. Open M-Th 9:30am-6pm, F 9:30am-7pm, Sa 9:30am-2pm. **Cyber King** (☎03 6334 2802) at the corner of York and George St. $5 per hr., $8 per 2hr. Open M-F 8:30am-7:30pm, Sa-Su 9:30am-6:30pm.

**Post Office:** 111 St. John St. (☎03 6331 9477). Open M-F 9am-5pm, Sa 9:30am-1pm. **Postal Code:** 7250.

# 🏠 🏕 ACCOMMODATIONS AND CAMPING

🏅 **Arthouse,** 20 Lindsey St. (☎03 6333 0222; www.arthousehostel.com.au). From downtown, cross the river on Tamar St. and turn left at the roundabout (10min.). A delightful hostel, in a newly renovated 1888 building. The pine floors and antique dressers gives it a historic charm, though it provides important modern comforts: a flat-screen TV in the lounge and a well-stocked, gorgeous kitchen. Outdoor terrace. Free Wi-Fi. Internet $5 per 30min., $8 per hr. Bike $15 per day. Reception 8am-9pm. 8-bed dorms $23, 6-bed $25, 4-bed $27; singles $55; twins and doubles $65; family rooms $89. ❷

**Launceston Backpackers,** 103 Canning St. (☎03 6334 2327), across from Brickfields Reserve, off Bathurst St., a 7min. walk from the city center. Clean dorms await travelers in this restored brick home, although the cinderblock walls are a little less than appealing. Large industrial kitchen, long-term storage ($2 per day), and laundry. Internet access $2 per 30min. Key deposit in summer $10. Free parking. Female-only dorms on request. Reception 8am-10pm. 6-bed dorms $18, 4-bed $19; singles $44; twins $24; doubles $50, ensuite $60; triples $20. VIP. ❶

**Batman Fawkner Inn,** 35-39 Cameron St. (☎03 6331 7222), only a few blocks from town center. If you don't need cooking facilities, hop on over to the Inn to get a clean bed, duvet, and towel. Complimentary tea and coffee in each room. Backpackers rooms M-F only $40; twins and doubles M-F $75, Sa-Su $85, extra bed $15. ❸

**Glen Dhu Treasure Island Caravan Park,** 94 Glen Dhu St. (☎03 6344 2600), 2km south of downtown. Follow signs for South Launceston, then Glen Dhu and the caravan park. BBQ, showers, laundry, outdoor campers' kitchen with kettle, hot plate, and toaster-oven. Overlooks the city, but the nearby highway makes things noisy. Reception 8:30am-7pm. Sites for 1 $14, for 2 $21, powered $20/25; caravans $50; cabins $82. ❶

# 🍴 FOOD

Like so much of Australia, Launceston is a city gone mad for coffee. There seems to be a different cafe on every street corner, from chains such as Hudson's to local hole-in-the-walls with great lattes. If you need a java fix, you've come to the right place. There is a **Coles** supermarket at 198 Charles St. (☎03 6334 5744. Open daily 7am-10pm.), and an **Organic Wholefoods** at 54 Frederick St. (☎03 6331 7682. Open M-F 10am-6pm.)

🏅 **Konditorei Cafe Manfred,** 106 George St. (☎03 6334 2490). Old-world patisserie serving excellent baked goods (the hazelnut chocolate rings are to die for; $3) and light meals such as ocean trout frittata ($3-5) for a pre-dessert munch. Cake and coffee combo $6. Open M-Tu 8am-6pm, W-Su 8am-late. ❶

**The Metz Cafe and Bar,** 119 St. John St. (☎03 6331 7277; www.themetz.com.au), on the corner of York St. Upscale pizza pub and wine bar attracts a mixed crowd of local yuppies and travelers with innovative wood-fired pizzas such as satay chicken and mango ($17.50); you can even see your dinner being cooked in the open pizza oven. Open M-Th 10am-late, F-Su 9am-late. ❸

**Red Pepper Cafe** (☎03 6334 9449), in Centreway Mall, a quarter-block off Brisbane St. Cheap, healthful, light meals (chicken and almond burger $10) served in cramped surroundings. The low-fat breakfast muffins ($3.50), baked fresh every day, are suspiciously addictive. Open M-Sa 8am-4pm. ❶

**Elaia** (☎03 6331 6766), in the Quadrant Mall. Second location at 238-240 Charles St., 2 blocks south of Princes Sq. Colorful Mediterranean decor and classy food. Popular wraps and open sandwiches, such as steak with chili jam ($13.50-18.50). Outdoor seating available. Wi-Fi. Main courses $13-20. Open daily 9am-3pm. ❸

**Indian Empire,** 64 George St. (☎03 6331 2500). Your basic Indian restaurant, with cheap, yummy meals from $10-17. Eat-in or takeaway. BYOB. Open daily 5pm-late. ❷

## 👁 🏔 SIGHTS AND ACTIVITIES

■**CATARACT GORGE RESERVE.** The most spectacular sight in Launceston is the handiwork of the South Esk River: the awesome sheer cliffs of the **Cataract Gorge Reserve** hold the river flow. The cliffs are a 20min. walk from Paterson St. toward King's Bridge. Don't expect pristine wilderness; the **First Basin** of the gorge has been popular since the town's settlement and now hosts peacocks, an exotic tree garden, a restaurant, and a gorgeous ■**free swimming pool. Walking tracks** run on either side of the river from King's Bridge to the First Basin; the one on the north side is easy, while the more difficult **Zig-Zag track** on the south climbs to the gorge's rim for excellent views of the cataracts (20min.). A **chairlift** connects the two sides at the First Basin. *(Open daily 9am-4:30pm. $12 round-trip, $10 one-way; children $8/7.)* The **Band Rotunda,** on the First Basin's north side (cross the Basin on the swinging **Alexandra Suspension Bridge;** 5min.), and the **Duck Reach Power Station,** 45min. down from the First Basin, provide info about the Gorge's history. Those making the worthwhile walk from the First Basin to Duck Reach should be aware that the track on the south side of the river is much easier and better maintained than the return track on the North side. *(Rotunda and power station open daily in summer 8am-8pm; winter in 8am-5pm.)*

**QUEEN VICTORIA MUSEUM AND ART GALLERY.** The museum, which is quite impressive for a not-very-impressive collection of art, is split between the exhibits at **Royal Park** and at **Inveresk.** Royal Park, on the corner of Cameron and Wellington St., houses a local and natural history display focusing on Tasmania's wildlife. The upstairs gallery offers a brief but sweet peek at Tasmanian sculpture, paintings, ceramics, and textile art. A highlight is the Chinese temple **(Joss House)** built by immigrant miners in a nearby town in the 19th century. The **Planetarium** is part of the complex. The **Inveresk Museum** (across the river on Tamar St.) houses a Tasmanian art gallery, which has a fantastic display of ■**Aboriginal shell necklaces.** Be sure to check out the pearly Maireener shells. *(☎03 6323 3777. Royal Park open M-Sa 10am-5pm, Su 2-5pm; Inveresk open daily 10am-5pm. Both museums free; $5 suggested donation. Planetarium shows Tu-F 3pm, Sa 2 and 3pm. $3.50, children $2.20, families $7.70. No children under 5.)*

**BOAG'S BREWERY.** For an illuminating overview of the beer-brewing process, as well as a few free samples, take the **Boag's Brewery tour,** 21 Shields St. The tour will give you an excellent comparison point to **Cascade Brewery** (p. 540) in Hobart; besides, you get four free samples here, as opposed to three there. *(☎03 6332 6300; www.boags.com.au. Tours every hr. M-F 9am-4pm. Fully enclosed shoes required. Book ahead. $18, concessions and children $14.)*

🔲 **DAYTRIP FROM LAUNCESTON:** ■**PLATYPUS HOUSE.** Didn't get to see a platypus in the wild? Ever wanted an echidna to lick your toes? In this conservation center, the elusive monotremes are on full view. The animals were rescued and are being studied by researchers trying to combat the fungus decimating the platypus population. *(☎03 6383 4884. The complex is 1hr. by car from Launceston on the West Tamar Hwy. Open daily 9:30am-4:30pm. Tours every 30min.; all tours include feedings. $18, concessions $15, children $9.)* The adjacent **Seahorse World** also has tours of its vast collection of seahorse species. *(☎03 6383 4111. Tours daily every 30min. 9:30am-4pm. $20, concessions $16, children $9, families $50.)*

## SCOTTSDALE

☎ 03

Scottsdale (pop. 7500), though maybe not worth a stopover by itself, lies midway along the A3 between St. Helens and Launceston, thus serving as a good base from which to explore Tassie's northeast, including **Mount William National Park. Redline** (☎ 1300 360 000) buses run from Launceston to Scottsdale ($12). The tourist office is in the building that houses the **Forest EcoCentre**, 46 King St., an exhibit run by Forestry Tasmania. (☎ 03 6352 6520. Open daily 9am-5pm, in winter 10am-4pm.) **Postal code:** 7260.

**Northeast Park Campground ❶** (☎ 03 6352 2017), along the A3 to Derby, has laundry facilities, a playground, and free sites. **Lords Hotel ❷**, 2 King St., offers budget hotel rooms with electric blankets, but guests should expect to share a bathroom. (☎ 03 6352 2319. Singles $30; doubles $50.) Twenty-two kilometers west of Scottsdale, just off B81, is the **Bridestowe Estate Lavender Farm,** 296 Gillespies Rd., the largest lavender oil farm in the Southern Hemisphere. Travelers who are in the region in December or January shouldn't miss the chance to enjoy these beautiful lavender fields in bloom. (☎ 03 6352 8182. Open Dec.-Jan. daily 9am-5pm. $4, children free.)

## LAUNCESTON TO THE SUNCOAST

**MOUNT VICTORIA FOREST RESERVE.** The reserve is a 45min. drive past Scottsdale. From the A3, follow signs south to Ringarooma and continue 15km on mostly unsealed roads to the carpark. The single-drop **Ralph Falls,** the tallest in Tassie, is a 10min. walk from the carpark. ⧉**Norm's Lookout** provides a fantastic view of the gorge and falls below. The tough hike up **Mt. Victoria** passes through a variety of ecosystems and offers panoramic views of the Northeast.

**SAINT COLUMBA FALLS.** Thirty minutes from St. Helens, the 90m Saint Columba Falls unleashes 42,000L of water per minute. Drive 20min. off the A3 (follow signs for the Pub in the Paddock) on an unsealed road ending at a carpark, then walk 15min. to the falls. Keep an eye out for the supposedly extinct Tasmanian tiger while in the area; a ranger allegedly spotted one here in 1995.

## MOUNT WILLIAM NATIONAL PARK

More a hill than a mountain, Mt. William overlooks a quiet stretch of coast in the sunny northeast corner of the park, east of Bridport. Travelers flock to Mt. William to camp near the park's extraordinary beaches—widely considered the best in the state—and to bushwalk among marsupials. Wallabies are everywhere, and echidnas pop up in the daytime. At dusk, Forester kangaroos are common, as well as pademelons and wombats. After dark, flashlight-equipped visitors can spot brushtail possums, spotted-tail quolls, and Tasmanian devils.

Mt. William is a relatively isolated national park with no facilities. Bringing drinking water is essential; food and petrol can be found in Gladstone or St. Helens but not in Anson's Bay. In an emergency, call the **ranger** (☎ 03 6376 1550) at the north entrance. Depending on weather conditions, the road to the park is frequently accessible only to 4WDs; check ahead before going up. Park entrance fees apply. The park is accessible via the north entrance, at the hamlet of Poole; follow the signposts through the gateway of Gladstone (17km southwest), or from St. Helens to the southern entrance at Ansons Bay via the C843 and C846. From St. Helens, the drive to the southern entrance takes about 1hr. The gravel access roads are a bumpy ride even at slow speeds. No buses run to the park. Both ends of the park offer ample free coastal **camping ❶** (only at designated sites), short hikes, and beach walks. The northern access road leads to Forester Kangaroo Dr., past the turnoff for Stumpy's Bay and its camping areas (pit toilets), and on to the trailhead for the Mount William Walk (1hr. round-trip; moderate). Starting along the road to campsite four, a short track passes through coastal heath to the extraordinary coastline at Cobbler Rocks (1hr. round-trip; moderate). At the south end of the park, campsites are located at Deep Creek. Farther south, across the Anson River and outside park boundaries (thus not subject to fees), **Policeman's Point** has delightfully secluded coastal camping, but no toilets or clean water.

# THE SUNCOAST

Tasmania's east coast is the island's softer side, where the weather is milder and the majority of people are on vacation. Tasmania's mountainous interior shelters this side of the island from the storms that pound the west, and summer travelers come to fish, swim, and loaf in the sun on some of the best beaches in the world, which are still shockingly undiscovered.

## ST. HELENS         ☎03

St. Helens, located off the A3 south of **Mt. William National Park** (p. 562), is the largest and northernmost of the coastal fishing and vacation villages on Tasmania's east coast. Peaceful and easygoing, the town is an excellent base from which to visit the nearby Bay of Fires, which is one of Tasmania's must-sees.

▐ **TRANSPORTATION.** Tassielink (☎1300 300 520) runs **buses** from the St. Helens Travel Centre to Hobart (4hr.; F, Su 2:15pm; $44) via Bicheno (70min., $12), the highway turnoff for Coles Bay (1hr., $14), and Swansea (1hr., $17). Calow Coaches run from the video store, across the street from the travel center, to Hobart and Launceston daily (prices vary).

▐ **PRACTICAL INFORMATION.** The **St. Helens Travel Centre,** 20 Cecilia St., books for Tassielink. (☎03 6376 1533. Open M-F 9:30am-4:30pm.) **St. Helens History Room,** 61 Cecilia St., offers history and information. (☎03 6376 1744. Open daily 9am-5pm. History room by donation.) A 24hr. **ATM** is available at ANZ, at the corner of Cecilia and Quail St. **Service Tasmania,** 23 Quail St., has free **Internet** on one terminal. (☎1300 135 513. Max. 30min. Open M-F 8:30am-4:30pm.) The **post office** is at 46 Cecilia St. (Open M-F 9am-5pm.) **Postal Code:** 7216.

▐ **ACCOMMODATIONS.** One of the biggest perks of St. Helens is ▓**St. Helens Backpackers ❷,** 9 Cecilia St., which features beautiful Tasmanian woodworking, an excellent kitchen, clean and comfortable rooms and transportation and outfitting ($25) for backpackers looking to see the Bay of Fires up close. (☎03 6376 2017; www.sthelensbackpackers.com.au. BBQ. Laundry $3. Bike rental $20 per day. Free parking. Dorms $22; doubles $55, ensuite $60.) Quiet **St. Helens YHA ❷,** at 5 Cameron St., off Quail St, has everything a backpacker could desire in a family home setting. (☎03 6376 1661. Reception 8-10am and 5-8pm. Dorms $25, YHA $22; doubles $55/50.) Beautifully landscaped **St. Helens Caravan Park ❶,** 1.5km from the town center on Penelope St., just off the Tasman Hwy. on the southeast side of the bridge, is nice enough to verge on luxury. (☎03 6376 1290. Reception 8am-8pm. Sites for 2 $27, powered $28; cabins $95.)

▐ **FOOD.** ▓**East Coast Providore ❶,** 32c Cecilia St., offers delicious gelato in fruity flavors like apricot nectar ($3.50), smoothies ($5), and exotic milkshakes like Ferrero Rocher ($5) for those hot summer days. (Open M-Sa 10am-5pm,

Su 10am-4pm.) **Cafe 57 ❶**, around the corner from the visitor's center on Cecilia St., is a Mom-and-Pop breakfast joint. Get there early enough to snag a fresh-baked blackberry muffin ($2.50) while they're still warm. (☎03 6376 2700. Eggs on toast $4. Gourmet Tassie pies such as rabbit and bush spice $6. Open M-Sa 8:30am-4pm.) South of the Scamander Township, just off the A3, on C421 between St. Helen's and Coles Bay, is **Eureka Farm ❷**, 89 Upper Scamander Rd. This is a great place to stop for lunch, and Eureka's fresh fruit and outstanding homemade ice cream ($3.50) are delicious. A small cafe located within the farm also serves superb dishes, like fresh salmon and focaccia, for $8-12. (☎03 6372 5500. Open Nov.-May M-F 10am-5pm. Cash only.) The **Supa IGA** supermarket is at 33 Cecilia St. (☎03 6376 1177. Open daily 8am-7pm.)

**⬛ SIGHTS.** The closest of the outdoor sights are out of town but only a 15min. drive away. **▨Binalong Bay**, gateway to the **▨Bay of Fires Coastal Reserve**, is 15km northeast of town and is one of the most magnificent beaches you will ever see; it's popular with bathers and sunbathers alike but is still remarkably quiet. The reserve itself stretches northward from Binalong Bay; the Gardens, 13km north of the bay, is the last section of road in the reserve and leads to numerous beautiful hidden bays. The entire area is named for the red rocks Capt. Tobias Furneax mistook for fire, and the area has a number of great walks and a few basic, free campsites for those looking to sleep by the beach. Humbug Point, on Binalong Bay Rd. just before the bay, offers great views over the whole area, giving an impression of why Capt. Tobias made his fiery mistake. As you leave town heading south on A3, signs direct you to St. Helens Point, which has numerous unsealed roads leading to isolated beaches; similar roads lead to the Peron Dunes, which cover a large expanse of coast and attract dune buggies. The point itself has a boat ramp and public toilets.

# BICHENO ☎03

The spectacular 75km drive south from St. Helens along the A3 traces the coastline's sand dunes and granite peaks to the small town of Bicheno (BEE-shen-oh; pop. 750). The community's beautiful, rocky seashore, friendly community, proximity to Freycinet National Parks, and a made-for-postcard colony of fairy penguins make Bicheno well worth a visit.

**▣▨ TRANSPORTATION AND PRACTICAL INFORMATION.** Redline **buses** (☎03 6376 1182) leave from the main bus stop at Four-Square Store on Burgess St. (open M-Sa 8am-6:30pm, Su 8am-6pm) and run to the Coles Bay turnoff (10min., M-F 1 per day, $5.50) and continue to Swansea (35min., $9), with connections to Hobart (5hr., M-F 1 per day, $38) and Launceston (2hr., M-F 1 per day, $28). Tassielink (☎1300 300 520) runs from the bus stop to the Coles Bay turnoff (5min.; W, F, Su 1 per day; $2.50); Hobart (3hr.; W, F, Su 1 per day; $27); Launceston (2hr.; F, Su 1 per day; $25); St. Helens (1hr.; F, Su 1 per day; $10.10); Swansea (40min.; W, F, Su 1 per day; $5.50). Bicheno Coach Service (☎03 6257 0293) runs to Coles Bay (40min., M-Sa 1-4 per day, $9.50) and Freycinet National Park (50min., $9), making Redline and Tassielink connections from the Coles Bay turnoff. The visitors center, on Burgess near the town center, is a useful source of brochures. (☎03 6257 4792. Open daily 10am-4pm.) **Internet access** is available at **Swell Cafe** (see below) and at the **Online Access Centre**, on Burgess St. near the primary school. (☎03 6375 1892. $5 per 30min. Open W 1-4pm, Th 9am-noon and 1-5pm, F 11am-1pm and 2-4pm, and Sa 10:30am-12:30pm.) The **Festival IGA** supermarket (open daily 7:30am-7pm) and the **post office** (open M-F 9am-5pm) are near the A3 "elbow" in the town center. **Postal Code:** 7215.

**TASMANIA**

**⬛⬛ ACCOMMODATIONS AND FOOD.** Because of its popularity as a holiday destination, Bicheno has very comfortable accommodations, but they fill up quickly, so be sure to book ahead. The above-average **Bicheno Backpackers Hostel** ❷, 11 Morrison St., just off the A3 behind a little white church near the post office, provides guests with comfortable bunks, excellent service, and lots of information on things to do in the area. (☎03 6375 1651; www.bichenoback-packers.com. Kitchen. Laundry $2. Free parking. Bike rental $10 per hr., $30 per day. Kayak rental $15 per hr., $35 per day. 10% penguin tour discount available. Dorms $22; doubles $60. Cash only.) **Swell Cafe** ❶, in the town center, offers fresh juice ($4.50), meal ($11-13) and dessert ($8) crepes, and Wi-Fi for $2.50 per 15min. (☎03 6375 1076. Open Tu-Sa 10am-10pm, Su 10am-8pm.)

**⬛ SIGHTS.** The best short walk in the area, the 3km **Foreshore Footway** coastal track begins at the bottom of Weily Ave., left off Burgess St., where there is a lovely beach for those who don't want to walk farther, and leads past a blow-hole, a marine reef around Governor Island, and numerous opportunities for swimming, snorkeling, and diving. To see Bicheno from an underwater per-spective, check out **Bicheno Dive Centre**, 2 Scuba Court, which takes boats out and rents gear. (☎03 6375 1138; www.bichenodive.com.au. Boat leaves daily 9:30am, 1:30pm. Boat dives $32, full gear rental $70.) For a view of the fish with-out the inconvenience of water, a glass-bottom boat runs 40min. tours. (☎03 6375 1294. Departs daily 10am, noon, 2pm. $15, children $5.) A highlight of the area is the fairy penguin colony. ⬛**Penguin Tours** leave from the scuba shop in the town center; book ahead, as they're wildly popular. The tours explore the area of shore where the penguins make their homes each night and include close-up encounters with the birds. This is the oldest species of penguin on Earth at 40 million years; they are also the smallest, which doesn't hurt their cuteness factor. Watching them waddle across the sand is truly a magical experience. Dress warmly; even in summer it can be cold and windy. (☎03 6375 1333. Tours 1hr. Depart nightly 5:30-9pm, depending on the time of sunset. Closed footwear recommended, as penguins are known to bite toes. $18, children $9.)

# COLES BAY                                                                    ☎03

The tiny township of Coles Bay (pop. 100) is the service and lodging center for the marvelous Freycinet National Park and is the closest civilization gets to the famous Wineglass Bay. Its sunny location in Great Oyster Bay makes it popular with summer vacationers, while its remote location (27km south on the C302, off the A3 between Bicheno and Swansea) ensures inflated prices.

The YHA-affiliated **Iluka Holiday Centre** ❷ is a lovely campground and hostel at the west end of The Esplanade, just off the beach, with excellent facilities. Book ahead; the entire complex fills up in summer. (☎03 6257 0115 or 1800 786 512. Reception 8am-6pm. Internet and Wi-Fi $5 per 30min. Sites $23, powered $28; dorms $27; twins and doubles $67.50; on-site vans for two $60; cabins $55-160. 10% YHA discount.) For a rustic experience, travelers can try the **Coles Bay Youth Hostel (YHA)** ❶, in the national park at Parsons Cove, which has 10 bunks with pit toilets, cold showers, and a bare-bones kitchen. (☎03 6234 9617. Open Dec. 15-Feb. 15 and Easter. Bunks $10; cabins $50. Book ahead.)

**Freycinet Sea Cruises** (☎03 6257 0355; www.freycinetseacharters.com) offers three excursions on which dolphins and seals are often seen; call ahead to book the Wineglass Bay Cruise (daily 9am-12:30pm; adults $110, children $65) or the Explorer Cruise (daily 2-4:30pm, $75/40). **Freycinet Air** offers 30min. flights over the park and Wineglass Bay. (☎03 6375 1694; www.freycinetair.com.au. From $82.) **Freycinet Adventures** (☎03 6257 0500; www.freycinetadventures.com) runs half- to four-day sea kayak tours ($90-990), and rents out kayaks and mountain bikes. **All4Adventures** (☎03 6257 0018; www.all4adventure.com.au) leads 2hr. 4WD motorbike tours of the park ($105, children $65; book ahead).

Tassielink (☎1300 300 520) runs **buses** from the Coles Bay turnoff to Hobart (3hr., M-F 1 per day, $29). Redline (☎1300 360 000) buses run as close as the turnoff for Coles Bay on the A3 south toward Hobart (3-5hr., M-F 1 per day, $28) and north to Launceston (3hr., M-F 1 per day, $34). From the highway turnoff, take Bicheno Coaches (☎03 6257 0293) to town (20min.; M-F 3 per week. connect with Tassielink and Redline.) The **supermarket** in the Iluka complex on the Esplanade has a coffee shop (open 8am-5pm) and a **visitors center** (open 8am-8pm). Info on the park can also be found at the **Visitors Centre** at the park's entrance. The supermarket on Garnet Ave. sells pricey petrol and houses the **post office**. (☎03 6257 0383. Open daily 7am-7pm.) **Postal Code:** 7215.

# FREYCINET NATIONAL PARK

Freycinet (FRAY-sin-nay) National Park is famous for mountains, beaches, and outdoor activities; it has plenty to do for days, including doing nothing on one of the many beautiful stretches of sand. A 3hr. drive from Hobart or Launceston, the park is home to the striking red-granite Hazards and photogenic ◨**Wineglass Bay**, making it the best of what Tassie's East Coast has to offer.

**Campsites** ❶ are available throughout the park; sites serviced with water and basic toilets dot the coast ($12), and there are powered sites at Richardson's Beach (sites 1-8 and 13-18; $15). During summer, all park campsites are available only by ballot system; register by July and expect to hear in August. Free campsites with pit toilets are available at Isaacs Point, just past Friendly Beach. Be sure to bring your own drinking water.

Nearly all the short walks in the park are extraordinary. Just past the Freycinet Lodge, there's a turnoff on a sealed road for **Sleepy Bay** (1.8km) and the ◨**Cape Tourville Lighthouse** (5.5km). It's an easy 20min. round-trip walk from the carpark to the bay, which, while rocky, offers good swimming and snorkeling. The lighthouse provides amazing views of the Hazards, cliffs, and endless ocean and is accessible by an easy boarded track from its carpark (10min.). **Honeymoon Bay,** popular for snorkeling, and **Richardson's Beach,** a long stretch of white sand popular for swimming, are also on the main road. All major walking tracks begin at the carpark at the end of the road; a moderate 33km hike around the whole peninsula takes two to three days; campsites for overnight hiking are free. Be sure to bring water on dayhikes. The ◨**Wineglass Bay Lookout Walk** (1-2hr.) is a very popular hike, and for good reason: the steep, well-maintained trail, mostly a series of steps, climbs up through the Hazards and has fabulous views of the bay and the peninsular Freycinet mountains. Continuing down to the Bay itself makes the hike a 2½hr. round-trip. The 4-5hr. loop by Wineglass Bay and Hazards Beach (11km) is a nice alternative that provides great swimming opportunities, though you should wear insect repellent, as the mosquitoes and extremely persistent flies are brutal in the summer. The **Mount Amos Track** (3-4hr. round-trip) is the most difficult walk in the park, involving a fair amount of boulder-scrambling, but has spectacular views. The white sands and good surf of **Friendly Beach** can be accessed via the unsealed Friendly Beaches Rd., 18km north of Coles Bay.

**Bicheno Coaches** stops in Coles Bay en route to the park's tracks. (☎03 6257 0293. M-Sa 1 per day. $8.80.) They also offer service between Coles Bay, the Coles Bay turnoff (30min., $6.30), and Bicheno (40min., $7.50). At the turnoff, you can connect with Tassielink and Redline services to other destinations (see **Coles Bay**, p. 565). An hour's walk away, Coles Bay is the service and lodging center for Freycinet, but for information on the park, stop at the **visitors**

**center** near the park entrance. Register and pay at the center; park fees apply. (☎03 6356 7000. Open daily 8am-5pm.)

# TRIABUNNA

☎03

On Prosser Bay, 50km southwest of Swansea and 87km northeast of Hobart, Triabunna (try-a-BUN-na; pop. 1200) is a tiny but delightful port town where you can stock up on food and spend the night before heading to Maria Island. Tassielink (☎1300 300 520) runs **buses** to Hobart (1½hr., M-F 1 per day, $18.20) and Swansea (45min., M-F 1 per day, $7.60). It also connects to the Maria Island Ferry in Triabunna. The **Tourist Information Centre,** at the Esplanade, has **Internet** and all the information you could ever want on Maria Island. (☎03 6257 4772. $2 per 10min. Open M-Tu and Sa-Su 10am-4pm, W-F 9am-4pm.) Budget accommodation is limited. **Triabunna Caravan Park ❶,** 6 Vicary St., is the only place to stay; it is cramped but friendly. (☎03 6257 3575; www.mariagateway.com. Sites $15, powered $17.) **Value Plus** supermarket is at Charles and Vicary St. (Open daily 8am-6:30pm.) The **post office** is on Vicary St. **Postal Code:** 7190.

# MARIA ISLAND NATIONAL PARK

A surprisingly undertouristed treasure, Maria (muh-RYE-uh) Island has housed penal colonies, a cement industry, whalers, and farmers. The ruins of an 1825 settlement at Darlington—along with the area's unique wildlife and natural beauty—are the island's main attraction, and it is also a center for birdwatching. Sea eagles, dolphins, whales, and seals all use the area, making the area a truly special wildlife haven. There are no roads on Maria, but there are excellent walking tracks, some of which can be biked.

Park brochures are available from the **Tourist Information Centre** in Triabunna; the ferry has descriptions of walking tracks, and the crew can advise you on the best way to use your time. Walks meander through the Darlington Township ruins (30min.), past Fossil Cliffs, where sea critters from long ago dot the rocks (1½hr.), over the textured sandstone of the Painted Cliffs (2hr., best at low tide; check schedule at the **Tourist Information Centre**), and to the rock-scramble up Bishop and Clerk (4hr.). The toughest walk in the park is to **Mount Maria** (6hr.), and the summit affords the best views of the island. The longest walks are to the French's Farm (8hr.) and Encampment Cove (8½hr.) campsites.

To reach Maria, travelers can take the Maria Island Ferry, which departs from "downtown" Triabunna, 50m from the Tourist Information Centre. (☎04 1974 6668. 30min. Runs from late Dec. to Apr. 9am, 3:15pm from Triabunna; 9:30am, 4pm from Maria. Round-trip $50, children $25; bikes and kayaks $10.) Many travelers bring a bicycle with them on the **ferry,** as it's a great way to traverse the island's 30km of roads. On the island itself, there are no shops or facilities save a tourist office at the stone Commisariat Store and a ranger station in "central" Darlington with a telephone (☎03 6257 1420). Pick up the free pamphlet *Historic Darlington* for an outline of the island's extensive history. The **Old Darlington Prison ❶** houses nine six-bed units, each with a table, chairs, and fireplace. (Book ahead with the ranger station ☎03 6257 1420. Shared toilets, sinks, and hot showers for $1. Beds $15; doubles $40, extra person $5.) The island has three **campsites ❶: Darlington** (sites $12, extra person $5); **French's Farm,** 11km south down the main gravel road, with a pit toilet and rainwater tanks; and **Encampment Cove,** 3km down a side road near French's Farm, with a small bunkhouse and pit toilet. The cove's campsites are free. For all park accommodation, bring your own food, bedding, lighting, and cooking gear. Park entry fees apply; day passes are available at the ranger station.

# VICTORIA

Victoria may be mainland Australia's smallest state, but it's blessed with far more than its fair share of fantastic cultural, natural, and historical attractions. The landscape varies widely, from the empty western plains of the Mallee to the inviting wineries along the Murray River, from the ski resorts of the Victorian Alps to the forested parks of the Gippsland coast. No other part of Australia packs in so much ecological diversity into so little space.

Sleek and sophisticated, Melbourne overflows with eclectic ethnic neighborhoods, public art spaces, back-alley bars, and verdant gardens. It's no wonder that many Aussies claim Melbourne as Australia's best-kept secret. Hewn from the limestone cliffs west of Melbourne, the Great Ocean Road winds past roaring ocean, lush rainforests, and geological wonders like the Twelve Apostles rock formation. East of the capital, the coastline unfolds past Phillip Island's penguin colony and the beach resorts on the Mornington Peninsula, before heading into Gippsland. Here, crashing waves collide with granite outcroppings to form the sandy beach edge of Wilsons Promontory National Park.

Victoria is remarkable for its rich history and natural grandeur. The jaw-dropping ranges of Grampians National Park offer unparalleled opportunities for rock climbing, abseiling, and other adventure sports, and the park holds the state's most important Aboriginal rock-art sites. Victoria's historical heart, meanwhile, beats to the drum of the mid-19th-century gold rush. When the ore waned, a host of dusty country towns were left in its wake—the Goldfields and the Murray River towns are defined by a fascinating past of rugged miners and antiquated riverboats. The 20th century brought agricultural and commercial development, including massive hydroelectric public works projects that still impact the state's ecosystems. Still, Victoria's physical beauty prevails, tempered by a refined sensibility and cosmopolitan flair.

## HIGHLIGHTS OF VICTORIA

**STEEP** yourself in the heady atmosphere of **Melbourne,** Australia's cultural, culinary, and sporting capital (p. 570).

**ABSEIL** 60m down the Ledge in **Grampians National Park** (p. 636).

**PAMPER** your palate at **Rutherglen Wineries** with free tastings (p. 662).

**EXPERIENCE** a diverse array of terrain at Sealers Cove dayhike in **Wilsons Promontory,** a UNESCO World Heritage Site (p. 671).

# ⌐ TRANSPORTATION

Getting around Victoria is a breeze, thanks to the thorough, efficient intrastate train and bus system run by V/Line. For more extensive national service, Greyhound Australia, Country Link, and Great Southern **buses** depart from Southern Cross Station (for more information, see **Intercity Transportation,** p. 570). Renting a car allows for more freedom, and Victoria's highway system is the country's most extensive and navigable. To cut down on rental costs, check hostel ride-share boards. The **Royal Automobile Club of Victoria (RACV),** 438 Lt. Collins St.,

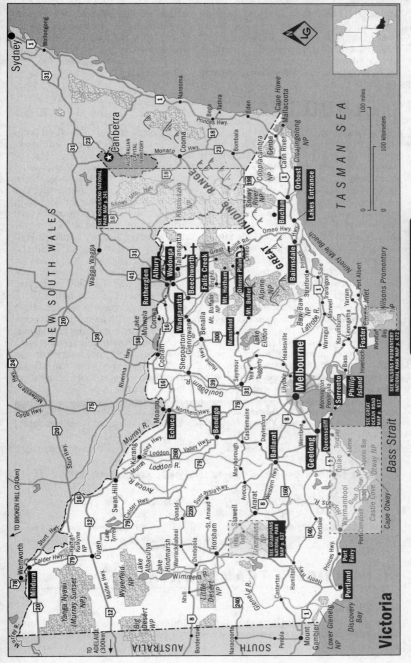

Melbourne (☎03 9944 8808 or 13 19 55; roadside assistance ☎13 11 11; www.racv.com.au), has great maps and sells short-term traveler's insurance. Members of other automobile clubs may already have reciprocal membership. The RACV Roadside Care package (including 8 free service calls annually and 20km of free towing in the metropolitan area) costs $73, plus a $42 joiner's fee. For more information see **Costs and Insurance**, p. 31.

# MELBOURNE
☎03

Melbourne (pop. 3.9 million) began rather inauspiciously in 1825 when John Batman (yes, Batman) sailed a skiff up the Yarra, got stuck on a sandbank, and justified his blunder by claiming he had found the "ideal place for a village." Originally named Batmania, the small town underwent a phenomenal growth spurt at the onset of the Victorian Gold Rush three decades later. "Marvelous Melbourne" celebrated its coming-of-age in 1880 by hosting the World Exhibition, which attracted over a million people. When the Victorian economy collapsed after bank failures in the 1890s, Melbourne's infrastructure followed suit, and its fetid open sewers earned it the nickname "Marvelous Smellbourne." By the dawn of the 20th century, however, the city had improved enough to challenge Sydney for the honor of being Australia's capital. While the Canberra compromise deprived both of this status, Melbourne was happy to serve as the government's temporary home until the Parliament House in Canberra was completed. The city's 20th-century zenith was the 1956 Olympics, which brought the its competitive passions to an international audience.

Today, Australia's second-largest city (projected to surpass Sydney in 2020) has blossomed into an impressive cosmopolitan center with an active arts community, a fierce love of sports, and an appetite for gourmet dining and streetside cafes. Recent years have witnessed population growth and an increased international flavor. Melbourne's neighborhoods (called "precincts") invite exploration and are easily accessible by tram. With its picturesque waterfront, epic sporting events, happening bar scene, and world-class culture, Melbourne offers big city attractions with a refreshing lack of tourist hype.

---

### ◨HIGHLIGHTS OF MELBOURNE

**SHOP** at the giant **Queen Victoria Market,** which offers everything from fresh produce to souvenirs and bric-a-brac (p. 587).

**EXPERIENCE** some seriously chill cafe culture and shopping on **Brunswick Street,** the main drag of youthful, artsy Fitzroy (p. 595).

**CATCH A GAME** of Aussie Rules Football, Melbourne's obsession, at the historic **Melbourne Cricket Ground** (p. 583).

**SUN YOURSELF** outside the city limits in **St. Kilda;** the laid-back, beach-bumming atmosphere makes for a great escape from the hectic city (p. 602).

**PARTY** at the **swanky back-alley bars**. Don't leave town without spending a night roving the streets of the city center in search of the poshest digs (p. 591).

---

## ◨ INTERCITY TRANSPORTATION

### BY PLANE

There are two main airports that service Melbourne. The boomerang-shaped **Tullamarine International Airport,** located 25km northwest of the city center (25min.

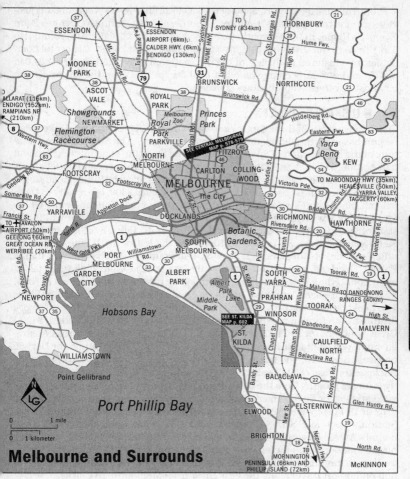

**Melbourne and Surrounds**

by car), hosts both domestic and international flights. **Qantas International** (☎13 12 11) operates from Terminal 2. **Virgin Blue** (☎13 67 89; www.virginblue.com. au) is in Terminal 3, and **Qantas** (☎13 13 13; www.qantas.com.au) is in Terminal 1. Each airline flies to all state capitals at least once daily. Virgin Blue has last-minute specials that often rival the price of bus tickets. **Travelers Information** (☎03 9297 1805), near International Arrivals, books same-day accommodations and has maps, brochures, and a backpacker bulletin board. **Avalon Airport** (www. avalonairport.com.au) is a newer airport, located on the Princes Hwy., 50min. south of the city toward Geelong. Travelers can take **Jetstar** (www.jetstar.com. au) flights from Avalon to anywhere in the country. For more information on airport services, visit www.melair.com.au.

From Tullamarine airport, **Skybus** (☎03 9335 2811; www.skybus.com.au) provides ground transport to Melbourne's Southern Cross Station. (Operates 24hr. Every 10-15min. in both directions, every 30min.-1hr. at night; $16, round-trip $26.) Taxis to the CBD cost roughly $45 and take about 25min. Car rental companies are clustered to the left of the international arrival terminal (see **By Car,** p. 575) and generally charge an additional fee for pickup at the airport. Some city hostels offer complimentary shuttles.

## BY BUS AND TRAIN

Train transportation throughout Victoria is run by V/Line services. Tickets can be purchased at the station, online, or over the phone. The Southern Cross Station, at the intersection of Spencer and Bourke St., is the main intercity **bus** and **train** station. The station spans several city blocks, with cafes and outlet stores filling most of the building; for the ticket counters and platforms, head to the southern end of the station. (**Travel info booth** ☎03 9619 2300; open daily 6:30am-8:30pm. Shops/cafes open M-Th and Sa-Su 10am-6pm, F 10am-9pm.) **V/Line** (☎13 61 96; www.vline.com.au) offers the most extensive service within the state of Victoria. (Ticket offices open M-Th 5:40am-10:15pm, F 5:40am-midnight, Sa 6:15am-midnight, Su 7:15am-10:15pm.) To the left of the V/Line booths, an office sells tickets for CountryLink and Great Southern (which operates Indian Pacific, Overland, and Ghan). (Open daily 7am-8pm.) Countrylink (☎13 22 32; www.countrylink.nsw.gov.au) has multiple-day passes to destinations in NSW, as well as Brisbane, and also offers discounted fares for ISIC-card holders. The Backtracker Pass provides unlimited journeys on the Countrylink network for those with foreign passports. (1-month $275, 3-month $298, 6-month $420.) Great Southern (☎13 21 47; www.gsr.com.au) has destinations across Australia, but if you want to travel from Melbourne to Perth, Alice Springs, or Darwin on Great Southern, you must go via Adelaide. Great Southern also offers the Backpacker Pass ($590), valid for all Ghan, Indian Pacific, and Overland train trips for six months from the date of purchase (must have foreign passport and valid student or backpacker association ID). Greyhound Australia (☎03 9642 8562 or 13 14 99; www.greyhound.com.au) also operates out of Southern Cross Station. (Open M-F 8am-8:30pm, Sa 8:30am-12:30pm, Su 4:30-8:30pm.) Greyhound's Aussie Pass, allows you to hop on and off at different stops, depending on the number of kilometers you purchase (from 2000-20,000km). The Traveller Pass (6 months, $429) and Mini-Travellers Pass (45 days, $397) are valid for hop-on/hop-off travel along the east coast from Melbourne to Cairns.

## ◪ ORIENTATION

Melbourne lies along the Yarra River near Port Phillip Bay. The river splits Melbourne into northern and southern regions. The city center, North Melbourne, Carlton, Fitzroy, Collingwood, Richmond, and the Docklands are on the northern bank; South Yarra, Prahran, Southbank, Windsor, St. Kilda, Williamstown, and Brighton are on the southern bank. Each of these precincts has its own well-trodden thoroughfares and unique style. South of the Yarra River, several communities boast popular beaches and bayside vistas. While the city center has impressive architecture and most of the museums, the diverse array of attractions in the other precincts is not to be missed.

**OUR COVERAGE OF MELBOURNE.** Since Melbourne is divided into several precincts, we have grouped together each area's accommodations, food, sights, entertainment, and nightlife listings. General information on these aspects of the city, as well as information about entertainment, sports and recreation, and annual festivals, appears after the practical information. A list of daytrips from Melbourne appears at the end of the section.

# ▣ LOCAL TRANSPORTATION

## PUBLIC TRANSPORTATION

Melbourne's public transportation system, the **Met** (☎ 13 16 38 or 1800 652 313; www.metlinkmelbourne.com.au), consists of three modes of transportation: light-rail trains, buses, and trams, and is divided into two zones. Most attractions and points of interest are within Zone 1. Tickets can be used on buses, trams, or trains, and are valid for unlimited travel over a specified period of time. (Zone 1 $3.50, Zone 2 $5.50 per 2hr.; $6.50/10.10 per day; $28/47.40 per week; $104.40/161 per month; $1117/1722 per year.) ▨**The Sunday Saver Metcard** is a great deal, as it allows unlimited Sunday travel through both zones ($2.90). If you're going to be in town for a while, the month-long and year-long passes save time and money; buy them at a station machine or ticket counter. There are train stops at Melbourne Central, Flagstaff Gardens, Parliament, and Southern Cross Station, though the main hub is the Flinders St. Station at the southern end of Swanston St., identifiable by its big yellow clock. A free tourist shuttle stops at key tourist attractions with informative commentary; hop on and off the 11 stops, including Fed Sq., Melbourne Museum, Lygon St., Queen Victoria Market, Southbank, and the Royal Botanic Gardens (every 15-20min. 9:30am-4:30pm). For additional information and route maps, grab Metlink's free *Fares and Travel Guide* at any station. Check the back of the brochure for helplines, including lost property inquiries and translated information.

## BY TRAM

Tram routes crisscross the metropolitan area. Although slow, they are the most useful means of navigating the city and its outskirts. (Trams run M-Th 5am-midnight, F-Sa 5am-2am, Su 8am-11pm; weekdays every 3-12min., nights and weekends approx. every 20min.) When the tram stops running at 2am on Friday and Saturday nights, the **Night Rider buses** take over, running every 20min. until 4am. For more information and routes, check out www.metlinkmelbourne.com.au. Passengers can purchase tram tickets at various stations, on trams (coins only), at 7-11 stores, and at the Met Shop, located in the old town hall building on the corner of Lt. Collins and Swanston St. (Open M-F 9am-5:30pm, Sa 9am-1pm). Although some report that it may be possible to ride the trams without a ticket, inspectors do random checks, usually around tram junctions and during peak hours; *Let's Go* recommends always purchasing a ticket, as fines can cost as much as $150. Similar fines apply if you do not validate your ticket once onboard. To validate a ticket, place it in one of the green electronic boxes near the bus and tram stops, which will stamp and return it to you. The burgundy and gold City Circle Tram circumnavigates the city in both directions, providing running commentary on the city's sights and history, and stopping at 48 city highlights. (Daily, every 12min. 10am-6pm; free.)

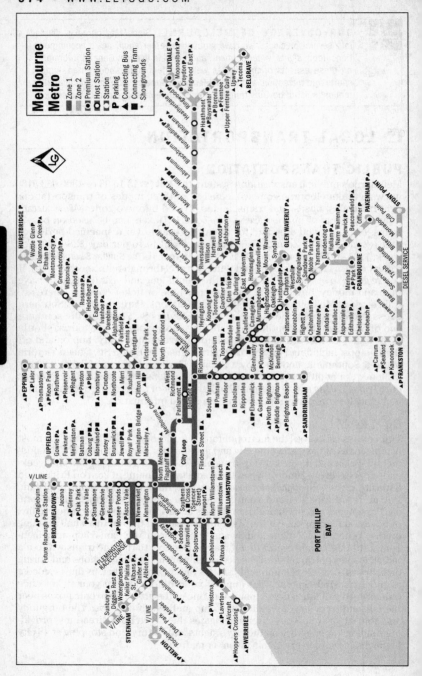

# BY CAR

National car rental chain offices are located in Melbourne city and at the airport, but it's usually cheaper to rent in the city, as the airport offices often include a 9% airport tax. Prices for all vehicles will fluctuate seasonally; be sure to take advantage of special deals, and save money by booking online (see **Getting Around Australia,** p. 29 for more information on the car rental process). The **RACV** (p. 568) is a comprehensive driving resource with good maps for sale. Members receive emergency roadside assistance. For more information on driving in Australia, see **Great Outdoors,** p. 63.

## NATIONAL AGENCIES

**Avis,** 2/8 Franklin St. (☎03 9663 6366, airport 03 9338 1800). Under 25 age surcharge $28.35. Open M-Th 7:30am-6pm, F 7:30am-7pm, Sa-Su 8am-5pm.

**Budget,** 3/8 Franklin St. (☎03 9204 4851 or 13 27 27, airport 03 9241 6366). Age surcharge $16.50. Open M-Th 7:30am-6pm, F 7:30am-7pm, Sa-Su 8am-5pm.

**Europcar,** 89 Franklin St. (☎13 13 90; www.deltaeuropcar.com.au). Age surcharge $16. Open M-F 8am-6pm, Sa-Su 8am-5pm.

**Hertz,** 97 Franklin St. (☎03 9663 6244, airport 03 9338 4044). Age surcharge $27.50. Open M-Th 7:30am-6pm, F 7:30am-7pm, Sa 7:30am-5pm, Su 8am-5pm.

**Thrifty,** 390 Elizabeth St. (☎03 8661 6000, airport 03 9241 6111). Age surcharge $16.50. Open M-Th 7:30am-6pm, F 7:30am-6:30pm, Sa-Su 8am-5pm.

## BUDGET AGENCIES

The benefit of budget agencies is the standardization of prices. Expect to get a car for a standard rate year-round, whether it be a 2-3 day rental or one that's several weeks long. For longer trips, some national agencies can beat these budget agency prices. For shorter trips, you won't find anything cheaper than the listings below. There are several bargain agencies, like Rent-a-Bomb, that are only half-joking about car quality. Still, it's a good idea to weigh the savings against the potential costs of breaking down in the middle of nowhere.

**Southern X Rentals,** 228 Flinders Ln. (☎03 9639 6057), on the ground fl. of Greenhouse Backpackers. Operated by Friendly Backpacker Travel on the hostel's ground fl., Southern X is known for having the cheapest rates in town, ideal for those under 25 as there is no surcharge. Free pickup in CBD. Standard daily rate: 2-door manual $39, 4-door automatic $45. Open M-F 9am-5pm.

**MetroCar,** 58 Franklin St. (☎03 9663 0700; www.metrocar.com.au). Standard daily rate: 2-door manual with 100km $19, with unlimited km $29. Surcharge ages 21-22 $20; 23-24 $14. Open M-F 8am-6pm, Sa-Su 8am-3pm.

**Rent-a-Bomb,** 149 Clarendon St., South Melbourne (☎03 9696 7555; www.rentabomb. com.au). Week- and month-long rental deals. Open M-F 9am-6pm, Sa-Su 9am-3pm.

## LONG-TERM RENTALS

For information about buying a car, see p. 31.

**Travellers Auto Barn,** 67 Roden St., North Melbourne (☎03 9326 3988; www.travellersautobarn.com). Compact, station wagon, campervan, and 4WD long-term rentals, as well as car sales with guaranteed buyback. Open M-F 9am-5pm, Sa 9am-1pm.

**Car Connection** (☎03 5472 2731; www.carconnection.com.au), near Castlemain, 120km northwest of Melbourne. Though out of the way, Car Connection is a good budget option. Rent a station wagon for up to 6 months for $2700 plus $825 insurance charge. A 6-month 4WD pick-up is $6545, with $1265 insurance. Free pickup from Melbourne airports or any city hostel as well as free first-night lodging in Castlemaine.

**VICTORIA**

**Wicked Campers,** 496 Geelong Rd., West Footscray (☎1800 246 869; www.wicked-campers.com.au), 20min. outside of the city. Rents campervans, with bed and kitchen, for about the price of a regular car rental (from $30 per night).

## BY TAXI

After the Met stops running at midnight during the week and 2am on the weekends, taxis are one of the only options left. (For Night Rider bus services that run until 4am on weekends, see p. 573). Cabs can be hailed at any time of day on the street. Varying surcharges apply when traveling between midnight and 6am, when riding with luggage, or if you book the cab in advance. Try **Silver Top** (☎13 10 08), **Arrow Taxi Service** (☎13 22 11), or **Embassy Taxis** (☎13 17 55). Wheelchair-accessible taxis are available at **13 Cabs** (☎13 27 27).

## BY BICYCLE

If you don't fear oncoming traffic, biking is an economical way to get around; practically every major thoroughfare in the greater Melbourne area has a bike lane. An extensive bike trail also runs along the Yarra River, and others loop through Albert Park and Middle Park, along the Port Phillip beaches, and around North Melbourne's gardens. Southern Melbourne's flat bayside roads are perfect for low-impact, scenic riding. The shore of Port Phillip Bay is a popular destination for serious bikers who can spend the entire day cycling around the bay. Riders can then take the **ferry** (p. 614) between Queenscliff and Sorrento and return to the city on the other side of the bay. Before finding a rental shop, check if your accommodation offers cheap rentals. **RentaBike** (☎03 9654 2762; www.byohouse.com.au/bikehire), in Vault 14 at Federation Wharf under Princes Bridge, (believe it or not) rents bikes. (Open daily 10am-5pm. Bike rental 1hr. $15, ½-day $30, full-day $35, week $100. Guided bike tours $89, children $69.) **Bike Fun,** 12 Carlisle St., St. Kilda, has great rates. (☎03 9534 3074. Cruiser 1hr. $15, full-day $40, week $80. Open M-Sa 9am-6pm, Su 9am-5pm.) **Carlton Borsari Cycles,** 193 Lygon St., can also find you a ride. (☎03 9347 4100; www.borsaricycles.com.au. Bike rental ½-day $30, full-day $50, week $150. Open M-Th 9:30am-6pm, F 9:30am-7:30pm, Sa 9:30am-5pm.)

# ▨ PRACTICAL INFORMATION

## TOURIST AND FINANCIAL SERVICES

**Tourist Offices:** ▨**Melbourne Visitor Centre** in Federation Sq., across from Flinders St. Station at the corner of Flinders St. and Saint Kilda Rd. The sprawling center offers Internet ($1 per 10min.), transport, entertainment ticket sales, the **Best of Victoria** accommodations and tour booking service (☎03 9928 0000 or 1300 760 045), and the Melbourne Greeter Service, which gives free 2-4hr. tours of the city tailored to your personal interests. Tours are offered in many languages to groups of 1-4. Affiliated "roving ambassadors" wearing red jackets canvass nearby streets offering free tourist advice. (Visitors center ☎03 9658 9658; www.melbourne.vic.gov.au. Open daily 9am-6pm.) Smaller info booth at the **Bourke Street Mall.** Open daily 9am-6pm.

**Budget Travel:**

▨**The Friendly Backpacker Travel,** 228 Flinders Ln. (☎03 9639 6057), on the ground fl. of Greenhouse Backpackers. Rents cars (see **Southern X,** p. 575), books Australia, NZ, and Fiji tours; offers 5-20% discounts for the aquarium, zoo, museum, Rialto towers, and movies. No need to call ahead; just pop in and ask for the discount card.

**STA Travel,** 240 Flinders St. (☎03 9654 7266; www.statravel.com.au). Open M-F 10am-6pm, Sa 10am-4pm. Another branch is located at 208 Swanston St. (☎03 9639 0599). Open M-F 10am-6pm, Sa 11am-4pm, Su 1am-3pm.

**YHA Victoria,** 359b Lonsdale St. (☎03 9670 9611; www.yha.com.au), between Elizabeth and Queen St. Provides info on YHA hostels and booking service. YHA member international booking charge $6, domestic charge $5 after 2 free bookings. Open M-F 9am-5:30pm, Sa 10am-1pm.

**Consulates: Canada** (☎03 9653 9674). **France** (☎03 9602 5024). **Greece** (☎03 9866 4524). **Italy** (☎03 9867 5744). **UK,** 90 Collins St., Level 17 (☎03 9652 1600). Open M-F 9am-4:30pm. **US,** 553 St. Kilda Rd., Level 6 (☎03 9526 5900; http://usembassy-australia.state.gov). Open M-F 9am-12:30pm and 1:30-4pm.

**Currency Exchange:** All banks exchange money during regular operating hours. Several banks have offices at the airport. 24hr. **ATMs** are all over. **Travelex,** 261 Bourke St. (☎03 9654 4222), near Swanston St., has an average 2% commission on checks and cash. Open M-F 9am-5pm, Sa 10am-5pm, Su 11am-4pm.

**American Express:** 233 Collins St. (☎03 9633 6318). Buys all traveler's checks (no charge, except for non-AmEx AUS$ traveler's checks: min. $10 or 1% fee); $8 fee on cash exchanges. *Poste Restante* for AmEx card or Travelers Cheques holders. Wire transfers. Open M-F 9am-5pm, Sa 10am-1pm.

**Work Opportunities:** Most accommodations listed in *Let's Go* have employment bulletin boards; some help find jobs or offer work to travelers in exchange for accommodation (must have Australian working visa). **Down Under Jobs,** in the lobby of **Discovery Hotel** (see **Accommodations,** p. 586; ☎1800 154 664), can help find jobs at no charge, for hostel guests and non-guests alike. Open M-F 9am-5pm, Sa noon-3pm. Melbourne's biggest daily, *The Age,* has classifieds on Sa and can be accessed online at www.theage.com.au. See **Beyond Tourism,** p. 81 for more work and volunteer opportunities.

### MEDIA AND PUBLICATIONS

**Newspapers:** The main newspapers are *The Age* ($1.40) and *The Herald Sun* ($1.10) for local coverage, and *The Australian* ($1.30) for national news. *B.News* (www.bnews.net.au; free, released every other Th).

**Nightlife:** See *Beat* (www.beat.com.au), Melbourne's biggest street paper, and *InPress* (free, released W). For gay nightlife, check out *B.News* (above) or *MCV* (by subscription, but found in most gay establishments).

**Entertainment:** Check out *The Age's* Entertainment Guide as well as *The Herald Sun's* Gig Guide (released F).

**Radio:** Top 40, Triple M 105.1FM and MixFM 101.1FM; classic hits, Vega 91.5FM and Gold 104.3FM; alternative underground music, Triple J 107.5FM; news, 1116AM; gay and lesbian radio, Joy 94.9FM.

# LOCAL SERVICES

**Outdoors Information: Information Centre and Bookshop,** Dept. of Sustainability and Environment, 8 Nicholson St., at Victoria Pde., East Melbourne (www.dse.vic.gov.au). Maps, books, and info on licenses. Open M-F 8:30am-5:30pm. **Parks Victoria** (☎13 19 63; www.parks.vic.gov.au) has state and national park information.

**Disabled and Elderly Travelers Information: Travellers Aid,** 169 Swanston St., 2nd fl. (☎03 9654 2600), has a tearoom with great services. Open M-F 8am-5pm. Branch at Southern Cross Station (☎03 9670 2873). Open M-F 9am-3pm. Representatives will meet and assist elderly and disabled travelers on trains and buses M-F 7:30am-7:30pm, Sa-Su 7:30am-11:30am. Arrange in advance.

## Central Melbourne

### ACCOMMODATIONS

Discovery Hotel, **25**
Elephant Backpacker, **32**
Greenhouse Backpacker, **39**
King Street Backpackers, **33**
Kingsgate Hotel, **27**

Melbourne Metro YHA, **6**
Melbourne Oasis YHA, **1**
NOMADS Industry, **28**
The Nunnery, **23**
Urban Central, **45**

VICTORIA

VICTORIA

FOOD
Arcadia Café, **52**
Bimbo Deluxe, **15**
Brunetti Restaurant, **7**
Builder's Arm Hotel, **53**
Casa del Gelato, **8**
Crossways, **20**
Gopals, **37**
Jimmy Watson's Wine Bar, **3**
Journal, **29**
Lemongrass, **14**
Mario's, **12**
MoVida, **42**
Nyala, **26**
Pho Mekong Vietnam, **16**
Retro Café, **5**
Shanghai Dumplings, **44**
Soul Food, **51**
The Aussie Indian, **50**
The Meat & Wine Co., **55**
The Waiter's Restaurant, **22**
Tiamo, **4**
Toto's, **21**
Trampoline, **9**
Trotters, **48**
Vegie Bar, **10**

NIGHTLIFE
Bar Open, **11**
Black Cat, **17**
Blue Diamond, **18**
Bond, **41**
Cookie, **40**
Croft Institute, **34**
e:fiftyfive, **38**
Gin Palace, **36**
Loop, **49**
Night Cat, **54**
Peel Hotel, **33**
Riverland, **19**
Rooftop Bar, **35**
Section 8, **31**
St. Jeromes, **47**
Strike Bowling Bar, **30**
The Melbourne Supper
    Club, **46**
The Provincial, **13**
Transit, **43**

**Library: State Library of Victoria,** 328 Swanston St. (☎03 8664 7000; www.slv.vic.
gov.au), located on the corner of La Trobe St. Open M-Th 10am-9pm, F-Su 10am-6pm.
There's also a smaller **City Library,** 253 Flinders Ln. (☎03 9658 9500). Open M-Th
8am-8pm, F 8am-6pm, Sa 10am-1pm.

**Gay and Lesbian Resources: The Alternative Life Styles Organization (ALSO) Founda-
tion,** 6 Claremont St., South Yarra (www.also.org.au).

**Ticket Agencies: Ticketek** (☎13 28 49; www.ticketek.com.au) and **Ticketmaster**
(☎1300 136 166; www.ticketmaster.com.au) for sports, performances, and other
events. Fee for phone booking. Both open daily 9am-9pm. **Halftix** (☎03 9650 9420;
www.halftixmelbourne.com), in Melbourne Town Hall on Swanston St., sells cut-rate tickets for shows on the day of the performance (Su performances sold Sa). Open M 10am-
2pm, Tu-Th 11am-6pm, F 11am-6:30pm, Sa 11am-4pm. Cash only; no phone orders.

**Laundromat: Flinders Lane Dry Cleaning,** 165 Flinders Ln. (☎03 9639 0477), just
west of Russell St. Open M-F 7am-6pm. 1hr. express service available.

## EMERGENCY AND COMMUNICATIONS

**Emergency:** ☎000.

**Fire:** ☎000.

**Police:** 24hr. hotline ☎03 9427 6666; www.police.vic.gov.au. 637 Flinders St. (☎03
9247 6491), at Spencer St.; 226 Flinders Ln. (☎03 9650 7077), between Swanston
and Elizabeth St.; 412 St. Kilda Rd. (☎03 9865 2102), south of Toorak Rd.; 92 Chapel
St., St. Kilda (☎03 9536 2666); and 330 Drummond St., Carlton (☎03 9347 1377).

**LET'S NOT GO.** Though locals consider the city of Melbourne to be quite
safe, it is a metropolitan area, and as in any other big city, street smarts are
necessary to stay out of trouble. At night and in the early morning, avoid
walking through Melbourne's parks, including Fitzroy Gardens, Carlton Gardens, and Albert Park. King St., in the city, is where most late-night scuffles
and brawls occur and should be avoided unless you're in the mood for a
fight. Professional pickpockets operate along Brunswick St. in Carlton, so
keep a tight watch on your valuables as you stroll through the area.

**Crisis Lines: Victims of Crime Helpline** 24hr. ☎1800 819 817; www.justice.vic.gov.au/
victimsofcrime. **Centre Against Sexual Assault** ☎1800 806 292. **Lifeline Counseling
Service** ☎13 11 14. **Poison Information Centre** ☎13 11 26. **Coast Guard Search
and Rescue** ☎03 9598 7003. **Youth Substance Abuse Service** 24hr. ☎1800 014
446. **Suicide Helpline** 24hr. ☎1300 651 251 (www.suicidehelpline.org.au).

**Sexual Health: Melbourne Sexual Health Centre,** 580 Swanston St., Carlton (☎03
9347 0244; www.mshc.org.au). Free counselling on sexually transmitted diseases.

**Sexual Assault:** 24hr. ☎03 9346 1766 or 1800 806 292.

**Helpful numbers: Directory assistance** ☎12 23, international ☎12 25; **collect calls**
☎1800 REVERSE; **translation and interpretation** 24hr. ☎13 14 50. **City of Melbourne
Language Link** ☎03 9280 0716 or 9280 0726. **VicRoads** 24hr. ☎13 11 70.

**Pharmacy: Elizabeth Street Pharmacy,** 125 Elizabeth St. (☎03 9670 3815). Open M-F
7:30am-6:30pm, Sa 9:30am-5:30pm. **Melbourne Boulevard Pharmacy,** 403 St. Kilda
Rd. (☎03 9866 1284), near Toorak Rd. Open M-F 8:30am-6pm, Sa 9am-1pm.

**Hospital: Saint Vincent's Public Hospital,** Princes St. Fitzroy (☎03 9288 2211, emergencies ☎03 9288 4364; www.svhm.org.au). To get there, take any tram east along
Bourke St. to stop 9. Royal Melbourne Hospital, 34-54 Poplar Rd., Parkville (☎03 9342
7000; www.rmh.mh.org.au). Take tram #19 from Elizabeth St. to stop 16.

**Locksmiths: API Security** (☎13 15 39). Available 24hr. **A Locksmiths** (☎1300 651 478). Available 24hr. Specializes in car locks.

**Internet Access:** Internet cafes are fairly easy to find; some bars even have hidden terminals. Most budget accommodations offer Internet access, and prices throughout the city tend to be about $4 per hr. There are free terminals at the **State Library** (p. 590). Sign up in advance for 15min. sessions; limit 1 session per day. Unlimited free Wi-Fi is available after registering at the Book Desk for a library card. **Global Gossip,** 440 Elizabeth St. (☎03 9663 0511), between A'Beckett and Franklin St. Phone cards, CV and resume editing and formatting, mailbox rentals, CD burning, fax machines, scanner, and printers. Internet $4 per hr. Open daily 9am-midnight.

**CYBER MELBOURNE**

**www.visitvictoria.com.** Comprehensive government website with tons of info on food, nightlife, accommodations, and events in Melbourne and all of Victoria. Events searchable by type, town, and date.

**www.mdg.com.au.** A selection of the best restaurants in Melbourne, searchable by location and cuisine, with online booking.

**www.melbournepubs.com.** A comprehensive website listing and reviewing hundreds of local bars, pubs, and nightclubs.

**Post Office:** 250 Elizabeth St. (☎13 13 18; www.post.com.au). Open M-F 8:30am-5:30pm, Sa 9am-4pm. **Postal Code:** the city 3000, North Melbourne 3051, Carlton 3053, Fitzroy 3065, Southbank 3006, South Melbourne 3205, South Yarra 3141, Prahran and Windsor 3181, St. Kilda. 3182.

# ▛ ACCOMMODATIONS

As most major Australian sporting events take place in Melbourne, including the 2006 Commonwealth Games, budget accommodations are popping up all over the city, and the competition has encouraged a considerable number of impressive budget deals. The largest concentration of lodgings is within the city and southern St. Kilda. The YHA-affiliated hostels in North Melbourne are slightly removed from the action and so tend to be quieter and more sedate. South Yarra and Prahran lie farther afield, but these pretty "boonies" are full of chic shopping and nightlife. Prices for accommodations change seasonally; during high season (roughly November to March), most hostels raise their prices (by up to $10) and availability drops, so be sure to book well in advance. Prices may also fluctuate during long weekends and festivals.

**LONG-TERM STAYS.** Many hostels allow stays of several weeks, or even months, often with discounted rates. For a more comfortable stay in a studio apartment, contact **UniLodge** (☎03 9224 1500 or 03 9224 7888; www.unilodge.com.au). Catering to those studying abroad (min. 6 months), UniLodge has several apartment buildings in the city (238 Flinders St., 39 Lonsdale St., and 339 Swanston St.) and Carlton (9 Earl St., 139 Bouverie St., and 740-746 Swanston St.). Rates from $1087 per month.

Most accommodations in Melbourne are wheelchair-accessible and accept MasterCard and Visa. Many allow guests to work in return for lodging if they stay for an extended period of time (Australian working visa required; see **Beyond Tourism,** p. 81). Standard budget lodging in Melbourne usually includes common bathrooms, common spaces with TV, a kitchen, and laundry facilities.

## ☐ FOOD

Melbourne's international influences explode in the city's kitchens, where tantalizing fusion feasts combine virtually every culture on the planet. In the city center, it's impossible not to stumble across small Japanese restaurants, while Italian eateries line Carlton's not-so-Little Italy. Enjoy a frothy latte in the cafe kingdoms of Fitzroy and South Yarra, or hunt down fresh produce in the Queen Victoria Market, where prices go down as the day goes on. For travelers looking to take advantage of hostel kitchens, there are numerous grocery stores, including a 24hr. **Coles**, 2-26 Elizabeth St. (☎03 9654 3830), at the corner of Flinders St.; **Safeway** on the corner of Swanston and Lonsdale St. (☎03 9663 5181; open daily 7am-midnight); and **IGA Southbank** at 89-91 City Rd. (☎03 9682 0489; open M-W 7am-9pm, Th-Sa 7am-11pm, Su 8am-8pm.)

## ☐ ENTERTAINMENT

Melbourne prides itself on its style and cultural savvy, and these two traits are most evident in the city's extensive and always-happening entertainment scene. The range of options can be overwhelming; take a deep breath and check www.melbourne.citysearch.com.au for listings.

### PERFORMING ARTS

The hard-to-miss **Victoria Arts Centre**, 100 St. Kilda Rd., sports an Eiffel-like spire right on the Yarra across from Flinders St. Station. It houses five venues: the State Theatre for major dramatic, operatic, and dance performances; the Melbourne Concert Hall for symphonies; the George Fairfax Studio and the Playhouse, largely used by the Melbourne Theatre Company; and the Black Box for cutting-edge, low-budget shows targeting an under-35 audience. (**Victoria Arts Centre switchboard** ☎03 9281 8000, Ticketmaster 1300 136 166; www.vicartscentre.com.au. Tickets range from free to $180; $2.50 transaction fee when not purchased at the box office. Box office open M-Sa 9am-9pm.)

### CINEMA

Melbourne has long been the focal point of Australia's independent film scene, and the city holds dozens of old theaters that screen arthouse flicks as well as cinema classics. The arthouse crowd logs on to www.urbancinefile.com.au, for flip reviews of the latest films. The annual **Melbourne International Film Festival** showcases the year's international indie hits, and the **St. Kilda Film Festival** highlights shorts. An especially select crew of home-grown flicks can be viewed in September at the **Melbourne Underground Film Festival** (www.muff.com.au), an eccentric screening by local students in Fitzroy. (See **Festivals**, p. 584, for more information.) Plenty of cinemas in the city show mainstream first-run movies as well. For screenings under the stars, don't miss the **Moonlight Cinema** (p. 599) at the Royal Botanic Gardens or screenings of classic films at the popular **Rooftop Bar** (p. 591). At the theater, try a "choc-top," the chocolate-dipped ice-cream cone ($2-4) that's a staple of Australian movie-going.

### SPORTS AND RECREATION

Melbournians refer to themselves as "sports mad," but it's a good kind of insanity—one that causes fans of footy (Australian Rules Football), cricket, tennis, and horse racing to skip work or school, get decked out in the colors of their favorite side, and cheer themselves hoarse. Their hallowed haven is the **Melbourne Cricket Ground (MCG)**, adjacent to the world-class **Melbourne Park Tennis**

**Centre** (p. 583). A new ward, **Colonial Stadium,** right behind Southern Cross Station, has begun to share footy-hosting responsibilities with the more venerable MCG and also hosts most local rugby action. The lunacy peaks at yearly events: the **Australian Open,** a Grand Slam tennis tournament in late January; the **Australian Grand Prix Formula-One** car-racing extravaganza in March; the AFL Grand Final in late September; the **Melbourne Cup,** the "horse race that stops the nation," in early November; and cricket's **Boxing Day Test Match** on December 26.

**A GOOD ROOT.** Make this crucial mental note: in Australian slang, "to root" means to have sexual intercourse. Thus, when referring to "rooting on" a sports team, use the term "to barrack." However passionate your feelings for your favorite team and its members might be, the use of "rooting" is not to be used in conjunction with sports terminology, as it will most assuredly bring about snickers from any local overhearing your blunder.

**MELBOURNE CRICKET GROUND (MCG).** With a 92,000-seat capacity, the MCG functions as the sanctum sanctorum of Melbourne's jolly cricket culture. The season runs from October to April and gets particularly crazy during the test matches between Australia and South Africa, England, New Zealand, Pakistan, and the West Indies. The north side of the MCG contains the **National Sports Museum,** another celebration of Australia's love of sport. The venue houses the Australian Cricket Hall of Fame (which requires some understanding of the game to appreciate), a feature on extreme sports, and the Olympic Museum, with a focus on Australian athletes and the 1956 Melbourne games. The best way to see the stadium and gallery is with a guided tour. Tours offer unique insight into the MCG's history and bring you to both the players' changing rooms and the hallowed turf itself. Entertaining guides make the 1hr. tour worthwhile, even if you don't have the slightest idea what a wicket or a googly is. (☎03 9657 8879; www.mcg.org.au. Tours run on all non-event days 10am-3pm, and depart from Gate 3. $15, concessions $11, families $45. Admission includes tour and access to galleries with audio.) Australian Rules Football (AFL) games bust into town every weekend in winter, including the Grand Final the last Saturday in September. To achieve—or at least mimic—authenticity, order a meat pie and beer, choose a favorite team, and blow out your vocal chords along with the passionate crowd. Make sure you stay long enough to hear the winning team's song played after the game. (The MCG is in Yarra Park, southeast of Fitzroy Gardens across Wellington Pde. Accessible via trams #48, 70, and 75. AFL game tickets $34; sold through Ticketmaster.)

**MELBOURNE PARK (NATIONAL TENNIS CENTRE).** Across the railroad tracks from the MCG and Yarra Park sits ultramodern Melbourne Park. The tennis complex, composed of the domed Rod Laver Arena, sleek Hisense Arena, and numerous outer courts, hosts the **Australian Open** every January. You can't play on the center court, but the outer courts get you close to greatness for a steep fee. During the Open, a $29 ground pass will get you into every court except center. (Take tram #70 from Flinders St. Australian Open tickets ☎02 8736 2711 or 1300 888 104. Courts available M-F 7am-11pm. For upcoming events, check www.mopt.com.au.)

**TELSTRA DOME.** Embark on an informative tour of one of the largest venues in sport-crazy Melbourne. The new Dome hosts an astonishing number of events, from Australian Rules Football to a regular Catholic mass. (☎03 8625 7277; www.telstradome.com.au. 1hr. tours depart from the Customer Service Centre at Gate 2 M-F 11am, 3pm. $14, students/concessions $11, children $7.)

## HEN IN MELBOURNE...

f you plan on doing as Austra-
ians do, you may have to forget
what you thought you know about
antipodean culture. The following
products aren't as "Aus-thentic" as
you thought.

1. **Foster's** is actually *not* "Aus-
ralian for beer." Ask for a Foster's
n any bar in Australia and the
bartender will ask where you're
rom—because it can't possibly
be Australia. Popular in the UK
and the US, Foster's is brewed in
Australia but quickly boxed and
exported, since the lager isn't
popular among Aussies. Accord-
ng to recent statistics, 30 pints
of Foster's are consumed every
second in the UK.

2. **Aussie Haircare Products**
use the slogan "Put some 'roo in
your do," and their commercials
feature a purple 'roo playing
beach volleyball. They play up the
cliché like no other. So, this quintessential Australian shampoo
s meant to give you shiny locks
down under, right? Wrong. Aussie
Haircare is sold only in the US, UK,
and Canada, so don't expect the
Australian pharmacy to sell your
avorite line of kangaroo-covered
shampoo bottles.

3. **Outback Steakhouse** serves
he oh-so-typical Bloomin' Onion,
Coral Reef Crab Dip, and Kookaburra Wings. But ask for an Outback burger or Boomerang shrimp
n a Melbourne restaurant and
we're not responsible for whatever jokes the offended waitstaff
decides to play on you.

**RECREATION.** Melbourne's sporting spirit is not limited to spectator events. City streets and parks are packed with joggers and skaters, although sports are officially prohibited in the Royal Botanic Gardens. Great jogging routes include the gravel track encircling the Royal Botanic Gardens, the pedestrian paths along the Yarra, the Port Phillip/St. Kilda shore, and the Albert Park Lake. These wide, flat spaces also make for excellent in-line skating; you can rent equipment at sport shops throughout Melbourne. The beach in St. Kilda, accessible by tram #16 and 96, is not Australia's finest, but it'll do for sun and swim-ming. The lake in Albert Park is good for sailing but not for swimming. The **Melbourne City Baths,** 420 Swanston St., on the corner of Franklin St., packs pools, a sauna, a spa, squash courts, and a gym (fitness classes, too) into a single restored Victorian building. (*☎03 9663 5888; www.melbour-necitybaths.com.au. Open M-Th 6am-10pm, F 6am-8:30pm, Sa-Su 8am-6pm. Pool $5, Australian uni students $4, conces-sions $2.25; 20-ticket pass $88.20/70.20/40.50; gymnasium $18/16 /10; group fitness class $16/12.50/8.*)

## ✳ FESTIVALS

Melbournians create excuses for city-wide street parties all year. Below are the city's major events, ordered by date. For a complete guide to Mel-bourne's goings-on, grab a free copy of *Melbourne Events* at any tourist office, or do an events search online at www.visitmelbourne.com.

**Midsumma Gay and Lesbian Festival,** late Jan. to mid-Feb. (☎03 9415 9819; www.midsumma.org.au). 3 weeks of hijinks all over the city ranging from the erotic to the educational, with lots of parades, dance parties, and general pandemonium.

**Yarra Valley Grape Grazing,** late Feb. (passes and info ☎03 5962 6600). Many wineries in the Yarra Valley region participate in this annual Dionysian festival.

**Australian Grand Prix,** early Mar. (www.grandprix.com.au). Albert Park, St. Kilda. Formula One racing frenzy holds the city hostage.

**Moomba,** early Mar. (☎03 9658 9658; www.moomba-waterfest.com.au). This 4-day citywide fête with food and performances is a great way to get your party on with all the locals.

**Melbourne Food and Wine Festival,** mid-Mar. (☎03 9823 6100; www.melbournefoodandwine.com.au). A delicious way to celebrate Australia's "culinary capital."

**International Comedy Festival,** April (☎03 9245 3700; www.comedyfestival.com.au). A huge laugh-fest featuring over 1000 performances.

**St. Kilda Film Festival,** early May (☎03 9209 6490; www.stkildafilmfestival.com.au), Palais Theatre and George Cinemas, St. Kilda. Features Australia's best short films; documentaries, comedies, and experimental movies are all screened.

**International Film Festival,** late July to early Aug. (☎03 9662 3722; www.melbournefilmfestival.com.au). The cream of the international film crop, plus local work.

**Royal Melbourne Show,** mid-Sept. (☎13 28 49; www.royalshow.com.au). At Ascot Vale. Sideshow alleys, rides, entertainment, and animal exhibitions for judging.

**Melbourne Fringe Festival,** late Sept. to early Oct. (☎03 9660 9600; www.melbourne fringe.com.au). Features local artists; performances and parties across town.

**Melbourne Festival,** mid-Oct. (☎03 9662 4242; www.melbournefestival.com.au). A 3-week celebration of the arts, attracting world-famous actors, writers, and dancers for over 400 performances, workshops, and parties in 30 different venues.

**Spring Racing Carnival,** Oct.-Nov. (☎1300 139 401; www.springracingcarnival.com.au). Flemington Racecourse. Australia's mad love for horse racing stretches over 50 days and includes the fancy, famous Melbourne Cup.

**Melbourne Boxing Day Test Match,** Dec. 26-30 (☎03 9653 1100). More than 100,000 cricket fans pack the MCG to root for the boys in green and gold.

# ▉ NIGHTLIFE

Some cities blare Top-40 hits on the thoroughfare, but Melbourne jams to live bands and funky DJs hidden away in back alleys. Each year, several dozen new locales pop up while several dozen close down, ensuring a spectacularly wide array of establishments. In this city, the distinction between bar, pub, and nightclub is blurry at best. Many venues belong to all three categories, while others swap out their weekday chairs and tables in favor of raucous weekend grind-fests. Some unique venues deserve a category all on their own. For a list of venues throughout the metropolitan area, check out www.melbournepubs. com. Expect a small cover charge on the weekends ($5-10) at venues offering live music or a dance floor. Gay nightlife in Melbourne isn't restricted to one portion of the town, but is peppered throughout the city, with a little more spice along Commercial Rd. in Prahran and Smith St. in Fitzroy.

## MELBOURNE BY PRECINCT

# THE CITY

The city center is located just north of the Yarra and reaches its northern limit at Victoria St., just north of the Queen Victoria Market. Its western border is the recently-gentrified Docklands and to the east the ever-popular Carlton Gardens. The city is laid out in a grid, with most of the action near the river's edge at Federation Sq. and along Swanston St. The city is the transit hub for Melbourne's outlying neighborhoods, with numerous tram and railway stations.

# ▉ ACCOMMODATIONS

The perfect jumping-off point to explore any neighborhood of Melbourne, hostels in the city are at the heart of the action. A 20min. walk to Federation Sq., accommodations in the northern portion of the city tend to be slightly cheaper and close to several grocery stores and the Queen Victoria Market.

**NOMADS Industry,** 196-198 A'Beckett St. (☎03 9328 4383 or 1800 447 762; www. nomadsindustry.com), just west of Queen St. Clean but party-prone hostel. The quietest rooms are on the higher floors facing the front of the hostel. Hallway bathrooms are separated into individual units for privacy. Wheelchair-accessible. Free dinner; bigger portion $4, with beer $7. The sleek bar-lounge serves thirsty travelers pots and basic spirits at cheap prices, with happy hour daily 5-7pm. Laundry $3. Internet access $4 per hr. Reception 24hr. Female-only dorms available. 14-bed (NOMADS only) dorms $21; 10-bed $28, NOMADS $25; 6- to 8-bed $30/27, ensuite $32/29; 4-bed $34/31, ensuite $36/33; singles and doubles $90/85, ensuite $105/95. MC/V. ❷

**Greenhouse Backpacker,** 228 Flinders Ln. (☎03 9639 6400 or 1800 249 207; www. friendlygroup.com.au), just west of Swanston St. Reception on 6th fl. Continuously gar-nering tourism awards, this gem is the most centrally located hostel in the city. Vast common spaces, kitchen, and rooftop sundeck. For a sunnier stay, request a room with a window. A/C and heating in all rooms. Wheelchair-accessible. Tu 6pm free pasta or BBQ dinner, Th pub crawl, M free city walking tours. Organizes ½-price trips to footy games May-Nov. Coffee, tea, and a small breakfast are included (offered 7-9am). Laundry $6. Free Internet (max. 30min. per day). Reception 24hr. 4- to 8-bed dorms $27-30, weekly $182; singles $65; doubles $78. MC/V. ❷

**Discovery Hotel,** 167 Franklin St. (☎03 9329 7525 or 1800 645 200), between Eliza-beth and Queen St. This boozy bastion of backpackers sleeps 700. With a cozy movie theater, cafe, bouncin' Velvet Underground bar, travel desk, job desk, free breakfast and airport pick-up. The main drawback: no A/C leaves summer travelers sweaty. However, during winter, the hotel cools down to a comfortable temperature. Paper-thin walls may compromise privacy (and sleep). Laundry $6. Internet $4 per hr. Reception 24hr. 10- to 16-bed dorms $25, weekly $154; 8-bed $26/161; 6-bed $27/168; 4-bed $28/175; doubles $85/525, ensuite $100; family $110/700; 14-bed female-only ensuite dorms $32 (no weekly rate). VIP discount. MC/V. ❷

**King St. Backpackers,** 197-199 King St. (☎03 9670 1111 or 1800 671 115; www. kingstreetbackpackers.com.au), corner of Lt. Bourke and King St. The comfortable rooms have A/C, heat, and oversize lockers (BYO lock). 16-bed dorms are partitioned for added privacy. Dark hardwood floors and quaint TV nooks. Coffee, tea, and breakfast included. Tu free big breakfast, W free pasta dinner, Su free pancakes. Free luggage storage. Laundry $6. Free Internet (30min. per day). Key deposit $10. Large car sales board. Wheelchair-accessible. Reception 24hr. 16-bed dorms $24, weekly $168; 4- to 6-bed $28/168; singles and doubles $78; triples $90. MC/V. ❸

**Kingsgate Hotel,** 131 King St. (☎1300 734 171; www.kingsgatehotel.com.au), between Bourke and Lt. Collins St. A break from raucous dorms with private ensuite rooms with TV and A/C. Ground-floor cafe serves inexpensive breakfast and dinner. Laundry $3. Internet $3 per 30min. Wheelchair-accessible. Reception 24hr. Singles and doubles $109-139; triples $135-165; quads $181-211. AmEx/MC/V. ❺

**Elephant Backpacker,** 250 Flinders St. (☎03 9654 2616 or 1800 002 616; www. elephantbackpacker.com.au). In an ideal location, Elephant Backpacker offers slightly aging facilities with less than ample lounge spaces at record-low prices. Large kitchen. Laundry $6. Internet $4 per hr. Key deposit $25. Reception 24hr. 2- to 4-bed dorms $25, weekly $140; 6-bed $19; singles $40; doubles $50. MC/V. ❷

## ▶ FOOD

Every tantalizing taste from around the world can be found in the city center, a veritable culinary UN. Neon Chinatown fills the stretch of Lt. Bourke St., hemmed in by red gates between Swanston and Exhibition St. Blink and you'll miss the Greek Precinct, on Lonsdale St. between Swanston and Russell St. It consists of only a half-dozen or so expensive Greek restaurants and taverns, but each serves transcendent baklava. Experiencing cramped cafe culture is a must; Degrave St. and Centre St., between Elizabeth and Swanston St. near Flinders Station, are stuffed to the gills with locals and tourists alike. Above all, the city center rewards the adventurous gourmet; wander around with your nose and palate as guides and you're sure to strike culinary gold.

**Shanghai Dumpling,** 23-25 Tattersalls Ln. (☎03 9663 8555), off Lonsdale St. between Swanston and Russell St. The secret is finally out, and locals are still shaking their fists. Off a hidden alleyway, the best dumplings in town await at low prices and in huge portions. Mushroom and veggie dumplings 20 pieces for $6.50. Steamed pork dumplings 15 pieces for $5.80. Beer $4.80. Rice and noodle mains $6-10. Open M and Su 10am-9pm, Tu-Sa 11am-10pm. Cash only. ❶

**LONG LIVE THE QUEEN.** The royal heritage has given its name to Melbourne's best open-air market and mall complex with restaurants, shops, and bars. **Queen Victoria Market (QVM),** west of Elizabeth St. and south of Victoria St, is a glorious, old-fashioned market that teems with locals and tourists. Venture deep into the bustle for bargain produce, dairy products, fish, and meat. Be sure to bargain with vendors; note that prices drop as the day goes by—somehow, everything costs only a buck at closing time. (☎03 9320 5822; www.qvm.com.au. Open Tu and Th 6am-2pm, F 6am-6pm, Sa 6am-3pm, Su 9am-4pm.) The mall complex known as QV, at the corner of Lonsdale and Swanston St., houses a large food court offering budget-friendly fare, as well as shops, restaurants, and a couple of bars. Ride the elevator underground to the Safeway for the cheapest groceries in the city center. (Open daily 7am-midnight.)

**Crossways,** 123 Swanston St., upstairs (☎03 9650 2939). Founded by the Hare Krishna Food for Life charity, Crossways serves delicious vegetarian food at unbeatable prices. Catch the all-you-can-eat lunch buffet ($6.50, students $5). Also offers yoga classes in the evening (www.urbanyoga.com.au; M, W, F 6:15pm; $15, students $12, includes dinner). Open daily 11:30am-2:30pm. MC/V. ❶

**Gopals,** 139 Swanston St. (☎03 9650 1578), Crossways's sister restaurant just a few doors down, has longer hours and serves a great Chef's Special (a vegetarian dish, soup or rice, salad, and a lassi drink; $12.) Open daily 11am-8:30pm. MC/V. Every Su 4:30pm, enjoy Mantra Meditation and a sumptuous vegetarian feast at the temple (free). Breakfast 9am. Lunch 1pm. Dinner 6pm. ❶

**MoVida,** 1 Hosier Ln. (☎03 9663 3038; www.movida.com.au), off Flinders St. just west of Russell St. Located in an alleyway with some of the city's best graffiti, MoCida is a locally renowned *tapas y vino* bar. Extensive wine list; glasses $7-15. Tapas $3-7.50, mains $10-20. Open daily noon-late. Reservations essential. MC/V. ❸

**The Waiters Restaurant,** 20 Meyers Pl., upstairs (☎03 9650 1508), off Bourke St. Started 25 years ago by a nonna serving heaping plates of pasta to hungry waiters and bar staff after work, this unassuming hole-in-the-wall has become one of the most popular Italian restaurants in town. Pasta and steak mains $14-22. Open M-F noon-2:30pm and 6pm-late, Sa 6pm-midnight. MC/V. ❸

**Pho Mekong Vietnam,** 241 Swanston St. (☎03 9663 3288), just south of Lonsdale St. Avert your eyes from the tacky paper dolls, purple garlands, and silver and gold balls: Mekong offers the most authentic *pho* fare in Melbourne at startlingly low prices with extremely fast service. The crowds attest to the food's popularity and authenticity. Spring rolls $4. All mains under $9. Open M-Sa 9am-1pm, Su 10am-10pm. Cash only. ❶

**Journal,** Shop 1, 253 Flinders Ln. (☎03 9650 4399). Housed in the same building as the City Library, Journal is a mini-library in itself, with encyclopedias and magazines hanging from suspended shelves. The perfect spot to study or relax with a cappuccino. Coffee $3. Muffins $3.50. Bruschetta $6-7. Mains and salads $12-13. Open M-Th 7am-8:30pm, F 7am-9:30pm, Sa 7am-6pm, Su 7am-5pm. Cash only. ❶

## 👁 SIGHTS

**FEDERATION SQUARE.** This explosion of post-modern architecture repositioned the center of the city and now acts as the host to all major public spectacles. "Fed Square" is stuffed with museums, bars, and restaurants, but its crazy amalgam of copper, glass, and metal is worth a stop simply for the design. Fed Square is also your one-stop shop for tourist information, located underground at the incredibly helpful **Melbourne Tourist Office.** *(Located at the corner of Flinders and Swanston St., which becomes St. Kilda Rd.)*

 **CHI-TOWN.** Every Tuesday morning at 7:30am, free Tai Chi sessions are held in Federation Square for those that want to relax mind and body. (Held in the Atrium during rain.)

**THE RIALTO TOWERS.** The Rialto Towers complex rises 253m above the city. The 55th-floor observation deck provides spectacular 360° views of the city and surroundings. The "Zoom City" binoculars allow voyeurs to zoom in and see people crossing the street all the way across town. With unabashedly cheesy music and dramatic, wide-angle shots, Rialtovision Theatre plays a 20min. film called *Melbourne, the Living City,* which highlights city attractions as well the Yarra Valley, Phillip Island, and other daytrip destinations. Before you leave, get your ticket stamped and signed for free re-entry at night. *(525 Collins St., between King and William St. ☎03 9629 8222; www.melbournedeck.com.au. Open daily 10am-10pm. Film shows every 30min. Film and deck $14.50, concessions $10, children $8, families $9.50.)*

 **THE REAL DEAL.** At the top of the Rialto Towers, visitors pay a hefty fee for their stroll above the skyline. But at the other end of Flinders St., at the Collins Centre, visitors can sneak a bird's-eye peek for free. A second lobby on the 35th floor of the Sofitel boasts a glitzy restaurant called Cafe La; the bistro's views are more delicious than the food, and diners pay accordingly. The adjacent bathroom windows, however, are free, and offer sweeping panoramas. Grungy backpackers, fear not; the hosts at Cafe La are all-too familiar with gawking tourists and politely direct them to the lavatories.

**IMMIGRATION MUSEUM.** Chronicling 200 years of Australian immigration, the Immigration Museum combines various artifacts with moving soundtracks, most of which are triggered by visitors' footsteps in the gallery. A mock ship recreates typical living quarters aboard ocean-going vessels from the 1840s to the 1950s. The museum space alone is well worth a visit; high ceilings, a grand staircase, and cool marble floors entice casual passersby. The ground-floor Immigration Discovery Centre contains links to immigrant ship listings as well as a genealogy database. *(400 Flinders St., in the Old Customs House on the corner of William St. ☎03 9927 2700; www.immigration.museum.vic.gov.au. A City Circle Tram stop. Wheelchair-accessible. Open daily 10am-5pm. $6, concessions and children free; free after 4:35pm.)*

**PARLIAMENT OF VICTORIA AND OLD TREASURY.** Victoria's Parliament building is a grand, pillared 19th-century edifice. Free tours discuss Victorian government and detail the architectural intricacies of the chambers. *(On Spring St. north of Bourke St. A City Circle Tram stop. ☎ 03 9651 8568; www.parliament.vic.gov.au. Daily guided tours when Parliament is not in session leave every hr. 10am-3pm and 3:45pm. Call ahead.)* Designed in Italian palazzo style by a 19-year-old prodigy, the City Museum at the Old Treasury Building chronicles Melbourne's past, with some great stories about the city's first years. The gold vaults in the basement were built to combat a crime wave during the Victorian Gold Rush; they now house a multimedia exhibit detailing daily life and events in the gold-rush era. *(On Spring St., at Collins St. ☎ 03 9651 2233; www.oldtreasurymuseum.org.au. Guided 2hr. Grand Tour $11; arrange ahead. Open M-F 9am-5pm, Sa-Su 10am-4pm. $8.50, concessions $5, families $18.)*

**MELBOURNE AQUARIUM.** This impressive facility offers a unique look at Australia's lesser-known wildlife. Its three levels include an open-air billabong and an "Oceanarium" with a glass tunnel that allows visitors to walk beneath roaming sharks and rays. Glass-bottom boat tours run daily and offer another perspective on the watery wildlife. *(On the corner of Flinders and King St. ☎ 03 9620 0999; www.melbourneaquarium.com.au. Open daily 9:30am-6pm; Jan. 1-26 9:30am-9pm; last entry 1hr. before closing. $25, concessions $17, children $15, families $70. Boat tours M-F 11am, noon, 1, and 2:15pm; Sa-Su 11am, 12:30, 1:15, and 2pm. $13.50, children $7.50.)*

**OLD MELBOURNE GAOL.** Opened in 1845, this former prison is now a macabre testament to criminal history. The creepiest displays feature the stories and death masks of the most notorious criminals executed here. Ned Kelly, Australia's most infamous bushranger, was hanged in the jail in 1880, and a scruffy wax likeness stands on the original scaffold. Downstairs is the suit of armor that Kelly, or one of his cohorts, wore in the gang's final shoot-out with police. A free live stage performance is held on Saturday (12:30 and 2pm). Visit on Sunday to participate in a reenactment of the trial of Elizabeth Scott, the first Victorian woman to be hanged for conspiracy to murder her husband (Su noon, 1, 2:30, and 3:20pm). Wonderfully spooky evening tours led by candlelight by Michael Gateley, "Melbourne's most prolific and brutal hangman," provide a chillingly vivid sense of its horrible past. *(On Russell St. between La Trobe and Victoria St. A City Circle Tram Stop. ☎ 03 8663 7228, group bookings 8663 7222; www.oldmelbournegaol. com.au. Open daily 9:30am-5pm. $18, concessions $14, children $9.50, families $44. Night tours 4 times per week Nov.-Feb. 8:30pm, Mar.-Oct. 7:30pm. $30, children under 15 (not recommended for those under 12) $22.50. Bookings required; call Ticketek ☎ 13 28 49.)*

**CATHEDRALS.** The immense Anglican **St. Paul's Cathedral,** completed in 1891, impresses with its detail and stained glass. Keep an eye out for the beautifully stenciled pipes of the 19th-century Lewis organ. They're easy to miss; look up to the right of the altar. Evensong choral services echo through the hall M-F at 5pm and Su at 6pm. *(On the corner of Flinders and Swanston St., diagonal to Flinders St. Station. Enter on Swanston St. Open daily 8am-6pm. Services M-F 7:45am, 12:15, 5:10, 6pm; Sa 12:15pm; Su 8, 9:15, 10:30am, 6pm. Free. Avoid taking pictures during mass.)* Guarded by two lonesome gargoyles, Catholic **St. Patrick's Cathedral** is a beautiful product of the Gothic revival, with elaborate stained glass, a magnificent altar, and a painting of John Paul II. In addition to the more traditional Catholic relics housed in the cathedral is an Aboriginal message stick and stone inlay, installed as a gesture of welcome to—and reconciliation with—Aboriginal Catholics. The cathedral is most spectacular at night, when its 106m spires are illuminated. *(West of the Fitzroy Gardens' northwest corner on Cathedral Pl. ☎ 03 9662 2233. Open daily 7:30am-6pm. Free guided tours M-F 10am-noon; advanced bookings essential. No tourists allowed during Mass M 7am and 1pm; Tu-F 7, 8am, 1pm; Sa 8am, 6pm; Su 8am-12:30pm and 6:30pm.)*

VICTORIA

**FITZROY GARDENS.** These gardens, originally planted in 1848 and laid out in the shape of the Union Jack, bloom year-round. The closest to the city of the many public parks in Melbourne, they offer a bucolic break from the city rush without requiring an all-day commitment. On the south end is Cook's Cottage, a small stone home constructed by Captain James Cook's family in England in 1755 and moved to Melbourne in 1934 to celebrate the city's centennial. Next door, the colorfully stocked Conservatory Greenhouse overflows with plants and flowers; a few wrought-iron benches nestle amid the blooms. In January and February, Sundays in the Park bring a variety of music and revelry. Evening sightings of possums are guaranteed. *(Gardens bordered by Lansdowne, Albert, Clarendon St., and Wellington Pde. Tram #48 or 75 from Flinders St. www.fitzroygardens.com. Free garden tour W 11am, starting from Sinclair's Cottage. Cook's Cottage ☎03 9419 4677. $4.50, concessions $2.70, children $2.20. Conservatory ☎03 9419 4118. Both open daily 9am-5pm.)*

**STATE LIBRARY OF VICTORIA.** The State Library is worth a visit, if you appreciate elegant interior design; it's also a great space to read. Check out the Cowen Gallery, which presents 150 portraits and busts of famous Victorians. *(328 Swanston St., on the corner of La Trobe St. ☎03 8664 7000; www.slv.vic.gov.au. Free tours M-F 2pm. Open M-Th 10am-9pm, F-Su 10am-6pm.)*

**CHINATOWN.** The colorful gates at the corner of Swanston and Lt. Bourke St. signal your arrival in Chinatown, a lively two-block stretch of Asian restaurants, grocery stores, and bars first settled by Chinese immigrants in the 1870s. This area is now one of the hippest niches in the city center. A block and a half east, and left down Cohen Pl., the Chinese Museum houses the Dai Loong (Great Dragon). This is the largest imperial dragon in the world—so large it has to be wound around two entire floors—and a staple of Melbourne's Moomba festival. *(22 Cohen Pl. ☎03 9662 2888; www.chinesemuseum.com.au. Open daily 10am-5pm. $7.50, concessions $5.50. Wheelchair-accessible.)*

## 🎭 ENTERTAINMENT AND CINEMAS

- 🎬 **Australian Center for the Moving Image (ACMI),** Federation Sq. (☎03 8663 2200; www.acmi.net.au), at Swanston and Flinders St. The ACMI screens an eclectic array of film and video works and displays installation pieces and multimedia exhibitions. Also houses the nation's largest public collection of film, video, and DVD titles, as well as the world's largest screen gallery (spanning most of Federation Sq. underground). Open M-W and F-Su 10am-6pm, Th 10am-9pm. Permanent collection free.

- 🎬 **The Forum,** 150 Flinders St. (☎03 9299 9700). Built in 1928, The Forum looks like a cross between an Arabian palace and a Florentine villa. Big-budget dance and drama ($50-100), as well as periodic concerts (around $40) and movies. Inside, enjoy the performance from cozy booths. Bookings through Ticketek (in Regent Theatre; see below).

- **Princess' Theatre,** 163 Spring St. (☎03 9299 9800). Home to an annual line-up of big-budget musicals. A 1500-seat venue that has been around since 1885. Tickets $50-170. Book through Ticketek (☎13 28 49) or at the theater's box office.

- **Regent Theatre,** 191 Collins St. (☎03 9299 9500), just east of Swanston St. Affiliated with The Forum, the dazzlingly ornate Regent Theatre, founded in 1929, was once a popular movie house dubbed the "Palace of Dreams." It now hosts big-name touring musicals and international celebrity acts. Tickets $50-120. Box office open M-Tu 10am-5pm, W-Sa 10am-8pm, Su 10am-7pm.

- **Last Laugh at the Comedy Club,** 188 Collins St. (☎03 9650 1977, booking 03 9650 6668), in the Athenaeum Theatre. Boasts a 3-course dinner and show package for $35. Hosts local and international acts. Prices vary. Book ahead by phone (M-F 9am-5pm,

Sa 10am-5pm) or online at www.thecomedyclub.com.au; the website also has monthly schedules and information about upcoming acts.

**KinoDendy Cinemas,** 45 Collins St. (☎03 9650 2100), downstairs in the Collins Place complex. Independent and foreign films. $15, students $10; M $7.

## 🍸 NIGHTLIFE

The nerve-center of nightlife in Melbourne, the city has the best bars in Australia. The most popular venues are usually tucked away in alleys and obscure lanes, sometimes with no more than a lightbulb outside a black door to announce the happening scene inside. With each successive drink, they seem to get harder and harder to find. Fear not: simply follow our guide below or check out our **Marvelous Melbourne Pub Crawl** to the left.

■ **Rooftop Bar,** 252 Swanston St., 6th fl. (☎03 9654 5394). With no signs on street level, the easily missed Rooftop Bar is in the same building as Cookie (see below). Up 6 flights, Rooftop Bar offers unparalleled views of the Melbourne skyline. Complemented by martinis, screenings of the classics on the bar's huge projector are always a hit (Oct.-Mar. Tu-Su 8:30pm; $18, concessions $15). Pint of beer $8. Wine by the glass $5. Open M-Sa 11am-1am, Su noon-1am.

■ **Riverland,** Vaults 1-9 Federation Wharf (☎03 9662 1771; www.riverlandbar.com). Hidden behind the mega-complex of Transport/Transit in Federation Sq., Riverland lies on the bank of the Yarra in a desolate vault once used for shipping storage. The glass elevator will bring you down to the water's edge, revealing a superb beer garden. Packed on weekends with both sophisticated and casual crowds, Riverland is an excellent spot to kick off the night. Beer $4-10. Wine by the glass $6-9. Open daily 7am-midnight.

■ **Section 8 Container Bar,** 27-29 Tattersalls Ln. (☎04 3029 1588), off Lonsdale St. between Swanston and Russell St. Put an obscure alleyway, a vacant lot, a few crates and umbrellas, and excellent drinks together and you may be lucky enough to get Section 8. This temporary, makeshift bar will last as long as some entrepreneur doesn't buy out the lot to build a high-rise, so enjoy this creative scheme while it lasts. Dressed up with graffiti-covered walls and potted plants, Section 8 has offbeat music and a casual vibe. Come by on weekday mornings for excellent coffee ($3). Beer $5.50-11. Wine by the glass $7.50. Open M-Th 8am-11pm, F 8am-1am, Sa noon-1am, Su noon-11pm.

**The Melbourne Supper Club,** 161 Spring St., upstairs (☎03 9654 6300). Hidden behind a narrow, wooden doorway and marked with a tiny sign, the Supper Club

## THE MARVELOUS MELBOURNE PUB CRAWL

It would be criminal of us not to give you a guide to an evening out in this happening city. The following may seem ambitious: hitting every spot on this treasure map may take multiple nights.

**1. Riverland,** 27-29 Tattersalls Ln. (☎04 3029 1588).

**2. Transit,** Level 2 Federation Sq. (☎03 9654 8808).

**3. Bond,** 24 Bond St. (☎03 9629 9844).

**4. e:fiftyfive,** 55 Elizabeth St. (☎03 9620 3899).

**5. Gin Palace,** 10 Russell Pl. (☎03 9654 0533).

**6. Loop** 23 Meyers Pl. (☎03 9654 0500).

**7. Croft Institute,** 21-25 Croft Alley. (☎03 9671 4399).

**8. Section 8,** 27-29 Tattersalls Ln. (☎04 3029 1588).

**9. Cookie,** 252 Swanston St., 2nd. fl. (☎03 9663 7660), and **Rooftop Bar,** 252 Swanston St., 6th fl. (☎03 9654 5394).

is arguably the finest wine bar in town. The 85-page menu (including 1 of light food, $7.50-13.50) is a wine education in itself. Leather couches, dim lighting, and relaxed jazz standards set the mood for a sophisticated experience among a classy, mostly older clientele. But don't write it off as just an after-dinner stop; the wine bar stays open until dawn on the weekends. Wines by the glass $9-19.50; by the bottle $28-10,500. Open M-Th 8am-4pm, F 5pm-6am, Sa 8pm-6am.

**St. Jeromes,** 7 Caledonian Ln. (too cool for a phone number), off Lonsdale St. between Swanston and Elizabeth St. The ultimate cache of the grunge and scunge crowd head to this Melbourne institution. Delicious beats are spun nightly by DJs in the dance pit, while tables of contented regulars sip on a small selection of alcohol in this back-alley hole-in-the-wall. Beer from $4.50, coffee from $2.50. Open daily 8pm-1am.

**Transit,** Level 2 Federation Sq. (☎03 9654 8808; www.transporthotel.com.au), in the Transport complex marked by the huge yellow T. Pass ground-floor Transport bar and 2nd-floor Taxi restaurant to settle in at comfortable and classy Transit on the top floor. Warm red lights and inviting couches tempt crowds indoors, but the true treasure is the balcony, with stunning views of the Yarra, the Southbank skyline, and the Arts Centre spire. Smart casual dress. Live music Th 9:30pm, F-Sa 10:30pm. Beer $7.50. Wine by the glass $11. Blended "luxury" martinis $18. Open W-Su 5pm-latenight.

**Cookie,** 252 Swanston St., 2nd. fl. (☎03 9663 7660). Previously known as Kookoo, the large bar is packed on F-Sa nights with suits and students alike, attended to by cravat-wearing barkeeps. Stocks pretty much every beer known to humankind, with rows and rows of international liquors. Beer from $4. Open daily noon-latenight.

**Gin Palace,** 10 Russell Pl. (☎03 9654 0533), off Lt Collins. Slightly out of the budget price range but worth the splurge. Caters to a professional crowd lounging on tassled pillows after a hard day's work. Many of the mixed drinks are made with fresh fruit, and the martinis ($17) are exquisite—all ingredients in the Surrealist Martini, for example, are frozen for 2 days before serving. Large selection of Australian microbrew beers and an extensive collection of bourbon. Open daily 4pm-3am.

**Loop,** 23 Meyers Pl. (☎03 9654 0500; www.looponline.com.au). Not many bars can boast their own art curator; this chill art space blends booze with a moving image show of experimental video media. Eclectic range of music, from Depeche Mode to Blondie. Regulars never get tired of this ever-changing venue and its creative martinis. Occasional indie film screenings and art talks; check website for details and dates. Beer from $5. Cover some F-Sa, depending on DJ. Open M-Sa noon-late.

**Blue Diamond,** 123 Queen St., 15th fl. (☎03 8601 2720; www.bluediamondclub. com.au). Classy cocktail bar with live music on the dance floor, excellent martinis, and insane views of Melbourne's rooftops. The city-slicker crowd varies in age, but everyone comes decked in sequins, glitter, and gold. Live music nightly from 10:30pm. Bottled beers $6-7. Martinis $15-18. Wines by the glass from $8. F-Sa night cover $10. Open Th-F 5pm-3am, Sa 7pm-3am, Su 5pm-3am.

**Croft Institute,** 21-25 Croft Alley (☎03 9671 4399; www.thecroftinstitute.com.au), off tiny Paynes Pl. between Russell and Exhibition St. Croft defines "laboratory-chic," serving various flavors of ethanol in test tubes and beakers. Not packed to the gills like many city bars, and makes a great place for a relaxed chat. If the talk makes you drowsy, head to the hospital beds on the 2nd fl. for a cat nap, or visit the restrooms (rather, the "Departments of Male and Female Hygiene"). Beer $5-7. Mixed drinks from $6.50. Cover some F-Sa $5-10. Open M-Th 5pm-1am, F 5pm-3am, Sa 8pm-3:30am.

**e:fiftyfive,** 55 Elizabeth St. (☎03 9620 3899; www.efiftyfive.com), just north of Flinders Ln. Looks like someone transported a '60s living room into a chill coffee shop, then added cheap alcohol to the chaotic mix. Internet $1 per 20min. Lattes $2.80. Beer from $3.50. Open M-Th and Su 10am-1am, F-Sa 10pm-3am.

**Bond,** 24 Bond St. (☎03 9629 9844), between Queen and Elizabeth St. Patrons soak up the sleek, futuristic atmosphere with a little more privacy than in other establishments. DJs spin house F-Sa. Beer from $5. Wine $7. Open Th-Sa 5pm-late.

**Strike Bowling Bar,** 245 Little Lonsdale St. (☎1300 787 453; www.strikebowlingbar. com.au), at the corner of Swanston St. Music videos pulse at the end of each fluorescent lane. $13-16 per person per game on the lanes. M-F 10am-4pm uni students $5 per game. Tu 5pm-1am $8 bowling and free popcorn. W 5:30pm-1am $5 margaritas with a game. Su free game with purchase of drink (min. $5). Open daily 10am-1am.

# NORTH MELBOURNE

An older, quiet residential area, North Melbourne is a neighborhood where everybody knows everybody. The action is in the southern precinct, near bustling Queen Victoria Market and the University of Melbourne. The area doesn't draw many tourists; the main attraction is the Melbourne Zoo.

## ▨ ACCOMMODATIONS

▨ **Melbourne Metro YHA,** 78 Howard St. (☎03 9329 8599). Take tram #55 north from William St. to stop 11 on Queensberry St. From there, walk 2 blocks west to Howard St. Don't miss the impressive rooftop hangout, still sparkling after a $2 million renovation. In addition to clean, same-sex accommodations, they offer free passes to the City Baths, a licensed bistro, a travel agency, a huge kitchen, pool tables, and free parking. Rooms have heating and fans. Laundry $3.60. Internet $4 per hr. Bike rental ½-day $20, YHA $10; full-day $30/15. Reception 24hr. Wheelchair-accessible. 8-bed dorms $29, YHA $26; 6-bed $30/27; 4-bed $33.50/30; singles $78/70, ensuite $89/80; doubles $89/80, ensuite $100/90; family rooms $110/99, ensuite $133.50/120; apartments for 5 $139/125. Book ahead in summer. MC/V. ❸

**Melbourne Oasis YHA,** 76 Chapman St. (☎03 9328 3595; www.yha.com.au). Take tram #57 north to stop 18 and turn right onto Chapman St. Catering to the quieter traveler, this eco-friendly hostel is situated outside the city. Worm-fertilized herb garden is available to guests, who are encouraged to recycle and compost virtually all waste. Rooms have heating and fans. Free parking and free passes to the City Baths available. Luggage storage $2. Laundry $3.60. Internet $4 per hr. Key deposit $5. Bike rental full-day $15. Reception 7:30am-11pm. 3- to 5-bed same-sex dorms $30.50, YHA $27; singles $62.50/56; doubles $74.50/67. MC/V. ❸

## ◉ SIGHTS

**MELBOURNE ZOO.** Many sections of this world-class, 143-year-old zoo consist of expertly designed habitats that allow animals to live almost as they would in the wild. The "Trail of the Elephants" and orangutan sanctuary exhibits in particular are both first-rate, and, of course, the lions, tigers, and bears can't be missed. From early January until early March, groove with the animals at Zoo Twilights, which features live bands as well as vocal performances of jazz, pop, swing, and rock. *(On Elliott Ave., north of the University of Melbourne. Take tram #55 from William St. to the Zoo stop, #25. ☎03 9285 9300; www.zoo.org.au. Free guided tours 10am-3pm; call ahead to arrange. Zoo Twilights early Jan.-early Mar. Sa-Su 6:30pm. $34, concession $27, children 4-15 $17; tickets include zoo entry and concert. Open daily 9am-5pm. $23, concessions $17.30, children 4-15 $11.50, families $52.40.)*

# CARLTON

Melbourne's unofficial "Little Italy," Carlton begins at Nicholson St. and extends west past the Carlton Gardens (home to the World Heritage Royal Exhibition Building and the informative Melbourne Museum and IMAX), ultimately reaching the University of Melbourne. On Lygon St., its primary thoroughfare, locals are lured by the numerous upmarket Italian bistros. While there are no budget accommodations, the food is draw enough. To get to Carlton's Lygon St., either take a tram up Swanston St. (#1, 3, 5, 6, 8, 16, 22, 25, 64, 67, or 72) and then walk east along Queensberry or Faraday St., or take #96 from Bourke St. up Nicholson St. and walk west along Faraday St.

## 📷 FOOD

🖼 **Tiamo,** 303 Lygon St. (☎03 9347 5759). Flavorful Italian cuisine at very reasonable prices, as well as the best coffee in town. Its next-door sequel, **Tiamo2** (☎03 9347 0911), is a *cucina antica* that is slightly more refined and serves a comparatively sophisticated menu. Pastas at both $13.50. Licensed and BYO. Tiamo open M-Sa 7:30am-11pm, Su 7:30am-10:30pm; Tiamo2 open M-Sa 9:30am-10:30pm. MC/V. ❷

🖼 **Trotters,** 400 Lygon St. (☎03 9347 5657; www.trotters.com.au), on the corner of Elgin St. Small, quirky, and packed with locals, Trotters has true character at superb prices. For breakfast, the crepes with lemon and sugar are a must ($7). The gnocchi with butternut pumpkin, pine nuts, and sage butter or the veal penne (both $15.50) are superb specialties. Lunch and dinner mains $12-21. Open M-F 7:30am-10:30pm, Sa 8am-10:30pm, Su 9am-10:30pm. Breakfast served until 3pm. AmEx/MC/V. ❸

**Brunetti,** 194-204 Faraday St. (☎03 9347 2801; www.brunetti.com.au) just east of the intersection with Lygon St. Great desserts. The most popular sweet is the scrumptious, flaky lobster tail pastry ($4.50), and the array of chocolates, tarts, and pies will astound any sweet tooth. Open M-Th and Su 6:30am-11pm, F-Sa 6:30am-midnight. MC/V. ❶

**Lemongrass,** 176 Lygon St. (☎03 9662 2244). A critically acclaimed restaurant serving some of the best Thai food in Melbourne. The all-you-can-eat lunch buffet ($20) will satisfy any Thai craving. Dinner mains $15-36. Open M-F noon-2:30pm and 5:30pm-11pm, Sa-Su 5:30-11pm. AmEx/MC/V. ❹

**Casa del Gelato,** 163 Lygon St. (☎9347 0220), near Argyle Sq. A local favorite, Casa has been around for nearly 30 years and makes frozen treats using only fresh produce. Try the popular *bacio* in a small cone or medium bowl (both $5.50). Open daily noon-midnight, closed M June-Aug. Cash only. ❶

**Jimmy Watson's Wine Bar,** 333 Lygon St. (☎03 9347 3985). A Lygon St. institution, Jimmy's is one of the oldest wine bars in Melbourne (est. 1932). Plays jazz classics and serves over 300 types of wine to a generally older crowd. The traditional Italian restaurant serves pizzas ($13-15) and mains ($20-35). Open M 10:30am-6:30pm, Tu-Sa 10:30am-late, Su 11am-4pm. AmEx/MC/V. ❹

**Toto's,** 101 Lygon St. (☎03 9347 1630). Self-proclaimed "first pizzeria in Australia." Cheap pies (small $8.80, large $14.80) and speedy delivery. Licensed and BYO wine. Open M-Th noon-11pm, F-Sa noon-midnight, Su noon-11:30pm. AmEx/MC/V. ❷

## 👁 SIGHTS

🖼 **CARLTON GARDENS AND MELBOURNE MUSEUM.** Spanning three city blocks, the peaceful Carlton gardens are criss-crossed with pathways and studded with spectacular fountains. Within the gardens is the Melbourne Museum, a stunning facility with an excellent Aboriginal art and culture center and exhibits on Australian wildlife. There's also an **IMAX theater** (see below), a children's museum, and a mind and body gallery. Next door to the museum is the grand World Heritage-listed **Royal Exhibition Building.** Built in 1879 for an international exposition and home to Australia's first parliament, the building is the last 19th-century exhibition hall left in the world that is still used for exhibitions. *(Bordered by Victoria, Rathdowne, Carlton, and Nicholson St. Take the free city tourist shuttle, the city circle tram, or trams #86 or 96. Museum ☎03 8341 7777; www.melbourne.museum.vic.gov.au. Open daily 10am-5pm. Free tours daily 1:30 and 2:30pm. $6, concessions and children free. Royal Exhibition Building tours daily 2pm; $5, children $3.50. Wheelchair-accessible.)*

## 🎵 ENTERTAINMENT AND CINEMAS

**La Mama,** 205 Faraday St. (☎03 9347 6948). Head east on Faraday St.; it's near the intersection with Lygon St., hidden down an alleyway and behind a carpark. Esoteric and modern Australian drama in a diminutive, black-box space. Sa afternoon poetry and play readings when no performances. Similar cutting-edge work is performed at the affiliated **Carlton Courthouse Theatre,** 349 Drummond St., just around the corner in the old courthouse building across from the police station. Wheelchair-accessible. Tickets $20, students $10. Free tea and coffee at performances.

**Cinema Nova,** 380 Lygon St., Carlton (☎03 9347 5331; www.cinemanova.com.au), in Lygon Ct. between Faraday and Elgin St. Indie and foreign films. A huge arthouse megaplex. $15, students $11. Sa after 6pm $13; M before 4pm $5.50, after $7.50.

**IMAX,** Melbourne Museum (☎03 9663 5454; www.imaxmelbourne.com.au), off Rathdowne St. in the Carlton Gardens. Daily screenings of 5 films. $17.50, concessions $14, children $12.50, families $50. Book tickets online. RACV discount 20%.

# FITZROY

A mecca for cutting-edge hipsters, Fitzroy does an impressive job of reconciling its grungy roots with a recent high-end influx. Tram #11 runs the length of **Brunswick Street,** Fitzroy's main artery. This main drag acts as a thoroughfare just west of Bohemia on the way to Pretention-ville. Generally, the area teems with a healthy mix of bohemians, families, and everyone in between. Grungy **Smith Street,** which runs parallel to Brunswick St., has recently become popular and features several gay bars and some unique boutiques. A small Spanish district has popped up along **Johnston Street** with top-notch tapas.

## 🏠 ACCOMMODATIONS

**The Nunnery,** 116 Nicholson St. (☎03 9416 2824; www.nunnery.com.au). Stop 13 on tram #96, at the northeast corner of Carlton Gardens. Housed in the beautiful former convent of the Daughters of Mercy with religious paintings plastering the walls. Cordial staff refer to themselves as nuns. Considerably calmer than other digs, with a real family feel; the attached guesthouses provide further privacy. Towel included. F wine and snacks night, Su morning pancakes. Continental breakfast included. Internet $2 per 20min. Reception daily 8am-12:30am. 10- to 12-bed dorms $28; 6- to 8-bed $30; 4-bed $32; singles $70; bunk twins $85; doubles $95; triples $105; guesthouse doubles $115; quad $185. Discounted weekly rates Apr.-Dec. ❷

## 🍴 FOOD

Food in the "Bohemian District" of Melbourne is alternative, trendy, and most importantly, tasty. Wander through the unique boutiques and vintage stores of Brunswick St. for an unbeatable breakfast. Try Johnston St. for tapas; Smith St. offers an extended sampling of grunge-inspired eateries.

**ORGASMIC ORGANIC.** The CERES Organic Food and Craft Market is held in East Brunswick every Saturday morning (9am-1pm) at 8 Lee St. From the city, take Tram #96 to the last stop.

**Retro Cafe,** 413 Brunswick St. (☎03 9419 9103; www.retro.net.au), on the corner of Westgarth St. The bright yellow facade is hard to miss; check out the TV-turned-aquarium inside. Try the gourmet pizzas ($13) or the delicious foccacias ($10-11). Happy hour daily 3-6pm, $3 wine and beer. Open fire in winter. Breakfast served until 6pm ($8-15). Open daily 8am-1am. MC/V. ❷

**Bimbo Deluxe,** 376 Brunswick St. (☎03 9419 8600). Bright walls and a garden out back enhance the trendy vibe of this classy, healthy establishment popular with local uni students. You can't beat the $4 pizza specials (M-Th noon-4pm and 7-11pm, F noon-4pm, Su 7-11pm). Open daily noon-3am. MC/V. ❶

**Vegie Bar,** 380 Brunswick St. (☎03 9417 6935; www.vegiebar.com.au). So tasty that it even draws the general meat-eating populace, Fitzroy's top vegetarian option lives under the wood-beamed roof of a converted textile factory. Mains from $11.50. Try the popular Mexican Burrito ($12.50). Pizzas from $7. Fresh fruit juices $5-6. Loads of vegan and gluten-free options. BYO. Open M-F 11am-10pm, Sa-Su 9am-10pm. ❷

**The Aussie Indian,** 25 Johnston St. (☎03 9419 2118; www.aussieindian.com.au), just east of Smith St. Pay no mind to the kitschy lime-green sign above the door and the plastic tablecloths: Aussie Indian is renowned for its traditional Hyderaba biryana. Melbourne's Indian cabbie population trickles in all day and packs the place at night. Practically everything goes for under $10. 10% takeaway discount. BYO. Open daily 11:30am-3pm and 5:30pm-late. AmEx/MC/V. ❶

**Soul Food,** 273 Smith St. (☎03 9419 2949; www.soulfoodcafe.com.au). This vegetarian cafe has beeen making soy lattes (fair trade coffee beans, of course; $3.50), organic tofu burgers ($10), and vegan pizzas ($11.50) for over 30 years. Check out the new bar out back. Open M-Sa 7am-10pm, Su 10am-4pm. MC/V. ❷

**Trampoline,** 381 Brunswick St. (☎03 9415 8689; www.trampolineHQ.com.au). Traditional Italian gelato made with chocolate and fresh fruit churned in the back kitchen; arguably the city's best. Flavors include Caramel Pear, White Chocolate and Raspberry, and Violet Rumble, with honey comb and chocolate swirls. Small $4.30, medium $5.30, monster $6.30. Franchises throughout the city. Open daily 11am-11pm. ❶

**Arcadia Cafe,** 193 Gertrude St. (☎03 9416 1055), just east of George St. Great coffee and delicious muffins ($3.50). The menu changes daily; check out the chalkboard for creative sandwiches and breakfast rolls. Coffee $3. Fresh-squeezed juices $4.80. Breakfast $5-15. Open M-F 8am-5pm, Sa-Su 9am-5pm. Cash only. ❶

**Nyala,** 131 Brunswick St. (☎03 9419 9128). Mostly Kenyan and Sudanese fare with a dash of Gambian and Moroccan flavor. Try the *kuk na nazi* (Kenyan coconut chicken $17.50). BYO ($2 corkage fee). Open daily 6-10pm. AmEx/MC/V. ❸

**Builders Arms Hotel,** 211 Gertrude St. (☎03 9419 0818). Once one of the roughest pubs in town, Builders is now popular with the uni crowd. This artist's hub has transformed into a retro space, with cozy lounges and a great little beer garden. Gourmet pub grub (lemon garlic chicken wings $10) and generous Su BBQ ($15, 2-9pm). M night ½-priced bar menu. Su $10 jugs, $5 Bloody Marys. Mixed drinks $6.50. Wines by the glass $6-9. Open M-Th 3pm-1am, F-Sa noon-1am, Su noon-11pm. MC/V. ❷

**Mario's,** 303 Brunswick St. (☎03 9417 3343). A small neon sign in a cluster of cafe fronts marks one of the best breakfast deals in town, served all day. Try Mario's homemade blend of muesli ($7) or toast with one of the delicious homemade jams ($4.50-5). Later in the day, grab one of the pasta dishes ($12.50 and up). Fully licensed. Beware: 10% surcharge on Su. Open daily 7am-11pm. Cash only. ❷

## ▣ NIGHTLIFE

▨ **Black Cat,** 252 Brunswick St. (☎03 9419 6230). A small cafe-lounge with remarkably discerning musical taste and a gorgeous sidewalk beer garden. Great for an afternoon beer in the setting sun or for a nightcap. DJs nightly; M-Tu open decks, W hip hop, Th breaks, F-Sa eclectic (jazzy funk, hip hop, breaks, drum 'n' bass), Su reggae and hip hop. Happy hour after 4pm: M-Tu Coopers $5, local beers $4.50; W Becks $5.50; Su Coronas $5.50. Open M-F 10am-1am, Sa 11am-1am, Su noon-4pm.

**Bar Open,** 317 Brunswick St. (☎03 9415 9601). Portraits of the Queen Mum, JFK, and baby Jesus overlook the youngish mix of students and locals in this intimate bar. W-Sa nights local jazz, gypsy, rock, and funk. Open M-Sa 2pm-3am, Su 2pm-2am.

**The Night Cat,** 141 Johnston St. (☎03 9417 0090; www.thenightcat.com.au), just west of Brunswick St. This institution blends the Fitzroy feel with the Spanish flair of Johnston St.'s. tapas block. Th and Su salsa classes from 7:30pm for beginners and intermediates ($15). Live music F-Su nights; wide range of hip hop, reggae, funk, and soul. Beer $6-8. Wine by the glass $6-8. Open daily 10pm-2:30am.

**The Provincial,** 299 Brunswick St. (☎03 9810 0042; www.provincialhotel.com.au), at the corner of Johnston St. The peeling paint outside belies the sleek interior and hip beats inside. The "Prov" is the perfect place to jumpstart a night out in Fitzroy. The menu devotes a whole page to food and 7 to liquor. Snack on eggplant chips ($7.50) or the tempura veggie plate ($11.50). Large selection of beers on tap (from $3.60). Mixed drinks $10. Tu trivia, F-Sa DJs. Open daily noon-1am.

**The Peel Hotel,** (☎03 9419 4762), corner of Peel and Wellington St.; turn left up Wellington coming from Gertrude St. and Fitzroy. An institution in Melbourne's gay nightlife, the Peel is more down-to-earth than its Commercial Rd. counterparts. The club pumps house to an almost exclusively gay male crowd. The attached pub is more laid-back, with cheap drinks (beer from $2.80, spirits $8) and relaxed conversation. Cover for special events from $10. Open Th-Su 9pm-dawn.

# SOUTHBANK AND SOUTH MELBOURNE

Set between the bustling beaches of St. Kilda and the urban activity of the city, industrial Southbank is growing increasingly commercial. The riverside Southbank Promenade, which begins across Clarendon St., is known for its shopping and sidewalk-dining. It's most crowded on sunny Sundays, when an odd mix of skater kids, health nuts, and executives gather to show off and conspicuously consume. South Melbourne, west of St. Kilda Rd. and stretching south from the West Gate Freeway to Albert Park, is more working-class than either the northern suburbs or its neighbors to the southeast but offers some quality (though pricey) restaurants and nightspots along its main thoroughfare, Cecil St.

## ▣ ▣ ACCOMMODATIONS AND FOOD

One of the newest lodgings in town, ▨**Urban Central ❸,** 334 City Rd., is a 15min. walk south of the city. Guests are shown to their rooms and given a welcome package. Thick walls block out noise from nearby highway traffic. Amenities include free breakfast, A/C in all rooms, a huge bar on ground level open until 3am (happy hour daily 7pm-8pm, occasional live music), library, game room, plasma TV room, travel desk, massive kitchen, electrical outlets within lockable compartments, and nightly dinner deals. (☎1800 631 288; www.urbancentral. com.au. Laundry $6. Internet $4 per hr. Key deposit $10. Reception 24hr. 4-bed dorms $29, ensuite $35; doubles $89-99; family room $119-129. MC/V.)

The promenade lining Southbank is full or pricey, elegant restaurants catering to corporate lunches. For cheap eats, head into the city. If a juicy steak at the price of a night's accommodation is your thing, though, head to the **Meat & Wine Co. ❺**, 3 Freshwater Pl., in Queensbridge Sq. off Queensbridge St. (☎03 9696 5333; www.themeatandwineco.com. Open M-Th and Su noon-3pm and 6-10pm, F-Sa noon-10pm. AmEx/MC/V.)

## 👁 SIGHTS

**▓KING'S DOMAIN AND ROYAL BOTANIC GARDENS.** Over 50,000 plants fill the 36 acres stretching along St. Kilda Rd. east to the Yarra and south to Domain Rd. Stately palms share the soil with oaks, rainforest plants, possums, wallabies, and a rose pavilion. There's also a steamy **tropical glasshouse** and lake where you can have tea and feed the ducks. *(Open daily 10am-4pm.)* Special events, such as outdoor film screenings, take place on summer evenings (see **Cinema,** p. 582). The **Aboriginal Heritage Walk** explores the use of plants by local Aboriginal groups in ceremony, symbol, and food. *(Th-F and alternate Su 11am. $18, concessions $14. Book ahead.)* Near the entrance closest to the Shrine of Remembrance are the visitors center and observatory. The visitors center houses an upscale cafe, the Terrace Tearooms, and a garden shop. *(Open M-F 9am-5pm, Sa-Su 9:30am-5pm.)* The observatory includes an original 1874 telescope accessible by day tours; night tours let visitors use the instruments. *(Admission by night tour only M 7:30pm, later in summer. $18, concessions $14. Book ahead.)* La Trobe Cottage, by Gate F, was home to Victoria's first lieutenant governor, Charles Joseph La Trobe. *(Open M, W, and Sa-Su 11am-4pm.)* Tours depart from the cottage to Government House, the Victorian Governor's residence. *(348 St. Kilda Rd. Gardens ☎ 03 9252 2300; www.rbg.vic. gov.au. Wheelchair-accessible. Open daily Nov.-Mar. 7:30am-8:30pm; Apr.-Oct. 7:30am-6pm. Free garden tours depart the visitors center Tu-F 11am and 2pm.)*

**NATIONAL GALLERY OF VICTORIA (NGV: INTERNATIONAL).** Housing what many consider to be the finest collection in the Southern Hemisphere, the NGV has re-opened as National Gallery of Victoria: International after a $136 million renovation. Galleries exhibit 14th- to 20th-century European art, as well as Asian and Oceanic antiquities and 20th-century international art and photography. *(180 St. Kilda Rd. ☎ 03 8620 2222; www.ngv.vic.com.au. Free guided collection tours M and W-Su 11am and 2pm. Free guided 19th-century focus tours M and W-F 10:30am. Free guided Asian art focus tour M and W-F 11:30am. Wheelchair-accessible. Admission to permanent collection free. Open M and W-Su 10am-5pm.)* On the north side of the river, the postmodern facilities of the **▓Ian Potter Centre,** in the Federation Sq. building on the corner of Russell and Flinders St., house three levels of Aboriginal, colonial, and contemporary Australian art. This striking complex of glass and steel prisms contains the only entirely Australian collection of art anywhere in the world. *(Federation Sq., on the corner of Russell St. ☎ 03 9208 0222; www.ngv.vic.gov.au. Free guided collection tours Tu-F 11am, noon, 2pm; Sa-Su 11am and 2pm. Free guided Marvelous Melbourne tour Tu-F 10:30am. Free guided Indigenous focus tour M-F 1:30pm. Open Tu-W and F-Su 10am-5pm, Th 10am-9pm. Admission to permanent collection free. Wheelchair-accessible.)*

**SHRINE OF REMEMBRANCE.** This imposing temple, with columns and a Ziggurat roof, commemorates fallen Australian soldiers from WWI. Crowning the central space are a stepped skylight and the stone of remembrance, which bears the inscription "Greater Love Hath No Man." The skylight is designed so that at 11am on November 11 (the moment of the WWI armistice), a ray of sunlight illuminates the word "Love." Ascend to the balcony for spectacular views of the Melbourne skyline, or venture into the crypt to view the colorful division flags and memorial statues. Outside, veterans of subsequent wars are honored with a memorial that includes the perpetual flame, burning continuously since ignited by Queen Elizabeth II in 1954. *(On St. Kilda Rd. www.shrine.org. au. Open daily 10am-5pm. Donations encouraged.)*

**VICTORIA ARTS CENTRE.** This enormous complex is the central star of Melbourne's performing arts galaxy. The 162m white-and-gold latticed spire of the Theatres Building is a landmark in itself. Home to the Melbourne Theatre Company, Opera Australia, and the Australian Ballet, this eight-level facility holds three theaters (see **Performing Arts**, p. 582) that combined can seat over 3000. The Theatres Building also serves the visual arts; the space that once belonged to the Performing Arts Museum is now used for free public gallery shows. Next door is 2600-seat **Hamer Hall,** which hosts the renowned Melbourne Symphony and the Australian Chamber Orchestra. Its chic **EQ Cafebar** (☎03 9645 0644) is a bit pricey but offers award-winning meals and great views of the Yarra. Finally, the third tier of the Victorian Arts conglomerate, the **Sidney Myer Music Bowl,** is across St. Kilda Rd. in King's Domain Park. After extensive renovations, the bowl will be the largest capacity outdoor amphitheater in the Southern Hemisphere, sheltering numerous free and not-so-free summer concerts. Its "Carols by Candlelight," in the weeks before Christmas, draws Victorians by the sleighloads. The Centre hosts a free arts and crafts market Su 10am-5pm. *(100 St. Kilda Rd., at the east end of Southbank, just across the river from Flinders St. Station. ☎03 9281 8000; www.vicartscentre.com.au. Guided tours leave from the Theatres Building desk M-Sa 11am; $11, concessions $7.50. Special Su 12:15pm backstage tour $13.50.)*

 **CINEMAS**

> **Moonlight Cinema** (☎03 9869 8222 or 1300 551 908; www.moonlight.com.au), in the Royal Botanic Gardens. Special tour-and-movie nights, including a complimentary glass of sparkling wine, a guided tour of the gardens, and a movie screening on the central lawn (mid-Dec.-early Mar.). Tour begins 6pm, films start at sundown (approx. 8:45pm); purchase tickets at the visitor center. $22, concessions $20.

# SOUTH YARRA, PRAHRAN, AND WINDSOR

The suburbs of South Yarra, Prahran (per-RAN), and Windsor span the area enclosed by the Yarra River to the north, St. Kilda Rd. to the west, Dandenong Rd. to the south, and William St. to the east. Divided by High St., South Yarra borders Prahran, which arches over the tiny surburb of Windsor in the southeast, just an 8min. walk to **St. Kilda** (p. 602). Chapel St. runs from South Yarra through Prahran to Windsor. This happening stretch of pavement is lined with over 1000 storefronts, offering an unbeatable locale for an eclectic assortment of one-of-a-kind trinkets as well as more standard goods. Following Chapel St. over the Yarra, it becomes Church St. in hip Richmond. Although Melbourne's gay community doesn't have a center per se, Commercial Rd. is home to a significant number of gay-friendly venues.

**▛ TRANSPORTATION**

> **Trains:** From Flinders St. Station in the city's Federation Sq., take the Sandringham Line train to South Yarra, Prahran, or Windsor Stations—each lies just west of Chapel St.

**Trams:** #78 and the nighttime #79 run along Chapel St. #8 travels below the Botanic Gardens, then along Toorak Rd. to Chapel St., while #5 and 64 head south along St. Kilda Rd., and then go east along Dandenong Rd. to Chapel.

# ACCOMMODATIONS

Clean, charming accommodations, only a few minutes by train from the city, are nestled within the vibrant mix of trendy boutiques and cafes.

**Chapel Street Backpackers,** 22 Chapel St., Windsor (☎03 9533 6855; www.csback-packers.com.au), just north of Dandenong Rd. across from Windsor train station, on tram routes #78 and 79. A friendly 13-room retreat in the southern end of the Chapel St. action. Impeccably maintained. TV lounge and courtyard with BBQ. Breakfast included. No laundry or Internet, but both coin laundry and Internet cafe are just a few doors down. Ensuite dorms $28, weekly $170; ensuite doubles $85/550. MC/V. ❷

**Claremont Guest House,** 189 Toorak Rd., South Yarra (☎03 9826 8000; www.hotelcla-remont.com), close to the intersection of Toorak Rd. and Chapel St. From the city center, take the train (7min.) or tram #8 (20min.) to the South Yarra train station; walk 1 block east. Built in 1886, the building retains much of its Victorian charm while still providing modern amenities. Feels much more like a quaint hotel than a budget accommodation. Spotless hallway bathrooms and toilets. Towels and breakfast included. Ceiling fans and heating. Kitchen for light fare (no stove or oven). Laundry $6. Internet $6 per hr., Wi-Fi $8 per hr. Dorms (with skylights instead of windows) $42; singles $79; doubles $89; triples $129; quads $169; add $12 for dorms and $20 for private rooms during special events, holidays, and festivals. Advanced bookings required. AmEx/MC/V. ❸

**Lord's Lodge,** 204 Punt Rd., Prahran (☎03 9510 5658). Take tram #3, 5, 6, 16, 64, or 67 south on St. Kilda Rd. to stop 26, then walk 2 blocks east along Moubray St. Easily accessible on foot from Prahran or St. Kilda. Older mansion with a carefree spirit on a beautiful, residential street; enjoy the croquet on the front lawn. All rooms have heater, locker, fan, and fridge. 3 private bungalows with TV and DVD. Sa free BBQ and sangria. Free Internet and Wi-Fi. Coffee and tea included. Small kitchen. Reception daily 8am-1pm and 5-7pm. 6-bed all-female dorms available. 8-bed dorms $22, weekly $132; 6-bed dorms $24/144; 4-bed dorms $26/156. MC/V. ❷

# FOOD

Preened, pricey South Yarra aggressively markets itself as the place to see and be seen in Melbourne, and its chic Mod Oz bistros with sidewalk seating experience their share of black-clad fashion mavens. There are some excellent budget options, however, particularly south of Commercial St. in more down-to-earth Prahran and Windsor. Check out the Prahran Market, on Commercial Rd. at Izett St., for cheap fresh produce, meat, and multicultural food.

**Borsch Vodka and Tears,** 173 Chapel St. (☎03 9530 2694). Distressed bohemian vibe, complete with eerie antique lamps, makes the Polish borsch ($8.50), pierogis (from $13.50), Hungarian lamb stew ($12), and potato blintzes (from $9.50) taste all the more authentic. Indulge in any of 60 vodkas ($6-12) served in a tall shot glass sunk in a bed of ice. The Spirytus is 160-proof rocket fuel. Breakfast and lunch until 6pm. Open M-W 8:30am-1am, Th-Sa 9:30am-3am, Su 9:30-11am. AmEx/MC/V. ❷

**Yellow Bird,** 122 Chapel St. (☎03 9533 8983). With red velvet couches, a stuffed bird, and a male mannequin (sometimes) wearing paper briefs, Yellow Bird defines eccentric. Started by the drummer of popular Australian band Something for Kate, this place sings with rock, indie, and garage anthems. On F and Sa nights, the cafe transforms into a happenin' bar, though Yellow Bird is most renowned for its breakfasts, served all day. Try the green eggs and ham ($13). Lunch sandwiches, salads, and risottos $8-16. Dinner specials $8-12. Wi-Fi $5 per hr. Open daily 8am-11pm. MC/V. ❷

**Grill'd,** 157 Chapel St., Windsor (☎03 9510 2377; www.grilld.com.au). These "fast food gone upmarket," burgers are made with fresh ingredients and 95% fat-free, preservative-free patties. Try the Mighty Melbourne, with cheese, trim bacon, free-range egg, beetroot, and herbed mayo ($11.50). Range of chicken, lamb, and veggie burgers too. Open M-Th 11am-10:30pm, F-Sa 11am-midnight, Su 11:30am-10:30pm. MC/V. ❷

**Gurkha's Brasserie,** 190 Chapel St. (☎03 9510 3325; www.gurkhas.com.au). Delicious Nepalese cuisine comes at a reasonable price in a dim, lantern-lit restaurant permeated by South Asian music. It might take a while to figure out what to order; try the Dal Bhat Masu, which comes with your choice of meat curry, soup, and rice or bread. Main dishes $10-16. Licensed and BYO wine; $2 corkage per person. Check out the other 4 locations, each with unique decor. Open daily 5:30-10:30pm. AmEx/MC/V. ❷

**Orange,** 124-126 Chapel St., Windsor (☎03 9529 1644), south of High St. An inviting orange awning and smooth dark hardwood interior provides a chill setting for coffee sippers. Refreshingly attentive and friendly staff makes dining a pure pleasure. Though mains ($27-37) are pricey, the breakfast ($7-16) and lunch ciabatta ($9) are satisfyingly affordable. Coffee $3. 2-course lunch and glass of wine $20, 3-courses plus wine $25. Open daily 6:30am-late. AmEx/MC/V. ❷

## ▣ NIGHTLIFE

▨ **Lucky Coq,** 179 Chapel St., Prahran (☎03 9525 1288). Delicious and cheap mixed drinks using vodkas infused with flavors like lychee, apricot, and ginger. Uni students crowd in for the $4 pizzas and hipster scene. M-Th and Su all-day entire menu $4. Local boutique microbrews from $4.50. Spirits $6.50. Vodka $7.50. Open daily noon-3am.

**Electric Lady Land,** 265 Chapel St., 2nd fl., Prahran (☎03 9529 6499). Head up the long, gray staircase to this classy bar and lounge. One of the newest places on the block, Electric Lady Land seduces you with its comfy couch corners and red chandeliers. DJs spin on F and Sa nights. Beer from $7. Spirits from $8. Open daily 5pm-3am.

**Revolver,** 229 Chapel St., 1st fl., Prahran (☎08 9521 5985; www.revolverupstairs.com. au). Once you get past the long lines, you can pretty much stay the entire weekend. Authentic Thai food ($8-11) available at the in-house restaurant. Beer from $4.50. Spirits from $7.50. Live music F-Sa, sometimes M. Cover F-Su 9pm-midnight $8, later $12-15. Open M-Th noon-3am, F noon-noon, Sa 5pm-noon, Su 5pm-5am.

**Revellers,** 274 Chapel St., Prahran (☎03 9510 3449). The friendliest spot on Chapel St. Crowds of locals crams in every weekend for all-night romps. Excellent playlists and live music Th-Sa keep the party going until breakfast. Don't leave without trying their popular Marc-E-marc, a massive cocktail in a huge pint glass ($11). Happy hour Th 9-11pm, half-priced drinks. Beer on tap from $4. Spirits from $8. Open Th-Sa 9pm-7am.

**Hoo Haa,** 105 Chapel St., 2nd fl., Windsor (☎03 9529 6900; www.hoohaa.net.au). With cheap drinks, cozy alcoves, and a great beer garden, Hoo Haa is for relaxing. The modern decor sends heads spinning with aqua and turquoise, as do the strong mixed drinks. Tu any pasta and glass of wine $12. W-Th 2 courses plus wine $25. Su parma and 2L jugs $15. Spirits $7.50. Open Tu-Th 4pm-1am, F-Sa 4pm-2am, Su 1pm-1am.

**La La Land,** 134 Chapel St., Windsor (☎03 9533 8972). Plush recliners and a low-key atmosphere. Beers from $6.50. Spirits from $7. Happy hour daily 5-8pm; wine and bubbly $2, spirits $4, beer on tap $3. Open M-Th and Su 5pm-1am, F-Sa 5pm-3am.

**Bridie O'Reilly's,** 462 Chapel St., South Yarra (☎03 9827 7788), with other branches at 62 Lt. Collins St. in the city (☎03 9650 0840) and Sydney Rd., Brunswick (☎9387 2600). Wooden booths, stag's heads, and Guinness posters: Irish to the bone. Enjoy pints in the sunny beer garden. Beer from $3.50. Spirits from $7.50. Live music W-Sa and traditional Irish Su. Open M-Th and Su 11am-1am, F-Sa 11am-3am.

**The Market,** 143 Commercial Rd., South Yarra (☎03 9826 0933; www.markethotel. com.au), attracts a mixed crowd—gay, lesbian, and straight. The Market's hard-working dance floor changes faces each night. F is "Grind" night, featuring underground house; DJs spin dance house for Sa "Late Night Shopping." F drag shows, Sa acrobat performance artists. The Market promotes international DJs and live vocalists as well. Cover F $15, Sa $20. Open F 10pm-8am, Sa 10pm-11am.

# ST. KILDA

Officially a part of Port Phillip, St. Kilda is a budget hot-spot just a little ways away from Melbourne. Although officially separated from the city proper, the area is easily accessible by tram and is a thriving, self-sustained community. The annual, popular St. Kilda Festival features multiple stages of live music, with everything from house and rave to classical (takes place the second week in February). If you're coming in March, book way ahead to avoid the hassle of finding accommodations along with the rest of the Grand Prix crowd; for more information on the **Grand Prix,** see p. 584.

# TRANSPORTATION

**Trams:** From Southern Cross Station, trams #12 and 96 head to St. Kilda (stops 131-134), while #16 runs from Flinders St. Station. You can catch these three tram lines from numerous points in the city center as well.

**Bike Rental:** Bike Fun, 12 Carlisle St. (☎03 9593 9137 or 1300 245 338; www.bike-fun.com.au). Choice of cruisers, mountain bikes, hybrids, road racers, and even folding bikes. Additions like baskets, luggage trailers, audio tour guides, trail maps, beach goods available. Cruiser 1hr. $15, full-day $40, week $80. Mountain bike $20/35/100. Open M-Sa 9am-6pm, Su 9am-5pm.

# ORIENTATION AND PRACTICAL INFORMATION

The precinct is focused around the beach, with the Esplanade following the curve of the coastline. About a block inland is infamous **Acland Street,** with loads of tasty pastry joints and scrumptious restaurants. To the north, **Fitzroy Road** offers shopping opportunities, many of St. Kilda's budget accommodations, and a host of cheap eateries.

**Internet Access: Hello International,** 22-28 Fitzroy St. (☎03 9534 9535). $3 per hr. Backpacker discounts on international calls. Free tea and coffee. Open M-Th 10am-7:30pm, F 10am-6:30pm, Sa 12:30pm-6pm, Su noon-6:30pm.

**Post Office:** 2-3 Shakespeare Grove (☎13 13 18), next to Luna Park. Open M-F 9am-5pm. **Postal Code:** 3182.

# ACCOMMODATIONS

A hub for hostels, St. Kilda offers budget travelers the cheapest deals in the area. Many book up months ahead during the Grand Prix in March, so plan your stay early, and expect hiked rates.

**St. Kilda Beach House,** 109 Barkly St. (☎03 9525 3371; www.stkildabeachhouse.com), on the corner of Inkerman St. From the city, take tram #16 or 96 and get off at Luna Park (stop 138); walk towards Greasy Joes up Fawkner St. and turn left onto Barkly St. Ensuite dorms, A/C, large kitchen, several flat-screen TV lounges, lockers, Internet ($3 per hr.), and 24hr. reception. The popular bar serves cheap drinks (Happy hour daily 5-7pm; pints $3.50, sparkling wine $3, and jugs $11), $5 breakfasts, and $5 pizzas. Su free BBQ. Wheelchair-accessible. Free parking. 8- to 10-bed dorms $28; 4- to 6-bed $32; 7th night free; doubles and triples with TV and balcony $110-113. Prices drop as much as $10 June-July, but rise during summer holidays and festivals. MC/V. ❷

**Olembia,** 96 Barkly St. (☎03 9537 1412; www.olembia.com.au), tucked behind a canopy near the intersection with Grey St. Follow the directions to St. Kilda Beach House (above) and cross Barkly St.; Olembia is on the left. This small sanctuary provides quiet, comfortable quarters in a beautiful mansion. Well-informed, friendly staff will point you to all the best spots in town. Key deposit $10. Bike rental $12 per day. Free car and bicycle parking. Reception 8am-1pm and 5-7pm. Max. stay 2 weeks. Book ahead in summer. 3-, 4-, and 6-bed dorms $30-33; singles $60; doubles $84. MC/V. ❸

**Base Backpackers,** 17 Carlisle St. (☎03 8598 6200 or 1800 24 BASE; www.stayatbase.com). From the city, take tram #16 or 96 to the Luna Park stop, and follow Carlisle St. to the corner of Barkly St. Shiny red facade and super-sleek interior. Bar music stays loud all night, so request a room on a higher floor. All rooms ensuite with heat and A/C. 6-8 bed "Sanctuary" all-female dorms available, with free towels, shampoo, champagne (daily 6-7pm), hair dryer and straightener, and tea and coffee on weekend mornings. Travel desk and job assistance. Laundry $6. Locker rental $2. Internet $5 per 75min.

Reception 24hr. Wheelchair-accessible. 10-bed dorms $24-30; 6- and 8-bed dorms $28-35, all-female $32-37; 4-bed dorms $34-40; doubles from $99. VIP. MC/V. ❷

**Cooee,** 333 St. Kilda Rd. (☎03 9537 3777; www.cooeeonstkilda.com). From the city, take tram #3 or 67 to stop 34. Built in 2006, Cooee's modern, clean amenities will satisfy any traveler. Full-time Entertainment Manager publishes weekly schedules of activities, including theme parties, historical tours, and more. Pool tables, large lounges, and outside deck with lounge chairs. Travel desk and work assistance. Laundry $4, dry $1. Reception 24hr. Wheelchair-accessible. 10-bed dorms $22-28; 6-bed dorms $24-31; 4-bed dorms $29-34; doubles $89-129, extra person (up to 5) $30. MC/V. ❷

**The Ritz for Backpackers,** 169 Fitzroy St. (☎03 9525 3501 or 1800 670 364; www.ritzbackpackers.com). Tram #16 lets off at stop 132 out front. A smaller hostel with comfy lounges. TV room with a huge projection screen, large kitchen, and sunny deck. Free pancake breakfast daily 9am. Internet $3 per 40min. Free bike use. Reception 24hr. 10-bed dorms $23; 6-bed dorms $26; 3-bed dorms $29; doubles $70. VIP. MC/V. ❷

**Tolarno Boutique Hotel,** 42 Fitzroy St. (☎03 9537 0200 or 1800 620 363; www.hotel-tolarno.com.au). Take tram #16 to stop 133. Built in 1884, this sassy boutique hotel is decked out in modern art. Internet $2 per 10min. All rooms with TV, heat, and queen-sized beds; balconies, kitchenettes, and Japanese baths available. Small doubles $110; balcony suites for 2 $180, for 3 $200; 4-person apt. $385. AmEx/MC/V. ❺

**Coffee Palace Backpackers Hotel,** 24 Grey St. (☎03 9534 5283 or 1800 654 098; www.coffeepalacebackpackers.com.au), 1 block east of Fitzroy St. Recently renovated, with large common area and spotless kitchen (cleaned 5 times per day). Free pancake breakfast daily. M movie night, Tu pool competition, F night $5 BBQ. Vouchers for cheap drink deals to bars on Fitzroy St. Lockers $5 for 3 days. Laundry $8. Internet $4 per hr. Key deposit $20. Pickup available from city bus stations or airport. 8- to 10-bed dorms $20-22; 4- to 6-bed $24-27, ensuite $25-29; doubles $50-70. VIP. MC/V. ❷

# 🔆 FOOD

As hip as those in South Yarra and Chapel St., St. Kilda's less-pretentious eateries are still mostly overpriced traps for bronzing beauties. Generally, the closer to the beach, the more expensive the eatery, but some good deals can be found farther north along Fitzroy St. The Barkly St. end of Acland St. is legendary among locals for its divine cake shops. A **Coles** supermarket is in the Acland Court shopping center on Barkly St. (Open daily 6am-midnight.)

🔲 **Lentil as Anything,** 41 Blessington St. (☎03 9534 5833; www.lentilasanything.com). Diners can pay whatever they think their meal was worth at this startlingly refreshing enterprise. The organic menu is unbelievable, with currries, udon noodles, lentil burgers, *okonomiyaki,* and more. Chai, bambu, and homemade mango *lassi.* All meals can be made gluten-free or vegan. Open daily noon-9:30pm. Cash only.

🔲 **Soul Mama,** 10-18 Jacka Blvd., at the St. Kilda Seabaths, on the 2nd fl. (☎03 9525 3338; www.soulmama.com.au). The mama-lode of incredible vegetarian options, from gourmet pizza to Indian curries. Once you snag a table, wait in the buffet line to stock your plate with healthful treats. Love the earth and your meal while looking out over the ocean. Desserts $9 (try the chocolate espresso pot). Salad/soup bowl $10. Medium plate $15.50, large $17.50. Open daily noon-late. AmEx/MC/V. ❷

**Apples,** 74 Acland St. (☎03 9537 3633; www.7applesgelato.com). You'll rarely find a time when there isn't a line around the corner for this gelato. Add fresh fruit to your cup for $1.50. 2 flavors $4.20, 3 flavors $5.20. Open daily 10:30am-11pm. Cash only. ❶

**Banff,** 145 Fitzroy St. (☎03 9525 3899). Banff has been serving hungry locals in this relaxed, Parisian-style cafe since 1942. Conveniently located near most of the hostels on Fitzroy St. A perfect breakfast stop, with fresh muffins ($3) and gigantic breakfast sandwiches (bacon, egg, arugula, and chutney; $6.50). Don't miss the ridiculously cheap gourmet pizzas ($8-9). Head here on M and Tu (all day/night) or W and F before 5:30pm; all in-house pizzas are only $5.50. Happy hour daily 3-6pm; pots $2, jugs $8, spirits $4-5, wine $3. Open daily 8am-10pm. MC/V. ❶

**Cicciolina,** 130 Acland St. (☎03 9525 3333). Named for an Italian-Hungarian porn star who was elected to the Italian parliament in 1979. Serves tasty Italian fare that gives Lygon St. a run for its money. Delicious main courses (lunch $16-37, dinner $23-38) and affable service keep patrons coming back for more. Lunch bookings only, expect a wait at dinner. Chill out in a dimly lit bar behind the restaurant while waiting for a table. Local beer $4-6, imported $8-10.50. Wine by the glass $4.50-20. Open M-Sa noon-11pm, Su noon-10pm. Bar open M-Sa noon-1am, Su noon-11pm. AmEx/MC/V. ❹

**Monarch Cake Shop,** 103 Acland St. (☎03 9534 2972). The oldest and arguably best cake shop on Acland St.'s cake-shop row. Blissful chocolate *kugelhopf* is the most popular (mini $6; regular from $16, priced by weight), but the plum cake and the polish cheesecake ($4.50 per slice) are delicious as well. Open daily 7am-10pm. MC/V. ❶

**Kat Balhoo,** 107 Acland St. (☎03 9593 8855). A tasty and cheap cafe. Serves fluffy pancakes ($6.50-8) and a variety of *schnitzels,* sandwiches, burgers, and wraps, all under $11. Coffee and muffin deal $5. Salads $9-15. Pastas and risottos $12-13. Free Wi-Fi; bring your own laptop or use theirs. Open daily 8:30am-10pm. MC/V. ❶

**Spud Bar,** 51 Blessington St. (☎03 9534 8888; www.spudbar.com.au). Half come for the food, half for the friendly service. A simple and brilliant concept: design your own potato. Choose from 30 toppings to smother your spud. Takeaway $8, eat-in $8.50. Cuppa soup $4. Open daily noon-9:30pm. MC/V. ❶

## 📷 SIGHTS

Quirky St. Kilda has shifted away from its image as a den of drugs and prostitution, embracing instead its offbeat shops, sandy shoreline, and mixed population. St. Kilda Beach is easily accessed by any number of trams (see **Transportation,** p. 603) and swarms with swimmers and sun bathers during the summer. On Sundays, the Esplanade craft market sells art, toys, and more.

**LUNA PARK.** Built in 1912 by a trio of American entrepreneurs hoping to replicate the fame of Coney Island's successful Luna Park, Melbourne's Luna has a slew of classic carnival rides, including the largest wooden rollercoaster in the world. The entrance gate of this St. Kilda icon is a grotesque clown mouth that devours visitors. *(On the Lower Esplanade. ☎03 9525 5033 or 1300 888 272; www. lunapark.com.au. Open in summer F 7-11pm, Sa 11am-11pm, Su 11am-6pm; Victorian school holidays M-Th 11am-6pm, F 11am-11pm; in winter Sa-Su 11am-6pm. Unlimited ride tickets $36, ages 4-12 $26; family pass $109. Single ride tickets $7, ages 4-12 $5.)*

**JEWISH MUSEUM OF AUSTRALIA.** The Jewish Museum outlines the history of the Jewish people as a whole and the 200-year history of Australia's Jewish community from the time of the First Fleet. A captivating hallway display draws a timeline of Jewish history, complete with fascinating multimedia displays and gorgeously illustrated texts from the Roman era and the Middle Ages. The Belief and Ritual Gallery provides a thorough overview of Judaism's basic tenets. There are also rotating displays of art and Judaica, and an extensive reference library and archive, available for use upon request. *(26 Alma Rd., east of St. Kilda Rd. near stop 32 on tram #3 or 67. ☎03 9534 0083; www.jewishmuseum.com.au. Museum open Tu-Th 10am-4pm, Su 11am-5pm. Wheelchair-accessible. $10, students and children $5, families $20. Present a print-out of the front page of the website and get a 50% discount on admission. 1hr. tours of the adjacent synagogue Tu-Th 12:30pm, Su 12:30 and 3pm; included in museum entrance fee. Open services F 6pm at the Reform synagogue on Alma Rd. Inquire for details.)*

VICTORIA

## ♫ ENTERTAINMENT

**Astor Theatre** (☎03 9510 1414; www.astor-theatre.com), on the corner of Chapel St. and Dandenong Rd. Art Deco cinema still has many of its original furnishings. Mostly repertory and reissues. Seats 1100; no bookings. Runs much as it did when it opened in 1936, showing mostly double features. Box office opens 1hr. prior to each session. $11; double feature $13, concession $12, children $11; book of 10 tickets $100.

**National Theatre,** 20 Carlisle St. (☎03 9534 0221), on the corner of Barkly St. Converted 1920s cinema now hosts off-beat, cosmopolitan performances of modern dance, drama, opera, and world music. The National Theatre Drama School and Ballet School operate here as well. Tickets $10-100, depending on show.

**Palais Theatre** (☎03 9534 0651), on the Esplanade. Holds the largest chandelier in the Southern Hemisphere. Seats 3000. Tickets around $50. Tickets through **Ticketmaster** (☎13 61 00; www.ticketmaster.com.au) or through newsagencies (closest: Village Belle Newsagency, 600m away on Acland St. Open M-F 9am-5pm, Sa 9am-2pm).

## ♬ NIGHTLIFE

**The Vineyard,** 71a Acland St. (☎03 9534 1942; www.thevineyard.com.au), near Luna Park. Home away from home for a varied clientele. Warm and friendly, a great place for a post-beach beer ($5.50-11). Live music Tu-Su nights, anything from house to rock to reggae. Main courses $15-26. Open daily 7:30am-3am; kitchen open 9am-10pm.

**Esplanade Hotel,** 11 Upper Esplanade (☎03 9534 0211; www.espy.com.au). Multi-faceted seaside hotel known as the "Espy." Down-to-earth bar with gorgeous sea views offers live music daily, from local Australian bands to international names. Pots from $4, spirits from $7. Open M-Th and Su noon-1am, F-Sa noon-3am.

**Belgian Beer Cafe,** 557 St. Kilda Rd. (☎03 9529 2899; www.belgianbeercafemelbourne.com), on the corner of Beatrice St. From St. Kilda, take tram #16 just past High St. to stop 26. Bordering Prahran, Belgian Beer Cafe is easily accessible from St. Kilda (10min. tram ride) and embodies the breezy, relaxed spirit of the beachside town. Best on F nights after work and Su afternoons, relaxing under the trees and enjoying the setting sun. This cafe is the biggest Stella Artois seller outside of Belgium, and you can also find other delicious, lesser-known labels like the amber Kwok and the blonde Westmalle Trappist. Open M-Th and Su 11am-11pm, F-Sa 11am-1pm.

**Amello,** 10-18 Jacka Blvd., at the St. Kilda Seabaths (☎03 8598 9055; www.amello.com.au). Open all day to serve meals to beachgoers too lazy to leave the sand, Amello heats up on Su nights as Melbourne's best salsa venue. Free salsa lessons Su from 4pm. Happy hour M-F 5-7pm; $2 pots. M 5-7pm and Tu 5pm-late $5 pizza and $10 steak. Beers on tap $3.50-6. Wine by the glass $6.50-20. Open daily 9am-10pm.

**The George Public Bar (GPB),** 127 Fitzroy St. (☎03 9534 8822). The subterranean style of this local haunt's old-fashioned fittings pack the place on weekend nights. Try their "world-famous" chili mayo chips ($6 for a big basket). M-Th $10 lunch or dinner plus free beer or wine. Live music Sa 4-7pm and Su 6-9pm. Beer from $3.40. Spirits from $6.50. Open M-Th and Su noon-1am, F-Sa noon-3am.

# OTHER PRECINCTS

**BRIGHTON.** For the serious beach bum, Brighton is far removed, but offers calmer waters and less commercial hoo-ha. Located south of St. Kilda, Brighton offers a nice mix of technicolor beach boxes and unbeatable views of the distant city. Take the train south from Flinders Station along the Sandringham Line and get off at Brighton Beach, then walk west toward the water.

**DOCKLANDS.** Long ago, the area was a dank and marshy port, but in anticipation of the 2006 Commonwealth Games, the once-industrial warehouses were transformed into sparkling commercial venues. Head here for chic shopping and restaurants that cater to Melbourne's filthy rich. Take the free city tram to the eastern edge of the Docklands near Southern Cross Station.

**RICHMOND.** East of the city, sedate Richmond is dubbed "Little Saigon" for the numerous Vietnamese establishments along Victoria St., between Church St. and Bridge Rd. Bridge Road runs perpendicular to Victoria St. and has a large shopping district and significant cafe culture. Take the tram east from Flinders Station to reach Richmond Station or East Richmond Station.

**PORT MELBOURNE AND ALBERT PARK.** West of South Melbourne along Port Phillip Bay are two of Melbourne's quietest, poshest suburbs. Station Pier marks the division between Port Melbourne, the more commercial side of the area, and Albert Park, an urbane residential neighborhood. Ferries to Tasmania (p. 554) depart from Station Pier at the terminus of tram #109.

**WILLIAMSTOWN.** Originally intended to be the main port of Port Phillip Bay, this peninsular precinct is now one of Melbourne's quieter districts, characterized by manicured gardens and charming coastal photo-ops. Although mostly residential, Williamstown is extremely tourist-friendly and offers delicious dining and modestly priced accommodations ideal for a weekend away from city life. From the city, head west on the Melton or Sydenham line and switch at Footscray station to the Williamstown line. Alternatively, catch the ferry from Southgate which departs for Williamstown every 30min.

# 🔎 DAYTRIPS FROM MELBOURNE

There are a variety of opportunities to escape the city and head out on exciting expeditions just a stone's throw away. Popular trips include visits to the **Yarra Valley** (see below) and **Phillip Island** (p. 609). Several tour companies also offer round-trip daily service to seemingly distant destinations. Don't be put off by perceived travel time; many travelers who are strapped for time have enjoyed day-long journeys through the picturesque **Great Ocean Road** (p. 616) or into the depths of the **Grampians National Park** (p. 636). Stop by the 🗗**Melbourne Visitor Centre** in Federation Sq., across from Flinders St. Station for a bevy of brochures and helpful agents who can provide additional information about daytrips (☎03 9658 9658; open daily 9am-6pm). Also, check out www.backpackerking. com.au for information on budget trips and activities.

## YARRA VALLEY WINERIES

Just 60km (1hr.) from Melbourne, the Yarra Valley is home to over 70 award-winning cellar doors. The unending supply of booze is a definite plus, but it's the scenery that keeps the crowds coming. Since 1835, Yarra's vineyards have been famous for their Chardonnays, Pinot Noirs, and Cabernet Sauvignons, which flourish in the valley's cool climate. Don't miss the quality bubblies that these grapes produce, too. Year-round, the Yarra Valley hosts dozens of concerts, festivals and events. One of the most famous is the unbeatable **Melba Festival,** held in March, with live music, drama performances, excellent food, and of course, wines. For more info, check out www.melbafestival.com.au.

**⊡☑ TRANSPORTATION AND PRACTICAL INFORMATION.** Public transportation to the wineries is practically nonexistent. Lilydale, 10-20km outside the Yarra, is on the Met train line, but after that there's no way to get to the wineries without renting a car; make sure you've got a designated driver. There are several tour options from Melbourne; the best and most affordable is **Backpacker Winery Tours** (☎03 9419 4444; www.backpackerwinerytours.com.au), recipients of the "2007 Best of Wine Tourism Award" for being the best daily tour operators. The tour offers free tastings at four wineries, and a gourmet lunch overlooking the valley, not to mention knowledgeable commentary on wine. ($95. Departs daily 9am, return 4:30pm. Pickup and dropoff near major hostels in CBD and St. Kilda. Approx. 20 passengers in group. Book online.) Most accommodations in the Yarra are pricey B&Bs and luxury resorts, which makes a day visit ideal. If you do choose to stay in the Yarra, call the **Yarra Tourist Association** in Healesville for accommodation information (☎03 5962 2600).

**◪ CELLAR DOORS.** Before you head out, pick up a free copy of *Wineries of the Yarra Valley* or *Wine Regions of Victoria* at the Melbourne tourist office, or check out www.yarravalleywineries.asn.au. In the valley, there are three main routes lined with cellar doors: **Melba, Maroonda,** and **Warburton Highways.** Wander into any winery that piques your curiosity; the listings below have free tastings. Many cellar doors throughout the valley have an average price of $2 for a taste of the whole selection (usually refundable upon purchase of a bottle). To make a full day of it, head to the **Healesville Sanctuary** (p. 609) in the Yarra Valley.

▨ **Domaine Chandon** (☎03 9738 9242; www.greenpointwines.com.au), "Green Point" on Maroondah Hwy. Founded in 1986 by Moët & Chandon, this lavishly landscaped vineyard produces the company's signature sparkling wine, as well as Green Point stills. Owned and operated under the Louis Vuitton corporate umbrella, the most polished vineyard in the Yarra offers an in-depth exhibit on wine production and breathtaking views from its restaurant. ($8-9.50 flutes with a free bread, cheese, and chutney plate. Bottles $20-40. Free tours daily 11am, 1, 3pm. "Sunday School" wine discovery lesson, 11am-1pm, $55; booking essential. Open daily 10:30am-4:30pm.

▨ **Yering Station,** 38 Melba Hwy. (☎03 9730 0100; www.yering.com). Founded in 1838, Yering Station is located on the site of Yarra's first vineyard. With an elegant modern touch, the cellar door is housed in an art gallery. Next door, the Station has a spectacular **restaurant ❺** with phenomenal views of the valley through floor-to-ceiling glass walls; take advantage of the views and have an indulgent dessert, like the rhubarb and currant pie with Pinot Gris syrup ($13.50). Bottles $15-64; the Mr. Frog Pinot Noir is an excellent value for its quality ($15). Open M-F 10am-5pm, Sa-Su 10am-6pm. Restaurant open M-F noon-3pm, Sa-Su noon-4pm.

**Seville Hill,** 8 Paynes Rd. (☎03 5964 3284; www.sevillehill.com.au), off Warburton Hwy. in Seville. Simple, unpretentious, and family-owned, Seville Hill is serious about its hand-crafted wines. The vineyard was planted on an old cherry orchard, and from Nov. to early Jan., you can complement your wines with tart, fresh cherries. Bring a picnic and eat under the grounds' 150-year-old elms. Bottles $18-45. Open daily 10am-6pm.

**Rochford Wines** (☎03 5962 2119; www.rochfordwines.com), on Maroondah Hwy. and Hill Rd. in Coldstream. This large estate hosts a summer concert series; see website for concert dates. The beautiful winery has an excellent gourmet **restaurant ❹.** Bottles $20-54. Restaurant open daily 10am-3pm; cafe and cellar door 10am-5pm.

**St. Huberts** (☎03 9739 1118), on St. Huberts Rd. off Maroonda Hwy. Founded in 1863. Small winery offering a very popular Cabernet, and one of only 4 Australian wineries to produce Rhone River Valley Roussanne, a unique flavor. The vineyard hosts regular musical events Nov.-Apr.; call for details. All its wines are sold only in Australia. Bottles $19-40. Open M-F 9:30am-5pm, Sa-Su 10:30am-5:30pm.

## OTHER DAYTRIPS

**HEALESVILLE SANCTUARY.** An open-air zoo that has won numerous awards for ecotourism, the Healesville Sanctuary lies in the Yarra Valley, 65km from Melbourne, a place better known for its wineries than its wildlife. The sanctuary's daily "Meet the Keeper" presentations allow visitors to interact with and ask questions about native animals *(Keeper talks: wombats 11am, roos 11:30am, reptiles 11:30am and 2pm, tasmanian devils and pelican feed 1pm, platypus 1:15pm.)* The popular "Birds of Prey" presentation has been revamped to include more birds with double the seating capacity *(daily noon and 2:30pm).* The sanctuary also has programs on Warundjeri Aboriginals and indigenous culture, with talks on Saturdays, following the Birds of Prey presentation. *(On Badger Creek Rd. By car, take the Maroondah Hwy. and follow signs. By public transport, take the Met's light rail to Lilydale, then take McKenzie's tourist service bus #659 for about 35min. Sanctuary ☎03 5957 2800; www.zoo.org.au. Open daily 9am-5pm. $23, concessions $17.30, children 4-15 $11.50, families $52.40-70.40. Free guided tours 10:30am-3:30pm; bookings required.)*

**WERRIBEE PARK AND OPEN RANGE ZOO.** The mansion at Werribee Park is a great, relaxing daytrip from Melbourne, with serene sculptured gardens, an imposing billiards room, and an expansive nursery. From October to May, the bloom of 5000 roses colors the garden. *(On K Rd. 30min. west of Melbourne along the Princes Hwy., or take the Werribee line to the Werribee train station, then bus #439. ☎03 9741 2444 or 13 19 63. Open daily 10am-5pm. Wheelchair-accessible. $13, concessions $8, children 3-15 $7, families $31.)* Animals from the grasslands of Australia, Africa, and Asia give the Open Range Zoo the feel of a safari, with a recently-opened hippo home. The zoo also runs an overnight "safari slumber" program from September to April that includes dinner, craft workshops, night spotting, accommodations, and breakfast. To explore on your own, take the two 45min. walking trails; covering the 200 hectare park takes about three hours. *(By the mansion on K Rd. ☎03 9731 9600; www.zoo.org.au. Open daily 9am-5pm, last entry 3:30pm, 45min. safaris daily 10:30-3:40pm. Wheelchair-accessible. Zoo entrance with safari tour $23, concessions $17.30, ages 4-15 $11.50 families $52.40.)*

# PORT PHILLIP AND WESTERNPORT BAYS

Two strips of land—the Bellarine Peninsula to the west and the Mornington Peninsula to the east—curve south from Melbourne around Port Phillip and Westernport Bays. Travelers short on time should head straight to Phillip Island's plentiful wildlife attractions and excellent surf beaches, while Mornington Peninsula offers tranquil picnics, water activities, and scenery.

## PHILLIP ISLAND ☎03

A whopping 4 million visitors gather on Phillip Island (pop. 8000) every year to witness the smallest species of penguin scamper back to their burrows nightly in a "Penguin Parade" on the southwestern corner of the island. In addition to the little waddlers, the island has beaches, seal rocks, hikes, and wildlife centers where you can get meet plenty of koalas, kangaroos, and emus.

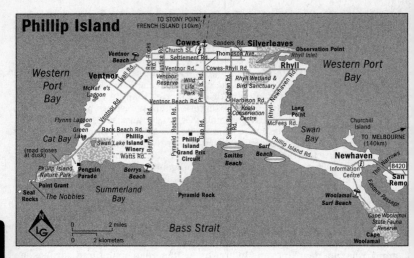

Phillip Island

**TRANSPORTATION.** V/Line **buses** serve Cowes from Melbourne (3hr.; M-F 2 per day, Sa-Su 1 per day; $10). Public transportation on the island is limited. From December 26 to the end of January, Phillip Island Bus Lines (☎03 5952 2500) runs an hourly loop around the island ($1.70); the rest of the year, it operates only from Cowes to the Penguin Parade each night ($15 roundtrip). Dozens of companies run backpacker tours to the island; for info, talk to your Melbourne hostel, most of which offer daytrip deals for guests. Phillip Island is 2hr. from Melbourne; take the South Eastern Arterial (M1) to the Cranbourne exit to the South Gippsland Hwy. (M420), then turn onto the Bass Hwy. (A420) and onto Phillip Island Tourist Rd. (B420). This road becomes Thompson Ave. when it reaches Cowes, the island's biggest township. For **bike rentals,** head to **Ride On Bikes,** 2/17 The Esplanade in Cowes. (☎03 5952 2533; www.rideonbikes. com.au. 1hr. $10, ½-day $18, full-day $25, week $99. Open M-Sa 9am-5pm, Su 9am-3pm.) For a **taxi,** call **Cowes Taxi** (☎03 5952 2200). From the Mornington Peninsula, **Inter Island Ferries** offers a passenger-only (no cars) service between Stony Point and Cowes. (☎03 9585 5730; www.interislandferries.com.au. 30min., 2-3 per day; one-way $10, children $5.)

**PRACTICAL INFORMATION.** Phillip Island lies just across a narrow strait from San Remo. Just after you pass the bridge, you'll see the **Phillip Island Information Centre** in the island's gateway town of New Haven. (☎03 5956 7447 or 1300 366 422; www.penguins.org.au or www.visitphillipisland.com. Open daily 9am-5pm.) There's also a smaller **visitors center** in Cowes, convenient for those who don't have a car. (Open daily 9am-5pm.) At either info center, buy tickets for the **Penguin Parade** to avoid long lines, or the **3 Parks Pass,** which offers entrance to the Penguin Parade, the Koala Centre, and Churchill Island ($32; children $16; family $80). Most services are in Cowes, including: **ATMs** on Thompson Ave.; **police,** 92 Chapel St. (☎03 5952 2037); **Internet** at **Waterfront Computers,** 130 Thompson Ave. (☎03 5952 3312; www.waterfront.net.au; $1.50 per 15min. Open M-F 9am-5pm, Sa 10am-1pm.) If your car breaks down, call **RACV** (☎13 11 11) for 24hr. emergency service. The **post office** is at 73 Thompson Ave. (Open M-F 9am-5pm.) **Postal Code:** 3922.

**ACCOMMODATIONS.** A hostel and several caravan parks on the island meet the needs of most campers and backpackers, and those who want a more luxurious stay can try one of the dozens of B&Bs or resorts. The **Amaroo Park (YHA) ❶**, 97 Church St., Cowes, on the corner of Douglas Rd., is just a 2min. walk to the center of town. Driving toward the water on Thompson Ave. turn left on Church St. and take the first left onto Douglas Rd. The Amaroo has clean and comfortable four-bed dorms, tidy cabins and camping sites, a deliciously free continental breakfast with fresh fruit, a pool table, a pub with cheap drinks, and a swimming pool. (☎03 5952 2548; www.amaroopark.com. Internet $2 per 20min. Sites for 1 $15, for 2 from $25, powered $60; dorms $30, YHA $25, ensuite $40/30; singles $60/50; doubles $45/35; cabins from $135. MC/V.) With sites directly on the beach, **Cowes Caravan Park ❷**, 164-188 Church St., is conveniently located near the center of Cowes (10min. walk) and has a playground, BBQ and camp kitchen, rec room with an open fire, laundry, and showers. (☎03 5952 2211. Sites high season $44, low season $29; cabins $75-145. MC/V.) If you're looking to splurge, it doesn't get much better than the beautiful **Holmwood Guesthouse ❸**, on Chapel St. in Cowes, at the corner of Steele St. Accommodation options include a traditional guesthouse, cottages (with kitchenette and wood fire), and townhouses (with full kitchen, laundry, and 2 bedrooms) for groups or families. Relax in the guest lounge next to a fire or on the sunny veranda overlooking the lush garden. Guesthouse and cottages (not townhouse) rates include home-cooked breakfast. (☎03 5952 3082; www.holmwoodguesthouse.com.au. Guest rooms for 2 people $195; self-contained cottages for 2 $215-250; townhouses for 4 people $240. AmEx/MC/V.)

**FOOD.** Virtually all food options in Cowes are clustered along the two blocks of Thompson Ave. approaching the northern beach. For delicious baked goods and deli fare (from $7), steer to **MadCowes ❶**, 17 The Esplanade. Try the delicious breakfast egg and bacon sandwich ($7.50), or the lunchtime smoked salmon sandwich with capers and cream cheese. (☎03 5952 2560. Breakfast $4-10. Foccacia $8-9. Open daily 8am-5pm. MC/V.) A few doors down, **Kristos ❶**, Shop 5, 15/16 The Esplanade, serves excellent and cheap Greek meals like souvlaki ($8.50) or warm lamb salad for $10.50. (☎03 5952 3355. Roasted chicken and chips $6. Rolls $5-7. Beef, chicken, fish, and veggie burgers $4.50-6.50. Open daily 10:30am-9pm. Cash only.) A **Coles** supermarket is at the corner of Thompson and Chapel St. (☎03 5952 2244. Open daily 7am-10pm.)

**PHILLIP ISLAND WINES.** Several vineyards share space with the abundant wildlife and beautiful forests of Phillip Island. The **Phillip Island Vineyard and Winery** has free cellar door tastings, as well as a beautiful courtyard to enjoy the wines during summer, or a cozy indoor lounge with a fireplace for wintertime. The woody Chardonnay or the Pinot Noir (only opened on weekends) are excellent and made from island grapes. Complement the wines with a local cheese platter ($17). The winery is located on Berry's Beach Rd., just off Back Beach Rd. which connects the Nobbies to the eastern end of the island. (☎03 5956 8465; www.phillipislandwines.com.au. Bottles $19-50. Open daily 11am-5pm.)

**WILDLIFE.** Phillip Island's tourist magnet is the **Little Penguin Parade** at the **Phillip Island Nature Park.** Each night, up to 1000 fairy penguins return to their burrows after lengthy fishing expeditions to rest or tend to their hungry chicks. These dark-blue, wobbly little creatures are the world's smallest variety of penguin. People await the penguins from a large grandstand along the board-walk at sunset. Get there early for a good position; bring a coat, as you may have to wait a while. Eventually, the penguins emerge and their "parade" lasts nearly an hour. The **Penguin Information Centre** provides extensive information about the penguins, including interactive exhibits. (☎03 5951 2800; www.penguins.org.au. Wheelchair-accessible. Open daily 10am-10:30pm. $18, children $9, families $44.80. Included in the **3 Parks Pass,** see p. 610. Buy tickets during the day to avoid long lines at the island's visitors centers or at the Penguin Info Centre.)

Although the penguins are the main draw, Australia's largest colony of Aus-tralian **fur seals** lives offshore from the **Nobbies** volcanic rock formation. The colony has over 24,000 seals, and up to 10,000 can be found on **Seal Rocks** at any given time. These are the largest fur seals in the world (the male seals can exceed 350kg). A boardwalk approaches the Nobbies, enabling you to take in the beautiful eroded hills of volcanic rock and crashing sea. The Seal Rocks are quite a distance from the lookouts at the Nobbies, so bring powerful bin-oculars or a $2 coin for the boardwalk telescopes. Don't miss the live feed of the action on Seal Rocks in the brand-new **Nobbies Centre,** which also houses informative displays on the slippery swimmers. (Boardwalk open daily 7:30am-dusk. Centre open daily 11am-dusk. Both free.) The **Koala Conservation Centre,** south of Cowes on Phillip Island Rd., is a sanctuary housing about 35 koalas in eucalyptus canopies, and elevated boardwalks will ensure a close-up view of the sleeping creatures. From August to February, the joeys are around. (☎03 5952 1316. $9.50, children $5, families $24. Included in the **3 Parks Pass,** see p. 610. Open daily 10am-6pm.) Farther toward Cowes, **Phillip Island Wildlife Park** has a few koalas of its own, as well as a wide cross-section of other Aussie wild-life favorites. Visitors have little choice but to hand-feed wallabies, wombats, kangaroos, and emus—the animals come to you. (☎03 5952 2038. Open daily in summer 10am-6pm; in winter 10am-5pm. Bag of animal feed included with admission. $15, children $7.50, families $40.)

**BEACHES AND HIKES.** Originally home to the Bunurong Aboriginal people, the tiny 57-hectare **Churchill Island** became one of the first European settlements in Victoria in 1801. The pleasant grounds include a number of walk-ing tracks and a working farm, where you can meet the horses, cattle, sheep, ducks, peacocks, and pet the baby animals in the nursery. If you're lucky, you might even be able to milk a cow. The island is accessible by bridge from Phil-lip Island at Newhaven. (☎03 5956 7214. $9, children $4.50, families $22.50. Included in the **3 Parks Pass,** see p. 610. Open daily 10am-4:30pm.)

The rugged pink granite of **Cape Woolamai,** on the southeast corner, contrasts with the island's volcanic rock. The Cape is the island's highest point, and a series of hikes (running the gamut from easy to difficult) and platforms let you take in the island and the ocean in all its beauty, including the **Pinnacles,** the **Woolamai Lighthouse,** and the old granite quarry. Cape Woolamai's golden beach is one of the most popular surfing beaches in Australia, and is patrolled from December 26 to the end of January, and irregularly the rest of the year. Other popular surfing beaches are **Surf Beach** and **Smith's Beach. Island Surfboards,** 147 Thompson Ave. and 65 Smith's Beach Rd., can set you up with a board and instruction. (☎03 5952 2578, Smith's Beach Rd. location ☎03 5952 3443. 2hr. lesson $50. Board rental $12.50 per hr., full-day $40. Open daily 9am-5pm.)

**RACING.** The island has a strange fascination with everything on wheels, hosting the **Island Classic** motorcycle race in January, the **Superbike World Champi-onship** in March, the **V8 Supercar Championship** in September, the **Australian Motor-cycle Grand Prix** in October, and the **Island Magic** car race in November. Note that

VICTORIA

accommodations are prebooked for months. The **Phillip Island Grand Prix Circuit,** Back Beach Rd., Cowes, offers the chance to feel the fuel-injected frenzy for yourself as you get behind the wheel of a Go-Kart or wander the racing displays. (☎03 5952 2710; www.phillipislandcircuit.com.au. 10min. Go-Kart ride $25. Tours daily 11am and 2pm; $18, children $9. Open daily 10am-5pm.)

# SORRENTO                                                    ☎03

Named after a famous seaside resort town on Italy's Amalfi Coast, the Sorrento (pop. 1600) in Australia has inherited chic cappuccino-serving cafes and trendy boutiques selling Italian designers. Luckily, relaxed Sorrento does have some affordable options as well. The beautiful bay is popular for swimming and sailing in summer, but exercise caution: the riptides here change rapidly. Just across the peninsula on the ocean side, **Back Beach** has decent surf and is only a 5min. walk from town. For board rentals, head to **Been Surfing,** Shop 4, Coppins Arcade, on the corner of Ocean Beach and Melbourne Rd. (☎03 5984 5199. Boards ½-day $20, full-day $40. Open daily 10am-5pm, later in summer.) To flounder with flippers, swim with wild dolphin and seal colonies with ☒**Polperro Dolphin Swims.** Environmentally- and safety-conscious Polperro limits group size for a more private experience. (☎03 5988 8437 or 04 2817 4160; www.polperro.com.au. Swims run Oct.-Apr. 8:30am and 1:30pm. Booking required. 3-4hr. $110; observers $50; children observers $30.)

Ideally located 1min. from town and 5min. from Back Beach, **Sorrento Beach House YHA ❸,** 3 Miranda St., is the only budget accommodation around. Clean and comfortable, the Beach House has a large kitchen, cozy lounge area, and a great outdoor patio with BBQ. From the roundabout at Melbourne and Ocean Beach Rd., follow the YHA signs up Ossett St.; Miranda St. is the first right. (☎03 5984 4323. Book ahead in summer. Dorms in summer $40, YHA $30; in winter $30/25.) The main promenade in town which leads down the hill to the ocean is **Ocean Beach Road,** lined with upscale eateries and the aforementioned Italian boutiques. For delicious fish and chips at unbeatable prices, head to **Fish Fetish ❶,** 27 Ocean Beach Rd. The seafood pack with fish, calamari, scallops, crab sticks, and chips is only $8.50. (☎03 5984 1479. Fish from $4.20. Hamburgers $4.50. Open M-Th and Su 11:30am-8pm, F-Sa 11:30am-9pm. Cash only.)

From Melbourne, board a **train** at Flinders Station in Federation Sq. to Frankston (1hr., Zone 1 and 2 all-day Met pass $10.10). Then catch bus #788, which departs from just outside the Frankston train station, in the direction of Portsea; Sorrento is the second-to-last stop. (80min.; every 45min. M-F 5:30am-9:30pm, Sa 7:45am-10:30pm, Su 9am-9:40pm; included from last leg, plus $3.) If you're coming from the Great Ocean Road, you can reach Sorrento via ferry from **Queenscliff** (p. 614), on the Bellarine Peninsula. (☎03 5258 3244; www.searoad.com.au. 40min.; daily every hr. 7am-6pm; $9 for passengers. Cars $44-50 plus additional $7 per person.) The tiny **visitors center** is easily missed and not always manned in winter; from where the bus drops you off on the corner of Melbourne and Ocean Beach Rd., turn right toward the water; it is on your left, next to Commonwealth Bank. (Open daily 10am-4pm.) Along this same road, you'll find numerous **ATMs** and a **post office,** 16 Ocean Beach Rd. (Open M-F 9am-5pm.) **Postal Code:** 3943.

# QUEENSCLIFF                                                 ☎03

Tiny Queenscliff retains its Victorian elegance, enticing mostly older visitors who seek a relaxing holiday vacation to its rambling, rocky shores. Queenscliff, 120km southwest of Melbourne, overlooks the **Rip,** renowned among sailors for its strong current and perilous shoreline. The grand old architecture and lei-

**VICTORIA**

surely ambience, well-suited for beach-sitting and twilight strolls, inspire some to start their journey on the **Great Ocean Road** (p. 616) in Queenscliff.

Take the **V/Line train** from Melbourne to Geelong (1hr., daily every hr., $6.20) and then **McHarry's Buslines** (☎03 5223 2111; www.mcharrys.com.au) to Queenscliff (1hr.; M-F 14 per day, Sa 8 per day, Su 4 per day; $3.20). **Ferries** run from the Sorrento Pier, just across the bay. (☎03 5258 3244; www.searoad.com.au. 40min.; daily every hr. on the hr. 7am-6pm; $9 for passengers. Cars $44-50, plus additional $7 per person.) The **Visitor Information Centre** at 55 Hesse St. has Internet for $3 per 30min. (☎03 5258 4843 or 1 300 884 843; www.queenscliff. org. Open daily 9am-5pm.) The **library,** in the same building as the information center, has two free **Internet** terminals: 1hr. with advanced booking, or a 15min. fly-by. (Open M-Tu 2-5pm, Th-F 10am-1pm and 2-5pm, Sa 9:30am-noon.) The ANZ **bank** is at 71 Hesse St. (24hr. **ATM**), and the **post office,** 47 Hesse St., is right nearby. (☎03 5258 4219. Open M-F 9am-5pm, Sa 9am-noon.) **Postal Code:** 3225.

Inexpensive lodging is scarce in Queenscliff; book well in advance in the summer. If you can't get a room, contact the information center for assistance with finding accommodations in Point Lonsdale, 6km west of Queenscliff. It's a 1hr. walk west along the coast, but public buses also cover the distance. Located in a 1906 Edwardian building, the YHA-affiliated **Queenscliff Inn B&B** ❸, 59 Hesse St., has a drawing room with an open fire, outdoor BBQ, and kitchen facilities. Breakfast ranges from continental ($10) to fully cooked meals ($145). (☎03 5258 4600. Towels $2. Dorms $30, YHA $26; singles $65/60; doubles $80/70. MC/V.) The **Queenscliff Dive Centre** ❸, 37 Learmonth St., has bright and comfortable backpacker accommodations, with a huge kitchen, access to the center's pool and spa, and free laundry. (☎03 5258 1188. Continental breakfast included. Dorms $33, if taking the dive course, $20. MC/V.)

Set in a beautiful and lush garden, ◪**Hobson's Garden Cafe** ❷, 2 Hobson St., has an array of tasty and trendy foods with a variety of vegetarian options. Having one of their excellent desserts on the back patio is a true indulgence. (☎03 5258 4945. Cappuccino $3.20. Breakfast $4-11, served 9-11:30am. Lunch $9-13. Open daily 9am-5pm. MC/V.) **Beaches Cafe** ❶, 1/84 Hesse St. at the roundabout with Stokes St., serves the best smoothies ($6) around, as well as a reasonably-priced and very filling breakfast for $12. (☎03 5258 4470. Open daily 8am-5pm. Cash only.) At **Queenscliff Fish and Chips** ❶, 77 Hesse St., the fish are as fresh as they boast, unbeatably tasty, and inexpensive at $4-9. (☎03 5258 1312. Open daily 11am-8:30pm.) There's a **Foodworks** supermarket at 73 Hesse St. (☎03 5258 1727. Open M-Sa 9am-8pm, Su 9am-7pm.)

# GEELONG ☎03

The second-largest city in Victoria, Geelong (jih-LONG; pop. 200,000) is an hour southwest of Melbourne on the Princes Hwy. (Hwy. 1). Historically a hub for the wool trade, today the city is trying to reinvent itself as an up-and-coming tourist destination. Most travelers on a tour of the Great Ocean Road still bypass the town, but those who don't will find an industrial town with some hidden gems, such as the famous boardwalk bollards and some excellent drinking and eating establishments in the downtown area.

**▮ TRANSPORTATION.** At the V/Line Station (☎13 61 96) on the western edge of the downtown area, **trains** run to Melbourne (1hr., daily every hr., $6.20) and Warrnambool (2 hr., 3 per day, $17.80). V/Line **buses** depart for the Great Ocean Road, stopping in Torquay, Anglesea, and Lorne before arriving in Apollo Bay

(2hr., 2-3 per day, $13 ). Buses also head to Ballarat (1 hr., M-F 1 per day, $7.10). From late December to Easter, a free **shuttle bus** circles town. Route maps and schedules are available at visitors centers and the train station.

**⊞ 🚺 ORIENTATION AND PRACTICAL INFORMATION.** Geelong is situated on the northern side of the **Bellarine Peninsula,** and **Corio Bay** forms the northern border of the city. **Princes Highway (Latrobe Terrace)** runs north-south along the western edge of town. **Moorabool Street** heads south from the waterfront, and its intersections with **Malop** and **Little Malop Street** host most of the town's action. Detailed maps of the city are available at the visitors centers.

There are **four visitors centers** in Geelong, all providing the same helpful information. An excellent visitors center is located in the **Wool Museum.** (☎03 5229 9000. Open daily 9am-5pm.) **Banks** with **ATMs** line Moorabool St., and free **Internet** is available at the city **library,** 49 Little Malop St., on the south side of Johnston Park. (☎03 5222 1212. Open M-F 10am-8pm, Sa 9:30am-noon, Su 2-5pm. Book at reception desk.) The **police** are located on the corner of Mercer St. and Railway Terr., directly in front of the railway station. **Geelong Hospital** (☎03 5226 7111) is on Ryrie St. between Bellarine and Swanston. The **post office,** 99 Moorabool St., is located in the Market Square Mall. (Open M-F 9am-5:30pm, Sa 9am-1pm.) **Postal Code:** 3220.

**🚹 🏠 ACCOMMODATIONS AND FOOD.** The city has no true backpacker hostels, and the cheapest digs are semi-clean rooms above loud pubs. The **Carlton Hotel ❸,** on Malop St. near the park between Gheringhap and Moorabool St., offers decent private rooms with shared baths above a pub. Amenities include a large, clean kitchen as well as free laundry, Internet, and Wi-Fi. (☎03 5229 1955. Singles $49; doubles $69. MC/V.)

In the center of town just a couple blocks from the waterfront sits the **National Hotel ❷,** 191 Moorabool St., which accommodates backpackers with basic dorm rooms and lockers. Downstairs is an inexpensive noodle bar as well as a pub. (☎03 5229 1211 or 04 1052 9935; www.nationalhotel.com.au. Pub open Tu-Su nights. Dorm $26; doubles $55. MC/V.)

Noodle bars cluster together on Malop St., while Little Malop St. features slightly more upscale cafes and restaurants. A variety of eating options line Moorabool St. as it approaches the bay. The colorfully decorated **Wayans ❷,** 82A Little Malop St., in the center, has authentic Balinese food in a small and lively setting. (☎03 5222 5422. Noodles and rice mains $11-16. Open Tu-Su 5:30pm-latenight.) Gourmet beer lovers pack the relaxed **Scottish Chief's Tavern Brewery ❸,** 99 Corio St., where even the fish are battered in amber ale. Enjoy the bright, conservatory-like setting or attached beer garden. From the city center, head down Malop St, pass Bay City Plaza on the left, and turn left on Yarra St. (☎03 5223 1736. Lunch from $10. Dinner $17-27. Open M-Th 11am-11pm, F-Sa 11am-1am. No dinner M. Live bands F-Sa.)

**🅖 SIGHTS.** The **Wool Museum,** 26 Moorabol St., displays the history of Geelong's love affair with wool through an abundance of revealing exhibits, including a stuffed descendant of Oz's first flock. (☎03 5227 0701. Open M-F 9:30am-5pm, Sa-Su 1-5pm. $7.30, concessions $6, children $3.65. Allow 30-40min.; taxidermy enthusiasts and wool aficionados may require longer.)

**🎭 NIGHTLIFE.** The **National Hotel** (see **Accommodations,** p. 615) has a raucous pub that uses its stage to showcase local bands on the weekend. (Pub open Tu-Sa noon-late, Su 4pm-late.) **Lamby's,** 26 Moorabol St., abutting the wool museum at Brougham St., has in-house bands F 5pm-3am, Sa-Su 8pm-3am.

(☎03 5223 2392; www.lambys.com.au. Wine-tastings on F 5-8pm. Cover $5, free before 10pm; more on holiday weekends.) Chain **Irish Murphy's,** 30 Aberdeen St., features Guinness and live music Th-Su nights. (☎03 5221 4335. Pub open M-W 11am-midnight, Th-Sa 11am-1am, Su 11am-11pm.)

# GREAT OCEAN ROAD

On your list of Things to Do Before You Die, the ⬛**Great Ocean Road** should be up there. Rivaling Australia's other prized attractions like Sydney's opera house, the Great Barrier Reef, and Uluru, you can't leave Australia without driving one of the most spectacular scenic coastlines in the world. The world's largest war memorial, the 175km highway project provided work for Australian soldiers returning home after WWI. Over 3000 veterans carved the coastal road into the crumbling cliffsides, creating a masterpiece that runs from world-famous surf beaches through rainforests to idyllic beach hamlets. Beside the road, the turbulent waves of the Southern Ocean—angrily tossed about by Antarctic winds blown from 3000km away—have sculpted the coast's impressive rock formations, which stand as highlights of the Great Ocean Road.

## ⬛HIGHLIGHTS OF THE GREAT OCEAN ROAD

**RIP IT UP** on **Bells Beach,** which draws thousands for the world-famous Rip Curl Pro Classic every Easter (p. 620).

**VIEW** the **Shipwreck Coast** and the spectacular limestone rock formations that took hundreds of vessels to their grave (p. 628).

**HIKE** through rainforests and under waterfalls in the **Great Otway National Park,** wedged between Lorne and Apollo Bay (p. 625).

**KAYAK** with fur seals—who get up close and personal—in **Apollo Bay** (p. 623).

**GALLOP** on golden sands in **Airey's Inlet** or **Warrnambool,** as trusty steeds take riders on the most picturesque beach trail ride of their lives (p. 629).

# ✦ ORIENTATION

Though the road itself runs from **Torquay** to **Warrnambool,** the Great Ocean Road region encompasses the entire serene and spectacular southwestern coast of Victoria, from Geelong to Nelson. Stretching from **Torquay** to **Lorne,** the **Surf Coast** is the road's first segment, and it hosts some of the country's best surfing. The **Great Otway National Park,** on the 73km stretch from **Anglesea** to **Apollo Bay,** is home to one of Victoria's most breathtaking rainforests, with spectacular pines and waterfalls. Rejoining the shoreline on the other side of the park, the Great Ocean Road follows **Shipwreck Coast,** where unrelenting winds and unpredictable swells made the region a 19th-century ship graveyard and shaped the famous ⬛**Twelve Apostles** rock formations. Continuing west, visitors can discover Southern Right Whales off **Warrnambool** (from late May to September), seal colonies at **Cape Bridgewater,** and stunning caves in **Lower Glenelg National Park.** Though visitors have been known to complete the entire Road in just a day or two, it's worth as much time as you've got; a week on the Great Ocean Rd. is a week well spent. Most travelers drive the road from Melbourne heading west toward Adelaide, so *Let's Go* lists towns and attractions east to west.

VICTORIA

**Great Ocean Road**

VICTORIA

TO MELBOURNE (73km)
TO QUEENSCLIFF (31km)
Surf Coast Hwy
Princes Hwy
Geelong
Torquay
Jan Juc
Bells Beach
Point Addis
Marine NP
Anglesea
Airleys Inlet
Eastern View
Lorne
Winchelsea
Lake Murdeduke
Barwon R.
Dry Lakes
Lake Colac
Lake Corangamite
Colac
Gellibrand
Beech Forest
Great Otway NP
Lavers Hill
Gellibrand R.
Tomahawk R.
Aire R.
OTWAY RANGES
Great Otway National Park
Wye River
Kennett River
Cape Patton
Skenes Creek
Great Ocean Rd
Apollo Bay
Marengo
Shelly Beach
Point Franklin
Great Otway NP
Glenaire
Cape Otway
Johanna Beach
Great Otway NP
Melba Gully
Moonlight Head
Bass Strait
Surf Coast
SOUTHERN OCEAN
Camperdown
Lake Colongulac
Cobden
Terang
Timboon
Princes Hwy
Princetown
Gibson Steps
Twelve Apostles
Loch And Gorge
Twelve Apostles Marine NP
Port Campbell
Peterborough
Bay of Martyrs
Bay of Islands
The Grotto
London The Arch
Bridge
Great Ocean Rd
Curdies R.
Warrnambool
Allansford
Childers Cove
Logans Beach
Hopkins R.
Merri R.
Hopkins Hwy
TO TOWER HILL RESERVE (15km), PORT FAIRY (26km)
Shipwreck Coast

C140 C145 C151 C146 C147 C155 C161 C165 C164 A1 C168 C167 C163 C164 C119 C151 B100

Bass Strait

10 miles
10 kilometers

N

**WHEN TO GO.** High season for the Great Ocean Road lasts from December to January, during school holidays. To avoid the crowds but still catch the best of Victoria's moody weather, try to plan a trip in late November or Feb.-Mar. In winter, the crowds are gone from the Great Ocean Road, but so is the sun. If winter is all you've got, head to **Warrnambool** (p. 629), where a population of Southern Right whales stops to give birth to their calves in late May, staying near the beach until September. Surfing season in Australia's surfing capital, **Torquay** (p. 619), is Mar.-Sept.

# ☰ TRANSPORTATION

Known as one of the world's greatest scenic drives, the Great Ocean Road is meant to be driven—in your own car. Because the demand is not high, public transport along the road is infrequent and doesn't serve the national parks and other more remote, scenic areas. Adding up the bus tickets and headaches, it often proves cheaper to rent a car or a caravan for the trip. For information on renting a car from **Melbourne**, see p. 575; from **Adelaide**, see p. 461.

Even so, with schedules from the visitors office in hand and lots of planning, making your way along the Great Ocean Rd. using public transportation is not impossible. V/Line **trains** (☎13 61 96) from Melbourne will get you as far as Geelong ($6.20, daily every hr. 5am-midnight), where the less-frequent V/Line **bus service** connects you to towns further west along the coast. Buses run both ways along the Great Ocean Road between Geelong and Apollo Bay, passing through Torquay, Bells Beach, Anglesea, and Lorne, (in both directions M-Th 4 per day, F 5 per day, Sa-Su 2 per day). The "Coastal Link" V/Line bus has newly extended service, running M, W, and F year-round from Apollo Bay to Warrnambool, with a 30min. stop at the Twelve Apostles, a 15min. stop at Loch Ard Gorge, and 10min. stops at London Bridge and Bay of Islands. Other than this Coastal Link service, it is difficult to progress farther west than Apollo Bay via public buses, which often run only once per week.

## BY BIKE

Breathtaking in both senses of the word, bicycling along the highway is becoming increasingly popular. For those with the time and the motivation, it may well be the best way to get off-the-beaten path on one of the most trafficked roads in Australia. Cyclists should be well prepared, as the narrow, winding road (with no protective shoulder in most places) and the steep hilly topography of some sections of the route make for difficult riding conditions. Bikes can be rented in several towns along the way. In Torquay and Anglesea, call **Hire-A-Bike** for bike delivery to any accommodations between the two towns. (☎03 5261 4807. Full-day $20, week $100.) The **Warrnambool Visitors Centre** rents bikes. (☎03 5559 4620 or 1800 637 725; www.warrnamboolinfo.com.au. Bikes ½-day $20, full-day $30. Open daily 9am-5pm.) Further west, the **Portland Visitors Centre** also rents bikes. (☎03 5523 2671 or 1800 035 567. Bikes ½-day $12, full-day $20. Open daily 9am-5pm.) **Apollo Bay Backpackers** (p. 623) in Apollo Bay, **Warrnambool Beach Backpackers** (p. 630), and **Emoh YHA Hostel** (p. 632) in Port Fairy allow guests free use of their mountain bikes.

Satisfy your competitive streak with the **Great Ocean Road Marathon,** which combines sport and tourism like no other event in the world. For more info on the G.O. Marathon, check out www.greatoceanroadmarathon.com.au.

# BY TOUR

Those without a car should consider a bus tour. Tours offer more flexibility than public transport and generally come in two varieties: those that make a loop starting and ending in Melbourne and those that run between Melbourne and Adelaide. The loop option is less scenic, leaving the Great Ocean Road for the relatively nondescript Princes Hwy. at Port Campbell. For those heading west from Melbourne to Adelaide, there are a number of three-day tours connecting the cities via the Great Ocean Rd. at prices rivaling air or rail travel. Those short on time can choose to do the trip all at once, while some companies allow those with more time to get on and off as often as they want.

**Otway Discovery** (☎03 9654 5432; www.otwaydiscovery.primetap.com) is the most affordable and flexible of the loop tours. The friendly drivers run along the Road from Melbourne to Port Campbell and then back to Melbourne via the inland route, with the option to hop on and off. There is no time limit for those paying for the hop-on, hop-off option, but you only get to do the loop once. Hostel pickup daily 7-8am. Day tour $85; hop-on, hop-off $95. They also run a 3-day Melbourne-Adelaide or Melbourne return-trip that runs along the Great Ocean Rd. with a detour north to the Grampians National Park. Melbourne-Adelaide $190, Melbourne return $175.

**Wildlife Tours** (☎1300 661 730; www.wildlifetours.com.au) runs a 1-day tour of the Great Ocean Road (Melbourne to Port Campbell), as well as 3-day round-trip tours that include the Grampians and 2- or 3-day Melbourne-to-Adelaide trips. Stopovers may be allowed, if the next bus has room for you. 1-day Great Ocean Road tour $75, departs daily; 2-day Great Ocean Road and Grampians tour $160, departs M, Th, Sa; 2-day Melbourne-Adelaide $190, departs M, Th, Sa; $10 off with ISIC/NOMADS/VIP/YHA.

**Groovy Grape Getaways** (☎1800 661 177; www.groovygrape.com.au) runs a back-packer-oriented all-inclusive 3-day trip in either direction between Melbourne and Adelaide, hitting all the main sights and providing all accommodation, meals, park entrance fees. $340. Departs Melbourne year-round Tu and F 7am, additional tour in summer Su; departs Adelaide Tu and Sa 7am, additional tour in summer Th. No hop-on or hop-off.

**Goin' South** (☎1800 009 858; www.goinsouth.com.au) does a tour similar to the Groovy Grape, plus caving at Naracoorte and hiking in the Grampians. 3-day trips include everything except lunches. From $325. Departs from Adelaide and Melbourne M and Th.

**CYBER GREAT OCEAN ROAD.** For more info on the spectacular coastline and its attractions, check out www.greatoceanroad.org. To check up on surf conditions along the Surf Coast, head to www.magicseaweed.com.

# TORQUAY ☎03

On the Great Ocean Road, Torquay (tor-KEY; pop. 10,000) is the spot to rip it up and whip it out (your credit card, that is). A mecca for surfers during the summer months, boarders from all over the world make the pilgrimage to nearby Bells Beach every Easter for the Rip Curl Pro Classic. Surf shops line the main boulevard, appropriately named Surf Coast Hwy. (also known as Torquay or Geelong Rd.), to gear you up with boards and wetsuits for the surf.

**TRANSPORTATION AND PRACTICAL INFORMATION.** V/Line **buses** (☎13 61 96) leave from the Torquay Holiday Resort by Bells Beach Lodge on the Surf Coast Hwy. Buses head north to Geelong (30min.; M-F 4 per day, Sa-Su

2 per day; $2.50) and west on the Great Ocean Rd., making numerous stops, before arriving in Apollo Bay (2hr.; M-F 3-5 per day, Sa-Su 2 per day; $11). Most commercial activity takes place along the Surf Coast Hwy. (Geelong Rd.), a continuation of the Great Ocean Rd., or just off the highway on the pedestrian Gilbert St., where there is a well-marked shopping district with **ATMs** and food options. The **Visitors Centre,** on Beach Rd., is in the Surfworld Museum in the Surf City Plaza retail center. (☎03 5261 4219. Open daily 9am-5pm. **Internet access** $7 per hr.) Free Wi-Fi is available at **Soul Fuel,** p. 620. For bike rental, **Hire-A-Bike** delivers to any accommodation in Torquay. (☎03 5261 4807. Full-day $20, week $100.) In case of emergency, contact the **police,** 122 Surf Coast Hwy. (☎03 5264 3400.) The **Torquay Pharmacy** is at 18 Gilbert St. (☎03 5261 2270. Open M-Sa 9am-6pm, Su 10am-5pm.) The **post office** is located at 23 Pearl St., on the corner of Bristol St. (Open M-F 9am-5pm.) **Postal Code:** 3228.

**⌖ ACCOMMODATIONS.** Book ahead in summer and for the Easter surfing competition. **Bells Beach Lodge ❸**, 51-53 Surf Coast Hwy., is a brightly painted, bungalow-style bunkhouse with surfing posters, magazines, and nearly constant screenings of surf documentaries. You'll meet professional surfers from around the world as well as beginners trying to absorb some skills through osmosis. Bells Beach has lockers, surf equipment rentals, Internet access ($6 per hr.), and good vibrations. (☎03 5261 7070; www.bellsbeachlodge.com.au. Key and linen deposit $10. Dorms $30; doubles $60. MC/V.) **Torquay Holiday Resort ❷**, 55 Surfcoast Hwy., next to Bells Beach Lodge, has a pool, spa, minigolf, and tennis court, as well as a host of activities for kids. (☎03 5261 2493. Check-in 3-8pm. Powered sites $26-62; cabins $58-242. MC/V.)

**⧉ FOOD.** Hordes of surfers with the munchies provide a large market for the takeaway joints that dominate Torquay's food scene and are centered on the pedestrian Gilbert St. in the town center as well as and Bell St. near the beach. There are also a few notable options on Surf Coast Hwy. **Soul Fuel ❷**, 1/57 Surfcoast Hwy., is a hip eatery with eclectic fare and tons of healthy veggie options, like the double soy burger ($11.50) or the lentil burger for $9.50. (☎03 5261 4999. Free Wi-Fi. Iced coffees and fruit smoothies $5.50-7.50. Wraps $7.50. Open daily 7:30am-4pm.) Near the pedestrian strip on Gilbert St., **Las Olas ❶**, 10 Pearl St., serves up fresh and spicy Mexican food. Cure a hangover or get ready for a big day on the surf with a classic burrito ($7.20) or a heaping tostada basket for $11.50. (☎03 5264 8877. Tacos $4.50-5.50. Quesadillas $6-10.50. Open daily 11am-8pm. MC/V.) There's a **Safeway** supermarket with an attached LiquorWorks on Gilbert St. (open daily 7am-midnight). Every third Sunday (10am-3pm) between September and April, the local **Cowrie Market** lines the Torquay Esplanade with live music, food, and artwork.

**ADRENALINE RUSH GUARANTEED.** For an aerial view of Bells Beach, why not jump out of a plane thousands of meters in the air, reaching falling speeds of up to 220km per hr.? **Australian Skydive,** 325 Blackgate Rd. just off Surfcoast Hwy., can hook you up with tandem jumps for novices as well as lessons for wanna-be pros. (☎1800 557 101; www.australianskydive.com.au. Tandem jump $380. DVD with stills $145. Booking required.)

**⚐ SURFING.** Peak surfing season is from March to September. The **Torquay Surf Beach,** off Bell St., a 10min. walk from Bells Beach Lodge, is the first in a string of surfable beaches that stretch down the coast. The king of them all is **▨Bells Beach,** the first surfing reserve in the world, where the reef breaks attract top professional surfers for the Easter Rip Curl Pro Classic. Beware: Bells is for advanced surfers only. It's a 10min. drive from town, though the most scenic way to reach it is via the ◪**Surf Coast Walk,** a trail that begins at the beach in Torquay. The pedestrian trail, also great for mountain biking, follows the coast for nearly 35km, passing **Jan Juc,** composed of reef and beach breaks, and the second-best surfing site after Bells. The trail continues to Bells, then Point Addis, Anglesea, and Airey's Inlet. For closer swimming beaches, cross the highway from Bells Beach Lodge and continue 10min. down Zeally St. to **Zeally Bay,** where **Cozy Corner, Torquay Front Beach,** and **Fisherman's Beach** await.

Surf lessons are available from **Go Ride a Wave,** 1/15 Bell St. (☎1300 132 441; www.gorideawave.com. Standard 2hr. surf lesson $70; $55 with advance payment. Booking required.) **Southern Exposure,** 55b Surfcoast Hwy., rents surfboards ($30) and wetsuits ($10) and offers 2hr. surf clinics classes. (☎03 5261 2170; www.southernexposure.com.au. Surf clinic $55. Booking required.) **Offshore Surf Tours,** 55b Surfcoast Hwy., also has lessons and equipment hire; the office is located between Bells Beach Lodge and Torquay Holiday Resort. (☎04 2235 3723; www.offshoresurftours.com. Board and wetsuit hire $25. 2hr. surf lesson $55. Full-day "Surf Tour" including transport, surf lesson, and lunch $85.) The **Torquay Surfworld Museum,** on Beach Rd., located in the Surf City Plaza, has a higher concentration of boards than most of the area shops. The museum pays tribute to surfing history and culture, providing interactive video tours, explanations of waves, and a history of the surfboard. (☎03 5261 4219. Open daily 9am-5pm. $9, concessions and children $6.)

# LORNE ☎03

If you had to choose only one town to visit along the Great Ocean Road, Lorne should be it. The population jumps from 900 to 20,000 in summer, as Australians set up shop in their million-dollar vacation homes. With the best hostels on the Great Ocean Road, wicked surf on one side of town and the rainforests and waterfalls of the **Great Otway National Park** (for more info, see p. 625) bordering the other, and a host of trendy spots, you'll never want to leave.

◪◪ **TRANSPORTATION AND PRACTICAL INFORMATION.** The Great Ocean Rd. becomes **Mountjoy Parade** as it passes through town. You don't need a car to get around the town itself, but public transportation does not reach the nearby sights of the Great Otway National Park. V/Line **buses** depart three to four times daily during the week and twice daily on weekends from the Commonwealth Bank at 68 Mountjoy Pde. to Apollo Bay (1hr., $3.50), Geelong (1hr., $8.10), and Melbourne (2hr., $15). In January, there's a free shuttle bus service along Mountjoy Pde. from the supermarket to the Lorne pier. (Every 30min., daily noon-8pm.) The **Lorne Visitors Centre,** 15 Mountjoy Pde., has excellent maps and information on activities, hiking, and camping in the area as well as **Internet access.** (☎03 5289 1152; www.visitsurfcoast.com or www.lornelink.com.au. Internet access $6 per hr. Open daily 9am-5pm.) In case of emergency, contact the **police** on Smith St. (☎03 5289 2712). The **post office** is located in the massive gray complex called the Cumberland Resort, on the west end of town. (☎03 5289 1405. Open M-F 9am-5pm.) **Postal Code:** 3232.

◪ **ACCOMMODATIONS.** ◪**Great Ocean Backpackers (YHA)** ❷, 10 Erskine Ave., is a colony of wooden cabins set amid the trees on the hillside behind the supermarket, just before the bridge. Free amenities include Wi-Fi, laundry, BBQ, boogie board loan, and birdseed to feed the native cockatoos that perch on the cabin balconies. (☎03 5289 1809. Book months in advance for school holidays. Dorms $23.50, YHA $20; doubles $65/60; family rooms $90/75. MC/V.) The **Erskine River Backpackers ❷**, 6b Mountjoy Pde., on the right just over the bridge as you enter town from Geelong, sports airy facilities and a large, tidy kitchen. A balcony with hammocks and picnic tables overlooks a leafy courtyard on one side and the town on the other. (☎03 5289 1496. Pool table, TV, and table tennis. Dorms $25-40; doubles $60-70. Weekly rates available. Cash only.) **Free camping ❶** without amenities is available inside the **Great Otway National Park** (p. 625). **Lorne Foreshore Caravan Parks ❷** runs paid camping facilities, powered and unpowered, next to the visitors center in town. (☎03 5289 1382 or 1300 736 533; www.gorcc.com.au. Reception 8am-8pm. Sites $20, powered $25; caravans $50; cabins from $60. Prices almost double in summer. Open M-Th and Su 8am-8pm, F-Sa 8am-9pm.) Complete camping facilities are available 7km west of town at the **Cumberland River Camping Reserve ❷**. Several short walks originate here and there's a swimming beach across the road. (☎03 5289 1790. Sites for 2 $20-28, extra person $10; cabins for 2 $85-105, extra person $28. MC/V.)

**❏ FOOD.** Trendy 🔲**Qdos ❸**, 35 Allenvale Rd., just out of town on the way to Erskine Falls, oozes chic from every corner. Nestled in the woods overlooking a small pond, Qdos is a relaxed eatery/modern art gallery, serving creative meals ($14-22) amid unique statues, paintings, and jewelry. Signs lead you from town to Qdos; take Otway St. from Mountjoy Pde., then Allenvale Rd. at the rotary. The atmosphere is chic but relaxed. If you can't get enough of this place, splurge for a night (from $180) in the attached compound. (☎03 5289 1989; www.qdosarts.com. Open Jan. daily 9am-5pm; Feb.-Dec. M and Th-Su 9am-5pm. MC/V.) **Grandma Shields Bakery ❶**, in the Cumberland Resort complex on Mountjoy Pde., has award-winning pies ($4) that are the best budget meal in town. (☎03 5289 1525. Open daily 7am-6pm, later in summer. Cash only.)

**⚑🏄 SURFING AND OUTDOOR ACTIVITIES.** Lorne has good surf right in town—both beach and reef breaks—although the area is not as famous for surfing as Torquay or Apollo Bay. Prime spots with parking are available all along the Great Ocean Rd. toward Apollo Bay. Beginners who want to rent a board should head to **Lorne Surf Shop**, 130 Mountjoy Pde., on the corner with William St. The shop rents foam boards for new surfers, as well as wetsuits and boogie boards. (☎03 5289 1673. Boards $25 per ½-day, $40 per day. Wetsuit $15/20. Boogie boards $15/20. Open daily 9:30am-5:30pm.)

The opportunities to explore Victoria's best rainforests are limitless. Reaching the trailheads and waterfalls with a car is easiest, though you can take a long walk to some of them. For those without a car, try **No Hurry No Worries,** which runs a private tour with a stop at Erskine Falls, a drive through the national park to Gentle Annie, fruit picking and trout fishing, and a grand finale at Deans Marsh and an art gallery. (☎03 5236 3481 or 04 2906 0646. 4-5hr. tour, pickup from Lorne visitors center 10am. Booking required.)

**⚑ NIGHTLIFE. The Lorne Hotel,** 176 Mountjoy Pde., is the place to be on Friday and Saturday nights. Lorne's entire 20-something population turns out to dance the night away at this hip locale with floor-to-ceiling picture windows and pool tables. (☎03 5289 1409; www.lornehotel.com.au. Ages 18+. F nights DJ, Sa nights live band or DJ. Cover $5-10, more for special events. Open 10am-late, usually until 1-3am.) Locals pour into **Ba Ba Lu,** 6a Mountjoy Pde., around 7:30pm on Sundays, when local bands and Melbourne groups start their show. Enjoy the featured paella, or just chill to the music with a glass of wine from their extensive list—Australian labels only, of course. (☎03 5289 1808. Tapas $9-11. Dinner mains $12-32. Open 8:30am-1am. MC/V.) Another popular Sunday night music scene is at **Kostas,** 48 Mountjoy Pde. (☎03 5289 1885. Dinner mains $15-27, reservations recommended. Open daily 6pm-late.)

> **KOALA SIGHTING.** On the drive westward from Lorne to Apollo Bay, you'll have a guaranteed koala sighting because they lounge in the gum trees. Just after the Kennet River sign and the bridge, turn right on Grey River Rd. Follow the road only a couple hundred meters (if you pass the BBQ of the caravan park, you've gone too far). And then, just look up!

# APOLLO BAY                                                            ☎03

In an idyllic cove at the base of the rolling Otway mountains, Apollo Bay (pop. 1400) is a beach hamlet that has seen a boom in tourism in recent years. As increasing numbers of sun-lovers gather at beachfront cafes, waves lap at the shore, and glowworms light up the quiet nights. Apollo Bay remains a placid setting with great budget accommodations, making it a good choice for a few days' rest on the Great Ocean Road. The town also boasts one of Australia's largest summer music festivals in April (see **Outdoor Activities**).

**▐ TRANSPORTATION.** V/line **buses** leave from the front of the visitors center (M-F 3 per day; Sa-Su 2 per day) going to Geelong (2hr., $13), Lorne (1hr., $3.50), and Melbourne (3hr., $19.40). The "Coastal Link" buses also runs Warrnambool with a 30min. stop at the Twelve Apostles, a 15min. stop at Loch Ard Gorge, and 10min. stops at London Bridge and Bay of Islands (3hr.; M, W, F 1:30pm; $15).

**▐▐ ORIENTATION AND PRACTICAL INFORMATION.** The **Great Ocean Road** is the main street through town. Helpful volunteers will book accommodations and tours and advise on road closures and campsite availability in the Otways at the **Visitors Centre,** 100 Great Ocean Rd. (☎03 5237 6529 or 1800 689 297. Internet access $4 per 30min. Open daily 9am-5pm.) The stretch of highway through town also has two 24hr. **ATMs. Internet access** is available at **Nautigals Cafe,** 57-59 Great Ocean Rd. (Open daily 8:30am-5pm. $5 per 30min.) In case of emergency, contact the **police,** 31 Nelson St. (☎03 5237 6750) or the **hospital** on McLachlan St. (☎03 5237 8500). The **post office** is located at 155-161 Great Ocean Rd., Shop 1. (☎03 5237 6205. Open M-F 9am-5pm.) **Postal Code:** 3233.

**▐ ACCOMMODATIONS.** Apollo Bay has the highest concentration of great hostels in one town on the Great Ocean Road. **Surfside Backpacker ❷,** on the corner of the Great Ocean Rd. and Gambier St., provides guesthouse comfort at backpacker prices with two kitchens and lounge areas, a record player and TV, and great ocean views. Robyn, the owner, is one of the friendliest, most helpful people you're likely to meet. (☎03 5237 7263, 04 1932 2595, or 1800 357 263; www. surfsidebackpacker.com. Wheelchair-accessible. Internet access $2 per 15min. Book ahead in summer. Reception 8am-10pm. Sites in courtyard $12 per person; dorms from $20-25; doubles from $50, ensuite from $70. MC/V.) Billing itself as "the chilled-out cottage by the sea," the relaxed **Apollo Bay Backpackers ❷,** 47 Montrose Ave., is on a quiet residential street, a 10min. walk from the Great Ocean Road. For surfing enthusiasts, the owner provides lessons and free transport to the ocean. (☎03 5237 7360, 1800 113 045, or 04 1934 0362; www.apollobaybackpackers.com.au. Continental breakfast included. Free use of bikes and golf clubs. Surfboard rental $20 per day. Internet access $5 per hr. Dorms $22; singles and doubles in neighboring cottage $55; 2-bedroom self-contained unit $120-140, can sleep 5. MC/V.) For the backpacker who wants to relax in posh digs, head to the more expensive **Eco Beach YHA ❸,** 5 Pascoe St. Located in a large modern beach house with tons of amenities and spotless, new facilities. To get a free bed in this amazing hostel, put in 2hr. of work per day in housecleaning and chores; you must have an Australian working visa. (☎03 5237 7899. Dorms $30-37, YHA $27; singles $72/65; doubles $83.50-89/75; family room $106-109/95. Internet access $6 per hr. Luggage locker rental $2. Reception 8-10am and 5-9:30pm. MC/V.) While most nearby campsites are free, there are few places where you can set up a tent directly on the beach. **Skenes Creek Beachfront Caravan Park ❶,** about 5km east of Apollo Bay, has hot showers, BBQ, laundry, a TV lounge, and a basic camp kitchen. (☎03 5237 6132 or 04 0293 7819; www.skenescreek.com. Sites $19-27, powered $22-34. MC/V)

**⬛ FOOD.** The **Bay Leaf Cafe ❷,** 131 Great Ocean Rd., has a creative menu for great prices. Try the roasted pumpkin, caramelized onions, and goat cheese tart ($14.80) or the lamb and olive burger ($15.80) on warm turkish bread. (☎03 5237 6470. Breakfast $4-14. Lunch and dinner $10-18. Open Oct.-Mar. M and Sa-Su 8am-3:30pm, Tu-Sa 8am-late; Apr.-Sept. daily 8am-3:30pm. MC/V.) The cosmic center of Apollo Bay's hippie culture is The **Sandy Feet Cafe & Health Foods ❶,** 139 Great Ocean Rd., where you can get your own astrological calendar for $10, along with a veggie burger or salad. Award-winning pies are $5.50. (☎03 5237 6995. Breakfast $6.50-10. Open daily 7:30am-4:30pm. Cash only.)

**◪ ◩ BEACHES AND SIGHTS.** While the Otways get all the attention, there are plenty of things to see right around town, starting with the gently curving bay itself, best viewed from the **Marriners Lookout.** From the carpark on Marriners Lookout Rd., about 1.5km from Apollo Bay toward Lorne, a short, steep trail (1km, 20min. roundtrip) leads to the lookout. The best surf beach in the area for advanced surfers is **⬛Johanna Beach,** 30min. of Apollo Bay west along the Great Ocean Rd. Johanna Red is a sealed road leading to the beach, while Johanna Blue, farther from Apollo Bay, is unsealed. For non-surfers, the beach is an excellent, and often underestimated, scenic stop amid rolling green hills. There is also surf for all levels, within walking distance from town and Skenes Creek east of town, at Marengo; catch the bus to Geelong to reach Skenes Creek. **Hodgy's Surf Center,** 143 Great Ocean Rd., rents boards and wetsuits. (Surfboard $20 per 2hr.; wetsuit $10 per 2hr.)

**⬛ OUTDOOR ACTIVITIES AND TOURS.** There are so many tours and trips that take advantage of Apollo Bay and its surroundings that it would take weeks (and a lot of cash) to do them all. Highly recommended is **⬛Apollo Bay Seal Kayak Tours,** which kayaks to the nearby Marengo Marine Sanctuary to visit the seal colony in their natural environment. (☎04 0549 5909; www.apollobaysurf-kayak.com.au. 2hr. tour $55 per person.) The same company runs the **Apollo Bay Surf School** (1hr. lesson $45) and rents out beach gear (full-day prices: surfboard $50, wetsuit $11, fishing rod $14) and camping gear (2-day camping package for 2, including sleeping bags and liners, inflatable roll mats, cooking utensils, hand torch, stove, 2-person tent, and backpacks $85.)

Recreational fishing is a popular activity in Apollo Bay, both from the beach (fishing permit required, purchase at visitors center) and with **Apollo Bay Fishing & Adventure Tours.** (4hr. inshore fishing $85, children $77; 6hr. deep-sea shark fishing $200 per person.) They also organize scenic tours to the seal colony and sunset cruises to the Cape Otway lighthouse ($30, children $20) and shark fishing. (☎03 5237 7888 or 04 1812 1784; www.apollobayfishing.com.au. Booking required.) For an airborne adventure, **Wingsports** has hang-gliding and parasailing, and on a sunny day a flight off Marriners Lookout can't be beat. (☎04 1937

8616; www.wingsports.com.au. Tandem paragliding $150; tandem hang-gliding $250.) **Apollo Bay Aviation** does 45min. round-trip flights to the Twelve Apostles (☎1800 538 735; www.apollobayaviation.com.au. $190 per person with 2 passengers; rates drop with more passengers. Booking required.) Those looking for a bit of exercise might want to try a mountain biking tour with **Otway Expeditions** through the lush Otway forest to the ocean. (☎03 5237 6341 or 04 1900 7586; 2-3hr. tour $55 per person, min. 6 people, max. 10. Booking required.) The same company also offers 6- and 8-wheel buggy adventure tours that take you across dams and through fern gully tracks in the national park ($40 per person, min. 2). **Otway Eco Tours** runs "Paddle with the Platypus" guided canoe tours for a chance to see a platypus in the wild. (☎03 5236 6345. 4hr. canoe tour $85, children $50.) Among Apollo Bay's most illuminating features are its glowworms. **Sunroad Tours,** 71 Costin St., leaves just after dark for a 1hr. tour to the Otways to spot the bright bugs. (☎03 5237 6080 or 04 2900 2296. Pickup and dropoff at accommodation. Tours daily $30, under 12 free.) Each year in April, the town grooves to the sounds of the ⓜ**Apollo Bay Music Festival,** which attracts groups from all over the world and a crowd that books every available bed and campsite in town. (☎03 5237 6761; www.apollobaymusicfestival.com. All-weekend tickets around $30, concessions $10. Early-bird ticket prices available at the end of January, about $20 cheaper.) On Saturday mornings (9am-1pm) the **Apollo Bay Market** sets up on the foreshore and sells local handicrafts.

# GREAT OTWAY NATIONAL PARK

Starting as far east as Anglesea and continuing to Cape Otway, 60km west of Apollo Bay, the Great Otway National Park encompasses a wide variety of terrain from Victoria's most beautiful rainforests, waterfalls, and the rugged coastal hikes of the Great Ocean Walk. The park's highlights center around the Redwood forest west of Apollo Bay and the rainforest and waterfalls near Lorne. Before heading off on any adventures, stop at the **Lorne** (p. 621) or **Apollo Bay** (p. 623) visitors centers if arriving from the east, or the Port Campbell visitors center if entering the park from the west. The centers have the latest information on trail and campsite closures and conditions, as well as the invaluable **map** of the Otways, covering the National Park, the Otway Forest Park, the Great Ocean Walk, and the Old Beech Rail Trail ($16). If you arrive after visitors center hours, the YHA hostel in Lorne has maps for its guests. There is also a permanent map posted outside the Lorne visitors center beside a list of hotel vacancies that is updated nightly.

**LORNE OTWAY HIKES AND SIGHTS.** Bordering Lorne, the northeastern section of the park, which used to be Angahook-Lorne State Park, has more than 64km of walking trails that meander through temperate rainforests, cool fern gullies, and past striking waterfalls. It is helpful to have a car to access most of the trailheads, though several walks do start from the town center. **Erskine Falls** (7.5km, 4hr. one-way) begins at the bridge over the Erskine River in Lorne and follows the river through the rainforests of the park and past Splitter and Straw Falls before arriving at the 38m Erskine Falls, the most famous in the area. The falls are also accessible by car; follow signs from town. Those without a ride can get a **taxi** from Lorne (☎04 0989 2304; approximately $21). A much shorter walk from town will bring you to **Teddy's Lookout,** a high point at the southern edge of town that presents sweeping views of forested mountains abutting wide-open ocean. (30min. walk; go up Bay St. from the Great Ocean Road in Lorne and make a left on George St.) The **Allenvale Mill Site,** a 30min. walk or 10min. drive from town along Allenvale Rd., is a good jumping-off point for a beautiful trail that leads to Phantom Falls, the Canyon, Henderson, and Won Wondah Falls before winding up at the Sheoak carpark. From there, walk back along the road to Allenvale carpark (9km, 4hr. round-trip).

The other main trailheads in the area, the Blanket Leaf Picnic Area and the Sheoak Picnic Area, are best reached by car, though you can also walk to them from Lorne. Various easy tracks begin at the Sheoak Picnic Area, a 1hr. walk up Allenvale Rd. from Lorne. The walk to **Sheoak Falls** (1hr.) follows a gentle track by the creek and eventually reaches the ocean, while the **Lower Kalimna Falls Walk** (1hr.) leads beneath a waterfall. From there you can continue on to the **Upper Kalimna Falls Walk** (additional 30min.). A little farther, ▨**Phantom Falls** (1hr. one-way) is one of the most stunning hikes in the park, providing a sense of the majesty and isolation of the rainforest. The trail is for experienced hikers and dangerous after a heavy rain, as it involves a lot of slippery rock-hopping. The trail ends at Allenvale Rd., close to the Allenvale Mill Site.

**LORNE OTWAY CAMPING. Allenvale Mill ❶**, a 200m walk from the carpark, is among the park's nicest spots and has pit toilets. Take Otway St. from Lorne center; at the rotary, follow Allenvale Rd. The carpark is past Qdos Cafe on the left. The largest free facility is on Hammonds Rd., in Airey's Inlet, a 30min. drive east of Lorne. Take Banbra Rd. from the Inlet.

**APOLLO BAY OTWAY HIKES AND SIGHTS.** A number of highlights can be seen by making a counterclockwise loop from Apollo Bay toward Melba Gully. From Apollo Bay, start your tour by heading east along the Great Ocean Road and turn left onto Skenes Creek Rd., which offers views of the surrounding mountains. Follow the sign for the Sabine Picnic Ground, starting point for the trail down to **Sabine Falls** (1.5km, 1hr. roundtrip), a moderate walk through the rainforest. The unspectacular falls at the hike's conclusion are overshadowed by the exotic foliage and bubbling brooks en route. Another 10min. back down the same road will bring you to the turnoff for Beech Forest, C159. This is the start of **Turton's Track** (30min.), a 12km stretch of gravel switchbacks through the heart of the rainforest—driving down this one-lane, two-way road is a not-to-be-missed experience. Signs lead to two more waterfalls at the end of Turton's: **Hopetourn Falls** (1km, 25min. roundtrip), whose roaring waters are visible from the carpark and the valley below, and the moderately difficult trail to **Beauchamp Falls** (3km, 1hr. round-trip). The three-tiered **Triplet Falls** (1.8km, 40min. loop) are nearby, just off Beech Forest Rd., on Phillip's Rd. heading west.

Along Beech Forest Rd., signs lead to the brand new steel structure, **The Otway Fly Tree Top Walk,** which is the longest (600m) and highest (25m) forest canopy walk in the world, from where you can climb to the top of a spectacular 47m high lookout to see the giant Redwoods from above. A ranger is always on hand to answer any questions. Allow 45min. for the walk. (☎03 5235 9200 or 1800 300 477; www.otwayfly.com. Open daily 9am-5pm. Last ticket 6pm in summer. $19.50, children $9; discounted adult tickets available from Apollo Bay visitors center, $17.) In Melba Gully, **Madsen's Track,** 5km past Lavers Hill and 40min. from Apollo Bay, is a short walk (30min. round-trip) through a spectacular section of rainforest that contains the grand and imposing "Big Tree," a 300-year-old Otway Messmate. Glowworms are prolific along this track at night. The **Mait's Rest Rainforest Walk** (1km, 30min. loop), one of the best-known rainforest walks in Victoria, is 17km west of Apollo Bay, halfway to the cape. Check out the Myrtle beech, whose roots sprung from three trees and grew together. Shortly after Johanna's Beach, heading east toward Apollo Bay, is the turnoff for the **Cape Otway Lightstation,** the mainland's oldest lighthouse (built in 1848). Take the tour to view the Bass Strait to the east and the Southern Ocean to the west. (☎03 5237 9240. Open daily 9am-5pm, last admission 4:45pm. $114, concessions $912, children $7.50. Guided tours daily 11am, 2, 3pm included with admission.) Lining the southern portion of the park is the 91km **Great Ocean Walk** (www.greatoceanwalk.com.au). With step-on and step-off points, the walk is ideal for short day walks or longer trips; the entire walk would take about eight days, starting in Apollo Bay and ending in Princetown.

**APOLLO BAY OTWAY CAMPING.** For camping, check into the vast private **Bimbi Park ❶** (☎03 5237 9246; www.bimbipark.com.au; sites from $15, on-site vans from $40, cabins from $56), or use one of the five **camping areas ❶** in Otway National Park. Get information at the tourist office in Apollo Bay (see below) for bookings at Bimbi, or call **Parks Victoria** (☎13 19 63; open daily 9am-5pm) for information on the campsites around the park. All camping facilities in the Otways are free, except during peak times when fees may apply. Camping in picnic areas or carparks results in a fine. There are powered sites at caravan parks but none at the campgrounds. **Blanket Bay** has nice, remote sites. Follow Lighthouse Rd., then watch signs for a left turn. The area is safe for swimming. The **Aire River camping areas** can be reached from the Great Ocean Rd., another 5km west by way of the Horden Vale turnoff. The Aire River is suitable for swimming and canoeing, and three walks diverge from the grounds. **Johanna Beach** also has basic campsites (p. 624).



## PORT CAMPBELL ☎03

Stuck in the middle of the beautiful rock formations lining the Shipwreck Coast, Port Campbell (pop. 300) provides a convenient rest stop with great budget accommodations; however, nothing else about the town is budget, and the cheapest eats are pricier than the most expensive restaurants in other Great Ocean Road towns. Port Campbell is located west of the Twelve Apostles and Loch Ard Gorge, and east of the Arch, London Bridge, and the Grotto.

**TRANSPORTATION AND PRACTICAL INFORMATION.** V/Line **buses** depart from Ocean House Backpackers and head east to Melbourne via Apollo Bay (M, W, F; $27.20) and west to Warrnambool (M, W, F 10:15am; $5.40) with stops at the Twelve Apostles, Loch Ard Gorge, London Bridge, and the Bay of Islands. Call a **taxi** (☎04 3840 7777; approx. $25) to visit the Twelve Apostles.

In town, the Great Ocean Road becomes **Lord Street,** where most restaurants and shops can be found. The **visitors center,** on the corner of Morris and Tregea St., one block south of Lord St., has information on the Great Ocean Road as well as on nearby Otway National Park. (☎03 5598 6089. Open daily 9am-5pm.) Wi-Fi ($5 per 30min.) is available at **Loch Ard Motor Inn,** on Lord St. The **post office** is in the **Port Campbell General Store,** Lord St., which also has basic groceries. (☎03 5598 6379. Open daily 8am-7pm.) **Postal Code:** 3269.

**ACCOMMODATIONS.** With a porch facing the Cairns St. beach, **Ocean House Backpackers ❷** has a cozy, log-cabin feel and spotless facilities. The common area even has a fireplace. There is no on-site reception at the hostel; check in at the camping park around the corner. (☎03 5598 6223; www.portcampbell.nu/oceanhouse. Dorms $27. AmEx/MC/V.) The **Port Campbell Hostel ❷,** 18 Tregea St., one block south of Lord St., around the corner from the beach, has a huge kitchen and great location but a vacant feel, as the staff is often out. Laundry facilities and a BBQ area with picnic tables are available. Weary travelers are also offered free tea, coffee, and soup. (☎03 5598 6305; www.portcampbellhostel.com.au. Key deposit $5. Towels $1. Internet access $2 per 15min. Reception 8-10am and 5-10pm. Dorms $24; doubles $55; cabins $70. The annex has dorms for $21 and camping facilities for $10 per person, $15 for 2.) The **Port Campbell National Park Cabin and Camping Park ❷**, on Morris St. next to the visitors center, has BBQ, showers, and laundry, and serves as the booking office for the Ocean Beach Backpackers. (☎03 5598 6492; www.portcampbell.nu/camping. Reception 8:30am-9pm. Sites $25-27, powered $28-30; ensuite cabins $110-125, extra adult $12, extra child $6. AmEx/MC/V.)

**⬛ FOOD.** The throngs of tourists passing through Port Campbell have created a demand for all kinds of restaurants; many are pricey. Closing hours fluctuate depending on the crowds. The cheapest eatery is **Cafe on Lords ❶**, hidden behind The Splash complex. It has great pies ($3-3.50), sandwiches ($4-7.50) and lots of veggie options, like the spinach and ricotta burger for $6.50. (☎03 5598 6489. Cappuccino $3.50. Open daily 8am-3:30pm. Cash only.) The breakfasts ($5.50-14.50) at **12 Rocks Beach Bar and Cafe ❷**, on Lord St., are an excellent start to the day, while the smoothies ($5) are the perfect refreshment after a day on the beach. (☎03 5598 6123. Wraps and rolls $8. Lunch mains $14-18. Open daily 7am-late. Kitchen open 7-11am, noon-3pm, and 6-9pm. MC/V.) Nearly everything at **Nico's Pizza and Pasta ❸**, 25 Lord St., is delicious. The large pizza ($16-22.50) will satiate a standard lunch appetite, while the mediums are much smaller. (☎03 5598 6131. Open daily 6pm-late.)

**⬛ OUTDOOR ACTIVITIES.** The gentle **Port Campbell Discovery Walk** (4.7km) begins at the cliff base at the western end of the beach or at the carpark west of the bay. There are several reef breaks for more advanced surfers along the rocky coast, while the small beach along Cairns St. is good for swimming and has lifeguards on duty Sa-Su during school holidays. **Port Campbell Boat Charters,** headquartered at the service station on Lord St., offers crafts for diving, fishing, or sightseeing. (☎03 5598 6366. $50-150 per person, 4-person min.)

# THE SHIPWRECK COAST

Stretching from Princetown in the east to Warrnambool in the west, the Shipwreck Coast has panoramic views that attract thousands of visitors each year. The jagged formations and rocks jutting up from the sea took down more than 160 ships through the decades, and a few 19th-century anchors are still embedded in the beach. From the Twelve Apostles to Childers Cove, tourists pull out their cameras to get a snapshot of the picturesque coastline. Though most of the big sights can be covered in a day of driving, slowing down to get to the lesser-known sights or hikes will afford a chance to encounter this stretch of coastline without the crowds. The sights below are listed from east to west.

**TWELVE APOSTLES.** Those who aren't overeager to get to the Twelve Apostles themselves can appreciate their enormous scale from sea level by taking the The **Gibson Steps** to the shore; the turnoff is 2km east of the famed rock formations. **Gibson Beach** is beautiful, though the waters have dangerous riptides. The ⬛**Twelve Apostles** are the most famous of the rock formations in the area, and with good reason. At sunset, the stones blaze red before fading slowly to shadows in the waning light, and the spectacular vista will be enough to make you forget the hordes of tourists jostling for a view. The **Interpretive Centre** has displays that give more information about the rocks, and from the center a walkway goes under the highway to the Twelve Apostle boardwalk. (www.12apostlesnatpark.org. Open daily 9am-5pm.)

**THE ARCH, LONDON BRIDGE, AND THE GROTTO.** These three limestone oddities are the greatest testament to the natural forces of the Southern Ocean and the unrelenting Antarctic winds whipping from 3000km away that shape the coastline. The most visited of the three, **London Bridge,** isn't much of a bridge at all. In 1990, the bridge collapsed into the surf below, stranding two shocked but somehow unharmed tourists on the seaward pillar. London Bridge has fallen down, and some now refer to it as the London Stacks.

**BAY OF MARTYRS AND BAY OF ISLANDS.** After passing **Port Campbell** (p. 627), you'll reach the Bay of Islands Coastal Park, stretching 33km west along the coast. The Bay of Martyrs and Bay of Islands (both turnoffs clearly labeled on the Great Ocean Road) offer stunning views and walks among smaller limestone formations on the beach; in general, the crowds are thinner than at Twelve Apostles. **Worm Bay,** a poorly-marked turnoff directly before the Bay of Martyrs, is perhaps the best viewpoint along this stretch. ◨**Childers Cove** is the last notable limestone formation on this beautiful stretch of coast. Despite the fame of the Twelve Apostles, Childers Cove makes the statement "Saving the best for last" true. Located at the end of a narrow, 7km dead-end road, the cove is composed of three private inlets with access to deserted beaches. Paths from the carpark meander along the craggy coast leading to stunning views—each more spectacular than the last—of limestone cliffs and aqua waters.

---

 **THE BIG CHEESE.** Though the Great Ocean Road is famous for its coastline, the highway also runs through farmland full of grazing sheep and cows. These farm animals are the source of delicious local cheeses, which you can sample at a few cheese factories just off the highway. The **Timboon Farmhouse,** 15min. west of Port Campbell and 13km off the Great Ocean Rd., offers free samples of its homemade organic cheeses in the Mousetrap shop. You can enjoy a cheese platter ($123-36) along with local wines (from $5 per glass) and cheesecake in the garden seating area. (☎03 5598 3387. Open Oct-Apr. daily 10:30am-45pm; May-Sept. W-Su 10:30am-10:45pm. Follow the well-marked signs from Port Campbell or the Great Ocean Road) In the small township of Allansford, 13km east of Warrnambool, **Cheese-world** provides the perfect pit stop directly off the Great Ocean Road with free samples of half a dozen varieties of local cheeses with interesting flavors (try the curry cheddar or tomato and basil cheddar), as well as a small 1850s farm museum. (☎03 5563 2130; www.cheeseworld.com.au. Open M-F 8:30am-5pm, Sa 9am-4pm, Su 10am-4pm.)

---

# WARRNAMBOOL ☎03

The largest city on the Great Ocean Road, Warrnambool (WAR-na-bull; pop. 32,000) is just developed enough to support nightlife and amenities not found elsewhere along the coast. While its natural attractions lag behind some of the other stops along the Great Ocean Road, it does have a number of beautiful beaches as well as southern right whales off the coast from June to September. The variety of activities like whalewatching, excellent surfing, horseback-riding on the beach, miniature golf, and park-visiting makes Warrnambool a popular holiday destination for Australians and foreigners alike.

▐ **TRANSPORTATION.** The **V/Line Railway Station** (☎03 5561 4277) is on the south end of town, just north of Lake Pertobe on Merri St. V/Line **trains** run to Melbourne (3hr. 20min.; daily 5:45am, 11:45am, 5:08pm; $24.70) via Geelong (1hr. 20min. $17.80). V/Line **buses** run to: Ballarat (3hr.; M 6am and Tu 5:50am

$13); Mount Gambier (3hr.; M-F 11:30am, Sa 11:35am, Su 10:30am; $19.40); Port Fairy (25-40min.; daily 11:30am, 4:55, 10pm; $3.10); and Portland (1hr.; M-F 10:30am and 10pm, Sa 11:35am and 10pm, Su 10pm; $8.80). The "Coastal Link" bus runs to Apollo Bay, with brief stops at the Bay of Islands, London Bridge, Loch Ard Gorge, and the Twelve Apostles (3hr.; M, W, F 9am; $15). In town, **Transit Southwest** runs seven bus routes across the city, with stops at each location roughly on the hour; pick up a timetable from the visitors center or buy one at a newsstand for $0.20. (☎03 5562 1866. $1.80, concessions $0.90. Tickets good for 2hr. of unlimited rides.) For a **taxi,** call ☎13 10 08.

**▓▓ ⁊ ORIENTATION AND PRACTICAL INFORMATION.** The **Princes Highway**, which eventually becomes **Raglan Parade** in town, runs along the top edge of the downtown area. The town's main streets run south toward the sea from **Raglan Parade,** with **Banyan Street,** on the east side of downtown, turning into **Pertobe Road** to round the lake (before heading down to the bay, the beach, and then the breakwater). **Liebig Street,** the town's main drag, heads south from Raglan Pde. at the McDonald's, crossing Lava St., Koroit St., and Timor St. before finally winding up at **Merri St.** on the southern edge of downtown. The street is lined with restaurants, pubs, **banks,** and **ATMs.** The **visitors center,** in the Maritime Museum at Flagstaff Hill on Merri St. near Banyan, provides free maps of the area, has a message board filled with current events, and rents out mountain bikes to visitors. (☎03 5559 4620 or 1800 637 725; www.warrnamboolinfo.com.au. Internet access $5 per 30min. Bikes ½-day $20, full-day $30. Open daily 9am-5pm.) Other services include: **police,** 214 Koroit St. (☎03 5560 1333); **hospital** on Ryot St. (☎03 5563 1666); **library,** in the city council building at the south end of Liebig St. near the intersection with Timor St., with free **Internet access** (☎03 5562 2258; open M-Th 9:30am-5pm, F 9:30am-8pm, Sa 10am-noon); and two **post offices,** one on Koroit St. and the other on Timor St., both between Kepler and Liebig. (Open M-F 9am-5pm.) **Postal Code:** 3280.

**⁊ ACCOMMODATIONS.** Book well ahead in summer for the **Warrnambool Beach Backpackers ❷,** 17 Stanley St., as their colorful rooms close to the beach are undoubtedly the best in town. The friendly owners provide everything a backpacker could want, including Internet ($6 per hr.; Wi-Fi $10 for 3hr.), a licensed tiki bar, big-screen TV with DVD, a pool table, a full kitchen, coin laundry, and soda and snack machines. Guests can use mountain bikes, boogie boards, and fishing rods for free. The owners can also set you up with short-term work at local farms. To reach the backpackers, follow signs through town to the info center; at the corner of the info center, turn down Pertobe Rd. toward the beaches; follow until a roundabout at waters edge and turn right onto Stanley St. (☎03 5562 4874; www.beachbackpackers.com.au. Key deposit $10. Pickup and dropoff at train station. Reception daily until 11pm. Dorms $23; ensuite doubles $70, extra person $20. Weekly rate for short-term workers $120. MC/V.) For basic pub rooms at the cheapest rates in town, head to **Victoria Hotel ❷,** 90 Lava St., on the corner with Liebig St. in the center of town. (☎03 5562 2073. $20 per person, key deposit $20. MC/V.) There are six caravan parks in and around Warrnambool, and all are surprisingly expensive. **Surfside Holiday Park ❷,** on Pertobe Rd., has the best location, just steps from the surf beach; the prices are comparable, if not cheaper, than those of the other parks farther from the beach. (☎03 5559 4700; www.surfsidepark.com.au. Only unpowered sites offered from Christmas to Easter $35; powered Easter to Christmas $27, the rest of the year $40. 1-room cabins and cottages $72-128, 2-room $101-133. MC/V.) **Hotel Warrnambool ❸,** 185 Koroit St., on the corner with Kepler, is an old-fashioned hotel with a nice popular pub downstairs. (☎03 5562 2377; www.

hotelwarrnambool.com.au. Free Wi-Fi for guests. Breakfast included. Double rooms $100, ensuite $140. Pub open daily 11am-late.)

**FOOD.** The bottom half of Liebig St. has a cluster of great restaurants and bars. It's worth coming to Warrnambool just to eat the food at ⬛Bojangles ❷, 61 Liebig St. Award-winning, gourmet wood-fired pizzas ($12-19) come laden with delicious, creative toppings. (Restaurant ☎03 5562 8751, takeaway ☎03 5562 0666; www.bojangles.com.au. Open daily 5pm-late. MC/V.) A few doors up Liebig, **Figseller's Cafe ❷**, 89 Liebig St., has beautiful outdoor seating hidden behind the kitchen in the back. The cafe serves breakfast all day (fluffy pancakes with fresh fruit $9.50-11) and loads of veggie options. (☎03 5562 7699; www.figsellers.com. Open M-F 7am-5:30pm, Sa-Su 8am-5:30pm. MC/V.) Next door to Bojangles, hip **Fishtales ❶**, 63 Liebig St., cooks up a varied menu of fish, vegetarian pasta, and Asian food for under $13. (☎03 5561 2957. Breakfast $5-14. Open daily 7am-late. MC/V.) **Coles** supermarket is on Lava St. between Liebig and Kepler St. (Open daily 7am-10pm.)

**NIGHTLIFE.** With a student population studying at Deakin University, Warrnambool has the best nightlife on the Great Ocean Road. The neighborhood around the bottom of Liebig St. is where the students hit the pubs. The **Seanchai Irish Pub**, 62 Liebig St., is popular with university students and backpackers. Even on slow nights, the casual atmosphere makes for a good time, with drinks that are as cheap as they are strong (spirits $6.50). It's the only place in town with live music during the week—and, it has 10 different beers (pots $3.70, pints $7) on tap. (☎03 5561 7900. Free Internet. Open Tu-Sa 2pm-1am.) For more pub action, **Hotel Warrnambool,** 185 Koroit St, has a cool scene with live jazz on Thursday nights. (☎03 5562 2377; www.hotelwarrnambool.com.au. Pub open daily 11am-late.) Across the street, the **Whaler's Inn,** 53 Liebig St., has a contemporary style for the discerning drinker with live music on Friday and Saturday nights. The attached dance club, **C59,** has two dance floors playing Top 40, techno, and house music. (☎03 5562 8391; www.whalersinn.com.au. Pints $6, cocktails from $7.50. Bar open M-Sa 11:30am-late; club open W and F-Sa 10pm-late, last entry 1:30pm.) The diehard latenighters hit **The Gallery Nightclub,** 214 Timor St. on the corner of Kepler St., and dance to funk and soul downstairs, or acid and trance upstairs. (☎03 5562 0741. Open W-Sa 9pm-3am. Cover W $5, F $8, Sa $10.)

**SIGHTS AND ACTIVITIES.** Whale watching is the thing to do in Warrnambool from June to October; the info center has booklets on Southern Right Whales. Every winter in late May or June, a population of whales stops just off **Logans Beach**, to the east of the Bay, to give birth. They stay until September, when the calves are strong enough to swim south to Antarctica. To watch these beautiful beasts blow and breach, tourists gather on viewing platforms built above the beach's delicate dune vegetation. **Dive Inn Charters** is Warrnambool's catch-all tour company and leads whale watches as well as fishing or diving tours. (☎03 5562 5044 or 04 1934 9058; www.diveinncharters.com.au. Whalewatching from $40. 3hr. fishing tour $65, includes equipment.) Boasting ample beach space and parks, Warrnambool is a great spot for outdoor recreation. Though a wildly cliché image, horseback riding on the beach is an unforgettable experience with ⬛Rundell's Beach Trail Rides. Even beginners who have never mounted a horse before will learn to trot and canter on the shore. (☎08 5565 9111. 1hr. $45, 2hr. $60. Ask about the *Let's Go* discount. Booking required.) The protected bay has a beautiful beach. **Easyrider Surf School** offers surf lessons at good prices. (☎03 5521 7646; www.easyridersurfschool.com.

au. 2hr. group lessons $40, min. 3 people; 3 group lessons for $99. 1hr. private lessons $69. Boards, wetsuits, and sunscreen included. Book ahead.)

At low tide, it's possible to cross the breakwater over to **Middle Island,** where a colony of fairy penguins returns at dusk to roost. (Guests at nearby Warrnambool Beach Backpackers can borrow flashlights from the front desk.) Be careful wading to the island as tides change, making the walk dangerous. The 5.7km **promenade** lining Warrnambool Bay is popular with cyclists, in-line skaters, and evening strollers. West of the bay, the lookout at **Thunder Point** has trails along the coast and inland along the Merri River. Step off the path to find a secluded spot to watch the sun meet the sea. Families will enjoy **Adventure Playground,** adjacent to Lake Pertobe. The park, built over 35 hectares of former swampland, features a maze, giant slides, BBQ, picnic area, and leisure walks.

If your visit doesn't coincide with that of the whales, don't despair; the **Flagstaff Hill Maritime Museum,** overlooking Lady Bay on Merri St., is fascinating even for those not usually intrigued by nautical history. The huge museum is an outdoor recreation of a late-19th-century coastal village. "Shipwrecked," the museum's spectacular light show, is not to be missed. (☎03 5559 4600; www.flagstaffhill.com. Open daily 9am-5pm, last entrance 4pm. $16, children $6. Light shows daily at sundown, $25.50/14; advance booking required.)

# PORT FAIRY ☎03

There's not much to do in Port Fairy (pop. 2600)—which is exactly its appeal.

📟 **TRANSPORTATION.** Southwest Roadways **buses** leave from the bus depot next to the visitors center on Banks St. (☎03 5568 1355; office open M-F 9:10am-3pm) and head to Hamilton (M-Th 4:05pm, F 12:20pm) via Warrnambool (M-F 7 per day, Sa 4 per day, Su 2 per day; $5.40).

🔳🇮 **ORIENTATION AND PRACTICAL INFORMATION.** Most of the action in this sleepy town occurs on **Banks Street** and **Sackville Street,** which intersect a few blocks from the water. Tour maps are available from the **Port Fairy and Region Visitor Info Centre,** on Bank St. (☎03 5568 2682; www.port-fairy.com. Open daily 9am-5pm.) The **library,** 65 Sackville St. (☎03 5568 2248), has free **Internet.** (Open M, W, F 10:30am-1pm and 1:30-5pm.) The **post office,** 22 Bank St., Shop 2, also has Internet. (Open M-F 9am-5pm. $5 per hr.) **Postal Code:** 3284.

🗝 **ACCOMMODATIONS.** Budget travelers are welcomed by the hospitable couple at the **Emoh YHA Hostel ❷,** 8 Cox St. Located in a lovely old house built by Port Fairy's first official settler, William Rutledge, the Emoh has satellite TV, a pool table, BBQ, laundry, and Internet access ($2 per 20min.). Free use of bikes, boogie boards, and fishing rods is available to guests, and the owners sometimes leave out fresh herbs and tomatoes from their garden. (☎03 5568 2468. If reception isn't in when you arrive, just pick up the free blue phone to connect directly to the owners. Book ahead Dec.-Apr. Dorms $26.50, YHA $22; singles $41.50/37; doubles $72/62; apartment for 4 with kitchen and lounge $150. Cash only.) For basic pub rooms in the center of town, head to **The Star of the West Hotel ❷,** 76 Sackville St. (☎03 5568 1715; www.thestarhotel.com.au. Singles $30; doubles $40. MC/V.) In Yambuk, 17km west of Port Fairy, **Eumarella Backpackers ❷,** on High St., is the perfect spot to relax. The remote hostel is a converted 19th-century schoolhouse, run by the Peek Whurrong people. Amenities include a kitchen, free laundry, and free canoe rental for guests. (☎03 5568 4204. Dorms and doubles $20 per person. Cash only.)

**FOOD.** With a creative gourmet menu, reasonable prices, and large windows overlooking the ocean, **Time and Tide Cafe ❷**, 21 Thistle Pl., down a dirt road just out of town toward Portland, is without a doubt the best place to eat on the Great Ocean Road. (☎03 5568 2134. Filling sandwiches from $9. Open Th-Su 10am-5pm.) One of the most popular breakfast spots in town, **Rebecca's Cafe ❶**, 70-72 Sackville St., sells omelettes and quiches as well as pastas and risottos ($12-16) for lunch. Try the ice cream next door at **Rebecca's Ice Creamery ❶**. (☎03 5568 2533. Breakfast $6-15. Open daily 7am-6pm. Cash only.)

**OUTDOOR ACTIVITIES.** Activities in Port Fairy are lowkey and center around the waterfront. The beach is excellent for swimming (lifeguards on duty daily in Jan. and Sa-Su in Dec. and Feb.), and the wharf is a great place to watch the ships coming in while enjoying fresh seafood. **Lady Julia Percy Island,** 19km out to sea, is home to seals, fairy penguins, and peregrine falcons. Visits can be arranged at the wharf. **Port Fairy Boat Charter,** stationed at the harbor, goes to Lady Julia for $55. The **Surf Shop Port Fairy,** 33 Bank St., runs surfing and diving lessons at great prices, and also rents wetsuits, body boards, water skis, and snorkel gear. (☎03 5568 2800; www.daktarisport.com.au. Open daily in summer 9am-5:30pm; otherwise 11am-5:30pm. Board rental $5 per hr. 2hr. group surf lesson $33, private $60. 2hr. 1-on-1 diving lesson for beginners or guided diving tour for experienced divers $99; book surfing and diving lessons/tours ahead by email or phone.) The **Kitehouse,** 27 Cox St., sells all kinds of kites, wind socks, and other high-flying toys. Free kite-flying workshop during school holidays at George Dodd's Reserve daily 3-5pm. (☎03 5568 2782 or 04 0831 2422. Open daily Jan. 9am-6pm; Feb.-Dec. 10am-5pm.)

**FESTIVALS.** Port Fairy has made a name for itself as the unlikely host for some of the world's best music. Almost every bed on the Shipwreck Coast is booked during the **Port Fairy Folk Festival,** held during Australia's Labor Day weekend in March. The festival attracts folk, blues, and country music acts from all over the world. During the weekend, the population of the town jumps from 2600 to over 30,000. In addition to the main ticketed program, music lines the streets in free venues. (☎03 5568 2227; www.portfairyfolkfestival.com. Order tickets months in advance. Tickets around $160.)

# PORTLAND                                                        ☎03

Portland (pop. 10,000) was the first town settled in Victoria, and its modern industrial feel betrays its age. Before the Henty brothers and their sheep enterprise permanently settled the area in 1834, this area was a base for whalers, sealers, and escaped convicts. Its harbor is still active, and maritime history buffs may take pleasure in its storied past; however, most travelers use the town as a departure for the Great South West Walk and Cape Bridgewater. The budget accommodations are definitely lacking, so a quick stop is adequate time to explore what the town has to offer.

**TRANSPORTATION.** V/Line **buses** (☎13 61 96; www.viclink.com.au) depart from the north side of Henty St., just west of Percy St. Buses pass through Port Fairy (50min., 2 per day, $6.20) to Warrnambool (1hr., 2 per day, $8.80), where Melbourne connections stop. Heading west, buses go to Mount Gambier (55min.; M-Th 1:10pm, F 6:30 and 11:20pm, Sa 1:15pm, Su 11:50pm; $8.10).

**ORIENTATION AND PRACTICAL INFORMATION.** The two main north-south streets in town are the waterfront **Bentinck Street,** with cafes, takeaway

**VICTORIA**

joints, and pubs, and **Percy Street,** one block up, which has the majority of the town's commercial activity. Percy is the continuation of the Henty Hwy., which enters the city from the north. Percy and Bentinck St. are connected in the center of town by Henty, Julia, and Gawler St. At the town's southern end, Bentinck St. becomes Cape Nelson Rd. and heads to Cape Nelson State Park.

The **Portland Visitors Centre,** on Lee Breakwater St., down the hill by the bay, provides Internet ($3 per 30min.) and rents bikes. (☎03 5523 2671 or 1800 035 567. Bikes ½-day $12, full-day $20. Open daily 9am-5pm.) If there's a crowd at the visitors center, you can learn about outdoor attractions at the **Parks Victoria office,** 8-12 Julia St. (☎13 19 63. Open M-F 8am-5:30pm, Sa-Su 9am-6pm.) **Internet** and Wi-Fi are available at the **library,** 40 Bentinck St., across from the large Mac's Hotel (☎03 5523 1497. Open M-Th 10am-5:30pm, F 10am-6pm, Sa 10am-1pm. $3 per 30min.) In case of emergency, contact the **police** (☎03 5523 1999) or the **hospital,** on the corner of Bentinck and Fern St. (☎03 5521 0333). The **post office** is at 108 Percy St. (open M-F 9am-5pm). **Postal Code:** 3305.

**▐ ACCOMMODATIONS.** The **Royal Hotel ❸,** 119 Percy St., provides clean and comfortable pub rooms at the cheapest prices in town. (☎03 5521 1111. Singles $30; doubles $55. MC/V.) Close to the waterfront in town, the **Gordon Hotel ❸,** 63 Bentinck St., provides pub accommodations with great harbor views. (☎03 5523 1121. Backpackers $40 per person. Singles $45; doubles $65. MC/V.) For those willing to venture farther afield, **Bellevue Backpackers ❷,** Sheoke Rd., on the way to Cape Nelson, provides cozy trailers with small dining area, kitchen, and TV. From Portland, follow signs to Cape Nelson Lighthouse; after the left-hand turn near the cemetery, look for the white sign on the left just before Yellow Rock. (☎03 5523 4038. Campsites $10. Trailer $25 per person. Cash only.)

**▐ FOOD.** Just across the street from the port, laid-back **Kopi on the Beach ❶,** 49 Bentinck St., provides delicious and healthful tortillas, wraps, and focaccia for great prices ($7-8.50). Breakfast is served all day; you can't beat fluffy pancakes with fresh fruit and ice cream for $6-8. (☎03 5523 1822. Open M-F 7am-3pm, Sa-Su 9am-3pm. MC/V.) **Kokopelli's Kafe and Ice Bar ❸,** 79 Bentinck St., is a trendy lounge with a layer of ice lining the top of the bar to keep drinks cold. There are tapas ($2.70-6), plus pasta and risotto mains for $13-14. (☎03 5521 1200. All-day breakfast $3.20-10. Open Tu-Sa 8am-late, M and Su 8am-5pm. MC/V.) With advertisements for yoga classes covering the door, you can align your Chi at **Sunstream Wholefoods Takeaway ❶,** 49 Julia St., with vegetarian options. (Near the corner with Gawler St. ☎03 5523 4895. Open M-Tu and Th-F 9am-5:30pm, W 9am-5pm. Cash only.) A **Safeway** supermarket, 95-97 Percy St., is across from the post office. (Open daily 7am-10pm.)

**▣ SIGHTS.** Though the Portland Harbor area is safer today, many ships became intimately acquainted with its ocean floor. The **Maritime Discovery Centre,** in the same building as the visitors center, memorializes some of those ships and celebrates the city's fishing and whaling history. The prized display is the reconstructed skeleton of a sperm whale beached in 1987, complete with a bench built under the rib cage (☎03 5523 2671. Open daily 9am-5pm. $5.50, concessions $4.50, children free.) Behind the Maritime Centre, a restored 1885 **cable tram** will take you on a waterfront ride to several of Portland's tourist attractions. (Runs daily 10am-4pm. Buy tickets onboard or at the visitors center. $12, concessions $10, children $6.) The **Powerhouse Motor and Car Museum,** on the corner of Glenelg and Percy St., has a beautiful collection of privately owned antique cars and a restored tram. (☎03 5523 5795. Open daily 10am-4pm. $5, concessions $4, children $1.)

## CAPE BRIDGEWATER

Stretching 65km from Portland to the South Australia border, the beautiful **Discovery Bay Coastal Park** provides bush walks along the Great South West Walk, the Blowholes, the Petrified Forest, and the Springs. Access to the coastal park is easiest from Cape Bridgewater, just 18km west of Portland.

From Portland, take Otway St. west until it becomes Bridgewater Rd. On the right, you will reach a lovely stretch of sand, the **Cape Bridgewater Beach,** which has great surf and safe swimming. Continue up the road another 200m to reach the higher carpark, from where you can embark on the spectacular ⊠**seal walk.** The winding cliff trail (2hr. round-trip) is steep, but the effort is worth it for unbelievable ocean views from atop the cliffs. A **longer hike** (9km, 3hr.) to the seals runs in the opposite direction, following the Great South West Walk from the blowholes carpark to the seal walk carpark, but requires you to find a way back to your car. To avoid the hard work altogether, ⊠**Seals By Sea** runs 45min. boat tours to the seal colony and its caves, allowing you to get up close and personal. To reach the Seals by Sea jetty, park at the higher carpark and follow the seal walk partway; the 20min. walk down to the jetty is just as beautiful as the boat tour itself. (☎03 5526 7247 or 1800 267 247. $30, concessions $25, children $20. Booking required.) Straight up from the higher car park, waves crash into the **Blowholes** at the foot of the sea cliffs. To the left is the **Petrified Forest,** eerie rock formations in cavities left when trees rotted away centuries ago. Virtually indistinguishable from tidal pools, the **Springs** (45min. round-trip) are in fact freshwater springs formed as rainwater seeps through limestone farther inland. If the surf at Cape Bridgewater has left you wanting more, head to **White's Beach** on the northern side of the cape, which provides a nice surf break as well. On the way, you'll pass the freshwater **Bridgewater Lakes,** a popular swimming, boating, and picnicking area. From Cape Bridgewater, the Bridgewater Lakes Rd. will lead you back to the Nelson-Portland Rd., passing by the Amos Rd. turnoff, which heads to White's Beach.

The unmanned kiosk on the Cape Bridgewater beach has limited tourist info, but the Portland visitors center can give you ample information about Cape Bridgewater and the Discovery Bay Coastal Park. The **Cape Bridgewater Holiday Camp ❶,** another 100m past the higher carpark, offers great views of the bay and beach as well as a range of accommodation options from camping to more upscale rooms in the town's first church, dating from 1870. (☎03 5526 7267; Sites $20, powered $25, extra person $8. Dorms $20; doubles $60; triples $68; quads $76. Self-contained cabins for 4 $120. Cash only.) The **Bridgewater Bay Cafe ❶,** 1661 Bridgewater Rd., just next to the beach at the lower carpark, has all-day breakfast, cheap sandwiches, burgers ($7-10), and of course, fish and chips. (☎03 5526 7155. Cappuccino $3.10. Open M-Th 9am-6pm, F 9am-9pm, Sa 9am-7pm, Su 9am-8pm. Cash only.)

# THE WIMMERA AND MALLEE

The Wimmera and Mallee regions fill the remote northwestern part of Victoria. Mountains, lakes, swamps, wildlife reserves, rich farmland, and rugged bushland can all be found in this area. West of the Goldfields, inland Victoria rises with the rugged peaks of **Grampians National Park** before gradually settling into an immense plain that stretches west into South Australia and north into New South Wales. The Wimmera region takes its name from the river that begins in the Grampians and wanders north past the **Little Desert National Park.** North of Little Desert and west of the Sunraysia Hwy., all the way up to Mildura, is the semi-arid expanse of the Mallee, named for the mallee eucalyptus, a hardy water-hoarding tree that thrives in the rugged plains.

# GRAMPIANS (GARIWERD) NATIONAL PARK

In 1836, Major Mitchell, in command of a British expedition, was hiking through seemingly endless plains, when he suddenly spotted a range of majestic hills. He named them the Grampians after a range in his home country of Scotland; the ensuing rush of settlers steadily pushed the Jardwadjali and Djab Wurrung Aboriginal people out of their ancestral home of Gariwerd. A park visit affords travelers insight into indigenous cultural history (80% of the rock art sites in Victoria can be found here, including five major sites open to the public), as well as access to breathtaking ranges, peerless rock climbing and hiking, abundant wildlife, rare birds, and a springtime carpet of technicolor wildflowers. In early 2006, a devastating fire tore through the park, scorching much of the landscape. Though the ecosystem is slowly regenerating, complete recovery will take many years; be sure to consult **Parks Victoria** (see below) and their updated maps to verify which trails and camp sites have reopened to the public.

| GRAMPIANS NATIONAL PARK AT A GLANCE | |
|---|---|
| **AREA:** 167,000 hectares. | **GATEWAYS:** Halls Gap (east); Horsham (north); Dunkeld (south). |
| **FEATURES:** Lookouts, waterfalls, hiking, rockclimbing, and lakes. | **CAMPING:** 110 campgrounds, each with dozens of sites. Camping $12.50 for up to 6 people and 1 car. $5.30 per additional car. |
| **HIGHLIGHTS:** Koori rock paintings, 160km of hiking tracks, the lookouts in the Wonderland, extensive rock climbing opportunities. | |

## TRANSPORTATION AND ORIENTATION

The northern approach passes through **Horsham,** at the junction of Western and Henty Hwy., roughly 18km north of the park. From the south, the town of **Dunkeld,** on the Glenelg Hwy., provides access via Mt. Abrupt Rd. From the east, the town of **Stawell** (rhymes with "shawl") is 26km away. The most convenient point of entry is on the eastern edge of the park at **Halls Gap** (**Budja Budja;** pop. 350), is the only town in the park itself. Nestled in a crevasse between two mountains, the tiny settlement has an overpriced grocery store, budget accommodations, a petrol station, and that's about it. Everything is clustered together in a small strip on **Grampians Road,** also called **Dunkeld Road, Stawell Road,** and sometimes even **Main Road,** which runs from Halls Gap to Dunkeld.

One V/Line **bus** per day leaves from opposite the **newsagency** in Halls Gap bound for Ararat (1hr.; $8.10) via Stawell (30min.; $5.40), Ballarat (2hr.; $17.80), and Melbourne (4hr.; $25.60). Several companies also run 2-3 day tours from Melbourne and Adelaide, with day stops in the Grampians. For a 1-day tour in the Grampians, **Eco Platypus Tours** runs a round-trip bus from Melbourne that stops at Reeds Lookout, the Balconies, and MacKenzie Falls. (☎03 9419 5950 or 1800 819 091; www.ecoplatypustours.com. Depart Melbourne W, F, Su 8:15am; return 9pm. $90 per person; group discounts.) From late Feb. to early Nov. you can hitch a ride on the **Sandlant schoolbus** between Halls Gap and Stawell (☎03 5356 9342; 30min., M-F 3 per day, $7.70).

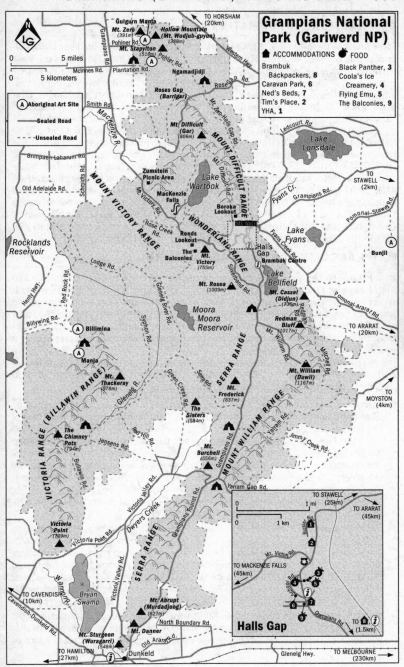

# Grampians National Park (Gariwerd NP)

🏕 ACCOMMODATIONS 🍴 FOOD

Brambuk
  Backpackers, 8
Caravan Park, 6
Ned's Beds, 7
Tim's Place, 2
YHA, 1

Black Panther, 3
Coola's Ice
  Creamery, 4
Flying Emu, 5
The Balconies, 9

Ⓐ Aboriginal Art Site
— Sealed Road
--- Unsealed Road

0    5 miles
0    5 kilometers

VICTORIA

Halls Gap

## 🔋 PRACTICAL INFORMATION

**The Brambuk Centre** (a.k.a., **National Park and Cultural Centre** and **Brambuk Living Cultural Centre**), 2.5km south of Halls Gap town center on Dunkeld Rd., is the best resource for those interested in the local Aboriginal culture. For handicapped travelers, the Brambuk Centre has a handy pamphlet listing wheelchair-accessible routes throughout the park. (☎03 5361 4000. Open daily 9am-4:45pm. Hiking maps $3.30, Riding and Touring map $6; donations appreciated.) Though the ranger office is not open to the public, **Parks Victoria** (☎13 19 63; www.parkweb. vic.gov.au) publishes helpful *Park Notes*, available at the Brambuk Centre. The **Halls Gap Visitors Centre** in the town center can answer many questions about the park as well, though it is geared toward accommodation and dining options. (☎03 5356 4616 or 1800 065 599; www.grampianstravel.com. Open daily 9am-5pm.) The **Mobil petrol station** has basic camping and food provisions and an **ATM.** (☎03 5356 4206. Open daily 7am-8pm.) If your car breaks down, **Stawell & Grampians Towing** (☎03 5358 4000) is open 24hr. The Halls Gap **police station** (☎03 5356 4411) is located just north of the town center, at the intersection of Grampians and Mt. Victory Rd. The **post office** is rather small and located just beside the general store. (Open M-F 9am-5pm.) **Postal Code:** 3381.

## 🏠 🏕 ACCOMMODATIONS AND CAMPING

In addition to the excellent hostels in and around Halls Gap, there are 140 major **camping ❶** areas in the park, all with toilets and fireplaces and most with water. Rangers advise stopping at the Brambuk Centre first for a map of the park's campsites and new information. All sites operate on a first come, first serve basis; campers must pay $12.50 (up to 6 people and 1 vehicle) for permits available at the Brambuk Centre. Those who arrive after-hours can pick up a permit and drop off the money in a box outside the center's doors. Bush camping is free but prohibited in certain regions including the Wonderland Range and the Lake Wartook watershed. Other prohibited areas are demarcated on maps; check with the park center before camping.

🏠 **Grampians YHA Eco-Hostel** (☎03 5356 4544), 700m north of the town center on Grampians Rd., at the corner of tiny Buckler St. Friendly managers take great care of the immaculate complex. Highlights include a sparkling kitchen, several cozy dens with TV or fireplace, and quaint bedrooms, each with balconies or doors into the backyard brush. Solar-heating, compost, and an herb garden and chicken coop are just some of the eco-friendly amenities. Internet $6 per hr. Free use of mountain bikes. Wash $2, dry $1. Wheelchair accessible. Reception 8-10am and 3-10pm. Book ahead, as its reputation alone attracts a steady stream of visitors year-round. For a free bed, do 2hr. of light duties each day; must have Australian work visa. 3- to 4-bed dorms with lockers $29, YHA $26; singles $62/56; doubles $75/65. MC/V. ❷

🏠 **Tim's Place** (☎03 5356 4288; www.timsplace.com.au), on Grampians Rd., 500m north of town center. Stay at Tim's cozy digs and meet the owner, who is committed to providing a paradise for budget travelers. Several new units, including immaculate 2-bedroom ensuite apartments with kitchens and dining areas. Free amenities include unlimited Internet and Wi-Fi, use of mountain bikes, golf cubs, tennis and badminton racquets, petanque equipment, and a pass to Brambuk Centre's Dreaming Theatre. Laundry $4. Dorms $25; singles $45; doubles $60; triples $75. Cash only. ❷

**Brambuk Backpackers** (☎03 5356 4250; www.brambuk.com.au/backpackers.htm). Located directly across the street from the Brambuk Centre. Run by the friendly Stephanie and Alan, Brambuk has a comfy lounge with A/C, fireplace, TV, and suede couches.

Large, clean kitchen. Includes continental breakfast and free pass to the Brambuk Centre's Dreaming Theatre. Laundry $4. Internet $6 per hr. Dorms 7- to 12-bed $19, 4-bed $23; doubles $55; family $80. Cash only. ❷

**Ned's Beds (Grampians Backpackers),** 2 Heath St. (☎03 5356 4296), just south of the Halls Gap Information Centre. Ned's collection of quaint cabins offers casual lodging and extras including TV/DVD player, kitchen, game room, laundry, and BBQ. Ned recently acquired a 2nd unit of cabins next to Tim's Place, which is called **Ned's Other Beds.** Internet $6 per hr. If you can't find the manager, walk over to the public pool (open daily 7-9am and 1-6:30pm) across the street from the Mobil station and ask for Blanche. Dorms $23-24; doubles $60. Cash only. ❷

**Halls Gap Caravan Park** (☎03 5356 4251; www.hallsgapcaravanpark.com.au), in the center of Halls Gap across from the Mobil station. Many walking trails start just behind the campground. Reception 8:30am-7pm. High season sites for 2 $25, low season $20; powered $30/25; extra person $5. On-site caravans for 2 $53/47. Units from $75. 7th night free during low season. MC/V. ❷

##  FOOD

Budget-savvy travelers purchase food at a supermarket before arriving in the Grampians, since even the General Store will cost you an arm and a leg for a decent meal. There is a large **Safeway** in Stawell in the town center at 26-32 Scallon St. (Open M-Sa 9am-10pm, Su 10am-10pm.) Groceries can also be purchased at the **Halls Gap General Store,** although high prices drive the locals elsewhere; you'll get a pack of hot dogs and some Tim Tams for the price of a night's stay in town. (Open daily 8am-7:30pm.) For those on the go, the **Brambuk Centre** (p. 638) offers authentic bush tucker ($10-15) for lunch.

 **OLIVE EXTRAVAGANZA.** About 40km out of Halls Gap, Mount Zero is one of Australia's premier olive and olive-oil producing regions, and ▓**Mt. Zero Olives** (☎03 5383 8280; www.mountzeroolives.com) sells award-winning extra virgin olive oil, black olive tapenades, spiced chutneys, and olive oil soaps. From Halls Gap, the farmgate can be reached by following Mt. Victory Rd. and passing Reeds Lookout and then MacKenzie Falls; follow the road for about 20min., turn right on Plantation Rd., then turn left on Winfields Rd. until you see signs. Note: do not take the turnoff marked "Mt. Zero" directly from the main road in Halls Gap; that will take you on a roundabout 38km, unsealed road to Mt. Zero. (Farmgate open daily 10am-5pm.)

**Coolas Ice Creamery,** Stoney Creek Stores (☎03 5356 4466). The 1st shop in the complex; bakes fresh waffle cones and offers an assortment of ice cream flavors. Try the popular Honeycomb or Bailey's with scorched almonds. Cheap hotdogs ($3) and spuds ($6). Waffle cone with 1 scoop $3, 2 scoops $4.30, 3 scoops $5.50; sundaes $6. Open daily 9am-6pm or later. Cash only. ❶

**The Balconies** (☎03 5356 4430; www.thebalconies.com), at the Mountain Grand Hotel, right next to the caravan park in town. Elegant meals and friendly service accompanied by live jazz on Saturday nights. Try the "Kangaroo Experience" ($26), Tuscan lasagna ($22), or salmon ($26). Live Jazz Saturdays also offers a $45, 3-course meal. Open daily 6:30pm-late. Bookings essential. MC/V. ❹

**The Flying Emu,** Stoney Creek Stores (☎03 5356 4400), has a respectable selection of vegetarian and gluten-free options for $8-13, with lighter fare starting at $4. Spinach

and feta quiche $12. Coffee and hot chocolate $3.50. Open daily 9am-4pm, sometimes later. 10% YHA discount. Cash only. ❷

**Black Panther Cafe,** Shop 6, Stoney Creek Stores, (☎03 5356 4511) is a licensed bar
that offers a wide selection of pizzas ($12-20) and mains ($10-24). $10 specials. Iced
coffees and milkshakes $4.50. Fresh fruit smoothies $6.50. Open M-Th 8am-9pm, F-Su
8am-late. Meals served 8am-3pm and 5-9pm. MC/V. ❸

## 🅒 SIGHTS

Most of the Grampians' most noteworthy lookouts and waterfalls lie along
**Mt. Victory Rd.** in the Wonderlands region, making for streamlined scenic tours.
Unfortunately, these sights are a good distance from Halls Gap and require a
car. From Halls Gap, take the turnoff at Mt. Victory with signs for MacKenzie
Falls. The first stop along the way (10km from Halls Gap) is the **Boroka lookout.**
Follow the marked turnoff on Mt. Difficult Rd. for about 5km until you reach
the carpark with the lookout directly in front of it, offering an excellent view
of the eastern side of the range. Continuing up Mt. Victory Rd. for another 8km,
the next lookout is **Reeds Lookout** (also spelled Reids). From the Reeds Lookout
carpark, an easy, mostly flat trail (1km, 20min.) to Grampians icon **Balconies
(Jaws of Death)** ends in sweeping panoramas. The Balconies themselves, a pair
of parallel slabs of sandstone, jut out over the steep sides of Mt. Victory and are
a superb spot to watch the sunset. From the Reeds Lookout carpark, continue
up Mt. Victory Rd. another 7.5km until the turnoff for ⬛**MacKenzie Falls.** Those
who brave the 1.1km steep, downhill path to MacKenzie Falls (and remember,
what goes down must come up), are rewarded with one of Victoria's most
spectacular waterfalls—a 25m wall of crashing water. There is a wheelchair-
accessible approach to the top of the falls (1.75km), but not to the base. From
here, most tourists turn around and head back to Halls Gap, unaware that
**Aboriginal rock art sites** lie just 20min. further up Mt. Victory Rd. For more info
on the **Gulgurn Manja and Ngamadjidj shelters,** see p. 641.

**ABORIGINAL ROCK ART.** Before the intrusion of Major Mitchell and his British army, Gariwerd (the Grampians) was home to the Aboriginal Jardwadjali
(yard-wa-JA-li) and Djab Wurrung people for thousands of years. There are
about 60 Aboriginal rock shelters scattered through the Grampians, where
indigenous people camped and painted over 4000 motifs of their life and law
on the sandstone walls. Very few sites in the Grampians have been investi-
gated, but research shows that Aboriginal people have camped in the Grampians rock shelters for the last 22,000 years and have lived in the area now called
Victoria for at least 40,000 years. Five of the most impressive sites are open
to the public: one in Central Grampians **(Bunjil)**, two in the Northern Grampians **(Gulgurn Manja** and **Ngamadjidj)**, two in the western end of the Southern
Grampians **(Billimina** and **Manja)**. Before heading into the park, visit the **Brambuk
Aboriginal Culture Centre** (see p. 638). The invaluable information available at
the center includes displays about the cultural history of the Jardwadjali and
Djab Wurrung people. The **Dreaming Theatre's** 30min. light-and-sound show tells
a traditional dreaming story explaining the creation of Gariwerd, and offers a
geographic perspective of the national park. The Brambuk Centre also offers
a guided rock-art tour to the Bunjil site. (☎03 5361 4000. Open daily 9am-5pm. Entry
free. Shows every 30min.; $5, concessions and children $3, families $12. 2hr. tours depart M-F
9:30am; bookings essential. $20, concessions $5, children $8.)

**LOST IN TRANSLATION.** Over the last 150 years, European names have been given to Aboriginal places, like Cave of Ghosts for the Ngamadjidj shelter. However, the shelter is not in fact a cave, and there is no evidence that the painted white figures were meant to resemble ghosts. In 1991, the traditional names of 49 places and features within Gariwerd (the Grampians) were restored to recognize the important heritage and mythology of western Victoria's Aboriginal people. Local indigenous words are gaining ground once again, and are now preferred.

**Bunjil** (150m, 15min. one-way). The closest to Halls Gap in Central Grampians, the Bunjil shelter is the most important rock art site in the Grampians and in Victoria. Visit the site either with the Brambuk guided rock-art tour (see above) or on your own. The site depicts Bunjil, the traditional creator of the land, and his 2 dingoes. When his work on earth was finished, he turned into an eagle that then flew into the sky to become a brilliant star. From Halls Gap, head south on Lake Fyans Rd. to Pomonal. In town, Lake Fyans Rd. (here a.k.a. Pomonal-Stawell Rd.) curves left in the direction of Stawell. The Bunjil Shelter is well-marked, 11km before Stawell.

**Ngamadjidji** (300m, 10min. round-trip). From Halls Gap, turn down Mt. Victory Rd. (the same road that leads you past the Balconies and MacKenzie Falls). About 20min. past MacKenzie Falls, turn left on Plantation Rd. The sealed road ends, leading straight to Ngamadjidj or left to **Mt. Zero Olives** (p. 639) and **Gulgurn Manja** (below). The Ngamadjidj shelter is a gentle 100m walk from the carpark; this is the easiest and shortest walk to any of the 5 rock art sites. Translating to "white person," the paintings at this shelter are unusual only because the motifs were painted with white clay, while elsewhere red pigment was favored. The remnants of 16 painted figures are on the panel, but some are becoming very faint. Stone tools and remains of campfires have also been found at this shelter, suggesting it was a favored camping place.

**Gulgurn Manja** (1km, 20-40min. round-trip). Following the same directions from Halls Gap to Ngamadjidji, turn left when the sealed road ends, which will lead you to Gulgurn Manja and Mt. Zero Olives. The shelter lies .5km from the carpark, and the beautiful 15min. walk ends in amazing views over the valley below. Translating to "hands of young people," the Gulgurn Manja (GOOL-koorn MAHN-ya) shelter is located at the northern tip of Gariwerd. For the groups of Jarwadjali, this shelter was used to scout the fires of other groups on the plains to the north. They also chiseled stone tools from the fine-grained sandstone in the area, and marks where the stone was broken from the wall can still be seen. The paintings depict bars, emu tracks, and handprints, many made by Aboriginal children, hence the name of the shelter. The handprints here were made by pressing a painted hand directly to the rock, as opposed to the stenciled hands at Manja.

**Billimina** (1.7m loop, 45min. round-trip). Billimina and Manja, the two shelters in the Southern Grampians, are the least convenient to reach from Halls Gap. However, if you make the trek, the serene sites will reward your effort. From Halls Gap, follow Mt. Victory Rd. past MacKenzie Falls. Just past Wartook Valley, turn right on Brimpaen-Laharum Rd. toward Brimpaen. When this road ends, turn left onto Henty Hwy., following arrows to Hamilton. At signs for Buandik Campground, turn left on Billwing Rd. The Billimina shelter is just past the Buandik campground. The walk from the carpark to the shelter is the only walk graded "medium," while the other 4 are graded "easy." The steady uphill walk (20min., 1.3km) leads to the massive rock overhang. A common camping area for the Jardwadjali people, excavations in 1976 revealed stone tools and remains of plant and animal food. Over 2500 motifs cover the walls here, painted with ochre strokes. The most noteworthy are the many bars arranged in horizontal rows; it is believed that these were used to count events in retelling stories or record the number of days spent at a place. Though difficult to see, there are also emus, kangaroo and emu tracks, and 55 human stick-figures painted in the shelter.

**Manja** (2.6km, 1hr. round-trip). Follow the same directions to the Buandik Campground as above. Before the campground, a turnoff leads you to the Manja shelter 10min. farther up the road. The 1.3km walk to the rock shelter site is easy. Manja has more hand stencils than any other site in Victoria, a total of 90. Conveying the link between the Jardwadjali people and their land, the hand stencils were a way of recording a visit to the rock overhang, renewing the ties to the rock with each visit and each stencil. Animal tracks and many human stick-figures are also depicted on the sandstone walls.

## HIKING

Indescribably beautiful and rugged, the park has easy tracks for those seeking beautiful scenery, as well as difficult tracks for more experienced hikers and rock-climbers looking for racing heartbeats. Some **Wonderland walks** lead to serene waterfalls and rock formations. To the south, **Victoria Valley** is carpeted with red gum woodlands and is home to emus and kangaroos. Experienced hikers might want to tackle some of the steep trails on the range's highest peak, **Mount William** (1168m), at the park's extreme eastern end; the "trail" to the summit is fully paved and well traveled. The Wonderland hikes vary by difficulty and duration (from 30min. to 6hr. to several days). The trails below start near Halls Gap; all distances are round-trip, although budget extra time if you want to ponder the meaning of life at the summit.

**Wonderland Trail** (11.5km, 4-5hr. round-trip). The trail starts behind the town center carpark; walk past the swimming pool and rear asphalt road and turn left before the Botanical Gardens. Moderately difficult, this hike traverses many of the most-touristed sites; slightly more strenuous detours abound. The ½-day loop along well-formed tracks leads first to the **Venus Baths,** a series of rock pools popular for swimming in summer (when water levels are high enough), then to **Splitters Falls.** The trail continues through the lush forest along a creek to the Wonderland carpark, then up the spectacular **Grand Canyon** and eventually to the narrow rock tunnel **Silent Street.** At the awe-inspiring **Pinnacle,** sweeping views of the valley reward breathless hikers. The trail is well-marked (and well-traveled). To reach the Pinnacle, follow the orange arrows that point up into the rock. At the Pinnacle, the short **Forest Loop** joins back to the original trail at Bridalveil Falls, returning to Halls Gap.

**Mount Rosea Loop** (12km, 4-5hr. round-trip). A more difficult hike that should be attempted only with a copy of the *Wonderland Walks* map ($3.30), sold at the Brambuk Centre. Starts at the **Rosea Campground,** located on Silverband Rd. off Mt. Victory Rd. The hike ascends through forest to a sandstone plateau. The orange markers are somewhat difficult to follow in this area; be careful not to lose the trail. After a bit of scrambling over rocky ledges, turn left at the sign for Mt. Rosea and continue to a summit with one of the most spectacular vistas in the Grampians. Follow the trail back to the intersection and head left, away from the Rosea Campground, through a forest, then onto a 4WD track, which leads to the **Burma Track.** Keep left around the outlying portions of the Sierra Range. At Silverband Rd., turn right and walk for 200m to the **Dellys Dell Track,** then uphill for about 700m to the Rosea Campground.

**Boronia Peak Trail** (6.6km, 2-3hr. round-trip). Starts past the kangaroo fields next to the Brambuk Centre or, alternatively, from the narrow path by the bridge just north of Tim's Place (add roughly 2km to the latter route). This trail is more difficult than the Wonderland Trail, but shorter. For the first half of the hike, the dense forest provides plentiful opportunities to observe birds and other wildlife. The moderate terrain ends in a short, unmarked scramble to the peak. With a lake to the south, flat bush country to the east, and the jagged Wonderland range to the west, the view is worth the haul to the top.

**Chatauqua Peak Loop** (Shi-TA-kwa; 5.6km, 2-3hr. round-trip). Starts from behind the Recreation Oval on Mt. Victory Rd., 150m from the intersection with Grampians Rd. The hike opens with an up-close view of tranquil **Clematis Falls,** best seen after rain. The final 400m climb to the peak is long and strenuous, but the views of Halls Gap and the valley are perfect. Or, skip the boulder hop; the main trail continues on through to **Bullaces Glen,** a green fern gully. At the glen, cross Mt. Victory Rd. and continue on the forest trail (many accidentally follow the road) to the botanical gardens in Halls Gap.

**Mount Stapylton Summit** (4.6km, 2-3hr. round-trip). A challenging hike that requires a bit of scrambling over elevated ledges, as well as some basic navigation skills. Starts at the Mount Zero picnic area in the northern Grampians; before setting off, purchase the *Northern Walks* map ($3.30) from the Brambuk Centre. The hike begins with a long uphill walk over unshaded **Flat Rock,** then passes through a wooded area to the base of **Mt. Stapylton.** The hike to the summit is extremely strenuous; beware of crevasses and stay close to the trail markers. The view from the top includes many of the surrounding mountain ranges and plains. On the way back down, you have the option of returning to the Mt. Zero Picnic area directly or turning the outing into a ½-day hike by tackling the entire **Mount Stapylton Loop** (12.2km, 5-7hr.). Follow the signs for the trail to the **Stapylton Campground** (4.4km), which passes through dense scrub. From the campground, signs mark the trail back to the Mt. Zero Picnic Area. The loop and summit can also be attempted by starting from—and returning to—the Stapylton Campground.

## ⚡ ROCK CLIMBING AND ABSEILING

The Grampians offer thousands of routes to some of the best rock climbing in the entire world, and there are plenty of companies in the area to hook you up with your next adrenaline rush. Nearby **Mount Arapiles** is the best bet for diehard climbers; most routes are accessible from a central location. Those who prefer the crags of the Grampians will need a car to get from site to site. Several small adventure companies operate in the region and offer guided climbs at all skill-levels in the northern section of the park at crags such as "Asses Ears," "Wall of Fools," "Manic Depressive," "Golden Shower," and "Group Sex." While many have offices in Halls Gap, they are more often than not unattended, since the guides are out on tours. Last-minute types beware: you must book at least a week in advance to secure a trip. **Grampians Mountain Adventure Company** (☎03 5383 9218 or 04 2774 7047; www.grampiansadventure.com.au) is run by an adventurous Aussie named Troy who strikes an excellent balance between good times and safety. (Climb/abseil combo ½-day; full-day $110). **Absolute Outdoors,** shop four in Stony Creek Stores (☎03 5356 4556; www.absoluteoutdoors.com.au), hasn't been quite the same since the brush fires, but enthusiastic guides still offer adventures of every type. Their selection of adventures includes canoe trips, mountain biking, abseiling, and bushwalking. (½-day abseil $65, full-day $130. Groups tend to be larger here than at Grampians Mountain Adventure Company.) **Hangin' Out** (☎03 5356 4535 or 04 0768 4831; www.hanginout.com.au) is another one-man company which offers half-day or full-day single-pitch and multi-pitch climbing tutorials for individuals or small groups. (4hr. climb $65; 6hr. climb/abseil combo $90, 9hr. $120. Private guiding for groups of 1-3 more expensive. Full-day guided bush walking $125.) The **Grampians Personalized Tours and Adventures,** in the Halls Gap newsagency, offers abseil and climb trips along Watchtower Mountain, as well as mountain biking, 4WD nature tours, and an intense 8hr. Big Day Out, with rock climbing, abseiling, mountain biking, and bushwalking. (☎03 5356 4654 or 04 2995 4686; www.grampianstours.com. ½-day abseil or climb $69, full-day abseil/climb combo $125. Big Day Out $125.)

> **GRAPE-IANS.** Sprinkled throughout the Grampians and the Goldfields, more than 50 cellar doors uncork their bottles of delicious reds and whites and offer the public free tastings. The vineyards cover a vast expanse of land, with about a dozen cellar doors near **Ballarat** (p. 644), a few dozen in the Pyrenees ranges clustering around the towns of Avoca and Moonambel, and a dozen on the eastern edge of the **Grampians** (p. 636) that line the road from Stawell to Ararat. Pick up a free map of the **Great Grape Touring Route,** with cellar door locations and hours, at the visitors centers in Melbourne, Ballarat, Ararat, Halls Gap, Stawell, or Avoca.

# GOLDFIELDS

In 1851, the first year of Victorian statehood, a group of miners unearthed one of the largest gold nuggets ever to be discovered by humans. A year later, the London Times reported that over 50,000 impatient diggers had converged upon Victoria's goldfields, shovels in hand. As paupers prospered, the Australian government began taxing the nouveau riche, igniting the brief and bloody Eureka Rebellion of 1854. The chaotic hustle of the Goldrush has dissipated in recent times, and today's visitors can enjoy a relaxed stay amid picturesque historical townships. Sovereign Hill, a large living museum in Ballarat, offers a vivid portrayal of what life was like in the 1850s. Looking beyond the rich regional history, tourists have come to savor the region's picturesque vistas and soothing spa region. Although most of the gold has been harvested, towns like Ballarat and Bendigo remain prominent centers in Victoria.

## BALLARAT ☎03

Ballarat (pop. 90,000) is the self-appointed capital of the Goldfields and, as the site of the infamous 1854 Eureka Rebellion, is also commonly held to be the birthplace of Australian democratic idealism. Like America's Boston Tea Party, the Eureka Rebellion was one of Australia's first acts of defiance against the motherland, Great Britain. Although the area's gold is now long gone, much of the 19th-century architecture has been preserved, and the city's golden past has been channeled into a bustling tourist trade that centers on the acclaimed **Sovereign Hill,** a large theme park dedicated to transporting visitors back in time to the gold rush era. Most of the gold in the region came from the deep alluvial deposits in town, and at the height of the gold rush, over 60,000 miners camped out around town hoping to strike it rich.

### ▬ TRANSPORTATION

**Trains and Buses:** V/Line (☎13 61 96) runs buses and trains, depending on destination, from Ballarat Station, 202 Lydiard St. N., reached from Curtis St. by bus #2. To: **Ararat** (1hr., 3-5 per day, $8.10); **Bendigo** (2hr.; M-F 2 per day, F and Su 1 per day; $12); **Castlemaine** (1hr., F and Su 1 per day, $8.10); **Daylesford** (40min., 1 per day, $6.20); **Geelong** (1hr., M-F 1 per day, $7.10); and **Melbourne** (1hr., 5-6 per day, $10-14.20). Frequency varies Sa-Su.

**Public Transportation:** (☎03 5331 7777). The city loop bus runs from Sturt St. and the railway station to all of Ballarat's attractions. Pick up a helpful transit guide ($0.50) from a bus driver. (Every 35min. M-F 7am-6pm, Sa limited schedule; $1.70 ticket valid

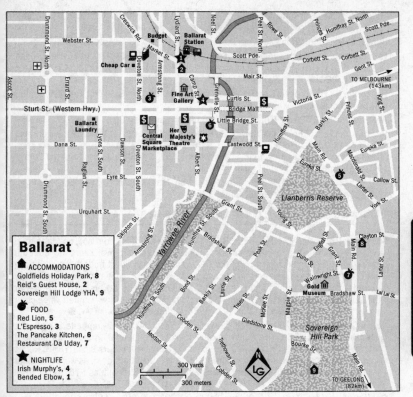

**Ballarat**

🏠 ACCOMMODATIONS
Goldfields Holiday Park, **8**
Reid's Guest House, **2**
Sovereign Hill Lodge YHA, **9**

🍎 FOOD
Red Lion, **5**
L'Espresso, **3**
The Pancake Kitchen, **6**
Restaurant Da Uday, **7**

⭐ NIGHTLIFE
Irish Murphy's, **4**
Bended Elbow, **1**

for 2hr. use. Buy from driver.) **Ballarat Taxis** (☎13 10 08 or 03 5329 0000) line up in the city center and run tours of Ballarat and nearby wineries. Wheelchair-accessible.

**Car Rental: Avis,** 1113 Sturt St. (☎03 5332 8310), between Talbort St. and Ascot St. **Budget,** 106 Market St. (☎03 5331 7788). **Cheap Car and Ute,** 209 Doveton St. (☎03 5333 7206). **Europcar,** 206 Burnbank St., Wendouree (☎03 5339 1058).

# 🔆 🔢 ORIENTATION AND PRACTICAL INFORMATION

The name Ballarat comes from a local Aboriginal word meaning "resting place," and was originally spelled "Ballaarat." Recently, the city has begun to revert back to its original spelling; several signs and maps have added the double "a," so don't be too alarmed if you feel as if you've suddenly entered a different city. The town straddles the **Western Highway,** which becomes **Sturt Street** as it runs through town east to west. The railway station is a few blocks north of Sturt on **Lydiard Street.** At its eastern end, Sturt becomes the pedestrian **Bridge Mall,** which has shops, restaurants, and supermarkets.

**Tourist Office: Eureka Centre** (☎1800 446 633; www.visitballarat.com.au), on the corner of Eureka and Rodier St. The well-stocked facility is located 2km east of the city center along Eureka St. The large Southern Cross flag makes it very hard to miss. Internet $2 per 15min. Bike rental ½-day $15, full-day $25; $100 deposit. Open daily

**9am-5pm. Ballarat Fine Art Gallery** (☎03 5320 5858), across from the railway station. Walk through gallery to the helpful info desk. Open daily 9am-5pm.

**Banks: Banks** and **ATMs** line Sturt St.

**Laundromat: Ballarat Laundry,** 711 Sturt St. (☎03 5331 6476). Coin-operated wash $3, dry $1 for 8min.; open daily 6am-midnight. Dropoff wash/dry/fold $13 per load; open M-F 7:30am-6pm, Sa 8am-1pm.

**Police:** (☎03 5336 6000), on the corner of Dana and Albert St., is located just behind the tourist center.

**Hospital:** (☎03 5320 4275), on the corner of Sturt and Mair St.

**Internet Access:** Free at the **library,** 178 Doveton St. (☎03 5331 1211), which also offers Wi-Fi. Open M-Th 9:30am-6pm, F 9:30am-7pm, Sa 9:30am-1pm, Su 1:15-4pm. Book ahead. **Guf,** 121 Dovetone St. North (☎03 5331 5303), across from the library. $5 per hr. Open daily 11am-11pm.

**Post Office:** (☎03 5336 5736), in the Central Sq. Marketplace. Fax services. Open M-F 9am-5pm, Sa 9am-noon. **Postal Code:** 3350.

## ACCOMMODATIONS AND CAMPING

**Sovereign Hill Lodge YHA** (☎03 5333 3409; www.sovereignhill.com.au), on Magpie St. a block uphill from the main carpark for Sovereign Hill. Located over 3km away from the train station. Elegant Victorian bungalows that are by far the best budget option in Ballarat. The YHA cottage next door to the Lodge offers 4 small, spotless rooms positioned around a cozy kitchen and sitting area. Discounted tickets to Sovereign Hill events for YHA members. Reception daily 7am-11pm. Book well in advance. Limited wheelchair access. Dorms $25, YHA $22; singles $38/34; doubles $58/50. MC/V. ❷

**Reid's Guest House,** 128 Lydiard St. North (☎03 5331 3461; www.rcpballarat.com.au), just 1 block north of Sturt St. Finally, a backpacker accommodation that's not above a dirty pub blasting karaoke late into the night. Welcoming travelers since 1886, Reid's Guest House offers spotless 6-bed dorms with an attached bathroom, as well as ensuite private rooms, in the center of town. Dorms $26; singles $65; doubles $75; triples $88. Reception M-F 9am-10pm, Sa 10am-10pm, Su 1-10pm. MC/V. ❷

**Goldfields Holiday Park,** 108 Clayton St. (☎03 5332 7888 or 1800 632 237; www. ballaratgoldfields.com.au). One of the finest holiday park sites in all of Victoria, located only 300m from Sovereign Hill. Offers modern kitchens, recreation rooms, a playground, a heated pool, and heated communal bathrooms. 4- to 6-person ensuite cabins with A/C, kitchenette, and TV. Reception 8am-8pm. Try to book cabins well in advance. Sites for 2 $29-35; cabins from $85. MC/V. ❷

## FOOD

**Sturt Street,** which defines the CBD, is the mecca for trendy cafes with outdoor seating, and the pedestrian **Bridge Mall** is lined with great restaurants. Around town, a cheap eat can be found every couple of doors, appealing to the town's student population. A 24hr. **Coles** supermarket lies at the eastern end of Sturt St. The **Buninyong Farmers Market** occurs on the third Sunday of each month.

**L'Espresso,** 417 Sturt St. (☎03 5333 1789). Sip on a glass of wine or a delicious cappuccino at this trendy cafe, with its black decor and giant wall covered with CDs. Patrons can request music from the lengthy playlist, and a chalkboard announces the cafe's newest CD arrivals. Espresso $3. Wines by the glass $6.50-10. Breakfast $5-14. Lunch $9-19. Open daily 7am-6pm. MC/V. ❷

**Red Lion,** 217-229 Main Rd. (☎03 5331 3393; www.redlionhotel.biz). Located en route from the town center to Sovereign Hill on the east side of the road. The Red Lion is part of a larger conference center that includes a bar and casino. The restaurant is modern and polished. The cafe mains ($8-17) are less expensive than those served in the bistro ($16-27). Cafe open daily 8am-10pm. Bistro open daily noon-2pm and 6-9pm. Pub open M-W and Su 8pm-1am, Th-Sa 8pm-3am. ❸

**Restaurant Da Uday,** 7 Wainwright St. (☎03 5331 6655), at the corner of Grant and Wainwright St., just a stone's throw from the Sovereign Hill guest carpark. Set in a colorful bungalow covered with iron-wrought frills, the budget-friendly joint serves a smorgasbord of nearly 200 dishes of Indian, Thai, or Italian origin ($7-20). Open M 5:30-10:30pm; Tu-Su noon-2pm and 5:30-10:30pm. Reservations required F-Su. MC/V. ❸

**The Pancake Kitchen,** 2 Grenville St. South (☎03 5331 6555). Savor pancakes with fruit and ice cream ($11.50-14) and crepes with cheese, veggies, and meat ($18-24) in this restored 1870s building. Offers a retro atmosphere that's enhanced by the decor. Open M-Th 9am-10pm, F-Sa 7:30am-11pm, Su 7:30am-10pm. AmEx/MC/V. ❷

## ◐ SIGHTS

The 100-year-old **Ballarat Begonia Festival** (www.ballaratbegoniafestival.com) is an open-air arts and crafts fair that draws thousands of flora fans over the Victoria Labour Day long weekend every March. **Royal South Street** music, debate, and performance competitions attract top talent (late August to mid-October). The tree-lined pathways of **Victoria Park,** south of Lake Wendouree, offer good views of the city, and the **Black Hill Lookout** can be a peaceful nighttime stroll.

▥**SOVEREIGN HILL.** Sovereign Hill is a living museum that gives visitors a taste of what life was like during the region's gold rush in the 1850s. Sovereign Hill staff, dressed in period attire, roam about town pretending to be miners and townfolk. Demonstrations and exhibits include smelting, musket-firing, and the pouring of over $70,000 worth of gold. A 40min. tour of the mine reveals the often brutal conditions in which miners worked. Pan for gold or ride a horse-drawn carriage through the streets. In the evening, tourists can enjoy the 90min. **Blood on the Southern Cross** interactive light show set under the stars, which reenacts the events leading up to the infamous Eureka Rebellion. *(☎03 5337 1100. Open daily 10am-5pm. Day pass combined with Gold Museum admission $35, concessions $27, children $16, families $90. Blood on the Southern Cross $43, concessions $33.50, children $23, families $115. Advanced booking required; ☎03 5333 5777.)*

**EUREKA STOCKADE.** From afar, the museum looks like a giant sailing ship which has run aground. On the inside, this informative space carefully documents the events of the Eureka Rebellion through a multimillion-dollar exhibit. The self-guided tour ambles through larger-than-life exhibition spaces with an archeology area where you can piece together artifacts recovered from the mining towns. Ballarat's main **information center** is located at the entrance. *(Eureka St. at Rodier St. Drive 2km out of town on Main Rd. and turn right at the Eureka St. roundabout; it's 1km up the road. Or, take bus #8. ☎03 5333 1854; www.eurekaballarat.com. Open daily 9am-5pm. Last entry 4pm. $8, concessions $6, children $4, families $22.)*

## ◧ ♫ ENTERTAINMENT AND NIGHTLIFE

With a lively student population of 19,000 attending the University of Ballarat, the city's nightlife will keep you up until the wee hours of the morning. To start your nightly festivities, head to the pedestrian **Bridge Mall** at the east end of Sturt St., filled with street musicians on the weekends. A few doors down from Reid's Guest House, **Bended Elbow,** 120 Lydiard St. (☎03 5332 1811) is a classy pub with events nearly every night, awesome dinner deals, and great happy hour specials on drinks. (Open M-Th and Su 11:30am-late, Th-Sa

11:30am-4:30am.) **Irish Murphy's,** 36 Sturt St. (☎03 5331 4091), is a popular Aussie pub chain with live music Th-Su nights starting at 9:30pm and Irish dancers on Sunday afternoons. A casual dress code is enforced after 7pm. (Open daily noon-late. Cover F-Sa after 10pm $4-5.)

Although it first opened its doors in 1875, the elegant **Her Majesty's Theatre,** 17 Lydiard St. (☎03 5333 5888; www.hermaj.com/cms), is still the center of Ballarat's performing arts and culture, presenting professional touring and local productions. (Box office open 9:15am-5pm.)

# BENDIGO
☎03

Like almost all Victorian Goldfields towns, "the Go" (pop. 100,000) sprang into existence in the 1850s, when the region was flooded by miners lured by tales of striking it rich. While many of its neighbors fell from prosperity to obscurity in the boom-and-bust cycle, Bendigo continued to prosper into the 20th century thanks to a seemingly endless supply of gold-rich alluvial quartz. Today, it's a lovely commercial center with a plethora of street-side sculptures and private galleries. The grand main street and pedestrian-only shopping arcades make it a pleasant stopover for travelers headed elsewhere.

## ⌐ TRANSPORTATION

**Trains and Buses: Bendigo Station** is behind the Discovery Centre at the south end of Mitchell St. V/Line (☎13 61 96) has trains and buses, depending on destination, to: **Adelaide** (8hr., 1 per day, $36.10); **Ballarat** (2hr.; M-F 2 per day, F and Su 1 per

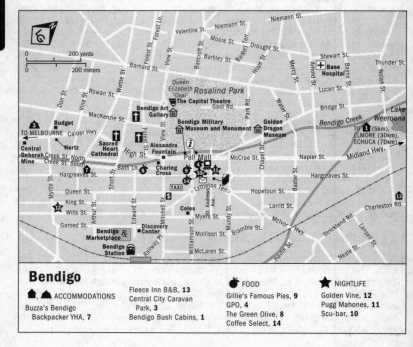

## Bendigo

**▲,▲ ACCOMMODATIONS**

Buzza's Bendigo
  Backpacker YHA, **7**

Fleece Inn B&B, **13**
Central City Caravan
  Park, **3**
Bendigo Bush Cabins, **1**

**🍎 FOOD**

Gillie's Famous Pies, **9**
GPO, **4**
The Green Olive, **8**
Coffee Select, **14**

**★ NIGHTLIFE**

Golden Vine, **12**
Pugg Mahones, **11**
Scu-bar, **10**

day; $12); **Daylesford** (1hr., M-F 6:59am, $6); **Maldon** (2hr., 10 per day, $15-21.40) via **Castlemaine** (22min., 10 per day, $3-4.40); **Melbourne** (2hr., 13-17 per day, $15-21.40); **Mildura** (5hr.; M-Th and Su 1 per day, F 2 per day; $30).

**Public Transportation: Bendigo Airport Bus** (☎03 5439 4044; www.bendigoairportservice.com.au) transports visitors to and from the Melbourne airport 3 times per day, with several stops along the way (2hr.; $38). A much cheaper ride with **V/Line** will also get you to Melbourne airport, but with a transfer; trains depart from Bendigo Station with transfer buses in Sunbury. (2hr.; 9 per day 5:18am-4:25pm; $10-14.) Within the city, public transportation is limited to the **Tram** route, which runs from Calder Hwy. in the west through the center of town (Pall Mall) and up to the north of Lake Weerona. For more information on the **tram,** see p. 651.

**Taxis: Bendigo Taxis** (☎13 10 08).

**Car Rental:** A small group of car rental centers are located around the Central Deborah Mine and Tram Depot. **Hertz,** 141 High St. (☎03 5443 5088), at Thistle St. Open M-F 8am-5pm, Sa 8am-noon, Su 9-noon. **Budget,** 150-152 High St. (☎03 5442 2766). Open M-F 8am-6pm, Sa-Su 8am-noon. There is free 3hr. **parking** on the roof of the Coles supermarket on the corner of Myers St. and Williamson St.

## ⚡🗺 ORIENTATION AND PRACTICAL INFORMATION

In Bendigo, neatly planned streets intersect with winding gullies packed down by diggers' feet. Most points of interest are near the city center, bounded on the south and east by railroad tracks and on the north by Rosalind Park. The **Calder Highway (Hwy. 79)** from Melbourne runs into the city center, becoming **High Street,** then **Pall Mall** (at Charing Cross), then **McCrae Street,** and finally **Midland Highway,** which leads to Elmore and Echuca. The popular pedestrian **Hargreaves Mall** runs one block along Hargreaves between Mitchell Street and Williamson Street.

**Tourist Office:** 51-67 Pall Mall St., at Williamson (☎03 5434 6060 or 1800 813 153), in the ornate post office building. A mini-museum details Bendigo's history. Extensive information about nearby towns also available. Open daily 9am-5pm.

**Police:** (☎03 5440 2510), on High St. near Golden Sq.

**Hospital:** (☎03 5454 8100), on Arnold St. between Stewart and Lucan St.

**Pharmacy: Toni Riley Pharmacies** (☎03 5443 3319), in the Bendigo Marketplace Shopping Center. Open M-F 9am-6pm, Sa 9am-4pm, Su 11am-3pm.

**Internet Access: Library,** 259 Hargreaves St. (☎03 5449 2700). Free 15min. or 1hr. slots. Open M-F 10am-7pm, Sa 10am-1pm. **Renaissance Computers,** 70 Pall Mall St. (☎03 5442 5856). Brand-new computers and fast connections. $1 per 10min. Open M-F 9am-5:30pm, Sa 9am-1:30pm.

**Post Office:** (☎13 13 18), on the corner of Hargreaves and Williamson St. Poste Restante. Open M-F 9am-5pm, Sa 9:30am-12:30pm. **Postal Code:** for *Poste Restante* 3552; for addresses in Bendigo 3550.

## 🏠🛏 ACCOMMODATIONS AND CAMPING

Lodging in Bendigo is a colorful array of B&Bs, backpackers, and beds for big-spenders. Accommodation is also available at the **Golden Dragon Museum** (p. 651), which is perfect for small groups or families.

**Buzza's Backpacker YHA,** 33 Creek St. South (☎03 5443 7680), on the narrow one-way road parallel to Hargreaves St. The only hostel in the center of town welcomes visitors with its colorful facade. Comfortable reading den, pretty courtyard, and bathrooms. Linen and towels included. Internet $2 per 30min. Laundry $6. Lockers; bring your own lock. Free parking. Wheelchair accessible. Reception 8-10am and 5-10pm. Dorms $26, YHA $22; singles $44/40; doubles $64/56. AmEx/MC/V. ❷

**The Fleece Inn B&B,** 139 Charleston Rd. (☎03 5443 3086 or 04 0705 2986; www. thefleeceinn.com.au), on the corner of Nolan St. on the east end of town. 10min. walk to the CBD. This comfortable B&B has spotless rooms, cozy lounges with TV, a beautiful backyard with BBQ, and kitchen facilities. Free continental breakfast and laundry. 4-bed dorms $33; singles, doubles, and family rooms $37 per person. MC/V. ❸

**Bendigo Bush Cabins** (☎03 5448 3344; www.bwc.com.au/ironbark), on Watson St. Located 5km from the city center on a large plot of wooded land. By car, follow the Midland Hwy. out of town toward Echuca and turn left at the lights at Holdsworth Rd., where there's a sign directing you to Long Gully. Make a right on John St., which curves into Crane Rd., and then make a right onto Watson St. Open-air bar and fire pit. Basic backpacker accommodations with private cabins available. Try the monstrous green 75m waterslide. The **Bendigo Goldfields Experience** (p. 650) runs on the premises. Dorms $22; cabins for 1 $40-55, for 2 $61-73. NOMADS discount. MC/V. ❷

**Central City Caravan Park,** 362 High St. (☎03 5443 6937), at the corner with Beech St. Take bus #1 from Hargreaves Mall. With BBQ facilities and a playground. Wheelchair accessible. Reception daily 8am-8pm. Sites from $26. Cabins $62-92. MC/V. ❶

## 🍴 FOOD

Although small in size, Bendigo has a considerable cafe culture; just look around the tourist office, particularly on **Pall Mall** and **Hargreaves Street.** Several pubs offer cheap eats as well. The **Hargreaves Mall** has a food court that bustles during lunch hours. **Coles** supermarket (☎03 5443 6311; open 24hr.) is on the corner of Myers and Williamson St. The third Saturday of each month brings the **Bridge Street Market,** featuring the best of the Bendigo region (8am-2pm).

**GPO,** 60-64 Pall Mall (☎03 5443 4343; www.gpobendigo.com.au). The hippest place in town proves that trendy can be cheap. Smooth beats and sleek decor lure locals and visitors alike. Most come for the creative assortment of delicious flat-bread pizzas ($8-18). Don't miss the calm courtyard in the back. Salads $8-13, handmade pasta $20-25. Open daily noon-1am. AmEx/MC/V. ❷

**Coffee Select,** 234 Hargreaves St. (☎03 5443 2233). For those needing a jolt, this popular roasthouse and shop will satisfy your caffeine cravings with beans from Brazil, Ethiopia, and East Timor, to name a few. The Grazing Plate with veggies, meats, and cheeses supplements the java to perfection (for 1 $12.50, for 2 $17.50). Coffee $3-3.20. Pot of tea $3.50. Foccacia $8.50. Open M-F 8:30am-4pm, Sa 9am-1pm. MC/V. ❶

**Gillie's Famous Pies** (☎03 5443 4965), on the corner of Hargreaves Mall and Williamson St. A tasty way to clog an artery. Locals love meat pies and fried food (from $2.25). Cappuccino $3. Open M-F 8am-6pm, Sa 9am-4pm, Su 10am-4pm. Cash only. ❶

**The Green Olive,** 11 Bath Ln. (☎03 5442 2676), a one-way lane parallel to Hargreaves St. A good choice for those seeking hearty breakfasts, served all day. Outdoor seating. Fluffy pancakes with maple syrup and fruit $9.50. Eggs Benedict $12.50. Lunch salads $11-16. Wraps and foccacias $12.50-14. Fresh-squeezed juices $5-5.50. Open M-F 7am-5pm, Sa 7am-3:30pm, Su 8am-3pm. AmEx/MC/V. ❷

## 👁 SIGHTS

The budget-savvy way to see Bendigo is to purchase the ◪**Bendigo Experience Pass,** available at tourist centers such as the Central Deborah Mine or Bendigo Tram office. It includes the Mine Experience Tour at Deborah Mine, a two-day pass on the Tram Tour, entry into the Golden Dragon Museum, and Bendigo Pottery Museum, as well as discounts for the mine's adventure tour, the

Discovery Science and Technology Centre, and wheel-throwing lessons at Bendigo Pottery. ($39.50, concessions $33.50, children $22.50, families $99.50.)

**CENTRAL DEBORAH MINE.** The **Mine Experience Tour** (1hr.) take visitors 61m down the last mine that operated commercially in Bendigo. Explanations of mining history and techniques are interactive; volunteer and you may even get to show off your skill with the drill. The **Underground Adventure Tour** allows participants to don miner's garb and go down one extra level to use real mine equipment for 2hr. The headquarters of the historic **Bendigo Trams** are located just next door to the mine, and trams operate every hour through town. Discount combo tickets are available at the mine, tram office, or the tourist office. *(76 Violet St. ☎ 03 5443 8322; www.central-deborah.com. Open daily 9:30am-5pm. Mine Experience Tours 10am, 11:10am, 12:20pm, 1:30pm, 2:40pm, 3:50pm. $19, concessions $16, children $10; combined package with tram tour $28.50/24.50/15.50. Underground Adventure Tour daily 9:30am, noon, 2pm, booking essential; $58/53/33.)*

**LANDMARKS.** Tours with recorded commentary cover the town in the restored, turn-of-the-century **Talking Trams.** Trams run every hour, picking up tourists from the elaborate Alexandra Fountain near the tourist office or from the Central Deborah Mine. Each tram pass is valid for two consecutive days, and you can hop on and hop off as you like. *(1hr.; $12.50, concessions $11.50, children $7.50, families $37.)* The late-Victorian feel of Bendigo's architecture is most pronounced along Pall Mall. Most impressive are the old post office building (which now houses the visitors center) and the adjacent Bendigo Law Courts, both with ornate facades on all four sides. The stunning ▣**Sacred Heart Cathedral,** on High St. between Wattle and Short St., sends its spires soaring toward heaven from atop a hill overlooking town. Details about prominent landmarks are available at the information center. The **Shamrock Hotel,** at the corner of Williamson St. and Pall Mall, began as a roaring entertainment hall in the golden 1850s. **Rosalind Park,** on the site of the old 1850s police barracks north of Alexandra Fountain, is a vast expanse of greenery scattered with winding pathways, trees, and statues—including a fairly unflattering likeness of Queen Victoria. If you brave the long climb up its observation tower, you'll be rewarded with a view of Bendigo and surrounding gold country.

**GOLDEN DRAGON MUSEUM.** When news of the gold rush hit Asia, hundreds of Chinese miners flocked to Bendigo to cash in, creating a cultural legacy that lives on in Bendigo to this day. This collection provides an overview of both Chinese culture in Australia and the culture's particular impact on Bendigo. Displays offer a look at the Chinese-Australian experience in the place dubbed Dai Gum San (Big Gold Mountain) but remain notably silent on the racism that Chinese-Australians often faced. The collection's highlight is the fantastically ornate **Sun Loong,** the longest imperial (five-clawed) dragon in the world at just over 100m. The adjacent gardens are a recreation of the imperial water garden in China. The **tearoom ❷** serves light meals and snacks for $6-12. *(5-9 Bridge St. ☎ 03 5441 5044; www.goldendragonmusem.org. Tearoom open during museum hours. Open daily 9:30am-5pm. $8, concessions $6, children $54, families $20.)*

**DISCOVERY SCIENCE & TECHNOLOGY CENTRE.** With over 100 hands-on exhibits, the colorful museum is a haven for curious children. Attractions include Australia's largest vertical slide, a planetarium with regular showings, and a dazzling water vortex. Tickets can be purchased along with the Central Deborah Mine and Bendigo Tram tour. *(7 Railway Pl. ☎ 03 5444 4400; www.discovery.asn.au. Open daily 10am-4pm. $9.50, concessions $8, children $6.95, families $30.)*

## 🎵 🎭 ENTERTAINMENT AND NIGHTLIFE

Pubs are everywhere in Bendigo. Most are tame local hangouts that close around midnight, but weekends can be rowdier as tourists funnel into the small watering holes and live music pubs. With the nearby La Trobe University, "Uni" nights can get ridiculous, and pubs lower their prices to lure the local students. The main late-night entertainment options are on Pall Mall and Hargreaves St. between Williamson and Mundy St.

**Scu-bar,** 238 Hargreaves St. (☎03 5441 6888). This club caters to the trendy by employing a "No effort, no entry" dress code. Beer flows freely from behind the chic stainless steel bar, as a late-night crowd lounges on foamy blue chairs and dances the night away to the in-house DJs. Tu and Th Uni Night, with $2.50 pots of beer and $4 spirits. Su $2.50 pots. Open Tu, Th, F-Su 8pm-3am.

**Golden Vine Hotel,** 135 King St. (☎03 5443 6063). A bit more out of the way; this hotel attracts a young local crowd with some of the best live music Bendigo has to offer. Great beer garden. Tu jam sessions, $2.20 pots, $4 spirits. W Trivia night and $12 Parma and Pot night. F-Sa live bands. Open M-Sa noon-1am, Su noon-11pm.

**Pugg Mahones,** 224 Hargreaves St. (☎03 5443 4916), on the corner of Bull St. Offers a selection of Irish beers on tap and live music (Th 9:30pm, F-Sa 11pm) in a dark green and hardwood interior. Locals love the hearty pub grub, such as chicken parm ($115). Pool tables. Happy hour F 4:30-6:30pm. Open daily M-Sa 10am-3am.

# MURRAY RIVER AREA

Home to the few population clumps in the mostly arid stretch of northwestern Victoria is Australia's longest river, the Murray, which defines the border between New South Wales and Victoria and completes its 2600km journey by spilling out into the salty ocean near Adelaide. The ashen eucalyptus trees that haunt the banks of its muddy waters have been a hallowed home to Indigenous Australians for years. The river was an essential artery in the late 19th century, its waters traveled by giant freight-toting paddle steamers, but extensive rail and road networks rendered these boats obsolete by the end of the 1930s. Today, its only real draw for budget travelers is the many farms that call the region home, providing almost year-long work for those short on cash. If you're stuck here, there are a few things that might hold your interest, but otherwise, this is one corner of Victoria that you can easily skip.

**BUGGAH.** The crops in the Murray area are guarded by a fruit-fly exclusion zone, which means that no fresh fruit or vegetables can enter the region. Several postings along major roads will remind travelers; those who are caught can face fines from $250 to $2000.

# ECHUCA ☎03

The self-appointed "Paddle Steamer Capital of Australia," Echuca was founded at the site where the Campaspe and Goulbourn Rivers meet the gushing Murray (Echuca is the Aboriginal word for "meeting of the waters"). Founded by an ex-con in 1853, Echuca quickly became the biggest inland port in all of Australia, transporting supplies halfway across the nation. In its prime, the port precinct stretched over a 1km distance and boasted a whopping 79 pubs. However, due

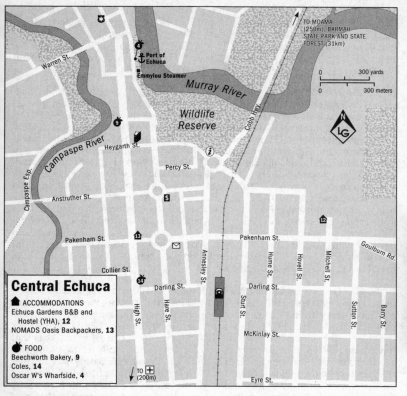

**Central Echuca**

🏠 **ACCOMMODATIONS**
Echuca Gardens B&B and
  Hostel (YHA), **12**
NOMADS Oasis Backpackers, **13**

🍴 **FOOD**
Beechworth Bakery, **9**
Coles, **14**
Oscar W's Wharfside, **4**

to general stoogery, a drinking ban was enacted. Although the ban has long
been lifted, Echuca remains quiet, and even its made-for-tourists port draws
few to this hot, dusty town. If you travel here, you'll want to immerse yourself
in the Murray riverboat culture by boarding a cruise or taking a stroll along one
of the town's several authentic riverside walks. But if you're thinking about
making a special trip to Echuca, think twice.

▶ **TRANSPORTATION.** V/Line **buses** run from the visitors center or the Ampol
Road House on the Northern Hwy. to: Albury-Wodonga (3-4hr., 1-3 per day,
$25-50); Bendigo (1hr., 1-3 per day, $8); Melbourne (3-4hr., 4-6 per day, $34);
Mildura (5hr.; 1 per day M, W-Th, Sa; $42); Swan Hill (2hr., 1-2 per day, $25).

▶ **ORIENTATION AND PRACTICAL INFORMATION.** Echuca and Moama
(across the Murray) lie about 200km north of Melbourne. Two highways
intersect in the region as well—the **Murray Valley Highway** and **Northern Highway.**
Echuca's main thoroughfares are Hare and High St., parallel roads that run
north-south from the Murray River to the Murray Valley Hwy. The **visitors center,**
2 Heygarth St., is on the Echuca side of the Echuca-Moama bridge. (☎03 5480
7555 or 1800 804 446; www.echucamoama.com. Open daily 9am-5pm.) ANZ,
National, and Commonwealth banks with 24hr. **ATMs** are side-by-side on Hare

St., just south of Anstruther St. (All open M-Th 9:30am-4pm, F 9:30am-5pm.) The **library,** at the corner of Heygarth and High St. across the intersection from McDonald's, offers Internet access. (☎ 03 5482 1997. Research free, email $2.60 per 30min. Book at desk. Open M-Tu and Th-F 10am-5:30pm, W noon-8pm, Sa 10am-1pm, Su 2-4:30pm.) The **post office** is on the corner of Hare and Pakenham St. (Open M-F 9am-5pm, Sa 9am-noon.) **Postal Code:** 3564.

**ⵎ ACCOMMODATIONS.** Only a handful of budget accommodations lurk among several dainty B&Bs and overpriced motels. The best option in town is **Echuca Gardens B&B and Hostel (YHA) ❷,** 103 Mitchell St., 8 blocks east from the CBD. Located in the second-oldest building in Echuca, the quiet backpackers' cottage behind the B&B has a homey feel, with only 10 beds, antique uphol-stered furniture, and a garden. (☎ 03 5480 6522; www.echucagardens.com. Key deposit $10. Reception 7:30-8:30am and 5-10pm. Cottage: high season $45, chil-dren $20; low season $25/10. B&B: high season $130-160, low season $100-140. YHA discount.) Catering to fruit pickers and other long-term guests, **NOMADS Oasis Backpackers ❷,** 410-422 High St., on the corner of Pakenham St., has bright, cheery dorms and a delightful garden. Request the suite with its own kitchen and bathroom; avoid the room across from the front desk. (☎ 03 5480 7866; www.backpackersechuca.com. $10 key deposit. Kitchen, TV lounge, and outdoor courtyard. Internet $5 per hr. Alcohol strictly prohibited. Transporta-tion to work sites $5.50 per day. Reception 9am-8pm. 4- to 12-bed dorms $25; doubles $55. $3 NOMADS discount.)

**ⵎ FOOD.** Don't miss **◪Oscar W's Wharfside ❷,** 101 Murray Esplanade, which promises an unforgettable dining experience with amazing views of the Mur-ray. All of the scrumptious servings are created on a red gum grill. The twice-cooked boned duck ($32) is their signature dish. The deck bar, hovering over the river, offers cheaper fare ($7.50-16.50), and guests can sit in old kegs that have been refitted into surprisingly comfortable seats. (☎ 03 5482 5133; www.oscarws.com.au. Open daily 11am-10pm.) The **Beechworth Bakery ❶,** 513 High St., has also set up shop in Echuca. The fabulous snickerdoodles ($3) and beestings ($3.50) are just as good as those in Beechworth itself. (☎ 03 5480 6999. Open daily 6am-6pm.) A **Coles** supermarket is on the corner of High and Darling St. (Open daily 6am-midnight.)

**ⵎ SIGHTS.** The main attraction in Echuca is its **historic port,** which consists of the wharf and several historic buildings, although the small area can be seen in an hour and holds only limited appeal. The 1865 red gum wharf has three levels to accommodate changing river conditions. Blacksmith and woodturn-ing shops sell handmade wares, and a steam display explains the workings of the invention that brought on the Industrial Revolution. (Entrance at 52 Murray Esplanade. ☎ 03 5482 4248; www.portofechuca.org.au. Open daily 9am-5pm.) Several paddlesteamers still ply the waters off the old port and are now open to the public for leisurely cruises. The **Port Authority** runs 1hr. cruises on *PS Pevensey, PS Alexander Arbuthnot,* and the *PS Adelaide,* the oldest wooden paddlesteamer in Australia. (The Historic Port building, 52 Murray Esplanade. ☎ 03 5482 4248. 5 per day. $20, concessions $15, children $9, families $42. Joint port and cruise: $23/19/13/57.) Just across the street are the paddlesteamers *Pride of the Murray* and *Emmylou;* the *Emmylou* is worth the slightly higher price, and so are its overnight accommodations, if you really want to splurge. (Tickets available at the Customs House or at 57 Murray Esplanade. ☎ 03 5480 2237 or 03 5482 5244. *Pride of the Murray:* 1hr.; 6 per day; $18.50, seniors $15, children $8, families $48. *Emmylou:* 1hr.; 5 per day; $20, children $10; 1½hr.

*VICTORIA*

$24.50/12.) The same company also operates 1hr. cruises on the steamer *PS Canberra*. ($18.50, seniors $15, children $8, families $48.)

# MILDURA                                            ☎ 03

A palm-lined oasis in dry Mallee country, Mildura can hit record-breaking temperatures during the summer. The town is mostly working-class; it's a haven for hungry backpackers with its 11 months of reaping and planting each year.

**⌐ TRANSPORTATION.** For those seeking transportation to farming jobs, note that hostels can assist you finding suitable means. The **train and bus station** is on 7th St., across from the northern end of Langtree Ave. **V/Line** runs to: Albury-Wodonga (10hr.; 1 per day Tu-W, F, Su; $67); Echuca (5hr.; 1 per day Tu-W, F, Su; $42); Melbourne (7-9hr., 2-3 per day, $67) via Bendigo (5-7hr., $58); Swan Hill (3-4hr., $37). **Countrylink** runs to Sydney (15hr., daily 4am, $120). **Tom Evans coaches** (☎03 5027 4309) services Broken Hill (3hr.; M, W, F 9am; $52). **Sunraysia Bus Lines** (☎03 5023 0274; www.sunbus.net.au) runs local routes and is a useful service for people working in the area. For car rentals, **Avis** (☎03 5022 1818), **Budget** (☎03 5021 4442), **Hertz** (☎03 5022 1411), and **Thrifty** (☎03 5023 2989) are in the airport, 8km out of town on the Sturt Hwy., with rentals from $55-70 per day. Avis also has a branch at 7th and Madden St. (☎03 5023 1263).

**◼◪ ORIENTATION AND PRACTICAL INFORMATION.** The commercial center of Mildura is the strip of Langtree Ave. from 7th to 10th St., which includes a pedestrian mall chock-full of retail and dining options. The **Mildura Visitor Information and Booking Centre**, on the corner of Deakin Ave. and 12th St. can assist with any queries. (☎03 5018 8380; www.mildura.vic.gov.au/tourism. Open M-F 9am-5:30pm, Sa-Su 9am-5pm.) The attached **library** offers free Internet ($2 per 30min.) for research. (☎03 5018 8350. Book ahead. Max. 1hr. Open M and Su 1-5pm, Tu-F 10am-7pm, Sa 10am-2pm.) For work opportunities, ask for the free *Working Holiday and Backpacker Information Sheet* from the visitors center, or contact **MADEC Jobs Australia**, 95 Lime Ave., off 10th St. (☎03 5021 3359. Open M-F 8am-7pm.) Work can often be found in the *Sunraysia Daily*'s employment section. There are also over a dozen hostels in town that can help guests lock down farming work. The **police** are on Madden Ave. between 8th and 9th St. (☎03 5023 9555) and the **post office** is on the corner of 8th St. and Orange Ave. (Open M-F 9am-5pm.) **Postal Code:** 3500.

**⌐ ACCOMMODATIONS.** Hostels in Mildura serve the constant influx of travelers searching for fruit-picking jobs; there are more than a dozen basic budget options scattered around town, as well as in nearby Red Cliffs and Wentworth. These self-proclaimed "working hostels" offer shelter and help find work. However, be aware that they take their "working" motto seriously; if you're only passing through, don't expect to find a bed. In terms of the work available, the local garlic farm and vineyards provide the bulk of it; expect to work about 8hr. per day and earn around $16 per hr. ▨**Oasis Backpackers ❷**, 230-232 Deakin Ave., is located past the visitors center when heading up Deakin Ave. from the train station and Murray River. This sparkling hostel is an oasis for weary fruit pickers; they are invited to laze in the pool, frequent the on-site bar, or chill out in front of a plasma TV. Be aware that it fills up quickly during harvest season. (☎04 1738 0744 or 04 1723 0571; www.milduraoasis.com.au. On-site licensed bar. Transport to work $5 per day. Free Internet. F free dinner. Laundry $3. Reception 8-10:30am and 3:30-5:30pm. Check-out 9am. Weekly rent due Th at 5pm. 4-bed ensuite dorms $20, weekly $140.) **Mildura City Backpackers ❷**, at 50

Lemon Ave., has tidy bungalows with smooth hardwood floors; just try to avoid the bedroom with a skylight instead of a window. (☎03 5022 7922 or 04 0750 2120; www.milduracitybackpackers.com.au. Lockers $2 per day. Key deposit $10. Transport to work $6 per day. F free dinner. Dorms $22, weekly $13; twins $25/150; doubles $55/330.) **Riverboat Bungalow Backpackers ❷** is located at 27 Chaffey Ave. This is the original working hostel in Mildura. The Riverboat consists of three neighboring bungalows. (☎03 5021 5315. Transport to work $3 per day. Dorms $22, weekly $132. VIP discount $1.)

**⬛ FOOD.** The best option for a night out is the Langtree Avenue Mall, one block west of Deakin Ave. between 7th and 9th St. Be aware that on weeknights, the streets are deserted after 5pm (though the pubs are not). **Pizza Cafe at the Grand ❶**, 18 Langtree Ave., dishes out gooey slices of wood-oven pies. (☎03 5022 2223. Small pizzas $12-16, large $16-19. Open M-Th 11am-11pm, F-Sa 11am-midnight, Su 11:30am-11pm.) **Fasta Pasta ❷**, 30 Langtree Ave., serves decent and quickly prepared pastas ($8-13) and pizzas. (☎03 5022 0622. Open M-Sa 11:30am-3pm and 5-10pm, Su 11:30am-3pm and 5-9:30pm.) There is a 24hr. **Coles** supermarket at 8th St. and Lime Ave.

**⬛ SIGHTS.** Mildura is the base camp for nearby national parks and other outback sights. The **visitors center** (see **Orientation** above) books all commercial tours. **Harry Nanya Tours** runs full-day trips to Mungo and Wentworth focusing on Aboriginal history and the Dreaming. (☎03 5027 2076; www.harrynanyatours.com.au. $75-300.) As is often the case for the towns along the Murray River, the main summertime attraction is the local swimming hole. Apex Park, a sandbar in the Murray, is perfect on hot days, as it's shaded by ash trees and red gum trees. From town, take 7th St. past the train station and turn right across the tracks on Chaffey Ave., which winds its way to the park.

# HUME CORRIDOR

The Hume Hwy. links Melbourne and Sydney via 872km of relatively unspectacular scenery; intrepid travelers who venture off the Hume, however, are rewarded. Quaint mining towns and ski resorts are sprinkled throughout the sunburnt hills. Farther west along the Murray Valley Hwy. are the billabongs of Yarrawonga and Cobram, perfect for fishing, swimming, and relaxing, especially as the towns themselves snooze in the summer.

## MANSFIELD ☎03

Mansfield's *raison d'être* is its proximity to Mt. Buller, allowing tourists to rent skis and chains before ascending 45km to Victoria's most popular ski resort.

**⬛ TRANSPORTATION.** The **Mansfield Passenger Terminal** is at 137 High St. V/Line buses (☎03 13 61 96) serve Melbourne (3hr., 1-2 per day, $34) and Mt. Buller (1hr., 7 per day, $72) during ski season. Law requires all vehicles heading to Mt. Buller to carry snow chains from June until September. You can leave them in the trunk, but there are spot checks and hefty fines ($135) for not carrying them at all. Drivers heading to the top of the mountain should be careful to fill their cars with petrol in Mansfield, as it is not widely available at the summit.

**⬛ PRACTICAL INFORMATION.** The brand-new **Mansfield Visitors Centre** is just outside town at 167 Maroondah Hwy. and offers endless information on Mt.

Buller and High Country. (☎03 5775 7000; bookings 1800 039 049. Open daily 9am-5pm.) Heading east into town on High St., the town's main drag, you'll find ski rental stores and a few **ATMs.** The **library,** at the corner of High and Collopy St., has **Internet access;** you must fill out a form, even for one-time use. (☎03 5775 2176. $2 per 30min. Open Tu 9:30am-6pm, W 9:30am-1pm, Th-F 9:30am-5:30pm, Sa 9:30am-noon.) The **police station** is at 92-94 High St. (☎03 5775 2555). **Discount Ski Hire,** 131 High St. (☎03 5775 2859 or 1800 647 754), and its nearby affiliate, **Ski Centre Mansfield,** 149 High St. (☎03 5775 1624), rent chains (full-day $15) and a range of ski equipment and clothing. (Open June-Oct. M-Th, Sa-Su 6am-7pm, F 6am-midnight.) There are similar ski rental shops all along High St., all offering comparable deals (full-day skis, boots, and poles from $25; snowboard and boots from $45). The **post office** is next door at 90 High St. (☎03 5775 2248. Open M-F 9am-5pm.) **Postal Code:** 3722.

**⌐☐ ACCOMMODATIONS AND FOOD.** The best budget beds in town are at the ▦**Mansfield Backpackers Inn ❷,** 116 High St., part of the brick bungalows at the Travellers Lodge Motel. The small dorms are spic and span, and there's a large common area for backpackers that includes a tidy kitchen and lounge with ping-pong table and a mural by local schoolchildren, lockers, and TV, as well as a lovely garden and BBQ area. (☎03 5775 1800; www.mansfieldtravel-lodge.com. Only the motel portion has A/C, but dorms have fans. Book ahead in winter. Reception 8am-9:30pm. Dorms $25; singles $85; doubles $95-105; family rooms $145-155.) The **Hotel Delatite ❸,** on the corner of High and Highett St., offers simple accommodations with a fresh coat of paint above a popular bar. The porch is a plus, although be aware that rooms can get stuffy in hot weather. (☎03 5775 2004. Shared bath and toilet. Continental breakfast included. Bar open daily 10am-1am. Singles $35; doubles $70.)

Mansfield doesn't offer many non-fast food culinary options; the few that exist are definitely not budget. Your best option is self-catering. There are two supermarkets: **FoodWorks,** 117-119 High St. (☎03 5775 2255), and **IGA,** 47-51 High St. (☎03 5775 2014. Both deliver to Mt. Buller. Both open daily 8am-8pm.)

# MOUNT BULLER ☎03

Victoria's largest and most accessible ski resort, Mt. Buller is a 3hr. drive from Melbourne and has arguably the best terrain in Victoria. While it may not compare to popular skiing destinations in the US or Europe (despite the local moniker "Aussie Alps"), it's a mecca for skiers and snowboarders between mid-June and early October. Though quiet in the low season, several summer weekends attract large groups of tourists; look for the luxury car races at the end of January or the annual Easter weekend art show.

**⌐ TRANSPORTATION.** Along with V/Line (see **Mansfield,** p. 656), Mansfield-Mount Buller Bus Lines operates coach service to Mt. Buller from Mansfield. (☎03 5775 6070; www.mmbl.com.au. 1hr., 6-8 per day, $40.) V/Line (☎03 13 61 96) offers round-trip service from Melbourne to Mt. Buller ($115, including ski fees). **Snowcaper Tours** departs from Melbourne and offers packages that include round-trip transport, entrance fees, and a full-day lift ticket. Participants leave Melbourne at 4am and return by 9:30pm. (☎03 5775 2367, reservations ☎1800 033 023. Mid-week $115, Sa-Su $130.) Only Mansfield-Mt. Buller and V/Line buses pull into the Cow Camp Plaza, in the center of Mt. Buller village; all others stop at the base of the mountain, making a cab ride to the top necessary ($14). If going by car, bring snow chains (cars without chains will be fined $135 and given 3 demerit points) and take Buller Rd. (Hwy. 164)

## YOU SNOOZE, YOU LOSE

"Rest or die." "A powernap could save your life." "Fatigue kills." "The only cure for fatigue is sleep." When driving down the long, flat, straight roads of eastern Victoria—with only the occasional sheep or cow to keep you entertained—the highway commission's signs are the only things to look at for miles. And they're really getting their message out there. With billboards every few hundred meters, frequent rest stops and messages intended to scare some sense into drivers, Victoria is trying its hardest to combat one of the biggest killers on Australia's highways: chronic fatigue.

Because of those long, flat, straight stretches, drivers who are already tired are more likely to fall asleep, even if only for a moment. However, loss of control for just a second can cause a car to veer off the road or into another lane, endangering the driver and others around him, which is a point that the sign "A microsleep can kill" hammers home pretty well. Victoria's message is simple: take a break from the monotony of the road, treat yourself to a quick nap, and take at least some of the danger out of driving. So the next time you feel your eyes drooping on the road, take the sign's advice: "Droopy eyes? Pull over." It's possible that a brief powernap could save your life.

east to Mt. Buller. (Car admission $32 per day; overnight fee $6.) There is free parking at the bottom of the mountain. To get to the village from the carpark, visitors without luggage can take a free shuttle; those with bags must take a taxi ($14). Beware: these daily charges add up fast. Consider taking the bus, especially if you're staying on the mountain for a while.

🛈 **PRACTICAL INFORMATION.** The village is the hub of accommodations, food, and ski services. The **Cow Camp Plaza** houses lockers, ATMs, and Cow Camp Alpine Ski Rentals. (☎03 5777 6082. Skis, boots, and poles $32-70; snowboard and boots $45-70.) The **information center,** located in the nearby post office in summer and opposite the plaza in winter, has maps of the resort and slopes, as well as info on work and long-term accommodations options. (☎03 5777 7800, reservations ☎1800 039 049; www.mtbuller.com.au. Open M-F 8:30am-5pm.) The **lift ticket office** sits across the village center from the info tower. (☎03 5777 7800 or 5777 7877. Day pass $94, children and high school students with valid ID $53; university students with valid ID receive 50% discount Tu, 20% M and W-Su.) For the latest snow conditions, call the official **Victorian Snow Report** (☎1902 240 523; www.vicsnowreport.com.au. $0.55 per min.) or tune into 93.7FM. The Resort Management Building in the village center has a **post office.** (☎03 5777 6013. Open daily 8:30am-5pm.) **Postal Code:** 3723.

🏠 **ACCOMMODATIONS.** Mt. Buller is tough for budget travelers; in the summer, no budget accommodations are open, and in the winter, they're less budget than one would hope. In the winter, **Buller Backpackers ❹** is the least expensive lodging on the mountain, and you can ski to its front door. (☎1800 810 200. 2-night min. stay on weekends. Open only during ski season. Book at least 3 weeks ahead July-Aug. Ski lockers available. Reception 8-10am and 5pm-10pm. Dorms $60-85.) Next door, the **Kooroora Hotel ❺** has more intimate four-person dorms with showers. There's a 15% guest discount for on-site ski rental. (☎03 5777 6050. Open only during ski season. Ages 18 and up. Reservations require a 50% deposit. Dorms M-Th $85, F-Su $100.)

🍴🍷 **FOOD AND NIGHTLIFE.** Food options abound, but in summer, almost all the restaurants close. A polar bear guards the doorway at **ABOM ❷,** on Summit St., a convivial lodge that offers both affordable bistro fare and an ideal refuge from the cold. (☎03 5777 7899; www.mtbuller.com/abom.

Lower-end lunch fare of sandwiches and soups around $10.) The campy Cow Camp Plaza houses **Uncle Pat's** ❷, with second-floor decks overlooking the valley and the only budget dining option in the village open all year. (☎03 5777 6949. Focaccia $8. Pizzas $7-16.) Though only open during ski season, **Kooroora's Pub** is hands-down the place to go for nightlife. Besides the pub's great atmosphere, it's also the only place on the mountain that regularly stays open past midnight. (Sa live music, M-F and Su DJs. Open daily until 3am; kitchen open until 10pm.) A newly opened **Foodworks,** 349 Athletes Walk, in the village square, caters to all your grocery needs. (☎03 5777 6133. Open June-Sept. daily 7am-8pm; closed in summer.)

⛷ **SKIING.** Nearly half of Mt. Buller's terrain is classified as "intermediate," but several expert trails traverse the southern slopes, including **Fanny's Finish,** which separates the skiers from the snow-bunnies. First-time skiers have plenty of long runs to choose from, as well as numerous lesson packages. Twenty-five lifts service the mountain, and lift lines are usually short; the pride of the mountain is the brand-new Holden lift, Australia's first high-speed, six-seater chair. Those who prefer the flatlands will find 75km of cross-country skiing trails (approx. half of which are groomed) and an entire mountain, **Mount Stirling,** set aside for their use. (Ticket office ☎03 5777 5624. Open June-Sept. dawn-dusk. No overnight accommodations on Mt. Stirling except camping, which is free.) The information center (next to the carparks) contains a public shelter with fireplace, ski and toboggan rental, and food. (Car entry $23; trail $10; cross-country ski rental $35; telemark $47.)

🥾🚵 **HIKING AND MOUNTAIN BIKING.** After many of its trails were destroyed by bushfire, Mt. Buller is slowly regaining its status as a prime mountain biking and hiking destination, although the lack of open accommodations, restaurants, or transport options can make things difficult. In summer, it is easiest to daytrip from Mansfield. The Horsehill chairlift near the carpark operates intermittently in January and the end of December (subject to bushfires), transporting bikers and hikers to higher-altitude trails. The **Summit Walk** (3.6km; 2hr. round-trip; easy), beginning and ending at the Arlberg Hotel at the western edge of town, has informative plaques on local flora and fauna and rewards hikers with views of blue-green mountains and cattle country rolling to the horizon. The summit can also be reached by driving to the end of Summit Rd. and following a marked unsealed road to the base of the final leg of the summit hike (200m). Popular with mountain bikers, a longer hike to Mount Stirling via **Corn Hill and Howqua Gap** (16.4km; 5-7hr. round-trip; moderate) offers a grand view of Mt. Buller. The shortest of the hikes, the **Blind Creek Falls walk** (40min. round-trip; moderate), is accessible from Boggy Corner, 3.5km below the village. The path leads down a switchback to the Chalet Creek and then to the falls. Detailed descriptions of all the hikes in the area are available in the information center's free *Walking Trails Guide*.

Downhill mountain biking is a must for any adrenaline junkie, and Mt. Buller is prime terrain for those who enjoy throwing themselves down big hills. All downhill bike trails start at Spurs Restaurant and are marked with the same colors and symbols as ski trails (black diamond, etc.). **Buller Sports** (☎03 5777 7884), in the village center, rents bikes. All downhill bikers must purchase a pass, which includes use of the Horse Hill chairlift ($45). The **Abom Downhill Track** (2.2km) is the original downhill track, offering intermediate thrills with a lot of switchbacks. Reserved for pros or the truly insane, the **International Track** (2km) offers extremely technical terrain.

# WANGARATTA ☎03

Referred to endearingly as "Wang" by locals, Wangaratta (pronounced WANG-uh-RET-ta) was erected at the junction of the Hume Hwy. and the Great Alpine Rd. Wangaratta, an Aboriginal word meaning "resting place of the cormorant," is a pleasant place to live but not an exciting place to visit. That said, it is definitely worth a stop for the great daytrips.

**TRANSPORTATION.** Schedules and prices vary; contact the **train station** (☎03 5721 3641) for up-to-date info. V/Line (☎03 136 196) runs from the station at 51 Norton St. to: Albury station (1hr., 1 per day, $13); Beechworth (30min., 1 per day, $7); Bright (1hr., 1 per day, $13); Melbourne (2hr., 3 per day, $40); Rutherglen (30min., 1 per day, $6); Wodonga station (50min., 1 per day, $10). Countrylink runs to Sydney (9hr., 2 per day, $100).

**PRACTICAL INFORMATION.** Visit the **Worktrainers Employment Services** on the corner of Ovens and Faithful St. for assistance with finding available farmhand work. (☎1800 062 332; www.worktrainers.com.au. Open M-F 9am-5pm.) The **visitors center** at 100 Murphy St. in the CBD has a useful, free map of town and significant information about fruit-picking opportunities and nearby activities, as well as **Internet access.** (☎03 5721 5711 or 1800 801 065. Internet $2 per 30min. Open daily 9am-5pm.) Free Internet can also be found at the **library,** 62 Ovens St. (☎03 5721 2366. Book ahead. Open M-F 8:45am-6pm, Sa 9:30am-1pm. **Police** can be reached at ☎03 5723 0888. The **post office** is by the intersection of Murphy and Ely St. (Open M-F 9am-5pm.) **Postal Code:** 3677.

**ACCOMMODATIONS.** The best budget digs in town are at the **Hotel Pinsent ❸**, 20 Reid St., known by locals as the "Pino." With an expansive bar and restaurant, the Pino has newly refurbished ensuite rooms that are great value for the money, with A/C, TV, and continental breakfast. (☎03 5721 2183. Singles $45; doubles from $60; triples $70; quads $80.) Just around the corner is the **Billabong Motel ❸,** 12 Chisholm St., at the end of Reid St. The rooms are always prim and proper, although the kitschy trinkets and preponderance of pink may discourage some. (☎03 5721 2353. Singles $45; doubles $60-70.) Across the Ovens River on Pinkerton Cres., just north of Faithful St., is **Painters Island Caravan Park ❶,** with a swimming pool and a playground. (☎03 5721 3380. Reception 8am-8pm. Sites $22, powered 25; cabins from $55.) The visitors center has color-coded handouts with additional accommodation options.

**FOOD.** **Scribbler's Cafe ❶,** 66 Reid St., is so-named because patrons are given bits of paper and encouraged to leave their words behind. Scribbler's serves breakfast ($10-13) and dessert all day (cakes $7) and draws crowds for lunch as well. Vegeterians and coeliacs will find plenty of options here. (☎03 5721 3945. Open M-Sa 8am-5pm, Su 9am-3pm. BYO.) **Casual Hollywood's Pizza Cafe ❷,** 1 Murphy St., is as classy as Wang gets. Vast outdoor seating, fresh coffee, and tasty pizzas ($12-21) keep the locals happy. (☎03 5721 9877; www.hollywoods.com.au. Open Tu-Th 9am-11pm, F 9am-late, Sa 8am-late, Su 8am-11pm.) Groceries are available at **Safeway,** on Ovens St. between Reid and Ford St. (open daily 7am-midnight) and **Coles,** on Tone Rd., south of the CBD (open 24hr.).

**SIGHTS.** Visitors can bike, hike, or ride horses on the **Murray to the Mountains Rail Trail.** (☎1800 801 065; www.railtrail.com.au.) The 94km paved trail begins next to the Painters Island Caravan Park and follows historical railway lines, passing through Bowser, Beechworth, and Myrtleford before ending in Bright. Wangaratta's renowned **Jazz Festival** (☎03 5722 1666 or 1800 803 944;

www.wangaratta-jazz.org.au), the weekend prior to the **Melbourne Cup** in fall, is among Australia's best; accommodations are often booked by June.

**✷ DAYTRIP FROM WANGARATTA: THE MILAWA GOURMET REGION.** The Milawa Gourmet Region is the area that contains all of the towns, vineyards, and eateries of interest; it centers out from Wangaratta and encompasses 50km of roads in a rough circle. Milawa itself is a sleepy village with a well-preserved town center and a smattering of pricey B&Bs. The highlights are just outside' town. The ▨**Milawa Cheese Factory,** on Factory Rd., has generous free samples of over 20 gourmet cheeses, handmade from the milk of local goats and cows. If the samples don't sate your appetite, there is a snazzy **restaurant ❸** (Milawa 3-cheese pizza $15; main courses from $26) and a first-rate bakery that has a 15-year-old sourdough culture named George. (✆ *03 5727 3589. Cheese tasting room open daily 9am-5pm. Bakery open daily 9am-5pm. Lunch daily noon-3pm. Dinner Th-Sa starting at 6:30pm. Book ahead for dinner. From Wangaratta, take Oxley Flats Rd. to reach the area.)*

**✷ DAYTRIP FROM WANGARATTA: BROWN BROTHERS VINEYARD.** About 1km down the road, the classy ▨**Brown Brothers Vineyard** could satisfy a small nation with its five tasting bars. Though the experience doesn't come cheap, it is worth every penny. The rustic, wood-beamed tasting room offers a sample of regionally famous wines (from $13) and is wildly popular. Each course at its **Epicurean Centre Restaurant ❸** includes an accompanying glass of wine; the attached lounge serves lighter fare. (✆ *03 5720 5500. 2 dishes $42, extra dish $14. Vineyard open daily 9am-5pm. Restaurant open daily 11am-3pm. Lounge open daily 9am-4pm.)*

# RUTHERGLEN ☎ 02

"Sydney may have a beautiful harbor, but Rutherglen has an excellent Port," says a billboard in the center of the sleepy town. Known for some of the world's best fortified wines, the Rutherglen area offers the finest varieties of Muscats and Tokays, and the charming central village is the perfect base for sampling these drinkable delights. Stop at the informative visitors center and a grab a meal at one of the town's restaurants before strolling through the vineyards.

**◪✷ TRANSPORTATION AND PRACTICAL INFORMATION.** In Rutherglen, the **Murray Valley Highway (Hwy. 16)** is called **Main Street** and runs from Yarrawonga (45km west) through the town to Albury-Wodonga (50km east). Several private wine tours run from Rutherglen and Albury-Wodonga; call the **visitors center** for further details. Wine de Tour operates from Albury-Wodonga ($50), Yarrawonga ($50), Rutherglen ($30), and Melbourne ($130) and offers daily tours of the region's best wineries (☎ 1300 3685 22; www.winedetour.com.au). V/Line **buses** leave Rutherglen's BP service station for Melbourne via Wangaratta (3hr.; M, W, F 6:35am; $40). Purchase tickets from the newsagency on Main St. Webster buses shuttle to Albury-Wodonga at 9:30am on weekdays from the BP station west of the city center (☎ 02 6033 2459; $7). The **visitors center** (officially called the **Rutherglen Wine Experience**) is located on the town's central roundabout at 55 Main St. and is the place to go for wine literature and bike rental. It also stocks the **Official Visitor's Guide,** an indispensable map of the region's vineyards. (☎ 02 6032 9009 or 1 800 622 871. Open daily 9am-5pm. ½-day bike rental $20, full-day $30.) The **post office** is at 83 Main St. (Open M-F 8am-5pm.) **Postal Code:** 3685.

**▮ ACCOMMODATIONS.** The **Star Hotel ❸**, 105 Main St., is the best option for budget digs in town offering large, private ensuite motel units with TV, A/C, and continental breakfast for a reasonable rate. (☎ 02 6032 9625. Singles $45;

doubles $75.) If the Star is full, try the **Victoria Hotel ❸**, 90 Main St., where you'll find cozy, older rooms. Its **bistro ❺** serves meals on a gorgeous balcony. (☎02 6032 8610. Breakfast included. Singles $45; twins and doubles $60.)

**❏ FOOD.** Before heading out to the wineries, stop for lunch at 🍴**Parker Pies ❶**, 86-88 Main St. This famous meat pie shop has garnered nationwide awards including "Best Game Pie" in 2003 (for a savory buffalo pie) and 2005 (for an emu pie), and for good reason. The *pièce de résistance* is the less-exotic, but spectacularly delicious chicken pie with mustard, avocado, and ham— winner of "Best Chicken Pie in Australia" in 2000. The sweets are also out of this world—the lemon and passionfruit cheesecake is of particular note. The ultra-friendly staff deserves national recognition as well. (☎02 6032 9605. Pies $3.80. Open M-F 9am-5pm, Sa 8:30am-5pm, Su 9am-4pm. Cash only.) The **Poachers Paradise Hotel ❶**, 120 Main St., serves pub lunches from $7. (☎02 6032 9502. Open M-Sa 10am-1am, Su 10am-11pm.) The **IGA** supermarket, 95 Main St., caters to all your budget dining needs. (☎02 6032 9232. Open M-W and Sa 7:30am-7pm, Th-F 7:30am-7:30pm, Su 8:30am-6pm.)

# WINERIES NEAR RUTHERGLEN

Rutherglen's temperate climate allows vineyards to keep grapes on their vines longer and favors full-bodied red wines and fortified varieties of Tokay and Muscat. Choosing from among the excellent local wineries can be difficult, especially since they all offer free tastings. For those in cars, the **Official Visitor's Guide,** available at the **Rutherglen Wine Experience** (see **Transportation and Practical Information,** p. 661) and most wineries, is essential. Also get the **Touring Rutherglen** map, which makes finding the wineries significantly easier (both brochures are free). If traveling by bike, pick up the free *Muscat Trail Map* as well.

The Rutherglen vineyards sponsor several festivals throughout the year. The most popular is the carnival-like **Rutherglen Winery Walkabout** (on the Queen's Birthday weekend in June), featuring food and entertainment at the estates and a street fair downtown. Be aware that hordes flock to the area during this time, and accommodations are scarce. True connoisseurs would probably prefer to skip the big production and instead sample the impressive food and wine combinations during **Tastes of Rutherglen,** held the second and third weekends in March. Remember, the local specialty is fortified wine, which indicates an alcohol content far greater than that of wine from other parts of Australia. If you are driving, be responsible when tasting, and remember that the country's super-low blood-alcohol legal limit is 0.05%.

## WINERIES

If you want good vino, we recommend you check out the following.

- 🍷 **All Saints Estate** (☎02 6035 2222; www.allsaintswine.com.au). Posh, 120-year-old vineyard offers fantastic Tokays ($31 per bottle), incredibly knowledgeable staff, and a setting from a storybook. The tree-lined entrance to the estate is irrefutably majestic, as is the red-brick castle that hosts the tasting room. The **Indigo Cheese Company** is located on the premises and offers homemade cheeses. (☎02 6035 2250; www. indigocheese.com. Open M-F 11am-4pm, Sa-Su 10am-5pm.) A self-guided tour takes you past picture-perfect gardens filled with roses and huge display casks; pick up a map from the cellar door. Winery open Sept.-Apr. daily 10am-5pm; May-Aug. hours vary. Restaurant open W-Su 10am-5:30pm, Sa 10am-11pm. Book ahead on weekends.

- **St. Leonards Vineyards** (☎02 6033 1004; www.stleonardswines.com) on St. Leonards Rd. just off All Saints Rd. Same owners as All Saints. Combines an idyllic setting with delicious, unique flavors. Enjoy the signature Orange Muscat (crisp, light, and dry) while lounging near a placid billabong fed by the Murray River. **St. Leonards Cafe** offers warm BBQ meals that go perfectly with the fruity fortifieds. The vineyard also features twilight movies in the vines once a month ($10). Live music 1st and 3rd Su of the month. Frequent art expositions. Cellar open for tastings M and F-Su 10am-5pm.

**Cofield Wines** (☎02 6033 3798; www.cofieldwines.com.au), northwest of Rutherglen on Distillery Rd., just off Corowa Rd. Smaller than nearby vineyards and family-run. Its signature press is a fantastic sparkling Shiraz. The superb 2002 Quartz Vein Shiraz is also popular. The **Pickled Sisters Cafe,** located next door, is a local favorite. Cellar open M, W-Th, Su 10am-4pm, F-Sa 6:30pm-late. Cafe open M and W-Su 10am-4pm.

**Pfeifer Wines** (☎02 6033 2805), next to Cofield Wines on Distillery Rd. A small, unpretentious, and family-run winery that has recently been collecting national awards for its vintage Port-style wines. Taste the sumptuous table wines, the 2002 Merlot, and the 2006 Riesling. Open M-Sa 9am-5pm, Su 10am-5pm.

# HIGH COUNTRY

Tucked between the Murray River and Gippsland's coastal forest is high country, a lush contrast to the iconic ocean vistas and scorched red rocks of the Outback. Mere hills compared to the skyscraping ranges of other continents, Victoria's high country is nonetheless a favored destination for Australian winter sports enthusiasts. In the summer, the region's terrain challenges even the most seasoned hikers, climbers, and mountain bikers. Bright is the only budget hub in the area, although the Falls Creek Resort has a hostel and is somewhat open in summer; the other resorts more or less shut down after ski season.

# BEECHWORTH ☎03

Beechworth, Victoria's best-preserved gold town, lies off Owens Hwy. in the northeast. Traces of gold were discovered here in February 1852, and by 1866, over 128 tons had been found. Today, the town has become a haven for weekend getaways at endearing B&Bs. Some visit to immerse themselves in the history of Australia's most famous crook, Ned Kelly, who stood trial in the mining town for theft and murder. Some make the trek just to sample the delicious treats at the noteworthy Beechworth Bakery.

**▐ TRANSPORTATION.** The **bus stop** is on Camp St., just west of Ford St. V/ Line **buses** (☎03 13 61 96) run to: Bright (1hr., 1-2 per day, $6.10); Melbourne (3hr., 1-4 per day, $58); Wangaratta (35min., 1-6 per day, $5.30); Wodonga (1hr., 1-4 per day, $21). Wangaratta Coachlines (☎03 5722 1843) run between Beechworth and Albury-Wodonga (1hr., M-F 2 per day, $7.20), making stops in Yackandandah (15min., 2 per day, $3.60), and Wodonga (45min., 2 per day, $7.20). **Taxis** can be reached at ☎03 5728 1485. Beechworth Cycles and Saws, 17 Camp St., rents **bicycles.** (☎03 5728 1402. Open M-F 9am-5pm, Sa 9am-noon. $20 per ½-day, $30 per day; $100 deposit.)

**▐ PRACTICAL INFORMATION.** The **Visitors Information Centre** is in Shire Hall on **Ford Street,** Beechworth's main north-south thoroughfare, and offers a plethora of information about the town. Pick up the official **Beechworth's Visitors Guide** for a handy map and a list of attractions. (☎03 5728 8064 or 1300 366 321; www.beechworthonline.com.au. 2-day museum pass $12.50, concessions $8, ages 5-16 $6. Ned Kelly tour departs daily 10:30am; 1hr; $7.50, concessions and under 18 $5, family $15. Goldfields tour departs daily 1pm; 1hr.; $7.50/5/15. Open daily 9am-5pm.) The **police station** (☎03 5728 1032) is located on Williams St., around the corner from the visitors center.

**⌕ ACCOMMODATIONS.** Centrally located **Tanswell's Commercial Hotel ❹**, 30 Ford St., offers freshly refurbished rooms with wrought-iron balconies. (☎03 5728 1480. Shared bath and toilet. Singles $45; doubles $65.) Simple bedrooms are available above the **Empire Hotel ❸**, a betting bar on the corner of Camp and High St. (☎03 5728 1030. Singles $30; doubles $50.) The sprawling **Old Priory ❹** is a B&B built in an old stone-and-brick Brigidine convent. Beautiful gardens, wrap-around porches, and an antique feel make this hotel worth the extra money. Rooms have wood panelling and antique washstands. The dorms, however, hark back to the convent's past, crammed with metal bunks sporting thin foam mattresses. (☎02 5728 1024; www.oldpriory.com.au. Dorms for groups $40 per person; singles $50; doubles and twins $80; ensuite cottages $115. Call ahead.) **Lake Sambell Caravan Park ❷**, 1.5km outside of town, has lovely lake views. Take Ford St. north, veer right on Junction St., and follow the blue signs which guide visitors toward the left at the fork in the road. (☎03 5728 1421; www.caravanparkbeechworth.com.au. Reception 8am-8pm. Laundry, BBQ, playground, and minigolf. Sites $21-29, powered $24-36; 4-person caravans $45-60; 4-person cabins $65-85.)

**▢ FOOD.** It's worth going to Beechworth simply to try the divine desserts at the acclaimed **▨Beechworth Bakery ❶**, 27 Camp St. Don't miss the popular almond, honey, and custard bee stings ($3.50) or the raspberry snickerdoodles ($3). Enjoy a focaccia sandwich ($7.50) or Ned Kelly pie (steak, egg, cheese, and bacon; $4.50) in their street-side seating area or quiet upper level. (☎03 5728 1132. Open daily 6am-7pm.) For a memorable splurge, try the elegant **Bank Restaurant ❹**, 86 Ford St. Situated in the old Bank of Australasia building and attached to a luxurious B&B, the dining rooms have high ceilings and period decor. Although dinner portions start at $27 and extend far beyond the budget traveler's wallet, weekend brunches (starting at $12.50) are worth the price. (☎03 5728 2223. Open M-F 6:30-9:30pm, Sa-Su 9am-noon.)

**◪ SIGHTS.** Inquire at the visitors center about 1hr. **Ned Kelly and Goldfields walking tours** in historic Beechworth (see above). Behind the visitors center, on Loch St., the rather unimpressive **Burke Museum** displays gold-rush era artifacts, a collection of Victorian Aboriginal weapons, and animal and bird specimens, including the Thylacine, a now-extinct Tasmanian marsupial. (☎03 5728 8067. Open daily 10am-5pm. $5, concessions $3, families $10.) The town's highlight is the stone government buildings across the street from the visitors center, which include the **Beechworth Historic Court House,** 94 Ford St., where the courtroom has been preserved in its 19th-century condition, right down to the dock where bushranger Ned Kelly stood during his trials and the cells in which he and his mother were (at separate times) detained. The courthouse saw over 40 trials involving various members of the Kelly family. A back room displays Kelly's famous self-made armor; when he was finally captured, it took 28 bullets to bring him down. The trial is recreated in surround-sound as you walk through. (☎03 5728 8066. Open daily 9am-5pm. $5, concessions $3, families $10.) At the **Beechworth cemetery,** north of the town center on Cemetery Rd., you'll find the **Chinese Burning Towers** and rows of headstones with epitaphs in Chinese characters—reminders of the Chinese presence in gold-rush Beechworth. Chinese miners once outnumbered whites five to one. After growing resentment of their perceived success exploded in the violent Buckland riots of 1857, many moved to Beechworth's relatively peaceful Chinese community.

# MOUNT BUFFALO NATIONAL PARK

Located off of the Great Alpine Rd., Mt. Buffalo dominates the landscape, signaling the site of a rich sub-alpine ecosystem with plenty of outdoor adventure opportunities year-round. Check out *Discovering Mount Buffalo*, a small book published by the Victorian National Parks Association, for a detailed guide to walks and camping areas within the vast park. Founded in 1898, Mt. Buffalo is one of Australia's oldest national parks. Sadly, in the summers of 2006 and 2007, devastating bushfires swept through the region, wiping out most of the park's infrastructure, formal lodgings, and downhill ski industry. Cross-country skiing and snowtubing keep the park popular in winter, but most options are now limited to mild daytrip activities. In addition to the country's best rock-climbing, the summer months offer numerous easy-to-moderate hikes, leading to a cool lake, winding falls, and mesmerizing outlooks over Buckland Valley.

**⚡ PRACTICAL INFORMATION.** The **park entrance gate** (☎03 5756 2328) serves as the primary information source on site, while the actual **Parks Victoria Office** is 20km beyond the entry. (☎03 5755 1466, 24hr. 13 19 63. Snowshoe tours July-Aug. daily at 1pm. Open daily 8:30am-4:30pm.) The entrance, 5km north of Bright (p. 666), is just off the Great Alpine Rd. roundabout by Porepunkah. (Entrance fee $10.) There is no public transportation to Mt. Buffalo, but **Northeast Off Road Tours** (☎04 1857 9218 or 04 2010 3382; www.neoffroadtours.com. au) shuttles visitors to the park in 4WD vehicles. If driving, be aware that there's no petrol on the mountain, so fill up in Bright.

**⛏ ACCOMMODATIONS.** The Mount Buffalo Chalet is the only lodging left by the fires, but its future, including room rates, is still uncertain. Great **campsites ❶** exist throughout the park, including one beside **Lake Catani ❶**, 2km beyond the park office, with toilets, water, hot showers, and a laundry basin. (High season $19 per night for 4 people; extra person $4, extra vehicle $5. Low season $14/4/5; in winter $6 per site. Peak periods are Dec.-Feb., Easter, Melbourne Cup weekend, Apr. school holidays, and Labour Day weekend. Open year-round.) There are remote camping sites with pit toilets and water at **Rocky Creek Track ❶**, 6.5km from Reservoir Area carpark ($3.50).

**⛷ SKIING.** In the park, 11km of groomed (and 2km of ungroomed) cross-country ski trails lie across the road from the Lodge carpark. Cross-country skiing is free; an information sheet is available at the entrance gate. (On-site rental of cross-country skis and boots $20 per day.)

**🥾 HIKING.** Mt. Buffalo is also an excellent choice for hikers. Within the park are numerous walking tracks with spectacular lookouts, which are described at length in *Discovering Mount Buffalo* and in the park notes, available at the parks office. The most challenging hike is the **Big Walk** (11.3km, 4-5hr. from park entrance to the Gorge Day Visitor Area). It ascends over 1km in only 9km of trail as it climbs the plateau. The **Eurobin Falls track** (1.5km, 45min. round-trip), starts approximately 1km past the park entrance. Beginning with an amble and ending in a steep clamber, the walk features views of the falls as they careen down bare rock. Several trailheads are by the Mt. Buffalo Chalet, where Bent's Lookout dazzles with a panoramic sweep across the Buckland Valley. On clear days, Mount Kosciuszko is visible. The terminus of **View Point Nature Walk** (4km,

1hr. round-trip) offers a similar—but grander—view from a boulder seemingly balanced on a point the size of a pancake. Driving past the park office toward the Mt. Buffalo Lodge, you'll see numerous marked walking trails. The steep, relatively short **Monolith Track** (1.8km, 1hr. round-trip), with a trailhead across from the park office, is definitely worth the effort. Information and descriptions of the walks are available at the park entrance and the visitors center.

**OTHER SUMMER ACTIVITIES.** Mt. Buffalo supports a wealth of activities for the adventurous traveler. Abseilers go over the edge near Bent's Lookout year-round, and rock climbers come from far and wide to test themselves against sheer granite walls. The climbing on the north wall of the gorge is world-renowned. **Adventure Guides Australia** (☎03 5728 1804; www.adventureguidesaustralia.com.au) in association with the **Mount Buffalo Chalet Activities Centre** (☎03 5755 1500; www.mtbuffalochalet.com.au) runs rock climbing, abseiling, caving, and rugged mountaineering expeditions (see **Bright**, p. 666). The site of several World Championships, Mt. Buffalo has superb hang gliding and paragliding. Lake Catani is a small manmade lake perfect for swimming, fishing, and canoeing. If you prefer to limit your activity to getting in and out of the car, a 3km unsealed road at the end of the park's one sealed road leads to the Horn, which offers sweeping views and a picnic area.

# BRIGHT ☎03

An ideal jumping-off point for any adrenaline junkie, full of skiers in the winter and paragliders in the summer, Bright is an apt name for this town of radiant natural beauty. Most streets are lined with majestic European oaks that change colors with the seasons, a rarity in Australia. Bright has the best collection of discount digs in high country, making it ideal for those on tight budgets.

**ORIENTATION AND PRACTICAL INFORMATION.** Bright is located 79km southeast of Wangaratta on the **Great Alpine Road** (called Gavan St. and then Delaney Ave. within town). The town center lies along **Ireland Street,** just off the highway behind a roundabout with a clock tower. Public transportation in and out of Bright is limited. However, **V/Line** (☎03 13 61 96) serves Melbourne (4hr.; M, W, F 1 per day; $47.40) and Wangaratta (1hr.; M, W, F 1 per day; $12). The **Bright Visitors Centre** is at 119 Gavan St. (☎03 5755 2275 or 1800 500 117. $5 booking fee for V/Line. Open daily 8:30am-5pm.) and has **Internet** ($3 per 10min). The **post office** is at the bottom of Ireland St. in an arcade, near the roundabout at Cobden St. (Open M-F 9am-5pm, Sa 10am-noon.) **Postal Code:** 3741.

**ACCOMMODATIONS AND FOOD.** Bright's centrally located backpacker accommodation is the **Bright Hikers Backpackers Hostel ❷**, 4 Ireland St., two doors down from the town library. Guests of the hostel are welcome to borrow from a limited selection of snow chains and skiing gear. Although the rooms are small, spacious common areas, plus a kitchen, and wooden veranda with hammocks will be sure to please. (☎03 5750 1244; www.brighthikers.com.au. Towels $1. Laundry $6. Non-suspension mountain bikes $15 per ½-day, $20 per day. Internet $6 per hr. Reception 11am-10pm. Dorms $25; doubles $38, ensuite $52.) The **Star Hotel ❺**, 91 Gavan Rd., located in the town center, is a good option if you want privacy and more amenities. Refurbished ensuite rooms (including heat, A/C, TV, fridge, and tea) stand in contrast to the motel's bleak facade. (☎03 5755 1277. Singles $50; doubles $70.)

Bright is peppered with enticing little cafes and restaurants, but very few of them fall under a budget heading. Throwing something together with ingredients from the supermarket is probably your best bet: the **Bright Supa IGA** supermarket is at 16 Ireland St. (☎03 5755 1666. Open daily 8am-9pm.), and **Foodworks** is a few storefronts away (open M-Sa 7am-7pm, Su 8am-7pm).

**⛷ SKIING.** At the center of town, a handful of ski-rental establishments will outfit you with a full range of skiing and snowboarding equipment, snow chains, and clothing; prices here are considerably lower than at the resorts, so it's advisable to rent in town. **Adina Ski Hire,** 15 Ireland St., offers both new and used budget skis for rent. (www.adina.com.au. Downhill skis, boots, and poles $43 per day, $137 per week; snowboard and boots $43/137. $100 deposit required for snowboards. 10% YHA discount. Open daily in winter 7:30am-6:30pm; in summer daily 9am-5pm.) **Bright Ski Centre,** 22 Ireland St. (☎03 5755 1093), and **JD's for Skis** (☎03 5755 1557), on the corner of Burke and Anderson St., have the same owners and similar services. (Open in winter M-Th and Sa-Su 7am-7pm, F 7am-10pm; in summer M-Sa 9am-6pm, Su 10am-4pm.)

**🪂 OTHER OUTDOOR ACTIVITIES.** Thermal air currents make the valleys surrounding Bright ideal for hang gliding and paragliding—the area was host to the 1986 World Hang Gliding Championships, and every year gliding buffs return to hone their skills. **Bright Microlights** (☎03 5750 1555), out at Porepunkah airfield, offers a 20min. "Mt. Buffalo Flight" ($125) that takes you over the gorge before gliding back to earth. The local ranges are perfect for mountain biking. **Cycle-Path Adventures,** 74 Gavan St., has customized and fully supported one- to five-day high-country and single track bike tours, although they are mostly aimed at large groups. They also offer rentals. (☎03 5750 1442 or 04 2750 1442; www.cyclepath.com.au. ½-day $20-30, full-day $28-40. For groups of 5 or more, ½-day tours $40, with bike rental $54; full-day $65/90. Credit card required for security deposit.) **Adventure Guides Australia** (☎03 5728 1804 or 04 1928 0614; www.adventureguidesaustralia.com.au) conducts abseiling (from $45), caving (from $99), rock climbing (from $99), and bushwalking and camping excursions. All except rock climbing are year-round, subject to weather.

# MOUNT HOTHAM ☎03

With Victoria's highest altitude and highest average snowfall, 13 lifts, and a partnership with nearby **Falls Creek** (p. 669), Mt. Hotham is Victoria's intermediate and advanced skiing and snowboarding headquarters. With a constant flow of university groups filling lodges in the ski season, the mountain skews younger than nearby Falls Creek, though après-ski offerings are more or less on par with those of its rival. In the summer, Hotham is quiet, with nature trails and only a few shops and lodgings open for visitors. The magnificent 50km drive from Bright on the Great Alpine Rd. is worth a trip at any time of year.

**🚌 TRANSPORTATION.** Mt. Hotham is accessible by a sealed road from the north. Entrance from Omeo in the south is safer and more reliable but is inconvenient for those coming from Melbourne or Sydney. **Buses** to Mt. Hotham depart from Melbourne's **Spencer St. Station** (6hr.; 1 per day; $80, round-trip $130) and **Bright's Alpine Hotel** (1hr., 2 per day, $30). Book with Trekset Tours (☎03 9370 9055 or 1300 656 546; www.mthothambus.com.au). There is also shuttle service between Mt. Hotham and Dinner Plain. (☎03 5156 7320; July-Aug. every 20min., June and Sept. every 1hr. 20min.) Tickets for round-trip helicopter rides to Falls Creek are $140 or $90 with a valid lift ticket. Trips must be booked in person on the day of travel. A free village **shuttle** runs in winter, although you can't bring luggage on board (7am-3pm). There is no petrol on the mountain; fill up in Omeo or Bright.

**⚡ PRACTICAL INFORMATION.** From the Queen's Birthday in June to mid-October, there is an entrance fee, payable at the tollbooth 1hr. from Bright on the Great Alpine Rd.; the fee is waived if you're driving through without stopping. ($10 per person; season pass $95. Cars 3hr. $20, 24hr. $29.50; season pass $250-290. Lift tickets not included.) Drivers coming from Bright can rent mandatory snow chains from Hoy's **A-Frame Ski Centre,** on the right just after the school bridge in Harrietville. (☎03 5759 2658. $30 per day, 2 days $40. Deposit $50. Chain-fitting service free.) These can be returned to the BP petrol station in Omeo, on the south side of Mt. Hotham. Omeo does not have chain service.

The resort is constructed around the Great Alpine Rd., which scales the mountain. The lodges are clustered to the south, with ski lifts and services farther north. Village **buses** transport folks for free around the resort. The **visitors center** (☎03 5759 3550; www.hotham.com.au) is on the first floor of the resort management building, just above the Corral carpark. (Open daily 8am-5pm.) Directly across the street, Hotham Central houses the **Snowsports Centre** (☎03 5759 4424), ski rental shops (skis/boots/poles or snowboards/boots $59, children $41; pants and parka $40/30. Open daily 8am-5:30pm), a small grocery store, and a lift ticket office, which sells passes valid both here and at Falls Creek. (Full-day ticket $90, students $70, children $45; lift and lesson packages $149/136/86.) The **Big D** lift hosts night skiing. (Open W and Sa 6:30-9:30pm. Without lift ticket $11, with lift ticket $6.)

**⌂♨ ACCOMMODATIONS AND FOOD.** Lodging on Mt. Hotham is pricey; the excellent hostels in Bright and Falls Creek offer inexpensive alternatives. The cheapest accommodation on the hill is the **Shepard and Alpine Club ❺.** (☎03 5759 3597. Shared rooms M-F $75 during peak season.) Call **Hotham Holidays** for accommodation booking and availability (☎1800 354 555). There are several supermarkets atop Hotham: the Alberg and Jack Frost general stores are in Hotham Central, and there is one at Davenport Village. The **Summit Bar ❶,** in the Snowbird Inn, features outstanding views, live bands (Th and Sa), and happening crowds. (☎03 5759 3503. Open daily during high season 3:30pm-2am.)

**⛷ SKIING.** The mountain is considered the hottest place in Victoria for all varieties of thrill-seekers, but it is held in especially high regard by snowboarders. The slopes are more challenging than those in the rest of Australia, with short, steep double-black diamonds cutting through the trees in the Extreme Skiing Zone. Beginner skiing is limited, though lessons are available.

**⚑ HIKING.** The challenging **Mount Loch trail** (8km, 2½hr.) leaves from the Mt. Loch carpark and leads to the summit. An easier hike is the **Dargo Lookout Circuit** (1.5km, 30min.), which leads from the Wire Plain Nordic Shelter Hut to picnic tables with views over the Dargo High Plains.

# DINNER PLAIN                                          ☎03

A mere snow-bunny hop (14km) from Hotham's hills lies the only village in prime snowfields that isn't corporate-run. When describing Dinner Plain (www. visitdinnerplain.com), visitors often allude to the Hansel-and-Gretel-like cottages of the resort. Although the chalets are not made of candy and there is a noticeable dearth of witches, this bewitching little haven exudes a fairy-tale essence. It is an excellent base for cross-country skiing and offers more to do during the summer than nearby Hotham, although with only one lift and at an altitude of 1590m, the resort is best for intermediate and beginner skiers. Fittingly, lift tickets cost considerably less than at nearby resorts ($45).

The most affordable accommodation in Dinner Plain and Hotham is the **Currawong Lodge ❺** on Big Muster Dr. Guests enjoy a huge kitchen, billiard room, fireplace, and large spa. (☎03 5159 6452; www.currawonglodge.com.au. High season from June 29 to Aug. 30. 4- to 6-person rooms $130 per 2 nights, $405 per week; low season $60 per night.) In winter, a free shuttle bus runs between Dinner Plain and Mt. Hotham. (July-Aug. every 20min.; June and Sept. every 1hr. 20min.) General information on the resort is available at www.visitdinnerplain. com. An up-to-date weather report is accessible at ☎1300 734 365. There is no fuel at the resort; fill up in Bright.

# FALLS CREEK ☎03

An hour's drive from Bright along serpentine roads, Falls Creek Ski Resort peaks at 1842m. Falls's ambience is more family-oriented than nearby **Mt. Hotham's** (p. 667), though their partnership gives multi-day skiers the chance to try both (all lift tickets allow access to both resorts). The ample snowfall, both natural and manmade, is a selling point at Falls, and the spread of trails means that bad weather conditions in one area can still allow for good skiing in another. Although quiet in summer, Falls is one of the only resorts that keeps running, and it offers wonderful hiking and cross-training opportunities.

**TRANSPORTATION AND PRACTICAL INFORMATION.** Driving to the slopes from June to October requires carrying snow chains (24hr. rental in Tawonga and Mt. Beauty $20-25) and paying a hefty entrance fee ($25 per day). Note that there's nowhere to get fuel on the mountain, so fill up in Mt. Beauty. It is more practical to stay in Bright and use public transport to reach the resort for the day. **Pyle's Falls Creek Coach Services** (☎03 5754 4024; www.fallscreek-coachservice.com.au) runs a ski-season service from Melbourne (6hr., 1-2 per day, $140 round-trip), Albury-Wodonga (3hr., 1-2 per day, $78 round-trip), and Mt. Beauty (50min., 5-8 per day, $47 round-trip). All prices include an entrance fee. There is a free **shuttle** that runs throughout the village in winter (8am-6pm), but if you have luggage, you'll probably need to use a snow **taxi** (☎03 5758 3285; $5 per person) to get where you're going. Depending on where your accommodations are, you can also think about using oversnow transport ($17.10, round-trip $31). Entry fees to the park will add a hefty chunk to your skiing budget ($28 per car per day), so it may make more sense to use the coach services and park your car with them ($7-15 per night).

The only major center of information for Falls Creek is in Mt. Beauty, a winter haven with no prospects for budget travelers that is en route from Bright. The **Alpine Discovery Centre**, at 31 Bogong High Plains Rd., has a museum about the local ecology and offers comprehensive information and booking services for accommodations and activities in High Country. (☎1800 111 885; www. visitmtbeauty.com. Open daily 9am-5pm; hospitality specialists work M-F.) The resort's website, www.fallscreek.com.au, also has all the information you could ever need. **Police** ☎03 5758 3424; **ski patrol** ☎03 5758 3502.

**ACCOMMODATIONS AND FOOD.** The best option for local accommodations is the **Alpha Lodge ❸**, at the back left corner of the resort on 5 Parallel St. After settling into the Alpha, you may well mistake your hostel for a luxury lodge. Open year-round, the Alpha spoils its guests with extravagant facilities, including large balconies extending from its odd-numbered dorm rooms. Also available is a huge kitchen, a spacious common area with TV and video games, a laundry, a drying room, a miniature beer garden, and a cedar-paneled sauna. (☎03 5758 3488. Linen $10. 4-bed dorms $28-100; 2- to 3-bed ensuite dorms $36-120.) Inquire within the Alpine Discovery Centre for other moderately priced lodges spread throughout the village.

**The Man ❷**, 20 Slalom St., a mainstay on the mountain, has several bar areas, billiards, and offers the cheapest options in town for dining out. (☎03 5758 3362. Delicious personal pizzas $13. Open daily in winter noon-late.) **The Frying Pan Inn ❹**, 4 Village Bowl Cir., at the base of the Summit and Eagle chairlifts, is the place to be on winter weekends, when there are bands, dance parties, and drink specials to fuel the debauchery. (☎03 5758 3390. Happy hour 5-6pm. Pub open daily in winter 5pm-late. Bistro open daily in winter 8am-8pm.) **Falls Creek Licensed Supermarket** (☎03 5758 3355) is on Falls Creek Rd.

**⛷ SKIING.** Lift ticket prices are comparable to other resorts and include entrance to the nearby Mt. Hotham resort as well. (☎1800 232 557; www. fallscreek.com.au. Tickets $90 per day, students $70, children $45; lifts with lessons $149/136/86.) Few trails are very long and most are intermediate—advanced skiers can expect to spend more time on the chairlifts than on the slopes. However, with over 92 alpine trails and 14 lifts, few visitors complain. Just over 23% of Falls Creek is advanced terrain, and the black diamond trails are clustered in an area known as The Maze; a snowboarding terrain park with Australia's only superpipe opens when snowfall permits. A Kat service transports skiers in heated Kassbohrers up the back-country slopes of Mount McKay for black- and double-black-diamond bowl runs.

**🥾 SUMMER ACTIVITIES.** In the summer, a comparatively quiet Falls Creek offers bushwalking opportunities, tennis, fly-fishing, hiking, and extensive high-altitude cross-training trails open from October to June (many of Australia's Olympians come to the region to train). Scenic walks include the **Home and Away Circuit** (6km round-trip), which is quite narrow and steep but eventually leads to the top of the Summit Chair, and the **Mountain and Castle Adventure Trail** (7km round-trip), which follows the cliffs during an ascent to Mt. McKay and provides sweeping views of Mt. Hotham. Both hikes start at Ory's Trail. The visitors center has the free *Summer Walks Guide*, which offers detailed descriptions of nearly all the area's hikes.

# GIPPSLAND

Southeast of Melbourne, the Princes Hwy. snakes toward the border of neighboring New South Wales, loosely following the contours of the Victoria coast through verdant wilderness that is interspersed with small, quiet towns and extensive lake systems. Gippsland is largely rural and sparsely populated; its towns aren't a huge draw for tourists. But many of the area's national parks and coastal reserves are magnificent enough to warrant a trip through the boring towns and farmland that make up the rest of Gippsland.

## FOSTER                                                                    ☎03

While gold-hungry miners used to flock to Foster (pop. 1000) in search of supplies and a warm bed, most of today's visitors who make momentary stops in town are on their way to Wilsons Promontory National Park. Foster is just 30km north of the entrance to the Prom, and it's really the only place to stay near the park without booking accommodations months in advance. To drive there from Melbourne (170km), take the South Eastern Arterial (M1) to the

South Gippsland Hwy. (M420), following signs to Phillip Island and then to Korumburra, where the road becomes A440 and finally leads to Foster. V/Line (☎13 61 96) **buses** run to Foster from Melbourne (2hr.; M-F 4:30pm, Sa 6:45pm; returns M-Sa 7:50am, Su 3:25pm; $28). **Tourist information,** as well as a telephone for booking accommodations, can be obtained at the Stockyard Gallery building on Main St. Additionally, **Parks Victoria** has an office in the same building. (☎1800 630 704. Open M-F 8am-4:30pm.)

🛏**Prom Coast Backpackers ❷**, 50 Station Rd., in a purple colonial house, is a lovely place for budget travelers to hang their hats. (☎03 5682 2171. Free tea and coffee. Free parking. Free washing machine. Unlimited Internet access $5. Book ahead. Dorms $30, YHA members $27; doubles $70/67.) There's mostly just fast food in Foster, so unless you want a hamburger or fish and chips, be prepared to self-cater. **FoodWorks,** on the corner of Main St. and Station Rd., sells groceries. (Open M-Sa 8am-8pm, Su 9am-5:30pm.)

# WILSONS PROMONTORY NATIONAL PARK

The southernmost tip of the Australian mainland, Wilsons Promontory National Park attracts nearly 400,000 visitors a year and is one of Victoria's most astonishing natural highlights. Thankfully, it's also virtually unspoiled thanks to local enthusiasm for conservation. Its beauty is due in large part to the wonderful meeting of two natural majesties: the mountains and the sea.

---

### THE PROM AT A GLANCE

**AREA:** 490 sq. km of parkland, 83 sq. km of marine parks.

**FEATURES:** A UNESCO World Biosphere, home to Mt. Oberon and Sealers Cove.

**HIGHLIGHTS:** Easy to challenging hikes and walks, from day to overnight routes, the meeting of mountains and the sea.

**GATEWAYS:** Foster and Yanakie.

**CAMPING:** Must register with the ranger. Fees vary across the park.

**FEES:** $10 per vehicle, 2-day pass $15.80. Fishing permits are required; all payments and inquiries at Tidal River.

---

## TRANSPORTATION AND PRACTICAL INFORMATION

From Foster, turn left at the end of Main St. onto the Foster Promontory Rd., which snakes 30km to the park entrance. ($10 per car, 2-day pass $15.80). Some touring companies offer trips into the park. **Duck Truck Tours** has two-day tours leaving from Phillip Island. (☎03 5952 2548. Summer only.)

From the entrance station, the park's only sealed road, Wilsons Promontory Rd., winds 30km along the Prom's western extremity, providing glimpses of breathtaking coastal vistas and numerous opportunities to turn off for picnics and hikes. The grassy airfield between Cotter's Lake and Darby River is the best place in the park to spot wildlife, particularly around dawn and dusk. The road ends at Tidal River, a township with basic facilities, camping, and lodging. During its busiest periods (Christmas, January school holidays, and weekends through to Easter), the park runs a free **shuttle bus** between the Norman Bay carpark, at the far end of Tidal River, and the Mt. Oberon carpark.

Visitors who wish to stay overnight, obtain a fishing license, or get weather updates should go to the **Tidal River Information Centre** at the end of the main road. (☎03 5680 9555. Open daily 8:30am-4:30pm.) A 24hr. Blue Box phone for contacting a ranger is outside the info center. Tidal River offers free storage for superfluous gear, along with the only toilets, pay phones, petrol, and

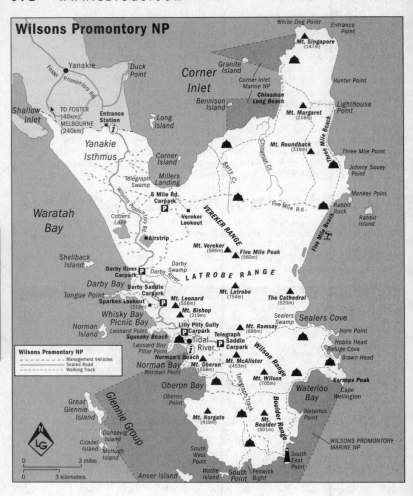

groceries available in the park. During the summer and Easter holiday period, Tidal River's amenities include an open-air cinema with nightly screenings of recent releases. For more information on Wilsons Promontory, contact **Parks Victoria** (☎ 13 19 63; www.parkweb.vic.gov.au).

## ACCOMMODATIONS AND CAMPING

While **campsites ❶** at Tidal River function on a first come, first served basis most of the year, booking is recommended for holidays and Melbourne Cup weekend. Bookings for the Christmas and January school holiday period are subject to a ballot, with applications accepted only in June.

Formal lodging is considerably more difficult to come by and always requires booking in advance. Options in Tidal River range from basic cold-water **huts ❶** to ensuite **cabins ❺** with appliances. Try to reserve three to six months in advance, and even earlier for summer weekends. Bookings here also operate under a ballot system for the Christmas holiday and January (1 week min., 3 week max.), and ballots are accepted only in May. Cabins have bath, kitchen, and living room, and include towels and linen. (☎03 5680 9555. Sites Nov.-Apr. $23 for up to 3 people, additional adult $5; May-Oct. $19/5; cabins Sept.-Apr. $154, additional adult $20.50; May-Aug. $141/20.50; 4-bed huts Sept.-Apr. $59; May-Aug. $57; 6-bed huts Sept.-Apr. $89; May-Aug. $85.) For **camping ❶** outside the Tidal River camping area ("outstation camping") there's no need to book ahead, but you must obtain a permit and pay nightly fees ($7). All sites have a two-night maximum stay, except southern sites November through April, which have a one-night maximum stay. There are no toilets at northern sites, toilets in outstation sites have no toilet paper, and no sites are powered.

## 🅗 HIKING

To best experience the Prom, tackle a few bushwalking areas or take a dip in the crystal-clear water. Although some visitors sample the Prom in a day, consider allowing at least three to five days to take in the entire park. A terrific assortment of tracks enables walkers of all abilities to explore the diverse landscape. The info center's free parknotes give detailed descriptions, distances, and duration of short hikes, dayhikes, and overnight hikes and include useful maps and emergency information. The center also sells *Discovering the Prom* ($15), which details over 100km of trails in the park, and *Down Under at the Prom* ($20), which lists sites for scuba diving and snorkeling. One of the most popular swimming beaches is at Norman Bay, past the Tidal River, which has its own carpark and is accessible from the second ramp.

### SHORT HIKES

Past the entrance to the park, the first left leads to the Five Mile Road Carpark. Originating at the carpark, the Millers Landing Nature Walk (4km, 3hr. round-trip, easy) leads to mangroves at Corner Inlet. Several short walks depart from Tidal River, including **Pillar Point** (3.6km, 1hr. round-trip, easy to moderate), a loop track winding gradually uphill through tea trees, banksias, and sheoaks to a granite outcrop with delightful views of Norman and Squeaky Beaches, and **Loo-Errn Track** (2km, 1hr. round-trip, easy), a wheelchair-accessible boardwalk leading through swamp paperbark and fishing stations. For a longer walk with decent views, try **Squeaky Beach Nature Walk** (4.2km, 1hr. round-trip, moderate), which passes through dunes, coastal scrub, and granite outcroppings before descending to the beach. Be careful when swimming off Squeaky Beach, as there is a strong undertow and a rip. Look for wombats in the scrub, and once on the beach, slide your feet to hear the white-grained quartz sand squeak. **Lilly Pilly Gully Nature Walk** (5.2km, 2hr. round-trip, easy), starting from the Lilly Pilly carpark 2km up the road from Tidal River, follows a slight incline through coastal woodlands into the rainforest. This walk can be extended by leaving from **Tidal River** (7.2km, 2hr. round-trip, easy); the section between Tidal River and Lilly Pilly Gully is wheelchair-accessible. About 5km on the main road from Tidal River is a turnoff for the Telegraph Saddle carpark, where the 🅜**Mount Oberon Summit Walk** begins. The walk (6.8km, 2hr. round-trip, moderate to hard) climbs steadily up to the summit (558m), where you'll find fantastic 360° views. For rare sunset views from eastern Australia, nothing beats **Whisky Bay** (600m, 30min., easy), which is a quick stroll from the carpark and provides a perfect lookout to watch the sun sink below Norman Island.

## DAY HIKES

For more ambitious hikers, two incredible dayhikes cover some of the Prom's most beloved spots. Departing from the Telegraph Saddle carpark, the **Sealers Cove Track** (20.4km, 6-7hr. round-trip, moderate to hard) traverses most of the peninsula, taking you across nearly every ecosystem found in the Prom. Camping is available at the cove. **Tongue Point Track** (11.2km, 5hr. round-trip, moderate to hard) starts from **Darby Saddle** (6.7km north of Tidal River) and proceeds, sometimes steeply, past two scenic lookouts to a small granite peninsula with a stunning view of the coast. The track is also accessible from the **Darby River** carpark (7.6km, 4hr. round-trip, easy to moderate).

## OVERNIGHT HIKES

The overnight hikes in the south are definitely worth the time and extra preparation, as they allow hikers to enjoy many terrains and spectacular secluded spots. The less-traveled northern part of Wilson's Prom has a circuit but lacks toilets, and many of the trails fade out in places. Only experienced hikers with a compass should attempt overnight hikes in the North. The most popular multi-day hike sweeps 36km around the eastern coastal areas along well-maintained trails to **Sealers Cove** (10.2km), **Refuge Cove** (6.4km), and **Waterloo Bay** (7km). An extra two or three days will allow access to the Prom's full beauty with a hike down to the lighthouse on South East Point. Overnight campsites are near walking tracks. Make sure to carry a stove, as fires are not allowed at any time. All sites have water, but it is from the creek and should be boiled or treated. The legs of the southern overnight hike are outlined below; distances, times (round-trip), and difficulty levels listed are from one campsite to the next. All overnight hikers require a permit ($7 per night); purchase one at the Tidal River parks office, online at www.parkweb.vic.gov.au, or by calling ☎03 5680 9555.

**CUTGRASS AND LEECHES AND SNAKES, OH MY!** Make sure to take extra caution in order to avoid the less-savory parts of nature on these routes. Watch for raised roots, sharp rocks, leeches, and overhanging snakes, among other outdoors dangers.

**Telegraph Saddle Carpark to Sealers Cove** (10.2km, 3hr. one-way, moderate). This track leads through a burnt-out stretch of rainforest filled with brown stringy bark and banksia, then into a Messmate forest of austral mulberry and musk daisy-bush before arriving at Windy Saddle, between Mt. Latrobe and Wilson. It's all downhill from there. The forest gets darker and the terrain muddier as the trail heads into Sealers Swamp. Keep an eye out for colorful fungi. The track switches to a boardwalk before opening out to the magnificent cove. Check tide times to ensure you don't get stranded in a high-water crossing of Sealers Creek. The overnight campground is 0.7km down the beach.

**Sealers Cove to Refuge Cove** (6.4km, 2hr. one-way, easy to moderate). This track offers beautiful views, and the coast eventually merges with the lush forest. Climbing a few large rocks rewards you with a stunning view. A short detour along the coast heads inland again into stringy bark and a rainforest. A decline leads you to the beach before heading briefly back into forest, ending at a campground with water and a flush toilet.

**Refuge Cove to Little Waterloo Bay** (7km, 2hr. one-way, moderate to difficult). The track ascends steeply through stringy bark woodland, dipping briefly into a gully before heading up again to reach the Kersops Peak lookout. Leave your pack at the signpost to catch a glimpse of the bay (look for humpback whales) via the detour (600m, 10min. round-trip). The track then heads steeply down to the beach and traces the coast on an extremely narrow path with raised roots and large rocks. After a quick bend around the coast, the track inclines before heading briefly back into the forest. The beach, directly in front of the Little Waterloo Campground, is available for a quick dip. From here, you can follow the lower part of the circuit, which joins up with Telegraph Track (5.8km, 2hr.), taking you north to return to the carpark (6.1km, 2hr.), or south to Roaring Meg camp (6km, 2hr.), or farther west to Oberon Bay (3.4km, 1hr.). The fit and ambitious can continue directly to the lighthouse from Little Waterloo camp.

**Little Waterloo Bay to Lighthouse** (10.9km, 3hr. one-way, difficult). This long uphill stretch is exposed to the sun, has sword-grass, and is rocky. Heading inland, the track opens onto a large-faced rock with an amazing view, then passes through a eucalyptus forest. The track then rolls through fern forests to the turnoff for the lighthouse.

**The Lighthouse to Roaring Meg** (7.2km, 2hr. one-way, moderate to difficult). This portion of the track is a rollercoaster of ups and downs. The track mostly winds its way through moist rainforest, so be wary of leeches. Turn right where the track empties onto the Telegraph Track and follow the road 700m until the walking track to Roaring Meg splits off on your left. Deceptively flat at the beginning, the track later presents hikers with extreme uphill climbs followed by steep descents, ending at the bridge over the creek.

**Roaring Meg to Halfway Hut and Oberon Bay** (3.3km, 1hr. one-way, easy to moderate). Though the road is shorter, the walking track has better views. After a short, steep incline, the track is relatively flat before opening into a short growth forest. A left at Telegraph Track will go downhill to the Halfway Hut. This campground has a compost toilet, water, and a stone hut. The flat track leading to Oberon Beach crosses shaggy forest. Walk along the beach and cross over a small tidal pool to find the track to Tidal River.

# BAIRNSDALE ☎03

Bairnsdale (pop. 11,000) is a useful place to refuel before exploring Mitchell River National Park, the Australian Alps, and Gippsland Lakes. It is also the base for a delightful daytrip to Raymond Island.

**⌨❼ TRANSPORTATION AND PRACTICAL INFORMATION.** About 275km east of Melbourne and 35km west of Lakes Entrance, Bairnsdale is accessible by the **Princes Hwy. (A1),** called **Main St.** in town. V/Line **buses** go to Lakes Entrance (1hr.; M-F 4 per day, Sa 3 per day, Su 2 per day; $9.30) and **trains** to Melbourne (4hr.; M-Sa 3 per day, Su 2 per day; $43.20). **Bairnsdale Visitors Centre,** 240 Main St., has a knowledgeable staff. (☎03 5152 3444. Open daily 9am-5pm.) The **library,** 22 Service St., around the next block, has **Internet access** available for free by prior booking. (☎03 5152 4225. Open M 10am-5pm, Tu 10am-1pm, W and F 9am-6pm, Th 9am-7pm, Sa 9:30am-noon.) Other services include: a **hospital** on Day St. (☎03 5150 3333); **police,** 155 Nicholson St. (☎03 5152 0500); and a **post office,** 16-18 Nicholson St. (Open M-F 9am-5pm.) **Postal Code:** 3875.

**▐❑ ACCOMMODATIONS AND FOOD.** Accommodation in Bairnsdale is limited to camping or splurging. Of the many motels in town, **Travellers Rest Motel ❹,** 49 Main St., is the best, offering a well-maintained, family-down atmosphere as well as free Internet, free coffee and tea, DVD players and free DVD rental, and a toaster, water kettle, and fridge, all of which make the clean rooms more like tiny studio apartments. (☎03 5152 3200; www.travellersmotel.com.au. Singles $69; doubles $79.) **Mitchell Gardens ❷,** a few blocks past the supermarket on Main St., has pleasant campsites on the banks of the river, as well as a pool. (☎03 5152 4654; www.mitchellgardens.com.au. Linen $6. Sites for 2 during high season $22, shoulder season $21, low season $20; powered sites $30/25/23; cabins $84/62/50, extra person $8/7/7.)

Cheap takeaways clutter Main St., broken up by the occasional panini vendor. Bairnsdale is not a culinary mecca, and the array of options is unimpressively

VICTORIA

homogenous. There is a **Coles** on Nicholson St., around the corner from Main St. (☎03 5152 2743. Open daily 6am-midnight.)

**◨ ⚠ SIGHTS AND OUTDOOR ACTIVITIES.** Bairnsdale is the starting point of the **Great Alpine Road,** a 300km drive through the Australian Alps to Wangaratta. Walhalla (approximately 50km from Bairnsdale) is the start of the epic **Australian Alps Walking Track,** which ends in Mount Tennent (655km), outside Canberra. This monster bushwalk, which traverses many of the area's highest mountains, can be completed in 10 weeks. For more info, contact **Parks Victoria** (☎13 19 63). Fifteen kilometers from Bairnsdale, the charming, if somewhat elderly, community of Paynesville is the departure point of the **ferry to Raymond Island,** a great daytrip destination for wildlife watching. (☎04 1851 7959. 2min. Ferry runs M-Th 7am-10:45pm, F-Sa 7am-midnight, Su 8am-11:15pm; service after 6pm is not continuous. Cars $7, pedestrians and bicyclists free.) The tiny island boasts a huge population of wild koalas, which are most-easily spotted off the rocky, unsealed Centre Rd. True to its name, Centre Rd. runs straight ahead down the center of the island from the ferry landing. While you may not spot a reclusive koala, the small community of holiday cottages, picturesque port, and large population of black swans and pelicans are sure to please.

## MITCHELL RIVER NATIONAL PARK

Flowing from the alpine high country down to the Gippsland Lakes, the Mitchell River bisects 12,200 hectares of warm temperate rainforest and rugged gorge land. Canoeing, rafting the Class III and IV rapids, and hiking through the Mitchell River Gorge are the best ways to see the park's splendors. To reach the park from Bairnsdale (45km), turn right about 3km west of town onto Lindenow Rd., which becomes Dargo Rd., and follow the many signs to the park. Most roads through Mitchell River are unsealed and are navigated most safely in a 4WD, although three major attractions—the Den of Nargun, Billy Goat Bend, and Angusvale—are accessible via extremely narrow 2WD unsealed roads. On these roads, drive slowly and look out for debris.

The ominously-named **Den of Nargun** and its walk are the park's biggest draws. Local indigenous legend describes Nargun as a giant stone female, said to abduct children and to kill attackers by reflecting their spears back at them. The **Den of Nargun Circuit** (5km, 1hr. round-trip) loops around Bluff Lookout, sweeping down to the Mitchell River and the Den of Nargun before heading back up to the carpark. Chilly rainforests dominate much of the walk; be careful, as many of the rock steps can be slippery when wet. At the Den, the Gunnai/Kurnai people ask that visitors respect the space and not enter the actual cave. Ambitious hikers can tackle the two-day **Mitchell River Walking Track** (18km one-way), which traces the river from Angusvale past Billy Goat Bend to the Den, taking in the scenery along the way.

There are two free campsites, one accessible by 2WD. **Angusvale ❶** can be reached by turning right off Dargo Rd. onto unsealed Mitchell Dam Rd. (Pit toilets. No camping within 50m of the water.) **Billy Goat Bend ❶** must be reached on foot: turn right off Dargo Rd. onto Billy Goat Bend Rd. and go 1km past the picnic area. A natural amphitheater at the Bend yields vistas of the Mitchell River Gorge. **Bairnsdale Parks Victoria** (☎03 5152 0600) has more info.

# LAKES ENTRANCE ☎03

In good weather, its array of outdoor activities makes Lakes Entrance a paradise, but when the conditions turn sour, you'll be on the first bus out of town.

With inviting beaches, excellent fishing, and numerous boating opportunities, it's no surprise that Lakes Entrance is heavily touristed in the summer.

## ◨ ▸ TRANSPORTATION AND PRACTICAL INFORMATION

The Princes Hwy. becomes The Esplanade in town, a waterfront strip lined with shops, eateries, and motels.

**Buses:** V/Line buses leave near the post office to **Melbourne** (5hr.; M-F 3 per day, Sa-Su 1 per day; $52.10) via **Bairnsdale** (30min., $9.30). For reservations or schedules, call **Esplanade Travel,** 317 The Esplanade (☎03 5155 2404). Open M-F 9am-5pm.

**Tourist Office:** Lakes Entrance Visitors Centre (☎03 5155 1966), on the corner of Marine Pde. and The Esplanade. Open daily 9am-5pm.

**Tours:** Peels Tourist and Ferry Service (☎03 5155 1246) offers boat tours with excellent views. Departs daily from the post office. $26-34. Book ahead at the visitors center.

**Financial Services:** Banks and **ATMs** can be found all along The Esplanade and opposite the footbridge on Myer St.

**Library:** Lakes Entrance library, 18 Mechanics St. (☎03 5153 9500), in the Mechanics Institute building. Free **Internet.** Open M-F 8:30am-5pm.

**Post Office:** Lakes Entrance post office, 287 The Esplanade (☎03 5155 1809). Open M-F 9am-5pm. **Postal Code:** 3909.

## ⌂ ACCOMMODATIONS

Tempting as it may be, beach camping is illegal, and the area is frequently patrolled. Luckily, reasonably priced alternatives abound.

**Riviera Backpackers (YHA),** 669 The Esplanade (☎03 5155 2444). Has clean facilities, including laundry, kitchen, large lounge with TV, solar-heated pool, and billiards. Parking. Internet access $2 per 15min. Bike rental $15 per day. Dorms $22; doubles $47, ensuite $57. $3.50 discount for YHA members. Book weeks ahead Dec.-Jan. ❷

**Echo Beach Tourist Park,** 33 Roadknight St. (☎03 5155 2238; www.echobeachpark. com). Kitchen, BBQ, laundry, pool, playground, TV, and billiards. The 3-bedroom flat sleeps up to 6 people. Powered sites $27, high season $40; cabins $70/140; self-contained, 1-bedroom flats $80/150; 3-bedroom with spa bath $120/240. ❷

## ◖ FOOD

The Esplanade brims with mediocre takeaways. **FoodWorks,** 30-34 Myer St., has groceries. (☎03 5155 1354. Open M-W and Su 8am-8pm, Th-Sa 8am-9pm.)

**Pinocchio Inn Restaurant,** 569 The Esplanade (☎03 5155 2565). One of the few places in town that serves dinner, with a full menu of Italian fare. Entrees $13.50-28.50. Open M-Th and Su 5-9:30pm, F-Sa 5-9pm. ❹

**Lakes Entrance Bakery,** 537 The Esplanade (☎03 5155 2864). Has a large selection of goodies to tempt your sweet tooth. Meat pies $3.50 Open daily 6:30am-5pm. ❶

**Riviera Ice Cream Parlour** (☎03 5155 2972), opposite the footbridge on The Esplanade. Sells huge portions of delicious homemade ice cream. 1 scoop $4. Open daily 9:30am-5:30pm; in summer 8am-midnight. ❶

## ◗ BEACHES

**Ninety Mile Beach,** accessible via the footbridge by Myer St. The town's biggest attraction—a long, thin stretch of sand enclosing the region's lakes and swampland. From the snack bar, a 1hr. walking track follows the coast to the boat entrance to the deep waters of the Bass Strait. **Lakes Entrance Paddleboats** (☎04 1955 2753) rents canoes ($10 per 20min.), paddle boats ($15), aquabikes ($15), and catamarans ($40 per hr.).

# BUCHAN ☎03

Large numbers of visitors pass through the tiny town of Buchan (BUCK-in; pop. 200), 58km north of Lakes Entrance, on the Snowy River scenic drive through the austere Snowy River National Park. Surrounded by rolling hills, Buchan is also a great base for exploring the spectacular limestone Buchan Caves. The tiny town doesn't have any restaurants, so be prepared to fend for yourself.

**⊏⊐ TRANSPORTATION AND PRACTICAL INFORMATION.** No public transport serves Buchan; either drive in or take a tour bus from Melbourne or Sydney. From Lakes Entrance, take the Princes Hwy. 23km east to Nowa Nowa, turn left onto C620, right onto C608, and follow signs to Buchan. From Orbost, turn left off Princes Hwy., veer under the overpass and turn right at the T, then take the next right onto Buchan Rd. The **Buchan General Store,** on Main St. in the town center, has tourist brochures and groceries. It is also the town's **post office.** (☎03 5155 9202. Open M-F 8:30am-5pm, Sa 9am-noon.) **Postal Code:** 3885.

**⋔ ACCOMMODATIONS. Buchan Lodge ❷,** left after the bridge on Saleyard Rd. just north of the town center, provides a genuinely welcoming environment in a beautiful wooden building. The grand main room houses a lounge, dining area, and a well-stocked kitchen with an enormous, old copper stove hood. The lodge is a 5min. walk to town. (☎03 5155 9421; www.buchanlodge.com. Breakfast included. Dorms $25.) The **Parks Victoria office,** right before the caves, has the most info on camping and the national parks, as well as tickets for the caves and reservations for the 100 closely packed **campsites ❶** in the area. (☎03 5162 1900. Sites $13, powered $18; cabins $58, high season $17/22/71.)

**◪ SIGHTS.** Over the past 25 million years, underground rivers have formed over 300 caves in the **Buchan Caves Reserve.** Rain falling down the surface has left behind trace deposits of calcite, adding an impressive array of stalactites, stalagmites, curtains, and flowstone to the caves. **Fairy Cave** and **Royal Cave** are open for guided tours. Though the caves are similar in size and ornamentation, Fairy has more narrow passages. (1hr. Oct.-Easter 10, 11:15am, 1, 2:15, and 3:30pm; Easter-Sept. 11am, 1 and 3pm. $13, children $7, families $32.50.) The reserve has a few pleasant bushwalks, none longer than 2hr. The **Spring Creek Walk** (3km, 1hr. round-trip) travels past limestone, old volcanic rock, and fern-filled forest to Spring Creek Falls. Watch for lyrebirds on the creekside portion of the walk. The Parks Office has information on other short walks.

# SNOWY RIVER NATIONAL PARK

Stark, unspoiled, and jaw-droppingly beautiful, Snowy River National Park surrounds the river with jagged hills dressed in alpine ash and pine. The park is underrated and thus isolated, making it one of Victoria's best-kept secrets.

**⊏ TRANSPORTATION.** The park is best seen via the Snowy River scenic drive, a driving tour loop beginning in Orbost. Two days will allow plenty of time for bushwalking and sightseeing, although the drive can be done as a long daytrip, if you don't stray too far from the set path (7hr. round-trip Orbost loop, 6hr. Orbost to Buchan). If driving from Buchan, take the **Buchan-Jindabyne Road (C608)** north through Gelantipy and veer right onto the **Gelantipy-Bonang**

VICTORIA

**Road,** which leads into the park. If starting in Orbost, the scenic drive is clearly marked, starting from the visitors center. It's debatable which direction is better, but many locals claim starting from Orbost and ending in Buchan is preferable, since you will be on the inner curve of the mountain during the scarier bends and thus less likely to fall off a cliff. The park road is mostly unsealed from Bonang to Gelantipy and involves some serious white-knuckle driving in some of the scarier sections around MacKillop Bridge. The road is generally fine for 2WD vehicles, but only in dry weather. Check in with **Parks Victoria** in Orbost (☎03 5161 1222), Buchan (☎03 5155 9264), or their central info center (☎13 19 63) for up-to-date driving reports.

**▖▛ ACCOMMODATIONS AND CAMPING.** On-site, **Snowy River Expeditions ❷** has many adventure options including whitewater rafting trips (from $135) and full-day horseback trail rides (from $130). Oz Experience stops here; call ahead for pickup from Lake's Entrance. (☎03 5155 0220; www.karoondapark. com. Wheelchair-accessible. Dorms $26; motel singles $45; doubles $70; cabins $105.) Those doing the scenic drive in two days often stop to camp at **MacKillop Bridge ❶.** Farther into the park are **Raymond Falls ❶** and **Hicks Campsite ❶,** which can be reached off Yalmy Rd. on dirt tracks suitable for 2WD. All have pit toilets and are free. Bush camping is also permitted.

**▟ OUTDOOR ACTIVITIES.** The area around MacKillop Bridge, the only portion of the river accessible by conventional vehicle, is the starting point for many of the park's most popular activities. A canoe launch sets rivergoers downstream to explore rocky gorges; the most popular part of the Snowy River for canoeing and kayaking is the three- to four-day stretch between MacKillop Bridge and the Buchan River junction; those considering going downriver should check in with a local Parks Victoria office beforehand. Several dayhikes start from MacKillop Bridge, as well as the 18km **Silver Mine Trail.** Just upstream, river beaches invite swimming. West of MacKillop Bridge, a turnoff from Bonang Rd. leads to a 400m track overlooking Victoria's deepest gorge, **Little River Gorge.**

# ORBOST ☎03

Orbost, a logging and service town 60km northeast of Lakes Entrance, is a commercial hub for locals as well as a good pit stop for visitors on the way to nearby beaches and national parks. The town is the start and finish of the Snowy River National Park Scenic Drive and the base for the beautiful, abandoned beaches of Cape Conran Coastal Park.

**▛▟ TRANSPORTATION AND PRACTICAL INFORMATION.** Orbost is just off the Princes Hwy. via Lochiel or Salisbury St.; both exits intersect Nicholson St. V/Line **buses** between Melbourne and Canberra run to Orbost from Bairnsdale (1hr., 1 per day, $22) and Melbourne (5hr., 1 per day, $57). Buy tickets at **Orbost Travel Centre,** 86 Nicholson St. (☎03 5154 1481. Open M-F 9am-5:30pm, Sa 9am-noon.) The **visitors center,** 152 Nicholson St., provides information on East Gippsland's national parks. (☎03 5154 2424. Open daily 9am-5pm.) The **Parks Victoria office,** just down the street, is your best bet for getting the low-down on both weather conditions and park information. (☎03 5161 1222. Open M-F 9am-5pm.) In town, find **ATMs; a library,** just off Nicholson on Ruskin St., with free **Internet** access (☎03 5153 9500; open M-F 8:30am-5pm); and a **post office,** 84 Nicholson St. (Open M-F 9am-5pm.) **Postal Code:** 3888.

VICTORIA

**ACCOMMODATIONS AND FOOD. Snowy River Orbost Camp Park ❶,** 2-6
Lochie St. at Nicholson, has basic facilities in a nice garden. A trail along the
Snowy River starts nearby. (☎03 5154 1097. Sites $18.50, powered $21.50; cara-
vans $40; cabins for two $60-70. Prices for sites vary by $1 depending on the
season; for caravans and cabins by $10.) The **Orbost Club Hotel ❸,** 63 Nicholson
St., has unremarkable budget rooms. (☎03 5154 1003. Singles $30; doubles $40;
twins $45.) Nicholson St., the main drag in town, is home to a number of cafes.
The **FoodWorks** is opposite the Club Hotel. (Open daily 8am-8pm.)

# CAPE CONRAN COASTAL PARK ☎03

Just 35km southeast of Orbost, Cape Conran Coastal Park offers lovely sandy
beaches, a network of walks, and many opportunities for water sports. French's
Narrows, where the Snowy River meets the sea, is 5km east of Marlo.

**ORIENTATION.** To reach the park from Orbost, go south on Nicholson
Street, which becomes the **Marlo-Cape Conran Road.** From the east, turn left off
Princes Hwy. onto Cabbage Tree Rd., 30km east of Orbost, and avoid the right
fork to Marlo. The road ends at Marlo-Cape Conran Rd.

**ACCOMMODATIONS AND FOOD.** Parks Victoria operates **cabins ❺** and
**campsites ❶** at Banksia Bluff, near East Cape Beach. Turn left off Cape Conran
Rd. onto Yeerung River Rd., just before East Cape Beach. The eight wooden
self-contained cabins, one of which is wheelchair accessible, are right next to
the beach and feature toilets, hot showers, laundry, and outdoor BBQs. Bring
sleeping gear, pillows, towels, and food. (☎03 5154 8438; www.conran.net.au.
Book ahead. Sites for up to 4 $20.50; cabins for 4 $128.) Food supplies, as well
as standard accommodation options, are available in Marlo.

**OUTDOOR ACTIVITIES.** Two thin strips of land divide the river's end from
its shallow estuary and the breaks of the Bass Strait. Farther down the road
is Point Ricardo, a popular fishing beach a mere 2min. walk from the carpark
lot. The main beach is **East Cape Beach,** a long stretch of sand with crashing
waves and its own carpark. The primary walking options both begin at the
carpark, where there is a map. The **Dock Inlet Walk** (14km; 5-6hr.) along the coast
is for the fit and ambitious. The track leads to the Dock Inlet, a body of fresh
water separated from the sea by dune barriers, and continues to Pearl Point
(11km farther), known for its rock formations and surf fishing. The **Cape Conran
Nature Trail** goes inland (2.5km, 2hr.), and there's a map and info sheet for markings along the way. Check with rangers (☎03 5154 8438) before leaving. The
trail connects with the East Cape Boardwalk, also accessible from East Cape
Beach, which leads around the East Cape to Cowrie Bay. The trail continues
past the West Cape as far as Salmon Rocks. The Yeerung River is good for fishing and swimming. The best places to swim in the area are Sailors Grave (East
Cape Beach) and Salmon Rocks (near West Cape Beach).

# CROAJINGOLONG NATIONAL PARK

Temperate rainforest opens to a wild coastline stretching from the New South
Wales border to Sydenham Inlet in the phenomenal Croajingolong (crow-
a-JING-a-long) National Park. Recognized as a UNESCO World Biosphere
Reserve, it covers 87,500 hectares, encompassing a remarkable diversity of
landscapes. Much of the park is only accessible via bumpy, unsealed roads.

VICTORIA

## ⌐ ◣ TRANSPORTATION AND ORIENTATION

V/Line **buses** from Melbourne stop at the intersection of Cox St. and Princes Hwy. in Cann River (6hr., 1 per day, $62.70); no public transportation makes the turnoff to Mallacoota. Croajingolong is located 450km east of Melbourne and 500km south of Sydney. **Cann River** and **Mallacoota** serve as the park's gateway towns; they both provide services to the park. The Princes Hwy. passes through Cann River and Genoa before crossing the border into New South Wales. At Cann River, the highway connects with Tamboon Rd., leading south into the park. The 45km drive down unsealed roads leads to the **Thurra** and **Mueller Inlet,** ending at a trail to the **Point Hicks Lighthouse.** The turnoff for the unsealed West Wingan Rd., which leads to Wingan Inlet, is about 30km east of Cann River on Princes Hwy. The unsealed roads are rough and closed after rain, so check the weather forecast before heading out. At **Genoa,** farther east along the Princes Hwy., the Mallacoota-Genoa Rd. forks south toward Mallacoota, the only sealed access to the park and the coast.

## ⚠ PRACTICAL INFORMATION

Snag groceries at **FoodWorks** on Maurice Avenue (open daily 8:30am-6:30pm).

**Tourist Offices: Parks Victoria Information Centre** (☎03 5158 6351), on Princes Hwy. in the east end of Cann River. Info on the park's road and trail conditions, and area accommodations. Open M-F 10am-4pm depending on ranger availability. **Parks Victoria office** (☎03 5158 0219), on the corner of Buckland and Allan Dr. Info on local walks. Open M-F 9:30am-noon and 1-3:30pm, but hours vary due to volunteer staffing.

**Emergency:** ☎03 5158 6202.

## ⛺ CAMPING

There are five main **camping ❶** areas within the park as well as several in the immediate surrounds. The campgrounds at **Thurra River,** a shallow river and good swimming spot, and **Mueller Inlet** are run by **Point Hicks Lighthouse** (☎03 5158 4268). Both have fire pits, river water, and pit toilets. Thurra is more popular because of its private sites, caravan access, overnight parking, and proximity to trailheads. Between Cann River and Genoa is a turnoff for the park's best sites at **Wingan Inlet,** with popular bushwalking as well as fire pits, a water source, and pit toilets ($15.50). The park's two other campsites at **Peachtree Creek** ($11.50) and **Shipwreck Creek** ($15.50) also have fire pits, a water source, and pit toilets. (Contact the **Cann River Parks Victoria office** at ☎03 5158 6351 or the **Mallacoota Parks Victoria office** at ☎03 5161 9500 for permits. Bookings are required for the Christmas and Easter holidays.) For more outdoor comforts, head to **Mallacoota Shady Gully Caravan Park ❶,** on Genoa Rd. in Mallacoota, which has a pool and laundry. (☎03 5158 0362; www.mallacootacaravanpark.com. Sites $18, high season $22, powered $20/28; cabins from $40, ensuite $50-60.)

# WESTERN AUSTRALIA

In many ways, Western Australia represents both the nation's future and its past. Until recently, the region was the country-bumpkin relative of its city-slicker eastern cousins; only the hardy and adventurous would venture here to work, surf, and experience the outback in its vast, most isolated glory. But consistent growth over the last forty years—particularly in the thriving iron ore and gold mining industries—has helped transform the region into a major player on Australia's economic stage and a tourist destination in its own right.

These days, there's something here for everyone. Perth, the region's biggest city with a population of 1.5 million, offers cafes, concerts, and cosmopolitanism on par with any of the East's biggest metropolises. The Ningaloo Reef and Shark Bay World Heritage Region both give the Great Barrier Reef a run for its money; the massive forests of the Southwest house some of Australia's biggest, oldest, and most beautiful trees; and the Margaret River vineyards produce some of the nation's most highly esteemed vintages.

Despite recent growth, sophistication, and a new emphasis on tourism, Western Australia has largely maintained its country, small-town feel. Jaded, urbanite attitude melts away in these humble towns. Westralians promote their lifestyle, their region, and its strengths with a pride that's truly old-school.

---

## HIGHLIGHTS OF WESTERN AUSTRALIA

**SWIM** with whale sharks at **Ningaloo Reef** along 250km of coral (p. 744).

**ENJOY** white sand beaches at **Cape Le Grand National Park,** a deserted paradise of unrivaled natural beauty (p. 728).

**HANG** with quokkas in **Rottnest Island,** one of the few places on Earth where these little wallabies are found (p. 702).

**SINK** your toes in the pearly white sand of **Cable Beach,** Western Australia's most famous stretch of sand (p. 758).

**STUMBLE** through the **Gibb River Road** and find a tropical gorge and other surreal wonders along this untouched desert track (p. 762).

---

## ⊏ TRANSPORTATION

Because of the vast distances between towns and the dearth of long-haul transportation, many travelers—even those on a budget—buy cars or campervans for long visits (see **Buying and Selling Used Cars,** p. 31). The thriving market for used vehicles is fueled by message boards and *The West Australian* classifieds. Used car dealerships line Beaufort St. in and around Mt. Lawley, north of Northbridge, while used and new campervans can be found in Northbridge at **Wicked Campervans** on Shenton St., and **Traveller's Auto Barn** on Newcastle St. Before paying, have the vehicle checked by a mechanic; some car dealers prey on backpackers. The **Royal Automobile Club (RAC),** 832 Wellington St., offers

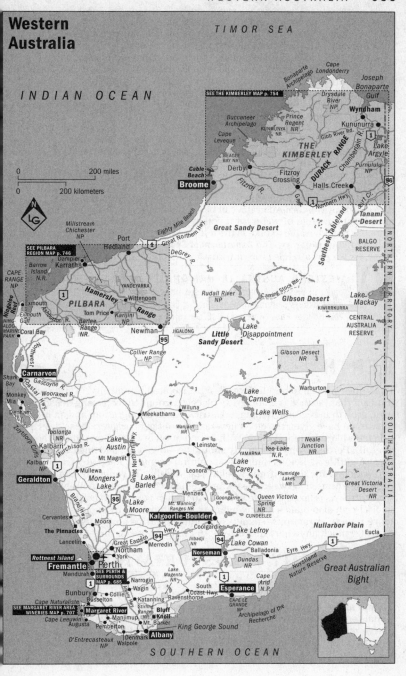

# Western Australia

TIMOR SEA

INDIAN OCEAN

Bonaparte
Archipelago

Cape
Londonderry

Joseph
Bonaparte
Gulf

SEE THE KIMBERLEY MAP p. 754

Drysdale
River
NP

Wyndham

Buccaneer
Archipelago

Prince
Regent
NR

KUNMUNYA
NR

Kununurra

Cape
Leveque

Gibb River Rd.

Lake
Argyle

THE
KIMBERLEY

DURACK RANGE

Chamberlain R.

Purnululu
NP

BEAGLE
BAY NR

Cable
Beach

Derby

Fitzroy
Crossing

Halls Creek

95

Broome

Fitzroy R.

Gr'gy

Northern Hwy.

Tanami
Desert

0        200 miles
0        200 kilometers

Eighty Mile Beach

Great Sandy Desert

Southesk Tableland

BALGO
RESERVE

Millstream
Chichester
NP

Port
Hedland

Great Northern Hwy.

DeGrey R.

SEE PILBARA
REGION MAP p. 746

Dampier

Barrow
Island
N.R.

Karratha

YANDEYARRA

Hamersley

Wittenoom

Rudall River
NP

Canning Stock Rte.

Gibson Desert

Lake
Mackay

KIWIRRKURRA

CENTRAL
AUSTRALIA
RESERVE

CAPE
RANGE
NP

Exmouth

Ningaloo
Reef

Exmouth
Gulf

NING
ALOO
MARINE
PARK

Coral Bay

Asharton R.

PILBARA

Tom Price

Karijini
NP

Barlee
Range
NR

Range

Newman

JIGALONG

Little
Sandy
Desert

Lake
Disappointment

Gibson Desert
NR

Warburton

Collier Range
NP

Carnarvon

Gascoyne

Shark
Bay

Wooramel R.

Monkey
Mia

Denham

Coastal Hwy.

Meekatharra

Wiluna

Lake
Carnegie

Lake Wells

Wanjarri
NR

Zuytdorp
Cliffs

Toolonga
NR

Murchison R.

Lake
Austin

Mt Magnet

Leinster

YAMARNA
N.R.

Lake
Carey

Yeo Lake
N.R.

Neale
Junction
NR

Kalbarri

Kalbarri
NP

Mullewa

Mongers
Lake

Lake
Barlee

Leonora

Plumridge
Lakes
NR

Great Victoria
Desert
NR

Geraldton

Brand Hwy.

95

Lake
Moore

Menzies

Mt. Manning
Ranges NR

Goongarrie
NP

CUNDEELEE

Queen Victoria
Spring
NR

Cervantes

Moora

Kalgoorlie-Boulder

Coolgardie

Lake Lefroy

Nullarbor Plain

Eucla

The Pinnacles

Lancelin

Great Eastern

Northam

Hwy.

Merredin

94

Jilbadji
NR

Norseman

94

Lake Cowan

Balladonia

Eyre Hwy.

1

Rottnest Island

Fremantle

Mandurah

SEE PERTH &
SURROUNDS
MAP p. 685

Perth

York

Lake
Magenta
NR

Dundas
NR

Nuytsland
Nature Reserve

Great Australian
Bight

Bunbury

Collie

Narrogin

Wagin

South
Coast Hwy.

Esperance

Cape
Arid
N.P.

Busselton

Katanning

Ravensthorpe

CAPE LE
GRANDE
NP

Archipelago of the
Recherche

SEE MARGARET RIVER AREA
WINERIES MAP p. 707

Cape Naturaliste

Margaret River

Stirling
Ranges
NP

Bluff
Knoll

Cape Leeuwin

Augusta

Manjimup

Pemberton

Mt. Barker

King George Sound

D'Entrecasteaux
NP

Denmark

Albany

Walpole

SOUTHERN OCEAN

inspections for members and provides roadside assistance. (☎13 17 03, roadside assistance 13 11 11. 1yr. roadside assistance $108, includes $36 joining fee.) For more info on cars and driving, see **On the Road,** p. 77.

For budget-conscious backpackers, the most popular and reasonably-priced way to get around Western Australia is on **Easyrider** bus tours, which offer "jump on, jump off" service to nearly all towns worth visiting. Drivers are usually young and act as de facto tour guides; they work with local hostels to arrange convenient pickup and drop-off times, and have deals with some restaurants to offer cheaper food for Easyrider clients.

Passenger rail service is virtually nonexistent, with the exception of the Kalgoorlie-Perth route, serviced by **Indian Pacific** and **Transwa Prospector,** and a commuter train from Perth to Bunbury. **South West Coach Lines** operates bus services southwest of Perth. **Transwa** buses operate in the southwest as well as north to Kalbarri, while **Integrity Buslines** runs to Port Hedland. **Greyhound Australia** offers flexible travel options and runs buses to Adelaide, Darwin, and Exmouth, with stops at major cities along the way. For more info, see **By Bus,** p. 686.

Portions of Western Australia can be toured by bicycle, but you should carry significant amounts of water with you at all times. In northern reaches of the state, it's not advisable to bike in the hot, wet months (Nov.-Apr.). Alert regional police of your itinerary. The **Department of Sport and Recreation** (☎08 9492 9700; www.dsr.wa.gov.au) has more information on traveling by bicycle.

**WESTERN AUSTRALIA NATIONAL PARKS.** Access to national parks in Western Australia requires a pass, available from DEC offices and most visitors centers. Individual parks: Day Pass $10 per vehicle. All parks in WA: Holiday Pass (4 weeks) $35 per vehicle.

# PERTH                                                      ☎08

What does it mean to be "the world's most isolated capital city?" Until recently, it meant that Perth was a hot, gritty place, surrounded by blazing desert. However, growth in regional mining industries, Asian immigration, and an increase in tourism have given the city a new cosmopolitan character; these days isolation feels like a beautiful thing. With a population of 1.5 million (90% of the state overall), Perth is everything a city should be—big, busy, and flush with enough great nightlife, delicious dining, and cultural events to keep any traveler busy and satisfied for days, if not weeks. The weather is generally beautiful, the location—nestled between the Swan river and the sea—is generally great, and the attitude is relaxed in spite of it all. And when you've had enough of the city itself, Perth also makes a convenient base from which to explore the region's more remote attractions—many companies run trips and tours from this hub to pretty much anywhere in Western Australia a traveler might want to visit.

## ✈ INTERCITY TRANSPORTATION

### BY PLANE

Flights arrive at and depart from **Perth Airport,** east of the city. The international terminal is 8km away from all domestic terminals; keep this in mind if you're planning a connection. If you are flying with Qantas, they offer a free shuttle between terminals; non-Qantas passengers can use the service for $8.

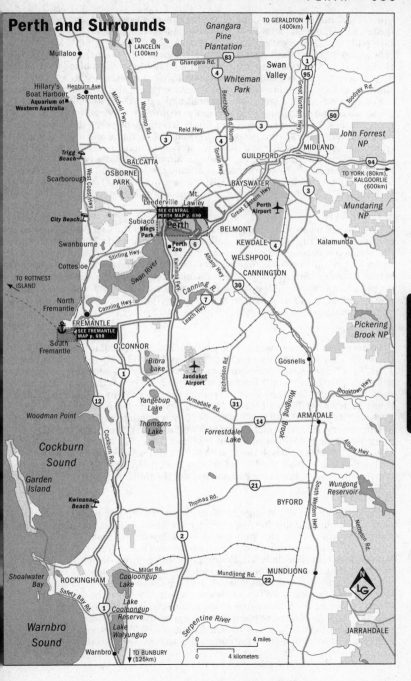

# Perth and Surrounds

For details and schedules, contact **Ground Transport Services** at ☎08 9365 9777. **Qantas,** 55 William St. (☎08 13 13 13; www.qantas.com.au; open M-F 9am-5pm), flies daily to: Alice Springs (2hr.), Brisbane (4hr.), Darwin (3hr.), Melbourne (3hr.), and Sydney (4hr.). Also services Kalgoorlie (1hr.), Karratha (2hr.), Port Hedland (2hr.), and Broome (2hr.) all on a daily basis. **Virgin Blue** (☎08 13 67 89; www.virginblue.com.au) connects Perth with the eastern states, as well as Kununurra (3hr.), Broome (2hr.), Port Hedland (2hr.), and Kalgoorlie (1hr.).

For trips within the state, try regional **SkyWest** (☎08 1300 660 088; www.skywest.com.au). Most major towns in the region are serviced by one or all of these airlines. There are a few transportation options between the city and airport. **TransPerth bus #37** runs between the domestic terminal and the city, leaving from the north side of St. Georges Terr., stop 39 (45min., every 20min. 6:20am-6:45pm, every hr. 7:15-11:15pm; $3.40) An **Airport-City Shuttle** (☎08 9277 7958) runs between most city accommodations and the domestic ($15) and international ($20) terminals. A **taxi** to the CBD costs around $25-30 from the domestic terminals (20min.) and $30-35 from the international terminal (30min.).

## BY TRAIN

All eastbound inter- and intrastate trains depart from the **East Perth Terminal,** on Summer St. off Lord St., a 30min. walk northeast of the CBD. **TransPerth** Midland line trains run between the station and the CBD every 15min. on weekdays and every 30min. on weekends. **Transwa** (☎1300 6622 05; www.transwa.wa.gov.au) serves Bunbury (2hr., $25.60) on the Australind line and Kalgoorlie (6hr., $76.85) on the Prospector line. The **Indian Pacific** runs east on Wednesday and Saturday to: Adelaide (43hr.; $395, backpackers $203), Melbourne (55hr., $484/253; change trains to the Overland in Adelaide), and Sydney (70hr., $690/315).

## BY BUS

**Easyrider** offers flexible budget tours to the major sights and towns throughout the state, and will pick you up at your hostel. (☎08 9227 0824, outside WA 1300 308 477; www.easyridertours.com.au. Open M-F 8:30am-6pm, Sa 9:30am-2:30pm, Su 10:30am-6pm.) **Transwa** (☎1300 662 205; www.transwa.wa.gov.au) runs buses from the East Perth Terminal, as does the more expensive **Greyhound Australia** (☎08 13 14 99 or 13 20 30; www.greyhound.com.au). **Integrity Buslines** (☎1800 226 339 or 08 9226 3665; www.integritycoachlines.com.au) departs every Thursday night from the Wellington St. Bus Station in the CBD and goes through the interior to Port Hedland (22hr.; $215, YHA/VIP/NOMADS/ISIC $194). **Southwest Coach Lines** (☎08 9324 2333) services the Margaret River region and leaves from the Perth City Bus Port, 3 Mounts Bay Rd., next to the convention center. For more **destinations,** see the table on p. 687.

## BY CAR

There are over 100 rental companies in greater Perth. Some quote dirt-cheap daily rates, but read the fine print: many have limited driving radii and/or limitations on where their cars may travel, voiding your insurance if you venture outside their boundaries. Sometimes for an additional fee you can increase your distance and/or daily kilometers, but make sure your contract doesn't preclude you from traveling on unsealed roads if you plan on visiting any national parks. All companies listed rent 2WDs to drivers over 21. Though there are exceptions, 4WD vehicles are generally the only way to explore unsealed areas; these are often more expensive than 2WDs, starting at $65 per day for longer-term rentals. Regardless of the type of car you rent, you will probably have to pay a surcharge for unlimited kilometers. For insurance reasons, it is extremely rare for companies to rent 4WDs to drivers under 25;

but most of the companies listed below do, including **Action Car Hire** (☎08 9277 4522) and **Britz** (☎08 9478 3488). **Backpackers World Travel,** 236 William St. (☎08 9328 1477 or 1800 67 67 63; www.backpackersworld.com; open M-F 9:30am-6pm, Sa 10am-4pm), helps with rentals and insurance.

The **Royal Automobile Club (RAC)** (832 Wellington St., West Perth; insurance ☎08 9436 4999; travel ☎08 9436 4840) offers roadside assistance to members and those of several associated overseas associations, including AAA.

**Action Hire Cars,** 343 Great Eastern Hwy. (☎08 9277 4522; www.actionhirecars.com. au). Rents cars and 4WDs to drivers ages 21-75. Surcharges apply to go to certain areas. Pickup service is available from most of the area's accommodations.

**Drive West,** 205 West Coast Hwy., Scarborough (☎08 9245 1200; www.drivewest.com. au), hires 2WDs and 4WDs to 21+ drivers and are generally reasonable and straight-forward about their policies. Renters can choose 100km per day, 200km per day, or unlimited; rates start at $28 per day. Under 25 surcharge $5.50 per day. Free delivery to accommodation in the Perth metro area and to airport hotels. MC/V.

**Europcar,** 3-5 Gordon St., West Perth (☎08 9237 4330), allows its cars to go farther north than many other companies for no extra charge, so long as you inform them beforehand. Under 25 surcharge $13.20 per day.

**M2000,** 166 Adelaide Terr. (☎08 9325 4110), guarantees that it will beat any other quote, and extends radii to include Exmouth, Monkey Mia, Kalgoorlie, Esperance, and points in between for $80. Under 25 surcharge $7 per day.

**Travellers Auto-Barn,** 365 Newcastle St., Northbridge (☎08 9360 1500; www.travellers-autobarn.com), is perhaps the only option for backpackers under 21—they rent cars, 4WDs, campervans, and station wagons stocked with camping gear to drivers 18+.

## BUSES AND TRAINS FROM PERTH TO:

| DESTINATION | COMPANY | DURATION | FREQUENCY | PRICE |
|---|---|---|---|---|
| Adelaide | Indian Pacific | 2 days | 2 per wk. (W, Sa) | $395 |
| Albany (via Bunbury) | Transwa | 8-12hr. | 1 per day (F 2) | $61 |
| Albany (via Mt. Barker) | Transwa | 6hr. | 1-2 per day | $41.70 |
| Augusta | Southwest | 5hr. | 1 per day (Sa, Su 2) | $39.65 |
| Broome | Greyhound Australia | 34hr. | daily except Tu, Su | $366 |
| Bunbury | Southwest | 2hr. | 3 per day | $23 |
| Busselton | Southwest | 3hr. | 3 per day | $27 |
| Carnarvon | Greyhound Australia | 13hr. | 1 per day M and W-Su | $145 |
| Darwin | Greyhound Australia | 2½ days | 1 per day | $719 |
| Dunsborough | Southwest | 4hr. | 1 per day | $29 |
| Esperance | Transwa | 10hr. | M, Tu, W, F | $71.65 |
| Exmouth | Greyhound Australia | 18hr. | 1 per day F, Sa, Su | $219 |
| Geraldton | Transwa | 6hr. | 1-2 per day | $50.05 |
| Kalbarri | Transwa | 8hr. | 1-2 per day M, W, F | $62.45 |
| Kalgoorlie | Transwa (Prospector Train)/Goldfields Express | 6hr./7hr. | 1 per day (M, F 2)/M, Th, F, Su | $77/70 |
| Margaret River | Southwest | 5hr. | 2 per day | $31 |
| Monkey Mia | Greyhound Australia | 12hr. | 6 per wk. (2 per day M, W, F) | $156 |
| Pemberton (via Bunbury) | Transwa | 5-8hr. | 1 per day M, T, W, Th (2 Su) | $41.60 |
| Port Hedland | Integrity | 22hr. | 1 per week | $215 |
| York | Transwa | 1hr. | 1-2 per day M-F and Su | $13.20 |

# ◪ ORIENTATION

Although Perth's streets are not quite aligned north-south or east-west, it helps to think of them as such, and locals will understand what you mean if you refer to them that way. The north-south streets run parallel to **William Street.** The east-west avenues run parallel to **Wellington Street.** The railway cuts east-west through town, separating the **Central Business District (CBD)** to the south from the cultural, culinary, and backpacker center of Northbridge. Near the center of the city, east-west streets **Hay** and **Murray Streets** become pedestrian malls between William and Barrack St. Shopping arcades and overhead walkways connect the malls to each other and to the Perth Railway Station. The Wellington Street Bus Station is a block west of the railway station, across William St.

**Central Perth** is relatively safe, but poorly lit; it empties after dark, so avoid walking alone at night. In **Northbridge,** restaurants, nightclubs, travel agencies, and budget accommodations cluster in the square bounded by Newcastle St. to the north, James St. to the south, Beaufort St. to the east, and Russel Sq. to the west. Upmarket **Subiaco,** west of the city, is a hotspot for chic cafes and cuisine, and has weekend market stalls on either side of the Subiaco train stop on the Fremantle line. The Subiaco Oval is home turf for two AFL teams: the Fremantle Dockers and West Coast Eagles.

A few blocks north of Northbridge on Beaufort St., the up-and-coming **Mount Lawley** neighborhood offers wonderful restaurants and more sophisticated nightlife. Just west of Northbridge, **Leederville,** one stop north of Perth on the Currambine line, is a pleasant place to spend the day, with plenty of pubs, cafes, and funky shops centered on Oxford St.

The green expanse of **Kings Park** rises just southwest of downtown, overlooking the city and the Swan River. The train to nearby **Fremantle** (30min., p. 697) passes through the lively beach suburbs of Swanbourne and Cottesloe.

# ◪ LOCAL TRANSPORTATION

Northbridge and the CBD are both compact and easy to navigate on foot. Free **CAT buses** whisk passengers around central Perth and Fremantle, and central Perth is a free transit zone for all buses and trains (though you must have a Smartrider card for the latter). The blue CAT runs a north-south loop from the Swan River to Northbridge; the red CAT runs east-west; and the yellow CAT connects West Perth and East Perth via Wellington St. The Free Transit Zone is bounded by the Swan River to the south and east, Newcastle St. to the north, and Thomas St. to the west. (☎ 13 62 13. Blue CAT: every 7min. M-F 6:50am-6:20pm; every 15min. F 6:20pm-1am, Sa 8:30am-1am, Su 10am-6:15pm. Red CAT: every 5min. M-F 6:50am-6:20pm; every 25min. Sa-Su 10am-6:15pm. Yellow CAT: every 10min. M-F 6:50am-6:20pm; every 30min. Sa-Su 10am-6:10pm.)

The **TransPerth** network of buses, trains, and ferries is divided into nine fare zones connecting to outlying areas; a 2-zone ride costs $3.40 and will get you from the CBD to the airport, Fremantle, or the beach. Save your ticket stub; it allows transfer between bus, train, and ferry services. Tickets are valid for 2hr. or more depending on how far you are traveling. All-day passes ($8.10) and SmartRider cards, which can be credited with any amount of money after the initial $10 to activate one, are available at TransPerth InfoCentre machines and newsagents. It may be tempting to ride without paying, but $50-$250 penalties await freeloaders who get caught, and ticket-checking officers abound.

Maps, timetables, and additional information are available by phone, online, (☎13 62 13; www.transperth.wa.gov.au) or at the four **TransPerth InfoCentres:** Plaza Arcade, Wellington St. Bus Station, City Busport, and the train station.

It's also easy to get around by taxi; a ride between the international airport terminal and Northbridge costs $30-40. **Swan Taxi** (☎13 13 30), **Independent Taxi** (☎08 9375 7777), or **Black and White Taxi** (☎13 10 08) can be hailed around the city, especially along Wellington or William St. Fares start at $3.40 on weekdays and $4.90 on weeknights and weekends, and then increase by $1.39 per km. The visitors center has maps of bike routes. The **Bicycle Transportation Alliance,** 2 Delhi St. (☎08 9420 7210; www.multiline.com.au/~bta), has information, maps, and advice on bike routes. (Open M and W 8:30am-4pm.) Bikes can be rented through **About Bike Hire** (☎08 9221 2665), at the corner of Plain St. and Riverside Dr., for $10 per hr. and $33 per day and $70 per week. (Open daily 9am-5pm; 9am-6pm during daylight saving time.)

# ◪ PRACTICAL INFORMATION

## TOURIST AND FINANCIAL SERVICES

**Tourist Office: Perth Visitors Centre** (☎1300 361 351), on the corner of Wellington St. and Forrest Pl. Books tours and sells maps of WA. Open Sept.-Apr. M-Th 8:30am-6pm, F 8:30am-7pm, Sa 9:30am-4:30pm, Su noon-4:30pm; May-Aug. M-Th 8:30am-5:30pm, F 8:30am-6pm, Sa 9:30am-4:30pm, Su noon-4:30pm.

**Outdoors Information: DEC,** 17 Dick Perry Ave. (☎08 9334 0333; www.naturebase. net), near the corner of Hayman Rd. and Kent St., Kensington. Take bus #33 east to stop 19. Has info on WA parks and sells park passes. Open M-F 8am-5pm.

**Budget Travel:** There are a number of budget travel agencies in Perth.

**YHA Western Australia,** 300 Wellington St. (☎08 9427 5100), next to the train station. Arranges travel and sells memberships. Open M-F 9am-5pm.

**STA Travel,** 100 James St., Northbridge (☎08 9227 7569). Open M-F 9am-5pm, Sa 10am-3pm.

**Peter Pan Travel,** 225 Williams St., Northbridge (☎1800 672 156; www.peterpans.com). Travel customers can get a bracelet which entitles them to 15min. free Internet on every return visit. Open M-F 9:30am-6pm, Sa 10am-5pm, Su noon-5pm.

**Student Flights,** 75 Barrack St. (☎08 9237 0600; www.studentflights.com.au). Guarantees to beat any written quote. Open M-F 9am-5:30pm.

**Consulates: Canada,** 267 St. Georges Terr. (☎08 9322 7930); **Germany,** 16 St. Georges Terr. (☎08 9325 8851); **Ireland,** 10 Lilika Rd., City Beach 6015 (☎08 9385 8247); **United Kingdom,** 77 St. Georges Terr. (☎08 9224 4700); **United States,** 16 St. Georges Terr. (☎08 9202 1224).

**Currency Exchange and Banks:** Pedestrian malls are the place to head for currency exchange—both Hay and Murray St. have multiple desks. ATMs are omnipresent, especially on William St. in Northbridge and on Hay St. between Barrack and William St.

**American Express,** 645 Hay St. Mall (☎08 9221 0777), London Court. YHA no commission. Foreign exchange open M-F 9am-5pm, Sa 9am-noon.

**Flight Centre Travel Money,** 645 Hay St, next to the AmEx desk. No fees or commission. Open M-Th 9am-6pm, F 9am-7pm, Sa 9am-5pm, Su noon-4pm.

**Travelex:** (☎08 9481 7900), 267 Murray St. near the corner of Murray and William St. Open M-F 8:45am-4:45pm, Sa 10am-2pm.

**Work Opportunities:** WA is full of high-paying work opportunities, thanks to its booming natural resources industry. Most hostels maintain notice boards with job openings. Seasonal fruit picking opportunities abound; check www.jobsearch.gov.au/harvesttrail

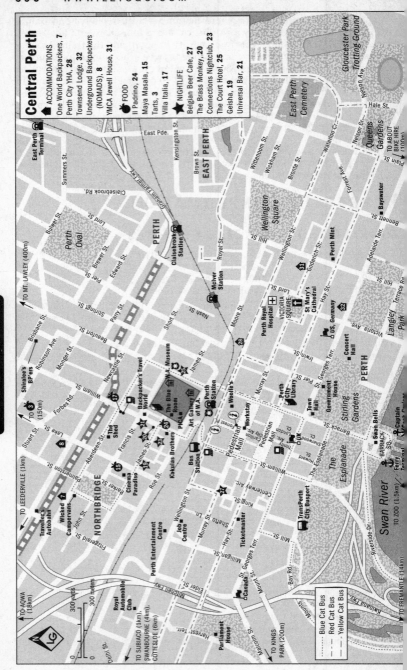

# Central Perth

**ACCOMMODATIONS**
One World Backpackers, **7**
Perth City YHA, **28**
Townsend Lodge, **32**
Underground Backpackers
(NOMADS), **8**
YMCA Jewell House, **31**

**FOOD**
Il Padino, **24**
Maya Masala, **15**
Tarts, **3**
Villa Italia, **17**

**NIGHTLIFE**
Belgian Beer Cafe, **27**
The Brass Monkey, **20**
Connections Nightclub, **23**
The Court Hotel, **25**
Geisha, **19**
Universal Bar, **21**

WESTERN
AUSTRALIA

—— Blue Cat Bus
---- Red Cat Bus
–·–· Yellow Cat Bus

or call ☎1800 062 332. Note: Employment agencies are generally uninterested in backpackers staying less than a couple of months.

**Workstay,** 9th fl. of Carillion City Office Tower in Murray St. Mall. (☎08 9226 0510; www.workstay. com.au). Great resource for work in the WA countryside. Arranges live-in work at country pubs, farms, and cattle stations. Min. committment 6 weeks; 12 weeks for visa extension farmwork. Also a resource for skilled workers looking for long-term or permanent work in Perth itself, and runs an internship program for university graduates. Open M-Th 9:30am-4:30pm, F 9:30am-4pm

**The Job Shop,** 224 William St., Northbridge (☎08 9228 1457; www.thejobshop.com.au), in the Easyrider office. A backpacker-oriented, free job placement service; caters to people of all levels seeking all nature of work (skilled, unskilled, office, field, in Perth, well outside). Prearranges placements at country pubs, stations, and harvest work throughout the WA region.

## LOCAL SERVICES

**Public Markets:** Head to Subiaco to find shops and an international food court at the Pavilion at Rokeby and Roberts Rd. Open Th-F 10am-9pm, Sa-Su 10am-5pm. Produce and plants can be found at the Station St. market. Open M and F-Su 9am-5:30pm.

**Library:** The **State Library of Western Australia** (☎08 9427 3111), is located at the north end of **Perth Cultural Centre** (p. 695). Although this is a reference library only—meaning no lending—entry is free (no membership required), as is its Internet use (although you may get booted off your terminal if a patron needs to perform a database search). Open M-Th 9am-8pm, F 9am-5:30pm, Sa-Su 10am-5:30pm. Bookshop open M-F 10am-5pm and Sa-Su noon-5pm.

**Ticket Agencies:** For sports events, try **Ticketmaster,** 200 St. George's Terr. (☎13 61 00; www.ticketmaster.com.au), located above Schmeer's Cafe in the Old Cloisters Building. Open M-F 9am-4:30pm. For other events, contact **BOCS Tickets,** Perth Concert Hall, 5 St. Georges Terr. (☎08 9484 1133; www.bocsticketing.com.au. Open M-F 9am-5pm.)

### MEDIA AND PUBLICATIONS
**Newspapers:** *The West Australian* ($1.10).
**Nightlife:** *XPress* and *Drum Media* come out weekly (free). For gay nightlife, try the weekly *Out in Perth* (free).
**Radio:** Rock, 97.3FM and 92.9FM; mix 94.5FM; Triple J (alternative mix) 99.3FM; news ABC 585 AM; tourist Info 87.6FM.

## EMERGENCY AND COMMUNICATIONS

**Emergency:** ☎000.

**Police:** ☎13 14 44. 60 Beaufort St.

**Crisis Lines: Crisis Care** (☎08 9223 1111 or 1800 199 008). **Sexual Assault** (24hr. ☎08 9340 1828 or 1800 199 888). **AIDS/STD Line** (☎08 9429 9944 or 9482 0044). **Suicide Emergency Service** (24hr. ☎08 9223 1111 or 9381 5555). **Poisons Information Centre** (☎13 11 26). **Gay Counseling Services of WA** (24hr. ☎08 9420 7201 or 1800 18 4527).

**Pharmacy:** 647 Beaufort St. (☎08 9328 7775), next to the IGA on the corner of Beaufort and Walcott St. in Mt. Lawley. Open 24hr.

**Hospital: Royal Perth Hospital** (☎08 9224 2244), on Wellington St. near Lord St. Fremantle Hospital (☎08 9431 3333), corner of Alma St. and South Terr.

**Central City Medical Centre,** (☎08 9221 0747), in the Perth Railway station, corner of Wellington & Barrack streets. Dive medicals, vaccinations, emergencies, general appointments. Open daily 8am-6pm.

**Internet Access:** In general, Barrack St. between Hay and Murray St. and William St. between James and Aberdeen are flush with Internet cafes. There is free Wi-Fi at the **State Library** in the cultural center, or you can buy it at **Backpacker's World Travel** or **Easyrider. Netcom,** 146 Barrack St. $3 per hr., $10 for 4hr. Open Su-Th 8-midnight, F-Sa 8-2am. The **Internet Station,** 271 William St., has fast connections ($3 per hr., YHA/VIP $2.40; open daily 9am-midnight), as do many of the cafes along Beaufort Street in the Mt. Lawley area, including Caffissimo, 595 Beaufort Street, and Exomodo, 615 Beaufort Street. The latter is open 24hr. on Fridays and Saturdays in the summer.

**Post Office:** 3 Forrest Pl. (☎08 9237 5460). Poste Restante M-F before 5pm. Open M-F 8am-5:30pm, Sa 9am-12:30pm. **Postal Code:** 6000 (Perth); 6004 (Northbridge).

# ☗ ACCOMMODATIONS

Most of Perth's hostels are located in Northbridge, though hostels in the CBD may offer more privacy and space. Kitchen, laundry, Internet, and linen are all standard in hostels; many also offer 24hr. check-in (for pre-booked accommodation) and a free breakfast. A/C makes a big difference in the hot summers, so ask—not all places are equipped. Book ahead in the summer.

**Hotel Bam'bu,** 75-77 Aberdeen St., Northbridge (☎08 9328 1211; www.hotelbambu. com.au). Northbridge's most exotic and unique hostel with southeast Asian themes and decor. A great option for couples—all doubles are ensuite with TV/DVD, fridge, and 4 poster bed. Continental breakfast included. Free Wi-Fi. Live DJs spin up on the roof every F and Sa. 8-bed dorm $27 per night, 2+ nights 25, weekly $155; 6-bed dorm $28/$26/$160; doubles $75/69/425. ❷

**Underground Backpackers (NOMADS),** 268 Newcastle St., Northbridge (☎08 9228 3755 or 1800 003 089; www.nomadsworld.com). This hostel's strongest asset is its great location—close enough to central Northbridge to be convenient, but removed enough to be quiet. Further perks include licensed bar, pool, A/C, and basement lounge with big-screen TV. Internet $4 per hr. Continental breakfast included. Free beer upon check-in. 6- to 10-bed dorms $25 per night, $150 per week; 4-bed $28/162; doubles $65/390, with TV/DVD, $70/420. MC/V. ❷

**One World Backpackers,** 162 Aberdeen St., Northbridge (☎08 9228 8206; www.one-worldbackpackers.com.au). Eco-friendly backpackers on the fringe of Northbridge with a relaxed, family-style environment. Greenies will appreciate things like solar water heating and biodegradable cleaning products. Continental breakfast 7-10am. Cheap Internet and Wi-Fi ($5 per 2hr.). 24hr. reception for bookings. 4-, 5-, 6- and 8-bed dorms $24-30, YHA/VIP $23-29. Doubles $71/70. Weekly rates available. MC/V. ❷

**Townsend Lodge,** 240 Adelaide Terr., East Perth (☎08 9325 4143; www.townsend. wa.edu.au). A great deal for singles in a quiet location. The rooms are popular with students, so book ahead. Internet and Wi-Fi $5 per 2hr. Singles $42, 2-6 nights $35, over 7 nights or students $28; doubles $48. MC/V. ❸

**The Old Swan Barracks,** 6 Francis St. (☎08 9428 0000; www.theoldswanbarracks. com), next to cultural center. Now under new management, this hostel has undergone massive renovations. The castle-like building now boasts an on-site cafe, a backpackers bar, a gym, and Wi-Fi. All dorms have lockers as well as new mattresses. Multiple kitchens, TV rooms and dining areas. Great location close to CBD, nightlife and restaurants. Internet $3 per hr. Luggage storage $5 per item per day, weekly rates available. Parking ($13 per 24hr.; weekly rates available. Dorms $21-26; singles $59; doubles $69, executive $75; triples $86. AmEx/MC/V. ❷

**Governer Robinson's,** 7 Robinson Ave., Northbridge (☎08 9328 3200; www.govrobin-sons.com.au). Small, elegant hostel in a restored colonial home on a quiet sidestreet in

Northbridge. Short walk to nightlife and restaurants. Good option for those who prefer privacy; more like a B&B than a backpackers. Dorms $25; doubles $70. MC/V. ❷

**Perth City YHA,** 300 Wellington St. (☎08 9287 3333; www.yha.com.au). Renovated firehouse located next to the train station. Pool and cafe. Internet $3 per hr. Dorms $31.50, YHA $28; singles, twins, and doubles $83.50/75, ensuite $100/90; family rooms $122.50/110. MC/V with 3% surcharge. ❷

**YMCA Jewell House,** 180 Goderich St. (☎08 9325 8488; www.ymcajewellhouse.com). For those who need budget accommodations with privacy. Small TV room and kitchenette on every fl. Maid service daily. Towels provided. Singles $39, students $26, with TV and fridge $44; doubles $50, with TV and fridge $55; family rooms $80. MC/V. ❸

# ▧ FOOD

Perth has received many accolades for its multicultural cuisine. Northbridge is full of Asian restaurants, particularly along William St. Meanwhile, James St. takes you from Greece to Thailand and back again through China and Italy as you walk from William St. towards Russel Sq. Mt. Lawley is also a good place to find cafes and restaurants. There is dining in the CBD, but it's generally either chains or posh places; if you're on a budget, it's not the best option. Grab meats and produce at **City Fresh Gourmet Deli,** 375 William St. (☎08 9237 5659; open M-Sa 7am-8pm, Su 7am-7pm), or head to **Woolworths** in the Murray St. Mall directly across from the bus station (open M-Th 8am-7pm, F 8am-9pm, Sa 8am-5pm, Su noon-6pm). For cheap pasta, cereals, and deli foods, elbow through the crowds at **Kakulas Brothers Wholesale Importers,** 183-187 William St. (Open M-F 8am-5:30pm, Sa 8am-5pm. Cash only.)

 **WORK IT.** With so much fine dining available around the corner of Lake St. and James St., it can be hard to choose. Go on a slow night (Mondays for example) and let the hostesses fight for your business. At the very least you can expect to be offered a free beer or glass of wine.

▨ **Il Padrino,** 198 William St. (☎08 9227 9065; www.ilpadrinocafe.com). Perth's best pizza ($16-25), even complimented by Pope John Paul II. $13.50 pizza and pasta at lunch Tu-F and dinner Tu. All pizzas $13 to take-away, all pasta $12.50 to take-away. Open Tu-F 11:30am-3pm and 5pm-late, Sa 5pm-late. AmEx/MC/V. ❷

**Tarts,** 212 Lake St. (☎08 9328 6607). A fantastic neighborhood cafe that buzzes during lunch hour. Ginormous homemade pastries ($5), smooth green avocado with olive oil and cracked pepper on thick toast ($8), and scrumptious panini ($11). The servings are generous, and the quality is worth every penny. Open daily 7am-6pm. AmEx/MC/V. ❶

**Valentino's,** corner of Lake and James St. This bright blue Italian eatery serves one of the cheapest breakfasts in Northbridge (pancakes with bacon and maple syrup; $9). Wood-fired pizzas start at $10. Open M-Th 10am-11pm, F 10am-midnight, Sa 7am-midnight, and Su 7am-11pm. MC/V. ❶

**Chef Han's Cafe,** 245 William St. or 546 Hay St. (☎08 9328 8122). Chef Han is the emperor of local budget cuisine. Speedy and delicious heaps of vegetarian-friendly noodles and stir-fry ($9-14). Open daily 11am-10pm. AmEx/MC/V. ❶

**Villa Italia,** 279 William St. (☎08 9227 9030). In a city addicted to caffeine, the espresso ($3) here stands out. M-W pasta $12.90, otherwise $14-19; M-W after 5:30pm pizza $12.90, otherwise $13-18. Open M-Th 11:30am-late, F 7am-late, and Sa 8-11:30am and 6pm-late. AmEx/MC/V. ❷

## PRICELESS PERTH

Unfortunately, it seems that money tends to disappear faster in cities than it does in small towns. The good news is that the Perth hospitality scene seems savvy to the fact that most backpackers would rather spend their precious dollars partying than eating, and accordingly, offer "backpacker nights" during the week. Below is a guide for making the most out of Perth's dinner deals.

**Monday:** The **Deen** (84 Aberdeen St.; ☎08 9227 9361) hosts Manik Monday. Free BBQ (chicken, sausage, salad) and one drink 7-9pm. Drink specials can vary.

**Tuesday:** The **Hip-E Club** (Newcastle and Oxford St.; ☎08 9227 8899) has free BBQ, drink, and entry for everyone who arrives between 8-10pm. Drink specials last all night.

**Wednesday:** Try the **Mustang Bar** (46 Lake St.; ☎08 9328 2350), where $5 gets you BBQ (steak, sausage, 2 salads, and a roll), a pint or mixed drink, and entry into a prize drawing. From 6pm until late.

**Thursday:** **Eurobar** (108-114 Aberdeen St.; ☎08 9227 5244) provides partiers with a free sausage BBQ at 8pm, as well as $2 middies, $4 wines, $5 bourbons and vodkas all night long.

**Friday:** Check for happy hour specials at any pub in the afternoon/early evening for surefire savings on food and drink.

**Maya Masala** (☎08 9328 5655), at the corner of Francis and Lake St. An "Indian brasserie," dishing up curry plates ($17-21), tandoori ($10-20), and dosa ($9-16). Reduced prices for takeaway. Open daily 11:30am-2:30pm and 5:30pm-late. ❷

**The Beaufort Street Merchant,** 488-492 Beaufort St. (☎08 9328 6299), in Mt. Lawley. A combination grocer, bottle shop, gift shop, and cafe, this classy but rustic-looking stop is a delight to peruse. Much of the food is made on premises; savory pastries from $8.50-11 (watch as they write your order on the stainless steel countertop in permanent marker!). Try the delicious sweet potato fritter with hummus and artichoke ($9.50). Open M-Th 8am-9pm, F 8am-9:30pm, Sa 7:30am-9pm, Su 7:30am-7:30pm. ❶

# ◙ SIGHTS

**SWAN BELLS.** Perth's most recognizable landmark is also one of the world's largest musical instruments—a glass bell tower designed to recall the city's ship-building past. Perched like a swan on the river's shores, the tower houses 12 bells cast in 14th-century England and given to Perth on Australia's bicentenary in 1988. The bells have commemorated everything from Britain's 1588 victory over the Spanish Armada to the more recent 9/11 attacks. The bells now ring Mondays, Tuesdays, Thursdays, and on weekends from noon to 1pm. Bell demonstrations are given Wednesday and Friday from 11:30am to 12:30pm. *(Barrack Sq., at the river end of Barrack St. Take the blue CAT to stop 19. ☎08 9218 8183; www.swanbells.com.au. Open daily 10am-4:30pm. $10; under 15, seniors, and students $7.)*

**AQUARIUM OF WESTERN AUSTRALIA.** Leafy sea dragons, saltwater crocodiles, and eight kinds of sharks live at AQWA, where visitors walk through an underwater tunnel surrounded by fish from all of Western Australia's diverse seascapes. Watch divers feed the sharks by hand (daily 1pm and 3pm) or interact with squid and stingrays in the discovery pools. Those 18 and older can book ahead to dive or snorkel with the sharks, turtles, and stingrays off the coast. *(North of Perth along the Mitchell Fwy. at Hillary's Harbour, off the Hepburn Ave. exit. Take the Joondalup train to Warwick, then bus #423 to Hillary's. ☎08 9447 7500; www. aqwa.com.au. Open daily 10am-5pm. $26, concessions $19. Dive/snorkel $125, additional $25-40 for gear.)*

**PERTH ZOO.** Missed the chuditches and diblers in Fitzgerald River National Park? Want to see the quokkas that gave Rottnest ("Rat's nest," in Dutch) Island its name? If you won't be seeing these Aussie animals in their natural habitats, the Perth Zoo is an essential stop. An Australian bushwalk leads you past koalas and echidnas, and leaves nothing but a "stay on the path" sign between you and the kangaroos. The reptile exhibit lets you safely see some of the region's most dangerous natives, and the new orangutan treetop walk places you right next to these gentle giants. *(20 Labouchere Rd. in South Perth. Take the blue CAT to the jetty and then ferry across the river for $1.20, or take bus #30 or 31 from the Wellington St. Bus Station. 24hr. infoline ☎ 9474 3551; www.perthzoo.wa.gov. au. Free walking tour daily 11am. Open daily 9am-5pm. $18, children $9, under 4 free.)*

**PERTH MINT.** Several million dollars worth of gold lies just beyond your fingers at this historic mint, which is Australia's biggest gold refinery. The world's largest display of gold bars moved here from Singapore in 2004. Marvel at molten gold, and then relax outside over traditional tea ($20) in the posh Tea Garden. *(310 Hay St., East Perth. Take the red CAT to stop 3 or 11. ☎ 08 9421 7223. Open M-F 9am-5pm, Sa-Su 9am-1pm. Gold pours 10am-4pm, guided heritage walk 9:30am-3:30pm; both on the hr. $15, concessions $13. Tea Garden ☎ 08 9421 7205. Open M-F 10am-4pm.)*

**KINGS PARK.** Perched atop Mt. Eliza just west of the city, Kings Park offers spectacular views of Perth and the Swan River. Larger than New York's Central Park, it contains a War Memorial, Botanic Gardens featuring over 1000 plant species, and the DNA tower, with views of Rottnest Island. Free guided walks (1-3hr.) depart from the karri log opposite the War Memorial daily at 10am and 2pm. Don't miss the **Lotterywest Federation Walkway,** a raised boardwalk through the trees and an arched, glass-sided bridge with gorgeous river views at its peak. *(20min. walk west from the CBD up St. Georges Terr., or take the #37 bus free to Fraser Ave., #39 on weekends. Free parking. Info center ☎ 08 9480 3600; www.bgpa.wa.gov.au. Open daily 9:30am-4pm. Gardens open daily 9am-4pm; treetop walk 9am-5pm.)*

**BEACHES.** Perth's beaches are easily accessible from the city, yet far enough away to make you forget that they're there. Families flock to Cottesloe Beach (on the Fremantle line) for swimming and mild surf, and Swanbourne Beach is a perennial favorite. *(Bus #102 towards Cottesloe, or a 2km walk from the Swanbourne stop on the Fremantle train.)* City Beach is a great swimming spot. *(Bus #81, 84, or 85 from the stop in front of Hobnobs on Wellington St.)* Scarborough has bigger surfing waves and crowds of twentysomethings. *(Bus #400 from Wellington St. Station.)* The best surfing is through the tubes at Trigg Beach, just north of Scarborough; the waves here can get a bit rough. *(Joondalup train to Warwick, then bus #423.)*

**CULTURAL CENTRE.** The Perth Cultural Centre packs several good museums, performance centers, and the state library into one block. The **Art Gallery of Western Australia** has collections of modern and classical Australian art, including Aboriginal carvings, and hosts international exhibits. *(☎ 08 9492 6600; www. artgallery.wa.gov.au. Open daily 10am-5pm. Free, except for special exhibitions. Free guided tours available.)* The **Perth Institute of the Contemporary Arts (PICA)** houses hit-or-miss multimedia exhibits, and the art ranges from the very intriguing to baffling at best. Pick up a booklet of events or call for schedules. *(☎ 08 9227 6144. Open Tu-Su 11am-6pm. Gallery free, performance prices vary.)* The **Western Australian Museum** showcases the state's natural history. Don't miss "diamonds to dinosaurs" and the Aboriginal exhibits. *(☎ 08 9427 2700; www.museum.wa.gov.au. Open daily 9:30am-5pm. Suggested donation $2.)* The **Blue Room** provides a great venue for local theater. Productions range from classic plays to more experimental pieces by local playwrights. *(☎ 08 9227 7005; www.pacs.org.au. $22.)*

**EARTH, SEA, AND SKY. Captain Cook Cruises,** Pier 3 Barrack Sq., runs a variety of tours, including a wine cruise ($135, YHA/VIP/NOMADS $130), a Fremantle explorer cruise ($38/34), and the "Zoocrooz" ($46/40) to Perth Zoo. *(☎ 08*

**FOOTY NATION**

Two teams of men, clad in short shorts and sleeveless shirts, run madly across a cricket pitch and battle for a leather ball. There are few rules, less padding, and a stadium full of waving flags and fans.

The game is Aussie Rules Football or "Footy," as it is commonly known. It is the quintessential Australian sport: physically demanding, high-scoring, and injury-inflicting. Head to Perth's Subiaco Oval to watch the West Coast Eagles—difficult to get tickets for—or the upstart Freo Dockers. If you make it to a game, grab a beer and take note of these next few guidelines.

A game consists of four quarters with almost no break in the action. If a player has the ball, he can run with it as long as he bounces it once every 15 steps, or he can pass it by kicking or punching it toward a teammate. If a player catches the ball within 50m of the goal, he has a free kick. Scoring occurs when a ball is kicked between the goalposts; 6 points for the central posts or 1 for the outer posts.

*The best way to appreciate the sport is to see it live. Tickets at the Subiaco Oval, located in East Subiaco on Wellington Rd., start at $11 if purchased at the gate. Tickets also available through Ticketmaster (☎13 61 00; ticketmaster.com.au.)*

9325 3341; *www.captaincookcruises.com.au.*) **Malibu City Dive** has diving tours to Rottnest Island (p. 702), noted for its unique coral and fish; the company also offers a four-day scuba certification class. *(126 Barrack St. ☎08 9225 7555; www.rottnestdiving.com.au. Rottnest trips including equipment start at $150, without equipment $105; scuba certification class $395.)* Nearby **Western Australia Dive Centre** offers cheaper certification courses, with the option of completing the 4-day course over 2 weekends. *(37 Barrack St. ☎08 9202 1999. Weekday course $305. 2-weekend course $325.)* **Planet Perth** has several trips, including wine tours (from $55) and trips to Broome (from $1235); Exmouth (from $640); Monkey Mia (YHA/VIP/NOMADS/students $495); and Swan Valley. *(☎08 9225 6622; www.planettours.com.au.)* **Western XPosure** offers comparable tours *(☎08 9371 3695; www.westernxposure.com.au. Broome from $1299. Exmouth incl. Pinnacles from $625.)* For Pinnacles tours (see **Nambung National Park,** p. 735), popular options are **Australian Pinnacle Tours** *(☎08 9417 5555; www.pinnacletours.com.au. Daytrip to Pinnacles from $139)* or the **Planet Perth option** *(from $125).*

# 🎭 NIGHTLIFE

Perth's laid-back attitude keeps the pubs, clubs, and cafes hopping. Northbridge starts partying around 10pm and rages late into weekend nights. Mt. Lawley and Subiaco have more upscale, subdued nightlife. Pick up the free weekly *XPress* or *Drum Media* to find out what's going on. Cover charges are infrequent, but queues are not, particularly on weekends. Formal dress codes are rare, but jeans may get the occasional scowl and most places require closed-toed shoes. Most places require ID to enter, and some will not accept foreign drivers' licenses, so be sure to bring along a passport. Tuesdays are generally dead, so take advantage of cheap eats and take a night off.

Perth is gay- and lesbian-friendly. **The Cinema Paradiso,** 164 James St. *(☎08 9227 1771; open daily 10:30am-11pm.),* posts a variety of local events, and is a good place to pick up *Out*, a monthly gaylesbian publication, and the *Q Pages*, a directory of gay- and lesbian-friendly and -run establishments and events (both free). The website www.gayinWA.com.au is also a great resource.

◪ **The Brass Monkey,** 209 William St., Northbridge (☎08 9227 9596; www.thebrassmonkey.com.au). Fantastic ex-hotel serves local microbrews. Billiards, an indoor courtyard, leather sofas, and an airy veranda. Connects to swanky **Grapeskins,** a suave wine bar and brasserie. Open M-Tu 11am-midnight, W-Th 11am-1am, F-Sa 11am-2am, Su noon-10pm.

**The Belgian Beer Cafe,** 347 Murray St. (☎08 9321 4094). A bar for any who feel that Australian beers leave them deprived of good head. Sip Stella Artois, Hoegaarden, and other Belgian brews through creamy foam out of goblets and chalices. Open M-F 11am-midnight, Sa 11am-1am, Su 11am-10pm.

**The Shed,** 69-71 Aberdeen St. (☎08 9228 2200; www.the-shed.com.au). Big open-air venue with live music and DJs every night, beer-of-the-month specials, and plenty of $10 meals for starving backpackers. Th and Su pints $4, jugs $8. Be prepared to queue after about 10pm on a Friday or Saturday. No cover except for infrequent ticketed concert events. Open Th-Su noon-midnight.

**Universal Bar,** 221 William St., Northbridge (☎08 9227 9596). Frequent live bands and a slightly older, sophisticated crowd. No jeans; closed-toed shoes required. Open W-Th 5pm-1am, F 4pm-2am, Sa 5pm-2am, Su 5pm-midnight.

**Connections Nightclub,** 81 James St., Northbridge (☎08 9328 1870; www.connectionsnightclub.com). Popular gay-friendly club with DJ-spun beats. Theme nights like "Lesbian Mud Wrestling." Open W, F (cover $10), Sa ($12) 10pm-6am.

**Geisha,** 135a James St., Central Perth (☎08 9328 9808). Pulsates with various genres of dance music, sometimes from celebrity guest DJs. (Heath Ledger once spun here.) Attracts a more eclectic crowd than other Northbridge clubs. Open F-Sa 11pm-6am.

**The Court Hotel,** 50 Beaufort St., Northbridge (☎08 9328 5292), on the corner of James St. The scene at this gay-friendly bar varies from Latino to disco inferno, including amateur drag nights on Wednesdays, to standard dance pub during the rest of the week. Open M-Th and Su noon-midnight, F-Sa noon-2am.

**The Elephant and Wheelbarrow,** Northbridge (☎08 9228 4433), cnr. Lake and Francis St. Classic English pub with nice British beers on tap and a leafy, shaded veranda full of tables. Good option for those who prefer pubs to clubs. Beer of the month is always on special; $6 pints of Kilkenny and Guinness on backpacker night Thursdays. Open M-Th 11-1am, F-Sa 11-3am, Su noon-midnight.

# FREMANTLE ☎08

Fremantle is in many ways Perth's younger, cooler sibling—it remains in the shadow of its larger, more populous counterpart, yet outshines it by being hip and relaxed in ways that only a small beach town can. Its inviting blend of Victorian architecture and vibrant cafe culture—check out the famous "cappuccino strip" of South Terr.—makes Fremantle an attractive destination. Traditionally a popular port, "Freo" gained international attention with the arrival of the America's Cup race in the 1980s, when the city sailed into a new era and upscale improvements were made to the waterfront area and the shopping district. These days, the waterfront boasts state-of-the-art museums, while the town's main drags are populated by graceful old hotels and civic buildings.

## TRANSPORTATION AND PRACTICAL INFORMATION

**TransPerth trains** regularly travel into Freo from Perth (30min.; M-F approx. every 15min. 6am-midnight, then every 30min. until 2:30am F and Sa; $3.20). The **Fremantle Airport Shuttle** goes to both terminals of the Perth Airport and departs from the Fremantle Railway Station regularly until midnight; pickup at Fremantle accommodations is available 24hr. when booked ahead. (☎08 9335 1614; www.fremantleairportshuttle.com.au. $25 for the 1st person, $5 per additional passenger.) Although downtown Freo is easily walkable, the free **Fremantle CAT buses** trace a figure-eight around the harbor and through the town's main sights. (☎13 62 13. Every 10min. M-Th 7:30am-6:30pm, F 7:30am-9pm, Sa-Su 10am-6:30pm.) Car rentals are widely available in this region; **Bayswater,** 13 Queen Victoria St. (☎08 9430 5300), allows drivers to travel within a 500km radius with no extra fees. **Free parking** is available on Ord St., off of High St. roughly 1km from town center; you can also park for the day for $2.80 in the lots on Victoria Quay Rd. opposite the ferry passenger terminal.

**Tourist Office: Fremantle Tourist Bureau** (☎08 9431 7878; www.fremantlewa.com.au), on the corner of High and William St., Kings Sq. Offers free accommodation and tour bookings. Open M-F 9am-5pm, Sa 10am-3pm, Su 11:30am-2:30pm.

**Budget Travel: STA Travel,** 53 Market St. (☎08 9430 5553). Open M-F 9:30am-5:30pm, Sa 10am-3pm. **Student Flights** (☎08 9289 2800; www.studentflights.com.au), on the corner of Cantonement & Market St. Open M-F 9am-5:30pm.

**Police:** ☎08 9430 1222. Corner of Queen St. and Henderson St.

**Hospital: Fremantle Hospital** (☎08 9431 3333, after hours ☎08 9480 4960), corner of Alma St. and South Terr.

**Internet Access:** Typically $5 per hr. Try the **Travel Lounge,** 16 Market St. (☎08 9335 4822). Internet available M-F 7:30am-8pm, Sa 8am-8pm, Su 9am-8pm. **Croissant Express,** on South Terr. next to the Sail & Anchor has Wi-Fi ($5 per 15min.)

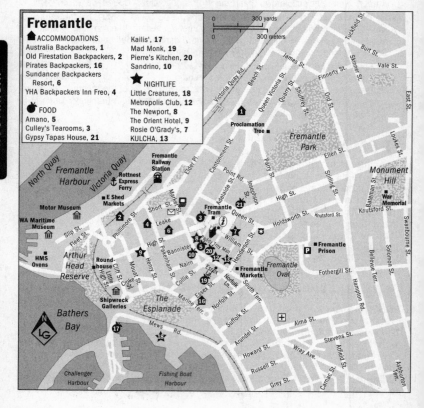

**Crisis Care Hotline (24hr):** ☎08 9325 1111.

**Taxi: Swan** (☎13 13 30), **Black & White** (☎13 10 08).

**Post Office: Fremantle GPO** (☎08 9335 1611), on the corner of Market St. and Short St. Open M-F 8:30am-5pm. Another branch at 142 High St. (☎08 9336 3466). Open M-F 8:30am-5pm, Sa 8am-1pm. **Postal Code:** 6160.

# ACCOMMODATIONS

In general, you're going to want to book a room in advance—there aren't many hostels, and they fill up quickly with long-term backpackers seeking work in the area. The tourist office books apartment rentals that offer comfortable accommodations for two at a budget rate, but you can do it yourself through their website. An apartment with a kitchen, TV, and laundry facilities typically starts from $70, but you may have to stay a minimum of 2 nights.

- **Sundancer Backpackers Resort,** 80 High St. (☎1800 061 144; www.sundancerbackpackers.com). This centrally located, social hostel is a restored turn-of-the-century resort and has one of the most interesting lobbies around. Has a pool, free Internet for guests, and an in-house bar. 8-10 bed dorms $22; 6-bed dorms $23; 4-bed dorms $24; singles $45; doubles $60, ensuite $70. NOMAD discounts available. MC/V. ❷

- **Old Firestation Backpackers,** 18 Phillimore St. (☎08 9430 5454; www.old-firestation.net), at Henry St. Short walk from cafes and nightlife, this hostel more than makes up for its location with free Internet, videos, digital jukebox, and video games. Separate female wing with kitchen and lounge. Curries available from the attached Indian restaurant ($4-11). Dorms $23; doubles $65. MC/V. ❷

- **Pirates Backpackers,** 11 Essex St. (☎08 9335 6635). A smaller, low-key hostel with the best location in town. Offers BBQ, job information, monthly social events, and free lockers. Check-in 24hr. Internet $4 per hr., first 30min. free. 6-8 bed dorms $26; 4-bed dorms $28; doubles and twins $85. VIP discount. MC/V. ❷

- **YHA Backpackers Inn Freo,** 11 Pakenham St. (☎08 9431 7065). From the train station, turn right on Phillimore St., then left on Pakenham St. Attractive, renovated warehouse space. Big-screen movie showings nightly at 8pm; 2 kitchens; free breakfast. Bike rental $10 per day. Reception 7am-11:30pm. Check-in 24hr. Dorms $24.50-$31.50; singles $67; doubles and twins $72.50. NOMAD, VIP, and YHA discounts. MC/V. ❷

- **Australia Backpackers,** 4 Beach St. (☎08 9433 2055; www.austbackpackers.com). Turn left down Elder St. from train station (becomes Beach St.) or take the Freo CAT to stop 8. A friendly, affordable hostel in an old hotel building. Take advantage of discounted drinks at the bar next door or in the shady back courtyard. There is also a jobs board and a free bus to and from the beach. Internet access $2 per 30min. or $5 per 2hr. 5-8 bed dorms $20, YHA/VIP $18; 3-4 bed dorms $22/20; singles $35/30; twins $45/40; doubles $50/45. Weekly rates available. MC/V. ❷

# FOOD

The soothing sunny weather and laid-back attitude of Fremantle make it an ideal place to capitalize on al fresco dining opportunities. Sidewalk cafes line many of the streets. Don't miss the **Fremantle Markets** on the weekend for fresh produce at rock-bottom prices (see below). During the week, try **Kakulas Sister** (☎08 9430 4445), a quaint Italian grocery store at 29-31 Market St.

**HONE YOUR PICNICKING SKILLS.** Many restaurants offer the same meals for slightly cheaper takeout prices, and Fremantle has a beautiful park along the waterfront. Take your food with you for a chance to enjoy the Freo doctor, the oceanic wind rumored to cure whatever's ailing you.

**Gypsy Tapas House** (☎08 9336 7135), on the corner of High & Queen St. An affordable culinary wonderland hiding in a strip mall. Open only 3 nights a week and run by an expat Frenchman, this unassuming little restaurant has a menu of 30 different beautifully prepared tapas, each for only $7 (the gorgonzola bruschetta and the grilled cut of lamb are tasty). Live music F and Sa, with a focus on local artists and gypsy stylings. It's best to book at night—the small courtyard fills up quickly. Open Th-Sa 11am-11pm. ❷

**Pierre's Kitchen** (www.pierreskitchen.com), opposite Collie St. in the Fremantle Malls off of South Terr. For $7.50-12, enjoy authentic savory crepes and wash them down with a European-styled coffee or an ice cream crepe ($4.50-5.50). ❶

**Mad Monk,** 33 South Terr. (☎08 9336 3100; www.madmonk.com.au). A sprawling, sunny veranda is the main draw for this restaurant cafe on South Terr. Seat yourself on a stool or a lounge cushion and watch people stroll to and from the market as you sip your latte or nibble on a gourmet sandwich ($5.50) and tapas ($6-12). Open daily 8:30am-midnight. ❸

**Kailis',** 46 Mews Rd. (☎08 9335 7755; www.kailis.com). A step above the standard fish and chips joint. Enjoy the sun (or shade) on their expansive veranda and munch on lightly battered fish while watching the pearl ships return to harbor. Bar and cafe. Fish and chips $9.25. Open daily 8am-8:30pm. Cash only; in-house ATM. ❶

**Sandrino,** 95 Market St. (☎08 9335 4487; www.sandrino.com.au). Stands out with a popular patio and a unique take on classic Italian fare. Their artisan pizzas are especially tempting; try the pumpkin pizza ($19). Open daily 11:30am-late. AmEx/MC/V. ❸

**Culley's Tearooms,** 116 High St. (☎08 9335 1286). Serves full meals from crepes to salads to meat pies ($6-15) in addition to bakery fare. Shelf of ½-price items. Open M-F 8:30am-5pm, Sa 8:30am-4:30pm, Su 10am-4:30pm. ❶

**Amano,** 6 South Terr. (☎08 9336 1695). If your wallet is feeling a bit light, grab one of their massive slices of sicilian pizza ($5) and you'll be satisfied for hours. Add a gelato and get both for $7. Open daily 8am-11pm. ❶

## 👁 SIGHTS

**WESTERN AUSTRALIA MARITIME MUSEUM AND SUBMARINE OVENS.** Fremantle's maritime museum, housed in a striking building at the mouth of the Swan River, tells the unique history of sailboat racing, warships, and fishing practices from Aboriginal times to today. Particularly popular is the exhibit on *Australia II*, the famed sailboat that captured the America's Cup racing trophy in 1983. The real highlight is the tour, sometimes led by former captains of the Oberon-class submarine *Ovens*, which was in active service until 1997. A path marked by anchors leads from the museum to the other must-see: the Shipwreck Galleries on Cliff St., which showcase restored pieces of major wrecks like the Batavia. (*'A' Shed Victoria Quay.* ☎08 9431 8444; www.museum.wa.gov.au/maritime. *Open daily 9:30am-5pm. Sub tours every 30min. 10am-3:30pm; sign up early before tours fill up. Museum $10, concessions $5, children $3, families $22. Sub $8/5/3/5/22. Museum and sub $15/8/5/8/35. Shipwreck Galleries $2 suggested donation.*)

**FREMANTLE PRISON.** Get a thorough look at a maximum-security prison without committing a felony. The prison, which opened in the 1850s, closed in 1991.

Excellent guides recall daring tales of escape as well as the horrors of incarceration, while works of art left on the walls by convicts reveal a different side of life behind bars. The Torchlight Tour is especially thrilling and may scare the daylights out of the easily-spooked. A limited portion of the prison is wheelchair-accessible. *(1 The Terrace. ☎08 9336 9200. 75min. tours depart every 30min.; last tour 5pm. Torchlight tours W and F; book ahead. Open daily 10am-6pm. Day tour $16.50, concessions $13, children 4-15 $8.50, families $44; candlelight tour $21/16.50/11/56.)*

**FREMANTLE MOTOR MUSEUM.** Highlights include a never-refurbished 1914 Rolls Royce, the world's only 1904 Napier Samson (hand-built from drawings after the six 2.5L cylinder engines were discovered in a sunken boat), and also the car from the film *Crocodile Dundee* (signed, of course, by Paul Hogan). The massive collection of vintage automobiles, racecars, and motorbikes is as much a snapshot of cultural history as it is a celebration of mechanical innovation. *(B Shed Victoria Quay. ☎08 9336 5222; www.fremantlemotormuseum.net. Open daily 9:30am-5pm. $9.50, seniors $8, children $5, families $23. AmEx/MC/V.)*

**FREMANTLE MARKETS.** The place to be on a weekend afternoon in Freo. One can find just about anything among its stalls (which number more than 150), from massages to marsupials. Fresh veggies abound; produce prices hit rock bottom Sunday around closing time. *(On the corner of South Terr. and Henderson St. ☎08 9335 2515. www.fremantlemarkets.com.au. Open F 9am-9pm, Sa 9am-5pm, Su 10am-5pm.)*

## 📷 NIGHTLIFE

The emphasis shifts from cafe to club as the sun sets, giving Freo one of the most active latenight scenes in Western Oz. Look for old hotels; many have been converted into bars under a national law that lets hotels sell alcohol.

**Little Creatures,** 40 Mews Rd. (☎08 9430 5555). This microbrewery offers the best beer in town, great views of the harbor, and the trendiest set of Freo locals. Once a crocodile farm, the building now lends itself to late-evening conversation. Open M-F 10am-midnight, Sa 9am-midnight, Su 9am-10pm.

**The Newport,** 2 South Terr. (☎08 9335 2428). A converted hotel that's popular with students, catering to sports and music fans. Has drink specials and local music many nights. Open M-Th 11am-midnight, F-Sa 11am-1am, Su noon-10pm.

**Bar Orient,** 39 High St. (☎08 9336 2455). A relaxed venue that offers live music 6 nights per week. Cap-

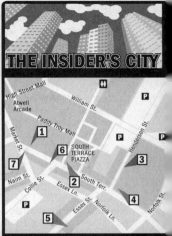

## THE INSIDER'S CITY

## OH SO FREO

Fremantle's famous "Cappucino Strip" is a cosmopolitan oasis where you can sip lattes, dig through literary treasure chests, and catch a concert or poetry reading. Below is a daylong itinerary with some of the town's must-see stops.

**1.** Peruse the extensive collection of up-to-date overstock books at **Elizabeth's Bookshop.**

**2.** Grab a crepe at **Pierre's Kitchen** and check out the shops in **Fremantle Malls.**

**3.** Wander through the bursting bookcases of **Magpie Books** for rare and old gems.

**4. Fremantle Markets** has pretty much everything you could ever want, from capes to capers.

**5.** Indulge your cultural side by catching an artsy independent flick at the **Luna on SX** theater.

**6.** Grab dinner at **Dome,** one of South Terrace's sophisticated sidewalk cafes.

**7.** Unwind with a dessert and cocktail at **Gino's.**

tures Freo's artsy vibe well. Th open-mic night (jugs of beer $10). Su poker tournaments. Open M-Th 10am-midnight, F-Sa 10am-1am, Su 10am-10pm.

**Rosie O'Grady's,** 23 William St. (☎08 9335 1645). Irish pub in the town center, with live music on most weekend nights. Open M-Th 11am-midnight, F-Sa 11am-1am, Su 11am-10pm.

**Metropolis Club,** 58 South Terr. (☎08 9228 0500). Glitzy, multi-level dance club. Expect long waits in line at the door. Cover $15. Open F-Sa 9pm-4 or 5am.

**KULCHA,** 13 South Terr. (☎08 9336 4544); www.kulcha.com.au), above the Dome Cafe. This multicultural artspace has shows and concerts most weekends for $10-20. Expect anything from French dance troupes to Canadian songstresses to "global groove" DJs. Grab a brochure or call to find out what's on; sometimes there are art exhibitions and workshops or classes running being offered the day.

# ROTTNEST ISLAND ☎08

Dubbed a "rat's nest" by Dutch explorers who mistook the island's quokkas (small marsupials) for giant rodents, Rottnest Island is anything but. Just 30min. from Fremantle and 90min. from Perth, the island is a spectacular haven for wildlife and visitors; peacocks roam freely and vacationers cycle, swim, snorkel, surf, and kayak. The coastline is a beautiful setting for water sports: white beaches meet rolling green hills. Remnants of a darker past, however, linger in the form of buildings constructed by Aboriginal prisoners who were incarcerated on the island in the 19th century.

**█ TRANSPORTATION.** Several companies offer similarly priced ferry service to Rottnest from Fremantle, Hillary's Harbour, and Perth; call ahead to make sure that all boats are running. **Oceanic Cruises** (☎08 9325 1191) departs from Pier 5 of the Barrack St. Jetty, Perth (daily 8:45, 10am; also noon, Dec.-Apr.; $68, concessions $63, students $54, children $26) and from the B Shed on Victoria Quay, Fremantle (daily 7:30am, 10, 11:30am, 3:30pm; Dec.-Apr. also 8:45am, 2, 5:15pm; $54/48/42/21). Overnight packages are also available (ticket and YHA dorm bed $94 from Perth, $85 from Fremantle). **Rottnest Express** (☎1300 467 688; www.rottnestexpress.com.au) has several daily departures from the Barrack St. Jetty in Perth (daily 8:45, 9:45am, 2pm; round-trip $69, students $54, children $29, concessions $60) and from the Victoria Quay, C Shed, Fremantle (7:30, 9:30, 11:30am, 3:30pm, M-Th 5:15pm; F 6pm; same-day round-trip $53, concessions $46, students $43, children $22; extended-stay $58/51/48/24). Free pickup is available from Perth and Fremantle accommodations.

Once on the island, visitors can explore by bus, bike, or foot. Free transfer **shuttle buses** can get travelers to the airport, Geordie Bay and Kingstown; these depart from the main bus stop near the museum every 30min. between 8am and 5pm, with additional buses every hour between 6 and 9pm. The **Bayseeker Bus** shuttles passengers between all of the island's bays, hop-on, hop-off style (day pass $10; buses every ½-hour between 8:30am-4:30pm) and offers a full-commentary 2-hr. tour (daily 11am, 1:30, 1:45pm; $25.50). In line with its vaguely Dutch ancestry, Rottnest is an island of **bicycles.** And indeed, the best way to see Rottnest is by biking—the island is only 11km long and 4.5km wide, although the terrain is slightly hilly. **Rottnest Island Bike Hire,** 300m left of the jetty, has a massive fleet of bikes for hire and is a better option than renting before you arrive. (☎08 9292 5105. Open daily in high season 8:30am-5pm; in low season 8:30am-4pm. Fixed-gear $18 per day, 18-speed $24.10; deposit $25. Locks and helmets included. AmEx/MC/V.)

**7** **PRACTICAL INFORMATION.** The **Visitors Centre,** which provides maps and books accommodations, is at the end of the jetty at Thomson Bay. (☎08 9372 9732. Open M-Th and Sa-Su 7:30am-6:15pm, F 7:30am-7pm.) Free tours of Rottnest leave the Salt Store to the left of the visitors center. To the right of the jetty is a pedestrian mall with an **ATM.** A half-kilometer north of the mall is a **nursing post.** (☎08 9292 5030. Open daily 8:30am-4:30pm.) The **police station** (☎08 9292 5029) is across the street. The **post office** is inside the Rottnest Island Gift Shop at Thomson Bay (open M-F 9am-1pm and 1:30-4pm). **Postal Code:** 6161.

**7** **ACCOMMODATIONS AND FOOD.** Booking for all accommodations on the island is handled through the visitors center; all overnight guests must check in here upon arrival. The **YHA Kingstown Barracks Youth Hostel ❷** is in Kingstown, a 20min. walk from the visitors center or short shuttle ride via the transfer bus (see above). Though there are meals available in the barracks complex ($7), travelers who do not want to relive the noise and chaos of their primary school cafeterias may prefer to cook in the hostel's kitchen. (☎08 9372 9780, or try central booking at 08 9432 9111. Linen $5. Internet access 1 per 10min. Lockers $2-5. Dorms $25.20, YHA $23). Other accommodation choices can be booked trough the central reservation service (☎08 9432 9111) and include 4-6 bed bungalows ($33-63 per night), tent sites ($9), and self-contained units ($97-152) as well. (Lower prices midweek. Book ahead in summer.) In the Thomson Bay settlement, fish and chips ($9.50), milkshakes ($5), or a midday drink at the bar can be found at **Rottnest Tearooms and Cafe ❶.** (Open M-F 8am-late, Sa-Su 8am-8:30pm; takeaway 8:30am-4:30pm.) Next door, **Dôme Cafe ❶** serves up Anzac biscuits or biscotti ($2-2.60), gourmet coffee ($4), and soups and salads ($8.50-16) to satisfy the hungry traveler. (☎08 9292 5026. Open M-Th and Su 7am-7pm, F-Sa 7am-8pm. MC/V.) Both afford views of Thomson Bay.

**S** **SIGHTS.** Rottnest Island's beaches get emptier as you head away from settled areas—go far enough and you may have a cove to yourself. **Narrow Neck** and **Salmon Bay** offer good fishing, as does the jetty. The **Basin, Pinky Beach,** and **Parakeet** are nice swimming spots near the settlement. **Little Salmon Bay** and **Parker Point** are ideal for snorkeling, while **Strickland Bay** boasts Rottnest's best surfing. Whales and dolphins are often seen from the windy cliffs at **West End,** where 3m high waves crash upon the limestone, ending their long journey across the Indian Ocean. **Rottnest Malibu Diving,** located below Dôme Cafe, hires all the necessary gear for a variety of water sports. (☎08 9292 5111; www.rottnestdiving. com.au. Single dive including gear $80; snorkel gear $16.50; surfboard $20 per day; fishing rod $12.50 per day; beach umbrella $10 per day. Open daily 8am-5:30pm. MC/V.) For those who would prefer to stay dry, Oceanic Cruises runs **Underwater Reef & Wreck Explorer** tours October-April. Guests on the 45min. cruise can enjoy views of 100-year-old shipwrecks and tropical aquatic life from the safety and comfort of a boat. (Daily cruises at 11, 11:45am, 2:15pm. $23, concessions $21, students $18, children $15.) The **Catholic Church** also offers a break from sun and surf; visitors can ring the bells every day 3-4:30pm.

**WESTERN AUSTRALIA NATIONAL PARKS.** Access to national parks in Western Australia requires a pass, available from DEC offices and most visitors centers. Individual parks: day pass $10 per vehicle. All parks in WA: holiday pass (4 weeks), $35 per vehicle.

# SOUTHWEST

Tourism in the Southwest is booming, and it's not hard to see why—Mother Nature has been kind to the region. The adventurous can hike in the Stirling and Porongurup ranges, dive with dolphins in Bunbury, scale sky-scraping trees in the Walpole-Narnalup park and Pemberton areas, and—as always—relax on quiet, pristine beaches with stunningly clear coastal waters. To boot, the region's cultural offerings—particularly in the fine food and wine areas—are among the country's best in quality and reputation. In the low season, the crowds depart and rates go down, but many activities—including surfing, whale-watching, spelunking, and wine-tasting—are still available.

## ◰ TRANSPORTATION

The easiest way to see the Southwest is by car; many sights are well off the bus routes, and public transportation is often inadequate or nonexistent. Once completely out of Perth, the 3hr. drive south toward Margaret River takes you past shoreline, cattle stations, and the occasional limestone quarry. Options do exist for those without cars. The **Easy Rider Backpackers bus** offers a three-month pass that covers service between most regional hostels as far as Albany. (Dec.-Mar. 3 per week, Apr.-May and Sept.-Nov. 2 per week., June-Aug. 1 per week. 24hr. notice required for pickup. $269; $10 YHA discount.) **Transwa's** (☎1300 662 205) handy 28-day **Southern Discovery Pass** allows for travel in a one-way loop to most destinations in the region, including Albany, Esperance, and Kalgoorlie.

## BUNBURY                                          ☎08

Dolphins are the main attraction in Bunbury (pop. 55,000), 2hr. south of Perth, where over 100 bottlenoses have made their home. Though there's no shortage of dolphin-admirers, Bunbury has escaped the deluge of tourists that drowns Monkey Mia. This may be due to the fact that many visitors feel they've seen all the town has to offer after visiting the **Dolphin Discovery Centre,** (p. 705).

◰ **TRANSPORTATION.** Downtown Bunbury is located 3km from the Wollaston **train station** on the southern end of Western Australia's **train** network. Trains depart for Perth daily on the "Australind" line (2hr., 6am and 2:45pm, $25.60). There is a free shuttle between the station and the visitors center. South West Coachlines is in the **Old Railway Station** at Carmody Pl. and Haley St. (☎08 9791 1955. Open M-F 8am-6pm, Sa-Su 8am-2pm and 3:30-6pm.) **Buses** run to Perth (2hr.; 8:45am, 2, 6:30pm; $23, YHA $20.70) and Augusta via Busselton and Margaret River (2hr.; M-F 11:35am and 4:20pm, Sa-Su 8:45am and 4:05pm; $17, seniors $9.60, 10% YHA/VIP discount. Cash only). Transwa also offers service to Perth (3hr.; M, W, F 11:40am; Tu, Th, Sa 11:15am; and M-F and Su 5:40pm; $24, YHA/VIP discount 10%) and Augusta (3hr.; M-Th and Su 3:45pm, M-F and Su 12:05pm, F also 8:20pm; $21.40, YHA/VIP $18). **Local buses** circle the city (☎08 9791 1955. M-F 7am-9pm, Sa 8am-5pm. $2.20, outlying areas $3.40; all destinations for students, children, and seniors $1-1.40.)

◪ **PRACTICAL INFORMATION.** The **Old Railway Station,** off Blair St., houses the **Bunbury Visitors Centre** (☎08 9721 7922; www.visitbunbury.com.au; open M-F 9am-5pm, Sa 9:30am-4:30pm, Su 10am-2pm), the bus station, and the **Bunbury Internet Cafe** (☎08 9791 1254; $5 per hr.; open M-Sa 8am-4:30pm). Other services include banks along Victoria St., **police** (☎ 13 14 44) on the corner of Wittenoom St. and Stephen St., and a **hospital** (☎ 08 9722 1000) located south of town at Bussell Hwy. and Robertson Dr. There is a **post office** on the corner of Victoria and Stirling St. (☎ 13 13 18. Open M-F 8:30am-5pm). **Postal Code:** 6230.

**ACCOMMODATIONS.** The **Dolphin Retreat YHA** ❷, 14 Wellington St., is a friendly hostel with free bikes and boogie boards, billiards, a ping-pong table, and Internet access for $5 per hr. (☎ 08 9792 4690. Dorms $21, non YHA $24; singles $35/40; doubles $54.60; family rooms $85/95. MC/V with 2% surcharge.) The **Wander Inn YHA** ❷, 16 Clifton St., near Wittenoom St., has free breakfast, free cake and coffee, movie nights on Wednesday, $8 BBQs every Friday, and bikes to rent for $10 per day. (☎ 08 9721 3242. Internet access $4 per hr., 1st 10min. free. Coin laundry. Dorms $25, VIP/YHA $22; singles $38/35; doubles and twins $60/56; triples $28/25. MC/V.) **Koombana Bay Holiday Resort** ❷, just across Koombana Dr. from the Dolphin Discovery Centre, has impeccable grounds and extensive facilities including a pool, laundry, tennis courts, Wi-Fi, and a convenience store. (☎ 08 9791 3900. High-season sites for 2 $32, powered $34; ensuite $42; cabins for 2 $85. Low season $30/37/80. MC/V.)

**FOOD.** The stretch of Victoria St. between Wellington and Clifton St. has a collection of restaurants that locals refer to as "the cappuccino strip." After dark this street boasts Bunbury's nightlife. Customers sip smooth cappuccinos ($3.70) while sitting on plush leather couches at **Benesse** ❶, 83 Victoria St. (☎ 08 9791 4030. Open daily 7am-5pm. MC/V min. $10.) **Buck's Diner** ❶, at the corner of Symmons and Victoria St., serves up hearty meals to a local crowd. A chicken breast fillet, salad, fries, and coffee costs just $10. (Open M-W 7:30am-8pm, Th-Sa 7:30am-9pm, Su 8am-3pm. Cash only.) The more frugal should try **Orfa Kebabs and Turkish Bakery** ❶, 57-59 Victoria St. (☎ 08 9791 2440. Kebab combo with tabouleh and soda $9.30. Open daily 8am-late. Cash only.) There's a **Coles** supermarket in the Centrepoint Shopping Center behind the visitors center. (☎ 08 9795 1800. Open M-W and F 8am-6pm, Th 8am-9pm, Sa 8am-5pm.)

**SIGHTS.** The **Dolphin Discovery Centre,** on Koombana Dr., is the best way to learn about the local dolphins. It's run by a friendly volunteer staff. (☎ 08 9791 3088; www.dolphindiscovery.com.au. Open daily Nov.-Apr. 8am-4pm, May and Oct. 8am-3pm, June-Sept. 9am-3pm. $6, children and concessions $3, families $9.) **Naturaliste Charters,** located on the adjacent jetty runs dolphin-watching and swimming tours. (☎ 08 9791 3088, must book through the Discovery Centre. 1hr. tours daily 11am and 3pm. Dolphin-watching tour $37, YHA $35, children $27; 3hr. swim tour Dec.-Apr. $125.) Across the street from the discovery center, the 200m **Mangrove Boardwalk** weaves through the southernmost mangrove ecosystem in Western Australia. The **Big Swamp Wetlands** on Prince Philip Dr., just south of the CBD, is home to over 60 species of birds. The **Big Swamp Wildlife Park,** also on Prince Philip Dr., lets you interact with a number of white kangaroos, tawny frogmouths, and exotic birds. From Ocean Dr., turn onto Hayward St. and look for the sign at the next roundabout. (☎ 08 9721 8380. Open daily 10am-5pm. $5.50, seniors $4.50, ages 2-12 $3.50.) The **Marlston Hill Lookout,** near the intersection of Victoria St. and Koombana Dr., provides panoramic views of the area from atop a spiral staircase. There are also beautiful beaches along **Ocean Dr.,** including the popular **Back Beach.**

# MARGARET RIVER AREA ☎08

The coastline, caves, and cuisine of the Margaret River Area make the region a popular year-round destination for vacationing Perthites. The vast cave systems, beaches, and dramatic rock and coral formations of the Leeuwin-Naturaliste National Park are complemented by an overwhelming selection of celebrated vineyards, orchards, farms, and galleries that cover the countryside. Perhaps even more remarkable than the region's wide variety of landscapes and activities is that they're all contained within a small area—the drive from northernmost point Dunsborough to southern tip Augusta takes only an hour.

## ▣ ORIENTATION

Margaret River lies 100km south of Bunbury on the **Bussell Highway (Hwy. 10)**, which becomes the town's main street. The scenic **Caves Road** branches off the Bussell Hwy. at Busselton, 52km from Bunbury, and winds its way by Margaret River through the towns of **Yallingup** and **Dunsborough.** About 45km south of Margaret River, the **Blackwood River** meets the ocean at Augusta.

## ▣ LOCAL TRANSPORTATION

The lack of centralized attractions means transportation can be a hassle. **Buses** run by South West Coachlines depart Margaret River from Charles West St., two blocks from the Bussell Hwy., and goes to Perth (4hr.; 2 per day; $31, YHA $28). Transwa (☎1300 662 205) uses **Margaret River Travel,** 109 Bussell Hwy., as its area agent. (☎08 9757 2171. Open M-F 9am-5pm, Sa 9am-noon.) The best way to get around is by **car.** Rental is most easily arranged in Perth or Bunbury before arriving in Margaret River. In Busselton, Avis (☎08 9754 1175) operates out of the Toyota dealership at the west end of Peel Terr. Dunsborough Car Rentals (www.dunsburoughcarrentals.com), based out of the Dunsbuourgh YHA, also rents budget cars to drivers 25+. Margaret River Car Hire (☎08 1794 4485) is your best option with small cars and 4WDs from $55 per day. You can also rent **bikes** at various places in town, including Margaret River Cycles, 31 Station Rd. off Wallcliffe Rd. (☎08 2145 0677; www.westozbikes.com.au. Open M-F 9am-5pm, Sa 9am-1pm. $25 per 24hr.)

## ▣ PRACTICAL INFORMATION

**Tourist Offices:**

**Augusta Visitor Centre** (☎08 9758 0166), on the corner of Bussell Hwy. and Ellis St. Free accommodation booking. Open daily 9am-5pm.

**Busselton Tourist Bureau,** 38 Peel Terr. (☎08 9752 1288). Free booking service for accommodations and tours. Open M-F 9am-5pm, Sa 9am-4pm, Su 10am-3pm, public holidays 10am-4pm.

**DEC,** 14 Queen St., Busselton (☎08 9752 5555). Hiking and camping info. Open M-F 8am-5pm.

**Dunsborough Visitor Centre** (☎08 9755 3299), in the shopping center on Seymour Blvd., Dunsborough. Books tours and accommodations. Open M-F 9am-5pm, Sa 9am-4pm, Su 10am-4pm.

**Margaret River Visitor Centre** (☎08 9757 2911; www.margaretriver.com), on the corner of Bussell Hwy. and Tunnbridge St. Maps, brochures, and a wine showroom. Open daily 9am-5pm.

**Work Opportunity:**

**Labour Solutions,** 24 Fearn Ave (☎08 9758 8136). Vineyard work agency. Min. 6-week commitment during harvest and pruning seasons. Carpools for $5 per day. Open M-F 8:30am-5pm.

**Vine Power,** 33 Fearn Ave (☎08 9757 2547). Vineyard work agency.

Margaret River Area Wineries

**Police:** 42 Willmott Ave., Margaret River (☎08 9757 2222).

**Hospital:** on Farrelly St. just off of Wallcliffe Rd. (☎08 9757 2000).

**Internet Access: Cybercorner Cafe,** Shop #2, 72 Willmott Ave., Margaret River (☎08 9757 9388). $6 per hr; laptop connection $14 per hr. Open M-F 8am-8pm, Sa-Su 9am-5pm. **The Bookshop,** Shop #1, 109 Bussell Hwy. Internet and Wi-Fi $7 per hr. Open daily 9am-5pm in winter, 9am-7pm in summer.

**Post Office:** Wilmott St., Margaret River (☎08 9757 6200), 1 block up Willmott Ave. from Bussell Hwy. Open M-F 9am-5pm. **Postal Code:** 6285.

# ACCOMMODATIONS AND CAMPING

Visitors to the Margaret River area can choose to stay in a wide range of settings, from vineyards to beaches to tuart forests. Upscale options tend to be the norm—with wine comes money, and luxury accommodations abound in the Margaret River area. Those looking to splurge can contact the **Margaret River Visitor Centre** (☎08 9757 2911) to book a room in one of the many wonderful B&Bs, chalets, apartments, or cottages. Backpacker rooms fill up quickly from October to March; be sure to book ahead for summer weekends. From June to August, more bargain options are available. Contact **DEC** (☎08 9752 5555) if you want to camp in **Leeuwin-Naturaliste National Park.**

## MARGARET RIVER

**Inne Town Backpackers,** 93 Bussell Hwy. (☎08 9757 3698 or 1800 244 115; www. innetown.com). Great location. Internet access $5 per hr. Laundry. Bike hire $10 per 3hr., $25 per day. Dorms $25-27; singles $60; doubles $65; triples $75. MC/V. ❷

**Surfpoint Resort** (☎1800 071 777; www.surfpoint.com.au), on Riedle Dr. south of Prevelley, about 500m from Gnarabup Beach. Clean, simple rooms around a small courtyard and pool; a beautiful beach escape. Internet access $6 per hr. BBQ. Dorms high season $24, low season $22; doubles $79/67; ensuite $99/85. Book ahead in summer. ❷

**Riverview Tourist Park,** 8-10 Wilmott Ave. (☎08 9757 2270; www.riverviewtouristpark. com). Camping and cabins within reasonable walking distance (800m) to town. Free Wi-Fi; well-equipped campers kitchen. Offers one of the cheapest wine tours in town, with discounted rates for guests. Powered sites for 2 $30; cabins from $60, ensuite $70-120. Higher in summer and during long weekends. ❸

**Prevelly Park Beach Resort** (☎08 9757 2374), turn right on Mitchell Rd. off Wallcliffe Rd. west out of Margaret River. Close to great surfing. Check in at the adjoining general store. Only BBQ equipment for campers. Linen $4.50-6.50. Sites high season $17, low season $11; basic on-site vans $90/50; 5-person cedar cabins $110/60. ❶

## BUSSELTON, DUNSBOROUGH, AND YALLINGUP

🖾 **Dunsborough Beach House YHA,** 201-205 Geographe Bay Rd., Dunsborough (☎08 9755 3107). Excellent location on beach gives this social hostel a laid-back vibe. Manager Andy is both knowledgeable and amiable, providing guest-friendly services like daily shuttles to town for grocery shopping, in-house car hire, free rice, free herbs from the garden, and free boogie boards and snorkel gear. Internet access $4 per hr. Bike rentals $10 per day, free for quick trips. Dorms $27, YHA $24; doubles and twins $66/60. Weekly rates available. MC/V. ❷

**Hideaway Holiday Homes,** 24 Elsegood Ave., Yallingup (☎08 9755 2145). Cabins just a 10min. walk from the beach. Bathrooms, laundry, TV, and kitchen. No linen. Doubles from $60. Weekly rentals only in high season, from $500 per week. Cash only. ❹

**Yallingup Beach Holiday Park,** 1 Valley Rd. (☎1800 220 002 or 08 9755 2164), as you drive down to Yallingup Beach. Great location across from the area's biggest surf. High-season sites for 2 $50; low-season $28; cabins for 2 $175-255/80-120. MC/V. ❷

## AUGUSTA

🖾 **Baywatch Manor Resort YHA,** 88 Blackwood Ave. (☎08 9758 1290; www.baywatch-manor.com.au). Cozy atmosphere and gorgeous, well-maintained facilities. Native jarrah-wood dining tables. Knowledgeable owners arrange whale watching trips at 10% discount. Internet access $5 per hr. Bikes ½-day $8, full-day $12. Free lockers. Dorms $24, YHA $22; doubles and twins high season $70/65, low season $60/55; ensuite doubles high season $95/88, low season $80/75. MC/V with 3% surcharge. ❷

**Leeuwin House Backpackers** (☎08 9758 1944; www.augusta-resorts.com), across Blackwood Ave from the Augusta Hotel-Motel (book through the hotel). Basic bunk rooms with standard amenities, available to book any night except M, Th, or Sa. High season $28 per bed, low season $24. AmEx/MC/V. ❷

**Flinders Bay Caravan Park** (☎08 9758 1380), 2.5km south of the visitors center. Sites for 2 Dec.-Jan. $20-22, powered $25; Feb.-Nov. $18/20. ❶

# ◗ FOOD

Because of the high standards for food and wine in the Margaret River area, eating out can be sensational. Cafes, bistros, restaurants, and gourmands line Bussell Hwy. and its few side streets in town. Not surprisingly, most eateries are BYO, meaning guests can bring their own wine to drink with their meal (though beware the corkage fee, which can be steep).

BYO-ers can choose between the **Riverfresh IGA** supermarket next to the visitors center on the Bussell Hwy. in Margaret River (open daily 7:30am-8pm) or the **Coles** supermarket opposite the public restrooms off of Bussell Hwy. (open daily 7:30am-7pm). Margaret River also hosts a **market** every Sunday (10am-1pm) on Bussell Hwy. across from the pharmacy. In Augusta, there is an **IGA** grocery store on Blackwood Ave. across the street from the visitors center, and a **fruit market** about 500m north. Small restaurants line Dunn Bay Road, which runs through Dunsborough. Many area wineries also have restaurants which serve lunch, though expect to pay top dollar. Margaret River's laid-back nightlife begins in the evenings at Corner Bar in town on the corner of Bussell Hwy. and Willmott St. or Settlers Tavern farther along Bussell.

## MARGARET RIVER

▣ **Wino's,** 85 Bussell Hwy. (☎08 9758 7155). This trendy wine bar is the quintessential end to a Margaret River day; enjoy local shiraz under the cascading grape vines around the veranda. Serves light tapas appropriately named "bar grits" ($5-14), gourmet pizzas ($13.50), and more expensive main courses. Open daily 3pm-late. MC/V. ❷

**Green Planet,** 113b Bussell Hwy. (☎08 9757 3644; www.vegism.org). Wholesome, fresh vegan foods from curries to salads. Open W-Su 11:30am-9pm. ❶

**Sails Cafe,** 2/117 Bussell Hwy. (☎08 9757 3573). The terrace has great views for people-watching over Margaret River's busiest street. Seels scrumptious homemade scones; lunch meals $7.50-18. Breakfast available all day (pancakes $9). Open daily 7am-4:30pm (kitchen open until 3pm). Cash only. ❶

**Settler's Tavern,** 114 Bussell Hwy. (☎08 9757 2398). At the end of the night, all roads lead to Settler's. Live bands 4 nights per week. Billiards and big-screen TV. Healthful, innovative dishes like spicy baja tacos ($12) until 8:30pm. YHA discount 10%. Cover varies. Open M-Th 11am-midnight, F 11am-1am, Sa 10am-1am, Su noon-10pm. ❷

## BUSSELTON, DUNSBOROUGH, AND YALLINGUP

**Dunsborough Bakery** (☎08 9755 3137), in the Centrepoint Shopping Center on Dunn Bay Rd., Dunsborough, is legendary for its meat pies. The "surfer's" bacon and egg pie ($4.60) is popular. Open daily 6:30am-5pm. Cash only. ❶

**Evviva** (☎08 9755 3811), on the corner of Cyrillean Way and Naturaliste Terr., Dunsborough. Take a break from tired breakfasts and indulge in muesli with yogurt and stewed fruit ($9). While most other spots stock their display cases with cakes and tarts, lovely Evviva's is filled with fresh carrots, mangos, beetroot, and other ready-to-juice fruit and vegetables. Open daily 7am-2:30pm. Cash only. ❶

**The Food Farmacy,** Shop 9 in Dunsborough Park Shopping Centre, Dunn Bay Rd., Dunsborough (☎08 9759 1877). With menu titles like $C6H12O6$ (glucose), and salt, pepper, oil, and spice "shakers" that are actually test tubes displayed in racks on the table, it's a modern gourmet joint with a keen sense of humor. Breakfast and lunch $6-40, pricier dinner $15-40. Open M-Tu and Th-Su 8am-late. ❹

### AUGUSTA

**Augusta Bakery and Cafe,** 121 Blackwood Ave. (☎08 9758 1664). A bakery with superb pastries and meat pies ($2-4). Gigantic, topping-laden pizzas F nights (small $7.50-10). Open daily; bakery 7am-4pm; cafe 7:30am-3:30pm, F also 5-8:30pm. ❶

**Colourpatch Cafe** (☎08 9758 1295), on Albany Terr., just south of town. Specializes in fish and chips ($9-10). The patio boasts a great view of the Blackwood River flowing into Flinders Bay. Open daily 8am-8pm, except Tu evenings. ❶

# ◉ SIGHTS

The Margaret River area boasts numerous farms that offer food tastings, demonstrations, and farmstays. There are also dozens of regional art galleries around the wine country. In Dunsborough, these are localized near the town center, while in Busselton they're housed in the unique **ArtGeo Center** in the old Court House complex on Queen St.

**BUSSELTON JETTY.** At 2km, this is the longest wooden jetty in the Southern Hemisphere. An underwater observatory at the end of the jetty allows visitors to view sea life below the water's surface without getting wet. *(At the end of Queen St. in Busselton. ☎08 9754 3689; www.busseltonjetty.com.au. Observatory open daily, weather permitting. Open daily in summer 8:30am-5:30pm, in winter 10:30am-3:30pm. Wheelchair accessible. Jetty access $2.50, under 15 free; 40min. tour and trolley ride $20, children $11.50.)*

**WARDAN ABORIGINAL CENTRE.** The Wardan Aboriginal Centre, run by the native Wardandi People, is the only facility of its kind in Western Australia. Cultural custodians lead bushwalks and demonstrate spear and boomerang throwing. *(Head 6km south on Caves Rd. from Yallingup, turn right on Wyadup Rd. and then left on Injidup Springs Rd. ☎08 9756 6566. Open daily 10am-4pm. $12-25. AmEx/MC/V.)*

**EAGLES HERITAGE RAPTOR WILDLIFE CENTRE.** Located on Boodjidup Rd. 5km southwest of Margaret River, the Centre houses Australia's largest collection of birds of prey. It is dedicated to the rehabilitation of injured birds, breeding projects, and public education. Be sure to catch a flight display, when you may get to handle an eagle. *(☎08 9757 2960; www.eaglesheritage.com.au. Open daily Sept.-May 10am-5pm, June-Aug. 10am-4pm. Flight displays daily 11am and 1:30pm. Wheelchair accessible. $11, seniors $9, children $5, families $28.)*

## ⚡ WINERIES AND WINE TOURS

### WINERIES

The Margaret River area boasts over 80 wineries, most of which are clustered in the region between Yallingup and Margaret River. The biggest varietals are Shiraz, Cabernet Sauvignon, Chardonnay, Sauvignon Blanc, and Riesling, so both red and white fans find satisfaction around here. Smaller wineries generally offer more personal tasting experiences.

**Vasse Felix** (☎08 9756 5014; www.vassefelix.com.au). Posh gourmet restaurant with a raised dining room that overlooks the vines. All the pretension you'd expect from the oldest vineyard in the region. Open daily 10am-5pm; restaurant 11am-3:30pm.

**Cullen** (☎08 9755 5277; www.cullenwines.com.au). Fully organic since 1988. In 2004 became one of only a few biodynamic vineyards in the world. The vineyard's principal winemakers have both been women, mother Diana and daughter Vanya Cullen. The flagship wine is called "Diana Madeline" and is considered one of Australia's best. Cellar and restaurant open daily 10am-4pm. MC/V.

**Settler's Ridge** (☎08 9755 5883; www.settlersridge.com.au), at 54b Bussell Hwy. in Cowaramup, has fairly priced, award-winning organic wines. Open daily 10am-5pm.

**Gralyn** (☎08 9755 6245; www.gralyn.com.au). One of the region's first vineyards; remains the gold standard in fine ports. It's still a friendly, family-run operation, in a beautiful modern facility. Open daily 10am-5pm.

**Woody Nook** (☎08 9755 7547; www.woodynook.com.au), on Metricup Rd., north of Cowaramup. This vineyard is a relaxed option with its cafe and several award-winning wines, including its flagship Gallagher's Choice Cabernet Sauvignon, or the more playful Nooky Delight tawny port. Open daily 10am-4:30pm.

**Howard Park** (☎08 9756 5200; www.howardparkwines.com.au, www.madfishwines. com.au), on Miamup Rd., offers 2 different lines—the stately Howard Park wines for experts, and the drink-and-enjoy it now Mad Fish line. The vineyard also hosts the Sony Tropfest, an annual short film festival over a long weekend in early Mar., and the largest of its kind in the world. Although there is no restaurant, guests are welcome to bring a picnic to enjoy with their wine purchase at one of the large wooden tables overlooking the grounds. Open daily 10am-5pm.

 **EAT, DRINK, AND BE WARY.** Although wineries are a major attraction in the Margaret River area, visitors should be careful of driving between tastings. Australia's legal blood alcohol limit for driving is a very low 0.05%. Walking, going on a wine tour, or riding with a designated driver (called "the skipper" in Oz) are all good ways to avoid run-ins with the law (and trees).

**Laurance Estate** (☎08 9321 8015; www.laurancewines.com). Offers 2 ranges of non-intimidating wines—Laurance and Aussie Jeans Rock—that come in artistically curvy bottles and purse-like carrying cases. There are platters available to order with tastings, and guests can relax to the sounds of lounge tunes as they enjoy the rose gardens. You'll know you've reached this one when you see the massive fountain with the golden figure on Caves Rd. Taster trays available with bread and oils. Open daily 10am-5pm.

**Chateau Xanadu** (☎08 9757 2581; www.xanaduwines.com), off Boodijup Rd. Welcomes a younger crowd with a variety of trendy wines. Walkers and bikers can take Railway Terr. 3km south to Terry St. Open daily 10am-5pm; restaurant daily noon-4pm.

**Cape Mentelle** (☎08 9757 0888), off Wallcliffe Rd. west of town. A relaxed, friendly winery, and one of only a few to grow zinfandel grapes. Tours $25. Vineyard and winery tours available daily at 11am. Open daily 10am-4:30pm.

**Voyager** (☎08 9757 6354). One of the most beautiful estates in the entire region. A long walk or a short bike ride away from town, this vineyard rewards visitors with beautiful gardens and award-winning wines. Open daily 10am-5pm; restaurant daily noon-3pm.

**Leeuwin Estate Winery** (☎08 9759 0000; www.leeuwinestate.com.au), off Gnarawy Rd. Boasts sweeping, picnic-perfect grounds. The estate hosts a wildly popular concert in February or March every year. Past performers have included luminaries such as Diana Ross, Dionne Warwick, and Ray Charles. Winery tour $12.50, children $2.20. For non-touring guests, some tastings incur a small fee of $2.20. Open daily 10am-4:30pm. 1hr. tours at 11am, noon, and 3pm; includes tasting.

## WINE TOURS AND WINE EDUCATION

While renting a car makes area wineries more accessible, drinking and driving don't mix. Wine tours are a popular alternative; they generally cost about $65-80 per person. Most tours run 11am-6pm and include lunch, pickup and dropoff from most locations in Margaret River, at least one brewery, and visits to the local cheese and chocolate factories.

WESTERN AUSTRALIA

**Dirty Detours** (☎04 1799 8816; www.dirtydetours.com). Hosts a Sip and Cycle bike trip that visits all of these vineyards over the course of a day. From $80. Departs 9:30am.

**Wine for Dudes** (☎04 2777 4994; www.winefordudes.com). Exists to make wine culture accessible to everyone. Don't be fooled by the guides' laid-back attitudes—all of them have experience and education in the industry. Tour includes 4-5 wineries, contemporary vineyard lunch, and unique wine blending session. $75. MC/V.

**Margaret River Vintage Wine Tours** (☎08 9757 1008). A more economical option. This mini-tour visits Voyager, Leeuwin, Watershed, and Xanadu. $45. Tours depart daily 2pm.

**Deluxe Margaret River Wine Tour** (☎08 9757 9084). The other side of the spectrum. Visits some of the more exclusive wineries and offers a seafood lunch and complimentary wine on the bus. It concludes with a sightseeing tour of nearby beaches and forests, with a sunset toast to top it all off. Tours daily 11-5:30pm. $110. MC/V.

**Margie's Big Day Out Beer & Wine Tour** (☎04 1618 0493; www.margaretriverbigdayout. com). Splits its attention more evenly between vineyards and breweries, visiting 2 of each, plus a 3rd of the party's choice. Guests also enjoy a didjeridu performance during their vineyard lunch. Tours daily. $65 per person. MC/V.

# ⚐ ACTIVITIES

Although Australian wine can stand on its own, many food artisans peddle their wares around Margaret River, providing samples of their own to accompany any vintage. Begin your behind-the-scenes culinary quest at ⬛**Olio Bello**, which produces an impressive line of organic extra virgin olive oils, including a delicious range of citrus varieties. During pressing season (Apr.-June), visitors can watch the pressing. Olio's restaurant is also a treat—all food is $13-18 and includes delicious house-made fettuccine. (☎08 9755 9771 or 1800 982 170; www.oliobello.com. Off Cowaramup Bay Rd. on Armstrong Rd. Open daily 10am-4:30pm; kitchen open 11:30am-3:30pm.) The **Margaret River Chocolate Company** will entice you with free tastings; it's a great place to find discount chocolates and fudges. (Corner of Harman's Mill Rd. and Harman's South Rd. ☎08 9755 6555; www.chocolatefactory.com.au. Open daily 9am-5pm.) Find the perfect cheese to complement your wine at the **Margaret River Dairy Company**, which has free tastings daily at their store just north of Cowaramup on Bussell Hwy. (☎08 9755 7588. Open daily 10am-5pm.) A popular—though distant—spot is **The Berry Farm**, southeast of town off Rosa Glen Rd. It offers samples of jams and fruit wines, and has a reasonably priced cafe with a mouth-watering menu. (☎08 9757 5054; www.berryfarm.com.au. Open daily 10am-4:30pm.)

There are also several breweries in the region. **Bootleg Brewery** off of Johnson Rd. is one of the most well-established, famed for its Raging Bull stout. To complement the brews, the restaurant has platters (veggie platter $23.50), meals, and sweets at reasonable prices. (☎08 9755 6300; www.bootlegbrewery. com.au. Open daily 10am-4.30pm; lunch noon-3pm.)

The beaches and surf along the coast are stunning, and **Caves Road** south of Margaret is one of the area's most spectacular drives. It runs through karri forests, beside verdant pastures, and past hundreds of hidden caves, six of which are open to the public. **Biking** is a good way to get around, and there are many rewarding trails. One of the best hiking and biking trails is the 15km round-trip walk east to **10 Mile Brook Dam** along the Margaret River. (Trailhead less than 1km north of Margaret River on Bussell Hwy. at the Rotary Park.)

# LEEUWIN-NATURALISTE NATIONAL PARK

Spanning much of the coast from Cape Naturaliste to Cape Leeuwin, ◙**Leeu-win-Naturaliste National Park** encompasses beaches with jagged rock formations rising from the water, imposing forests, yawning caves, and whale-watching spots. The **DEC offices** in Busselton (☎08 9752 5555) and Margaret River (☎08 9780 5500) service the park. Generally speaking, the majority of the park's best natural sites—beaches, caves, snorkel spots, forests—are below Margaret River, though the park's northern half is home to a plethora of vineyards and artisanal eateries. The park offers a few basic **camping ❶** sites. Stay at **Conto's Spring** where thundering waves crash on enormous boulders rising from the sea. From the site, you can walk north along ocean cliffs or south through the majestic Boranup forest. (At the Lake Cave turnoff from Caves Rd. south of Margaret River. Pit toilets. Sites $6, children $2.) **Boranup Campground** provides secluded sites ($6, children $2; pay ranger) at the southern end of the ◙**Boranup Forest scenic drive,** a 45min. drive that is an attraction in itself. Those who get out of their cars can stand next to a towering karri tree and listen to the sounds of the forest. Three kilometers from the drive's southern entrance, the **Boranup Lookout** peaks over treetops with views of the nearby rocky coast.

◙ **SIGHTS.** **Whales** can be seen north of Margaret River at **Cape Naturaliste, Gracetown, Canal Rocks,** and **Injidup Beach** in the spring, and in **Flinders Bay** near Augusta in late fall and winter. Beware when standing on the rocks near breaking surf—locals warn about "King Waves" that come in unexpectedly from the Indian Ocean and wash away victims to a watery grave. There are also many bushwalks along the coast and near Margaret River. Cape Naturaliste's walks wind past the lighthouse to cliff lookouts. The best hiking in the region is the **Cape to Cape Walk** from Cape Leeuwin in the south to Cape Naturaliste in the north. The 130km trail includes everything from soaring forests to towering cliffs and isolated beaches, and takes five to seven days. For a glimpse of one of the more spectacular segments of the walk, go to **Prevelly Beach** just above Calgardup cave on Caves Rd. and hike north along the **Cape Walk,** following it across the Margaret River mouth for 3km. The **Cape Leeuwin Lighthouse** is at the southwesternmost point of the park (and Australia), and has a great view of the Indian Ocean. (☎08 9758 1920. Drive south on Hwy. 10 through Augusta and continue to follow it after it changes to Leeuwin Rd. Free to walk grounds; tour $10, children $6. Open daily 8:45am-5pm; last entry 4:20pm.)

◙ **CAVES.** A network of caves runs through the Margaret River region, containing fossils of extinct species and evidence of Aboriginal occupation dating back some 32,000 years. Six caves are open to visitors, displaying an amazing underground world. They are all located along Caves Rd. The most readily accessible caves are **Lake Cave** and **Jewel Cave**—both of which offer multiple daily guided tours—and **Mammoth Cave,** where visitors can rent audio guides to learn about the area as they go spelunking through caves. These caves all have the same entry fee, and grant access to the **CaveWorks Eco-centre,** an informative display area at the Lake Cave site. (☎08 9757 7411. Jewel and Lake tours daily every hr. on the hr. 9:30am-4pm. Mammoth open daily 9am-5pm. Each cave $19, children $9.50; all 3 $45/22.) Near Yallingup, **Ngilgi Cave** (☎08 9755 2152), named after a spirit believed by Indigenous Australians to inhabit the cave, offers guided, lighted tours (daily every 30min. 9:30am-3:30pm; $15.50, children $6.50), and guided flashlight "adventure" tours. (By request. Max. 6 people. Ages 16 and up. 3hr. $90; 1hr. short adventure $30.)

**SURFING. Surf reports** are posted at surf shops or at www.srosurf.com/thereport.html. October through April is the best time for surfing, though it gets very crowded, especially in December and January. Packs of grommets (young surfers) and beginners can learn the ropes at **Rivermouth** near Prevelly Beach in Margaret River, **Smith's Beach** on the way into Yallingup, and **Bunker Bay** just east of the Cape Naturaliste lighthouse. More experienced surfers delight in the breaks off **Surfer's Point** near Prevelley, or head farther north to **Gracetown**—a good surfing beach protected from southern winds—and **Moses Rock. Yallingup Beach** was one of the first breaks surfed in Western Australia in the 1950s, and the namesake **Yallingup Surf School** gives daily lessons on nearby Smith's Beach. (☎08 9755 2755; www.yallingupsurfschool.com. 1hr. group lesson $50, daily at 7:45am and 9:45am). In Dunsborough, surfboards can be rented from **Yahoo Surfboards,** at the corner of Clark St. and Naturaliste Terr. (☎08 9756 8336. Open M-Sa 9am-5pm. $40; 2 or more days $30 per day.)

**DIVING AND SNORKELING. Eagle and Meelup Bays** in Dunsborough both have great beaches for snorkeling and surfing; turnoffs are well marked on Cape Naturaliste Rd., north of town. **Cape Dive,** 222 Naturaliste Terr., Dunsborough, runs diving trips to the wreck of the *HMS Swan* off Cape Naturaliste. (☎08 9756 8778 or 04 1892 3802; www.capedive.com. Open Nov.-Apr. daily 9am-5pm. Double dive to wreck with gear $135; intro dive $150; PADI course $425.) Farther south, **Canal Rocks, the Yallingup Reef,** and **Hamelin Bay** all provide great snorkeling opportunities. Hamelin Bay in particular is beautiful to the point of distraction—the area has seen some 11 shipwrecks since 1882. You can scuba dive or go snorkeling at the four visible wrecks, but you have to swim from shore to get there. Check with someone before diving; the wrecks are old and shift around a bit. Swimming here is sheltered, and fishing in the area is superb. Stingrays often feed below the boat ramp. **Augusta X-treme Outdoor Sports,** at the corner of Ellis St. and Blackwood Ave., has info and gear for diving and fishing. (☎08 9758 0606. Open M-F 9am-5pm, Sa 8:30am-4pm.)

**OUTDOOR TOURS.** Several companies organize half- or full-day adventure tours of the area, most of which can be booked through tourist bureaus. **Naturaliste Charters** runs whale-watching tours that bring sightseers to the humpback whales off Augusta in the winter (June-Aug.) and Dunsborough in the spring (Sept.-Dec.). In addition to humpbacks, southern right whales frequent the area in August, while December brings blue whales. (☎08 9755 2276; www.whalesaustralia.com. Departs daily at 10am from the boat ramp on Geographe Bay Rd. in Dunsborough or Davies Rd. in Augusta. 3hr. $60, students 13-17 $44, seniors $55, children $33, under 4 free. YHA 10% discount.) **Augusta Eco Cruises** (☎08 9758 4003) has boats that depart daily at 11am for dolphin observation river cruises (1hr.; $30, backpackers $25.) on the Blackwood River; they leave from Fishermans Jetty off Ellis St. **Bushtucker River Tours** gives guided canoe trips up the Margaret River to historical sights, with native flora, fauna, and bush medicine recipes identified along the way. (☎08 9757 1084. Departs daily at 9:45am from the Margaret River mouth off Wallcliffe Rd. in Prevelly Beach. Tour 10am-2pm, lunch included. $75, children $30.) **Dirty Detours** (☎04 1799 8816; www.dirtydetours.com) organizes bike tours of the region for various skill levels. The **Boranup Forest ride** (departs 9am or 2pm, $70) is a good challenge for beginners, while the **Sip and Cycle wine tour** (departs 9:30am, $80) visits Cape Mentelle, Chateau Xanadu, Leeuwin Estate, and Voyager Estate.

# PEMBERTON                                    ☎ 08

Encircled by national parks, massive trees, and boutique vineyards, the sleepy hamlet of Pemberton (pop. 800) manages to have a fair bit going on year-round. Though it was once filled with timber mills, the town has since learned to embrace the trees it once shredded for gain. Nearby national parks offer good hiking, fishing, and opportunities to scale massive karri trees. In recent years, food and wine have increasingly come into focus: the local trout, marron, wine, and produce make this town a delight. Even a simple drive among the local farms and forests is well worth the views of rolling countryside.

**🚆🚍 TRANSPORTATION AND PRACTICAL INFORMATION.** Transwa **buses** (☎1300 6622 05; www.transwa.wa.gov.au) run once per day to **Albany** (3hr., $31) and **Bunbury** (3hr., $24), and three times per week to **Perth** (8hr., $44). The **Pemberton Visitors Centre,** on Brockman St., the town's main artery, provides a comprehensive guide to the town and surrounding region. It also contains a small **Pioneer Museum** and informative **Karri Forest Discovery** ($1 suggested donation). The center sells passes to the local national parks and books tours and accommodations. (☎08 9776 1133; www.pembertontourist.com. Open daily 9am-5pm.) The **DEC office,** on Kennedy St., also sells passes and has info on nearby national parks. (☎08 9776 1207. Open M-F 8am-5pm.) The **Telecentre,** 29 Brockman St., offers **Internet access.** (☎08 9776 1745. $6 per hr. Open M-F 9am-5pm, Sa 9am-noon.) The **police** (☎08 9776 1202) are at the corner of Ellis St. and Jamieson St. on the way to the **Gloucester Tree** (p. 716). There is an **IGA** supermarket on Dean St. with an **ATM.** (Open M-Sa 8am-6pm, Su 9am-6pm.) **Public restrooms** and a **post office** are located on Brockman St. at the crest of the hill. (☎08 9776 1034. Open daily 8am-5pm.) **Postal Code:** 6260.

**🛏 ACCOMMODATIONS. Pemberton Backpackers YHA ❷,** 7 Brockman St., has basic rooms on Pemberton's main street, within a 10min. walk of the town center. It has Internet access ($5 per hr.), bike rental ($10 per day), and free dropoff at the Gloucester Tree. Weekly rates are available for backpackers working in nearby orchards or vineyards. (☎08 9776 1105. www.pemberton-backpackers.com.au. Dorms $24, YHA $18, weekly $112; singles $38; twins $29; doubles $59; cottage $69. MC/V.) **Pemberton Caravan Park ❷,** 1 Pump Hill Rd., is situated within walking distance of local services. (☎08 9776 1300; www.pembertonpark.com.au. Sites for 2 $25, extra person $10; cabins for 2 with kitchen $70, low season $60, extra person $8; ensuite cabins $85, extra person $12. MC/V.) The **Pemberton Hotel ❸,** 66 Brockman St., offers ensuite rooms or singles with shared amenities. (☎08 9776 1017. Rooms $30. AmEx/MC/V.)

**🍴 FOOD.** Trout and marron are the most popular local freshwater fare, and at **King Restaurant & Marron Farm ❷,** on the corner of Northcliffe Rd. and Old Vasse Rd. (en route to the Bicentennial Tree), guests can fish for both ($6 rod rental), and then have the kitchen staff cook their catch. The restaurant also offers tours ($10 per person) of its hatchery and grow-out area where the trout are reared. (☎08 9776 1352. Main courses $12-25. Open daily 9:30am-5pm; closed W-Th in winter. MC/V.) The **Cafe Mazz ❷,** in the Pemberton Hotel, serves breakfast (7-10am), lunch (noon-2pm) and dinner (6-8.30pm) to hotel patrons and locals alike, while its adjacent bar provides nightlife for the quiet town. (☎08 9776 1017. Bar open M-Th 11am-11pm, F 11am-midnight, Sa 10am-11pm, Su 2-9pm. MC/V.) **Jan's Cafe ❶,** on Brockman St., has hearty "farmer" and "hiker" breakfasts ($11-13) along with equally satisfying lunch offerings ($4-15). (☎08 9776 0011. Open daily 8am-3pm.) The **Coffee Connection ❶,** on Dickinson St.,

1km southeast of Brockman St., has a shaded patio and serves crepes ($9), focaccia ($12), and other wholesome foods. (☎08 9776 1159. Open daily 9am-5pm.) The Pemberton region has a growing number of excellent wineries; the **Woodsmoke Estate** off Golf Links Rd. north of town has a boutique cafe and also brews Jarrah Jacks beer. (☎08 9776 1333 or 08 9776 0225; www.woodsmoke-estate.com.au. 6-beer sampler $10. Open M-F 9am-5pm, Sa-Su 9am-6pm.)

**GUIDED TOURS. Pemberton Tramway Co.** has tram tours to Warren River Bridge on an old logging rail line, which passes over trestle bridges with magnificent views of the forest. Stops are made at a picnic area on the banks of Lefroy Brook. Steam trains to Eastbrook and Lyall are also available from Easter to November. (☎9776 1322; www.pemtram.com.au. 1hr.; departs daily at 10:45am and 2pm from Pemberton Station; $18, children $9.) **Pemberton Discovery Tours** offers half-day 4WD treks to D'Entrecasteaux and Warren National Parks. (☎9776 0484; www.pembertondiscoverytours.com.au. Tours 9am and 2pm. 4hr. tour includes tea; $85, children $50. YHA $15 discount. MC/V.)

**OUTDOOR ACTIVITIES.** Three national parks lie within a 10km radius of Pemberton, and the number of opportunities they afford for fishing, swimming, and hiking can be overwhelming. The 86km **Karri Forest Explorer** self-guided driving tour is a convenient way to hit all the highlights of the area's natural wonders as well as its local businesses; maps are available at the visitors center and DEC. Travelers can listen to 100FM to learn about the history of the area and its forests while they complete the drive.

**Gloucester Tree** boasts an unparalleled view of the surrounding forests from a former fire-lookout platform 61m in the air. The climb up is not for the faint of heart; you must carefully navigate the pegs that wind around the tree, and there is no safety net. (Located 3km southeast of town; take Ellis St. off Brockman until it turns left into Kennedy St., then follow the signs. Park entry fees apply.) Three trails also originate at the site: the 400m **Duke's Walk,** the 800m **Karri Views Walk,** and the 10km **Gloucester Route.** The latter is steep and difficult in sections, so be prepared. Another dizzying climb is up the **Bicentennial Tree.** This 60m lookout tree takes its name from the 200th anniversary of European settlement in Australia, celebrated in 1988, and has a platform halfway up that is a good goal for novice climbers. It is also the origin of several short **walking trails** (200m, 1km, and 2.4km) that meander through the 3000 hectares of karri forest in Warren National Park. Stately karris tower over the tranquil reservoir at **Big Brook Dam,** which has a 4km paved, wheelchair-accessible walk along its banks. (Take Golf Links Rd. off Vasse Hwy., just north of town.) **Beedelup National Park,** 18km west of town on Vasse Hwy., features a cable bridge walk over the clear, rushing waters of **Beedelup Falls.**

**TIP**

**A DIFFERENT POINT OF VIEW.** In the 1930s and 40s, the pegged karri lookouts were constructed as a means of spotting forest fires. Today, adventurous tourists are the only ones gazing from the rickety platforms atop the Gloucester, Bicentennial, and Diamond Trees. It is well worth the dizzying climb, but climbers should take their time, especially when headed down.

**DAYTRIPS FROM PEMBERTON.** Southwest of Pemberton sprawls the mammoth **D'Entrecasteaux National Park.** Most of it is inaccessible without a 4WD, except for the paved **Windy Harbour Road,** heading south out of Northcliffe to the aptly named Windy Harbour. Fifteen kilometers south of Northcliffe on this road, **Mount Chudalup,** a 188m high granite rock, rears up above the surrounding bush, allowing views of up to 30km on a clear day. Visitors can access these views by attempting the steep 1.5km hike from the carpark. If you're heading on to Denmark and wish to see more of the park, turn off Windy Harbour Rd. onto **Chesapeake Road** 5km south of Northcliffe. The gravel track winds through the heart of the park and is usually 2WD accessible, although make sure to check on road conditions in Northcliffe.

---

 **A TEMPERAMENTAL MISTRESS.** Little has changed in the years since D'Entrecasteaux charted the coast that now bears his name. The tides were rough then, and they're still rough now. There is a reason for all those shipwrecks; swimmers and seafarers beware.

---

# GREAT SOUTHERN

The beautiful, diverse region known as the Great Southern earns its title from the scale of the area's natural offerings, from the sprawling karri and tingle forests on the rugged mountain ranges in the west, to the vast nothingness of the Nullarbor Plain in the east, and the pristine scalloped coastline, which dips in and out of the region's southern harbours. The South Western Highway links most of the region's attractions, and Albany functions as an urban hub for the less-populated southern coast. While the Great Southern has been growing in popularity with Australians, offering gourmet food and many boutique wineries, the region's wonders remain under appreciated by the world at large, allowing visitors to enjoy its natural beauty in relative peace.

## WALPOLE-NORNALUP NATIONAL PARK  ☎ 08

Officially settled only 100 years ago, tiny, congenial Walpole (pop. 500) lies along the northern shore of the Nornalup Inlet and makes a great base for exploring Mt. Frankland, Shannon, and Walpole-Nornalup. Walpole-Nornalup National Park boasts inlets from the ocean, sand dunes, beaches, and the Franklin River, but the highlight is the forest of giant tingle trees.

**TRANSPORTATION AND PRACTICAL INFORMATION.** Transwa **buses** (☎1300 6622 05; www.transwa.wa.gov.au) run once daily (twice on F) to **Albany** (1hr., $19) and **Bunbury** (4hr., $38). The volunteer-staffed **Walpole-Nornalup Visitors Centre**, in an old pioneer's cabin off the highway, is a great source of information about many of the nearby natural wonders and can also book tours. (☎08 9840 1111. Open M-F 9am-5pm, Sa-Su 9am-4pm.) The **Telecentre** on Latham St. offers **Internet.** (☎08 9840 1395. Open M-F 9am-5pm, Sa-Su 10am-noon.) Around the corner on Vista St. is the **police station** (☎08 9840 1618). Nockolds St., a service road adjacent to the South Coast Hwy. which is also the town's main street, has a **post office.** (☎08 9840 1048. Open M-F 9am-5pm.) **Postal Code:** 6398.

**ACCOMMODATIONS AND FOOD. Walpole Lodge ❷,** on the corner of Pier St. and Park Ave., has rooms around a spacious common area. (☎08 9840 1244. Internet $8 per hr. Dorms $22; singles $38; doubles $55, ensuite $77. Extra person $15. MC/V.) For camping, head west to **Rest Point Holiday Village ❷,** which sits on the water's edge at the junction of Walpole and Nornalup Inlets, at the end of Rest Point Rd. (☎08 9840 1032; www.restpoint.com.au. Sites for 2 $24, low season $22, extra person $11-12; ensuite cabins for 2 $95/75, extra adult $28, extra child $11.) The **Coalmine Beach Holiday & Caravan Park ❷,** on the road toward the Knoll Scenic Dr. just across from the Hilltop Dr., has cozy, shaded sites, a playground, Internet, satellite TV, and multiple access points to Coalmine Beach. (☎1800 6700 26; www.coalminebeach.com.au. Sites for 2 $22, powered $25; standard cabins $105-115, low season $68; ensuite $110-150/$100-110. MC/V.)

Nockolds St. has a number of cafes and restaurants. The **Top Deck Cafe ❶,** 25 Nockolds St., serves breakfast ($9-16) and lunch ($7-14) in a sun-filled room with a stove in the winter and on a sheltered patio in the summer. (☎08 9840 1344. Open M-Sa 9am-4pm. MC/V.) Next door, **Ras Lunch Bar ❶** is open for breakfast and lunch, serving burgers, fish and chips, and deli sandwiches. (☎08 9840 1344. Open M-F 9am-2pm.) Nearby is an **IGA** supermarket. (☎08 9840 1031. Open M-Sa 7:30am-6pm, Su 8am-5:30pm.)

**◙ SIGHTS.** The park's claim to fame is undoubtedly the **Tree Top Walk,** 13km east of town. A 600m state-of-the-art metal catwalk lets visitors scale dizzying heights through the canopy of tingle trees. The views are incredible, but acrophobics beware: the swaying walkways reach heights of 40m. (☎08 9840 8263. Open daily 9am-5pm; school holidays 8am-6pm; last entry 45min. before close. $8, children $4, families $22.) Visitors to the Tree Top Walk can also stroll along the **Ancient Empire boardwalk,** which passes through a grove of red tingle trees, some of which are hollowed out, allowing visitors to stand inside or pass through. Another way to visit these giants is on Hilltop Rd., which passes the **Giant Tingle Tree,** the largest known eucalypt in the world.

In addition to the Hilltop drive, the **Valley of the Giants Road** winds through towering forests and the **Knoll Drive** snakes through dunes with dramatic views of the inlet. The **Coalmine Beach Heritage Trail** is a leisurely and educational 3km walk which originates at the visitors center and meanders its way to Coalmine beach, a popular swimming spot. Along the way, in addition to looking for wildflowers and birdlife, hikers can read plaques with information about what life was like for Walpole and Narnalup's earliest European settlers in the early 20th Century. (2hr. round-trip.) The **Nuyts Wilderness Peninsula** portion of the park is accessible by way of the superb ◙**Wow Wilderness Cruises,** which offers a 2hr. cruise through the double inlets, punctuated by an 800m hike across the peninsula and a traditional tea. Gary, the captain and guide, is an energetic encyclopedia of local lore. (☎08 9840 1036; www.wowwilderness.com.au. Departs daily at 10am from the Jones St. Jetty in Walpole. Book at tourist bureau in Walpole. $40, ages 6-14 $15, under 5 free.)

# STIRLING RANGE AND PORONGURUP NATIONAL PARKS

These two parks, separated by just 40km, differ dramatically in their geological history. The **Porongurups** date back over a billion years, making them one of the oldest mountain ranges on Earth. By comparison, the **Stirlings** are newcomers, emerging later than 100 million years ago. Giant eucalyptus trees and the occasional karri fill the sides of the Porongurups, while in the higher Stirling Range hardier scrub predominates. In spring, over 1200 species of wildflowers electrify the hills. The town of **Mount Barker** is the gateway to both parks.

## ⌐ TRANSPORTATION

Transwa **buses** (☎ 1300 662 205; www.transwa.wa.gov.au) run to **Mt. Barker** from Albany (40min., $8) or Perth (5hr., $44.50) once per day. However, the best way to see the parks is by **car**. Rental is easily arranged in **Albany** (p. 720).

## ◣ 🛈 ORIENTATION AND PRACTICAL INFORMATION

From Albany, the Porongurups are 40km north on the **Chester Pass Road.** The Stirling Range is another 40km along the road. **Porongurup Road** is a sealed road running west through its namesake to Mt. Barker, 20km away. **Stirling Range Drive** is a pretty but corrugated road running west through the Stirlings from Chester Pass. Most of the park's best walks can be reached from Chester Pass.

**Tourist Office: Mount Barker Tourist Bureau,** in a renovated train station located on Albany Hwy. (☎08 9851 1163; www.mtbarkertourismwa.com.au). Open M-F 9am-5pm, Sa 9am-3pm, Su 10am-3pm.

**Ranger stations:** In **Stirling Range National Park** at **Moingup Spring** (☎08 9827 9230) and Bluff Knoll (☎08 9827 9278), and in the **Porongurup** on **Bongalup Rd.** just before the picnic area (☎08 9853 1095).

**Police:** On Mt. Barker Rd. between Marion St. and Montem St.

## ⌐ ⌐ ACCOMMODATIONS AND CAMPING

Both parks can easily be visited as daytrips from Albany, but there are plenty of accommodations in the area as well. **Moingup Springs,** off Chester Pass Rd. just south of Toolbrunup, offers basic **camping** ❶ facilities with toilets, BBQs, and park information, though there are no showers or electricity.

**Porongurup Shop and Tearooms,** on Porongurup Rd. (☎08 9853 1110; www.porongu-rupinn.com.), at the main entrance to Porongurup National Park. Family-run hotel offers budget accommodations and good meals ($12-17). Restaurant open daily 8am-5pm. Doubles $60; self-contained flat for 2 $80; ensuite cabin with kitchen, lounge area, and bedroom for 4 $100. Extra person $10. MC/V. ❷

**Porongurup Range Tourist Park,** 1304 Porongurup Rd. (☎08 9853 1057; www.poronguruprangetouristpark.com.au). Tidy and well-equipped tourist park with lovely hosts. Offers a tennis court, pool, kitchen, and beautiful views of the mountains across the road. Sites for 2 $22, powered $25; cabins $70-95. Cash only. ❷

**Stirling Range Retreat,** Chester Pass Rd. (☎08 9827 9229. www.stirlingrange.com.au.), less than 500m beyond the turnoff for Bluff Knoll. Offers scenic camping at the base of the mountains and an inviting pool (open Nov.-Mar.) for weary hikers. Daily wildflower tours ($35) and bird walks ($20) available Sept.-Oct. Tent sites for 2 $22, powered $25; dorms $25; singles and doubles $60; triples $75; cabins for 2 $62-135. ❶

## ⌐ FOOD

The **Supa IGA** supermarket on Lowood Rd. sells groceries. (☎08 9851 3333; open M-W and F 8:30am-5:30pm, Th 8:30am-6:30pm, Sa 8am-4pm.)

**Maleeya's Thai Cafe,** on Porongurup Rd. (☎08 9853 1123), between Chester Pass and Mt. Barker. Thai food ($18-28) that's often organic and flavored with home-grown herbs. Open F-Su noon-3pm and 6:15-9pm. Reservations recommended. MC/V. ❹

**The Sail-Inn Cafe,** 39 Lowood Rd. (☎08 9851 1477), in Mt. Barker. Offers trusted favorites ($11-20) at budget-friendly prices in a laid-back atmosphere. Takeout options are slightly cheaper. Open M-Th 10:30am-3pm and 6-9pm, F 10:30am-3pm and 6-10pm, Sa 9:30am-9:30pm, Su 9:30am-9pm. MC/V. ❶

**The Old Station Cafe,** on Albany Hwy. (☎08 9851 2984). Serves breakfast and lunch ($5-17) in a small house. Check out the daily specials. Open Tu-W 10am-4pm, Th-F 10am-4pm and 5-8pm, Sa-Su 8:30am-4pm. MC/V. ❷

**Wing Hing Chinese Restaurant,** 26 Albany Hwy. (☎08 9851 1168). Lunch $9-11. Dinner $11-18. Open Tu and Sa 5-9:30pm, W-F noon-2pm and 5-9:30pm, Su 5-9pm. ❷

## 🝔 HIKING

Visitors to both the Porongurups and the Stirlings must display **national park passes** (day pass $10, 4-week "holiday" pass $35), which can be purchased at park entry points, DEC offices, or www.naturebase.net. All of the trails listed here are accessible by sealed or smooth gravel roads shorter than 10km. The others require longer drives along the corrugated Stirling Range Dr. Many of the walks originate at the **Tree in the Rock picnic area** at the end of Bolganup Rd., across from the caravan park on Porongurup Rd. The namesake karri tree sprouting from a crack in a boulder is an easy 100m walk from the **carpark,** which offers toilets, BBQs, and picnic facilities.

### STIRLINGS

🝔 **Bluff Knoll** (6.2km, 3-4hr. round-trip). This Stirlings hike is more rugged than the Porongurups and features multiple opportunities to scale massive peaks and enjoy truly awesome panoramic views. The most popular is Bluff Knoll (1094m), which is best described by its Aboriginal name Bullah Meual, which means "Great Many-Faced Hill." The trail that climbs its sides is well maintained and has stairs, but is a steep climb and windy at points on the southwestern face. The views of the surrounding formations are exhilarating, and the contrast with the flat, vast surrounding farmlands is impressive. The beautiful scenery and views begin immediately on the walk, making this one a worthwhile hike even for those who don't make it all the way to the summit.

**Stirling Ridge Walk** (20km, 3 days). Links Bluff Knoll to Mount Ellen. This hike promises 3 days of narrow ledges, jagged rocks, and steep climbs. Those planning to tackle this trek should register with the park ranger beforehand by stopping by the registration station near the Bluff Knoll turnoff, or by calling ahead (☎08 9827 9278).

**Toolbrunup Peak** (2km, 3hr.). Toolbrunup (1052m), the second highest in the park, is a challenging climb. The first half winds through the trees, climbing gently but steadily. The second half is a bit more difficult. Toolbrunup is less crowded than Bluff Knoll, even though it also offers unobstructed 360° views from the top.

**Mount Trio** (3km, 2hr.). This hike, off Formby South Rd. (which intersects Chester Pass about 5km north of Toolbrunup) is shorter, beginning quite steeply and leveling off for the 2nd half of the climb. Look for the turnoff on Fromby South Rd.; it's easy to miss.

### PORONGURUPS

**Castle Rock trail** (3km, 1hr. round-trip). Those who scramble up the granite behemoths will be rewarded with great views and a nice spot to relax after the climb. Don't miss the **Balancing Rock,** an enormous boulder that looks like it will tumble at any second.

# ALBANY     ☎08

Albany (pop. 32,000) was the first colonial settlement in Western Australia, founded in 1826 to protect the western half of the continent, then called New Holland, from the possibility of French annexation. From 1800 until 1978, whaling was a major industry here; today the migrating humpbacks are caught only on camera. The town sits at the base of Mounts Clarence and Adelaide, with access to beaches, mountains, and wineries. Many Perthites use Albany as a

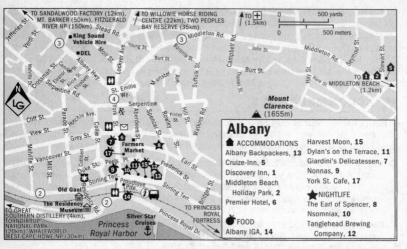

TO SANDALWOOD FACTORY (12km),
MT. BARKER (50km), FITZGERALD
RIVER NP (150km) Stead Rd.

TO WILLOWIE HORSE RIDING
CENTRE (22km), TWO PEOPLES
BAY RESERVE (35km)

TO (1.5km)

TO MIDDLETON BEACH (1.2km)

TO GREAT
SOUTHERN DISTILLERY (4km),
TORNDIRRUP
NATIONAL PARK
(20km), WHALEWORLD—
WEST CAPE HOWE NP (30km)

TO PRINCESS
ROYAL
FORTRESS

King Sound
Vehicle Hire
DEL

Mount
Clarence
(1655m)

Farmers
Market

Old Gaol

The Residency
Museum

Princess
Royal Harbor

Silver Star
Cruises

**Albany**

ACCOMMODATIONS
Albany Backpackers, **13**
Cruize-Inn, **5**
Discovery Inn, **1**
Middleton Beach
Holiday Park, **2**
Premier Hotel, **6**

FOOD
Albany IGA, **14**

Harvest Moon, **15**
Dylan's on the Terrace, **11**
Giardini's Delicatessen, **7**
Nonnas, **9**
York St. Cafe, **17**

NIGHTLIFE
The Earl of Spencer, **8**
Nsomniax, **10**
Tanglehead Brewing
Company, **12**

summer retreat, and the city has responded with trendy new restaurants and a wide range of accommodations that make it the perfect getaway.

# TRANSPORTATION

**Transwa** buses (☎1300 662 205; www.transwa.wa.gov.au) depart from the visitors center to: Bunbury (6hr.; M and Th 8:35am, Tu-W and F-Su 8am; $45.60) via Augusta, Margaret River, Pemberton, and Walpole; Esperance (6hr., M and Th 11:45am, $57.25); and Perth (6hr.; M-Sa 9am and Su 3pm, extra buses F 5:30pm and Sa 11am; $51.15). The two hostels in town have a steady stream of travelers sharing rides; hitchhikers usually wait by the "Big Roundabout" on the Albany Hwy., 2km west of the north end of York St. Despite the convenience of this option, *Let's Go* does not recommend hitchhiking. **Love's Bus Service** provides city transport for $2.20-3.40 per trip; schedules are available at the tourist bureau. (☎08 9841 1211. Open M-Sa.) Multiple taxi companies service the Albany area; try **Amity Taxis** (☎08 9844 4444) or **Albany City Cabs** (☎ 131 008). Most are based around the intersection of Stirling Terr. and York St. Car rental companies include **Budget,** 360 Albany Hwy. (☎08 9841 7799; the office is behind the Toyota dealership) and **Avis,** 557 Albany Hwy. (☎08 9842 2833). Prices range $55-70 per day with daily $25 surcharges for those under 25. Bike rental is available at **Albany Bicycle Hire** for hourly, daily, or weekly use. (☎08 9842 2468. Free drop off/pick up to the visitors center or any accommodation in Albany City or Middleton Beach. $18 per day; $50 per week.)

# ORIENTATION AND PRACTICAL INFORMATION

York Street is the main strip and runs north-south through the center of town. Middleton Beach Road, which branches off of the roundabout at the top end of York St., is the most direct route to Middleton beach. Alternatively, Marine Drive, which becomes Stirling Terrace, connects the two centers via a scenic coastal route with lovely lookouts. The **visitors center** is in the Old Railway Station, just east of the southern end of York St. near Stirling Terr. (☎08 9841 9377; www.amazingalbany.com. Open daily 9am-5pm.) York St. also has several ATMs. The **police** (☎08 9841 0555) are located on Stirling Terr. west of York

St., while the **Albany Regional Hospital** (☎08 9892 2222) is northeast of town in Spencer Park on Warden Ave. off Collingwood Rd. There are plenty of Internet cafes along York St.; the going rate is $6 per hr. **Albany Backpackers** offers **Internet access** to the public for $6 per hr. and to guests for $4 per hr. There is Wi-Fi for $3 per hour at **Bar Cino,** in the Middleton Loop just off the northern end of York St., or at the McDonald's on Albany highway. The **post office** is on the corner of York St. and Grey St. (Open M-F 8:30am-5pm.) **Postal Code:** 6330.

# ACCOMMODATIONS

Albany has excellent budget accommodations, split between two districts: the old town of Albany, with its historic buildings and ample amenities, and the laid-back Middleton Beach, a waterside escape away from major attractions.

**Cruize-Inn,** 122 Middleton Rd., Middleton Beach (☎08 9842 9599; www.cruizeinn. com). A step up from your average hostel with beautiful, homestyle accommodations. Kitchen, TV lounge, and a superb stereo system. Free bikes, surf boards, and fishing rods. Perfect for a group getaway. Twins/doubles $85; ensuite $95; triple $105; family room $120; entire house from $220 for 4, $20 per extra person. MC/V. ❺

**Discovery Inn,** 9 Middleton Rd., Middleton Beach (☎08 9842 5535; www.discoveryinn. com.au), 100m from the water. Comfortable rooms. Top-notch Internet $5 per hr. All-you-can-eat 3-course "Cook's table" meal $10 (W-Sa 7-9pm; order by 5pm.) Dorms $25; singles $45; twins/doubles $70; queen with TV $75. MC/V. ❷

**Albany Backpackers** (☎08 9841 8848; www.albanybackpackers.com.au), corner of Stirling Terr. and Spencer St. Lively hostel with common spaces and free coffee and cake each evening at 6:30pm. Cheap home-cooked meals ($5) every night at 7pm. Internet access $4 per hr., first 10min. free. Bike rentals, weekly movie screenings. Weekly all-you-can-eat sausage BBQs $2. Dorms $25-26, with discount $23-24; singles $40/36; doubles $60/56; triples $84/78. VIP/YHA. MC/V. $1 surcharge. ❷

**Premier Hotel,** 208 York St. (☎08 9841 1544). The best option for those seeking a little more privacy right in the heart of town. Located above a lively bar and restaurant. Singles $25; twins and doubles $45; motel units $80. MC/V. ❷

**Middleton Beach Holiday Park,** Middleton Beach (☎08 9841 3593 or 1800 644 674; www.holidayalbany.com.au), at the end of Middleton Rd. Puts the holiday back in holiday park: free Hydrospa, theater, rec room, solar-heated pool, and beachfront access; golf course next door. High season sites for 2 $47; powered $48; cabins $240. Low season $30/32/90. Extra adult $10, child $8. MC/V. ❸

# FOOD

**FOR HIP FOOD, ASK THE HIPPIES.** A short hop west of Albany lies Denmark, a town notorious for its sizeable "alternative" population and large number of organic farms and fine wineries. If you cannot make the 35km trip to sample their famous Riesling and Shiraz, go by the Albany Farmers Market on Saturday 8am-noon for fruit, meat, and other gourmet produce.

The Great Southern region is blessed with some of the best pastures and farmlands in the entire continent, and Albany showcases the bounty of the harvest. Most restaurants can be found near York St.; for a market try the Albany **IGA** at the south end of York St. on Proudlove Pde. (Open daily 7am-9pm.) Cheaper groceries can be found at **Coles** in the Albany Plaza Shopping Centre at the intersection of York St. and Albany highway (open M-Sa 8am-6pm) or at **Woolworths** in the Dog Rock Shopping Centre at the top of York St. (open

M-Sa 8am-6pm). In addition, the **Albany Farmer's Market** takes place in town on every Saturday, and includes local fruit, vegetables, meats, dairy products, and seafood. (Located on Collie St. between Duke and Grey Sts. ☎08 9841 4312; www.albany-farmersmarket.com.au. Open Sa 8am-noon.)

**Dylan's on the Terrace,** 82-84 Stirling Terr. (☎08 9841 8720; www.dylans.com.au). Top-notch food and atmosphere. Serves salads, sandwiches ($5-10), burgers ($11-12.50), and breakfast. Discount takeaway menu. Open Tu-Sa 7am-late, Su 8am-5pm. MC/V. ❷

**Harvest Moon,** 86 Stirling Terr. Easy to miss but worth finding—look for a moon sign and "cafe" written in knives and forks. Inside you'll find homemade gourmet vegetarian fare ranging from pizzas to nachos to curries ($7.50-14.50). There are books to read, a fireplace with couches, and plenty of light. Dinner served on Thursdays. Open M-W 10am-5pm, Th 10am-8pm, F 10am-6pm, Sa 11am-4:30pm. Cash only. ❷

**Nonna's,** 135 York St. (☎08 9841 4626). Lively Italian restaurant with a certain Aussie flair. Famous for its "15 for 15" deal: main course and drink for $15 (mostly burgers, pies, and pastas). Be sure to go by for Fish Fridays, a local favorite. Open M-F 11am-latenight, Sa 5pm-latenight. AmEx/MC/V. ❷

**York St. Cafe,** 184 York St. (☎08 9842 1666). The generic looking facade of the York St. Cafe hides this culinary gem. York St. strives to use local, organic ingredients and to support sustainable consumption wherever possible. Their housemade pastries are impeccable. Try the savory brioche with bacon, poached eggs, and avocado ($13.50) for a great breakfast. Open M-Th 8:30am-4pm, F-Sa 8:30am-9pm, Su 8:30am-2pm. ❷

**Giardini's Delicatessen,** 189 York St. (☎08 9841 2532). This gourmet grocer has aisles of high-quality cheeses, meats, and rolls. Makes a mouth-watering deli sandwich ($4) using all local ingredients. Open daily 7am-8pm. MC/V. ❶

**The Squid Shack,** Emu Point Boat Pens (☎08 9844 9771). Seafood doesn't get much fresher than this off-the-boat-into-the-deep-fryer cafe; it's something of a local institution. In the winter they keep a fire going to warm your fingers as you snack on fish and chips, as well as other succulent seafood items. Meals $6-17.50. Fish and chips $10. Open Tu-Su 10am-7pm in winter; 10am-9pm in summer. ❷

## 🅢 SIGHTS

Albany boasts many historic sites; the visitors center provides a free map with a walking tour, or you can take a guided walk with **JJ Tours.** (☎08 9841 3180. Tours M-Sa 10am and 2:30pm; $15.) The

## GREAT TASTE, GREAT SOUTHERN

By now it's tradition: every year over a long weekend in February or March, the Great Southern Coast takes a few days to focus on the two things it does best: food and drink. The **Great Southern Taste** festival, which will celebrate its fifth anniversary in 2009, is a regional festival with cooking classes, special meals, and a number of events.

Most events are ticketed and carry a price tag between $15 and $150, but as a well-calculated splurge, they're pretty much guaranteed to provide guests with the best produce, meats, and wines that the region has to offer. The **Porongorup Wine Festival** is a day-long event with music, food and art stalls, a grape stomp, and (of course) wine tastings; **Mount Barker Grazes** are progressive lunches that meander from cellar to cellar in the region, with specially paired wine-and-dish offerings at each stop. The weekly, free **Albany Farmers Market** also has a particularly special session on the Saturday during the festival, and many shops feature sales on local food and wine. Master cooking classes with local and visiting chefs are between $50 and 80 and include a meal and often cocktails afterward.

*Ask at the Albany Visitors' Centre for information on bookings and events.* www.greatsoutherntastewa.com

Forts Rd. turn off of Marine Drive leads up to the twin peaks of Mount Clarence and Mount Adelaide. The former was the last glimpse many soldiers had of home soil before deployment to Gallipoli in WWI. A monument to the ANZAC (Australia New Zealand Army Corps) troops who died in WWI stands at the start of the walk to the summit, which offers a lookout with stunning views of Princess Royal and Oyster Harbours. On Mt. Adelaide to the east is the Princess Royal Fortress. It was built in 1893 as a coastal defense, and later used by the American Navy as a base in WWII. The site today includes the **Military Heritage Centre and Australian War Memorial Gallery,** both of which complement the monument at Mt. Clarence. (☎08 9841 9333. Open daily 9am-5pm. $5.20, seniors $3.10, children $1.10, families $12.)

Among its many crowning achievements, Albany is also the Australian sandalwood oil capital of the world. The **Mt. Romance Sandalwood Factory,** 15km out of town, offers free tours of the oil distillery, and a variety of alternative healing sessions like reiki, reflexology and massage. Its central offerings are gong relaxation sessions three times a day at 11am, 1, and 2:30pm; lose yourself in the scent of sandalwood oil and the rhythmic melody of the gong. (On Down Rd., off Albany Hwy. just past the airport. ☎08 9845 6888; www.mtromance.com. au. Open daily 9am-5pm. Gong session $15.) Albany also houses the world's largest whaling museum, **Whaleworld,** on Frenchman Bay Rd. past the Gap and Blowholes. It may be the only place in the world where you can watch a 3D video in an (empty) blubber vat. Access to all of its features—guided tours, three different films (all in oil vat theatres), access to a real former whaling ship, and photo galleries on the history of whaling in Albany—are all included in the entry price. The photos of dead whales being processed are not for those with weak stomachs. (☎08 9844 4021; www.whaleworld.org. Open daily 9am-5pm. 30min. tours every hr. 10am-4pm. $20, concessions $18, students $15.)

## ☒ NIGHTLIFE

Although the nightlife in Albany isn't exactly raging, the abundance of backpackers and vacationing cityfolk has contributed to a lively late-night scene.

◪ **The Earl of Spencer** (☎08 9841 1322; www.earlofspencer.com.au), on the corner of Earl and Spencer St. Historic pub with cozy English feel and great foreign beer selections. The hearty "Earl's Famous Pie and Pint" ($18) shares the menu with lighter fare including soups and salads. Open M-Sa noon-midnight, Su 2-9pm. AmEx/MC/V.

**Tanglehead Brewing Company,** 72 Stirling Terr. (☎08 9841 1733; www.tanglehead. com.au). Demure storefront contrasts with trendy modern microbrewery inside. Handcrafted brews on tap for $7-8.50 per pint. Th open mic night. Live music most Fridays and Saturdays. Open M-Sa 11am-midnight, Su 11am-10pm.

**Nsomniax Lounge** (☎08 9841 7688), corner of York St. and Stirling Terr. For those hoping to shake it. Open late on weekends and keeps the party going when the pubs have closed. Cover $8 when busy (roughly after 11:30pm). Open F-Sa 11pm-3:30am.

**The Premier Hotel,** 208 York St. (☎08 9841 1544). This hotel has two bars—the bar in front offers some variety in its tap beer selection, and looks out on the street. The back bar has pool tables and a big screen for sporting events. Live music on weekends (check for cover price). M-Th noon-6pm "down 3, get 1 free" promo for all of their tap beers.

**The Hotel Albany,** York St. (☎08 9842 3337). Pleasant al fresco veranda and an airy indoor bar and restaurant. Happy hour M-Th 11am-noon, 5-6pm; middies $2.50. Open M-W and Su 10am-late, Th-Sa 9:30am-late.

# ◢ OUTDOOR ACTIVITIES

Albany's most impressive natural formations are in **Torndirrup National Park,** 20km south of town on Frenchman Bay Rd (follow York St. to the southern end, make a right onto Princess Royal Dr., and then left at the sign for Frenchman Bay Rd.). The **Natural Bridge**—a rock formation that spans 24m above crashing waves—and **the Gap**—a sheer 30m drop into a surging, frothy inlet—are reminders of the inexorable powers of water and wind. The rock formations here align with some in Antarctica, a remnant of Pangaea. Further up the road, rough weather can force the surf through porous granite, creating blowholes that spray heights of up to 10m. Do not go beyond the blowholes; people have died trying to get a photo. The **Middleton Bay Scenic Path** runs from Middleton Beach to Emu Point. **West Cape Howe National Park,** roughly 30km west of town on the way to Denmark, offers good snorkeling and diving at Shelley and Dunsky beaches, both accessible by 2WD unsealed roads (as always, beware of strong riptides). Thirty-five kilometers east of town, the **Two Peoples Bay Nature Reserve** was the site where the Noisy Scrub-bird and Gilbert's Potoroo—two species once thought to be extinct—were rediscovered in the 1990s. Most of the beaches in the park have good fishing; Nanarup is quite popular.

To learn more about Albany's history and geological past, check out the **WA Residency Museum** off Stirling Terr., west of York St., next to the replica of the Brig Amity. (☎08 9841 4844. Open daily 10am-5pm. $5 suggested donation.) In addition to warm currents and tropical fish, Albany's waters also host the wrecks of the *HMAS Perth*, a Vietnam-era warship in King George Sound, and the whaling ships *Cheynes III* and *SS Cheynes*. **Albany Dive Company,** at the corner of York St. and Stirling Terr., does dives of all kinds, as well as daily courses during the summer. Highlights of the local sea life include rare Australian sea lions, western blue devils, and leafy sea dragons. (☎08 9842 6886; 0429 664 874; www.albanydive.com. Departs daily at 8:30am and 12:30pm. Dive with full gear rental $120; 2 dives $190. Snorkeling with full gear rental $75.

If you're sobered by the gravity of Whaleworld and the Torndirrup sights, stop off at the **Great Southern Distillery Company,** 252 Frenchman Bay Rd., on the way home. They offer cellar door tastings of gin, vodka, grappa, and single malt whiskey. (☎08 9842 5363; www.distillery.com.au. Open Su-Th 9:30am-5pm, F-Sa 9:30am-7:30pm.) Wine connoisseurs can sample the local and regional wines on **Grape Southern Tours,** which run through Albany, Denmark, Mt. Barker, Frankland, and the Porongurups. The tour includes 4-5 winery visits with tastings at each, plus a lunch of local food and produce. (☎08 0429 479 463. Tours W-Su 10am-5:30pm; $75.) Horseback riding along a 4km scenic trail is available at **Willowie Horse Riding Centre,** 20km east of Albany. (☎08 9846 4365. By appointment. Scenic ride $35. Cash only.) At **Albany Motorcycle Touring Co.,** Rob takes visitors on "joy rides" on Harley Davidson motorcycles (1 passenger), on trikes (2 passengers), and in convertibles (up to 4 passengers). Free pick-up from local Albany accommodations; routes can be determined when the tour is booked. (☎08 9841 8034. Motorcycle $65 per hr., trike $85 per hr., convertibles $115 per hr. Cash only.) **Albany Air Charter** offers scenic flights over Albany and the coastline. (☎04 2720 6210. Departs Albany airport and flies over Oyster Harbour, up Middleton Beach, past Frenchman's Bay over a windfarm and back across the town center. 30min. flight for 5 people $240. Cash or check only.) **Spinners Charters** offers deep-sea fishing. (☎08 9844 1906; wwww.spinnerscharters.com.au. Departs Emu Point at 7am. Full-day including lunch $180.)

# ESPERANCE ☎08

Esperance (pop. 14,500) is one of Western Australia's best-kept secrets. Although the town itself is rather basic, the beaches are almost too ideal to believe, especially in nearby Cape Le Grand National Park. Summer tourists flock to the area to swim, dive, and explore nearby parks.

## ▣ TRANSPORTATION

**Transwa** buses (☎1300 662 205; www.transwa.wa.gov.au) stop on Dempster St. at the Love of the Earth Photo Gallery between the visitors center (where tickets are sold) and the Municipal Museum. Buses offer a YHA/VIP 10% discount and run to Albany (7hr.; Tu and F 8am; $57.25), Kalgoorlie (5hr.; W and F 8:35am, Su 2pm), and Perth (10hr., M-F and Su 8am). **Skywest** (☎1300 660 088; www.skywest.com.au) flies between Esperance and Perth daily. Two major car rental companies operate in Esperance and both offer airport pickup: **Budget,** at the airport (☎08 9071 2775), and **Avis,** 63 the Esplanade (☎08 9071 3998). A cheaper option is **Hollywood Car Hire** on Sheldon Rd. off Norseman Rd., which hires used cars from $40 per day (☎08 9071 3144; 21+; MC/V). Otherwise, hire a taxi through **Esperance Taxi Service** (☎08 9071 1782).

## ✳▮ ORIENTATION AND PRACTICAL INFORMATION

The **South Coast Highway** (Monjingup Rd.) intersects Harbour Road, which circles the primary commercial area. **Dempster Street,** the main road through the city center, runs parallel to the Esplanade, which follows the bay. The **visitors center** is on the corner of Dempster and Kemp St. They're the place to buy national park passes. (☎08 9071 2330; www.visitesperance.com. Open Sept.-Apr. M-F 9am-5pm, Sa 9am-4pm, Su 9am-2pm; May-Aug. M-F 9am-5pm, Sa 9am-2pm, Su 9am-noon.) **Internet** is available at **Computer Alley,** 69c Dempster St. (☎08 9072 1293; $5.50 per hr.; open M-F 9am-5pm, Sa 9am-4pm.) or at the **library** on Windich St., parallel to Dempster St., one block north. (☎08 9071 0680. $6 per hr. Open M and W-F 10am-6pm, Tu noon-6pm, Sa 9-midnight.) Wi-Fi is available at the **Taylor Street Jetty Cafe Restaurant.** A variety of **banks** and **ATMs** are on the corner of Dempster St. and Andrew St. The **police** (☎08 9071 1900) are located at 100 Dempster St., while the **hospital** (☎08 9071 0888) is two blocks west of the visitors center on Hicks St. The **post office** is on the corner of Andrew St. and Dempster St. (Open M-F 9am-5pm.) **Postal Code:** 6450.

## ▮ ACCOMMODATIONS

**Esperance Guesthouse,** 23 Daphne St. (☎08 9071 3396), off Norseman Rd. Manages to feel both luxurious and homey at the same time. Dorms are spacious, doubles are palatial, and the lounge is furnished with antique leather furniture. Complimentary breakfast of homemade bread, coffee, and cereal. Internet $2 per 30min. Bike hire ($2) and a pool table. Dorms $25; singles $40; doubles $55. MC/V. ❷

**Blue Waters Lodge YHA,** 299 Goldfields Rd. (☎08 9071 1040), just before the intersection of Dempster and Norseman St. A 15min. walk from the town center along the harbor bike path. Right on the bay, this former Australian Army Corps building has Internet ($5 per hr.), a pool table, and bikes for $10 per day. Free bus station pickup and drop-off. Dorms $25, YHA $22; singles $38/34; twins and doubles $60/54. ❷

**Esperance Seafront Caravan Park** (☎08 9071 1251; www.esperanceseafront.com), next to the YHA at the base of Goldfields Rd. Great beachfront location. Wi-Fi available. Sites for 2 $22, powered $28, extra person $5; standard cabin for 2 $60, extra person $10; ensuite 2-bedroom cabin for 2 $90, extra person $10. MC/V. ❷

# FOOD

Great dining abounds in this cozy ocean town, but many restaurants have reduced hours in the winter. There is an **IGA** supermarket on Dempster St. between William and Andrew St. (Open M-W and F 8am-6pm, Th 8am-8pm, Sa 8am-5pm.) There's also a **Woolworth's** in the shopping center on Forrest St. (Open M-W and F 8am-6pm, Th 8am-9pm, Sa 8am-5pm.)

**Taylor Street Jetty Cafe Restaurant** (☎08 9071 4317), predictably located at the Taylor St. jetty, just off the Esplanade. Patrons enjoy good meals and spectacular views of Esperance Bay in a hip setting. Daily pizza ($12.50) and seafood specials, local art on display, and live music on Sundays. Reserve ahead for dinner. Breakfast $4-10. Lunch $9.50-26. Dinner $10-30. Open daily 7am-10pm. ❷

**Ocean Blues Cafe,** 19 the Esplanade (☎08 9071 7107). Ocean Blues is a good place to grab a bite after fun in the sun. At $12.50, the King prawn & avocado focaccia is still a delicious steal. Lunches $5.50-12.50. Open Tu-F 9:30am-8:30pm, Sa-Su 8am-8:30pm; hours vary in winter. MC/V. ❶

**Ollie's** (☎08 9071 5268), at the corner of the Esplanade and Andrew St. Offers cafe fare for breakfast ($3-18), lunch ($3-13), and dinner ($10-20). Take your grub across the street and eat beachside. Open Tu-F 10am-9pm, Sa-Su 8am-9pm. MC/V. ❷

# NIGHTLIFE

Several pubs can be found on Andrew St. and Dempster St.; **The Pier,** on the corner of Andrew St. and the Esplanade is a local favorite. They offer bar meals ($7-15), live music on Friday, karaoke on Thursday and Sunday, and two of the only nightclubs in town. ($6.50 cover. Open F-Sa 11pm-3am.)

# SIGHTS AND OUTDOOR ACTIVITIES

Esperance's greatest offerings are its beaches, tucked into the coastline extending southwest of the town center. The 38km loop on the Great Ocean Drive snakes along the coast before circling inward and past the Pink Lake. The drive begins at the southern end of Dempster St.; the visitors center has maps and the road is clearly marked. The coastal part of the loop is the highlight, with steep drop-offs into the bays and spectacular views. Make time to stop at least one beach as you make the loop—good choices include **Twilight Beach** and **Fourth Beach,** both of which offer fine white sand, turquoise water, and fascinating rock formations to enjoy. Beware that the water may be a bit chilly (average temperatures peak at 17-18°C), but it's worth going in anyway. The **Rotary Lookout,** off Orr St. at the beginning of the scenic drive on Wireless Hill, is a great place to watch the sunset. A 30min. round-trip walk down from the lookout leads to a gazebo with a picnic table overlooking the bay.

The wide variety of diving sites in Esperance make it suitable for nearly all levels of experience and income. The **Sanko Harvest,** the second-largest wreck dive in the world, is popular among experienced divers, and the plethora of islands just off its coast (of which the Recherche archipelago, with 105 islands alone, is only a small subset) provides great access to a variety of diving conditions and exciting sea life. **Esperance Diving and Fishing,** 72 the Esplanade, guides dives and charters fishing trips. (☎08 9071 5111; www.esperancedivingandfishing.com.au. Single dive with equipment $110; double dive including lunch and tea $210. Sanko Harvest dive min. 8 people; $235) **Mackenzie's Island Cruises,** 71 the Esplanade, runs daily 3hr. wildlife cruises. From September to April, they run tours of Woody Island in the Recherche Archipelago. (☎08 9071 5757. Departs 9am, weather permitting, from Taylor St. Jetty. ½-day $72, YHA/

students $65, ages 5-16 $25; full-day $102/95/48.) **Woody Island ❶** offers posh camping administered by Mackenzie's Island Cruises. (☎08 9071 5757. Sites $15 per person; single tents with foam mattresses $30; doubles $54; elevated safari huts with queen bed and private deck $102, with linen $120.)

The islands near Esperance are known for having some of the most difficult surfing in the world, including Cyclops, the "most hyped, least surfed wave in the world." Many 4WD opportunities on the beach and among the sand dunes north of town are incredible, but beware of quicksand. **Esperance Eco-Discovery Tours,** whose 4WD trips travel to Cape Le Grand and Cape Arid; packages include meals and park fees. It's also possible to tag along with your own 4WD. (☎04 0773 7261; www.esperancetours.com.au. ½-day $80, under 16 $60; full-day $150/125. 4WD tagalong, $145 per vehicle.)

## CAPE LE GRAND NATIONAL PARK

▨**Cape Le Grand National Park** is the stuff of postcards—cavernous granite, sandy sheltered bays, and dazzling aquamarine waters. Hiking trails of all lengths and difficulties will bring you to some breathtaking views and striking rocks, but beaches are Le Grand's finest asset. These stunning stretches are nearly deserted: locals complain that a beach is "crowded" if there are more than ten people enjoying it. To reach Cape Le Grand, take Goldfields Rd. north out of Esperance to Fisheries Rd., turn right on Merivale Rd., and right again on Cape Le Grand Rd.; signs point the way. Without a car, the best way to get to the park is with a tour from **Esperance Backpackers** or **Esperance Eco-Discovery Tours.** Most roads in the park are sealed; the handful of unsealed roads can be easily managed by careful 2WD drivers. There is **camping ❶** with full facilities at Cape Le Grand National Park, so consider staying onsite for a night or two to get the most out of the beaches and trails. There are sites at **Le Grand Beach** and **Lucky Bay;** the former has showers, and both have eco-toilets as well as camper kitchens with BBQ, stove, and running water. Keep in mind that sites cannot be booked and fill up quickly in the summer, so have a backup plan just in case. ($10 park pass. Sites $7.50 per person. Extra child $2).

A 15km coastal trail connects the park's five beaches: Le Grand Beach, Hellfire Bay, Thistle Cove, Lucky Bay, and Rossiter Bay, from west to east. The best are the middle three, with calmer waters and crazy rock formations. Despite the name, Hellfire Bay is particularly pleasant and offers fishing off the rocks on its east side. The stretch from **Le Grand Beach to Hellfire** (3hr.) is classified as a "hard walk" due to its steep, rocky areas. The path runs through sandy coastal plains and along the slopes of the lichen-encrusted Mount Le Grand. The challenging **Hellfire to Thistle track** (2hr.) weaves through low scrub and showy banksia flowers. The track from **Thistle to Lucky** (1hr.) is the easiest of the four legs, with humbling views of caves, waves, and granite formations. The moderate hike from **Lucky to Rossiter** (2hr.) features more granite outcrops and windswept dunes. Those attempting the entire walk should register with the ranger at the entrance to the park (☎08 9075 9072) or with the Esperance **parks office,** 92 Dempster St. (☎08 9083 2100. Open M-F 8:30am-4:30pm.) Perched above the bays and coastline is the impressive **Frenchman Peak,** a granite mound with a hollow cave through the top. In the Nyoongar dreaming for this area, the peak is a mother eagle, perched protectively on her nest. The 262m peak can be reached via a steep 3km track (2hr. round trip). **Hellfire Gallery,** on Tyrrell Rd., off Merivale Rd., 30km east of Esperance, displays local art inside and in its beautifully landscaped garden. There is a lovely **cafe ❶** attached that serves fabulous coffee, tea, scones, and cakes ($3-6). A variety of musicians perform on the grounds during spring and summer. (☎08 9075 9042; www.wn.com.au/hellfiregallery. Open M and Th-Su 10am-5pm. MC/V.)

At the eastern end of the park, Wharton is one of its most tantalizing beaches, a satisfying reward for those willing to make the 83km trek from Esperance. With on-site petrol, a convenience store, tennis court, playground, kitchen, and takeaways, **Orleans Bay Caravan Park ❷** has everything but linen. (Take Fisheries Rd. east and turn south on Orleans Bay Rd. at Condingup. ☎08 9075 0033. Powered sites for 2 $23; park homes for 2 $50; ensuite chalets for 2 $80. Extra person $6.) The park is also the base for **Duke Charters & Scenic Tours**, which offers whale and dolphin sight-seeing cruises and fishing charters for tuna, snapper, and harlequin. (☎08 9076 6223. Full-day fishing trip with lunch $200.)

On Fisheries Rd., 120km east of Esperance, remote **Cape Arid National Park** provides more surf-pounded granite headlands and white sand beaches. Entrance fees apply, but **camping ❶** is free; there are BBQ facilities and pit toilets, but you should bring your own water as none is available in the park.

# GOLDFIELDS

In 1893, hundreds of kilometers east of Perth, a group of Irish prospectors stumbled onto the Golden Mile, the most gold-rich square mile in the world. Thus the city of Kalgoorlie was born, and to this day it's churning out gold. Modern miners may wear uniforms and drive company 4WDs, but they still like to cut loose like cowboys in the local saloons. However, the road to Kal is nothing but 'roos and road trains, so unless you're particularly interested in gold mining, when heading west to Perth from Eyre you should consider taking the South Coast Hwy., which provides a much more relaxed and varied trip.

## GREAT EASTERN HIGHWAY

As you make the (long, flat, and lonely) 600km drive from Perth to Kalgoorlie, your travel buddy is the incredible "Golden Pipeline," an uphill pump system designed to get water from Perth out to the lucrative goldfields of Kalgoorlie. The traffic in Perth's eastern suburbs can be frustrating and slow, but the tension melts away as you drive through the woodland and wildflowers of the Darling Range. By the time you reach the towns of Merredin and Southern Cross, the only traffic is swaggering road trains bearing farm equipment or livestock. Roadhouses are spaced no more than 150km apart.

## KALGOORLIE-BOULDER                    ☎08

Kalgoorlie-Boulder's a two-headed beast. Kalgoorlie enjoys being the primary head; it's home to most of the major industry, nightlife, and accommodations. Growing awkwardly out of this urban animal's neck is the smaller Boulder, traditionally home to the working class in this mining metropolis. The two towns are officially merged, but they remain distinct even now, with different town centers (about 5km apart), different postal codes, and different atmospheres. If you're passing through, Kalgoorlie is likely the place you'll stay; if you have the time, though, check out Boulder's weekly markets.

### ▐ TRANSPORTATION

The **airport** is south of the city off Gatacre St. **Qantaslink** and **Skywest** offer daily flights to Perth (1-3 per day). **Goldfields Express** buses depart from the Goldrush Tours office on Lane Street. (☎1800 620 440; www.goldrushtours.com.au. 7hr.; M and F 3:15pm, Th and Su 1pm; $70, YHA $63.) Prospector trains (☎13 10 53) depart from the station, on the corner of Forrest and Wilson St., for Perth (6hr.; M-Sa 7:05am, also M and F 2.30pm, Su 2:05pm; $77, YHA $69.15).

## 🔳 🔢 ORIENTATION AND PRACTICAL INFORMATION

The Great Eastern Highway (Hwy. 94 from Coolgardie) becomes **Hannan Street,** the main drag running northeast through town. The town's hostels and famous brothels sit one block northwest on **Hay Street.** Lionel St., Wilson St., and Boulder Rd. are all major roads running perpendicular to Hannan and Hay St. To reach Boulder from downtown Kalgoorlie, turn right on Boulder Rd. at the north end of Hannan St. and follow it to Federal Road.

The **visitors center,** in the Town Hall at the corner of Hannan and Wilson St., books accommodations and tours. (☎08 9021 1966 or 1800 004653; www.kalgoorlietourism.com. Open M-F 8:30am-5pm, Sa-Su 9am-5pm.) **Internet access** is available at the **library** on Roberts St., near the Arts Center off Boulder Rd. (☎08 9021 7112. $3 per 30min. Open M-F 9:30am-8pm, Sa 9am-noon, Su 2-5pm.) Or try **NetZone,** on the corner of Hannan and Wilson St. (☎08 9022 8342. $10 per hr. Open M-F 10am-7pm, Sa-Su 10am-5pm.) The **Kalgoorlie Regional Hospital** (☎08 9080 5888) is northwest of Hannan St. on Piccadilly St; go across Maritana St. and turn east (right) on Picadilly. The **post office** is on Hannan St. (☎08 9024 1093. Open M-F 9am-5pm.) **Postal Code:** 6430 (Kalgoorlie); 6432 (Boulder).

The **police** (☎08 9021 9777), on Bookman St. behind the post office, maintain that no areas of Kalgoorlie-Boulder are particularly unsafe, although they do warn visitors to be careful of deep mining holes when bushwalking. However, theft has become common in recent years; locals are careful to keep their personal belongings under lock and key. Watch your wallet, use lockers, and don't leave valuables in your car. There are three brothels on Hay St. between Lionel and Lane St. Women should not walk alone in this area after dark. **Twin City Cabs** provides taxi service (☎13 10 08).

## 🔳 ACCOMMODATIONS

Many of Kalgoorlie's main-street hotels have elaborate, historical facades, but you may end up paying for the beauty. Those who are uncomfortable with prostitution should note that both hostels are close to the discreet-but-operational brothels on Hay St. The caravan parks on the way out of town toward Coolgardie or the Hannan St. hotels are a good alternative. Book ahead during the September horse races and the mining expo in October.

**Gold Dust Backpackers,** 192 Hay St. (☎08 9091 3737). A friendly, well-kitted backpackers hostel. Offers discounted weekly and monthly rates for long-term residents. Spacious common areas and kitchen. Pool and A/C. Many staying here work in Kalgoorlie; job notices and employment help available. Internet $6 per hr. Free shuttle to airport and bus terminals; free bikes for use. Dorms $28, with discount $24; singles $40/35; twins and doubles $60/55. VIP/YHA. MC/V. ❷

**Kalgoorlie Backpackers YHA,** 166 Hay St. (☎08 9091 1482), near the intersection with Lionel St. Shared kitchen, laundry, lounge, A/C, and swimming pool. Notice board for work opportunities. Internet $6 per hr. All rooms $26. Weekly rates available. MC/V. ❷

**The Palace Hotel** (☎08 9021 2788; www.palacehotel.com.au), on the corner of Hannan and Maritana St. Nice rooms and an in-house movie channel set within a historic building. The mirror in the foyer, along with a poem, was given to a barmaid by the young Herbert Hoover. Backpacker singles $35; doubles $45; twins $65 (men only); doubles $80, internal $75; singles $60/55; family room $110. AmEx/MC/V. ❸

**FOOD**

With miners working around the clock, Kalgoorlie's services cater to any schedule. Most cafes line Hannan St.; many open early and close late. A **Coles** supermarket is located at the corner of Wilson and Brookman St. (☎08 9021 8466; open M-W and F 8am-6pm, Th 8am-9pm, Sa 8am-5pm), and there is a **Woolworth's** on the corner of Hannan and Wilson St.

**Monty's** (☎08 9022 8288), at the corner of Hannan and Porter St. Head here to sate your munchies, or for a welcoming atmosphere complete with elegant and comfy leather chairs. Main courses $21-37. Pasta $15 on Tuesdays. Open daily 24hr. AmEx/MC/V. ❸

**Saltimbocca,** 90 Egan St. (☎08 9022 8028), behind the Palace Hotel. This chic restaurant is a welcome respite from pub grub. Travelers can order fine Italian food served in a trendy atmosphere. Main dishes $20-30. Open M-Sa 6pm-late. ❸

**Goldfields Bread Shop** (☎08 9091 9113), on Wilson St. between Brookman and Hannan St. Delicious meat pies ($2.20). Open daily 5am-5pm. ❶

**Peter Pan Milk Bar,** 312 Hannan St. (☎08 9021 2330). Renowned for its hearty breakfasts ($6-8). Open M-Sa 7am-3pm. ❶

## NIGHTLIFE

Kal boasts nearly 30 pubs, most of which line Hannan St., but nightlife here can be a bit of a bummer for anyone who doesn't want to compete for the attention of lingerie-clad barmaids, known as skimpies. Most pubs in Kal feature these ladies on most, if not all, nights of the week; it will usually be clearly announced on the outside. All of the establishments listed here are skimpy-free.

**Kalgoorlie Hotel** (☎08 9021 3046), on the corner of Hannan and Wilson St. A plain exterior hides a darn good-looking bar inside, with big wooden tables and a beer garden full of large, inviting cushions. Wood-fired pizzas ($20) are a good bet for budget eats. Live music most weekends; cover varies. Open M-Th and Su noon-midnight, F-Sa noon-1am. Lunch daily noon-2pm; dinner daily 6-9pm. AmEx/MC/V. ❷

**Paddy's Ale House** (☎08 9021 2833), on Maritana St. in the Exchange Hotel building. A popular, laid-back spot where many locals spend their Friday nights. Burgers $10-15. Live music M-Th. DJs F-Sa. Open daily 11am-late. ❷

**Cornwall Hotel,** (☎08 9093 2510), at the corner of Hopkins St. and Goldfields Hwy. in Boulder. A lively bar in an historic hotel. Su jazz nights start at 4pm in the outdoor beer garden. Open daily from 11am. Meals Th-Sa 6:30pm-late, Su 12:30pm-late. ❸

## SIGHTS

The best place to learn about the local industry is the extensive ⚑**Mining Hall of Fame,** located at Hannans North Historic Mining Reserve, a right turn off Goldfields Hwy., 2km north of Hannan St. It features new Chinese gardens, demonstrations of gold pouring and panning, and a tour of an underground mine. (☎08 9026 2700; www.mininghall.com. Open daily 9am-4:30pm. $24, without underground tour $17; concessions $18/14, children $14/9, families $60/45.) To see the industry in action, head to the enormous **Super Pit,** a 365m-deep open pit mine. Miners usually set off explosions once a day; check with the visitors center. The lookout is just outside town; head toward Boulder on Goldfields Hwy., then turn left at the sign for the pit. It's best to arrive a bit early, since the miners won't hold back for tourists if things are ahead of schedule. (Open daily 6am-7pm. Free.) The **WA Museum of Kalgoorlie-Boulder** sits primly under a massive mining tower. It contains a reconstructed miners' cottage, exquisitely rebuilt mining board rooms, and **British Arms,** once the Southern Hemisphere's narrowest pub. (17 Hannan St. ☎08 9021 8533; www.museum.wa.gov.au. Open daily 10am-4:30pm. Suggested donation $5.) The visitors center at the **Royal Flying Doctor Service,** located at the airport on Hart Kerspien Dr., gives tours explaining the organization's impressive medical service to isolated outback communities. Guests can check out the state-of-the-art plane used to transport patients and staff—provided it isn't out on a mission. (☎08 9093 7595. Open M-F 10am-3pm. Tours on the hr. Admission by donation.) Take a glimpse of Kalgoorlie's kinky side on a working tour of any of Hay St.'s brothels. As the oldest brothel, **Questa Casa,** 133 Hay St., offers tours that are as historically informative as they are naughty. Learn about the history, evolution and regulation of prostitution in Kalgoorlie from their dignified British madam. (Tours 2pm daily; $20.) **Langtree's Club 181,** 181 Hay St., is the newest brothel and offers a more jazzed-up theatrical tour. (☎08 9026 2111. 18+. Tours daily 1, 3, and 6pm; $35, randy seniors $25. Coffee, tea, and cake available 10am-6pm.) Merchants peddle some more conventional wares at the **Boulder Town Market,** held on the third Sunday of every month on Burt St. (Open 9:30am-1.30pm.)

## NORSEMAN                                                                    ☎08

About 100 years ago, "Hardy Norseman" was tethered here as his rider slept. The restless horse pawed at the ground, uncovering a chunk of gold. At the news of his discovery, prospectors rushed to the area and the town of Norseman was born. Today, most visitors are on their way elsewhere, and there's little to keep them in this one-horse town. For those heading north from Esperance, Norseman's the first encounter with the Goldfields. For those heading east across the Nullarbor Plain, it's the last bit of civilization for 1000km.

The family-run **Lodge 101 ❷** on Prinsep St. offers convenient, homey accommodations with a small kitchen and outdoor lounge area. Free local bus pickup is also available. (☎08 9039 1541. Dorms $24; singles $45; doubles $65. Cash only.) Another option is the **Gateway Caravan Park ❷,** off of the highway just before McIvor Street on the way into town. They have Wi-Fi, in addition to standard facilities like showers, laundry, kitchen, etc. (☎08 9039 1500; www.acclaimparks.com.au. Sites $23.50; backpacker rooms $15 per person; cabins $69; ensuite $82-87.) There aren't many cheap options for dining out in Norseman. **Cafe on Roberts ❶,** next to the IGA in the "shopping district," has nice coffees, sandwiches ($3.50-7), pasties ($3.20), coffees, pastries, and A/C. (Open daily 8:45am-3:30pm.) There are two 24-hour Travelstops on Highway 94 on the northern way into town: a **BP** and a **Caltex.** Both offer hot food, showers ($2), Internet, convenience stores, ATMs, and petrol. The BP has a laundromat as well, and so does the **Shell Station** on the corner of Robert & Ramsay Sts. in town. The **IGA,** 89 Robert St., is your best bet for buying groceries. (Open M-F 8:30am-6pm, Sa 8:30am-5pm, Su 9:30am-1pm.)

The **visitors center,** on Robert St., one block east on the highway between Sinclair and Richardson St., has information about driving the Eyre Hwy; they also do bookings for buses and trains to Perth or Kalgoorlie. (☎08 9039 1071. Open daily 9am-5pm.) An ATM is also on Roberts St., and the Telecentre, which offers **Internet access,** is on the corner of Talbot and Prinsep St. (the Coolgardie-Esperance Hwy.) next to the town hall. (☎08 9039 0538. Open Tu, W, F 9:30am-5pm.) Also on Prinsep St. are the **post office** (☎08 9039 1211; **postal code:** 6443) and **police station;** the **hospital** is 1km west of town on Talbot St.

## CROSSING THE NULLARBOR

**The Eyre Highway,** running between Norseman and Adelaide across the Nullarbor (null-a-BORE) Plain, is a grueling 1200km desert haul with little to entertain you on your way. Ninety Mile Straight, the longest completely straight stretch of highway in the world, is just west of Cocklebiddy. The Plain can be crossed by car or by the Indian Pacific train out of Perth (see **Intercity Transportation,** p. 684). For information on crossing into South Australia, call the agriculture department. Fruit and vegetables are not permitted, nor are plants or soil; violators get slapped with a hefty $2500 fine. (☎08 9039 3227 in WA or ☎08 8625 2108 in SA; www.agric.wa.gov.au.) The visitors center in Norseman has helpful info and handles train bookings. When you reach Ceduna at the eastern corner of SA's Eyre Peninsula, pick up a Nullarbor certificate of completion at the visitors center; or, if Norseman marks the completion of your trek from east to west, get your certificate at the Norseman visitors center. See **Crossing the Nullarbor,** p. 530, in the **South Australia** chapter, for more information.

# BATAVIA COAST AND MIDLANDS

The region just northeast of Perth represents different things to different people. For windsurfers, Lancelin and Geraldton offer world-class gusts; for fishermen, Batavia's treacherous coast promises a bountiful harvest; and for the Dutch mariners of the vessel Batavia, which wrecked upon its reefs in the 17th century, it was the first European glimpse of the land down under. Those who take the time to explore will be treated to a beautiful coastal road, thrilling water sports, a glorious wildflower season (June-Nov.), and coastal dunes.

# LANCELIN ☎08

Lancelin (pop. 800), 126km north of Perth, is considered by many to be the windsurfing capital of Australia, with thrill-seekers flocking here from October to March. The famed four-day Ledge Point Sailboard Classic is held during the second week of January, but even in the low season there's almost always a good breeze. The region's indigenous people called it *Wangaree,* meaning "Good Fishing Place," and this small village thrives on the ocean's bounty; the season runs from September to June.

## ▐ TRANSPORTATION

There is no public transportation to Lancelin, but YHA has pickups from Perth for $30 (generally on M,W, and F, though they're flexible for groups). If you're staying elsewhere, you can call the day before to see if they have spots on their van. The easiest way to reach Lancelin is by car; from Perth, take Bulwer St. to Charles St., which becomes Hwy. 60 (Wanneroo Rd.) before hitting Lancelin.

## ▐ PRACTICAL INFORMATION

The **visitors centre** is at 102 Gingin Rd. (☎08 9655 1100. Open daily 9am-6pm.) There are **ATMs** in the adjacent store (open daily 7am-7pm), at the Gull petrol station (open daily 7am-7pm), at the Lancelin Beach Hotel at the corner of Gingin St. and North St. (past Harold Park), and in the Endeavour Tavern. The **police** (☎13 14 44) are down Hammersly Rd., and the **hospital** (☎1800 022 222) is north on Gingin Rd. **Internet access** is available at the **telecenter** off Vins St. for $5 per 30min. (Open M-F 10am-4pm, Sa 10am-2pm.) The **post office** is located in the main shopping center (M-F 7am-5pm, Sa 7am-4pm.) **Postal Code:** 6044.

# ACCOMMODATIONS

**Lancelin Lodge YHA,** 10 Hopkins St. (☎08 9655 2020; www.lancelinlodge.com.au). Get ready: 2 comfy lounges, free bikes, boogie boards, fishing rods, a lovely kitchen, wonderful showers, beach volleyball, and a new pool make this sparkling hostel the pick of the town. The sound of crashing waves is a happy reminder that Lancelin's beautiful beach is only a short walk away. Internet $5 per hr. Dorms $28; doubles Mar.-Oct. $60, Oct.-Mar. $70. Cheaper rates for weekly rentals; YHA discounts. MC/V. ❷

**Lancelin Caravan Park** (☎08 9655 1056), just down the street from the YHA. Although the park offers no cooking or refrigeration facilities, you can use the free BBQ in Harold Park on Gingin Rd. Sites $9, powered $11; on-site 4-person van $75. MC/V. ❶

**Lancelin Holiday Accommodation** (☎08 9655 1100), in the visitors center. Budget self-contained units. Linen is not provided (it can be rented), but bathroom, kitchen, and washing machine are. One-bedroom apartment $75; two-bedroom $85. ❺

# FOOD

Food options in Lancelin are fairly limited. Several fish and chips joints are located on Lancelin's self-proclaimed "cappuccino strip" in the shopping center. A supermarket is located in the shopping center on Gingin Rd. (☎08 9655 1172. Open daily summer 7am-8pm, winter 7am-7pm.)

**Lancelin Bay Restaurant** (☎08 9655 2686), off of Gingin Rd. on Miragliotta Rd., toward the waterfront. This cafe-bistro opened in 2007. Although their dinner mains may break the budget traveler's bank, their $8 lunch sandwiches with fries and bruschetta salad are a steal. Coffees and pastries are available all day. Open daily 9am-6pm. MC/V. ❶

**Endeavour Tavern,** on the corner of Cray St. and Gingin Rd. Pub fare for $9-14. Open M-F noon-2pm and 6-8pm, Sa-Su noon-2:30pm and 6-9pm. MC/V. ❷

# ACTIVITIES

**WINDSURFING AND SURFING.** Windsurfing lessons and equipment are available Oct.-Mar. at **Werner's Hotspot** on the South End beach (☎08 9655 1553). Lancelin Beach Surf School is based both in Perth and Lancelin and offers group lessons, 5-day surf courses, and 2-5 day all-inclusive surf camps. (☎1800 198 121; www.surfschool.com. 1-day group lesson in Lancelin $50; 5-day all-inclusive surf camp $580). If you want to learn to wind- or kitesurf, try **Wedge Island Surf Co.** They can also provide transport up from Perth if you aren't already in Lancelin (☎08 9336 6773; www.wedgeislandsurfco.com.au. Kitesurfing lesson from Lancelin $195, from Perth $235; windsurfing lesson $85/$125). **Lancelin Surfsports,** 127 Gingin Rd., rents sandboarding and surfing gear. (☎08 9655 1441. Sandboards $10 per 2hr., surfboards $25 per ½-day, $40 per full-day, 24hr. overnight rental $50. Open daily 9am-5pm. MC/V.)

**SAND DUNES.** The dunes, which extend for kilometers northeast of town, are a 4WD playground and a practice area for the Australian military; check with the visitors centre before going. **Desert Storm Adventures** lets you cruise in a schoolbus with monster truck tires and an equally monster stereo. (☎08 9655 2550; www.desertstorm.com.au. $45, concessions $40, children $30.) **Lancelin Off Road Motor Bike Hire** lets you jump on a dirt bike and explore on your own. (☎04 1791 9550; www.dirtbikehire.com.au. $45 per 30min., $80 per hr.)

# NAMBUNG NATIONAL PARK: THE PINNACLES

Between Lancelin and Geraldton, the Pinnacles Desert, in Nambung National Park, is an accessible and bizarre attraction. The barren, jagged landscape isn't really a desert at all, but an expanse of deep golden sand dunes with thousands of wind-eroded limestone pillars up to 4m tall. Climb the Pinnacles Lookout at the northernmost edge of the vehicle loop for gorgeous views of the contrasting Red Desert to the east and the White Desert to the west. Try to visit at dawn or sunset when the hordes of daytrippers from Perth are gone, the heat is bearable, and the sand and pillars glow in the changing light.

**Greyhound Australia** (☎ 13 14 99 or 13 20 30) drops off right in town (3hr.; daily 3:30pm; $46, concessions $42). Driving to Nambung means a national park pass, sold at the Pinnacles Visitor Centre and at the Pinnacles Desert loop. (Day pass $10 per vehicle; 4-week holiday pass for all national parks $35.)

There aren't many advantages to a guided tour over a self-guided walk around the Pinnacles—the track is easy and no 4WD is necessary. Renting a car is the cheapest way to see the park and allows the most flexibility. Travel 1hr. west from Brand Hwy.; turn left into the park just before Cervantes. Once inside the park, the Kangaroo Point and Hangover Bay turnoffs provide beach access, as well as picnic areas and toilets. **Lake Thetis,** between the park turnoff and Cervantes, is home to ancient stromatolites. To learn more about the area, try the **Pinnacles Visitors Centre,** inside the Post Office on Cadiz St. in Cervantes, which has tour and accommodation info for both Cervantes and nearby Jurien Bay. (☎ 08 9652 7700. Open M-Sa 7:15am-5:30pm, Su 7:15am-5pm.

## ACCOMMODATIONS

**Cervantes Lodge and Pinnacles Beach Backpackers,** 91 Seville St. (☎ 08 9652 7377; www.cervanteslodge.com.au). Clean and cozy accommodations, a big bright kitchen, and a small adjoining cafe make this hostel a good pick, even if it's a bit out of the way. Internet $4 per hr. Wheelchair accessible. Dorms $25, doubles $75; ensuite $100; deluxe room with TV, fridge, and ocean views $110. Extra person $10. ❷

**Cervantes Pinnacles Caravan Park,** 35 Aragon St. (☎ 08 9652 7060). A waterfront location and cafe make this a nice option. Cafe open daily 8am-5pm. Sites $24, powered $27; "old style" caravans $45; cabins $80. All prices for 2 people. Extra adult $7, extra child $4; in cabins, extra person $10. MC/V. ❷

# GERALDTON

☎ 08

Geraldton (pop. 33,000) is the gateway to the beautiful Abrolhos Islands, where the scuba diving is superb. Thanks to consistent winds—particularly the southerlies that flow from November to March—Geraldton is also an international windsurfing and kitesurfing destination in the Australian summer months.

## TRANSPORTATION

**Greyhound Australia** (☎ 13 14 99 or 13 20 30; www.greyhound.com.au) runs **buses** to Perth (6hr.; M, W, F-Su 12:30pm; $60, concessions $54). **TransWA** (☎ 1300 662 205; www.transwa.wa.gov.au) also goes to Perth (6hr., 1 per day, $53.55/48.20). There's also a local bus that serves the greater Geraldton area ($2.10-3.20, concessions $0.90-1.30); use this service to reach some of the area beaches as well (including Sunset Beach, St. George's, Champion Bay, and Pointe Moore).

## ⚔️ 🔼 ORIENTATION AND PRACTICAL INFORMATION

If you come in from the Brand Hwy., head straight through the rotary and up Cathedral Ave. to the town center. From the North West Coastal Highway, turn right on Phelps St. and go left at the roundabout. Main drag Chapman Rd. and shop-lined Marine Terr. run parallel to the coast and intersect Cathedral Ave.

**Tourist Office: Visitors Centre** (☎08 9921 3999; www.geraldtontourist.com.au), in the complex at Bayly St. and Chapman Rd. Open M-F 9am-5pm, Sa-Su 10am-4pm.

**Police:** (☎08 9923 4555), downtown.

**Hospital** (☎08 9956 2222), off Cathedral St. on Shenton St.

**Internet Access: SunCity Books and Internet.** Internet $6 per hr.

**Post Office:** on Durlacher St., just off Chapman St. behind the art gallery. Open M-F 8:30am-5pm. **Postal code:** 6530.

## 🏠 ACCOMMODATIONS

**Geraldton YHA Foreshore Backpackers,** 172 Marine Terr. (☎08 9921 3275), a block southwest of Cathedral Ave., in an older building off the water in the center of town. The clean dorms here have 3-4 beds each, and some have patios overlooking the ocean. Free pickup and dropoff for bus arrivals. Internet $5 per hr. Key deposit $10. Dorms $24; singles $35; twins and doubles $55. MC/V. ❷

**Freemasons Hotel** (☎08 9964 3457; www.freemasonshotel.com.au), on the north end of Marine Terr. Another great option, with a lively pub and a central location on the city mall. Singles $30, with queen $60; ensuite doubles $80. AmEx/MC/V. ❸

**Batavia Backpackers** (☎08 9964 3001), next to the visitors center. This hostel holds large, 20-bed single-sex dorm rooms and is situated in a building which was once a hospital and, for a brief time, a jail. Internet access $3 per hr. Dorms $25, $120 per week; singles $30/150; doubles and twins $50/250; family rooms $60/300. ISIC, NOMADS, VIP, and YHA discounts. MC/V. ❷

**Cameliers Guest House** (☎08 9964 3725), across from the Freemason's Hotel on Marine Terr. Offers single and double rooms with shared facilities. Alcohol is not permitted. Key deposit $10. Singles $30, $110 per week; doubles $45/165. ❸

## 🍴 FOOD

There is a **Woolworths** supermarket on Sanford and Durlacher St. (☎08 9921 4088; open M-W and F 8am-6pm, Th 8am-9pm, Sa 8am-5pm.)

**Planet Bean** (☎08 9965 2233), in the Marine Terr. mall. This budget standout has good breakfasts and lunches for $7-14. Open M-F 6:30am-2:30pm, Sa 6:30am-noon. ❶

**Tanti's Restaurant** (☎08 9964 2311). Exquisite Thai meals for $11-17.50 and lunch specials W-F. Open M-Sa 5-9:30pm, W-F 11am-2pm. MC/V. ❸

**The Camel Bar** (☎08 9965 5500), on Chapman St. next to the Art Gallery. Camel blends a popular nightlife atmosphere with tasty oven-baked pizzas. Try the Pollo pizza ($18) with chicken, avocado, sun-dried tomatoes, and mango for a different, but delicious blend. Open daily 11:30am-2pm and 6-9pm. ❸

## 🐪 ACTIVITIES

Geraldton's two biggest attractions are its windsurfing and the beautiful scenery and diving available on the Abrolhos islands. The best wind- and kitesurfing conditions occur Nov.-Mar., though it is a great activity year-round in this area. The best windsurfing in the area is at Point Moore; the channel there known as "Hell's Gate" is the gnarliest spot around. Surfers prefer Greys Beach, Sunset Beach, and Back Beach. If you just want to swim, the three foreshore beaches—recently renamed as Front Beach, Champion Bay, and Jambinbirri Beach—are sheltered, deep spots that are easy to reach from town.

**Sailwest** (☎08 9964 1722; www.sailwest.com.au), at the Point Moore Lighthouse on Willcock Rd. west of town. Windsurfing equipment rental. Windsurfing gear $90 per day, $50 per day. Group lessons $59 per person. Open M-F 9:30am-5pm on clear days, 9:30am-3pm on windy days; Sa 10am-1:30pm. MC/V.

**Midwest Surf School and Tours** (☎04 1998 8756; www.surf2skool.com). Surf lessons available from $30 per person. You can also book through the visitors center.

# KALBARRI

The main draw of Kalbarri (kal-BERRY) is the national park, with its collection of coastal cliffs and spectacular river gorges, carved out over millions of years. The diverse landscape looks even more beautiful in the late winter and early spring with its stretches of wildflowers.

## ▣ TRANSPORTATION

Transportation in town or to the coastal cliffs and inland gorges is available through **Kalbarri Taxi** (☎08 9937 1888). **Greyhound** and **TransWA** bus services run both north and south nearly every day of the week. (Greyhound $128 to Perth M, W, F; Transwa $66 to Perth T, Th, Sa.)

## ▰ ▱ ORIENTATION AND PRACTICAL INFORMATION

The township of Kalbarri, with its grassy riverfront and picturesque view of the mouth of the Murchison River, is the primary starting point for exploring this natural wonderland. Most services lie on or near Grey Street, which follows the river and turns into Red Bluff Road and Ajana-Kalbarri Road at either end of town. The former leads to Geraldton via a newly sealed road, making for a great coastal drive; the latter goes to the North West Coastal Hwy.

**Tourist Office: Visitors Centre** (☎08 9937 1104; www.kalbarriwa.info), on Grey St. between Woods and Porter St. Open daily 9am-5pm.

**Tours:** There are a number of companies offering various types of tours out of Kalbarri.
**Kalbarri Adventure Tours** (☎08 9937 1677; 0427 371 677; www.kalbarritours.com.au).
**Kalbarri Coach Tours** (☎08 9937 1161).
**Kalbarri Air Charters** (☎08 9937 1130).
**Kalbarri Wilderness Cruises** (☎08 9937 2259 or 9937 1393).

**Police: Station** (☎08 9937 1006) in the shopping center.

**Pharmacy:** (☎08 9937 1026), in the shopping center on the corner of Grey and Porter St. Open M-F 8:30am-5:30pm, Sa 8:30am-12:30pm.

**Medical Services: Medical Center** (☎08 9937 1000).

**Internet Access: Book exchange** (☎08 9937 2676), next to the pharmacy. $6 per hr. Open M-F 9am-5pm, Sa 9am-12:30pm; reduced hours in low season.

**Post Office:** (☎08 9937 2212), past Ajana Kalbarri Rd. on Grey St., next to the marina jetty. Open M-F 8am-5pm, Sa 8am-noon. **Postal Code:** 6536.

## ACCOMMODATIONS AND CAMPING

**Kalbarri Backpackers,** 52 Mortimer St. (☎08 9937 1430). From the visitors center, turn right on Grey St., then right on Woods St. The comfortable hostel offers a pool, cozy lounges, BBQ, bike rental ($10 per day), and free use of its snorkel gear and boogie boards. Most of the dorms are ensuite, but there are some communal bathrooms as well. The kitchen is relatively new; kitchen gear can be hired for a $10 deposit. 8-bed dorms $25, YHA $22; twins or doubles $65/60. YHA discounts available on nearby self-contained chalets and cabins as well. MC/V. ❷

**Kalbarri Tudor Caravan Park** (☎08 9937 1077; www.kalbarritudor.com.au), on Porter St. Offers doubles with bed, TV, fridge, A/C, and full-service kitchenette. Other amenities include pool, kitchen, BBQ area, and TV room. Linen $10 per night. Free Wi-Fi throughout the park. Sites for 2 $22; powered $27; tudor cabin for 2 $50; standard cabin for 2 $70; ensuite cabin for 2 $95; motel unit for 2 $120. ❷

**Kalbarri Anchorage Caravan Park** (☎08 9937 1181), across from the jetty at the north end of Grey St. This park sits on a grassy knoll with great views of the surrounding area, and has an enclosed kitchen, a pool, and $3 "Snagga Roll" BBQ nights every Th at 6pm. Sites for 2 $23, powered $26. Cabins high season $65, low season $50, ensuite $80/$90. Extra adult $10, extra child $5. MC/V. ❷

## FOOD

**Finlay's Fresh Fish BBQ** (☎08 9937 1260). From Grey St., turn left at Porter St., right on Walker St., then right onto Magee Cres. Finlay's serves up huge portions of delicious seafood with a folksy flare ($10-25). Open Tu-Su 5:30-8:30pm. BYO. ❸

**Black Rock Cafe** (☎08 9937 1062), on Grey St. next to the visitors center. A classy but subdued cafe/bistro with heaps of outdoor, riverfront seating, really good morning coffees ($4), and a variety of filling meals on offer. Breakfast features a great selection of crepes ($6-12.50); the crusty Italian toast with salsa, avocado, and poached eggs ($14) is also a good pick. Open daily 7am-8pm. ❶

**Gorges Cafe** (☎08 9937 1200), next to the post office on Grey St. Come here to enjoy cooked breakfasts (from $7.50), souvlaki, burgers, focaccia, panini, and coffees. Internet $3 per 15min. Open M and W-F 8am-4pm; Sa-Su 8am-2pm. ❶

**Kalbarri Cafe and Takeaway** (☎08 9937 1045), in the Kalbarri Shopping Centre on the corner of Porter and Walker St. This joint is always jam-packed and has tasty burgers (from $8), pizzas, fish and chips (from $8), sandwiches (from $4.30), and rolls (from $5). Internet $1 per 5min. Open daily 8.30am-8pm. MC/V. ❶

> **TIP**
>
> **PELICANS!** Daily pelican feedings take place at 8:45am in the informal amphitheatre on Grey St. across from the GrassTree restaurant. The feedings are a 35-year-old tradition; bring coins for a small donation.

## SIGHTS

**KALBARRI NATIONAL PARK.** The park is divided into two main sections: the coastal cliffs and the river gorges. The river gorges were etched by the waters of the Murchison River, and boast a number of jagged hikes. Access to the river gorges area costs $10 per vehicle. Bring exact change in case no one's on duty. The park's unsealed roads are generally in good 2WD condition, but the 25km to the Loop and Z Bend can be corrugated and caravans should be left behind. It's always a good idea to check with DEC (☎08 9937 1140) for current reports.

WESTERN AUSTRALIA

**Kalbarri Auto Centre** hires older cars that renters can take on unsealed roads to the Loop Trail and Z Bend. Don't worry about their location; they'll pick you up. *(☎08 9937 1290; open daily 8am-5pm. 2WD $50 per day; 4WD $80 per day. Cash only.)*

**KALBARRI RAINBOW JUNGLE PARROT SANCTUARY.** Just beyond the cliffs on the way back to town from the Rock Island formations, the sanctuary houses hundreds of colorful cockatoos and pretty parrots. Visit the aviary during a feeding to see over 100 bird species. On the weekends they also show films in their outdoor "Cinema Parrotisso" and serve wood-fired pizzas. *(☎08 9937 1248; www.rainbowjunglekalbarri.com. Open M-Sa 9am-5pm, Su 10am-5pm; no entry after 4pm. Call for times and showings. $12.50, children $4.50. Cinema entry $14, concessions $12, children $5.)*

**HUTT RIVER PROVINCE.** Hutt River seceded from Australia in 1970, and though the province resembles a small farm/caravan park, it's about the same size as Hong Kong (though the population, around 20, makes it feel a bit less crowded). Visitors to this independent principality can go on a tour given by the ruler, Prince Leonard, purchase official currency and stamps, and get their passport stamped. *(www.hutt-river-province.com. 35km south of Kalbarri, then another 40km on the unsealed Ogilvie Rd. West. Open daily 9am-4pm.)*

## ⬛ HIKES

Along the 10km of the coastal road just south of Kalbarri, numerous side streets lead to dramatic cliffs dropping into the Indian Ocean. If you plan on taking an overnight hike, alert DEC (☎08 9937 1140) beforehand, and bring a satellite phone and 5L of water per person per day.

**LOOP TRAIL.** A challenging but rewarding climb that runs along clifftops, down to the river bed, and then along river-level ledges before climbing again to the top of the gorge, **Loop Trail** (8km, 4hr.) starts near **Nature's Window,** a red rock arch that frames a river landscape behind it. Keep the river on your right and stay close to water level, even if it seems like you're not on the trail.

**ROSS GRAHAM LOOKOUT.** This is an intensive 38km hike that runs alongside the river. Allow four days and hike in groups (DEC requires parties of 5 or more). For those who would prefer not to carry several liters water on their back, Ross Graham is also accessible by car; it's 38km outside of Kalbarri along the Ajana-Kalbarri Rd. (turn left at the sign for the gorge). There is a well-marked 300m trail down to the riverbed, as well as two lookout points. Just up the road is **Hawk's Head,** another lookout point with similar amenities.

**MELALEUCA CYCLE/WALK TRAIL.** This 5km trail connects a number of swimming/surfing/fishing spots on the way out of town. Out along the coastal road, the first available sights belong to **Red Bluff**—first a beautiful, secluded beach about 4km out of town with bathrooms and gorgeous rocky sea views, as well as a sandy shore, then the lookout point, another 0.5km further along.

# OUTBACK COAST AND GASCOYNE

The Outback Coast is a mind-numbing expanse of bushland, broken only by termite mounds and the occasional befuddled emu crossing the road. Although the distances between towns are daunting, the sights and activities that lie hidden off the coast of this apparent wasteland can rejuvenate road-weary travelers. The dazzling ocean that abuts this semi-desert counters its sparseness with an impressive abundance of marine life, from the dolphins and dugongs of

Shark Bay to the whale sharks and coral of the Ningaloo Marine Park. Winter is high season, when Perthites park themselves along the sunny coast.

# SHARK BAY

Shark Bay, Western Australia's popular World Heritage area, was the site of the earliest recorded European landing in Australia. Today, Shark Bay is known for the dolphins at Monkey Mia, tranquil Shell Beach, and the "living fossils" (stromatolites) at Hamelin Pool. The pool is 34km from the North West Coastal Hwy., while Monkey Mia lies beyond Denham towards the end of the peninsula. Shark Bay is a slow-paced destination, where travelers come to relax and enjoy the palms, lovely water, and marine life. The best way to see the area is by car or on a tour, as buses to the area are infrequent.

## MONKEY MIA

At Monkey Mia (pronounced my-UH), the Indian bottlenose dolphins of Shark Bay swim right up to the shore to be fed by herds of tourists. The dolphins have been visiting Monkey Mia since it was nothing but a sheep-farming area, but in the past 10 years the playful creatures have become an international sensation. Some think Monkey Mia provides an unparalleled opportunity to interact with intelligent, sociable animals; others find it a contrived and exploitative show. Tour groups flock to this area by the dozens, but their high head-counts and squished time frames can sometimes detract from the dolphin experience itself. There are three feedings daily between 7:30am and noon. The earliest feeding is when visitors are most likely to spot some dolphins. Access to the site costs $6 per person or $12 per family.

The **Monkey Mia Visitors Centre** has displays on local marine life and history. (☎08 9948 1366. Open daily 7:30am-4pm.) There's also an easy walking trail (1.5km round-trip, 1hr.) that starts at the carpark and proceeds along the coast and up a ridge. **Shark Bay Camel Safaris** offers a chance to explore the beaches of Denham and Monkey Mia on camelback, an interesting alternative to usual resort activities (☎08 9948 3136 or 04 0419 6798). After dark, don't miss the hot tub at the **Francois Peron National Park** homestead. It's filled with a natural hot spring, and allows bathers to bask under the Milky Way amid bubbles.

The backpackers lodging at **YHA Monkey Mia Dolphin Resort ❶**, next to the dolphin interaction site, is really a resort with a beachside location and many amenities, including a tennis court, hot tub, and pool. The rooms are simple, with little more than beds and lockers, but everything is fresh and new. There is also a general store (open daily 7am-6pm), snorkel hire ($25 per day with a $50 deposit), and 24hr. Internet access next to the general store ($1 per 10min.; $10 per 90min. card). Resort guests must still pay park entrance fees, so if you're staying longer than two days, get a week pass ($9) and avoid paying the $6 daily fee. (☎08 9948 1320 or 1800 653 611; www.monkeymia.com.au. Powered sites for 2 $29; dorms $24; doubles $78. AmEx/MC/V.)

The road to Monkey Mia from Denham is well marked and departs from the western tip of Knight Terr. Those without a car can take Denham YHA's shuttle. ($5; guests free. Departs daily 7:45am, returns 4:30pm.) About 4km outside of Denham on the road to Monkey Mia, Little Lagoon is about as pristine and private a beach as possible. Stop off for a swim, a sunbathe, or a snack on your way from point A to point B. You may well be the only person in sight.

# CARNARVON                                    ☎ 08

Carnarvon (pop. 7000) manages to feel at once like an agricultural city and a small beach town. Based on its size compared to what lies to the North, this can be a good place to restock and refuel between destinations on the coast. Most backpackers come here looking for work at one of the local fruit plantations, or to see the 30m-high blowholes north of town.

**TRANSPORTATION.** Greyhound Australia (☎13 14 99 or 13 20 30) runs **buses** to **Perth** (13hr.; M, W, F-Su; $165) and **Broome** (20hr.; M, W-Sa; $253).

**ORIENTATION AND PRACTICAL INFORMATION.** A big yellow banana welcomes visitors as they head into town along Robinson St. from the North West Coastal Hwy. The main road through Carnarvon is **Robinson Street,** while major sights are also on **Babbage Island Road** and **Olivia Terrace,** which run along the water. The **visitors center** is in the **Carnarvon Civic Centre** on Robinson St., and has a guide to the town's history and services. (☎08 9941 1146. Open M-F 9am-5pm, Sa 9am-12pm, Su and public holidays 10am-1pm.) Also located on Robinson St. are multiple **ATMs** and the **police** (☎08 9941 1444). The **hospital** is one block south on Johnston St. (☎08 9941 0555), and the fire station (☎08 9941 1222) is across from the library on Stuart St. **Internet access** is available in the **library** on Stuart St. ($1 per 10min.; open M-F 9am-6pm, Sa 9am-noon), in the visitors center ($1 per 10min.), and at **Carnarvon Computers** across from the library ($2.50 per 30min., $5 per hr.; open M-F 9am-5pm). The **post office** (open M-F 9am-5pm) is located in the town center. **Postal Code:** 6701.

> **TIP**
> **WORKING IN CARNARVON.** There are only two consistently successful ways to find work in Carnarvon. Those with their own transportation can visit the plantations that line the north and south sides of the Gascoyne River and inquire about work. Those without transportation are dependent on their accommodation. Both the **Port Hotel** and **Carnarvon Backpackers** help their guests find work and provide transportation when possible.

 **ACCOMMODATIONS.** Just off the corner of Robinson St. and Olivia Terr. at the waterfront, you'll find **Carnarvon Backpackers ❷.** Overlooking the water, this hostel has hand-painted murals and lush grounds. The owners will help with job placement (in a variety of industries, from plantations to hospitality), and offer Internet access ($6 per hr.), bike rentals ($30 per week), work transport, and free fruit and vegetables in season. They also have self-contained units, which can be rented as flats for workers who wish to stay longer-term. (☎08 9941 1095. Dorms $20 per night, $100 per week; private room in 2- or 3-bedroom self-contained unit $25 per person). The **Port Hotel ❷,** on Robinson St., is also known also as the **Fish and Whistle Backpackers** and is a converted old hotel that houses many of the working backpackers in Carnarvon. The building's former life as a hotel means it has a large kitchen, but beware the lack of A/C. (☎08 9941 1704; www.theporthotel.com.au. Dorms $22 per night, $125 per week, $140 per week with work transport; singles $35/154/169; motel-style singles $77 per night, $385 per week; doubles $85/425. Extra person $11. MC/V.) On the way into town, Robinson St. is lined with half a dozen caravan parks. The closest is the **Coral Coast Tourist Park ❷,** which offers standard amenities, including that oh-so-important pool. (☎08 9941 1438. Sites for 2 $23, powered $24; extra adult $7, extra child $3. Standard cabin for 2 in high season $75, $65 per night for stays longer than 1 week; in low season $70/60.)

📱 **FOOD.** There are a few cute cafes and restaurants along Robinson St. in the block between Stuart St. and Olivia Terr., all of which offer pleasant sidewalk seating. **River Gums Cafe ❶** is a popular local hangout with main courses from $4 and delicious mango smoothies for $4; turn at the big banana on Boundary Rd. and follow the signs. (☎08 9941 8281. Open W-Su 10am-3pm.) For good coffee and a huge variety of fresh sandwiches, try the pirate-themed **Galleon Cafe ❶** at 26 Robinson St. The focaccias ($8.50) are big, the salads (from $7) are fresh, and the burgers (from $8) get pirate names like "the Veggie Lubbers." (☎08 9941 2531; open M-F 7am-4pm, kitchen closes at 3pm; Sa 7:30am-1pm. Cash only.) A few storefronts toward the water is the slightly more upscale **Avocadeau Tree ❷**, 12-14 Robinson St. In addition to the artisanal jams, spreads, and sauces on offer, they serve cooked breakfasts (from $7), focaccias (from $9.50), and a variety of pastries and coffees. (☎08 9941 4888. Open M-F 8am-3pm; kitchen closes at 2pm. Open some Sa. Cash only). For a dinner option, the **Old Post Office Cafe and Pizzeria ❸** has big rustic outdoor tables on a wooden veranda just steps away from the waterfront. They serve pizzas ($18-23) and a la carte food (from $21); it's wise to book ahead. (☎08 9941 4231. Open Tu-Sa 5-10pm; a la carte served 6-9:30pm. MC/V.) For a taste of the fresh seafood in Carnarvon, head over to **Hacienda Crab ❶**, at the Snapper Jetty, for a steamed crab ($4) or some prawns. (☎08 9941 4078. Open M-Sa 10am-6pm). **Woolworths** supermarket, in the shopping center on Robinson St., has cheap groceries. (☎08 9941 2477. Open M-W and F-Sa 8am-8pm, Th 8am-9pm, Su 8am-6pm.)

🔲 📷 **SIGHTS AND ACTIVITIES.** 📷**The Blowholes** are natural, wave-driven water jets that spurt 30m high as water slams against the rocky shore. Attacking the porous coastline, they're a wondrous sight that shouldn't be missed. Time your visit so you arrive between tides for the largest jets. A lovely beach is located just 1km south. (Take the North West Coastal Hwy. 24km north of North River Rd. and turn left onto Blowholes Rd.; follow it for 49km to the blowholes. The road is sealed to the blowholes, but not beyond.)

**Stockman Safaris** visits the area's fruit plantations, prawn factory, boat harbor, salt mine, blowholes, and jetty, as well as the OTC—an out-of-use NASA communications center located on the town's outskirts. (☎08 9941 1146. Town tour $50, children $25. All trips include lunch.) Carnarvon is also a popular base for trips to **Mount Augustus,** the largest rock in all of Australia, which is twice the size of **Uluru** (p. 311), with a summit at 1105m. The trip is 430km from Carnarvon via Gascoyne Jct. on an unsealed road; check road conditions at the visitors center before leaving, or consider going to the area with a tour group. **Outback Coast Safaris** operates two-day all-inclusive trips to both Mt. Augustus and the Kennedy Ranges. (☎08 9941 3448; www.outbackcoastsafaris.com.au. 2-day Mt. Augustus trip leaves Apr.-Oct. every Su 7am, returns M 5pm. $280; other months, min. 4 travelers required).

# EXMOUTH ☎08

For anyone who has come to Australia in hopes of seeing an emu in the wild, a majestic whale shark, or the massive manta ray, Exmouth (pop. 3500) is your prime destination. This small town is the scuba diving epicenter of the west coast, nestled comfortably between two national parks—the famed Ningaloo Reef Marine Park and its terrestrial counterpart, the Cape Range National Park. The main township area is inland and is not much to look at, conveniently leaving you with the real attractions: diving and fishing around the Cape.

**TRANSPORTATION.** Getting out of Exmouth to points north (like Broome) or south (like Perth) on Greyhound Australia **buses** (☎13 20 30) requires making a connection at the Minilya roadhouse. After the connection, the trip to either city takes about 18hr. (to **Broome** $295; to **Perth** $238). Both services make intervening stops at towns along the way. Red Earth Safaris also offers a "Perth Express" service ($160), which departs at 7am on Sunday and arrives in Perth at 1:30pm on Monday. It only takes 18 passengers, so book ahead. Allen's, at the Autopro on Nimitz St., provides **car rentals.** (☎08 9949 2403. 1 day from $60, 2-6 days from $55 per day, 7+ from $50 per day. 2WD only. Rentals allow 130km per day and charge $0.33 per km after. Credit card and license required.) Tours & Travel Ningaloo, south of town on the corner of Pellew St. and Murat Rd., rents scooters ($20 per hr, $53 per day, $27 per day for a 1-week rental) and 4WD vehicles (from $125 per day; 25+; 100km per day, $0.25 per km after) through Avis (☎08 9949 4748). **Bikes** can be rented from Exmouth Mini Golf on Murat Rd. (☎08 9949 4644. $4 per 4hr., $20 per day. Open 9am-late.)

**ORIENTATION AND PRACTICAL INFORMATION.** Most action takes place around **Maidstone Crescent,** where the shopping center is located. The **Exmouth Visitors Centre,** on Murat Rd., has info on Cape Range National Park as well as helpful sheets that summarize available accommodations, tours, and transportation services. (☎08 9949 1176; www.exmouthwa.com.au. Open daily 9am-5pm, holidays 9am-1pm.) The shopping center just off Maidstone has a **pharmacy.** (Open M-F 9am-5:30pm, Sa 9am-1pm.) Two blocks west, on Lyon St., is a **hospital,** the only medical facility until Carnarvon. (☎08 9949 3666. Dive medicals $100-$170; call ahead.) Westpac, on Learmonth St. next to the shopping center, has an **ATM. Internet access** is available at most hotels and many dive centers as well (including all that are mentioned here); expect to pay $4-6 per hr. Across the street is the **police station** (☎08 9949 2444) and the **post office.** (Open M-F 9am-5pm.) **Postal Code:** 6707.

**ACCOMMODATIONS.** Most of the backpacker joints in Exmouth are part of sprawling tourist villages that also contain campsites, cabins, various amenities, and sometimes hotel rooms. Few dorms provide blankets, so come prepared during the winter months. There are many **campsites ❶** within Cape Range National Park as well ($6.50; $9 vehicle entry fee), and rangers patrol the area. Keep in mind that shade is a precious commodity that most campers do without. Fires are prohibited, and there is no drinkable water in the park. **Excape Backpackers ❷,** within the Potshot Resort on Murat Rd., is a 5min. walk from the town center. This social hostel boasts the best location, as well as two lively pubs, ensuite dorms, and a pool. Head here if you get into town late: reception is open until 9pm daily. (☎08 9949 1200. Internet access $4 per hr. Key deposit $20. Dorms $25, with YHA/VIP $22; doubles $59. MC/V.) **Exmouth Cape Tourist Village ❷,** on the right as you enter town, offers the newest and most picturesque setting for backpackers; their refurbished **Blue Reef Backpackers ❷** is a wonderland of palm trees, outdoor tables, and brand-new amenities. With a refundable deposit, you can rent kitchenwares. A free bus service runs to Bundegi Beach from the tourist village. (☎08 9949 1101 or 1800 621 101. Sites for 2 Nov.-Mar. $20, Apr.-Oct. $25; powered $23/33. Blue Reef: 4-bed dorms $25; twins/doubles $55. MC/V.) **Winstons Backpackers ❷,** part of the Ningaloo Caravan and Holiday Resort, is conveniently located right across from the visitors center on Murat Rd. Amenities include a pool, restaurant, Wi-Fi, luggage storage, and an on-site dive shop. (☎08 9949 2377; www.exmouthresort.com. Sites Nov.-Mar. $19, Apr.-June $22, July-Oct. $23; powered $22/26/28. Dorms $27, weekly $162; doubles $75/450. AmEx/MC/V.)

**FOOD AND NIGHTLIFE.** Exmouth offers an impressive selection of quality dining at reasonable prices. On Kennedy St., behind the shopping center, **Whaler's Restaurant ❸** serves delicious gourmet food in an upscale setting. They also offer small plates that let you savor the food while saving cash. (☎08 9949 2416. Lunch $10-$19; dinner from $19. Open daily.) Right next door, a treat for both your tastebuds and your health can be found on the tempting menu at **Ningaloo Health Foods ❶.** The vegetarian flatbread ($9.50) is especially good. (☎08 9949 1400. Open daily 8am-4:30pm. MC/V.) There is also an Italian restaurant, **Pinocchio's ❷,** in the Ningaloo Caravan & Holiday Resort. (☎08 9949 4905. Pizzas from $14.50, pasta from $14. Open T-Su 6-10pm). **Grace's Tavern ❷,** at 829 Murat Rd. across from the Exmouth Tourist Village, is a pleasant hangout with an outdoor area and excellent takeaway pizza. (☎08 9949 1000. Open M-Sa 10am-midnight, Su 4-10pm.) The shopping center off Maidstone has two supermarkets—an **IGA Express** (open daily 6:30am-7pm) and an **IGA** (open daily 7am-7pm). The **Potshot Resort,** on Murat Rd., includes an elegant main bar, the Bamboo Room, and the more crowded Vance's Bar. Friday is the big night here; beer flows until the wee hours. (☎08 9949 1200. Open M-Th 10am-midnight, F 10am-1:30am, Sa 9:30am-1:30am, Su 10am-10pm.)

## NINGALOO MARINE PARK

Most people come to Exmouth to see the impressive Ningaloo Reef, which begins south of Coral Bay and stretches over 250km around the Northwest Cape and back into Exmouth Gulf. The town is full of dive shops catering to all experience levels. The standard price for an introductory PADI course is $550. Arrange a medical check-up in advance, or pay $100 in cash at the local hospital. Shop around before choosing a dive shop; all have certified instructors and good equipment, but shops will differ in class size, quality of instruction, add-on bonuses, and personality. For veteran divers, there are many great dives in the area, including **Lighthouse Bay, Navy Pier** (one of the top 10 dive sites in the world), the **Muiron Islands,** and the **Hole-in-the-Wall.**

> **TIP**
>
> **SNORKEL FOR LESS.** If you plan on snorkeling on the Ningaloo, purchase a mask, snorkel, and flippers before you come. Rentals can add up, and purchasing even a basic set can cost you over $60.

**Ningaloo Reef Dreaming,** in the shopping center, offers the funkiest, most independent attitude in town, not to mention the best value. Their dive course is standard for price and duration ($550 for 4 days), but they have many perks. They are the only company licensed to include the Navy Pier (one of the top 10 dive sites in the world) in their PADI course. They also do three dives per day (standard is 2), and students get an hour of free Internet, plus 25% off food in the shop's cafe for the duration of their course. (☎08 9949 4777; www.ningaloodreaming.com. 3 Murion Island dives including equipment $185; 3 Ningaloo Reef dives including equipment $160; PADI $550.) **Village Dive,** in the shopping centre, currently boasts the newest dive boat in town, and PADI students don't need to lug their gear to and from the boat every day. Certified graduates can do a dive for half-price the day after they finish their course, and Tu and Th offer "3-dive specials." (☎08 9949 1116; www.ningaloowhalesharkndive.com.au; PADI $550; full-day 2-dive scuba trip $185; half-day 2-dive scuba trip $145). **Exmouth Dive Centre** has storefronts at both Winston's and Excape Backpackers. Their PADI runs $550 and lasts five days; graduates can get discounts on Reef and Murion Island dives. (☎08 9949 1201; www.exmouthdiving.com.au. 2

Murion Island dives including equipment $185, $150 for graduates; 2 Ningaloo Reef dives including equipment $145/115; PADI $550.)

One of the biggest draws of the Ningaloo Reef, whale shark snorkeling, is expensive (usually about $350) but offers a unique chance to swim with the world's largest fish. Whale sharks appear most frequently from April to July. A variety of companies schedule tours, but **Ningaloo Reef Dreaming** has an edge over the competition: they have a private spotter plane, so they don't have to "share" the sharks they locate with other tour groups. They also donate $10 from each tour booked toward whale-shark research.

The best surfing is found at Surfers Beach at Vlamingh Head, at the northern end of the cape. Surf lessons are available through **Surf Ningaloo,** starting at $60 for a 3hr. lesson. (☎04 2920 2523; www.yallingupsurfschool.com. Booking available through the Exmouth Visitors Centre.)

# CAPE RANGE NATIONAL PARK

West of Exmouth, the rugged limestone cliffs and long stretches of sandy white beach of Cape Range National Park provide a haven for bungarras, emus, and Stuart's desert peas. Although you can camp at various spots within the park itself, the lack of water and shade leads many people to base themselves in Exmouth and enter the park by day for snorkeling and swimming trips.

In general, water is a limited resource throughout the park, but bore water is available at Ned's and Mesa Campgrounds. Try to bring your own drinking water. The highlight of the park is its beautiful coastline, which grants access to the Ningaloo Reef Marine Park. Swimming and snorkeling are popular activities in the aquamarine waters along the tropical coast; though water-goers should beware the riptides caused by the coral reef, as these can make swimming very dangerous outside of the park's sheltered coves. For swimmers, nearly any beach off of Yardie Creek Rd. (including those above where the Cape Range officially begins) will grant access to the same view—clear green waters and sand dunes—and basic day recreation facilities (picnic tables, perhaps a toilet) or campsites. The most popular beaches for swimming and camping include **Mesa & Neds Camps, Sandy Bay,** and **Tulki Beach.** Because the reef stops most wave motion in the coves, surfing is generally better above the park on the coast; the appropriately named Surfer's Beach by Vlamingh Head Lighthouse is the considered the best. For snorkeling, **⚑Turquoise Bay** is the spot travelers will hear about most—and unfortunately, it most likely will be crowded during the high season. Beginners will be comfortable in the "bay snorkel area," and more seasoned ones will appreciate the "drift loop." Even if you do pull up to see 11 tour buses crammed into the parking lot, make sure to wade out and take your turn to see all manner of exciting marine fauna, including clown fish, dories, and the oh-so-impressively-named humahumanukanukaapuaa.

For the hydrophobic visitor, the park has a few short walking trails that reveal ocean views and the jagged sandstone characteristic of the area. Accessible from Yardie Creek Rd., the best of the walking trails is the **Mandu Mandu Gorge Walk** (3km, 2hr. round-trip), which treks along the gorge ridge to a nice lookout before descending. Further south, the shorter **Yardie Creek Walk** (1.5km, 1hr.) lets visitors explore a limestone ledge overlooking a creek.

To get to Cape Range from Exmouth, continue North on Murat St. until you see a left-hand turnoff for the park onto Yardie Creek Rd. This is the main (and only sealed) road within the park and will get you to all of the park's main attractions, as well as the visitors centre. Keep an eye out for kangaroos, echidnas, and perenties (large lizards) on the road, especially at night. Note that the speed limit in the park is only 80kph—this may feel slow. If you're coming from the South, **Shothole Canyon** and **Charles Knife Rd.** (both unsealed) enter the eastern section of the park before you reach Exmouth. It can be rough going; check (☎08 9949 1676) before heading into the park. Use of the unsealed roads in the park is discouraged except for drivers who are confident in their 4WD abilities and are prepared for potential damage to their cars. If you don't have a car, you can use the Cape's shuttle service, **Ningaloo Reef Bus,** which collects passengers from most accommodations in town and carries them to the park's main attractions. Not all tours run every day, so check for exact schedules (☎1800 999 941. $20 to Turquoise Bay, $30 to Yardie Creek; $70 for both with lunch at Ningaloo Reef Retreat. All prices includes park entry.) The solar- and wind-powered **Milyering Visitors Centre** is located 52km from Exmouth, on Yardie Creek Rd. and takes about 45min. to reach from the town center. It even has a dive shop where you can hire snorkel gear for $10 per person and a $50 deposit (☎08 9949 2808. Open daily 9am-3:45pm.)

# PILBARA REGION

The beauty of the Pilbara is rugged and dramatic. The land is harsh to unprepared travelers: hundreds of kilometers of arid bush separate the region's small industrial towns, and summer temperatures are searing. In the late winter and early spring, however, the heat becomes bearable and the landscape explodes into fields of pale yellow spinifex, red Stuart peas, and purple mulla-mulla flowers. The Pilbara has recently seen an increase in mining, resulting in some of the most lucrative seasonal work opportunities in Australia.

## KARRATHA                                                                   ☎08

Karratha (17,000), the closest thing to a city between Carnarvon and Broome, is a good supply station for anyone heading to Karijini National Park.

■ 7 **ORIENTATION AND PRACTICAL INFORMATION.** The town's spine is **Dampier Road,** which runs parallel to the North West Coastal Hwy.; to the north

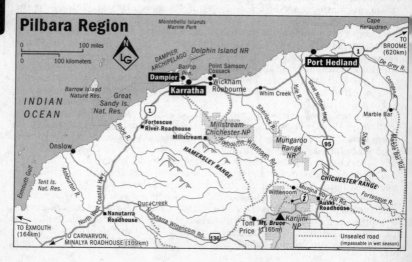

is Karratha's CBD. A good first stop is the **Tourist Bureau** on Karratha Rd. 1km before you enter town. (☎08 9144 4600. Open Nov.-Mar. M-F 9am-5pm, Sa 9am-noon; Apr.-Oct. M-F 8:30am-5pm, Sa-Su 9am-4pm.) Although Karratha is still a fairly bare-bones kind of place, nearly anything a traveler could want or need can be found in the town's sizeable shopping center (the **Centro,** as it is called) located below Welcome St. between Sharpe St. and Searipple Rd. (☎08 9185 4288. Open M-F 9am-5:30pm, Th 9am-9pm, Sa 8:30am-5pm, Su and holidays 10am-2pm). In addition to over 50 shops, the Centro holds several **ATMs,** a **pharmacy** (☎08 9185 7316; open M-F 9am-5:30pm, Th 9am-9pm, Sa 8:30am-5pm, Su 10am-2pm), and two supermarkets: **Woolworths** (☎08 9185 2322; open daily 7am-9pm) and **Coles** (☎08 9185 4633; open daily 6am-9pm). The **library,** in the TAFE campus, located west of the town center off Dampier Rd., has **Internet.** ($4 per 30min. Open M, W, F 8:30am-5pm; Tu and Th 8:30am-8:30pm; Sa 9am-noon.) The **police** (☎08 9144 2233) and fire station (☎08 9185 2580) are clustered between Balmoral and Searipple Rd. The **Nickol Bay Hospital** is located west of town center off of Dampier Rd. (☎08 9144 0330). The post office is adjacent to the Centro (Open M-F 9am-5pm). **Postal Code:** 6714.

**⛏ ACCOMMODATIONS.** Like many of the towns in the Pilbara region, Karratha is short on budget accommodation options: many backpackers choose to continue on to Port Hedland or to camp in the nearby national parks. **Karratha Backpackers ❷,** 110 Wellard Way, off Searipple Rd., has a great social atmosphere. While the cinderblock building is less than picturesque and the dorms lack lockers, the inside spaces are tidy and air-conditioned. The only bummer is the $1 hourly charge for A/C. There's free pickup and dropoff from the bus station, and Garth will take you on an entertaining 3hr. tour of the Dampier Archipelago for $25. Short-term housing is available for those working in the area. (☎08 9144 4904. Dorms $22; doubles $55.) **Pilbara Holiday Park ❷** has pleasant, shaded sites and the most inexpensive motel-style accommodations in town. To get there, take Dampier Rd. west out of the city and turn right on Rosemary Rd. (☎08 9185 1855 or 1800 451 855; www.aspenparks.com.au. Powered campsites for 2 $35; camper sites for 2 $42; ensuite campervan site for 2 $62; motel unit for 2 $190; studio unit for 2 $215; holiday unit for 2 $240. Extra adult $25 for cabins, $18 for sites, extra child $20/15; MC/V.)

**🍴 FOOD.** Karratha doesn't offer a particularly tantalizing or original array of options for dining out, but in a town like this, the old favorites are always safe. **Karratha Pizza Bar ❷,** on the corner of Balmoral Rd. and Morse Ct., is a bustling little pizza shop with hearty pizzas for delivery or takeaway for $10-20. (☎08 9185 2780. Open M and W-Su 5pm-late.) **Al's Burgers and Kebabs ❷,** across the street, fittingly sells burgers (from $6) and kebabs from $8. (☎08 9144 1419. Open M-Sa 11am-9pm. Cash only.) For a cold escape from the Pilbara sun, **Elephant Juice ❶,** in the Centro, offers gelato for $4 and fresh-squeezed juices and smoothies from $5. (☎08 9144 4914. Open M-W and F 9am-5:30pm, Th 9am-9pm, Sa 8:30am-5pm, Su 10am-2pm.) **Jamaica Blue ❶,** across from Elephant Juice in the centro, offers fresh sandwiches (from $6.40) and wraps from $8. (☎08 9185 4555. Open M-Sa 8am-5pm, Su 9am-2pm.) For something a little different, try the **Karratha Chinese Garden Restaurant ❷,** in the Centro. It's BYO and they have savory lunch specials from $12. (☎08 9185 2469; open M-Sa 11:30am-2pm and 5-10pm, Su 5-10pm. AmEx/D/MC/V.)

**🔅 DAYTRIPS FROM KARRATHA.** An easy daytrip from Karratha is **Point Samson,** with beaches on the peninsula off the east side of the Pilbara coast. A bus runs between Dampier, Karratha, and Point Samson several times a day on weekends. Point Samson is well-known for its fishing, and **Moby's Kitchen** ❷, at the end of Samson Rd. on Miller Ct., serves some of the northwest's best seafood. (☎08 9187 1435. Open daily 11am-8:30pm; holidays 11am-3pm and 5-8:30pm. MC/V.) Another nice way to beat the heat is to visit the freshwater **Miaree Pool,** about 25km west of the city along the North West Coastal Hwy. From the highway, make a left at the small sign. Spend the afternoon swimming, jumping off the rope swing, and cooking up sausages on the BBQ.

# KARIJINI NATIONAL PARK

Welcome to the ancestral home of the Banyjima, Yinhawangka, and Kurrama peoples. Aboriginal legend has it that the gorges of Karijini National Park were formed by giant serpents who snaked through the rocks and now reside in the park's glistening waters. For today's visitors, the park is a place marked by highs and lows. The sky-scraping heights of Mt. Bruce and Mt. Nameless are complemented by the plunging gorges of Joffre and Weano. The searing heat and bumpy, unsealed roads may try your patience, but the gorgeous combination of brick-red rock and cooling, sea-green water will compensate for any harm done by this rugged, natural wonderland in the heart of the Pilbara.

---

### KARIJINI NATIONAL PARK AT A GLANCE

**AREA:** 100,000 sq. km.

**FEATURES:** Various deep gorges (Dales, Joffre, Weano, Hamersley, Kalamina), high peaks (Mt. Bruce, Mt. Nameless), and vast expanses in between.

**HIGHLIGHTS:** Hiking the scenic gorges and swimming in the rock pools.

**GATEWAY:** Tom Price.

**CAMPING:** At Dales Gorge, $5 per adult and $2 per child; at Savannah Campground, $10/5 per child; max. $25 per family.

**FEES:** $10 vehicle entry fee.

---

 ## TRANSPORTATION

From Port Hedland, the 350km drive to the Karijini visitors center takes about 4hr. Karijini's northern entrances through Yampire Gorge and Wittenoom are closed, for good reason: both are contaminated by asbestos. The sealed **Karijini Drive** cuts across the park from the Great Northern Hwy. to Marandoo Rd., which leads to Tom Price. Most attractions are accessed by **Banjima Drive,** which meets Karijini Dr. at two points: 30km west of Great Northern Hwy. (the Park Entrance East) and 5km east of Marandoo Rd. (the Park Entrance West). Banjima Dr. is unsealed and at times corrugated, but a 2WD should be able to navigate it with care during the dry season. A 4WD is safer. Check road conditions before heading to the park by calling the **visitors center** (☎08 9189 8121).

**Car Rental:** At Paraburdoo Airport, about 80km outside of Tom Price. Try **Thrifty** (☎08 9189 6512), **Budget** (☎08 9189 5414), **Avis** (☎08 9189 5225), or **Hertz** (☎08 9189 6910). You may pay upward of $65 per day, and potentially twice that.

---

**TIP** **THE SHORT AND THE LONG OF IT.** When driving, keep in mind that your maximum speed should be much lower on an unsealed road than on a sealed one. As a result, travel times over deceptively short distances may be longer than expected.

## PRACTICAL INFORMATION

Karijini is a big place with limited infrastructure, so come prepared. **Untreated water** is available in the park at the fork between Dales Gorge area and the new visitors centre as well as on Banjima Dr. near the turnoff for Weano Gorge and the Eco Retreat, but it's best to bring plenty with you. **Petrol** and **supplies** are available in Tom Price, about 50km west of the Park Entrance West, and at the Auski Roadhouse to the northeast.

Karijini NP

**Tourist Offices: Tom Price Tourist Bureau** (☎08 9188 1112). Maps, road conditions, and weather forecasts. Internet $3 for 15min., $5 per 30min. Open Apr.-Sept. M-F 8:30am-5:30pm, Sa-Su 9am-noon; Oct.-Mar. M-F 9:30am-3:30pm, Sa 9am-noon. **Karijini visitors center** (☎08 9189 8121), on the sealed part of Banjima Dr, is an impressive structure with exhibits on local flora and fauna, geology, and history, as well as trail maps for the few marked trails in the park. Public phone, ice, and hot showers ($2). Also sells various park passes—helpful if you plan on visiting multiple parks during your time in Western Oz. Open daily Nov.-Apr. 10am-2pm; May-Oct. 9am-4pm.

**Tours: Lestok Tours** (☎08 9188 2032; www.lestoktours.com.au), out of Tom Price. Runs daytrips to the major gorges and provides lunch. $130, $120 with 3-day advance booking; under 15 $65. **Pilbara Gorge Tours** (☎08 9188 1534; www.pilbaragorgetours.com.au). A similar trip with a focus on ecotourism—and a smashing cup of morning tea. Full tour adults $120, ages 6-14 $60, under 6 free; part tour $90/45/free.

**Road Conditions: Main Roads** (☎138 138; www.mainroads.wa.gov.au). Available 24hr.

**Ranger Stations: CALM ranger station** (☎08 9189 8147 or 9189 8157). Or just ask attendants at park entrances and campsites.

**Library:** Adjacent to the Tom Price Tourist Bureau. Internet $3 per 30min. Open M-Tu and F 10am-1pm and 2pm-5pm, Th 10am-1pm and 3:30-6:30pm, Sa 9am-noon.

**Emergency: CALM ranger station** (after-hours emergency ☎08 9189 8101/8102/8103). There is also an **emergency radio** in the Weano Gorge day-use area.

**Police and Fire:** ☎000, or access them in person in Tom Price on Central Rd. across from the Tom Price Hotel/Motel right as you enter town.

**Medical Services:** The **hospital** (☎08 9159 5222) is a left turn off Mine Rd.

**Internet Access: Nameless Coffee House & Internet** (☎08 9188 1768), in Tom Price. $3 per 15min. Open Tu-F 9am-3pm.

**Post Office:** In the Stadium St. shopping complex behind Coles. Open M-F 9am-5pm. **Postal Code:** 6751.

## ACCOMMODATIONS AND CAMPING

**Karijini Eco Retreat** (☎08 9425 5591; www.karijniecoretreat.com.au), on and around the former Savannah Campground. This little village is tidy, new, and eco-friendly. All guests have access to flushing toilets, eco-showers, outdoor BBQ, and the lodge restaurant. Joffre Gorge is just a convenient walk away from the grounds. Tent sites for 2 $25.

Mar.-Oct. standard cabins ("Eco Tents") $175, deluxe $270; Nov.-Apr. standard cabins $97/149. 10% discount with online booking. AmEx/MC/V. Camp ❸/Lodge ❺

**Tom Price Tourist Park** (☎08 9189 1515; tompricetouristpark@westnet.com.au), 3km outside of Tom Price. Comfortable quarters with showers, laundry, camp kitchen, and playground. Small, blissfully cool pool. Spacious dorms with mini-fridge and A/C. Guests can pet the kangaroos who come to graze at dusk and feed wild corellas (native cockatoos) by hand. Tent sites $11 per person; caravan sites $25, powered $30. 4-bed dorms $29; budget doubles $79; cabins for 2 $107; 2-story chalets $133. AmEx/MC/V. ❶

**Dales Gorge campsite.** Among the only accommodations in the park itself. Comes with gas BBQs, pit toilets, and power. $6.50 per person, children $2. Cash only. ❶

## █ FOOD

There's a large **Coles** in Tom Price on Central Rd. (Open M-W and F-Sa 8am-6pm, Th 8am-9pm, Su 10am-6pm.) The following eateries are all in Tom Price.

**Bistro/Uncle Tom's Cabin** (☎08 9189 1101), attached to the Tom Price Hotel/Motel, just next to Coles on Central Rd. 2 restaurants with matching menus. Pizzas ($10-24) may be the best deal. For something different, the Aussie Pizza is topped with bacon, onion, and egg, drizzled in barbecue sauce ($16). Uncle Tom's also has a bar. Kitchen open daily noon-1:30pm and 6-8:30pm. Pizza served 6-9pm. ❷

**Nameless Coffee House & Internet Cafe** (☎08 9188 1768). Best coffee around (from $3.50) along with coffeehouse-staple pastries. Nachos and focaccia seem to be house specialties. Tuna melt ($8.50) with avocado and sun-dried tomato is a winner. Entrees $5-13. Milkshakes from $3. Internet $3 per 15min. Open Tu-F 9am-3pm. ❶

**Moon Palace Chinese Restaurant** (☎08 9189 1331). A change of pace from the standard fare of the Outback. Open M-Th and Su 5-9pm, F-Sa 5-10pm.

## ▣ HIKING

Before you set out, internalize this mantra: in order to enjoy any gorge, you must finish by climbing out of it. Keep this in mind and make peace with it.

**KEEP YOUR COOL.** Since a summer day in Karijini may be hot enough to steam through even the thickest cooler insulation, freeze bottles of water overnight and use them as icepacks when you set out to explore. They'll keep your lunch cool, and you'll have cold water to drink when they melt.

**▨DALES GORGE.** Particularly from the Park Entrance East (off Great Northern Hwy.), **Dales Gorge** is the most accessible and user-friendly of Karijini's gorges. Those following in Dale's footsteps can get there via sealed roads, and there's even a campsite nearby. A 30min. walk and a steep descent will lead you to the Circular Pool, a cool, green, lagoony relief for the sweaty, dust-weary traveler. While you're there, also check out **Fortescue Falls** (800m; 30min. round-trip), a spring-fed watercourse that runs year-round and cascades into a deep turquoise pool. From there, the **Fern Pool**, hidden down an unmarked track through the trees, is considered the best swimming hole in the park. If you don't have the time or energy to descend into Dales Gorge itself, backpack the **Rim Trail**, following it past some gorgeous views.

**KALAMINA FALLS.** This little gorge, 25km west of the visitors center, is a good introduction to the park. The formula is simple: well-marked stairs plus a 2min. descent equals the foot-soaking, sightseeing delights of the gorge bottom. A walk through the lush valley of the gorge (3km, 2hr. round-trip) leads past a small waterfall and along a creek to Rock Arch Pool, which sits beneath a natural archway. The sure-footed traveler can climb up the gorge wall through a doorway aided by a tree that clings miraculously to the rock. If you don't have time to do the walk, bring a sandwich and a bathing suit to have a leisurely lunch on the broad rocks overlooking the pool and waterfalls.

**JOFFRE GORGE.** Head to Joffre by car via Banjima Dr. or by foot from the Eco Retreat. Joffre's waterfall is the tallest in the park, and, though the flow is often fairly weak, its downward cascade is endlessly picturesque. The walk (2km, 2hr. round-trip) down to the pool at the base of the falls is a steep descent and may require you to climb along the rock walls for the last stretch. This trail is one of the trickier options that is still doable for casual climbers. Be sure to wear sturdy shoes or bring a buff Aussie to carry you when you're tired.

**WEANO GORGE.** This gorge is the deepest in the park, plunging into shadowy depths reached by the sweltering Australian sun only at high noon. The **Oxers Lookout** and **Junction Pool** overlook the area where Weano, Joffre, Red, and Hancock gorges meet; the scope of the view is truly jaw-dropping. A walk (1.5km, 2hr. round-trip) runs to the base of Hancock, while a longer, more difficult trail takes you to **Kermit's Pool,** another great swimming hole. This spot is so dwarfed by its towering rock walls that the pool almost feels enclosed from above.

**MOUNT BRUCE.** The turnoff to Mt. Bruce, the second tallest peak in Western Australia, is 3km east of the western entrance to the park. The walk (9km, 5hr. round-trip) to the summit (1235m) should be started in the morning, but there are several excellent vantage points along the way if you don't have the time or energy for the full ascent. That said, the views from the top are breathtaking.

**HAMERSLEY GORGE.** By far the most isolated gorge in the park, Hamersley offers an interesting bit of variety from its gorge brothers and sisters. It's worth seeing if you can handle the very long, very unsealed approach (55km on unsealed roads, plus another 50km from Tom Price). Hamersley is probably best experienced as a full-day (or at least full-morning) trip, given its distance from everything else. The descent and ascent are relatively short and painless, and the rock formations and their wave-like, color-banded patterns can be downright psychedelic. A series of waterfalls creates rock "spa pools" that are lovely to relax in, but watch out for the slippery surfaces and bot-

## GIVING BACK

### HELPING TURTLES SURMOUNT HURDLES

One of the best reasons to visit Port Hedland might be to play turtle nursemaid and protector for a few weeks in the summer. Every year from November to February, the beaches of Port Hedland become thriving turtle nurseries, as flatback sea turtles return to their native nesting sites to lay and bury clutches of eggs in the sand. Australia is thought to be the only country in which this species of turtle nests. In a given year, the turtles may lay up to 160,000 eggs; even so, it's estimated that only 1 in 10,000 hatchlings will survive to adulthood if they come from a beach in a developed area like Port Hedland.

**Care for Hedland** (☎04 3994 1431) accepts volunteers to help monitor and track turtle activity on Port Hedland's beaches and has no minimum stay requirement for people who want to get involved. The main responsibility of a volunteer is to get up at 6:30am each morning and look for new egg-laying evidence, generally indicated by tracks left at the previous night's high tide line. It's advisable to get in touch as early as October to secure a spot and organize details. Regardless, anyone passing through Port Hedland for even two days in the summer can probably help out if they call ahead, and onlookers are welcome at any time to accompany the volunteers as they make their morning treks.

toms. You can swim a fair ways along the gorge bottom to see more rocks and waterfalls farther along. Because of the gorge's location, be sure to check the weather before leaving to avoid getting caught on unsealed roads in the rain.

# PORT HEDLAND                                    ☎08

Port Hedland is a tough place—and we mean that both literally and figuratively. In this baking-hot, windblown industrial port, most of the hardy residents are somehow linked to the Pilbara's booming mining industry. But while iron ore might be easy to unearth here, digging up a good deal is another matter. Trying to stay even one night in this town may well break the bank, since budget accommodations and food are difficult—sometimes well-nigh impossible—to find. Unfortunately for your wallet, Port Hedland is often a necessary stopping point for travelers heading to or from **Broome** (one of Australia's most renowned beach oases; p. 754), over 600km north. But don't ignore the shores near Port Hedland; some early mornings, you might be lucky enough to see its famous baby sea turtles scuttling down the beach toward the sea.

> **⊓TIP** **CALL AHEAD.** Once you enter the interior of Western Australia, you may find yourself utterly cut off from communication for long stretches at a time. Cell-phone service is basically nonexistent, and pay phones are few, far between, and often unusable. As such, it's best to book accommodations ahead of time; even if you arrive and there is a number to call for after-hours arrival, you may not have any way to dial.

 **TRANSPORTATION AND PRACTICAL INFORMATION.** From Port Hedland, the Great Northern Hwy. winds 621km along the coast to Broome. Roadhouses can be up to 300km apart, so fuel up whenever you get the chance. Although humans are scarce, kangaroos, cows, sheep, and wild camels populate the scrubland, so take your time. There is also a **local bus service** (☎08 9172 1394) that runs between Port Hedland and its neighbor, South Hedland ($3), as well as within each town ($2). Service stops at night and on Sundays; full timetables are available at the visitors center, which is also the dropoff point for any travelers arriving via the **Greyhound Bus** (service from Broome: 1 per day, 8hr., $97). If you prefer your transportation a little closer to the ground, call a cab from **Car Lindy** (☎08 9140 1313) or **Hedland Taxis** (☎08 9172 1010).

At the western edge of the peninsula, the town's main drag is Wedge St., with the usual must-haves, including the endlessly helpful **Port Hedland Visitor Centre.** It generously helps backpackers find the cheapest accommodations available upon their arrival. (☎08 9173 1711. Internet $2 for 1st 5min., $0.50 for each 5min. thereafter. Open Nov.-Apr. M-F 9am-4pm, Sa 10am-2pm; May-Oct. M-F 8:30am-4:30pm, Sa-Su 10am-2pm.) The street also has about half a dozen **24hr. ATMs** and a **convenience store.** (☎08 9173 3098. Open 24hr.) On a more serious note, Port Hedland also has **police** (☎08 9173 1444) and medical services. The **hospital,** on the corner of Howe and Kingsmill St., is a bit out of the way (☎08 9158 1666; open M-F 8am-3pm). After hours, call or go to the Accidents and Emergency entrance on Sutherland St. just above the main entrance. The **Port Hedland Seafarer's Centre,** at the corner of Wedge St. and the Esplanade, has the cheapest **Internet** in town. (☎08 9173 1315. $6 per hr. Open daily noon-10pm.) The **post office** (open M-F 9am-5pm) is also on Wedge St. **Postal Code:** 6721.

**WESTERN AUSTRALIA**

**◪◪ ACCOMMODATIONS AND CAMPING.** Since mining companies have bought out many of the former digs for their workers, budget accommodations in Port Hedland are rather scarce. The only budget option still available to casual travelers is the **Cooke Pointe Holiday Park ❸**, at the corner of Athol and Taylor St., about 5km east of town. The park (more of a little neighborhood of caravans and holiday units) has a pool, kitchen (for dorm residents), BBQ area (for campers), and beach access. The air-conditioned rec room has Internet ($2 per 15min.) and a TV. (☎08 9173 1271; www.aspenparks.com.au. Office open M-F 7:30am-6:30pm, Sa-Su 7:30am-5pm. Tent sites for 2 $35; RV sites for 1-2 $35. Extra adult $10, extra child $5. Bunkhouse singles $50; doubles $75-150, with kitchen $170.) If Cooke Point is booked, consider pressing on out of Port Hedland to the **Port Hedland Caravan Park ❶**, about 13km north of the town center on the Great Northern Hwy. opposite the airport. Amenities include a BBQ area, a pool, laundry, a supermarket, and a restaurant. (☎08 9172 2525. Reception open M-Th 7:30am-7pm, F 7:30am-6pm, Sa-Su 9am-5pm. $11 per person without electricity; powered tent sites for 2 $28. Doubles $90-200.)

**UNDER THE SMALL TOP.** Particularly during cyclone season (Nov.-Apr.), think twice before trying to save money by camping. The combination of blazing heat and constant, strong winds make pitching a tent a tricky, sticky ordeal—one whose only reward is a non-climate-controlled, non-shaded sack in which to sweat the night away.

**◪ FOOD.** The best budget option for food is probably just saving your cash and cooking for yourself. The shopping center at the south edge of town, on the corner of Wilson St. and McGregor St., has a **Woolworths.** (Open M-W and F 8am-7pm, Th 8am-9pm, Sa-Su 8am-5pm.) Otherwise, local favorite **Bruno's Pizza Bar ❷**, formerly located on Richardson St., was blown away in a cyclone in 2007, forcing the restaurant to relocate to a small metal shed on nearby Keesing St., next to the rec club. The pizza still gets good reviews despite the less-than-spectacular location overlooking some overgrown tennis courts. (☎08 9173 1440. Pizzas start at $10. Open daily 5:30pm-anywhere between 9pm and midnight, depending on the club's hours.) The **Hedland Harbour Cafe ❶**, on Wedge St., opens super early and serves standard sandwiches, burgers, coffees, and the like. The fruit salad (small $3.50, large $6.50) is delightfully fresh. (☎08 9173 2630. Open M-F 5am-4pm, Sa 6am-4pm, Su 7am-4pm.)

# THE KIMBERLEY

Known as one of the world's last great frontiers, the Kimberley is dominated by expansive natural preserves and enormous swaths of land with no signs of human development besides the occasional road. The first European visitors to the region thought they had discovered Australia's great freshwater source, a floodplain of seemingly endless waters; what they didn't realize was that they were only witnessing half the story. They had arrived during the Wet (Nov.-Mar.), the region's sticky summer, when monsoonal rains wash out roads and turn the region into a muddy mess. These frontiersmen must have thought they had misread their own directions when they returned during the Dry (Apr.-Oct.) to find a parched, dusty landscape extending in all directions. During the winter months, the lack of rain transforms the region into the arid scrubland now most commonly associated with the Australian Outback.

WESTERN AUSTRALIA

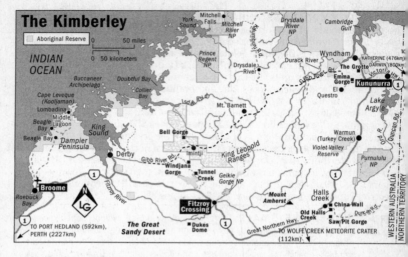

Today, the Kimberley is traversed west to east by two major roads: the Great Northern Highway and the highly enticing—but highly impractical—Gibb River Road. The latter offers few service stations and amenities but is the best way to truly experience the region; numerous turnoff paths can carry you to beautiful, remote gorges, waterfalls, and other natural wonders.

Tourists generally flock to the Kimberley during the Dry, when its dirt roads are more passable, and the perpetually hot air loses its suffocating humidity. However, the area's many pristine beaches remain appealing year-round, so the thrifty, adventurous tourist in search of surf and sand should take advantage of lower-priced accommodations throughout the Wet.

# BROOME
☎08

Operating as a gateway to the Kimberley, the shire of Broome (pop. 15,000) is a frontier town disguised as a beach resort. During the Dry, the population can double as tourists flood the town's clean, manicured streets to frequent comfortable restaurants, Aboriginal art galleries, and spiffy resorts. Historically, the town owes its foundation to the pearl industry, which arrived in the 1880s and today manifests itself in the form of jewelry shops and pearl-related tourist attractions. However, the town's greatest lure is its proximity to immense beaches of unspoiled white sand. Broome's numerous travel agencies offer seemingly unlimited literature about wilderness adventure tours by land, air, and sea. The dusty 4WD vehicles that you see around town tell a story that the convenience of modern shops and amenities may well veil—it's hundreds of kilometers from here to the next settlement.

## ▐ TRANSPORTATION

**Airport: Broome International Airport** (☎08 9193 5455). A 10min. walk from downtown. Follow the signs from Coghlan St. in the city center to McPherson St. **Qantas** (☎08 9193 6022) flies to Melbourne (4hr.), Sydney (4hr.), and Perth (2½hr.); **Virgin Blue** (☎13 67 89) flies to Adelaide (3½hr.); **Skywest** (☎1300 660 088) has flights

**Broome**

🏠 **ACCOMMODATIONS**
Beaches of Broome, **12**
Broome's Last
    Resort, **1**
Broome Motel, **2**
Cable Beach
    Backpackers, **8**
Tarangau Caravan
    Park, **5**

🍴 **FOOD**
Matso's Brewery, **18**
Shady Lane Cafe, **14**
Old Zoo Cafe, **9**

⭐ **NIGHTLIFE**
Divers Tavern, **10**
Murphy's, **4**
Roebuck Bay Hotel, **17**

WESTERN AUSTRALIA

to Darwin (2hr.) with connections to other cities. Number of flights depends on season. Hostels run free shuttles to the airport based on demand and availability.

**Intercity Buses: Greyhound Australia** (☎13 14 99). Service to Perth (32hr., daily 8am) and Darwin (27hr., daily 7:30pm), via Kununurra (14hr.). Tickets are sold through local travel agencies—look for a sticker on the window or on the wall. The Pearl Diver Pass ($487) allows you to go all the way down to Perth, getting off at as many towns along the way as you like. The 7-day, 2000km pass ($247) is an option for getting to Darwin. Buses leave from the tourist office, but the pickup point can change.

**Public Transportation: Town Bus** (☎08 9193 6585; www.broomebus.com.au; 7:10am–6:05pm; service every hr.) connects Chinatown, Cable Beach, and several hotels. 1st bus of the day departs town at 7:10am and reaches Gantheaume Pt. with no round-trip service (walk back approx. 5km). During the Dry, the last bus leaves Cable Beach at

6:12pm and service is every 30min. from 8:40am to 4:40pm. $3.50, ages 6-16 and concessions $1.30, under 6 free. All-day pass $10.

**Taxis: Broome Taxis** (☎08 9192 1133); **Roebuck Taxis** (☎1800 880 330); **Chinatown Taxis** (☎1800 811 772); **Pearl Town Taxi** (☎1800 622 433). A trip from town center to Cable Beach runs approximately $15.

**Car Rental: Avis** (☎08 9193 5980), **Budget** (☎08 9193 5355 or 1800 649 800), **Europcar** (☎08 9193 7788), **Hertz** (☎08 9192 1428 or 1800 655 972), and **Thrifty** (☎08 9193 7712) all have offices at the airport carpark. **Broome Broome** (☎08 9192 2210 or 1800 676 725), corner of Hamersley and Napier St., offers 1-way rental options from $450. Broome Broome caters to backpackers with 3-door hatches for $63 per day (insurance included). **Britz** (☎08 9192 2647; www.britz.com), on Livingston St., has campervans starting at $95 per day plus a remote location flat fee of $450. All listed companies have 4WDs and will rent to drivers age 21-24 for an additional fee. Make sure to book ahead in high season (Apr.-Oct.).

## ◪ ORIENTATION

Broome occupies part of a kangaroo-shaped peninsula and is centered around two clusters of activity: one in the town and business center **(Chinatown)** and the other a few kilometers north around **Cable Beach.** From the east, the **Great Northern (Broome) Highway** runs into Chinatown, becoming Hamersley St. as it crosses Napier Terr. Most shops and restaurants in town cluster along **Carnarvon Street.** A block south of Napier Terr., Frederick St. heads west. To get to Cable Beach from Frederick, take a right on Cable Beach Rd. E., then a right onto Gubinge Rd. followed by a left on Cable Beach Rd. W., which runs along the beach to the carpark and snack bar area, a walk of about 45min. from the info center. A left on Gubinge Rd. will take you to the road to **Gantheaume Point.**

## ◪ PRACTICAL INFORMATION

**Tourist Office: Broome Visitor Center** (☎08 9192 2222; www.broomevisitorcenter.com. au), on Broome Hwy. at the corner of Short St. Offers souvenirs and maps for purchase, as well as massive numbers of pamphlets detailing tour options in town and the region at large. Open Oct.-Mar. M-F 9am-5pm, Sa-Su 9am-1pm; Apr.-Sept. M-F 8am-5pm, Sa-Su 9am-4pm, public holidays 9am-4pm.

**Budget Travel: Harvey World Travel** (☎08 9193 5599), Paspaley Shopping Centre in Chinatown. Serves as a broker for Greyhound, Qantas, and other carriers. Open M-F 8:30am-5pm, Sa 9am-noon. **Travelworld,** 9 Johnny Chi Ln. (☎08 9193 7233), off Carnarvon St., across from the movie theater. Open M-F 9am-5pm, Sa 9am-noon.

**Currency Exchange: ANZ Bank,** 16 Carnarvon St. (☎13 13 14). Open M-Th 9:30am-4pm, F 9:30am-5pm. **Commonwealth Bank** (☎08 9192 1103), on Hamersley and Barker St. Open M-Th 9:30am-4pm, F 9:30am-5pm. Each has an ATM. In Cable Beach, ATMs are in both Divers Tavern and the store next door (open daily 9am-6pm).

**Work Opportunities:** There is typically plenty of temporary food-service work in the Dry; check message boards at hostels for postings and requests, as well as the *Broome Advertiser,* which comes out on Th and can be bought at supermarkets in the various shopping centers. Broome also has several employment agencies. **Grunt Labour Services** (☎08 9192 8555; www.gruntlabour.com.au), on Weld St., is popular. Additionally, those looking specifically for work in the pearl industry can contact **Paspaley Pearling Support** (☎08 9192 1087) and **Clipper Pearls** (☎08 9193 6156).

**Police:** (☎08 9194 0200) on Frederick St. between Hamersley and Carnarvon St.

**Internet Access:** At many locations along Carnarvon St. Going rate hovers around $6 per hr. **Telecenter Network,** 40 Dampier Terr. (☎08 9193 7153), away from Pearl Luggers with the bay to your left. Offers Internet at $5 per hr. as well as fax, printing, CD burning, and copying services. Open Nov.-Apr. M-F 9am-5pm; May-Oct. M-F 9am-5pm, Sa 9am-1pm. **Galactica,** on Hamersley St. upstairs and behind the McDonald's offers Internet at $5 per hr. Open M-Tu and Su 8am-8pm, W-Th 8am-9pm, F-Sa 8am-midnight.

**Post Office:** (☎08 9192 1020) in Paspaley Shopping Centre on Carnarvon St. Poste Restante. Open M-F 9am-5pm. **Postal Code:** 6725.

# ACCOMMODATIONS AND CAMPING

During the Dry, book ahead for all accommodations. Cheaper rates are often available during the Wet. Most hostels have their own bars; alcohol purchased elsewhere is strictly prohibited. All hostels have a tropical resort feel, so choose based on whether you want to be close to Cable Beach—where camping is popular—or near the shops and nightlife of Chinatown.

**Cable Beach Backpackers,** 12 Sanctuary Rd. (☎08 9193 5511 or 1800 655 011; www.cablebeachbackpackers.com). Just 5min. from the shore. Isolated from town, but free shuttles to Chinatown and the airport. Intimate and lively, with friendly staff, pool, kitchen, bar (beer $5) with fabulous happy hour, laundry ($3), Internet access ($6 per hr.), billiards, and scooter rentals. Surfboard rental $20, bodyboard $8. Deposits: key $10; blanket, sheet, and pillow $10; plate set $10. Reception 7:30am-10pm. Check-out 9:30am. 7-bed dorms $20-25; 4-bed $22-28; singles $50; doubles $68. Book several days in advance. VIP discount. ❷

**Beaches of Broome,** 4 Sanctuary Rd. (☎1300 881 031; www.beachesofbroome.com.au). New, modern, and relaxing upscale backpackers' resort. 5min. from the beach. Pool and lounge area. Clean, high-ceilinged dorm rooms. A/C and continental breakfast. Facilities include a bar/eatery (beer $4-6.50, closes at 11pm), large communal kitchen, DVD room ($5 DVD rental), pool table ($2.20), laundry ($3 wash, $1 dry), scooter rental ($35 per day plus $10 insurance), boogie board rental ($5 per day), on-site ATM and Internet room ($6 per hr.; Wi-Fi $15 per day, $50 per week, $150 per month). Key and sheet deposit $20. Checkout 10am. Book any tours through front desk. 8-bed mixed dorm $30; 5-bed dorm $35; quad dorm $38; triple mixed dorm $45. ❸

**Broome's Last Resort,** 2 Bagot St. (☎08 9193 5000; www.broomeslastresort.com.au). Has the feel of a beach lodge with the conveniences of the town center. Fast Internet access ($6 per hr.), pool tables, an attractive pool with small cascades, and a popular bar that's open daily until 11pm. Breakfast is included. Key deposit $10. 3- and 4-bed dorms $28; 6- and 8-bed dorms $23-25. ❷

**Broome Motel,** 34 Frederick St. (☎08 9192 7775; www.broomemotel.com.au), near Robinson St. Just outside of Chinatown. Total convenience with none of the latenight ruckus. Spacious ensuite rooms with A/C. Free parking. Has a pool, BBQ, and laundry facilities. Wheelchair-accessible. Reception daily 7am-8pm. Motel $125, self-contained $165. Discounts during the Wet. MC/V. ❺

**Tarangau Caravan Park,** 16 Millington Rd. (☎08 9193 5084), on the corner of Millington Rd. and Lullfitz Dr. A quieter, cheaper alternative, but a 15-20min. walk from the beach. Unpowered sites $15 per person; powered for 2 $32, extra person $10. ❶

# FOOD

Food offerings in Chinatown are varied and enticing, though—ironically—mostly non-Chinese and often expensive.

**Shady Lane Cafe** (☎08 9192 2060), on Johnny Chi Ln. off Carnarvon St. Hidden away in a pedestrian alley, this cafe serves great flapjacks ($10, with ice cream $12), toasted focaccia ($13), and fresh juice blends ($5). Open daily 7am-2pm. ❷

**Old Zoo Cafe** (☎08 9193 6200), at the intersection of Sanctuary, Koolama, and Challenor Dr. 16 years after the zoo closed, this cafe serves samples of its former residents to guests. Features outdoor seating in a lush, tropical setting. Try the Kimberley Taste Plate, a "fushion of flavors" with pearl meat, barramundi, croc, kangaroo, and camel (for 2, $29). Main courses $27-33. Vegetarian menu substitutions on request. Open for breakfast daily 7am-noon, for lunch and dinner 1pm-9pm. ❺

**Matso's Broome Brewery** (☎08 9192 7751; www.matsosbroomebrewery), corner of Carnarvon St. and Hamersley. The shop-turned-cafe-turned-restaurant love-child of a Japanese-Aboriginal couple. Enjoy breakfast (eggs any style $8.50), lunch (grilled chicken skewers in homemade peanut sauce $16), or dinner (seared kangaroo with pumpkin salad $26) outside on the quiet patio or inside in the large, comfortable dining room and bar adjacent to the brewing room. Matso's biggest draws are its 9 beers on tap, all brewed on-site. Mains $24-56. Open daily 7am-late. Kitchen closes 9pm. ❷

**Zander's,** on Cable Beach Rd. W. (☎9193 5090; www.zanders.com.au), adjacent to pedestrian access to the beach. Prices are steep, but the location can't be beat. A snack stand sells ice cream ($3.50-4.60) and melts ($9.60), while the restaurant serves meals of the surf and/or turf variety ($21-37). Say hello to your friends back home on the webcam pointed at the beach (www.broomecam.com). Open daily 8am-9pm. ❶

## 🦪 🏊 BEACHES AND ACTIVITIES

🦪**CABLE BEACH.** The soft blues of the Indian Ocean lapping against the fine sand of Cable Beach makes for an inviting scene year-round. Swim between the flags, where a lifeguard protects bathers from the perils of the tropical deep, or meander along 22km of pristine beach and find a place to enjoy a day all by yourself—clothing optional past the rocks to the north, although 4WD vehicles are also given free reign here. **The Beach Hut,** located at the trailer by the swimming area, rents chairs and gear daily 8am-5pm (including surfboards $10-15 per hr). Another option is to pace the water's edge on the back of a camel. **Ships of the Desert** (☎08 9193 7912 or 04 1995 4311) offers morning (40min.; $45, ages 6-16 $30, under 6 $10), afternoon (30min.; $35/25/10), and sunset (1hr; $60/40/10) rides. **Broome Camel Safaris** (☎04 1991 6101; www.broomecamel-safaris.com.au, or book through the visitors center M-Sa), offers pre-sunset (30min.; $30, children 5-15 $20, under 5 $10) and sunset (1hr.; $55/40/10) tours and the opportunity to feed your carrier a carrot afterward for his good work.

**TOWN BEACH.** Town Beach is farther south than Cable Beach on the Roebuck Bay shore, at the end of Robinson St. Though you can't swim here, the mix of blue hues in the water is spectacular. For three days each month from March to October (check tourist bureau for exact dates), Broome's 10m tide is so low that the exposed mudflats stretch for kilometers, reflecting the light of the full moon in a staircase pattern. The city celebrates with the **Staircase to the Moon Market** at Town Beach, with local foods, arts and crafts for sale, and entertainers performing for crowds. At the lowest tides, the waters off the beach recede to uncover skeletons of sunken WWII boats.

**REPTILES AND DINOS.** Get up close and personal with some aggressive 5m saltwater crocodiles at **Malcolm Douglas Broome Crocodile Park,** started by the eponymous TV naturalist and icon. (200m from the beach access on Cable Beach Rd., next to Divers Tavern. ☎9192 1489. In the Dry: guided feeding tours M-F 11am and daily 3pm. Open M-F 10am-5pm, Sa-Su 2-5pm. In the Wet: call for times. Adults $25, students and concessions $22.50, children $20, families $65.) On the far west of Broome Peninsula, 5km from Cable Beach, **Gantheaume Point** serves as a home to a set of dinosaur footprints preserved in the rocks. These 120-million-year-old prints only surface during very low ocean tides. At high tide, you can watch the small, circular basin called **Anastasia's Pool** fill with the rising water. This site was carved into the rock by a former lighthouse keeper for his arthritic wife so that she could take a dip without walking to the bottom of the rocks. Take a left onto Gubinge Rd. from Cable Beach Rd. E., then a right onto the Gantheaume Point access road.

**PEARLS.** You can't come to Broome without encountering the pearl industry. Pearl shops line the streets of Chinatown, restaurants serve pearl meat, and tours run daily during the the Dry. To get your fill of pearl history, try a tour at **Pearl Luggers** (☎08 9192 2059; www.pearlluggers.com.au) on Dampier Terr. and get a free taste of pearl shell meat. The outfit also organizes other pearl-related events such as film nights, concerts, and appreciation evenings (daily tours 1hr., call for times. Adults $18.50, concessions $16.50, ages 10-18 $9). The **Willie Creek Pearl Farm** (☎08 9192 0000; www.williecreekpearls.com.au) offers the opportunity to see how pearls are produced with tours of their farm, 37km outside of Broome. (Coach tours 4hr., including hotel pickup/dropoff and transfer, farm tour, cruise, and refreshments $80, concessions $75, children 6-16 $40; self-driven tours 2hr., including farm tour, cruise, and refreshments $40/35/20. Note that 4WD vehicles are recommended for the drive to the farm.

## 🎵 🎎 ENTERTAINMENT AND FESTIVALS

For information on local events, pick up a copy of the weekly *Broome Happenings* (in hostels and the visitors center), or visit www.makecentsbroome.com.au to read an online guide detailing attractions and tips for making the most out of Broome. No visit is complete without catching a feature at the world's oldest operating outdoor movie theater. **Sun Pictures Outdoor Cinema,** on Carnarvon St., spun its first reel in 1916. (☎08 9192 1077. Shows nightly at 6:30 and 8:30pm. $15, concessions $11.50, children $10, families $42.) Broome racing (that's horses, not witches) comes alive on Saturdays from May to August, and is especially popular in July during the **Broome Cup**. (Buses depart Chinatown for track 12:15pm and 1:15pm, $4. Entrance $10+). The **Shinju Matsuri Pearl Festival** runs for 10

## THE LOCAL STORY

### LONG-DISTANCE LEARNING

While some modern schools teach courses online, the Kimberley School of the Air was born in 1960, long before the Internet, in order to provide isolated students with a public education.

One of five Schools of the Air within Western Australia, Kimberley teachers broadcast to their students each day from studios in the school headquarters building at Derby. Thirty-minute lessons each day bring together tiny classes of young students from small outposts of the Kimberley. Monday through Thursday broadcasts supplement the children's reading materials, while Fridays are music days.

Teachers of the school frequently express their satisfaction with the unorthodox system. The school provides 4WDs for their semi-regular trips to visit pupils and will even fly them out to the most remote stations, where isolated students eagerly await the day when they can show their teacher their homes.

In 2004, the school switched to a satellite system and now supplies its students with a computer, printer, and lesson materials. Meanwhile, alumni of the school consistently place among the upper levels of students on Australia's standardized tests and at Universities. It would seem that in Australia, parents may best serve their children by moving far away from the best school districts.

days in August or September. The **Mango Festival** (last weekend in Nov.) marks the harvest with a Mardi Gras celebration and mango tastings.

## NIGHTLIFE

For a such a small town, Broome makes an impressive attempt at nightlife. Per local tradition, the soirée venue changes nightly, probably because if each bar or club were equally attended, there wouldn't be much of a party anywhere. All bars take major credit cards. The **Roebuck Bay Hotel,** or "Roey," on Carnarvon St., has a de facto monopoly on nightlife options in Chinatown (☎08 9192 1221; www.roey.com.au). Each of its three bars offers different entertainment. The Sports Bar starts off the week, with karaoke night on Monday and a lyrics competition on Tuesday. The **Pearler's Lounge** takes over with live bands Wednesdays through Sundays. **Oasis Bar** stays open until 2am Thursdays, when they host a wet t-shirt competition ($5 cover for males), through Saturdays, when there's a $5 cover for everyone. Tuesdays and Fridays bring live music to **Murphy's,** an Irish bar in the Mercure Inn on Weld St. If you have ever dreamed of being a rock star, you can sign up to play a hit for the packed crowd—Tuesday is open mic night. Get there early to grab a place in line (☎08 9192 1002; open daily noon-midnight, Tu and F until 1am). **Divers Tavern,** on Cable Beach Rd., is the mainstay of the nightlife scene in the Cable Beach section of town. Saturdays are popular here after the races, which finish around 5pm, although bands often play until 8pm. (☎08 9193 6066. W jam night. Su live bands. Beers from $4.30. Open M-Sa 10am-midnight, Su 10am-10pm, later for sporting events.)

# FITZROY CROSSING ☎08

Sitting alongside the Fitzroy River, Fitzroy Crossing (pop. 1500) is an important mining and Aboriginal resettlement center. It's also an obvious stop for tourists along the Great Northern Hwy. and sits in the middle of prime cattle country. The town still celebrates the amazing pioneering feat of the MacDonald broth-

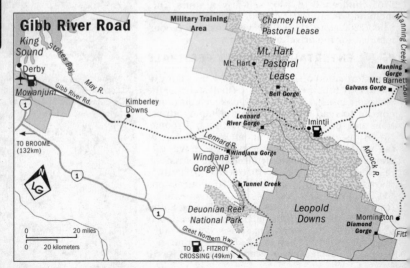

ers, 19th-century pastoralists who dragged their horses and cattle on a three-year, 3500 mi. journey from Goulburn, New South Wales.

**TRANSPORTATION.** The **Shell** station, across Forrest Rd. from the Tourist Office, offers gas and a **Coles Express** (☎08 9191 5005; open daily 6am-9pm).

**ORIENTATION AND PRACTICAL INFORMATION.** The **Tourist Office** (☎08 9191 5355; open M-F 8:30am-4:30pm, Sa 9am-1pm) is located just off the highway on Forrest Rd. **Fitzroy Crossing Hospital** (☎08 9166 1777) can be found just off Flynn Dr. on Fallon Rd. **Postal code:** 6765.

**ACCOMMODATIONS AND FOOD.** Those looking for a resort-like atmosphere can stay at the **Fitzroy River Lodge ❶**, across the river and slightly east of town. The Fitzroy provides a pool, tennis courts, and on-site lounges and restaurants for guests of the lodge and caravan park. (☎08 9191 5141; www. kimberleyhotels.com.au. Internet $6 per hr. Unpowered sites $11 per person, powered $27 for 2; lodge options $135-285 for 2 people, extra person $35.) Campers in the area can also set up at the **Tarunda Caravan Park ❶**, 1km down Forrest Rd. (☎08 9191 5330. Unpowered sites $11 per person, ages 8-12 $5; powered sites $25 for 2, $11 per extra person, ages 8-12 $5; self-contained units $130 per night for 2, extra person $30. Office open daily 7:30am-8:30pm.)

**SIGHTS AND ENTERTAINMENT.** Only 20km from Fitzroy Crossing, **Geikie Gorge National Park** is a photographer's dream come true. This chasm was once a limestone barrier reef, but the Fitzroy River has since bleached and split these massive rocks. The Tourist Office offers information about cruises on the Fitzroy River (June-Sept., 3-4 cruises per day, 8am-3pm; $25, concessions $20, under 16 $5; make bookings at the Park). Additionally, **Darngku Heritage Cruises** feature lessons about Aboriginal law and medicine. (2hr., $55; 3hr. including a walk, $70. Make bookings through the tourist office.) The **Fitzroy River Lodge** also offers 3hr. tours of the Gorge, including a cruise and visits to some of Fitzroy Crossing's oldest sites (☎08 9191 5141; 8am and 2pm; $60,

**WESTERN AUSTRALIA**

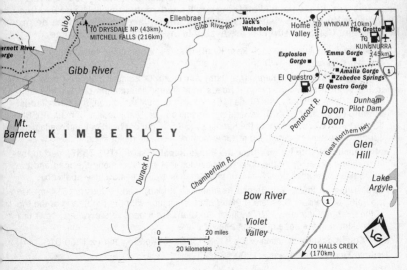

children $30). The lodge also offers an all-day group tour of **Windjana Gorge and Tunnel Creek** ($160, children $80; min. number of tourists necessary).

# GIBB RIVER ROAD

For anyone who has ever dreamed of trekking across one of the world's last frontiers, the Gibb River Road is a perfect opportunity to fulfill your fantasy—provided you have a 4WD vehicle. It's one of the wildest, roughest tracks left in Australia for the adventurous-at-heart to explore.

| GIBB RIVER ROAD AT A GLANCE | |
|---|---|
| **LENGTH:** 659km. | **GATEWAYS:** Derby and **Kununurra** (p. 763). |
| **FEATURES:** Windjana Gorge, Tunnel Creek NP, King Leopold Range. | **DURATION:** In good conditions, the road can take as few as 2 days to drive, but it takes 4-5 days to enjoy the primary gorges and the more remote turnoffs. |
| **HIGHLIGHTS:** Dips into pristine, massive gorges, unpopulated walks, and wicked cliff-jumping for the foolhardy. | |

## ORIENTATION AND PRACTICAL INFORMATION

The Gibb River Road begins 6km south of **Derby** off the Derby Hwy. and ends at the **Great Northern Highway,** halfway between **Wyndham** (48km from end) and **Kununurra** (45km from end). The most commonly visited gorges are concentrated anywhere from 120 to 220km east of Derby, as well as in the privately-run **El Questro,** 35-45km from the road's eastern end. Gorges along the 400km between the two regions are harder to get to; if you have limited time, you may want to drive straight through. Those with extra time might consider a detour on the **Kalumburu Road,** which intersects the Gibb 416km east of Derby and continues northward to **Drysdale National Park** and **Mitchell Falls.**

Services along the way are limited. Roadhouses and stations with accommodations may have groceries and supplies—and, occasionally, EFTPOS facilities—but you should pack everything you'll need, including cash. The Broome, Derby, and Kununurra visitors centres are good places to get advice before heading out. Camping supplies are available in Kununurra and Broome.

**Tours:** Many people do the Gibb River Road via small private group tours, which can be cheaper than renting a 4WD and going it alone.

**Guides:** Visitors centers in Kununurra, Derby, and Fitzroy Crossing sell the *Traveler's Guide to the Gibb River and Kalumburu Roads,* with limited information on distances and services along the roads. The Guide ($5) can also be purchased from the **Derby Tourist Bureau.** (☎08 9191 1426; www.derbytourism.com.au. Derby Tourist Bureau, P.O. Box 48, Derby WA 6728.) A map of the Kimberley ($8.50), put out by HEMA and available at visitors centers, is essential and includes summaries of all major sites.

**Auto Repairs: Neville Heron's Over the Range Repairs** (☎08 9191 7887), next to the Imintji store (222km), is the only repair service that operates along the road and the only place to get used tires. A callout tradesman is available—travel fee applicable.

**Petrol:** Diesel at Imintji, Mt. Barnett Roadhouse (306km), and El Questro (614km). On the Kalumburu Rd. at Drysdale (59km from the junction with the Gibb), and at the top of the road at Kalumburu (267km from the Gibb). It's expensive everywhere; don't risk not making it in the hope of saving a few dollars.

**Road Conditions:** Derby office (☎08 9158 4333). WA Road Report (☎1800 013 314).
**Medical Emergency Phone:** ☎1800 625 800.

# KUNUNURRA ☎08

Founded in 1960 and just a few kilometers east of the Ord river dam, heavily irrigated Kununurra (kuh-nah-NAR-ah; pop. 5500) is quite literally a modern oasis. The town stays lush and green even well into the Dry, and the surrounding farmland is notable for existing at all in the Kimberley's arid climate. Local farms attract young foreigners—who fulfill an Australian visa requirement by working for a few months at a time as regional laborers—in large numbers. In the Dry, tourists inundate the town, as Kununurra makes a logical base for exploration of **Purnululu National Park, Lake Argyle,** and the **Gibb River Rd.** Summitting any of the sandstone monoliths that ring the town to the north and east opens up vistas beyond the green lawns and fields of Kununurra to the rugged rocky landscape beyond, reminding you in dramatic fashion that you are, indeed, still in the Kimberley.

**TRANSPORTATION.** The **airport** is 5km down the Victoria Hwy. toward Wyndham. **Air North** (☎08 9168 2111, for reservations 1800 627 474) flies daily to Broome (from $248) and Darwin (from $248). **Buses** arrive and depart from the BP station and roadhouse on Messmate Way, just off the highway. **Greyhound Australia** (☎13 20 30) departs for Broome (13hr., daily 6:50pm, $236), Katherine (5hr., daily 10:15am, $129), and Darwin via Katherine (13hr., daily 10:15am, $208). Greyhound also offers discounts and package deals. There are several **car rental** companies in town: **Budget,** 947 Mango St. (☎08 9168 2033) and at the airport; **Avis** (☎08 9169 1258; for reservations, 13 63 33) at the airport; **Thrifty Territory Rent-a-Car,** 26 Bandicoot Dr. (☎08 9169 1911), and at the airport; **Europcar,** 24 Konkerberry Dr. (☎08 9168 3385) and at the airport; and **Hertz** (☎08 9169 1424), on Coolibah Dr. and at the airport. Three **taxi** companies operate: **Berts Taxi** (☎08 9168 2553), **Yellow Taxi** (☎08 9168 2356), and **Alex Taxi** (☎13 10 08).

**ORIENTATION AND PRACTICAL INFORMATION.** **Messmate Way** turns off the Victoria Hwy. at a petrol station and heads into town, where it crosses Konkerberry Dr. and ends at Coolibah Dr. The **Kununurra Visitor Centre** is on Coolibah Dr. near the windmill. (☎08 9168 1177. Open in the Dry M-F 8am-5pm, Sa-Su 8am-4pm; call for times in the Wet.) The **Commonwealth Bank**, on the corner of Coolibah Dr. and Cotton Tree Ave. near the tourism office, has a **24hr. ATM** (☎13 22 21; open M-Th 9:30am-4pm, F 9:30am-5pm), as does the **National Bank** on Ebony St. (☎13 22 65. Open M-Th 9:30am-4pm, F 9:30am-5pm.) **Police** are located at the corner of Coolibah Dr. and Banksia St. (24hr. ☎08 9166 4530.) **Internet access** is available at **Kimberly Croc Backpackers** (see below) for $5 per hr. **Telecentre,** in the same building as the visitors center, has Internet access for $6 per hr., as well as faxing, photocopying, and Wi-Fi. (☎08 9169 1868. Open M-F 9:30am-5pm.) The **post office** is across from the police station. (☎08 9168 1072. Open M-F 9am-5pm.) **Postal Code:** 6743.

**ACCOMMODATIONS AND FOOD.** All accommodations in town fill up quickly during the Dry, so book ahead. Backpacker accommodations are often full of seasonal laborers staying for months at a time and waking up early in the morning for work. **Kimberley Croc Backpackers,** 120 Konkerberry St., two blocks from the shopping center on Tristania St., has a pool, patio, lounge areas surrounded by pleasant tropical gardens, A/C, free sunset tour to **Kelly's Knob** (see below) nightly if requested, spacious kitchen, and laundry. It offers free pickup and dropoff as well as the option of booking tours of the area through reception. (☎08 9168 2702. Internet $5 per hr. Key deposit $10. 8-bed dorms $22-25, weekly $147; 4-bed $23-27; twins and doubles $55-99; family room $120-160.

YHA discounts.) **Kununurra Backpackers Adventure Centre ❷**, 24 Nutwood Cres., is a 10min. walk from the visitors center; follow Konkerberry Dr. away from the highway, then turn right on Nutwood. With an in-ground pool, large kitchen, small DVD-equipped theater, a pool table, an Internet room ($5 per hr.), and a modest waterfall, the Adventure Centre has great facilities and draws a young crowd. It also provides free pickup and dropoff for bus and plane journeys and can book tours at the front desk. (☎1800 641 998. Key deposit $20. 3-4 bed dorm $25, $142 per week; 8-10 bed dorm $22/132; twins and doubles $56. VIP $2 discount.) Food options are limited. The main pub is **Gulliver's Tavern ❷**, on Konkerberry Dr. at Cotton Tree Ave. The stars of its menu are the fisherman's basket (fried fish, prawns, and calamari served on top of chips; $14.50) and the $10.50 steak sandwich. (☎08 9168 1666. Open daily noon-10pm. MC/V.) Across from Croc Backpackers and next to the tavern is a **Tuckerbox IGA** supermarket. (☎08 9169 1270. Open M-Sa 6:30am-7:30pm, Su 7:30am-7:30pm.)

**◧ SIGHTS. Kelly's Knob** stands erect over the stunning terrain of Kununurra. Take Konkerberry Dr. to its end; turn left onto Ironwood, right onto Speargrass, and right again at the large stone tablet. ◪**Mirima (Hidden Valley) National Park,** 2km east of town, is a sandstone valley of undeniable aesthetic appeal. Despite its convenience just outside of town, accessibility—there are steps and railings abounding—and the outstanding panoramas afforded by its 350-million-year-old rock formations, the park is quite sparsely touristed. Reach Mirima by turning off the highway at Weaber Plain Rd., which runs up the eastern edge of Kununurra, then take a right on Barringtonia Ave. The **Derdebe-Gerring Banan Lookout Trail** (800m return) ascends a steep hill for a view of the Ord Valley and nearby sandstone ranges. The **Demboong Banan Gap Trail** (500m return) heads through a gap in the range and a small valley, and ends up at a lookout over Kununurra. Ranger-led walks meet at the carpark at the end of Hidden Valley Rd. and at the secluded retreat of Lily Pool in Hidden Valley. (☎08 9168 4200 or 9168 7300 for details). Female travelers should avoid Lily Pool, along with the area that extends away from it down Lily Creek; they are sacred men's places for the Miriwoong people. **Wild Adventure Tours** (☎08 0945 6643; www.gowild. com.au) offers travelers a more interactive and ecologically friendly take on the Kununurra area, with abseiling tours and lessons at local sites, including Kelly's Knob ($80) and the Grotto ($150). Take the edge off at the **Hoochery,** the oldest continuously operating distillery in Western Australia, where tours illustrate the fermentation, distillation, and maturation processes. Relax in their bar and enjoy tastings of bourbon, five different grades of rum, and the popular Cane Royal Liqueur, a chocolate/coffee affair. To reach the Hoochery, continue on Weaber Plains Rd. for about 10km. (☎08 9168 2467. Open M-F 9am-4pm, Sa 9am-noon during the Dry. Tours 11am and 2pm; $7.50, children free. Tastings $1 each.) Six kilometers west of town, a turnoff from Packsaddle Road brings visitors to the **Zebra Rock Gallery.** While geologists have yet to explain the terrestrial phenomenon that creates "zebra" rock—stone with black and white stripes unique to Oz—all can agree that it makes for beautiful pieces of art, on display at the gallery. Also on-site is a cafe (mango smoothies $5, sandwiches $4), an expansive lawn conducive to picnicking, and a pond full of catfish. If you're feeling lonely, have a chat with one of the numerous multilingual birds on-site. Fourteen kilometers west of town and 5km down a quality dirt road (in the Dry only), **Valentine Springs** is a tranquil swimming hole.

# LAKE ARGYLE

Australia's largest manmade lake was created in 1971 with the completion of the Ord River Irrigation Project. Unfortunately, numerous sacred sights of the Miriwoong people were relegated to its murky depths in the process. **Lake Argyle's** cruises now allow tourists to feel like riders on a yellow ducky in one of mankind's truly spectacular tubs. As the Argyle station was flooded and the gorges filled, canyon walls became etched sandstone slides into the bathwater, and former escarpment peaks decorate the upper rim. Even local wildlife has adapted enthusiastically to the sudden appearance of freshwater in the unforgiving Kimberley environment. To reach Lake Argyle, drive 37km east of Kununurra on the Victoria Hwy. and turn onto the access road. Another 34km on the open road leads to the **Lake Argyle Tourist Village.**

**Lake Argyle Cruises** has a booking office that's located at the Lake Argyle Tourist Village. (☎08 9168 7687; www.lakeargylecruises.com. Tours May-Sept. daily, Oct.-Apr. by demand. 2hr. morning cruise $65, children $40; 2hr. sunset cruise $85/50; 4hr. Best of Lake Argyle cruise $145/87. Pickup in Kununurra $30/20.) **Kimberley Eco-noeing** offers a three-day self-guided tour of the region. (☎1300 663 369. $165, includes pickup, dropoff, canoe, and camping gear; min. 2 people.) The **Lake Argyle Tourist Village ❶** has accommodations, including a caravan park with showers and laundry facilities. (☎08 9168 7777; www.lakeargyle. com. Sites $10 per person. $5 per site for power.)

# PURNULULU (BUNGLE BUNGLE) NATIONAL PARK

Purnululu, unknown to the outside world until 1983, is famous for its towering orange-and-black rock domes, which have eroded to look like giant beehives. While an oft-repeated sentiment holds that the domes' grandeur can only be appreciated from the air, the view from the bottom at this World Heritage sight is equally impressive. The name "Bungle Bungle" is thought to be either a corruption of the Kija word *purnululu*, meaning "sandstone," or a misspelling of a common grass in the area, Bundle Bundle.

WESTERN AUSTRALIA

## PURNULULU AT A GLANCE

**AREA:** 209,000 hectares.

**FEATURES:** Bungle Bungle Range, Ord River, and the Western Hikes.

**HIGHLIGHTS:** Scenic helicopter flights, walks through gorges, and the unique sandstone domes.

**GATEWAYS: Kununurra** (p. 763) and Warmun.

**CAMPING:** At Walardi and Kurrajong campsites, or registered overnight bush camping ($10 per person).

**FEES:** Entry $10 per vehicle.

## TRANSPORTATION AND PRACTICAL INFORMATION

There are two ways into Purnululu: by road and by air. The drive into the park is flanked by wonderful scenery, and the independence of having a car while traveling is enviable, but the road can be grueling. Flying in provides spectacular aerial views, but it doesn't come cheap. Book with **Alligator Airways** at the Kununurra Airport. (☎1800 632 533 or 9168 1333; www.alligatorairways. au. 2hr. scenic flight $265, ages 3-12 $185. Departs daily. Book in advance.) **Helicopter flights** through the park are also available from Turkey Creek (Warmun), on the Northern Hwy. by the Purnululu turnoff (Heliwork Turkey Creek ☎08 9162 7337), or Bellburn Airstrip within the park (Heliwork in Purnululu ☎08 9168 7335). To drive to Purnululu, you need a high-clearance 4WD. The **Spring Creek Track** leaves the Great Northern Hwy. 250km south of Kununurra and 109km north of Halls Creek. For 53km, the track rumbles and grinds its way to the visitors center. Allow 5hr. driving time from Kununurra (or 4hr. from Halls

Creek) to reach the park; the Spring Creek Track alone takes 1-3hr. depending on conditions and traffic. The vehicle entry fee is $10; fees are payable 24hr. at the **visitors center** (☎08 9168 7300; open from early Apr. to mid-Oct. daily 9am-noon and 1-4pm) near the entrance to the park.

## 🏕 CAMPING

The only two public campsites available within the park have untreated water, toilets, and firewood. A left at the T-intersection after the visitors center leads 7km to the **Kurrajong campsite ❶**, on the road toward Echidna Chasm and Frog-hole Gorge. After a right at the T, it's 12km to the quieter **Walardi campsite ❶**, closer to the domes. (Sites $10 per person.) **Bellburn,** a private campground 15km from the visitors center, off the road toward Walardi, offers campers increased comfort and more facilities. Booking ahead is essential; call **Kimberley Wilderness Adventures** (☎08 9192 7022) or **East Kimberley Tours** (☎08 9168 2213). Pay entrance fees at the visitors center if you've already booked.

## 🥾 HIKING

### BUNGLE BUNGLE RANGE

In order to protect this natural wonder, visitors are not allowed to scale the fragile limestone to the top of the range, although fantastic walking trails wind around and through the formations. These trails can occasionally be difficult to find, but nearly all follow dry stream beds. When wandering away from the stream bed, stay on marked and well-worn trails, as moving off the trail can damage plant life. Also, don't forget to bring plenty of water. Three walks depart from **Piccanninny Gorge carpark,** 27km south of the visitors center.

**Piccanninny Creek and Gorge Trail** (30km round-trip). The longest walk; hiking the entire length requires overnight camping (register with the ranger station or the visitors center at the park entrance before departing). The first 7km is a smooth trail over bedrock and makes a nice day hike. From there, the trail turns into a much more difficult, rocky track. A lookout point offering a great view of the domes is located at the end of a 600m walk from the start of the trail (branches off the main trail to the right).

**Domes Walk** (1km; 30min.-1hr. round-trip). The only trail which actually passes the famous domes, this relaxed circuit links up with the Cathedral Gorge Walk.

**Cathedral Gorge Walk** (3km; 1-2hr. round-trip). This easy trail follows a river bed up the gorge to the immense waterfall at the end. The hollowed-out pool and surrounding amphitheater are of a humbling scale and beauty. The Domes Walk loops into the Cathedral Gorge Walk; the hikes are best done together.

### WESTERN HIKES

The western section of the park is marked by an imposing escarpment. Though none of the famous domes are to be found here, the walks through the gorges are just as awe-inspiring as their counterparts to the east.

**Echidna Chasm** (2km; 1hr. round-trip). Begin from Echidna Chasm carpark, 20km north of the visitors center. A flat gravel path threads an almost impossibly narrow crevasse cut into the towering red rock by millions. The passage squeezes past a pair of boulders and leads up a ladder to a chamber at the end of the crack. At midday, the spectacle is heightened by the sun's rays probing the tops of the walls along the path.

**Mini Palms Gorge** (5km; 2-3hr. round-trip). Begins at Mini Palms carpark, 19km north of visitors center. A difficult day trail follows rocky riverbeds to a steep, boulder-strewn final ascent up to an observation platform. The view from the top is less captivating, looking as much back over the trail as forward into an area of palms.

# APPENDIX

## CLIMATE

Tropical in the north, temperate in the south, Australia is blessed with a bevy of different climates. In many areas of Oz, the parched deserts of the Outback get a welcome drink as the Dry gives way to the Wet; but not all regions experience such extremes and remain pleasant year-round. Temperatures and precipitation vary based on time and place; pack accordingly.

| AVG. TEMP. (LOW/ HIGH), PRECIP. | JANUARY | | | APRIL | | | JULY | | | OCTOBER | | |
|---|---|---|---|---|---|---|---|---|---|---|---|---|
| | °C | °F | mm | °C | °F | mm | °C | °F | mm | °C | °F | mm |
| Adelaide, SA | 17/29 | 63/84 | 21 | 12/22 | 54/72 | 38 | 7/15 | 45/59 | 82 | 11/22 | 52/72 | 43 |
| Alice Springs, NT | 21/36 | 70/97 | 31 | 13/28 | 55/82 | 13 | 5/20 | 41/68 | 15 | 15/31 | 59/88 | 20 |
| Brisbane, QLD | 21/29 | 70/84 | 131 | 17/26 | 63/79 | 41 | 9/21 | 48/70 | 13 | 16/26 | 61/79 | 86 |
| Cairns, QLD | 24/31 | 75/88 | 416 | 21/29 | 70/84 | 191 | 17/26 | 63/79 | 28 | 21/29 | 70/84 | 38 |
| Canberra, ACT | 14/27 | 50/81 | 44 | 7/20 | 45/67 | 32 | 1/11 | 33/52 | 35 | 7/19 | 44/65 | 41 |
| Darwin, NT | 25/32 | 77/90 | 406 | 24/33 | 75/91 | 97 | 19/30 | 66/86 | 1 | 25/33 | 77/91 | 71 |
| Hobart, TAS | 12/26 | 54/79 | 42 | 9/20 | 48/68 | 46 | 4/13 | 39/55 | 47 | 7/20 | 45/68 | 49 |
| Melbourne, VIC | 14/26 | 57/79 | 49 | 11/20 | 52/68 | 58 | 6/13 | 43/55 | 48 | 9/20 | 48/68 | 68 |
| Perth, WA | 17/32 | 63/90 | 7 | 13/25 | 55/77 | 42 | 9/18 | 46/64 | 163 | 10/22 | 50/72 | 47 |
| Sydney, NSW | 18/26 | 64/79 | 104 | 15/22 | 59/72 | 126 | 8/16 | 46/61 | 99 | 13/22 | 55/72 | 77 |

To convert from degrees Fahrenheit to degrees Celsius, subtract 32 and multiply by 0.55. To convert from Celsius to Fahrenheit, multiply by 1.8 and add 32.

| °CELSIUS | -5 | 0 | 5 | 10 | 15 | 20 | 25 | 30 | 35 | 40 |
|---|---|---|---|---|---|---|---|---|---|---|
| °FAHRENHEIT | 23 | 32 | 41 | 50 | 59 | 68 | 77 | 86 | 95 | 104 |

## MEASUREMENTS

Australia uses the metric system. The basic unit of length is the meter (m), which is divided into 100 centimeters (cm) or 1000 millimeters (mm). One thousand meters make up one kilometer (km). Fluids are measured in liters (L), each divided into 1000 milliliters (mL). A liter of pure water weighs one kilogram (kg), the unit of mass that is divided into 1000 grams (g). One metric ton is 1000kg. Pub aficionados will note that an Australian pint is closer in size to the larger Imperial pint (20 oz.) than its US counterpart (16 oz.).

| MEASUREMENT CONVERSIONS | |
|---|---|
| 1 inch (in.) = 25.4mm | 1 millimeter (mm) = 0.039 in. |
| 1 foot (ft.) = 0.305m | 1 meter (m) = 3.28 ft. |
| 1 yard (yd.) = 0.914m | 1 meter (m) = 1.094 yd. |
| 1 mile (mi.) = 1.609km | 1 kilometer (km) = 0.621 mi. |
| 1 ounce (oz.) = 28.35g | 1 gram (g) = 0.035 oz. |
| 1 pound (lb.) = 0.454kg | 1 kilogram (kg) = 2.205 lb. |
| 1 fluid ounce (fl. oz.) = 29.57mL | 1 milliliter (mL) = 0.034 fl. oz. |
| 1 gallon (gal.) = 3.785L | 1 liter (L) = 0.264 gal. |

# AUSSIE BEVERAGE GUIDE

## TERMS OF EMBEERMENT

While, contrary to popular belief, the word "beer" is actually Australian for beer, Aussies do have their own unique way of talking about the amber stuff. Refer to the following phraseology; or, if you've imbibed too much to remember the proper term, order by the ounce. On the mainland, call for a "5," "7," "10," or "15;" in Tasmania, order a "6," "8," "10," or "20."

| REGION | BRING ME A... | STATE BEER |
|---|---|---|
| New South Wales | Pony 140mL (5 oz.), Beer/Glass 200mL (7 oz.), Middy 285mL (10 oz.), Schooner 425mL (15 oz.) | Tooheys, Victoria Bitter |
| Northern Territory | Handle 285mL (10 oz.), Darwin Stubbie 1.25L (40 oz.) bottle | (None) |
| Queensland | Pot 285mL (10 oz.), Schooner 425mL (15 oz.), Jug 1.125L (40 oz.) | XXXX |
| South Australia | Pony 140mL (5 oz.), Butcher 200mL (7 oz.), Middy/Schooner 285mL (10 oz.), Pint 425mL (15 oz., smaller than the British or American pint), Real Pint 560mL (20 oz.) | Coopers, Lion Nathan's West End Brand |
| Tasmania | Real Pint 560mL (20 oz.) | Boag's, Cascade |
| Victoria | Pot 285mL (10 oz.), Pint 568mL (20 oz.) | Victoria Bitter, Canton Draught |
| Western Australia | Shetland 115mL (4 oz.), Bobbie/Beer 200mL (7 oz.), Middy 285mL (10 oz.), Pot 425mL (15 oz.) | Emu Bitter, Swan |

## COOL BEANS

Australia loves coffee, so much so that Melbourne boasts the Coffee Academy at the William Angliss Institute of Technical and Further Education. Their coffee beverages are generally espresso-based, meaning black coffee tends to be stronger than elsewhere. Whole milk is always used unless you specify low-fat. "Cream" is generally not used in Australia.

| WHAT TO ORDER... | ...AND WHAT YOU'LL GET |
|---|---|
| short black | 60mL of espresso |
| long black | 120-200mL of espresso |
| flat white | espresso with cold milk |
| cafe latte | espresso, hot milk, and froth |
| cappuccino | espresso, hot milk, and heaps of froth |
| macchiato | espresso with a bit of froth |
| vienna coffee | espresso, whipped cream, and powdered chocolate |

# HOLIDAYS AND FESTIVALS

Banks, museums, and other public buildings are often closed or have reduced hours during holidays and festivals. Tourism generally peaks during school holidays. Although dates differ between regions, summer holidays typically run from mid-December through January, and winter holidays run from late June through early July. Virtually every Australian town boasts a festival of some sort during the year; listed below are only a few of the major ones. More specific festival info can be found in the Festivals sections throughout this book.

| 2009 DATE | HOLIDAY | DESCRIPTION |
|---|---|---|
| Jan. 1 | New Year's Day | National public holiday |
| Jan. 16-25 | Tamworth Country Music Festival (Tamworth, NSW) | Over 2500 performances and golden guitars galore in Australia's country music capital (www.tamworthcountrymusic.com.au) |
| Jan. 26 | Australia Day | National day to commemorate the arrival of the First Fleet in 1788, with festivities centered in Sydney (www.australiaday.com.au) |
| Feb. 14-Mar. 7 | Sydney Gay and Lesbian Mardi Gras | Famous display of pride that culminates in a spectacular street parade (www.mardigras.org.au) |
| Late Feb. to mid-Mar. | Adelaide Fringe Festival | The largest independent alternative festival in Australia; held annually to showcase cutting-edge artists (www.adelaidefringe.com.au) |
| Mar. 17-22 | Australian Surf Life Saving Championships | Grueling ironman and ironwoman contests, as well as the world's biggest surf party (www.slsa.asn.au) |
| Apr. 10 | Good Friday | National public holiday |
| Apr. 13 | Easter Monday | National public holiday |
| Apr. 25 | ANZAC Day | National commemoration that marks the anniversary of WWI ANZAC troops in Gallipoli (www.anzacday.org.au) |
| June 8 | Queen's Birthday | National public holiday |
| Mid July to early Aug. | Melbourne International Film Festival | Once a year, buffs, stars, and critics flock to this exhibition of world film (www.melbournefilmfestival.com.au) |
| Nov. 3 | Melbourne Cup | The horse race that entrances the nation (www.melbournecup.com) |
| Dec. 25-26 | Christmas Day and Boxing Day | National public holiday |

# GLOSSARY OF 'STRINE

**'Strine** is 'stralian for "Australian." The main thing to remember when speaking Australian slang is to abbreviate everything: **Oz** for Australia, **brekkie** for breakfast, **cuppa** for cup of tea, **uni** for university. Australian pronunciation is harder to learn than the lingo—with Aboriginal words especially, but even with English-derived proper nouns, it's difficult to pin down any definite "rules."

**ablution block:** shower/toilet block at a campground

**abseil:** rappel

**ace:** awesome

**aggro:** aggravated

**ANZAC biscuits:** honey-oat cookies

**arvo:** afternoon

**Aussie:** Australian (pronounced "Ozzie"—thus, Australia is "Oz")

**backpackers:** hostel

**bagged:** criticized

**barbie:** barbecue (BBQ)

**bathers:** bathing suit (primarily Western Australia)

**beaut:** positive exclamation, as in "You beaut!"

**beetroot:** beet, a common hamburger filling

**belt bag:** known to Americans as a "fanny pack"

**billabong:** a water hole

**biro:** pen

**biscuit:** cookie

**bitumen:** a rough, black asphalt used to pave roads
**bloke:** guy, man (familiar), "chap"
**bludger:** malingerer
**bluey:** someone with red hair (um...)
**bonnet:** hood of a car
**boofhead:** fool
**to book:** to make reservations
**boot:** trunk of a car
**bottle shop:** liquor store
**bottle 'o:** a drive through liquor store
**brekkie:** breakfast
**Brizzy:** Brisbane, QLD
**bugger:** damn
**Bundy:** Bundaberg, QLD, as in the rum
**bush:** scrubby countryside
**bush tucker:** traditional Aboriginal wild foods
**bushwalking:** hiking
**BYO:** bring your own (booze)
**campervan:** mobile home, RV
**capsicum:** bell peppers
**caravan:** a trailer; term for any sort of cabless campervan
**carpark:** parking lot
**Central Business Distict (CBD):** a city's commerical center or "downtown"
**chap:** guy, man, "bloke"
**chemist:** pharmacy
**chips:** thick french fries, often served with vinegar and salt
**chock-a-block:** crowded
**chook:** chicken
**chunder:** vomit
**coldie:** a cold beer
**concession:** discount; usually applies to students, seniors, or children, sometimes only to Australian students and pensioners
**cordial:** concentrated fruit juice
**cossie:** swimsuit, primarily NSW
**crook:** sick
**crow eater:** South Australian (a tad disparaging)
**D&M:** deep and meaningful talk
**dag:** often used in familial context as an affectionate version of "daggy"
**daggy:** unfashionable, goofy
**damper:** a term for traditionally unleavened bread
**dear:** expensive
**dill:** silly person (affectionate)
**dobber:** tattle-tale

**dodgy:** sketchy
**doona, duvet:** comforter, down blanket
**drink driving:** driving under the influence of alcohol
**drongo:** idiot
**dunny:** toilet, often outdoors
**ensuite:** with bath
**entree:** appetizer (not a "main")
**esky:** cooler
**excess:** deductible (i.e. car insurance)
**fair dinkum:** genuine
**fair go:** equal opportunity
**fairy floss:** cotton candy
**to fancy:** to like, as in "would you fancy...?"
**feral:** wild, punky, grungy
**flash:** fancy, snazzy
**free call:** toll-free call
**full on:** intense
**full stop:** period (punctuation)
**furphy:** tall tale, exaggerated rumor (as in, "tell a furphy")
**g'day:** hello
**to give it a go:** to try
**good onya:** good for you
**glasshouse:** greenhouse
**grommet:** young surfer
**ground floor:** American first floor ("first floor" is second floor, etc.)
**grog:** booze
**to hire:** to rent
**hitching:** hitchhiking
**hoon:** loud-mouth, show-off
**icy-pole:** popsicle (any sweet frozen treat on a stick)
**jackaroo:** stationhand-in-training
**jersey:** sweater, sweatshirt
**jillaroo:** female "jackaroo"
**journo:** journalist
**jumper:** "jersey"
**keen:** enthusiastic
**Kiwi:** New Zealander
**knackered:** very tired
**lad:** guy, man, "chap"
**licensed:** serves alcohol
**like hen's teeth:** rare
**lollies:** candies
**magic:** really wonderful, special
**mate:** friend, buddy (used broadly)
**milk bar:** convenience store
**Milo:** chocolate product in bar and drink varieties
**mobile:** cell phone

**moke:** an open-air, golf cart-esque vehicle

**mozzie:** mosquito

**nappy:** diaper

**narky:** annoyed

**newsagent:** newsstand

**nibblies:** snacks

**no worries:** sure, fine, or "you're welcome"

**ocker:** boorish hick, *Crocodile Dundee* type

**ordinary:** bad; an "ordinary" road is full of potholes

**'Ow yer goin'?:** How are you?

**Oz:** Australia

**pavlova:** a creamy meringue dessert garnished with fruit

**pensioner:** senior citizen

**perve:** a pervert, also used as a verb, "to perve"

**petrol:** gasoline

**piss:** beer (usually)

**pokies:** gambling machines

**polly:** politican

**Pom, pommy:** person from England

**powerpoint:** power outlet

**prawn:** jumbo shrimp

**raging:** partying

**ratbag:** corrupt, unethical person

**rego:** car registration papers

**return:** round-trip

**'roo:** as in kanga-

**roobar:** bumper protecting your car from 'roo damage

**roundabout:** traffic rotary

**rubber:** eraser

**sauce:** usually tomato sauce; closest equivalent to ketchup

**serviette:** napkin

**sheila:** woman

**shout:** buy a drink or round of drinks for others; also a noun, as in an evening's worth of everyone buying rounds for each other

**side:** team

**singlet:** tank top or undershirt

**skivvie:** turtleneck sweater

**sook:** crybaby

**spider:** ice cream float; or, arachnid (pay close attention to context)

**squiz:** a look, as in "take a squiz at something"

**sticky beak:** nosy person

**'strine:** Aussie dialect (from Australian)

**'straya:** Australia

**swimmers:** swimsuit

**sunnies:** sunglasses

**to suss:** figure out, sort out

**ta:** short for thank you—said softly

**TAB:** shop to place bets, sometimes in pubs

**takeaway:** food to go, takeout

**Tassie:** Tasmania (TAZ-zie)

**tea:** evening meal

**thongs:** flip-flops

**throw a wobbly:** get angry

**Tim Tams:** chocolate-covered cookie

**togs:** swimsuit, in Queensland

**torch:** flashlight

**tucker:** food

**uni:** university (YOU-nee)

**unsealed:** unpaved roads, usually gravel, sometimes dirt

**ute (yute):** utility vehicle, pickup truck

**upmarket:** upscale, expensive

**Vegemite:** yeast-extract spread for toast and sandwiches

**veggo:** vegetarian

**wanker:** jerk (rude term)

**winge:** to whine or complain

**yakka:** hard work

**yobbo:** slobby, unthinking person

**zed:** Z (American "zee")

# INDEX

## A

AAA. See automobile assistance.

AANT. See automobile assistance.

Aboriginal
art 103, 162, 174, 190, 223,
  229, 262, 273, 293, 302, 305,
  307, 388, 443, 450, 469, 540,
  561, 594, 598, 640, 641, 695
cultural centers 139, 223, 285,
  310, 388, 428, 469, 556, 640,
  695, 710
Dreaming 58, 169, 285, 441, 748
history 48
music 59
tours 43, 170, 257, 283, 430,
  437, 443, 498, 656, 713, 761

Abrolhos Islands, WA 736

accommodations 38
bed and breakfasts 40
camping 41
hostels 38
hotels 40
other types of accommodations 40
short-term housing 93

Adelaide River, NT 288

Adelaide, SA 459
accommodations 465
activities 470
daytrips 472
entertainment 470
food 466
museums 469
orientation 460
practical information 464
pubs 471
sights 468
transportation, intercity 459
transportation, local 461

AFL. See Australian Rules Football

Agnes Water, QLD 383

AIDS 24

Airey's Inlet, VIC 621

Airlie Beach, QLD 395

airmail 37

airplanes. See flights

Albany, WA 720

Albury, NSW 246

Aldgate, SA 475

Alexandra Headlands, QLD 358

Alice Springs Cup Carnival,
  NT 303

Alice Springs, NT 298

animal reserves
Billabong Sanctuary 407
Blackbutt Reserve 185
Currumbin Wildlife Sanctuary 344
Hanson Bay Sanctuary, SA 485
Kaiser Stuhl Conservation Park,
  SA 495
Kalbarri Rainbow Jungle Parrot
  Sanctuary, WA 739
Koala Hospital 195
Lone Pine Koala Sanctuary,
  QLD 331
Tucki Tucki Nature Reserve 207

animals
dangerous species 66
introduced species 65

Apollo Bay, VIC 623

Apsley Gorge, NSW 224

Arkaroola, SA 518

Armidale, NSW 222

Arnhem Highway, NT 278

Arnhem Land, NT 294

Arno Bay, SA 523

Art Gallery of New South
  Wales, Sydney, NSW 133

Art Gallery of South Australia,
  Adelaide, SA 469

Art Gallery of Western Australia, Perth, WA 695

arts 57

Arve Road Forest Drive,
  TAS 547

Atherton, QLD 430

Atherton Tablelands, QLD 429

Auburn, SA 495

Augusta, WA 708

Australian Alps, VIC 676

Australian Capital Territory
  (ACT) 96

Australian Celtic Festival 221

Australian Football League.
  See Australian Rules Football

Australian Formula One Grand
  Prix 584

Australian Open 583

Australian Rules Football 57
Adelaide, SA 471

Darwin, NT 275
Gabba, Brisbane, QLD 333
Melbourne Cricket Ground 583
Subiaco Oval, Perth, WA 688
Sydney, NSW 126

automobile assistance 33
AANT 267

Automobile Association of the
  Northern Territory. See automobile assistance

Ayers Rock, NT. See Uluru.

Ayers Rock Resort, NT.
  See Yulara.

## B

Bairnsdale, VIC 675

Bald Rock National Park,
  NSW 220, 357

Ballarat, VIC 644

Ballina, NSW 204

Bamaga, QLD 450

Bangalow, NSW 208

Barossa Valley, SA 490

Barron Gorge National Park,
  QLD 430

Batavia Coast, WA 733

Batemans Bay, NSW 234

Bathurst, NSW 250

Battery Point, TAS 535

Bay of Islands, VIC 629

Bay of Martyrs, VIC 629

beach driving 379

Beachport, SA 501

bed and breakfasts. See accommodations

Bedarra Island, QLD 415

Beechworth, VIC 663

beer 56, 768

Beer Can Regatta, NT 274

Bellingen, NSW 198

Bendigo, VIC 648

Beyond Tourism 81

Bicheno, TAS 564

Billabong Koala Breeding
  Centre 195

Billimina, VIC 641

Binna Burra, QLD 352

INDEX

# SMART TRAVELERS KNOW:
## GET YOUR CARD BEFORE YOU GO

An HI USA membership card gives you access to friendly and affordable accommodations at over 4,000 hostels in more than 85 countries around the world.

HI USA Members receive complementary travel insurance, airline discounts, free stay vouchers, long distance calling card bonus, so its a good idea to get your membership while you're still planning your trip.

Get your card online today:

# hiusa.org

# MAP INDEX

## MAP LEGEND

| | | | | | | |
|---|---|---|---|---|---|---|
| ■ Point of Interest | ✝ Church | ℞ Pharmacy | Beach | Park |
| ⌂ Accommodations | ⚑ Consulate | ✪ Police | Building | Water |
| ⌂ Camping | ⚓ Ferry Landing | ✉ Post Office | | |
| ● Food | ❀ Garden | ⛰ Ranger Station | ·········· 4WD Road | |
| ★ Nightlife | ⛳ Golf Course | ▥ Restrooms | – – – – Ferry Line | |
| ▮ Shopping | ✛ Hospital | Shipwreck | Pedestrian Zone | |
| Winery | ▯ Internet Café | ✡ Synagogue | Railroad | |
| ✈ Airport | Library | ☎ Telephone Office | – ∙ – ∙ – State Boundary | |
| $ Bank | ⚑ Lighthouse | Theater | Unsealed Road | |
| ⚘ Beach | ☪ Mosque | (i) Tourist Office | Walking Trail | |
| ⛟ Bus Station | ▲▲ Mountain | Train Station | | |
| ⌃ Cave | 🏛 Museum | ∫ Waterfall | LG The Let's Go compass always points NORTH. | |